ISBN: 9781407758039

Published by:
HardPress Publishing
8345 NW 66TH ST #2561
MIAMI FL 33166-2626

Email: info@hardpress.net
Web: http://www.hardpress.net

Yours sincerely

H. J. Johnston Lavis

BIBLIOGRAPHY

OF THE

GEOLOGY AND ERUPTIVE PHENOMENA

OF THE MORE IMPORTANT

VOLCANOES OF SOUTHERN ITALY

COMPILED WITH THE ASSISTANCE OF

MADAME ANTONIA JOHNSTON-LAVIS

BY

HENRY JAMES JOHNSTON-LAVIS

M.D., D.CH., M.R.C.S., F.G.S., ETC.

LATE PROFESSOR OF VULCANOLOGY IN THE ROYAL UNIVERSITY OF NAPLES

SECOND EDITION

COMPLETED AFTER THE AUTHOR'S DEATH

BY

MISS B. M. STANTON

AND EDITED WITH A PREFACE AND SHORT LIFE OF THE AUTHOR

BY

B. B. WOODWARD, F.L.S., F.G.S., ETC.

OF THE BRITISH MUSEUM (NATURAL HISTORY)

London : The University of London Press, Ltd.

AT ST. PAUL'S HOUSE, WARWICK SQUARE, E.C. 4.

1918

DEDICATED TO THE MEMORY

OF THE

AUTHOR AND HIS WIFE

BY THEIR FAMILY

PREFACE

THE " Congrès Géologique International " having arranged to hold its second session at Bologna in 1881, the " Comité d'Organisation " in that town decided, in their *Séance* of March 17th, 1879, to undertake the compilation of a " Bibliographie géologique et paléontologique de l'Italie " as a contribution towards the success of the meeting. For many unavoidable reasons that list was an imperfect one. Still, a very considerable number of works and papers were recorded, the total number of entries amounting to 6,566.

Dr. Johnston-Lavis naturally availed himself of those sections that concerned his special pursuits and set to work to supply deficiencies and to add the titles of further publications as issued. In this he was cordially aided by Mme. Lavis, who, working under her husband's directions, industriously transcribed the fresh titles and incorporated them with the entries from the older bibliography.

By the time that the Geologists' Association paid its visit to Southern Italy in the months of September and October, 1889, the bibliography had grown to almost twice the size, and Lavis happily seized upon the occasion to publish it in 1891 as an appendix to the account of the excursion, which was reprinted from the Proceedings of the Association. The whole thus formed a valuable manual of information on the Volcanoes of Southern Italy.

From that time onwards no opportunity was lost for working at this bibliography and endeavouring to render it as complete as such a work can ever be.

When the war broke out, depriving him at once of his practice, he had determined to employ his enforced leisure from professional duties till happier times should return in systematically revising and augmenting the whole bibliography and in ransacking every available source with this object in view.

His tragic death cut this project short, and all the loving labour of years of patient research seemed likely to be thrown away had not his family most felicitously conceived the idea of completing the work so far as might be possible and publishing it as a worthy offering to his memory.

Fortunately, this has been rendered practicable through the cordial co-operation of his secretary, who during recent years had been closely associated with Dr. Johnston-Lavis in the work and was thoroughly acquainted with his scheme and method. Miss Stanton accordingly continued the researches that had been begun in the Library of the Geological Society of London, where the index catalogue prepared by Mr. C. Davies Sherborn proved invaluable, the Reading Room of the British Museum, and the Libraries in the Natural History Museum, extending them to the Library of the Société Géologique de France, where she met with cordial assistance, especially from the President, M. Maurice Cossmann, and the former President, M. Emmanuel de Margerie, and the Bibliothèque Nationale de France, where, as unhappily customary in that establishment, all spirit of practical help was conspicuous by its absence.

In this way the present bibliography was completed, so far as at present practicable, as regards all the more important volcanoes. To have extended its scope and to have embraced all volcanic records for the region would have entailed many more years of labour, whilst the value of the bibliography would not have been materially increased thereby. Nor has it been possible in all cases to incorporate in their entirety the individual contents of previous bibliographies in the body of the present one. The existence of such sources of reference is, however, duly recorded, and the inquirer will, therefore, be furnished with the necessary clue towards the object of his research.

On account of the war, all access to Dr. Johnston-Lavis's own library was cut off, and hence many entries that might have been completed have perforce had to be included in a less perfect state than could have been wished. The whole bibliography must therefore, under the circumstances of its production, be leniently judged and regarded as a stage only towards that ideal work one would like to see.

The editor has to acknowledge much kindly assistance and advice given during the progress of the work by Sir Lazarus Fletcher, LL.D., F.R.S.

The subject-matter has been subdivided, as in the previous edition, according to the different volcanic groups, but some modifications in these have been introduced that approximately follow the author's known intentions in that respect. Where a given book or memoir treats of more than one of these districts the title is repeated in the separate divisions concerned.

The growth of this bibliography is well shown by comparing the number of titles cited for these subdivisions in the publication for the Congrès Géologique International, in Lavis's previous edition and in the present one.

	Congrès Géol.	*Lavis, 1891.*	*Present Edition.*
Lipari Islands ⎫			
Graham's Islands ⎬	739	1,027	2,061
Etna ⎭			
Vesuvius	667	1,552	3,050
Campi Phlegræi ⎫			
Ponza and Ventotene Islands ⎬	290	572	1,602
Roccamonfina ⎭			
Mte. Vultura	—	—	71
Colli Albani, etc.	125	210	469
Pantelleria	—	—	56
General Maps	—	—	40
	1,821	⁝3,361	7,349

ARRANGEMENT AND ABBREVIATIONS

1. ALL titles of publications are classed under the names of their respective authors, and these last are arranged alphabetically.

2. Publications written by two or more persons are placed under the name of the writer that stands first and ranged in the chronological order of his writings.

3. Publications not bearing the name of an author or of a responsible editor are placed under *Anonymous*.

4. The entries under Nos. 1 and 2 are ranged in chronological order, followed by those whose dates cannot be ascertained, these last being in alphabetical order by the titles. Those under No. 3 are ranged in alphabetical order, without regard to articles, prepositions, etc.

⁎ Publications upon earthquakes are included only when these appear to be of a volcanic nature, or limited to the immediate vicinity of a volcanic district.

[B.N.]	Biblioteca Nazionale di Napoli.
[O.V.]	Osservatorio Vesuviano.
[C.A.]	Club Alpino, Sezione di Napoli.
[B.N.P.]	Bibliothèque Nationale, Paris.
[B.M.]	British Museum.
[B.M.-N.H.]	British Museum—Natural History.

A SHORT SKETCH OF THE LIFE OF

HENRY JAMES JOHNSTON-LAVIS

BY

B. B. WOODWARD, F.L.S., F.G.S., ETC.

WITH APPRECIATIONS BY

FRANCES E. HOGGAN, M.D. Zurich ; LOUIS W. SAMBON, M.D. Naples ; and
G. OLIVER, M.D. London.

JOHNSTON-LAVIS was born in London, 1856. He was descended from a
Huguenot member of the old French family " de Lévis," who, on account of the religious
persecutions, migrated to Britain in the seventeenth century and eventually settled in
Devonshire, where land, still in the possession of the family, was acquired. The name
became anglicised and transformed into Lavis.

Johnston-Lavis received his primary education at the Grammar School, Iver, Bucks,
then under the headmastership of the Rev. W. E. Oliver, afterwards Vicar of Ealing. Full
of high spirits, he was ever in trouble with his masters over some innocent prank or other
during school hours, so his old school-fellow, Mr. Harry Kimber, writes, " and in consequence
received more canings than all the boys put together, yet withal he soon forgot his woes and
kept the classes on the alert for further jokes, followed by more punishment."

It was at Iver that the simple incident occurred which determined his lifelong interest
in geology. A stone thrown at him by a school-fellow chanced to be the flint cast of an
Echinoderm shell. Johnston-Lavis was struck by the curious appearance of the stone and,
on inquiry, made it the first specimen of a collection which ultimately evolved into one
unique of its kind. This stone is now among the family relics.

On the conclusion of his school career he resolved to enter the medical profession. With
that view, and having resorted to the South of France for the benefit of the health of his
mother, whom he attended with great filial devotion, he sought to pass through the medical
course at the University of Montpellier. That institution, however, having had to be closed
on account of a revolt of the students, he attended, instead, at the University of Marseilles,
where he studied for a year.

At the beginning of the session 1873-74 he transferred to University College, Gower
Street, London, and also attended for some subjects at the neighbouring St. Mary's Hospital,
Paddington. In the University he was placed in the First Class for Practical Chemistry
in 1874, and was also First Class in Clinical Medicine in 1878.

His geological bent received further stimulus at this time, for he came under the teaching
of Prof. John Morris, who was then at the summit of his fame. Lavis joined the Geologists'
Association in 1874, and was elected a Fellow of the Geological Society in 1875, having by
an oversight been admitted before the full age.

His first paper, " On the Triassic Strata which are exposed in the Cliff Sections near Sidmouth," was read before that Society in the following year. The amphibian bones which
he had discovered whilst working there, proving to belong to a new species, were described
at the same time by Prof. H. G. Seeley, who gave them the name of " *Labyrinthodon Lavisi.*"
These specimens have since been deposited in the Geological Department of the British
Museum (Natural History).

For several years Lavis made a careful study of the Lower London Tertiaries exposed
in the pits at Charlton and at Lewisham, in Kent, which resulted in a paper attempting
a correlation of the two sections, read before the Geologists' Association in 1877.

On these and other geological excursions, sometimes with a third friend, or on some trip
of the Geologists' Association, the writer was his frequent companion, and has a vivid

recollection of the enjoyment they brought, and how Lavis, who in those days was greatly taken with Shakespeare, would declaim whole passages with great glee in the open country.

Other studies, more immediately connected with his destined profession, were not neglected, although his tutor, Prof. G. W. Thane, " soon found out that his interest was in Geology and Fossils, while of medical work Physiology had much more attraction for him than Anatomy." Nevertheless, Lavis turned his medical knowledge to practical account by conducting evening classes on Animal Physiology at the old Polytechnic, in Regent Street, during the sessions between 1875 and 1878, being " exceptionally allowed " by the Science and Art Department " to earn payments on the results of . . . instruction." (Letter from the Department dated October 30th, 1875.)

Johnston-Lavis obtained his M.R.C.S. on April 17th, 1878, the certificate of the R.C.P. on June 4th and the L.S.A. on August 8th of the same year.

At this time (April, 1878) he went as an assistant to Dr. R. G. Long at Stalbridge, Dorset, where he took considerable part in the social and scientific gatherings, especially in connection with the Dorset Field Club, and first turned his attention to ecclesiastical archæology, of which he obtained an extensive acquaintance in subsequent years.

In January, 1879, he married Mlle. Antonia Françoise Bourdariat de Saint-Aupre, whose acquaintance he had formed when at Marseilles, and who, he testifies in the dedication to his last published work, " through a long married life encouraged me in my medical and scientific work, affording me valuable help and appreciation and aiding me to overcome almost insurmountable difficulties."

Quitting Stalbridge about February, he spent most of 1879 as an assistant to a doctor in Plaistow, and after taking the degree of " B.-ès-Sci. Paris," he went out at the end of the year to Naples and established a practice among the members of the English and American colonies and the visitors.

One of the earliest of his observations in the course of his medical work there was to trace the connection between certain prevalent gastric complaints and the consumption of molluscan shell-fish, a subject which was more fully dealt with by him at a later period.

The year 1882 found him further acting as consulting medical adviser to the Naples Sailors' Rest, of which Mme. Johnston-Lavis was secretary.

Opportunity offering, he took a trip to the United States in June (3rd to 28th), 1883, signing on the company of the s.s. *Trinacria*. Unfortunately, he suffered so severely from *mal de mer* himself, he was wont to relate, that, when attending the sole case requiring his professional services, he had to be supported by a sailor on either side.

He received his discharge from the *Trinacria* at New York and took the opportunity to visit various geologically interesting localities, including Niagara.

In order better to carry on his professional work Johnston-Lavis obtained the diploma of " Dottore di Medicina e Chirurgia " at the Naples University in January, 1884, whilst in March, 1887, he was appointed Chief Medical Officer to the works of Sir W. Armstrong, Mitchell & Co., Ltd., at Pozzuoli.

In the autumn of 1887 cholera broke out and raged fiercely at Pozzuoli. " Lavis," Dr. Sambon writes, " himself attended the stricken foreign employees and took all necessary sanitary measures for the protection of the Italian workmen. I know that he was dreadfully afraid of the Gangetic disease, insidious, swift, and deadly like the very cobra, but no one would have thought it seeing with what apparent contempt of life he laboured day and night, often without food, always tired out, to save others. When his Italian colleague contracted the infection he came to me. I shall never forget, he looked ghastly, and I promised to go that very night on condition that he would take some rest."

Exacting as his professional occupations were, they fortunately did not absorb the whole of his time, and it was at Naples that he was started on his vulcanological studies. To the young, energetic, and ardent geologist, Vesuvius, with its many fascinating problems, was a powerful loadstone, and consequently all his spare time was devoted to its study and survey.

His first important memoir on the subject was laid before the Geological Society in 1884. The paper was a long one and the author not then an acknowledged authority on the subject, so some condensation was insisted on before publication. Unfortunately, in his absence from England this was not too wisely or sympathetically done, and the omission of some portions spoilt the continuity of the work, a fact which involved the author subsequently in much useless discussion. The views embodied in the memoir have, however, been widely accepted on the Continent by competent authorities, as have those in many subsequent papers, which, not meeting with approval at Burlington House, were all published elsewhere.

The above memoir and the fact that he was living so near the volcano led to his being appointed in the autumn of 1884 secretary of the British Association Committee " for the purpose of investigating the Volcanic Phenomena of Vesuvius." The first report of the committee was made to the Association the following autumn, and subsequent reports appeared regularly up to the eleventh and final one in 1895.

In 1884, also, he spent about a fortnight investigating the geological structure of the Ponza Islands. Cholera was then raging at Campobasso on the mainland, and the islanders, not comprehending the ways of a man who broke off pieces of rocks with a hammer and wrapt them up in paper " like cheeses," concluded that he had been sent over by the Government (then a widespread belief) to spread " the Cholera Powder," and ordered him to leave the islands by the next steamer, which for safety's sake he was compelled to do.

Johnston-Lavis's work received acknowledgment from the Geological Society by the award of the Barlow-Jameson Fund in February, 1886, but the higher award of one of the Society's medals, to which his work fully entitled him, was never vouchsafed.

Numerous writings on subjects connected with Vesuvius and the southern Italian volcanoes flowed from his pen during the succeeding years, including an exhaustive study of, and monograph on, the great earthquake at Ischia, published in 1885, but his chief and, perhaps, most important work was the completion under great difficulties of his survey of Vesuvius during 1880–88, and publication in 1891 of the Geological Map in six sheets on the scale of 1 : 10,000. Save for the addition of some lava streams during the eruption of 1906, there is but little to alter in the map to-day.

In his zeal to make his work thorough and complete he never spared himself and often took great risks. His frequent companion of those days, Dr. L. Sambon (now Lecturer to the London School of Tropical Medicine), writes : " Many a time did I fear that Lavis's name would have to be inscribed on the tablet which bears those of Empedocles, Pliny the Elder, and Louis Coutrel. I have seen him fall from dangerous heights, whilst trying to reach some particularly interesting petrological specimen ; on two occasions the irate volcano threw stones at him whilst he was photographing the eruptive cone at close range ; but the narrowest escape of which I am cognisant occurred on June 7th, 1891. On the afternoon of that day, having noticed strange appearances of eruptive activity between the Vesuvian cone and the summit of the older encircling crater of Monte Somma, I ran to inform Lavis, and, of course, a few minutes later we were both hurrying to the seat of activity. What a night we spent in the Vesuvian inferno ! Having reached the lava-plain of the Atrio, we began ascending the eruptive cone, which looked like a huge pile of yellow corn-meal owing to sublimates of ferric perchloride which coated its surface materials. A considerable portion of the cone had already fallen in, and the widened crater measured about three hundred feet in its widest diameter. The broken edge was all fissured and dangerous to approach; other great rents scored the cone in every direction. Vast quantities of tumultuous white steam escaped from this great cauldron, which was no longer an eruptive crater, but a gaping fumarole. We struggled over the incoherent scoriæ, rounding the cone in an easterly direction in order to reach the opening from which the lava was issuing, but great gusts of choking sulphurous acid prevented our progress, and although lower down we had dared to jump over the fissure where it was only three or four feet wide, we were obliged to make a hasty retreat to avoid being scalded or suffocated by the heated, stifling vapours. The Atrio was also fissured in many places and covered by great patches of variegated sublimates, which contrasted sharply with the gloomy grey of the old lavas and scoriæ. At about 2.30 a.m. the ground beneath our feet trembled violently and, amidst flashes of lightning, a new gap burst open at the very foot of the eruptive cone, pouring forth a great stream of molten lava, which seemed to bear down upon us precipitously. Terrified by the sudden, unexpected explosion, we retreated as fast as we could, but found our way barred by the earlier stream, which was still copiously gushing out. Believing ourselves entirely cut off, and fearing lest we should be overwhelmed by either the scorching lava or the scalding, irrespirable vapours, we proceeded to clamber up the almost perpendicular face of the Somma escarpment. Fortunately, Lavis had climbed it on a former occasion, whilst studying its exposed lava dykes, and we managed to reach safety in a piteous condition of exhaustion. From the summit of the Somma, still gasping, we witnessed the grand spectacle of the eruption. The lava gushed out in waves, thundering just like a tempestuous sea bursting upon a rocky coast, and the lashing boom of the incandescent billows was followed by a mighty sound of clattering as parts of the eruptive cone fell within the blocked-up crater at the summit of the Vesuvian cone. In his masterly account of the Vesuvian eruption of April, 1906, Lavis dismisses this episode by saying : ' Dr. L. Sambon, who was then my assistant, and myself were nearly overwhelmed,' but the danger was very real, and we had sought it like Semele, who, wishing to behold Zeus in all his thundering glory, was consumed by lightning.''

Johnston-Lavis became a member of the Società Geologica Italiana in 1889, and during the autumn of that year the Geologists' Association paid a visit to the South Italian volcanoes, mainly at the instigation of Johnston-Lavis, on whom fell the brunt of conducting the party. A full account of the excursion appeared in the " Proceedings " of the Association (Vol. xi., 1890, pp. 389–423), and a yet more ample account in volume form in 1891. This last was published by Johnston-Lavis at Naples and contains the germ of the " Bibliography of the South Italian Volcanoes."

Among other activities of a more social description appertaining to this Naples period of Johnston-Lavis's life may be named the delivery of lectures to the Naples branch of the now well-known " Y.M.C.A.," and participation in the establishment in March, 1889; of the " Anglo-American Institute " in Naples.

In 1890 Johnston-Lavis visited Iceland in company with Dr. Tempest Anderson. The trip was confined to the south-western and, vulcanologically, most interesting portion of the island, and his observations were published in a paper read before the Scottish (now Royal Scottish) Geographical Society in 1895.

In the spring of 1891, accompanied by Dr. L. Sambon and by his eldest son Marcus, he investigated for the Italian Government the mineral sparkling waters of Sujo, and made a general survey of the valley of the Garigliano. An account of this expedition is included in his " South Italian Volcanoes."

Recognition then began to come to him from his Italian confrères, for the " Accademia di Scienze, Lettere ed Arti dei Zelanti di Acireale " elected him a corresponding member in April, 1891, while on December 14th, 1892, he was appointed Professor of Vulcanology in the Royal University of Naples. In 1893 he was elected an Honorary Member of the Edinburgh Geological Society.

Finding that his patients were, for the most part, migratory, consisting of those who only wintered in Naples, Lavis took up a consultative practice for the summer season at Harrogate, beginning in 1891 and continuing annually (except for 1895) till 1897.

The summer of 1895 was spent in company with his wife and his sons Marcus and Walter in Auvergne, where he made a careful study of the remarkable volcanic system of the Puys, as well as of the innumerable mineral waters with which the district abounds.

At Harrogate he immediately exerted himself in the interests of the place and was able from his ripe experience of foreign watering-places to offer criticisms and suggestions for the improvement of the spa, all of which were subsequently carried out.

He wrote the " Prescriber's Guide to Harrogate Mineral Waters " in 1892, and, delegated to represent the spa at the International Medical Congress held at Rome in 1893, gained for it the " Silver Medal " with his " Guide de Harrogate," especially prepared for the meeting.

Deciding to remove from Italy to the South of France, Johnston-Lavis quitted Naples in December, 1894, and practised for one season at Monte Carlo, while qualifying himself for the exercise of his profession in France by going through a medical course *de novo* at the Lyons University. He took his diploma on December 9th, 1895, his thesis being a complete résumé of the part played by edible mollusca in the propagation of gastro-intestinal diseases. He then made Beaulieu his headquarters, practising both there and at Nice, till, the work becoming excessive, he gave up the latter, while retaining his interest in the place and especially in the Queen Victoria Memorial Hospital.

Johnston-Lavis had first conceived the idea in 1899 of building an international, non-sectarian hospital at Beaulieu, and he published the scheme in March, 1902.

About the same time in the latter year Dr. A. W. Gilchrist thought of erecting an English Cottage Hospital at Nice. This idea was taken up by Mr. Alec McMillan, H.B.M. Consul, whilst Mr. E. Colston Keevil (late R.N.) suggested that it should be built as a memorial to the late Queen Victoria. Sir Blundell Maple then recommended that the two schemes should be amalgamated, and, since at that time the subscribers were all English, that it should be for British people, with facilities for American visitors. Sir Blundell also generously gave £3,000 to the cause. Johnston-Lavis gave his assent to this suggestion on March 1st, 1903, and on the 20th of that month ground was bought on Mont Boron, within the jurisdiction of Nice. The building was completed and opened on March 24th, 1906. The hospital was further decreed of "public utility" by the French Government on August 28th in the same year. Johnston-Lavis remained the Senior Consulting Physician to the hospital to the last.

His private consulting practice in popular and fashionable resorts naturally brought him into contact with many persons of note, including such widely divergent characters as the Rt. Hon. W. E. Gladstone, when at Naples, and the late Marquess of Salisbury at Beaulieu, and many valuable friendships were the outcome. With increased professional work opportunities for following his favourite study were diminished; nevertheless, he was a constant attendant at the annual meetings of the British Association and seized upon other opportunities for the pursuit of his favourite hobby. Thus in the summer of 1904, accompanied by his son Marcus, he visited and studied the ancient volcanic region of the Eiffel and Rhenish Prussia, and in 1913, guided by Prof. Lajos Lóczy von Lócz, Director of the Royal Hungarian Geological Survey, he paid a visit to the extinct volcanic regions around Lake Balaton; whilst in May, 1906, he visited Vesuvius to study the effects of the great eruption of the previous month. He was one of the first to ascend the altered crater and had the honour of explaining the whole phenomenon to His Majesty King Edward VII., who, with Queen Alexandra, visited the volcano at the time. Another visit to Vesuvius was paid by him in 1909.

More practical diversions were those of 1897, when he was President of the "British Chamber of Commerce for the Alpes Maritimes and Principality of Monaco," and of 1908, when he attended the ninth "International Congress of Geography" at Geneva and delivered the opening address to Section III. (Vulcanology and Seismology), entitled "Mécanisme de l'Activité Volcanique." The address itself was not published till 1910, but the substance of it was given in English in the *Geological Magazine* for October, 1908.

In 1904 he had accepted for the summer season the post of English Consulting Physician to the celebrated "Etablissement de la Société Générale des Eaux Minérales de Vittel" in the Vosges, France, a position which he still held at the time of his death.

Here, as at Harrogate, he at once associated himself with the welfare of the place, and by word and pen did his best to make this most charming of French spas known to his compatriots, especially such as stood in need of its revivifying waters. His wide experience suggested many improvements, some of which were gradually accepted, and he would probably have succeeded in more but that, being keen of intellect himself, he never realised that others were not like gifted, and was sometimes tempted to display a certain amount of impatience at delayed acceptance that did not tend to allay opposition to a given project.

He was at Vittel, where the present writer had left him but three days before, when the war broke out. Dismissing his patients, he started on August 1st and hastened to his son-in-law's country seat, Château de la Doultre, near Château Thierry, Aisne, to join his wife, then an invalid owing to a recent operation conducted with a view to alleviating a long-standing chronic complaint. (Mme. Johnston-Lavis passed away February 2nd, 1917.)

Misadventure then followed misadventure : he was called away to Paris, leaving his wife in charge of their devoted secretary and companion, Miss Stanton, who just succeeded in getting her away in time from the advancing Germans, and who then assisted the departure of both, with a friend, in apparent safety from Paris. The railways being blocked, the intention was to go by motor-car southwards, and so reach Beaulieu by a safe, if circuitous, route ; unhappily, their own car breaking down, recourse had to be had to another, the owner of which drove it at too high a speed and, a tyre bursting, the party was overset near Bourges (Cher) on September 10th, 1914. Whilst the rest of the occupants escaped with bruises, Johnston-Lavis was pitched forward on his head and instantaneously killed, the car falling over on the top of him. Such was the too sad end to a busy, useful life, that had every prospect of many fruitful years still before it.

Of his medical qualifications the following appreciation, written by Dr. G. Oliver at the instance of Sir Lauder Brunton, Bart., will be the best testimony :—

"My first acquaintance with Johnston-Lavis was made at Naples in the early 'eighties, shortly after he settled there as consulting physician to the English and American colony and visitors. Being myself somewhat interested in geology, I sought out Johnston-Lavis, who even in these early days was quite an authority on Vulcanology and other departments of Geology. I had the pleasure and advantage of going through his fine collection, which was rich in Vesuvian specimens of lava of various dates. Though as a physician he was popular among the visitors, I had no opportunity at that time of estimating his professional worth ; but that was afforded me when he in 1892 resorted to Harrogate for the summer season and for several subsequent seasons. There I frequently met him and discussed with him medical subjects of mutual interest. I found him keenly interested in these and in the new lines of clinical research which were at that time advancing and have since advanced to a prominent position. In these discussions I was always struck by the openness of his mind to the reception of new ideas—his attitude being that of the critical receptivity which is the natural outcome of scientific training. But he differed from most men who devote much time to the study of unapplied science in being thoroughly practical in applying his medical knowledge. His proclivity was decidedly in the direction of physiological medicine and treatment ; therefore he preferred to practise his profession in watering-places, in which such treatment takes a prominent part. In fact, his views on what he denominated ' physiological disequilibrium ' form an important part of his contributions to practical medicine. At Vittel his loss must be severely felt, for his clinical work there has done much to raise the reputation of that watering-place to a high level. As a physician he was endowed with a good presence and a reassuring and sympathetic manner, which naturally win the confidence of patients ; and as a friend his geniality and keen intelligence will be a grateful memory to all who had the pleasure of his acquaintance."

A conspicuous trait in Lavis's character was strong adhesion to the justice of giving women fair and equal play in all matters for which they were fitted, and not least in their suitability to take their share in the medical world. On this point we have the testimony of Dr. Frances Hoggan, herself one of the pioneer lady doctors, a sincere and valued old friend, who writes as follows :—

" Dr. Johnston-Lavis was one of the Emergency Guard organised by my husband to protect medical women in Edinburgh [at first] from being attacked by their rowdy fellow-students. That, as far as I know, was his only contribution to the active assistance of medical women. I myself became first acquainted with Dr. Lavis and his gifted wife in Naples in 1891, the year of my husband's death. The acquaintance soon ripened into friendship, all three of us having so many interests in common. For nearly a quarter of a century I found in Dr. Lavis a staunch friend, a man of consistently wide and liberal views, ever ready to be practically helpful to all who needed sympathy or help. The open-handed hospitality of the Lavis household will be sadly missed by a large circle of friends. To sit at their table and listen to the genial, sparkling conversation of Dr. Lavis and the quick and witty repartees of his wife was delightful, and Dr. Lavis's death will, I am sure, be widely felt as a personal sorrow.

" Dr. Lavis was too true a liberal to make any invidious distinctions in his treatment of medical men and women. His mind simply refused to recognise anything of the nature of a sex barrier between professional colleagues. How grateful such an attitude was to the first generation of medical women, accustomed to the endurance of slights and to all manner of setbacks and hindrances in their professional life, only those older women can fully know. To the many and varied mental gifts Dr. Lavis possessed must be added great kindliness of disposition, of which his patients had ample proof, and wholehearted devotion to his professional and civic duties."

Although endowed with seemingly inexhaustible energy, it was still wonderful how much Lavis accomplished without relaxing for a moment the scrupulous and unwearied attention he devoted to his very numerous patients. Some 200 books, memoirs, etc., including many important medical theses and articles, in addition to numerous vulcanological writings, stand to his credit ; whilst his latest important memoir, " On the Effects of Volcanic Action in the Production of Epidemic Diseases in the Animal and Vegetable Creation, etc." (1914), gained the Parkin Prize of £100, triennially offered by the Royal College of Physicians of Edinburgh, in May, 1914. From the touching dedication to this work we have already quoted.

A man of great force of character, with wide interests, practical ever, rather than what is known as scholarly, he numbered amongst his pursuits an extensive acquaintanceship with ecclesiastical architecture, and the carved woodwork in the little English Protestant church at Vittel, in which he took so lively and so keen an interest, was executed by local workmen from his exceedingly tasteful and in some respects unique designs.

He was also from early days deeply interested in prehistory and anthropology, hobbies keenly shared afterwards by his eldest son, Marcus. Much excavating was carried out or conducted by them, more especially on the Riviera, resulting in the discovery of a Neolithic plateau in the Beaulieu area, and of the probable site of the ancient Olivula. Many fine prehistoric Gallo-Roman and Roman remains were discovered by them, including that of a Gallo-Roman " kitchen-midden " containing some ten cubic yards of broken pottery, the whole of which was carefully collected and taken home. Some of the vases and plates reconstituted by them, after months of patient search among this enormous mass of material, are exceedingly fine and beautiful.

Never a moment seemed wasted by him. The odd minutes were devoted to looking after the fittings and furnishing of his laboratory or of his museum, in examining and cataloguing new accessions to his vulcanological library or furbishing the bookbindings with a special preparation he had invented, or in framing after a method of his own some one or other of the valuable engravings he had acquired relating to his favourite subject.

The whole of his valuable collection of vulcanological specimens, books, engravings, and photographs were offered by him in 1913 to the University of London for the purpose of creating a geodynamical section of the Geological Museum at University College. The offer was cordially accepted by the Senate, but the outbreak of the war has postponed transference to London, where ultimately it should serve the double purpose of materially assisting students along a road which Johnston-Lavis had largely to cleave for himself, and of perpetuating the memory of a keen and zealous geologist and vulcanologist.

Such, in brief, were the main features in the career of one whose loss is greatly deplored, and whose memory will ever be cherished, not only by his bereaved family, but also by a very wide circle of friends, English, French, and Italian. He was a man, take him for all in all, on whose like we ne'er shall look again.

B. B. W.

LIST OF BOOKS, MEMOIRS, ARTICLES, ETC.

DR. H. J. JOHNSTON-LAVIS

1876.

On the Triassic Strata which are exposed in the Cliff sections near Sidmouth, and a Note on the occurrence of an Ossiferous Zone containing Bones of a Labyrinthodon. —*Quart. Journ. Geol. Soc. xxxii, pp.* 274–77, *2 figs., 1 pl.*

Notes on the Geology of Lewisham.—*Proc. Geol. Assoc. iv, pp.* 528–43, *4 figs.*

1878.

A glass-eating Lichen.—" *Science Gossip,*" *No.* 162, *pp.* 128–30, *4 figs.*

1879.

A short history of the town of Stalbridge, Staplebridge, Stawbridge, or Stapleford, Dorsetshire. — *Stalbridge Almanack (Meader's) for* 1878, *pp.* 1–3.

1880.

A Visit to Vesuvius during an eruption.— " *Science Gossip,*" *xvi, pp.* 9–10.

Iron and Hydrogen.—" *Nature,*" *xxii, p.* 220.

Hardening of Steel.—" *Nature,*" *xxii, p.* 511.

Volcanic cones, their structure and mode of formation.—" *Science Gossip,*" *xvi, pp.* 220–23, *1 fig.*

1881.

On the origin and structure of volcanic cones.—" *Science Gossip,*" *xvii, pp.* 12–14, *4 figs.*

The Earthquake in Ischia.—" *Nature,*" *xxiii, pp.* 497–98.

The late changes in the Vesuvian Cone.— " *Nature,*" *xxv, pp.* 294–95.

1882.

Notes on the comparative specific gravities of molten and solidified Vesuvian lavas. [Abstr.]—*Quart. Journ. Geol. Soc. xxxviii, pp.* 240–41.

Earthquakes in Naples.—" *Nature,*" *xxvi, p.* 151.

Diary of Vesuvius from January 1 to July 16, 1882.—" *Nature,*" *xxvi, pp.* 455–56, *2 figs.*

1883.

[The Ischian Earthquake of July 28th, 1883.]—" *Nature,*" *xxviii, pp.* 346–48.

Observations scientifiques sur le tremblement de terre du 28 juillet, 1883, à l'Île d'Ischia. —" *L'Italie,*" Rome, 13 *août.*

Il parere d'uno scienziato.—" *Il Piccolo,*" Napoli, 2 *Settembre.*

Prévision de futures catastrophes dans l'Île d'Ischia.—" *L'Italie,*" Rome, 2 *septembre.*

The Disaster in Ischia.—" *Indianapolis Journal,*" Sept. 6th.

Una Risposta al Prof. Palmieri.—" *Il Piccolo,*" Napoli, 8 *Settembre.*

Étude sur l'emplacement des nouvelles villes à l'Île d'Ischia.—" *L'Italie,*" Rome, 15 *septembre.*

Le Costruzioni a Casamicciola.—" *Il Piccolo,*" Napoli, 20 *Settembre.*

Rapport préliminaire sur le tremblement de terre du 28 juillet, 1883, à l'Île d'Ischia. —" *L'Italie,*" Rome, 22 *septembre.*

The Ischian Earthquake of July 28th, 1883. —" *Nature,*" *xxviii, pp.* 437–39, *1 map.*

Notices on the Earthquakes of Ischia of 1881 and 1883, with a Map of the Isoseismal.—8°, *pp.* 56, *1 map. Naples.*

The remarkable Sunsets.—" *Nature,*" *xxix, p.* 152.

1884.

The late eruption of Vesuvius.—" *Nature,*" *xxix, pp.* 271, 291.

[Note on the eruption of Vesuvius.]— " *L'Italie,*" Rome, 12 *janvier.*

La dernière éruption du Vésuve.—" *L'Italie,*" Rome, 15 *janvier.*

The Geology of Monte Somma and Vesuvius, being a study in Vulcanology.—*Quart. Journ. Geol. Soc. xl, pp.* 35–119, 2 *figs.,* 1 *pl.*—[Abstr. in] *Geol. Mag. pp.* 379–80. 1883.

Volcanoes on the shore of Lake Nyassa, Africa.—" *Nature," xxx, pp.* 62–63.

Earthquakes and Seismographs.—" *Nature," xxx, pp.* 608–12, 5 *figs.*—[Rept. in] *Peterm. Mitth. xxxi, p.* 33. *Gotha,* 1885.

Brevi considerazioni intorno alla relazione del Professore L. Palmieri sul terremoto dell' Isola d'Ischia.—" *Il Piccolo," Napoli,* 31 *Marzo e* 1 *Aprile.*

Preliminary Notice of the Earthquake of [March 4th,] 1881, in the Island of Ischia. —*Rept. British Assoc.* 1883, *pp.* 499–501.

Preliminary Notice of the Earthquake of July [28th], 1883, in the Island of Ischia.—*Rept. British Assoc.* 1883, *pp.* 501–3, 1 *fig.*

Seismographs. An Apology.—" *Nature," xxxi, p.* 29.

Earthquake Measurements.—" *Nature," xxxi, pp.* 53–54.

1885.

A plea for the experimental investigation of some Geological Problems.—" *Nature," xxxi, p.* 338.

Meteorite o Ciottolo ?—" *Il Piccolo* " and " *Il Pungolo," Napoli,* 8–9, 9–10 *Dicembre.* —" *Roma* " and " *Corriere del Mattino," Napoli,* 9, 10 *Dicembre.*—" *L'Italie," Rome,* 9, 10, 12 *décembre.*—" *The Times," London, December* 17*th, p.* 6, *col.* 3.—" *Nature," xxxii, p.* 153.
    An amusing incident in which two of the Professors of the University of Naples described what was supposed to be the fall of a meteorite, a fragment of the comet of Biela, but which the author proved to be a cobbler's greasy lapstone, made of a large pebble of Vesuvian lava, and thrown from some neighbouring roof.

The physical conditions involved in the injection, extrusion and cooling of Igneous Matter. [Abstr.]—*Quart. Journ. Geol. Soc. xli, Proc. pp.* 103–6.—*Geol. Mag. p.* 282.

Monograph of the Earthquakes of Ischia, a Memoir dealing with the Seismic Disturbances in that Island from Remotest Times, with Special Observations on those of 1881 and 1883, and some calculations by Rev. Prof. Samuel Haughton.—*roy.* 4⁰, *pp.* x+112, 20 *photo-engrav.,* 2 *maps col.,* 4 *pls.* (1 *col.*). *London and Naples.*— [Review in] *Geol. Mag. pp.* 369–71. 1886.

The new outburst of lava from Vesuvius.— " *Nature," xxxii, pp.* 55, 108.

Notice of a Geological Map of Monte Somma and Vesuvius.—*Rept. British Assoc.* (1884), *p.* 730.—*Geol. Mag. pp.* 27–28.

Some speculations on the phenomena suggested by a geological study of Vesuvius and Monte Somma.—*Geol. Mag. pp.* 302–7. —[Rept. in] *Peterm. Mitth. xxxi, p.* 401. *Gotha.*

On the preparation of sections of pumicestone and other Vesicular Rocks.—*Journ. R. Micro. Soc. S.* 2, *vi, pp.* 22–24.

1886.

[First] Report of the Committee . . . for the Investigation of the Volcanic Phenomena of Vesuvius.—*Rept. British Assoc.* (1885), *pp.* 395–96.—" *Nature," xxxii, pp.* 505–6. 1885.

Krakatào.—" *Nature," xxxiii, p.* 6.

Nouvelle éruption du Vésuve du 4 février, 1886.—" *L'Italie," Rome,* 9 *février.*

Vesuvian eruption of February 4th, 1886.— " *Nature," xxxiii, p.* 367.

The relationship of the structure of Igneous Rocks to the conditions of their formation. —*Scient. Proc. R. Dublin Soc. N.S. v, pp.* 113–55.

On the Fragmentary Ejectamenta of Volcanoes.—*Proc. Geol. Assoc. ix, pp.* 421–32, 1 *pl.*

Notes on Vesuvius from February 4 to August 7, 1886.—" *Nature," xxxiv, pp.* 557–58.

The Volcanic Eruption in New Zealand.— *Geol. Mag. pp.* 523–24.

The relationship of the activity of Vesuvius to certain Meteorological and Astronomical Phenomena.—*Proc. R. Soc. xl, pp.* 248–49.

L'Eruzione del Vesuvio nel 2 Maggio 1885. —*Ann. Acc. Aspir. Nat. Era,* 3, *i, pp.* 87–94, 2 *pls. Napoli.*

Sounding a crater, fusion points, pyrometers, and seismometers.—" *Nature," xxxv, p.* 197.

1887.

Diario dei fenomeni avvenuti al Vesuvio da Luglio 1882 ad Agosto 1886.—" *Lo Spettatore del Vesuvio e dei Campi Flegrei," nuova serie pubblicata a cura e a spese della Sezione Napoletana del Club Alpino Ital.*—4⁰, *pp.* 81–103, 13 *photo-engrav. Napoli.*

Discorso, il 8 Febbrajo al Cinquantesimo Anniversario dell' Insegnamento di Arcangelo Scacchi come rappresentante la Società Geologica di Londra e la Società Mineralogica della Gran Bretagna.—*See Rendiconto pub. by the Tipografia della R. Università di Napoli, 4°, pp. 39-40.*

1892.

Harrogate as seen by an Outsider.—*Two letters reproduced from the " Harrogate Herald," Jan. 12 and 27, pp. 15.*

The Prescriber's Guide to the Harrogate Mineral Waters.—*12°, pp. 46, 2 tables of analyses.*

International, Geological, and other Records. —" *Nature," xlvi, pp. 441-42.*

Notes on the Gulf of Naples as a Winter Resort.—*Forming a chapter in " Mediterranean Winter Resorts," edited by E. A. Reynolds Ball, 2nd ed. 1892 ; 3rd ed. 12°, pp. 20, 3 figs. London.*

Earthquake Sounds.—*Geol. Mag. pp. 280-82.*

Note on the Lithophyses in Obsidian of the Rocche Rosse, Lipari.—*Geol. Mag. pp. 488-90.*

[Seventh] Report of the Committee . . . appointed for the Investigation of the Volcanic Phenomena of Vesuvius and its Neighbourhood.—*Rept. British Assoc.* (1891), *pp. 312-20, 3 figs., 1 pl.*

Street Numbering.—" *Harrogate Herald," 5 October.*

1892-93.

Vivisection.—" *Harrogate Advertiser,"* 24 *Dec. 1892 and 14 Jan. 1893.*

1893.

Dr. Allinson.—" *Naples Echo," 1 April and 27 May.*

A new Seismograph.—" *Nature," xlvii, pp. 257-58.*

Stromboli.—" *Nature," xlvii, p. 453.*

[Rise of Lava in Etna.]—" *Nature," xlviii, p. 179.*

Remarkable Hailstones.—" *Nature," xlviii, p. 294, 1 fig.*

Harrogate at the International Congress in Rome.—"*-Harrogate Herald," August* 9 *and 12.*

Naples and the Cholera.—" *Naples Echo,"* 26 *August.*

The Pestilence of Street Noises.—" *Harrogate Advertiser," 19 August.*

The Ejected Blocks of Monte Somma ; Part I. Stratified Limestones.—*Trans. Edinb. Geol. Soc. vi, pp. 314-51, 3 pls., 1 fig.*

[Remarks on Eozoonal Structure in Ejected Blocks from Monte Somma.]—*Quart. Journ. Geol. Soc. xlix, Proc. pp. 149-50.*

Guide de Harrogate, compilé sur les données recueillies par l'auteur, et par la Société Médicale de Harrogate pour la Municipalité, à l'occasion du Congrès International de Médecine tenu à Rome.—*12°, pp. 27, 9 figs., 2 tables. Harrogate.*

Guida di Harrogate.
   Italian edition of last.

Notes on the Pipernoid Structure of Igneous Rocks.—" *Natural Science," iii, pp. 218-23.*

[Eighth] Report of the Committee . . . appointed for the Investigation of the Volcanic Phenomena of Vesuvius and its Neighbourhood.—*Rept. British Assoc.* (1892), *pp. 338-43.—Geol. Mag. 1892, pp. 507-13.*

On the occurrence of Pisolitic Tuff in the Pentlands.—*Rept. British Assoc.* (1892), *p. 726.*

The Crescent Estate : Town Music : House Foundations.—" *Harrogate Advertiser,"* 28 *Oct.—" Harrogate Herald," 1 Nov.*

A Museum for Harrogate.—" *Harrogate Advertiser," 16 Dec.*

1894.

The Spa Gardens.—The Public Library.— " *Harrogate Advertiser," 17 Feb.*

The causes of variation in the composition of Igneous Rocks.—" *Natural Science," iv, pp. 134-40.*

The Basic Eruptive Rocks of Gran (Norway) and their Interpretation. A Criticism.-- *Geol. Mag. pp. 251-54.*

With J. W. Gregory.—Eozoonal Structure of the Ejected Blocks of Monte Somma.— *Scient. Trans. R. Dublin Soc. N.S. v, pp.* 259-86, 5 *photo-engrav.—*[Abstr.] *Scient. Proc. R. Dublin Soc. N.S. viii, p. 280.—Proc. Geol. Soc. xlix, pp. 149-50. —Abstr. Proc. Geol. Soc. 1892-93, 610, pp. 107-8.*

The Science of Vulcanology [being the introductory Address to a course of lectures on that subject in the R. University of Naples].—" *Nature," l, pp.* 66-68.— " *Science," 16 March.*

[Ninth Report of the Committee appointed for the Investigation of] The Volcanic Phenomena of Vesuvius and its Neighbourhood.—*Rept. British Assoc.* (1893), *pp.* 471–73.

On Quartz Enclosures in Lavas of Stromboli and Strombolicchio, and their effect on the Composition of the Rock.—*Rept. British Assoc.* (1893), *pp.* 759–60.—*Geol. Mag.* 1894, *pp.* 47–48.—*Quart. Journ. Geol. Soc. l, Proc. p.* 2.

Sulle Inclusione di Quarzo nella lave di Stromboli, ecc. e sui cambiamenti da ciò causati nella composizione della lava.— *Boll. Soc. Geol. Ital. xiii, pp.* 32–41, 1 *pl.* *Roma.*

1895.

The Relationship of Oysters to Typhoid Fever and Gastro-enteritis.—*British Med. Journ.* i, *pp.* 559–60.—In French : " *Lyon Médical,*" *lxxix*, 33, *pp.* 525–28.

On the Formation at Low Temperatures of certain Fluorides, Silicates, Oxides, etc. in the Pipernoid Tuff of the Campania. With a note on the determination of some of the Species by Prof. Pasquale Franco.— *Geol. Mag. pp.* 309–14.

Notes on the Geography, Geology, Agriculture and Economics of Iceland.—*Scottish Geog. Mag. pp.* 441–66, 11 *pls.* *Edinburgh.*

The Eruption of Vesuvius, July 3, 1895.— " *Nature,*" lii, *pp.* 343–45, 4 *figs.*

With E. Flores.—Notizie sui depositi degli antichi laghi di Pianura (Napoli) e di Melfi (Basilicata) e sulle ossa di mammiferi in essi rinvenute.—*Boll. Soc. Geol. Ital. xiv, pp.* 111–18, 1 *pl.* *Roma.*

Du Rôle des mollusques alimentaires dans la propagation des infections gastro-intestinales (fièvre typhoïde, choléra, etc.). Mesures prophylactiques. Thèse présentée à la Faculté de Médecine et de Pharmacie de Lyon, et soutenue publiquement le 9 décembre 1895, pour obtenir le grade de Docteur en médecine français.—4⁰, *pp.* 64. *Lyon.*—*Also issued in* 8⁰.

[Tenth Report of the Committee appointed for the Investigation of] The Volcanic Phenomena of Vesuvius and its Neighbourhood.—*Rept. British Assoc.* (1894), *pp.* 315–18.—*Geol. Mag.* 1894, *pp.* 513–16.

With J. W. Dawson and J. W. Gregory.— Eozoon and the Monte Somma Blocks.— " *Natural Science,*" vi, *pp.* 398–404.

1896.

Les Médecins étrangers en France.—" *Le Concours Médical,*" 24 *octobre.*

[Eleventh and final Report of the Committee appointed for the Investigation of] The Volcanic Phenomena of Vesuvius and its Neighbourhood.—*Rept. British Assoc.* (1895), *p.* 351.

The Highwood Mountains of Montana and Magmatic Differentiation : A Criticism.— *Rept. British Assoc.* (1896), *pp.* 792–93.

1897.

A Question of Nomenclature : Chemical Name for H_2O.—*Geol. Mag. pp.* 526–27.

1899.

Medical Notes on Beaulieu and Cap St. Jean. —*In* " *Mediterranean Health Resorts,*" *by* E. Reynolds Ball, 12⁰, *pp.* 85–86. *London.*

The Boycott of the Riviera.—" *Westminster Gazette,*" 14 *Dec.*—" *Leeds Mercury,*" 14 *Dec.*—" *Pall Mall Gazette,*" 15 *Dec.*

1900.

Calcareous Confetti and Oolitic Structure.— *Rept. British Assoc.* (1899), *pp.* 744–46.

1901.

Découverte de l'Emplacement d'Olivula et d'Antiquités Gallo-romaines à Beaulieu.— *Ann. Soc. Lettres, Sci. et Arts des Alpes Maritimes, pp.* 268–69. *Nice.*

Italian Geology. [A Review.]—" *Nature,*" lxiv, *pp.* 640–41, 2 *figs.*

1905.

Origin of Lunar Formations.—" *Nature,*" lxxi, *p.* 256.

1906.

Beaulieu.—" *The Queen,*" 2 *photos by the author, Jan.* 30.

Some Truths about Vittel, Contrexéville, and Martigny. Practical Hints to my Medical Brethren.—*Journ. Balneology and Climatology,* x, *pp.* 92–96, 1 *fig.*—Extended Reprint with preface : 8⁰, *pp.* 14, 3 *figs.* *Doherty & Co., London.*

Note sur une Plateforme Néolithique à Beaulieu.—" *Journ. de la Corniche,*" 22 *avril.*

* A New Vesuvian Mineral, " Chlormanganokalite."—" *Nature,*" lxxiv, *pp.* 103–4.

* [Remarks and Explanation of an Exhibit of Views of Vesuvius, taken after the eruption of Vesuvius in April, 1906. Also quoted as " The Recent eruptive phenomena of Vesuvius."]—*Quart. Journ. Geol. Soc. lxii, Proc., p. cxxxiv.—Abstr. Proc. Geol. Soc.* 1905–6, *No.* 830, *pp.* 107–9.—" *Nature," lxxiv, pp.* 165–66.

The New Vesuvius.—Its unrecognizable Aspect. Five photographs of the altered cone, obtained and described for the " Sphere," by H. J. J.-L., Prof. of Vulcanology at Naples, who described to King Edward the effects of the great eruption.—" *Sphere,*" 3 *views and text. London,* 2*nd June.*

* Another new Vesuvian mineral, " Chlornatrokalite."—" *Nature," lxxiv, p.* 174.

A Reprint of the articles marked *.—8°, *pp.* 4. *Saint Dizier.*

The Springs of Vittel. Their use in derangements of Physiological Equilibrium, such as Gout, Albumenuria, Diabetes, etc. —*Paris Medical Journ.* i, *pp.* 105–7, 4 *figs.*

Vittel ; the Vosges Spa.—" *The Queen,*" 21 *July, p.* 135, 3 *photos by the Author.*

Hæmoptysis in Pulmonary Tuberculosis.— *Paris Medical Journ.* i, *p.* 180.

Sur une Plateforme Néolithique à Beaulieu, Alpes Maritimes.—*Compt. Rend. Congrès Internat. Anthrop. & Archéol. Préhist. Sess.* XIII, i, *pp.* 174–77.

Recent observations at Vesuvius. [Title only.]—*Rept. British Assoc.* (1906), *p.* 579.

1907.

De la relation existant entre l'activité du Vésuve et certains phénomènes météorologiques et astronomiques.—*Bull. Soc. Belge Géol. xxi, Mém. pp.* 303–24, 1 *pl. Bruxelles.*

1908.

With L. J. Spencer.—On Chlormanganokalite, a new Vesuvian mineral ; with notes on some of the associated minerals.— *Min. Mag.* xv, 68, *pp.* 54–61.

Vittel.—" *The Practitioner," special number devoted to Health Resorts and Climatic Treatment, lxxxi,* 1. *July.*

1909.

The Eruption of Vesuvius in April, 1906.— *Scient. Trans. R. Dublin Soc. S.* 2, ix, *pp.* 139–200, 21 *pls.,* 2 *figs.,* 2 *col. maps.* —[Reviewed in] *Geol. Mag. p.* 281, [and in] " *Nature," lxxx, pp.* 289–90, 3 *figs.*

Beaulieu and its Climate.—*A Chapter in the " Sunny South," being a Picturesque Guide to the Riviera.—Pall Mall Press, London.*

Vittel ; the most up-to-date Spa in France.— " *Continental Daily Mail,*" 2 *figs. June* 27*th. Also* 1910, 1911, 1912, 1913, 1914.

With A. Bourdariat.—Note sur le remarquable volcan de Tritriva au centre de l'Île de Madagascar, avec des observations sur l'origine du Quartz dans les Basaltes et autres Roches Basaltiques.—*Bull. Soc. Belge Géol. xxii, pp.* 103–15, 3 *pls.,* 4 *figs. Bruxelles.*

The mechanism of Volcanic Action, being the opening address to Section III. (Vulcanology) of the Int. Geographical Congress at Geneva, 1908.—*Geol. Mag. pp.* 433–43, 2 *pls.,* 1 *fig.*—[Reprinted in] *Smithsonian Report for* 1909, *pp.* 305–15, 3 *pls. Washington,* 1910.

1910.

Some examples illustrating cases of Chronic Toxæmia at Vittel.—*British Med. Journ.* ii, *pp.* 190–93, 6 *figs.*

Mécanisme de l'Activité Volcanique.—*C.R. Travaux* IX. *Congrès Internat. Géographie* (1908), *pp.* 187–200, 5 *pls. Genève.*

Notes Archéologiques sur Beaulieu. A contribution of local notes to " Les Voies Romaines depuis Vintimille, où soit la Roya jusqu'au Var, et leurs Bornes Militaires," par le Dr. A. Barety.—" *Nice Historique," pp.* 11–12. *Nice.*

Osmotic Metamorphism : *See discussion of* paper on Dedolomitization in Marble of Port Shepstone (Natal), by F. H. Hatch. —*Quart. Journ. Geol. Soc. lxvi, pp.* 520–22.

Vittel, Vosges, with Notes on the Medical Use of the Waters. [A popular Guide to this Spa, prepared at the request of the Soc. Générale des Eaux Minérales de Vittel, and published by them with emendations and new editions each year.] —8°, *pp.* 22, *many pls. and maps. Saint Dizier.*

1911.

Hypertension and Neurasthenia.—*British Med. Journ. p.* 169, *Jan.* 21*st.*

Renal Calculi and Calcium Metabolism.— *British Med. Journ. pp.* 966–67(*April* 22*nd*), *p.* 1406 (*June* 11*th*).

Therapeutics of Aconite.—*Proc. R. Soc. Medicine,* iv, *Sect. Therapeutics and Pharmacol. p.* 190.

Hypertension, Blood Viscosity and Capillary Spasm.—*Brit. Med. Journ. July* 10*th.*

Physiological Disequilibrium, or Chronic Toxæmias and the principles of their treatment.—*Amer. Journ. Physiol. Therapeutics, ii, pp.* 84–91.—[Reprint] 8⁰, *pp.* 14. *Saint Dizier.*

1912.

Sphygmomanometry and Pachon's Oscillometer.—*British Med. Journ. p.* 72, *Jan.* 13*th.*

Further Examples illustrating cases of Chronic Toxæmias at Vittel.—*British Med. Journ. p.* 231, *Feb.* 3*rd.*—[Reprint] 8⁰, *pp.* 8, 6 *figs.*

Vittel ; the most up-to-date, bracing and fashionable of Spas in France.—"*Guide through Europe,*" *of the Hamburg-Amerika Linie,* 16⁰, *pp.* 733–36, 2 *figs. Berlin.*

List of Books, Memoirs, Articles, Letters, etc.—8⁰, *pp.* 24. *Doherty & Co., London.*

With Dr. H. Géraud.—A Case of Gonococcic Empyema.—*Proc. R. Soc. Medicine, v,* 8, *pp.* 217–23, 4 *figs.*

[Successful treatment of Glycosuria at Vittel.]—*British Med. Journ. ii, p.* 104, *July* 13*th.*

Archéologie de Beaulieu-sur-Mer.—*Guide des Étrangers à Beaulieu-sur-Mer,* 8⁰, *pp.* 14–21. *Paris (Doin).*

Medical Science and Weights and Measures : a protest.—*British Med. Journ. ii, p.* 527, *Aug.* 31*st.*

1913.

Sea-water and Critical Temperatures.—*Geol. Mag. pp.* 143–44, 239.

An Analysis of a series of cases of Hypertension and Hypotension treated at Vittel.—*British Med. Journ. i, pp.* 1050–52, *May* 17*th.*

The Treatment of Neurasthenia.—*British Med. Journ. ii, p.* 282, *Aug.* 2*nd.*

1914.

System of Rays on the Moon's Surface.—"*Nature,*" *xcii, pp.* 631–32, *Feb.* 5*th.*

Zonal Structure in Colloids.—"*Nature,*" *xcii, p.* 687, *Feb.* 19*th.*

Saturation of Minerals and Genesis of Igneous Rocks.—*Geol. Mag. pp.* 381–83.

Oxaluria.—*British Med. Journ. i, p.* 744.

On the Effects of Volcanic Action in the Production of Epidemic Diseases in the Animal and in the Vegetable Creation, and in the Production of Hurricanes and Abnormal Atmospherical Vicissitudes.—8⁰, *pp. xii* + 67.—*J. Bale, Sons and Danielsson, London.*

This Essay gained the Parkin Prize of £100, offered triennially by the Roy. College of Physicians of Edinburgh.

LECTURES

1880.—Dec. 1st.   " Volcanoes and allied Phenomena."
To the Naples Branch of the Y.M.C.A.

1881.—March 9th.   " How we catch Fevers."
To the same as above.

March 30th.   " Earthquakes."
To the same as above.

1890.—Dec. 17th.   " Recent Discoveries in Bacteriology."
To the same as above.

1892.—Feb. 3rd.   " On Iceland."
To the same as above.

Oct. 3rd.   " The History and Geology of Vesuvius."
To the Leeds Naturalists' Club and Scientific Association.

1894.—Sept. 14th.   " Vesuvius and other volcanoes near Naples."
At Cairn. *See* " Cairn Times."

Oct. 31st.   " On Thermo-mineral Springs in Naples and its Neighbourhood."
To the Naples Branch of the Y.M.C.A.

1903.—July 16th.   " Vesuvius, the type Volcano."
To the Devonshire Association at Sidmouth.

1906.—Oct. 8th.   " Vesuvius."
To the Margate Lecture Society at Margate.

1907.—Jan. 19th.   " Vesuvius."
To the Société des Arts, Sciences et Lettres at Nice.

March 26th and 28th.   " Vesuvius."

To the Association Polytechnique des Alpes Maritimes at Nice.

April 13th and 15th.   [The same.]

Repeated in French to the above Association.

BIOGRAPHICAL NOTICES

L'Encyclopédie Contemporaine Illustrée, *Ann. xxviii, pp.* 65–66, *portrait.* 10 *July,* 1904.
Nice Illustré, *jan.-fév.,* 1906 ; *avril,* 1907.
Nature, 1 *Oct.,* 1914, *p.* 119.
The Times, 5 *Nov.,* 1914.
The Standard, 5 *Nov.,* 1914.
British Medical Journal, *ii, p.* 862, 14 *Nov.,* 1914.
Geological Magazine, *pp.* 574–76, *Dec.,* 1914.
Riviera Scientifique, *Ann. xii, pp.* 10–12. 1915.

CONTENTS

ERRATA

P. 37, col. 1. *Dele* ANON.—Parthenope terræmotu vexata.

P. 41, col. 2. ARAGO, D. F. J. *Dele* " J."

P. 48, col. 2. BUCH, C. L. VON.—Physikalische Beschreibung, etc.—*Gesammelte Schriften, etc.* 1877 (*not* 1887).

P. 61, col. 2. FOUQUÉ, F. A.—Sur les phénomènes éruptifs, etc. " Septième Lettre "
(*not* " Sixième ").

P. 68, col. 2. HAMILTON, SIR W.—Remarks upon the Nature of the Soil of Naples,
etc.—*Phil. Trans. R. Soc. lxi, etc.* (not *lxxi*).

P. 80, col. 1. MAJONE.—*See* MAIONE under VESUVIUS for correct version.

P. 92, col. 1. POLEHAMPTON, E., and GOOD, J. M.—The Gallery of Nature and Art,
etc. For correct pagination *see* VESUVIUS.

P. 92, col. 2. QUARANTA, B. . . . AYOLA, M. *Should be* AYALA, M.

P. 97, col. 1. SALLE, DE LA. *Should be* LASALLE, A. É. GIGAULT DE.

P. 121, col. 1. ANON.—Parthenope terræmotu vexata, *etc.* Add : *See* MISCELLANEA
POETICA.

P. 133, col. 2. ANSTED, B. T. *Should be* ANSTED, D. T.

ARAGO, D. F. J. *Dele* " J."

P. 134, col. 2. ARTAUD, CHEV. DE, etc. *Should read* ARTAUD DE MONTOR, CHEV.
A. F.—Italie.—*See* L'Univers, ou Histoire et description de tous les
peuples, *etc. pp.* 384, 96 *pls.*, 2 *maps. Paris*, 1835.
See plate at p. 324.

P. 139, col. 2. BIANCONI, A. *Should be* BIANCONI, G. G.

P. 140, col. 2. BLAKE, J. F.—A Visit to the Volcanoes of Italy.—*Proc. Geol. Assoc.
xi, pp.* 145–76. *London*, 1891 (not *ix*, 1889).

P. 145, col. 2. BULIFON, A.—Compendio istorico, *etc.*—2nd ed. *pp.* 152 (*not* 116).

P. 223, col. 2. OSTERLAND, C., WAGNER, P.—Beitrag zur Kenntniss der Vesuvasche.
—To ref. " *Bull. Soc. Chim. Paris* " add *xx, p.* 263.

P. 279, col. 1. ARAGO, D. F. J. *Dele* " J."

P. 364, col. 2. ARAGO, D. F. J. *Dele* " J."

COLLI ALBANI, VULCANI ERNICI,
AND DISTRICT

ANON.—Bibliographie géologique et paléontologique de l'Italie, par les soins du Comité d'Organisation du 2e Congrès Géologique International à Bologne.— 8⁰, pp. 630. *Bologne*, MDCCCLXXXI.

ANON.—Carta geologica della Campagna Romana e regioni limitrofe.—*R. Uffic. Geol. Ital. Roma*, 1888.
   1 : 100,000, in 6 sheets with 1 section. *See* sheet " Rome " (150) for Alban Hills.

ANON.—Carta (Corografica) d'Italia.—*Ist. Geog. Milit. Ital.* 1889.
   1 : 1,000,000, in 7 sheets.—3 ed. 1st, in 3 colours, with mountains shaded in brown and water in blue ; 2nd, mountains in grey ; 3rd, without mountain shading. *See* sheets 3 and 4.

ANON.—Carta (Corografica) d'Italia.—*Ist. Geog. Milit. Ital.* 1889.
   1 : 1,800,000, in 6 sheets.—2 ed. 1st in 3 colours as in preceding ; 2nd, without the mountains shaded. *See* sheets 3 and 4.

ANON.—Carta geologica del Regno alla Scala di 1 : 100,000.—*R. Uffic. Geol. Ital.* 272 sheets.

ANON.—Carta Topografica della Lombardia, del Veneto e dell' Italia Centrale.—*Ist. Geog. Milit. Ital.* 1829–1889.
   1 : 75,000, in 159 half-sheets. Mountains shown G 15, H 15, G 16, H 16 (Alban Hills).

ANON.—Carta Topografica del Regno d'Italia.—*Ist. Geog. Milit. Ital.* 1889.
   1 : 100,000. Chromolithographic ed. in 3 colours without line shading of mountains. *See* sheet 150.

ANON.—Carta Topografica del Regno d'Italia.—*Ist. Geog. Milit. Ital.* 1889.

1 : 100,000, in 277 photo-engraved sheets, in course of publication (1889). The orography is shown by contour lines of 50 m. as well as by zenith-light shading. *See* sheet 150.

ANON.—Carta Topografica del Regno d'Italia.
   1 : 75,000. Economic ed. similar to above.

ANON.—Carta Topografica di Roma e dintorni.—*Ist. Geog. Milit. Ital.* 1883.
   1 : 100,000, in 1 sheet similar to sheet 150 of Cart. Topog. d. Regno d'Italia.

ANON.—[An outline engraving without any inscription, but with 29 reference numbers. Possibly a view in the Alban Hills ?]
   405 × 188 mm.

ANON.—[Dr. Bleicher.]—La Géologie de Rome.—*Revue Britannique*, S. 9, vi, 12, pp. 405–420. *Paris*, 1867.

ANON.—Sull' incendio di un combustibile fossile al Monte delle Piche.—*Corrisp. scient. vi. Roma*, 1863.

ANON.—L'Italia.—4⁰, pp. 326, num. maps. *Torino*, 1896.

ANON.—L'Italie.—8⁰, 243 engrav., 5 maps. *Paris*, — ?

ANON.—Raccolta di storia naturale.—4⁰, pl. *Roma*, 1784.

ANON.—Tavolette rilevate per la costruzione della carta del Regno d'Italia.—*Ist. Geog. Milit. Ital.* 1873–1879.
   Part to the scale of 1 : 50,000 and part 1 : 25,000. *See* sheet 150, i–iv.

ANON.—Vestigi del Settizonio di Seuero Imperatore, detto la Scola di Vergilio in Roma.
   Engrav. octag. : 143 × 115 mm.

ABICH, O.W.H.VON.—Geologische Beobachtungen über die vulcanischen Erscheinungen und Bildungen in Unter- und Mittel-Italien.—Bd. i, Lief. 1: Ueber die Natur und den Zusammenhang der vulkanischen Bildungen.—4º, pp. viii + 134 + xi, maps 3, lith. pls. 2. (Atlas to same bound separately, pls. 5.) Braunschweig, 1841.

AGAMENNONE, G.—Il terremoto laziale dell' 8 maggio 1897.—Boll. Soc. Sismol. Ital. iii, 6, pp. 133-147. Modena, 1897.

AGAMENNONE, G.—Il terremoto laziale del 10 aprile 1911.—Atti R. Acc. Lincei, S. 5, Rend. xx, sem. 2, pp. 12-18. Roma, 1911.

ANCA, F.—Sull' elefante africano rinvenuto fra i fossili post-pliocenici presso Roma.—Atti R. Acc. Lincei, xxv, pp. 353-6. Roma, 1872.

ANGELIS D'OSSAT, G. DE.—Sopra un giacimento di roccie vulcaniche nel territorio di Rocca S. Stefano (prov. di Roma).—Riv. Ital. Sci. Nat. xii, pp. 81-4. Siena, 1892.

ANGELIS D'OSSAT, G. DE.—Storia fisica dell' Agro Romano.—" Cosmos," S. 2, xii, pp. 65-82. Torino, 1894-95.

ANGELIS D'OSSAT, G. DE.—Nuovi fatti geologici nella provincia romana.—Boll. Soc. Geol. Ital. xvii, 4, pp. 199-200. Roma, 1898.

ANGELIS D'OSSAT, G. DE.—Sulle condizioni sfavorevoli per i pozzi artesiani tra Roma ed i Colli Laziali.—Atti R. Acc. Lincei, S. 5, Rend. xiii, sem. 2, pp. 394-402. Roma, 1904.

ANGELIS D'OSSAT, G. DE.—Bonifica idraulica del Pantano di Granaraccio nella Campagna romana.—Boll. Soc. Ing. e Arch. Ital. xiii, pp. 785-788. Roma, 1905.

ANGELIS D'OSSAT, G. DE.—Sulla geologia della provincia di Roma.—Boll. Soc. Geol. Ital. xxviii, 1, pp. 169-172. Roma, 1909.

ANGELIS D'OSSAT, G. DE.—Azione caolinizzante delle radici sulle roccie laviche romane.—Atti R. Acc. Lincei, S. 5, Rend. xix, sem. 1, pp. 154-157. Roma, 1910.

ANGELIS D'OSSAT, G. DE.—Le rocce e le acque dell' Agro Romano rispetto alla calce.—Atti R. Acc. Lincei, S. 5, Rend. xx, sem. 1, pp. 259-266. Roma, 1911.

ARTINI, E.—Contribuzioni alla mineralogia dei vulcani Cimini.—Atti R. Acc.

Lincei, S. 5, Mem. vi, pp. 88-93. Roma, 1889.

AUDOT, L. E. (père).—L'Italie, la Sicile, les Îles Éoliennes, l'Île d'Elbe, etc.— 8º, 5 Pts. in 4 Vols. Pt. i, pp. 370, 1 map; Pt. ii, pp. 280 + 128; Pt. iii, pls. 140 on steel; Pt. iv, pls. 141-291. Paris, 1834.—[Also] Pt. i, pp. 270, pls. 1-94; Pt. ii, pp. 271-370, pls. 95-118; Pt. iii, pp. 280, pls. 119-207; Pt. iv, pp. 108, pls. 208-252; Pt. v, pp. 109-179, pls. 253-291, 1 map. Paris, 1834-37.

See Pls. 119, 120, 120 bis, 121, 170.
2nd ed. ? 8º, pp. 267, 94 pls. Paris, 1835.

BAGLIVI, G.—De terraemotu romano et urbium adjacentium anno 1703. Opera omnia medico-practico et anatomica.— ii, pp. 192-265. Lipsiae, 1828. [C.A.]

BARATTA, M.—Il terremoto laziale del 22 gennaio 1892.—Boll. Soc. Geol. Ital. xi, 1, pp. 36-62. Roma, 1892.

BARATTA, M.—Sulla distribuzione topografica dei terremoti in Italia durante il quinquennio 1887-91.—Atti Primo Congr. Geog. Ital. Genova, 18-25 sett. 1892. Mem. sez. scient. ii, Pt. 1, pp. 180-189, tav. v. Genova, 1894.

BARATTA, M.—Materiali per un catalogo dei fenomeni sismici avvenuti in Italia (1800-1872).—Mem. Soc. Geog. Ital. vii, Pt. 1, pp. 81-164. Roma, 1897.

BARATTA, M.—Saggio dei materiali per una storia dei fenomeni sismici avvenuti in Italia raccolti dal Prof. Michele Stefano de Rossi.—Boll. Soc. Geol. Ital. xviii, pp. 432-460. Roma, 1899.

BARATTA, M.—Il terremoto laziale del 19 luglio 1899.—Boll. Soc. Geog. Ital. S. 3, xii, pp. 359-361. Roma, 1899.

BARATTA, M.—I Terremoti d'Italia.— 8º, pp. 950, pls. Torino, 1901.
Gives, in Pt. iii, an extensive bibliography of the earthquakes of Italy.

BARBIERI, G.—I vulcani Cimino e Vulsinio.—Viterbo, 1877.

BARLOCCI, S.—Ricerche fisico-chimiche sul lago Sabatino, e sulle sorgenti di acque minerali che scaturiscono nei suoi contorni.—Roma, 1816.—Giorn. Arcad. Sci. xlvi, pp. 18-46. Roma, 1830.——3rd ed. Roma, 1843.

BARNARD.—See MAPEI, C.—Italy, Classical, Historical, and Picturesque.

BATTY, C. (del.).—Lago di Albano, [part of Pl.] 21, Aubert sc. Audot ed.
Fine engrav. : 109×82 mm.

BATTY (del.).—La Riccia. 120.—Audot ed. [Part of Pl. 120.]
Line engrav. : 117 × 80 mm.

BATTY, E. F.—Italian Scenery from Drawings made in 1817.—8°, *pp.* 197. *London*, 1820.

BELLEVUE, FLEURIAU DE. — Mémoire sur les cristaux microscopiques et en particulier sur la séméline, la mélilite, la pseudosommite et le selce-romano.—*Journ. Phys. Chim. et Hist. nat. li, pp.* 442–461. *Paris*, 1800.

BERTELLI, T.—Intorno ad un articolo dei periodici " Nature " e " Cosmos " sui moti microsismici di Rocca di Papa in ordine al terremoto di Aquila dell' 8 febbraio 1892.—*Atti. Acc. Pont. N. Lincei, xlv, pp.* 121–135. *Roma*, 1892.—*Moncalieri Oss. Boll. xii, pp.* 103–108, 117–119. 1892.

BERTELLI, T.—Di alcuni moti tromometrici osservati in Sicilia nelle eruzioni Etnee del 1883, 1886 e 1892 e di quella sottomarina della Pantelleria nell' ottobre 1891.—*Atti Acc. Pont. N. Lincei, xlvi, pp.* 17–24. *Roma*, 1893.

BLEICHER, M. G.—Essai d'une monographie géologique du Mont-Sacré.—*Bull. Soc. Hist. nat. Colmar, v, pp.* 147–160. *Colmar*, 1865.

BLEICHER, M. G.—Sur la géologie des environs de Rome.—*Bull. Soc. géol. France*, [S. 2, xxiii, pp.* 645–654. *Paris*, 1866.

BLEICHER, M. G.—Recherches géologiques faites dans les environs de Rome.—*Bull. Soc. Hist. nat. Colmar, vi, pp.* 65–99, *pl.* 1. *Colmar*, 1867.

BLEICHER.—*See* GUINARD.

BONWICK, J.—The Volcanic Rocks of Rome and Victoria compared.—*Trans. R. Soc. Victoria, vii, pp.* 149–165. *Melbourne*, 1866.

BORKOWSKY, S. DUNIN.—Geognostische Beobachtungen in der Gegend von Rom.—*Taschenb. gesammt. Min. x, pp.* 352–395. *Frankfurt-am-Main*, 1816.

BRANCO, W.—I Vulcani degli Ernici nella Valle del Sacco.—*Atti R. Acc. Lincei, S. 3, Trans. i, p.* 180. *Roma*, 1877.

BRANCO, W.—Die Vulkane des Herniker Landes bei Frosinone in Mittel-Italien.—*N. J. f. Min. pp.* 561–589, 1 *geol. map. Stuttgart*, 1877.

BREISLAK, SC.—Voyages physiques et lithologiques dans la Campanie, suivis d'une mémoire sur la constitution physique de Rome.—*Paris*, 1801.—In Germ. : 4°. *Vol. i, pp.* 300 + xvi, *pls.* 3 ; *Vol. ii, pp.* 324, *pls.* 3. *Leipzig*, 1802.

BROCCHI, G. B.—Sopra una sostanza fossile contenuta nella lava di Capo di Bove presso Roma.—*Giorn. Fis. Chim. e Stor. nat. dir. da L. Brugnatelli, S.* 1, vii, *pp.* 386–396. *Pavia*, 1814.—*Taschenb. gesammt. Min. ix, pp.* 126–134. 1815.

BROCCHI, G. B.—Catalogo Ragionato di una raccolta di rocce disposto con ordine geografico per servire alla geognosia dell' Italia.—8°, *pp. xl*+346. *Milano*, 1817.

BROCCHI, G. B.—Osservazioni sulla corrente di lava di Capo di Bove presso Roma e su quella delle Fratocchie sotto Albano.—*Bibl. Ital. Giorn. Lett. Sci. vii, pp.* 102–118. *Milano*, 1817.

BROCCHI, G. B.—Risposta a una lettera del sig. Riccioli intorno all' olivina della lava basaltina di Capo di Bove.—*Bibl. Ital. viii, pp.* 347–9. *Milano*, 1817.

BROCCHI, G. B.—Lettera intorno ad uno scavo interessante la geognosia, fatto in Roma a Campo Vaccino.—*Bibl. Ital. xiii, pp.* 114–5. *Milano*, 1819.

BROCCHI, G. B.—Dell' antica condizione della superficie del suolo di Roma.—*Roma*, 1820.

BROCCHI, G. B.—Sopra una particolare varietà di lazialite trovata in una lava di monte Vulture in Basilicata.—*Bibl. Ital. xvii, pp.* 261–265. *Milano*, 1820.

BROCCHI, G. B.—Dello stato fisico (geologico) del suolo di Roma e carta fisica geologica del medesimo.—*Roma*, 1820.

BROCCHI, G. B.—Dello stato fisico del suolo di Roma ad illustrazione della carta geognostica di questa città.—*Roma*, 1820.

BROCKEDON.—*See* MAPEI, C.—Italy, Classical, Historical, and Picturesque.

BRONGNIART, A.—On the freshwater formation of the environs of Rome. (Translation.)—*Phil. Mag. N.S. ii, pp.* 172–6. *London*, 1827.

BUCH, L. VON.—Geognostische Ueber-sicht der Gegend von Rom.—*Neue Schrift. Gesellsch. naturf. Freund. iii, pp.* 478-536. *Berlin,* 1801.

BYLANDT PALSTERCAMP, A. DE.—Théorie des Volcans.—3 vols. 8⁰. *Vol. i,foll. ii + pp.* 470; *Vol. ii, foll. ii + pp.* 438; *Vol. iii, foll. ii + pp.* 459. Atlas, 17 *pls., fol. Paris,* 1835.

CANCANI, A.—I rombi laziali del 16 febbraio 1900.—*Atti R. Acc. Lincei, S.* 5, *Rend. ix, sem.* 1, *pp.* 304-309. *Roma,* 1900.

CANCANI, A.—Terremoto laziale del 19 luglio 1899.—*Boll. Soc. Sismol. Ital. v,* 8, *pp.* 244-258, *tav. Modena,* 1900.

CAPPELLO, A.—Saggio sulla topografia fisica del suolo di Tivoli.—*Giorn. Arcad. Sci. xxiii, pp.* 137-158, 257-277. *Roma,* 1824.

CAPPELLO, A.—Riflessioni geologiche sugli avvenimenti recentemente accaduti nel corso dell' Aniene.—*Giorn. Arcad. Sci. xxxv, pp.* 261-295. *Roma,* 1827.——2ᵃ ed. *Opusc. Scelti Scient. Roma,* 1830.

CAPPELLO, A.—Réflexions géologiques sur les événemens arrivés récemment dans le cours de l'Anieno.—*Bull. Sci. nat. et Géol. p. l. Baron de Ferussac, xvi, pp.* 42-3. *Paris,* 1829.

CAPPELLO, A.—Ulteriori schiarimenti intorno il fiume Aniene presso Tivoli.—*Giorn. Arcad. Sci. lv, pp.* 89-125, 257-282. *Roma,* 1832.

CARLUCCI, C.—Sulle condizioni fisiche e stato civile della provincia romana.—*Relaz. espost. al consigl. super. d. sanità d. Roma. Roma,* 1876.

CARLYLE, REV. GAVIN.—*See* MAPEI, C. Italy, Illustrated, &c.

CARPI, P.—Lettera al Brocchi contenente nuove notizie sulla corrente di lava di Capo di Bove.—*Bibl. Ital. vii, pp.* 524-5. *Milano,* 1817.

CARPI, P.—Osservazioni chimico-minera-logiche sopra alcune sostanze che si trovano nella lava di Capo di Bove.—*Bibl. Ital. xxv, pp.* 302-5. *Milano,* 1822.—*Mem. Soc. Ital. Sci. Modena, xviii, pp.* 217-231. *Modena,* 1827.

CARPI, P.—Sopra un' antica corrente di lava scoperta nelle vicinanze di Roma.—*Giorn. Arcad. Sci. xli, pp.* 158-171, 2 *tab. Roma,* 1829.

CASORIA, E.—Studio analitico di alcune Lave e Pozzolane dell' Agro Romano.—*Ann. R. Scuola Agric. Portici, S.* 2, *vi,pp.* 1-10. *Portici,* 1905.

CASSINIC, G. M.—Carta generale dell' Italia divisa ne' suoi stati e provincie delineata sulle ultime osservazioni ed incisa dal P. D . . .—*fol. tav.* 26. *Roma, Presso la Calcografia Camerale,* MDCCXCIII. *See* Tav. 24 and 25.

CAVAZZI, A.—Analisi chimica completa della pozzolana di S. Paolo di Roma e della pozzolana delle maremme toscane.—*Bologna,* 1875.

CERMELLI, P. M.—Carte corografiche e memorie riguardanti le pietre, le miniere e i fossili, per servire alla storia naturale delle provincie del Patrimonio, Sabina, Lazio, Marittima, Campagna e dell' Agro Romano.—*fol. pls.* 4. *Napoli,* 1782.

CERULLI-IRELLI, S.—Escursione ai Monti Albani (21 settembre 1908).—*Boll. Soc. Geol. Ital. xxvii,* 4, *pp. cxxxvii-cxl. Roma,* 1909.

CESELLI, L.—Memoria geologica sopra i colli gianicolensi.—*Roma,* 1848.

CESELLI, L.—Esposizione descrittiva ed analitica su i minerali dei dintorni di Roma, e della quiritina nuovo minerale.—*Corrisp. scient. vii,* 30-31. *Roma,* 1866.

CESELLI, L.—Tavola topografica e clima-tologica di Roma e sua campagna.—*Roma,* 1875.

CESELLI, L.—Sui prodotti minerali utili della Provincia Romana.—*Giorn.* " *Il Popolo Romano,*" 246 e 248. *Roma,* 1877.—*La Giovane Roma,riv.econ.amministr. ecc. ii,* 17. *Roma,* 1877.

CHANAVARD, ARCH. A. M.—Vues d'Italie, de Sicile et d'Istrie.—*obl.* 4⁰, *pls.* 15. *Lyon,* 1861. *See* Pl. iv.

CHECCHIA, G.—Escursione geologica ai Colli Laziali.—*Boll. Nat. xix, pp.* 78-79. *Siena,* 1899.

CLEMENT-MULLER, J. J.—Documents historiques et géologiques sur le Lac d'Albano.—*Bull Soc. géol. France, S.* 2, *xi, pp.* 526-8. *Paris,* 1854.

CLERICI, E.—Sopra alcuni Fossili recentemente trovati nel tufo grigio di Peperino presso Roma.—*Boll. Soc. Geol. Ital. vi, pp.* 20–22. *Roma,* 1887.

CLERICI, E.—La Vitis vinifera, fossile nei dintorni di Roma.—*Boll. Soc. Geol. Ital. vi, pp.* 403–8. *Roma,* 1887.

CLERICI,E.—Il travertino di Fiano Romano. —*Boll. R. Com. Geol. Ital. xviii,* 3–4, *pp.* 99–121. *Roma,* 1887.

CLERICI, E.—Sopra i resti di Castoro finora rinvenuti nei dintorni di Roma.— *Boll. R. Com. Geol. Ital. xviii,* 9–10, *pp.* 278–284. *Roma,* 1887.

CLERICI, E.—Contribuzione alla flora dei tufi vulcanici della provincia di Roma. [1888.]—*Boll. Soc. Geol. Ital. vii, pp.* 413–415. *Roma,* 1888.

CLERICI, E.—Notizie intorno ai tufi vulcanici della Via Flaminia dalla Valle del Vescovo a Prima Porta.—*Atti R. Acc. Lincei, S.* 5, *Rend. iii, sem.* 1, *pp.* 89–97. *Roma,* 1894.

CLERICI, E.—Sulla origine dei tufi vulcanici al Nord di Roma.—*Atti R. Acc. Lincei, S.* 5, *Rend. iii, sem.* 1, *pp.* 407–415. *Roma,* 1894.

CLERICI, E.—Ancora sulla origine e sulla età dei tufi vulcanici al nord di Roma.— *Atti R. Acc. Lincei, S.* 5, *Rend. iii, sem.* 1, *pp.* 605–611. *Roma,* 1894.

CLERICI, E.—[Orvieto e sui blocchi di argilla marina contenuti nei materiali vulcanici sostenuti questa città.]—*Boll. Soc. Geol. Ital. xiv, pp.* 294–296. *Roma,* 1895.

CLERICI, E.—Per la storia del systema vulcanico Vulsinio.—[Bagnorea, Italy.]— *Atti R. Acc. Lincei, S.* 5, *Rend. iv, sem.* 1, *pp.* 219–226. *Roma,* 1895.

CLERICI, E.—La nave di Caligola affondata nel lago di Nemi e la geologia del suolo romano.—*Boll. Soc. Geol. Ital. xv,* 3, *pp.* 302–309. *Roma,* 1896.

CLERICI, E.—Contribuzione alla conoscenza dei capisaldi per la geologia dei dintorni di Roma.—*Atti R. Acc. Lincei, S.* 5, *Rend. x, sem.* 1, *pp.* 77–83. *Roma,* 1901.

CLERICI, E.—Sulla Stratigrafia del Vulcano Laziale.—*Atti R. Acc. Lincei, S.* 5, *Rend. xiii, sem.* 2, *pp.* 614–618. *Roma,* 1904.

CLUVERIUS, PHILIPPUS.—P. Cluverii Italia antiqua . . . Ejusdem Sicilia, Sardinia et Corsica . . . (Cum epistola dedicatoria

Danielis Heinsii).—3 Pts. in 2 Vols. *fol. Vol. i, pp.* 786; *Vol. ii, pp.* 787–1338+510, *portrait, maps and plans. Lugduni Batavorum,* 1624.

"Sicilia antiqua" is dated 1619 and has special title and pagination. [B.N.P.]

COHN, F.—Ueber die Entstehung des Travertin in den Wasserfällen von Tivoli.— *N. J. f. Min. pp.* 580–610. *Stuttgart,* 1864.

COIGNET, M.—Vues Pittoresques de l'Italie, dessinées d'après nature par . . . et lithographiées par . . . &c. &c. 6me livraison.—*fol., pls.* 36. *A Paris,* MDCCCXXV. [B.N.P., Ub. 45.]

COIGNET (del.).—Vue du Lac de Némi. Joly Lith.—Litho. de Langlume (4me Liv^re).
334 × 288 mm.

COIGNET (del.).—Vue du Lac de Némi. Joly Lith.—Litho. de Langlume.
Litho. on single paper: 335 × 288 mm.

COLLET-DESCOTILS, H. V.—Mémoire sur les Alunières de la Tolfa.—*Ann. Mines, i, pp.* 319–368. *Paris,* 1816.

COMITÉ D'ORGANISATION DU 2ME CONGRÈS GÉOLOGIQUE INTERNATIONAL À BOLOGNE, 1881.—Bibliographie Géologique et Paléontologique de l'Italie.—8°, *pp. viii*+630. *Bologne,* 1881.
See No. x. ZEZI, P.—La Campagne de Rome (1934–2206).

CONDAMINE, DE LA.—Extrait d'un journal de voyage en Italie.—*Hist. Acad. R. Sci. Mém. Math.* 1757, *pp.* 6–16. *Paris,* 1762.

CONTARINI, G. B.—Bibliografia geologica e paleontologica della provincia di Roma, pubblicata per cura del R. Ufficio Geologico.—8°, *pp.* 116. *Roma,* 1886.

COOK, H.—The Scenery of Central Italy drawn from Nature and on Stone.—*fol., pls.* 26. *Haymarket,* 1846.
See Pls. 9 and 10.

COOPER, R. (del. et sculp.).—View of the Campagna of Rome, taken from the Villa d'Este at Tivoli. Published as the Act directs by R. Cooper, and at J. Boydell's, London. [B.M. Portfolio of Rome.]
710 × 529 mm.

COOPER, Ric^r. ad vivum del. et sculp.— View of part of Tivoli and adjacent Hills 20 miles from Rome, taken from the Villa d'Este. Published as the Act directs, Feb. 1779, by R. Cooper, Great Russell Street, Bloomsbury, and J. Boydell, 90,

Cheapside, London. [B.M. Portfolio of Rome.]
699 × 525 mm.

COOPER, Ric⁺. ad vivum del⁺. et fec⁺.— View of Rome, with the adjacent Villas and Country, taken from the Villa Madama two miles distant from the City. Published as the Act directs by R. Cooper, No. 24, Edward Street, Cavendish Square, and at J. Boydell's, Cheapside, London. [B.M. Portfolio of Rome.]
712 × 528 mm.

CROS, Du (pin.).—Le Lac d'Albano. An outline engraving. Man, woman, sheep, goat, and dog in foreground :
347 × 241 mm.

DAINELLI, G.—Contemporaneità dei depositi vulcanici e glaciali in provincia di Roma.—*Atti R. Acc. Lincei, S. 5, Rend. xv, sem. 2, pp.* 797–801. *Roma,* 1906.

DAMOUR, A.—Nouvelles analyses et réunion de la Mélilite et de la Humboldtilite. —*Ann. Chim. Phys. S. 3, x, pp.* 59–66. *Paris,* 1844.

DAUBENY, C. G. B.—A Description of active and extinct Volcanos ; with remarks on their origin, their chemical phenomena, and the character of their products, as determined by the condition of the earth during the period of their formation.— 8⁰, *pp.* 466, *figs., maps* 2, *pl.* 1. *London,* 1826.—8⁰, *pp.* 743, *figs., maps* 10, *pls.* 4. *London,* 1848.

DAVIES, W.—The Pilgrimage of the Tiber, from its mouth to its source : with some account of its tributaries.—8⁰, *pp. xii + 346, 23 illustr. London,* 1873.

DEECKE, W.—Bemerkungen zur Entstehungsgeschichte und Gesteinskunde der Monti Cimini.—*N. J. f. Min. Beil.-Bd. vi, pp.* 205–240. *Stuttgart,* 1889.

DEECKE, W.—Italien.—8⁰, *pp. xii+514, maps, pl. and fig. Berlin,* 1898.

DEGLI ABBATI, Fr.—Del suolo fisico di Roma e suoi contorni, sua origine e trasformazione.—*Cosenza,* 1869.

DELTA (Pseud. for FORBES, J. D.).— On the cold Caves of the monte Testaccio at Rome.—*Edin. Journ. Sci. viii, pp.* 205–216. *Edinburgh,* 1828.

DELTA (Pseud. for FORBES, J. D.).— Observations on the style of buildings employed in Ancient Italy and the materials used in the city of Rome.—*Edin. Journ. Sci. ix, pp.* 30–48. *Edinburgh,* 1828.

DEMARCHI, L.—I prodotti minerali della provincia di Roma.—*Ann. Statist. S. 3, ii. Roma,* 1882.

DESCLOIZEAUX.—Note sur la détermination de la forme primitive de la Humboldtilite.—*Ann. Chim. Phys. S. 3, x, pp.* 69–72. *Paris,* 1844.

DESOR, P.J. E.—Compte rendu d'une excursion faite à une ancienne nécropole des Monts Albans, recouverte par un dépôt volcanique.—*Bull. Soc. Sci. Nat. xi, pp.* 134–141. *Neuchâtel,* 1877.

DIES, A. C., REINHART, Ch., MECHAN, J. —Collection de Vues Pittoresques de l'Italie dessinées d'après nature et gravées à l'eau forte à Rome par trois peintres allemands. Contenant lxxii planches. *Nuremberg,* MDCCIC.
See Pls. 43 and 44.

DIES, A. C., REINHART, C., MECHAN, J.—Collection ou Suite de Vues Pittoresques de l'Italie dessinées d'après nature et gravées à l'eau forte à Rome par trois peintres allemands. . . . Contenant lxxii planches. — *fol. Nuremberg,* MDCCLXXV.
See Pls. 25, 43, 44.

ESCHINARDI, F.—Descrizione di Roma e dell' Agro Romano.—*Roma,* 1750.

ESPIN, T. E.—The Volcanoes of Central Italy.—*Trans. Weardale Nat. F.C. i, pp.* 87–90. 1900.

FANTAPPIÈ, L.—Nuove osservazioni su minerali dei blocchi erratici nella Regione Cimina.—*Riv. Min. Crist. Ital. xviii, 1 and 2, pp.* 3–19. *Padova,* 1897.

FANTAPPIÈ, L.—Sopra alcuni blocchi erratici a granato ed idocrasio nella regione Cimina.—*Riv. Min. Crist. Ital. xx, 1–4, pp.* 14–19. *Padova,* 1898.

FANTAPPIÈ, L.—Su i projetti minerali vulcanici trovati nell'alti piano tufaceo occidentale dei Vulsinii da Farnese a San Quirico e Pitigliano.—*Atti R. Acc. Lincei, S. 5, Mem. ii, pp.* 546–575, *tav.* 3. *Roma,* 1898.

FANTAPPIÈ, L.—Contribuzioni allo studio dei Cimini.—*Atti R. Acc. Lincei, S. 5, Rend. xii, sem.* 1, *pp.* 443–451, 522–529 ; *sem.* 2, *pp.* 33–39. *Roma,* 1903.

FAUJAS DE ST.-FOND.—Essai de Géologie, ou Mémoires pour servir à l'histoire naturelle du globe.—8⁰, *Paris,* 1803–9. 3 tomes illustr.
See T. i, pp. 291–4, *and T. ii,* 2nd part.

FEA, C.—Varietà di notizie economiche fisiche antiquarie sopra Castel Gandolfo, Albano, Ariccia, Nemi, loro laghi ed emissarii.—8⁰. *Roma*, 1820.

FERBER, J. J.—Briefe aus Welschland über natürliche Merkwürdigkeiten dieses Landes. Traduz. del barone Dietrich.—*Prag*, 1773.

FISCHER, TH.—Das Halbinselland Italien. —*In Kirchhoff's* "Länderkunde von Europa," *pp.* 285-515. *Prag, Wien, Leipzig*, 1890.

FLEURIAU DE BELLEVUE. — See BELLEVUE, FLEURIAU DE.

FLOTTES, M. L.—Géologie des environs de Rome.—*Bull. Soc. Hist. nat. Toulouse, xiii, pp.* 252-4. *Toulouse*, 1879.

FODERA, O.—See MARCHI, L. DE. 1882.

FORBES, J. D.—Ueber die Vulcane Latiums.—1849.

FORBES, J. D.—On the volcanic formation of Monte Albano.—*Edinb. New Phil. Journ. xlviii, pp.* 360-2. *Edinburgh*, 1850. —[Extr.] *N. J. f. Min. xix, pp.* 466-7, *Stuttgart*, 1851.

FORBES, J. D.—See DELTA.

FORTIS, G. B.—Dei vulcani spenti della Maremma Romana.—*Venezia*, 1772.

FOUGEROUX DE BONDAROY, A. D.— Mémoire sur les Aluminières, Alumières ou Alunières de la Tolfa aux environs de Civita-Vecchia.—*Hist. Acad. Sci., An.* 1766, *pp.* 16-21. *Paris*, 1769.

FOUGEROUX DE BONDAROY, A. D.— Mémoire sur les solfatares des environs de Rome.—*Hist. Acad. Sci., An.* 1770, *pp.* 1-5. *Paris*, 1773.

FRANCO, P.—Ancora del Vesuvio ai tempi di Spartaco e di Strabone.—*Boll. Soc. Geol. Ital. xvii*, 1-2, *pp.* 76-80. *Roma*, 1898.

FUCHS, C. W. C.—Ueber die erlöschenen Vulcane in Mittel-Italien.—*Verhandl. Naturhist. Medic. Vereins zu Heidelberg, iii, pp.* 117-122. *Heidelberg*, 1862-63.

FUCHS, C. W. C.—Les Volcans et les Tremblements de Terre.—8⁰, *pp. viii* + 279, *fig. and map. Paris*, 1876.——2nd ed. 1878.

GARRUCCI, P.—On the Alban Necropolis said to have been covered by a Volcanic Eruption.—4⁰. — ? , 1879.

GATTI, A.—Discorso sull' Agro Romano e cenni economico-statistici sullo stato pontificio.—*Roma*, 1840.

GEIKIE, A.—Recent Studies of Old Italian Volcanoes.—"*Nature*," *lxiv, pp.* 103-106. *London*, 1901.

GEIKIE, A.—The Roman Campagna.— *International Quarterly, London, June* 1904. Landscape in History and other Essays.— *Ch. x, pp.* 308-352, 8⁰. *London*, 1905.

GELL, SIR W.—The Topography of Rome and its vicinity.—2 vols. 8⁰. *Vol. i, pp.* 456; *Vol. ii, pp.* 414, *map bound separately London*, 1834.

GENTILE, G.—Escursione geologica a San Polo dei Cavalieri (Roma).—*Boll. Nat. xix, pp.* 43-45. *Siena*, 1899.

GIORDANO, F.—Cenni sulle condizioni fisico-economiche di Roma e suo territorio. —8⁰. *Firenze*, 1871.

GIORDANO, F.—Cenni sulla costituzione geologica della Campagna Romana.—*Boll. R. Com. Geol. Ital. ii, pp.* 11-27. *Firenze*, 1871.

GIORDANO, F.—Condizioni topografiche e fisiche di Roma e Campagna Romana. (Monografia archeologica e statistica di Roma e della Campagna Romana.)— 8⁰. *Roma*, 1878.

GISMONDI, C.—Osservazioni sopra alcuni particolari minerali dei contorni di Roma. —*Bibl. Ital. Giorn. Sci. v. Milano*, 1817. —*Taschenb. gesammt. Min. xi*, 1, *pp.* 164-8. *Frankfurt am Main*, 1817.

GLANGEAUD, PH.—Les volcans du Latium et la Campagne Romaine (1900).—*Bull. Soc. géog. iii, pp.* 461-471. *Paris*, 1901.

GMELIN, L. — Observationes oryctognosticae et chimicae de Hauyna et de quibusdam fossilibus quae cùm hac concreta inveniuntur, praemissis animadversionibus geologicis de montibus Latii veteris.— *Heidelbergae*, 1814.—*Ann. Phil., or Mag. Chem. Min. etc. by T. Thomson, iv, pp.* 115-22, 193-9. *London*, 1814.—*Journ. Chem. u. Phys. v. I.S.C. Schweigger, xv, pp.* 1-42. *Nürnberg*, 1815.

GMELIN, L.—Carte géologique des environs d'Albano.—*Tubingen*, 1816.

GOSSELET, J.—Observations géologiques faites en Italie. (I. Vésuve, II. Champs Phlegréens, III. Etna, IV. Latium.)—*Mem. Soc. Imp. Sci. S.* 3, *vi, pp.* 417-475, 7 *pls. Lille*, 1869.

GRUNDMANN (del.).—Lago di Nemi, 120 bis., Aubert sc. Audot ed.
Fine line engrav. : 151 × 101 mm.

GUINARD & BLEICHER.—Note sur un gisement nouveau de Diatomacées dans le terrain quarternaire des environs de

Rome.—*Rev. Sci. nat. i, pp.* 315–319. *Montpellier and Paris,* 1872.

GUSSONE E TENORE.—3 articoli risguardanti le peregrinazioni fatte in alcuni luoghi del regno di Napoli. —?, 1838.

HACQUET, B.—Ueber Versteinerungen des ausgebrannten Vulkans bei Rom offenbar in dortigem Basalttuff.—*Leipzig,* 1780.

HAKEWILL, J.—A Picturesque Tour of Italy, from drawings made in 1816–1817. —*fol., pls.* 63, *with text. London,* 1820.

HARDING (del.). — Gensano. Aubert sc. [Part of Pl. 120], Audot ed. Fine line engrav. : 108 × 82 mm.

HARDING.—*See* MAPEI, C.—Italy, Classical, Historical, and Picturesque.

HESSENBERG, F.—Haüyn von Marino am Albanergebirge bei Rom.—*Min. Notiz. v. F. Hessenberg. N.F., v. Frankfurt-am-Main,* 1868. Pleonast, mit Hexaederflächen.—*Senckenberg. Naturf. Gesellsch. Abhandl. vii, pp.* 43–45. 1869–70.

HOFFMANN, F.—Ueber die Beschaffenheit des römischen Bodens, nebst einigen allgemeinen Betrachtungen über den geognostischen Charakter Italiens. — *Ann. Phys. u. Chem. xvi. pp.* 1–40. *Leipzig,* 1829. —*Edinb. Phil. Journ. iii, pp.* 76–98. *Edinburgh,* 1830.

HOFFMANN, F.—Auszüge aus Briefen des Hrn. Prof. . . .—*Archiv. f. Min. Geognos. &c. v. C. J. B. Karsten, iii, pp.* 361–412. *Berlin,* 1831.

HOFFMANN, F.—On the Scenery of Italy, as contrasted with that of Germany ; the Geognosy of Albano, near Rome, and the General Structure and Trachytic Rocks of Etna.—*Edinb. New Phil. Journ. xii, pp.* 370-7. *Edinburgh,* 1832. This is a transl. of most of the 1st letter of the foregoing.

HOFFMANN, F.—Geognostische Beobachtungen. Gesammelt auf einer Reise durch Italien und Sicilien, in den Jahren 1830 bis 1832.—*Archiv. f. Min., Geognos. &c. v. C. J. B. Karsten, xiii, pp.* 3–726, *pl.* 1, *map* 1. *Berlin,* 1839. [Sep. publ.] *Berlin,* 1839.

HULLMANDEL, C.—Twenty-four views of Italy drawn from Nature, and engraved upon stone.—*obl.-fol.* [*London*], 1818.

INDES (frère).—Sur la formation des tufs et sur une caverne à ossements des environs de Rome.—*Bull. Soc. géol. France, S.* 2,

xxvi, pp. 11–28. *Paris,* 1869.——2ᵉ éd. ·*Béthune,* 1875.

INDES (frère).—Sur la formation des tufs des environs de Rome.—*Bull. Soc. géol. France, S.* 2, *xxvii, pp.* 410–426. *Paris,* 1870.——2ᵉ éd. *Béthune,* 1875.

JACCOTEL, J.—*See* RONMY.

JERVIS, G.—The mineral resources of central Italy.—*London,* 1862.—Also *London,* 1868.

JERVIS, G.—I tesori sotterranei dell' Italia. Parte seconda : Regione dell'Appennino e vulcani attivi e spenti dipendentivi.—*Torino,* 1874.

JOHNSTON-LAVIS, H. J.—Viaggio scientifico alle regioni vulcaniche italiane nella ricorrenza del centenario del " Viaggio alle due Sicilie " di Lazzaro Spallanzani.—8°, *pp.* 1–10. *Naples,* 1889. This is the programme of the excursion of the English geologists who visited the South Italian volcanoes under the direction of the author. It is here included as it contains various new and unpublished observations.

JOUSSET, P.—L'Italie illustrée.—*fol., pp.* 370, *col. maps and plans* 14, *engrav. maps* 9, *pls.* 12, *photos* 784. *Paris,* 1829.

JUDD, J. W.—Contributions to the Study of Volcanos.—The Great Crater-lakes of Central Italy.—*Geol. Mag. Dec.* II, *ii, pp.* 348–356. *London,* 1875.

KARRER, F.—Der Boden der Hauptstädte Europa's, Rome.—*Wien,* 1881.

KELLER, F.—Contributo allo studio delle roccie magnetiche dei dintorni di Roma.—*Atti R. Acc. Lincei, S.* 4, *Rend. v, sem.* 1, *pp.* 519–526. *Roma,* 1889.

KELLER, F.—Guida itineraria delle principali rocce magnetiche del Lazio.—*Atti R. Acc. Lincei, S.* 4, *Rend. vi, sem.* 2, *pp.* 17–19. *Roma,* 1890.

KEPHALIDES.—Reise durch Italien und Sicilien.—2 vols., maps, 8°. *Leipsic,* 1818.

KIRCHER,A.—Latium. Id est,nova et parallela Latii tum veteris tum novi descriptio. —*pp.* 263, *maps, pls. Amstelodami,* 1671.

KLAPROTH, M. H.—Chemische Untersuchung des krystallisirten schwarzen Augits von Frascati.—*Journ. Chem. u. Phis. v. A. F. Gehlen, v, pp.* 199–202. *Berlin,* 1808.—*Ann. Chim. lxvii, pp.* 225–257. *Paris,* 1808.—*Journ. Nat. Phil. Chem. & Arts, by W. Nicholson, xxvii, pp.* 148–155, 225–231. *London,* 1810.

KLEIN, C.—Beiträge zur Kenntniss des Leucits.—*N. J. f. Min. ii, pp.* 234–6. *Stuttgart,* 1885.

KLEIN, C.—Optische Studien am Leucit.— *N. J. f. Min. Beil.-Bd. iii, pp.* 540–575. *Stuttgart,* 1885.

KLITSCHE DE LA GRANGE, A.—Sulla formazione di alcuni vulcanetti di fango nei dintorni di Civitavecchia.—*Roma,* 1880.

KLITSCHE DE LA GRANGE, A.—Eruzione nei vulcanetti di fango presso Civitavecchia durante il periodo sismico dell' isola d'Ischia.—*Bull. Vulc. Ital. xi. Roma,* 1884.

KLITSCHE DE LA GRANGE, A.—Sulla formazione dei tufi vulcanici nell' Agro Romano e nel Viterbese.—*Roma,* 1884.

KOBELL, I. VON.—Ueber den Spadaït, eine neue Mineralspecies und über den Wollastonit von Capo di Bove.—*Gelehrte Anzeig. herausg. v. Mitgliedern d. Königl. Bajerischen Akad. Wissensch. xvii, coll.* 945–950. *München,* 1843.—*Journ. prakt. Chem. xxx, pp.* 467–471. *Leipzig,* 1844.— *Giorn. Arcad. Sci. xcix, pp.* 162–4. *Roma,* 1844.—*Ann. Acc. Aspir. Nat. ii, pp.* 177–180. *Napoli,* 1844.

LACROIX, A. F. A.—Etude sur le Métamorphisme de contact des roches volcaniques. —4°, *pp.* 88. *Paris,* 1894.

LALANDE, DE LA.—Voyage en Italie, contenant l'Histoire et les Anecdotes les plus singulières de l'Italie, etc.—*Paris,* 1779.——2nd ed., 9 *vols. atlas,* 12°. *Paris,* 1786. *See pp.* 364–375.

LAPI, G. G.—Lezione accademica intorno l'origine dei due Laghi Albano e Nemorense.—4°. *Roma,* 1781.

LARTET, ED.—Sur les débris fossiles de divers Eléphants découverts aux environs de Rome.—*Bull. Soc. géol. France, S.* 2, *xv, pp.* 564–569. *Paris,* 1857–58.

LEAR, E.—Views in Rome and its Environs ; Drawn from Nature and on Stone by Edward Lear.—*fol., pls.* 25. [*London*], 1841.

LEITCH.—*See* MAPEI, C.—Italy, Classical, Historical, and Picturesque.

LOCCHI, ING. D.—Roma e dintorni.— *Pub. G. B. Paravia e C., Torino, Roma, Milano, Firenze, Napoli,* 1876.

1 : 100,000. Raised map, coloured, in two ed.—1st, physical and political ; 2nd, geological (Alban Hills).

LUDWIG, R.—Geologische Bilder aus Italien. —*Bull. Soc. Imp. Naturalistes,* 1874, *pp.* 42–131. *Moscou,* 1874.

MANTOVANI, P.—L'epoca diluviale nella Campagna, osservazioni geologiche e paleontologiche risguardanti le vallate del Tevere e dello Aniene.—*Boll. naut. e geog. xx,* 4. *Roma,* 1867.

MANTOVANI, P.—Osservazioni geologiche sul terreno pliocenico della campagna romana.—*Corrisp. scient. vii,* 39. *Roma,* 1867.

MANTOVANI, P.—Descrizione mineralogica dei Vulcani Laziali.—8°, *pp.* 87. *Roma,* 1868.

MANTOVANI, P.—*See* VERNEUIL, E. DE. 1872.

MANTOVANI, P.—Descrizione geologica della Campagna Romana.—*Large col. map and pls.* 4. *Torino,* 1874.—*Roma,* 1875.

MANTOVANI, P.—Escursione fatta dalla sezione romana del Club Alpino Italiano al Monte Pila nell'aprile 1876.—*Corrisp. scient. viii,* 29. *Roma,* 1876.

MANTOVANI, P.—Is Man tertiary ? The antiquity of Man in the Roman Country.— *Geol. Mag. iv, pp.* 433–9. 1877.

MANTOVANI, P.—Descrizione geologica dei Monti Laziali.—*Ann. R. Liceo E. Q. Visconti,* 1876–77. *Roma,* 1878.

MANTOVANI, P.—Uno sguardo alla costituzione geologica del suolo Romano.— *Monograf. Archeolog. Statist. Roma e Campagna Romana. Roma,* 1878.

MANTOVANI, P.—Descrizione geologica della Campagna Romana.—2a ed. 8°, *pp.* 115, *map. Torino,* 1884.

MANZONI, A.—Intorno alle ultime pubblicazioni del Prof. Ponzi sui terreni pliocenici delle Colline di Roma, e specialmente intorno ad una così detta Fauna Vaticana.—*Boll. R. Com. Geol. Ital. vi, pp.* 368–371. *Roma,* 1875.

MAPEI, C.—Italy, Classical, Historical and Picturesque. Illustrated in a series of views from drawings by Stanfield, R.A., Roberts, R.A., Harding, Prout, Leitch, Brockedon, Barnard, &c. &c., with descriptions of the scenes. Preceded by an Introductory Essay, on the recent history and present conditions of Italy and the

Italians.—fol., pp. cviii + 164, pls. 163. London, 1859.——2nd ed., pp. viii+cxlvi, pls. 65. 1864. See p. 97 (1st ed.).

MAPEI, C.—Italy, Illustrated and Described, in a series of views, from drawings by Stanfield, R.A., Harding, Prout, Leitch, Brockedon, Barnard, &c., &c. With Descriptions of the scenes, and an introductory essay, on the political, religious, and moral state of Italy. And a sketch of the History and Progress of Italy during the last fifteen years (1847-62), in continuation of Dr. Mapei's essay, by the Rev. Gavin Carlyle, M.A.—4°, pp. viii + cxlvi+ 168, pls. 65. London, 1864.

MARCHI, L. DE.—I prodotti minerali della provincia di Roma.—Ann. Statist. S. 3, ii, 1883.—Journ. Soc. Arts, xxx, pp. 398, 556. 1881.

MARCHI, L. DE, and FODERA, O.—Notes on the Production of Puzzolana in the Provinces of Rome and Naples.—Eng. & Min. Journ. xxxiv, p. 45. 1882.

MARTINORI, E.—I vulcani laziali.—Rassegna di alpinismo, ii, 9. Rocca S. Casciano, Firenze, 1880.

MAURO, FR.—Ricerche chimiche sulle lave di Montecompatri, del Tuscolo, di Villa Lancellotti e di Monte Pila.—Atti R. Acc. Lincei, S. 3, Trans. iv, pp. 226-230. Roma, 1880.

MAZEAS, L'ABBÉ.—Mémoire sur les solfatares des environs de Rome ; sur l'origine et la formation du vitriol romain. —Mém. Math. Phys. présent. Acad. R. Sci. v, pp. 319-330. Paris, 1768.

MECHAN, J.—See DIES, A. C.

MEDICI SPADA, L. DE.—Sopra alcune specie minerali non in prima osservate nello Stato Pontificio.—Racc. lett. ecc. int. Fis. & Mat. d. C. Palomba, i, pp. 114-120. Roma, 1845.

MEDICI SPADA, L. DE, e PONZI, G.—Profilo teorico dimostrante la disposizione dei terreni della Campagna Romana. —Roma, 1845.

MELI, R.—Notizie ed osservazioni sui Resti Organici rinvenuti nei tufi leucitici della provincia di Roma.—Boll. R. Com. Geol. Ital. S. 2, ii, 9-10, pp. 428-457. Roma, 1881 ; iii, pp. 260-280, 358-368. 3 photographic plates. 1882.

MELI, R.—Rinvenimenti di Ossa fossili nei dintorni di Roma.—Boll. R. Com. Geol.

Ital. S. 2, ii, 11-12, pp. 580-582. Roma, 1881.

MELI, R.—Ulteriori notizie ed osservazioni sui Resti Fossili rinvenuti nei tufi vulcanici della provincia di Roma.—Boll. R. Com. Geol. Ital. xiii, 9-10, pp. 260-280, e 11-12, pp. 358-366. Roma, 1882. See Tav. 1-3 and 7.

MELI, R.—Bibliografia riguardante le acque potabili e minerali della Provincia di Roma.—8°, pp. 108. Roma, 1885.

MELI, R.—Sopra i Resti Fossili di un grande Avvoltoio (Gyps) racchiuso nei peperini Laziali.—Boll. Soc. Geol. Ital. viii, 3, pp. 490-544. Roma, 1889.

MELI, R.—Sul rinvenimento dei resti fossili di un grande avoltoio, racchiuso nel peperino Laziale.—Boll. Soc. Geol. Ital. viii, 3, pp. 562-4. Roma, 1889.

MELI, R.—Elenco bibliografico delle più importanti pubblicazioni in cui trovasi fatta parola dei Manufatti e specialmente delle Terrecotte rinvenute nelle Deiezioni Vulcaniche de Lazio.—8°, pp. 32. Roma, 1890.

MELI, R.—Notizie bibliografiche sulle rocce magnetiche dei dintorni di Roma.—Boll. Soc. Geol. Ital. ix, pp. 609-670. Roma, 1891.

MELI, R.—Relazione sommaria delle escursioni geologiche eseguite con gli allievi della R. Scuola d'applicazione per gli ingegneri di Roma nell'anno scolastico 1894-95 al Monte Soratte e nel Viterbese (prov. di Roma).—Ann. R. Scuola Roma 1895-96. Roma, 1895.

MELI, R.—Alcune Notizie di Geologia riguardanti la Provincia di Roma.—Boll. Soc. Geol. Ital. xv, pp. 281-287. 1896.

MELI, R.—Un minerale nuovo per i dintorni di Roma. Atacamite riscontrata nella lava leucitica di Capo di Bove presso Roma.—Riv. Ital. Sci. Nat. xviii, 3-4, pp. 25-27. Siena, 1898.

MELI, R.—Sulla corrente di Lava Leucitica (Leucitite) di Lunghezza presso Roma.— Boll. Soc. Geol. Ital. xxvii, pp. 485-490. Roma, 1908.

MELI, R.—Intorno l'origine dei due Laghi Albano e Nemorense.—Ristampa di una dissertazione scritta nel 1758 dal dott. Giovanni Girolamo Lapi, romano, con indicazioni dei naturalisti che nella seconda metà del secolo XVIII. parlarono dei

Monti vulcanici dell'antico Lazio.—*Boll. Soc. Geol. Ital. xxx, 4, pp.* 981–1006. *Roma,* 1912.

MERCALLI, G.—Vulcani e fenomeni vulcanici in Italia.—8⁰, *pp.* 376, *pls.* 13. *Milan,* 1882.

MERCALLI, G.—Osservazioni petrografico-geologiche sui Vulcani Cimini.—*Rend. R. Ist. Lomb. S.* 2, *xxii, pp.* 139–147. *Milano,* 1889.

MERCALLI, G.—Contribuzione allo studio geologico dei vulcani viterbesi.—*Mem. Acc. Pont. N. Lincei, xx, pp.* 301–334. *Roma,* 1903.

MERCATOREM GERARDUM. — Italiæ, Sclavoniæ et Græciæ tabule geographice.—*fol., col. maps* 23. *Duysburgi,* 1589.

MICHALLON (del.)—Lac d'Albano. Villeneuve, Lith. Imp. Lith. de Villain. Chez Hilaire Sazerac, Passage de l'Opéra. Lith. on straw-col. film : 208×190 mm.

MICHALLON (pinxt.).—Vue de Frascati. Marchais delt. Desaulx sculp. Liv. 7ᵐᵉ. Pl. 28. Déposé. Engraving : 222 × 210 mm.

MILLOSEVICH, F.—Di alcuni giacimenti di alunogeno in provincia di Roma.—*Boll. Soc. Geol. Ital. xx,* 2, *pp.* 263–270. *Roma,* 1901.

MODERNI, P.—Rocche eruttive dei Vulcani Sabatini.—*Boll. R. Com. Geol. Ital. xxvii,* 1 *& 2, pp.* 57–112, 129–160, *tab. Roma,* 1896.

MODERNI, P.—Contribuzione allo studio geologico dei Vulcani Vulsini.—*Boll. R. Com. Geol. Ital. xxxiv,* 2, *pp.* 121–147 ; 3, *pp.* 177–244, *tav.* 5 ; 4, *pp.* 333–375 ; *e xxxv,* 1, *pp.* 22–72, *tav.* ; 2, *pp.* 198–230, *tav.* 2 ; 3, *pp.* 253–262. *Roma,* 1904.

MODERNI, P.—Carta geologica dei Vulcani Vulsini, nella scala di 1 per 100,000 (un foglio a colori).—*Roma,* 1904.

MODERNI, P.—Alcune osservazioni geologiche sul Vulcano Laziali e specialmente sul Monte Cavo.—*Atti R. Acc. Lincei, S.* 5, *Rend. xv, sem.* 1, *pp.* 462–469. *Roma,* 1906.

MOROZZO, C. L. Dɪ.—Sopra i denti fossili di un Elefante trovato nelle vicinanze di Roma (1802) ed analisi chimica di un dente fossile fatta dal dott. Morecchini.—*Mem. Soc. Ital. Sci. x, p.* 1. *Modena,* 1803.

MORTILLET, G. Dᴇ.—Géologie des environs de Rome.—*Atti Soc. Ital. Sci. Nat. vi, pp.* 530–8. *Milano,* 1864.

MORTILLET, G. Dᴇ.—[Sur l'âge des tufs volcaniques de la Campagne de Rome.]—*Bull. Soc. géol. France, S.* 2, *xxii, p.* 69. *Paris,* 1865.

MURCHISON, R. J.—Ueber die älteren vulkanischen Gebilde im Kirchenstaate, und über die Spalten welchen in Toscana heisse Dämpfe entsteigen und deren Beziehung zu alten Eruptions- und Bruche-Linien.—*Stuttgart,* 1851.—In Eng.: *Quart. Journ. Geol. Soc. vi, pp.* 281–310. 1858.

NECKER-DE-SAUSSURE, L. A.—Note sur la Gismondine de Carpi, et sur un nouveau minéral (Berzéline) des environs de Rome.—*Bibl. Univ. Sci. S.* 1, *xlvi, pp.* 52–9. *Genève, Paris,* 1831.

NEUMAYR, M. — Erdgeschichte. — *Allgemeine Naturkunde, i, pp.* 42 + *xii* + 653, very num. illustr. *Leipzig,* 1886.

NUVOLI, I.—Topografia medico-statistica di Viterbo e triennio clinico.—*Viterbo,* 1866.

OMALIUS D'HALLOY, J. B. F.—Note sur l'existence du calcaire d'eau douce dans les départements de Rome et de l'Ombrone et dans le royaume de Würtemberg.—*Journ. Mines, xxxii, pp.* 401–410. *Paris,* 1812.

OMBONI, G. — Geologia dell'Italia. — 8⁰. *Milano,* 1869.

ORIOLI, F.—[Ragguagli e riflessioni su di un singolar vulcano acquoso malamente creduto dai più il Vadimone etrusco.]—*Bibl. Ital. xii, p.* 430. *Milano,* 1818.

ORIOLI, F.—Sul vero sito dell'antico Lago di Vadimone.—*Bibl. Ital. xiv, pp.* 35–44. *Milano,* 1819.

PARETO, L.—Memoria sulla costituzione geognostica del paese di Viterbo e delle vicinanze di Roma.—*Atti 4a. Riun. Sci. Ital.* (1842). *Padova,* 1843.

PARETO, L.—Osservazioni geologiche dal Monte Amiata a Roma.—*Giorn. Arcad. Sci. c, pp.* 3–53, *pl.* 2. *Roma,* 1844.

PARETO, L.—Della posizione delle roccie pirogene ed eruttive dei periodi terziario quaternario ed attuale in Italia.—8⁰, *pp.* 35. *Genova,* 1852.

PARRAVANO, N.—Contributo allo studio chimico dei pirosseni della provincia di Roma.—*Atti R. Acc. Lincei, S.* 5, *Rend. xxi, sem.* 2, *pp.* 469–471. *Roma,* 1912.

PARRAVANO, N.—Sulla composizione chimica della Haüynite dei Colli Albani.—*Atti R. Acc. Lincei, S.* 5, *Rend. xxi, sem.* 2, *pp.* 631–633. *Roma,* 1912.

PELLATI, N.—I travertini della Campagna Romana.—*Boll. R. Com. Geol. Ital. S.* 2, *iii, pp.* 196–221, *map. Roma,* 1882.—*Ing. Civ. Arti Industr. ix,* 1882.
See Tav. vi.

PENTLAND, G. B.—On the geology of the country about Rome.—*London,* 1859.

PERREAU, L.—Il sottosuolo dell' Agro Romano.—" *Il Popolo Romano,*" *xii,* 339. *Roma,* 1884.

PETRINI.—Gabinetto mineralogico del Collegio Nazzareno.—*Roma,* 1791.

PICCINI, A.—Analisi di un' Augite del Lazio delle vicinanze di Roma.—*Atti R. Acc. Lincei, S.* 3, *Trans. iv, pp.* 224–6. *Roma,* 1880.

PILLA, L.—Osservazioni geognostiche che possonsi fare lungo la strada da Napoli a Vienna attraversando lo Stato Romano, la Toscana, lo Stato Veneto, la Carintia, la Stiria ed Austria.—*Napoli,* 1834.

PIRANESI (del.).—Via Appia e sepolcro di Pompeo. [Part of Pl.] 121. Aubert sc. Audot edit.
Fine line engrav. : 109 × 82 mm.

PONZI, G.—*See* MEDICI SPADA, L. DE. 1845.

PONZI, G.—Mémoire sur la zone volcanique d'Italie.—*Bull. Soc. géol. France, S.* 2, *vii, pp.* 455–469, *pl.* 1. *Paris,* 1850.

PONZI, G.—Carta geologica della Valle latina da Roma a Monte Cassino.—*Roma,* 1850.

PONZI, G.—Storia fisica del bacino di Roma. —Memoria da servire di appendice all' opera il suolo fisico di Roma.—*Ann. Sci. Nat. Fis. i, pp.* 281–302. *Roma,* 1850.

PONZI, G.—Osservazioni geologiche fatte lungo la Valle Latina da Roma a Monte Cassino.—*Atti Acc. Pont. N. Lincei, i* (1847–48), *pp.* 182–193. *Roma,* 1851.

PONZI, G.—Sulle correnti di lava e sopra un nuovo cratere vulcanico nelle vicinanze di Roma.—*Atti Acc. Pont. N. Lincei, iv, pp.* 116–121. *Roma,* 1852.

PONZI, G.—Descrizione della carta geologica della provincia di Viterbo.—*Atti. Acc. Pont. N. Lincei, iv, pp.* 153–164. *Roma,* 1852.

PONZI, G.—Sulla Valle Latina. Appendice alla memoria pubblicata nella sessione xvii del 31 dicembre 1848 (anno I.).—*Atti Acc. Pont. N. Lincei, iv, pp.* 612–615. *Roma,* 1852.

PONZI, G.—Sopra un nuovo cono vulcanico rinvenuto nella Valle di Cona.—*Atti Acc. Pont. N. Lincei, v, pp.* 263–7. *Roma,* 1852.

PONZI, G.—Descrizione della Carta geologica della Cormaca di Roma.—*Atti Acc. Pont. N. Lincei, vi, p.* 125. *Roma,* 1855.

PONZI, G.—Sui terremoti avvenuti in Frascati nei mesi di maggio e giugno 1855. —*Atti Acc. Pont. N. Lincei, vi, pp.* 230–6. *Roma,* 1855.

PONZI, G.—Sulla eruzione solforosa avvenuta nei giorni 28, 29, 30 ottobre [1856], sotto il paese di Leprignano, nella contrada denominata il Lagopuzzo.—*Atti Acc. Pont N. Lincei, x, pp.* 71–7. *Roma,* 1856.

PONZI, G.—Rinvenimento dei vulcani spenti degli Ernici nella valle Latina.—*Atti Acc. Pont. N. Lincei, xi, pp.* 61–2. *Roma,* 1857.

PONZI, G.—Sull'origine dell'Alluminite e Caolino della Tolfa.—*Atti Acc. Pont. N. Lincei, xi, pp.* 339–343. *Roma,* 1857.

PONZI, G.—Nota sulla carta geologica della provincia di Frosinone e Velletri.—*Atti Acc. Pont. N. Lincei, xi, p.* 441. *Roma,* 1857.

PONZI, G.—Sur les diverses zones de la formation pliocène des environs de Rome. —*Bull. Soc. géol. France, S.* 2, *xv, pp.* 555–561. *Paris,* 1858.

PONZI, G.—Sullo stato fisico del suolo di Roma.—*Giorn. Arcad. Sci. N.S. ix, pp.* 28–49. *Roma,* 1858.

PONZI, G.—Storia naturale del Lazio.—*Giorn. Arcad. Sci. N.S. xii, pp.* 104–143. *Roma,* 1858.

PONZI, G.—Sulle correnti di lava scoperte dal taglio della ferrovia di Albano.—*Atti Acc. Pont. N. Lincei, xii, pp.* 113–117. *Roma,* 1859.

PONZI, G.—Carta geologica e montanistica dei monti di Allumiere e di Tolfa, &c.—*Atti Acc. Pont. N. Lincei, xiii, p.* 432. *Roma,* 1860.

PONZI, G.—Storia geologica del Tevere.—*Giorn. Arcad. Sci. N.S. xviii, pp.* 129–149. *Roma,* 1860.

PONZI, G.—Sul sistema degli Appennini.— *Giorn. Arcad. Sci. N.S. xxiii, pp.* 110–138. *Roma,* 1861.

PONZI, G.—Catalogo ragionato di una collezione di materiali da costruzione e di marmi da decorazioni dello Stato Pontificio.—*Roma,* 1862.

PONZI, G.—Osservazioni geologiche sui Vulcani Sabatini.—*Atti Acc. Pont. N. Lincei, xvi, pp.* 845–852. *Roma,* 1863.

PONZI, G.—Sui diversi periodi eruttivi determinati nell'Italia centrale.—*Atti Acc. Pont. N. Lincei, xvii, pp.* 133–163. *Roma,* 1864.

PONZI, G.—Quadro geologico dell'Italia centrale.—*Atti Acc. Pont. N. Lincei, xix, pp.* 107–8. *Roma,* 1866.

PONZI, G.—Storia fisica del bacino di Roma. —*Atti Acc. Pont. N. Lincei, ii* (1849), *pp.* 27–44. *Roma.* (*reprint* 1867.) [B.M.—N.H.]

PONZI, G.—Sopra un nuovo ordinamento geologico dei terreni subappennini.—*Atti Soc. Ital. Sci. Nat. xi, pp* 181–192. *Milano,* 1868.

PONZI, G.—Le volcanisme romain. Remarques sur les observations géologiques faites en Italie par M. Gosselet.—*Bull. Soc. géol. France, S.* 2, *xxvi, pp.* 903–912. *Paris,* 1869.

PONZI, G.—See ROSSI, M. S. DE, 1870.

PONZI, G.—Storia fisica dell'Italia Centrale. —*Atti R. Acc. Lincei, xxiv, pp.* 191–224. *Roma,* 1871.

PONZI, G.—Sulle oscillazioni sismiche diluviali.—*Atti R. Acc. Lincei, xxiv, pp.* 253–8. *Roma,* 1871.

PONZI, G.—Les relations de l'homme préhistorique avec les phénomènes géologiques de l'Italie centrale.—*Compt. Rend. Congr. internat. anthropol. etc.,* 1871, *Sess. v. Bologne,* 1873.

PONZI, G.—Del bacino di Roma e della sua natura.—*Ann. Minist. Agr. Ind. e Comm. Firenze-Genova,* 1872.

PONZI, G.—Carta geologica del bacino di Roma.—*Boll. Soc. Geog. Ital. viii, pp.* 26–52, *map. Roma,* 1872.

PONZI, G.—Il bacino di Roma. (In the collection entitled : Studi sulla geografia naturale e civile d'Italia.)—*Roma,* 1875.

PONZI, G.—Cronaca subappennina od abbozzo di un quadro generale del periodo glaciale.—*Atti* XI. *Congr. Sci. Ital.* 1873. *Roma,* 1875.

PONZI, G.—L'Italia e gli Appennini.—In " Studi sulla geografia naturale e civile d'Italia."—*Roma,* 1875.

PONZI, G.—Storia dei Vulcani Laziali.— *Atti R. Acc. Lincei, S.* 2, *i, pp.* 26–42, 1 *map. Roma,* 1875.

PONZI, G.—Dei Monti Mario e Vaticano e del loro sollevamento.—*Atti R. Acc. Lincei, S.* 2, *ii, pp.* 545–556, *pls.* 2. *Roma,* 1875.

PONZI, G.—Panorama della catena Lepino-Pontina visto dalla città di Anagni.—*Boll. Club Alp. Ital. ix. Torino,* 1876.

PONZI, G.—La Tuscia Romana e la Tolfa.— *Atti R. Acc. Lincei, S.* 3, *Mem. i, disp.* 2, *pp.* 875–928, 1 *map. Roma,* 1877.

PONZI, G.—Sulle epoche del vulcanismo italiano.—*Atti R. Acc. Lincei, S.* 3, *Trans. ii,* 1, *pp.* 35–7. *Roma,* 1878.

PONZI, G.—Le Ossa Fossili subappennine dei dintorni di Roma.—*Atti R. Acc. Lincei, S.* 3, *Mem. ii, disp.* 2, *pp.* 709–736. *Roma,* 1878.

PONZI, G.—Le Acque del bacino di Roma.— *Riv. Agr. Rom. Roma, Luglio,* 1879.

PONZI, G.—I terremoti delle epoche subappennine.—*Boll. R. Com. Geol. Ital. S.* 2, *i, pp.* 175–183. *Roma,* 1880.

PONZI, G.—I tufi della Tuscia Romana, loro origine, diffusione ed età.—*Boll. R. Com. Geol. Ital. S.* 2, *ii, pp.* 251–2. *Roma,* 1881.

PONZI, G.—I tufi vulcanici della Tuscia Romana.—*Atti R. Acc. Lincei, S.* 3, *Mem. ix, pp.* 17–30. *Roma,* 1881.

PONZI, G.—Sui tufi vulcanici della Tuscia Romana a fine di togliere qualunque discordanza di opinione emessa sulla loro origine, diffusione ed età.—*Atti R. Acc. Lincei, S.* 3, *Trans. v, p.* 132. *Roma,* 1881.

PONZI, G.—Intorno alla Sezione geologica scoperta al Tavolato sulla via Appia-nuova, nella costruzione del Tramway per Marino, con una nota dell'ing. R. Meli, sulle fenditure delle mura del Panteon.—*Atti R. Acc. Lincei, S.* 3, *Mem. xiii, pp.* 10–18. *Roma,* 1882.

PONZI, G.—Sulle ossa fossili rinvenute nella cava dei tufi vulcanici della Sedia del Diavolo sulla via Nomentana presso Roma. —*Boll. R. Com. Geol. Ital. S.* 2, *iv,* 3–4, *pp.* 91–3. *Roma,* 1883.

PONZI, G.—Del bacino di Roma e della sua Natura ; per servire d'illustrazione alla Carta geologica dell'Agro Romano.—8°, pp. 35. Roma, 1884.

PONZI, G.—Conglomerato del Tavolato ; Pozzo artesiano nella lava di Capo di Bove ; Storia dei Vulcani Laziali accresciuta e corretta.—Atti R. Acc. Lincei, S. 4, Mem. i, pp. 349-365. Roma, 1885.—Rend. id., pp. 319-320. 1885.

PONZI, G.—Contribuzione alla geologia dei Vulcani Laziali sul cratere tuscolano.—Atti R. Acc. Lincei, S. 4, Rend. i, pp. 772-3. Roma, 1885.

PONZI, G., e MELI, R.—Molluschi fossili del Monte Mario presso Roma.—Atti R. Acc. Lincei, S. 4, Mem. iii, pp. 672-698, 1 pl. Roma, 1886.

PORTIS, A.—Contribuzione alla storia fisica del bacino di Roma, e studi sopra l'estensione da darsi al Pliocene superiore.—Torino, 1893.

PROCACCINI RICCI, V.—Viaggi ai vulcani spenti d'Italia nello Stato Romano verso il Mediterraneo.—2 Pts. 4°. Firenze, 1814, 1821-24.

PROCACCINI RICCI, V.—Descrizione metodica di alquanti prodotti dei vulcani spenti nello Stato Romano.—8°. Firenze, 1820.

PROUT.—See MAPEI, C.—Italy, Classical, Historical, and Picturesque.

RATH, J. J. G. VOM.—Mineralogisch-geognostische Fragmente aus Italien. I. Rom und die Römische Campagna. II. Das Albaner-Gebirge. III. Die Gegend von Bracciano und Viterbo. IV. Das Bergland von Tolfa. V. Monte di Cuma, Ischia, Pianura.—Zeitschr. deutsch. geol. Gesellsch. xviii, pp. 487-642. Berlin, 1866.

RATH, J. J. G. VOM.—Geognostisch-mineralogische Fragmente aus Italien. VI. Die Umgebungen des Bolsener Sees.—Id. xx, pp. 265-307. Berlin, 1868.

RATTI, F.—Sul laghetto di recente formatosi nelle vicinanze di Leprignano.—Corrisp. scient. v, 8. Roma, 1857.

RECLUS, E.—Les Volcans de la Terre.—Soc. Astronom. Bruxelles, 1906.

REINHART, CH.—See DIES, A. C.

RICCIARDI, L.—Ricerche chimiche sulle rocce vulcaniche dei dintorni di Viterbo.—Atti Soc. Ital. Sci. Nat. xxviii, pp. 127-131. Milano, 1886.

RICCIARDI, L.—Genesi e successione delle rocce eruttive.—Atti Soc. Ital. Sci. Nat. xxx, 3, pp. 212-237. Milano, 1887.

RICCIARDI, L.—Sull'allineamento dei vulcani italiani. . . . Sul graduale passaggio delle roccie acide alle roccie basiche. Sullo sviluppo dell' acido cloridrico dell' anidride solforosa e del jodio dai vulcani.—8°, pp. 1-45. Reggio-Emilia, 1887.

RICCIARDI, L.—Ricerche di chimica vulcanologica sulle rocce dei Vulcani Vulsinii.—Gazz. Chim. Ital. xviii, pp. 268-288. Palermo, 1888.

RICCIARDI, L.—Genesi e Composizione Chimica dei Terreni Vulcanici Italiani.—8°, pp. 155. Firenze, 1889.

RICCIOLI.—Lettera al Sig. Brocchi intorno all'Olivina della lava basaltina di Capo di Bove.—Bibl. Ital. viii, p. 347. Milano, 1817.

RIGACCI, C.—L'origine atmosferica dei Tufi vulcanici della Campagna Romana trovata dall'Abate Carlo Rusconi il di 11 novembre 1864.—Roma, 1865.

RIZZO, G. B.—Sulle emanazioni vulcaniche dell'età presente nella Campagna Romana.—Atti R. Acc. Sci. Torino, xxxiii, disp. 1, pp. 48-54. Torino, 1897.

ROBERTS, R. A.—See MAPEI, C.—Italy, Classical, Historical, and Picturesque.

RODRIGUEZ, J. S.—Note sulle rocce vulcaniche e principalmente su i Tufi dei dintorni immediati di Roma.—4°, pp. 18, pls. 4. Roma, 1893.

RONMY (pinxt.).—Vue près du Lac d'Albano. Des Religieux administrent l'Aqua Santa à une jeune fille malade. Arnout del. 1824. Bonnemaison dirext.—Litho. on tinted film : 244 × 227 mm.

RONMY (pinxt.), JACCOTEL, J. (delt.).—Vue du Lac Némi.—Bonnemaison direxit. Imp. Lith. de Villain. Lith. lightly tinted. Horses, camp, and soldiers in foreground ; ab. 1824 : 321 × 215 mm.

ROSATI, A.—Contributo allo Studio petrografico del Vulcano Laziale. Rocce erratiche del Colle di Fonte Molara, sulla via Monte Compatri-Zagarole (Lave).—Atti R. Acc. Lincei, S. 5, Rend. xvii, sem. 2, pp. 183-190 and 240-247, fig. 1908.

ROSSI, D. DE.—Maps of Italy.—*gd. fol.* 10 *maps.* *Roma,* 1694.

ROSSI, M. S. DE.—Analisi geologica ed architettonica delle catacombe di Roma. (Nota inserita nell' opera di G. B. De Rossi intitolata " Roma Sotterranea " i.)— *Roma,* 1864.

ROSSI, M. S. DE.—Etudes géologico-archéologiques sur le sol Romain.—*Bull. Soc. géol. France, S.* 2, *xxiv, pp.* 578–591. *Paris,* 1867.

ROSSI, M. S. DE.—Saggio degli studii geologico-archeologici fatti nella Campagna Romana.—*Roma,* 1867.

ROSSI, M. S. DE, and PONZI, G.—Vulcane von Latium.—*Zeitschr. gesammt. Nat. xxxv, pp.* 509–514. 1870.

ROSSI, M. S. DE.—Nuova ed importante scoperta fatta nella necropoli preistorica dei Colli Albani coperta dalle eruzioni del Vulcano Laziale.—*Giorn.* " *L'Opinione,*" No. 12. *Roma,* 1871.

ROSSI, M. S. DE.—Le fratture vulcaniche laziali ed i terremoti del genn. 1873.— *Atti Acc. Pont. N. Lincei, xxvi, pp.* 136–179. *Roma,* 1873.

ROSSI, M. S. DE.—Sull'Uranolito caduto nell'Agro Romano il 31 Agosto 1872.— *Atti Acc. Pont. N. Lincei, xxvi, pp.* 346–353, 419–426. *Roma,* 1873.—*Les Mondes, xxxii, pp.* 681–684, 724–731. 1873.

ROSSI, M. S. DE.—Intorno al seppellimento vulcanico della necropoli ed abitazioni albane.—*Bull. Vulc. Ital. i,* 8. *Roma,* 1874.

ROSSI, M. S. DE.—Terra Cotta primitiva rinvenuta entro la massa del peperino vulcanico nei colli tusculani.—*Bull. Vulc. Ital. i, p.* 34. 1874.

ROSSI, M. S. DE.—Attività straordinaria della mofete nella solfatara delle acque Albule presso Tivoli, verificata a di 26 Aprile.—*Bull. Vulc. Ital. i, pp.* 84–85. 1874.

ROSSI, M. S. DE.—Piccolo periodo sismico nel sistema vulcanico laziale nel giugno e luglio 1874.—*Bull. Vulc. Ital. i, pp.* 128–130. 1874.

ROSSI, M. S. DE.—Analisi dei tre maggiori terremoti italiani avvenuti nel 1874 in ordine specialmente alle fratture del suolo 1874.—*Atti Acc. Pont. N. Lincei, xxviii, pp.* 14–87. *Roma,* 1875.

ROSSI, M. S. DE.—I terremoti di Romagna dal settembre 1874 al maggio 1875.—*Atti Acc. Pont. N. Lincei, xxviii, pp.* 308–333. *Roma,* 1875.

ROSSI, M. S. DE.—Quadro generale statistico topografico giornaliero dei terremoti avvenuti in Italia nell'anno meteorico 1874 [& 1877] col confronto di alcuni altri fenomeni.—*Atti Acc. Pont. N. Lincei, xxviii, pp.* 514–536. *Roma,* 1875. [& *xxxi, pp.* 479–482. 1878.]

ROSSI, M. S. DE.—Fenomeni aurorali e sismici della regione laziale confrontati coi terremoti di Casamicciola, Norcia, e Livorno. Notizie ed osservazioni.—*Bull. Vulc. Ital. ii,* 6, 7 *e* 8, *pp.* 49–54. *Roma,* 1875.

ROSSI, M. S. DE.—I terremoti nella città di Roma.—*Bull. Vulc. Ital. xviii–xx,* 1–6, *pp.* 9–21. *Roma,* 1897.

ROZET, LT.-COL.—Addition à la note de M. Ponzi sur l'époque de soulèvement des Appennins.—*Bull. Soc. géol. France, S.* 2, *x, pp.* 196–9. *Paris,* 1853.

RUSCONI, C.—Sulla origine atmosferica dei tufi vulcanici della Campagna Romana.— *Corrisp. Scient. vii,* 19–20. *Roma,* 1865.—*Bull. Soc. géol. France, S.* 2, *xxii, pp.* 68–9. *Paris,* 1865.

RUSCONI, C.—Nuovo deposito di Ossa fossili trovato nella Campagna Romana. —*Corrisp. scient. vii,* 38. *Roma,* 1867.

RUSSEGGER, J.—Geognostische Beobachtungen in Rom, Neapel, am Aetna, auf den Cyclopen, dem Vesuv, Ischia ecc.— *N. J. f. Min. pp.* 329–332. *Stuttgart,* 1840.

RUTILI-GENTILI, A.—Cenni sui sollevamenti dell'Appennino dello Stato Romano.—*Corrisp. Scient. ii. Roma,* 1853.

SABATINI, V.—Relazione del lavoro eseguito nel biennio 1893–94 sui Vulcani dell' Italia Centrale e i loro Prodotti.—*Boll. R. Com. Geol. Ital. xxvi,* 3, *p.* 325. *Roma,* 1895.

SABATINI, V.—Sull' origine del Felspato nelle Leucititi Laziali.—*Boll. Soc. Geol. Ital. xv* (1896), 1, *pp.* 70–74. *Roma,* 1896.

SABATINI, V.—Relazione del lavoro eseguito nell'anno 1895 sui vulcani dell'Italia centrale e loro prodotti.—*Boll. R. Com. Geol. Ital. xxvii,* 4, *pp.* 400–405. *Roma,* 1896.

SABATINI, V.—Relazione sul Lavoro eseguito nel triennio 1896–97–98 sui Vulcani dell' Italia Centrale e i loro Prodotti.— *Boll. R. Com. Geol. Ital. xxx* (*S.* 3, *x*), *pp.* 30–60, *figs.* 1899.

SABATINI. V.—I Vulcani dell' Italia Centrale e i loro Prodotti. Parte prima : Vulcano Laziale.—8⁰, *Mem. Carta Geol. Ital. x, pp. i–xv*, 1–392, *geol. maps* 1 : 75,000, *pls.* 10, *figs.* 79. *Roma*, 1900.

SABATINI, V.—De l'État actuel des Recherches sur les Volcans de l'Italie centrale.—8⁰ [*Paris*], 1901. —*C. R. Congrès Géol. internat. de Vienne, viii, pp.* 366–376 ; *ix, pp.* 665–684, *figs., pls. i and ii* (*geol. maps*). *Vienne*, 1904.

SABATINI, V.—Il Peperino dei Monti Cimini.—*Boll. R. Com. Geol. Ital. S.* 4, *iii, pp.* 245–254. *Roma*, 1902.

SABATINI, V.—Relazione sul Lavoro eseguito nel periodo 1899–1903 sui Vulcani dell' Italia Centrale e i loro Prodotti.— *Boll. R. Com. Geol. Ital. xxxv, pp.* 179–198, *fig., pl. iv* (*geol. map*). 1904.

SABATINI, V.—Cronologia delle Eruzione dei Vulcani Cimini.—*Boll. R. Com. Geol. Ital. xli, pp.* 401–405, *fig.* 1911.

SABATINI, V.—I Vulcani dell' Italia Centrale e loro Prodotti. Parte II. Vulcani Cimini. —*Mem. Carta Geol. Ital. xv, pp.* 1–369, *figs., pls. i–xviii* [*geol. map*]. 1912.

SACCO, F.—L'Appennino settentrionale e centrale.—8⁰, *pp.* 400, *tav. and map. Torino*, 1904.

SALMON, U. P.—Mémoire sur un fragment de basalte volcanique tiré de Borghetto, territoire de Rome.—*Rome*, 1799.

SAUSSURE, NECKER DE, L. A.—*See* NECKER-DE-SAUSSURE.

SCACCHI, A.—I composti fluorici dei vulcani del Lazio.—*Rend. R. Acc. Sci. S.* 2, *i, pp.* 19–24. *Napoli*, 1887.

SCACCHI.—*See* STOPPANI, A.

SCHMIDT, J. F. J.—Die Eruption des Vesuv im Mai 1855 nebst Beiträgen zur Topographie des Vesuv, der phlegräischen Crater, Roccamonfina's und der alten Vulkane im Kirkenstaate mit Benützung neuer Charten und eigener Hohenmessungen.—8⁰, *pp.* xii + 212, 37 *figs. Wien u. Olmütz*, 1856.—*Peterm. Mitth., pp.* 125–135. *Gotha*, 1856.

SCHMIDT, J. F. J.—Die Eruption des Vesuvs in ihren Phänomaenen in Maj 1855, nebst Ansichten und Profilen der Vulkane des phlegräischen Gebietes, Roccamonfina's und des Albaner Gebirges.—*gd.* 4⁰, *pls.* 9. *Wien und Olmütz*, 1856. Album to foregoing.

SCHMIDT, J. F. J.— Neue Höhenbestimmungen am Vesuv, in den phlegräischen Feldern, zu Roccamonfina u. im Albaner-Gebirge.—4⁰, *pp.* 41. *Wien u. Olmütz*, 1856.

SESTINI, F.—Studio sui tufi della Campagna Romana.—*Boll. Com. Agr. iv*, 4. *Roma*, 1873.

SESTINI, F.—Analisi diverse. Travertino della Campagna Romana ; minerale manganesifero di Subiaco.—*Boll. Com. Agr.* 3–4. *Roma*, 1874.

SICKLER, F. CH. L.—Carte géographique et géognostique des environs de Rome. —1816.

SICKLER, F. CH. L.—Pantogramme ou vue descriptive générale de la Campagne de Rome.—*Rome*, 1821.

SICKLER, F. CH. L.—Plan topographique de la Campagne de Rome, considérée sous les rapports de la géologie et des antiquités. —*Rome*, 1821.

SIGNORILE, G.—Nuovi studii e ricerche sulla origine delle pozzolane vulcaniche e sulle cause della loro idraulicità, con un confronto delle pozzolane di Roma e Napoli, nell'interesse dei lavori marittimi. —*Roma*, 1877.

SILLIMAN, B. (JUNIOR).—Miscellaneous notes from Europe : 1⁰. Present condition of Vesuvius ; 2⁰. Grotta del Cane and Lake Agnano ; 3⁰. Sulphur Lake of the Campagna, near Tivoli ; 4⁰. Meteorological observatory of Mount Vesuvius ; 5⁰. Light for illumination obtained from the burning of hydrogen.—*Amer. Journ. Sci. S.* 2, *xii, pp.* 256–261. *New-Haven*, 1851.

SMITH, J.—Lake of Nemi. Engraved by W. Byrne. Plate 43.—London. Published 15 Sept. 1796 by John Smith, William Byrne and James Edwards. Same as Pl. 43 in Smith's Views in Italy, but with details of publication added. Fine engrav. : 190 × 128 mm.

SPADONI, P.—Osservazioni mineralo-vulcaniche fatte in un viaggio per l'antico Lazio.—*Macerata*, 1802.

SPECIALE, S.—Ricerche di chimica mineralogica sulle lave dei Vulcani degli Ernici nella Valle del Sacco.—*Atti R. Acc. Lincei, S. 3, Trans. iii, pp.* 181–183. *Roma*, 1879. —*Boll. R. Com. Geol. Ital. x, pp.* 301–302. *Roma*, 1879.—*Gazz. Chim. Ital. ix, pp.* 393–395. 1879.

STANFIELD, R. A.—*See* MAPEI, C.—Italy, Classical, Historical, and Picturesque.

STEFANI, C. DE.—I vulcani spenti dell' Apennino settentrionale.—*Boll. Soc. Geol. Ital. x, pp.* 449–555. *Roma*, 1891.

STOLBERG, F. L.—Reise in Deutschland, der Schweiz, Italien und Sicilien.—4 vols. 8°. *Königsburg und Leipzig*, 1794.—Atlas, 4°.—In Eng.: 2 vols. 4°. *London*, 1796–97. *See* Vol. i.

STOPPANI, A.—Corso di Geologia.—*Milano*, 1871–73.

STOPPANI, A., and SCACCHI.—Sopra la Memoria del dott. Guglielmo Terrigi intitolata " Le formazioni vulcaniche del bacino Romano."—*Atti R. Acc. Lincei, S. 3, Trans. vi, pp.* 12–14. 1882.

STRUEVER, G.—*See* STRUEVER, J. K. T.

STRUEVER, J. K. T.—Ueber das Albaner Gebirge und über Somma-Bomben mit der schönsten Zonen-Structur.—*N. J. f. Min. pp.* 619–620. *Stuttgart*, 1875.

STRUEVER, J. K. T.—[Ueber die erste Abtheilung seiner Studien über die Mineralien des Albaner Gebirges.]—*N. J. f. Min. p.* 413. *Stuttgart*, 1876.

STRUEVER, J. K. T.—Studi petrografici sul Lazio. Parte 1a (1876).—*Atti R. Acc. Lincei, S. 3, Mem. i, pp.* 46–58, 2 *pls. Roma*, 1877.

STRUEVER, J. K. T.—Studi sui minerali del Lazio.—*Atti R. Acc. Lincei, S. 2, iii, Pt. 2, pp.* 205–224, *pl.* 2. *Roma*, 1876 ; *S.* 3, *Mem. i, pp.* 93–111. 1877.—*N. J. f. Min. i, pp.* 641–3. *Stuttgart*, 1877.

STRUEVER, J. K. T.—Die Mineralien Latiums (darunter Sanidin vom Vesuv).—*Zeitschr. f. Kryst. i, p.* 246. *Leipzig*, 1877.

STRUEVER, J. K. T.—Contribuzioni alla mineralogia dei Vulcani Sabatini. Pte. I. Sui projetti minerali vulcanici trovati ad Est del lago di Bracciano.—*Atti R. Acc. Lincei, S. 4, Mem. i, pp.* 3–17. *Roma*, 1885.

STRUEVER, J. K. T.—Forsterite di Baccano. —*Atti R. Acc. Lincei, S. 4, Rend. ii, pp.* 459–461. *Roma*, 1886.

STRUEVER, J. K. T.—Sopra alcune miche del Lazio.—*Atti R. Acc. Lincei, S. 5, Rend. ii, pp.* 111–114. *Roma*, 1893.

TELLINI, A.—Carta geologica dei dintorni di Roma (Regione alla destra del Tevere). —*Roma*, 1893.

TENORE, G.—Sunto d'una memoria sulla riunione della Melilite alla Humboldtilite de Signori A. Damour et Descloizeaux.— *Ann. Acc. Aspir. Nat. ii, pp.* 140–144. *Napoli*, 1844.

TENORE, G.—Sulla Spadaite, nuove specie minerale, e sulla Wollastonite del Capo di Bove del Signor Kobell.—*Id. pp.* 177–180.

TENORE.—*See* GUSSONE.

TERRIGI, G.—Le formazioni vulcaniche del bacino romano considerate nella loro fisica costituzione e giacitura.—*Atti R. Acc. Lincei, S. 3, Mem. x, pp.* 389–418, *pls.* 3. *Roma*, 1881.

TERRIGI, G.—Ricerche microscopiche fatte sopra frammenti di marna inclusi nei peperini laziali.—*Boll. R. Com. Geol. Ital. S. 2, vi, pp.* 148–156. *Roma*, 1885.

TERRIGI, G.—Relazione della commissione per lo studio delle acque del sotto-suolo della città di Roma.—*Boll. R. Acc. Medica, xiii, pp.* 316–328. *Roma*, 1887.

TESTA, D.—Lettere sopra l'antico vulcano delle Paludi Pontine.—*Roma*, 1784.

TEXIER, CH.—Considérations sur la géologie des sept collines de Rome.—*Bull. Soc. géol. France, iii, pp.* 264–7. *Paris*, 1833.

TITTONI, T.—Studi geologici sulla regione trachitica dell'Agro Sabatino e Cerite.— *Roma*, 1885.

TITTONI, T.—La regione trachitica dell' Agro Sabatino e Cerite.—*Boll. Soc. Geol. Ital. iv, pp.* 337–376. *Roma*, 1886.

TSCHERMAK, G. VON.—Ueber Leucit [von Acquacetosa bei Rom.]—*Min. Mitth. pp.* 66–7. *Wien*, 1876.

TUCCI, P. DI.—Un' escursione alla Sempreviva e nei dintorni della medesima (Monti Lepini).—*Boll. Club Alp. Ital. x,* 1. *Torino*, 1876.

TUCCI, P. DI.—Dell'antico e del presente stato della Campagna Romana in rapporto alla salubrità dell'aria e alla fertilità del suolo.—*Roma*, 1878.

TUCCI, P. Di.—Saggio di studî geologici sui peperini del Lazio.—*Atti R. Acc. Lincei, S.* 3, *Mem. iv, pp.* 357-392, 1 *map. Roma,* 1879.

TUCCIMEI, G. A.—La geologia del Lazio.— *La Rassegna Italiana, pp.* 24. *Roma,* 1882.

TUCCIMEI, G. A.—Sopra i terreni incontrati nei recenti scavi dell'Oppio in Roma. —*Atti Acc. Pont. N. Lincei, xxxvi, pp.* 191-4. *Roma,* 1883.

TUCCIMEI, G. A.—Sulla costituzione geologica del Colle Esquilino in Roma.—*Mem. Acc. Pont. N. Lincei, i, pp.* 99-112. *Roma,* 1887.—[Extr. in] *Atti id. xxxvii, pp.* 155-7. *Roma,* 1884.

TUCCIMEI, G. A.—Contribuzione alla geologia dell'interno di Roma.—*Atti Acc. Pont. N. Lincei, Mem. i, pp.* 323-9. *Roma,* 1887.

TUCCIMEI, G. A.—Sulla presenza del manganese nei dintorni di Roma.—*Boll. Soc. Geol. Ital. xxv, pp.* 857-862. *Roma,* 1906.

UNGERN-STERNBERG, W. H. C. R. A. Von.—Werden und Seyn des Vulkanischen Gebirges. Mit 8 Abbildungen.— 8°, *pp. xi* + 320. *Carlsruhe,* 1825.

UZIELLI, G.—Sopra lo zircone della costa tirrena.—*Atti R. Acc. Lincei, S.* 2, *Mem. iii,* 2, *pp.* 862-877. *Roma,* 1876.

VERNEUIL, E. De.—Renseignements sur le terrain diluvien des environs de Rome.— *Bull. Soc. géol. France, S.* 2, *xxii, pp.* 521-2. *Paris,* 1865.

VERNEUIL, E. De, e MANTOVANI, P.— Carta geologica della Campagna Romana. —1872.

VERRI, A.—Sulla cronologia dei vulcani tirreni, e sulla idrografia della Val di Chiana anteriormente al periodo pliocenico. —*Rend. R. Ist. Lomb. S.* 2, *xi, pp.* 144-163, 1 *pl. Milano,* 1878.

VERRI, A.—I vulcani Cimini.—*Atti R. Acc. Lincei, S.* 3, *Mem. viii, pp.* 3-34, *map. Roma,* 1880.

VERRI, A.—Seguito delle note sui terreni terziari e quaternari del bacino del Tevere. —*Atti Soc. Ital. Sci. Nat. xxiii, pp.* 281-8. *Milano,* 1881.

VERRI, A.—Due parole sui tufi leucitici dei vulcani tirreni.—*Boll. Soc. Geol. Ital. ii, pp.* 40-43. *Roma,* 1883.

VERRI, A.—Sui tufi dei vulcani tirreni.— *Boll. Soc. Geol. Ital. v, pp.* 46-52. *Roma,* 1886.

VERRI, A.—Osservazioni geologiche sui crateri Vulsinii.—*Boll. Soc. Geol. Ital vii, pp.* 49-99. *Roma,* 1888.

VERRI, A.—I tufi vulcanici da costruzione della Campagna di Roma.—*Boll. Soc. Geol. Ital. xi, pp.* 63-75. *Roma,* 1892.

VERRI, A.—Note per la storia del Vulcano Laziale (Gruppo dei Crateri).—*Boll. Soc. Geol. Ital. xii, pp.* 39-80, 559-585, *map. Roma,* 1893.

VERRI, A.—Osservazioni sulla successione delle Rocce vulcaniche nella Campagna di Roma.—*Boll. Soc. Geol. Ital. xvii, pp.* 121-122. *Roma,* 1898.

VERRI, A.—Sulla Trivellazione di Capo di Bove. (Volcano Laziale).—*Boll. Soc. Geol. Ital. xix, pp.* 376-380. 1900.

VERRI, A.—Sul Vesuvio e sul Vulcano Laziali.—*Boll. Soc. Geol. Ital. xxi, pp. xxxi-xxxv,* 411-412. *Roma,* 1902.

VERRI, A.—Rapporti tra il Vulcano Laziale e quello di Bracciano.—*Boll. Soc. Geol. Ital. xxii, pp.* 169-180, *figs. Roma,* 1903.

VERRI, A.—La Nota del Prof. G. de Angelis d'Ossat : " Sulle Condizioni sfavorevoli per i Pozzi artesiani tra Roma ed i Colli Laziali."—*Boll. Soc. Geol. Ital. xxiii, pp.* 465-466. *Roma,* 1904.

VERRI, A.—Le Eruzioni della Montagna Pelée, e del Vulcano Laziale.—*Boll. Soc. Geol. Ital. xxiv, pp.* 84-88. *Roma,* 1905.

VERRI, A.—Il bacino al nord di Roma.— *Boll. Soc. Geol. Ital. xxiv, pp.* 195-236, 700-719. *Roma,* 1905.

VERRI, A.—Sui grandi giaciamenti delle Pozzolane di Roma.—*Giorn. Genio Civile, pp.* 12. *Roma,* 1907.

VERRI, A.—Sulle Pozzolane ed altri materiali da costruzione della Campagna Romana.—*Giorn. Lav. Pubbl.* 22, *pp.* 14, *Roma,* 1907.

VERRI, A.—Origine e trasformazioni della Campagna di Roma.—*Boll. Soc. Geol. Ital. xxx, pp.* 263-311. *Roma,* 1911.

VIOLA, C.—Osservazioni fatte sui Monti Lepini e sul Capo Circeo in provincia di Roma, nell'anno 1893.—*Boll. R. Com. Geol. Ital. xxv, pp.* 152–9. *Roma,* 1894.

VIOLA, C.—Sopra l'Albite di Secondaria Formazione, quale Prodotto di Metamorfismo di Contatto della Diabasi e dei Gabbri in Basilicata.—*Boll. R. Com. Geol. Ital. xxv, p.* 301. 1894.

VIOLA, C.—La Metamorfosi dinamica nelle lave leucitiche dei Vulcani estinti degli Ernici in Provincia di Roma.—*Atti Soc. Tosc. Sci. Nat. x, Proc.-verb. pp.* 170–182. *Pisa,* 1896.

VIOLA, C.—Osservazioni geologiche fatte sui Monti Ernici (Provincia di Roma) nel 1895.—*Boll. R. Com. Geol. Ital. xxvii, pp.* 300–313 (1–14). *Roma,* 1896.

VIOLA, C.—La struttura carsica osservata in alcuni monti calcarei della provincia romana.—*Boll. R. Com. Geol. Ital. xxviii,* 2, *pp.* 147–183. *Roma,* 1897.

VIOLA, C.—Porosità, Permeabilità e Metamorfismo delle Roccie in genere e delle Roccie eruttive degli Ernici (provinc. di Roma) in ispecie.—*Atti Soc. Tosc. Sci. Nat. xii, pp.* 15–23. *Pisa,* 1898.

VIOLA, C.—Mineralogische und petrographische Mittheilungen aus dem Hernikerlande in der Provinz Rom (Italien).—*N. J. f. Min. i,* 2, *pp.* 93–137, *tav.* 8. *Stuttgart,* 1899.

VIOLA, C.—Nuove Osservazioni geologiche fatte nel 1898 sui Monti Ernici e Simbruini (Appennino Romano).—*Boll. R. Com. Geol. Ital. S.* 3, *x, pp.* 325–345. *Roma,* 1899.

VIOLA, C.—I principali Tipi di Lave dei Vulcani Ernici (Prov. di Roma).—*Boll. R. Com. Geol. Ital. S.* 4, *iii, pp.* 104–124, *pls. v* and *vi. Roma,* 1902.—*N. J. f. Min. ii, pp.* 371–2. *Stuttgart,* 1903.
 Ref. note by Deecke.

VOLPICELLI, P.—Sulla Memoria del sig. Cav. M. S. de Rossi intitolata : Analisi geologica ed architettonica delle catacombe romane.—*Atti Acc. Pont. N. Lincei, xviii, pp.* 130–2. *Roma,* 1865.

WASHINGTON, H. S.—Italian petrological sketches. II. The Viterbo region.—*Journ. Geol. iv,* 7, *pp.* 826–849. *Chicago,* 1896.

WASHINGTON, H. S.—Italian petrological sketches. V. Summary and Conclusion.—*Journ. Geol. v,* 4, *pp.* 349–377. *Chicago,* 1897.

WASHINGTON, H. S.—Some Analyses of Italian Volcanic Rocks.—*Amer. Journ. Sci. S.* 4, *viii, pp.* 286–294, 1899 ; *ix, pp.* 44–54. *New Haven,* 1900.

WASHINGTON, H. S.—Chemical Analyses of Igneous Rocks published from 1884 to 1900, with a critical discussion of the character and use of analyses.—*U.S. Geol. Surv., Prof. Paper* 14, *pp.* 495. 1903.

WASHINGTON, H. S.—The Roman comagmatic region.—1 vol. 8°, *pp.* 200. *Washington,* 1906.

WESTPHAL.—Carte géognostique des environs de Rome.—1828.

ZAMBONINI, F.—Ueber den Olivin Latiums.—*Zeitschr. f. Kryst. xxxii, pp.* 153–156, *pl. iv. Leipzig,* 1899.

ZAMBONINI, F.—Ueber den Pyroxen Latiums.—*Zeitschr. f. Kryst. xxxiii, pp.* 39–56, *figs., pl.* 1. *Leipzig,* 1900.

ZAMBONINI, F.—Sul sanidino (Viterbese, Tombe dei Nasoni, Lazio, Vesuvio).—*Riv. Min. e Crist. Ital. xxv, pp.* 33–69, *tav.* 6. *Padova,* 1900.

ZAMBONINI, F.—Mineralogische Mittheilungen. 1. Ueber Müllerit, Melit, und Schrötterit. 2. Olivin von Latium. 3. Chemische Zusammensetzung des Forsterit der Albaner Gebirge. . . . 10. Anhang zu meiner Abhandlung " Ueber den Pyroxen Latiums."—*Zeitschr. f. Kryst. xxxiv, pp.* 225–260, 549–562, *figs., pls. iv–v. Leipzig,* 1901.

ZAMBONINI, F.—Amphibol von Cappuccini di Albano.—*Zeitschr. f. Kryst. xxxvii, pp.* 369–378, *pl. vi. Leipzig,* 1903.

ZAMBONINI, F.—Sulla vera natura della pseudonefelina di Capo di Bove, presso Roma.—*Rend. R. Acc. Sci. S.* 3, *xvi, pp.* 83–86. *Napoli,* 1910.

ZEZI, G. P.—Osservazioni geologiche fatte nei dintorni di Ferentino e di Frosinone, nella provincia di Roma.—*Boll. R. Com. Geol. Ital. vii, pp.* 360–388. *Roma,* 1876.

ZEZI, G. P.—Escursione ai monti Laziali.— *Progr. R. Scuola Applicaz. ingegn. Roma*, 1877.

ZEZI, G. P.—Indice bibliografico delle pubblicazioni italiane e straniere riguardanti la mineralogia, la geologia e la paleontologia di Roma, con un appendice per le acque potabili, termali e minerali.—[Estr.] *Mon. Arch. e Stat. Roma e Camp. Rom. Roma*, 1878.

ZEZI, G. P.—*See* COMITÉ D'ORGANISATION, &c.—Bibliographie Géologique, &c., x. 1881.

ZEZI, G. P.—La lava di Capo di Bove presso Roma.—*Boll. R. Com. Geol. Ital. S.* 2, *viii, pp.* 257–9. *Roma*, 1887.

ZEZI, G. P.—The Travertine and the Acque Albule in the neighbourhood of Tivoli.— *pp.* 83–88. *Naples*, 1891.
    See JOHNSTON - LAVIS : " South Italian Volcanoes," pp. 83-8.

ZOPPI, G.—Le acque sotterranee dei Colli Laziali.—*Mem. illustr. Carta idrograf. Ital.* 12. *Roma*, 1892.

ROCCAMONFINA

ANON.—Carta (Corografica) d'Italia.—*Ist. Geog. Milit. Ital.* 1889.
1: 1,000,000 in 7 sheets.—3 ed. 1st in 3 colours, with mountains shaded in brown and water in blue ; 2nd, mountains in grey ; 3rd, without mountain shading. *See* sheet 4.

ANON.—Carta (Corografica) d'Italia.—*Ist. Geog. Milit. Ital.* 1889.
1 : 1,800,000 in 6 sheets.—2 ed. 1st in 3 colours as in preceding ; 2nd, without mountain shading. *See* sheet 4.

ANON.—Carta della Provincia di Napoli e delle parte contigue di Caserta, Salerno e Benevento.—*Napoli*, 1861–1875.
1 : 10,000, in 6 sheets, copper engraving. *See* sheet 2 (Roccamonfina).

ANON.—Carta Topografica del Regno d'Italia.—*Ist. Geog. Milit. Ital.* 1869.
1 : 100,000.—Chromolithographic edition in 3 colours without line shading of mountains. *See* sheets 160, 161, 171, 172.

ANON.—Carta Topografica del Regno d'Italia.—*Ist. Geog. Milit. Ital.* 1889.
1 : 100,000 in 277 photo-engraved sheets, in course of publication (1889). The orography is shown by contour lines of 50 m. as well as by zenith-light shading. *See* sheets 160, 161, 171, 172.

ANON.—Carta Topografica del Regno d'Italia.
1 : 75,000.—Economic edition similar to above.

ANON.—L'Italia.—4°, *pp.* 326, *num. maps. Torino*, 1896.

ANON.—Tavolette rilevate per la costruzione della carte del Regno d'Italia.—*Ist. Geog. Milit. Ital.* 1873–1879.
Part to the scale of 1 : 50,000 and part 1 : 25,000. *See* sheets 160, 161, 171, 172 (*i–iv*).

ABICH, O. W. H. VON.—Ueber Erhebungskratere und den Volcan von Roccamonfina.—*Berlin*, 1841.

ABICH, O. W. H. VON.—Geologische Beobachtungen über die vulkanischen Erscheinungen und Bildungen in Unter- und Mittel-Italien.—Bd. i, Lief. 1 (all that appeared) : Ueber die Natur und den Zusammenhang der vulkanischen Bildungen.—4°, *pp. viii + 134 + xi, maps* 3, *lith. pls.* 2. *Braunschweig*, 1841.

ABICH, O. W. H. VON.—Die Vulkane in Unter- und Mittel-Italien. (1. Die Vulkane Neapels ; 2. Roccamonfina ; 3. Vultur ; 4. Blick auf den Vesuv ; 5. Ansicht von Roccamonfina.) 5 Karten aufgezogen.
Atlas to above (bound separately).

ANDREA, D.—Anno Domini 1688. Immani Terremotu Furente Munimen Hoc Concussum, etc.
A photograph in Dr. Johnston-Lavis' collection of a fresco inscription at Sessa Aurunca of 1693.

BARATTA, M.—Saggio dei materiali per una storia dei fenomeni sismici avvenuti in Italia raccolti dal Prof. Michele Stefano de Rossi.—*Boll. Soc. Geol. Ital. xviii, pp.* 432–460. *Roma*, 1899.

BREISLAK, S.—Topografia fisica della Campania.—8°, *pp. xii + 368 + iii, pl. Firenze*, 1798.
See pp. 69 to 104.

BUCCA, L.—Il monte di Roccamonfina, studio petrografico.—*Boll. Com. Geol. Ital. xvii*, 7–8, *pp.* 245–265. *Roma*, 1886.

CASORIA, E.—Sui processi di mineralizzazione delle acque in rapporto con la natura geologica dei terreni e delle rocce.—8°, *pp.* 197. *Portici*, 1902.
See pp. 189–197.

CASORIA.—Analisi delle acque di Sujo. *See* ROCCATAGLIATA.

CHERUBINI, CAV. C.—Carta Fisica dell' Italia.—*Pub. G. B. Paravia e C., Torino, Roma, Milano, Firenze, Napoli*, 1876.
1 : 750,000 horiz. ; 1 : 150,000 vert. Raised map.

COVELLI, N.—Memoria per servire di materiale alla costituzione geognostica della Campania (1827).—*Atti R. Acc. Sci.* iv, Mineralogia, *pp.* 33–69. *Napoli,* 1839.

DAUBENY, C. G. B.—A Description of active and extinct Volcanos ; with remarks on their origin, their chemical phenomena, and the character of their products, as determined by the condition of the earth during the period of their formation.— 8⁰, *pp.* 466, *figs., maps* 2, *pl.* 1. *London,* 1826.—8⁰, *pp.* 743, *figs., maps* 10, *pls.* 4. *London,* 1848.

DAUBENY, C. G. B.—On the Ancient City of the Aurunci (Rocca Monfina) and on its Volcanic Phenomena ; with Remarks on Craters of Elevation, on the Distinctions between Plutonic and Volcanic Action and on the Theories of Volcanic action at present most in Repute.—*Trans. Ashmol. Soc. pp.* 3–51. *Oxford,* 1846.—*Edinburgh New Phil. Journ.* xli, *pp.* 213–255, 1 *pl.* 1 *map.* 1846.

DEECKE, J. E. W.—Zur Geologie von Unteritalien : 4. Das System des Monte Maggiore bei Pignataro in Campanien.—*N. J. f. Min.* i, *pp.* 51–74, 1 *pl.* *Stuttgart,* 1893.

DEECKE, J. E. W.—Italien.—8⁰, *pp.* xii + 514, *maps, pl. and fig. Berlin,* 1898.

FERRERO, L. O.—Sopra i Metamorfismi chimici che le roccie esistenti nei pressi delle acque di Sujo presentano, in dipendenza delle mofete e sorgive locali.—*See* ROCCATAGLIATA.—Analisi, etc., *pp.* 21–45.

FERRERO, L. O.—Cenni stratigrafici e geologici sul luogo di Sujo.—*Ibid. pp.* 47–51.

FERRERO, L. O.—Analisi delle più rinomate acque minero-termali di Sujo.— *Ibid. pp.* 65–99.

FIORILLO.—*See* TARTARO.

FISCHER, TH.—Das Halbinselland Italien. —*In Kirchhoff's* " Länderkunde von Europa," *pp.* 285–515. *Prag, Wien, Leipzig,* 1890.

FUCHS,￪ C. W. C.—Les Volcans et les Tremblements de terre.—8⁰, *pp.* viii + 279, *fig. and map. Paris,* 1876.——2nd ed. 1878.

FUSCO, M. DE.—Le acque di Sujo sulla sponda destra del Garigliano.—*Il Movimento Medico-Chirurgico,* xvi, 5–6, *pp.* 7. *Napoli,* 1884.

FUSCO, M. DE.—Le acque di Sujo.—8⁰, *pp.* 8. *Napoli,* 1889. Chiefly medical.

GALDIERI, A.—Su di una leucofonolite haüynitica del vulcano di Roccamonfina. —*Rend. R. Acc. Sci., S.* 3, xix, *pp.* 107–112. *Napoli,* 1913.

GATTULA.—Hist. Abbatiae Cassinensis. See Vol. ii, p. 759.

JERVIS, W. P.—Tesori sotterranei dell'Italia. —4 vols. 8⁰, *num. pls. Torino,* 1873–1889.

JOHNSTON-LAVIS, H. J.—The Physical Conditions involved in the Injection, Extrusion and Cooling of Igneous Matter. [Abstr.]—*Quart. Journ. Geol. Soc. xli, Proc. pp.* 103–106. 1885.—*Geol. Mag. p.* 282, 1885.

JOHNSTON-LAVIS, H. J.—The Relationship of the Structure of Igneous Rocks to the Conditions of their Formation.—*Scient. Proc. R. Dublin Soc., N.S.* v, *pp.* 112–156. *Dublin,* 1886.

JOHNSTON-LAVIS, H. J.—Il Pozzo Artesiano di Ponticelli.—*Rend. R. Acc. Sci. S.* 2, iii, *pp.* 142–148. *Napoli,* 1889.

JOHNSTON-LAVIS, H. J.—Viaggio scientifico alle regioni vulcaniche italiane nella ricorrenza del centenario del " Viaggio alle due Sicilie " di Lazzaro Spallanzani. (This is the programme of the excursion of the English geologists who visited the South Italian volcanoes under the direction of the author. It is here included as it contains various new and unpublished observations.)—8⁰, *pp.* 1–10. *Naples,* 1889.

JOHNSTON-LAVIS, H. J.—Excursion to the South Italian Volcanoes.—[Read Jan. 3, 1890.]—*Proc. Geol. Assoc.* xi, 8, *pp.* 389–423. *London,* 1891. See pp. 412–415.

JOHNSTON-LAVIS, H. J.—Thermo-mineral and gas-springs of Sujo.—In JOHNSTON-LAVIS.—S. Italian Volcanoes, etc. Naples, 1891.

JOHNSTON-LAVIS, H. J.—The Science of Vulcanology. [Being the Introductory Address to a Course of Lectures on that Subject in the R. University of Naples.]— " Nature," l, *pp.* 66–68. 1894.—" Science," 16 *March* 1894.

JUDD, J. W.—Contributions to the Study of Volcanoes.—The Great Crater-lakes of Central Italy.—*Geol. Mag. Dec.* II, ii, *pp.* 348–356. *London,* 1875.

KRANZ, W.—Vulcanismus und Tektonik im Becken von Neapel.—*Peterm. Geogr. Mitth.* 1912, *Märzheft, pp.* 131–135; *Aprilheft, pp.*203–206; *Maiheft,pp.*258–264, 2 *maps.* 1912.

LACROIX, A. F. A.—Étude sur le Métamorphisme de contact des roches volcaniques. —4°, *pp.* 88. *Paris*, 1894.

LOCCHI, ING. D.—Italia ; Carta Fisica.— *Pubbl. G. B. Paravia e C., Torino, Roma, Milano, Firenze, Napoli*, 1876. 1 : 200,000. Raised map.

LORENZO, G. DE.—Studi di geologia nell' Appennino meridionale.—*Napoli,* 1896. —*Atti R. Acc. Sci. S.* 2, *viii, Mem.* 7, *pp.* 128. *Napoli*, 1896.

LORENZO, G. DE.—Geologia e geografia fisica dell'Italia meridionale.—8°, *pp.* 241. *Bari*, 1904.

MODERNI, P.—Note geologiche sul gruppo vulcanico di Roccamonfina.—*Boll. Com. Geol. Ital. xviii, pp.* 74–100, *geol. map* 1. *Roma*, 1887.

MONACO, E.—Sull'impiego delle roccie leucitiche nella concimazione.—*Le Staz. Speriment. Agrar. Ital. xxxvi,* 7, *pp.* 577–583. *Modena*, 1903.

MONACO, E.—Sull'impiego delle rocce leucitiche nella concimazione.—*Le Staz. Speriment. Agrar. Ital. xxxvii, pp.* 1031–1034. *Modena*, 1904.

MONACO, V.—Saggio analitico ed uso Medico delle acque medicinali fredde e termali di Sujo in Terra di Lavoro. —*Piedimonte di Cassino ?*, 1798.

MONTORIO, SERAFINO.—Zodiaco di Maria, ovvero le dodici provincie del Regno di Napoli.—4°, *pp.* 728. *Napoli*, 1715.

PARETO, L.—Della posizione delle roccie pirogene ed eruttive dei periodi terziario, quaternario ed attuale in Italia.—8°, *pp.* 35. *Genova*, 1852.

PEROTTA, G.—Storia del Regno di Napoli. This is identical with the following, except the title page. In Dr. Johnston-Lavis' copy both the author's portrait and the folding plate of S. Maria di Lattini are absent in the former, but present in the latter.
La Sede degli Aurunci antichissimi d'Italia, etc.—4°, *w. portrait, pp.* 33 + 366 + 15 + 5. *Napoli*, 1737.
See pp.147–155 : Tremuoto spaventevole da cui fu gravemente crollata la Rocca Monfina nell'anno 1728, etc.

PILLA, L.—Geologia vulcanica della Campania.—*Napoli*, 1823.

PILLA, L.—Sur le groupe volcanique de Rocca Monfina.—*C. R. Acad. Sci. x, pp.* 767–770. *Paris*, 1840.—*Ann. Mines, xviii, pp.* 127–144. *Paris*, 1840.—*N. J. f. Min. ix, pp.* 162–175. *Stuttgart*, 1841.

PILLA, L.—Applicazione della teorica dei crateri di sollevamento al vulcano di Rocca Monfina. — *Atti 3a. Riun. Sci. Ital. Firenze*, 1841.—*Boll. id.* [Extr.] *xiii, pp.* 169–171. *Firenze*, 1841.—*Mem. Soc. géol. France, S.* 2, *i, pp.* 163–180, *pl.* 3. *Paris*, 1844.—German transl. in ROTH: " *Vesuv und die Umgebung von Neapel." Berlin*, 1857.

PILLA, L.—Sur quelques minéraux recueillis au Vésuve et à la Roccamonfina.—*C. R. Acad. Sci. xxi, pp.* 324–327. *Paris*, 1845.

PILLA, N.—Saggio litologico dei vulcani estinti di Rocca Monfina, Sessa e Teano.— 8°, *pp. xiii* + 77, *maps* 2. *Napoli*, 1795.

PILLA, N.—Primo viaggio geologico per la Campania eseguito nelle Contrade volcaniche della Rocca.—*Napoli*, 1814.

PLINIUS.—*See* Lib. 2, Cap. 103.

POMBA. CAV. C.—L'Italia nel suo Aspetto Fisico.—*Pubbl. G. B. Paravia e C., Torino, Roma, Milano, Firenze, Napoli*, 1890.
1 : 100,000 horiz. and vert. Raised map on section of globe.

RATH, J. J. G. VOM.—Il vulcano di Roccamonfina. (Transl.)—*Boll. R. Com. Geol. Ital. iv, pp.* 385–388. *Roma*, 1873.

RATH, J. J. G. VOM.—Zwei Gesteine der Rocca Monfina.—*Zeitschr. deutsch. geol. Gesellsch. xxv, pp.* 245–7. *Berlin*, 1873.

RECLUS, E.—Les Volcans de la Terre.— *Soc. Astronom. Bruxelles*, 1906.

RICCIARDI, L.—Sull'allineamento dei Vulcani Italiani. Sulle roccie eruttive subaeree e submarine e loro classificazione in due periodi. Sul graduale passaggio delle roccie acide alle roccie basiche.—8°, *pp.* 1–40. *Reggio-Emilia*, 1887.

RICCIARDI, L.—Genesi e successione delle Rocce Eruttive.—*Atti Soc. Ital. Sci. Nat. xxx*, 3, *pp.* 212–237. *Milano*, 1887.

RICCIARDI, L.—Genesi e composizione chimica dei Terreni Vulcanici Italiani. —8°, *pp.* 155. *Firenze*, 1889.

ROCCATAGLIATA, P., FERRERO, L. O., CASORIA.—Analisi delle acque Minero—termali di Sujo in Provincia de Terra di Lavoro.—*pp.* 99 + 2, 4 *col. pl.*, 2 *maps. Aversa,* 1877.

ROGGERO, CAV. G.—Carta in rilievo dell' Italia.—*Pubbl. G. B. Paravia e C., Torino, Roma, Milano, Firenze, Napoli,* 1876. 1 : 2,800,000 horiz.; 1 : 320,000 vert. Raised map.

SCACCHI, A.—Lezioni di Geologia. Vulcani di Roccamonfina, Campi ed Isole Flegree, M. Somma e Vesuvio.—8⁰, *pp.* 178. *Napoli,* 1843. *See* pp. 155-174.

SCHMIDT, J. F. JULIUS.—Die Eruption des Vesuv in Mai 1855. Nebst Beiträgen zur Topographie des Vesuv, der phlegräischen Crater, Roccamonfina und der alten Vulkane in Kirchenstaate.—8⁰, *pp.* xii + 212, 37 *figs. Wien und Olmütz,* 1856.—*Peterm. Mitth., pp.* 125-135. *Gotha,* 1856.

SCHMIDT, J. F. J.—Die Eruption des Vesuv in ihren Phänomenen im Mai 1855 nebst Ansichten und Profilen der Vulkane des Phlegräischen Gebietes, Roccamon-finas und des Albaner Gebirges, etc.—*gd.* 4⁰, 9 *pls. Wien & Olmütz,* 1856. Album to foregoing.

SCHMIDT, J. F. J. — Neue Höhen-Bestimmungen am Vesuv, in den phle-gräischen Feldern, zu Roccamonfina und im Albaner Gebirge.—4⁰, *pp.* 41. *Wien, Olmütz,* 1856.

SCROPE, G. J. POULETT.—Considerations on Volcanos, the probable causes of their phenomena . . . and their connection with the present state and past history of the globe ; leading to the establishment of a new Theory of the earth.—8⁰, *pp.* xxxi + 270, 2 *pls.*, 1 *map. London,* 1825. [Another ed. entitled :] Volcanos : the character of their phenomena. With a descriptive Catalogue of all known Vol-canos.——2nd ed. 8⁰, *pp.* xi+490, 1 *pl.*,

1 *col. map. London,* 1862.—In French (transl. by Endymion) : *col. pls.* 2. *Paris,* 1864.—In Germ. (transl. by G. A. v. Klöden) : 1 *pl.*, 65 *figs. Berlin,* 1872.— Extr. in Ital. : *Bibl. Ital. xlv, pp.* 70-83, 211-226. *Milano,* 1827.

TARTARO E FIORILLO.—Analisi delle acque di Sujo. Società Economica della Provincia di Caserta.— ?, 1866.

TENORE, G.—Ragguaglio di un breve viaggio geologico alla contrada vulcanica di Sessa e di Roccamonfina.—*Ann. Acc. Asp. Nat. ii, pp.* 203-210. *Napoli,* 1844.

TENORE, G.—Saggio di Carta geologica della Terra di Lavoro.—*Napoli,.*1872. 1 : 20,000. Includes Roccamonfina.

THUILLIER FILS. (Gravé par).—Carte Physique de la Campanie. Écrit par Miller. *See* BREISLAK, S.—Voyages Physiques et Lithologiques, i, pl. i. Paris, 1801.

WASHINGTON, H. S.—The Rocca Monfina region. W. Italian Petrological Studies.—*Journ. Geol. v, 3, pp.* 241-256. *Chicago,* 1897.

WASHINGTON, H. S.—Italian petrological sketches. v. Summary and Conclusion.—*Journ. Geol. v, 4, pp.* 349-377. *Chicago,* 1897.

WASHINGTON, H. S.—Some Analyses of Italian Volcanic Rocks, II.—*Amer. Journ. Sci. ix, Art.* 6, *pp.* 44-54. *New-Haven, Jan.* 1900.

WASHINGTON, H. S.—Chemical Analyses of Igneous Rocks published from 1884 to 1900, with a critical discussion of the character and use of analyses.—*U.S. Geol. Surv. Prof. Paper* 14, *pp.* 495. *Washington,* 1903.

WOLFFSOHN, L.—Sujo on the Garigliano. —*Gentleman's Magazine, pp.* 265-279, *Sept.* 1890.—In Italian in *L'Araldo. Giornale di Terra di Lavoro, Feb. e Marzo,* 1891.

ZARLENGA, F.—Le Acque di Sujo ?—*See Filiatre Sebezio, Settemb.* 1852.

MONTE VULTURA

ANON.—Carta geologica del Regno alla
Scala di 1 : 100,000.—*R. Uffic. Geol. Ital.*
272 sheets.

ANON. [CLERMONT ?].—Carte de l'Italie
Méridionale et de la Sicile Ancienne, Pays
autrefois connus sous le nom de Grande
Grèce. Rédigée et corrigée d'après les
observations les plus récentes, et que
l'on croit les plus certaines. — ?, — ?

ANON.—Giornale letterario di Napoli per
servire di continuazione all'Analisi ragionata de' libri nuovi.—112 vols. 8⁰. *Napoli,*
1793–98.
    See Vol. xciv, pp. 3–45 : Discorso
meteorologico dell'anno 1796 : di Luca
Cagnazzi.

ANON.—L'Italia.—4⁰, *pp. 326, num. maps.*
Torino, 1896.

ANON.—L'Italie.—8⁰, 243 *engrav.,* 5 *maps.*
Paris, — ?

ABICH, O.W. H. Von—Geologische Beobachtungen über die vulkanischen Erscheinungen
und Bildungen in Unter- und Mittel-Italien.
Bd. i, Lief. 1 : Ueber die Natur und den
Zusammenhang der vulkanischen Bildung-
en.—4⁰, *pp. viii* + 134 + *xi, maps* 3, *lith.*
pl. 2. *Braunschweig,* 1841.

ABICH, O.W.H. Von—Die Vulkane in Unter-
und Mittel-Italien. (1. Die Vulkane
Neapels ; 2. Roccamonfina ; 3. Vultur ; 4.
Blick auf den Vesuv ; 5. Ansicht von
Roccamonfina.) 5 Karten aufgezogen.
    Atlas to foregoing.

ANTONELLIO, C. De.—Il canto del Bardo
su le rovine di Melfi.—1 *pl. Napoli,*
1852.

BAEDEKER, K —Italien. Handbuch für
Reisende. 3 Theil : Unter-Italien und
Sicilien nebst Ausflügen nach den Liparischen Inseln.—8th ed. 16⁰, *pp. xlviii*
+ 412, *maps* 26, *plans* 17. *Leipzig,* 1887.
    See pp. 194-5.

BARATTA, M.—Sulla distribuzione topografica dei terremoti in Italia durante il
quinquennio 1887–91.—*Atti Primo Congr.*
Geog. Ital. Genova, 18-25 *Sett.* 1892.
Mem. sez. scient. ii, Pt. 1, *pp.* 180–189,
tav. v. Genova, 1894.

BARATTA, M.—I Terremoti d'Italia.—8⁰,
pp. 950, *pls. Torino,* 1901.
    Gives, in Pt. iii, an extensive biblio-
graphy of the earthquakes of Italy.

BROCCHI, G. B.—Sopra una particolare
varieta di Lazialite trovata in una lava di
monte Vulture in Basilicata.—*Bibl. Ital.*
xvii, pp. 261–265. *Milano,* 1820.

CAGNAZZI, L.—Osservazioni Meteorologiche fatte in Altamura.—*Giorn. Lett.*
iii, pp. 104-7 ; *iv, pp.* 105-8 ; *v, pp.* 104-7,
1793 ; *vi, pp.* 105-8 ; *vii, pp.* 110–114 ;
viii, pp. 103-6 ; *ix, pp.* 100-4 ; *x, pp.*
103-6 ; *xiii, pp.* 104-8 ; *xiv, pp.* 107–110 ;
xv, pp. 103-6 ; *xvi, pp.* 108–116 ; *xvii,*
pp. 103-7, 1794 ; *xix, pp.* 54-7 ; *xxiii,*
pp. 50-3 [34–7] ; *xxv, pp.* 73-6, 1795.

CASORIA, E.—Le acque carboniche delle
falde orientali del Vulture in relazione alla
costituzione chimica dei materiali vulcanici.—8⁰, *pp.* 40. *Portici,* 1901.

CASORIA, E.—Sui processi di mineralizzazione delle acque in rapporto con la
natura geologica dei terreni e delle rocce.—
8⁰, *pp.* 197. *Portici,* 1902.
    See pp. 167–189.

DAUBENY, C. G. B.—A Description of
active and extinct Volcanos ; with remarks
on their origin, their chemical phenomena,
and the character of their products, as determined by the condition of the earth during
the period of their formation.—8⁰, *pp.* 466,
figs., maps 2, *pl.* 1. *London,* 1826.—8⁰,
pp. 743, *figs., maps* 10, *pls.* 4. *London,*
1848.

DAUBENY, C. G. B.—Narrative of an Excursion to Lake Amsanctus, and to Mount Vultura in Apulia in 1834.—*Ashmol. Trans. pls. 3 and map. Oxford*, 1835.

DEECKE, J. E. W.—1. Zur Geologie von Unteritalien ; 2. Die sogenannte " erratischen Granite " in Apulien und in der Basilicata und ihre geologische Bedeutung.—*N. J. f. Min. ii, 1, pp. 49–61. Stuttgart*, 1891.

DEECKE, J. E.W.—Der Monte Vulture in der Basilicata (Unteritalien).—*N. J. f. Min. Beil.-Bd. vii, 4, pp.* 556–623, 1 *pl.*, 1 *map. Stuttgart*, 1891.

DEECKE, J. E.W.—Zur Geologie von Unteritalien.—Betrachtungen über das neapolitanische Erdbeben im Jahre 1857.—*N.J.f. Min. ii, pp.* 108–124, 1 *pl. Stuttgart*, 1892.

DEECKE, J. E. W.—Italien.—8⁰, *pp. xii* + 514, *maps, pl. and fig. Berlin*, 1898.

FANO, A.—Breve cenni mineralogici e botaniche sui dintorni del R. Istitut. Technico di Melfi e nota sul Museo di Storia Naturale dell'Istit. stesso.—8⁰, *pp.* 25. *Melfi*, 1887.

FARRAR, A. S.—The Earthquake at Melfi in 1851, and recent eruption of Vesuvius in 1855.—*Abstr. Proc. Ashmol. Soc. xxxiv, pp.* 91–6. *Oxford*, 1856.

FISCHER, TH.—Das Halbinselland Italien. —*In Kirchhoff's* " Länderkunde von Europa," *pp.* 285–515. *Prag, Wien, Leipzig*, 1890.

FITTIPALDI, E.—Una giornata sul Vultura.—*Tip. Santanello. Potenza*, 1877.

FLORES, E.—*See* JOHNSTON-LAVIS.

FONSECA, F.—Osservazioni geognostiche sul Vulture.—*Napoli*, 1846.

FONSECA, F.—Osservazioni intorno alle lave, conglomerati, e massi erratici del Vulture.—*Atti Sett. Adun. Sci. Ital. p.* 1156. *Napoli*, 1846.

FUCHS, C. W. C.—Les Volcans et les Tremblements de Terre.—8⁰, *pp. viii* + 279, *fig. and map. Paris*, 1876——2nd ed. 1878.

GATTA, L.—L'Italia, sua formazione, suoi vulcani e terremoti.—8⁰, *pp.* 539, 32 *woodcuts*, 3 *lithog. maps. Milano*, 1882.— *Boll. R. Com. Geol. Ital. pp.* 102–104 (*notiz. bibliog.*). *Roma*, 1882.

GEIKIE, A.—Recent Studies of Old Italian Volcanoes.—" *Nature*," *lxiv, pp.* 103–106. *London*, 1901.

GENTIL, L.—Sur l'existence de la Horneblende dans les tufs volcaniques du Monte Vulture (Basilicate).—*Bull. Soc. franç. Min. xvii, pp.* 81–4. *Paris*, 1894.

GENTIL, L.—Sur la microstructure de la mélilite.—*Bull. Soc. franç. Min. xvii, pp.* 108–119. *Paris*, 1894.

GIORGI, C. DE.—Note geologiche sulla Basilicata.—8⁰, *panorama of Mt. Vultura, maps and figs. Lecce*, 1879.

GIUSTINIANI, L.—La biblioteca storica e topografica del Regno di Napoli.—4⁰, *pp. xv* + 241. *Napoli*, 1793. *See* p. 104.

GUSSONE E TENORE.—Ragguaglio delle Peregrinazioni effettuate nella state del 1838 in alcuni luoghi delle provincie di Principato Citeriore e di Basilicata. Mem. I. Peregrinazioni da Salerno al Monte Vulture (1839–1840).—*Atti R. Acc. Sci. v, Pt.* 1, *pp.* 335–367. *Napoli*, 1843. Mem. II. Melfi.—*Id. pp.* 369–381; Mem. III. Il Vulture.—*Id. pp.* 383–407.

JOHNSTON-LAVIS, H. J.—The Physical Conditions involved in the injection, extrusion and cooling of Igneous Matter. [*Abstr.*]—*Quart. Journ. Geol. Soc. xli, Proc. pp.* 103–106. *London*, 1885.—*Geol. Mag. p.* 282. 1885.

JOHNSTON-LAVIS, H. J.—On the Fragmentary Ejectamenta of Volcanoes.— *Proc. Geol. Assoc. ix, pp.* 421–432, 1 *pl. London*, 1886.

JOHNSTON-LAVIS, H. J.—The Relationship of the Structure of Igneous Rocks to the Conditions of their Formation.—*Scient. Proc. R. Dublin Soc. N.S. v, pp.* 112–156. *Dublin*, 1886.

JOHNSTON-LAVIS, H. J.—Volcans et tremblements de terre. Revue de ce qui a été publié sur ces sujets durant l'année 1888.—*Ann. Géol. Univ. v, pp.* 629–655. *Paris*, 1889.

JOHNSTON-LAVIS, H. J., e FLORES, E.— Notizie sui depositi degli antichi laghi di Pianura (Napoli) e di Melfi (Basilicata) e sulle ossa di mammiferi in essi rinvenute.— *Boll. Soc. Geol. Ital. xiv, pp.* 111–118, 1 *pl. Roma*, 1895.

LORENZO, G. DE.—Studi di geologia nell' Appennino meridionale.—*Napoli*, 1896.— *Atti R. Acc. Sci. S.* 2, *viii*, 7, *pp.* 128. *Napoli*, 1896.

LORENZO, G. DE.—I grandi Laghi Pleisto-cenici delle Falde del Vulture.—*Atti R. Acc. Lincei, S.* 5, *Rend. vii, sem.* 2, *pp.* 326–330, *fig., map* (1 : 500,000). *Roma,* 1898.

LORENZO, G. DE.—Studio geologico del Monte Vulture (Basilicata).—4^0, *tab.* 8, *geol. map. Napoli,* 1900.—*Atti R. Acc. Sci. S.* 2, *x,* 1, *pp.* 1–207, *figs.* 20, *pls. ix* (1 *col.* and 1 *map*). *Napoli,* 1901.—*Id. Rend. S.* 3, *v, p.* 191. 1899.

LORENZO, G. DE.—Un paragone tra il Vesuvio e il Vulture.—*Rend. R. Acc. Sci. S.* 3, *vii, pp.* 315–320, *figs.* 2. *Napoli,* 1901.

LORENZO, G. DE.—Considerazioni sull' origine superficiale dei Vulcani.—*Atti R. Acc. Sci. S.* 2, *xi,* 7, *pp.* 1–19, 1 *pl. Napoli,* 1902.

LORENZO, G. DE.—Geologia e geografia fisica dell'Italia meridionale.—8^0, *pp.* 241. *Bari,* 1904.

LORENZO, G. DE.—La Basi dei Vulcani Vulture ed Etna.—*Congr. Ital. Geol., pp.* 6, 1 *pl. Mexico,* 1906.

LORENZO, G. DE.—Venosa e la regione del Vulture (la terra d'Orazio).—*Ist. Ital. Arti graf. pp.* 116, *fig.* 120, *pl.* 1. *Bergamo,* 1906.

MARIANI, E.—Una salita al Monte Vulture in Basilicata.—*Ann. R. Ist. tecn. Udine, S.* 2, *ix. Udine,* 1892.

MINERVINO, C. S.—Lettera al Signor Domenico Tata.—8^0, *pp.* 63–235, *foll.* 2, *pls.* 5. *Napoli,* 1778.
Paged consecutively to Tata, D.— Lettera, etc.

MONTANO, B.—[Memoria sulla topografia e geologia del Vulture].—*Ann. Acc. Aspir. Nat. ii, pp.* 161–174. *Napoli,* 1844.

NEUMAYR, M. — Erdgeschichte. — *Allgemeine Naturkunde, i, pp.* 42 + xii + 653, *very num. illustr. Leipzig,* 1886.

PALLOTTINO, F.—Il Vulture e la sua regione vulcanica.—*Rionero di Vultura,* 2a ed. 1880, [estr. d.] *Boll. Sez. Alpina Lucana, i, pp.* 42. 1880.

PALMIERI, L., SCACCHI, A. — Ueber die vulcanische Gegend des Vultur und das dortige Erdbeben vom 14 August 1851.—*Zeitschr. deutsch. geol. Gesellsch. v, pp.* 21–74, *geol. map. Berlin,* 1853.

PALMIERI, L.—*See* SCACCHI, A., 1852.

PARETO, L.—Della posizione delle roccie pirogene ed eruttive dei periodi terziario, quaternario ed attuale in Italia.—8^0, *pp.* 35. *Genova,* 1852.

RAMMELSBERG, C. F. A.—Ueber die Zusammensetzung des Hauyns und der Lava (Hauynophyr) von Melfi am Vultura. —*Zeitschr. deutsch. geol. Gesellsch. xiii, pp.* 273–276. *Berlin,* 1860.

RATH, J. J. G. VOM.—Erdbeben von Ischia von 4 März 1881.—Zustand des Vesuv in März 1881.—Ein Besuch des Vultur.—Krystallform des Cuspidin.— [Extr.] *Sitz. niederrhein. Gesellsch. Nat. pp.* 192–210. *Bonn,* 1881.

RECLUS, E.—Les Volcans de la Terre.— *Soc. Astronom. Bruxelles,* 1906.

RICCIARDI, L.—Sull' allineamento dei vulcani italiani. . . . Sul graduale passaggio delle roccie acide alle roccie basiche.—8^0, *pp.* 1–40. *Reggio-Emilia,* 1887.

RICCIARDI, L.—Ricerche di Chimica Vulcanologica sulle rocce e minerali del Vulture-Melfi.—*Gazz. Chim. Ital. xvii, pp.* 214–225. *Palermo,* 1887.

RICCIARDI, L.—Genesi e composizione chimica dei Terreni Vulcanici Italiani. 8^0, *pp.* 155. *Firenze,* 1889.

RICCIARDI, L.—La recente eruzione dello Stromboli in relazione alla frattura Capo Passero-Vulture e sulla influenza lunisolare nelle eruzioni.—8^0, *pp.* 12. *Reggio Calabria,* 1893.

SCACCHI, A.—Sul magnetismo polare di alcune lave del Monte Vultura.—*Rend. R. Acc. Sci. i, pp.* 23–24. *Napoli,* 1852.— *Corrisp. Scient. iii, pp.* 30–31. *Roma,* 1855.

SCACCHI, A., PALMIERI, L. — Della regione vulcanica de Monte Vulture e del tremuoto ivi avvenuto il 14 agosto 1851. Relaz. fatta per incar. d. R. Acc. Sci. —*pp.* 160, *pl.* vii. *Napoli,* 1852.

SCACCHI, A.—*See* PALMIERI, L., 1853.

SIMON, E.—Aracnidi raccolti da G. Cavanna al Vulture.—*Boll. Soc. Entomolog. Ital. xiv, pp.* 17. *Firenze,* 1882.

STEGAGNO, G.—I crateri-laghi del Vulture. —*Il Mondo Sottereaneo, iv.* [1908].

SWINBURNE, H.—Travels in the two Sicilies in the years 1777-78-9 and 80. —2nd ed. 2 vols. 8⁰. *Vol. i, pp. lxviii+307, pls. 5 ; Vol. ii, pp. xi + 359, pls. 3. London*, 1790.
See Vol. ii, p. 332 *et seq.*

TATA, D.—Lettera sul Monte Volture a sua eccellenza il Signor D. G. Hamilton.—8⁰, *figs.* 2, *pp.* 62. *Napoli*, 1778.

TENORE, M.—Sul Ciprino del Vulture (1838).—*Atti R. Acc. Sci. v*, 2 *Mem.*, Class. fis. e stor. nat. *pp.* 1-6. *Napoli*, 1844.

TENORE, M.—*See* GUSSONE.

TERRACCIANO, N. — Floræ Vulturis Synopsis, exhibens Plantas Vasculares in Vulture Monte ac finitimis locis sponte vegetantes.—*Atti R. Ist. Incorag. S.* 2, *vi, pp.* 241-446. *Napoli*, 1869.

WASHINGTON, H. S.—Chemical Analyses of Igneous Rocks published from 1884 to 1900, with a critical discussion of the character and use of analyses.—*U.S. Geol. Surv., Prof. Paper* 14, *pp.* 495. *Washington*, 1903.

ISOLE PONZA

ANON.—Description des Estats Naples, Sicille, Sardagne.—*fol.*, *pp.* 320, *num. plans, maps and engrav.* — ?, — ?

ANON.—Tableau topographique et historique des Îles d'Ischia, Vandotena, Procida, Nisida, du Cap Misène et du Mont Pausilipe. Par un Ultramontain. (M. Haller).—8⁰, *pp. viii + 216. Napoli,* 1822.

ANON.—Totius Italia noua et accurata Descriptio.—*In "Italie oder Welschland in gemeyn."* — ?, — ?

ANON.—[View of part of the inside of the harbour of the Island of Ponza.] Engrav. by Jˢ. Basire, from letter of Sir W. Hamilton to Sir Joseph Banks on the Present State of Vesuvius with an account, etc.—*Phil. Trans. R. Soc. lxxvi, Tab. xii, p.* 380. *London,* 1786.
Engrav.: 322 × 176 mm.

ABICH, O. W. H. Von.—Geologische Fragmente aus dem Nachlasse Hermann Abich's. . . . II. Zur Geologie der Ponza Inseln. . . . Mit einem Atlas.—*gd. fol., pp.* 46, 1 *pl. Wien,* 1887.

BAEDEKER, K.—Italien. Handbuch für Reisende. 3 Thiel : Unter-Italien und Sicilien nebst Ausflügen nach den Liparischen Inseln.—8th ed. 16⁰, *pp. xlviii + 412, maps 26, plans 17. Leipzig,* 1887.

BARATTA, M.—Materiali per un catalogo dei fenomeni sismici avvenuti in Italia (1800–1872).—*Mem. Soc. Geog. Ital. vii, Pt. 1, pp.* 81–164. *Roma,* 1897.

BARATTA, M.—I Terremoti d'Italia.—8⁰, *pp.* 950, *pls. Torino,* 1901.
Gives, in Pt. iii, an extensive bibliography of the earthquakes of Italy.

BEGUINOT, A.—L'Arcipelago Ponziano e la sua flora. Appunti di Geografia storica e di Topografia botanica.—*Boll. Soc. Geog. Ital. S.* 4, *iii, pp.* 214–243, 339–370, 408–438. *Roma,* 1902.
See pp. 346–351.

CERULLI, D.—In Metrobii titulum Pandatariae Insulæ jur. dic. Praefecti exercitatio in hac altera editione curis posterioribus auctior.—4⁰, *foll.* 4 + *pp.* 50, *figs.* 3. *Neapoli, Raimundi,* 1775.

DAUBENY, C. G. B.—A Description of active and extinct Volcanos ; with remarks on their origin, their chemical phenomena, and the character of their products, as determined by the condition of the earth during the period of their formation.—8⁰, *pp.* 466, *figs., maps* 2, *pl.* 1. *London,* 1826.—8⁰, *pp.* 743, *figs., maps* 10, *pls.* 4. *London,* 1848.

DOELTER, C.—Vorläufige Mittheilungen über den geologischen Bau der Pontinischen Inseln.—*Sitz. k. Akad. Wissensch. lxxi, pp.* 49–57, *pl.* 1. *Wien,* 1875.—*Boll. R. Com. Geol. Ital. vi, pp.* 154–162. *Roma,* 1875.

DOELTER, C.—Die Vulcangruppe der Pontinischen Inseln.—*Denkschr. k. Akad. Wissensch. xxxvi,* 2, *pp.* 141–186, *pls.* 6. *Wien,* 1875.

DOELTER, C.—Carta delle Isole Ponza, Palmarola e Zannone.—*R. Uffic. Geol. Ital. Roma,* 1876.
1 : 20,000.

DOELTER, C.—Il gruppo vulcanico delle Isole Ponza.—*Mem. p. serv. descriz. Cart. Geol. Ital. pubbl. d. R. Com. Geol. Ital. iii,* 1, *pp.* 1–43, 4 *pl. Roma,* 1876.

DOLOMIEU, D. G. S. T. G. De.—Mémoire sur les Îles Ponces et catalogue raisonné des produits de l'Aetna.—8⁰, *pls.* 2. *Paris,* 1788.—8⁰, *pp.* 4 + 412, *pl. iv. Leipzig,* 1789.

EIGEL, F.—Ueber einige Eruptivgesteine der pontinischen Inseln.—*Min. petr. Mitth. viii,* 1 *and* 2, *pp.* 73–100. *Wien,* 1886.

EMMONS, H.—Hebung der Insel Palmarola. —*Leipzig,* 1892.—*N. J. f. Min. ii, pp.* 82–84, *figs.* 2. *Stuttgart,* 1892.

FORTIS, G. B.—Osservazioni litografiche sulle isole di Ventotene e Ponza.—*Mem. Acc. Sci. Lett. ed Arti. Padova,* 1794.

FRANCO, P.—See FRIEDLAENDER, E. . . . Geologia delle Isole Pontine. 1900.

FRIEDLAENDER, E., and FRANCO, P.— Contribuzione alla Geologia delle Isole Pontine.—Boll. Soc. Geol. Ital. xix, pp. 672–676. Roma, 1900.

GALDIERI, A.—Osservazioni sui Terreni sedimentarii di Zannone. (Isole Pontine) —Rend. R. Acc. Sci. S. 3, xi, pp. 38–45, 1 pl. (geol. map.). Napoli, 1905.

GALDIERI, A.—Su di una Sabbia magnetitica di Ponza.—Rend. R. Acc. Sci. S. 3, xii, pp. 115–116. Napoli, 1906.

GIUSTINIANI, L.—Dizionario geografico ragionato del regno di Napoli.—8⁰, 8 tomes. Napoli, 1802–1805.

HALLER.—Tableau topographique et historique des Isles d'Ischia, Ponza, Ventotene, de Procida et de Nisida, du Cap de Misène et du Mont Pausilipe par un ultramontan.—8⁰, pp. viii + 216. Naples, 1822.

HAMILTON, W.—Some particulars of the present state of Mount Vesuvius ; with the account of a journey into the province of Abruzzo, and a voyage to the Island of Ponza.—Phil. Trans. R. Soc. lxxvi, pp. 365–381, folding map and 2 pls. by Basire. London, 1786.—In German : Dresden, 1787.

JOHNSTON-LAVIS, H. J.—The Relationship of the Structure of Igneous Rocks to the Conditions of their Formation.— Scient. Proc. R. Dublin Soc. N.S. v, pp. 112–156. Dublin, 1886.

JOHNSTON-LAVIS, H. J.—Notes on the Ponza Islands.—Geol. Mag., pp. 529–535, 3 woodcuts. London, 1889.

JOHNSTON-LAVIS, H. J.—Osservazioni geologiche sulle Isole Ventotene e Santo Stefano (Gruppo delle Isole Ponza).— Boll. R. Com. Geol. Ital. xxi, pp. 60–64. Roma, 1890.

JOHNSTON-LAVIS, H. J.—Volcans et tremblements de terre (Revue).—Ann. géol. univ. vi, pp. 355–381. Paris, 1890.

JUDD, J. W.—Contributions to the Study of Volcanoes. The Ponza Islands.—Geol. Mag. pp. 298–308, figs. London, 1875.

LIGORIO, P.—Nova Regni Neapolit. Descript. ecc.—Roma, MDLVIII. Shows Palmarola as a single island as big as Ponza. Very rough delineation.

LORENZO, G. DE.—Studi di geologia nell' Appennino meridionale.—Napoli, 1896 ; e Atti R. Acc. Sci. S. 2, viii, Mem. 7, pp. 128. Napoli, 1896.

MAGINI, G. A.—Italia. Data in luce da Fabio suo figliuolo al Serenissimo Ferdinado Gonzaga.—fol., pp. 24, maps 61. Bononiae, MDCXX. Map 51 : Palamarola and Faraglione are represented as two islands of equal size.

MAGINI, G. A.—Italia Nuova. — ?, — ? [B.N.P.] See sheet with " Meridies " at foot.

MATTEJ, P.—L'Archipelago Ponziano.— 2a ed. 4⁰, pp. 100 + v. num. figs. Napoli, 1857.

MERCALLI, G.—Note Geologiche e Sismiche sulle Isole di Ponza.—Atti R. Acc. Sci. S. 2, vi, pp. 27, pl. 1, fig. 1. Napoli, 1894.—Id. Rend. S. 2, vii, pp. 168–169. Napoli, 1893.

MERCALLI, G.—Le Isole Pontine.—Natura ed Arti, 7. Milano, 1894.

MORTIER, P. (publ.).—Terre de Labeur ou Campagna Felix.—Amsterdam, — ? [B.M.—K. 83, 44.] Shows Palmarola and Faraglione as separate isles of about equal size.

ORTELIUS, A.—Theatrum Orbis Terrarum. D. Philippo Austriaco Ded. Consecratque Adolphi Mekerchi. . . . Frontispicii explicatio Abrahamas Ortelius Antverpianus, benevolis Lectoribus. S.D. Catalogos Auctorum Tabulorum Geographicorum, etc.—1st ed. fol., maps 1-53 (engraved by many authors). Antwerpiæ, 1570. There were editions again in 1570, with col. pl., 1571, 1571 (in Dutch), 1572, 1573 (Additamentum), 1574, 1575, 1579, 1580, 1581, 1584 (with Additamentum), 1587, 1589, 1590, 1592, 1595, 1598 (the year of the Author's death). Further editions, edited by John Moretus, appeared in 1601 epitome, 1602 Tabulis Aliquot novis, 1603, 1606, 1609, 1612, 1619 Parergi, 1624, 1631, the last by Blaev. In all these editions in the map of S. Italy the I. of Parmarola is much exaggerated in size and there are no indications of its being divided. For further details on Ortelius, consult HESSELS, J. H.—Abraham Ortelii (Geographi Antverpiensis et virorum eruditorum ab eundem, etc.) — sm. fol. Cantabrigiæ 1887.

PARETO, L.—Della posizione delle roccie pirogene ed eruttive dei periodi terziario, quaternario ed attuale in Italia.—8⁰, *pp.* 35. *Genova*, 1852.

PILLA, L.—Application de la Théorie des Cratères de Soulèvement au volcan de Roccamonfina, dans la Campanie.—*Paris, Bertrand,* 1844.—[Abstr.] *Bull. Soc. géol. France, xiii, pp.* 402-3. *Paris,* 1842.— *Id. Mém. S.* 2, *i,* 3, *pp.* 163-179, *pls. iv, v, vi.* 1844.—*Atti 3a Riun. Sci. Ital. pp.* 169-171. *Firenze,* 1841.—German transl. in ROTH : " *Vesuv und die Umgebung von Neapel.*" *Berlin,* 1857.

PROGENIE, F. (del.).—[View taken from the outside of the harbour of the island of Ponza near the lighthouse.] Engraved by Js. Basire sc. from Letter from Sir W. Hamilton to Sir Joseph Banks on the Present State of Vesuvius, with an account, &c.—*Phil. Trans. R. Soc. lxxvi, Tab. xii. p.* 380. *London,* 1786.
An engrav. : 568 × 180 mm.

RATH, J. J. G.VOM.—Ueber einen Besuch der Insel Ponza.—*Sitz. niederrhein. Gesellsch. Nat. &c. pp.* 137-149. *Bonn,* 1886.

RECLUS, E.—Les Volcans de la Terre.— *Soc. Astronom. Bruxelles,* 1906.

RICCIARDI, L.—Sull'allineamento dei Vulcani Italiani. Sulle roccie eruttive subaeree e submarine e loro classificazione in due periodi. . . . Sul graduale passaggio delle roccie acide alle roccie basiche.—8⁰, *pp.* 1-40. *Reggio-Emilia,* 1887.

RICCIARDI, L.—Genesi e successione delle Rocce Eruttive.—*Atti Soc. Ital. Sci. Nat. xxx, pp.* 212-237. *Milano,* 1887.

RICCIARDI, L.—Genesi e composizione chimica dei Terreni Vulcanici Italiani.— 8⁰, *pp.* 155. *Firenze,* 1889.

RIZZI-ZANNONI, G. A.—Carta Geograf. della Sicilia Prima o sia Regno di Napoli. —*Parigi,* 1769. [B.M.—23880 (21).] A fine map of Palmarola, well-drawn.

RIZZI-ZANNONI, G. A.—General-Karte von dem Koenigreiche Neapel oder Napoli verfasst von . . . neu herausgegeben von Herrn F. A. Schræmbl.—4 *foll. Wien,* 1789. [B.M.—23880 (23).] Palmarola is fairly well represented.

ROTH, J. L. A.—Zur Kenntniss der Ponza Inseln.—*Sitz. k. Akad. Wissensch. xxix, pp.* 623-633. *Berlin,* 1882.—*Boll. R. Com. Geol. Ital.* 7-8, *pp.* 178, 189. *Roma,* 1883.

SABATINI, V.—Descrizione geologica delle Isole Pontine.—*Boll. R. Com. Geol. Ital. xxiv, pp.* 228-267, 309-329, *figs.* 18, *pls.* 2, *map* 1. *Roma,* 1893.

SABATINI, V.—Sulla Geologia dell'Isola di Ponza.—*Boll. Soc. Geol. Ital. xv, pp.* 384-414, *figs.* 9. *Roma,* 1896.

SABATINI, V.—Ueber die Geologie der Ponzainsel.—*Min. petr. Mitth., N. F. xvi, pp.* 530-535. *Wien,* 1897.

SABATINI, V.—Relazione sulle Escursioni alle Isole Pontine fatte dalla Società Geologica Italiana nei giorni 21 e 22 Febbraio 1898.—*Boll. Soc. Geol. Ital. xvii, pp. xl–lxi. Roma,* 1898.

SCHNEIDER, C. C.—Geologie der Ponzainsel.—*Min. petr. Mitth., N. F. xvi, pp.* 65-69. *Wien,* 1896.

SCHNEIDER, C. C.—Erwiderung auf Sabatini's : Ueber die Geologie der Ponzainsel.— *Min. petr. Mitth., N. F. xvii, pp.* 374-383. 1897.

SCHOEL, H. VAN.—Regno di Napoli.—H. v. S. formis.—*Romae,* 1602. Very sketchy map of Palmarola represented as a single island.

SCROPE, G. J. POULETT.—Notice on the geology of the Ponza Isles (1824).—*Trans. Geol. Soc. ii, pp.* 195-236. *London,* 1827.— *Zeitschr. f. Min. v, pp.* 324-343. *Heidelberg,* 1829.

SCROPE, G. J. POULETT.—Considerations on Volcanos, the probable causes of their phenomena . . . and their connection with the present state and past history of the globe ; leading to the establishment of a new Theory of the earth.—8⁰, *pp. xxxi* +270, 2 *pls.,* 1 *map. London,* 1825.— [Another ed. entitled :] Volcanos : the character of their phenomena. . . . With a descriptive Catalogue of all known volcanos.——2nd ed. 8⁰, *pp. xi* +490, 1 *pl.,* 1 *col. map. London,* 1862.—In French (transl. by Endymion) : *col. pls.* 2. *Paris,* 1864.—In Germ. (transl. by G. A. v. Klöden) : 1 *pl.,* 65 *figs. Berlin,* 1872. —Extr. in Ital. : *Bibl. Ital. xlv, pp.* 70-83, 211-226. *Milano,* 1827.

SENTIERI, M.—Neapolis Regnum quo continentur Aprulium Ulterius et Citerius.—*Augusta Vind[elicorum*, 1740 ?] [B.M. 23880(13).]
Palmarola is represented as a double island.

SWINBURNE, H.—Travels in the two Sicilies in the years 1778–80.—2 *vols. London*, 1783.——2nd ed. 2 vols. 8⁰. *Vol. i*, *pp. lxviii+307, pls. 5; Vol. ii, pp. xi+359, pls. 3. London, Nichols*, 1790.——3rd ed. 1795.—In French : *Paris, Didot*, 1785. —In German: 2 *Th., I. R. Forster, Hamburg*, 1785.

TACCHINI, P.—Il terremoto romano del 19 luglio 1899.—*Atti R. Acc. Lincei, S. 5, Rend. viii, sem. 2, pp.* 291–296. *Roma*, 1899.

TRICOLI, G. C.—Monografia per le Isole del Gruppo Ponziano.—8⁰, *pp.* 437. *Napoli*, 1855.

WASHINGTON, H. S.—Italian petrological sketches. v. Summary and Conclusion.—*Journ. Geol. v*, 4, *pp.* 349–377. *Chicago*, 1897.

WASHINGTON, H. S.—Some Analyses of Italian Volcanic Rocks.—*Amer. Journ. Sci. viii, pp.* 286–294. *New-Haven*, 1899.

WASHINGTON, H. S.—Chemical Analyses of Igneous Rocks published from 1884 to 1900, with a critical discussion of the character and use of analyses.—*U.S. Geol. Surv., Prof. Paper* 14, *pp.* 495. *Washington*, 1903.

WASHINGTON, H. S.—The Superior Analyses of Igneous Rocks, from Roth's Tabellen, 1869–1884, arranged according to the Quantitative System of Classification.— *U.S. Geol. Surv., Prof. Paper* 28, *pp.* 61. *Washington*, 1904.

CAMPI PHLEGRÆI

ANON.—Sulle acque balneolane dette di Bagnoli.—*Napoli*, 1863.

ANON.—Analisi dell'acqua raccolta dal vapore di una fumarola della Solfatara di Pozzuoli.—8⁰, *pp.* 27. *Napoli*, 1780. [C.A.]

ANON.—Arces Apollinis. Cittadella di Cuma. Æn. Lib. VI. 9.
A distant view of Ischia. A fine engrav.: 108 × 69 mm.

ANON.—Arriua an dem Lustgarten des Vice-Re zu Neapoli 14. (Over this, written in ink, is " 39.")
Engrav.: 230 × 136 mm.

ANON.—Arriva zu Neapoli in Angesicht desz Pallazzo Reale. 10.
Engrav.: 206 × 134 mm.

ANON.—Bibliographie géologique et paléontologique de l'Italie, par les soins du Comité d'Organisation du 2e Congrès Géologique International à Bologne.—8⁰, *pp.* 630. *Bologne*, MDCCCLXXXI.

ANON.—Breve descrizione della Città di Napoli e del suo Contorno.—8⁰, *pp.* 16 + 344. *Napoli*, 1792.

ANON. [THOMPSON, G.].—Breve notizia di un viaggiatore sulle incrostazioni silicee termali d'Italia, e specialmente di quelle de' Campi Flegrei nel regno di Napoli.—*Giorn. Lett. xli. pp.* 32–51. *Napoli*, 1793–1798.

ANON. [British Association Committee].—Report . . . changes of the land level of the Phlegræan Fields.—*Rep. Brit. Assoc.* (1901), *pp.* 382–383. 1901.

ANON.—[Camaldoli della Torre.]
View of monastery from road to it. Ischia in distance and three monks in foreground. Litho.: 273 × 197 mm.

ANON.—[Campi Phlegræi from the Camaldoli Monastery.]
Six monks, two civilians, and two spaniels in foreground. Engrav.: 600 × 415 mm.

ANON.—Carta (Corografica) d'Italia.—*Ist. Geog. Milit. Ital.* 1889.
1 : 1,800,000, in 6 sheets.—2 ed. 1st, in 3 colours as in preceding ; 2nd, without mountain shading. *See* sheet 4.

ANON.—Carta (Corografica) d'Italia.—*Ist. Geog. Milit. Ital.* 1889.
1 : 1,000,000, in 7 sheets.—3 ed. 1st, in 3 colours, with mountains shaded in brown and water in blue ; 2nd, mountains in grey ; 3rd, without mountain shading. *See* sheet 4.

ANON.—Carta Corografica del Regno d'Italia e delle Regioni Adiacenti.—*Ist. Geog. Milit. Ital.* 1889.
1 : 500,000, in 35 sheets.—3 ed. 1st, in 3 colours ; 2nd, in 2 colours ; 3rd, in black, without mountain shading. *See* sheet 24.

ANON.—Carta de' Crateri esistenti tra il Vesuvio e la Spiaggia di Cuma. [B.M.—K. 83, 52-2-b.]

ANON.—Carta dalla Gajola a Torre del Greco (piani Porte Granatello e Torre del Greco).—*Uffic. Idrograf. R. Mar. Ital.* 1885.
1 : 20,000.

ANON.—Carta geologica d'Italia nella scala di 1 : 1,000,000, in due fogli. 2a ed.—*R. Uffic. Geol. Ital. Roma*, 1889.

ANON.—Carta del Golfo di Pozzuoli.—*Uffic. Idrograf. R. Mar. Ital.* 1887.
1 : 20,000.

ANON.—Carta del Mare Jonio e Mar Tirreno.—*Uffic. Idrograf. R. Mar. Ital.* 1878.
1 : 1,000,000.

ANON.—Carta della Provincia di Napoli e parte delle contigue di Caserta, Salerno e Benevento.—*Napoli*, 1861–1875.
1 : 10,000, in 6 sheets, copper engrav. *See* sheet 3.

ANON.—Carta Topografica e Idrografica dei Contorni di Napoli.—*Napoli*, 1818–1870.
1 : 25,000, in 15 sheets, copper engrav. *See* sheet 8.

D

ANON.—Carta Topografica di Napoli e dintorni.—*Ist. Geog. Milit. Ital.* 1885.
1 : 100,000, in 1 sheet similiar to Cart. Topog. d. Regno d'Italia : Campi Phlegræi and Vesuvius.

ANON.—Carta Topografica del Regno d'Italia.—*Ist. Geog. Milit. Ital.* 1889.
1 : 100,000. Chromolithographic ed. in 3 colours without line shading of mountains. *See* sheets 183, 184.

ANON.—Carta Topografica del Regno d'Italia.—*Ist. Geog. Milit. Ital.* 1889.
1 : 100,000, in 277 photo-engraved sheets, in course of publication (1889). The orography is shown by contour lines of 50 m. as well as by zenith-light shading. *See* sheets 183, 184.

ANON.—Carta Topografica del Regno d'Italia.
1 : 75,000. Economic edition similar to above.

ANON.—Carte Géologique Internationale de l'Europe.
1 : 1,500,000.

ANON. [H. W.]—Casamicciola.—*"Athenæum,"* March 19, 1881.

ANON.—Casamicciola nella notte del 28 Luglio 1883. [C.A.]
3 loose sheets.

ANON.—Catalogo della Collezione Orittologica ed Oreognosica del fu chiarissimo Professore Cav. Matteo Tondi Direttore del Museo di Mineralogia di Napoli, ecc.—8⁰, *pp. viii* + 243. *Napoli,* 1837.

ANON.—Città, Fortezza, et Isola d'Ischia. [Vienna lib.]
With 6 ref. nos., ded. to Monsig. Trapani.— ? engrav. : 170×123 mm.

ANON.—La Città di Napoli Capitale del Regno. Tom. xxiii.
Naples from the sea. Engrav. : 363×164 mm.

ANON.—Continovazione al racconto dell' orribil terremoto seguito il dî 5 di Giugno 1688 nella città di Napoli e particolarmente nella città di Benevento ; co'nomi della Città . . . e de'castelli, che hanno patito simile sventure, etc.—4⁰. *Napoli et in Todi,* 1688. [B.M.]

ANON.—Contributo alla ricerca delle norme edilizie per le regioni sismiche.—*Atti R. Ist. Incorag.* MCMIX. *S.* 6, *lxi, d. Atti, pp. iii–xxv, tav.* 7. *Napoli,* 1910.
Per la Commissione del R. Ist. Incorag. di Napoli. (Bassani, F., Lorenzo, G. de, Masoni, V., Mercalli, G., Nitti, F., Pepe, G.) *See* pp. x–xiii.

ANON.—Corrispondenza da Fozio d'Ischia 14 settembre.—*"Liberta Cattolica,"* 16 *settem.* 1883.
Refers to water in well at Bajola becoming turbid before the earthquake.

ANON.—Cumæ Euboicæ. Città detta di Cuma. Æn. Lib. VI, 2.
Cuma from the woods. Fine engrav. : 110 × 69 mm.

ANON.—Description des Estats Naples, Sicille, Sardagne.—*fol. pp.* 320, *num. plans, maps, and engrav.* — ? — ?

ANON.—Descrittione di tutto l'amenissimo paese di Pozzuolo e luoghi convicini.— ?, [1600 ?] [B.M. 24120. 6.] .·
A bad copy of that of Cartaro, but with a longer printed reference.

ANON.—Disastri, Ischia-Giava.—8⁰, *pp.* 178. *Napoli,* 1883. [C.A.]

ANON.—Don Chisciotte. Catania Casamicciola.—*Catania,* 1881.

ANON.—The Earthquake in Ischia.—*"Illust. London News,"* 2183, *p.* 271, *figs.* 4, *March* 19, 1881. [C.A.]

ANON.—Dell Edificio di Pozzuoli volgarmente detto Il Tempio di Serapide.—8⁰, *pp.* 48, *pls.* 2, *tav.* 1. *Roma,* 1773.
See GUASCO.

ANON.—Das Erdbeben auf Ischia am 28 Juli 1883. Mit Ansicht und Karte der Insel und 4 autotypischen Darstellungen der Zerstörung in Kasamicciola nach Originalphotographien.—*Sonderabdr. aus* Nʳ 4 des *" Ausland "* J. 1883, 8⁰, *pp.* 40, *figs. München,* 1883. [C.A.]

ANON.—Die Erdbeben-Katastrophe von Ischia am 28 Juli 1883.—*Chronik der Zeit.* Heft 8, *pp.* 95, *pls.* 16, 1 *map. Vienna,* 1883.

ANON.—Statistica fisica ed economica dell'Isola di Capri.—*Esercitazioni Accademiche degli Aspiranti Naturalisti, ovvero Raccolta di Memorie dell' Accademia di tal nome. Fondata e diretta dal dottore O. G. Costa P. P. di zoologia nella R. Univ. di Napoli, ii, Pt.* 1, 8⁰, *pp.* 1–140. *Napoli,* 1840.
See Cap. i, Geologia, [by Pasquale La Cava] pp. 11–22, tav. 1.

ANON.—Extrait d'une lettre sur le tremblement de terre qui a eu lieu dans l'Île d'Ischia, le 2 fév. 1828.—*Bibl. Univ. Sci. xxxvii, pp.* 236–240. *Genève,* 1828 [C.A.]

ANON.—Fontana ausser Neapoli am Eingang des Furste Lustgarten, 35.
Engrav.: 206 × 138 mm.

ANON.—A General View of the City of Naples. *Vue générale de la Ville de Naples.* [B.M. Portfolio of Naples.]
Engrav.: 305 × 224 mm.

ANON.—Giornale letterario di Napoli per servire di continuazione all' Analisi ragionata de'libri nuovi.—112 vols. 8⁰. *Napoli,* 1793-8.
See Vol. xli, pp. 39-51.—Breve notizia di un viaggiatore sulle incrostazioni silicee termali d'Italia, e specialmente di quelle de'Campi Flegrei nel Regno di Napoli.

ANON.—Golfo di Napoli.— ? — ? [B.M.—K. 83, 75.]
A map of early date.

ANON.—Grotta di Posillipo.
Distemper showing Naples end of tunnel : 418 × 278 mm.

ANON.—La Grotte du Chien. [Source unknown, marked]. Tom. i, pag. 319.
Engrav.: 162 × 120 mm.

ANON.—Grotto of Posilippo, Naples [about 1850 ?].
Fine pencil drawing slightly tinted and touched with chalk: 142 × 98 mm.

ANON.—Guida descrittiva dei contorni di Napoli e sue isole.—12⁰, *pp.* 477, *num. woodcuts. Napoli,* 1865.
T. of Serapis, Grotta, etc.

ANON.—Guide du Voyageur pour les Antiquités et Curiosités naturelles de Pouzol et des environs.—8⁰, *pp.* 134. *Naples.*
See pp. 17-26 : De Campi Flegrei e della Solfatara.

ANON.—Hæc est nobilis et florens illa Neapolis Campaniæ ciuitas, antea Parthenope appellata, etc.—*Naples,* 1516.
Engrav. map with text at back in French, entitled "Naples" and dated 1516; 71 reference numbers : 481 × 337 mm.
This is Pl. 48 in Braun, G., and Hohenberg, F.: Théâtre des Principales Villes de tout l'Vnivers, Vol. i, Brussels, 1574; and is Pl. 47 in the Italian edition : Civitates Orbis Terrarum, Lib. ii, *Coloniæ Agrippinæ,* 1582-1618; and Pl. 47 of Lib. i of the ed. of 1523-1618 ; with 71 nos. of explanatory text in Gothic German characters on back and date 1516: 481 × 236 mm.

ANON.—A Handbook for Travellers in Southern Italy and Sicily ; comprising the description of Naples and its environs, Pompeii, Herculaneum, Vesuvius, Sorrento ; the islands of Capri and Ischia ; Amalfi, Pæstum, and Capua, the Abruzzi and Calabria ; Palermo, Girgenti, the Greek Temples, and Messina.—9th ed. in 2 pts. 8⁰. Pt. i, South Italy, *pp.* 288 + 20, *maps, plans, &c.;* Pt. ii, Sicily, *pp.* 289-418 + 11, *maps, plans, &c. London,* 1890.

ANON.—Interno della Grotta di Pozzuoli.
Distemper: 165 × 260 mm.

ANON.—Intorno all'acqua della Solfatara di Pozzuoli, storia e documenti.—*Napoli,* 1869.

ANON.—Intorno alle Acque Minerali delle provincie Napoletane.—*Atti R. Ist. Incorag. S. 2, ii, pp.* 161-222. *Napoli,* 1865.

ANON.—Per Ischia.—"*Corriere del Mattino*" *of Naples, loose sheets, pp.* 10. [C.A.]

ANON.—Isola d'Ischia.—*Pubbl. G. B. Paravia e C., Torino, Roma, Milano, Firenze, Napoli,* 1876.
Raised map : 1 : 15,000.

ANON.—L'Italia.—4⁰, *pp.* 326, *num. maps. Torino,* 1896.

ANON.—Von Italia. Die Statt Neapels, nach form und gestalt gantz Schoen abcontrasehtet, an Bewen, Palasten und herzlichen Platzen wie sie jetzundt zu unfern zeiten ist gestaltet Cc v Der.
Engrav.

ANON.—L'Italie.—8⁰, *pp.* 608, 243 *engrav.,* 5 *maps. Paris,* — ?

ANON.—Itinéraires et souvenirs d'un voyage en Italie en 1819 et 1820.—3 vols.: *Vol. i, pp.* 374; *Vol. ii, pp.* 390; *Vol. iii, pp.* 416. *Paris,* 1829.

ANON.—Itinerario per Pozzuoli, Baja, Miseno ed altri luoghi intorno colla descrizione delle cose più rare che ivi si rivengono, fatto colla massima brevita per comodo de'viaggiatori.—8⁰, *pp.* 47. *Napoli,* 1832.

ANON.—Lacus Anianus.—[S. Martino Mus. 5890.]
A plate, second half of 1500.

ANON.—Lacus Avernus.—[S. Martino Mus. 5891.]
A plate, second half of 1500.

ANON.—Le landscape français. Italie.—
8⁰, *pp.* 232, 12 *pls. Paris*, 1833.
See pl. at p. 172 : Mole of Caligula,
similar to others of same date.

ANON.—Loggia mit Statuen dess Card :
Mont Alto zu Neapoli. 11.
Engrav.: 206 × 138 mm.

ANON.—[Part of a large Map of the Kingdom
of Naples engraved at Naples 1785–1789.]
[B.M.—K. 83, 23.]
A good map of Vesuvius and Campi
Phlegræi for the date.

ANON.—Mappa di Pozzuoli. [B.M.—K.
83 (73, 74, 75).] Tempio di Giove e
Serapeo in Pozzuoli. [B.M.—K. 83 (78).]
The latter is a distemper painting.

ANON.—Das Mare Morto bei Neapel. [C.A.]
A plate ?

ANON.—1, Marochiaro ; 2, Scuola di Virgilio. D.D. a S.E. Madᵉ la Duchesse de
Calabritta.
Similar to Pl. 68 in Morghen's 84
Vedute, but does not bear " Pl. 13 " nor
inscript. " Con Priv. Reg." Engrav.:
250 × 134 mm.

ANON.—The Mediterranean Illustrated. Picturesque Views and Descriptions of its
Cities, Shores, and Islands.—4⁰, *pp.* xii +
373. *London*, 1877.
See pp. 125–142 and illustrations. Good
woodcuts of the Temple of Serapis.

ANON.—Memoria sui Monumenti di Antichita e di Belle Arti ch'existono in Miseno,
Baoli, Baja, Cuma, Napoli, Pompei, &c.—
pls. Napoli, 1812.

ANON.—Mirabilium Sulphureorum Motium
apud Puteolos (Campos Flegreos) Plin.
Vulcani forum Strabo Vulgo nunc Solfataria
vocantNeapolitani genuina accuratisimaq =
ad viuum depicta representatio. [On
top] ORIENS. [Below] Georgivs Dum
Expendar. [B.M. Portfolio of Naples.]
Col. view of the Solfatara: 540 × 400 mm.,
with description on top right-hand corner
and a note entitled " Forum Vulcani " at
the back.

ANON.—Monte S. Simone und die Eruption
von 1811.—*Morgenblatt*, 138, *pp.* 551. 1823.
Cited by Hoff Veränd. ii, S. 241.

ANON.—Mute History, or Documentary
Ruins of Nature and Art in Italy ; illustrated by a Volcanic and Antiquarian Map
of the Italian Continent and Islands.—
" *Gentleman's Magazine*," vii, *pp.* 249–
256 *and* 468–470, 1 *map. March, May,*
1837.

ANON.—Naples.—[Source unknown,marked]
Tom. 3, p. 34.
Small engrav. plan of Naples : 145 × 113
mm.

ANON.—Naples ville Capitale du Royaume
de Naples. 233.
Plate from a book with view engraved at
top and rest filled with sums : 147 × 101
mm.

ANON.—Naples from road to Capodimonte.]
Line engrav. hand-coloured. Peasant
woman, three sheep and cow in foreground :
267 × 186 mm.

ANON.—Napoli.
Small plan of Naples, probably first
half of 16th cent., fine engraving, with
text in Italian at back and on another
leaf, numbered 46, 47, 48: 172 × 113
mm.

ANON.—Napoli e luoghi celebri delle sue
vicinanze.—7ᵐᵒ Congr. scient. Ital. 8⁰.
Vol. i, pp. 8+542, num. lith. pls. and map;
Vol. ii, pp. 602 + 22, num. lith. pls. and
map. *Napoli*, 1845.
See Vol. ii, pp. 361–376, 415–468, pl. at
p. 425.

ANON.—Neapels. Napoli. Der koniglichen
State Abcontrafechung. 485, h h iii.folchen.
A view of Naples from the sea enclosed
in a fancy frame. Ships in foreground.
Woodcut : 326 × 262 mm., includ. frame.

ANON.—Der kinniglichen Statt Neapolis
Abcontrasetung (with a view of Naples).
This is a folio smaller by 2 × 2 cm.
than the above, and is attached to : Von
Italia. Neapels die, Haupstate des finni-
greichs [with a plan of Naples and descrip-
tion in Gothic characters in German.
The following page has a sword, and the
next page :] Von Italia Apulia und
Neapolis, &c. (with a map of Southern
Italy).

ANON.—Neapolis.
Bird's-eye plan of Naples from the
Sebeto to La Toretta. Below, on two sides
of a wreath, 30 reference numbers. Engraved map on thin paper : 354 × 274 mm.

ANON.—Neapolis.
Engraving. Bird's-eye view of town of
Naples, with 34 reference nos. and re-
ferences in Latin : 393 × 491 mm.

ANON.—Neapolis.
Hand-coloured engraved plan of Naples,
with text on back, ref. nos. (30) and
key at foot of map : 502 × 400 mm.

ANON.—Neapolis.
Plan of Naples with explanatory reference in Latin. Engrav.: 352 × 273 mm.

ANON.—Noticia .do fatal terremoto succedido no regno de Napoles em 29 de Novembro do anno de 1732. Tirado de cartas fide dignas escritas de Italia.— *Lisboa Occidental*, 4⁰, 1733.

ANON.—Observations diverses sur les Volcans.—*fol. pp.* 125.
MS. after 1808./ Many notes from other authors on Vesuvius, Campi Phlegræi, Etna, &c.

ANON.—Osservazioni su di un fenomeno avvenuto nel lago di Patria. Lettera 1a e 2a.—8⁰, *pp. x + 74. Napoli*, 1796.

ANON.—1. Palazzo della Rocella ; 2. Castel dell'Ovo ; 3. M. Vesuvio ; 4. M. di Somma. D.D. a Mᵉ André. Chloë regit. Dulces docta moclos et cytharæ sciens. Horat. Carm. III.
Similar to Pl. 71 of Morghen's 84 Vedute, but does not bear " Pl. 19." Engrav.: 248 × 133 mm.

ANON.—Parthenope terræmotu vixata, &c.
—*See* MISCELLANEA POETICA. [C.A.]

ANON.—A Perspective View of the City of Naples.—Vue Perspective de la Ville de Naples.—Published 12 May 1794 by Laurie and Whittle, 53, Fleet Street, London.
Similar to one publ. by Robt. Sayer, London. A carefully hand-coloured engraving of Naples from the sea : 385 × 286 mm.

ANON.—Piano d'Ischia e Procida.—*Uffic. Idrograf. R. Mar. Ital.* 1889.
Scale 1 : 25,000.

ANON.—Piano della Rada di Castellammare.—*Uffic. Idrograf. R. Mar. Ital.* 1889 *(pubbl. provvis.*).
Scale 1 : 20,000.

ANON.—[Piano di Sorrento from the South.]
Peasant, monk, and woman in foreground. Line engrav. hand-coloured : 263 × 182 mm.

ANON.—Plan de Naples.
Engrav. plan with ref. letters from A to N and nos. from 1 to 74 : 353 × 253 mm.

ANON.—[Plate of neighbourhood of Pozzuoli.]—[B.N.P.—Vb. 113, 2.]
Part of Caligula's Mole is shown with complete arches near the town and six sections with the arches broken.

ANON.—Ein Platz von Neapoli gegen der Sonenauffgang gelegen. 13.
Engrav. : 196 × 128 mm.

ANON.—Ponti Rossi (Naples).
Small distemper : 96 × 72 mm.

ANON.—Pozzvolo (with letters explan. A to G.)— ? — ? [Vienna lib.]
The Cappucini is shown on dry land and a row of houses beyond on shore of undercliff of the citadel of Pozzuoli : 175 × 124 mm.

ANON.—La Promenade utile et récréative de deux Parisiens en cent soixante-cinq jours.—2 tomes in 1 vol. 12⁰. *Vol. i, pp. xxiv*+323 ; *Vol. ii, pp.* 261. *Avignon*, 1768.

ANON.—A Prospect of Vulcan's Court, near Putzol, in Naples.
Engrav. : 195 × 146 mm.

ANON.—Puteoli. Baiæ.— *From* BRAUN, G., *and* HOHENBERG, F.: Civitates Orbis Terrarum — *Coloniæ Agrippinæ*. 1582-1618.
Two panoramas of the bay of Pozzuoli, probably by Houfnaglius, with one page of text in Latin. Engrav. : 492 × 292 mm.

ANON.—Puteoli. Kieser sc.
Circa 1630, from book by Meissner.
Inscriptions in German and Latin. A carpenter at work, with a monkey working a crane. A distant and good view of Pozzuoli and the Mole of Caligula. Said to be from Schatzkastlein, or, in French, Boîte à Passone. Very fine engrav. : 145 × 72 mm.

ANON.—Raccolta de Disegno.—*fol.* — ? — ?
Contains 107 water-colour sketches.

ANON.—Raccolta di Vedute del Regno di Napoli e suoi contorni disegnate dal vero.
—4⁰, *pls.* 47. *Presso Antonio Boggioli, Roma*, 1829.

ANON.—Raised Model of Vesuvius and Neighbourhood.—*Ist. Geog. Milit. Ital.* 1878.
1 : 50,000 horizontal and 1 : 25,000 vertical scale, cast in zinc and plated with copper.

ANON.—Relazione della commissione per le prescrizione edilizie dell'Isola d'Ischia istituita dal Ministero dei Lavori Pubblici (Genala) dopo il terremoto del luglio 1883.
—4⁰, *pp.* 86, col. pl. 2. *Roma*, 1883.

ANON.—Relazione distinta de'danni cagionati da passato tremuoti del Regno di Napoli e nello stato di Santa Chiesa, 1703.
—4⁰. *Napoli*, 1703. [B.M.]

ANON.—Relazione di un Fenomeno osservato nel Porto di Napoli a' 24 decembre 1798.—*Atti Acc. Sci. ix, pp.* 30–6. *Siena*, 1808.

ANON.—Relazione del terremoto accaduto in Napoli il giorno 8 settembre 1694.— *Napoli*, 1694.

ANON.—Relazione del tremuoto sentito in Napoli e altre provincie nel 29 novembre 1732.—*Napoli*, 1805.

ANON.—Ruina beii Pozzolo Nahe der Grossen Sibilla Cumana. 19.
Engrav.: 207 × 137 mm.

ANON.—Ruine antique, Golfe de Pauzzuoli, par M.
A tower with hazy view of coast and headlands? Rough litho.: 130 × 90 mm.

ANON.—[Sta. Lucia, Naples.]
Line engrav., hand-col. Franciscan monk, two women, and other figures in foreground: 263 × 183 mm.

ANON.—[Sorrento from house on edge of cliff.]
Line engrav., hand-col. Man, woman, and child in foreground : 263 × 182 mm.

ANON.—Tableau topographique et historique des îles d'Ischia, Vendatene, Procida, Nisida, du Cap Misène et du Mont Pausilipe. Par un Ultramontain [M. Haller]— 8⁰, *pp. viii* + 216. *Napoli*, 1822.

ANON.—Tavolette rilevate per la costruzione della carte del Regno d'Italia.— *Ist. Geog. Milit. Ital.* 1873–1879.
Part to the scale of 1 : 50,000 and part 1 : 25,000. *See* sheets 183, ii ; 184, i–iv.

ANON.—[Temple of Mercury at Baja.]
Line engrav. coloured by hand. Man with gun stooping in foreground: 263 × 182 mm.

ANON.—Terra Sulphurata Puteolana. Planiti Sulphurea a grecis " φαι.γ. ἀγορ." a hoc est Vulcani forum nūcupata. (With ref. nos. and expl.)
3 cavaliers, 2-horsed carriage and dog in foreground. Engrav.: 450 × 362 mm.

ANON.—Il terremoto del luglio 1883, nell-Isola d'Ischia.—Secondo la relazione ufficiale della Commissione Governativa presieduta dall'Ing. F. Giordano.—" Cosmos," *viii, pp.* 65–76, 113–19, 164–84, 1 *map. Torino*, 1884–85.

ANON.—Trattati dei Terremoti.—8⁰. *Bologna*, 1571. [B.M. 444, b. 20.]

ANON.—Veduta degli Avanzi di 13 Pile, che tra l'numero della 25 terminavano l'antico Porto di Pozzuoli, nella cui continuazione fu fatto fui a Baia il Ponte Sopra Navi dall Imperatore Ciligola.— —? , 1760. [B.M. 24125 (2).]
A plate.

ANON.—Veduta generale di Napoli da Capodichino.—Si vende presso Giorgio Glass dirimp¹⁰ S. Ferdinando. 54.
Outline engrav. about 1814 : 303 × 233 mm.

ANON.—Veduta del Golfo di Baja.—? , 1760. [B.M. 24129 (13).]

ANON.—Vera e distinta relazione dell' horribile . . . terremoto accaduto in Napoli & in piu parte del regno il giorno 5 Giugno, 1688, &c.—4⁰. *A. Parrino : Napoli*, 1688. [B.M.]—Also an English translation publ. by Randal Taylor.—4⁰, *pp.* 27. *London*, 1688. [B.M.]

ANON.—Vera e distinta relazione dello spaventoso e funesto terremoto accaduto in Napoli, e parte del suo regno, il giorno di 8 Settembre 1694, &c.—8⁰, *pp.* 8. *Roma and Napoli*, 1694. [B.M.]

ANON.—Vera e distinta relazione del terremoto accaduto in Napoli il giorno 8 di settembre 1694, &c.—4⁰. *A. Parrino e C. Cavallo, Napoli*, 1694.

ANON.—Veue magnifique du Port et de la Ville de Naples Capitale du Royaume de mesme nom, La Metropole est dediée a St. Janvier Patron de la ville. Elle renferme un très grand nombre d'Eglises et bastiments Superbes, les Italiens la nomment la Gentille par sa beauté et Sa belle et Riche Scituation : Le Royaume de Naples appartient à Philippe V. Roy d'Espagne.
Engrav.: 308 × 216 mm.

ANON.—A View of the Valley of the Sulfatara, otherwise called Vulcan's Cave, near Naples. Engraved for Middleton's Complete System of Geography.
Engrav.: 260 × 174 mm.

ANON.—A. Villa di Agrippina Julia figliuola di Germanicus Caesare e di Agrippina Agosto, &c. 46.
A view near Baja. Fine line engrav. in style of Silvestre: 272 × 144 mm.

ANON.—La Ville de Naples [reversed]. Vue Perspective de la Ville de Naples du côté du Port.—A Paris chés Huquier fils, Graveur, rue St. Jacques, au Gd. St. Rémy.
Naples from sea. A coloured " Vue d'Optique ": 410 × 254 mm.

ANON.—Voie des tombeaux à Pouzzoles. Engrav.: 189 × 121 mm.

ANON.—Vue de Naples prise du Phare.—Chez C. T. Muller à Naples. Line litho.: 572 × 422 mm.

ANON.—Vue de la Soufrière qui est près de Pozzuole au royaume de Naples, appelée Solfatara. [C.A.] ? A plate.

ANON.—Vue de la Ville de Sorrente.—Chez C. T. Muller à Naples. Very fine line engrav. View of the coast looking towards Vesuvius. Line litho.: 352 × 243 mm.

ANON.—Dei Vulcani o Monti Ignivomi più noti, e distintamente del Vesuvio osservazioni fisiche e notizie istoriche di Uomini Insigni di varj tempi, raccolte con diligenza. Divise in due Tomi.—12⁰. *Vol. i, pp. lxx+149; Vol. ii, pp. viii+228. Livorno*, 1779. Contains contributions from Targioni Tozzetti (Dei Monti Ignivomi della Toscana e del Vesuvio), Galiani, F., Plinio il Giovine, Magalotti, L., Strang, G., De Bomare, Darbie, F., Derham, G., Mead, R., Gennaro, A., Minervino, C. S. This work is attributed by some to Galiani, by others to Gentile. Two copies are in the Johnston-Lavis collection, one with the two tomes in one vol., containing a plate: " Prospetto del Vesuvio dal Palazzo Regio "; the other in two vols., in which the plate is missing.

ANON.—[A water-colour plan of the Naples fortifications with MS. notes, some in French.] [B.M.—K. 83, 54.] Monte Nuovo is shown vomiting flames and smoke.

ANON.—Wunderbarliche und erschreckliche neue Zeitung so sich neulich auf den xxiii sept. in 1533 in Welschland, nicht fern von Neapolis zugetraegen haben. —8⁰, foll. 3. — ? — ?

ANON.—Wunderbarliche und erschrockliche newe Zeitung so sich neulich auff den 28 tag Septembris im 1538 jar in Welschland nit fern von Neapolis zugetragen haben.—4⁰. — ? — ? [B.N.]

ABICH, O. W. H. VON.—Beiträge zur Kenntniss des Feldspathes.—*N. J. f. Min. pp.* 468–474. *Stuttgart*, 1841.—*Ann. Phys. u. Chem. [Pogg.]* l, pp. 125–149, 341–363. *Leipzig*, 1840.

ABICH, O. W. H. VON.—Geologische Beobachtungen über die vulkanischen Erscheinungen und Bildungen in Unter- und Mittel Italien : Bd. i, Lief. 1.—Ueber die Natur und den Zusammenhang der vulkanischen Bildungen.—4⁰, *pp. viii* + 134 + *xi, maps* 3, *lith. pls.* 2. *Braunschweig*, 1841.

ABICH, O. W. H. VON.— Die Vukane in Unter- und Mittel-Italien. (1. Die Vulkane Neapels ; 2. Roccamonfina ; 3. Vultur ; 4. Blick auf den Vesuv ; 5. Ansicht von Roccamonfina.) 5 Karten aufgezogen. Atlas to foregoing.

ABICH, O. W. H. VON.—Topografisch-geognostische Ubersichtskarte der continentalen vulcanischen Gegenden in Königreich Neapel, nach eignen Beobachtungen im Jahre 1838.—*Brunswick*, 1841. [B.M. 23891 (1).] In " Atlas zu den Geologischen Beobachtungen uber die vulkanischen Erscheinungen," &c.

ABICH, O. W. H. VON.—Recherches sur les Roches d'origine volcanique.—*Ann. Mines*, ii, *pp.* 579–612. *Paris*, 1842.—*Rend. Acc. Sci. ii, pp.* 457–477. *Napoli*, 1843.

ABICH, O. W. H. VON.—Geologische Fragmente aus Italien.— ? , 1863.

ACERBI, P. FRANCISCI. — Polypodium Apollineum.—*fol., viii, pp.* 352. *Neapoli*, 1674. [C.A.]

AC. f. —1. Fabrica antica chiamata la Scuola di Virgilio. D.D. a. S.A.S. Mgr. le Duc Louis de Würtemberg, &c., Sis felix ubicumque mavis, Horat. Carm. III. Similar to Morghen's 84 Views (Pl. 70), but does not bear " Con P. Re " in inscript. Engrav.: 250 × 135 mm.

ADAM (grav.).—Carte des environs de Naples : [and sections of] Terrains volcaniques des environs de Naples. Pl. iii.—*Ann. Mines*, S. 3, xi, p. 113. *Paris*, 1837. Engrav. coloured : 274 × 178 mm.

ADAM (grav.).—Terrains volcaniques des environs de Naples. Pl. viii.—*Ann. Mines*, S. 3, xi., p. 389. *Paris*, 1837. Engrav. : 268 × 175 mm.

ADAM, V.—*See* COGNET.

ADDISON, J.—Remarks on several parts of Italy, in the years 1701, 1702, 1703.—8⁰, *pp.* 534 *and index. London*, 1705.

40   *Bibliography of the South Italian Volcanoes—Campi Phlegræi*

ADLERHOLD, G.—Umständliche Beschreibung des anjetzo vom Krieg neu-bedrohten
sonst herrlichen Königreich Neapolis nach
dessen bewunderswürdigen Naturgütern,
Fruchtbarkeit, Flüssen, Seen, Meer-Busen,
und Häfen, dem stets rauchenden und
offtmals mit entsätzlichen Feuer wütenden
Vesuvio auch andern Bergen und Vorgebürgen Insuln, Höhlen, Warm- Sand- und
Gesund-Bädern, &c. Nebst vielen schönen
Kupfern auch mit und ohne Land-Carten.
—8°, *pp.* 18, *foll.* 952. *Nürnberg,* 1702.

AELST, N. VAN.—Puteoli.—*Roma,* 1560.

AGOSTINO, L. D'.—Sulle acque termo-
minerali balneolane dette dei Bagnoli di
proprietà di Gennaro Masullo.—*Napoli,*
1874.

AGUILAR, E.—Su di uno sprofondamento
avvenuto alla Solfatara di Pozzuoli.—
Boll. Soc. Nat. xix, pp. 52–3, *fig. Napoli,*
1905.

AGUILAR, E.—Notizie sulla presente attivita della Solfatara di Pozzuoli (a proposito di una nuova bocca apertosi nel
fondo di essa).—*Boll. Soc. Nat. xxi, pp.*
58–60, *fig.* 1. *Napoli,* 1907.

AGUILAR, E.—La Metavoltina tra le Sublimazioni della Solfatara di Pozzuoli.—
Boll. Soc. Nat. xxv, pp. 28–30. *Napoli,*
1911.

AJELLO, G.—*See* QUARANTA, B.

ALBERTI, F. L.—Descrittione di tutta
l'Italia & Isole pertinenti ad Essa . . . Nella
quale si contiene il sito di essa, l'Origine,
& le Signorie della Città, & de'Castelli ;
co i nomi antichi e moderni ; . . . i Monti, i
Laghi, i Fiume, le Fontane, i Bagni, le
Miniere, e tutte l'opere maravigliose in lei
dalla Natura prodotte, &c.—4°, *foll.* 32 +
foll. 502. *Gio. Batt. Porta. Venetia,*
1581.—Other ed.: *Bologna,* 1550 ; *Vineg.*
1551 ; *Vineg.* 1557 ; 1576 ; 1577 ; 1581 ;
1588 ; 1596. [In Latin] *Colonia Agrippinensi,* 1566 ; 1567.
See foll. 167–189, 1581.

ALBERTI, F. L.—Isole appartenenti all'
Italia, di nuovo ricorrette, e con l'aggionta
in piu luoghi di diverse cose occorsi fino
à nostri tempi adornate.—8°, *pp.* 97 + *iv.*
Venetia, 1581.
Frequently bound up with " Descrit. di
tutta l'Italia " of Alberti. *See* foll. 24–25.

ALFANO, G. M.—Sullo stato della questione circa la causa dei fori circolari nei
vetri, e largo contributo apportato allo
studio di essa dai professori F. Bassani e
A. Galdieri della R. Università di Napoli,
e dal Prof. Ignazio Galli di Velletri.—*Riv.
Fis. Mat. e Sci. Nat. xcvi, pp.* 558–576.
Pavia, 1907.

ALLEN, LIEUT.—*See* TEMPLE, SIR G.—
The Shores and Islands of the Mediterranean.

ALLEN.—*See* WRIGHT, G. N.

ALLERS, C. W.—La Bella Napoli.—*pp.*
214, *num. illustr. Stuttgart, Berlin, Leipzig* [1893].

ALOE, S. D'.—Naples, ses Monumens et ses
curiosités, avec une description de Pompéi,
Herculanum, Stabies, Pæstum, Pouzzoles, Cumes, Capoue et des autres endroits célèbres des environs.—12°, *pp.*
xv+435, 1 *plan. Naples,* 1847.——2nd ed.
pp. vii + 625. 1853.

ALOE, S. D'.—*See* QUARANTA, B.

ALOJA, V.—*See* FERGOLA, L., also
HACKERT.

ALVINO, F.—La Penisola di Sorrento descritta.—8°, *pp.* 52, *pls.* 3. *Napoli,* 1842.
In first note author quotes Pelliccia,
asserting Sorrento to have been an island
and that the region of Nocara, Sarno,
and Nola originated in an eruption of
Vesuvius that occurred two centuries
before the foundation of Rome, also that
Vesuvius rose from the sea in what, in
remote times, was a vast gulf.

ALVINO, F.—Il Regno di Napoli e Sicilia
descritto da Francesco Alvino con disegni
eseguiti dal vero ed incisi dall'artista
Achille Gigante. La Collina di Posilipo.
—8°, *pp.* 152 + *index, pls.* 41. *Napoli,*
1845.

AMBRA, A.—*See* QUARANTA, B.

AMENDUNI, G. — Dell'incendio dell'Agro
Puteolano. Epistola di Simone Porzio al
Viceré D. Pietro di Toledo. Traduzione
italiana preceduta da una illustrazione
critica.—*pp.* 24. *Napoli,* 1878. [C.A.]

AMODIO, M. (éditeur).—La Vittoria ed il
Castello dell' Ovo a Napoli.—A Milan,Galerie
de Cristoforis, 57. [Vienna lib.]
A litho. on yellow ground : 242 × 182
mm.

ANCORA, GAETANO D'.—Guida ragionata per le antichità e per le curiosità naturali di Pozzuoli e dei luoghi circonvicini.—8°, *pp. vi + 152, pls. 52, engrav. frontispiece. Napoli*, 1792. [C.A.]—French transl. by B. de Manville.—8°, *pp. vi + 142 + foll. li. Naples*, 1792. [B.M. 663. d. 27.] Contains many interesting views.

ANDERLINI, F.—*See* NASINI, R.

ANDERSON, TEMPEST.—The Volcanoes of the Two Sicilies.—*Rept. Brit. Assoc.* 1888, *pp.* 663–664. *London*, 1889.—*Geol. Mag.* 1888, *p.* 473.

ANDERSON, TEMPEST.—Volcanic Studies in many lands.—8°, *pp. xxii + 202, pls. cv. London*, 1903.

ANDREUCCI, O.—Reminiscenze storico geologiche sull'Isola d'Ischia.—[Estr.] *Giorn.* "*La Nazione," xxv, 246, p. 2, col. 5, to p. 3, col. 1. Firenze*, 1883.

ANDRIA, N.—Trattato delle Acque minerali. — ? , 1783.

ANGEL, F.—Ueber einen Porphyrpechstein vom Mte. Rotaro auf Ischia.—*N. J. f. Min. Beil. Bd. xxx, pp.* 447–466, *figs. Stuttgart*, 1910.

ANGELIS D'OSSAT, G. DE.—Casamicciola e le sue rovine.—8°, *pp.* 85. *Napoli*, 1883. [C.A.]

ANGELIS D'OSSAT, G. DE.—Il pozzo artesiano di Marigliano.—*Atti Acc. Gioen. Sci. Nat. S.* 4, *vii, Mem. vii, pp.* 50. *Catania*, 1894.

ANGELIS D'OSSAT, G. DE.—Un pozzo trivellato presso Napoli.—*Boll. Soc. Geol. Ital. xxi,* 1, *pp.* 33–35. *Roma*, 1902.

ANGELIS D'OSSAT, G. DE.—I coralli del calcare di Venassino (Isola di Capri).—*Rend. R. Acc. Sci. pp.* 139–140. *Napoli,* 1905.—*Id. Atti, S.* 2, *xii,* 16, *pp.* 1–48, *tav.* 2. 1905.

ANGELIS D'OSSAT,G.DE.—*See* TURSINI, A.

ANNA, A. R. DE.—Monografie intorno all'uso delle Acque termo-minerali del Tempio di Serapide in Pozzuoli.—*Napoli*, 1854.

ANNECHINO, R.—Pozzuoli e Dintorni. Note Storiche, evo antico.—8°, *pp.* 95 + 5. *Pozzuoli*, 1891.

ANTARINO, C. A.—Icon Sinus Baiarum uti nuper videbatur veterum testimoniis comprobatum. [Underneath] BE HARDI. [B.N.P. Vb. 113. B.M.—K. 83.62.]

ARABIA.—Le Acque d'Ischia.—? 1883.

ARAGO, D. F. J.—Rapport verbal sur les nouvelles recherches de M. Capocci, sur le phénomène connu de l'érosion du temple de Sérapis à Pouzzoles.—*C. R. Acad. Sci. iv, pp.* 750–753. *Paris*, 1837.

ARETINUS, FRANC.—Libellus de mirabilis Civitatis Puteolorum et locorum vicinorum : ac de nominibus virtutibusq. balneorum ibidem existentium, primo ponit epistole Franc. Aret. ad Pium pont m. (Eneas di Picolominis) [in fine] : Hoc opusculum p. eundem Augustinum Tyfernum cursim reuisum et auctum.—*foll.* 32. *Neapoli*, 1507.

ARNOLD, E. (publ.).—1te Ansicht von Neapel mit den Hafen nach einer Italienischen Zeichnung gestochen.—Dresde, chez —Erneste Arnold, ci-devant Rittner.

Hand-coloured litho. ; very poor drawing and incorrect : supposed to be from imaginary land facing Naples. : 430 × 340 mm.

ARTAUD DE MONTOR, CHEV.—Italie.— *In* "L'Univers Pittoresque. Histoire et description de tous les peuples," &c. *T. ii,* 96 *pls.,* 2 *maps. Paris*, 1834. *See* Pl. 56.

ARZRUNI, A.—Krystallographische Untersuchungen an sublimirtem Titanit und Amphibol (d. Insel Ponza).—*Sitz. k. preuss. Akad. Wissensch. i, pp.* 369–376. *Berlin,* 1882.

ASCIA, G. D'.—Storia dell'Isola d'Ischia divisa in quattro parte : Storia Fisica— Civile — Amministrativa — Monografica.— 4°, *pp.* 527. *Napoli*, 1867–68.

ASCIA, G. D'.—Fenomeni precursori del terremoto di Casamicciola del 4 marzo 1881. (Lettera.)—*Bull. Vulc. Ital.* 8, *pp.* 38–39. *Roma*, 1881.

ASCIA, G. D'.—Quesito agli scienziati pel terremoto d'Ischia.—"*Piccolo." Napoli,* 9 *Agosto*, 1883.

ASCIONE, G. DE.—I Campi Flegrei illustrati.—8°, *pp.* 95. *Pozzuoli*, 1895.

ASCOLI, DUC D'.—Earthquake at Naples.— *Phil. Mag. xxiii, pp.* 90–2. *London*, 1806.

ATTUMONELLI, M.—Mémoire sur les Eaux Minérales de Naples, et sur les Bains de Vapeurs, avec des Dissertations pathologiques et pratiques sur le traitement de diverses maladies par leur moyen et par les Eaux minérales en général.—8°, *pp.* 168. *Paris, An. xii* [1804].

ATTUMONELLI, M.—Delle Acque Minerali di Napoli, de'Bagni a Vapore, &c.—16°, *pp. xxii* + 168. *Napoli*, 1808.

AUDOT, L. E. (père).—L'Italie, la Sicile, les Îles Éoliennes, l'Île d'Elbe, la Sardaigne, Malte, l'Île de Calypso, &c., d'après les inspirations, les recherches et les travaux de Chateaubriand, Lamartine, R. Rochette, Piranezi, Napoleon, Denon, St. Non, Goethe, &c. Recueillis et publiés par Audot père.—5 Pts. in 4 Vols. 8°: *Vol. i, pp.* 370, 1 *map; Vol. ii, pp.* 280 + 128; *Vol. iii, pls.* 140 *on steel; Vol. iv, pls.* 141-291. *Paris,* 1834.
See Vol. i, pp. 95-119; Pls. 27, 49, 50, 52, 53, 54, 87, 91.

Other ed. are divided as follows:—*Pt. i, pp.* 270, *pls.* 1-94; *Pt. ii, pp.* 271-370, *pls.* 95-118; *Pt. iii, pp.* 280, *pls.* 119-207; *Pt. iv, pp.* 108, *pls.* 208-252; *Pt. v, pp.* 109-179, *pls.* 253-291, 1 *map. Paris,* 1834-37. Also:—*Pt.* 1, *pp.* 113, *pls.* 26, *Paris,* 1834; *Pt.* 2, *pp.* 370, *pls.* 27-118, 1835; *Pt.* 3, *pp.* 280, *pls.* 119-207, 1836; *Pt.* 4, *pp.* 108, *pls.* 208-252, 1836; *Pt.* 5, *pp.* 111-128, *pls.* 253-291, map 1, 1837. [B.M.]
See Pt. 2, pp. 95-119, Pls. 27, 33-38, 49, 50, 52-54, 87, 91.

2nd ed. ? 8°, *pp.* 267. *pls.* 94 *on steel. Paris,* 1835.

AUDOT, L. E. (père).—Royaume de Naples. —8°, *pp.* 370, *pl.* 117. *Paris,* 1835. [C.A.]

AUDOT, L. E. (père). (edit.).—[Views of the Campi Phlegræi.] Pl. 27, Salathé del. Collina di Posilippo. Sketton fils sc.— 150 × 92 mm.
Pl. 38. Sorrento. Casa di Torquato Tasso, Sorrento.—Each 114 × 80 mm.
Pl. 49. Ingresso della Grotta di Posillipo Interno della Grotta.—Each 105 × 80 mm.
Pl. 50. Pozzuoli. Tempio di Giove Serapida, Pozzuoli.—Each 105 × 73 mm.
Pl. 51. Pozzuoli Piazza.—160 × 108 mm.
Pl. 52. Lago Averno, Baja. Tempio di Venere.—107 × 72 mm.
Pl. 53. Lago d'Agnano e Grotta del Cane. Cuma, Grotta della Sibilla. (2 copies, one proof before letters).
Pl. 54. Ischia. Campi Elisei.—Each 112×78 mm.
Pl. 91. Napoli, Villa Reale. Napoli, Palazzo di Dogn' Anna. Napoli, Le Catacombe. Napoli, Cluostro di S Martino. —85 ⨰ 55 mm.
Pl. 92. Napoli, Sepolcro di Virgilio. —2 pls. 110 × 78 mm., 105×78 mm. Fine line engravings.

AVDEBER.—Le Voyage et observations de plvsievrs choses diverses qvi se pevvent remarquer en Italie.—12°, *pp.* 334. *Paris,* 1656.

AYOLA, M.—*See* QUARANTA, B.

BABBAGE, C.—On the geognostical phenomena at the Temple of Serapis.—*Edinb. Phil. Journ. xi, pp.* 91-99. *Edinburgh,* 1824.

BABBAGE, C.—Observations on the Temple of Serapis at Pozzuoli, near Naples, with remarks on certain causes which may produce Geological Cycles of great extent. —*Amer. Journ. Sci. Arts, xxvii, pp.* 408-411. *New-Haven,* 1835.—*Proc. Geol. Soc. ii, p.* 72. *London,* 1838.—*Quart. Journ. Geol. Soc. iii, Appendix, pp.* 213-217. *London,* 1847.

BABBAGE, C.—Observations on the Temple of Serapis at Pozzuoli, near Naples, with an attempt to explain the causes of the frequent elevation and depression of large portions of the Earth's surface in remote periods, and to prove that those causes continue at the present time. [With a supplement:] Conjectures on the Physical Condition of the Surface of the Moon.—8°, *pp.* 42, 2 *pls. London,* 1847.

BACCI, A.—De Thermis. Lib. vii.—*fol., pp. xxxii* + 509. *Venetiis,* 1571. Other ed.— *fol., foll. xxiii, pp.* 493. *Venetiis,* 1588.— *fol., pp. viii* + 425 + *xviii. Romæ,* 1622.— *fol., pp. viii* + *xxviii* + 366. *Patavii,* 1711.

BAEDEKER, K.—Italien. Handbuch für Reisende. 3 Theil: Unter-Italien und Sicilien nebst Ausflügen nach den Liparischen Inseln. 8th ed.—16°, *pp. xlviii* + 412, *maps* 26, *plans* 17. *Leipzig,* 1887. See pp. 100-112.

BALAGUER, A. M.—Los estragos del Tremblor, y subterranea conspiracion.— 4°, *pp.* 360. *Napoles,* 1697. [C.A.]

BALDACCI, L.—Alcune osservazione sul terremoto avvenuto all'isola d'Ischia il 28 luglio 1883.—*Boll. R. Com. Geol. Ital. S.* 2, *iv, pp.* 157-166. *Roma,* 1883. — " *Science,*" *ii, pp.* 396-399. 1883.

BALDACCI, L.—Tremblement de terre survenu à l'Île d'Ischia en juillet 1883.— " *La Meuse,*" *Liége,* 1, 2 *Dec.* 1883.
This is a transl. of 2nd note of author with introduction by M. Victor Buhy.

BALLERINI, G.—Viaggi sentimentali-istorici-istruttivi nel circuito del Cratere di Napoli da Pesto sino a Cuma, &c. Viaggio primo o gita sul Monte Posilippo.—8°, *pp.* 51, *pls.* 7, *map* 1. *Napoli,* 1842.

BALSAMO, F.—Sulla storia naturale delle Alghe d'acqua dolce del Comune di Napoli.—*Atti R. Acc. Sci. S.* 2, *i*, 14, *pp.* 84, *tav.* 2. *Napoli*, 1888.

BALZO, C. Del.—Cronaca del Tremuoti di Casamicciola.—8°, *pp.* 228, *foll. ix. Napoli*, 1883. [C.A.]—2nd ed. *pp. xi* + 240.— ?,— ?

BARATTA, A.—Fidelissima urbis Neapolitanæ cum omnibus vijs accurata et nova delineatio edita in luce ab. . . . [*Napoli*], 1627. [B.M. 24045, 2.]
A gigantic view, plan of Naples and Campi Phlegræi of high artistic merit.

BARATTA, M.—Carta sismica d'Italia per l'anno 1892.—*Boll. Soc. Geog. Ital. S.* 3, *vi*, *pp.* 313–323. *Roma, Aprile*, 1893.

BARATTA, M.—Sulla distribuzione topografica dei terremoti in Italia durante il quinquennio 1887–91.—*Atti Primo Congr. Geog. Ital. Genova*, 18–25 *Settembre* 1892, *Mem. sez. scient. ii*, 1, *pp.* 180–189, *tav. v. Genova*, 1894.

BARATTA, M.—Materiali per un catalogo dei fenomeni sismici avvenuti in Italia (1800–1872).—*Mem. Soc. Geog. Ital. vii*, 1, *pp.* 81–164. *Roma*, 1897.

BARATTA, M.—Saggio dei materiali per una storia dei fenomeni sismici avvenuti in Italia raccolti dal Prof. Michele Stefano de Rossi.—*Boll. Soc. Geol. Ital. xviii*, *pp.* 432–460. *Roma*, 1899.

BARATTA, M.—I Terremoti d'Italia.—8°, *pp.* 950, *pls. Torino*, 1901.
Gives, in Pt. iii, an extensive bibliography of the earthquakes of Italy.

BARBARO, A. T.—Il Pelegrino geografocronistorico da Napoli sino a Venezia.—12°, *foll.* 12 + *pp.* 588. *Venezia*, 1738.
See p. 8 for earthquake, 29 Sept. 1732.

BARBIERI (dis.).—Campania. I Campi Elisi. Lit. Berlotti.—Milano, Francesco Pagnoni Editore.
Very bad imaginary litho. on graduated tinted background : 166 × 99 mm.

BARBIERI (dis.).—Cuma. Il Lago d'Averno Lit. Berlotti.—Milano, Francesco Pagnoni Editore.
Very bad litho. on graduated tinted background : 166 × 99 mm.

BARNARD.—*See* MAPEI, C.—Italy, Classical, Historical, and Picturesque.

BARONE, G.—Ἡ ΚΑΤΑΣΤΡΟΦΗ ΤΗΣ CASAMICCIOLA, ΤΕΤΡΑΣΤΙΧΟΝ.—8°, *pp. Naples*, 1883. [C.A.]

BARRAL.—Mémoire sur des roches coquillères trouvées à la cime des Alpes dauphinoises et sur des colonnes d'un temple de Sérapis à Pouzol près Naples.—*Grenoble*, 1813.

BARTLETT, W. H. (drawn by).—The Bay of Baiae, Italy ; La Baie des Bayes, Italie ; Die Bucht zu Baiae, Italien. Engraved by T. A. Prior.—Fisher, Son & Co., London and Paris.
Steel engrav. : 194 × 164 mm.

BARTLETT, W. H. (drawn by).—The Fort and Bay of Baiae. Engraved by T. A. Prior.—The London Printing and Publishing Company, Limited.
Steel engrav. : 194 × 157 mm. Peasant man and woman under pine.

BARTOLO, S.—Breve ragguaglio dei bagni di Pozzuoli dispersi, investigati, &c.—4°, *pp.* 76. *Napoli*, 1667.

BARTOLO, S.—Thermologia Puteolana.—2 vols. *pp.* 304. 1679.

BASSANI, F., e LORENZO, G. De.—Per la geologia della penisola di Sorrento.—*Atti R. Acc. Lincei, S.* 5, *Rend. ii*, *sem.* 1, *pp.* 202–3. *Roma*, 1893.

BASSANI, F.—Di una piccola bocca apertasi nel fondo della Solfatara.—*Rend. R. Acc. Sci. S.* 3, *iv*, 12, *pp.* 441–2. *Napoli*, 1898.

BASSANI, F.—Di una nuova piccola Bocca nel fondo della Solfatara di Pozzuoli, con alcune considerazioni nella opportunità di uno studio sistematico di questo Cratere e dei lenti movimenti del suolo presso il Serapeo.—*Rend. R. Acc. Sci. S.* 3, *xiii*, *pp.* 60–65. *Napoli*, 1907.

BASSANI, F., e CHISTONI, C.—Relazione sulla opportunità di uno studio sistematico della Solfatara e dei lenti movimenti del suolo presso il Serapeo di Pozzuoli e sui mezzi piu adatti per attuarlo.—*Rend. R. Acc. Sci. S.* 3, *xiii*, *pp.* 121–124. *Napoli*, 1907.

BASSANI, F., LORENZO, G. De, MASONI, U., MERCALLI, G., NITTI, F., PEPE, G.—Contributo del R. Istituto d'Incoraggiamento di Napoli alla ricerca delle norme edilizie per le regioni sismiche.—*Atti R. Ist. Incorag.* MCMIX. *S.* 6, *lxi*, *d. Atti*, *pp. iii–xxv*, *tav.* 7. *Napoli*, 1910.
See pp. x–xiii.

BATTAGLIA TEDESCHI, A.—Le previsioni dei terremoti.—" *Corriere di Catania,*" N⁰ 193, e " *Piccolo di Napoli,*" 13 *Agosto,* 1883.

BATTY, E. F.—Naples from above the Grotto of Posilipo. Engrav. by Samuel Mitan.—*London,* 1819.

BATTY, E. F.—Italian Scenery from Drawings made in 1817.—8⁰, *pp.* 122, *pls.* 61. *London,* 1820.
See Pls. 42, 43, 45, 46, 47.

BATTY, E. F.—Naples from Capo di Chino. Engraved by Chᵉ. Heath. — ?, — ?
Steel engrav. Terrace and two umbrella pines with 4 ladies and 1 gentleman on terrace in foreground : 206 × 142 mm.

BEAUREGARD, J. DE.—Du Vésuve à l'Etna et sur le littoral de l'Adriatique . . . (Iᵉʳ juin, 1895).—8⁰. *Lyon,* 1895.

BELL, J.—Observations on Italy.—2nd ed. 2 vols. 8⁰, *Vol. i, pp. xx* + 202, *num. litho. pls.; Vol. ii, pp.* 260. *Naples,* 1834.
See pls. at pp. 195, 209, 215.

BELLICARD.—*See* COCHIN.

BELLINI, R.—La Grotta dello Zolfo nei Campi Flegrei.—*Boll. Soc. Geol. Ital. xx, pp.* 470–475. *Roma,* 1901.

BELLINI, R.—Alcuni appunti per la geologia dell'Isola di Capri.—*Boll. Soc. Geol. Ital. xxi,* 1, *pp.* 7–14. *Roma,* 1902.

BELLINI, R.—Ancora sulla geologia dell' Isola di Capri.—*Boll. Soc. Geol. Ital. xxi,* 3, *pp.* 571–576. *Roma,* 1902.

BELLINI, R.—Sul *Pecten medius,* Lam. (Citato da Philippi E. Scacchi tra i fossili della regione Flegrea.)—*Boll. Soc. Geol. Ital. xxvi, pp.* 340–342. *Roma,* 1907.

BENKOWITZ, C. J.—Reisen von Neapel in die umliegenden Gegenden, nebst einigen Notizen über das letzte Erdbeben in Neapel.—*Berlin,* 1806.

BENOIST, P. W.—Procida : Vue prise de la pointe de l'Île. Procida, Veduta presa dalla punta dell'Isola. Royaume de Naples. —Imp. Lemercier, Bulla, Paris.

BENOIST, PH.—Ischia : Vue prise du Château. Ischia : Veduta presa del Castello. Royaume de Naples.—Imp. Lemercier, Bulla, Paris.
Tinted litho.

BENOIST, PH. (des. et lith.).—Royaume de Naples. Ischia : Vue prise du Château. Ischia : Veduta presa del Castello.—Imp. par Lemercier à Paris. Paris, Bulla éditeur, rue Tiquetonne 18, et (Mᵒⁿ Aumont) François Delarue, succ., r. J. J. Rousseau 10. (Embossed stamp) Boulevart de Sebastopol 56, Rive Droite, Eugène Jouy éditeur.
Good litho. on tinted background : 275 × 196 mm.

BENOIST, PH. (des.).—Royaume de Naples. Naples : Grotte de Pouzzole. Napoli : Grotta di Pozzuoli. Lith. par J. Jacottet.—Imp. par Lemercier à Paris. Paris, Bulla éditeur, 18 rue Tiquetonne, et (Mᵒⁿ Aumont) François Delarue, succ., 10 rue J. J. Rousseau.
Fine litho. on tinted background : 275 × 215 mm.

BENOIST, PH. (des.).—Royaume de Naples. Naples : Vue générale prise de la Maison de Campagne de la Reine. Napoli : Veduta generale presa dalla casina della Regina. Lith. par Jacottet.—Imp. par Lemercier à Paris. Paris, Bulla éditeur, 18 rue Tiquetonne, et (Mᵒⁿ Aumont) François Delarue. succ., rue J. J. Rousseau. (Embossed stamp) Boulevard Sebastopol 56, Rive Droite. Eugene Jouy Editeur.
Litho. on col. background : 273 × 195 mm.

BENOIST, PH.—Royaume de Naples. Pouzzole : Vue générale. Puozzuoli : Veduta generale. Lith. par J. Jacottet. Fig. par Bayot.—Imp. Lemercier à Paris. Paris, Bulla éditeur, 18 rue Tiquetonne, et (Mᵒⁿ Aumont) François Delarue, succ., 10 rue J. J. Rousseau.
Good litho. on tinted background : 275 × 180 mm.

BENOIST, PH. (des. et lith.).—Royaume de Naples. Procida: Vue prise de la pointe de l'Île. Procida : Veduta presa dalla punta dell'Isola. 54.—Imp. par Lemercier à Paris. Paris, Bulla éditeur, rue Tiquetonne 18, et (Mᵉᵃ Aumont) François Delarue, succ., r. J. J. Rousseau 10.
Fine litho. on tinted background : 273 × 192 mm.

BERTAZZI, G.—*See* SACCHI, G. 1862.

BERTELLI, T.—Terremoto in Casamicciola (Ischia) avvenuto il 13 luglio (lettera).—*Bull. Vulc. Ital. ii, p.* 75. *Roma,* 1875.

BERTELLI, T.—Risposta ad alcune obbiezioni ripetute contro le osservazioni microsismiche in occasione del terremoto d'Ischia del 1883 ed opinioni che l'Autore ritiene probabili riguardo al vulcanismo antico e moderno della terra.—*Bull. Soc. Meteor. Ital. Luglio,* 1884, *and following nos.* Also *pp.* 26, 2 *tab. Torino,* 1885.

BERTHIER, P.—Analyse de la Pouzzolane de Naples et du trass des bords du Rhin.—*Ann. Mines, S.* 2, *i, pp.* 333–6. *Paris,* 1827.

BERTINI, C.—Disastri—Giava—Ischia—Albo.

BERTOLONI, A.—Su di un viaggio a Napoli nella estate del 1834.

BERTONI.—*See* MACAGNO, 1874.

BIANCHI, L.—*See* CUCINIELLO, D.

BIBBY, H.—Castle Ischia. A. H. Payne.—London, Brain & Payne, 12 Paternoster Row.
Land end of mole looking towards citadel; basket, jug, persons, and ship in foreground. Steel engrav.: 156 × 141 mm.

BILLMARK, C. J.—Pittoresk Resetour fran Stockholm till Neapel genom Sverge, Danmark, Tyskland, Holland, Belgien, Frankrike, Schweitz, Tyrolen, Savojen, Italien—100 vuer. Tecknade ester naturen, lithographierade och ulgisue.—*pp.* 24, *num. pls. Paris,* 1852.
See p. 23 and plate of Santa Lucia.

BLACHET et LECANU.—Note' sur une substance cristalline, recueillie sur les murs des bains de San Germano, près de Naples.—*Journ. Pharm. Sci. access. xiii, pp.* 419–420. *Paris,* 1827.

BLAEU, J. (excud.).—Lacus Anianus. Agnano, Lac de la Terre de Labour, Province du Royaume de Naples.—Se vend à Amsterdam chez Pierre Mortier avec privilège. [Vienna lib.]
Engrav. : 534 × 423 mm.

BLAEU, J. (excud.).—Puteolanus Ager. Le Golfe de Pouzol est une Partie du Golfe de Naples, elle est vers la Ville de Pouzol, & les Ruines de Baies.—Se vend à Amsterdam chez Pierre Mortier avec Privilège U.
Engraved map : 505 × 403 mm.

BLAEU, J.—Theatrum civitatum nec non admirandorum Neapolis et Siciliae Regnorum.—*fol., pp.* 78 + 30, *pls.* 34. *Amstelœdami,* 1602. [C.A. and B.M.—176, h. 4.]
Gives a good view of the Solfatara and views of the Camp. Phleg.

BLAEU, J.—Nouveau Théâtre d'Italie ou Description Exacte de ses Villes, Palais, Églises, &c. et les Cartes Géographiques de toutes ses Provinces.—3 vols. fol. *Amsterdam, Pierre Mortier,* 1704.
Vol. iii contains "Le Royaume de Naples et de Sicile." Map 2 shows Palmarola and Faraglioni as separate and equally large islands ; 11. is a map of the Campi Phlegræi ; 12. Ischia redrawn from Ortelius ; 13. Lacus Anianus. Agnano lac de la Terre de Labour, Province du Royaume de Naples (similar to that of Braun) ; 13. Forum Vulcani vulgo Solfatara. Les Soufrières, Montagne du Royaume de Naples ; 14. Pozzuoli (an impossible and imaginary view with overhanging cliffs, fishermen camping in foreground) ; 15. Le Lac d'Averno près de Pouzzol dans le Royaume de Naples ; 16. Redrawing of Pozzuoli and Baja of Ortelius. The French edition has some of the plates redrawn or additional title in French added to that of the earlier Latin edition.
Another French edition appeared at *La Haye,* 1724.

BLAEU, J.—Novum Italiae Theatrum, sive Accurata Descriptio Ipsius Urbium, Palatiorum, Sacrarum Aedium, &c., Juxta delineationes D. Joannis Blaeu. I. continens Longobardiam ; II. continens Statum Ecclesiasticum ; III. continens Regna Neapolis et Siciliae ; IV. continens Romam Antiquam et Novam.—4 vols. *fol. Hagæ Comitum, R. Ch. Alberts,* 1724.
Latin ed. of foregoing. Contains a large number of fine engraved views of towns, monuments, &c.

BLAKE, J. F.—A Visit to the Volcanoes of Italy.—*Proc. Geol. Assoc. ix, pp.* 145–176. *London,* 1889.

BOCCONE, P.—Osservazioni naturali ove si contengono materia medico-fisiche e di botanica, produzioni naturali, fosfori diversi, fuochi sotterranii d'Italia ed altra curiosità.—12⁰, *pp.* 400, 2 *pls. Bologna,* 1684. [C.A.]

BOIS, DE (fecit).—A View of the Salfatara, a remarkable mountain near Naples which continually sends forth streams of Smoke, and where Sulphur and Alum is made of the Earth.
Engrav.: 230×170 mm. This view is sometimes bound up with 33 views of Venice, Rome, Naples, Vienna, Paris, &c., most of them with the same ornamental margins by Canale, A., d'Ért, Silvestre, Israel, Parr, De Fer, Campbell, Smith, &c. Most of the other plates are marked "Printed for John Bowles at the Black Horse in Cornhill," cp. seq.
Vedute di Venezia, Roma, Napoli, Vienna, Parigi, ecc. del sec. xviii, dai migliori autori.—4⁰ obl.
33 tavole. Tav. 1–3: Vedute di Roma di DE BOIS. Tav. 4–16: Vedute di Venezia di Antonio Canale e J. Lereau. Tav. 17–20: Vedute di Napoli di DEBOIS. Tav. 21–24: Vedute di Vienna di I. E. F. d'Ért e R. Parr. Tav. 25: La solfatara di Pozzuoli in eruzione di De Bois. Tav. 26: Isle Louvrier et Notre Dame, di Silvestre e Israel. Tav. 27: Il Louvre, di Parr. Tav. 28: Le Luxembourg di Israel. Tav. 29 e 30: Due vedute dell'Isle Minorque di Fontaine e De Fehr. Tav. 31 a 33: Vedute dell'Inghilterra di Campbell e Smith.

BOIS, F. DU.—The Earthquakes of Ischia. —Trans. Seism. Soc. Japan, vii, 1, pp. 16 + 42, pl. 1. Yokohama, 1883–84. [C.A.]

BOIS, F. DU.—Further Notes on the Earthquakes of Ischia.—Trans. Seism. Soc. Japan. viii, pp. 95–99. Yokohama, 1885. [C.A.]

BONNEMAISON.— See TURPIN DE CRISSÉ et alii.—Vue de Naples.

BONNEY, T. G.—Volcanoes, their structure and significance.—8⁰, pp. 351, pl. 13, fig. 21. London, 1899.

BONUCCI, C.—See QUARANTA, B.

BORGIA, GIROLAMO (1538).—See GIUSTIN-IANI, 1812.

BORGIA, GIROLAMO.—Incendium ad Avernum lacum horribile pridie calendas octobris MDXXXVIII. nocte intempesta exortum.—4⁰, foll. 16. Naples, 1538. [C.A.]

BORGIA, GIROLAMO.—Carmina lirica et heroica quae extant.—12⁰, pp. 18 + 319. Venetiis, 1666.

BÖSE, E.—Contributo alla Geologia della Penisola di Sorrento.—Rend. R. Acc. Sci.

S. 3, ii, p. 177. Napoli, 1896.—Id. Atti, S. 2, viii, 8, pp. 18. Napoli, 1897.

BÖSE, E., & LORENZO, G. DE.—Zur Geologie der Monti Picentini bei Neapel.— Zeitschr. deutsch. geol. Gesellsch. xlvii, 1, pp. 202–215. Berlin, 1896.

BOSSIS, DESSOULAVY, & SANTOR-ELLI, F.—Raccolta di Vedute del Regno di Napoli e suoi contorni disegnate dal vero.—obl. 8⁰. Roma, 1829. [B.M.— S. 136 (22).]
Shows Palazzo Don'Anna with lower floor well out of water.

BOTTINI, E.—Sulla durata del tremuoto, 1883.

BOTTIS, G. DE.—Nuovi vulcani comparsi nel finire del 1760 presso Torre del Greco. —Napoli, 1761.

BOUÉ, A.—Ueber Solfataren und Kratererlöschener Vulcane.—Sitz. Akad. Wissensch. xlviii (Abth. 1), pp. 361–380. Wien, 1863.

BOURGEOIS, CH. (des.).—Intérieur d'une Grotte de pêcheurs, sous le Cap Pausilippe, à Naples. Vue prise à Puzzoli près de Naples.
Two figures on engrav. pl. before letters signed by C. Bourgeois in pencil. Engrav.: 212 × 135 mm., 148 × 100 mm.

BOURGEOIS, Cᵗ. (del.).—Vue de l'entrée de la Grotte de Pausilippe du côté de Naples. Vue près le Cap Misène dans le Golphe de Naples. Felipe Cardano Sculp. N⁰ 88.
Two sepia engrav.: 213 × 140 mm., 140 × 100 mm.

BOURGEOIS, Cᵗ.—Vue prise près de Naples. Imp. Lithog. de F. Delpech.
Rampa above Grotta di Posilippo looking upwards. Woman and child mounting in foreground: 288 × 220 mm.

BRACCI, G. (del.), CARDON, A. (scul.)— Icon Sinus Baiarum uti nunc videtur, 1772. [B.M.—K. 83.63, B.N.P. Vb. 113.]
Modernised map similar to that by Antarino of ancient times.

BRACCI, G. (del.), CARDON, A. (scul.)— Icon Crateris Neapolitari vti nvper videb, &c. [B.M.—K. 83.55.]

BRACCIO DA MONTONE, A.—Studio delle acque minerali dell'Isola d'Ischia.

BRAMB[ERGIUS], AMBR[OSIUS].—[Map of Pozzuoli and neighbourhood.]—Apud Claudij Ducheti, 1586.

BRAMB[ERGIUS], AMBR[OSIUS].—Explicatio aliquot Locorum quae Puteolis spectantur. Mappa di Pozzuoli. Apud heredes C. Ducheti.— — ?, 1586. [B.M.— K. 83 (72).]

A good map, but similar to that of Rossi Ant. and Cartaro.

BRAUN, G., & HOHENBERG, F.—Hæc est nobilis & florens illa Neapolis Campaniæ civitas . . . disciplinarum gymnasio clarissima.

One page of text dated 1516 and 71 ref. nos.—*From* "Civitates Orbis Terrarum." Engrav. map extend. from Sebeto to Toretta: 481 × 236 mm. 2 ed. of Latin text.

BRAUN, G., & HOHENBERG, F.—Civitates Orbis Terrarum.—6 vols. *fol. Coloniæ Agrippinæ,* 1523 [? 1573]—1618. Other ed.—5 vols.'| *fol.* 1612.—6 vols. *fol.* 1582 [-1618].—1 or 2 vols. *Coloniæ,* 1572 [*Cologne* ? 1575 ?]—In French : 6 vols. *fol. Brussels,* 1574-1617.

Vol. i, Pl. 47 is a plan of Naples, with half of back of plate forming text. (See above.) Vol. ii, Pl. 51 gives the double panorama of "Puteol" and Baiae with 1 p. of text at back. In the later edition of 1582, Vol. iii, Pl. 56 is entitled "Nullus, in orbe locus Baiis prælucet amœnis," &c. and has below : "Abrahamo Ortelio, Georgius Hoefnaglius &c. . . . 1580," and ref. letters to Y with fine view of Pozzuoli and Baiae and the 1 p. of text : "Campaniæ Felicis Deliciæ."

Pl. 57 in same vol. is entitled "Antrum Sibyllæ Cumanæ " . . . "Lacus Anianus " . . . "Schoronæ Scrobes " . . . "Sudatorium S. Germani," a multiple plate by Hoefnaglius, dated 1538.

Pl. 58 is entitled "Mirabilium Sulphureorum Motium," and simply signed Georgius [Hoefnaglius], while at back is a page of text entitled " Forum Vulcani." It is very ornate, and in foreground are a lady and page and palanquin with another lady.

Some ed. are in 2, some 5, and some in 6 vols. The numbering of the plates is often erroneous : thus Pl. 65 in Vol. v of one edition is marked 56. It is a view of Vesuvius and Naples from Posilippo with a rather fantastic view of that volcano entitled "Elegantissimus ad Mare Tyrrhenum ex Monte Pausilipo Neapolis Montisque Vesuvii Prospectus," with text at back.

In the later editions the text is reset and often covers both pages at back of plate.

One edition is badly and gaudily handcoloured, and other copies are to be met with having dabs of green on the trees.

The edition of Brussels 1574 is with a French text and consists of 6 vols. *See* Vol. i, Pl. 48 : "Naples " ; Vol. ii, Pl. 51 : "Pussol et Baye " ; Vol. iii, Pl. 56 : "Les Délices de la Champaigne heureuse du Royaume de Naples " ; Pl. 57 : "La Caverne de Sibylla Cumana," "Le Lacq d'Anian," "Les Fosses de Charon," "Le Sudatoire S. Germain " ; Pl. 58 : "Le Soufrière nommé Forum Vulcani " ; Vol. v, Pl. 65 : "L'Agréable et Plaisante veue de la Ville de Naples située sur la Mer Tyrrhenée."

BRAUNS, D. A.—Ueber die Niveauschwankungen an der Küste der Umgegend von Neapel.—*Ber. Naturf. Gesellsch. pp.* 48-51. *Halle,* 1882.

BRAUNS, D. A.—Das Problem des Serapeums von Pozzuoli.—*Leopoldina, xxiv, pp.* 15. *Halle,* 1888.

BREISLAK, S.—Essais minéralogiques sur la Solfatara de Pozzuole.—8°, *pp.* 240. *Naples,* 1792.

BREISLAK, S.—Topografia fisica della Campania.—8°, *pp. xii* + 368, *pl.* 3. *Firenze,* 1798.

See pp. 225-308.

BREISLAK, S.—Carta Topografica del cratere di Napoli e dei Campi Flegrei, colla pianta speciale del Vesuvio, secondo le ultime osservazioni del Abte. Breislak. Map in foregoing.

BREISLAK, S.—Voyages physiques et lithologiques dans la Campanie suivis d'un mémoire sur la constitution physique de Rome.—*Vol. i, pp.* 300 + *xvi, pls.* 3 ; *Vol. ii, pp.* 324, *pls.* 3. *Paris,* 1801.—*Leipzig,* 1802 (in German).

BREISLAK, S.—Carte physique de la Campanie.—*In* Voyage dans la Campanie, *Vol. i. Paris,* 1801.

BREISLAK, S.—Notice sur la fontaine de la fumarole à la Solfatare de Pouzzoles.—*Journ. Mines, xv, pp.* 118-127. *Paris,* 1803-1804.

BREUGHEL, G. (pinx.).—[Temple of Venus at Baja ?] G. Zino del. Dhoerty sc. —[Impressed stamp] L. Bassadonna. Torino. Vol. iii, tav. cxvi.

Personages in foreground in Turkish costume. Very fine engrav. on single paper : 219 × 182 mm.

BREUGHEL, G. (pinx.).—[Temple of Venus at Baja ?] G. Zino del. Dhoerty sc. Figures in Turkish costume and boat in foreground. Fine line engrav. on double paper. : 208 × 183 mm.

BRIVE, A. DE.—Extrait d'un voyage en Italie dans l'année 1831 ; Environs de Naples.—*Ann. Soc. Agr. pp.* 185–215. *Au Puy*, 1834.

BROCCHI, G. B.—Catalogo Ragionato di una raccolta di rocce disposto con ordine geografico per servire alla geognosia dell' Italia.—8⁰, *pp. xl* + 346. *Milano*, 1817.

BROCCHI, G. B.—Notizie di alcune osservazioni fisiche fatte nel Tempio di Serapide a Pozzuoli.—*Bibl. Ital. Giorn. Lett. Sci.* . *xiv, pp.* 193–201. *Milano*, 1819.

BROCKEDON, W.—Traveller's Guide to Italy, or Road-book from London to Naples.—16⁰, *pp. vi* + 208. *Paris*, 1835.

BROCKEDON, W.—*See* MAPEI, C.— Italy, Classical, Historical, and Picturesque.

BROECK, E. VAN DEN.—On some Foraminifera from Pleistocene beds in Ischia : preceded by some geological remarks by A. W. Waters.—*Quart. Journ. Geol. Soc. xxxiv, pp.* 196–8. *London*, 1878.

BRUIN (seu BRAUN, G.).—Civitates Orbis Terrarum. *See* Lib. ii of edition of 1582–1618. [In one panorama above.]—Puteoli, Pussol, Baiae, Bayne, Monte Sibilla. [In one panorama below.] Templv Fregana, Pvssol, Baiae. [With a page of explanation at back] Puteoli et Baiae. Two hand-coloured engravings : each 480 × 140 mm.

BRUIN, G., and HOHENBERGIUS, F.— Théâtre des Principales Villes de tout l'Univers.—2 vols. *fol. Brussels*, 1574. [B.M. 2058.f.] Gives the two identical views of Pozzuoli and Baia as that of Hoefnaglius. The plan of Naples is limited to the town.

BRUNO, FR. SAV.—L'osservatore di Napoli, ossia rassegna delle istituzioni civili, de' pubblici stabilimenti, dei monumenti storici ed artistici, e delle cose notabili di Napoli, con una breve descrizione de'suoi contorni, ecc.—12⁰, *pp.* 8 + 592. *Napoli*, 1854. *See pp.* 376–386.

BUCH, C. L. VON.—Scipio Breislak's physikalische Topographie von Campanien.—*Ann. Phys. v, pp.* 396–407. *Halle u. Leipzig*, 1800.

BUCH, C. L. VON.—Ischia.—*Jahrb. Berg.- u. Hüttenkunde. i, pp.* 343–353. *Nürnberg*, 1809.

BUCH, C. L. VON.—Physikalische Beschreibung der Canarischen Inseln.—*figs.* 2. *Berlin*, 1825.(*See* pp.338–347.)—*Gesammelte Schriften, Berlin*, 1887. (*See* Vol. iii, pp. 524 *et seq.*)

BUCH, C. L. VON.—Description Physique des Îles Canaries, suivie d'une indication des Principaux Volcans du Globe.—8⁰, *pp. vii* + 525. *Paris*, 1836.

BUCH, C. L. VON.—[Besuch und Entstehungsweise des Monte Nuovo.]—*Zeitschr. deutsch. geol. Gesellsch. i, pp.* 107–111. *Berlin*, 1849.

BUCH, C. L. VON.—Lettre à Naumann sur sa visite au Mte. Nuovo avec M. Pareto. — ?, — ?

BUFFA.—Le acque d'Ischia.— ?, 1883.

BULIFON, A.—Lettere storiche politiche ed erudite.—12⁰, *pp.* 482 + 10. *Pozzuoli*, 1685. [C.A.] *See* Raccolta 4a, pp. 177–188.

BULIFON, ANT. D. D.—Veduta della Città di Pozzuoli dall'Monte Nuovo.—[*Naples ?*] 1691. [B.N.P., Vb. 1141.] Shows Caligula's mole, with all arches broken.

BULIFON, A.—Regno di Napoli con le sue province distinte. Nuovamente date in luce. Accuratissima e nuova delineazione. No. 8.—*obl.* 4⁰. *Napoli*, 1692. 365 × 265 mm. Ischia, with view of Terra and Marina of Procida.

BULIFON, A.—Lettere memorabili, istoriche, politiche, ed erudite.—2nd ed. ded. F. D. Cocco-Palmeri.—12⁰. *Vol. i, pp.* 24 +460 + 11, *pls.* 4 ; *Vol. ii, pp.* 12 + 399 + 8, *pls.* 8 ; *Vol. iii, pp.* 12 + 355 + 5, *pls.* 5. *Pozzuoli*, 1693. (*See* Vol. ii, pp. 166–174.)—Also 4 vols. 12⁰, *Pozzuoli e Napoli*, 1693–8 ; 4 vols. 12⁰, *Pozzuoli e Napoli*, 1696–7 ; 12⁰, *Pozzoli e Napoli*, 1698.

BULIFON, A.—Lettera al sig. D. G. F. Pacceco sul terremoto del 5 giugno 1688 in Napoli.—*Napoli*, 1697.

BULIFON, A.—Le guide des étrangers curieux de voir et de connoître les choses les plus mémorables de Pouzzol, Bayes, Cumes, Misène et autres lieux des environs, de l'Abbé Sarnelli, traduite en français, avec le texte en regard, et la description des vertus et propriétés des bains d'Ischia par J. C. Capaccio.—12⁰, *pls.* 33, *portrait of Bulifon. Naples*, 1699. [C.A.]

BULIFON, A., LUIGI, DR. (nipote).—Carte de' Regni di Napoli e di Sicilia loro provincie ed isole adjacenti.—4⁰, 19 *maps*. *Napoli*, 1734.

BULIFON, A.—Campagna Felice. Neap. [1692] Dʳ Franc Cassianus de Silua sculpsit. [B.M.—K. 83. 52—1.] Map.

BULIFON, A.—Isola d'Ischia [with] Veduta della Terra e Marina di Procida.—[*Napoli?*,] — ? [B.M.—K. 83. 51.] Map.

BULIFON, A.—Terra del Lavoro. — ?, — ? [B.M.—K. 83. 45.] Map with small inset of Campi Phlegræi.

BULIFONE, N.—Distinta relazione del danno cagionato dal terremoto del 3 Novembre 1706.—*Napoli*, 1706.

BULLURA (del.).—Golfe de Baïa. Golfo di Baia. Lacauchie sculp., 216. Baja and Pozzuoli from above Arco Felice. Engrav.: 155 × 106 mm.

BUNONIS, JOH.—*See* CLUVERIUS, PH.

BURCHARDS, J.—Diarium, ecc. ann. 1483-1506.—*Edit. L. Thuasne, Paris*, 1884.

BURMANNUS, P.—*See* GRAEVIUS. J. G. —Thesavrvs Antiqvitatvm et Historicarvm Italiae.

BURNET, G.—Some Letters. Containing, an account of what seemed most remarkable in Switzerland, Italy, &c.—12⁰, *pp.* 310. *Rotterdam,* 1686.—Another ed. 2 Pts. 12⁰. *Amsterdam,* 1686.——2nd ed. 8⁰, *pp.* 336. *Rotterdam,* 1687.——3rd ed. 12⁰, *pp.* 321. *Rotterdam,* 1687.—Another ed. 3 Pts. 12⁰. *Amsterdam,* 1687.——3rd ed. with appendix, 12⁰, *pp.* 232. *Amsterdam,* 1688. —Other ed. 12⁰, *pp.* 400. *London,* 1689.— 8⁰, *pp.* 322. [*London* ?] 1708.—8⁰, *pp.* *xxvi* + 355. *London,* 1724.—12⁰, *pp.* 24 + 264. *London,* 1737.—12⁰, *pp. xxiv* + 258. *Edinburgh,* 1752.—In French : 2 Tom. in 1 Vol. 12⁰. *T. i, pp.* 235 ; *T. ii, pp.* 312. *Rotterdam,* 1687.——2nd ed. 12⁰, *pp.* 536. *Rotterdam,* 1688.—Another ed. [last, B.M.] 12⁰, *pp.* 468. *Rotterdam,* 1690.

BUSIN, P.—Terremoto del 28 Luglio 1883 nell'isola d'Ischia. — *Gazz. Ital. numero straordinario 5 Agosto* 1883.

BYLANDT PALSTERCAMP, A. DE.— Théorie des Volcans.—3 vols. 8⁰. *Vol. i, foll. ii, pp.* 470 ; *Vol. ii, foll. ii, pp.* 438 ; *Vol. iii, fol. ii, pp.* 459. *Paris,* 1835. Atlas, *fol.,* 17 *pls.*

BYRNE, W.—*See* SMITH, J. 1796.

CABELLA,A.—*See* OGLIALORO-TODARO, A. 1895, 1896.

CALAMAI, L.—Dell'acqua Medici di Castellamare.—*Pisa,* 1849.

CAMPILANZI, E. — Sulla corrispondenza dei cangiamenti di livello del mare osservati negli avanzi del tempio di Serapide con quelli avvenuti a Venezia.—*Ann. Sci. R. Ist. Lomb. Veneto, x, pp.* 51-67. *Padova e Venezia,* 1840.

CANGIANO, LUIGI.—Sul pozzo che si sta forando nel giardino delle Reggia di Napoli e di taluni induzioni geologiche di cui è stato occasione.—4⁰, *pp.* 23. *Napoli,* 1845. [C.A.]

CANGIANO, L.—Sul pozzo forato nel giardino della Reggia di Napoli.—*Atti Sett. Ad. Scienz. Ital. pp.* 1147-1148. *Napoli,* 1847.

CANGIANO, L.—Breve ragguaglio del perforamento dei due pozzi artesiani recentemente compiuti nella città di Napoli. —*Napoli,* 1859.

CANGIANO, L. — Sull'attuale condizione delle acque pubbliche in Napoli, e dei modi di migliorarla.—*Napoli,* 1859.

CANNIZZARO.—Analisi delle acque minerali Fornello e Fontana.

CAPACCIO, G. C.—Puteolana Historia a secretis et cive conscripta, accessit eiusdem de Balneis libellus.—4⁰, *foll.* 8, *pp.* 16+208, *num. woodcuts. Napoli, C. Vitalis,* 1604.

CAPACCIO, G. C.—Balnearum quæ Neapoli, Puteoli, Baiis, Pithecusis extant, virtutes, thermarum et balnearum apud antiquos structuræ, usus, ministeria ad ægrorum commoda.—4⁰, *pp.* 88. *Neapoli, C. Vitalem,* 1604. (Bound up with Puteolana Hist.)

CAPACCIO, G. C.—Puteolana Historia, accessit ejusdem de Balneis libellus.—8⁰, *fol.* 1, *pp.* 900, *num. woodcuts. Napoli, I. I. Carlinum,* 1607.

CAPACCIO, G. C.—Neapolitanæ Historiæ a . . . eivs vrbis a secretis et cive conscriptæ, tomvs primvs. In quo antiqvitas ædificio, ciuibus, republica, ducibus, religione, bellis, lapidibus, locis adiacentibus, qui totam ferè amplectuntur Campaniam, continetur.—4⁰, *pp.* 900, *figs. of coins, views of Solfatare, Avernus, Tritoli, Pausilippe. Neapoli, Apud Jo. Jacobum Carlinum.* M.DCVII.

E

CAPACCIO, G. C.—La vera antichita di Pozzuolo, con l'historia di tutte le cose del contorno, delle cose naturali, etc.—12°, figs. Napoli, 1607.

CAPACCIO, G. C.—Il Forastiero, dialoghi ne'quali oltre a quel, che si ragiona dell' origine di Napoli, ecc. siti e corpo della Città con tutto il contorno da Cuma al Promontorio di Minerva, varietà e costumi di habitatori, famiglie nobili, e popolari, con molti Elogii d'huomini illustri, aggiuntavi la cognitione di molte cose appartenenti all'istoria d'Italia, con particolari relationi per la materia politica con brevità spiegate.—pp. 56 + 1024.
Bound up with : Incendio del Vesuvio, Dialogo.—4°, pp. 86. Napoli, per Gio. Dom. Roncagliolo, 1634.

CAPACCIO, G. C.—La vera antichita di Pozzuolo descritta da G.C.C. secretario dell' inclita città di Napoli, ove e con l'istoria di tutte le cose del contorno, si narrano la bellezza di Posilipo, l'origine della Città di Pozzuolo, Baja, Miseno, Cuma, Ischia. Riti, costumi, magistrati, nobilita, statue, inscrittioni, fabbriche antiche successi, guerre, e quanto appartiene alle cose naturali di Terme, Bagni, e di tutte I Miniere.—12°, pp. 38 + 384, num. pls. and figs. Roma, 1652.

CAPACCIO, G. C. (Urbis Neapoleos a Secretis & Civis).—Antiquitates et Historiæ Neapolitanæ : in quibus antiquitas ædificii, civium, reipublicæ, ducum, religionis, bellorum, lapidum, adjacentiumque locorumque continetur : Novissima editione a mendis corruptelisque, quibus scatebant plurimis, repurgatæ, locisque compluribus restitutæ : & Nummis figurisque accuratissimè ornatæ. Cui vita auctoris effigiesque additæ sunt.—foll. 4, pp. 194 + 6 in two cols., portrait, maps 2, pls. 8. See GRAEVIUS, J. G.—Thesaurus Antiquitatum . . . Italiae, T. ix, Pt. 2. 1725, &c.

CAPACCIO, G. C. — Historiæ Neapolitanæ libri duo in quibus antiquitas ædificii, civium, reipublicæ, ducum, religionis, bellorum, lapidum, locorumque adjacentium, qui totam fere Campaniam complectuntur, continetur.—4°, Liber primus, foll. 4, pp. 312 ; Liber secundus, pp. 500, figs. Neapoli Sumptibus Joannis Gravier Typographi, et Bibliopolæ Galli, MDCCLXXI.

CAPACCIO, G. C.—See BULIFON, 1699.

CAPANO, COUNT G.—Rapporto dell'Ispettore della Provincia di Napoli (Capano) sul progetto di miglioramento della boscaglia del Monte Nuovo di Pozzuoli.—8°, pp. 40. Naples, 1823. [C.A.]

CAPMARTIN DE CHAUPY, ABB. B.—Découverte de la maison de Campagne d'Horace.—2 vols. 8°, topogr. map. Rome, 1767-9.
See Vol. i, pp. 101 & seq. de' Vulcani, del Vesuvio, de' Campi Flegrei, &c.

CAPOA, L. DI.—Lezione intorno alla natura delle Mofete.—4°, foll. viii, pp. 179. Napoli, 1683. Also an ed. at Cologne. 1714.

CAPOCCI, E.—Nuove ricerche sul noto fenomeno delle colonne perforate dalle Folladi nel Tempio di Serapide in Pozzuoli. —Il Progr. Sci. Lett. ed Arti. xi, pp. 66-76. Napoli, 1835.—Edinb. New Phil. Journ. xxiii, pp. 201-204. Edinburgh, 1837.

CAPOCCI, E.—Catalogo de'tremuoti avvenuti nella parte continentale del Regno delle Due Sicilie, posti in raffronto con le eruzioni vulcaniche ed altri fenomeni cosmici, tellurici e meteorici.—Atti R. Ist. Incorag. ix, pp. 335-378, 379-421. Napoli, 1861.—x, pp. 293-327. Napoli, 1863.—4°. pp. 45. Napoli, 1859.

CAPORALI, G.—Delle acque minerali Campane alla esposizione Italiana del 1861. —Napoli, 1861.

CAPPA, R.—Dell'analisi chimica e delle virtù medicinali dell'acqua termo-minerali di Gurgitello e di Castiglione.—8°, pp. 15. Napoli, 1863. [C.A.]

CAPPARELLI, L.—La causa dei terremoti secondo Lucrezio.—Albo-Napoli-Ischia.

CARAFA, G.—Mappa topografica di Napoli e dei contorni incominciata.—35 large sheets. Napoli, 1775. [B.M. 3, 149, 4.]
A very fine map including Astroni, Lago d'Agnano to Resina. Some profiles of interest.

CARDON, ANT. (fecit).—1. Grotta vicino a 2. S. Maria Capella Vecchia, D. Da. Mr. Changouin à Naples an 1764.
Engrav. the same as Pl. 20 in Morghen's 84 Vedute di Napoli 1777, but does not bear the pl. number : 240 × 154 mm.

CARDON, A. (inv. sculp.), PICCININO, F. (Math. Arch. Del. L.)—Icon Crateris Neapolitani.—Napoli, 1765. [B.M.—K.83. 56.]

CARDON, A.—See BRACCI, G.

CARDONE, A.—Saggio di poetici componimenti (Sul funestissimo tremuoto. avvenuto in Casamicciola. Ode).—8⁰, *fol.* 1, *pp.* 25. *Naples*, 1828. [C.A.]

CAREGA DI MURICCE, F.—*See*MURICCE, F. C.

CARLETTI, Nicolaus V. A. P., Ph. Ma. et Acca. Rom. Me. Mer.—Pianta topografica della Città di Napoli in Campagna Felice. Philip Morghen Sc. 1770 (apparently retouched out).—In Napoli presso Nic. Gervasi, &c.

Engrav. map extending from the Sebeto to Capodimonte and Mergellina with 92 reference numbers : 379×275 mm. This is the 5th plate in Morghen's " 84 Vedute di Napoli," but has the " Apud " and " 1770 " badly erased.

CARLETTI, N.—Mappa topografica (di Napoli). Gius. Aloja Nap. Reg. Incis.

An enormous map in 35 sheets with 580 ref. nos. : 656 × 498 mm. Begun in 1750 by Gio. Carafa, Duca di Noja, continued by Campana, Aloja, and Lamarra, Gio. Pignatelli in 1769, and completed in 1775 with additions and corrections up to date.

CARLETTI, N.—Storia della Regione abbruciata in Campagna Felice in cui si tratta il suo sopravvenimento generale, e la descrizione de'luoghi, de'Vulcani, de'Laghi, de'Monti, delle Città litorali e di popoli, &c.—4⁰, *pp. xliii* + 382, *pl.* 1. *Napoli*,1787. *See* GUICCIARDINI, C.

CARLYLE, Rev. Gavin.—*See* MAPEI, C., 1864.

CARRETO, G. Del.—Rapporto dei fenomeni di calore naturale nel littorale dei Maronti.

CARTARO, M.—Dissegno di Pozzuoli et luochi vicini. — *Napoli*, 1588. [B.M. 24120, 2.]

A good map of the Campi Phlegræi.

CARWITHAM (engrav. and publ.).—A Prospect of Vulcan's Court near Putzol in Naples, 1740. (With explanation.)

Engrav. : 190 × 136 mm.

CASORIA, E.—Sui processi di mineralizzazione delle acque in rapporto con la natura geologica dei terreni e delle rocce. —8⁰, *pp.* 197. *Portici*, 1902.

See pp. 153–167.

CASORIA, E.—Sulla composizione chimica delle Ceneri Vesuviane cadute a Portici nei giorni 9 e 10 aprile, 1906.—*Ann. R. Scuola Agric. S.* 2, *vi, pp.* 1–11. *Portici*, 1906.

CASORIA, E.—Le Sabbie e le Ceneri Vesuviane cadute a Portici nel mese d'Aprile dell'Anno 1906. Memoria II.— *Ann. R. Scuola Agric. S.* 2, *ix, pp.* 1–26. *Portici*, 1910.

CASSAS, L. F.—Vue près de Pouzzoles, 1784. Colombarium and distant view of Temple of Serapis. Engrav. : 198 × 253 mm.

CASSIANUS DE SILUA (sculp.).—*See* BULIFON, A.—Campagna Felice.

CASSOLA, F.—*See* PILLA, L., 1832–33.

CASSOLA, F.—*See* SEMENTINI, 1834 and 1835.

CASSOLA, F.—*See* RONCHI.

CASTALDO, A.—Istoria libri iv (in which are recounted the principal events that happened in the kingdom of Naples under the government of the Viceroy D. Pietro di Toledo and the Viceroys his successors till Cardinal Granvela).—4⁰, *pp.* 21-155. *Naples*, 1749. [C.A.]

CASTELLAN (del. and sculp.).—[Temple of Serapis.]

A sketchy engraving. : 147 × 111 mm.

CAVA, P. La.—*See* LA CAVA, P.

CAVE, La.—*See* LA CAVE.

CELANO, C.—Delle Notizie del bello, dell' antico, e del curioso della Città di Napoli, &c.——3rd ed. 4 vols. 8⁰. *Vol. i, pp.* x+281 +214 ; *Vol. ii, pp.* 346+174+*vi; Vol. iii, pp.* 172+96 ; *Vol. iv, pp.* 232+52+80 + 120, *num. figs.* (of no importance). *Napoli*, 1758-9. (Collect. H. Elliott, Esqr.). —Also : 5 vols. 8⁰, *figs., Napoli*, 1856-60 ; 5 vols., 1792.—Other ed. 1692, 1724.

CESTARI, Ab. G.—Anecdotti istorici sulle alumiere delli Monti Leucogei. — 12⁰. *Napoli*, 1790. [B.N.]

C. H. (ex Nat. Del.)—The Mole of Naples.— London : Published by C. Hullmandel. Gt. Marlbro' St., July 10, 1818.

Litho. : 309 × 231 mm.

C. H. (ex Nat. Del.)—The Port of Pozzuoli. Monte Nuovo. Supposed remains of Cicero's Villa.—London : Published by C. Hullmandel, Gt. Marlbro' St., July 10, 1818.

Litho. : 309 × 235 mm.

C. H. (ex Nat. Del.)—Sannazar's Tower, on the New Road of Posilippo near Naples. Capri (in distance).

Rough litho. : 310 × 210 mm.

E 2

CHACATON, H. De (pinxit).—Île de Procida. Galerie Durand Ruel. Litho-engrav. of no physical importance. Boats and figures in foreground : 215 × 142 mm.

CHARRIN, P. J.—*See* RICHARD DE SAINT-NON, J. C. 1829.

CHASTELET (des.).—Vue de l'Église de San Vitale en sortant de la Grotte de Pausilippe près de Naples. Gravé par Couchet. N⁰ 27. Engrav.: 219 × 170 mm.

CHASTELET (des.).—Naples. Vue Averne, des restes du Temple d'Apollon et de l'entrée de la Grotte de la Sibille de Cumes. L'on apperçoit dans l'éloignement le Château de Bayes et l'Isle de Capri. Gravé par Nicolet. N⁰ 49, A.P.D.R. Fine line engrav. (circa 1780) : 342 × 215 mm.

CHASTELET, L. (des. après nature).—Naples. Vue d'une partie des Champs Elisées prise sur les bords du Lac Acheron et dans l'éloignement les Îles de Procita et d'Ischia. Gravée à l'eau forte par Paris. Terminé par Du Parc. N⁰ 50, A.P.D.R. Engrav.: 350 × 233 mm.

CHASTELET (des.). — Naples. Vue du Lac d'Agnano et des Étuves de San Germano près de Naples. Gravé à l'eau forte par Bertheau. Terminé par Du Parc. A.P.D.R. N⁰ 51. Fine engrav.: 338 × 208 mm.

CHASTELET (des.). — Naples. Vue des sources d'eaux chaudes appellées le Pisciarelli près de la Solfatara. Vue d'une des Portes de l'ancienne Ville de Cumes appellée aujourd'hui l'Arco Felice près Bayes et Pouzzoles. Gravé par J. B. Racine. N⁰ 59, A.P.D.R. Two engrav. on same sheet : each 237 × 163 mm.

CHASTELET (des.). — Naples. Vue de l'Auberge et du Petit Golphe de Mare Piano entre Naples et Pouzzoles. Gravé par Le Veau. N⁰ 61, A.P.D.R. Engrav.: 350 × 223 mm.

CHASTELET (des.).—Grotte creusée dans la Montagne de Pizzofalcone à Naples appellée la Grotte des Cordiers. N⁰ 71. Gravé par Paris, A.P.D.R. Line engrav.: 220 × 148 mm.

CHASTELET.—Naples. Vue de l'Astrumi. Ancien Volcan éteint dans les environs de Pouzzoles. Gravé à l'eau forte par Marilier. Terminé par De Ghendt. N⁰ 90, A.P.D.R. Line engrav.: 342 × 213 mm.

CHASTELET (des.).—Vue prise au dessus de la Grotte de Pausilippe en allant au Tombeau de Virgile. Gravé par Auvrai. N⁰ 92, A.P.D.R. Engrav.: 225 × 174 mm.

CHÂTELET.—*See* CHASTELET.

CHAYS, S. (pinx. sculp.).—Le Posilipe du Côté de Poussolle. 12. A poor engraving : 250 × 178 mm.

CHERBUIN, L. (gravé). — Naples. Le Daguerréotype. Executé d'après le Daguerréotype.—Milan, chez Ferd. Artaria et Fils, Editeurs. [Vienna lib.] 215×207 mm. Dark sepia engrav. from beach opposite villa. (? 1846.)

CHERUBINI, Cav. C.—Carta Fisica dell' Italia.—*Pub. G. B. Paravia e C., Torino, Roma, Milano, Firenze, Napoli*, 1876. 1 : 750,000 horiz. 1 : 150,000 vert. Raised map.

CHEVALLEY DE RIVAZ, J. E.—Précis sur les eaux minéro-thermales, et les Étuves de l'Île d'Ischia.—4⁰, *foll.* 5, *pp.* 70. *Naples*, 1831. [C.A.]——2nd and 3rd ed. 8⁰, *pp. viii*+182, 1 *map. Naples*, 1837.—In Ital. [Trattati delle Acque.] 8⁰, *pp. xii* + 276, 3 *pls. Napoli*, 1838.

CHEVALLEY DE RIVAZ, J. E.—Analyse et propriétés médicinales des Eaux Minérales de Castellamare.—*pp.* 78. *Naples*, 1834.

CHEVALLEY DE RIVAZ, J. E.—Description des eaux minéro-thermales et des Étuves de l'Île d'Ischia.—*pp.* 182, 1 *map.* 1834 and 1837.

CHEVALLEY DE RIVAZ, J. E.—Descrizione delle acque termo-minerale e delle Stufe dell'Isola d'Ischia.—8⁰, *pp. xii*+276, *pl. iii. Napoli*, 1838. [C.A.]——5me ed. 8⁰, *pp. viii* + 206, *pl.* 1, *map* 1. *Naples*, 1846.

CHEVALLEY DE RIVAZ, J. E.—Voyage scientifique à Naples.—*Paris*, 1843.

CHEVALLEY DE RIVAZ, J. E.—[Comunicazione su di un Terremoto del 7 di giugno 1852 in Casamicciola.]—*Rend. R. Acc. Sci. N.S. i, p.* 88. *Napoli*, 1852.

CHEVALLEY DE RIVAZ, J. E.—Su di un terremoto ad Ischia.—*Boll. Meteor. Ital. ii, pp.* 20–21, 68. *Roma*, 1863.

CHIKHACHEV.—*See* TCHIHATCHEFF.

CHINNI, L.—Acque minerali Monte della Miseracordia.

CHISTONI, C.—*See* BASSANI, F., 1907.

CHUN, K.—Das Erdbeben auf Ischia.— "*Illustrirte Zeitung*," *pp.* 265–268, 3 *vignettes by B. Köhler, April 2nd,* 1881. [C.A.]

CIANCIO, A.—Ragionamento sulla privativa del Marchese Nunziante nella fabbricazione dell'Allume Vulcanico.—4⁰, *pp.* 60. *Napoli,* — ?

CICCONE, A.—Analisi delle acque minerali del Cotto e Sinigallia.

CIGLIANO, T.—Il 28 luglio nell'Isola d'Ischia.—"*Corriere del Mattino di Napoli,*" 218, 223, 9 *and* 14 *agosto,* 1883.

CIUTIIS, M. DE.—Casamicciola—8⁰, *pp.* 104. *Napoli,* 1883.
An account of the earthquakes of 1881 and 1883.

CIUTIIS, M. DE.—Discussioni scientifiche sulla previsione dei terremoti.
Letter, dated 30 agosto, published by several newspapers.

CLAUSON, C.—Saggio sulla topografia dell' antica Partenope.—8⁰, *pp.* 16, *map* 1. *Napoli,* 1889.

CLERIAN (fecit).—Grotte de Pausilippe à Naples. À Naples. Lith. de Marlet.
Sermon in church.—Litho. of two views : each. 124 × 89 mm.

CLERISEAU, C. (pinx.).—Temple of Serapis at Puzzoli in the Kingdom of Naples. Temple de Serapis situé à Pouzzoles dans le Royaume de Naples. D. Cunego Sc. Romæ.
Engrav.: 575 × 407 mm.

CLERISEAU, C. (p.).—Temple of Venus in the Kingdom of Naples upon the coast of Baja, the Fortress of which is seen on the left. (Title also in French.) D. Cunego Sc. Romæ.
Engrav.: 572 × 406 mm.

CLERMONT.—*See* WEBERT, C.

CLIUEN, HENRI (inven.).—Puteolj. Philipp Gall excud.
A view over the amphitheatre, Pozzuoli to Baja and Misenum. Greatly exaggerated. Fine line engrav.: 241 × 162 mm.

CLIUEN, H. (inven.).—Neapolitanæ vbis pars. Philipp Gall excud. — ?, — ?
An imaginary view of Naples, which appears reversed if the mountain in the distance be intended for Vesuvius: 238 × 169 mm.

CLIUEN, HENRI (inven.).—Neapolitanæ urbis pars. Philipp Gall excud.
W. end of Naples grossly exaggerated. Fine engrav. : 240 × 163 mm.

CLUVERIUS,PHILIPPUS.—Italiaantiqua . . . Ejusdem Sicilia, Sardinia et Corsica . . . (Cum epistola dedicatoria Danielis Heinsii). —3 pts. in 2 vols. *fol. Vol. i, pp.* 786 ; *Vol. ii, pp.* 787–1338 + 510, *portrait, maps, and plans. Lugduni Batavorum,* 1624. (" Sicilia antiqua " is dated 1619 and has special title and pagination.)—Also 2 vols. *fol.* 1624. (In this " Sicilia antiqua " is missing.) [B.N.P.]

CLUVERIUS, PHILIPPUS.—Italia Antiqua auctoris methodo, verbis, et tabulis geographicis retentis contracta opera Ioh. Bunonis.—4⁰, *pp.* 12 + 773 + (*index*) 48, *maps* 5. *Guelferbyti,* 1659.

COCCHI, D. F.—[Correspondenza.]—"*Roma di Napoli,*" 6–7 *Luglio,* 1884.
Interesting notes on modifications of mineral waters, fumaroles, and subterranean noises.

COCHIN et BELLICARD.—Observations sur les Antiquités d'Herculaneum, avec quelques reflections sur la Peinture et la Sculpture des Anciens ; et une courte description de plusieurs Antiquités des Environs de Naples.—8⁰, *pp.* 36 + 98+10, *num. figs. Paris,* 1754.——2nd ed. 8⁰, *pp.* 41 + 84, *pls.* 40. *Naples,* 1757. (reprint).
Good view of Temple of Serapis just after excavation in 1750.

COCKBURN, J. P.—[A Collection of Forty-one Sepia Drawings, chiefly of Italian and Roman Scenery.]—*About* 1820.

COCKBURN, MAJOR [J. P.] (drawn by).— Temple of Venus, otherwise called Bacchus. Engraved by W. B. Cooke.—London : Published July 21st, 1826, by W. B. Cooke, 9 Soho Square.
Engrav.: 424 × 298. mm.

COCKBURN, COL. [J. P.]—*See* WRIGHT, G. N.—The Rhine, Italy and Greece, &c.

COGNET (delt.).—Montagne de St. Nicolas à Ischia, Rᵐᵉ de Naples. Jacottet Lit : les Figures par V. Adam. Lith. de Mendouze.—A Paris chez Decrouan, rue St. Severin N⁰ 14, et chez Mendouze et Hauteceur, rue St. Pierre N⁰ 10.
Litho.: 345 × 237 mm.

COIGNET, M.—Vues Pittoresques de l'Italie, dessinées d'après nature par . . . et lithographiées par . . . &c. 6me livraison. —*fol., pls.* 36. *A Paris,* MDCCCXXV. [B.N.P., Ub. 45.]

COIGNET (del.).—Grotte de Pausilippe. Gué, Lith. fig. par V. Adam, Lith. de G. Engelmann [embossed stamp]. Sazerac et Duval [and Lyre]. Litho. on double paper : 286 × 208 mm.

COIGNET (del.).—Vue des Ravins de Sorente. Villeneuve Lith.—Imp. Lith. de Langlumé. Litho. on film : 317 × 213 mm.

COIGNET (del.).—Vue des Ravins de Sorente. Villeneuve Lith.—Imp. Lith. de Langlumé. Litho. on double paper : 320 × 214 mm.

COLACCI, O. DE.—Dialoghi intorno a'tremuoti di quest'anno 1783.—8⁰, pp. 79. Napoli, ? 1783. [C.A.]

COLLEGNO, G. P. DI.—Contrade vulcaniche delle vicinanze di Napoli.—Atti 6a Riun. Sci. Ital. 1844, pp. 1170–1173. Milano, 1845.

COLLENUCCIO, PANDOLPHO.—Compendio delle Historie del regno di Napoli composto da Messer Pandolpho Collenutio iurisconsulto in Pesaro. [Figure of Sibilla on title-page. At end :] Et infino a qui si troua scritto della historia di Napoli dal presente Auttore. Fine delle historie Napolitane, composte per lo Egregio Dottore messer Pandolpho Collenutio Iurisconsulto da Pesaro. Stampate in Vineggia per Michele Trame Zino, Nel anno. M.D.XXXIX. Nel Mese di Maggio—8⁰, foll. 204. Venetia, MDXXXIX. [B.N.P.] (This edition is extremely rare. See pp. 32–33.)—Other ed.: 8⁰, foll. iv+196, 1541; 8⁰, foll. 216, 1543; 8⁰, foll. iv + 196, 1548.

COLLENUCCIO, P.—Sommaire des Histoires du royaume de Naples, qui traicte de toutes choses advenues en iceluy . . . composé . . . en langage italien par M. P . . . C . . . et depuis n'aguères mis en françois par Denis Sauvage. . . . Avecques annotations.—8⁰, foll. 320. Paris, A. L'Angelier, 1546. [B.N.P.] See foll. 40–41. Another copy is on ruled paper with mosaic binding.

COLLENUCCIO, P.—Compendio dell'Historie del regno di Napoli, composto già da M. Pandolfo Collenucio da Pesaro, e nuovamente alla sincerità della lingua uolgare ridotto, e tutto emendato da Girolamo Rvscelli, con un brieue discorso del medesimo sopra l'istesso autore.—8⁰, foll. iv + 215. Vinegia, G. M. Bonelli, M.D.LII. See pp. 25–26.

COLLENUCCIO, P.—Compendio dell'Historia del regno di Napoli composto da M. . . . Iurisconsulto in Pesaro. Con la givnta di M. Mambrino Roseo da Fabriano delle cose notabili successe dopo. [On title-page figure of Sibylla with the inscription on 3 sides] : Qval piv fermo è il mio foglio è il mio presaggio.—2 vols. 8⁰. Vol. i, foll. vi + 344 ; Vol. ii, foll. 312. Vinegia, xv. di Ottobre, MDLVII. The date at end of 2nd vol. is 1558.

COLLENUCCIO, P.—Compendio de las Historias del reyno de Napoles, del famoso Doctor Pandolfo Colenucio . . . traduzido por Nicolas Spinosa . . .—8⁰, foll. 274. Valecia, impr. de J. Nauarro, 1563.

COLLENUCCIO, P.—Historiæ Neapolitanæ ad Herculem I, Ferrariæ ducem, libri vi. . . . Omnia ex Italico sermone in Latinum conuersa. Ioann. Nicol. Stvpano, Rheto Interprete. . . .—4⁰, pp. 325 and index, portrait. Basileæ, P. Pernam, 1572.

COLLENUCCIO, P.—Historia del reyno de Napoles, auctor Pandolfo Colenucio de Pesaro . . . traduzida de lengua Toscana por Juan Vasquez del Marmol. . . .—fol., foll. 167, fig. Seville, F. Diaz, 1584.

COLLENUCCIO, P.—Histoire du royaume de Naples, contenant les choses mémorables advenues depuis l'empire d'Auguste jusques à nostre temps . . . composée . . . en italien par Pandulphe Collenutio, et nouvellement traduite en langage vulgaire, reveue et augmentée de ce qui est advenu depuis l'année 1459 jusques à présent.— 8⁰, pp. 509. — ?, 1586. [Incomplete, B.N.P.]

COLLENUCCIO, P.—Del Compendio dell' Istoria del regno di Napoli, prima parte, di M. Pandolfo Collenuccio . . . e di Mambrin Roseo da Fabriano . . . seconda parte, di Mambrin Roseo da Fabriano, col settimo libro del Pacca. . . . Giunta overo terza parte del . . . Scritta da Tomaso Costo . . . —3 pts. in 1 vol. 4⁰. Venezia, B. Barezzi, 1591.

[COLLENUCCIO, P.] P? C.—Histoire du royaume de Naples, contenant les choses mémorables advenues depuis l'empire d'Auguste jusques à notre temps . . . reveue, et augmentée de ce qui est advenu depuis l'année 1459, jusques à présent, par P. C.— 8⁰, pp. 509. Tournon, G. Linocier, 1595. —8⁰, pp. 609. 1596.

COLLENUCCIO, P.—Compendio dell'Istoria del regno di Napoli, di Pandolfo Collenvccio da Pesaro, di Mambrino Roseo da Fabriano, et di Tomaso Costo Napolitano. Diuiso in tre parti. Con le Annotationi del Costo poste nouamente à suoi luoghi, da lui con diligenza, e fedeltà riuedute, & ampliate, le quali suppliscono a molte cose del Regno, da essi Autori tralasciate. Aggiuntovi in questa vltima editione il quarto libro alla terza parte, che serue per tutto l'anno MDCX. Arricchito di tutti i nomi delle Prouincie, Città . . . Famiglie Illustri e Magistrati di quel Regno . . .—3 pts. in 1 vol. 4⁰, *pp.* 443 + 407 + 264 *and index. Venetia, i Giunti,*1613.

COLLENUCCIO, P.—Historiæ Neapolitanæ ad Herculem I, Ferrariæ ducem, libri iv. . . .—8⁰, *pp.* 716 *and index. Roterodami, typis J. L. Berevvont,* 1617.
See pp. 46–47.

COLLENUCCIO, P.—Compendio dell'Istoria del regno di Napoli di P . . . C . . . di Mambrino Roseo, . . . e di Tommaso Costo, . . . con le annotationi del Costo . . . Aggiuntovi . . . il quarto libro alla terza parte che serve per tutto l'anno 1610 . . .—3 *vols.* 4⁰. *Napoli, stamp. G. Gravier,* 1771.

COLLENUCCIO.—Eruzione del 1301.

COLLEZIONE DI MONOGRAFIE ILLUSTRATE.—Italia Artistica.—*See* RICCI, C.

COLLOMB, E.—[Sur un voyage géologique en Corse, en Sardaigne et aux environs de Naples.]—*Bull. Soc. géol. France, xi, pp.* 63–75. *Paris,* 1854.

COLOMBO, A.—La Fauna sottomarina del Golfo di Napoli.—*Rivista Marittima, xx, pp.* 5–32, 413–443, *tav. i–vii. Roma, Ottobre-Dicembre,* 1887.

COMITÉ D'ORGANISATION DU 2ME CONGRÈS GÉOLOGIQUE INTERNATIONAL À BOLOGNE, 1881.—Bibliographie Géologique et Paléontologique de l'Italie.—8⁰, *pp. viii* + 630. *Bologne,* 1881.
See xi. ZEZI, G. P.—Les Provinces de Napoli, &c. (2207–2537).

COMMISSIONE DEL R. IST. INCORAG. DI NAPOLI.—*See* ANON : ˙ Contributo alla ricerca delle norme edilizie per le regioni sismiche.

CONCINA, G.—Casamicciola, ossia le acque minerali di Ischia.—*Venezia,* 1832.

CONSTANTIN, J.—Voyage scientifique à Naples avec M. Mangendie en 1843.—8⁰, *pp.* 103. *Paris,* 1844. [C.A.]

CONTE.—Saggio di sperimenti su le proprietà chimiche e medicamentose delle acque termo-minerali del Tempio di Serapide.—8⁰, *pp.* 4 + *xxxi* + 213. *Napoli,* 1826.

CONVITO, N.—Sul vulcanismo dell'Isola d'Ischia.

COOL, H.—Der Serapis-Tempel bei Pozzuoli. —*Centralbl. f. Min. pp.* 218–219. *Stuttgart,* 1906.

COPPOLA, M.—*See* PALMERI, P. 1875–76.

CORDIER, P. L. A.—Rapport sur le voyage de M. Constant Prévost à l'Île Julia, à Malte, en Sicile, aux Îles Lipari et dans les environs de Naples.—*C. R. Acad. Sci. ii, pp.* 243–255. *Paris,* 1836.—*Nouv. Ann. Voy. lxx, pp.* 43–64. *Paris,* 1836.

CORRERA, L.—De li bagni Napolitani de Puzolo e de Ischia.

COSTA, O. G.—Mammiferi viventi e fossile della fauna di Napoli.—*Napoli,* 1839.

COSTA, O. G., LA CAVE, ecc.—Statistica fiscia ed economica dell'Isola di Capri.— *Napoli,* 1840.

COSTA, O. G.—Sopra un erpetolite idrotermale con appendice di osservazioni intorno à depositi di avanzi organici a piè di Monte Nuovo presso Pozzuoli, e nelle marne argillose dell'Isola d'Ischia.—*Rend. Acc. Pontaniana, xviii, pp.* 65–88, 139– 145. *Napoli,* 1853.

COSTA, O. G.—Osservazioni ulteriori intorno ai fossili organici di Pozzuoli. —*Napoli,* 1853.

COSTA, O. G.—Cenni intorno alle scoperte paleontologiche fatte nel R. di Napoli durante gli anni 1854–55.—*Napoli,* 1856.

COSTA, O. G.—Intorno alle scoperte paleontologiche fatte nel regno di Napoli durante gli anni 1857–58.—*Napoli,* 1858.

COSTA, O. G.—Note geologiche e paleontologiche su taluni degli Appennini della Campania.—*Atti R. Ist. Incorag. S.* 2, *iii, pp.* 43–80, *tav. i–v. Napoli,* 1866.

COSTO, I.—Ragionamenti di . . . intorno alla descrizzione del regno di Napoli, et all' antichita di Pozzuolo di Scipione Mazzella.—4⁰, *pp.* 82. *Napoli,* 1595.

COSTO, T.—*See* COLLENUCCIO, 1591, 1613, 1771.

COURTOIS, H.—Les Champs Phlégréens.— *Bull. Soc. géog. comm. Bordeaux, xvii, pp.* 515–520. *Bordeaux,* 1880.

COVELLI, N.—Terremoto in Ischia, 2 febbrajo 1828.—foll. 3. [C.A.] Two autograph letters to Monticelli.

COVELLI, N.—Observations sur le tremblement de terre qui a eu lieu dans l'Île d'Ischia le 2 févr. 1828.—Bibl. Univ. Sci. xxxix, pp. 157-165. Genève, 1828. —Notiz. aus dem Gebiete der Natur. und Heilkunde, xxiii, coll. 177-182. Erfurt und Weimar, 1829.

COVELLI, N.—Cenno sul tremuoto d'Ischia. —"Il Pontano," 2, pp. 82. Napoli, 1828-29. [C.A.] See also an English translation in chap. iv of Johnston-Lavis' "Monograph of the Earthquakes of Ischia," &c. Naples, 1885.

COVELLI, N.—Memoria per servire di materiale alla costituzione geognostica della Campania (1827).—Atti R. Acc. Sci. iv, pp. 33-69. Napoli, 1839.

COX, J. C.—Hints for Invalids about to visit Naples ; being a Sketch of the medical Topography of that City. Also an account of the Mineral Waters of the Bay of Naples ; with Analyses of the most important of them derived from authentic Sources.— 8°, pp. 6 + 190, pls. 2. London, Paris, Nottingham, 1841.

CRAIG.—Grotto de Cane, on the Lake of Agnano, in Italy. Engraved by Deeble for the Gallery of Nature and Art.— Published by R. Wilks, 89 Chancery Lane, Sept. 1, 1814. Fine line engraving : 157 × 98 mm.

CREPY (publ.).—Naples, Ville Cap¹ᵉ du R⁼, &c.—A Paris chez Crepy, rue St. Jacques. Bird's-eye view of Naples from the sea, with explanation. 1713 or later. Engrav.: 226 × 140 mm.

CRISCIO, G. DI.—L'Antico Porto Giulio.— 8°, pp. 32. Napoli, 1856.

CRISCIO, G. DI.—Notizie istoriche archeologiche topografiche dell'antica Città di Pozzuoli e dei suoi due aquidotti Serino e Campano con modi onde accrescere il volume delle acque nel secondo Condotto. —8°. Napoli, 1881.

CROCE, B.—Veduta della città di Napoli nel 1479 e del trionfo navale per l'arrivo di Lorenzo de' Medici, con testo illustrativo di B. Croce.—Supplemento alla "Napoli nobilissima." Fascicolo di Aprile MCMI.V. 527 × 175 mm. process pl. with text.

CROIX, LA (pinx.), VEAU, LE (sculp.).— Vue près Pouzzol au Golfe de Naples. Tirée du Cabinet de Monsieur du Bocage. —Se vend à Paris chez Basan. Engrav.: 430 × 329 mm.

CUCINIELLO, DOM., and BIANCHI, L.— Viaggio pittorico, nel Regno delle due Sicilie (with drawings by R. Müller, L. Jely, F. Horner, G. Forino, F. Dura, F. Wenzel, P. de Leopold, C. Goetzloff, G. Gigante, A. Vianelly, A. Marinoni, A. Carelli).— gd. fol. Vol. i, Pt. i, pp. 128, pls. 60 ; Vol. ii, Pt. i, pp. 122, pls. 60 ; Vol. iii, Pt. ii, pp. 122, pls. 60. Napoli, [1833].

DALBONO, C.—See QUARANTA, B.

DANTONE, E.—Casamicciola illustrata da 55 incisioni.—Roma, 1883.

DARONDEAU, VIARD, PLOIX, LA-ROUSSE.—Plan de la Baie de Pouzzol levé en 1856.—[Paris], 1861.—Later ed. 1864. [B.M.—H.F. Sec. 7, 1931.] Scale 1 : 20,000. A well-drawn hydrographical chart with coast features well shown.

DARONDEAU, GAUSSIN, VIARD, MANEN, E. PLOIX, LAROUSSE, and VIDALIN.—Carte particulière des côtes d'Italie, partie comprise entre la tour Patria et le cap Sottile, golfe de Naples et îles. (Nr. 2058.)—Paris, Dépôt de la Marine, 1865.

DASCHER.—Eruptions Volcaniques. Notices abrégées relevées par . . . dans les ouvrages spéciaux.—16°, pp. 16. Paris, 1902.

DAUBENY, C. G. B.—A Description of active and extinct Volcanos ; with remarks on their origin, their chemical phenomena, and the character of their products, as determined by the condition of the earth during the period of their formation.—8°, pp. 466, figs., maps 2, pl. 1, London, 1826.— 8°, pp. 743, figs., maps 10, pls. 4. London, 1848.

DAUBENY, C. G. B.—On the volcanic Strata exposed by a section made on the site of the new thermal spring discovered near the town of Torre dell'Annunziata, in the Bay of Naples ; with some remarks on the gases evolved by this and other springs connected with the volcanoes of Campania. —Edinb. New Phil. Journ. xix, pp. 221-231. Edinb. 1835.—Proc. Geol. Soc. ii, pp. 177-179. London, 1838.

DAUBRÉE, G. A.—Rapport sur le tremblement de terre ressenti à Ischia le 28 juillet 1883 ; causes probables des tremblements de terre.—*C. R. Acad. Sci. xcvii, pp.* 768–778. *Paris,* 1883.—Also *Rev. Sci. xxxii, pp.* 465–468. *Paris,* 1883.

DAUTONE, E.—Casamicciola illustrata da 55 incisioni.—*Roma,* 1883.

DAVENPORT (sculp.).—Naples.—London : published by Thomas Kelly, 17 Paternoster Row, 1836.
Fine engrav. : 170 × 105 mm.

DAVY, SIR HUMPHRY.—Sur les Phénomènes des' Volcans.—*Ann. Chim. Phys. xxxviii, pp.* 133–150. *Paris,* 1828.

D. B.—L'Italia descritta e depinta con le sue isole di Sicilia, Sardegna, Elba, Malta, Eolie, di Calipso, ecc. Collected from numerous authors by D. B.——2nd ed. 5 vols. 8⁰, *with many (good) engravings. Turin, Gius. Pomba, e. c.* 1837.

DEECKE, J. E. W.—Über die Gestalt des Lukriner Sees vor dem Ausbruche des Mte. Nuovo im Jahre 1538.—*Jahresb. geog. Gesellsch. Greifswald, pp.* 18, *map* 1. 1887–1888.

DEECKE, J. E. W.—Il cratere di Fossa Lupara nei Campi Flegrei presso Napoli.—*Boll. R. Com. Geol. Ital. pp.* 233–245. *Roma,* 1888.—[Estr. d.] *Zeitschr. deutsch. geol. Gesellsch. xl, pp.* 166–172, 1 *pl. Berlin,* 1888.

DEECKE, J. E. W.—Zur Geologie von Unteritalien. 3. Der sog. campanische Tuff, seine Lagerung, Zusammensetzung u. Entstehung (1891).—*N. J. f. Min. ii, pp.* 286–330, 1891 ; *ii, pp.* 108–124, 1892.—4. Das System des Monte Maggiore bei Pignataro in Campanien.—*Id., i, pp.* 51–74. 1893.

DEECKE, J E. W.—Ueber den Sarno in Unteritalien (Provinz Neapel).—*Jahresb. geog. Gesellsch. v. Greifswald,* 1892.

DEECKE, J. E. W.—Italien.—*Bibl. der Länderkunde, iii and iv,* 8⁰, *pp.* 519, 33 *maps and pl.,* 79 *fig. Berlin,* 1899.

DEECKE, J. E. W,—Geologischer Führer durch Campanien.—12⁰, *pp.* 235, *figs.* 28, 1 *map. Berlin,* 1901.

D'ALEMBERT.—*See* DIDEROT.

DELTA (Δ) (Pseud. for FORBES, J. D.) —Remarks on the climate of Naples and its vicinity ; with an account of a visit to the Hot springs of la Pisavella, Nero's Baths.—*Edinb. Journ. Sci. vii, pp.* 263–267. *Edinburgh,* 1827.

DENOZZA, M.—Analisi dell'acqua di Sava Scura (Isola d'Ischia).—*Atti R. Ist. Incorag. S.* 6, *lix, pp.* 121–126. *Napoli,* 1908.

DENZA, F.—Il disastro di Casamicciola. Causa del disastro di Casamicciola.—*Bull. mens. Assoc. Meteor. Ital., agosto* 1883.

DEROY (lith.).—Vues de Naples. Vedute di Napoli. N⁰ 19. St. François de Paule. Vue Prise de Pausilippe. Ste. Lucie. Ruines du temple de Vénus à Bayes. Grotte de Pausilippe. Vue Générale prise des Carmes (also inscript. in Italian).— Paris, Bulla Frères et Jouy, rue Tiquetonne 18. Imp. Lemercier, à Paris. Milano, si vende da tutti Negozianti di generi di belli Arti.
6 lithos. : each 124 × 84 mm.

DEROY (lith.).—Vues de Naples. N⁰ 20. La Vittoria. Palais de la Reine Jeanne. Vue prise de Capo di Monte, Amalfi, Pouzzole, Temple de Serapis, Salerne.—Paris, Bulla Frères et Jouy, rue Tiquetonne 18. Imp. Lemercier, à Paris. Milano, si vende da tutti Negozianti di generi di belli Arti.
6 views in litho. : 121 × 83 mm. Inscriptions also in Italian.

DEROY (des. et lith.).—Pouzzole. Temple de Serapide. Italie. N⁰ 117. Imp. Lemercier, à Paris. Paris, publié par Jeannin, Place du Louvre 20. London, pub. by Gambert, Junin & Co., 25 Berners St., Oxf. St.
Fine litho. on tinted background : 284 × 183 mm.

DESMOULINS.—Vue prise de dessus le Cratère de Monte Nuovo. — ? , — ? [C.A.]

DESNOYERS, J. P. F. S.—Notice sur l'Île Julia, le Stromboli, les colonnes du Temple de Pozzuoli.—*Bull. Soc. géol. France, ii, pp.* 238–246. *Paris,* 1831-2.

DESPREZ.—Vue du Temple de Serapis à Pozzuoli.—Chez Piranesi. [B.M. Portf. II. Tab. K. 83 (78)b.]
A good distemper (photo'd).

DESSOULAVY.—Vedute Napolitane. 24 line drawings in pencil and sepia. 1826.
Of little interest as to Naples itself, (*See* N⁰ 2) but a drawing (24) of Valle di Amsanto is interesting.

DESSOULAVY.—*See* BOSSIS.

DEVERIA.—Île Bourbon, Île d'Ischia, &c. — ?, — ?.

DEVILLE, C. J. STE.-CLAIRE.—Recherches sur les produits des volcans de l'Italie méridionale.—*C. R. Acad. Sci. xlii, pp.* 1167–1171. *Paris*, 1856.

DEVILLE, C. J. STE.-CLAIRE.—Dixième et dernière Lettre à M. Elie de Beaumont sur les phénomènes éruptifs de l'Italie méridionale.—*C. R. Acad. Sci. xliii, pp.* 745–751. *Paris*, 1856.

DEVILLE, C. J. STE.-CLAIRE.—Mémoire sur les émanations volcaniques (premier mémoire).—*C. R. Acad. Sci. xliii, pp.* 955–958, *Paris*, 1856 ; *xliv, pp.* 58–62, 1857.—*Bull. Soc. géol. France, S.* 2, *xiv, pp.* 254–279. *Paris*, 1856-7.

DEVILLE, C. J. STE.-CLAIRE, et LE-BLANC.—Sur la composition chimique des gaz rejetés par les évents volcaniques de l'Italie Méridionale.—*Bull. Soc. géol. France, S.* 2, *xv, pp.*310–313, *Paris*, 1858 (2ᵉ *Mém.*). —*C. R. Acad. Sci. xliv, pp.* 769–773, *Paris*, 1857 (1ʳ *Mém.*); *Id. xlv, pp.* 398–402 (2ᵉ *Mém.*).—*Ann. Chim. lii, pp.* 5–63. 1858.— *Journ. Pharm. S.* 3, *xxxiii, pp.* 128–132. 1858.—*Mém. Sav. Étrang. xvi, pp.* 225–276. *Paris*, 1862.

DEVILLE, C. J. STE.-CLAIRE, et LE-BLANC.—Sur les émanations gazeuses qui accompagnent l'acide borique dans les Soffioni et Lagoni de la Toscane. (Extr. d'une Lettre à M. Elie de Beaumont.)— *C. R. Acad. Sci. xlv, pp.* 750–752. *Paris*, 1857.

DEVILLE, C. J. STE.-CLAIRE.—Sur les émanations volcaniques des Champs Phlégréens. Trois lettres à son frère M. H. Sainte-Claire Deville.—*C. R. Acad. Sci.* (1ʳᵉ) *liv, pp.* 528–536. *Paris*, 1862 ; (2ᵐᵉ) *lv, pp.* 583–590, 1862 ; (3ᵐᵉ) *lxi, pp.* 760–764, 820–827, 1865.

DEVILLE, C. J. STE.-CLAIRE, LEBLANC, F., et FOUQUÉ, F. A.—Sur les émanations, à gaz combustibles, qui se sont échappées des fissures de la lave de 1794, à Torre del Greco, lors de la dernière éruption du Vésuve.—*C. R. Acad. Sci. lv, pp.* 75–76, *Paris*, 1862 ; *Id. lvi, pp.* 1185–1189, 1863.

DEVILLE, C. J. STE.-CLAIRE. — [Remarques sur les émanations volcaniques et métallifères.].—*C. R. Acad. Sci. lviii, pp.* 329–333. *Paris*, 1864.

DEVILLE, C. J. STE.-CLAIRE. — Rapport sur un mémoire de M. Fouqué, intitulé : " Recherches sur les phénomènes chimiques des volcans."—*C. R. Acad. Sci. lxii, pp.* 1366–1377. *Paris*, 1866.

DEVILLE, C. J. STE.-CLAIRE.—[Remarks upon Fouqué's "Sur les phénomènes éruptifs," &c.] *See* FOUQUÉ, F. A.

DIDEROT and D'ALEMBERT.—Encyclopédie. Minéralogie. 6ᵐᵉ Collection, Volcans.—5 *pls.* 4⁰. *Paris*, 1770. *See* Pl. 5, Solfatara.

DIENER.—Das Erdbeben auf der Insel Ischia am 28 Juli 1883.—*Mitth. deutsch. geog. Gesellsch. pp.* 10. *Wien*, 1884

DIETRICH, Dr.—*See* FERBER

DONATO, A. DI.—Dell'analisi chimica e delle proprietà medicinali dell'acqua termominerale detta Subveni-homini.—8⁰, *pp.* 16. *Napoli*, 1854. [C.A.]

DUCOS, B.—Itinéraire et Souvenirs d'un Voyage en Italie en 1819 et 1820.—4 vols. 8⁰, *maps. Paris*, 1829. *See* Vols. ii and iii.

DUFLOS.—Vue de la Solfatara près de Pouzzole, ancien volcan nommé par Strabon Forum Vulcani.—*Naples*, — ? [C.A.]

DUFRÉNOY, O. P. A. P.—De la manière dont peut se former le terrain des environs de Naples.—*Bull. Soc. géol. France, viii, pp.* 218–220. *Paris*, 1836.

DUFRÉNOY, O. P. A. P.—Sur les terrains volcaniques des environs de Naples.—*C. R. Acad. Sci. i, pp.* 353–356. *Paris*, 1835.— *Notiz. aus d. Geb. d. Natur- u. Heilkunde. xlvi, coll.* 225–230. *Erfurt und Weimar*, 1835. —*Edinb. New Phil. Journ. xx, pp.* 126–130. *Edinburgh*, 1836.—*Ann. Mines, S.* 3, *xi, pp.* 113–158, 369–386, 389–434, *pls. ii and viii. Paris*, 1837.—*Proc. Verb. Acad. Philom. pp.* 61–64. *Paris*, 1837.— *Mém. pr. servir à une description géologique de la France*, 8⁰, *foll.* 4, *pp.* 227–386, *pls.* 9, *figs. Paris*, 1838.—*Nouv. Ann. Voyages, lxx, pp.* 64–70. *Paris*, 1836.

DUFRÉNOY, O. P. A. P.—Parallèle entre les différents produits volcaniques des environs de Naples et rapport entre leur composition et les phénomènes qui les ont produits.—*Bull. Soc. géol. France, ix, pp.* 334–337. *Paris*, 1837-38.—*Ann. Chim. lxix, pp.* 95–100. *Paris*, 1838.—*Ann. Mines, xiii, pp.* 565–584. *Paris*, 1838.— *C. R. Acad. Sci. vi, pp.* 813–816. *Paris*, 1838.

DUKERUS, A.—*See* PELLEGRINO, CAM-MILLO (THE YOUNGER).

DUPLESSIS, BERTEAUX (grav.).—Grotte du Chien près du Lao Agnano. Gravé à l'eau forte par Duplessis Berteaux. Terminé par De Ghendt. 221, N. Engrav.: 222 × 154 mm.

DURA, G. (dis.).—La Solfatara di Pozzuoli. La Solfatara à Pouzzoles. G. Gigante dip. Lit⁺ Cuciniello e Bianchi. Litho. on double paper: 309 × 210 mm.

DURIER, C.—Le Vésuve et Capri.—*Ann. Club Alp. Franç. xxii, pp.* 404–464, 7 *pls.* 1896.

ECHO, D.—Par Monts et par Vaux. La catastrophe d'Ischia (MM. Palmieri—De Rossi — Laur — Trison — Kuntz).—*Journ. Hygiène. Paris,* 23 août 1883.

EDWARDS, J.—*See* SMITH, J. 1796.

EHRENBERG, C. G.—Feststellung des Kalk-Ueberzuges am Serapis Tempel als Süsswasserkalk durch das Mikroskop.—*Monatsb. k. preuss. Akad. Wissensch. pp.* 585–602. *Berlin,* 1858.

EHRENBERG, C. G.—Ueber eine auf der Insel Ischia jüngst beobachtete, zur Erlauterung einer ungarischen aus Kieselorganismen bestehenden Felsart dienende Wirkung heisser Quellen.—*Monatsb. k. preuss. Akad. Wissensch. pp.* 488–497. *Berlin,* 1858.—Reprint, *pp.* 488–497. 1858.

ELISIUS.—Succincta instauratio de Balneis totis Capanie I. Elisij medici Neap. cum libello etro medicos serenissimo principii Bisiniani directa. Item Elisianu auxiliu in orribile flagellum morbi Gallici contra non nullos, barbaros ac vulgares Empericos.—4⁰, *fig.* 1. *Neapoli,* 1519.

ELYSIO, J.—*See* JASOLINUS—De Remedii Naturali.

EMILIO, L. D'.—*See* PIUTTI, A. 1904.

ENGELBRECHT, M.—Posilipo. (View from sea.) 1. 25. N. 7, excud. Aug. Vind. [Vienna lib.] Engrav.: 298 × 191 mm.

ENGELBRECHT, M.—Promontorio Miseno. Excud. Aug. Vind. 4, 28. [Vienna lib.] View of ruins, with storm. Engrav.: 302 × 191 mm.

ENGELBRECHT, M.—Cuma. Excud. Aug. Vind. 2, 26. — ?, — ? (18th cent. 2nd half.) [Vienna lib.] View of ruins, with setting sun. Engrav.: 297 × 188 mm.

ERBA, L. DELL'.—Sulla Sanidinite Sodalito-pirossenica di Sant'Elmo. Studio petrografico e considerazioni geologiche.—*Rend. R. Acc. Sci. S.* 2, *iv, pp.* 175–186. *Napoli,* 1890.

ERBA, L. DELL'.—Considerazioni sulla genesi del Piperno.—*Atti R. Acc. Sci. S.* 2, *v,* 3, *pp.* 22. *Napoli,* 1893.

ERBA, L. DELL'.—La Sanidinite Sodalito-Anortica di Monte Nuovo. Studio petrografico.—8⁰, *pp.* 12. *Napoli,* 1893.

ERBA, L. DELL'.—L'Andesite pirosseno-micacea di Posilippo.—*Atti Acc. Pont. xxiii,* 13, *pp.* 15. *Napoli,* 1893.

ERBA, L. DELL'.—Sulla presenza della Pirite presso Agnano nei Campi Flegrei.—*Atti Acc. Pont. xxv,* 4, *pp.* 4. *Napoli,* 1895.

ERBA, L. DELL'.—Studio e considerazioni Petrografiche sulla lava dell'Arso nell'isola d'Ischia.—*Atti R. Acc. Sci. S.* 2, *vii, pp.* 13. *Napoli,* 1895.—*Id. Rend. pp.* 181–182. 1895.

ESCARD, J.—Les Phénomènes Volcaniques, leurs causes, leurs effets.—[Extr]. *Science Catholique,* Oct. 1903, 8⁰, *pp.* 22, *fig. Arras,* 1904.

EUCHERII DE QUINTIIS.—*See* QUINTIIS.

FABRIS.—[Twenty Views of Naples and its Environs engraved by Sandby and Robertson.] — ?, 1777–1782.

FABRIS (pinxt.), P. SANDBY (fec.).—Castello dell' Ovo at Naples.—Published by Paul Sandby, St. George's Row, Oxford Turnpike, Jan. 1st, 1778. N⁰ 709. Carefully hand-painted on line engrav.: 513 × 328 mm.

FABRIS (pinxt.).—Castello dell'Ovo at Naples. Vue du Château des Œufes à Naples. P. Sandby fecit.—Publish'd as the Act directs by P. Sandby, St. George's Row, Oxford Turnpike, Jan. 1st, 1778. A sepia stipple engrav.: 509 × 346 mm.

FABRIS (pinxt.).—Part of Naples, with the Ruined Tower of St. Vincent. Vue de Naples, avec les débris de la Tour de St. Vincent. P. Sandby fecit.—Publish'd as the Act directs by P. Sandby, St. George's Row, Oxford Turnpike, Jan. 1st, 1778. Sepia engrav.: 512 × 357 mm.

FAIRBAIRN, R.—View of the Lake of Avernus and the Ruins of the Temple of Apollo, the Lucrin Lake, Monte Nuovo and the Island of Caprea, in the Bay of Naples.   Ziegler sculp.—*London,* 1798. [B.M.—K 83. 61—b.]
A fine mezzotint engrav.

FALCO, B. DI.—Descrittione de i lvoghi antichi di Napoli e del svo amenissimo distreto.—*16⁰, foll.* 57.   *Napoli* [1535 ?].— Other ed. 1548, 1568, 1580.—*In* 1679 *another edit. was published under the title :* Antichità di Napoli, e del svo amenissimo distretto.   Di nuouo in questa Sesta impressione corretta, & posta in luce.— 8⁰, *pp.* 64, 1 *fig. Napoli,* 1679.   *See also* PORFILE, C.—" Raccolta di Varii libri overo opuscoli del Regno di Napoli."— *Napoli,* 1680.

FALCO, B. DI.—Antiquitates Neapolis, atquae, &c.—*fol., coll.* 48. *Lug.Bat.*—? *See* GRAEVIUS, J. G.: Thesaurus Antiquitatum . . . Italiae, ix, Pt. i. 1723.
This is the oldest guide to Naples [1679] in which Vesuvius and the Solfatara are mentioned.

FALCONI, A. DELLI.—Dell'Incendio di Pozzvolo Marco Antonio delli Falconi all'Illustrissima signora, Marchesa della Padula nel M.D.XXXVIII.   Cum Gratia et Privilegio. [At the end :] Si venne per Marco Antonio Passaro Alliferri Vecchi.— 4⁰ (*pages of text :* 150 × 100 *mm.*), *foll.* 22, 1 *woodcut.* [*Napoli ?*] 1538.
See GIUSTINIANI, L.—I Tre Rarissimi Opuscoli.—8⁰, *pp.* 287–332. [Napoli ?] 1538.

FARINA, A.—Compendio delle cose piv cvriose di Napoli, e di Pozzvoli.   Con alcune notitie del Regno.—16⁰, *foll.* 5, *pp.* 111. *Napoli,* 1679.

FAUJAS DE SAINT-FOND, B.—Minéralogie des Volcans, ou Description de toutes les Substances produites ou rejetées par les Feux Souterrains.—8⁰, *pp. xviii* + 511, *pl. iii. Paris,* 1784.—German ed. 1786.

FAUJAS DE SAINT-FOND, B.—Notice sur une espèce de charbon fossile nouvellement découverte dans le territoire de Naples.— *Ann. Mus. Hist. Nat. xi. Paris,* 1808.

FAZZINI, G.—Cenno sulla pozzolana della Baja di Napoli.—4⁰, *pp.* 21. *Napoli,* 1857.

F. C. (del. 1734).—Golfo di Napoli (with 16 reference numbers and expl.). [Vienna lib.]
Engrav. map : 316 × 225 mm.

FER, N. DE.—Description de la ville de Naples. [Vienna lib.]
Engrav. descrip. in 30 lines : 227 × 162 mm.

FER, N. DE.—Les Merveilles de Pozzoli ou Pouzzol, Cume et Baja ou Bayes, dans le voisinage de Naples.—I. F. Benard. 100. Paris, 1701. [B.N.P., Vb. 113.]
Shows Caligula's Mole partly arched, also map on same page does likewise. An ed. (with description) in B.M. [K. 83 (76)] is dated 1705. Engrav. map : 330 × 219 mm.

FER, [N.] SR. DE.—Naples. (Bird's-eye view of N. and Camp. Phleg., with 31 reference nos.)—Dans l'Ile du Palais à la Sphère Royale, &c. 1705. [Vienna lib.]
Engrav. plan : 331 × 224 mm.

FER, N. DE.—Les Environs de la Ville de Naples dans la Province de Labour avec la Routte de cette Ville à Roma.—*Paris* [*after* 1705]. [B.M.—K. 83. 47.]
Map showing Palmarola divided into four islands.

FERBER, J. J.—Lettres à Mr. le Chev. de Born sur la Minéralogie et sur divers autres objets d'histoire naturelle de l'Italie, traduit de l'Allemand, enrichi de notes et d'observations faites sur les lieux par M. de Dietrich.—8⁰, *pp.* 16 + 508. *Strasbourg and Paris,* 1776.
See pp. 160–274, letter xi, Napoli, 17 Feb. 1772 : long description of Monte Nuovo, Solfatara, &c.

FERGOLA, L.—Recueil des Vues les plus Agréables de Naples et de ses Environs . . . dessinées d'après Nature par L. F. et gravées par V. Aloja.—*obl. fol. Naples,* 1817. [B.M. 551 e 49.]
See Pls. 5, 7, 15.

FERGOLA, L.—*See* HACKERT, PH.—Raccolta di xxv vedute.

FERRARI, G. B. DE.—Guida di Napoli, dei Contorni, di Procida, Ischia e Capri.— 8⁰, *pp.* 320, *pls.* 4. *Napoli,* 1826.
See pp. 193–262.

FERRARI, G. B. DE.—Nuova Guida di Napoli, dei Contorni, di Procida, Ischia e Capri, compilata su la Guida del Vasi, &c. —Iᵃ ed. 8⁰, *pp.* 319, *pls.* 3, *maps* 2. *Napoli,* 1826.
Another ed. (still called " Prima edizione "), Engl. and Ital. text, *pp.* 671, *pls.* 3, *maps* 2. *Napoli,* 1839.

FERRERO, O.—Relazioni sopra un minerale trovato a Lusciano.—*Ann. Staz. Agr. v. Caserta*, 1877.

FERRERO, O.—*See* ROCCATAGLIATA, P. 1877.

FERRERO, O., and MUSAIO.—Studii ed analisi sopra le Roccie Vulcaniche costitutive in alcuni punti del territorio della provincia di Caserta.—*Ann. Staz. Agr. vi. Caserta*, 1878.

FERRERO, O.—Esposizione regionale di Caserta. Contribuzioni allo studio del materiale litologico della Provincia.—*ii. Caserta*, 1879.

F. F. (dis. dal vero.).—Veduta nell'Isola di Nisita. Vinc. Aloja inc. N⁰ 15.
Engrav.: 267 × 219 mm.

FIESCHI-RAVASCHIERI, Dˢᵃ.—*See* MEURICOFFRE, O.

FINDEN, W. and E.—Naples [from Posilippo Grotto].—*From* Brockedon's "Road Book from London to Naples."—8⁰. *London*, 1835.
Two men leaning over wall.

FISCHER, Th.—Das Halbinselland Italien. —*In* Kirchhoff's "Länderkunde von Europa."—*pp.* 285–515. *Prag, Wien, Leipzig*, 1890.

FLAMMARION, N. C.—Le tremblement de terre d'Ischia.—*Rev. Mens. Astron. Pop.* 9, *pp.* 317–329, 3 *figs. Paris*, 1883. [C.A.]
Transl. from the Ital.

FLAMMARION, N. C.—Les Éruptions Volcaniques et les Tremblements de Terre.— 12⁰, *pp.* 433, *figs.* 34. *Paris*, 1902.

FLORES, E.—*See* JOHNSTON - LAVIS, H. J., 1895.

FLORES, E.—Polveri sciroccali e Pisoliti meteoriche.—*Boll. Soc. Geol. Ital. xxii, pp.* 81–84. *Roma*, 1903.

FODERA, O.—*See* MARCHI, L. DE.

FONSECA, F.—Descrizione e carta geologica dell'Isola d'Ischia.—*pp.* 40, *map. Napoli*, 1847.—See also : *Ann. Acc. Aspir. Nat. S.* 2, *i, pp.* 163–200. *Napoli*, 1847.

FONSECA, F.—Descrizione geologica dell' Isola d'Ischia.—*Torino*, 1866.

FONSECA, F.—Geologia dell'Isola d'Ischia (con carta geologica).—4⁰, *pp.* 31 *and map. Firenze*, 1870.

FORBES, J. D.—*See* DELTA (Δ), 1827.

FORBES, J. D.—Physical notices of the Bay of Naples : N⁰ 3. On the district of Posilippo and the Lago d'Agnano.—*Edinb. Journ. Sci. x, pp.* 245–267. *Edinburgh,* 1829.—*Zeitschr. f. Min. pp.* 717–729: *Frankfurt-am-Main*, 1829.
For Nᵒˢ 1 and 2 *see* VESUVIUS.

FORBES, J. D.—Physical notices of the Bay of Naples : N⁰ 4. On the Solfatara of Pozzuoli.—*Edinb. Journ. Sci. N.S. i, pp.* 124–141. *Edinburgh*, 1829.—*Floriep. Notiz aus dem Geb. der Natur- und Heilkunde, xxv, coll.* 113–121 *and* 132–138. *Erfurt und Weimar*, 1829.

FORBES, J. D.—Physical notices of the Bay of Naples : N⁰ 5. On the temple of Jupiter Serapis at Pozzuoli and the phenomena which it exhibits.—*Edinb. Journ. Sci. N.S. i, pp.* 260–286. *Edinburgh*, 1829.—Boué : *Journ. Géol. i. pp.* 354–373. *Paris*, 1830.

FORBES, J. D.—Physical notices of the Bay of Naples : N⁰ 6. District of the Bay of Baia. —*Edinb. Journ. Sci. N.S. ii, pp.* 75–101. *Edinburgh*, 1830.

FORBES, J. D.—Physical notices of the Bay of Naples : N⁰ 7. On the Islands of Procida and Ischia.—*Edinb. Journ. Sci. N.S. ii, pp.* 326–350. *Edinburgh*, 1830.— *Floriep. Notiz a. d. Geb. d. Nat. u. Heilkunde, xxvii, coll.* 243–250 *and* 257–264. *Erfurt und Weimar*, 1830.

FORBES, J. D.—Physical notices of the Bay of Naples : N⁰ 8. Concluding view of the volcanic formations of the district. —*Edinb. Journ. Sci. N.S. iii, pp.* 246– 278. *Edinburgh*, 1831.

FORTE, O.—*See* OGLIALORO-TODARO, A. 1895, 1896.

FORTIS, A.—Lettera economica su l'attuale stato dell'Allumiera della Solfatara di Pozzuoli. — ?, 1790. [B.N.]

FORTUNATO, GIUSTINO. *See* G. F.

FOUGEROUX DE BONDAROY.—Observation sur le lieu appelé Solfatare, situé près de la Ville de Naples.—*C. R. Acad. Sci. ii, pp.* 418–447, *pl. iii. Paris,* 1765. —*Hist. Acad. R. Sci., Mém. Math. Phys.* 1765, *pp.* 267–284, *pls.* 3. *Paris*, 1768.

FOUQUÉ, F. A.—Sur les phénomènes éruptifs de l'Italie méridionale. Sixième lettre à Ch. Sainte-Claire Deville.—*C. R. Acad. Sci. lxi, pp.* 734–737. *Paris*, 1865.

FOUQUÉ, F. A.—Recherches sur les phénomènes chimiques des volcans. (Résumé et conclusions.)—*C. R. Acad. Sci. lxii, pp.* 616–7. *Paris,* 1866.

FOUQUÉ, F. A.—*See* DEVILLE, C. J. STE.-CLAIRE.

FRANCIS, J. G.—Notes from a Journal kept in Italy and Sicily. With illustrations.—8⁰, *pp.* 309. *London,* 1847.
See pp. 149–193, with a fine view of " Il Fungo " at p. 174.

FRANCO, P.—Note Mineralogiche. Amfibolo e Sodalite della Trachite di Montesanto. —*Rend. R. Acc. Sci. S.* 3, *i, pp.* 124–129, *pl.* 1. *Napoli,* 1895.—*Zeitschr. f. Kryst. xxv, p.* 328. *Leipzig,* 1895.

FRANCO, P.—Note Mineralogiche. Minerali formatisi sulle Ossa Fossili nel tufo di Fiano.—*Rend. R. Acc. Sci. S.* 3, *i, pp.* 130–132. *Napoli,* 1895.

FRANCO, P.—. . . Pipernoid Tuff of the Campania. . . .
See JOHNSTON-LAVIS, 1895.

FRANCO, P.—Il tufo della Campania.—*Boll. Soc. Nat. S.* 1, *xiv, pp.* 19–33, *tav. Napoli,* 1901.

FRANCO, P.—Il Piperno.—*Boll. Soc. Nat. S.* 1, *xiv, pp.* 34–52, *tav. Napoli,* 1901.

FRANCO, P.—L'attività vulcanica nella Campania secondo la tradizione e la storia. —*Boll. Soc. Nat. S.* 1, *xvi, pp.* 260–288. *Napoli,* 1903.

FRANCO, P.—*See* FRIEDLAENDER, E.

FRANᶜᵒ LELIO, MARCHESE.—Narratione di molte Cose auuenute nel Regno di Napoli nel gouerno di Don Pierro di Toledo, e d'alcune fameglie nobili del Regno.—MS. 8⁰, *pp.* 116.
See p. 115.

FRANZETTI, A.—*See* MORELLI.

FREDA, G.—Sulla composizione del Piperno trovato nella collina del Vomero, e sull' origine probabile di questa roccia.—*Rend. R. Acc. Sci. S.* 2, *ii, pp.* 177–180. *Napoli,* 1888.

FREDA, G.—Sulle Masse Trachitiche rinvenute nei recenti trafori delle colline di Napoli.—*Rend. R. Acc. Sci. S.* 2, *iii, pp.* 38–46. *Napoli,* 1889.

FREEBAIRN, R. (pinxt.).—The Ruin of the Temple of Diana at Baie, nr. Naples. This view is humbly inscribed to Edward Bootle, Esqr., of Latham House, Lancashire, by his much obliged and faithful servant, Robert Fairbairn. I. Hill, sculpt.— London : Published March 30, 1800, and to be had of R. Freebairn, Hampstead.
Col. engrav.: 574 × 477 mm., of [no?] important interest.

FREEBAIRN, R. (pinxt.).—A View of the Bay of Naples, the City of Pozzuoli, the Elysian Fields, the Stygean Lake and Cape of Miseno. To the University of Oxford, this plate of Classic Scenery is dedicated by their very humble servants. I. C. Ziegler, sculpsit.—London : Published March 1, 1811, by J. Deeley, 95 Berwick St.
Col. engrav.: 566 × 454 mm., of no important interest.

FREEBAIRN (pinxt.).—A View of the Lake of Avernus, with the Ruins of the Temple of Apollo, the Lucrin Lake, Monte Nuovo, and the Island of Caprea, in the Bay of Naples. To the University of Cambridge, this plate of Classic Scenery is dedicated by their humble servant, Robert Freebairn. I. C. Ziegler, sculpt.—London : Published March 1, 1811, by J. Deeley, 95 Berwick St.
Col. engrav.: 558 × 453 mm., of no great interest.

FRIEDLAENDER, E., and FRANCO, P.— Contribuzione alla Geologia delle Isole Pontine.—*Boll. Soc. Geol. Ital. xxix, pp.* 672–676. *Roma,* 1900.

FRIEDLAENDER, E.—Uber die Kleinformen der vulkanischen Produkte.— *Zeitschr. f. Vulk. i,* 2. *Berlin, Mai* 1914.
See taf. xxxii, fig. 40.

FRIEDLAENDER, H.—Ansichten von Italien, während einer Reise in den Jahren 1815 und 1816.—2 vols. 12⁰. *Leipzig,* 1819–20.—In Eng. : 5 vols. 8⁰. *London,* 1820.
See Vol. ii.

FUCHS, C. W. C.—Notizen aus dem vulkanischen Gebiete Neapels.—*N. J. f. Min. pp.* 31–40. *Stuttgart,* 1865.

FUCHS, C. W. C.—Ueber die Entstehung der Westküste von Neapel.—*Verh. Nat.-hist. Medic. Ver. zu Heidelberg, iii, pp.* 171–6. *Heidelberg,* 1865.

FUCHS, C. W. C.—Die Insel Ischia.—*Jahrb. k.-k. geol. Reichsanst. xxii, Min. Mitth. pp.* 199–238. *Wien,* 1872.

FUCHS, C. W. C.—Carta geologica dell' Isola d'Ischia.—*Uffic. Geol. Ital. Firenze,* 1873.
Scale 1 : 25,000.

FUCHS, C. W. C.—Monografia geologica dell'Isola d'Ischia.—*Mem. R. Com. Geol. Ital. ii, Pt. 1a, pp.* 5–58. *Firenze,* 1873.

FUCHS, C. W. C.—Chemisch-geologische Untersuchung der Insel Ischia.—*Verh. allgem. Schweiz. Naturf. Gesellsch. p.* 57. *Chur,* 1874 ; *pp.* 64–68, 1875.—*Zeitschr. gesammt. Naturw. xii, pp.* 207–208. 1875.

FUCHS, C. W. C.—Les Volcans et les Tremblements de Terre.—8⁰, *pp. viii*+279, *fig. and map. Paris,* 1876.——2nd ed. 1878.

FUESSLI, H. (pinx.).—Le Port de Baja avec le Temple de Vénus, pour le Voyage des quatres parties du Monde, de Mr. Henri Vernon, Anglois. H. Troll, del. et sculp.—A Paris, chez Basset, rue St. Jacques, 64.
Line litho. : 408× — mm. [Circa 1828]

FURCHHEIM, F.—Bibliografia della Campania.—2 vols. 8⁰. 1897–99.

FURCHHEIM, F.—Bibliografia dell'Isola di Capri e della Penisola Sorrentina.—*Bibliografia della Campania, ii, pp.* 88. *Napoli,* 1899.

FUSCO, G.—Giunta al Comento critico-archeologico sul frammento inedito di Fabio Giordano intorno alle grotte del promontorio di Posilipo.—8⁰, *pp.* 118, *pl. Napoli,* 1842.

FUSCO, G. M.—*See* GMFATGGVF.

FUSCO, G. V.—*See* GMFATGGVF.

GALANTI, G. M.—Breve descrizione della Città di Napoli e del suo contorno.—8⁰, *pp. xvi* + 348. *Napoli,* 1792.—Also with appendix : *pp.* 28. *Napoli,* 1803.

GALANTI, G. M. and L.—Napoli e Contorni. Nuova edizione interamente riformata dall'Abate Luigi Galanti.—8⁰, *pp.* 7 + 381, 11 *pls.,* 2 *maps. Napoli,* 1838.
See pp. 271-308.

GALANTI, L.—*See* GALANTI, G. M. 1838.

GALANTI, L.—Guida di Napoli e suoi contorni.—*Napoli,* 1845.——4th ed. 8⁰, *pp.* 4 + 292, 11 *pls.,* 2 *maps. Napoli,* 1861.
See pp. 195-219.
Also : 8⁰, *pp.* 292, 11 *pls.,* 2 *maps. Napoli,* 1872.
See pp. 195-220.

G. A. (dit le maître à la chausse-trappe).—Il vero disegno del infelice paese di Posuolo e del Monte di Nuovo nato, cominciando a abattar fuoco, pietre e cenere a li 29 Dec. 1538 et ancor seghuita con minacci horribili.— ! , 1538 ?

Eau-forte engrav. : 293 × 428 mm., Nordenskiöld 121, N⁰ 116. Nagler, Monogramm. II, N⁰ 2679, p. 960. N⁰ 20. Unknown to Bartch xv, p. 540.

GAIZO, M. DEL.—Notizie intorno all'eruzione del 1301 ed all'industria dell'allume nell'isola d'Ischia.—*La " Rassegna Italiana," An.* 4, *ii, pp.* 51–62. *Roma,* 1884.

GALDIERI, A.—Su di un'Alga che cresce intorno alle fumarole della Solfatara.—*Rend. R. Acc. Sci. S.* 3, *v, pp.* 160–164. *Napoli,* 1899.

GALDIERI, A., e PAOLINI, V.—Il Tufo Campano di Vico Equense.—*Atti R. Acc. Sci. S.* 2, *xv,* 15, *pp.* 12, 1 *pl.,* 1 *geol. map. Napoli,* 1913.

GAMBA, B.—Lettere descrittive da celebri Italiani. 2ᵈᵃ. ed.—8⁰, *pp.* 8 + 262. *Venezia,* 1819.—Earlier ed. 1813.

GARRUCCIO, G.—Un simposio sul cratere di Baia, disquisizioni archeologiche di Guida da Miseno a Porto Giulio.—8⁰, *pp.* 32. *Napoli,* 1859. [C.A.]

GASPARIS, A. DE.—*See* PALMIERI, L. 1863.

GATTA, L.—L'Italia, sua formazione, suoi vulcani e terremoti.—8⁰, *pp.* 539, *figs.* 32, *maps* 3. *Milano,* 1882.—*Boll. R. Com. Geol. Ital., Notiz. Bibliog. pp.* 102–104. *Roma,* 1882.

GATTA, L.—Su alcuni fenomeni fisici relativi all'Isola d'Ischia.—*Boll. Soc. Geol. Ital. ii, pp.* 210–217. *Roma,* 1883.

GATTA, L.—Il disastro di Casamicciola.—*" Gazetta Letteraria di Torino,"* 11 *Agosto* 1883.

GATTA, L.—The disaster of Casamicciola.—*" The Roman News,"* Aug. 1883.

GATTA, L.—Il terremoto di Casamicciola. —*" Nuova Antologia," S.* 2, *xl,* 1 *Agosto* 1883.

GATTA, L.—Sismologia.—16⁰, *pp.* 175, 16 *figs.,* 1 *map. Milano,* 1884.

GATTA, L.—Vulcanismo.—16⁰, *pp.* 267, *figs. Milano,* 1885.

GATTA, L.—*See* ROSSI, M. S. DE.

GAUSSIN.—*See* DARONDEAU.—Carte . . . des côtes d'Italie.

GAUTHIER, V.—Il Bradisisma Flegreo all'Epoca Ellenica.—*Rend. R. Acc. Sci. S.* 3, *xviii, pp.* 91–94, 2 *pls. Napoli,* 1913.

GAVAUDAN, G.—Memoria sopra l'uso dei bagni minerali di Gorgitello.—8⁰, *pp.* 20. *Napoli,* 1845.
See CONTE.—Saggio di Sperimenti. .

GEIKIE, A.—Text-Book of Geology.—8°, pp. 971, 434 figs. London, 1882.

GEIKIE, A.—Recent Studies of Old Italian Volcanoes.—" Nature," lxiv, pp. 103–106. London, 1901.

GEMMELLARO, C.—Sui crateri di sollevamento e di eruzione.—Atti Acc. Gioen. S. 2, iii, pp. 109–133. Catania, 1846.

GENOINO, G.—Viaggio poetico pe' Campi Flegrei.—16°, pp. 122–3, Napoli, 1813.

GEORGIUS [HOUFNAGLIUS]. — Mirabilium Sulphureorum Motium apud Puteolis campos Flegreos Plin. Vulcani forum Strabo. Vulgo nunc Solfataria vocant Neapolitani genuina accuratissimaque ad vivum depicta representatio.
View of the Solfatara with carriage, litter, lady, and page and grotesque frame with 1 p. of text in Latin entitled Forum Vulcani.—Is from Braun, G., and Hohenberg, F.—Civitates Orbis Terrarum, Coloniae Agrippinae, 1582–1618.
Engrav.: 413 × 308 mm.
The text varies in the different eds.

G. F. [Fortunato Giustino].—I Campi Flegrei e Pompei. Ricordi dei dintorni di Napoli. —12°, pp. 54. Napoli, 1870. [C.A.]

GIACOMO, S. DI.—Napoli.—Part 1, 192 illustr. in " Collezione di Monografie Illustrate."—See RICCI, C.—Napoli, N° 32.— S. 1 Italia Artistica, 1902 &c.

GIANNETTASIIS, N. P.—Æstates Surrentinæ.—12°, foll. 6 + pp. 280, frontisp. Neapoli, 1696.

GIANNETTASIIS, N. P.—Annus eruditus in partes quatuor, seu stata tempora distributus. Ver Herculaneum, Æstates Surrentinæ, Autumni Surrentini, et Hyemes Puteolani.—4 vols. 4°. Vol. i, pp. 185 ; Vol. ii, pp. 193 ; Vol. iii, pp. 192 ; Vol. iv, pp. 185. Neapoli, 1722.

GIANPETRI, A. T.—See GMFATGGVF.

GIARRE, P. (inc.).—Veduta di Camaldoli nelle vicinanze di Napoli. N° 2.
View over Campi Phlegræi and Ischia. Poor engrav.: 290 × 196 mm.

GIGANTE, A.—Friso. (Signed Achille Gigante 1844.) [Vesuvius, Naples and Pal. Donn'Anna].
Open line or etching like engrav. on dark yellow paper : 294 × 190 mm. Lady and gentleman descending steps in foreground.

GIGANTE, A.—Frisio (View of Pal. D. Anna and Vesuvius.)—Naples?, 1844.
Fine line engraving on brown paper.

GIGANTE, A.—Viaggio da Napoli a Castellamare.—8°, pls. 42 (acqua forte), pp. 166, fol. 1. Napoli, 1845.

GIGANTE, A.—See ALVINO, 1845.

GIGANTE [A. ?].—[Lago d'Averno. Tempio di Apollo.] 1851 [or 1857 ?]
Fine litho.: 264 × 184 mm.

GIGANTE, A. (dis.).—Entrata della grotta di Pozzuoli. Presso l'editore, Strada di Chiaja. N° 58.
Litho. on yellow paper : 230 × 145 mm.

GIGANTE, ERCOLE.—Monte Epomeo in Ischia.
Line engrav. or litho. on yellowish paper : 298 × 194 mm.

GIGANTE, G.—Grotte de la Sibille de Cumes. G. Gigante dess. d'après nature.
Litho.: 170 × 148. mm.

GIGANTE, G. (dis.).—Lago d'Agnano. Lac d'Agnano.—Lit*. Cuchinello, e Bianchi.
Litho. on double paper : 307 × 207 mm.

GIGANTE, G. (dis.).—Vue de Pouzzolles, Lit*.—Cuciniello, e Bianchi.
Man and woman praying in foreground. Part of Pozzuoli and the Mole in the distance. Litho.: 215 × 147 mm.

GIGLI, G.—Discorso sulla Zona VulcanicaMediterranea.—8°, pp. 146. Napoli, 1857.

GIGLIOLI, I.—On the condensation of vapour from the fumaroles of the Solfatara of Pozzuoli.—" Nature," xxviii, pp. 83–84. 1883.

GIMBERNAT, C. DE.—Notice sur les colonnes du Temple de Serapis près de Naples qui sont percées jusqu'à une certaine hauteur par les vers marins ou les Pholades. —Bibl. Univ. Sci. x, pp. 295–299. Genève, 1819.

GIMBERNAT, C. DE.—Notizie intorno ad una sostanza particolare che trovansi presso le acque termali d'Ischia, ed intorno ad vapori dell'Vesuvio.—Giorn. Fis. Chim. e Stor. Nat. S. 2, ii, pp. 178–181. Pavia, 1819.

GIMBERNAT, C. DE.—Phénomène observé à Massa Lubrense près Capo Campanella. —Nouv. Ann. Voy. v, pp. 218–223. Paris, 1820.

GIMMA. G.—Della storia naturale delle Gemme, delle Pietre e di tutti i Minerali, ovvero della fisica sotterranea.—2 vols. 4°. Vol. i, pp. 46 + 551 ; Vol. ii, pp. 4 + 603. Napoli, 1730.

[GIORDANO, Fabio.]—Frammento inedito di uno scrittore napolitano del secolo XVI intorno alle grotte incavate nel promontorio di Posilipo in cui è parola di quella detta volgarmente di Sejano con un comento critico-archeologico di GMFATGGVF. [*i.e.* G. M. Fusco, A. T. Gianpetri, G. V. Fusco]. —8°, *pp.* 111. *Napoli*, 1841.

GIORDANO, F.—*See* ANON.—Il terremoto del luglio, 1883, etc.

GIRARDET, Karl (peint.). — L'Artiste. Sorrente. Royaume de Naples. Gravé par Paul Girardet.
Steel engrav.: 197×138 mm.

GIRAUD, E.—Le Grand Golfe de Naples par Giraud, ou Recueil des Plus Beaux Palais de la dite Ville. Le dit ouvrage renferme les plus beaux Restes d'Antiquité qui existent sur la Coste de Poussole Baja et Cuma. Le tout pittoresquement Gravé a un seul trait a lau (*sic*) forte dans le gout du Celebre Piranesi.—*gd. obl.* [*Naples ?*] 1771.
Dr. Johnston-Lavis' copy is in two albums with 28 pls. in one and 6 folding in the other. That of the B.M. (K. 7 Tab. 59.) cont. 30 views. (*See* Pls. 9, 19, 20, 21, 22, 24, 25, 28, 31, 33.)

GIRAUD, Ett.—Vue de la Ville et Côte de Poussole.
The Mole of Caligula is hardly seen, but I Capuccini is well shown with two stories of windows on a foundation of rock continuous with the mainland.

GIROND, A.—Observations Sur une Mine de Fer en Sable qui se trouve aux environs de Naples.—*Journ. Mines, An.* IV, *iii*, 17, *pp.* 15–22. *Paris*, 1796.

GIUDICE, N. Del.—Viaggio medico ad Ischia ed altrove all' oggetto di riconoscere ed analizzare le acque minerali e le stufe.— 2 tomes in 1 vol. *Napoli*, 1822–25.

GIUOCHI, A.—Ischia dalla sua origine fino ai nostri giorni.—8°, *pp.* 145. *Roma*, 1884.

GIUSTINIANI, L.—La biblioteca storica e topografica del Regno di Napoli.—4°, *pp.* 15+241. *Napoli*, 1793.

GIUSTINIANI, L.—Dizionario geografico ragionato del Regno di Napoli.—10 tomes, 8°. *Napoli*, 1797–1805.

GIUSTINIANI, L.—I tre rarissimi opuscoli di Simone Porzio, di Girolamo Borgia, e di Marcantonio delli Falconi, scritti in occasione della celebre eruzione avvenuta in Pozzuoli nell' anno 1538, colle memorie storiche dei sudetti autori.—8°, *foll. iii*, *pp.* 219. *Napoli*, 1812. [C.A. and B.N.]

GMELIN, W. F. (fec. 1792).—Grotta vulcanica alla punta di Posilipo nel Golfo di Napoli, I.
A tufa arch of marine erosion ; 3 men bathing. Engrav.: 333×258 mm.

GMELIN, W. F. (fec.).—Romitorio in cima del Monte Epomeo nell' Isola d'Ischia, II. 1792.
Line engrav.: 339×248 mm.

GMELIN, W. F. (sc. Romæ, 1798).—Das Mare Morte bei Neapel. Seiner Churfürstlichen Durchlaucht dem regierenden Churfürsten von Pfalz-Baiern Maximilian Joseph. Unterthänigst gewidmet von Johan Friedrich Frauenholz 1799.
Engrav.: 481×659 mm.

GMFATGGVF. [G. M. Fusco, A. T. Gianpetri, G. V. Fusco.]—Frammento inedito di uno Scrittore Napoletano del Secolo XVI intorno alle Grotte incavate nel promontorio di Posilipo in cui e parola di quella detta volgarmente di Sejano con un Comenti critico-archeologico di . . .—8°, *pp.* 111. *Napoli*, 1841.
See FUSCO, G.

GOETHE, J. W. Von.—Architektonisch-naturhistorisches Problem.—*Zur Naturwissenschaft überhaupt*, ii, *pp.* 79–88. *Stuttgard und Tübingen*, 1823.
An account of the geol. phenomena presented at the temple of Pozzuoli.

GOOD, J. M.—*See* POLEHAMPTON, E.

GORCEIX, H.—État du Vésuve et des dégagements gazeux des Champs Phlégréens au mois de Juin 1869.—*C.R. Acad. Sci.* lxxiv, *pp.* 154–56. *Paris*, 1872.

GORCEIX, H.—On the composition of the vapours or gas escaping in the Phlegrean Fields and other places near Vesuvius.— *Amer. Journ. Sci. S.* 3, *iv*, *pp.* 147. *New Haven*, 1872. [C.A.]

GORCEIX, H.—Sur les gaz des solfatares des Champs Phlégréens.—*Ann. Chim. Phys.* xxv, *pp.* 559–66. *Paris*, 1872.

GORINI, P.—Difendiamoci dai vulcani.— " *Riforma,*" *Roma*, 16 *Settembre*, 1883.

GOSSELET, J.—Observations géologiques faites en Italie. I, Vésuve ; II, Champs Phlégréens ; III, Etna ; IV, Latium.— *Mem. Soc. Imp. Sci. S.* 3, *vi*, *pp.* 417–75, 7 *pls. Lille*, 1869.

GRABLOVITZ, G.—Il terremoto di Casamicciola.—" *L'Independente di Trieste,*" 11–12 *Agosto*, 1883.

F

GRABLOVITZ, G.—Descrizione dell' Osservatorio Meteorologico e Geodinamico al Porto d'Ischia.—*Ann. Uff. Cent. Meteor. Geodinam. viii, pt.* 4, *pp.* 12.   *Roma,* 1888.

GRABLOVITZ, G.—Funzionamento degli apparecchi in occasione d'un terremoto (29 febbraio, 1892) nell' Isola d'Ischia.— *Ann. Uff. Cent. Meteor. Geodinam. viii. Roma,* 1888.

GRABLOVITZ, G.—Risultati delle osservazioni idrotermiche eseguite al Porto d'Ischia nel 1887.—*Ann. Uff. Cent. Meteor. Geodinam. viii, pt.* 4, *pp.* 12.   *Roma,* 1888. —*Atti R. Acc. Lincei, S.* 4, *Rend. iv, sem.* 1, *pp.* 177–79.   *Roma,* 1888.

GRABLOVITZ, G.—Studii mareometrici al Porto d'Ischia.—*Ann. Uff. Cent. Meteor. Geodinam. viii, pt.* 4, *pp.* 10, 1 *pl.   Roma,* 1888.

GRABLOVITZ, G.—Influenza dello stato orario delle marea sulle sorgive termali del porto d'Ischia.—*Atti R. Acc. Lincei, S.* 4, *Rend. iv, sem.* 2, *pp.* 220–24.   *Roma,* 1888.

GRABLOVITZ, G.—Sulle acque termali dell' Isola d'Ischia, con riguardo speciale a quelle del Bacino del Gurgitello in Casamicciola.—Livellazione del bacino del Gurgitello.—*Ann. Uff. Cent. Meteor. Geòdinam. xi, Roma,* 1889 ; *xii, pt.* 1, *Roma,* 1890.

GRABLOVITZ, G.—Sulle osservazioni mareografiche in Italia e specialmente su quelle fatte ad Ischia.—*Ann. Uff. Cent. Meteor. Geodinam. xii.   Roma,* 1890.

GRABLOVITZ, G.—Studi fatti in occasione dell' accidentale ostruzione di una Sorgiva termale (Ischia).—*Atti R. Acc. Lincei, S.* 4, *Rend. vii, sem.* 1, *pp.* 456–60.   *Roma,* 1891.

GRABLOVITZ, G.—Sulle sorgenti termali di Casamicciola.—*Ann. Uff. Cent. Meteor. Geodinam. S.* 2, *pt.* 3, *xi.   Roma,* 1892.— *Riv. Scient. ind. An.* XXIV, *ii.   Firenze,* 1892.

GRABLOVITZ, G.—Strumenti del R. Osservatorio geodinamico di Casamicciola.— *Beitr. Geoph. Erganz. i, pp.* 408–16.   1902.

GRABLOVITZ, G.—Bemerkungen über den Erdbebenbeobachtungsdienst auf der Insel Ischia.—[Sonderabdr.] *Monatsschrift* " *Die Erdbebenwarte,*" *iii Jahrg.,* 1 *und* 2, *pp.* 8, *tab.* 2.   *Laibach,* 1903.

GRABLOVITZ, G.—Terremoti Balcanici del 4 aprile, 1904, registrati ad Ischia.—[Estr.] *Boll. Soc. Sism. Ital. x, pp.* 9.   *Modena,* 1904.

GRABLOVITZ, G.—Un ventennio d'operosità in Ischia.—[Estr.]   *Boll. Soc. Sism. Ital. xii, pp.* 18.   *Modena,* 1907.

GRÆVIUS, J. G.—Thesaurus Antiquitatum et Historiarum Italiæ, Neapolis, Siciliæ . . . atque adjacentium terrarum insularumque . . . digeri atque edi olim cœptus cura et studio J. G. G. . . . continuatus et ad finem perductus cum præfationibus P. Burmanni, etc.—10 tom., 45 vol. *fol. Lugduni Batavorum,* 1725.

GRASSI, C.—*See* HACKERT, Ph.

GRASSI, M.—Relazione storica ed osservazioni sulla eruzione dell' Etna del 1865 e sui terremoti flegrei che la seguirono.—8°, *pp.* 92.   *Catania,* 1865.

GRASSUS BARTOLOMEŒUS, Typographus Romanus. — Explicatio. aliquot. locoro. quæ Puteolis spectantur.—*Romæ,* 1584. [B.N.P. Vb. 113, No. 3.]
Monte Nuovo well shown, also the Mole of Caligula partly arched and piers broken. A sort of mole between the promontory (Promontorium Penatæ) of Baja and Misenum, also many buildings along the beach between la Pietra and Pozzuoli.
Another ed. bears the inscription : Joannes Orlandi formis romæ 1602, Romæ apud Hære des Claudij Duchesi 1586 in Amb. Bramb. f. [B.N.P. Vb. 113, No. 4.]
There is a still later edition.

GRAVIER, G. (publ.).—Veduta del Golfo di Baja, e di Pozuolo, alla di cui imboccatura si ravissano le tre isole di Nisidi, di Procida, e d'Ischia come si vede dai Bagnoli. Dedicata A.S.E. il Sig. C⁹ᵉ M. Pignatelli, etc.— *Giovanni Gravier, Napoli,* 1760.
Engrav. panorama on 2 sheets : 1110× 373 mm.

GREVTER, M.—Le XII Provincie del Regno (di Napoli). — *Venecia,* 1657. — Also : " *nuouamente Ristampata, Riuista et Augmentata da Domenico de Rossi Herede di Gio. Giacomo de Rossi . . . l'anno* 1695."

GUARINI, G.—Analisi chimica della sabbia caduta in Napoli la sera de' 26 Agosto, 1834.—*Atti R. Acc. Sci. v, pt.* 2, *pp.* 233–37. *Napoli,* 1844.

[GUASCO, C.]—Dell' Edificio di Pozzuoli volgarmente detto Il Tempio di Serapide.— 8°, *pp.* 48, 2 *pls.,* 1 *tab.   Roma,* 1773.

GUENTHER, R. T.—The Phlegrean Fields. —*Geog. Journ. x, pp.* 412–32, *figs. and* 4 *maps ; pp.* 477–99, *figs. and pls.* v–vii (*maps, Camaldoli, near Naples*).   *London,* 1897. —" *Nature,*" *vii, pp.* 583–86, *figs.*   1898.

GUENTHER, R. T.—On the possibility of obtaining more reliable measurements of the Changes of Land-level of the Phlegræan Fields.—*Scot. Geog. Mag. xvi, pp.* 605–6. *Edinburgh*, 1900.

GUENTHER, R. T.—A possible new Petroleum Field near Naples.—" *Nature,*" *lxv*, p. 152. 1901.

GUENTHER, R. T.—Report of a Committee appointed to Investigate the Changes of Land-level of the Phlegræan Fields.— *Rept. Brit. Assoc.* 1901, *pp.* 382–83. 1901.

GUENTHER, R. T.—The Submerged Greek and Roman Foreshore near Naples.—*Westminster*, 1902.—" *Archeologia,*" *lviii*, 6 *col. maps, num. figs.* 1903.—(*See ref. to* " Contributions to the study of Earth-movements in the Bay of Naples " *in* " *Archivio Storico per le Province Napoletane,*" *xxix*, 1, *pp.* 148–50. *Napoli*, 1904.)

GUENTHER, R. T.—Earth-movements in the Bay of Naples.—*Geog. Journ. xxii, pp.* 121–49, 269–86, *figs.* 17, 1 *topogr. map. London*, 1903.

GUENTHER, R. T.—Contributions to the study of Earth-movements in the Bay of Naples.—4⁰, *pp.* 115, *tav.* 6. *Oxford and Rome*, 1903.—Also : 4⁰, *pp.* 1–62, 1–49, *figs.*, 8 *pls. Westminster*, 1903.
Is a reprint of the above two papers.

GUENTHER, R. T.—Changes in the level of the City of Naples.—*Geog. Journ. xxiv, pp.* 191–98, *figs. London*, 1904.—" *Nature,*" *lxix, pp.* 274–75, *figs.* 1904.

GUENTHER, R. T.—A Bibliography of Topographical and Geological Works on the Phlegræan Fields.—8⁰, *pp. vi*+100. *London*, 1908.

GUERRA, G. (inc.).—[Map of Gulf of Naples from Salerno to Lago di Patria with Capri and Ischia.] No. 14. Naples, 1794.
Map with plain border : 527 × 763 mm.

GUERRA, G.—Carta de' Crateri esistenti tra il Vesuvio e la spiaggia di Cuma.—*Napoli*, 1797. [C.A., B.M.—83.52.2.b.]

GUICCIARDINI, C.—Mercurius campanus præcipua Campaniæ felicis loca indicans et perlustrans.—12⁰, *pp.* 274, *figs.* 6. *Napoli*, de Bonis, 1667. [C.A.]

GUISCARDI, G.—Extrait d'une lettre sur les Étuves de Néron.—*C.R. Acad. Sci. xliii, pp.* 751–52. *Paris*, 1856. [C.A.]

GUISCARDI, G.—Note sur les émanations gazeuses des Champs Phlégréens.—*Bull. Soc. géol. France, S.* 2, *xiv, pp.* 633–35. *Paris*, 1856–57.

GUISCARDI, G.—Cenno intorno ad una memoria del prof. Ehrenberg relativa ad una roccia dell' Isola d'Ischia formata da Sorgente Calde.—*Rend. R. Acc. Sci. pp.* 69–72. *Napoli*, 1859.
See EHRENBERG.—Ueber eine auf der Insel Ischia . . . Wirkung heisser Quellen. 1859.

GUISCARDI, G.—Contribuzioni alla geologia dei Campi Flegrei.—*Rend. R. Acc. Sci. i, p.* 197. *Napoli*, 1862.—*Id. Atti, i,* 7, *pp.* 6, *pl.* 1. *Napoli*, 1863.

GUISCARDI, G.—*See* PALMIERI, L. 1863.

GUISCARDI, G.—Sul livello del Mare nel golfo di Pozzuoli.—*Rend. R. Acc. Sci. iv, pp.* 203–4. *Napoli*, 1865.

GUISCARDI, G.—Sulla età degli scisti calcarei di Castellamare.—*Rend. R. Acc. Sci. v, pp.* 122–23. *Napoli*, 1866.

GUISCARDI, G.—Il piperno [dei crateri di tufo dei Campi flegrei].—*Rend. R. Acc. Sci. vi, pp.* 221–26. *Napoli*, 1867.

GUISCARDI, G.—Communicazione sopra alcuni vulcanetti fangosi osservati nella Solfatara di Pozzuoli.—*Rend. R. Acc. Sci. xiv, pp.* 59–62. *Napoli*, 1875.

GUISCARDI, G.—[Sopra una nuova sorgente d'acqua minerale nella solfatara di Pozzuoli.]—*Rend. R. Acc. Sci. xiv, pp.* 62–63. *Napoli*, 1875.

GUISCARDI, G.—Sulla Leucilite dell' Averno.—*Rend. R. Acc. Sci. xviii, pp.* 146–47. *Napoli*, 1879.

GUISCARDI, G. (relatore), with SEMMOLA, E., SCHIAVONI, F., ZINNO, S.—Il terremoto di Casamicciola del 4 Marzo, 1881. Relazione.—*Atti Acc. Potaniana, xiv, pp.* 253–59, 1 *map. Napoli*, 1881.

GUISCARDI, G.—Il Terremoto d'Ischia del 28 Luglio, 1883.—*Atti R. Acc. Sci. S.* 2, *ii,* 3, *pp.* 8, *map* 1. *Napoli*, 1888.

GUSSONE, G.—Analisi delle acque minerali dell' Isola d'Ischia.—*Napoli*, 1819.

HAAGEN VON MATHIESEN.—Die Wiederherstellung der Stadt Pozzuolo.—*N. J. f. Min. pp.* 699–707. *Stuttgart*, 1846.

HAAGEN VON MATHIESEN.—Ueber die Entstehung des Monte Nuovo und die neueste Hecla-Eruption.—*N. J.f. Min. vii, pp.* 586–95. *Stuttgart*, 1847.—*Quart. Journ. Geol. Soc. iii, pt.* 2, *pp.* 19–22. 1847.— *N. Ann. Sci. Nat. vii, pp.* 362–68. *Bologna*, 1847.

F 2

HAAS, H. J.—Ueber die Solfatara von Pozzuoli.—[Separat-Abdr.] *N. J. f. Min. ii, pp.* 65–108, *Tab.* III–V. *Stuttgart,* 1907.

HAAS, H. J.—Unterirdische Gluten. Die Natur und das Wesen der Feuerberge im Lichte der neuesten Anschauungen für die Gebildeten aller Stände in gemeinverständlicher Weise dargestellt. 2te. Auflage. —8°, *pp.* 316, *fig. and pl. Berlin,* 1912.

HACKERT, PH.—La rada di Napoli, 1784.— *pl. in fol. mas.* [O.V.]

HACKERT, PH.—Veduta di Baja presa dal Monte Nuovo (Gmelin sc.).—*Napoli,* 1787. [B.M.—K. 83.63.] Fine engraving.

HACKERT, PH. (pinx. 1787).—Veduta di Marechiano appresso Posilipo a Napoli. Vin.. Aloja Sculp. Giorg* Hackert direx.— Si vende a Napoli da Giorgio Hackert Incisore di S.M. . . . Con Privilegio. 456 × 335 mm.

HACKERT, PH.—Veduta di Pizzo-falcone, e del Castel dell' Uovo a Napoli Gio. de Grado sculp. Giorg* Hackert direx.—1787. Si vende a Napoli di Giorgio Hackert Incisore di S.M. . . . Con Privilegio. Engrav. with sailors firing ; boat in foreground : 456 × 328 mm.

HACKERT, PH.—Veduta di Pozzuoli presa dal Monte, . . . intagliata da Gmelin.— *Napoli,* 1787. [B.M., K. 83(78) a.] A fine engraving.

HACKERT, PH., GRASSI, C., FERGOLA, L., etc.—Raccolta di XXV vedute dell' Città e Regno di Napoli. Incise da Vincenzo Aloja.—*obl.* 4°. *Napoli e Francoforte, presso G. F. Wenner.* ? 1810. [Flor. B.N., 9, 1, 6, 26.]

HACKERT, PH. (pinx.).—Veduta di Baja presa dal Monte Nuovo. A Sua Eccelenza Il Sigʳ Dⁿ Giovanni Acton, etc., W. F. Gmelin sculp.—Si vende a Napoli da Giorgio Hackert incisore di S.M., con privilegio. Fine engrav. : 555 × 370 mm.

HACKERT, PH. (pinx.).—Veduta del Porto dell' Isola d'Ischia. Preso dal Quadro originale che fa parte della Collezione dei Porti delle due Sicilie ordinata da S.M. il Re., Gio de Grado inc. G. Hackert direx. No. 4. Good view of Ischia town and Castle. Goats, peasant women, child and dog in foreground. Engrav. : 533 × ? mm.

HACKERT, PH. (pinx.).—Avanzi del Tempio di Giove Serapide a Pozzuoli. Vincenzo

Aloja sculp. Giorgio Hackert direx.—Si vende a Napoli da Giorgio Hackert. Incisore di S.M. Con Privilegio. [1789.] Fine engrav. : 540 × 370 mm.

HACKERT, PH.—*See* MORELLI, F.—Raccolta . . . nella Città di Pesto.

HACKERT, J. F. [? PH.] (dipin.).—Veduta dei Laghi d'Averno, e Lucrino delle Grotte di Cuma e di Baja. Franᶜᵉ Morelli inc. In Roma presso Agapito Franzetti Calcografo e Mercante di Stampe al Corso. Fine line engrav. : 209 × 144 mm.

HAKEWILL, J.—A Picturesque Tour of Italy, from drawings made in 1816–1817.— *fol., pls.* 63, *with text. London,* 1820.

HAKEWILL, J. (drawn by).—Grotto of Posilipo near Naples. Engraved by J. Landseer, F.S.A.—Published as the Act directs Aug. 1, 1819, by John Murray, Albemarle Street, London.—*From* "A Picturesque Tour of Italy from Drawings made in 1816–1817 by James Hakewill, Archᵗ."—4°, *pl.* 63, *vol.* v, *pp. of expl.* 126. *London,* 1820. Steel engrav. : 140 × 247 mm.

HALL, B.—On the want of perpendicularity of the standing pillars of the temple of Jupiter Serapis, near Naples.—*Phil. Mag.* vi, *pp.* 313–14. *London,* 1835.—*Proc. Geol. Soc. ii, p.* 114. 1835.

HALLER.—*See* ANON.—Tableau topographique, etc.

HAMILTON, SIR W.—Remarks upon the Nature of the Soil of Naples, and its Neighbourhood.—*Phil. Trans. R. Soc. lxxi, pp.* 1–47, 48–50, 1 *pl. London,* 1772.

HAMILTON, SIR W.—Campi Phlegræi. Observations on the volcanoes of the two Sicilies.—*fol. Vol.* i, *pp.* 90, 1 *pl.*, 1 *map ; Vol.* ii, 54 *pls. Naples,* 1776. [C.A.] [B.M.—Tab. 435a, with MS. notes, contains the original drawings, besides 11 others and 1 print.]

HAMILTON, SIR W.—Supplement to the Campi Phlegrei, being an account of the great eruption of Mount Vesuvius in August, 1779.—*fol., pp.* 29, 5 *col. pls. Naples,* 1779.—*Phil. Trans. R. Soc. lxx, pp.* 42–84, 1 *pl. London,* 1780. [B.M.—Tab. 435a, with original drawings and 8 coloured drawings of Vesuvius in eruption.]

HAMILTON, SIR W.—Œuvres complètes, traduites et commentées par l'Abbé Giraud-Soulavie.—8°, *pp.* xx+506, 1 *map. Paris,* 1781.

HAMILTON, SIR W.—Neuere Beobachtungen über die Vulkane Italiens und am Rhein, nebst merkwürdigen Bemerkungen des Absts Giraud Soulavie v. G.A.R.—8⁰, *pp. xvi+214*, 1 *map. Frankfurt und Leipzig,* 1784. [C.A.]

HAMILTON, SIR W.—Waarneemingen over deVuurbergen in Italie, Sicilie, en omstreiks den Rhyn als mede over de Aardbeevingen voorgevallen in Italie 1783.—8⁰, *pp.* 552. *Amsterdam,* 1784. [C.A.]

HAMILTON, SIR W.—Bericht vom gegenwaertigen Zustande des Vesuvs und Beschreibung einer Reise in die Provinz Abruzzo und nach der Insel Ponza.—4⁰. *Dresden,* 1787.—In Eng. : *Phil. Trans. R. Soc. lxxvi, pp.* 365–81, *folding map and* 2 *pls. by Basire.* 1786.

HAMILTON, SIR W.—Campi Phlegræi, ou observations sur les volcans des deux Sicilies.—2 vols. *fol., num. hand-coloured pls. Paris, Lamy, An* VII [1799–1800]. [C.A.]

HAMILTON, SIR W.—Voyages physiques e litologiques dans la Campanie.—*Paris,* 1801.

HARDING, J. D.—Castell-a-Mare. Bay of Naples. Engraved by J. Hendshall.— London, published Oct. 28th, 1831, by Jennings and Chaplin, 2 Cheapside. Printed by Fenner, Sears and Co.
Steel engrav. on film : 145 × 115 mm.

HARDING, J. D. (drawn by).—Castle and Bay of Baia. Engraved by J. T. Willmore. London. Published Oct. 28th, 1831, by Jennings and Chaplin, 62 Cheapside.
View from back of Temple of Venus looking S.E. Engrav. on double paper : 134 × 114 mm.

HARDING, J. D. (drawn by).—Puzzuoli with the mole of Caligula. Engraved by R. Brandard.—London. Published Oct. 28, 1831, by Jennings and Chaplin, 62 Cheapside. Printed by Fenner, Sears and Co.—*From* ROSCOE, T.—The Tourist in Italy illustrated from Drawings by J. D. Harding.—8⁰. *London,* 1832.
Pozzuoli from one of the piers of the mole. —Very fine engrav. : 142 × 101 mm.

HARDING, J. D. (drawn by).—Puzzuoli. Engraved by W. R. Smith. Printed by Fenner, Sears and Co. London. Published Oct. 28, 1831, by Jennings and Chaplin, 62 Cheapside.
Man on donkey, another digging, and other figures in foreground. Steel engrav. : 144 × 104 mm.

HARDING, J. D.—Santa Lucia, Naples. Engraved by James B. Allen.—London. Published Oct. 28, 1831, by Jennings and Chaplin, 62 Cheapside. Printed by Fenners, Sears and Co.
Engrav. : 145 × 108 mm.

HARDING, J. D.—Vico. Bay of Naples. Engraved by James B. Allen.—London, Published Oct. 28th, 1832, by Jennings and Chaplin, 63 Cheapside. Printed by Lloyd and Hennings.
A beautiful line engrav. : 147 × 98 mm., on thin semi-glazed paper.

HARDING, J. D. (drawn by).—Naples from the sea. Italy. Engrav. by F. J. Havell. Fisher, Son and Co., London and Paris. 1840.
Steel engrav. : 145 × 110 mm.

HARDING, J. D.—*See* ROSCOE, T. 1849–50.

HARDING, J. D.—*See* MAPEI, C.—Italy, Classical, Historical and Picturesque.

HARE, A. J. C., and ST. CLAIR BADDELEY.—Cities of Southern Italy.—8⁰, *pp.* 237, 24 *illustr.,* 2 *plans,* 1 *map. London,* 1911.

HAUGHTON, S.—*See* JOHNSTON-LAVIS, H. J.—Monograph of the Earthquakes of Ischia, 1885.

H., C.—*See* C. H.

HELLEMANNS, J. GEORG.—De Montibus ignivomis Vulgò Feuer-speyende Berge.— 4⁰, *pp.* 22. *Marburgi Cattorum, Typis hæred. Joh. Jodoc. Kürsneri Acad. Typogr.* 1698.

HENTZNER, P.—Itinerarivm Germaniæ, Galliæ, Angliæ, Italiæ.—8⁰, *foll.* 8, *pp.* 418 *and index. Norimbergæ,* 1612. [B.M., G. 2581.]
Of this book H. Walpole observes that only 3 or 4 copies were to be found in England. This is the first and best edit. It was reprinted, Breslæ, 1617, without addition or omission ; again Norimbergæ, 1629, omitting a copy of laudatory verses by Echard, and adding the useless " Monita Peregrinatoria et Epitome " by Gruberus and Plotius in order to swell the volume, but with a map. Walpole only translated an extract from this curious book. The Nuremberg edit. of 1629 was reprinted at Lipsiæ, 1661, but this of 1612 is the best edition.

HERDESIANI, C.—Antiquitatum Puteolanarum quæ in agro Puteolano, felicis Campaniæ, nunc Regni Neapolitani regiuncula, hucusque cum stupore visuntur, Synopsis Inlustrandæ priscæ Historiæ, etc. —16⁰, *foll.* 59. *Francofurtensium,* 1619.

H. G. (exc.).—Puteoli and Baja. Small engrav. trimmed so that explanation is lost, but letters from A to Z are scattered over view : 129×76 mm.

HOCHSTETTER, FERDINAND VON.—Die phlegräischen Felder und der Vesuv.—*Schrift. Ver. Naturw. Kennt. iv, pp.* 3–23. *Wien*, 1863–64.

HOEFNAGLIUS, A. O. G.—Puteoli Baiæ. 1578. [B.M.—24120 (1).] Two oblong views of these places.

HOEFNAGLIUS, A. O. G.—Nullus in Orbe Locus Baiis Prælucet Amœnis. Bavaria, 1580. [B.N.P., Vb. 114.] Shows well Caligula's Mole partly arched.

HOEFNAGLIUS, A. O. G.—*See* ORTELIUS, 1580, 1582–1618, etc.

HOEPLI, U.—Catalogue Nr. 14. Pompéi. Le Vésuve, Herculanum, etc. Avec un Appendice : L'Île d'Ischia.—8⁰. *Milan, U. Hoepli*, 1883.

HOERNES, R.—Aus den phlegraïschen Feldern.—*Wissenschaft. Mittheil. pp.* 19–31, 1 *pl. Wien*, 1875.

HOFF, KARL ERNEST ADOLF VON.—Chronik der Erdbeben und Vulcan-Ausbrüche mit vorausgehender Abhandlung über die Natur dieser Erscheinungen.—2 vols. 8⁰. *Vol. i, pp.* 6+470 ; *Vol. ii, pp.* 2+406. *Gotha*, 1840–41.

HOFFMANN, F.—Auszüge aus Briefen des Herrn. Prof. . . . —*Archiv. f. Min. Geognos. etc. iii, pp.* 361–412. *Berlin*, 1831.

HOFFMANN, F.—On the Scenery of Italy, as contrasted with that of Germany ; the Geognosy of Albano, near Rome ; and the general structure and Trachytic Rocks of Etna.—*Edinb. New Phil. Journ. xii, pp.* 370–78. *Edinburgh*, 1832. This is a transl. of most of the 1st letter of foregoing.

HOFFMANN, F.—Mémoire sur les terrains volcaniques de Naples, de la Sicile, etc.—*Bull. Soc. géol. France, iii, pp.* 170–80. —*Paris*, 1833. [Extr.] *C.R. Acad. Sci. xli, pp.* 872–76. *Paris*, 1855.

HOFFMANN, F.—Geognostische Beobachtungen. Gesammelt auf einer Reise durch Italien und Sicilien, in den Jahren 1830–32.—*Archiv. f. Min. Geognos. etc. xiii, pp.* 3–726, 1 *pl.*, 1 *map. Berlin*, 1839.—[Sep. publ.] *Berlin*, 1839.

HOHENBERG, F.—*See* BRAUN, G.

HOMANN, J. B.—Urbis Neapolis cum Præcipuis eius Ædificiis secundum Planitiem exacta delineatio.—*Coloured map and*

views. *Norimbergæ*, 1727. [B.M.—K. 83.57 and also 24045.12. This last photographed.] Similar to many other maps under names of other authors. One ed. probably 1730.

HOMBRES FIRMAS, L. A. D'.—Note sur la Grotte-du-Chien. —*Mém. Acad. pp.* 66–75. *Gard*, 1847–48.

HONDIUS, HENRICUS (excudit).—Terra di Lavoro olim Campania felix (with 2 pages of descript. text). Amstelodami.—*From* MERCATOR.—Atlas s. Cosmographica meditationes de fabrica Mundi.—10ᵃ ed. *Typis A. Hondii. Amst.* 1630. Engrav. map : 482×377 mm.

HONDIUS, HENRICUS (excudit).—Campaniæ Felicis descriptio vulgo Terra de Lavoro. —*Amstelodami,* —? Two pages of description in Latin, with a map.

HORNER, F. (dis.).—Veduta della Città di Pozzuoli. Vue de la ville de Pouzzoles. Lith. Cuciniello e Bianchi. Litho. on double paper : 317×205 mm.

HORNER, F.—Vedute del Lago Averno. Vue du Lac Averne. Lith. Cuciniello e Bianchi. Litho. on double paper : 318×204 mm.

HOUEL, J. P. L. L.—Voyage Pittoresque des Isles de Sicile, de Lipari et de Malte, où l'on traite des Antiquités qui s'y trouvent encore ; des principaux Phénomènes que la Nature y offre ; du Costume des Habitans, et de quelques Usages.—4 tomes, *fol. T. i, pp. vii*+138, 72 *pls., Paris*, 1782 ; *T. ii, pp.* 148, *pls.* 73–144, 1784 ; *T. iii, pp.* 126, *pls.* 145–204, 1785 ; *T. iv, pp.* 124, *pls.* 205–64, 1787.—In German : 4 Th. 8⁰. *Gotha*, 1797–1805.

HUBER, I. W. (fece).—Veduta di Chiaja. 1813. Si vende presso Giorgio Glass dirimpᵗᵉ. S. Ferdinando No. 54. Chiatamone, Pizzofalcone, C. del Uovo from Villa Gardens. Fine litho. : 299× 205 mm.

HULLMANDEL, C.—Twenty-four views of Italy, Drawn from Nature, and engraved upon stone.—*obl. fol.* [London] 1818.

HULLMANDEL, C.—On the subsidence of the coast near Pozzuoli (1839).—*Proc. Geol. Soc. iii, p.* 290. *London*, 1842.

HUOT, J. J. N.—Coup d'œil sur les Volcans et sur les phénomènes volcaniques considérés sous les rapports minéralogiques, géologiques et physiques.—*pp.* 588, *maps* 30–46 (*bound separately*). —?, 1831. *See* Pl. 33.

IOLIVET, M. L. (archit., fecit, del. et sculp.).
—Pianta della Città di Napoli formata a
spese di Giovanni Gravier.—[*Napoli*] —?
Engraved map, including mouth of Sebeto, Regia di Capodimonte and Mergellina,
with 136 ref. nos. : 761×498 mm.

IRTON, MAJOR.—*See* WRIGHT, G. N.
1839?, 1841.

ISABEY, J. B.—Naples. 24. Vue du Château
de l'Œuf. Mai 1822. Imprimé par Villain.
Litho. : 233×249 mm.

ISABEY J. B.—Voyage en Italie en 1822.
30 Dessins.—*fol. Paris*, 1823.
See Pls. 24, 25.

ISRAEL (ex.).—Veue de Pouzzole.—Israel
ex. cum privil. Regis. [Vienna lib.]
Style of Sylvestre, engrav. : 179×78 mm.
Camp and cauldron in foreground.

ITTIG, THOMÆ.—De montium incendiis, in
quibus post ardentium toto passim orbe
montium catalogum et historiam, ac variarum opinionum examen, non modo totius
naturæ cum in efficiendis tum in conservandis illis ignibus processus exponitur, etc.
—8°, *pp.* 16+347+*index. Lipsiæ*, 1671.
See pp. 90–96 and other refs.

IVANOFF.—Chemische Untersuchung des
in Neapel gebräuchlichen Formsandes.—
*Oesterreichische Zeitschr. f. Berg- u. Hütten-
wesen*, i, *pp.* 403–4. *Wien*, 1853.

JACONO, A.—Esplorazioni delle montagne
dell' Isola d'Ischia dopo il terremoto del
28 luglio, 1883.—" *Libertà Cattolica*," 19
agosto, 1883.

JAMES, C.—Untersuchungen über die Am-
monium-grotte bei Neapel. (Transl. from
the Gazz. Méd. de Paris, 1843.)—*Notiz. a.
d. Gebiete d. Nat.- und Heilkunde. xxviii,
coll.* 257–65. *Erfurt und Weimar*, 1843.

JAMES, C.—Voyage scientifique à Naples
avec Mr. Magendie en 1843.—8°, *pp.* 103.
Paris, 1844. [O.V.]

JANUARIO, F. DE.—Felicis Campaniæ hilaritas tumvolata.—*fol. Napoli*, 1632. [C.A.]

JANUARIO, R.—La solfatara di Pozzuoli.—
Ann. Meteor. Ital. iv, pp. 306–11. *Torino*,
1889.

JASOLINUS, G. DI.—De Remedii Naturali
che sono nell' Isola di Pithecusa; hoggi
detta Ischia.—Libri due.—Nelli quali si
dimostrano molti rimedi naturali dal detto
Autore nuouamente ritrouati, oltre quelli,
che lasciarono scritti gli Antichi. Con
molte esperienze, & historie, dal medesimo
osseruate ; come nel Sommario della
seguente faccia si legge. Con due tauole

copiose.—Con licenza, e privilegio.—4°,
pp. 40+381+46. *In Napoli, appresso Gio-
seppe Cacchij*, M.D.LXXXVIII.
Another ed. : " Et in questa seconda
impressione ricorretto, & accresciuto con
alcune annotazioni del Dottor Filosopho
Sig. Gio. Pistoya. E nell' ultimo aggiunti
li bagni d'Ischia di Gio. Elisio Medico, con
le note di Gio. Francesco Lombardo medico
Napolitano. Con due figure, e Pianta della
detta Isola e con due tavole copiose."—
pp. 40+274+38. *Napoli (F. Molla), Per
spese di Nicolo Rispoli*, 1689.
Another ed. *Napoli*, 1751.
Another ed. bearing the same title, pub-
lisher and date (1689) is : " *A spese di
Francesco Massaro libraro.*" It has a con-
ventional map of Ischia on frontispiece and
another figure on title-page of a quail-
catcher.—8°, *folded map of Ischia*, 2 *figs.,
pp.* 39+274+29.
[Another ed. is entitled :] De' rimedi
naturali che sono nell' Isola di Pithecusa,
oggi detta Ischia con note di G. Pistoya e
aggiunte di Giov. Elisio.—4°. *Napoli*,
1773.

JASOLINUS, G. DI.—Ischia quæ olim
Ænaria. Ab Æneœ classe hic appulsa sic
nominata. 1590. [B.M. 83.48.]
A hand-coloured map of Ischia with
printed description on back.

JASOLINUS, G. DI.—Ischia Isola olim
Ænaria.—Amstelodami Apud Ioannem
Ianssonium. [Map of Ischia, Procida and
of] Elba Isola olim Ilua [and a bit of Campagna Felice]. [*See* B.M.—K. 83.50.]
455×353 mm., with descriptive text of
Ischia and Elba on back. Later ed.,
redrawn, of last.

JASOLINUS, G. DI.—Ischia quæ olim Ænaria ab Æneœ classe hic appulsa sic nominata.
1590.—*From* ORTELIUS, A.—Theatrum
Orbis Terrarum. Ischia Isola. (1 page of
descript.)
A map of Ischia, Procida and Monte di
Procida with Cuma. Engraved map, hand-
col. : 480×360 mm.

JATTA, G.—Discorso sulla ripartizione Civile,
e Chiesastica dell' antico agro Cumano,
Misenese, Bajano, e Pozzuolano, sui famosi
Campi Flegrei, sul Promontorio di Miseno,
sul Monte di Procida, e sul luogo, ove secondo Virgilio fu sepolto Miseno trombettiere
di Enea, sulle acque della Bolla, e sull' antico acquedotto che da Serino conduceva
l'acqua in Napoli.—8°, *pp. viii*+242.
Napoli, 1843.

JAUVIN (pinxt.).—Château de l'Œuf, à Naples. Eug. Ciceri lith. Imp. Lith. de Cattier.
Litho., black on buff background : 257 × 187 mm.

JAUVIN (pinxt.).—Côte de Pausilipe à Naples. Eug. Ciceri Lith. Imp. lith. de Cattier.
Litho. on greenish background : 254 × 189 mm.

JAUVIN (pinxt.).—Ruines sur la Côte de Pausilipe à Naples. Eug. Ciceri Lith. Imp. lith. de Cattier.
Litho., black on yellow background : 254 × 189 mm.

JERVIS, G.—See JERVIS, W. P.

JERVIS, W. P.—Tesori sotterranei dell' Italia.—4 vols. 8⁰, *num pls. Torino*, 1873–89.

JERVIS, W. P.—The supposed Quaternary and since Submerged Volcano of Mergellina, at Naples.—" *Mediterranean Naturalist,*" *Malta, Oct.* 1, 1892.—*Geol. Mag. pp.* 235–38. *London*, 1893.

JOANNE, P.—Italie.—16⁰, *pp.* 514, 10 *maps*, 80 *plans. Paris*, 1909.

JOHNSTON-LAVIS, H. J.—On the Origin and Structure of Volcanic Cones.—" *Science Gossip,*" 193, *pp.* 12–14, *figs.* 4.   1881.

JOHNSTON-LAVIS, H. J.—The Earthquake in Ischia.—" *Nature,*" *xxiii, pp.* 497–98.   1881.

JOHNSTON-LAVIS, H. J.—[The Ischian Earthquake of July 28th, 1883.]—"*Nature,*" *xxviii, pp.* 346–48, 437–39, 1 *fig.*   1883.

JOHNSTON-LAVIS, H. J.—Observations scientifiques sur le tremblement de terre du 28 Juillet, 1883, à l'Île d'Ischia.—" *L'Italie,*" *Rome,* 13 *Août,* 1883.

JOHNSTON-LAVIS, H. J.—Il parere d'uno scienziato.—" *Il Piccolo,*" *Naples,* 2 *Sett.,* 1883.

JOHNSTON-LAVIS, H. J.—Prévision de futures catastrophes dans l'Île d'Ischia.—" *L'Italie,*" *Rome,* 2 *Sett.,* 1883.

JOHNSTON-LAVIS, H. J.—The Disaster in Ischia.—" *Indianapolis Journal,*" *Sept.* 6th, 1883.

JOHNSTON-LAVIS, H. J.—Una risposta al Prof. Palmieri.—" *Il Piccolo,*" *Naples,* 8 *Sett.,* 1883.

JOHNSTON-LAVIS, H. J.—Étude sur l'emplacement des nouvelles villes à l'Île d'Ischia.—" *L'Italie,*" *Rome,* 15 *Sett.,* 1883.

JOHNSTON-LAVIS, H. J.—Le costruzioni a Casamicciola.—" *Il Piccolo,*" *Naples,* 20 *Sett.,* 1883.

JOHNSTON-LAVIS, H. J.—Rapport préliminaire sur le tremblement de terre du 28 Juillet, 1883, à l'Île d'Ischia.—"*L'Italie,*" 22 *Sett.,* 1883.

JOHNSTON-LAVIS, H. J.—Notices on the Earthquakes of Ischia of 1881 and 1883, with a Map of the Isoseismal.—8⁰, *pp.* 56, 1 *map. Naples,* 1883.

JOHNSTON-LAVIS, H. J.—Brevi considerazioni intorno alla relazione del professore L. Palmieri sul terremoto dell' Isola d'Ischia.—" *Il Piccolo,*" *Naples,* 31 *Marzo e* 1 *Aprile,* 1884.

JOHNSTON-LAVIS, H. J.—Preliminary Notice of the Earthquake of [March 4th,] 1881, in the Island of Ischia.—*Rept. British Assoc.* 1883, *pp.* 499–501.   1884.

JOHNSTON-LAVIS, H. J.—Preliminary Notice of the Earthquake of July [28th], 1883, in the Island of Ischia.—*Rept. British Assoc.* 1883, *pp.* 501–3, 1 *fig.*   1884.

JOHNSTON-LAVIS, H. J.—The Physical Conditions involved in the injection, extrusion and cooling of Igneous Matter. [Abstr.]—*Quart. Journ. Geol. Soc. Lond. xli, Proc. pp.* 103–6.   1885.—*Geol. Mag. p.* 282.   1885.

JOHNSTON-LAVIS, H. J.—Monograph of the Earthquakes of Ischia, a Memoir Dealing with the Seismic Disturbances in that Island from Remotest Times, with Special Observations on those of 1881 and 1883, and some calculations by Rev. Prof. Samuel Haughton.—*roy.* 4⁰, *pp. x+*112, 20 *photoengrav.,* 2 *maps col.,* 4 *pls.* (1 *col.*). *London and Naples,* 1885.—[Review in :] *Geol. Mag. pp.* 369–71.   1886.

JOHNSTON-LAVIS, H. J.—[Panoramic photo-engraving of Casamicciola after the Earthquake of 1883 for book " Earthquakes of Ischia."]
Photo-engrav. proof before letters : 465 × 185 mm.

JOHNSTON-LAVIS, H. J.—Bay of Pozzuoli, 1886.
Panoramic photo. : 983 × 143 mm.

JOHNSTON-LAVIS, H. J.—The Relationship of the Structure of Igneous Rocks to the Conditions of their Formation.—*Scient. Proc. R. Dublin Soc. N.S. v, pp.* 113–55.   1886.

JOHNSTON-LAVIS, H. J.—On the Fragmentary Ejectamenta of Volcanoes.—*Proc. Geol. Assoc. Lond. ix, pp.* 421–32, 1 *pl.* 1886.

JOHNSTON-LAVIS, H. J.—[Second] Report of the Committee for the Investigation of the Volcanic Phenomena of Vesuvius and its Neighbourhood.—*Rept. British Assoc.* 1886, *pp.* 226–28. 1887.—" *Nature,*" *xxxiv, p.* 481. 1886.

JOHNSTON-LAVIS, H. J.—[Third] Report of the Committee for the Investigation of the Volcanic Phenomena of Vesuvius and its Neighbourhood.—*Rept. British Assoc.* 1887, *pp.* 226–29. 1888.

JOHNSTON-LAVIS, H. J.—On a remarkable Sodalite Trachyte lately discovered in Naples, Italy.—*Geol. Mag. pp.* 74–77. 1889.

JOHNSTON-LAVIS, H. J.—Il Pozzo Artesiano di Ponticelli.—*Rend. R. Acc. Sci. S.* 2, *iii, pp.* 142–48. *Napoli,* 1889.

JOHNSTON-LAVIS, H. J.—Volcans et Tremblements de Terre. Revue de ce qui a été publié sur ces sujets durant l'année 1888.—*Ann. géol. univ. v, pp.* 629–55. *Paris,* 1889.

JOHNSTON-LAVIS, H. J.—[Fourth] Report of the Committee appointed for the Investigation of the Volcanic Phenomena of Vesuvius and its Neighbourhood.—*Rept. British Assoc.* 1888, *pp.* 320–26. 1889.

JOHNSTON-LAVIS, H. J.—Nuove osservazioni fatte in Napoli e dintorni.—*Boll. R. Com. Geol. Ital. xix, pp.* 393–98. *Roma,* 1888.
Abstract of preceding.

JOHNSTON-LAVIS, H. J.—The Excursion to the Volcanoes of Italy.—Seismology in Italy.—" *Nature,*" *xl, p.* 294. 1889.

JOHNSTON-LAVIS, H. J.—Viaggio scientifico alle regioni vulcaniche italiane nella ricorrenza del centenario del " Viaggio alle due Sicilie " di Lazzaro Spallanzani.—8°, *pp.* 1–10. *Naples,* 1889.
This is the programme of the excursion of the English Geologists who visited the South Italian Volcanoes under the direction of the author. It is here included as it contains various new and unpublished observations.

JOHNSTON-LAVIS, H. J.—Excursion to the South Italian Volcanoes. [Read Jan. 3, 1890.]—*Proc. Geol. Assoc. Lond. xi; pp.* 389–423. 890.

JOHNSTON-LAVIS, H. J.—Osservazioni geologiche lungo il tracciato del Grande Emissario Fognone di Napoli dalla Pietra sino a Pozzuoli. Relazione alla Società Napoletana degli Ingegneri Costruttori di Napoli.—*Boll. R. Com. Geol. Ital. xxi, pp.* 18–27, 1 *fig. Roma,* 1890.

JOHNSTON-LAVIS, H. J.—Nuove osservazioni geologiche in Napoli e suoi dintorni. —*Boll. R. Com. Geol. Ital. xxi, pp.* 65–68. *Roma,* 1890.
On p. 67, lines 3, 6 and 9, for *verdi* read *rossi,* i.e. for *green* read *red.*

JOHNSTON-LAVIS, H. J.—Volcans et Tremblements de Terre (Revue).—*Ann. géol. univ. vi, pp.* 355–81. *Paris,* 1890.

JOHNSTON-LAVIS, H. J.—[Fifth] Report of the Committee appointed for the Investigation of the Volcanic Phenomena of Vesuvius and its Neighbourhood.—*Rept. British Assoc.* 1889, *pp.* 283–94, 5 *figs.* 1890.

JOHNSTON-LAVIS, H. J.—The South Italian Volcanoes, being the account of an Excursion to them made by English and other Geologists in 1889 under the auspices of the Geologists' Association of London, and the direction of the author, with papers on the Different Localities by Messrs. Johnston-Lavis, Platania, Sambon, Zezi, and Mme. Antonia Lavis, including the Bibliography of the Volcanic Districts.— 8°, *pp.* vi+342, 16 *pls. Furchheim, Naples,* 1891.—[Reviewed in] " *Nature,*" *xliv, pp.* 539–40. 1891.

JOHNSTON-LAVIS, H. J.—Bibliography of the Geology and Eruptive Phenomena of the South Italian Volcanoes, that were visited in 1889, as well as of the submarine volcano of A.D. 1831. Compiled by Madame A. Lavis and Dr. Johnston-Lavis. —8°, *pp.* 89–331. *Naples,* 1891.
Chapt. VII. of foregoing.

JOHNSTON-LAVIS, H. J.—[Sixth] Report of the Committee appointed for the Investigation of the Volcanic Phenomena of Vesuvius and its Neighbourhood.—*Rept. British Assoc.* 1890, *pp.* 397–410, 3 *figs. London,* 1891.

JOHNSTON-LAVIS, H. J.—Notes on the Pipernoid Structure of Igneous Rocks.— " *Natural Science,*" *iii, pp.* 218–21. *London,* 1893.

JOHNSTON-LAVIS, H. J.—[Eighth] Report of the Committee appointed for the Investigation of the Volcanic Phenomena of Vesuvius and its Neighbourhood.—*Rept. British Assoc.* 1892, *pp.* 338–43. *London,* 1893.—[Also in] *Geol. Mag. pp.* 507–13. 1892.

JOHNSTON-LAVIS, H. J.—[Ninth Report of the Committee appointed for the Investigation of] the Volcanic Phenomena of Vesuvius and its Neighbourhood.—*Rept. British Assoc.* 1893, *pp.* 471–73. *London,* 1894.

JOHNSTON-LAVIS, H. J.—The Science of Vulcanology [being the Introductory Address to a Course of Lectures on that Subject in the R. University of Naples].—" *Nature*," *l, pp.* 66–68. 1894.—" *Science*," 16 *March,* 1894.

JOHNSTON-LAVIS, H. J.—On the Formation at Low Temperatures of certain Fluorides, Silicates, Oxides, etc., in the Pipernoid Tuff of the Campania. With a note on the determination of some of the Species by Prof. Pasquale Franco.—*Geol. Mag.* 1895, *pp.* 309–14.

JOHNSTON-LAVIS, H. J., e FLORES, E.—Notizie sui depositi degli antichi laghi di Pianura (Napoli) e di Melfi (Basilicata) e sulle Ossa di Mammiferi in essi rinvenute.—*Boll. Soc. Geol. Ital.* xiv, *pp.* 111–18, 1 *pl. Roma,* 1895.

JOHNSTON-LAVIS, H. J.—On the Effects of Volcanic Action in the production of Epidemic Diseases in the Animal and in the Vegetable Creation, and in the production of Hurricanes and Abnormal Atmospherical Vicissitudes.—8°, *pp.* xii+67. *John Bale, Sons and Danielsson, London,* 1914.
Parkin Prize Essay for Dec., 1913.

JOLY (del.).—*See* TURPIN DE CRISSÉ, CTE.—Vue de Naples.

JONES, E. W. S.—The earthquake at Casamicciola, July 28th, 1883.—8°, *pp.* 143. *Naples,* 1883. [C.A.]

JORIO, ANDREA DE.—Pozzuoli et ses Environs.—4°, 8 *pls. Naples,* 1810. [B.N.P.]
Two very fine plates, dated 1810, show the Serapeum with platform and basis of columns exposed.

JORIO, A. DE.—Guida di Pozzuoli e Contorni.—8°, *pp.* vii+151, *topogr. map. Napoli,* 1817. [B.M. 10151. b. 7.]
A good, well-shaded map is appended and one plate of inscription.
2nd ed. 8°, *pp.* xvi+191. *Napoli,* 1822.
——3rd ed. *pp.* 128, 2 *maps and* 6 *pls.* 1830.

JORIO, A. DE.—Indicazione del più Remarcabile in Napoli e Contorni. Engr. by G. Rossi, 1819. Ed. Nuov.—8°, *portrait,* 9 *pls., pp.* 164. *Napoli,* 1835.
Map of coast from L. di Patria to Pestum on a smaller scale than that in his " Guida di Pozzuoli e Contorni."

JORIO, A. DE.—Ricerche sul Tempio di Serapide in Pozzuoli.—4°, *pp.* 68, 3 *pls. Napoli,* 1820. [B.M.—7820.9.31.]

JORIO, A. DE.—Avanzi dell' Antica Città di Rocca di Cuma.—[*Napoli,*] 1820 ? [B.M. 24120.7., sheet 2.]
A well-made map of the district.

JORIO, A. DE.—Plan de la Ville de Naples et ses indications. 1826.—*Naples,* 1826.—— 2nd ed. 1835.

JORIO, A. DE.—Pozzuoli und dessen Umgebungen aus dem Italienischen.—8°, *pp.* 100. *Zurich,* 1830.

JOUSSET, P.—L'Italie illustrée.—*fol., pp.* 370, 14 *col. maps and plans,* 9 *engrav. maps,* 12 *pls.,* 784 *photos. Paris,* 1829.

JOVENE, FR.—Note geologiche sull' Isola d'Ischia.—*Napoli,* 1903.

JUDD, J. W.—Contribution to the Study of Volcanoes.—*Geol. Mag.* ii, *pp.* 245–57, *figs. London,* 1875.

KADEN, W.—Der Insel Ischia in Natur, Sitten und Geschichts Bildern aus Vergangenheit und Gegenwart.—8°, *pp.* 115, 4 *pls.,* 1 *map. Lutzen, Prell.* —? [C.A.]

KAISER, F. (dis. e inc. dal vero l'anno 1829). —La Grotta di Posilippo longa piedi 2123, largo piedi 19. Si vende in Roma da Tommaso Cuccioni Neg^te. di Stampa in Via della Croce No. 25.
Outline engrav. : 185×134 mm. Char-à-bancs and donkeys in foreground.

KAISER, F. (dis. e inc. dal vero l'anno 1829). —Napoli, verso l'Occidente No. 1. Si vende in Roma presso Tommaso Cuccioni Negoziante di Stampe in Via della Croce No. 25.
Outline engrav. with fishermen pulling in Seine net, cooking, and boat, men and baby in foreground ; 9 ref. nos. : 188× 132 mm.

KAISER, F. (dis. e inc. dal vero l'anno 1829). —Il Sepolcro di Virgilio presso la Grotta di Posilippo a Napoli. No. 5. Si vendono in Roma da Tommaso Cuccioni Neg^e di Stampe in Via della Croce. No. 25.
Outline engrav., man, woman and baby in foreground : 180×134 mm.

KAISER, F. (dis. e inc. dal vero l'anno 1829). —Veduta di Napoli verso l'Oriente. No. 11. Si vendono in Roma da Tommaso Cuccioni Negoziante di Stampe in Via della Croce. No. 2 .
189×134 mm.

KALKOWSKY, L. E.—Der Leucitporphyr vom Averner See.—*N. J. f. Min. pp.* 727–29. *Stuttgart*, 1878.

KALKOWSKY, L. E.—Ueber den Piperno. —*Zeitschr. deutsch. geol. Gesellsch. xxx, pp.* 663–77. *Berlin*, 1878.

KALKOWSKY, L. E.—[Notice of Mercalli] Sulla natura del terremoto Ischiano del 28 luglio, 1883.—*N. J. f. Min. i, pp.* 258–59. *Stuttgart*, 1886.

KARSTEN, H.—Zur Geologie der Insel Capri.—*N. J. f. Min. i, 2, pp.* 139–61. *Stuttgart*, 1895.

KARSTEN, H.—Zur Geologie der Insel Capri. II.—*N. J. f. Min. ii, 1, pp.* 39–52. *Stuttgart*, 1898.

KIRCHER, A.—Mundus Subterraneus.— 3rd ed. *fol., foll. x, pp.* 368, *foll.* 2, *num. figs. Amstelodami, Janssonio-Wæsbergiana*, 1678.
    See pp. 189–91 and fig. of Solfatara and Agnano.
    Earlier ed. : 2 tom. *fol. Amstelodami*, 1665.—2 tom. *fol. Amstelodami*, 1668, 65. [Tom. 2 is a dup. of Tom. 2 of the preceding.]

KIRCHER, A.—The Vulcanos : or, burning and fire-vomiting Mountains, famous in the World : with their remarkables. Collected for the most part out of Kircher's " Subterraneous World."—8°, *foll.* 4, *pp.* 64, 1 *pl. London*, 1669.

KOPISCH, A.—Entdeckung der blauen Grotte auf der Insel Capri.—*See* REUMONT, A.—Italia, *pp.* 155–201.

KOSMAN, B. A.—De nonnullis lavis Arverniacis dissertatio inauguralis mineralogico-chimica.—8°. *Statis Saxoniæ*, 1864. [B.N.]

KRANZ, W.—Hohe Strandlinien auf Capri. —[Sonderabdr.] *Jahresb. Geog. Gesellsch. xiii, 2 tav. Greifswald*, 1911–12.

KRANZ, W.—Vulcanismus u. Tektonik im Becken von Neapel. (1912.)—2 pts. 4°, 2 *pls.*—[Abdr.] *Peterm. " Geogr. Mitth." pp.* 131–35, 203–6, 258–64. *Gotha*, 1912.

KRENNER, J. A.—Die Krystallform und optischen Eigenschaften des Schullerschen Argensulfides. Ueber den Dimorphin der Solfatara in den Phlegräischen Feldern.— *Zeitschr. f. Kryst. xliii, pp.* 476–84, *figs. Leipzig*, 1907.

KRESSNER.—[Geographisch-orographische Uebersicht über das vulcanische Terrain im Neapolitanischen.]—*Berg- u. hüttenmänn. Zeitung, xxii, pp.* 236–37. *Freiberg*, 1836.

LA CAVA, P.—[Solfuro nero e rosso di Mercurio ; Argilla bianca ; Solfato d'Allumina della Solfatara.]—*Ann. Acc. Aspir. Nat. S.* 2, i, *Bull. p. xlii. Napoli*, 1847.

LA CAVE.—*See* COSTA, O. G. 1840.

LA CROIX.—*See* CROIX, LA.

LACROIX, A. F. A.—Les enclaves des roches volcaniques.—*Ann. Acad. Mâcon, S.* 2, *x, pp.* 1–710, 8 *pls.* 1893.

LACROIX, A. F. A.—Etude sur le Métamorphisme de contact des roches volcaniques. —4°, *pp.* 88. *Paris*, 1894.

LAFRERY, A.—La nobile Cita di Napoli.— *Romæ*, 1566.

LAGORIO.—Ueber die Natur der Glasbasis, sowie der Krystallisationsvorgänge im eruptiven Magma. No. 58 : Die Analyse braunen Obsidians aus Trachyttuff von Punta di Ricciola auf Procida.—*Min. petr. Mitth. N.F. viii, pp.* 421–529. *Wien*, 1887.
    See pp. 475–76.

LALANDE, L. J. LEBOUIDRE DE.—Voyage en Italie, contenant l'histoire, et les anecdotes les plus singulières de l'Italie, etc., etc.—*Paris*, 1779.——2nd ed. 9 vols. and atlas, 12°. *Paris*, 1786. (*See* Vol. vii, pp. 302–89.)——Another ed. 7 vols. and atlas (35 *pls.*), 8°. *Genève*, 1790. (*See* Vol. vi, pp. 18–39, Solfatara di Pozzuoli.)

LALMAN (pinx.), SANDBY, P. (fecit).— Castello Nuovo and part of the Mole at Naples. Published by P. Sandby, Oxford Turnpike, Jan. 1st, 1778. No. 712.
    Careful, hand-painted on line engrav. : 512 × 330 mm.

LALMAN (pinxt.), SANDBY, P. (fecit).— Castello Nuovo and part of the Mole at Naples. Le Castello Nuovo, et une partie du Môle de Naples. Publish'd as the Act directs, by P. Sandby, St. George's Row, Oxford Turnpike, Jany. 1st, 1778.
    Sepia engrav. : 512 × 356 mm.

LANCELLOTTI, F.—Memoria sull' analisi e sintesi dell' acqua solfurea di Napoli.—*Atti Soc. Pontan. ii, pp.* 151–62. *Napoli*, 1812.

LANCELLOTTI, F.—Saggi analitici sulle acque minerali del territorio di Pozzuoli.— 4°. *Napoli*, 1819.

LANG, O.—Ueber zeitlichen Bestandwechsel der Vesuvlaven u. Ætnagesteine.—?, 1892.

LANG, O.—Die vulcanischen Herde am Golfe von Neapel.—*Zeitschr. deutsch. geol. Gesellsch. xlv, pp.* 177–94, 1 *tab. Berlin*, 1893.

LANZANI, N.—Breve dissertazione dell' acqua nuovamente rinvenuta nell' anno 1738 in Pozzuoli, dagli antichi chiamata del Cantarello.—*Napoli*, 1740.

LANZETTA, A.—Risposta alla 1ª di un anonimo sulle osservazioni di un fenomeno avvenuto nel lago di Patria.—*Napoli*, 1796.

LA PIRA.—Memoria sull' origine, analisi ed uso medico delle acque minerali di Terra di Lavoro.—*Caserta*, 1820.

LAROUSSE.—*See* DARONDEAU.

LASALLE, E.—1. Vésuve de Strabon ou Somma. 2. Somma et Vésuve après l'éruption de Pline. 3. Astrone vu des Camaldoli. 4. Astrone vu des bords du Cratère.—Lith. de C. Adrien, rue Richer 7. *See* BUCH, L. VON.—Geognostische Beobachtungen, etc., Pl. 9. Lith.: 385 × 252 mm.

LASAULX, A. C. P. F. VON.—Das Erdbeben von Casamicciola auf Ischia (4 marzo,1881). —" *Humboldt*," i, *pp.* 1–5. *Stuttgart, Jun.* 1882. [C.A.]

LASSELS, RICH.—The Voyage of Italy or A Compleat Iovrney Throvgh Italy aend the Holy Laend with the Characters of the People, and the description of the chief Townes, Churches, Monasteries, Tombes, Libraries, Pallaces, Villas, Gardens, Pictures, Statues, Antiquities : as also of the Interest, Gouerment, Riches, Force, etc. of all the Princes.—Opus posthumum : Corrected and set forth by his old friend and fellow Traveller S.W.—12⁰, *pp.* 447+4. *Paris, V. Dv. Movtier,* M.DC.LXX.——2nd ed. 8⁰. *London, for R. Wellington,* 1698. Second part of the Voyage in Italy, pp. 295–300, mentions several arches of Caligula's Mole intact before 1650.

LAURENTIIS, M. DE.—Universæ Campaniæ Felicis Antiquitates.—2 vols. 4⁰. *Vol. i, pp.* 7 + 188, 1 *pl. ; Vol. ii, pp.* 303, 1 *pl. Neapolis*, 1826. *See* Part ii, pp. 42 *et seq.* Monte Nuovo, etc.

LAURUS, JACOBUS.—Typografia Puteolarum.—*Romæ*, 1626. (Another very similar has no title.) [B.N.P., Vb. 113.] Shows piers of Caligula's Mole partly arched and partly broken.

LEBERT, H.—Le Golfe de Naples et ses volcans et les volcans en général.—8⁰, *pp.* 120. *Vevey, Lausanne, etc.*, 1876.

LEBLANC, F.—*See* DEVILLE, C. J. STE.-CLAIRE.

LECANU, L. R.—*See* BLACHET.

LEITCH, W. L.—The Castle and Rock of Ischia, Gulf of Naples. Il Castello e la Rocca d'Ischia, Golfo di Napoli. J. Sands. Fisher, Son and Co. London and Paris.

LEITCH, W. L. (drawn by).—Naples from the Santa Lucia. Engraved by J. B. Allen. Blackie and Son, Glasgow, Edinburgh and London. Careful, hand-col. engrav.: 225 × 189 mm.

LEITCH, W. L.—*See* MAPEI, C.—Italy, Classical, Historical and Picturesque.

LEITCH, W. L.—*See* WRIGHT, G. N. 1839 ?, 1841. *.*

LEMERCIER (Imp.).—Ischia. Environs de Naples. 10, T. IV. Imp. Lemercier et Cie., Paris. Chromolitho. : 276 × 197 mm.

LEONHARD, C. C. VON.—Geologie oder Naturgeschichte der Erde auf allgemein faszliche Weise abgehandelt.—5 vols. 8⁰. *Vol. i, pp.* 456, *lith. pls. i–xiv ; Vol. ii, pp.* 481, *pls. xv–xxxix ; Vol. iii, pp.* 628, *pls. xl–lxviii ; Vol. iv, pp.* 490, *pls. lxix–lxxx ; Vol. v, pp.* 712, *pls. lxxxi–lxxxvii. Stuttgart,* 1836–44. *See* Vol. i, Pl. vii and pp. 200–3 ; Vol. ii, Pl. xx, pp. 103–10 ; Vol. v, Pls. lxxxix, lxxxxii, and pp. 233–64, 286–88.

LE RICHE, M. J.—*See* M. J. L. R.

LE RICHE, M. J.—Vues des Monumens Antiques de Naples gravées à l'Aqua-tinta accompagnées de Notices et de Dissertations.—4⁰, *pp.* 110, 60 *pls.* [*Paris,*] 1827. *See* Pls. 47, Agnano ; 48, Grotto del Cane ; 50, Molo di Caligula ; 51, Serapis ; 56, Tritoli ; 57, Avernus.

LE RICHE, M. J. (del.).—L'Île de Caprée, vue de Naples. Melle Lavallée, sculp. 2ᵐᵉ Liv., Pl. 7ᵉ. Stipple engrav. dark sepia : 184 × 137 mm.

LE VEAU.—*See* VEAU, LE.

LIBELLUS.—De mirabilibus civitatis Puteolorum et locorum vicinorum : ac de nominibus virtutibusq. balneorum ibidem existentium.—4⁰, *foll.* 32. 1507.—Another ed. 4⁰, *foll.* 37. *Naples*, 1475. [C.A.]

LICOPOLI, G.—Su d'un pezzo di Legno rinvenuto nel tufo vulcanico appresso Napoli.—*Rend. R. Acc. Sci. xiii, pp.* 141–43. *Napoli*, 1874.

LINTON, W.—Sketches in Italy, drawn on stone. Facsimiles of Sketches during a Tour in 1828–29 in various Parts of Piedmont, the Milanese, Venetian and Roman States, Tuscany and the Kingdom of Naples.—*imp. fol.*, 96 *views. London*, 1832. Very fine views. *See* Pl. 30 : Bay of Naples.

LINTON, W.—Puteoli. Pozzuolo. Acts xxviii, 13, 14. Engraved by E. Finden. 53.
Shows Caligula's Mole in profile. Fine engrav. : 144 × 100 mm.

LINTON, W. (drawn and sketched on the spot).—Puteoli. Pozzuolo. Acts xxviii, 13, 14. No. 53. Engraved by E. Finden.
Hand-coloured steel engrav. : 145 × 118 mm.

LIPPI, C.—Fu il fuoco o l'acqua che sotterrò Pompei ed Ercolano ?—*8⁰, foll.* 2, *pp.* 384, *foll.* 2, 1 *pl. Napoli*, 1816.

LIPPI, C.—Lago Lucrino ed emissario di Claudio nella regione dei Marsi.—*Napoli*, 1818.

LIPPI, C.—Sul progetto di doversi analizzare le acque minerali d'Ischia da una commissione della Real Accademia di Scienze.—*8⁰. Napoli*, 1820.

LLORD Y GAMBOA, R.—Estudo químico-geognóstico de algunos materiales volcánicos del Golfo de Nápoles.—*Rev. R. Acad. Cienc. iv, pp.* 340–50, *figs.*, 1 *pl., Madrid*, 1906 ; *vi, pp.* 179–97, 250–57, 1907.

LOBLEY, J. L.—Mount Vesuvius. A descriptive, historical and geological account of the Volcano and its Surroundings.—2nd ed. 8⁰, *pp.* 385, 20 *pls. London, Roper and Drowley*, 1889.

LOCCHI, ING. D.—Italia : Carta Fisica.—*Pub. G. B. Paravia e C., Torino, Roma, Milano, Firenze, Napoli*, 1876.
1 : 200,000. Raised map.

LOCCHI, ING. D.—Napoli e Dintorni.—*Pub. G. B. Paravia e C., Torino, Roma, Milano, Firenze, Napoli*, 1876.
1 : 100,000. Raised map coloured, in two editions : 1st, physical and political ; 2nd, geological.

LOFFREDO, F.—Le antichità di Pozzuoli e luoghi convicini nuovamente raccolte.— 12⁰, *foll.* 24. *Napoli*, 1580. [C.A.]—Another ed. 12⁰, *pp.* 46, *fol.* 1. *Napoli, Horatio Salviani*, 1585.—Another ed. 4⁰, *pp.* 4+38. *Napoli*, 1675.—Another ed. 4⁰, *pp.* 54. *Napoli*, 1752.

LOFFREDO, F.—Antiquitas Puteolorum cum Balneorum Agnani Puteolorum, et Tripergolarum descriptionibus per generosissimum Dominum Joannum Villanum ex auctoris vero,& antiquissimo Libro desumptis Faucibus temporis ereptio per dominum Pompeium Sarnellum. Editio novissima, aliis auctior & emendatior Sigevertus Havercampus ex. Italicis Latina fecit. Præfationis & indicem adjecit Lugduni Batavorum. *fol.,—pp.* 3+27.—*See* GRÆVIUS.—Thesaurus Antiquitatum, etc. *T. ix, Pt.* 4. 1725, *etc.*

LOMBARDI, A.—Cenno sul tremuoto avvenuto in Tito, ed in altri luoghi della Basilicata il di 1 Febbraio, 1824.—*Potenza*, 1829.

LOMBARDUS, J. F.—Synopsis autorum omnium qui hactenus de Balneis, aliisque miraculis Puteolanis scripserunt.—*foll.* 124. *Napolis*, 1557. [C.A.]—Also 1559.

LOMBARDUS, J. F.—Synopsis eorum, quæ de balneis, aliisq. miraculis Puteolanis scripta sunt. Adiecto balneis Ænariarum, nec non locis obscurioribus non inutilibus scholiis.—4⁰. *Venetiis*, 1566.

LOMBARDUS, J. F.—Ænariarum Balnea ex Joanne Elysio, Medico Neapolitano, cum Scholiis. . . . Neapolitani.—8⁰, *pp.* 16.— *See* JASOLINUS, G. DI.—De Remedii naturali.

LONGRAIRE, M. D. DE.—Seismies et Volcans.—*Bull. Soc. Ing. Civil. France. Paris, Nov.*, 1894.

LORENZO, G. DE.—Studi di geologia nell' Appennino meridionale.—*Napoli*, 1896.— *Atti R. Acc. Sci. S.* 2, *viii, Mem.* 7, *pp.* 128. *Napoli*, 1896.

LORENZO, G. DE, e RIVA, C.—Il Cratere di Vivara nelle Isole Flegree.—*Atti R. Acc. Sci. S.* 2, *x,* 8, *pp.* 59, 3 *tav.*, 6 *figs. Napoli*, 1901.—*Id. Rend. p.* 152. 1900.

LORENZO, G. DE.—Considerazioni sull' Origine Superficiale dei Vulcani.—*Atti R. Acc. Sci. S.* 2, *xi,* 7, *pp.* 19, 1 *pl. Napoli*, 1902.

LORENZO, G. DE, e RIVA, C.—Il Cratere di Astroni nei Campi Flegrei.—*Atti R. Acc. Sci.S.* 2, *xi,* 8, *pp.* 87, *pls. i–vii*, 11 *figs.*, 1 *col. geol. map, index. Napoli*, 1902.

LORENZO, G. DE.—I Vulcani di Napoli.— *pp.* 16. *Roma*, 1902.—" *Nuova Antologia,*" *S.* 4, *xcviii, pp.* 684–95. *Roma*, 1902.

LORENZO, G. DE.—I Campi Flegrei. With 152 illustr.—*See* RICCI, C.—Napoli, No. 52, in " *Collezione di Monografie Illustrate.*"— *Italia Artistica.*—*S.* 1, 1902, *etc.*

LORENZO, G. DE.—The History of Volcanic Action in the Phlegræan Fields.—*Abstr. Proc. Geol. Soc. pp.* 77–79, 1903–1904, and *Quart. Journ. Geog. Soc. lx, pp.* 296–315, *pls. xxvi–xxviii (geol. maps).* 1904.

LORENZO, G. DE.—L'Attività vulcanica nei Campi Flegrei.—*Rend. R. Acc. Sci. S.* 3, *x, pp.* 203–21. *Napoli,* 1904.

LORENZO, G. DE.—Geologia e geografia fisica dell' Italia meridionale.—8⁰, *pp.* 241. *Bari,* 1904.

LORENZO, G. DE.—I crateri di Miseno nei Campi Flegrei.—*Rend. R. Acc. Sci. S.* 3, *xi, p.* 325. *Napoli,* 1905.—*Id. Atti, S.* 2, *xiii,* 1, *pp.* 25, *pls. i–iii, geol. map.* 1908.

LORENZO, G. DE.—L'Isola di Capri.—*Atti R. Acc. Lincei, S.* 5, *Rend. xvi, sem.* 1, *pp.* 853–57. *Roma,* 1907.

LORENZO, G. DE.—Il Cratere di Nisida nei Campi Flegrei.—*Rend. R. Acc. Sci. S.* 3, *i, p.* 124. *Napoli,* 1907.—*Id. Atti, S.* 2, *xiii,* 10, *pp.* 1–14, *pls. i–ii (geol. map.).* 1908.

LORENZO, G. DE.—Una monografia dei Campi Flegrei.—*Riv. Geog. Ital. xv,* 3, *pp.* 7. *Firenze,* 1908.

LORENZO, G. DE.—I Campi Flegrei.—*Ist. Ital. Arti Graf.* 4⁰, *pp.* 156, 147 *figs.,* 5 *pls. Bergamo,* 1909.

LORENZO, G. DE.—Relazione sulla memoria del dott. Francesco Stella Starrabba dal titolo : " Il Cratere di Santa Teresa nei Campi Flegrei."—*Rend. R. Acc. Sci. S.* 3, *xvi, p.* 19. *Napoli,* 1910.

LORENZO, G. DE.—*See* BASSANI, F. 1893 and 1910.

LORENZO, G. DE.—*See* BÖSE, E.—Zur Geologie der Monti Picentini.

LUCA, B. DE.—*See* MICHELE, P. DE.

LUCA, D.—Intorno all' Acqua della Solfatara di Pozzuoli. Storia e documenti.—8⁰, *pp.* 16. *Napoli,* 1869.

LUCA, S. DE.—Studii fisico-geografici sulla regione da Baia a Castellamare.—*Napoli,* 1865.

LUCA, S. DE.—Ricerche chimiche sopra un acqua di pozzo della Città di Napoli.— *Rend. R. Acc. Sci. v, pp.* 398–402. *Napoli,* 1866.

LUCA, S. DE.—Osservazioni sulla compo sizione dell' acqua termale della Solfatara di Pozzuoli.—*Rend. R. Acc. Sci. vii, pp.* 139–44, 169–70, 182. *Napoli,* 1868.—*Les Mondes, xviii, pp.* 432–35. 1868.

LUCA, S. DE.—Osservazioni sulla temperatura interna della grande fumarola della Solfatara di Pozzuoli.—*Rend. R. Acc. Sci. viii, pp.* 34–38. *Napoli,* 1869.

LUCA, S. DE.—Ricerche chimiche e terapeutiche sull' acqua termo-minerale della Solfatara di Pozzuoli.—*Rend. R. Acc. Sci. viii, pp.* 168–73. *Napoli,* 1869.—*Journ. Chim. méd. S.* 5, *vi, pp.* 210–13. *Paris,* 1870.—*C.R. Acad. Sci. lxvii, pp.* 909–12, 1868 ; *lxx, pp.* 408–10. *Paris,* 1870.— *Journ. Pharm. Chim. S.* 4, *xii, pp.* 33–36. *Paris,* 1870.

LUCA, S. DE, e SCIVOLETTO, P.—Ricerche analitiche intorno a talune varietà di calcari ed argille della provincia di Caserta.—*Rend. R. Acc. Sci. ix, pp.* 62–70. *Napoli,* 1870.

LUCA, S. DE.—Notizie intorno agli usi dell' acqua termo-minerale, della Solfatara di Pozzuoli.—1871.—*See* LUCA, S. DE.— Ricerche speriment. 1874, 1882.

LUCA, S. DE.—Ricerche chimiche sull' allume ricavata dall' acqua termo-minerale della Solfatara di Pozzuoli.—*Rend. R. Acc. Sci. x, pp.* 63–64. *Napoli,* 1871.—*Gazz. Chim. Ital. i, p.* 387. *Palermo,* 1871.

LUCA, S. DE.—Sulla composizione dei gaz che svolgonsi dalle fumarole della Solfatara di Pozzuoli.—*Rend. R. Acc. Sci. x, pp.* 181-88, 211–18. *Napoli,* 1871.—*C.R. Acad. Sci. lxxiv, pp.* 536–38. *Paris,* 1872.—*Ann. Chim. xxvi, pp.* 289–309. *Paris,* 1872.— *Gazz. Chim. Ital. ii, pp.* 63–64. *Palermo,* 1872.

LUCA, S. DE.—Ricerche chimiche sopra una produzione della Solfatara di Pozzuoli.— *Rend. R. Acc. Sci. x, pp.* 218–21. *Napoli,* 1871.—*Gazz. Chim. Ital. ii, p.* 64. *Palermo,* 1872.—*Riv. Scient. Industr. Firenze,* 1873.—*C.R. Acad. Sci. lxxvi, pp.* 357–59. *Paris,* 1873.

LUCA, S. DE.—Recherches chimiques sur un alun complexe, obtenu de l'eau thermo-minérale de la Solfatare de Pouzzoles.— *C.R. Acad. Sci. lxxiv, pp.* 123–24. *Paris,* 1872.

LUCA, S. DE.—Action de la terre volcanique de la Solfatare de Pouzzoles sur les maladies de la Vigne.—*C.R. Acad. Sci. lxxvi, pp.* 359-61, 1873 ; *lxxvii, pp.* 1431–32, *Paris,* 1873.

LUCA, S. DE.—Ricerche chimiche sulla terra della Solfatara di Pozzuoli.—*Rend. R. Acc. Sci. xii, pp.* 17–18. *Napoli*, 1873.

LUCA, S. DE.—Ricerche analitiche sopra talune produzioni stalammitiche della Solfatara di Pozzuoli.—*Rend. R. Acc. Sci. xii, pp.* 35–38, *Napoli*, 1873 ; *xiii, p.* 115, 1874.

LUCA, S. DE.—Ricerche chimiche sopra una produzione stalattitica della Solfatara di Pozzuoli.—*Rend. R. Acc. Sci. xii, pp.* 114–15. *Napoli*, 1873.

LUCA, S. DE.—Ricerche analitiche sopra quattro diverse terre della Solfatara di Pozzuoli.—*Rend. R. Acc. Sci. xii, pp.* 130–34. *Napoli*, 1873.

LUCA, S. DE.—Ricerche chimiche sopra una sostanza legnosa trovata nel tufo vulcanico. —*Rend. R. Acc. Sci. xiii, pp.* 15–17. *Napoli*, 1874.

LUCA, S. DE.—Ricerche sperimentali sulla Solfatara di Pozzuoli.—8⁰, *pp.* 106, 5 *pls. Napoli*, 1874. (Printed with : " Notizie intorno agli usi," etc.)

LUCA, S. DE.—Sopra una nuova sorgente d'acqua termo-minerale scoperta nella Solfatara di Pozzuoli.—*Rend. R. Acc. Sci. xiii, pp.* 175–76. *Napoli*, 1874.

LUCA, S. DE.—Ricerche chimiche sull' assorbimento dell' Ammoniaca contenuta nell' aria atmosferica per mezzo della terra della Solfatara di Pozzuoli.—*Rend. R. Acc. Sci. xiv, pp.* 51–53. *Napoli*, 1875.—*C.R. Acad. Sci. lxxx, p.* 674. *Paris*, 1875.

LUCA, S. DE.—Sulla presenza del litio nelle terre e nelle acque della Solfatara di Pozzuoli.—*Rend. R. Acc. Sci. xiv, pp.* 143–45. *Napoli*, 1875.—*Riv. Scient. Ind. Firenze*, 1875.—*C.R. Acad. Sci. lxxxvii, pp.* 174–75. *Paris*, 1878.—*Journ. Pharm. xxix, pp.* 224–25. 1879.

LUCA, S. DE.—L'application des terres volcaniques de la Solfatare de Pouzzoles pour combattre les maladies de la Vigne et d'autres plantes et pour fournir au sol un bon engrais minéral.—4⁰, *pp.* 26. *Naples*, 1877.

LUCA, S. DE.—Observations sur le Sulfure de Carbone, et sur le Sulfocarbonate de Potasse employés pour combattre le Phylloxera.—*See* LUCA.—L'application des terres volcan. de la Solfat. de Pouzzoles, *pp.* 18–21. *Naples*, 1877.

LUCA, S. DE.—Recherches chimiques sur les produits de la Solfatare de Pouzzoles. (Résumé de recherches.)—*C.R. Assoc. franç. pp.* 386–406. 1878.

LUCA, S. DE.—Recherches sur la présence du Lithium dans les terres et dans les eaux thermales de la Solfatare de Pouzzoles.— *C.R. Acad. Sci. lxxxvii, pp.* 174–75. *Paris*, 1878.

LUCA, S. DE.—Sulle variazioni di livello dell' acqua termo-minerale nel pozzo della Solfatara di Pozzuoli.—*Rend. R. Acc. Sci. xvii, pp.* 70–74, 149–50, *Napoli*, 1878 ; *xix, pp.* 38–39, 1880.—*Id. Atti, viii, pp.* 11, 14 *tab.*, 1879 ; *ix, pp.* 2, 1 *pl.*, 1882.

LUCA, S. DE.—Recherches chimiques et thérapeutiques sur l'eau thermale de la Solfatare de Pouzzoles.—8⁰. *Paris*, 1881.

LUCA, S. DE.—Ricerche Sperimentali con note e documenti sulla Solfatara di Pozzuoli. Seconda edizione riveduta ed ampliata.—8⁰, *pp.* 62+10 (cont. list of papers by the author). *Napoli*, 1882.

From pp. 67–101 : Notizie e documenti intorno agli usi dell' Acqua termo-minerale della Solfatara di Pozzuoli, 1 pl., 1 fig.

LUCHESI, A.—Contribuzione allo studio del grande terremoto napoletano del dicembre, 1857.—*Boll. Soc. Sismol. Ital. vi,* 3, *pp.* 67–70. *Modena*, 1900.

LYELL, C.—On the successive changes of the Temple of Serapis.—*Notice Proc. at meeting of members of R. Instit. ii, pp.* 207–14. *London*, 1856.—*Amer. Journ. Sci. S.* 2, *xxii, pp.* 126–29. *New Haven*, 1856.

M * * * (Avocat en Parlement).—Lettres écrites de Suisse, d'Italie, de Sicile et de Malthe, à Mlle. * *à Paris, En 1776, 1777 et 1778.—6 tomes in 3 vols. 12⁰. *T. i, pp.* 454 ; *T. ii, pp.* 509 ; *T. iii, pp.* 536 ; *T. iv, pp.* 418 ; *T. v, pp.* 550 ; *T. vi, pp.* 515. *Amsterdam*, 1780.
See T. ii and iv.

MACAGNO e BERTONI.—Analisi della terra della Solfatara di Pozzuoli.—*R. Staz. Enol. Sperim. ii. Asti*, 1874.

MACINTOSH, C.—The temple of Serapis at Pozzuoli.—"*Athenæum*," *p.* 801. 1848.

MACINTOSH, C.—[On the tides at Naples.] —*Quart. Journ. Geol. Soc. iv, pp.* 191–93. *London*, 1848.

MACKOWEN, J. C.—Capri.—16⁰, *pp. iv+*199, 1 *drawing*, 1 *lith. map* (*reduced from that of the Ist. Topogr. Milit. di Firenze*). [*Napoli*, 1884.]

MADIA.—*See* RONCHI.

MAFFEI, G. C.—Scala naturale, overo fantasia dolcissima intorno alle cose occulte e desirate nella Filosofia.—8⁰, *foll.* 140.

Vinegia, per Gio. Varisco e Compagni, 1573. —Another ed. 8⁰, Venetia, 1564; also: Venetia, appresso Marco Guarischo, 1600. —Another ed. " di nuovo con quella più accurata diligentia, che si è potuto corretta et ristampata." 8⁰, foll. 126. Venetia, appresso Lucio Spineda, 1601. (Nel primo grado della scala Cap. IV.—La Causa perchè in Pozzuolo, et in gran parte del Regno di Napoli piove cenere. Nel secondo grado Cap. I.—Cagion perchè in Pozzuolo sono bagni, puzzo di solfo e perchè ogni trent' anni vi si fanno scissure e voraggini.)

MAGINI, G. A.—Italia. Data in luce da Fabio suo figliuolo al Serenissimo Ferdinado Gonzaga.—fol., pp. 24, 61 maps. Bononiæ, MDCXX.

MAGNATI, V.—Notizie istoriche de terremoti succeduti ne' secoli trascorsi e nel presente. —8⁰, foll. 16+pp. 431. Napoli, 1688.

MAJO.—Trattato delle acque acidule che sono nella città di Castellammare di Stabia. —Napoli, 1754.

MAJONE.—Breve descrizione della Real Città di Somma.—Napoli, 1702.

MALLET, G.—Voyage en Italie dans l'année 1815.—8⁰, pp. 277. Paris, 1817.

MALLET, R.—The great Neapolitan Earthquake of 1857.—2 vols. 8⁰, num. pls. and figs. London, 1862.

MALLET, R.—On some of the conditions influencing the projection of discrete solid materials from Volcanoes, and on the mode in which Pompeii was overwhelmed.— Journ. R. Geol. Soc. Ireland, iv, pp. 144–69, pls. viii–x. Dublin, 1877.

MAMONE, CAPRIA D.—Analisi delle acque minerali del Cotto e Sinigallia.

MANARA.—Le acque d'Ischia.

MANASSE, E.—Rocce trachitiche del cratere di Fondo Riccio nei Campi Flegrei. 3 parti.—Atti R. Acc. Lincei, S. 5, Rend. xi, sem. 1, pp. 85–90, 125–30, 208–12. Roma, 1902.—N. J. f. Min. ii, pp. 369–70. Stuttgart, 1903. (Ref. note by Deecke.)

MANASSE, E.—Di alcune Leucotrefiti di Santa Maria del Pianto nei Campi Flegrei. —Atti Soc. Tosc. Sci. Nat. xiv, Proc. verb. pp. 171–74. Pisa, 1905.

MANEN.—See DARONDEAU.—Carte . . . des côtes d'Italie.

MANGINIE.—See PETRINI.—Campagna Felice, etc.

MANGONI, R.—Ricerche storiche sull' Isola di Capri colle notizie più rilevanti sulla vicina regione del Cratere. Parte Prima (e Seconda).—16⁰, pp. viii+531. Napoli, 1834.

MANGONI, R.—Ricerche topografiche ed archeologiche sull' Isola di Capri da servire di guida a' viaggiatori.—16⁰, pp. 272. Napoli, 1834.

MAPEI, C.—Italy, Classical, Historical and Picturesque. Illustrated in a series of views from drawings by Stanfield, R.A., Roberts, R.A., Harding, Prout, Leitch, Brockedon, Barnard, etc., etc., with descriptions of the scenes. Preceded by an Introductory Essay, on the recent history and present conditions of Italy and the Italians.—fol., pp. cviii+164, 163 pls. London, 1859.——2nd ed. 1864. See pp. 100–13, 163.

MAPEI, C., and CARLYLE, REV. G.—Italy, illustrated and described, in a series of views, from drawings by Stanfield, R.A., Roberts, R.A., Harding, Prout, Leitch, Brockedon, Barnard, etc., etc. With descriptions of the scenes. And an introductory essay, on the political, religious, and moral state of Italy. By Camillo Mapei, D.D. And a sketch of the History and Progress of Italy during the last fifteen years (1847–62), in continuation of Dr. Mapei's essay. By the Rev. Gavin Carlyle, M.A.—gd. 4⁰, pp. viii+cxlvi+168, 65 pls. London, MDCCCLXIV.

MARANTA, B.—De aquæ Neapoli, in Luculliano scaturientis (quam ferream vocant) metallica materia, ac viribus epistola.— 4⁰, parch. Neapoli, 1559. Very rare.

MARCARD.—Sulle stufe dell' Isola d'Ischia. —1778.

MARCELLO, M.—Ischia, canti 3.—Milano, 1863.

MARCHESINO, F.—Copia di una lettera di Napoli che contiene li stupendi e gran prodigii apparsi sopra a Pozzolo.—foll. 4, engrav. frontisp. Napoli, 1538. [C.A.]

MARCHI, L. DE, and FODERA, O.—Notes on the Production of Puzzolana in the Provinces of Rome and Naples.—Eng. and Min. Journ. xxxiv, p. 45. 1882.

MARCHINÆ, M.—Virginis Neapolitanæ Musa posthuma.—12⁰, pp. 12+144. Neapoli, 1701. See De incendio Montis Vesuvii. Ode. p. 118.

MARGERIE, E. DE.—*See* SUESS, E.

MARIENI, L.—*See* SACCHI, G.

MARINELLI, G.—Un ascesa al Monte Epomeo (789 m.) nell' Isola d'Ischia.—*Cronaca bimest. Soc. Alp. Friulana, iv, 4, pp.* 30. *Udine*, 1893.

MARINONI, C.—Contribuzione alla storia naturale della provincia di Terra di Lavoro. —*Ann. Staz. Agr. v. Caserta*, 1877.

MARONE, V.—Memoria contenente un breve ragguaglio dell' Isola d'Ischia e delle acque minerali, arene termali e stufe vaporose che vi scaturiscono colle loro proprietà fisiche chimiche e medicinali, etc.—8⁰, *pp.* 84. *Napoli*, 1847.

MARRA, F. LA.—Antichità di Pozzuoli.— Plates by Falciatore,Philip., Fischetti,Giof., Ricciardelli, Gab., La Marra, Franc., Natali, Gio. Bat., Cla. Nic., Rajola, Thom., Magri, Cajet., Nicole, C. F., De Dominicis, Ant.— *pp.* 107, 68 *pls. and explanation, index. Naples*, 1768.
Pl. xiii shows all the arches of the Mole broken through. Pl. xv shows the floor and platform of the Serapeum to perfection. It was drawn by G. Bat. Natali.

MARSHALL, SARAH.—Ischia.—*Nat. Hist. Notes, iii, pp.* 97–100, 109–11, 121–22, 133–35. 1883.

MARTINO, D. F. DE.—Lettera contenente notizie dei primi fenomeni osservati al ch. P. Denza in data 30 luglio, pubblicata dal Denza.—*Bull. Assoc. Meteor. Agosto*, 1883.

MASELLA, E.—Poesie latine istoriche colle note in italiano.—4⁰, *pp.* 74. *Napoli*, 1795.
Monte Nuovo, 29 Sept., 1538, and Solfatara.

MASINO DI CALVELLO, M. A.—Distinta relatione dell' incendio del sevo Vesuvio alli 16 di Decembre, 1631, successo, con la relatione della città di Pozzuoli, e cause delli terremoti, al tempo di D. Pedro de Toledo Vicerè in questo Regno nell' anno 1534 (1538).—4⁰, *pp.* 36. *Napoli*, 1632. [C.A.]

MASONI, U.—*See* BASSANI, F. 1910.

MAURAND, C.—Der Quai von Santa Lucia. Woodcut on thick paper : 235 × 167 mm.

MAURI, A.—9. Casamicciola. Panorama delle Rovine. Achille Mauri, Napoli, Via Roma, 256.
Photo. : 393 × 270 mm.

MAURI, A.—15. Casamicciola, Rovine. Piccola Sentinella, 1883.—Achille Mauri, Napoli, Via Roma 256.
Photo. : 393 × 270 mm.

MAURO, OGLIALORO-TODARO,ED ALTRI. —Analisi chimica completa delle acque minerali di Castellamare di Stabia.— *Napoli*, 1894.

MAZZELLA, S.—Descrizione del Regno di Napoli.—4⁰. *Napoli, Cappelli*, 1586.

MAZZELLA, S.—Sito ed antichità della città di Pozzuolo e del suo amenissimo distretto con la descrittione di tutti i luoghi notabili, e degni di memoria, e di Cuma, e di Baja, e di Miseno, e de gli altri luoghi conuicini, con le figure degli Edifici, e con gli Epitafi che vi sono . . . Positivi medesimamente tutti i Bagni, e lor proprietà non solo di Pozzuoli, e di Baja ; ma anco dell' Isola d'Ischia, col modo, e regole che quelli s'hanno a pigliare, & a quali infermità giouino, etc.— 8⁰, *pp.* 16+152, 12 *figs. Napoli, Horatio Saluiani*, 1591.—Another ed. 8⁰, *pp.* xvi+ 291, 18 *figs.*, 1 *map. Napoli*, 1595.— Another ed. 8⁰, *pp.* 16+288, *Latin and Italian text* 292. *Stigliola a spese di G. Bonfadini. Napoli*, 1596.——2nd ed. 8⁰, *pp.* xvi+216, 18 *figs.*, 1 *map. Napoli*, 1606.
In the 1606 ed. " Opusculum de Balneis " is paged continuously from 216 to 288. In the 1595 ed. it has separate pagination.

MAZZELLA, S.—Opusculum de Balneis Puteolorum, Baiarium, et Pithecusarum, cum additamentis auctorum omnium qui hactenus de his scripserunt.—8⁰, *pp.* 41. *Napoli*, 1593.
This is bound up with the same author's " Sito ed Antichità della Città di Pozzuoli," etc., 1595, and is called 2ᵃᵈᵃ edizione. In the issue of " Sito " in 1606 this again forms part of the volume, but is here paged from pp. 217–88. This is also denominated 2ᵃᵈᵃ edizione.

MAZZELLA, S.—Apparato delle Statue, nuouamente trouate nella distrutta Cuma, con la dichiarationi & discorfattini dal Sig. Ant. Ferro, della Città di Bitetto, etc.—8⁰, *pp.* ii+103. *Napoli*, 1606.
Forms part of the author's " Sito et antichità di . . . Pozzuoli," 1606 ed.

MAZZELLA, S.—Situs et antiquitas Puteolorum, locorumque vicinorum, etc., etc.— *fol., pp.* 4+92+6. *Lugduni Batavorum, —?*
Earthquakes in Pozzuoli of 1198, 1456 and 1538.

MAZZELLA, S.—Urbium Puteolorum, et Cumarum descriptio, etc., etc.—*fol., pp.* 4+20 +2, *topogr. map. Lugduni Batavorum, —?*

MEAD, R.—Delle Venefiche Esalazioni, etc. —*See* ANON.—Dei Vulcani, etc.

G

MEDNYANSZKY, D. Von.—[Beobachtungen in geologischer Beziehung auf einer Reise durch Italien bis Neapel.]—*Verhandl. Ver. f. Naturk. iv, Sitz. pp.* 95–100. *Presburg,* 1859.

MEISNERO, D.—Thesaurus Philo-Politicus, hoc est Emblemata sive moralia, politica, figuris Œneis incisa, etc.—*obl.* 8⁰, *pp. x. Francofurti,* 1625. [B.M.—Maps 27, a–l.]
Puteoli is represented with the arches of the Mole complete as a causeway and well out of the water.

MELI, R.—Escursioni geologiche al Vesuvio e nei dintorni di Napoli eseguite con gli allievi ingegneri della R. Scuola di Applicazione di Roma nell' anno 1909.—16⁰, *pp.* 15. *Roma,* 1909.

MELLONI, M., & PIRIA, R.—Recherches sur les fumeroles, les solfatares, etc.—*C.R. Acad. Sci. xi, pp.* 352–56. *Paris,* 1840.—*Ann. Chim. lxxiv, pp.* 331–35. *Paris,* 1840. —*Journ. f. Prakt. Chem. xxii, pp.* 52–57. *Leipzig,* 1841.—*Notiz. a. d. Gebiete d. Nat.-u. Heilkunde, xvi, coll.* 33–37. *Erfurt und Weimar,* 1840.

MELLONI, M.—Osservazioni termometriche fatte nel pozzo artesiano che si traforo nella reggia di Napoli.—*Atti Sett. Adun. Scienz. Ital. pp.* 1148–49. *Napoli,* 1846.

MÈNE, C., & ROCCATAGLIATA.—Analyses de quelques eaux des sources thermales d'Ischia près Naples.—*C.R. Acad. Sci. lxvi, p.* 370. *Paris,* 1868.

MERCALLI, G.—I terremoti dell' Isola d'Ischia.—*Atti Soc. Ital. Sci. Nat. xxiv. pp.* 20–37. *Milano,* 1881.—*Boll. R. Com. Geol. Ital. S. 2, ii, pp.* 354–55. *Roma,* 1881.

MERCALLI, G.—L'Isola d'Ischia ed il terremoto del 28 luglio 1883.—*Mem. R. Ist. Lomb. S. 3, vi, pp.* 99–154, 2 *pls.,* 1 *col. map. Milano,* 1884.

MERCALLI, G.—Sulla natura del terremoto Ischiano del 28 Luglio 1883.—*Rend. R. Ist. Lomb. S. 2, xvii, pp.* 842–56. *Milano,* 1884.

MERCALLI, G.—Notizie sullo stato attuale dei vulcani attivi italiani.—*Atti Soc. Ital. Sci. Nat. xxvii, pp.* 184–98. *Milano,* 1884.

MERCALLI, G.—Terremoti napolitani del secolo XVI ed un manoscritto inedito di Cola Anello Pacco.—*Boll. Soc. Geol. Ital. x, pp.* 179–95, 1 *map. Roma,* 1891.

MERCALLI, G.—Il terremoto sentito in Napoli nel 25 gennaio 1893, e lo stato attuale del Vesuvio.—*Boll. mens. Osserv. Centr. Moncalieri, S.* 2, *xiii,* 5. *Torino,* 1893.

MERCALLI, G.—Sul Vesuvio e sui Campi Flegrei.—"*Appennino Meridionale,*" ii, 1–2, *pp.* 6. *Napoli,* 1900.

MERCALLI, G.—Per lo studio dei lenti movimenti del suolo presso il Serapeo di Pozzuoli.—*Atti V. Congr. Geog. Ital. ii, sez.* 1, *pp.* 266–70. *Napoli,* 1904.

MERCALLI, G.—Sullo stato attuale della Solfatara di Pozzuoli.—*Atti Acc. Pontaniana, xxxvii, pp.* 16, 5 *figs. Napoli,* 1907.

MERCALLI, G.—I Vulcani attivi della terra (morfologia, dinamismo, prodotti, distribuzione geografica, cause).—8⁰, *pp. viii*+ 422, 82 *figs.,* 26 *pls. Milano,* 1907.

MERCALLI, G.—Osservazioni sulla temperatura del vapore emanante alla Solfatara di Pozzuoli.—8⁰, *pp.* 3. 1911.—*Atti Congr. Soc. Progr. Sci. Napoli, seduta* 19 *Dic.* 1910. —Also "*Natura,*" *pp.* 16, 1 *fig. Milano,* 1912.

MERCALLI, G.—See BASSANI, F. 1910.

MEUNIER, É. S.—Les Éruptions et les Tremblements de Terre.—[Extr.] *Bull. Soc. Normande Géog.* 3e *cahier de* 1906, 4⁰, *pp.* 173–90. *Rouen,* 1907.

MEURICOFFRE, O., and FIESCHI-RAVASCHIERI, Dᵐˢˢᵃ.—La Carità nell' Isola d'Ischia.—12⁰, *pp.* 175. *Napoli,* 1883.
Also a French ed. without tables of account.

MEYER, F. J. L.—Darstellungen aus Italien. —16⁰, *pp. xvi*+475. *Berlin,* 1792.

MEYER, F. J. L.—Voyage en Italie.—8⁰, *pp. xiv*+426. *Paris, An* x [1802].
See *pp.* 396–418.

MICHALLON.—Vues d'Italie et de Sicile dessinées d'après Nature et lithographiées par MM. Villeneuve, Deroi et Renoux.—*fol. Paris,* 1827.
Of no scientific interest.

MICHALLON.—Dans le Golfe de Naples. Renoux del. I. Lith. de Villain. —Publié par Lami Denozan, Libraire-éditeur, rue des Fosses Montmartre, No. 4. (*From* MICHALLON, A. E.—Vues d'Italie et de Sicile dessinées d'après Nature.—*Paris,* 1827.)
Litho. on straw-col. film, tarantella in foreground : 288×228 mm.

MICHALLON (delᵗ.).—Baie de Naples. Caminade Jne. lith. Lith. de Bichebois

aîné à Saint Denis. A Paris chez Chaillon Potrelle rue St. Honoré No. 140. London, John Spratt, 137 Tottenham Court Road.
Litho. on double paper, monks in foreground : 275 × 232 mm.

MICHALLON (del'.).—Grottes de Sorrente. Caminade Jne. lith. Imprimé par Bichebois aîné et Cie. à Paris chez Chaillon-Potrelle,' rue St. Honoré No. 140. Lith. de Vᵉ. Noël dirigée par Houbloup.
Litho. on double paper : 294 × 194 mm.

MICHALLON (del.).—A Ischia. Rᵐᵉ de Naples. Jacottet lit⁰, fig. par V. Adam. Lith. de Engelmann, rue du faub⁰. Montmartre No. 6.
Three men shooting in foreground, one sitting, and dog : 299 × 251 mm.

MICHALLON (del.).—Vendanges à Naples. Villeneuve, lith. Imp. Lith. de Villain. Chez Sazerac et Duval, éditeurs, Passage de l'Opéra.
Litho. on double paper : 286 × 230 mm. Pl. 3 of Michallon's " Vues d'Italie."

MICHELE, P. DE, e LUCA, B. DE.—La Solfatara di Pozzuoli.—8⁰, *pp.* 108, 4 *pls. Napoli*, 1895.

MICHETTI, P.—Circa l'eruzione di Monti Rotaro, storia dei Monumenti dell' ex reame delle Due Sicilie.

MIDDLETON (publ.).—A View of the Valley of the Sulfatara, otherwise called Vulcan's Cave near Naples. Engraved for Middleton's Complete System of Geography.
Engrav. : 260 × 154 mm.

MIGLIETTA.—Rapporti sull' uso medicinale delle acque minerali del Tempio di Serapide in Pozzuoli.—4⁰, *pp.* 88. *Napoli*, 1818. [C.A.]

MIGLIETTA.—Acqua minerale del Tempio di Serapide in Pozzuoli.—*Giorn. Arcad. Sci. etc. vii, pp.* 150–56. *Roma*, 1820.

MIRABELLA, V.—Notizie intorno all' Isola d'Ischia.

MIRON, F.—Étude des phénomènes volcaniques, tremblements de terre, éruptions volcaniques, le cataclysme de la Martinique, 1902.—8⁰, *pp. viii*+320, *fig. and map. Paris*, 1903.

MISSON, F. M.—Nouveau Voyage d'Italie, fait en l'année 1688. Avec un mémoire contenant des avis utiles à ceux qui voudront faire le mesme voyage.—2 pts. 8⁰. *La Haye*, 1691.——2nd ed. " beaucoup augmentée," etc. 3 vols. 12⁰, *copper engrav. La Haye*, 1694.——3rd ed. 3 vols. 12⁰. *La*

Haye, 1698.——4th ed. 3 vols. 12⁰. *La Haye*, 1702.——Another ed., also called 4th ed., 3 vols. 12⁰. *La Haye*, 1727. [*See* Vol. iii, pp. 72–106.]——5th ed. . . . " augmentée d'un quatrième volume traduit de l'Anglois, et contenant les Remarques que Monsieur Addisson a faites dans son voyage d'Italie."—4 vols. 12⁰. *Utrecht*, 1722.——Another ed., also called 5th ed., 3 vols. 8⁰. *La Haye*, 1731.——Another ed. 4 vols. 12⁰. *Amsterdam*, 1743.
See Vol. ii, pp. 124–57.

MISSON, F. M.—A new voyage to Italy : with a description of the Chief Towns, Libraries, Palaces, Statues, and Antiquities of that Country. Together with useful instructions for those who shall travel thither. Done into English, and adorn'd with figures.—2 vols. 8⁰. *London*, 1695.——Another ed. " with . . . observations on several other countries, as Germany, Switzerland, Savoy, Geneva, Flanders and Holland. . . . Done out of French. The second edition, enlarg'd above one third," etc. 2 vols. 8⁰. *London*, 1699.——4th ed. 2 vols. (4 pts.) 8⁰. *London*, 1714.—— Another ed. 4 vols. 8⁰. —?, 1739.—*See* also HARRIS, J.—Navigantium atque Itinerantium Bibliotheca, etc., *Vol. ii, pp.* 339 [639]–702. *London*, 1705.

MITSCHERLICH.—*See* ROSE, G.

M. J. L. R. [LE RICHE].—Antiquités des environs de Naples, et dissertations qui y sont relatives.—8⁰, *pp.* 392+5, 3 *maps. Naples*, 1820.
See pp. 281–88 : Solfatara.

M. J. L. R. (D. p.).—Grotte de Pausilype près Naples. Witting sc., 2ᵉ Cahier. 6ᵉ Planche.
Dark sepia stippled pl. circa 1820 : 183 × 137 mm.

M. J. L. R. (del.).—Pont dit de Caligula à Pozzuoli. Salathé sculp. 10ᵉ Cah. 50ᵉ Pl.
Stipple engrav. : 185 × 160 mm.

M. J. L. R. (del.).—La Fusaro anciennement Acherusia. Salathé sculp. 11ᵉᵐᵉ Cah. 54ᵉ Pl.
Dark sepia stippled engrav. : 184 × 135 mm.

M. J. L. R. (del.).—Grotte de la Sybille à Cumes. Salathé sculp. 11ᵉᵐᵉ Cahier. 55ᵉ Pl.
Dark sepia stippled engrav. : 183 × 134 mm.

M. J. L. R. (dcl.).—Vue des Étuves de Tritoli à Baja. Salathé sculp.   12ᵐᵉ Cah., 56ᵉ Pl. Dark sepia stippled pl. circa 1820 : 184 × 136 mm.

MONACO, DI.—Saggio analitico ed uso medico delle acque medicinali di Lujo in Terra di Lavoro.—*Napoli*, 1798.

MONACO, E.—Su di una blenda cadmifera del Monte Somma e su di un solfuro arsenicale della Solfatara di Pozzuoli.—*Ann. R. Scuol. sup. agric. S.* 2, iv, pp. 1–12. *Portici*, 1903.

MONTANI, B.—Carta Geognostica del Bacino dei Bagnoli lago di Agnano e loro dintorni Eseguita per ordine dell' Amministratione Gˡᵉ delle Opere di Bonifiche. Napoli, 1856. B. Colao incise sc.—*Ann. Bonificazione, i, tav. ix,* 1858. Hand-coloured engrav., maps and sections : 460 × 320 mm.

MONTEFERRANTE,R.—Analisi delle acque minerali del Cotto e Sinigallia.

MONTHELIER   (del.).   — Castellamare. Strutt sc., 37. Engrav. : 162 × 110 mm.

MONTICELLI, T.—Recherches sur le territoire de Pozzuoles et des Champs Phlégréens.—*Ann. Mines, S.* 2, v, pp. 293–94. *Paris,* 1817.

MONTICELLI, T.—In Agrum Puteolanum Camposque Phlegræos Commentarium.— 4⁰, foll. xiv, pp. 25. *Napoli,* 1826. [C.A.]

MONTICELLI, T.—Sulle origini delle acque del Sebeto di Napoli, etc. (1828).—*Atti R. Ist. Incorag. v, pp.* 1–56, 2 figs. *Napoli,* 1834.

MONTICELLI, T.—Note del Cav. . . . Lette . . . nella tornata de' 13 Marzo e 20 Marzo, 1832.—*Atti Acc. Sci. Sez. Borbonica, iv, pp.* 5–9. *Napoli,* 1839.

MONTICELLI, T. — Opere. — 3 vols. *Vol.* 1, foll. 4, pp. 295, 2 pls.; *Vol.* ii, pp. 335, 7 pls. ; *Vol. iii, pp.* 432, 19 pls., map. *Napoli,* 1841–43.

MORELLI (inc.).—Italia. Napoli. Castello dell' Uovo. Tav. xx, iv. Engrav. : 167 × 105 mm.

MORELLI, F.—Raccolta degli antichi Monumenti esistenti fra Pozzuolo, Cuma e Baja ; Luoghi nel Regno di Napoli. Roma, publ. by Franzetti, [1810 ?] [B.M.—S.136 (43).] Shows part of the Mole of Pozzuoli with some arches intact and well out of the water, and the Temple of Serapis with the central platform well isolated.

MORELLI, F.—Raccolta degli antichi Monumenti esistenti nella città di Pesto e di alcune altre vedute appartenenti alla medesima città. Roma, nella calcografia di Agapito Franzetti a Torsanguigna, ecc.— 20 pls. obl. The first eight refer to Pæstum, 9 to 17 to the Campi Phlegræi, and the two last to Sicily and Etna. The first plate is by Hackert ; it is presumable that the others are also.

MORGAN, LADY.—Italy.—3   vols.   8⁰. *London,* 1821. See Vol. iii, Chapt. 23.

MORGHEN, F.—Environs de Pouzzoles.— [Naples ?] 1766. Pl. 30. [B.N.P.] Shows Temple of Scrapis with upper floor clear ; the Mole of Caligula with all the arches broken.

MORGHEN, F.—[A collection of 84 Views and Plans of Naples and the Vicinity.]— fol. [*Naples,*] 1772–77. See 22 (1), 25 (4), 32 (11), 35 (14), 41 (20), 43 (22), 44 (23), 45 (24), 46 (25), 54 (33), 55 (34), 58 (37), 59 (38), 64 (6), 66 (10), 67 (11 and 12), 68 (13 and 14), 69 (15 and 16), 70 (17 and 18), 71 (19), 76 (29), 77 (31), 78 (32), 81 (35), 83 (37), 84 (38). A fine collection of large plates from different authors.

MORGHEN, F.—Pianta del cratere tra Napoli e Cuma, incisa da Filippo Morghen. — ?,   — ?   [C.A.]

MORGHEN, F. (Appo).—Veduta a Levante della Grotta denominata di Pozzuoli dalla parte di Napoli. A.S.E. il Sigʳ. Guglielᵐᵒ Hamilton, etc. With 4 ref. nos. and text to these. Engrav. : 375 × 262 mm.

MORGHEN, F.—Veduta del Foro di Vulcano denominato la Solfatara.—1 pl. fol. —?, — ?   [O.V.]

MORGHERA, V.—Le Terme dell' Isola d'Ischia prima e dopo gli ultimi Terremoti distruttivi (4 Marzo, 1881, e 28 Luglio, 1883). —8⁰, pp. 4+392. *Napoli,* 1890.

MORMILE, G.—Descrizione della città di Napoli e del suo amenissimo distretto e dell' antichità della città di Pozzuoli.—*Napoli,* 1617.——2nd ed. 8⁰, pp. 248, 3 pls., figs. 1625.——3rd ed. 8⁰, foll. 4, pp. 251+3, num. figs., map of Pozzuoli. *Napoli,* 1670.

MORMILE, G.—Nuovo discorso intorno all' antichità di Napoli, e Pozzuoli.—8⁰, pp. 69. *Napoli,* 1629.

MORO, G.—La grotta del Circeo e il Tempio di Serapide in Pozzuoli.—*Ateneo Veneto, S.* 13, *ii*, 1-2-3. *Venezia*, 1889.

MORO, G.—Dal Lido di Venezia al Tempio di Serapide in Pozzuoli.—8⁰. *Venice*, 1889.

MORTIER, P.—Forum Vulcani vulgo Solfatara. Les Soufrières Montagne du Royaume de Naples.—Chez Pierre Mortier avec Privil. A Amsterdam.—*From* BLAEU : Theatrum Civitatum, etc. 1663.
Very fine engrav. : 523 × 384 mm.

MORTIER, P.—L'Isle d'Ischia, dans le voisinage de Naples. Chez Pierre Mortier, Aamsterdam, avec Privilège. —? 11. Blaev.
A map of Ischia Procida, Misenum and Cuma. Engrav. map: 483 × 376 mm. From BLAEU : Theatrum Civitatum, 1663.

MORTIER, P. (publ.).—Le Lac d'Averno près de Pouzzol dans le Royaume de Naples. No. 15. Se vend à Amsterdam chez Pierre Mortier avec privilège.
Engrav. : 500 × 390 mm. From BLAEU: Theatrum Civitatum, 1663.

MORTIER, P. (publ.).—Puteolani Sinus Prospectus pulcherrimus sive Campaniæ Felicis deliciæ. Le Golfe de Pozzol, ou les Délices de la Campanie Heureuse, dans le Royaume de Naples. A Amsterdam chez Pierre Mortier. Avec privilège.
Two panoramic views of the gulfs of Pozzuoli and Baja with explan.—From BLAEU : Theatrum Civitatum, etc. 1663. No. 18. Engrav. : 519 × 382 mm.

MORTIER, P.—Napoli. A Amsterdam, par Pierre Mortier avec privilège. [Vienna lib.]
A beautifully engraved bird's-eye view of Naples and the Campi Phlegræi, with 29 ref. nos. : 1006 × 425 mm.

MORTIER, P.—Napoli.—*Amsterdam.*
Engraved panoramic plan of Naples in two sheets joined : 997 × 420 mm.

MORTIER, P.—Plan du Port de Naples tel qu'il étoit lors que le Comte d'Oliva estoit Vise-Roy.—A Amsterdam chez Pierre Mortier.
Engrav. plan : 461 × 382 mm.

MORTIER, P.—Pouzol Ville du Royaume de Naples. Pozzuolo.—A Amsterdam. Par Pierre Mortier avec Privilège. No. 14.
A fantastic view of Pozzuoli. Men smoking, fishing, camping and on horseback. Line engrav. : 566 × 413 mm.

MORTIER, P. (publ.).—Terre de Labeur ou Campagna Felix.—*Amsterdam*, —? [B.M. 83.44.]
Shows Palmarola and Faraglione as separate isles of about equal size.

MORYSON, FYNES.—An Itinerary written by . . . First in the Latine Tongue, and then translated by him into English : Containing His Ten Yeeres Travell Throvgh the twelve domjnions of Germany, Bohmerland, Sweitzerland, Netherland, Denmarke, Poland, Jtaly, Turky, France, England, Scotland and Ireland. Diuided into III Parts.—4⁰, *foll.* 6. *Pt. i, pp.* 295 ; *Pt. ii, pp.* 301 ; *Pt. iii, pp.* 292. *London*, 1617.
See Pt. i, Bk. 2.

MULLER, C. T. (publ.).—Ruines d'anciens Édifices appellées École de Virgile à l'extrémité de Pausilipe. No. 8.—Chez C. T. Muller à Naples.
Line litho. [circa 1828]. Monk sitting in foreground : 340 × 240 mm.

MULLER, C. T. (publ.).—Vue du Lac d'Agnano, No. 12. Chez C. T. Muller à Naples.
A line litho. [circa 1828] style Vianelly or Gigante : 347 × 242 mm.

MURICCE, F. C.—I vulcani d'Italia. (Etna, Vesuvio, Campi Flegrei, Isole Eolie, Stromboli.)—1877.

MUSAIO.—*See* FERRERO. 1878.

NAPOLI-CASAMICCIOLA (newspaper, 1 number).—Napoli ai danneggiati di Casamicciola.—*pp.* 6. *Napoli*, 1881. [C.A.]

NAPOLI-ISCHIA.—Numero unico, pubblicato a beneficio dei danneggiati di Casamicciola e Lacco Ameno dagli studenti della Facoltà di Lettere e Filosofia di Napoli.—*pp.* 21. *Napoli*, 1881. [C.A.]

NASINI, R., ANDERLINI, F., e SALVADORI, R.—Sulla probabile presenza del Coronio e di nuovi elementi nei gas della Solfatara di Pozzuoli e del Vesuvio.—*Atti R. Acc. Lincei, S.* 5, *Rend. vii, sem.* 2, *pp.* 73-74. *Roma*, 1898.—*Atti R. Ist. Veneto, S.* 7, *ix, pp.* 1371-72. *Venezia*, 1898.

NASINI, R., ANDERLINI, F., e SALVADORI, R.—Ricerche sulle emanazioni terrestri Ital. II. Gas del Vesuvio dei Campi Flegrei, delle Acque Albule di Tivoli, del Bulicamo di Viterbo, di Pergine, di Salsomaggiore.—*Gazz. Chim. Ital. xxxvi, Pte.* 1, *pp.* 429-57, 9 *tav. Roma*, 1906.

NERO, E. DEL.—Lettera a Niccolò del Benino sul terremoto di Pozzuoli, dal quale ebbe origine la montagna nuova nel 1538.—*Arch. Stor. Ital. ix, pp.* 93-96. *Firenze*,1846.[C.A.]

NEUMAYR, M.—Erdgeschichte.—*Allgemeine Naturkunde*, 8⁰, i, pp. 42+xii+653, very num. illustr. *Leipzig*, 1886.

NIBBY, A.—*See* VASI, M. 1826.

NICCOLINI, A.—Rapporto sulle acque che invadono il pavimento dell' antico edifizio detto il Tempio di Giove Serapide.—4⁰, pp. 7+46, pl. 1. *Napoli*, 1829.

NICCOLINI, A.—Tavola metrico-cronologica delle varie altezze tracciate dalla superficie del mare fra la costa di Amalfi ed il promontorio di Gaeta nel corso di diciannove secoli.—4⁰, pp. 52. *Napoli*, 1839. [C.A.]

NICCOLINI, A.—Sunto delle cose avvenute, e di quanto è recentemente operato nella gran cisterna del Tempio di Serapide per restituire e conservare l'acqua salutifera che in essa sorge.—*Rend. R. Acc. Sci. ii, p.* 339. *Napoli*, 1843.

NICCOLINI, A.—Annunzio di un opera sul Tempio di Serapide in Pozzuoli ed osservazioni sul livello del Mare in quel luogo.—*Atti Sett. Adun. Scienz. Ital. pp.* 487–88. *Napoli*, 1846.

NICCOLINI, A.—Descrizione della Gran-Terma Puteolana volgarmente detta Tempio di Serapide.—4⁰, pp. 95, num. col. and uncol. pls., maps, etc. *Napoli*, 1846.

NICOLOVIUS (des. ap. Nature).—A View in the Island of Ischia, and of the Mountain Epomeo. Letter XCVII.
Engrav. : 248×203 mm.

NICOLUCCI, G.—Analisi microscopica della pretesa muccilagine che si forma sulle acque termo-minerali del Tambura, di Senogalla e della Rete nell' Isola d'Ischia.—*Rend. R. Acc. Sci. i, pp.* 252–56. *Napoli*, 1842.

NISCO, N.—Lettere sull' Isola d'Ischia ed una su Portici cont. in 6 numeri di " Il Diritto."—1869.

NITTI, F.—*See* BASSANI, F. 1910.

NIXON, J.—An account of the Temple of Serapis at Pozzuoli in the Kingdom of Naples.—*Phil. Trans. R. Soc. l, pt.* 1, *pp.* 166–74, 1 pl. *London*, 1758.

NORTHALL, J.—Travels through Italy containing New and curious Observations on that Country ; etc.—8⁰, pp. 476+*index*. *London*, 1766.

NOVI, G.—Due Saggi del tufo vulcanico delle Fontanelle nei Campi Flegrei. [With vegetable remains and shells.]—*Atti Sett. Adun. Scienz. Ital. p.* 1151. *Napoli*, 1846.

NOVI, G.—Degli scavi fatti a Torre del Greco dal 1881 al 1883, primi indizii del probabile Sito di Veseri, Tegiano, Taurania e Retina.—*Atti Acc. Pontaniana, xvi, pt.* 1, pp. 1–36, tav. i–iii. *Napoli*, 1885.

NOVI, G.—Le arene del Volturno ed i terreni donde derivano.

NOVI, G.—Calcarea con *Cardium* contenuta nel tufo di Posilipo ?

NOVI, G.—Il teatro della guerra dal Sett. al Nov. 1860. (Descrizione del terreno tra Maddaloni e la riva diritta del Volturno.)

N. V. A. Formis Romæ.—Puteoli. explicatio. aliquot. locorum quæ Puteolis. Spectantur. — ?, — ?
Bird's-eye map of Posilipo, Astroni, Patria and M. di Procida with 20 ref. nos. Engrav. : 496×375 mm.

N. V. A.—*See* AELST, N. VAN.

OCHME (gem. v.).—Camaldulenser Kloster in Neapel. Jahr 1836. 1 Elle 13 Zoll breit, 1 Elle 8 Zoll hoch. Gest. v. Pescheck.
Engrav. on sheet with similar view of " Haffen von Gaeta " : 157×183 mm.

ODELEBEN, E. G. VON.—Reise in Italien.—2 vols. —?, 1821.

OESTREICH, K.—Die Phlegräischen Felder. —*Sitz. Gesellsch. Beförd. Naturwiss. pp.* 10. *Marburg*, 9 Januar, 1907.

OGLIALORO-TODARO, A.—*See* PALMIERI, L. 1888.

OGLIALORO-TODARO, A.—Tavole dei risultati analitici delle acque minerali di Castellammare di Stabia.—*Rend. R. Acc. Sci. S.* 2, viii, pp. 183–88. *Napoli*, 1894.

OGLIALORO-TODARO, A.—*See* MAURO, 1894.

OGLIALORO-TODARO, A., FORTE, O., CABELLA, A.—Analisi chimica completa qualitativa e quantitativa dell' acqua Amaturo sull' Irno presso Salerno.—*Rend. R. Acc. Sci. S.* 3, i, pp. 240–50. *Napoli*, 1895.

OGLIALORO-TODARO, A., FORTE, O., CABELLA, A.—Analisi chimica completa qualitativa e quantitativa dell' Acqua minerale di Marigliano, pozzo artesiano Montagna.—*Rend. R. Acc. Sci. S.* 3, ii, pp. 38–48. *Napoli*, 1896.

OGLIALORO-TODARO, A.—Acque del Gurgitello delle Terme Belliazzi nell' Isola d'Ischia. (Casamicciola.) Analisi chimica. —*Atti R. Acc. Sci. S.* 2, ix, 7, pp. 34. *Napoli*, 1899.—*Id. Rend. S.* 3, iv, pp. 190–91. 1898.

OPPENHEIM, P.—Beiträge zur Geologie der Insel Capri und der Halbinsel Sorrent. —*Zeitschr. deutsch. geol. Gesellsch. xli, pp.* 442–90. *Berlin,* 1890.

OPPENHEIM, P.—Die Insel der Sirenen von ihrer Entstehung bis zur Gegenwart. Eine populäre Darstellung der physischen und politischen Geschichte der Insel Capri. Mit einer geologischen Karte der Insel Capri.—8⁰, *pp.* 32. *Berlin,* [1890].

OPPENHEIM, P.—Die Geologie der Insel Capri ; eine Entgegnung an Herrn Johannes Walther.—*Zeitschr. deutsch. geol. Gesellsch. xlii, pp.* 758–64. *Berlin,* 1891.

OPPENHEIM, P.—Die Geologie der Insel Capri. Ein offener Brief an Herrn Joh. Walther in Jena. Nebst einigen Bemerkungen über Ausdehnung und Berichtigung der bei der Zeitschrift der deutschen geologischen Gesellschaft gehandhabten Censur.—8⁰, *pp.* 24. *Berlin,* 1891.

OPPENHEIM, P.—Ancora intorno all' Isola di Capri.—*Riv. Ital. Paleontol. i,* 4, *pp.* 152–56. *Bologna,* 1895.

O'REILLY, J. P.—The earthquake of Ischia, July 28, 1883.—" *Nature,*" *xviii, p.* 461. 1883.

ORLANDI, JOANNES.—*See* GRASSUS BARTOLOMEŒUS.

ORLICH, L. VON.—Die Insel Ischia.— *Zeitschr. f. allgem. Erdkund. ii, pp.* 388–416. *Berlin,* 1854.

ORTELIUS, A.—Theatrum Orbis Terrarum. D. Philippo Austriaco ded. consecratque Adolphi Mekerchi. . . . Frontispicii explicatio Abrahamas Ortelius Antverpianus, benevolis Lectoribus. S.D. Catalogos Auctorum Tabulorum Geographicorum, etc.—1st ed. *fol.,* maps 1–53 (engraved by many authors). *Antwerpiæ,* 1570.
There were editions again in 1570, with col. pl., 1571, 1571 (in Dutch), 1572, 1573 (Additamentum), 1574, 1575, 1579, 1580, 1581, 1584 (with Additamentum), 1587, 1589, 1590, 1592, 1595, 1598 (the year of the Author's death). Further editions, edited by John Moretus, appeared in 1601 epitome, 1602 Tabulis Aliquot novis, 1603, 1606, 1609, 1612, 1619 Parergi, 1624, 1631, the last by Blaeu. In all these editions in the map of S. Italy the I. of Parmarola is much exaggerated in size and there are no indications of its being divided. A special plate with map of Ischia appears for the first time in the Additamentum of 1584, and occurs in all subsequent editions. For

further details on Ortelius, consult HESSELS, J. H.—Abraham Ortelii (Geographi Antverpiensis et virorum eruditorum ab eundem, etc.).—*sm. fol. Cantabrigiæ,* 1887.

ORTELIUS, A., HOEFNAGLIUS, A. O. G. —Baiis. Nullus in orbe locus Baiis prælucet amœnis [with explanatory text at back]. —?, 1580 (looks like 1780). [Vienna lib.] 488 × 332 mm.

ORTELIUS, A., & HOEFNAGLIUS, A. O. G. —Baiis. Nullus in orbe locus prælucet amœnis, etc.—*From* BRAUN, G., and HOHENBERG, F.—Civitates Orbis Terrarum. Lib. III.—*Coloniæ Agrippinæ,* 1582–1618.
A view of Pozzuoli and Baja, with Monte Nuovo, Misenum, etc. Reference letters to Y, dated 1580, with groups of flowers, fruit and cornucopiæ, and one page of Latin text.—Engrav. panorama : 493 × 335 mm. Two copies with Latin text different in the two ed.

ORTELIUS, A., & HOEFNAGLIUS, A. O. G. —Hic est introitus Antri Sibylle Cumane, quod vulgo appellatur Grotta della Sibylla, etc. Lacus Agnianus piscibus, carens ranis ac serpentibus scatens, etc., Charoneum Antrum sine spiraculum, etc., Sudatorium S. Germani.—*From* BRAUN, G., and HOHENBERG, F.—Civitates Orbis Terrarum.—*Coloniæ Agrippinæ,* 1582–1618.
Views of Lakes Avernus and Agnano. One page of text in Latin.

ORTELIUS, A.—Theatro del Mondo nel quale distintamente si dimostrano, in Tavole, tutte le Provincie, Regni e Paesi del Mondo, etc. . . . Ridotto à intiera perfettione, e in questa picciol forma, per maggior commodità de' Viaggianti.—16⁰, *foll.* 2, *pp.* 232 *and index, num. maps. Venetia, per Sc. Banca,* 1667.
See map and text, p. 271 : Ischia.

ORTELIUS, A., HOEFNAGLIUS, A. O. G. —[Views of Lakes Avernus and Agnano surrounded by florid scroll frames and Latin references.] [Vienna lib.] Engrav. : 470 × 325 mm.

OWENSON, S.—*See* MORGAN, LADY.— Italy, 1821.

PACCA.—*See* COLLENUCCIO. 1591.

PACI, G. M.—*See* PETRUCCELLI, F.

PACICHELLI, G. B.—Memorie de' Viaggi per l'Europa Christiana scritte a diversi in occasione de' suoi Ministeri.—5 pts. 12⁰. *Pte. i, pp.* 40+743+53 ; *Pte. ii, pp.* 8+

827+40 ; *Pte. iii, pp.* 8+761+27 ; *Pte. iv, vol.* 1, *pp.* 4+541+20 ; *Pte. v, vol.* 2, *pp.* 4+438+18. *Napoli*, 1685.
See Pte. iv, vol. 1, pp. 196 *et seq.* : Della Solfatara.

PALATINO, L.—Storia di Pozzuoli e contorni con breve trattato istorico di Ercolano, Pompei, Stabia e Pesto.—8⁰, *pp.* 336, 9 *pls. Napoli*, 1826.

PALLOTTA, DOTT. G.—Brevi cenni sulla uniformità delle Terme di Casamicciola animate dall' unica acqua di Gurgitello.—*Napoli*, 1873.

PALMERI, P., & COPPOLA, M.—Acque minerali del Pio Monte della Misericordia in Casamicciola (Ischia). Analisi chimiche delle acque, delle concrezioni e dell' atmosfera delle stufe.—*Napoli*, 1875–76.

PALMERI, P.—Ricerche storiche sul nome e sul luogo e confronti delle analisi delle acque di Gurgitello.—*Napoli*, 1879.

PALMERI, P.—Le terme del Pio Monte della Misericordia in Casamicciola (Ischia) dopo il terremoto del 4 maggio 1881.—4⁰, *pp.* 11. *Napoli*, 1881. [C.A.]

PALMERI, P.—Il pozzo artesiano dell' Arenaccia del 1880 confrontato con quello del Palazzo Reale di Napoli del 1847.—*Lo Spettatore del Vesuvio e dei Campi Flegrei, N.S. i, pp.* 53–58, 1 *pl. Napoli*, 1887. [C.A.]

PALMIERI, L.—On some Volcanic Phenomena lately observed at Torre del Greco and Resina. [Abstr.]—*Quart. Journ. Geol. Soc. xviii, p.* 126. 1862.

PALMIERI, L.—Communicazione (sopra una scossa di terremoto avvenuta il 30 Gennaio 1863 nell' Isola d'Ischia).—*Rend. R. Acc. Sci. ii, pp.* 51–52. *Napoli*, 1863.

PALMIERI, L. (relatore), GASPARIS, A. DE, GUISCARDI, G.—Rapporto sulla proposta di nuove indagini sulle variazioni del livello del mare nel Golfo di Napoli.—*Rend. R. Acc. Sci. ii, pp.* 220–24. *Napoli*, 1863.

PALMIERI, L.—Sulle scosse di terremoto avvertite in Napoli il dì 24 Giugno [1870].—*Rend. R. Acc. Sci. ix, pp.* 127–28. *Napoli*, 1870.

PALMIERI, L.—Il Litio scoperto dal Prof. S. De Luca nelle terre della Solfatara, riveduto con lo spettroscopio.—*Rend. R. Acc. Sci. xiv, p.* 151. *Napoli*, 1875.

PALMIERI, L.—Intorno ad un piccolo terremoto accaduto in Napoli il 18 Febbraio [1876].—*Rend. R. Acc. Sci. xv, p.* 84. *Napoli*, 1876.

PALMIERI, L.—Le terme del Pio Monte della Misericordia in Casamicciola (Ischia) dopo il terremoto del 4 Marzo 1881.—*Ann. R. Scuola Agric. Portici, ii, pp.* 441–49. *Napoli*, 1880.

PALMIERI, L.—Sul terremoto di Casamicciola del 4 Marzo 1881.—*Rend. R. Acc. Sci. xx, pp.* 82–89. *Napoli*, 1881.

PALMIERI, L., & OGLIALORO-TODARO, A.—Sul terremoto dell' Isola d'Ischia della sera del 28 Luglio, 1883.—*Atti R. Acc. Sci. S.* 2, *i*, 4, *pp.* 28, 1 *map. Napoli*, 1888.

PALMIERI, L.—Osservazioni simultanee sul dinamismo del Cratere Vesuviano e della grande fumarola della Solfatara di Pozzuoli, fatte negli anni 1888–89–90.—*Rend. R. Acc. Sci. S.* 2, *iv, pp.* 206–8. *Napoli*, 1890.—*Ann. Meteor. Ital. vi, pp.* 141–44. *Torino*, 1891.

PALMIERI, L.—Il Vesuvio e la Solfatara contemporaneamente osservati.—*Rend. R. Acc. Sci. S.* 2, *v, pp.* 161–62. *Napoli*, 1891.

PALMIERI, L.—Analisi fisico-chimiche delle fumarole antiche e moderne dell' Isola d'Ischia.

PAMPALONI, L.—Le roccie trachitiche degli Astroni nei Campi Flegrei. I. Roccie del cratere scoriaceo centrale.—*Atti R. Acc. Lincei, S.* 5, *Rend. viii, sem.* 1, *pp.* 86–91. *Roma*, 1899.—II. Esemplari della corrente laterale.—*Idem.—pp.* 133–39. 1899.

PAMPALONI, L.—Scorie trachitiche dell' Averno nei Campi Flegrei.—*Atti R. Acc. Lincei, S.* 5, *Rend. x, sem.* 1, *pp.* 151–56. *Roma*, 1901.

PANVINI, P.—Il forestiere alle antichità e curiosità naturali di Pozzuoli, Cuma, Baja e Miseno in tre giornate.—8⁰, *pp. viii*+156, 53 *pls. Napoli*, 1818.

PAOLI, P. ANT.—Le antichità di Pozzuoli.—*Napoli*, 1768.—*See* MARRA.

PAOLINI, R.—Memorie sui Monumenti di Antichita e di Belli Arti ch'esistono in Miseno, in Baoli, in Baja, in Cuma, in Pozzuoli, in Napoli, in Capua Antica, in Ercolano, in Pompei ed in Pesto.—4⁰, *foll. v*+*pp.* 346. *Napoli*, 1812.

PAOLINI, V.—*See* GALDIERI, A. 1913.

PAONI, B.—Ischia e le sue Terme.—8⁰, *pp.* 26. *Napoli*, 1877.

PAONI, B.—*See* ZINNO, S. 1880.

PARASCANDOLO, M.—Cenni storici intorno alla Città ed Isola di Procida.—8⁰, *pp.* 306. *Napoli*, 1892.

PARASCANDOLO, M.—Procida dalle origini ai tempi nostri.—8⁰, *pp.* 527, 1 *map.* *Benevento*, 1893.

PARBONI, A. (inc.).—Italia. Napoli. Tav. XLIII. Pozzuoli. Tempio di Giove Serapide.
Coarse line engrav. : 155 × 106 mm.

PARENTE, M.—Parthenope terræmotu vexata Magnam Matrem publicæ securitatis sospitem diligit, et ejusdem dolorum cultui se addicit. Carmen.—4⁰, *pp.* 11. *Neapoli*, 1830.

PARETO, L.—Rapporto sopra la gita ai Campi Flegrei.—*Atti Sett. Adun. Scienz. Ital. pp.* 1117-24. *Napoli*, 1846.

PARETO, L.—Della posizione delle roccie pirogene ed eruttive dei periodi terziario quaternario ed attuale in Italia.—8⁰, *pp.* 35. *Genova*, 1852.

PARIS (del.).—IIᵉ Vue du Temple de Serapis à Pouzzols tel qu'il existe actuellement, dessinée d'après Nature par Paris Architecte. Ch. Guttemberg sculp. No. 5, A.P.D.R.
Fine line engrav. : 215 × 144 mm.

PARKIN, J.—The remote cause of epidemic diseases ; or, the influence of volcanic action in the production of general pestilences. Part II.—8⁰, *pp.* 16+*foll.* 4, *pls.* 3. *London*, 1853.

PARONA, C. F.—Sulla presenza dei calcari a Toucasia carinata nell' Isola di Capri.—*Atti R. Acc. Lincei, S.* 5, *Rend. xiii, sem.* 1, *pp.* 165-67. *Roma*, 1904.

PARONA, C. F.—Nuove osservazioni sulla fauna dei calcari con ellipsactinidi dell' Isola di Capri.—*Atti R. Acc. Lincei, S.* 5, *Rend. xiv, sem.* 1, *pp.* 59-69. *Roma*, 1905.

PARRINO, A. — Moderna distintissima descrizione di Napoli, Città nobilissima, antica e fedelissima, e del suo Seno Cratere.—Aggiunte, osservazioni e correzioni a questo primo tomo della nuova descrizione di Napoli.—2 vols. 12⁰. *Vol. i, pp.* 20+438+54+46+2 ; *Vol. ii, pp.* 16+292+23, 28 *pls.* *Napoli*, 1703-4.

PARRINO, A.—Nuova Guida dei Forestieri per osservare e godere le curiosità più vaghe della Fedelissima Gran Napoli.—38 *pls.* *Napoli*, 1709.—Also : 1712.—Also : 12⁰, *pp.* 16+371, *index,* 28 *figs. and frontisp.* 1714. (The views are very rough and incorrect, none of Pozzuoli.)—Also : 12⁰, *foll.* 18+*pp.* 382, 31 *maps,* 30 *pls.* 1725. [C.A.]—Also : 8⁰, *pp.* 4+269+14. 1727.

—Also : 12⁰, *foll.* 2+*pp.* 269, 30 *pls.,* 9 *maps.* 1751. [C.A.] (The views of Pozzuoli are very poor and sketchy.)

PARRINO, A.—Nuova Guida de' Forastieri per osservare, e godere le curiosità più vaghe, e più rare della Real Fedeliss. Gran NAPOLI, città antica, e nobilissima, In cui si dà distinto ragguaglio delle varie opinioni dell' origine di essa, e Strade, Fabbriche, Chiese, Pitture, Statue, Dogi regnanti, Vescovi, & Arcivescovi, che la governarono, con tutto ciò, che di più bello, e di più buono della medesima città si trova; Ricavato dagl'Autori impressi, e manoscritti che di essa trattano ; Adornata con Figure delle sue più nobili Vedute, intagliate in Rame. Opera . . . consecrata Agl'Illustriss. ed Eccellentiss. Signori Li Signori ELETTI Della Fedelissima Gran Città di Napoli.—12⁰, *foll.* 17+*pp.* 371+*foll.* 30, 17 *pls.* *Napoli, Appresso Domenico-Antonio Parrino,* 1712.

PARRINO, A.—Nuova Guida de' Forastieri, per l'Antichità Curiosissime di Pozzuoli ; dell' Isole aggiacenti d'Isca, Procida, Nisida, Capri, Colline, Terre, Ville, e Città, che giaccioni intorno alle Riviere dell' uno, e l'altro lato di Napoli, detto Cratero. Colla descrizione della città di Gaeta. Il tutto epilogato dagli Autori impressi, e manoscritti, che ne han trattato. Adornata di 38. bellissime Figure intagliate in Rame. Dedicata all' Illustrissimo Signore Il Signor D. Diego Ripa De' Baroni di Pianchetella.—12⁰, *pp.* 257+*foll.* 4, 30 *pls.* *Napoli, Presso il Parrino,* MDCCXXV.

PARRINO, A.—Nuova Guida de' Forastieri per l'Antichità Curiosissime di Pozzuoli : dell' Isole adjacenti d'Ischia, Procida, Nisida, Capra, . . . e città, che sono intorno alle Riviere dell' uno, e l'altro lato di Napoli, detto Cratere. Colla Descrizione della Città di Gaeta.—8⁰, *pp.* 4+269+14, 30 *pls., map.* *Napoli, Parrino,* 1727. [B.M. 719.]
Dedicated to Diego Ripa di Pianchetella.

PARRINO, A.—Nuova Guida de' Forestieri per l'Antichità di Pozzuoli, e di tutte le Città, e Luoghi, et Isole, che sono alla veduta presso il mare dalla parte destra della città di Napoli.—12⁰, *num. figs.* *Napoli, Parrino,* 1727.

PARRINO, A.—Nuova Guida de' Forestieri per l'Antichità Curiosissime di Pozzuoli ; Dell' Isole adjacenti d'Ischia, Procida Nisida, Capri, Colline, Terre, Ville, e Città, che sono intorno alle Riviere dell' uno, e l'altro lato di Napoli, detto Cratero. Colla descrizione della città di Gaeta. Il tutto epilogato dagli Autori impressi e manoscritti, che ne han trattato. Adornate di 30. bellissime Figure intagliate in Rame. Ed in questa ultima Edizione di nuovo ricorretta, ed aumentata.—12°, *foll.* 2+*pp.* 269+*foll.* 9, 29 *pls. Napoli, A spese di Giuseppe Buono,* MDCCLI.

PARRINO, A.—Nuova Guida de' Forastieri per osservare, e godere la curiosità più vaghe, e più rare della Fedelissima Gran NAPOLI città antica, e nobilissima In cui si dà anco distinto ragguaglio delle varie opinioni dell' origine di essa ; Dogi, regnanti, Vescovi, ed Arcivescovi, che la governarono : Con tutto ciò, che di più bello, e di più buono nella medesima si ritrova. Ricavato dagl'Autori impressi, e manoscritti, che di essa trattano. Adornata con Figure delle sue più nobili Vedute, intagliate in Rame. Accresciuta con moderne notizie da NICCOLO' suo Figlio. —12°, *foll.* 2+*pp.* 409+*foll.* 14, 35 *pls. Napoli, A spese di Giuseppe Buono,* 1751.

PASCA, W.—Intorno ad una pozzolana rinvenuta presso Itri e delle pozzolane in generale.—*Napoli, Tip. Bonis.*

PASCALE, V.—Descrizione storico-topografico-fisica delle Isole del regno di Napoli. —16°. *Napoli,* 1796. *See* Cap. VI, pp. 95–107.

PASINI, L.—[Sul pozzo artesiano di Napoli.] —*Atti I.R. Ist. Veneto, v, pp.* 234 *et seq. Venezia,* 1845–46.

PASQUALE, G. A.—Flora Vesuviana, o catalogo ragionato delle Piante del Vesuvio confrontate con quelle dell' Isola di Capri e di altri luoghi circostanti.—*Atti R. Acc. Sci. iv,* 6, *pp.* 142. *Napoli,* 1869.—*See* VESUVIUS.

PELLÉ, C.—Il Mediterraneo illustrato le sue Isole e le sue Spiagge comprendente la Sicilia, ecc. ecc.—4°, *pp.* 512, *num. pls. Firenze,* 1841.

PELLEGRINO, C.—Discorsi sulla Campania Felice.—4°, *foll.* 56, *pp.* 780, 1 *pl. Napoli,* 1631. [C.A.]

PELLEGRINO, CAMILLO, figl. di ALESS.— Descrittione della Campania Felice nella maniera dimostrata ne' suoi Discorsi. Jacob' Thoneno Lotharing ? sculp.—1651. [B.N.P.—Vb. 113. No. 3.] Vesuvius is represented as a symmetrical, large-mouthed crater. *See* also in GRÆVIUS, J. G.—Thesaurus Antiquitatum et Hist. Italiæ.

PELLEGRINO, CAMILLO (the younger).— Dissertationes de Campania Felice. Ex Italico in Latinum transtulit et animadversionem adjecit A. Dukerus.—*See* GRÆVIUS.—Thesaurus Antiquitatum et Historiarum Italiæ, *T. ix, pt.* 2. 1725, *etc.*

PELORITANO, PENSANTE (pseud.) [*i.e.* I. V. Paterno, Prince di Biscari].—Descrizione del terribile terremoto de' 5 Febraro, 1783, che afflisse la Sicilia, distrusse Messina, e gran parte della Calabria. [Edited by M. Torcia.]—8°, *pp. xi*+118. *Napoli,* 1784.

PENTLAND, B.—Osservazioni intorno al Tempio di Serapide in Pozzuoli.—*Atti Sett. Adun. Scienz. Ital. pp.* 1125–27. *Napoli,* 1846.

PEPE, G.—*See* BASSANI, F. 1910.

PEPE, V.—Sunto delle analisi praticate nell' Isola d'Ischia.

PERRIER (gravé par).—Plan de la ville de Naples. A.P.D.R. No. 46. With 60 ref. nos. : 351 × 243 mm.

PERRONE, C.—Ricordi. Casamicciola e le sue rovine. Cenni storico-geografico-cronologici editi per cura del tipografo Prete.— 8°, *pp. xlvii*+52, 1 *pl. Napoli,* 1883.

PETER, J.—L'Italie inconnue.—Aux Îles Ponza.—8°, *pp.* 39. *Genève,* 1895.

PETERMANN, A. H.—Uebersicht des vulkanischen Heerdes im Mittelmeer. Maasstab 1 : 15,000,000.—*Peterm. Mitth. Taf.* 7. *Gotha,* 1866.

PETIT-RADEL, P. — Voyage historique, chorographique et philosophique dans les principales villes de l'Italie, en 1811 et 1812. —3 vols. 8°. *Vol. i, pp. xlviij*+348, 1 *map ; Vol. ii, pp.* 578 ; *Vol. iii, pp.* 592. *Paris,* 1815. *See* T. 3, pp. 204–5 : concerning state of Temple of Scrapis.

PETRACCONE, E.—L'Isola di Capri.—*pp.* 124, 130 *illustr.—See* RICCI, C.—Napoli, No. 72, in " *Collezione di Monografie Illustrate.*"—*Italia Artistica.—S.* 1. 1902, *etc.*

PETRINI (publ.).—Campagna Felice e Terra di Lavoro Meridionale delineata gia dal Manginie.—*Napoli* ? [B.M.—K. 83.46 b.]

PETRINI, N.—Mappa di Pozzuoli secondo lo stato presente 1750. [B.M.—K. 83–77.]

PETRINI, P. (publ.).—Pianta ed alzata della città di Napoli, fatti con ogni essatezza nuovamente data alla luce.—*Napoli*, 1718. A good view-map of Naples and Elysian Fields. Another ed. 1748. [B.M. 24045. 13 and 29.]

PETRINI, P.—Vedute delle antichità dell città di Pozzuoli, etc.—*obl. 4⁰, 16 pls. and frontisp. Naples*, 1718. [B.N.P.] Shows the Mole of Caligula with a few remaining arches.

PETRONIO, F.—Analisi delle acque minerali Cotto e Sinigallia.

PETRUCCELLI, F., e PACI, G. M.— Memoria chimico-medica su l'acqua termo-minerale del Bagnolo nelle vicinanze di Napoli.—*8⁰, pp.* 18. *Napoli*, 1832. [C.A.]

PETTERUTI, G.—La Solfatara di Pozzuoli. —*L'Idrologia medica, ii*, 9, 10 e 11.—Il Golfo di Napoli.—*Idem*, 40. *Bassano*, 1880.

PFLAUMERN, J. H. A.—Mercurius Italicus hospiti fidus per Italiæ et urbes, etc.—*8⁰, pp.* 32+484+2. *Augustæ Vindelicorum*, 1625. *See* pp. 371 *et seq.* Campi Phlegræi.

PHILIPPI, R. A.—Ueber die subfossilen Seethier-Reste von Pozzuoli bei Neapel und auf der Insel Ischia.—*N. J. f. Min. v, pp.* 285–92. *Stuttgart*, 1837.

PHILIPPI, R. A.—Notizie geologiche e con-chiologiche ricavate da una lettera del Dr. . . . ad A. Scacchi.—*Rend. R. Acc. Sci. i, pp.* 86 *bis*–90 *bis*. *Napoli*, 1842.

PHIPSON, T. L.—On the medicinal muds of the Island of Ischia, Bay of Naples.—*Rept. British Assoc.* (1864), *Not. and Abstr. pp.* 38–39. 1865.—*Chemical News, x, p.* 186. 1864. —*Journ. Chim. Med. ii, pp.* 274–76. 1866.— *C.R. Acad. Sci. lxii, pp.* 59–60. 1866.

PIGNATELLO, A.—Rime date nuovamente alle stampe, e dedicate al sig. Principe di S. Severo.—*4⁰, pp.* 8+94. *Napoli e Gallipoli*, 1593. *See* Sonetto C. alla Solfatara di Pozzuoli, pp. 69.

PIGRATELLI, J. (del.).—Residenz Stadt und Hafen von Neapel. Wizani jun. sc. Im Kunstverlag von L. v. Kleist zu Dresden. Hand-col. litho. very incorrect and sketchy, of no value : 534×401 mm.

PILLA, L., & CASSOLA, F.—Lo Spetta-tore del Vesuvio e dei Campi Flegrei.—*8⁰. Fasc. i, Nos.* 1–3, *pp.* 35+24+31 ; *Fasc. ii, Nos.* 1–3, *pp.* 92. *Napoli*, 1832–33.

PILLA, L.—Osservazioni geognostiche sulla parte settentrionale ed orientale della Campania.—*Ann. Civ. Reg. Due Sicilie, iii, pp.* 117–47. *Napoli*, 1833.

PILLA, L.—Bollettino geologico del Vesuvio e dei Campi Flegrei, destinato a far seguito allo Spettatore del Vesuvio.—*Ann. R. Oss. Vesuv. 8⁰, 1–5, pp.* 35+30+28+31+40. *Napoli*, 1833–34.—*Il Progr. Sci. viii, pp.* 129–56 ; *ix, pp.* 126–49 ; *x, pp.* 262–89 ; *xvi, pp.* 223–53. *Napoli*, 1834–37.—Also in German : *See* ROTH, J.—Der Vesuv und die Umgebung von Neapel.

PILLA, L.—Nota sulla quistione del Serapeo toccata dal Cav. Tenore.—*Il Progr. Sci. etc. xix, pp.* 242–45. *Napoli*, 1838.

PILLA, L.—Application de la Théorie des Cratères de Soulèvement au volcan de Roccamonfina (Ponza).—*Paris, Bertrand*, 1844.—*Mém. Soc. géol. France, S. 2, i, pt. 1, pp.* 163–79, *pls. iv–vi. Paris*, 1844.— [Abstr.] *Bull. id. xiii, pp.* 402-3. 1842.— *See* VESUVIUS.

PILLA, L.—Trattato di geologia.—2 vols. 8⁰. *Vol. i, pp. xiv+*549, *num. figs., Pisa*, 1847 ; *Vol. ii, pp.* 614, *num. figs., Pisa*, 1847–51. *See* Vol. i.

PILLA, N.—1° e 2° viaggio geologico per la Campania.—*8⁰. Napoli*, 1814.

PILLA, N.—Geologia vulcanica della Campania.—2 vols. 8⁰. *Vol. i, pp. xix+*125 ; *Vol. ii, pp.* 160. *Napoli*, 1823.

PINELLI, B.—Nuova raccolta di venti-quattre vedute de' Contorni di Napoli incise da Bartolomeo Pinelli.—*sm. obl. 8⁰. Roma*, 1823.

PINI, E.—Viaggio geologico per diverse parti meridionali dell' Italia.—2nd ed. *pp.* 2+ 156, 2 *pls. Milano*, 1802 [?1803]. *See* Temple of Serapis. He discusses Monte Nuovo.

PIRANESI.—*See* GIRAUD. 1771.

PIRIA, R.—*See* MELLONI. 1840.

PIRIA, R.—Sull' azione che alcuni corpi riscaldati esercitano sui vapori che si sviluppano da' fumaroli della Solfatara.

PISTOLESI, E.—Guida metodica di Napoli e suoi contorni per vedere con nuovo metodo la città, adornata di pianta e vedute litografate.—12⁰, *pp. xi+*706. *Napoli*, 1845. *See* pp. 433–82 and pl. at p. 453 of Temple of Serapis.

PIUTTI, A., & EMILIO, L. D'.—Analisi dell' acqua Apollo delle Sorgenti di Agnano.—*Rend. R. Acc. Sci. S.* 3, x, pp. 91–108. *Napoli*, 1904.

PIUTTI, A.—L'Elio nei minerali recenti.—*Rend. R. Acc. Sci. S.* 3, xvi, pp. 30–32, 1 tab. *Napoli*, 1910.

PLOIX, E.—*See* DARONDEAU.—Carte ... des côtes d'Italie.

POLEHAMPTON, E., and GOOD, J. M.—The Gallery of Nature and Art, in six volumes, illustr. with one hundred engravings.—2nd ed. 8⁰. *Vol. i, pp.* vi+x+527 ; *Vol. ii, pp.* vi+488 ; *Vol. iii, pp.* iv+441 ; *Vol. iv, pp.* vi+552 ; *Vol. v, pp.* vi+685 ; *Vol. vi, pp.* vi+600+24. *London*, 1818.
See Vol. ii, pp. 103–13, and Vol. iii, pp. 56–63.

POLI, G. S.—Memoria sul tremuoto de' 26 Luglio del corrente anno 1805.—*foll.* 3. *Napoli*, 1806.

POMBA, Cav. C.—L'Italia nel suo Aspetto Fisico.—*Pub. G. B. Paravia e C., Torino, Roma, Milano, Firenze, Napoli*, 1890.
Scale 1 : 100,000 horiz. and vert. Raised map on section of globe.

PONZI, G.—Osservazioni geologiche fatte lungo la Valle Latina da Roma a Monte Cassino.—*Atti Acc. Pont. N. Lincei, i, pp.* 182–95. *Roma*, 1851.—*Corrisp. Scient.* ii. *Roma*, 1853.—*N. Ann. Sci. nat. x.* 1848.

PORRO, C.—La Campania. Studio geografico, 1898.—*2 maps and 1 geol. sketch* (autogr.). — ?, — ?

PORTA, LEONARDO.—Memoria Geologica sull' Isola d'Ischia (title only).—*Atti Sett. Adun. Scienz. Ital.* p. 1126. *Naples*, 1846.

PORTII, S.—*See* PORZIO, S.

PORZIO, S.—De conflagratione Agri Puteolani.—8⁰, pp. 8, frontisp. *Napoli*, 1538.
The only known copy of this ed. is in C.A.
Another ed. : 4⁰, pp. 8. *Florentiæ*, 1551. [B.N.]—*See also* GIUSTINIANI, L. 1812.

PRELLER.—Collection of plans and views in Italy. Photos of M.S., 1860–61.—[B.M. $\frac{20660}{2101}$]
Good outline drawing of Cap Misenum.

PRÉVOST, L. C.—Voyage à l'Île Julia, à Malte, en Sicile, aux Iles Lipari et dans les environs de Naples.—*C.R. Acad. Sci.* ii, pp. 243–54. *Paris*, 1836.

PRÉVOST, L. C.—Théorie des soulèvements.—*Bull. Soc. géol. France, xi, pp.* 183–203. *Paris*, 1839–40.

PRIMAVERA, G.—Analisi delle acque minerali Cotto Sinigallia.

PROCTOR, R. A.—Le Vésuve et Ischia.—*Rev. mens. Astron. pop. pp.* 340–43. *Paris, Sept.* 1883. [C.A.]—In English : *"Knowledge,"* iv, pp. 81–82. *London*, 1883.

PROUT, S.—*See* ROSCOE, T. 1849–50.

PROUT, S.—*See* MAPEI, C.—Italy, Classical, Historical and Picturesque, 1859.

PUGGAARD, C.—Description géologique de la Péninsule de Sorrento.—*Bull. Soc. géol. France, xiv, pp.* 294–342, map. *Paris*, 1857.

PUGGAARD, C.—Notice sur les calcaires plutonisés de la péninsule de Sorrento.—*Bull. Soc. géol. France, xvii, pp.* 93–100. *Paris*, 1859–60.

PUOTI, F.—*See* QUARANTA, B.

PYRRHO, LIGORIO.—Regni Neapolitani Verissima secundum Antiquorum et Recentiorum Traditionem descriptio, Pyrrho Ligorio auct. Maris Hadriatici sive Superi pars nunc Golfo di Vinetia.—*See* ORTELIUS, A.—Theatrum Orbis Terrarum.
One page of descript. entitled : Il Regno di Napoli. Engraved map of S. Italy, hand-col. : 485×365 mm.

QUARANTA, B., AJELLO, G., ALOE, S. D', AMBRA, A., AYOLA, M., BONUCCI, C., DALBONO, C., PUOTI, F.—Napoli e sue Vicinanze. Napoli e Luoghi celebri, etc.—*Sett. Congr. Scient. Ital.* 4⁰. *Vol. i, pp.* 12+542, 15 pls., 1 map ; *Vol. ii, pp.* 602+xxii, 11 pls., 1 map. *Napoli*, 1845.

QUATTROMANI, G.—Itinerario delle Due Sicilie.—8⁰, pp. 249+xxii, 1 map. *Napoli*, 1827.

QUINTIIS, C. EUCHERII.—Inarime seu de balneis Pithecusarum ; libri sex.—8⁰, foll. 22, pp. 320, foll. 12, 7 pls., frontisp. *Neapoli*, 1726. [C.A.]

RAFFELSBERGER, F.—Gemälde aus dem Naturreiche Beyder Sicilien.—8⁰, pp. 164, 8 pls. *Wien*, 1824.
See pp. 1–12.

RAMMELSBERG, C. F. A.—Ueber den Bianchetto der Solfatara von Pozzuoli.—*Zeitschr. deutsch. geol. Gesellsch.* xi, pp. 446–47. *Berlin*, 1859.

RANIERI, A.—Documenti storico-geologici sulle antichità delle acque termali e sulle arene scottanti del littorale dei Maronti nell' Isola d'Ischia.—4⁰, pp. 59. *Napoli*, 1871.

RANIERI, C.—Sul funesto avvenimento della notte del 21 al 22 gennaio 1841 nel comune di Gragnano.—*Napoli*, 1841.

RASPE, R. E.—*See* FERBER.—Lettres à Mr. le Chev. de Born, etc.

RATH, J. J. G. VOM.—Mineralogisch-geognostische Fragmente aus Italien.—v. Monte di Cuma, Ischia, Pianura.—*Zeitschr. deutsch. geol. Gesellsch. xviii, pp.* 607–39. *Berlin*, 1866.

RATH, J. J. G. 'V.—(Tridymit im Neapolitanischen Vulcan Gebiete.)—*Ann. Phys. Chem. cxlvii, pp.* 280–81. *Leipzig*, 1872.

RATH, J. J. G. V.—(Ueber das Erdbeben von Ischia vom 4 März 1881, über den Zustand des Vesuv am 18 März 1881 und über einen Besuch des Vultur bei Melfi in der Prov. Basilicata. Krystallform des Cuspidin.)— *Sitz. niederrhein. Gesellsch. xxxviii, pp.* 192–210. *Bonn*, 1881.

RATH, J. J. G. V.—(Ueber vulkanische Auswürflinge im Tuffe von Nocera und Sarno 4 Meilen O.S.O. von Neapel.)—*Sitz. niederrhein. Gesellsch, xxxix, pp.* 26–27, 226–29, 230–31, 1882; *xliv, pp.* 146–47, *Bonn*, 1887.

RATH, J. J. G. V.—(Einige mineralogische und geologische Mitteilungen bez. von Vesuv und von den Tuffbrüchen von Nocera.)—*Sitz. niederrhein. Gesellsch. xliv, pp.* 132–49. *Bonn*, 1887.

REALE, N.—*See* VERDE, M.

RECLUS, E.—Les Volcans de la Terre.— *Soc. Astronom. Bruxelles*, 1906.

REMOND.—Ruines du Palais de la Reine Jeanne. (Golfe de Naples.) Imp. Lith. de Delpech. 1828.
Litho. : 254 × 198 mm.

RENARD, Architecte (des.).—Vue de la Place de Pouzzoles, où l'on voie encore le Pied d'Estal d'une Statue élevée à Tibère. Gravé à l'eau forte par Paris. Terminé par de Ghendt. No. 112, A.P.D.R.
Engrav. : 226 × 177 mm.

RENZI, S. DE.—*See* RONCHI.

REUMONT, A. (publ. by).—Italia. (With contributions by A. Hagen, A. Kopisch, H. Leo, C. Fr. von Rumohr, K. Witte and others.)—12⁰, *pp. xii*+298, *frontisp. Berlin*, 1838.

REZZADORE, P.—I disastri d'Ischia e di Giava.—*Riv. Marittima, xvi*, 11, *pp.* 35, 2 *maps. Roma*, 1883.

RICCI, C.—Napoli.—" *Collezione di Monografie Illustrate.*"—*Italia Artistica.*—1902, etc.

RICCI, G.—Analisi chimica dell' acqua ferrata e solfurea di Napoli . . . con un appendice sopra un nuovo liquido Vesuviano.—8⁰, *fol.* 1, *pp.* 27. *Napoli.* [C.A.]—*Giorn. Arcad. Sci. xii, pp.* 313–15. *Roma*, 1821. —*Giorn. Enciclop. iii, pp.* 285–301. *Napoli*, 1820. [O.V.]

RICCI, G.—Sopra un nuovo corpo (anacaprico) che si raccoglie sulla superficie della grotta dell' Arco nell' Isola di Capri.— *Atti 6a Riun. Sci. Ital. Milano*, 1845.

RICCIARDI, L.—Ricerche chimiche sui depositi di tufi vulcanici nella provincia di Salerno (1881).—*Atti Acc. Gioen. xvi, pp.* 107–14. *Catania*, 1882.—*Gazz. Chim. Ital. xi, pp.* 480–85. *Palermo*, 1881.

RICCIARDI, L.—I tufi vulcanici del Napoletano.—*Atti Acc. Gioen. S.* 3, *xviii, pp.* 37–46. *Catania*, 1885.

RICCIARDI, L.—Sull' allineamento dei vulcani italiani. Sulle roccie eruttive subaeree e submarine e loro classificazione in due periodi. Sullo sviluppo dell' acido cloridrico dell' anidride solforosa e del jodio dai vulcani. Sul graduale passaggio delle roccie acide alle roccie basiche.—8⁰, *pp.* 1–45. *Reggio-Emilia*, 1887.

RICCIARDI, L.—Genesi e composizione chimica dei Terreni Vulcanici Italiani.— *L'Agricoltura Italiana, xiv–xv, pp.* 155. *Firenze*, 1889.

RICCIARDI, L.—Per una critica del Prof. Sigismondo Guenther. Earthquakes and Volcanoes.—*Boll. Soc. Nat. xxiii (S.* 2, *iii), pp.* 17–50. *Napoli*, 1909.

RICHARD, A.—Notice sur les eaux thermales de l'Île d'Ischia.—*Journ. Chim. Méd. ii, pp.* 126–30. *Paris*, 1836.

RICHARD DE SAINT-NON, J. C.—Voyage Pittoresque, ou Description des royaumes de Naples et de Sicile.—*fol. Vol. i*, Naples et Vésuve, *foll. ii, pp.* 252, 2 *engrav. frontisp.*, 4 *maps*, 16 *text figs.*, 50 *pls.* ; *Vol. ii*, Herculaneum, Phlegrean Fields and Campania, *foll.* 16, *pp.* 283, 2 *maps*, 26 *text figs.*, 24 *col. text figs.*, 80 *pls.* ; *Vol. iii*, Italie Méridionale, *foll.* 24, *pp.* 201, 15 *text figs.*, 4 *maps*, 57 *pls.* ; *Vol. iv*, Sicile, 1*st Pt., foll.* 14, *pp.* 266, 13 *figs.*, 65 *pls.*, 2 *maps* ; 2nd *Pt., foll. v, pp.* 267–430, *frontisp.*, 4 *figs.*, 32 *pls. Paris*, 1781–86.

RICHARD DE SAINT-NON, J. C.—Neapel und Sizilien. Ein Auszug aus dem grossen und kostbaren Werke : Voyage pittoresque de Naples et Sicile.—12 *pts. 8⁰, num. pls. Gotha*, 1789–1806.

RICHARD DE SAINT-NON, J. C.—Voyage pittoresque à Naples et en Sicile. Nouvelle édition, corrigée, augmentée, mise dans un meilleur ordre par P. J. Charrin. —4 vols. 8⁰, and one atlas, *fol.* [containing 558 very fine large engraved plates divided into :] I. Naples et ses environs, *pls.* 1–285 ; II. Grande-Grèce, *pls.* 286–400 ; III. Sicile, *pls.* 401–558. *Paris, Dufour*, 1829.

Amongst the artists who drew and engraved the plates are Berteaux, Nicollet, Germain, Deny, Longueil, Marillier, Desmoulins, Berthault Queverdo, Cochin, De St. Aubin, Fraganard, Varin, Desprez, and many others, who mostly engraved " all' acqua forte."

Another ed. 4 vols. 8⁰. *Paris*, 1836.

RICHTER & CO (publ.).—Naples.—*From Tariff of Parker's Hotel ab.* 1910 (though Vesuvius is represented about 1905).

View from Parker's Hotel. Very fine colour-print : 131 × 55 mm.

RIDDELL, R. A.—*See* WILSON, J.

RIVA, C.—Sopra due Sanidiniti delle Isole Flegree (Vivara & Procida) con alcune considerazioni intorno all' impiego di liquidi a noto indice di refrazione per la determinazione dei minerali componenti.—*Atti R. Acc. Lincei, S.* 5, *Rend. ix, sem.* 2, *pp.* 170–76, 206–9. *Roma*, 1900.—*Riv. Min. e Crist. Ital. xxvi*, 1–4, *pp.* 21–34. *Padova*, 1901.

RIVA, C.—*See* LORENZO, G. DE. 1900 and 1902.

RIZZI-ZANNONI, G. A.—Carta Geograf. della Sicilia Prima o sia regno di Napoli.— *foll.* 4. *Parigi*, 1769. [B.M.—23880 (21).]

A fine, well-drawn map of Palmarola.

RIZZI-ZANNONI, G. A.—General - Karte von dem Koenigreiche Neapel, oder Napoli herausgegeben von Herrn F. A. Schraembel. —*foll.* 4. *Wien*, 1789. [B.M.—23880(23).]

Palmarola is fairly well represented.

RIZZI-ZANNONI, G. A.—Pianta della Città di Napoli come esiste nel presente Anno Gius. Guerra Nap. Reg. Inc.—*Napoli*, 1790.

A beautiful map of the town, showing the physical features of the hills behind it ; a column of ref. nos. on each side of the map and an elaborate border with names in scrolls : 808 × 564 mm.

RIZZI-ZANNONI, G. A.—Topografia del Agro Napolitano con le sue adjacenze.— [*Naples*,] 1793. [B.M.—23890(4).]

A very good map of the Campi Phlegræi.

RIZZI-ZANNONI, G. A.—Topografia fisica. —*See* BREISLAK, S. 1798.

RIZZI-ZANNONI, G. A.—Carta del regno di Napoli con parte della Sicilia e dell' Isola di Malta.—*Vienna*, 1806. [B.M.—23880 (24).]

Much the same as the " General-Karte " of 1789.

RIZZI-ZANNONI, G. A.—Carta del regno di Napoli, indicante la divisione delle xv sue Provincie.—[*Naples*,] 1807. [B.M. 23880 (25).]

A good map for the scale.

RIZZI-ZANNONI, G. A.—Carte du royaume de Naples.—*Paris ?*, 1830 ?

ROBERT (del.).—Vue des débris des Bains de Néron sur le bord de la mer entre Bayes et Puozzuoles à 6 milles de Naples. Adelaide Allon Sc. 1771. 66.

Engrav. : 234 × 181 mm.

ROBERT, H. (des.).—Naples. Ruines d'un ancien Palais bâti par la Reine Jeanne près de Naples sur le bord de la Mer du Côté du Pausilippe. Dessiné d'après nature par H. Robert, Peintre du Roi. Gravé à l'eau forte par Germain. Terminé par Desquauvilliers. A.P.D.R. [B.N.P.—Vb. 119.]

A fine view of Pal. Donn' Anna and the platform on which it is built. Engrav. : 347 × 229 mm.

ROBERTS, R. A.—*See* MAPEI, C.—Italy, Classical, Historical and Picturesque.

ROCCATAGLIATA, P.—*See* MÈNE. 1868.

ROCCATAGLIATA, P.—Analisi dell' acqua termo-minerale del Gurgitello.—*Napoli*, 1870.

ROCCATAGLIATA, P., & FERRERO, O.— Studii analitici sulle acque minerali e mineralo-termali di Sujo in prov. di Terra di Lavoro.—*Aversa*, 1877.

ROCCATAGLIATA, P.—Aquano e le sue numerose Sorgenti di acqua termo-minerali. —*fol.*, *pp.* 26. *Napoli*, 1890.

ROCCIO, ANT.—Ager Puteolanus sive prospectus eiusdem insigniores.—4⁰, 22 *pls. and map with short explanation. Romæ*, 1620.

$$\left[\text{B.M.—S.} \ \frac{95}{13} \right]$$

A most interesting and valuable reference-work for all the localities of the Campi Phlegræi. Maps 3 and 7 are very similar to those of Cartaro and Bramb.

ROCKWOOD, C. G. Fr.—The Ischian earth-quake of July 28th, 1883.—*Amer. Journ. Sci. xxvi, pp.* 473–76. *New Haven,* 1883.

RODWELL, G. F.—South by East : Notes of Travel in Southern Europe.—8⁰, *pp.* 274. *London,* 1877.

ROGGERO, Cav. G.—Carta in Rilievo dell' Italia.—*Pub. G. B. Paravia e C., Torino, Roma, Milano, Firenze, Napoli,* 1876.
Raised map. 1 : 2,800,000 horizontal ; 1 : 320,000 vertical.

ROGISSARD, De.—Les Délices de l'Italie ou description exacte de ce Pays, de ses princi-pales villes, et de toutes les raretez, qu'il contient.—3 vols. 12⁰. *Vol. i, foll.* 8, *pp.* 275, *num. pls.* ; *Vol. ii, pp.* 277–554, *num. pls.* ; *Vol. iii, pp.* 555–718, *foll.* 31, *pp.* 10. *Leide,* 1706.
See Vol. iii, pp. 555–601.
Another ed. 6 tom. 12⁰. *Leide,* 1709.
Another ed. 4 tom. 8⁰. *Amsterdam,* 1743.
In German : *Berlin,* — ?

ROHAN, Le Duc De.—Formation du Monte Nuovo.—*See* " Voyage du Duc de Rohan fait en l'an 1600," *pp.* 102–3. *Amsterdam,* 1646.

ROLLER, I.—Un tremblement de terre à Naples et la charité du gouvernement Napolitain.—*Genève,* 1860.

ROMANELLI, D.—Viaggio a Pompei, a Pesto e di ritorno ad Ercolano e Pozzuoli.— 8⁰. *Napoli,* 1811.——2nd ed. 2 pts. 12⁰. *Pte. i, pp.* 228, *2 pls.* ; *Pte. ii, pp.* 276, *2 pls. Napoli,* 1817.
3rd ed. *Milano,* 1831. *See* Pte. ii, pp. 116–23 : Della Solfatara.

RONCHI, S., MADIA, A., CASSOLA, F., RENZI, S. De.—Sulle acque termo-miner-ali Balneolane.—8⁰, *pp.* 79. *Napoli,* 1831. [B.M. 7462, ee. 5. (2).]——2nda ed. 8⁰, *pp.* 61. *Napoli,* 1863.

ROSA, D. T.—Ragguagli storici della origine di Napoli della Campagna Felice d'Italia.— 4⁰, *foll. ii, pp.* 118, *fol.* 1. *Napoli,* 1702.

ROSA, G. De.—Terra Insanguinata. Memo-riale storico-geologico e scientifico-etno-grafico sull' Isola d'Ischia, còmpilato sulle migliori opere di varî autori e preceduto di un ceno storico intorno all' Istituzione Inter-nazionale " La Croce Rossa," e seguito della cronaca esatta della catastrofe.—8⁰, *pp.* 128. *Napoli,* 1884.

ROSCIUS HORTINUS, Julius.—De rebus mirabilis Puteolorum.
Epigram on the map of Grassus Bar-tolomeœus.

ROSCOE, T.—The Tourist in Italy. Illus-trated from drawings by J. D. Harding.— " *The Landscape Annual,*" 8⁰, *pp.* 286. *London,* 1832 *and* 1833.
See pp. 173–256 and 7 plates therewith. 1832.

ROSCOE, T., SOSSON, A., PROUT, S., and HARDING, J. D.—The Continental Tour-ist. Views of Cities and Scenery in Italy, France and Switzerland. From original drawings by S. Prout and J. D. Harding, with descriptions in English by T. Roscoe, and in French by A. Sosson.—3 vols. 8⁰. *London,* 1849–50.

ROSE, G., & MITSCHERLICH.—Vorkom-men von Granit- und Porphyrgeschiebe auf dem hohen Neapolitanischen Apennin in der Nähe von Neapel.—*Bericht über die zur Bekanntm. geeign. Verhandl. k. preuss. Akad. Wissensch. pp.* 599–602. *Berlin,* 1851.— In French : *Arch. Sci. Nat. Genève,* 1852.

ROSEO DA FABRIANO, M.—*See* COLLE-NUCCIO, 1591, 1613, 1771.

ROSINI, (D.) P.—Lettera sui terremoti di Monte Oliveto Maggiore.

ROSSI, G. J. De.—[A Bird's-eye View of Pozzuoli and the surrounding country with] Explicatio aliquot locorum quæ Puteolis spectantur.—*Romæ* [1660 ?]. [B.M.— 24120.3.]
A separate plate of map. *See also* ROCCIO, Ant., and BRAMB[ERGIUS].

ROSSI, G. J. De (publ.).—Fidelissimæ urbis Neapolitanæ cum omnibus viis accurate nova delineatio anno 1649.—*Roma,* 1649. [B.M.—24045(3).]
View - map with references of little importance.

ROSSI, M. S. De.—Bulletino del Vulcanismo Italiano.—8⁰. *Roma,* 1873 *to* 1888. [C.A.]

ROSSI, M. S. De.—Fenomeni aurorali e sismici della regione laziale confrontati coi terremoti di Casamicciola, Norcia, e Li-vorno. Notizie ed osservazioni.—*Bull. Vulc. Ital. ii,* 6, 7 e 8, *pp.* 49–54. *Roma,* 1875.

ROSSI, M. S. De.—Quadro generale statis-tico topografico giornaliero dei terremoti avvenuti in Italia nell' anno meteorico 1874 [and 1877] col confronto di alcuni altri fenomeni.—*Atti Acc. Pont. N. Lincei, xxviii, pp.* 514–36, *Roma,* 1875 ; [*and xxxi, pp.* 479–82, 1878.]

ROSSI, M. S. DE.—Altri fatti analoghi [ai fenomeni precursori del terremoto di Casamicciola del 4 marzo 1881] raccolti sul luogo in una escursione fattavi nel luglio.— *Bull. Vulc. Ital. viii, p.* 38. *Roma,* 1881.

ROSSI, M. S. DE.—Rombo e scossa in Casamicciola ai 18 luglio 1881.—*Bull. Vulc. Ital. viii, pp.* 40–41. *Roma,* 1881.

ROSSI, M. S. DE.—Intorno all' odierna fase dei terremoti in Italia e seguatamente sul terremoto in Casamicciola de 4 Marzo 1881. —*Boll. Soc. Geog. Ital.* 5, *pp.* 23, 1 *map,* 1 *pl.* *Roma,* 1881.

ROSSI, M. S. DE.—[Sono da temersi prossimamente nuovi grandi terremoti in Casamicciola? Riposta alla lettera di G. Dombre.]—*Bull. Vulc. Ital. viii, pp.* 71–74. *Roma,* 1881.

ROSSI, M. S. DE.—Che cosa e geologicamente la catastrofe di Casamicciola.—*Castellamare-Casamicciola, numero unico,* 26 *Agosto,* 1883.

ROSSI, M. S. DE.—Studii sul Terremoto di Casamicciola.—*Rassegna Ital. pp.* 17. *Roma,* 15 *Oct.,* 1883.

ROSSI, M. S. DE.—Rivista sismica del lúglio, agosto, settembre 1883.—*Bull. Mens. Assoc. Meteor. Ital., nov.* 1883.
See " Raccolta di Fatti," etc. 1884.

ROSSI, M. S. DE.—La Catastrofe di Casamicciola.—*Gaz. Uffic. d. Regno, i,* 13 *agosto,* 4, 5 *settemb.,* 3 *dec.* 1883.

ROSSI, M. S. DE.—Comunicazione sul terremoto di Casamicciola.—*Boll. Soc. Geol. Ital. ii, p.* 92. *Roma,* 1883.

ROSSI, M. S. DE.—Comunicazione sulla questione dei segni precursori del terremoto di Casamicciola.—*Boll. Soc. Geol. Ital. ii, pp.* 217–20. *Roma,* 1883.

ROSSI, M. S. DE.—Raccolta di fatti, relazioni, bibliografie sul terremoto di Casamicciola del 28 luglio 1883, con brevi osservazioni.—*Bull. Vulc. Ital. xi, pt.* 2, *pp.* 175, 1 *map. Roma,* 1884.

ROSSINI, P. DE.—*See* ROSINI, (D.) P.

ROTH, J.—Der Vesuv und die Umgebung von Neapel.—8⁰, *pp. xliv*+540, 9 *pls. Berlin,* 1857.

ROTH, J.—Zur Geologie der Umgebung von Neapel.—*Monatsb. k. preuss. Akad. Wiss.* 1881, *pp.* 990–1006. *Berlin,* 1882.

ROUX, J.—Recueil des principaux plans des ports et rades de la Mer Méditerranée (par

A. R. Zannoni, Ayronard Condamine, Soper, J. Wilson, G. Peckam Michelot, T. Clements, Young, R. Nelson, etc.).—*obl.* 4⁰, 121 *pls. Gênes, Gravier,* 1779.

ROVERE, F.—Bagni e sorgente termominerali nell' isola d'Ischia.—8⁰. *Napoli,* 1865.

ROZET.—Sur les volcans des environs de Naples.—*Bull. Soc. géol. France, S.* 2, i, *pp.* 255–66. *Paris,* 1844.

RUFFO, G.—Sulla Grotta Azzurra di Capri. —*Il Progr. Sci. xiv, pp.* 208–12. *Napoli,* 1836.—*Atti Acc. Sci.* v, *pt.* 1, *pp.* 147–55. *Napoli,* 1843.

RUFFO, G.—Sulla Fata Morgana nel Lago di Averno.—*Atti Acc. Sci. iv, Mem., Class. fis., stor. nat. pp.* 19–41. *Napoli,* 1839.

RUGGIERO.—Analisi delle acque minerali dell' Isola d'Ischia.

RUGGIERO.—Lavoro geologico sull' Isola d'Ischia.

RUSCONI, C.—[L'origine atmosferica dei tufi vulcanici della Campagna Romana.]— *Corrisp. scient. vii,* 19–20. *Roma,* 1865.— *Bull. Soc. géol. France, S.* 2, *xxii, pp.* 68–69. *Paris,* 1865.

RUSSEGER, J.—Geognostische Beobachtungen in Rom, Neapel, am Ætna, auf den Cyclopen, dem Vesuv, Ischia, etc.—*N. J. f. Min. viii, pp.* 329–32. *Stuttgart,* 1840.

RUSSO, G. DEL.—Pianta della città di Napoli delineata nel 1815 da Giosuè Russo. Inc. da Dom. Guerra., Gen. Galiani Scris. Scala 1 : 20,000.—[*Napoli,* 1815.]
Finely engraved map extending from Sebeto to La Grotta and Castel dell' Uovo to Pal. Reale di Capodimonte. 104 ref. nos. : 255×323 mm.

SABATINI, V.—Osservazioni sulla profondità dei focolari vulcanici.—*Boll. R. Com. Geol. Ital. xxxiii, pp.* 26–45. *Roma,* 1902.

SABATINI, V.—Vulcani e terremoti.—*Riv. Ital. An.* 5, *ii, pp.* 353–79, 10 *figs. Roma,* 1902.

SACCHI, G., BERTAZZI, G., MARIENI, L.—Sulla statistica del agro Acerrano e sulle memorie intorno alle acque minerali della Campania del dotto G. Caporali.—*Atti de Ateneo, xvii. Milano,* 1862.

SADELER, ÆGID.—Vestigi delle antichità di Roma, Tivoli, Pozzuolo et altri luochi.— *obl.* 4⁰, 50 *pls. and frontisp. Praga da Ægidio Sadeler,* 1606.

SADELER, MARCO.—Vestigi delle Antichità di Roma, Tivoli, Pozzuolo et altri Luochi.— *Roma da I. di Rossi, [no date].*—Another ed. *obl. 4⁰, 50 pls. and frontisp.* 1680.
This book consists of the same views as that by Ægidio Sadeler, but re-engraved. Their average measurement is 264 × 155 mm., whereas in the early ed. the measurements are 270 × 150 mm. *See* Pl. 11.

SADELER, MARCO (excudit).—A. La Solfataria detta da Plinio Campi Flegrei da Strabone Forū Vulcani luocho di maruigliosa natura tutto solato di solfo et intorniato de alti colli eccetto dal lato. B. Oue si entra verso Pozzuolo. C. Fossa volgarmente detta galoza piena d'acqua nera et spessa, che di continouo bolli si che aggiatamente ui si cuoce qual si uoglia cosa. D. Della pietre et terra di questi monti se ne fa gran quantita di solfo. E. De queste et queta alume. F. Officine da stillare il solfo biancho. [B.M. Portfolio of Naples.]
Engraving : 265 × 156 mm.

ST. CLAIR BADDELEY.—*See* HARE, A. J. C.

SAINTE-CLAIRE DEVILLE, C. J.—*See* DEVILLE, C. J. SAINTE-CLAIRE.

SALATHÉ (fecit).—Vue de la Grotte de Pausilipe. Chez C. T. Muller à Naples.— [1810 *or* 1842 ?]
Line engrav. : 352 × 244 mm.

SALATHÉ (feci[t]).—Vue de Naples du Chemin neuf dit del Campo.—Chez C. T. Muller à Naples.
Naples from near Capodimonte ; woman, child and pitcher in foreground. Line litho. : 576 × 424 mm.

SALATHÉ (dis. e incisi.).—Vue de Naples du Côté de Capo di Monte.—Chez C. T. Muller à Naples.
Line litho. : 580 × 426 mm.

SALATHÉ (del.).—*See* AUDOT.—[Views of the Campi Phlegræi.]

SALLE, DE LA.—Sicile.—*In* " L'Univers pittoresque. Histoire et description de tous les peuples," etc., *T. ii*, 24 *engrav.* 1834.

SALVADORI, R.—*See* NASINI, R.

SALVI, V.—Ricerche storico-chemiche e considerazioni geologiche sulla fonte di Gurgitello.—*Napoli*, 1883.

SALVI, V.—Le Terme di Casamicciola son tutte Gurgitello ?—8⁰, *pp.* 62. *Napoli*, 1894.

SANCHEZ, G.—La Campania sotterranea, e brevi notizie degli edificii scavati entro Roccia delle Due Sicilie, etc.—8⁰, *pp.* 2+ 656. *Napoli*, 1833.

SANDBY, P. (fecit).—Monte Nuovo, with a distant View of the Coast and Castle of Baia. Monte Nuovo, avec la Côte et le Château de Baia, vûs dans l'éloignement. Fabris pinxt. Publish'd April 1777, by P. Sandby and A. Robertson, as the Act directs. [B.M. Portfolio of Naples.]
Sepia view : 542 × 304 mm.

SANDBY, P. (fecit).—The Town of Puzzuoli, with a View of the Ruins of Caligula's Bridge and the Island of Nisita. La Ville de Puzzuoli avec une vue des ruines du Pont de Caligula et de l'Isle de Nisita. Fabris pinxt. Publish'd April 1777, by P. Sandby, and A. Robertson, as the Act directs. [B.M. Portfolio of Naples.]
Sepia view : 539 × 311 mm.

SANDBY, P. (fecit).—View of the Isles of Proscita, Ischia and Baia. Vue des Isles Proscita, Ischia et de Baia. Fabris pinxt. Publish'd as the Act directs, by P. Sandby, and A. Robertson. Sepr. 1777. [B.M. Portfolio of Naples.]
Sepia view : 542 × 304 mm.

SANDBY, P. (fecit).—Sepulchral Monument at old Capua. Mausolée à l'Ancienne Capoué. Fabris pinxt. Publish'd by P. Sandby as the Act directs March 1778. St. Georges Row, Oxford Turnpike. [B.M. Portfolio of Naples.]
Sepia view : 444 × 313 mm.

SANDBY, P. (fecit).—View of the Lake of Avernus. Vue du Lac d'Averno. Fabris pinxt. Publish'd as the Act directs, by P. Sandby, and A. Robertson. [B.M. Portfolio of Naples.]
Sepia view : 544 × 303 mm.

SANDBY, P.—*See* LALMAN.

SANDRAST, IOACH (del.).—Forum Vulcani vocavit antiquitas, locum in agro Puteolano, quem hodie vulgo la Solfatara appelant.
A poor view of the Solfatara with four letters of reference in German. " No. 152 " added in ink. —? 17th cent. costumes. Said to be engraved by M. Merian *c.* 1640. Engrav. : 285 × 181 mm.

SANDYS, G.—A Relation of a Iourney begun An. Dom. 1610. Fovre Bookes. Containing a description of the Turkish Empire, of Ægypt, of the Holy Land, of the Remote parts of Italy, and Islands adioyning.—4⁰, *pp.* 309+1, *figs., frontisp. portrait of author. London*, 1615.

SANFELICIUS, A.—Campania Antonii Sanfelicii Monachi. Descripsit Matthias Cancer.—1st ed. 4⁰, foll. 20. Napoli, 1562.

SANFELICIUS, A.— Campania.—12⁰, pp.
8+64, 1 map, frontisp. Typis Joannis
Blaeu, Amstelædami, 1656. [C.A.]
Mentions specially M. Nuovo.

SANFELICIUS, A.—Campania notis illustrata.—4⁰, pp. 26+158, 1 pl. Neapoli,
Paci, 1726.

SANFELICIUS, A.—La Campania recata in
volgare italiano da Girolamo Aquino Capuano.—8⁰, pp. lxxi+117+3, 1 map, portrait.
Napoli, 1779. [C.A.]—Another ed. Napoli,
1796.

SANFELICIUS, A.—De situ ac origine
Campaniæ . . . etc.—See GRÆVIUS.—
Thesaurus Antiquitatum, etc. T. ix, pt. 1,
coll. 1–11.

SANTANGELO, N.—Osservazioni intorno
alle cose dette sopra il Tempio di Serapide
di Pozzuoli.—Atti Sett. Adun. Scienz. Ital.
p. 1125. Napoli, 1846.

SANTOLI, V. M.—De Mephiti et vallibus
Auxanti, libri 3. Cum observationibus super
nonnullis urbibus Hirpinorum, quorum
lapides ed antiquitatum relliquiæ illustr.—
4⁰, pp. viii+99+1, 6 pls. Neapoli, 1783.

SANTOLI, V. M.—Narrazione de Fenomeni
Osservati nel suolo Irpino.—8⁰, pp. vi+
160+43, 1 pl. Napoli, 1795.—Giorn. Lett.
xxx, pp. 84–85. Napoli, 1794.

SANTORELLI, F.—See BOSSIS.

SANTORO, P.—Descrizione del terremoto
avvenuto in Alvito e nei Comuni limitrofi
nel 1873.—Bull. Vulc. Ital. 11 e 12. Roma,
1874.

SARIIS, A. DE.—Termologio Puteolana a
vantaggio dell'uomo infermo.—8⁰, pp. xiv+
2+192. Napoli, 1800.

SARNELLI, P.—Guida de Forestieri per
Pozzuoli.—Napoli, 1669.

SARNELLI, P.—La vera Guida de' Forestieri
curiosi di vedere e d'intendere le cose più
notabili della Real città di Napoli e del suo
amenissimo distretto, etc.—12⁰, pp. 22+
3+8, num. pls. Napoli, 1685.
Another ed. 12⁰, foll. 17+pp. 401+foll.
15, 51 pls., frontisp. 1692.
Contains on title-page the addition :
" In questa nuova edizione da Antonio
Bulifon di vaghissime figure abbellita, e
dedicata all' Illustriss. e Reverendiss.
Monsignor Francesco Maria Pignatello,

Arcivescovo di Taranto, e Regio Consigliero. A spese di Antonio Bulifon."
Another ed. 12⁰, fol. 1+pp. 302. 1752.
(Separate vol. of pls.)
Has the addition : " con annotazioni di
tutto il circuito del Regno, e numero delle
città, terre, casali, e castelli d'esso, come
pure de' Fiumi, e Laghi. Vescovati Regj,
e Papalini : e il numero, e titoli de' Baroni
di esso Regno : con una distinta descrizione
di tutte l'eruzioni da volta in volta fatte dal
Monte Vesuvio. . . . Questa nuova edizione
viene ampliata con molte moderne fabriche
secondo lo stato presente, ed arrichita con
un altro tomo di Figure, per magior comodo
de' diletanti, che si dà separato. A spese di
Nicolò Petrini."
Another ed. 12⁰, fol. 1+pp. 312, 11 pls.,
frontisp. 1772.
Is entitled : " Nuova Guida de' Forestieri, e dell' Istoria di Napoli, con cui si
vede, e si spiegano le cose più notabil della
medesima, e del suo amenissimo distretto ;
con annotazioni di tutto il circuito del
Regno, etc. [as in the 1752 edit.]. In
questa nuova edizione ampliata delle
molte moderne fabbriche secondo lo stato
presente, ed arricchita di varie figure. A
spese di Saverio Rossi."
Another ed. 12⁰, pp. viii+364, 12 pls.,
frontisp. 1788.
Is entitled : " Guida de' Forestieri per la
città di Napoli. In cui si contengono tutte
le notizie topografiche della città, e degli
Edificj sacri, e pubblici da' tempi antichi
infino al dì di oggi, per istruire brevemente
l'umano, e prestante leggitore. Nuovamente spurgata dalle suiste, ed accresciuta
di quanto si osserva in sì famosa città. A
spese del Librajo Nunzio Rossi." (Anon.,
attributable to Sarnelli.)
Another ed. 12⁰, fol. 1+pp. 394, 10 pls.,
figs. 1791. [O.V.]

SARNELLI, P.—Gvida de' Forestieri, curiosi di vedere, e considerare le cose notabili
di Pozzoli, Baja, Miseno, Cuma, ed altri
luoghi convicini. Ritrovata colla lettura
de' buoni Scrittori, e colla propria diligenza
dall' Abate. . . .—Nova edit. 12⁰, foll. 10+
pp. 160+foll. 4, 13 pls., frontisp. In
Napoli, a spese di Antonio Bulifon. 1688.
/ Another ed. 12⁰, foll. 5+pp. 305+foll. 6,
32 pls., 2 frontisp. 1697.
This ed. is in Italian and French, the
title-page having the addition : " Tradotta
in Francese, accresciuta, e di vaghe figure
abbellita da Antonio Bulifon, giontovi
ancora li Bagni d'Ischia. Dedicata all'

Illustrissimo Signor D. Giacomo Farelli Cavalier Gerosolimitano. Per Giuseppe Roselli."

Another ed. 12⁰, *foll.* 4+*pp.* 368+*foll.* 7, 34 *pls., frontisp.* 1702.

Also in Italian and French, but whereas edit. of 1697 had first title-page in Italian and second in French, this edit. has both in French, the first bearing the dedication to Victor Marie Comte d'Estrées by the translator (Antoine Bulifon), the second the addition : " Traduite en François par Antoine Bulifon, qui l'a enrichie de plusieurs figures en taille douce, et augmentée de quelques particularitez très-curieuses, et de la Description des Bains, et Étuves de l'Isle d'Ischia très-salutaires pour la guérison de diverses maladies." This ed. contains J. C. Capaccio's " Description des Vertus, et Proprietez des Bains d'Ischia " [French transl. by A. Bulifon] (pp. 313–45), and also " Brieve Descrittione delle cose più notabili della città di Gaeta cavata da quella di D. Pietro Rossetto " (pp. 346–68).

Another ed. 12⁰, *foll.* 7, *pp.* 192 (*pp.* 1–192 *in double*), 32 *pls., frontisp.* 1709.

Also in Italian and French, 2 title-pages, bearing the addition " Ed in quest' impressione data in luce da Michele-Luigi Muzio, arricchita di molte figure in Rame, ed accresciuta di alcune curiosissime particolarità, con la Descrizione de' Bagni, e Stufe dell' Isola d'Ischia molto salutevoli per guarire d'ogni sorte d'Infermità. Dedicata all' Eccellentiss. Sig. D. Girolamo Capece. A spese di Michele-Luigi Muzio."

Another ed. in French, 12⁰, *pp.* x+324, 15 *pls.*, 1 *map*. 1769.

Is called the 4th ed.

Another ed. 12⁰, *foll.* 2+*pp.* 190+*fol.* 1, 23 *pls.* 1770.

In Italian only, and with the addition : " E arricchita da Antonio Bulifone di molte figure in Rame, ed accresciuta di alcune curiosissime particolarità, con la Descrizione de' Bagni, e Stufe dell' Isola d'Ischia molto salutevoli per guarire ogni sorte d'Infermità. A spese di Saverio Rossi."

Is also called the 4th ed.

Another ed. 12⁰, *foll.* 2, *pp.* 190, *fol.* 1, 23 *pls.* 1782.

In Italian only, with the same addition as the 1770 edit., is : " A spese del Librajo Nunzio Rossi," and is called : " Nuova Guida . . . di Pozzuoli, Baja, Cuma, Misena, Gaeta, e dell' Isole adjacenti d'Ischia, Procida, Nisita, Capri, colline, terre, ville, e città, che sono intorno alle Riviere dell' uno, e l'altro lato di Napoli, detto Cratero."

Another ed. in Italian and French, 12⁰, *pp.* 12+324+*xxiii*, *pls.* *Naples, Ant.* Spano, Éritier di Xavier Rossi, 1784.

Is called the 5th ed.

Another ed. 12⁰, *pp.* *xi*+215, 20 *pls.* 1789.

Is called : " Guida de' Forestieri per Pozzuoli, Baja, Cuma, e Miseno. Si dà conto preciso di molti Edifizj sacri, pubblici, e privati non meno Greci, che Romani. Si descrivono i Bagni, e le Terme che vi esistono, colle regole necessarie per usarle ne' disgraziati successi. Edizione novissima corretta con diligenza ed arricchita di molte Note. A Spese del Librajo Nunzio Rossi." All these ed., excepting those of 1688, in Italian, and 1769, in French, contain J. C. Capaccio's " Descrizione delle Virtù, e Proprietà de' Bagni d'Ischia," and all but the 1688, 1697 and 1789 have the " Brieve Descrittione delle cose più notabili della città di Gaeta cavata da quella di D. Pietro Rossetto."

SARNELLI, P.—*See* BULIFON, A. 1699.

SASS, H.—A Journey to Rome and Naples, performed in 1817 ; etc.—8⁰, *pp.* 345. *London,* 1818.

SCACCHI, A.—Catalogus Conchyliarum Regni Neapoletani.— — ?, 1836.

SCACCHI, A.—Notizie geologiche sulle Conchiglie che si trovan fossili nell' Isola d'Ischia e lungo la spiaggia tra Pozzuoli e Monte Nuovo.—*Antol. Sci. Nat.* (1 vol. only), 8⁰, *pp.* 33–48. *Naples,* 1841.

SCACCHI, A.—Della Voltaite, nuova specie di minerale trovato nella Solfatara di Pozzuoli.—*Idem, pp.* 67–71. *Napoli,* 1841.

SCACCHI, A.—Lezioni di Geologia : Vulcani di Roccamonfina, Campi ed Isole Flegree, Mᵗᵉ Somma e Vesuvio.—8⁰, *pp.* 178. *Napoli,* 1843.

See pp. 155–74.

SCACCHI, A.—Osservazioni critiche sulla maniera come fu seppellita l'antica Pompei. Lettera al Cav. Avellino.—8⁰. *Napoli,* 1843.—*Bull. Archeol.* i, 6, *pp.* 41–45. *Napoli,* 1843.

SCACCHI, A.—Voltaïte und Periklas, zwei neue Mineralien ; mit Bemerkungen von Kobell.—*Gel. Anz. xvi, coll.* 345–48. *München,* 1843.—*Erdm. Journal f. prakt. Chem. xxviii, pp.* 486–89. *Leipsic,* 1843.

SCACCHI, A.—Notizie geologiche dei vulcani della Campania estratte dalle Lezioni di Geologia.—8⁰. *Napoli,* 1844.

SCACCHI, A.—Napoli e i luoghi celebri delle sue vicinanze.—2 vols. *Napoli*, 1845.

SCACCHI, A.—Campi ed Isole Flegree, etc.— *See* "Napoli e i luoghi celebri delle sue vicinanze," *pp.* 361-413. 1845.

SCACCHI, A.—Descrizione delle Carte geologiche dei Campi Flegrei.—*Atti Sett. Adun. Scienz. Ital. p.* 1126. *Napoli*, 1845.—Pte. 2ª, *pp.* 1176–81, 2 *pls. Napoli*, 1846.

SCACCHI, A.—Notice sur le gisement et sur la cristallisation de la Sodalite des environs de Naples. (Transl.)—*Ann. Mines, S.* 4, *xii, pp.* 385–89, *figs.* 11-14 *of pl.* 3. *Paris*, 1847.

SCACCHI, A.—Memorie geologiche sulla Campania. Introduzione. *Mem.* I.— Condizioni topografiche della regione Flegrea considerate in rapporto alle cagioni che le han prodotte.—*fol., pp.* 131, 4 *pls. Napoli*, 1849.—*Rend. R. Acc. Sci. viii, pp.* 41–65. *Napoli*, 1849.—Mem. II.—Descrizione geologica della regione Flegrea.— *Idem, pp.* 115–40, 235–61, 3 *pls.*—Mem. III.— Esam delle sostanze che si formano presso i fumaroli della regione Flegrea.—*Idem, pp.* 317–35; *ix, pp.* 84–114, 1 *pl.* 1850.— *Zeitschr. deutsch. geol. Gesellsch. iv, pp.* 162–79. *Berlin*, 1852.—*Journ. f. prakt. Chem. lv, pp.* 54–59. *Leipzig*, 1852.

SCACCHI, A.—Osservazioni di fenditure aperte nelle pianure di Aversa il 21 settembre 1852. Lettera al Sig. A. Perrey.— — ?, 1852 ? Original MS. in C.A.

SCACCHI, A.—Ueber die Substanzen die sich in den Fumarolen der Phlegraeischen, Feldern bilden.—[Abdr.] *Zeitschr. deutsch. geol. Gesellsch. iv, pp.* 162–89, *figs.* 1–6 *of pl.* 3. *Berlin*, 1852.

SCACCHI, A.—Notizie delle fenditure apertesi nella pianura di Aversa nell' autunno del 1852 e del piperno per le medesime messo allo scoperto.—*Rend. R. Acc. Sci. xx, pp.* 159–61. *Napoli*, 1881.

SCACCHI, A.—Sul legno carbonizzato del tufo di Lanzara.—*Rend. R. Acc. Sci. xx, pp.* 207–12. *Napoli*, 1881.

SCACCHI, A.—Notizie preliminari intorno ai proietti vulcanici del tufo di Nocera e di Sarno.—*Atti R. Acc. Lincei, S.* 3, *Trans. v, pp.* 270–73. *Roma*, 1881.

SCACCHI, A.—Breve notizia dei Vulcani Fluoriferi della Campania.—*Rend. R. Acc. Sci. xxi, pp.* 201–4. *Napoli*, 1882.

SCACCHI, A.—La regione Vulcanica Fluorifera della Campania.—*Rend. R. Acc. Sci. xxiv, pp.* 155–61. *Napoli*, 1885.—Seconda appendice : *S.* 2, *ii, pp.* 130–33. 1888.— *Id. Atti, S.* 2, *ii*, 2, *pp.* 108, 3 *figs. Napoli*, 1888.——2a ed. 4º, *pp.* 48+1, 1 *col. map*, 3 *lithos. Firenze*, 1890. [*Extr. fr. Mem. p. serv. descriz. carta geol. Ital. pubbl. R. Com. Geol. Ital. iv, pt.* 1, *pp.* 48+1. *Firenze*, 1891.]

SCACCHI, A.—Sulle Ossa Fossili trovate nel tufo dei Vulcani Fluoriferi della Campania. —*Atti R. Acc. Sci. S.* 2, *iii*, 3, *pp.* 9, 2 *pls. Napoli*, 1889.—*Id. Rend. S.* 2, *ii, pp.* 109–10. 1888.

SCACCHI, A.—Il vulcanetto di Puccianello. —*Rend. R. Acc. Sci. S.* 2, *ii, pp.* 478–80. *Napoli*, 1888.—*Id. Atti, S.* 2, *iii*, 7, *pp.* 14. 1889.

SCACCHI, P. E.—*See* BELLINI, R. 1907.

SCARPA, O.—Analisi della radioattività delle acque termali Fornello e Fontana di Porto d'Ischia e Manzi di Casamicciola.—*Atti R. Ist. Incorag. lxii, pp.* 1–26. *Napoli*, 1911.

SCERVINO, P.—La Sibilla Cumana. Poema Storico.—8º, *pp.* vii+329, 22 *pls.*, 1 *portrait*, 1 *map. Napoli*, 1912.

SCHENK, P. (exc.).—Napels, een Seen oude Zeestad in Italie, wegens de Pracht der Gebowen en Adeldom haarer Inwooneren, boven andere nit muntende. Neapolis, Italia antiquissima, ad Mare Mediterraneum ; hodie ædificiorum splendore ac incolarum nobilitate maxime celebris. Pet. Schenk exc. Amst. cum Privil. Carefully hand-coloured engrav. : 192 × 167 mm.

SCHERILLO, G.—Dei Laghi Lucrino e Averno tra la città di Cuma e Pozzuoli.— 4º, *pp.* 53. *Napoli*, 1859.

SCHIAVONI, F.—Relazione all' Accademia Pontaniana intorno allo studio delle Maree compiuto sul littorale di Napoli per dedurre il livello medio del mare.—*fol.*, 8 *pls. Napoli*, 1867.

SCHIAVONI, F.—*See* GUISCARDI, G. 1881.

SCHIO, A. DA.—I terremoti sono essi prevedibili ?—" *Gazetta di Vincenza*," 1-2 *agosto* 1883.

SCHIO, A. DA.—La prevedibilità dei terremoti.—" *La Provincia di Vincenza*," 21-22 *agosto*, 1883.

SCHIRLITZ, P.—*See* WALTHER, J.— Studi geologici sul Golfo di Napoli.

SCHMIDT, J. F. J.—Die Eruption des Vesuv im Mai 1855, nebst Beiträgen zur Topographie des Vesuv, der Phlegräischen Crater, Roccamonfina's und der alten Vulkane im Kirkenstaate mit Benützung neuer Charten und eigener Hohenmessungen.—8⁰, *pp. xii+212, 37 figs. Wien u. Olmütz,* 1856.—*Peterm. Mitth. pp.* 125-35. *Gotha,* 1856.

SCHMIDT, J. F. J.—Die Eruption des Vesuv in ihren Phänomaenen im Maj 1855, nebst Ansichten und Profilen der Vulkane des Phlegräischen Gebietes, Roccamonfina's und des Albaner Gebirges, etc.—*gd.* 4⁰, 9 *pls. Wien u. Olmütz,* 1856.
Album to foregoing.

SCHMIDT, J. F. J.—Neue Höhen-Bestimmungen am Vesuv, in den Phlegräischen Feldern, zu Roccamonfina und im Albaner-Gebirge.—4⁰, *pp.* 41. *Wien u. Olmütz,* 1856.

SCHMIDT, J. F. J.—Vulkanstudien. Santorin 1866-72 ; Vesuv, Bajæ, Stromboli, Ætna, 1870.—8⁰. *foll.* 4+*pp.* 235, 7 *tab.,* 1 *map,* 13 *figs. Leipzig,* 1874.——2nd ed. 8⁰. 1881.

SCHNEIDER, K.—Die vulkanischen Erscheinungen der Erde.—4⁰, *pp. viii+272,* 50 *figs., maps. Berlin,* 1911.

SCHOEL, H. VAN.—Regno di Napoli. H. v. S. formis.—*Romæ,* 1602.

SCHOTTI, ANDREAS.—*See* SCHOTTUS, ANDREAS.

SCHOTTUS, ANDREAS.—Itinerario ovvero nova descrittione de' viaggi principali d'Italia . . . di A. Scoto [or rather of F. Schottus].—8⁰. *Vincenza, Bolzetta,* 1622.—Another ed. 2 pts. 8⁰. *Padoa, Vicenza,* 1629, 28.
Has the addition : " Novamente tradotto del Latino . . . & accresciuto," etc. Another ed. 3 pts. in 1 vol. 8⁰. *Pt.* 1, 64 *pls. and frontisp.* ; *Pt.* 2, 43 *pls.* ; *Pt.* 3, 25 *pls.* (*pls. by F. Bertelli*). *Vicenza, Bolzetta,* 1638. [*On engrav. title :* " *Padova,* 1642."] Another ed. 3 pts. in 2 vols. 8⁰. *Vol.* i, *Pt.* 1, *pp.* 10+20, *foll.* 165, 98 *pls.* ; *Vol.* ii, *Pt.* 2, *foll.* 115, 47 *pls., Padova, Fr. Bolzetta,* MDCXLVIII ; *Vol.* ii, *Pt.* 3, *foll.* 83, 25 *pls., Padova, Fr. Bolzetta,* M.DC.XLVII (*with error of pag.*).
Has the addition : " nella quale si ha piena notitia di tutte le cose più notabili, & degne d'esser vedute. Et aggiuntoui in quest' ultima .impressione la Descrittion dell' Isole di Sicilia, & di Malta. [*At begin.* :] Padova appresso Francesco Bolzetta

Libraro., M.DC.XXXXIX, [*At, end* :] Padova, nella Stamparia del Crivellari, 1648." Another ed. Itinerarum Italiæ.—12⁰, *pp.* 606+11, 19 *pls. Amstelodami,* 1655. *See pp.* 529-70.

SCHOTTUS, FRANCESCUS.—Itinerario ovvero nova descrittione de' viaggi principali d'Italia . . . di A. Scoto [or rather of F. Schottus].—*See* SCHOTTUS, ANDREAS. Another ed. " Corretta, . . . abbellita, . . . & accresciuta della quarta parte."—8⁰. *Roma,* 1650.
Another ed. 3 pts. 8⁰. *Padova,* 1654.
Another ed. 8⁰. *Padova,* 1659.
Another ed. 12⁰. *Venetia,* 1665.
Another ed. 8⁰, *maps and pls. Padova, Bolzetta,* 1669.
Another ed. 8⁰. *Cadorin, Padova,* 1670.
Another ed. 8⁰. *Padova,* 1688.
Another ed. 12⁰. *Roma,* 1717.
Another ed. 12⁰. *Roma,* 1737.
Another ed.—Itinerario d'Italia. In questa nuova Edizione abbellito di rami, accresciuto, ordinato, ed emendato, ove si descrivono tutte le principali città d'Italia, e luoghi celebri, con le loro origini, antichità, e monumenti singolari, che nelle medesime si ammirano.—3 pts. in 1 vol. 8⁰, *foll.* 4, *pp.* 479, *foll.* 8, 1 *map,* 25 *pls., frontisp. Roma, a spese di Fausto Amidei Mercante di Libri al Corso. Nella Stamperia del Bernabò, e Lazzarini.* MDCCXLVII.
See pp. 444-48, pl. of Pozzuoli and of Cuma.
Another ed. *Roma,* 1761.

SCHROEDER (del. et sc.).—Naples. Vue du Jardin Royal. Italie. Imp^le Gilquip, Dupain r. de la Calandre 19, Paris.—Publié par Dufour, Mulat et Boulanger.
Fine engrav. : 148×98 mm.

SCHULTZ, A. W. F.—Die Heilquellen bei Neapel.—*Berlin,* 1837.

SCIARELLI, F.—Pozzuoli e suoi dintorni. Impressioni del presente e memorie del passato.—8⁰, *pp.* 1+100, 1 *pl. Napoli,* 1893.

SCIVOLETTO, P.—*See* LUCA, S. DE. 1870.

SCLOPIS, I.—Prospetto Generale della città di Napoli, dedicato a Sua Ecc^ra Georgiana Vicecontessa Spencer. Napoli, 15 Febb. 1764, dal suo Umil^mo Serv^re Ignazio Sclopis Conte del Borgo.
Panorama of E. Naples from sea near the Faro. Engrav. : 2108×423 mm.

SCOTO, A.—*See* SCHOTTUS, ANDREAS.

SCOTO, F.—*See* SCHOTTUS, FRANCESCUS.

SCOTTI, Ant.—Dissertazione . oorografica storica delle due antiche distrutte città Miseno e Cuma.—4⁰, *pp.* 255, *col. map. Napoli*, 1775.

SCOTTI, C.—Omero e l'Isola d'Ischia.—8⁰, *pp. vii+96+foll. ii. Napoli*, 1907.

SCOTTO, F.—*See* SCHOTTUS, FRANCESCUS.

SCROPE, G. J. POULETT.—Considerations on Volcanos, the probable causes of their phenomena . . . and their connection with the present state and past history of the globe; leading to the establishment of a new Theory of the Earth.—8⁰, *pp. xxxi+270*, 2 *pls.*, 1 *map. London*, 1825.——2nd ed. entitled : Volcanos : the character of their phenomena. . . . With a descriptive Catalogue of all known Volcanos, etc.—8⁰, *pp. xi+490*, 1 *pl.*, 1 *col. map. London*, 1862. —Another copy 1872.—In French (transl. by Endymion) : 2 *col. pls. Paris*, 1864.— In Germ. (transl. by G. A. v. Klöden) : 1 *pl.*, 65 *figs. Berlin*, 1872.—Extr. in Ital. : *Bibl. Ital. xlv, pp.* 70–83, 211–26. *Milano*, 1827.

SCROPE, G. J. POULETT.—On the volcanic district of Naples (1827).—*Proc. Geol. Soc. i, pp.* 17–19. *London*, 1834.—*Trans. Geol. Soc. ii, pp.* 337–52, 1 *pl. London*, 1829.— *Bull. Sci. nat. xiv, pp.* 412–14. *Paris*, 1828.

SEIP, JOH. PHILIP.—Relatio de Caverna vaporifera sulphurea in lapicidina Pyromontana, quæ similis est Forea Neapolitanæ Grotta del Cane dicloe à D^no Misson et aliis descriptæ.—*Miscellanea Berolinensia . . . Soc. Reg. Scient. etc. v, pp.* 102–5. *Magdelburgica*, MDCCXXXVII.

SELHEIN, J. (pin.).—Vue du Fond du Golfe de Baye, et des Étuves de Neron prise du côté du Lac Lucrin. Beauvarlet execud.— A Paris chez Alibert M^d d'Estampes, Rue Froidmanteau, No. 16. Engrav. : 423×312 mm.

SEMENTINI, L., VALPÈS & CASSOLA.— Analisi e proprietà medicinali delle acque minerali di Castellamare.—*Napoli*, 1834.— Extr. in French : *Journ. Chim. méd. etc. S.* 2, *i, pp.* 240–45. *Paris*, 1835.—*Ann. Pharm. xv, pp.* 173–77. *Heidelberg*, 1835.

SEMMOLA, E.—*See* GUISCARDI, G. 1881.

SEMMOLA, G.—Delle Mofete del lago d'Agnano.—*Rend. R. Acc. Sci. vi, pp.* 237–43. *Napoli*, 1847.—*Ann. Chim. S.* 3, *vi, pp.*187–92. *Milano*, 1848.

SEMMOLA, M.—Analisi chimica delle acque potabili dei dintorni del Vesuvio e del Somma.—*Il Giambattista Vico, i,* 3, *pp.* 413-28. *Napoli*, 1857.

SENAPE, A.—Panorama di Napoli al Palazzo Caramanico. View of Chiaja Posilippo and Capri, circa 1858.   Pen-and-two-ink sketch in four sections : 1220×218 mm.

SENAPE, ANTONIO (Romano).—Dis^ne di Paesi con la penna da Lezione nel' istesso genere. Abita Gradoni di Chiaja. No. 59, 2⁰ piano. Napoli. 28 pen-and-ink sketches of Naples and vicinity, obl. fol. *See* Nos. 1, 5, 6, 7, 8 and 9.

SENTIERI, M.—Neapolis Regnum quo continentur Aprulium Ulterius et Citerius.— *Augusta Vind[elicorum,* 1740 ?] [B.M.— 23880 (13).]

SERPIERI, P. A.—Sul terremoto dell' isola d'Ischia del 28 luglio 1883.—*Nota letta al R. Ist. Lomb.* 13 *decembre* 1883.—*Rend. R. Ist. Lomb. S.* 2, *xvi, pp.* 969–81. *Milano*, 1883.

SIANO, F. DE.—Brevi e succinte notizie di storia naturale e civile dell' isola d'Ischia.— 8⁰, *pp. vii+106. — ?, — ?*

SIGISMONDO, G.—Descrizione della Città di Napoli e Suoi Borghi.—3 vols. 8⁰. *Vol. i, pp.* 8+287, 1 *map ; Vol. ii, pp.* 8+367 ; *Vol. iii, pp.* 8+320, *foll.* 2. 1788–89.

SILLIMAN, B.—Miscellaneous notes from Europe : 1. Present condition of Vesuvius. 2. Grotto del Cane and Lake Agnano. 3. Sulphur Lake of the Campagna, near Tivoli. 4. Meteorological Observatory of Mount Vesuvius, etc.—*Amer. Journ. Sci. S.* 2, *xii, pp.* 256–59. *New Haven*, 1851.

SILVESTRE, ISRAEL (del. et sculp.).— Maison de Plaisance du Viceroy de Naple. Israel ex cum privit Regis. (Pal. Donn' Anna.) Very fine circular engrav. : 118 mm. (? from : " Gravures de 129 vues en 83 planches ").

SILVESTRE, I. (fecit).—Veüe du Chasteau Neuf, et partie de la Ville de Naple. Avec privilège. Le Blond excudit. Circular engrav. : 133 mm.

SILVESTRE, I. (fecit).—Veüe d'un Palais des enuirons de Naple. Avec priuilège. A Paris chez N. Langlois. Circular engrav. : 132 mm.

SILVESTRE, I. (fecit).—Veüe d'un Palais des enuirons de Naple. Avec priuilege le Blond excudit. Circular engrav. : 134 mm.

SIMOND, L.—A Tour in Italy and Sicily.— 8⁰, *pp.* 618. *London*, 1828.

SIVRY, M. L. DE.—Rome et l'Italie Méridionale. Promenades et Pélerinages suivi d'une description sommaire de la Sicile.— 8⁰, *pp.* 368, 14 *pls. Paris* [1841]. *See* pl. at p. 264 : Mole of Caligula.

SKETTON (fils).—*See* AUDOT.—Views of the Campi Phlegræi.

SKIPPON, P.—An Account of a Journey made through part of the Low Countries, Germany, Italy, and France.—*See* A. and J. Churchill's collection of voyages and travels, *Vol. vi, pp.* 597-601. *London*, 1732.

SMITH, J., BYRNE, W., EDWARDS, J.— Select Views in Italy with topographical and historical descriptions in English and French.—2 vols. *obl.* 4⁰, 72 *pls.* and text. *London*, 1792-96. *See* Pls. 50-58.

SMITH, J.—Cuma. Engraved by B. T. Pouncy. Plate 50.—London, Published 15 May 1797, by John Smith, James Edwards and Willᵐ Byrne. Identical with Pl. 50 in Smith's " Views in Italy," but has in addition details of publication. Fine line engrav. : 192 × 129 mm.

SMITH, J. (drawn by).—Bay of Pozzuoli. Engraved by B. T. Pouncy.—London, Published 15 May 1797, by James Edwards, Willᵐ Byrne and John Smith. Plate 52. Fine line engrav. : 190 × 130 mm. Same as Pl. 52 in Smith's " Views in Italy," but with details of publication.

SMITH, J. (drawn by).—Solfatara. Engraved by B. T. Pouncy.—London, Published 15 May 1797, by Willᵐ Byrne, John Smith and James Edwards. Pl. 53. Fine line engrav. : 190 × 129 mm. Same as Pl. 53 in Smith's " Views in Italy," but with details of publication.

SMITH, J.—Lake Agnano. Engraved by W. Byrne. Plate 54.—London, Published 15 May 1797, by Willᵐ Byrne, John Smith and James Edwards. Similar to Pl. 54 in Smith's " Views in Italy," but with details of publication. Fine line engrav. : 190 × 127 mm.

SMITH, J.—Entrance into the Grotto of Posilipo. Engraved by B. T. Pouncy. Plate 55.—London, Published 1 Jan. 1798, by John Smith, Willᵐ Byrne and James Edwards. Similar to Pl. 55 in Smith's " Views in

Italy," but with details of publication. Fine line engrav. : 191 × 127 mm.

SMITH, J.—On Mount Vesuvius above Portici. Engraved by B. T. Pouncy.— London, Published 24 March 1798, by Willᵐ Byrne, John Smith and James Edwards. Pl. 59. Line engrav. : 190 × 128 mm. Identical with Pl. 59 in Smith's " Views in Italy," but with details of publication.

SOSSON, A.—*See* ROSCOE, T. 1849-50.

SPADA-LAVINI, A.—Sur l'âge des tufs de l'Île d'Ischia.—*Bull. Soc. géol. France, S.* 2, *xv, pp.* 362-65. *Paris*, 1858.

SPALLANZANI, L.—Viaggi alle due Sicilie e in alcune parti dell' Appennino.—6 vols. 8⁰. *Vol. i, pp.* 55+292, *tav.* 1-2 ; *Vol. ii, pp.* 351, *tav.* 3-9 ; *Vol. iii, pp.* 364 ; *Vol. iv, pp.* 356, *tav.* 10-11 ; *Vol. v, pp.* 371 ; *Vol. vi, pp.* 288. *Pavia*, 1792-97.—Another ed. 3 vols. 8⁰, *portrait and pls. Milano*, 1825. —In German : 8 vols. *Leipzig*, 1794-96. —Another ed. 5 vols. *Leipzig*, 1795-98. —In French : 2 vols. *T. i, pp.* 44+299, *pls. i-ii ; T. ii, pp.* 273, *pls. iii-ix. Berne*, 1795.—Another ed., transl. by G. Toscan : " Avec des notes du cit. Faujas-de-St. Fond," 6 tom. 8⁰. *T. i, pp.* 10+311, *pls. i-ii ; T. ii, pp.* 280, *pls. iii-v ; T. iii, pp.* 291 ; *T. iv, pp.* 272, *pls. vi-vii ; T. v, pp.* 309 ; *T. vi, pp.* 215. *Paris, an* VIII [1800].—In English : 4 vols. 8⁰. *Vol. i, pp.* 50+315, *pls.* 1-2 ; *Vol. ii, pp.* 389, *pls.* 3-7 ; *Vol. iii, pp.* 402, *pls.* 8-9 ; *Vol. iv, pp.* 394, *pls.* 10-11. *London*, 1798.—*See also* Pinkerton's collection of voyages and travels, *Vol. v. London*, 1809.

SPUHLER, A.—Mon Voyage en Italie.— 800 photos. *Paris, Leipzig*, — ?

STANFIELD, C. (paint.).—The Castle of Ischia from the original painting in the possession of George Knott, Esq. Art Union of London 1844. Engraved by E. Goodall.—Printed by McQueen. Very fine engrav. : 570 × 345 mm.

STANFIELD, C. (pinx.).—Ischia from the picture in the Royal Collection. R. Brandart Sculpt. Size of picture 1 ft. 1¾ in. by 9 ft. ¾ in. (this must be an error).—*Art Journal, iv, p.* 197, *one column of text.* 1858. Steel engrav. London : James S. Virtue : 252 × 209 mm. The original is in R. collection at Osborne.

STANFIELD, R. A.—*See* MAPEI, C.—Italy. Classical, Historical and Picturesque.

STEFANI, C. DE.—La Villa Puteolana di Cicerone ed un fenomeno precursore all' eruzione del Monte Nuovo.—*Atti R. Acc. Lincei, S.* 5, *Rend. x, sem.* 1, *pp.* 128–31. *Roma*, 1901.

STEFANI, C. DE.—I proietti di Leucotefrite nei Campi Flegrei.—*Atti R. Acc. Lincei, S.* 5, *Rend. xiv, sem.* 1, *pp.* 598–603. *Roma*, 1905.

STEFANI, C. DE.—Die Phlegräischen Felder bei Neapel.—4⁰, *pp.* 290, 2 geol. maps, 67 figs. *Gotha*, 1907.—*Peterm. Mitth. Ergänzungsbd.* 156, *pp. i–iv*, 1–201, figs., 1 geol. map. *Gotha*, 1907.

STEFANI, C. DE.—Die Phlegräischen Felder bei Neapel.—67 figs., map. *Gotha*, 1908.

STEFANONI, L.—Le cause del Terremoto (Casamicciola 1883).—"*Messaggero*," 2 e 3 agosto, 1883.

STEINMANN, G.—Ueber das Alter des Apenninkalkes von Capri.—*Ber. Naturf. Gesellsch. iv,* 3, *pp.* 48–52. *Freiburg i. B.*, 1889.

STEINMANN, G.—Sulla età del calcare appenninico di Capri. (Traduzione dal tedesco con note di M. Canavari.)—*Boll. R. Com. Geol. Ital. xx, pp.* 25–31. *Roma*, 1889.

STELLA STARRABBA, F.—Il Cratere di Santa Teresa nei Campi Flegrei.—*Rend. R. Acc. Sci. S.* 3, xvi, *p.* 19. *Napoli*, 1910.—*Id. Atti, S.* 2, xiv, 7, *pp.* 1–21, *pls. i–iv.* 1910.

STIELER, C.—Italy from the Alps to Mount Etna. Translated by F. E. Trollope and edited by T. A. Trollope.—*fol., pp. xiii+*468, *num. pls. London*, 1877.

STINY, J.—Ueber die Entstehung einer neuen Bocca in der Solfatara bei Pozzuoli.—*Mitth. deutsch. Naturwiss.-vereines beider Hochschulen in Graz. H.* 2, *p.* 6. 1898.

STOLBERG, F. L.—Reise in Deutschland, der Schweiz, Italien und Sicilien.—4 vols. 8⁰. *Königsburg und Leipzig*, 1794. Atlas, 4⁰.—In English : 2 vols. 4⁰. *London*, 1796-97. *See* Vols. i and ii.

STOPPANI, A.—Corso di Geologia.—3 vols. 8⁰. *Milano*, 1871–73. *See* Vol. i : Dinamica Terrestre. *Milano*, 1871.

STOPPANI, A.—Corso di Geologia. 3a ediz. con note ed aggiunte per cura di Allessandro Malladra.—3 vols. 8⁰. *Vol. i, pp.* 695, 178 figs., 1 map, *Milano*, 1900 ; *Vol. ii, pp.* 883, 217 figs., 2 maps, 1903; *Vol. iii, pp.* 714, 60 figs., 1903. *See* Vol. i.

STRIDBECK, JOHAN (fecit et excudit).—Napoli. Bird's-eye view of Naples as seen from the sea with explan. in two columns, left in Italian, right in German. Engrav.: 316 × 167 mm.

SUESS, E.—Das Antlitz der Erde.—3 vols. 8⁰. *Prag, Wien, Leipzig,* 1883–1909.—In French, transl. by E. de Margerie, 3 tom. in 5 pts. 8⁰. *Paris, A. Colin,* 1897.—In English, 8⁰. *Oxford,* 1904.

SWAINE.—*See* TAYLOR.

SWINBURNE, H.—Travels in the Two Sicilies in the years 1777–80.—2 vols. 4⁰. *London*, 1783.——2nd ed. 2 vols. 8⁰. *Vol. i, pp.* lxviii+307, 5 pls. ; *Vol. ii, pp.* xi+359, 3 pls. 1790.——3rd ed. 1795.—In French, *Didot, Paris,* 1785.—In German, I. R. Forster, 2 pts. *Hamburg*, 1785.

SYMONDS, J. A.—Sketches and Studies in Italy and Greece.—3 vols. 8⁰. *London*, 1898. *See* Vol. iii.

TAINE, H.—Voyage en Italie.—2 tom. 8⁰. *Paris*, 1866. *See* Tom. i : Naples et Rome.

TARCAGNOTA, G.—Del sito et lodi della città di Napoli.—8⁰, foll. 12+174. *Napoli*, 1566. [C.A.]

TARDIEU, B. (gravé par).—Carte des Cratères Éteints entre Naples et Cumes. Écrit par Miller.—*See* BREISLAK, S.—Voyages Physiques et Lithologiques....—*T. ii, p.* 18, *pl. iv. Paris,* 1801.

TAULERI, B.—Discorsi familiari sopra le Meteore.—12⁰, *pp.* 24+252. *Napoli*, 1709. *See* pp. 196–208 : " De' fuocchi sotterranei," which refers to Vesuv. erupt. of 1631.

TAVRINESIS (del. et sculp.).—A panorama of the town of Naples from the Bay. [B.M. Portfolio of Naples.] Engraving in 2 sheets : 730 × 502 mm.

TAYLOR, A., and SWAINE.—An account of the Grotta del Cane ; with remarks on suffocation by carbonic acid.—*Med. Phys. Journ.* lxviii, *pp.* 278–85, 1 fig. *London*, 1832.—*Notizen a. d. Gebiete d. Nat. u. Heilkunde.* xxxvi, coll. 49–52. *Erfurt und Weimar*, 1833.

TCHIHATCHEFF, P. DE.—Coup d'œil sur la constitution géologique des provinces méridionales du Royaume de Naples et observations sur les environs de Nice.

Avec carte géologique de S. Germano (Cassino) jusqu'à l'extrémité méridionale de la Calabre.—*Berlin*, 1842.

TELLSII BERNARDINI CONSENTINI.— De hisquæ in Aere fiunt, et de terræmotibus. Liber unicus.—4⁰, *foll.* 13. *Neapoli*, 1570. [C.A.]

TEMPLE, Sir G.—*See* WRIGHT, G. N. 1839 (?).

TENORE, G.—[Tufo volcanico di Piedimonte d'Alife.]—*Ann. Acc. Aspir. Nat. S.* 2, i, *pp. lxxxii–lxxxiii* [*lxxii–lxxiii*]. *Napoli*, 1847.

TENORE,.G.—Il tufo vulcanico della Campania e le sue applicazioni alle costruzioni. —*Boll. Coll. Ing. Arch. x*, 5–8. *Napoli*, 1892.

TENORE, M.—Cenno sulla Geografia fisica, e botanica del regno di Napoli.—8⁰, *pp.* 121, 2 *geog. maps*. *Napoli*, 1827.—In French : 8⁰, *pp.* 130, 2 *col. maps*. *Naples*, 1827.

TENORE, M.—Relazione del Viaggio fatto in alcuni luoghi di Abruzzo Citeriore nella state del 1831.—8⁰, *pp.* 132, *geog. map*. *Napoli*, 1832.

TENORE, M.—Ragguagli di alcune peregrinazioni effettuate in diversi luoghi delle provincie di Napoli e di Terra di Lavoro, nella primavera e nell' estàt del 1832.— *Il Progr. Sci. iv*, *pp.* 177–95 ; v, *pp.* 41–63, 161–75 ; vi, *pp.* 187–211. *Napoli*, 1833.

TENORE, M.—Intorno ad un passo degli " Elementi di Geologia " del Sig. Lyell relativo al Serapeo di Pozzuoli.—*Rend. R. Acc. Sci. i*, *p.* 415. *Napoli*, 1842.

TENORE, M.—Polvere caduta in Napoli colla pioggia nella notte del 9 al 10 novembre 1842.—*Ann. Fis. Chim. xi*, *pp.* 60–61. *Milano*, 1843.

TENORE, M.—Due lettere sull' Isola d'Ischia. —*Napoli*, 1858.

THOMAS, T. H.—A Visit to the Volcanoes of South Italy.—*Trans. Cardiff Nat. Soc. xxiii*, *pp.* 10–19. *Cardiff*, 1892. *See* Pt. ii : The Neapolitan District.

THOMPSON, G.—*See* THOMSON, W.

THOMSON, J. E. H.—The Temple of Jupiter Serapis in Puteoli (Pozzuoli).—*Geol. Mag.* 1892, *p.* 282.

THOMSON, W.—Breve notizia di un viaggiatore sulle incrostazioni silicee termali d'Italia e specialmente di quelle dei Campi Flegrei.—8⁰, *pp.* 35. *Napoli*, 1795. [O.V.]

THOMSON, W.—Topografia fisica della Campania.

THUILLIER fils (gravé par).—Carte Physique de la Campanie. Écrit par Miller.— *See* BREISLAK, S.—Voyages Physiques et Lithologiques.—*T. i, pl.* 1. *Paris*, 1801.

TISCHBEIN (fecᵗ).—Puzzole. Water-colour painting of Pozzuoli and Baja about 1775 with 28 ref. nos. in ink. The Capucin monastery is seen standing on a reef joined to the mainland : 920 × 34 mm.

TISSANDIER.—Le tremblement de terre d'Ischia du 28 juillet 1883. Rapport de la Commission.—" *La Nature*," i, *pp.* 91–94, 1 *map.* 1885.

TOLEDO, P. G. DA.—Ragionamento del Terremoto, del nuovo Monte, del Aprimento di Terra in Pozuolo nel anno 1538 e dela significatione d'essi.—4⁰, *foll.* 16, 1 *pl.* *Napoli, per Giouani Sultzhab*, 1539.

TOLEDO, P. G. DA.—De Puteolani aeris natura, epistola.—*foll.* 4. *Napoli*, 1544. [C.A.]

TONDI, M.—Catalogo delle collezioni orittologica ed oreognostica del fu prof. M. Tondi.—8⁰, *pp. viii*+243. *Napoli*, 1837.

TONO, M.—Il terremoto dell' Isola d'Ischia. —*Ann. Astro-Meteor. Osservat. Patriarcale di Venezia*, 1884.

TORCIA, M.—*See* PELORITANO.

TRIBOLET, M. DE.—Ischia et Java en 1883. —*Conférence académique*, 8⁰, *pp.* 37. *Neuchâtel*, 1884.

TRIDON, L.—Lettera al Petit Journal, août 1883.

TROLL, H.—*See* FUESSLI.

TROLLOPE, F. E.—*See* STIELER, C.

TROLLOPE, T. A.—*See* STIELER, C.

TURLERUS, H.—De peregrinatione et Agro Neapolitano, Libri II. . . . Omnibus peregrinantibus utiles ac necessarii : ac in eorum gratiam nunc primum editi.—8⁰. *Argentorati*, 1574. [B.N.] *See* pp. 85–86.

TURPIN DE CRISSÉ, CTE.—Souvenirs du Golfe de Naples recueillis en 1808, 1818 et 1824.—4⁰, *pp.* 65, 2 *maps*, 38 *pls.*, 10 *figs.*, *frontisp.* (fine steel engrav.). *Paris*, 1828.

TURPIN DE CRISSÉ, CTE. (peint.).— [Temple of Venus looking towards Pozzuoli.] Gravé par Lemaître 1828. Fine engrav. on double paper : 205 × 150 mm.

TURPIN DE CRISSÉ, Cte. (des.).—I ponti Rossi. Gravé par Lemaître. 2ᵐᵉ Liv. Pl. 7.
Engrav. on double paper : 230×170 mm.

TURPIN DE CRISSÉ, Cte. (peint.).—Ravin de Sorrento. Gravé par Aubert. 5ᵐᵉ Liv. Pl. 21.
Fine engrav. on double paper : 135× 100 mm.

TURPIN DE CRISSÉ, Cte. (peint.) — Château d'Ischia. Gravé par Lemaître. 7ᵉᵐᵉ Liv. Pl. 31.
Steel engrav. : 203×167 mm.

TURPIN DE CRISSÉ, Cte. (pinxt.), JOLY (del.), BONNEMAISON, (direxit). —Vuo de Naples, prise du Quai Sᵗᵉ Lucie.—Imp. Lith. de Villain.
Coloured litho. : 288×235 mm.

TURSINI, A., e ANGELIS D'OSSAT, G. De. —Sulla presenza del litio nella Nocerina.— Lettera al Prof. L. Palmieri.—*Rend. R. Acc. Sci. xxi, pp.* 74–75. *Napoli,* 1882.

TYFERNUS, A.—*See* ARETINUS, Franc.

ULRICH (pinx.).—Naples. Ruines du Palais de la Reine Jeanne. Royaume de Naples. Martens sculp. A Paris chez Rittner et Goupil.
Aquatint : 210×198 mm.

URSUS, J. B.—Inscriptiones.—*fol., foll.* 11, *pp.* 350. *Napoli,* 1642. [C.A.]
See pp. 14, 24, 26, 39, 99, 100, 101, 111, 331, 332, 333, 334, 336.

VALENTIN, L.—Voyage en Italie fait en l'année 1820. Deuxième édition corrigée et augmentée de nouvelles observations faites dans un second voyage en 1824.—8⁰, *pp.* 400. *Paris,* 1826.
See pp. 42–49, 73–84.

VALENZIANI, M.—Indice spiegato di tutte le produzioni del Vesuvio, della Solfatara e d'Ischia.—4⁰, *pp. lii+135. Napoli,* 1783. [C.A.]

VALMONT DE BOMARE.—Dictionnaire raisonné universel d'Histoire Naturelle, etc. —9 vols. 8⁰. *Paris,* 1775.
See Tom. ix. *See also* Vesuvius.

VALPÈS.—*See* SEMENTINI. 1834 and 1835.

VANDER AA, Pierre.—La Galerie Agréable du Monde, etc. Partie . . . Roïaume de Naples, Pouzol, Baja, etc.—*pp.* 5, 43 *pls. Leide,* — ? [B.N.P.]
Two plates show the mole in three parts with arches intact.

VASI, M.—Itinerario istruttivo da Roma a Napoli ovvero descrizione generale de' più insigni monumenti antichi, e moderni, e delle opere più rimarchevoli di pittura, scultura, ed architettura di questa celebre città.—3rd ed. 12⁰, *pp. ix+264, pls.,* 2 *plans. Roma,* 1816.—Other ed. : 2 tom. *Roma,* 1814.—2 tom. *Roma,* 1818.—2 tom. *Roma,* 1820, 19.—2 tom. *Roma,* 1824.— 2 tom. *Roma,* 1830.—2 tom. *Roma,* 1844.

VASI, M.—A New Picture of Naples, and its Environs ; in the form of an itinerary.— 16⁰, *pp. xii+364, pls.,* 1 *map,* 1 *plan. London* [1820 ?].

VASI, M.—Itinéraire instructif de Rome à Naples et à ses environs, tiré de celui de feu M. Vasi, et de la Sicile, tiré de celui de M. de Haraczay [by A. Nibby].—12⁰, *pp.* 399. *Rome,* 1826.—Other ed. : 2 tom. *Rome,* 1797.—2 tom. *Rome,* 1816.—(4th.) *Rome,* 1817.—2 tom. *Rome,* 1820.—2 tom. *Rome,* 1824 ; *Naples,* 1824.—2 tom. *Rome,* 1829. —2 tom. *Rome,* 1838, 39.

VASQUEZ DEL MARMOL, J.—*See* COLLE-NUCCIO, 1584.

VEAU, Le.—*See* CROIX, La.

VEGA, Mrs. De La.—Carte du Golfe de Pouzzoles avec une partie des Champs Phlégréens dans la Terre de Labour. [B.N.P., Vb. 113.]
A most beautifully shaded, accurate map, showing 15 piers to Caligula's mole.

VEGNI, L. De (inc.).—Veduta dell' ingresso della Grotta di Pozzuoli nella provincia di Napoli. No. ii, Tavola 1.
This is fig. ii of Pl. 1 of Vol. iii of ZUC-CAGNI - ORLANDINI, A. — Corografia Fisica Storica, etc. dell' Italia. Engrav. : 278×183 mm.

VELAIN, C.—Le tremblement·- de terre d'Ischia du 28 juillet 1883.—" La Nature," ii, 533, *pp.* 183–87, 2 *pls.,* 2 *maps.* 18 *août,* 1883.

VELAIN, C.—Les cataclysmes volcaniques de 1883 ; Ischia, Krakatoa, Alaska.— *Bull. hebd. Assoc. Sci. France,* 288 *and* 289, *pp.* 27, *figs. Paris, Oct.* 1885.

VELDE, I. V. (fecit).—Neapolis caput regni Neapolitani urbs amplitudine et Magnificentia toto orbe clarissima. [B.M. Portfolio of Naples.]
Panorama : 2174×487 mm.

VERDE, M., e REALE, N.—Dell' analisi chimica di una nuova acqua termo-minerale nel comune di Forio d'Ischia, prec. da una descriz. natur. dell' Isola.—8⁰, *pp.* 3–26. *Napoli,* 1866.

VERNET, J.—Vue de Pausilype près de Naples. Dédié à Monsieur de Tolozan, etc., Robert Daudet sculpsit 1785. Le tableau original est dans le cabinet de Mr de Tolozan.—A Paris chez Basan et Poignant, Rue et Hôtel Serpente, etc. Much idealised engrav. : 614×433 mm.

VERNON, H.—*See* FUESSLI.

VERRI, A.—Studio geologico delle sorgenti del Sarno : " Sorgenti, estuario e canale del fiume Sarno."—4⁰, *pp.* 119–51, *tav. Roma*, 1902.

VETRANI, A.—Sebethi vindiciæ, sive dissertatio de Sebethi antiquitate, nomine, fama, cultu, origine, prisca magnitudine, decremento, atque alveis, adversus Jacobum Martorellium.—8⁰, *pp.* 8+213, 2 *pls. Neapoli*, 1767.

VIANELLI.—*See* VIANELLY.

VIANELLO.—*See* VIANELLY.

VIANELLY, A. (dis.).—Strada nuova di Posilipo costrutta nell' anno 1825.—T. Witting inc. in Napoli. [Vienna lib.] Sepia stipple engrav. : 401×268 mm.

VIANELLY, [A.]—[View of bay of Naples from summit of Monte Epomeo in Ischia.] —*Naples* ?, 1828. A line lithogr. plate.

VIANELLY, [A.]—Pestum. [B.M. Portfolio of Naples.] View : 415×305 mm.

VIARD.—*See* DARONDEAU.—Carte . . . des côtes d'Italie.

VIDALIN.—*See* DARONDEAU.—Carte . . . des côtes d'Italie.

VIENNELLY (dis.).—*See* VIANELLY.

VILLAMENA, F.—Ager Puteolanes, sive prospectus eiusdem insigniores.—4⁰, 24 *pls. Roma*, 1652. [C.A.]

VILLANO, G.—Chroniche de la inclyta cita de Napole emendatissime : con li Bagni de Puzolo et Ischia : nouamente ristampate : con la tauola.—8⁰, *foll. lxxxv*+6. *Neapoli*, M.D.XXVI.—*Raccolta di varii libri overo opusc. hist. Reg. Nap.* 4⁰, *pp.* 120+*viii*, 1 *fig. Napoli*, 1680.

VILLANO, G.—Trattato utilissimo de li Bagni Napolitani de Pozolo e di Ischia.— *Istorie Fiorentine, Lib.* VIII, *cap.* 53. *Napoli*, 1526.

VINALLY (dip.).—*See* VIANELLY.

VIRGILIO, G.—I Campi Flegrei. Ricordanze.—4⁰, *pp.* 24. *Napoli*, 1877. [C.A.]

VISCONTI, R.—Topografia dell' Isola d'Ischia.

VISSCHER, N.—Totius Italiæ. Tabula.

VIZIOLI, F.—Intorno le acque minerali del Golfo di Napoli.—*Notizie. Dal Morgagni. Napoli, giugno*, 1869.

VOLAIRE.—Naples. Vue de la Solfatara près de Pouzzole. Ancien Volcan nommé par Strabon Forum Vulcani. Peint d'après Nature par Volaire à Naples. Gravé par P. Duflos. No. 19, A.P.D.R. Fine engrav. [*circa* 1780] : 377 × 227 mm.

VOLPICELLA, S.—Studi di Letteratura Storia ed Arti, con le poesie e vita del Costanzo vita del Iansillo, la Madonna di Atella, il palazzo Donnanna a Posilipo, antichita di Amalfi, cenni storici su Amoretto, San Giorgio, San Sebastiano, Massa di Somma, Pollena, Trocchia, Lacco, Casamicciola, etc.—12⁰, *pp.* 534+2. *Napoli*, 1876.

WALTHER, J. K.—I vulcani sottomarini del Golfo di Napoli.—*Boll. R. Com. Geol. Ital. pp.* 360–70, 1 *pl. Roma*, 1886.

WALTHER, J. K., SCHIRLITZ, P.—Studi geologici sul Golfo di Napoli.—*Boll. R. Com. Geol. Ital. pp.* 383–96. *Roma*, 1886.—In German : *Zeitschr. deutsch. geol. Gesellsch. xxxviii, pp.* 295–341. *Berlin*, 1886.

WALTHER, J. K.—Ueber die Geologie von Capri.—*Zeitschr. deutsch. geol. Gesellsch. xli, pp.* 771–76. *Berlin*, 1890.

WARREN (sc.).—View in the Gulph of Naples (? coast of Posilippo). Engrav. : 203×135 mm.

WASHINGTON, H. S.—On some Ischian Trachytes.—*Amer. Journ. Sci. S.* 4. i, *pp.* 375–85. *New Haven*, 1896.

WASHINGTON, H. S.—Some analyses of Italian Volcanic Rocks (Mte. Nuovo and Mte. Cuma, Ischia).—*Amer. Journ. Sci. S.* 4, *viii, pp.* 286–94, 1899 ; ix, *pp.* 44–54, *New Haven*, 1900.

WASHINGTON, H. S.—Chemical Analyses of Igneous Rocks published from 1884–1900, with a critical discussion of the character and use of analyses.—*U.S. Geol. Surv. Prof. Paper* 14, *pp.* 495. *Washington*, 1903.

WASHINGTON, H. S.—The Superior Analyses of Igneous Rocks, from Roth's Tabellen, 1869–1884, arranged according to the Quantitative System of Classification.— *U.S. Geol. Surv. Prof. Paper* 28, *pp.* 61. *Washington*, 1904.

WATERS, A. W.—Remarks on the recent geology of Italy suggested by a short visit to Sicily, Calabria and Ischia [1877].— *Trans. Manchester Geol. Soc. xiv, pp.* 251–82. 1877.

WEBER, C.—De Agro et vino Falerno.— *Marburgi,* 1855.

WEBERT, C., et CLERMONT.—Carte des Environs de la Ville et du Golfe de Naples. [As insets :] Plan du Cratère, dessiné le 2 Janvier 1778. Coupe du Cratère sur la ligne A.B. Dessiné le 2 Janvier 1778. A good, engraved map of Vesuvius : 480 × 367 mm.

WENTRUP, F.—Der Vesuv und die vulkanische Umgebung Neapels.—8⁰, *pp.* 35. *Wittemberg,* 1860. [C.Á.]

WERNER, F. B. (delin.).—Neapolis. Hæred. Jer. Wolffij. execudit A.V. [Vienna lib.] Views of Naples to Solfatara from sea ; 72 ref. nos. : 1007 × 341 mm.

WERTHER.—[Ein Ausflug zur Solfatara bei Pozzuoli.]—*Schrift. k. phys.-ökonom. Gesellsch. x, Sitz. pp.* 8–9. *Königsberg,* 1869.

WESTPHAL, G. E.—Carta de' contorni di Napoli per uso de' Forestieri e Viaggiatore rettificata ed accresciuta in Napoli a tutto il 1880.—*Napoli, Detken e Rocholl,* 1880. Scale 1 : 90,000.

WICHMANN, A.—Angebl. Bezieh. zw. Solfataren u.d. granitisch-körnigen Structur saurer Eruptivgesteine. [1890.]

WILLIAMS, COOPER.—Vues de la Méditerranée.—2 *maps,* 18 *pls.* — ? [1820 ?]

WILLYAMS, REV. C.—A Selection of Views in Egypt, Palestine, Rhodes, Italy, Minorca and Gibraltar, from the original drawings, executed during a visit to those places : with a geographical and historical description to each view, in English and French.— *gd.* 4⁰, *pp.* 36. *London,* 1822. *See* p. 22 and plate.

WILSON, J.—A History of Mountains, Geographical and Mineralogical. Accompanied by a picturesque view of the principal mountains of the World, in their respective proportions of height above the level of the sea by Robert Andrew Riddell. —3 vols. *Vol. i, pp. lv*+368+176, *London,* 1807 ; *Vol. ii, pp.* 735, *London,* 1809 ; *Vol. iii, pp.* 906+*index, London,* 1810. *See* Vol. ii. Vols. ii and iii read : " A History . . . to accompany a picturesque view, etc."

WILSON, R. (del.).—Castle of Ischia. Jas. Gandon Sc. Published Jan. 29, 1776, by John Boydell, Engraver, in Cheapside, London. Engrav. : 243 × 172 mm.

WILSON, R. (del.).—Torre delle Grotte near Naples. W. Hodges Sc. Published Jan. 29, 1776, by John Boydell, Engraver, in Cheapside, London. Engrav. : 246 × 172 mm.

WOLF, H.—Suite von Mineralien aus dem vulcanischen Gebiete Neapels und Siciliens. —*Verh. k. k. geol. Reichsanst. pp.* 219–20. *Wien,* 1870.

WRIGHT, E.—Some Observations made in travelling through France, Italy, etc. In the Years 1720, 1721, and 1722.—2 vols. 4⁰. *London,* 1730.——2nd ed. *London,* 1764. *See* Vol. i, pp. 149–89.

WRIGHT, G. N.—The Shores and Islands of the Mediterranean drawn from Nature by Sir Grenville Temple, Bart., W. L. Leitch, Esq., Major Irton, and Lieut. Allen, R.E., with an analysis of the Mediterranean and description of the plates by the Rev. G. N. Wright.—4⁰, *pp.* 156, 65 *pls.* *London and Paris,* 1839 ? *See* pp. 137, 139, 143.

WRIGHT, G. N.—The Rhine, Italy and Greece illustrated. In a series of views from drawings on the spot. By W. L. Leitch, Col. Cockburn and Major Irton. With descriptions by the Rev. G. N. Wright.—2 vols. in 18 pts. 4⁰, 73 [beautiful] *steel-engraved pictures. London, Fischer, and Paris,* 1841.

WUTKY, M.—Ansicht der [Astroni, wrongly marked] Solfatara [seen from its W. side] bei Neapel. Oil painting (No. 326) : 620 × 490 mm. ; and a similar gouache (No. 404) : 580 × 460 mm. in the Akad. d. Bildenden Künste, Vienna.

WUTKY, M.—Die Solfatara und der Golf von Bajae (from opposite entrance of former). Large oil painting (No. 334) in the Akad. d. Bildenden Künste, Vienna.

WYLD, W. (del.).—Vue de Naples. Salon de 1841. W. Wyld, Imp. Petit Bertauts. Challamel et Cie., édit., 4 rue de l'Abbaye. F. Sᵗ Gᵃⁱⁿ. Litho. : 205 × 139 mm.

YOUNG, T. GRAHAM.—The gas of the Grotta del Cane [near Naples].—*Journ. Chem. Soc. xxxiii, Trans. pp.* 51–52. *London,* 1878.

ZAMBONINI, F.—Su alcuni Minerali della grotta dell Zolfo a Miseno [Campi Flegrei].—*Rend. R. Acc. Sci. S.* 3, *xiii, pp.* 324–31. *Napoli,* 1907.—*Riv. Min. e Crist. Ital. xxxvi, pp.* 27–37. *Padova,* 1908.

ZAMPARI, F.—Impressioni scientifiche sul disastro d'Ischia.—" *Pungolo di Napoli,*" 12 *agosto,* 1883.

ZARLENGA, R.—Breve annotazione sui terremoti della Valie di Sora del 1873.—*Il Piria, i. Napoli,* 1873.

ZARLENGA, R.—L'Isola d'Ischia.—"*Roma di Napoli,*" 16 *agosto,* 1883.

ZERBI, R. DE (relatore).—Relazione della commissione sul disegno di legge presentato alla Camera il 26 novembre, 1883. Provvedimenti a favore dei dannegiati dal terremoto del 28 luglio, 1883, nell' Isola d'Ischia.—*Gazz. Uffic.* 10 *marzo.*

ZEZI, P.—*See* COMITÉ D'ORGANISATION, etc.—Bibliographie Géologique, etc. No. XI. 1881.

ZINNO, S.—Sulle industrie delle roccie e minerali dei Campi Flegrei.—*Il Piria, i,* 2. *Napoli,* 1872.

ZINNO, S.—Nuova analisi delle acque minerali delle terme Manzi in Casamicciola d'Ischia, con brevi riflessioni del dott. B. Paoni.—*Napoli,* 1880.

ZINNO, S.—Analisi delle acque di Fornello e Fontana ai Bagni d'Ischia.—*Napoli,* 1881.

ZINNO, S.—*See* GUISCARDI, G. 1881.

ZONA, T.—Sopra operazioni che si dovrebbero fare ad Ischia.—*Riv. Scient. del Vimercati,* 1884.

ZUCCAGNI-ORLANDINI, A.—Atlante Illustrativo ossia Raccolta dei Principali Monumenti Italiani Antichi, del Medio Evo e Moderni e di alcune Vedute Pittoriche per servire di Corredo alla Corografia fisica storica e statistica dell' Italia.—3 vols. of pls. *gd. fol. Firenze,* 1845.

The first two are views of N. and Central Italy, the third of Naples and Sicily.

ZUCCAGNI-ORLANDINI, A. — Corografia fisica storica e statistica dell' Italia e delle sue isolec orredata di un atlante di mappe geografiche e topografiche e di altre tavole illustrative.—12 pts. in 17 vols. 8°. *Firenze,* 1845.

See Vol. ii.

Atlas.—4 vols. *fol., maps and views.*

VESUVIUS

ANON.—An Abstract of a Letter from an English Gentleman at Naples to his Friend in London, containing an Account of the Eruption of Mount Vesuvius May 18 and the following Days, 1737.—*Phil. Trans. R. Soc. xli, pp.* 252–61. *London,* 1744.

ANON.—Account of a descent into the crater of Mount Vesuvius by eight Frenchmen on the night between the 18th and 19th of July, 1801.—*Phil. Mag. xi, pp.* 134–40. *London,* 1801.

ANON.—Extract from "The Natural History of Mount Vesuvius, translated from the original Italian, compos'd by the Royal Academy of Sciences at Naples, by order of the king of the Two Sicilies."—[12⁰, *pp.* 239, *cuts, London.*]—"*Gentleman's Mag.*" *xvii, pp.* 417–20. *London,* 1747.

Account of the Eruption of Vesuvius, 1737, illustrated by 2 plates in Serao's account, but here shown as woodcuts entitled : " South West Prospect of Mount Vesuvius " and " The Section of Vesuvius, as if cut thro' its summit."

ANON.—An account of the eruption of Mount Vesuvius in Octob. 1751.—*Phil. Trans. R. Soc. xlvii, pp.* 409–12. *London,* 1753.

ANON.—An account of the eruption of Vesuvius, in 1767.—*Trans. Amer. Phil. Soc. i, pp.* 281–85. *Philadelphia,* 1771.

ANON.—Account of the late eruption of Mount Vesuvius May 31st.—*Moniteur, June 22nd,* 1806.—*Nicholson's Journ. Nat. Phil.* 58, *pp.* 345–50. *Aug.* 1806.

ANON.—The advices from Naples (Oct. 1834).

Newspaper cutting of 11 lines, in Johnston-Lavis collection.

ANON.—Análisis microscopico de las cenizas arrojadas por el Vesubio.—*Bol. Soc. mexic. geog. y estadist. xii,* 2. *Mexico,* 1862–65.

ANON.—Atlante di Vedute de' principali incendij del Monte Vesuvio, etc.—*See* TORRE, Duca Della. [C.A.]

ANON.—Atlante de' principali incendij del Monte Vesuvio, etc.—*See* TORRE, Duca Della. [C.A.]

ANON.—Aus dem alten Pompeji. Die Strasse zum Forum (S. 79).

Woodcut with view of Vesuvius through the ruins. Amphoræ in foreground. From a German illustr. paper : 247×163 mm.

ANON.—Ausbruch des Vesuvs von 1771.

A sepia engraving after Volaire's picture No. 872 in the Akad. d. Bildenden Künste in Vienna. Mounted on blue paper back, with printed black scroll frame : 295× 195 mm. Title separately mounted below on the blue paper and not included in measurement.

ANON.—Der Ausbruch des Vesuvs am 25 und 26 Dezember 1813. (Nach Herrn Monticellis Bericht.)—*Taschenb. gesammt. Min. xiv, pp.* 85–104. *Frankfurt,* 1820.

ANON.—Ausbruch des Vesuv.—*Taschenb. gesammt. Min. xxii, pp.* 480–81. *Frankfurt,* 1828.

ANON.—Der Ausbruch des Vesuv.— " *Globus,*" i, *pp.* 276–78. *Hildburgh,* 1861.

ANON.—Der Ausbruch des Vesuv am 8 December 1861.—*Illustrirte Zeitung,* 966, *p.* 8, 1 *illustr. Leipzig,* 1862.

ANON.—Der Ausbruch des Vesuv [1861]. I–III.—*Ueber Land u. Meer, pp.* 252–53, 1 *fig.* ; 265, 1 *fig.* ; 278, 1 *fig. Stuttgart,* 1862.

ANON.—Der Ausbruch des Vesuv am 26 April, 1872.—*Westermann's Monatshefte, xxxii, pp.* 447–48. *Braunschweig,* 1872.

ANON.—Ueber die Ausbrueche des Vesuv.— *Taschenb. gesammt. Min. iii, pp.* 211–12. *Frankfurt,* 1809.

ANON.—*See* AUTORI VARII, 1779.

ANON.—Avvisi e notizie sull' Eruzione del Vesuvio del 1631, provenienti da Roma e da Napoli dal di 27 dicembre 1631 al di 21 febbraio 1632.—*In the Cancelleria Ducale Estense.*

ANON.—Avviso al pubblico, sull' analisi della cenere eruttata dal Vesuvio (nel di 16 di Giugno 1794).—*loose sheet.* — ?, — ? [B.N.]

ANON.—La Baie de Naples, où aura lieu, le 29 Avril, la grande Revue Navale en l'honneur du Président de la République.— Supplément au No. 3191 de " L'Illustration," 23 Avril, 1904.
Photo. engrav. tinted blue: 504 × 320 mm.

ANON.—Beobachtungen am Vesuv.—*Westermann's Monatshefte, xxxiv, p.* 225. *Braunschweig,* 1872.

ANON.—Bibliografia dell' Incendio Vesuviano dell' anno 1631.—*See* SCACCHI.— Istoria delle eruzioni, etc. 1847.

ANON.—Bibliographie géologique et paléontologique de l'Italie, par les soins du Comité d'Organisation du 2e Congrès Géologique International à Bologne.—8⁰, *pp. viii*+630. *Bologne,* MDCCCLXXXI.

ANON.—Blauer vesuvischer Kalkstein.— *Taschenb. gesammt. Min. iii. pp.* 199–200. *Frankfurt,* 1809.

ANON.—Blick auf die Phlegraeischen Gefilde und den Vesuv von Epomeo auf Yschia [1834]. [B.M. 24043 (3).]

ANON.—Bollettino della Società Sismologica Italiana, pubblicato per cura del Prof. Pietro Tacchini in unione al Ministero di Agricoltura, Industria e Commercio.— 2 vols. 8⁰, *illustr. Roma,* 1895–96.

ANON.—Breve Catalogo di alcuni prodotti ritrovati nell' ultima eruzione del Vesuvio. —*Giorn. Lett. xli, pp.* 51–55. *Napoli,* 1795.

ANON.—Breve Descrizione della città di Napoli e del suo Contorno.—8⁰, *pp. xvi*+ 344. *Napoli,* M.DCC.XCII.

ANON.—Breve descrizione geografica del regno di Sicilia.—4⁰. *Palermo,* 1787. [B.N.]

ANON.—Breve descrizione del Monte Vesuvio, e suoi Incendj cavata fedelmente da cio, che ne scrive il P. Giulio Cesare Recupito della Comp⁰ di Gesù, & altri Autori. Anno D'ni 1737.—*pp.* 35. 1737. MS. : 185 × 126 mm.

ANON.—Breve Narratione de Maravigliosi Essempi, occorsi nell' Incendio del Monte Vesuuio, circa l'Anno 1038. Cauata dall' Opere del' Beato Pietro Damiano dell' Ordine Camaldolense Cardinale di Santa Chiesa.—16⁰, *foll.* 4. *Napoli, Matteo Nucci,* 1632. [B.N.]

ANON.—Breve resúmen historico de las erupciones del Vesubio.—*Mem. liter. instruct. y cur. de la Corte de Madrid, xxvii, pp.* 401–23. *Madrid,* 1794.

ANON.—*See* BRITISH ASSOCIATION COMMITTEE.

ANON.—Brücke la Nunziata unter den Berg Vesuvio. No. 72.
Engrav. with ref. letters and explan. text : 307 × 203 mm.—*See also* S. Martino Mus. 10009.

ANON.—Carta (Corografica) d'Italia.—*Ist. Geog. Milit. Ital.* 1889.
1 : 1,000,000, in 7 sheets.—3 ed. 1st, in 3 colours, with mountains shaded in brown and water in blue ; 2nd, mountains in grey ; 3rd, without mountain shading. *See* sheet 4.

ANON.—Carta (Corografica) d'Italia.—*Ist. Geog. Milit. Ital.* 1889.
1 : 1,800,000, in 6 sheets.—2 ed. 1st, in three colours as in preceding ; 2nd, without the mountains shaded. *See* sheet 4.

ANON.—Carta Corografica del Regno d'Italia e delle Regioni Adiacenti.—*Ist. Geog. Milit. Ital.* 1889.
1 : 500,000, in 35 sheets.—3 ed. 1st, in 3 colours ; 2nd, in 2 colours ; 3rd, in black, without mountain shading. *See* sheet 24.

ANON.—Carta Geologica d'Italia nella scala di 1 : 1,000,000 in due fogli. 2a ed.—*R. Uffic. Geol. Ital. Roma,* 1889.

ANON.—Carta della Provincia di Napoli e parte delle contigue di Caserta, Salerno e Benevento.—*Ist. Topogr. Milit. Napoli,* 1861–75.
1 : 10,000, in 6 sheets, copper engrav. *See* sheet 3.

ANON.—Carta della Regione perturbata dai Fenomeni Vesuviani, cominciati il di 8 decembre 1861.—*Napoli,* 1862.
1 : 20,000.

ANON.—Carta Topografica e Idrografica dei contorni di Napoli.—*Ist. Topogr. Milit. Napoli,* 1818–70.
1 : 25,000, in 15 sheets, copper engrav. *See* sheet 9 (Vesuvius).

ANON.—Carta Topografica del Monte Vesuvio.—*Ist. Geog. Milit. Ital.* Firenze, 1877. 1 : 10,000, in 6 sheets. Contour map with contours of 5 m.

ANON.—Carta Topografica di Napoli e Dintorni.—*Ist. Geog. Milit. Ital.* 1885. 1 : 100,000, in 1 sheet similar to Carta Topogr. d. regno d'Italia (in 277 photoengraved sheets).—Campi Phlegræi and Vesuvius.

ANON. — Carta Topografica del regno d'Italia.—*Ist. Geog. Milit. Ital.* 1889. 1 : 100,000. Chromo-lithographic edition in 3 colours without line shading of mountains. *See* sheets 184, 185.

ANON.—Carta Topografica del regno d'Italia.—*Ist. Geog. Milit. Ital.* 1889. 1 : 100,000, in 277 photo-engraved sheets, in course of publication (1889). The orography is shown by contour lines of 50 m. as well as by zenith-light shading. *See* sheets 184, 185.

ANON.—Carta Topografica del regno d'Italia. 1 : 75,000. Economic ed. similar to above.

ANON.—Carte de la Baie de Naples levée en 1817, 1818 et 1819.—Dépôt Général de la Marine, 1850. [B.M.—H.F. Sec. 7 (1235).] Shows a plan of the crater of that date.

ANON.—Carte Géologique Internationale de l'Europe. Scale 1 : 1,500,000.

ANON. (CLERMONT ?).—Carte de l'Italie méridionale et de la Sicile ancienne, pays autrefois connus sous le nom de Grande Grèce. Rédigée et corrigée d'après les observations les plus récentes, et que l'on croit les plus certaines.

ANON.—Carte d'une partie du Golfe appelée le Cratère tel qu'il devait être avant l'éruption de 79, etc. [O.V.] A very fine engrav. with no indication.

ANON.—Carteggio di due amanti alle faldi del Vesuvio.—8⁰, *pp.* 45. *Pompei*, 1783. [C.A.]

ANON.—Catalogo della collezione Orittologica ed Θreognosica del fu chiarissimo Professore Cav. Matteo Tondi Direttore del Museo di Mineralogia di Napoli, etc.— 8⁰, *pp. viii*+243. *Napoli*, 1837.

ANON.—Catalogo delle materie appartenente al Vesuvio contenute nel Museo [Borbonico], con alcune brevi osservazione.

Opera del celebre autore de Dialoghi sul commercio de' Grani [*i.e.* F. Galiani].—12⁰. *Londra*, 1772. *See* GALIANI.

ANON.—Cenere del 22 Ottobre 1822. Vesuvius by day from the shore between Posilippo and Mergellina. Miniature gouache on parchment : 98×69 mm.

ANON.—Cenere de 22 Obre. 1822. Vesuvius from Naples by day. Three men in foreground, two sitting. Gouache : 203×132 mm.

ANON.—Cenere del 1846.—*Naples* ? A rough gouache, showing a small lava stream on W. side of great cone and some dust being ejected.

ANON.—Cenere del 1846. Vesuvius by day from Naples : four fishermen in foreground. Rather rough gouache : 233×163 mm.

ANON.—Cenno storico dell' eruzione del Vesuvio avvenuta in ottobre 1822.—8⁰, *pp.* 29. *Napoli*, 1822. [C.A.]

ANON.—La chûte de feu du Mont de Vésuve. —*Augsbourg.* [B.N.P., Vb. 121.] A good sepia litho.

ANON.—Collection complète ou liste des différentes productions du Mont Vésuve. Raccolta compita o sia lista delle differenti produzioni del Monte Vesuvio che si trovano presso il signor Nicola Amitrano.—4⁰. — ?, — ? [B.N.]

ANON.—Compendio delle Transazioni filosofiche, ecc.—*Giorn. Lett.* v, *pp.* 78–89. *Napoli*, 1793.

ANON.—Cono Vesuviano. 1 : 10,000.—*Ist. Geog. Milit. Ital.* 1900.

ANON.—Delle Conseguenze arrecate alle campagne ed alle culture agrarie dalla Eruzione Vesuviana dell' aprile 1906.—*Atti R. Ist. Incorag. S.* 6, v, *p.* 19, 1 *tav. Napoli*, 1909.

ANON.—Considerazioni su i prodotti del Vesuvio.—*Compend. Trans. Filosof. Soc. Reale di Londra*, xvi, *pp.* 491–95. *Venezia*, 1793.

ANON.—Continùatione de' successi del prossimo Incendio del Vesuvio, con gli effetti della cenere, e pietre da quello vomitate, etc.—4⁰, 1 *pl. Napoli*, 1661. [B.N.] —8⁰, *foll.* 12, 1 *pl. Napoli*, 1661. [B.M.] With preface by G. A. Tarino. *See* following.

ANON.—Continuazione de' succcssi del prossimo Incendio del Vesuvio, con gli effetti della cenere, e pietre da quello vomitate, e con la dichiarazionc, ed espressione delle croci ineravigliose apparse in varii luoghi dopo l'incendio.—4⁰. *Napoli*, 1661. [O.V.]

Palmieri says of these two pamphlets : " Both are very rarc : the Duca della Torre did not possess them : no bibliographer of Vesuvius had seen thcm." Mecatti must have seen the second, because he reproduces the view of the crater contained in it, but cites it with the title " Giornàle dell' incendio del Vesuvio," and declares the author to be Dr. G. Carpano, or elsewhere he attributes it to Macrino and dedicated to Carpano. *See* SUPO, TARINO and ZUPO.

ANON.—Continuazione delle notizie de' monumenti antichi disotterrati a Ercolano, Pozzuoli, Pompei, e Stabie fino a tutto l'anno MDCCL. Trattè dalle Lettere (34) di varj dotti Napolitani, e di altri Letterati.— *See* GORI.—Admiranda Antiquitatum Herculanensium, etc. *ii, pp*. 55–158, 1 *pl*.

ANON.—Conto reso dalla Commissione centrale pei danneggiati di Torre del Greco dal di 16 Dicembre 1861 al 27 aprile 1862.—8⁰, *pp*. 28. *Napoli*, 1862. [C.A.]

ANON.—Convito di Carità adunato nell' istituto Torquato Tasso a favore de' danneggiati della terribile lava del Vesuvio dei XXVI Aprile MDCCCLXXII.—8⁰. *Napoli*, 1872.

ANON. — Copia eines Schreibens auss Ncapolis darinnen berichtet werden etliche erschreckliche Wunderzeitungen welche sich im end dess nechst abgelauffennen 1631 Jahrs in Welschland, benanntlich im Königreich Neapolis mit einem brennenden Berge (Monte Vesuvio genannt) zugetragen, etc.—4⁰, *foll*. 4. *Neapolis* ?, 1632.

ANON.—Copia della seconda relazione stampata in Napoli della spaventevole eruzione fatta dal Vesuvio nella appertura del nuovo vulcano, etc.—4⁰, *pp*. 4. *Roma*, 1794. [B.M.]

ANON.—Declectus Scriptorum rerum Neapolitanarum qui populorum, etc. etc.—*fol.*, *pp*. 6+986+36, *topogr. map, etc. Neapoli*, 1735.

See pp. 6 to 10 : Vesuvius.

ANON. — Descripcion del Monte Vesuvio, y relacion del incendio, y terremotos que empezaron a 16 di diziembre 1631.—*fol.*, *pp*. 7. — ?, — ? [C.A.]

ANON.—Description des estats Naples, Sicille, Sardagne.—*fol.*, *pp*. 320, *num. plans, maps and engrav.* — ?,— ?

ANON.—Descrizione delle due eruzioni, che ha fatte il Vesuvio l'una nel mese di Luglio, e l'altra nel mese di Dicembre dell' anno 1754.—4⁰. *Napoli*, 1755.

ANON.—Descrizione del grande incendio del Vesuvio.—*See* TATA, D. 1779.

ANON.—Una descrizione del Vesuvio dopo l'eruzione del 1737.—MS. [O.V.]

ANON. — Descrizione del Viaggio pittorico, storico e geografico da Roma a Napoli, e suoi contorni.—8⁰, *pp*. 190+4. *Napoli*, 1824.

See pp. 187–90 : Pianta di una parte dell' antico Cratere ed il Vesuvio.

ANON. — Dettaglio su l'antico stato ed eruzioni del Vesuvio, colla ragionata relazione della grande eruzione accaduta a 15 Giugno 1794 di T., F.M.D.C.A.—8⁰, *pp*. 16. [*Napoli*, 1794.]

See D'ONOFRIO.

ANON.—Dettaglio del torrente di acqua calato dal Vesuvio nel 5 Luglio 1794.—MS.

ANON.—Dettaglio dalle ultime eruzioni del Vesuvio (1794).—MS.

ANON.—Deux lettres sur l'éruption du Vésuve, 22 oct. 1822.—*Bibl. univ. xxi*, *pp*. 190–91, 226–28, *Genève*, 1822 ; *xxii*, *pp*. 138–39, 1823. [C.A.]

ANON.—Devotione per il terremoto.—*loose sheet*, 8⁰. *Napoli*, 1632.

ANON.—Dialoghi sul Vesuvio in occasione dell' eruzione della sera de' 15 giugno 1794.—*See* F. A. A.

ANON.—Diario della portentosa eruzione del Vesuvio nei mesi di luglio e agosto 1707.—4⁰. *Napoli*, — ?

ANON. — Discours von dem brennenden Berg Vesuvio, oder Monte di Somma, etc. —*foll. vii.* — ?, 1632. [C.A.]

ANON.—Dissertatio de Vesuvio 1773. MS. [O.V.]

Apparently an original MS., but name of author cannot be ascertained.

ANON.—Dissertatione della grande Eruttione fatta dal Vesuvio nel maggio del 1737.—MS. 4⁰, *pp*. 62, *in Library of St. Martino Museum, Napoli.* [C.A.]

ANON.—Dissertationis Isagogicæ ad Herculanensium voluminum explanationem. Pars prima.—*fol.*, *pp*. 5+104. *Neapolis*, 1797.

ANON.—Dissertazione della vera raccolta o sia museo di tutte le produzioni del monte Vesuvio, etc.—4⁰. — ?, — ? [B.N.]

ANON. — Distinta relatione dei portentosi effetti cagionati dalla maravigliosa eruzione fatta dal Monte Vesuvio detto di Somma, di pietre infuocate, e di fiumi di acceso bitume con mistione di minerali di tutte le sorti.—4⁰, foll. 4. *Napoli*, 1694. [C.A.]

ANON. — Distinta relazione del grande incendio e meravigliosa eruzione fatta dal Monte Vesuvio detto volgarmente la Montagna di Somma, nella quale si dà distintissimo ragguaglio di quanto ha eruttato dalli 29 di aprile per infino alli 10 del corrente giugno 1698 et il danno, spavento, e fuga, che ha apportato a' popoli.—4⁰, foll. 2. *Napoli and Roma*, 1698. [C.A.]— *Napoli e Modena*, 1698.

ANON.—Ad Divum Januarium. Elogi due. —*See* GIORGI URBANO.

ANON.—Die Drahtseilbahn auf den Vesuv. Siehe Seite 666.
Woodcuts of : 1⁰. View of Vesuv from sea. 2⁰. Railway and stations on cone. 3⁰. Plans of carriages and rails. From illustr. German paper : 333×215 mm.

ANON.—Un Dramma al Vesuvio.—*Article in the " Corriere di Napoli," 2 Luglio*, 1891, *reproduced in the journal " Vesuvio," Portici, 5 Luglio*, 1891.

ANON.—Due lettere concernenti la morte di Plinio il Vecchio, etc. ed a proposito dell' ultima eruzione de' 15 Giugno 1794 di cui da valente Persona anonima si da succinta relazione, con descrizione de' danni da essa cagionati e figure in rame.—8⁰, *pp.* 30, 1 *pl. Napoli*, 1794.

ANON.—Due Relazioni dell' incendio del 1632, inscrizioni ec. unite insieme.—8⁰. *Napoli*, 1632.

ANON.—Ein in Eisen gelegter Vulkan.— " *Die Gartenlaube," pp.* 517–18, 1 *woodcut. Leipzig*, 1874.

ANON. (Cit. by Duca della Torre (Sen.).—Enarratio funeste Vesuviane conflagrationis anni 1631.—8⁰.

ANON.—Epigrammata leges et carmina insculpta in Villula et hortulo Joh. Donatus Rogadeus ; eques hierosolymitanus emto prædio extruxit Villulam, Leges de Villula et circunerario regundis in

XII Tabulas digestæ. Carmen continens Breviarium legum ad hospites.—*Carmen de Vesuvio, fol., pp.* 24.

ANON.—Eruzione del Vesuvio del 1631.— tav. *fol. P. Mortier, Amsterdam,* — ?

ANON.—L'éruption du Vésuve en 1754.—*fol.*

ANON.— [Sur l'éruption du Vésuve en août 1756.]—*Journ. Étrang. pp.* 159–68. *Paris*, 1757.

ANON.—Eruzione del Monte Vesuvio nell' anno 1767 veduta da Portici.—pl. *fol.* [C.A.]

ANON.—Éruption du 8 Août 1779.
Circular, transparent water-colour view of Vesuvius from Naples at night·'during eruption : 150 mm.

ANON.—Eruzione accaduta in Napoli nel anno 1779.
Distemper view from Mergellina by night : 392×280 mm.

ANON.—Eruzione accaduta in Napoli nel anno 1779.
Well-painted gouache of the period of eruption of Vesuvius by night : 391× 279 mm.

ANON.—[Erupt. 1794.]—*Gazz. Civ. Napoletana*, 25 *and* 26, *pp.* 163–76. 21 *Giugno*, 1794.

ANON.—Eruption of 1794 of Vesuvius by night from Naples.
Three men in foreground. Gouache : 115×76 mm.

ANON.—L'Eruzione del Vesuvio, della notte de' 15 Giugno, 1794, poeticamento descritta, etc.—*See* T., C. F.—L'Eruzione, etc. [*Napoli*, 1794 ?] [B.M.]

ANON.—Sull' eruzione del Vesuvio del 1794 datata da Torre del Greco 1794.—MS.

ANON.—Eruzione de 1794.
Vesuvius by night from Castellamare ; two men, a fisherman and a net in foreground. Gouache : 405×270 mm.

ANON.—Eruption of Mount Vesuvius. Extract of a private letter, dated Naples, June 6.—*Phil. Mag. xxv, pp.* 184–88. *London*, 1806.

ANON.—Eruzione del Vesuvio accaduta a di 18 Agosto l'anno 1805.
Gouache from nr. Portici by night.

ANON.—Eruzione del Vesuvio accaduta a di 18 Agosto l'anno 1805 [? 1808].
From near Resina by night ; arch and houses in foreground. Gouache : 670× 465 mm.

ANON.—Eruzione del 1° 7bre 1806 [*sic*].
Vesuvius by night from Naples; boat with striped awning in foreground. Gouache : 400 × 264 mm.

ANON.—Eruzione del 1809.
Vesuvius by night from Naples; a soldier, two fishermen and net in foreground. Gouache : 420 × 262 mm.

ANON.—Eruzione de' 12 Settembre anno 1810.
Vesuvius by night from Naples; two men standing and two sitting in foreground. Gouache : 410 × 273 mm.

ANON.—Eruzione del 1810.
Vesuvius by night from Naples; one soldier and six men in foreground. Gouache : 430 × 272 mm.

ANON.—Eruzione del 1812.
Vesuvius seen from Naples by night; four men in foreground. Gouache : 412 × 256 mm.

ANON.—Eruzione dell' anno 1813.
Vesuvius by day. Good gouache : 178 × 102 mm.

ANON.—Eruzione dell' anno 1813.
Vesuvius by night. Good gouache : 178 × 102 mm.

ANON.—Eruzione del 22 Feb. 1820.
Vesuvius by night from Naples; two men on broken bridge in foreground. Gouache : 430 × 277 mm.

ANON.—Eruption of Mount Vesuvius. Letter from Naples, dated October 21.—*Phil. Mag. lv, pp.* 291–93. *London,* 1822.

ANON.—Eruzione de 22. 8bre. del anno 1822.
Vesuvius from Naples by day; lady, gentleman, three fishermen, boat and guardhouse in foreground. Gouache : 660 × 405 mm.

ANON.—Eruzione d' 22 Ottobre 1822.
Vesuvius from Naples by night; three men in foreground, one sitting. Gouache : 640 × 455 mm.

ANON.—Eruzione del 22 Ottobre 1822.
Vesuvius by night from S^a Lucia. Miniature gouache : 97 × 67 mm.

ANON.—Eruzione de 22 Ottobre 1822.
By night from about S. Lucia. Distemper : 427 × 292 mm.

ANON.—Eruzione del 1822.
Vesuvius by night from Chiatamone. Poor gouache : 198 × 138 mm.

ANON.—Eruzione del 1822.
Vesuvius by night, showing central cone and adventitious cones over a lava rift. Rough gouache : 198 × 143 mm.

ANON.—Eruz. del 1828.
Vesuvius by night. Gouache.

ANON. — Sur l'éruption du Vésuve en juillet et août 1832, extrait de l'*Observatore del Vesuvio*, No. 3. (Translation.)— *Bibl. univ. Sci. etc. lii, pp.* 350–56. *Genève,* 1833. [C.A.]

ANON.—Eruzione del 1832.
View of eruption of Vesuvius from W. limb of M. Somma ; numerous figures in foreground and on the Salvatore. This is very similar to Volaire's engrav. of eruption of 1771, with figures changed. Varnished gouache : 662 × 432 mm.

ANON.—Eruption of Mount Vesuvius 12 and 13 Aug. 1833.—" *Notizie del Giorn. Roma.*"
Copied into English paper, 21 lines.

ANON. — Eruzione del Vesuvio. — *Giorn. Farm.-Chim. xviii, pp.* 181–86. *Milano,* 1833.

ANON.—Eruzione di cristalli di Leucite avvenuta sul Vesuvio.—*Ann. Civ. Due Sicilie, xliv, pp.* 62–66. *Napoli,* 1833–47.

ANON.—Eruption of Mount Vesuvius. Aug. 1834.
Cutting from English paper, quoting " French Paper," 35 lines.

ANON.—[Extract of a letter from Sorrento at the moment of the last eruption of Vesuvius.]—" *The Times,*" 19 *Jan. p.* 7, *col.* 1, 101 *lines. London,* 1835.

ANON.—An eruption of Mount Vesuvius 13, 14 March, 1835.—" *The Times,*" *April* 8, *p.* 4, *col.* 6, 9 *lines. London,* 1835.

ANON.—Eruption of Vesuvius, January 3rd, 1839.—pl. *fol., with text.* [C.A.]

ANON.—Eruzione del 1847.
Vesuvius from Naples by night ; men in boats in foreground. Gouache : 625 × 415 mm.

ANON.—Eruption of Vesuvius.—" *Illustr. London News,*" *pp.* 2, 2 *views. March 2nd,* 1850.

ANON.—Eruption of Vesuvius 1855.—*Amer. Journ. Sci. xx, pp.* 125–28. *New Haven,* 1855.

ANON.—Eruption du Vésuve le 1ᵉʳ mai 1855.—*Cuttings from newspapers.* [C.A.]

ANON.—Eruzione de 30 Maggio 1858.
Vesuvius from Naples by night ; three men, two women and stranded ship in fore-ground. Rough gouache : 525 × 367 mm.

ANON.—Eruz. del 13 Giugno 1858.
Lateral craterets of Vesuvius on Atrio to the west by night. Gouache : 427 × 288 mm.

ANON.—Eruz. [Vesuvius] del 13 Giugno 1858.
From near the Croce del Salvatore. Gouache.

ANON. — Eruption of Mount Vesuvius, Naples, 1858. 1⁰. The Erupt. of M. Vesuvius as seen from Naples. 2⁰. The Eruption of Vesuvius, the mouths of the great stream of Lava.—" *Illustr. London News,*" *pp.* 631-32. *June 26, 1858.*
Two woodcuts with explan. text.

ANON.—The Eruption of Mount Vesuvius (1861) : The Craters at Midnight.—" *Illustr. London News,*" *pp.* 4+23 (*supplement*). *Jan. 4, 1862.*
Woodcut and explan. text.

ANON. — Éruption du Vésuve en 1855.
—" *Magasin Pittoresque,*" *p.* 376. *1863.*
Woodcut of view over Naples to Vesuvius with fine pine-like smoke column : 130 × 75 mm. Looks more like eruption of 1822.

ANON.—The Eruption of Mount Vesuvius (April, 1872).—" *Nature,*" *vi, pp.* 2-3, *1872 ; vii, pp.* 1-4, *London and New York, 1873.*

ANON. — Éruption du Vésuve des 25, 26 et 27 avril 1872.—" *La Presse Illustrée,*" *figs. and text. Paris, 4 mai, 1872.* [C.A.]

ANON.—Eruzione del Vesuvio dell' anno 1872.—*MS. documents in the archives of the municipality of Torre del Greco, foll.* 17, copy. [C.A.]

ANON.—The Eruption of Vesuvius. The Lava Stream, Dec. 2, 1880.—" *The Graphic,*" *pp.* 611-12. *Dec. 18th, 1880.*
Woodcut with explan. text.

ANON.—The Eruption of Vesuvius.—" *The Times,*" *April 17th, p.* 3, *col.* 2, *and p.* 4, *col.* 3. *1906.*

ANON.—The Eruption of Vesuvius.—" *Nature,*" *lxxiii, pp.* 565-66, 588. *1906.*

ANON.—Eruzione Vesuviana del 1906. Relazione del Comitato Centrale di Soccorso.—*4⁰, pp.* 80+*clxviii,* 1 *chromolith. pl. Portici, 1908.*

ANON.—Éruption du Mt. Vésuve . . . ?
[B.N.P. Vb. 121.]
A small circ. engrav. of no importance.

ANON.—Escursion al Vesubio en la primavera de 1838.—*Mem. Soc. Econom. Habana, xvii, pp.* 286-93. *Habana, 1843.*

ANON.—Estratto di una Lettera sottoscritta (apud Will. Budily) comunicata da,.Enrico Robinson intorno alla pioggia di cenere nell' Arcipelago nell' incendio del Vesuvio del 1631.—SAVONAROLA O LASOR A VAREA : " *Univ. terr. orb.*" *ii, p.* 651. *Patavii, 1713.*

ANON.—Explanation of the View of Naples exhibiting in the Panorama, Strand. Printed at C. Hullmandel's Lithographic Establishment. [B.M. Portfolio of Naples.] 440 × 283 mm.

ANON.—Extract of a letter from Naples dated 5th January, 1839. [Erupt. of Vesuvius.]
Cutting in English paper quoted from " French Paper," 22 lines.

ANON.—Eygentlicher Abriss und Beschreibung dess grossen Erdbebens und erschröklichen brennenden Bergs im Königreich Neapolis (Monte Vesuvio auch Monte Soma genannt), etc. [1632.] [B.M. 1750 b. 29 (101).]
An engraving with letterpress description ; the whole is reversed and very imaginary. There is smoke as if of a submarine eruption in bay.

ANON.—Fertigstellung der Drahtseilbahn auf den Vesuv.—" *Globus,*" *xxxvii, p.* 144. *Braunschweig, 1880.*

ANON. — Die Feureyferige Zorn Ruthe Gottes auff dem Brennenden Berg Vesuvio in Campania über Italien und alle südlichen Königreiche weit und breit aussgestrecket : nach ihren Eigenschafften etc. etc.—*4⁰, foll.* 28. *1633.*

ANON.—Gegenständ : xx. Mélanges. xx.
Hand-coloured stipple engrav. of erupt. of Vesuvius by night from Mergellina ; monks, dog, woman and child, with other people, in foreground : 166 × 217 mm.

ANON.—Die geographische Verbreitung der thätigen Vulkane. I. Die europäischen Vulkane.—" *Globus,*" *xxi, pp.* 311–13, 5 *illustr.* Braunschweig, 1872.

ANON.—Geschichte des Vesuv.—" *Vermischte Beiträge z. physikalischen Erdbeschreibung,*" i, *pp.* 92–114. *Brandenbourg,* 1774.

ANON.—Giornale dell' incendio del Vesuvio dell' anno 1660. Con le osservationi matematiche al molto illustre e molto eccellente Signor mio Padrone osservandissimo, il Signor D. Gius. Carpano, Dottore dell' una e dell' altra legge e nella sapienza di Roma primario professore. A. C.—*Roma,* 1660. [O.V.]
This is the Roman edition of the other articles under the head of ANON. (p. 113) (Continuazione de' successi, etc.) referring to the erupt. of 1660. The author was padre Supo as proved by a MS. *See* SUPO.

ANON.—Giornale di Napoli.—*See* 21 *Ott. to* 11 *Nov.* 1822, *fol.* 19. [O.V.]

ANON.—Giornale di Napoli.—*See* 22 *Dec.* 1854, 1 *to* 31 *Maggio* 1855, *fol.* 24. [O.V.]

ANON.—Golfe de Torre del Greco. Imp. Lemercier, Benard et C. [Paris ?, — ?] [B.N.P., Vb. 120.]
A small litho.; shows Vesuvius much truncated.

ANON.—Guida descrittiva dei contorni di Napoli e sue Isole.—12⁰, *pp.* 477, *woodcuts. Napoli,* 1865.
Includes : " Relazione istorica dell Incendio com. nel giorno 25 Maggio . . . 1858," and details of state of Vesuvius before then. *See* pp. 196 *et seq.*

ANON.—Guida de' Forestieri per la città di Napoli. In cui si contengono tutte le notizie topografiche della città, e degli Edificj sacri, e pubblici da' tempi antichi infino al dì di oggi, per istruire brevemente l'umano, e prestante leggitore. Nuovamente spurgata dalle suiste, ed accresciuta di quanto si osserva in sì famosa città.—12⁰, *pp. viii+*364, *num. pls., frontisp. Con licenza de' Superiori. A spese del Librajo Nunzio Rossi, e dal medesimo si vendono nella sua Libreria a due porte sotto il Palazzo dell' Eccmo Sig.Duca di Monteleone. Napoli,* MDCCLXXXVIII.
Attributable to Sarnelli. *See* p. 310.
Another ed. : " nuovamente spurgata dalle sviste, ed accresciuta di quanto si

osserva in sì famosa Città."—12⁰, *pp. viii+*364. *A spese, etc. con antiporto, Napoli,* 1801.
See pp. 310–27.

ANON.—Guide nouveau de Naples en abrégé (érupt. 1834).—12⁰, *pp.* 84. *Naples,* 1841.

ANON.—A Handbook for Travellers in Southern Italy and Sicily ; comprising the description of Naples and its environs, Pompeii, Herculaneum, Vesuvius, Sorrento ; the islands of Capri and Ischia ; Amalfi, Pæstum, and Capua, the Abruzzi and Calabria ; Palermo, Girgenti, the Greek Temples, and Messina.—9th ed. 2 pts. 8⁰. *Pt. i.,* South Italy, *pp.* 288+20, *maps, plans, etc.; Pt. ii.,* Sicily, *pp.* 289–418+11, *maps, plans, etc. London,* 1890.

ANON.—Histoire complète de la grande éruption du Vésuve de 1631, avec la carte, au 1: 25,000, de toutes les laves de ce volcan, depuis le seizième siècle jusqu'aujourd'hui. —*Bruxelles,* 1866.

ANON.—Histoire du Mont Vésuve, avec l'explication des phénomènes qui ont coûtume d'accompagner les embrasements de cette montagne ; le tout traduit de l'Italien [of F. Serao] . . . Par M. Duperron de Castera.—12⁰. *Paris,* 1741.
See SERAO.

ANON.—Historiola incendii Montis Vesevi mense Februario anni 685. [In Greek.]
Found by N. C. Falcone at the end of a Greek MS. of the Atti di S. Gennaro, and printed by him at the end of his : " L'Intera Istoria della Famiglia, Vita, Miracoli, Traslazioni, e Culto del Glorioso Martire S. Gennaro," p. 488. Napoli, 1713.

ANON.—Homilia di S. Januario Episc. & Mart. ante annum 800. conscripta, in qua primum de Vesuvianis incendiis fusius agitur.—*Printed with* ENGENIO CARACCIOLO : Monum. Eccl. Neap. p. 276.

ANON.—L'incendio del Monte Vesuuio, rappresentatione spirituale composta da un devoto Sacerdote.—16⁰, *pp.* 185. *Napoli, L. Scoriggio,* 1632.
This is the first ed.; the second was publ. under the author's name, Ant. Glielmo [*q.v.*].

ANON.—Un incendio sconosciuto del Vesuvio.—*Archiv. Stor. Prov. Nap. xv,* 3, *pp.* 642–46. *Napoli,* 1890.

ANON.—Los incendios de la Montana di Soma.—*fol., pp.* 38. *Napoles,* 1632. [B.N.]

ANON.—Influence probable de la Lune à l'intérieur du Globe terrestre. [With a figure of] Éruption du Vésuve 1855.— "*Magasin Pittoresque,*" p. 376. *Paris,* 1863.

ANON.—Intorno del Vesuvio nel 1830.
Distemper view of crater and central cone of eruption : 627×412 mm.

ANON. [CAPOCCI, E., GIORDANO, G., SCHIAVONI, F., CAPPA, R., GUISCARDI, G., PALMIERI, L. (relatore).]—Intorno all' incendio del Vesuvio cominciato il di 8 dicembre 1861 ; relazione per cura dell' Accademia Pontaniana.—8⁰, *pp.* 36, 1 *tab.*, 1 *map,* 1 *pl.* *Napoli,* 1862.—*Rend. Acc. Pontaniana, x, pp.* 40–61. *Napoli,* 1862.

ANON.—Intorno del Vesuvio nel 1832.
Rough gouache of outer crater, crater plain and cone of eruption by day : 210× 144 mm.

ANON.—Istoria dell' incendio del Vesuvio accaduto nel mese di maggio dell' anno 1737. Scritta per l'Accademia delle Scienze.
See SERAO and DARBIE.

ANON. — Istruzione al forastiere, e al dilettante intorno a quanto di antico e di raro si contiene nel Museo del Real Convento di S. Caterina a Formiello˙de' P.P. Domenicani Lombardi in questa˙città di Napoli.—4⁰, *pp.* 19. *Napoli,* 1791. [B.N.]
Mentions the existence in that museum of about 300 specimens of different lavas, etc., from Vesuvius.

ANON.—L'Italia.—4⁰, *pp.* 326, *num. maps.* *Torino,* 1896.

ANON.—Italian Scenes, a series of interesting delineations of Remarkable Views and of the most celebrated remains of Antiquities. —4⁰, *pp.* 30, 27 *pls.* *London,* 1825.
Erupt. 1751 : descript. and 2 pls. *See* [CRAVEN, K.]

ANON.—Italian View. Mount Vesuvius in Eruption. New series. 3ʳᵈ plate of Views. — ?, — ?
An imaginary eruption from near the Darsena. Hand-col. engrav. of no interest : 220×176 mm.

ANON.—L'Italie.—8⁰, *pp.* 608, 243 *engrav.,* 5 *maps.* ˉ*Paris,* — ?

ANON.—Itinéraires et souvenirs d'un voyage en Italie en 1819 et 1820.—3 vols. *Tom. i, pp.* 374 ; *Tom. ii, pp.* 390 ; *Tom. iii, pp.* 416. *Paris,* 1829.

ANON.—Im Krater des Vesuv. (S. 194.)
View of crater of Vesuvius with cone of

eruption. Woodcut from a German illustr. paper, possibly about 1875 or 1876 : 215× 158 mm.

ANON.—Der Krater des Vesuv.—*Illustrirte Welt,* p. 194, *pl. at p.* 185. *Stuttgart u. Leipzig,* 1879.
Woodcut giving a view of the interior of the crater, with 25 lines of text : 228× 210 mm.

ANON. — Late eruption of Vesuvius.— "*Athenæum,*" p. 393. 18 *Apr.* 1828.
Letter from Italy, communicated for the " Athenæum."

ANON.—The latest eruption of Mount Vesuvius.—" *Graphic,*" *Sept.* 25, 1880.
Woodcut of cone and crater plain with pinnacle-like spiracles : 227×157 mm.

ANON.—Laves qui sortaient des flancs du Vésuve à la suite de l'éruption de 1754.—pl. *fol.* [C.A.]

ANON.—Lettera autentica in cui si da un succinta ragguaglio della strepitosa eruzione del Vesuvio accaduta nella notte dei 12 de corrente Agosto 1805.—8⁰, *fol.* 1. *Gioacchino Puccinelli vicino la Piazza di St. Andrea delle Valle,* 1805 (?).

ANON.—Lettera riguardante la relazione dell' eruzione Vesuviana del 1794.—MS.

ANON.—Lettera seconda del danno accaduto nel paese detto Somma non già del foco ; ma di acqua pietre arena e saette che hanno spianato detto paese con Ottajano sin' oggi li 27 giugno 1794.—8⁰. [O.V.]

ANON.—Lettera sopra le pitture di Ercolano oggi Portici.—*See* GORI.—Admiranda Antiquitatum Herculanensium, etc., ii, *pp.* 188–203.

ANON.—Lettere, avvisi e notizie diverse sulla eruzione del Vesuvio del 1631.

ANON.—Lettera datata del 17 Luglio 1794 in done un anonimo descrive ad un tal D. Ciro l'eruzione Vesuviana.—MS.

ANON.—[Letters from Naples describing eruption of Vesuvius beginning on 20 Oct. 1822.]—*Journ. des Débats,* 12, 14, 19, 21 *novembre,* 1822.

ANON.—Letters from a Young Painter abroad to his friends in England.—8⁰, *pp.* 283, *index. London,* 1748.
Views of Vesuvius. Pl. IV : general view from·Naples with lava of 1737. Pl. v : 1742.

ANON.—Lettre sur une éruption du Vésuve. —*Journ. Phys. lviii, pp.* 58–59, 203–6. *Paris,* 1806.

ANON.—Lettre touchant le Mont Vésuve et tremblement à Naples le 5 juin 1688.—*In :* Voyage fait en Italie en 1688, *T. iii, pp.* 391–418. *La Haye,* 1727.—*See* MISSON.

ANON.—Luigi Palmieri.—*Ueber Land u. Meer, xxviii,* 38, *pp.* 8–10, *portrait. Stuttgart,* 1872.

ANON. — Madrigale sopra l'incendio del Vesuvio.—*See* PERROTTI, A.—Discorso astronomico, etc. 1632.

ANON.—[Part of a large Map of the Kingdom of Naples.]—*Engraved at Naples* 1785–89. [B.M.—K. 83. 23.]
A good map of Vesuvius and Campi Phlegræi for the date.

ANON.—Del medesimo narrazione istorica dell' eruzione cominciata a' 3 di dicembre 1754. Non è finita di stampare.—*See* GALIANI, F.—Osservazioni sopra il Vesuvio, Note.

ANON.—The Mediterranean Illustrated. Picturesque Views and Descriptions of its cities, shores and islands.—4⁰, *pp. xii*+373. *London,* 1877.
See pp. and illustr. 125–42 ; good woodcuts of Vesuvius.

ANON.—Mémoire historique et critique sur la ville souterraine découverte au pied du Mont Vésuve.—8⁰, *foll.* 4, *pp.* 74. *Avignon,* 1748.—Another ed. : Mémoire sur la ville souterraine découverte au pied du Mont Vésuve.—8⁰, *foll.* 2, *pp.* 38. *Gottingue,* 1748. [B.M.]

ANON.—Memoria sui Monumenti di Antichita e di Belle Arti ch'existono in Miseno, Baoli, Baja, Cuma, Napoli, Pompei, etc.—*pls. Napoli,* 1812.

ANON.—Memoria per la remissione della strada che dal comune di Resina conduce al Monte Vesuvio.—4⁰, *pp.* 20. *Napoli,* 1841.

ANON.—La miracolosa immagine di nostra Signora del Carmine della Torre del Greco.—[O.V.]

ANON.—*See* MISCELLANEA POETICA.

ANON.—Delle Mofete eccitate dall' incendio del Vesuvio.—*See* ANON.—Dei Vulcani o Monti Ignivomi, 1779.

ANON.—Molo di Napoli con principio della terribile eruzione accaduta la sera de 15 Giug⁰ 1794.
A distemper picture.

ANON.—Molo di Napoli con terribile eruzione del Vesuvio mandata fuori la sera de' 15 del mese di Giugno 1794 ad ore 2 (? 4) di Notte. [B.M.—K. 83. 61-k.]

ANON.—Le montagne di basalto sono prodotti vulcanici, o effetti di una cristallizzazione ?—*Compend. Trans. Filosof. Soc. Real. Londra, xvi, pp.* 495–98. *Venezia,* 1793.

ANON.—Le Mont Vésuve. [B.N.P., Vb. 121.]
A small damaged print, very fantastic.

ANON.—Le Mont Vésuve. Tom. 2, p. 389.
A rather fantastic engraving.

ANON.—Mont Vésuve. Costumes Napolitains. Tʳ du Mᵈᵉ. Tome 3, p. 177.
Line engrav. : 91 × 64 mm.

ANON.—Le Mont Vésuve en éruption. [B.N.P., Vb. 121.]
A fantastic engraving.

ANON.—De Monte Vesuvio, disquisitionis.—*Acta Helvetica, i, pp.* 97–104. *Basilea,* 1751.

ANON.—La morte di Plinio nell' incendio del Monte Vesuvio e l'effetto che fece.—8⁰, *foll.* 2. *Napoli,* 1632. [O.V.]

ANON. — Mount Vesuvius. Letter from Naples Aug. 18th, 1832.
Newspaper cutting : 15 lines.

ANON. — Mount Vesuvius.—" *The Penny Magazine,*" *pp.* 345–46 *and fig.,* 355–56. *London, Dec.* 1st, 1832.

ANON.—Mount Vesuvius.
An imaginary eruption of Vesuvius. View obviously copied from Sandrart. Engraving of no scientific value : 206 × 164 mm.

ANON.—*See* MUNICIPIO DI NAPOLI.

ANON. — Mute History or Documentary Ruins of Nature and Art in Italy ; illustrated by a Volcanic and Antiquarian Map of the Italian Continent and Islands.—" *Gentleman's Magazine,*" *vii, pp.* 249–56, 468–70, 1 *map. London,* 1837.

ANON. — Naeckte Beschrijvinge van de schrickeligijcke Aerd-bevinge ende afgrijsselicken Brandt van den Bergh Soma gelegen in Italien, twee Mijlen van de Stadt Napels geschiet den 15, 16 ende 17 december 1631 geextraheret utenen Brief van date den 13 Januarij 1632, geschreben upt Napels by een hoffwaerdlich Personen, die dese ellendich ept aengesien heeft ende verkondigt aen zijne Drienten tot Leyden 1632.—4⁰, *pp.* 8. *Leyden,* 1632.

ANON.—Naples en Souvenir. Album du Journal des Jeunes Personnes Page 128, No. 13.
  Naples from Mergellina, but very imaginary. Litho. surrounded by a brown ink frame : 210×250 mm.

ANON.—[Naples and Vesuvius as seen from Camaldoli.]
  Hand-coloured litho. ; two monks and two other men in foreground : 272× 188 mm.

ANON.—[Naples and Vesuvius from Mergellina.]
  A line litho. col. by hand.

ANON.—Napoli [1895].
  Multiple post-card photo. engrav. : 560× 87 mm.

ANON.—Napoli e luoghi celebri delle sue vicinanze. Al settimo Congresso Scientifico degl'Italiani, 1845.—8⁰. *Vol. i, pp.* 8+542, *num. lith. pls. and map ; Vol. ii, pp.* 602+22, *num. lith. pls. and map. Napoli, 1845.*
  See pl. at p. 516 and pp. 377–413, 468–526 of Vol. ii.

ANON. — I Napolitani al cospetto delle nazioni civili, con appendice contenenti, etc.—*See* FRANCESCO II.

ANON.—The Natural History of Mount Vesuvius, with the explanation of the various Phenomena that usually attend the Eruptions of this celebrated Volcano. Transl. fr. the orig. Ital., composed by the R. Acc. Sci. at Naples [entitled " Istoria dell' incendio del Vesuvio, etc.," by F. Serao] by order of the King of the Two Sicilies.—12⁰, *pp.* 231, 2 *pls. London,* 1743.
  See [SERAO, FRANCESCO.]

ANON.—Neapel, Ansicht vom Grabe Virgils. Nach einer photographischen Aufnahme.
  Woodcut from a German illustr. paper : 237×165 mm.

ANON.—Neapolitanæ Scientiarum Academiæ de Vesuvii conflagratione quæ mense Majo anno MDCCXXXVII accidit commentarius.—4⁰, *pp. viii*+118, 2 *pls. Neapoli,* 1738.—*See* SERAO. [B.M. 664. b. 25(1).]

ANON.—Neuer Ausbruch des Vesuvs, ein feuerspeiender Berg des Königreichs Neapel in der Nähe der Hauptstadt.—8⁰, *pp.* 8. *Mulhausen,* 1855.

ANON.—The New Railway up Mount Vesuvius.—" *The Graphic,*" *p.* 521, *May* 22, 1880 ; *p.* 569, *June* 5, 1880 ; *p.* 633, *June* 19, 1880.

ANON.—The next Eruption of Vesuvius. Designed for that Enlightened Monarch, King Bomba.
  Caricature of Ferdinand running away from eruption of Vesuvius, which is ejecting daggers, bayonets, swords and cannon-balls. A pen-and-ink sketch intended for " Punch " : 305×222 mm.

ANON.—Notes on Vesuvius.—*Amer. Journ. Sci. S.* 2, *xiii, pp.* 131–33. *New Haven,* 1852. [C.A.]

ANON.—Notizie dell' alluvione del Vesuvio [1794].—MS.

ANON.—Notizie in data di Cerignola si descrive i fenomeni dell' eruzione Vesuviana del 1794.—MS.

ANON.—Notizie dell' eruzione del Vesuvio in Maggio e Giugno 1858.—*Cont. in* 21 *nos. of:* " *Giornale del Regno delle due Sicilie," from* 29 *Maggio. Napoli,* 1858. [C.A.]

ANON.—Notizie intorno alla Città Sotteranea, etc.—*See* D'ARTHENAY.

ANON.—Notizie del memorabile scoprimento dell' antica città Ercolano, etc., fino al corrente anno 1718, etc. [Per Anton. F. Gori.]—8⁰, *pp. xx*+106, 2 *pls. Firenze,* 1748. [B.N.]

ANON.—Nouveau Guide de Naples en abrégé.—2nd ed. 12⁰, *pp.* 84. *Salv. de Marco, Naples,* 1841.
  See p. 41.

ANON. — Novissima relatione dell' incendio successo nel Monte di Somma a dì 16 Decembre 1631, con un avviso di quello successo nell' istesso, dì nella Città di Cattaro nelli parti d'Albania.—8⁰, *pp.* 16. *Venetia,* [reprinted in] *Nàpoli,* 1632. [C.A.]

ANON.—Nuova descrizione de' danni cagionati dal Monte Vesuvio dalla sera de' 15 sino al giorno 28 giugno dell' anno 1794.— 8⁰, *pp.* 8. *Napoli,* 1794. [O.V.]

ANON. — Nuova istoria di una grazia particolare ottenuta da Dio alla città di Napoli, per intercessione di Maria Ss. ed il glorioso S. Gennaro per il Terremuoto sortito la sera dei 12 Giugno, e la grand eruzione del Monte Vissuvio la sera de' 15 del sudetto mese ; giorno di Domenica alle ore 2 della notte del 1794. A qual' effetto allagò di foco molti villaggi intorno stendendosi sino al mare con rovinare la gran terra della Torre del Greco.—12⁰, *foll.* 4. [*Napoli,* 1794.] [B.N.]

ANON.—Observations diverses sur les Volcans.—*MS. fol., pp.* 125. [*After* 1808.]
Many notes from other authors on Vesuvius, Campi Phlegræi, Etna, etc.

ANON.—D'Onfetcking en frant des Berghs met d'omleggende gelegentheyt af gilekant door I.—*Sandra*, 1631. [S. Martino Mus. No. 10,007.]
A plate.

ANON.—1. Palazzo della Rocella. 2. Castel dell' Ovo. 3. M. Vesuvio. 4. M. di Somma, D.D. a Mᵉ Andrè. Chloë regit. Dulces docta moclos et cytharœ sciens. horat, Carne. III.
Similar to Pl. 71 of Morghen's 84 Vedute, but does not bear "Pl. 19." Engrav. : 248 × 133 mm.

ANON.—[Panorama of Naples from S. Martino *circa* 1895.]
Bromide photo. panorama in eight sections : 1953 × 183 mm.

ANON.—Panorama di Pompei.
Good outline of Vesuvius in distance from an unknown Italian paper. Woodcut : 240 × 170 mm.

ANON.—Parere su le Facoltà salutifere dell' acqua termominerali Vesuviana Nunziante.—*Ann. Civ. Reg. Due Sicilie, vi, pp.* 109–11. *Napoli*, 1833–47.

ANON.—Parthenope terræmotu vexata.—Copy MS. *foll.* 6. [C.A.]

ANON.—A Particular Account of the Eruption of Mount Vesuvius. [Dec. 1754.]—"*Gentleman's Magazine,*" *p.* 79. Feb. 1755.

ANON.—Phénomènes observés au Vésuve.—"*La Science pour tous,*" i, 15, *pp.* 119–20. *Paris, août*, 1856. [C.A.]

ANON.—[Photographic Views in Italy, about 1873. Mounted photos.] [B.M.—S. $\frac{157}{4}$]
No. 17 gives a good view of the great cone.

ANON.—Physical Notices of the Bay of Naples. No. I.—On Mount Vesuvius.—*Edinb. Journ. Sci. ix, pp.* 189–213, 1828 ; x, *pp.* 133–36, 1829.
Signed Δ.—*See* FORBES, J. D.

ANON.—Physical Notices of the Bay of Naples. No. II.—On the Buried Cities of Herculaneum, Pompei and Stabiæ.—*Edinb. Journ. Sci. x, pp.* 108–33, 1829.—*Bibl. Univ. xl, pp.* 411–26. *Genève*, 1829. [C.A.]
Signed Δ.—*See* FORBES, J. D.

ANON.—Pianta delli confini tra Portici e S. Giorgio a Cremano fatta per ordine del Presidente della S. R. C. di S. Chiara.—pl. *roy. fol.* [O.V.]

ANON.—Pompei.—47 *photos.*

ANON.—Pompei. Library of Entertaining Knowledge.—8⁰, *pp.* x+323, 4 *pls.*, 139 *figs.* London, C. *Knight*, 1831.
See pp. 1–52 and figs. at pp. 33 and 52.

ANON.—Pompei e la regione sotterrata dal Vesuvio nell' anno LXXIX. Memorie e notizie pubblicate dall' Ufficio Tecnico degli Scavi delle Provincie Meridionali.—*fol. Pt. i, pp.* 291, 2 *pls.* ; *Pt. ii, pp.* 243. *Napoli*, 1879. [C.A.]

ANON.—Pompeii Temple of Jupiter.
With good drawing of Vesuvius about 1850. Fine pencil drawing, slightly tinted and touched with chalk : 160 × 105 mm.

ANON.—Preghiera al glorioso martire S. Gennaro. [Erupt. 1855.]—*loose sheet. Napoli*, 1855.

ANON.—Principio del Eruzione del 1794.
Vesuvius by night from Naples ; four men, one sitting, in foreground. Gouache : 423 × 263 mm.

ANON.—Principio e progressi del fuoco osservati giorno per giorno dalli 3 fino alli 25 di Luglio di questo anno 1660 ed esposti alla curiosità de' forestieri. [O.V.]

ANON. — Prodigioso miracolo del nostro gran santone e difensore S. Gennaro di averci liberati dall' incendio del Vesuvio e dal terremoto nell' anno 1794. [O.V.]

ANON.—Prodigium Vesuvii Montis per Carolum incarnatum.—*pp.* 4. *Neap. typis Ægidii Longhi*, 1632.
See GALIANI, F.—Osservazioni sopra il Vesuvio, Note.

ANON.—Il Prodromo Vesuviano.—*See* VETRANI, A.

ANON.—La Promenade utile et récréative de deux Parisiens en cent soixante cinq jours.—2 tomes in 1 vol. 12⁰. *Tom. i, pp.* xxiv+323 ; *Tom. ii, pp.* 261. *Avignon*, 1768.

ANON.—A Prospect of Mount Vesuvius with its irruption in 1630 [*sic*].
A poor reduction of P. Mortier's plate in BLAEU : Theatrum Civitatum. Engrav. : 194 × 150 mm.

ANON.—Prospetto del Vesuvio veduto dal Molo di Napoli, etc. 5.—[*Naples* ?, 1779 ?] [B.N.P. Vb. 121.]

ANON. — Prospetto del Vesuvio dal Palazzo Reale.—*See* ANON.—Dei Vulcani o Monti Ignivomi, 1779.

ANON.—Raccolta compita ossia Lista delle differenti produzioni del Monte Vesuvio. [On title-page :] Collection complète ou Liste des différentes productions du Mont Vésuve.—*fol.* (*in Ital. and French*). — ?,—?

ANON.—Raccolta di Disegno.—*fol.* — ?,— ? [B.N.P., Vb. 43 b.] Contains 107 water-colour sketches, one of which is a quaint drawing of Vesuvius.

ANON. — Raccolta di lettere scientifiche ed erudite dirette dall' abate Genovesi a diversi suoi amici.—8°, *foll.* 3, *pp.* 247. *Napoli,* 1780. [C.A.] Letter VII : an account of the Vesuvian eruption of 1779 ; Letter VIII : (by Padre Ant. de Sanctis) that of 1631.

ANON.—Raccolta di monumenti sopra l'eruzione del Vesuvio seguita nell' Agosto 1779. —*Giorn. Arti, Commercio, i. Macerata,* 1780. [At pp. 141 *et seq.* :] Una lettera di Antonio de Gennaro ; due lettere di un tale P. R. ; una lettera di Melchiorre Delfico ; un estratto dalla memoria del P. della Torre.

ANON. — Raccolta di osservazioni chimiche sull' uso dell' acqua termominerale Vesuviana Nunziante.—*Fascicolo Primo,* 8°, *pp.* 76. *Napoli,* 1833. [C.A.] *See* RICCI, G.

ANON.—Raccolta di Storia naturale.—4°, 1 *pl. Roma,* 1784.

ANON.—Raccolta di tutte le vedute che esistevano nel Gabinetto del Duca della Torre rappresentanti l'eruzioni del Monte Vesuvio fin oggi accadute, etc.—*obl. fol., pp.* 20, 50 *pls. Napoli,* 1805. [B.N.]

ANON.—Raccolta di Vedute del Regno di Napoli e suoi contorni disegnate dal vero.— 4°, 47 *pls. Presso Antonio Poggioli, Roma,* 1829.

ANON.—Ragguaglio di una nuova eruzione fatta dal Monte Vesuvio nei primi giorni del corrente agosto 1779.—4°, *foll.* 2. *Roma,* 1779. [C.A.]

ANON.—Ragionamento historico intorno a nuovi vulcani.—*Napoli,* 1761.

ANON.—Raised Model of Vesuvius and Neighbourhood.—*Ist. Geog. Milit. Ital.* 1878. 1 : 50,000 horiz. and 1 : 25,000 vert. scale, cast in zinc and plated with copper.

ANON.—The recent eruption of Vesusius [*sic*].—" *The Graphic,*" *p.* 538. *London, May 30th,* 1885.

ANON.—Recherches sur les ruines d'Herculanum.—*Paris,* 1770. [O.V.]

ANON.—Récit véritable et mémorable accident arrivé en la descente de la très renomée [*sic*] Montagne de Somma, autrement la Vésuve, . . . 1631.— *Merc. François, xvii, pt.* 2, *pp.. 67–73. Paris,* 1633. *See* RAZZANTI, F.

ANON.—Recueil de toutes les vues qui existaient dans le cabinet du Duc de la Tour et qui représentaient les incendies du Mont Vésuve arrivés jusqu'à présent.— 4°, *foll.* 2, *pp.* 20, 25 *pls. Naples,* 1805. [O.V.]

ANON.—Reisen eines Offiziers durch die Schweiz und Italien.—8°, *pp.* 12+356. *Hannover,* 1786. State of the crater of Vesuvius in Nov. 1783 ; *see* pp. 282.-83. Of little importance.

ANON. — Relacion del incendio de la Montaña de Soma.—*fol., pp.* 8. — ?, 1631.

ANON.—Relation de l'irruption du Mont Vésuve depuis son commencement jusques en l'etat quelle est aujourdhuy 28. 8bre 1751.—MS. 4°, *foll.* 2. [B.M.—Add. 4439. 527.]

ANON.—Relation oder Gründliche Beschreibung dess erschröcklichen Erdbebens vnd e bärmlichen grossen Feuersbrunst, so im Königreich Neapolis bey dem Berg Soma vnd vmb dessen gegent entstanden, im Monat Decemb. dess vergangenen 1631 Jars etc.—*foll. vi, woodcut frontisp.* —?, 1632.

ANON.—Relatione e curioso racconto del nvovo incendio del Vesvvio cauato da diffusa relatione venuta da Napoli.—*pp.* 8, 1 *fig.* (fancy fig. of burning house). *Roma, Fr. Moneta,* MDCLX.

ANON.—Relatione dell' incendio del Monte Vesuvio del 1631.—*See* RICCIO, L.— Nuovi Documenti, etc., *pp.* 27–35.

ANON.—Relatione dell' incendio successo nel Monte Vesuvio detto di Somma. L'anno 1631. Il mese di Dicembre.—8°, *foll.* 10. *Gio. Pietro Pinelli, Venetia,* 1631.

ANON. — Relazione fisico-storica della eruzione Vesuviana de' 15 Giugno 1794. —*Gazz. Civ. Napoletana*, 25 and 26, *pp.* 171–75. 1794. [B.N.]

ANON. — Relazione della Giunta comunale di Napoli al Consiglio su' provvidimenti adottati per la eruzione del Vesuvio del 1872 ed atti relativi.—4⁰, *pp.* 31. *Napoli*, 1872. [C.A.]

ANON.—Relazione dell' inaugurazionc dell' Osservatorio Meteorologico sul Vesuvio il 28 Settembre 1845.—*Giorn. Reg. Due Sicilie*, 30 *Settembre* 1845.

ANON.—Relazione dell' incendio del Vesuvio seguito l'anno 1682 dalli 14 di Agosto sino alli 26 del medemo.—4⁰, *foll.* 2, *fig.* (fancy fig. of a temple). *Roma*, 1682.

ANON.—Relazione dei meravigliosi effetti cagionati dalla portentosa eruzione del Monte Vesuvio detto di Somma, di pietre infocate, gorghi di fuoco, tuoni saetti e pioggia infinita di arenosa cenere seguita dal dì 26 del caduto luglio per tutti li due del corrente agosto 1707.—4⁰, *foll.* 2. *Napoli*, 1707. [C.A.]

ANON.—Relazione per le osservazioni del Monte Vesuvio del 29 Luglio 1794.—MS.

ANON.—Relazione ragionata della eruzione del nostro Vesuvio, accaduta a' 15 giugno 1794, etc.—*See* ONOFRIO.

ANON.—Relazione o sia descrizione della spaventevole eruzione del Monte Vesuvio distante alcune miglia da Napoli verso Levante, seguita la sera delli 8 del corrente mese d'agosto (1779) avendo la stessa cagionati grandissimi danni a tutti que' luoghi, a cui si è estesa.—4⁰, *foll.* 2. *Bologna*, 1779.

ANON.—Relazione del Tremuoto intesosi in questa città di Napoli, ed in alcune provincie del regno nel dì 29 Novembre 1732, ad ore tredici e mezza.—*pp.* 8. *Napoli*, M.DCC.XXXII.

ANON.—Relazione del Vesuvio.—4⁰. — ?, — ? [B.N.]

ANON.—Remarques sur le Vésuve.—*Bull. Sci. nat. Géol.* p. 39. *Paris*, 1837.— *Edinb. Journ. Sci. vii*, *pp.* 11–18. 1827.

ANON.—Rilievo Geologico dell' Isola di Capri. Scala orizz. 1 : 50,000, vert. 1: 5,000. —*R. Uffic. Geol. Roma*, 1886.

ANON.—Riscontro di un avvocato napoletano ad un suo amico di provincia della eruttazione del Vesuvio dei 15 giugno 1794.—8⁰, *pp.* 40. *Napoli*, 1794.

ANON.—Risposta di un regnicolo ad un suo amico in Napoli sull' eruzione del Vesuvio.—8⁰, *pp.* 7. *Napoli*, 1794. [B.N. and O.V.]

ANON.—Risultato dell' analisi di alcune sostanze minerali fatta dal Sig. Klaproth al Vesuvio.—*Giorn. Lett. xc*, *pp.* 81–104. *Napoli*, 1797.

ANON.—[S. Lucia from the South about 1850 (?) before the S. Lucia breakwater was made.]
Fine pencil drawing, touched with colour and chalk : 237 × 137 mm.

ANON.—Il Sebeto che piange, canzone d'incerto autore.—*See* GIORGI URBANO.

ANON. — Seconda lettera di un legista napoletano ad un suo fratello in provincia, in cui gli dà distinto 'ragguaglio di quanto è avvenuto in Napoli in occasione dell' orribile eruzione del Vesuvio avvenuta ai 15 giugno 1794.—8⁰, *pp.* 16. *Napoli*, 1794. [C.A.]

ANON.—Serenata per celebrare il patrocinio del glorioso apostolo S. Matteo per la prodigiosa liberazione di Salerno dell' oribile tremuoto de 5 Giugno 1688.—8⁰, *pp.* 12. *Napoli*, 1688.

ANON.—[A series of gouaches, or distempers bound up in the original copy of Sir W. Hamilton's Campi Phlegræi in the B.M., including eruptions of 1737, 1751, 1777, 1779, 1794.]

ANON.—Somma [with view of Vesuvius, dedic. Sig. Francesco Fasano with explan. letters A to P]. [Vienna lib.]
180 × 126 mm.

ANON.—Sommet du Vésuve ; autre vue du même sommet durant une petite éruption.—pl. *fol.* — ?, — ? [C.A.]

ANON.—Sostanze date fuori o sviluppate nelle eruzioni del Vesuvio. — *Il Propagatore Sci. Nat. i*, *pt.* 2, *pp.* 366. [B.N.]

ANON.—Souvenir de mon pélerinage à Rome. Excursions : Naples, Vésuve, Pompéi. 1899.—8⁰, *pp.* 116. *Versailles*, 1900.

ANON.—Souvenir du Vésuve.—8⁰, *pp.* 12. *Naples*, 1841. [O.V.]

ANON.—Lo Spettatore del Vesuvio e dei Campi Flegrei. Nuova Serie pubblicata a cura e spese della Sezione Napoletana del Club Alpino Italiano.—*fol.*, *pp.* 103, 13 *photo-engrav. Napoli*, 1887.
Contains writings by Palmieri, L., Comes, O., Palmieri, P., Riccio, L., Scacchi, A., Johnston-Lavis, H. J.

124   Bibliography of the South Italian Volcanoes—Vesuvius

ANON.—Statuto e regolamento organico dell' Associazione Vesuviane di mutuo soccorso per assicurare le proprietà dai danni delle lave vulcaniche.—4⁰, *pp.* 42. *Napoli*, 1873. [C.A.]

ANON. — La Storia dell' anno 1751.— Estratta per l'eruzione del 1755, *pp.* 7; Ibid. dell' anno 1760, *pp.* 2; Ibid. dell' anno 1779, *pp.* 3; Ibid. dell' anno 1794, *pp.* 5. 8⁰. *Amsterdam.* [O.V.]

ANON.—Studi sul Vesuvio ed altre località nel contorno di Napoli.—16⁰. *Roma*, 1885.
Forms part of the " Biblioteca scientifica dai Prof. Mario Lessona e Lorenzo Camerano."

ANON.—Succinta relazione dell' incendio del Vesuvio accaduto alla fine di luglio e progresso di agosto 1696.—4⁰, *foll.* 2. *Napoli*, 1696.

ANON.—Supplica alla Maestà del Re delle Due Sicilie [Carlo III.] in nome de' possessori de' territori ne' contorni del Vesuvio.—16⁰, *pp.* 14. — ?, — ? [O.V.]

ANON.—Taschenbuch für Freunde der Gebirgskunde.—8⁰, *pp.* 161, 1 *pl.* *Göttingen*, 1798.

ANON.—Tavola cronologica delle principali eruzioni del Vesuvio dall' anno 79 al 1850.—*Atti R. Ist. Incorag.* ix, at *p.* 8, *foll.* 7. *Napoli*, 1861.—See GIUDICE, F. DEL.—Brevi Considerazioni . . . Fenomeni Vesuviani.

ANON.—Tavolette rilevate per la costruzione della carte del regno d'Italia.—*Ist. Geog. Milit. Ital.* 1873–79.
Part to the scale of 1 : 50,000, and part 1 : 25,000. *See* sheets 184, i–ii ; 185, iii–iv.

ANON.—Terme Vesuviane Manzo (Torre Annunziata). Acqua termo-minerale " Cestilia." Premiate ecc.—16⁰, *pp.* 22. *Torre Annunziata*, 1894.

ANON.—Terremoto.—" *La Valigia*," *xiii*, *pp.* 215–17. 12 *Luglio*, 1891.
With a woodcut of the crater of Vesuvius.

ANON.—La Torre del Greco. Ode.—*fol.*, *fol.* 1. — ? [1794]. [O.V.]

ANON.—Torre del Greco distrutta dall' eruzione del 1794.
Lava flowing over houses into the sea ; four men in foreground. Varnished gouache : 66 × 437 mm.

ANON.—Le torrent de lave du Mont de Vésuve. Augsbourg. [B.N.P., Vb. 121.]
A good sepia litho.

ANON.—Touchant le Mont Vésuve et tremblement à Naples le 5 juin ·1688. Lettre écrite le 12.—*From :* " Voyage en Italie en 1688," 4ᵐᵉ éd. 4⁰, *T. iii*, *pp.* 391–418. *La Haye*, 1717. [C.A.]

ANON.—Touchant le M. Vésuve.—Extr. from : *Mélanges d'Histoire naturelle*, iv, *foll.* 13. — ?,— ? [O.V.]

ANON.—Tragedia Vesuviana.—MS. in Latin verse, 1794. [O.V.]

ANON.—Eine traurige Anmerkung und Ode, über die schrecklichen Begebenheiten welche sich in Neapel durch starke Windstürme, grosze Erdbeben und schrekliche Überströhmungen kürzlich zugetragen haben.—*pp.* 4. *Neapel, August*, 1805.

ANON.—Ueber den Zusammenhang des Meereswasser mit den Herden der Feuerberge.—*Taschenb. gesammt. Min.* xiii, *pp.* 194–98. *Frankfurt*, 1819.

ANON.—Untergang der Stadt Messina. Ingleichen eine kurze Beschreibung von den beiden feuerspeyenden Bergen Vesuv und Ætna.—4⁰, *pp.* 28, 2 *copper pls.* — ?, 1783.
See pp. 14–27.

ANON.—Uvaerachtige Af-beeldinge van den schricklijcken brandende Bergh Somma (anders genoemt Bergh Vesuvi) gelegen vande wijtberoemde Stadt Neapolis, ecc. C. Passe inc.
Erupt. 1631 with three columns of text.

ANON.—Vedute della eruzione del Vesuvio del 1631.—*fol.* 1. *Amsterdam.* [C.A.]

ANON.—Veduta dell' eruzione del Monte Vesuvio accaduta li 15 di Giugo [*sic*] 1794.
A beautiful contemporary‑gouache of erupt. by night : 323 × 243 mm.

ANON.—Veduta dell' eruzione del Monte Vesuvio accaduta li 15 Giugo [*sic*] 1794.
A very fine distemper by night from Mergellina : 325 × 244 mm.

ANON.—Veduta interiore del Vesuvio nel 1755.
Copper pl. obl. 4⁰.—*See* CARDON, A.

ANON.—Veduta del Monte Vesuvio disegnata dal mare dirempetto alla Torre del Greco dopo che la medesima fu quasi interamente distrutta dalla formidabile eruzione avvenuta la sera dei' xv Giugno MDCCXCIV. [*See* pl. in O.V.]
View from imaginary land opposite Torre del Greco ; ref. nos. and explan. Engrav. : 350 × 220 mm.

ANON.—Veduta del Monte Vesuvio e parte della città di Napoli.—*Napoli* ?, — ? [C.A.]

ANON.—Veduta di parte delle lave di bitume che nelle eruzione vomitate dal Vesuvio coprirono l'antichissima città di Ercolano ; prima della nostra era posta al di sotto di questi luoghi, tra il presente Portici e la Torre del Greco.—*Napoli* ?, — ? [C.A.]

ANON.—Veduta del Porto di Napoli dalla parte di Chiaja. [B.M.—K. 83. 61. e.]
Distemper with good outline of Vesuvius, but no date.

ANON.—Veduta del Vesuvio. [O.V.]
Three small views attached together.

ANON.—Veduta del Vesuvio con l'epigrafe : Oblatis ad Sebeti pontem simulacro Januari Cœlestis patroni contra erumpentes flammas stetit incendium Vesuvianum ; tantique beneficii ergo anno 1767 statua martyri dicatur quam cultor eius Gregorius Roccus Dominicanus populo in spem salutis demonstrat.—pl. 4⁰. [O.V.]

ANON.—Veduta del Vesuvio in eruzione con fuga dei Torresi.—pl. *roy. fol.* [O.V.]
Probably of the year 1794 ; excellently drawn.

ANON.—Vedute del Vesuvio in grande eruzione.—*roy. fol.* [1779 ?] [O.V.]

ANON.—Vera e distinta relazione dell' incendio ed eruzione del Monte Vesuvio cominciato al primo di Luglio per fino li 13 del presente anno 1701. Per quello che n'ha ocularmente osservato, e diligentemente notato un Curioso de' Deputati della Terra di Ottajano.—8⁰, *foll.* 2. *Napoli*, — ? [B.N.]

ANON.—Die Veränderungen des Vesuv-Gipfels.—*Peterm. Mitth. pp.* 206–7. *Gotha*, 1859.

ANON.—Il vero disegno in sul proprio luogo ritratto del infelice paese di Posuolo quale, E.M. 60 et del Monte di Nuovo nato in mare et in terra con danno et morte di molti habitatore e spaventi di di chiv che lo vede, comincio a butar fuoco poetre e cenere ali 29 Setembre 1538 et ancor' seghuita con minacci horribili.—[B.M.—K. 83 (71).]
Plate, giving quaint view of Vesuvius.

ANON.—Vero e distinto Ragguaglio di ciò che operossi dal Procurador Fiscale, etc. in render vuota la Regal Polveriera

della Torre nel di 7 dello scaduto mese di Dicembre su' l' terribil annunzio, che una spaventevol Fiumana di fuoco scoppiata dal Monte Vesuvio incaminavasi al di lei danno, e sterminio, etc.—4⁰. *Napoli*, 1755. [B.N.]

ANON.—Vero ritratto dell' incendio nella Montagna di Somma altramente detto Mons Vesuui, distante da Napoli sei miglia, successo alli 16 Xᵇʳᵉ 1631.—di Napoli alli 22 di Xᵇʳᵉ 1631. *Napoli*, 1632.
An engrav. of Vesuvius from S. Maria di Costantinopoli and Casale di S. Gio Ateduccio : 311×172 mm. Beneath this are title and explanation of engraved text, total dimensions being : 311×432 mm., constituting a *folio volante*.

ANON.—De Vesevo Monte.—*See* GIORGI URBANO.

ANON.—Vesuv. [B.N.P., Vb. 121.]
A very bad, incorrect litho. view of Vesuvius.

ANON.—Der Vesuv.
View of crater and cone of eruption *circa* 1876–77. Woodcut from a German illustr. paper : 142×95 mm.

ANON.—Der Vesuv, von dem Forum zu Pompeji aus gesehen. (S. 14.)
Woodcut from a German illustr. paper, " Ueber Land u. Meer," xiv, 40, with text : 230×317 mm.

ANON.—Der Vesuv, Pompeji und Herculanum, übersetzt von Franz Kottenkamp. —8⁰, *pp.* 40. *Stuttgart*, 1852.—*Wochenbände f. d. geistige u. materielle Wohl d. deutsch. Volkes, etc.* 121.

ANON.—Der Vesuv seit dem Ausbruch im December 1861 und die Zerstörung von Torre del Greco.—" *Globus*," ii, *pp.* 106–13, 7 *illustr.* Hildburghausen, 1862.

ANON.—Vesuv im Winter.
An anon. sepia print of Vesuvius covered with snow, from Hamilton's 84 views, with tower, men, donkeys and trap in foreground ; mounted on blue paper with printed black scroll frame : 292×210 mm. Title separately mounted below on the blue paper and not included in measurement.

ANON.—Le Vésuve.—*Journ. d. l'Empire*, 7 *et* 16 *nov. Paris*, 1807.

ANON.—N° 1438. Le Vésuve Sᵗ Sébastien : la nuit du 26 Avril 1872.
A hand-coloured photo. : 245×168 mm.

ANON.—Le Vésuve (Sicile). [B.N.P., Vb. 121.]
A minute litho.

ANON.—Le Vésuve [under snow]. Se vend à Augsburg dans le négoce de l'Académie de Hersberg. [B.N.P., Vb. 121.] Sepia engraving.

ANON.—Le Vésuve.
Unfinished pencil sketch on grey paper, showing details of cone and valleys of Somma taken from Mergellina : 500 × 380 mm.

ANON. — Vesuviani incendii elogium.—4⁰, *foll.* 2. [*Napoli*, 1631.] [C.A.]
See RICCIO, L.—Nuovi Documenti, etc.

ANON.—De Vesuvii conflagratione quæ mens. Majo 1737 accid. commentarius.—
See SERAO.

ANON. [SERAO].—Vesuvii prospectus ex Ædibus Regiis.
Erupt. of Vesuvius 1737, from SERAO'S "Ist. Incend. Vesuvio," 1737, with ref. nos. and explan. Engrav. : 402 × 174 mm.

ANON. — Il Vesuvio. — *Album di Roma*, *pp.* 105–7. 1834.

ANON.—Il Vesuvio. Foglio periodico.— i, 1–16, *fol.* Napoli, 1835.

ANON.—Vesuvio.—*Gazz. Comuni Vesuviani*, *xx.* Portici, 1897.

ANON.—Il Vesuvio Anacreontica.—8⁰, *pp.* 8, 1 *pl.* — ?, — ? [B.N.]

ANON.—Vesuvio ed Etna. S. Giorgio a Cremano Agosto 1892.—*fol., pp.* 25. 1892.

ANON.—De Vesuvio Monte nunc scimus fuisse Franciscum Mariano Suaresium Bibliotecharium Cardinalis Barberini. Copiato dal sig. Camillo Minieri dal MS. che si conserva nella Biblioteca Brancacciana.—MS. [O.V.]

ANON.—Il Vesuvio. Un Sonetto ed un Ode.—*foll.* 2. — ?, — ? [C.A.]

ANON.—Vesuvio. Strada di Portici-Resina e il romitorio del Vesuvio.—*Monibus pittoresco*, ii, 51 *and* 52, 2 *copper pls.* Napoli, 1840.

ANON.—Il Vesuvio. Strenna pel capo d'anno del 1844. Anno primo.—16⁰, *foll.* 3, *pp.* 72. Napoli.
See pp. 1–4.

ANON.—Il Vesuvio. Strenna pel 1869, pubblicata a pro dei dannegiati dell' eruzione del 1868.—8⁰, *pp.* 200. Napoli, 1869. [C.A.]
See CECI, G. (ed.).

ANON.—Vesuvio 1890.
View from Naples by day ; five men and two women in foreground. Gouache : 287 × 198 mm.

ANON.—Vesuvius.—" *Cornhill Mag.*," *xvii*, *pp.* 282–92. London, 1868.

ANON.—Vesuvius.—*Journ. Sci.* vi, *pp.* 188–96. London, 1869.

ANON.—Vesuvius seen from Naples, Nov. 30th, 1800.
Gouache : 245 × 172 mm.

ANON.—Vesuvius.—" *Liverpool Advertiser*," 76 *lines, Oct.* 13, 1831.

ANON.—Vesuvius. [In a letter from Naples, dated the 2nd inst. (April, 1835).]—*Newspaper cutting, 9 lines.*

ANON.—Vesuvius. View of cone of eruption and crater plain from the edge of the S.W. (1872) crater as it appeared in October, 1880.
Gouache : 250 × 177 mm.

ANON.—Vesuvius, by night. Eruption of Nov. 13th, 1880.
Gouache : 264 × 183 mm.

ANON. — Vesuvius. — *Encycl. Britannica*, *xviii*, pt. 2, *pp.* 728–34, — ? ; *xviii*, *pp.* 648–50, 1797.

ANON.—Vesuvius No. 2.
View of an explosion from Vesuvius from direction of Posilippo ; ruins, perhaps of Palazzo Donn' Anna, in foreground. Handcol. lith. of no scientif. importance : 116 × 191 mm.

ANON.—Vesuvius Morum Magister.—MS.
See RICCIO, L.—Nuovi Documenti, etc.

ANON.—[Eruption of Vesuvius, 1631.]
Very fine engrav. in style of I. Silvestre, with two large galleys in foreground : 151 × 183 mm.

ANON.—[An old painting of the Eruption of Vesuvius of August 8th, 1779.]
Water-colour, probably orig. of gouache : 405 × 291 mm.

ANON.—[Vesuvius from Naples by day, three men in foreground.]—1794.
Gouache : 115 × 76 mm.

ANON.—[Eruption of Vesuvius by day] Aug. 9, 1797.—*Naples ?*
Gouache.

ANON.—[Eruption of Vesuvius by night] Dec. 22, 1820.—*Naples ?*
Gouache.

ANON.—[Crater of Vesuvius, 1822.] [S. Martino Mus. No. 6692.]
Distemper painting.

ANON.—[Eruption of Vesuvius, 1822, by night.] [S. Martino Mus. No. 9969.]
Distemper painting.

ANON.—[Eruption of Vesuvius, 1822, by day.] [S. Martino Mus. No. 9970.]
Distemper painting.

ANON.—[Erupt. of Vesuvius, March 14th, 1828.]—*Gaz. di Napoli, Marzo 21*, 1828.
Copied into English papers, 49 lines.

ANON.—[Pencil sketch of Crater of Vesuvius in 1832.] [S. Martino Mus. No. 3832.]
This view is very similar to that of Auldjo, though not so careful as to perspective.

ANON.—[Erupt. of Vesuvius.] From Naples, Dec. 22nd, 1832.—*Cutting from English newspaper*, 9 *lines*.

ANON.—[Eruption of Vesuvius, Jan. 1st, 1839.]—" *Athenæum,*" p. 94. 1839.

ANON. — [Crater of Vesuvius by day.] 1847.
Two women, two men and guide in foreground. Gouache : 640×410 mm.

ANON.—[Vesuvius, in a quiet state, from Naples by night, 1848.]
Gouache : 470×314 mm.

ANON.— [5 Views of Naples :] 1. Mergellina to Vesuvius ; 2. Marinella at Castello di Carmine ; 3. Chiatamone and Pal. Crocelle ; 4. Molo and Vesuvius ; 5. Santa Lucia before the breakwater was built.
Pencil sketches, *circa* 1850 ? : 311× 222 mm.

ANON.—[A well-finished sepia sketch of Vesuvius from above Castellamare, looking from a Roman archway.]
Dated 1859. Vesuvius incorrectly detailed : 295×214 mm.

ANON. — [Eruption of Vesuvius, 1861, by day from Mergellina.]
Oil painting : 93×57 mm.

ANON.—[An idealized view of Vesuvius (?). In Roman times from S.W. foot of Camaldoli ?]
Water-colour : 265×185 mm.

ANON.—[Lateral rift and lava outflow with spiracles on slope of great cone of Vesuvius.]
Sepia water-colour : 292×215 mm.

ANON.—[Small view of Vesuvius in eruption from lighthouse.]
Oval stipple engrav. : 108×75 mm.
Rocks, faro, boats, men and piles in foreground.

ANON.—[Vesuvius in distance. Ruins of Pompei and man with staff on piece of cornice in foreground.]
Stipple engrav. without any inscription : 184×135 mm.

ANON.—[Vesuvius from ditch of Castel St. Elmo.]
Stipple engrav. with ox-cart, sheep and peasants in foreground. No inscription of any kind : 208×157 mm.

ANON.—[Vesuvius and mountains of Castellamare seen from the mole or fort de la Lanterne.]
This is a reduction of an engrav. by Chastelet, " Vue du Mosle, etc." Stipple engrav. or litho. : 162×117 mm.

ANON.—[Vesuvius with Pizzofalcone and Castel del Uovo in Foreground and seen from shore of Chiaja (? Toretta) with fishing-boats.]
Hand - colour. line - engraving : 262× 187 mm. (No margin.)

ANON.—[A view of I Camaldoli with cone of Vesuvius.] [B.N.P., Vb. 121.]
A picturesque engrav.

ANON.—[View over Naples and Vesuvius from above Grotto.]
Oil-painting : 93×57 mm.

ANON.—[A view of people escaping from an eruption of Vesuvius over the Ponte della Madalena.] [B.N.P., Vb. 120.]
A much damaged engrav. of no special interest.

ANON.—[No inscription of any kind. A view of Vesuvius from St. Elmo in dark sepia.]

ANON.—[View of Vesuvius from the Sea.]
Sepia stipple, well drawn ; fishing-boat in foreground : 400×276 mm.

ANON.—[Views of Pompei, especially Tempio di Ercole, with a view of Vesuvius in distance.]
Cutting from an unknown Italian paper. 4 woodcuts : 120×79 mm. each.

ANON.—View of the Eruption of Mount Vesuvius in 1767 from Portico. [Potter's collection.]
Pl. obl. 8⁰, with initialled letters.

ANON.—A View from the Garden of the Camaldulians near Puzzoli.
An engrav. with view of Vesuvius smoking in the distance, but very imaginary in outlines and detail ; three monks with two men regarding an inscription : 227×155 mm.

ANON.—View of His Majesty's Squadron under the Command of Rear Admiral Lord Nelson in line of Battle in the Bay of Naples when His Sicilian Majesty's Royal

Standard was hoisted on board the Foudroyant on His Majesty's arrival on board from Salerno on the 10th of June 1799. The Neapolitan Frigates, Brigantines and Hulks anchored astern the Squadron were full of Neapolitan Rebels taken from the Castles of Naples. [B.M. —K. 83. 60 h.]
A beautiful distemper with a detailed view of Vesuvius, bound in the original copy of Hamilton's Campi Phlegræi.

ANON.— A View of the late eruption of Mount Vesuvius.—See HINTON, I.

ANON.—View of Mount Vesuvius in the Kingdom of Naples.
A small, bad reproduction, reversed, of the eruption of 1757 by Lacroix. Engrav. : 171 × 117 mm.

ANON.—View of Mount Vesuvius in Naples with the eruption of Smoke, Fire, Lava, etc. Engraved for Moore's Voyages and Travels.
Shows eruption on S.W. flank of Vesuvius by night. Line engraving : 268 × 162 mm.

ANON.—View of the New Gate in the Suburbs of Naples with a distant prospect of Mt Vesuvius.
Engrav. with two soldiers in foreground on site now Strada Municipio : 177 × 120 mm.

ANON.— Volcans en éruption.—Art. of 14 lines in the "Matin," [11 ?] novembre 1906, dated Rome, 10 novembre [1906].

ANON.—Voyage en France, en Italie et aux Isles de l'Archipel, ou lettres écrites de plusieurs endroits de l'Europe et du Levant en 1750, etc.—12°. Tom. i, pp. 12+348 ; Tom. ii, pp. 8+340 ; Tom. iii, pp. 8+376 ; Tom. iv, pp. 7+379+4. Paris, 1763.
See pp. 205-17, state of Vesuvius 1750.

ANON.—Voyage d'un Françoi en Italie.— 8°, vii, foll. 2, pp. 475. 1769. [O.V.]

ANON.—Vor dem Ausbruch des Vesuvs.— " Die Gartenlaube," p. 492. 1869.

ANON.— Vue de l'église de Resina et de l'éruption du Vésuve du 23 oct. 1822.— A plate ? [C.A.]

ANON.—Vue d'une éruption volcanique du Vésuve depuis le 23 Dec. 1760 jusqu'au 5 Janv. 1761, etc. Se vend à Augsbourg in le Négoce de l'Académie de Herzberg.
Sepia print, well drawn.

ANON.—Vue de l'éruption du 8 Août 1779 prise de Pausilippe. [B.N.P., Vb. 121].
Probably reversed.

ANON.—Vue générale du Vésuve en 1757.— pl. fol. [C.A.]

ANON.—Vue du Mont Vésuve. Abrégé des Voyages en Europe. Tom. 9.
Lava in Atrio and rift on N. side of great cone : Somma escarp. to left, Salvatore to right, sea in distance. Copper engrav. : 274 × 177 mm. A poor copy of plate by Volaire of erupt. of 1771.

ANON.—Vue de Naples et du Vésuve.— Paris : Instit. Bibliographique XVIII.
Vesuvius and Naples from Posilippo ; peasant by tank, dog, shepherd and sheep in foreground. Very fine but dark engrav. : 148 × 89 mm.

ANON.—Vue du Temple de Jupiter à Pompéi. Dessiné d'après Nature.
Stipple engrav., with cone of Vesuvius in background : 274 × 204 mm.

ANON.—(3) Vue de Vésuve prise à Castellamare.—Paris [after 1840].
Another, simply entitled Castellamare, is much the same ; both show Vesuvius much truncated.

ANON.—Vue prise de Vésuve de la Vallée de Grognano. Lemercier, Benard et Cie. (deposit. 1840). [B.N.P., Vb. 121.] [Another entit. :] Dans la vallée de Grognano (deposit. 1840).
Both show Vesuvius.

ANON.—Vue du Vésuve et du Mosle ou Fort de la Lanterne à Naples.—Augsbourg, etc. — ? [B.N.P., Vb. 121.]
Sepia engraving of an erupt. probably between 1779 and 1812.

ANON.—Vulcani di Europa.—Il Propagatore Sci. Nat. i, pt. 2, pp. 328.

ANON.—Dei Vulcani o Monti Ignivomi più noti, e distintamente del Vesuvio. Osservazioni Fisiche e Notizie Istoriche di Uomini Insigni di varj tempi, raccolte con diligenza. Divise in due Tomi.—12°. Tom. i, pp. lxx+149 ; Tom. ii, pp. viii+ 228, 1 pl. [?Vesuvius, 1737]. Livorno, 1779.
Contains contributions from Targioni Tozzetti (Dei Monti Ignivomi della Toscana e del Vesuvio), Galiani, F., Plinio il Giovine, Magalotti, L., Strange, G., De Bomare, Darbie, F., Derham, G., Mead, R., Gennaro, A., Minervino, C. S. This work is attributed by some to Galiani, by others to Gentile. There are two copies in the Johnston-Lavis collection, one with the two

tomes in one vol. containing a plate : " Prospetto del Vesuvio dal Palazzo Regio " ; the other in two vols., from which the plate is missing.

A . . .—[Raised map of Vesuvius.]

ABATI, A.—Il Forno, Poesia heroica burlesca e latina sopra il Monte Vesuvio, etc.— 8⁰. *Napoli*, 1632. [B.N.]

ABBATI, B.—Epitome meteorologica di tremuoti con la cronologia di tutti quelli che sono accorsi in Roma dalla creatione del mondo sino agli ultimi successi sotto il pontificato del regnante pontefice Clemente XI il dì 14 Gennaro giorno di Domenica su le due della notte meno un quarto, e 2 di Febbraio del corrente anno 1703.— — ?, — ? [C.A.]

A.B.C.D.—Raccolta di quanto è stato pubblicato nelle novelle letterarie di Firenze sopra le antichità di Ercolano dall' anno 1748 a tutto 1750.—*Roma*, MDCCLI.—*See* GORI.—Admiranda Antiquitatum Herculanensium, etc., *2nd part of Vol. ii, pp.* 16+ 68.

ABICH, O. W. H. VON.—Der Krater des Vesuv, aufgenom. im Juli 1834.—[*Berlin*, 1834 ?] [B.M. 24058 (2).]
See Pl. i in his : " Erläuterndc Abbildungen, etc." Berlin, 1837.

ABICH, O. W. H. VON.—Sur les phénomènes volcaniques du Vésuve et de l'Etna.—*Bull. Soc. géol. France, vii, pp.* 40–48. *Paris*, 1835.

ABICH, O. W. H. VON.—Sur la formation de l'Hydrochlorate d'Ammoniaque à la suite des éruptions volcaniques et en particulier de celle du Vésuve en 1834.—*Bull. Soc. géol. France, vii, pp.* 98–102. *Paris*, 1835.

ABICH, O. W. H. VON.—Vues illustratives de quelques phénomènes géologiques prises sur le Vésuve et l'Etna, pendant les années 1833 et 1834.—*gd. fol. pp.* 4, 10 *pls. Paris*, 1836.

ABICH, O. W. H. VON.—Erläuternde Abbildungen geologischer Erscheinungen beobachtet am Vesuv und Aetna in den Jahren 1833 und 1834.—With French and German text, *roy. fol., pp.* 8, 10 *pls. Berlin*, 1837. —Also *Braunschweig*, 1841.
Very fine and correct views.

ABICH, O. W. H. VON.—Vulkanische Forschungen in Italien.—*N. J. f. Min. pp.* 439– 42. *Stuttgart*, 1837.

ABICH, O. W. H. VON.—Ueber Erhebungskratere, etc.—*N. J. f. Min. p.* 334. *Stuttgart*, 1839.

ABICH, O. W. H. VON.—Beiträge zur Kenntniss des Feldspathes.—*N. J. f. Min. pp.* 468–74. *Stuttgart*, 1841. — *Ann. Phys. Chem. l, pp.* 125–49, 341–63. *Leipzig*, 1840.

ABICH, O. W. H. VON.—Geologische Beobachtungen über die vulkanischen Erscheinungen und Bildungen in Unter- und Mittel-Italien. Bd. i, Lief. 1 : Ueber die Natur und den Zusammenhang der vulkanischen Bildungen.—4⁰, *pp. viii+134+ xi, 3 maps, 2 lith. pls. Braunschweig*, 1841. Atlas to same, bound separately, 5 *pls.*

ABICH, O. W. H. VON.—Topografisch-geognostische Uebersichtskarte der continentalen vulcanischen Gegenden im Königreich Neapel nach eigenen Beobachtungen und den besten vorhandenen Hülfsmitteln im Jahre 1838 entworfen.—*taf.* 1, *in* " Atlas zu den Geologischen Beobachtungen über die vulkanischen Erscheinungen und Bildungen in Unter- und Mittel-Italien." *Braunschweig*, 1841. [B.M. 23891 (1).]

ABICH, O. W. H. VON.—Ueber Lichterscheinungen auf dem Kraterplateau des Vesuv im Juli 1857.—*Zeitschr. deutsch. geol. Gesellsch. ix, pp.* 387–91. *Berlin*, 1857.

ABICH, O. W. H. VON.—Ueber die Erscheinung brennenden Gases im Krater des Vesuv im Juli 1857, und die periodischen Veränderungen, welche derselbe erleidet. (1857).—*Bull. Class. Phys. Math. Acad. Imp. Sci. xvi, coll.* 258–70. *St.-Pétersbourg*, *Leipzig*, 1858.

ABICH, O. W. H. VON.—Vues illustrées . . . sur le Vésuve et l'Etna.—*Paris*, 1887.

ACCADEMICO INCANTO.—Incendio del Vesuvio, pubblicato per cura di Vincenzo Bove.—8⁰, *foll. x. Napoli*, 1632. [C.A.] *See* MORMILE, G.

ACERBI, F.—De Vesvviano incendio anno 1631.—*In* " Polypodium Apollineum," 8⁰, *foll.* 8, *pp.* 1–10. *Napoli*, 1674.

ADAM (grav.).—Carte des environs de Naples [and sections of] Terrains volcaniques des environs de Naples. Pl. III.—*Ann. Mines, S.* 3, *xi, p.* 113. *Paris*, 1837. Engrav. coloured : 274×178 mm.

ADAM (grav.).—Terrains volcaniques des environs de Naples. Pl. VIII.—*Ann. Mines, S.* 3, *xi, p.* 389. *Paris*, 1837. Engrav. : 268×175 mm.

ADAM, VICTOR. — *See* COIGNET, M. — " Voyage en Italie " *and* " Pausilippe."

K

ADAMI, P.—Napoli liberata dalle stragi del Vesuvio.—8⁰. *Napoli*, 1633. [O.V.]

ADAMO, F. M. D'.—L'avampante ed avampato Vesuvio, in ottava rima.—12⁰, *foll. xii. Napoli*, 1632. [C.A.]

ADAMS, D.—*See* DAVENPORT ADAMS, W. H.

ADDATO, N.—Operetta Spirituale sopra il grande prodigio operato dal Glorioso S. Gennaro con averci liberato dall' orrendo incendio del Vessuvio.—16⁰, *woodcut frontisp. Napoli* [1632 ?].

ADDISON, J.—Remarks on several parts of Italy, in the years 1701, 1702, 1703.—8⁰, *pp.* 534 *and index. London*, 1705.

ADLERHOLD, G.—Umständliche Beschreibung des anjetzo vom Krieg neu-bedrohten sonst herrlichen Königreich Neapolis, nach dessen bewunderswürdigen Naturgütern, Fruchtbarkeit, Flüssen, Seen, Meer-Busen, und Häfen, dem stets rauchenden und offtmals mit entsätzlichen Feuer wütenden Vesuvio, auch andern Bergen und Vorgebürgen, Insuln, Höhlen, Warm-Sand- und Gesund-Bädern, etc. Nebst vielen schönen Kupffern, auch mit und ohne Land-Carten. . . .—8⁰, *pp.* 18, *foll.* 952. *Nürnberg*, 1702.

AFELTRO, O. DE.—De Monte Vesuvio ac ejus eruptione.—MS. *in the* [Biblioteca Brancacciana]. *Copy in* [C.A.].

AGADAMI, P. P.—Napoli liberata dalle stragi del Vesuvio. Diaria sacra.—8⁰. *Napoli*, 1632.

AGNAN D'ORBESSAN, LE MARQUIS A. M. D'.—Mélanges historiques, critiques, de physique, de littérature, et de poésie, etc.— 3 tom. 8⁰. *Paris*, 1768.

[AGNAN D'] ORBESSAN, [LE MARQUIS A.] M. D'.—Description du Mont Vésuve. Compita relazione di quanto e succeduto insino hoggi, (24 Dic.).

AGNELLO DI SANTA MARIA.—Trattato scientifico delle cause che concorsero al fuoco e terremoto del Monte Vesuvio, vicino Napoli.—8⁰, *pp.* 100. *Napoli*, 1632. [C.A.]-

AGRESTA, G. D.—Il Monte Vesuvio.—*In vol. " Delle Rime d'illustri Ingegni Napoletani,"* 12⁰, *pp.* 37–48. *Venezia*, 1633. [C.A.] Song.

AGRESTI, A.—Pochi versi sulla Torre del Greco nel 1861.—8⁰, *pp.* 12. *Napoli*, 1862. [C.A.]

AGRICOLA, G.—De natura eorum quæ effluunt ex terra.—*See* JUNTA, T.—De balneis, etc.—*foll.* 273–88. 1553.

AGUILAR, E.—Escursioni al Vesuvio.— *Boll. Soc. Naturalisti, xxi, pp.* 1–4, 1 *fig. Napoli*, 1908.

AJELLO, G.—*See* QUARANTA, B. 1845.

ALBERTI, F. L.—Descrittione di tutta Italia . . . nella quale si contiene il sito di essa . . . et più gli huomini famosi che l'hanno illustrata.—*fol., foll.* 4+469+29. *Bologna*, 1550.—4⁰, *foll.* 38+424. *Vinegia*, 1551 ; *Vinegia*, 1557.
Another copy of the 1550 ed. is stamped with the arms of Gaston d'Orléans.[B.N.P.]

ALBERTI, F. L.—Descriptio totius Italiæ . . . ex italica lingua nunc primum in Latinam conversa, interprete Guilielmo Kyriandeo Hæningeno.—*fol., foll.* 10, *pp.* 815, *foll.* 24. *Colonia Agrippinensi*, 1566. —*fol., foll.* 9, *pp.* 815, *foll.* 26. 1567.

ALBERTI, F. L.—Descrittione di tutta Italia. Aggiuntavi la Descrittione di tutte l'Isole all' Italia appartenenti . . . (Edizione curata da Antonio Cheluzio da Colle). —4⁰, *foll.* 42+504+100+5, 7 *maps. Venetia*, 1568.—Other ed. : 1576 ; 4⁰, *foll.* 32+501+ 69+4, 1577.

ALBERTI, F. L.—Descrittione di tutta l'Italia . . . Aggiontovi di nuovo . . . tutto quello chè successo sino l'anno 1581. E di più accresciutà d'altre additioni . . . da M. Borgaruccio Borgarucci.—4⁰, *foll.* 32+501+96+4. *Venetia*, 1581.—4⁰, *foll.* 34+495+100+5. *Vinegia*, 1588.—4⁰, *foll.* 34+495+91+4. *Venetia*, 1596. *See* foll. 191–93 of 1581 ed.

ALBINUS, F.—Dialogus de Vesuvij incendio. [C.A.]—*See* FALCONE, S.

ALDERANI, C. (dis.).—Veduta del R. Palazzo di Caserta. Lit. A. Fattalini. LIVORNO.
Vesuvius in distance, palace of Caserta and cascade in foreground. Litho. on tinted paper : 212×148 mm.

ALEMBERT, D'.—*See* DIDEROT.

ALEXANDER, C.—Practical remarks on the lavas of Vesuvius, Etna, and the Lipari Islands.—*Proc. Scient. Soc. i, pp.* 31–32. *London*, 1839.

ALFANI, P. G., ALFANO, G. B., SCOTTO DI PAGLIARA.—La Sezione Geodinamica, sua inaugurazione e suoi apparecchi. Il Museo Vesuviano, sua inaugurazione e sue collezioni. Osservatorio Meteorico-Geodinamico Pio x in Valle di Pompei (Napoli). —8⁰, *pp.* 128, *foll.* 2. *Valle di Pompei*, 1912.

ALFANO, G. [B.]—Rilievo del Monte Vesuvio.
Model : 400×420 mm., executed in 1896 on the Carta dell' Ist. topogr. milit. Scale 1 : 25,000, coloured by hand, with MS. explanation.

ALFANO, G. B.—I fenomeni geodinamici della Sorgente minerale di Valle di Pompei. —*Riv. Fis. Mat. Sci. Nat. x*, 112, *pp.* 350–65 ; 113, *pp.* 416–34 ; 114, 115, 4 *figs. Pavia*, 1909.

ALFANO, G. B.—Sulle Cause che determinano la traiettoria dei detriti del Vesuvio durante le sue eruzioni.—*Mem. Pontif. Acc. Rom. N. Lincei, xxix, pp.* 203–28. *Roma*, 1911.

ALFANO, G. B.—*See* ALFANI, P. G.

ALFANO, G. M.—L'incendio vesuviano dell' aprile 1906.—*Riv. Fis. Mat. Sci. Nat. vii*, 83, *pp.* 432–53, *tav.* ; 84, *pp.* 539–60. *Pavia*, 1906.

ALFANO, G. M.—Sullo stato della questione circa la causa dei fori circolari nei vetri, e largo contributo apportato allo studio di essa dai professori F. Bassani e A. Galdieri della R. Università di Napoli, e dal Prof. Ignazio Galli di Velletri.—*Riv. Fis. Mat. Sci. Nat. viii*, 96, *pp.* 558–76. *Pavia*, 1907.

ALLAUX.—*See* COIGNET, M.—Vues pittoresques de l'Italie, etc.

ALLEN.—*See* WRIGHT, G. N. 1839 (?).

ALLERS, C. W.—La Bella Napoli.—*fol., pp.* 214, *num. illustr. Stuttgart, Berlin, Leipzig*, 1893.

ALLERS, C. W.—Der Vesuv.—*In his* " La Bella Napoli," *pp.* 125–30. *Stuttgart*, 1893.

ALOE, S. D'.—*See* QUARANTA, B. 1845.

ALOE, S. D'.—Naples, ses Monumens et ses curiosités, avec une description de Pompéi, Herculanum, Stabies, Pœstum, Pouzzoles, Cumes, Capoue et des autres endroits célèbres des environs.—12⁰, *pp. xv*+435, 1 *plan. Naples*, 1847.——2nd ed. *pp. vii*+625. 1853.

ALOE, S. D'.—Les Ruines de Pompéi.—12⁰, *pp. xxxvi*+155. *Naples*, 1852.

ALOE, S. D'.—Les Ruines de Pompéi jusqu'en 1860. Suivies d'une excursion au Vésuve, à Herculaneum, à Stabia et à Pæstum avec les plans de la ville de Pompéi et de la maison de Marcus Lucrétius.—12⁰, *pp. lii*+196, 2 *plans. Naples*, 1860.——5e ed. 8⁰, *pp.* 130, 2 *plans. Naples*, 1866.—Another ed. 8⁰. *Naples*, 1873.

ALOIA (engraved by).—Eruzione del Vesuvio nella notte degli 8 agosto 1779. [C.A.] Plate.

ALOJA, R. (inc. 1805).—Veduta della 27ᵐᵒ eruzione del Monte Vesuvio accaduta l'anno 1766. Vue de la 27ᵉ éruption du Mont Vésuve en 1766. T. ix. In Napoli presso Franc. SCAFA. Str. S. Biagio de' Librari. N° 117.
Engrav. : 253×198 mm.

ALOJA, V.—*See* FERGOLA, L., also HACKERT, F.

ALSARIUS CRUCIUS [or DELLA CROCE], VINCENTIUS.—Vesvvivs Ardens siue Exercitatio Medico-Physica Ad Ριγοπύρετον, idest motum et incendium Vesuuij montis in Campania. xvi. Mensis Decembris, Anni MDCXXXI. Libris ii comprehensa.—4⁰, *pp. viii*+317+3. *Romœ*, 1632.

ALVINO, F.—Il Vesuvio. Cenno brevissimo sugli antichi suoi nomi, sue dimensioni, istorie di tutte l'eruzioni, ragioni fisiche di tal fenomeno, ed uno sguardo sul cratere (eruzione del 1794).—8⁰, *pp.* 18, *col. fig. Napoli*, 1841. [C.A.]

ALVINO, F.—La Penisola di Sorrento descritta.—8⁰, *pp.* 52, 3 *pls. Napoli*, 1842.
In first note author quotes Pelliccia, asserting that Sorrento was an island and that the region of Nocara, Sarno and Nola originated in an eruption of Vesuvius that occurred two centuries before the foundation of Rome ; also that Vesuvius rose from the sea in what in remote times was a vast gulf.

AMARO, F. DE.—Ærumni (Vesuvii) anni 1822. Epistola.—4⁰, *pp.* 12. *Neapoli*, 1823.
Poetry concerning Vesuvius. Frontisp., a vignette, with view of Vesuvius engr. by Spani.

AMARO, F. DE.—Ejusdam. Ode (de Vesuvio).—4⁰, *pp.* 7. *Neapoli*, 1824. [B.N.]
Poetry concerning Vesuvius.

AMATO, P. G. D'.—Giudizio filosofico intorno ai fenomeni del Vesuvio.—4⁰, *pp.* 38. *Napoli*, 1755.

AMATO, P. G. D'.—Divisamento critico sulle correnti opinioni intorno ai fenomeni del Vesuvio e degli altri vulcani.—8⁰, *pp.* 90, 1 *pl. Napoli*, 1756.

AMATO, P. G. D'.—Opinions sur le Vésuve. —*See* TORRE, G. M. DELLA. 1760.

AMBRA, R.—*See* QUARANTA, B. 1845.

AMBROSIO, F. DE.—La Torre del Greco. (Erupt. 1861.)—8⁰, *pp.* 8. *Napoli*, 1862. [B.N.]

AMITRANO, A.—Encomium sacri sanguinis gloriosi martyris et pontificis Januarii.—8°, *foll. iv. Neapoli*, 1632. [O.V.]

AMODIO, G.—Breve Trattato del Terremoto. Scritto . . . in occasione dell' incendio successo nel Monte Vesuuio nel giorno 16 di dicembre 1631, etc.—8°, *pp.* 60, 1 *fig. Napoli*, 1632.

AMODIO, [G.?](édit.).—Panorama de Naples. Chez M. Amodio, Éditeur, à Milan, Galerie De Cristoforis. N° 57.
 Stippled sepia engrav. : 470×185 mm.

A. M. S.—Lettera su i Vulcani al sig. Guglielmo Thomson.—*Giorn. Lett. xcvii, pp.* 3–26. *Napoli*, 1798.

ANCORA, G. D'.—Prospetto storico-fisico degli Scavi d'Ercolano e di Pompei e dell' antico e presente stato del Vesuvio.—8°, *pp.* 137, 2 *pls. Napoli*, 1803.

ANCORA, G. D'.—Lettera a S.E. il sig. priore Francesco Seratti consigliere e segretario di stato di S.M. Siciliana.—*Mag. Lett. Sci. Arti, pp.* 29–36. *Firenze, Agosto,* 1805.

ANDERLINI, F.—*See* NASINI, R.

ANDERSON, T.—Volcanic vapours of Mount Vesuvius. [1872.]—*Proc. Phil. Soc. viii,* 2, *pp.* 268–78. *Glasgow*, 1872–73.

ANDERSON, T.—The Volcanoes of the Two Sicilies.—*Geol. Mag. p.* 473. 1888.—*Rept. Brit. Assoc.* 1888, *pp.* 663–64. *London,* 1889.

ANDERSON, T.—Vesuvius, a Note on the Eruption of September, 1898.—*Alpine Journ. pp.* 1–4, 2 *pls.* 1899.

ANDERSON, T.—The Eruption of Vesuvius of 1898.—*Rept. Brit. Assoc.* 1899, *p.* 749. *London,* 1900.

ANDERSON, T.—Volcanic Studies in many lands.—8°, *pp. xxii*+202, 105 *pls. London,* 1903.

ANDERSON, T.—The Physical Geography of Volcanoes. (Erupt. 1906.) Lecture Brit. Assoc. Advanc. Sci. York, 1906.—"*Nature,*"*lxxiv, pp.* 527–28, 2 *figs. London,* 1906.

ANDOSILLA LARRAMENDI, IVAN DE.—Al Vesuvio. Soneto.—*See* QUINONES.—El Monte Vesvvio.

ANDREA, A. DE (publ.).—Eruzione del Vesuvio di Napoli nel giorno 22 Ottobre 1822. dis. dal vero ed inc. in Napoli. Pubb. in Milano da A. de Andrea. Deposto all' I.R. Biblioteca. [Vienna lib.]
 A stipple sepia engrav. : 443×380 mm.

ANDREA, A. DE (publ.).—Eruzione del Vesuvio di Napoli nella notte 22 Ottobre 1822. dis. dal vero ed inc. in Napoli.—Pubb. in Milano da A. de Andrea. Deposto all' I.R. Biblioteca. [Vienna lib.]
 A stipple sepia engrav. : 441×378 mm.

ANDREÆ, J. L.—Dissertatio inauguralis de montibus ignivomis sive Vulcanis, etc.—4°, *pp.* 32. *Altdorpi*, 1710.

ANDRINI.—La grande éruption du Vésuve, Naples, 17 Décemb.—*Press. Scient. des Deux Mondes, i, pp.* 114–19. *Paris,* 1862. [C.A.]

ANGELIS D'OSSAT, G. DE.—Il pozzo artesiano di Marigliano (1882).—*Atti Acc. Gioen. S.* 4, *vii,* 7, *pp.* 50. *Catania*, 1894.

ANGELO, R. D' (inc.).—Veduta della grande eruzione accaduta il giorno de 22 Ottobre 1822. Vue de la grande éruption du jour du 22 Octobre en 1822. Tav. XXVIII. In Napoli, presso Franc. Scafa.
 Engrav. : 247×197 mm.

ANGELO, R. D' (inc.).—Veduta della grande eruzione accaduta la sera de' 22 Ottobre 1822. Vue de la grande éruption du soir du 22 Octobre en 1822. Tav. XXIX. In Napoli, presso Franc. Scafa.
 Engrav. : 251×196 mm.

A. N. M.—Un Papiro, ossia i gladiatori nella caverna del Vesuvio.—4°, *pp.* 197. *Venezia*, 1826. [C.A.]

ANNA, ALÈSA D'—Eruzione del Vesuvio accaduta alli 8 d'Agosto del Anno 1779. Aloja inc. [B.N.P., Vb. 121.]
 A beautiful engraving.

ANNA, A. D'.—Eruzione del Vesuvio di 1779. Gravé d'après le dessin original de A. d'Anna, peintre du Roi de Naples (J. B. Chapuy sc.).—*Paris* [1779 ?].
 Mezzotint engrav., gd. fol.

ANNA, A. D' (pinxit).—Éruption du Mont Vésuve de 1779.—Gravé d'après le dessin original de Signor Alexandre d'Anna, peintre du Roi de Naples. J. B. Chapuy Sculpt. Se vend à Paris à la manufacture de papiers peints chez Arthur et Comp° sur le Boulevard.
 Mezzotint : 682×498 mm.

ANNA, A. D'.—Éruption du Mont Vésuve [1779 ?] gravé d'après le dessin original de Signor Alexandre d'Anna, peintre à Naples. Gravé par Fr. Weber. Se vend chez Fossari & Comp. et chez Fr. Weber.
 Hand-colour. engrav. on yellow paper : 542×387 mm.

ANNA, A. D'.—Éruption du Mont Vésuve [1779 ?]. Gravé d'après le dessin original de Signor Alessandro D'Anna, peintre à Naples. Gravé par F. R. [*i.e.* Fr.] Weber. Zu finden bei Steingriebel in Augsburg.— [Deutsches Museum, geol. sec. Munich.] Hand-coloured engrav.: 386×542 mm.

ANNA, A. D'.—Éruption du Mont Vésuve 1794. Peint par A. d'A. Gravé par Mixelle. Paris, chez Gamble & Coipel. [S. Martino Mus. 5975.] A coloured engraving.

ANNA, A. D'.—Eruzioni Vesuviane dal 1779 al 1794.—pl. *fol. Napoli.* [O.V.]

ANNA, A. D'.—Veduta del Torre del Greco incendiata e distrutta nella maggior parte dall' eruzione, che fece il Monte Vesuvio, alle 15 di Giugno 1794, essendo arrivata la lava al mare. (G. Morghen inc.)—[O.V. Also S. Martino Mus. 2908.] Two ed., one in sepia publ. by P. P. Gervasi, dedicated to Perelli; the other dedicated to F. Scafa. A fine engraving.

ANNA, A. D' (depin.).—Eruzione di cenere accaduta nel Monte Vesuvio alli 19 di Giugno 1794 la quale continuò sino al' giorno 21, etc. Vincenzo Aloja inc. In Napoli presso Vincenzo Talani, Strada del Gigante di Palazzo N° 7. [B.N.P. Vb. 121.] Fine engrav. like that in BOTTIS, but much larger : 412×281 mm.

ANNA, A. D' (dis.).—Veduta dell' eruzione di fumo e cennere disegnata li 11 Sett^bre 1804.—Vue de la éruption de fumée et de cendres dessinée dunt le nuit du 10 Sett^bre 1804. Gennaro Bartoli inc. T. XXIII. In Napoli presso Franc. Scafa. Str. S. Biagio de' Librari. N° 117. Engrav.: 257×198 mm.

ANNA, A. D' (pin.).—Veduta del Monte Vesuvio e parte della città di Napoli. A.S.E.D. Girolamo Settimo Çalvello, etc., Vincenzo Talani D. D. D., V. Aloja inc. N° 3. In Napoli presso Vincenzo Talani strada del Gigante di Palazzo, N° 7. Engrav.: 406×278 mm.

ANNA, OLIVA D' (dis.).—Veduta della 13ª Eruzione accaduta li 16 Decembre del 1631. —Vue de la 13me Éruption arrivée le 16 Décembre en 1631. Pietro Toro inciso T. II. In Napoli presso Franc. Scafa. Str. S. Biagio de Librari. N° 117. Engrav.: 252×196 mm.

ANNA, O. D' (dis.).—Veduta quarta della 23ª Eruzione accaduta nell' anno 1751.—

Vue quatrième de la 23me éruption arrivée dans l'année 1751. Raffael Aloja incise. T. IV. In Napoli presso Franc. Scafa. Str. S. Biagio de' Librari. N° 117. Engrav.: 254×198 mm.

[ANNA, O. D' (dis.).] ?—Veduta della stessa 23ª eruzione del 1751 presa dalla parte di Mezzogiorno.—Vue de la même 23me éruption en 1751 prise de la partie qui regarde le midi. T. V. In Napoli presso Franc. Scafa. Str. S. Biagio de' Librari. N° 117. Engrav.: 253×195 mm.

ANNA, O. D' (dis.).—Veduta della 26ª Eruzione accaduta li 23 Decembre 1760.—Vue de la 26me éruption arrivée le 23 Décembre en 1760. P. Toro incise. T. VIII. In Napoli presso Franc. Scafa. Str. S. Biagio de' Librari. N° 117. Engrav.: 253×199 mm.

ANNA, O. D' (dis.).—Veduta della 29ª eruzione del Monte Vesuvio accaduta l'anno 1771.—Vue de la 29e éruption du Mont Vésuve en 1771. T. XI. Pietro Garboni inc. in Roma. In Napoli presso Franc. Scafa. Str. S. Biagio de' Librari. N° 117. Engrav.: 256×198 mm.

ANNA, O. D' (dis.).—Veduta della 31ª eruzione accaduta nel mese di Settembre 1790. —Vue de la 31e éruption arrivée dans le mois de Septembre en 1790. Pietro Parboni inc. T. XV. In Napoli presso Franc. Scafa. Str. S. Biagio de Librari. N° 117. Engrav.: 253×197 mm.

ANNALI DI ROMA. Opera periodica.—*See Vol. ii, pp.* 109–13. *Roma,* 1791. An article on the eruption of 1790.

ANSTED, B. T.—The last eruption and present state of Vesuvius.—"*Good Words,*" *vii, pp.* 592–95. *London,* 1866.

ANTICI, S.—Sonctto (1631). [C.A.]—*See* GIORGI URBANO.

APOLLONI, G.—Il Vesuvio ardente.—2nd ed. 12°, *foll.* 15. *Napoli,* 1632.

ARACRI, G.—Altra relazione della pioggia di cenere avvenuta in Calabria ulteriore nel detto giorno [27 marzo 1809].—*Atti Soc. Pontaniana, i, pp.* 167–70. *Napoli,* 1810.

ARAGO, D. F. J.—Liste des Volcans actuellement enflammés.—*Ann. Bur. Longit. pp.* 167–89. *Paris,* 1824. [C.A.]—English trans. by Thomson.—*Ann. Phil. N.S. vii, pp.* 201–14. *London,* 1824.

ARAGONA, N. M. D' (PRINCE OF CASSANO).— On the eruption of Mount Vesuvius in May 1737, in Italian, with a translation.—MS. [B.M. Add. 4434]

ARAGONA, N. M. D' (PRINCE OF CASSANO).— A Letter from . . . to the President of the Royal Society, containing an Account of the eruption of Vesuvius in May 1737. Translated from the Italian by T. S. M. D., F.R.S.—*Phil. Trans. R. Soc. xli* (1739), *pp.* 237–52. *London,* 1744.

ARCONATI-VISCONTI, G. M.—Appunti sull' eruzione del Vesuvio del 1867–68.—*Il Politecnico, v, pp.* 237–53. 1868.—Also *Torino,* 1872.

ARDINGHELLI, MLLE.—Observation sur une violente éruption du Mont Vésuve le 23 oct. 1767 dans la quelle la cendre fut portée jusqu'à Naples.—*Mém. Acad. Sci. Hist. pp.* 26–27. *Paris,* 1767.

ARENA, F.—*See* OGLIALORO-TODARO, A., ET ALII. 1908.

ARENA, M.—*See* COMANDUCCI, E.

ARFVEDSON, J. A.—Analys af Meionit dioctaèdre och af Leucit fran Vesuvius.— *Afhandl. Fysik. vi, pp.* 255–62. 1818.— *Journ. f. Chem. Phys. xxxix, pp.* 347–48. *Nürnberg,* 1823.

ARISTIDE, A. (signed in ink).—Vue prise dans le royaume de Naples.
Vesuvius in distance, with Castello di Lettere in foreground. Same as views by Coignet, but redrawn and reversed. Litho. on double paper : 285×196 mm.

ARMFIELD, H. T.—At the crater of Vesuvius in eruption. A word picture.— *Salisbury,* 1872.

ARMINIO, I. D'.—De terremotibus et incendiis eorumque causis, et signis naturalibus et supranaturalibus. Item de flagratione Vesuvii ejusque mirabilibus eventis et auspiciis.—8°, *pp.* 16, *frontisp.* (a vignette of Vesuvius). *Neapoli,* 1632.

ARNALD, G.—Bay of Naples with Mount Vesuvius. From an Original Painting by G. Arnald, A.R.A. Engraved by E. Benjamin.—London, Simpkin & Marshall, Stationers Court : and T. W. Stevens, 10 Derby Street, King's Cross. 1832.—*No.* 309 *in* " *The R. Academy Exhibition,*" *Vol. i,* 1769–1904. *London,* 1905.
Fine engrav. : 160×111 mm. View of town and Vesuvius from above Grotto ; five umbrella pines, goats and personages in foreground. This is almost identical with one by H. Bibby.

ARTARIA ET COMP. (publ.).—Napoli. Dissegnata dal vero nel 1816. Vienna, presso Artaria et Compagnie. [Vienna lib.]
Outline, slightly shaded, engrav. : 675× 441 mm.

ARTAUD, CHEV. DE, et SALLE, DE LA.— L'Univers. Histoire et Description de tous les peuples. Italie par Chev. Artaud, Sicile par de la Salle.—8°, *pp.* 5+384+96, 120 *pls.,* 2 *maps. Paris,* 1845.
See pls. 55, 81.

ARTHENAY, D'.—*See* MOUSSINOT. 1748.

ARTHENAY, D'.—Des laves et des inondations qui accompagnent quelquesfois les embrasements du Vésuve.—*In* MOUSSINOT. — Mémoire sur la ville souterraine découverte au pied du Mont Vésuve, *pp.* 10–15. *Paris,* 1748.

ARTHENAY, D'.—Notizie intorno alla città sotteranea discoperta alle falde del Monte Vesuvio. Tradotte dal Franzese.—8°, *pp. xvi*+80. *Firenze,* 1749.—*See also* GORI.— Admiranda Antiquitatum Herculanensium, etc. *Vol. ii, pp.* 2+51, 1 *pl.* (good view of Vesuvius).

ARTHENAY, D'.—Journal d'observations, dans les différens Voyages qui ont été faits pour voir l'éruption du Vésuve.—*Mém. Math. Phys. présent. Acad. Roy. Sci. iv, pp.* 247–80. *Paris,* 1763.

ARTHOIS, H. D' (D.D.D.).—Vero ritratto della Marravellosa Montagna di Somma overo Vesvvio verso la parte de Mare la dievi bocca e distante da Napoli sei Miglia.
View of Vesuvius from commemorative stone at Portici, 1683. Engrav. : 500× 292 mm.

ARZRUNI, A.—Krystallographische Untersuchungen an sublimirtem Titanit und Amphibol.—*Sitz. k. preuss. Akad. Wissensch. i, pp.* 369–76. *Berlin,* 1882.—*Zeitschr. f. Kryst. Min. viii, pp.* 296–97. *Leipzig,* 1884.

ARZRUNI, A.—Vergleichende Beobachtungen an künstlichen und natürlichen Mineralien.—*Zeitschr. f. Kryst. Min. xviii, pp.* 44– 63. *Leipzig,* 1891.

ARZRUNI, A.—Forsterit von Monte Somma. —*Zeitschr. f. Kryst. Min. xxv, pp.* 471–76. *Leipzig,* 1895.

ASCIONE, C.—Breve compendio della descrizione della Torre del Greco antica e moderna, delle sue chiese esistenti prima e dopo 1631.—12°, *pp.* 108. *Napoli,* 1836. [C.A.]

ASTERIO, P.—Discorso Aristotelico intorno al terremoto, etc.—4°. *Napoli,* 1632. [Bibl. Vit. Eman. Roma.]

ASTORE, F. A.—Eruzione del Vesuvio del 1794.—*Napoli,* 1794.

ATTUMONELLI, M.—Della eruzione del Vesuvio accaduta nel mese d'agosto dell' anno 1779. Ragionamento istorico-fisico. —8⁰, *foll. v, pp.* 147, 1 *pl. Napoli,* 1779. [C.A.]

AUBERT, D', & CIE. (imp.).—Chiatamone. (Naples.) Tirpenne Litho. Litho. of Vesuvius, Pal. Caramanico and Castel del Uovo in foreground, with paddle-steamer ; litho. floral frame : 137 × 100 mm.

AUDOT.—Quattro vedute del Vesuvio riguardanti le eruzioni del 1751, 1804, 1822.—8⁰. *Napoli* ?, — ?

AUDOT, L. E. (père).—L'Italie, la Sicile, les Îles Éoliennes, etc.—2 vols. of text and 2 vols. of steel engravings, 8⁰. *Vol. i, pp.* 370, 1 *map ; Vol. ii, pp.* 280+128 ; *Vol. iii, pls.* 140 ; *Vol. iv, pls.* 141-291. *Paris, Audot fils,* 1834.
See Vol. i, pp. 51-78 and pls. 28-30, 39-44, 55, 56.
Other ed. are divided as follows :—*Pt. i, pp.* 270, *pls.* 1-94 ; *Pt. ii, pp.* 271-370, *pls.* 95-118 ; *Pt. iii, pp.* 280, *pls.* 119-207 ; *Pt. iv, pp.* 108, *pls.* 208-252 ; *Pt. v, pp.* 109-179, *pls.* 253-291, 1 *map. Paris,* 1834-37. —Also *Pt. i, pp.* 113, *pls.* 1-26, *Paris,* 1834 ; *Pt. ii, pp.* 370, *pls.* 27-118, 1835 ; *Pt. iii, pp.* 280, *pls.* 119-207, 1836 ; *Pt. iv, pp.* 108, *pls.* 208-252, 1836 ; *Pt. v, pp.* 111-128, *pls.* 253-291, 1 *map,* 1837. [B.M.]
See Pt. ii, pp. 51-78, pls. 28-30, 39-44, 55-56, 66.
2nd ed. ? 8⁰, *pp.* 267, 94 *pls. on steel. Paris,* 1835.

AUGER, H.—*See* NORVINS. 1737.

AUGEROT, A. D'.—Le Vésuve ; description du volcan et de ses environs.—8⁰, *pp.* 206, 1 *litho. Limoges,* 1877.

AUGUSTI, D. M.—Dei Terremoti di Bologna opuscoli. Seconda edizione accresciuta, ricorratta, e corredata di Note.—8⁰, *fol.* 1, *pp.* 182. *Bologna,* 1780.
Refers specially to erupt. 1779.

AULDJO, J.—Vues du Vésuve, avec un précis de ses éruptions principales depuis le commencement de l'Ere Chrétienne jusqu'à nos jours.—*Spettatore del Vesuvio, i, pp.* 102, *pl. xvii,* 1 *map. Napoli,* 1832.

AULDJO, J.—Sketches of Vesuvius with a short account of its principal eruptions from the Commencement of the Christian Era to the Present Time.—*foll. iii, pp.* 96, 1 *map,* 17 *pls. Naples,* 1832 ; *London,*

1833. ' [B.M. copy hand-coloured. 7109. f.17.]

AULDJO, J.—Veduta del Capo Uncino presso Torre dell' Annunziata, della cosi detta sorgente del Vesuvio, e degli avanzi di un cipresso giacente nel tufo a quaranta palmi di profondità.—*Spettatore del Vesuvio, ii. Napoli,* 1832.—English ed. 4⁰. 1833.

AULDJO, J.—Source jaillissante d'eau minérale, découverte, en 1831, près du Cap Uncino, dans le royaume de Naples.—*Bibl. univ. Sci., partie d. Sci. S.* 1, *lii, pp.* 323-26. *Genève,* 1833.—*Amer. Journ. Sci. xxv, pp.* 194-96. *New Haven,* 1834.

AULDJO, J. (abboz.).—Veduta del Capo dell' Uncino ; del Sorgente dell' Acqua Vesuviana, e degli Avanzi d'un cipresso scoperto in piede, e mezzo carbonizzato 40 palmi sotto la superficia della terra. Lit. A. Ledoux.
Litho. : 321 × 221 mm.

AULISIO, G. D. D'.—Diuotissime Orationi ecc.—*Mentioned in the catalog. of Vinc. Bove.*—*See* MORMILE.—L'Incendii del Monte Vesvvio.

AUTORI VARII.—Dei vulcani o monti ignivomi più noti, e distintamente del Vesuvio.—*Livorno,* 1779. — *See under* ANON.

AVDEBER.—Le Voyage et observations de plvsievrs choses diverses qvi se pevvent remarquer en Italie.—12⁰, *pp.* 334. *Paris,* 1656.

AVELINE, J.—Le Vésuve vu du Palais du Rois. Tome IV, p. 315. [B.N.P. Vb. 121.] An interesting engraving.

AVRIL, R. Du.—*See* JARDMET, C.

AYALA, M.—*See* QUARANTA, B. 1845.

AYALA, S. D'.—Copiosissima y verdadera relacion del incendio del Monte Vesuvio, donde se da cuenta de veinte incendios que ha auido sin este último.—4⁰, *pp.* 28. *Napoles,* 1632.

AYELLO, F. A. DE.—De ingenti ac repentino in hoc tempore Veseui Montis lamentabili incendio. Epistola.—*foll.* 4. *Neapoli,* 1632.

AYROLA, F. L.—L'Arco celeste, overo il trionfo di Maria dell' Arco e suoi miracoli.— 4⁰, *foll. xii, pp.* 328, *foll.* 12. *Napoli,* 1688. [C.A.]

BACCARINI, P.—Studio comparativo sulla flora Vesuviana e sulla Etnea.—*Nuov. Giorn. Bot. Ital. xiii,* 3, *pp.* 150 *et seq.* 1881.

BACCI, A.—De Thermis libri septem, etc.—*fol., pp. xxxii*+509. *Venetiis,* 1571.—Other ed. : *fol., foll.* 23, *pp.* 493. *Venetiis,* 1588.—*fol., pp. viii*+425+*xviii. Romæ,* 1622.—*fol., pp. viii*+*xxviii*+366. *Patavii,* 1711.

BÄCKSTRÖM, H.—*See* BROEGGER, W. C.

BADILY, W.—A Relation of the raining of ashes, in the Archipelago, upon the eruption of Mount Vesuvius, some years ago.—*Phil. Trans. R. Soc. i, p.* 377. *London,* 1666.—[Extr.] *Giorn. Lett. pp.* 146–47. *Roma,* 1674.—In French : *Mem. Phys. toutes Acad. Sci. Lausanne,* 1754.

BAEDEKER, K.—Italien. Handbuch für Reisende. 3. Theil : Unter-Italien und Sicilien nebst Ausflügen nach den Liparischen Inseln.—8th ed. 16⁰, *pp. xlviii*+412, 26 *maps,* 17 *plans. Leipzig,* 1887.
See pp. 116–24, 1 map.

BAGLIVUS, G.—Opera Omnia.—4⁰. *Lugduni,* 1704.
See pp. 502–4.

BAILLEUL.—Remarques sur quelques circonstances de la dernière éruption du Vésuve.—*C.R. Acad. Sci. xxxi, pp.* 8–9. *Paris,* 1850.

BAKUNIN, M.—*See* OGLIALORO-TODARO, A. 1910.

BALBASOR (delin.).—Vista del Monte Vesubio por la parte de la Real Fabrica de la Polborera de la Torre de la Anunciada en su ororoso incendio de los Dias 20, 21, 22, y 23 de Mayo de 1737. Pinga sculpt. - Engrav. : 329×253 mm.

BALDACCHINI, M.—Sulle eruzioni Vesuviane. Proposta.—*Rend. Acc. Pontaniana, x, pp.* 23–25. *Napoli,* 1862. [Report by Palmieri] *Id. pp.* 86–89. [Relazione by Gussone, G., Minervini, G., Giordano, G., Cappa, R., Guiscardi, G., relatore] *Id. pp.* 154–57.

BALDUCCI, F.—Gli incendi del Vesuvio. Discorso accademico.—At the end of his " Rime." *Venetia,* 1642. [C.A.]—Other ed. 1655, 1663 and 1762.
See Pt. 2, pp. 459–750.

BALSAMO, F.—Sulla storia naturale delle Alghe d'acqua dolce del comune di Napoli. —*Atti R. Acc. Sci. S.* 2, *i,* 14, *pp.* 84, 2 *tav. Napoli,* 1888.

BALZANO, D. L. M.—Succinta relazione dell' incendio cagionato nella Torre del Greco dal Vesuvio la sera del 15 Giugno 1794 fatta da B.D.L.M. testimone oculare perché uno di quei infelici Torresi.—MS.

BALZANO, F.—L'antica Ercolano, ovvero la Torre del Greco tolta all' oblio.—3 books in 1 vol. 4⁰, *pp.* 124. *Napoli,* 1688.
See pp. 92–124 : eruption of Vesuvius, 1680.

BALZANO, G.—Città di Torre del Greco. La popolazione e la mortalità del quinquennio 1889–1893.—8⁰. *Torre Annunziata,* 1894.

BANIER, A.—Des embrasements du Mont Vésuve.—*Mém. Acad. Inscript. et Bell. Lett. ix, pp.* 14–22. *Paris,* 1736. [MS. copy. C.A.]

BARATTA, M.—Alcune osservazioni su l'attuale fase eruttiva del Vesuvio.—*Ann. Uff. Cent. Meteor. Geodinam. xii, p.* 1. *Roma,* 1893.

BARATTA, M.—Sulla distribuzione topografica dei terremoti in Italia durante il quinquennio 1887–91.—*Atti Primo Congr. Geog. Ital., Mem. sez. scient. ii, pt.* 1, *pp.* 180–89, *tav. v. Genova,* 1894.

BARATTA, M.—Alcune osservazioni fatte sul Vesuvio il 21 Giugno 1895.—*Boll. Soc. Sismol. Ital. i, pp.* 101–11, 2 *figs. Roma,* 1895.

BARATTA, M.—Osservazioni fatte al Vesuvio il 22 Marzo 1896.—*Mem. Soc. Geog. Ital. vi, pt.* 2, *pp.* 199–208. *Roma,* 1896.

BARATTA, M.—Materiali per un catalogo dei fenomeni sismici avvenuti in Italia (1800–1872).—*Mem. Soc. Geog. Ital. vii, pt.* 1, *pp.* 81–164. *Roma,* 1897.

BARATTA, M.—Il Vesuvio e le sue eruzioni dell' anno 79 d.C. al 1896.—16⁰, *pp.* 202, *fig.,* 6 *maps. Roma,* 1897.

BARATTA, M.—Saggio dei materiali per una storia dei fenomeni sismici avvenuti in Italia raccolti dal Prof. Michele Stefano de Rossi.—*Boll. Soc. Geol. Ital. xviii, pp.* 432–60. *Roma,* 1899.

BARATTA, M.—I Terremoti d'Italia.—8⁰, *pp.* 950, *pls. Torino,* 1901.
Gives, in Pt. iii, an extensive bibliography of the earthquakes of Italy.

BARATTA, M.—L'Eruzione del Vesuvio (Aprile 1906).—8⁰, *pp.* 27. *Voghera,* 1906.

BARATTA, M.—L'Eruzione Vesuviana dell' Aprile 1906.—*Riv. Geog. Ital. xiii, pp.* 316–24. *Firenze,* 1906.

BARATTA, M.—La recente eruzione del Vesuvio.—*Boll. Soc. Geog. Ital. S.* 4, *vii,* 6, *pp.* 535–37. *Roma,* 1906.

BARATTA, M.—Il nuovo rilievo del Cono Vesuviano.—*Riv. Geog. Ital. xiv*, 8, *pp.* 385–95, 1 *fig. Firenze*, 1907.

BARATTA, M.—La nuova Carta del Vesuvio (1 : 25,000) dell' Istituto Geografico Militare.—*Boll. Soc. Geog. Ital. ix, pp.* 862–70, 1 *fig. Roma*, 1908.

BARBA, A.—Ragionamento fisico-chimico sull' eruzione ultima del Vesuvio accaduta ai 15 giugno 1794.—*Napoli*, 1794.

BARBAROTTA, L.—Il Vesuvio [a song]. (Il Fausto ritorno da Vienna di Ferdinando IV.)—*pp.* 13–19. *Napoli*, 1791. [C.A.]

BARBERIUS, F.—De prognostico cinerum quos Vesuuius Mons dum conflagrabatur eructauit.—4⁰, *pp.* 64. *Neapoli*, 1632.

BARBERIUS, F.—Manifestum eorum quæ omnino verificata fuerunt jam antea ab ipso prædicta in prognostico cinerum quos Mons Veseuus emisit dum comburebatur.— 4⁰, *pp.* 14. *Neapoli*, 1635. [O.V.]

BARNARD.—*See* MAPEI, C.—Italy, Classical, Historical and Picturesque.

BARONIUS, F., ac MANFREDI.—Vesvvii montis incendium.—4⁰, *pp.* 18. *Neapolis*, 1632.

BARRA, C.—Partenope languente per l'accaduto terremoto al 5 giugno 1688.—12⁰. *Napoli*, 1688. [C.A.]

BARTALONI, Dom.—Delle mofete del Vesuvio.—*Atti Acc. Sci. iv, pp.* 201–15. *Siena*, 1771.

BARTALONI, D.—Osservazioni sopra il Vesuvio.—*Atti Acc. Sci. v, pp.* 301–400. *Siena*, 1774.

BARTELS, J. H.—Briefe über Kalabrien und Sicilien.—*Göttingen*, 1781.—Also : 3 vols. 8⁰. *Vol. i, pp. xv*+428, 1787 ; *Vol. ii, pp. xxiii*+500, 1 *map*, 1789 ; *Vol. iii, Pt.* 1, *pp.* 38+472, 1792 ; *Pt.* 2, *pp.* 475–902, 1 *plan. Göttingen*, 1787–92. *See* pp. 314 *et seq.* 1781.

BARTLETT, W. H.—Pictures from Sicily.— 8⁰, *pp.* 200, 33 *engrav. on steel*, 16 *woodcuts. London*, 1853.

BARTLETT, W. H.—Naples, from the villa Falconnet, Italy. Napoli dalla villa Falconnette, Italia. S. Lacey. Steel engrav. with poor representation of Vesuvius ; road and agaves in foreground : 192 × 151 mm.

BARTOLI, P.—Continuazione dei successi del prossimo incendio del Vesuvio congli effetti delle ceneri, etc.—4⁰. *Napoli*, 1662.

BARTOLI, P. D.—Prose scelte. Nuova ediz. —3 vols. 16⁰. *Napoli*, 1859. *See* pp. 112–18.

BARUFFALDI, G.—Vesuvio. Baccanale. —12⁰, *pp.* 32. — ?, [*circa* 1820.] [C.A.]

BASILE, G. B.—Tre sonetti nelle rime d'illustri ingegni Napoletani.—12⁰, *pp.* 133– 36. *Venezia*, 1633. [C.A.]

BASSANI, F., LORENZO, G. DE.—Per la geologia della Penisola di Sorrento.—*Atti R. Acc. Lincei, S.* 5, *Rend. ii, sem.* 1, *pp.* 202–3. *Roma*, 1893.

BASSANI, F., GALDIERI, A.—Notizie sull' attuale eruzione del Vesuvio (Aprile 1906). —*Rend. R. Acc. Sci. S.* 3, *xii, pp.* 123–27. *Napoli*, 1906.

BASSANI, F., GALDIERI, A.—Sulla Caduta dei Projetti Vesuviani in Ottajano durante l'eruzione dell' Aprile 1906.—*Rend. R. Acc. Sci. S.* 3, *xii, pp.* 321–32, 4 *figs. Napoli*, 1906.

BASSANI, F., GALDIERI, A.—Sui Vetri forati di Ottajano nella eruzione Vesuviana dell' Aprile 1906.—*Rend. R. Acc. Sci. S.* 3, *xiii, pp.* 230–56, 8 *figs. Napoli*, 1907.

BASSANI, F., GALDIERI, A.—La Sorgente Minerale di Valle di Pompei. Relazione geologica.—*Rend. R. Acc. Sci. S.* 3, *xiv, p.* 159. *Napoli*, 1908.—*Atti, id. S.* 2, *xiv*, 2, *pp.* 8. 1910.

BASSI, B.—[Two songs referring to the Vesuvian eruption of June 15th, 1794.]— *Cont. in a vol. entitled :* " Opuscoli Varj." 8⁰, *pp.* 41–42. *Napoli*, 1794. [C.A.]

BASSI, U.—*See* PLANGENETO, U.

BASSO, L.—L'Eruzione del Vesuvio, XXI Marzo MDCCCXXVIII, Ode.—8⁰, *pp.* 15. *Padova*, 1831.

BATTANDIER, A.—L'Éruption du Vésuve. —" *Cosmos*," an. 49, *n.* 800, *p.* 658. *Paris*, 26 *mai*, 1900.

BATTY, E. F. (drawn by).—Naples from St. Elmo. Engraved by Edwᵈ Finden.— London, Published June 1st, 1819, by Rodwell and Martin, New Bond Street. [B.N.P. Vb. 119.] Engrav. with carefully drawn view of Vesuvius : 213 × 144 mm.

BATTY, E. F.—Naples from above the Grotto of Posilipo. Engraved by Samˡ Mitan. London ? [B.N.P. Vb. 119.] Coarser engrav.

BATTY, E. F.—Naples from above the Grotto of Posilipo.—Engrav. by Sam[1] Mitan. London, Published Dec[bre] 1, 1819, by Rodwell and Martin, New Bond Street. Fine line engrav. of Naples and Vesuvius; trees, rocks, stone terrace, women and child in foreground : 206×128 mm. In Batty's " Italian Scenery."

BATTY, E. F.—Italian Scenery from Drawings in 1817.—8⁰, *pp.* 122, 61 *pls. London,* 1820.
See pls. 40, 49, 50.

BATTY, E. F.—[View of Vesuvius in eruption.] Engrav. by Robt. Wallis.—*London?,* — ? [B.N.P. Vb. 119.]
A fantastic eruption.

BATTY, [E. F.] (drawn by).—[Imaginary view of Vesuvius in erupt., with columns and men in foreground.]—Engraved by Rob. Wallis.
Steel or copper engrav. from last page of Batty's " Italian Scenery " : 140 × 110 mm.

BAUER, M. H.—Wurfschlacken und Lava der Vesuv-Eruption von 1906.—*Centralbl. f. Min. pp.* 327–29. *Stuttgart,* 1906.

BAUMHAUER, H.—Studien über den Leucit.—*Zeitschr. f. Kryst.* i, 3, *pp.* 257–73. *Leipzig,* 1877.

BEALE, N.—Analisi qualitativa della cenere del Vesuvio, eruttata nella notte del 27 al 28 aprile p. p.—*Ann. Chim. S.* 3, liv, *p.* 375. *Milano,* 1872.

BEAUCE (del.). — Naples. Outhwaite sc. Garnier frères Éditeurs. Imp. F. Chardon aîné, 30 rue Hautefeuille, Paris.
Vesuvius and Naples from Mergellino. A fine engrav. : 129×91 mm.

BEAUREGARD, J. DE.—Du Vésuve à l'Etna et sur le littoral de l'Adriatique . . . (1er juin 1895).—8⁰. *Lyon,* 1895.

BEAUVOIE, R. DE.—*See* NORVINS. 1737.

BECKE, F. J. K.—Bemerkungen zur Thätigkeit des Vesuvs im Jahre 1894.—*Min. u. petr. Mittheil.* xv, *pp.* 89–90. *Wien,* 1895.

BECKE, F. J. K.—Ueb. d. gegenwärtigen Zustand des Vesuv. (1896.)—[Sonderabdr.] *Sitz. deutsch. naturwissensch.-medecin. Ver. f. Böhmen " Lotos,"* 1, *pp.* 10, 3 *figs.* 1896.

BECKE, F. J. K.—Optische Orientirung des Anorthits vom Vesuv.—*Sitz. k. Akad. Wissensch. cviii, pp.* 434–41, 1 *pl. Wien,* 1899.

BELGRADIUS, JACOBUS.—Epistole ii, iii & iv ad March. Scip. Maphejo.—*See* GORI.—Admiranda Antiquitatum Herculanensium, etc. i, *pp.* 33–90, 1 *pl. Also in same :* Epist. v, ad A. F. Gorio, *pp.* 90–98. *Parmœ,* MDCCIXL.

BELLANI, A.—Salita al Vesuvio.—*Soc. edit. Ann. Univ. Sci. etc. pp.* 36. *Milano,* 1835. —*Bibl. Farm.* iv, *pp.* 55–64, 115–24, 244–54. *Cattaneo,* 1835.

BELLATTI, G.—[Riviste sismiche e quadri sinottici delle osservazioni sui fenomeni endogeni col confronto di altri fenomeni.]—*Osserv. Spinea di Mestre, aprile* 1882 [*-giugno* 1883].—*Bull. Vulc. Ital.* x, *pp.* 152, 159, 165–66, 173, 182, 188, 196, 212, 219, 226, 249, 257, 265. *Roma,* 1883.

BELLI, G.—Applicazioni alle eruzioni vulcaniche.—[Estr.] *Giorn. Ist. Lomb.* ix, *pp.* 3–78. *Milano,* 1856.

BELLICARD, J. C., and COCHIN, C. N.—Observations upon the Antiquities of the town of Herculaneum, discovered at the foot of Mount Vesuvius.—8⁰, *pp. vii,* 42 *pls. London,* 1753.—Other ed. 1755, 1756 [C.A.], 1757.

BELLICARD, J. C.—Dissertation upon the eruptions of Mount Vesuvius.—*In his* " Observations upon the Antiquities of the town of Herculaneum, etc." *pp.* 3–11. *London,* 1753.

BELLICARD, J. C.—Exposition de l'état actuel du Mont Vésuve.—*In the French transl. of his* " Observations upon the Antiquities of the town of Herculaneum, etc." *pp.* 1–7. *Paris,* 1754.——2nd ed. 1757.

BELLINI, R.—Una nuova forma cristallina della Calcite Vesuviana.—*Boll. Nat. xvii, pp.* 105–6. *Siena,* 1897.

BELLINI, R.—Notizie sulle formazioni fossilifere Neogeniche recenti della regione Vulcanica Napoletana e Malacofauna del Monte Somma.—*Boll. Soc. Nat. S.* 1, xvii, *pp.* 1–16. *Napoli,* 1904.

BELLINI, R.—Spuren von Selen auf der Vesuvlava von 1906.—*Centralbl. f. Min. pp.* 611–12. *Stuttgart,* 1907.

BELLINI, R.—*See* GASPARIS, A. DE.

BELTRANO, O.—Vesuvio centone.—8⁰, *fol.* 1, *pp.* 30. *Napoli,* 1633. [O.V.]

BELTRANO, O.—Breve Descrittione del regno di Napoli, diviso in dodeci provincie . . . raccolti e dati in luce da . . . .—4⁰, *pp.* iv+341. *Napoli,* 1640.—4⁰, *pp.* iv+312, *engrav. frontisp.* 1644.

BELTRANO, O.—Descrittione del regno di Napoli, diviso in dodeci provincie . . . raccolta e data in luce da Cesare d'Engenio Caracciolo, Ottavio Beltrani e altri autori. Settima impressione.—4⁰, *pp. xii+288, maps. Napoli, 1671.*

BENETTI, F.—Sonetti tre.—*See* GIORGI URBANO.

BENIGNI, D.—Sonetti tre (1631).—*See* GIORGI URBANO. [C.A.]

BENIGNI, D.—La strage di Vesuvio. Lettera all' abate Perretti.—4⁰, *foll. 6. E. Longo, Napoli, 1632.*

BENOIST, PH.—Royaume de Naples. Naples. Sainte Lucie. Napoli. Santa Lucia. Dessiné d'après nature et litho. par P. B. Imp. Lemercier Paris. Paris (M⁰ⁿ Aumont) François Delarue Succ. Rue J. J. Rousseau. Paris. Bulla éditeur, 18 rue Tiquetonne.
Tinted litho. : 275×192 mm.

BENOIST, PH. (des.).—Royaume de Naples. Naples. Le Vésuve pris des Camaldules. Napoli. Il Vesuvio visto de Camaldoli. Dessiné d'après nature par Ph. Benoist. Lith. par J. Jacottet. Fig. par Bayot. Paris (M⁰ⁿ Aumont) François Delarue succ. Rue J. J. Rousseau et chez Bulla, éditeur, 18 rue Tiquetonne.
Litho. on tinted paper ; Naples and Vesuvius in distance, path in wood with monks and peasants : 274×192 mm.

BERGAZZANO, G. B.—Bacco arraggiato co' Vorcano, discurzo intrà dell' oro.—8⁰, *foll. 8. Napoli,* 1632. [C.A.]

BERGAZZANO, G. B.—I prieghi di Partenope durante l'eruzione del 1631. Idillio. —8⁰, *foll. 8. Napoli,* 1632. [C.A.]

BERGAZZANO, G. B.—Il Vesuvio fulminante. Poema.—8⁰, *foll. 8. Napoli,* 1632. [B.N.]

BERGAZZANO, G. B.—Vesuvio Infernal. Scenico avvenimento.—12⁰. *Napoli,* 1632. —*See* QUADRIO.—Della storia e della ragione d'ogni poesia, *Vol. iii, par.* 1, *p.* 88. *Bologna, Milano,* 1739–52.

BERGMANN, T.—Dei prodotti Vulcanici considerati chimicamente con note di Dolomieu.— 8⁰, *pp.* 254, 2 *tab. Napoli* [*circa* 1800]. [O.V.]

BERKELEY, E.—Extract of a letter, giving several curious observations and remarks on the eruptions of fire and smoak from Mount Vesuvio.—*Phil. Trans. R. Soc. xxx, pp.* 708–13. *London,* 1720.—

In Ital. : *Compend. Trans. Filos. Londra, pp.* 62–68. *Venezia,* 1793.

BERLIOZ, H.—*See* NORVINS. 1737.

BERNARDINO, FRATE.—Discorso istorico intorno all' eruzione del Monte Vesuvio accaduta a di 15 giugno 1794.—4⁰, *pp.* 22. *Napoli,* 1794.

BERNARDO, F.—L'incendio del Monte Vesuvio, etc.—4⁰, *pp.* 32 *in* 2 *col. Napoli,* 1632.

BERTEAUX (des.).—Naples. Vue de la ville de Naples, prise du Faubourg de Chiaija, peinte d'après Nature par M. Vernet, Peintre du Roy. Gravée par Nicollet. A.P.D.R.
Engrav. : 367×233 mm.

BERTELLI, P. D. T.—Delle cause probabili del Vulcanismo presente ed antico della Terra.—4⁰, *pp.* 28, 8 *figs. Torino,* 1886.

BERWERTH, F.—Magnesia-Glimmer vom Vesuv.—*Jahrb. Geol. Reichsanst. xxvii. Wien,* 1877.—*Zeitschr. f. Kryst. ii, p.* 521. *Leipzig,* 1878.

BETOCCHI, A.—Sulla cenere lanciata dal Vesuvio alla fine della passata straordinaria eruzione (24 aprile).—*Atti R. Acc. Lincei, xxv, pp.* 332–34. *Roma,* 1872.

BEULÉ, C. E.—Le drame du Vésuve.— *Revue des Deux Mondes,* 2e *pér., lxxxvii, pp.* 5–31. *Paris,* 1870.—*pp.* 368. *Paris,* 1871.——2nd ed. 12⁰, *pp.* 366, 1 *map. Paris,* 1872. [C.A.]

BIANCHI, L. (dis.).—Veduta di Napoli da sopra due porte. Lorenzo Bianchi dis. 1823. Napoli, Lit. della Guerra.
Lith. : 221×181 mm.

BIANCHI, L.—*See* CUCINIELLO, D.

BIANCHI, [L.]—*See* VIANELLY.

BIANCONI, A.—Storia naturale dei terreni ardenti, dei vulcani fangosi, delle sorgenti infiammabili, dei pozzi idropirici, e di altri fenomeni geologici ecc.—8⁰, *tav. Bologna,* 1840.

BIASE, DI.—Sonetto ed ode sul Vesuvio.— In the " Poesie " *of that author,* 16⁰, *pp.* 3. Thus reported in G. Dura's " Vulcani e Tremuoti." 1866.

BIBBY, [H.] (pinx.).—Naples. A. H. Payne sc. London : Brain and Payne, 12 Paternoster Row.
A view of town and Vesuvius in slight eruption from above Grotto, with peasants and six umbrella-pines in foreground. Fine line engrav. : 158×112 mm.

BIBBY, H.—Naples [from above the Grotto]. A. H. Payne sc. Brain and Payne, London.

BICCHIERAI, Fabio (editore).—Vesuvio veduto da Napoli. Eruzione 5 aprile 1906. [This is printed over an inscription :] Napoli-Vesuvio. Veduto da S. Giuseppe. Eruzione 12 aprile 1906. F. B., editore. Napoli. Proprieta riservata.
Gaudy chromolitho. of Vesuvius seen from the sea : 270 × 170 mm.

BICCHIERAI, Fabio (editore).—Vesuvio. Eruzione lavica 7 aprile 1906. [Printed over another inscription to same effect.] F. B. editore. Napoli. Proprieta riservata.
Gaudy chromolitho. of lava, apparently at foot of great cone; moon in sky : 270 × 170 mm.

BICCHIERAI, Fabio (editore).—Vesuvio veduto da mare, presso Torre del Greco. Eruzione 9 Aprile 1906. F. B., editore. Napoli. Proprietà riservata.
Gaudy chromolitho. of Vesuvius seen from the sea : 266 × 170 mm.

BICHEBOIS.—*See* COIGNET, M.—Vues pittoresques de l'Italie, etc., *and* Voyage en Italie, etc.

BIDERA, E.—Passegiata per Napoli e contorni.—2 vols. 8°. *Vol. i, pp.* 322 ; *Vol. ii, pp.* 254. *Napoli*, 1845.
See Vol. ii, pp. 201–18, popular descript. of crater *circa* 1844.

BILLMARK, C. J.—Pittoresk Resetour fran Stockholm till Neapel, genom Sverge, Danmark, Tyskland, Holland, Belgien, Frankrike, Schweitz, Tyrolen, Savojen, Italien. 100 vuer. Tecknade ester naturen, lithographierade och ulgisue.—*pp.* 24, *num. pls. Paris*, 1852.
See p. 22 and plate of Golfe de Naples.

BINNET-HENTSH, J. L.—Une excursion au Vésuve.—*Echo des Alpes*, 2. 1876.

BISCHOF, G.—On the natural history of Volcanoes and Earthquakes.—*Amer. Journ. Sci. xxxvi, pp.* 230–82 ; *xxxvii, pp.* 41–77. *New Haven*, 1839.

BISCHOFF, H.—Vulkane.—"*Vom Fels zum Meer,*" *pp.* 1792–1818. *Stuttgart*, 1888–89.

BITTINI, G.—Sonetto (1631).—*See* GIORGI URBANO. [C̆.A.]

BITTNER, A.—Beobachtungen am Vesuv.— *Verh. k. k. geol. Reichsanst. pp.* 287–88. *Wien*, 1874.

BLACK, C. C.—On the Smoke-rings of Vesuvius (1863).—"*Intellectual Observer,*" *iv, pp.* 326–27. *London*, 1864.

BLACK, J. M.—An account of the eruption of Mount Vesuvius of April, 1872.—*Proc. Geol. Assoc. iii, pp.* 253–65. 1874.—*See also : Trans. Manchester Geol. Soc. xiii, pp.* 361–69. 1876.
These were notes published by the author's brother, W. J. Black, from the observations of J. M. B. made on the spot. Reprinted at Salford by J. Roberts, Chapel Street, pp. 8, 1 pl. and 1 map. Photos. taken at the time were given to the Geol. Socs. of Manchester and Liverpool and to the Bolton Museum.

BLACK, W. J.—*See* BLACK, J. M. 1874.

BLACK, W. J.—Eruption of Vesuvius, 1872 (1875).—*Trans. Manchester Geol. Soc. xiii, pp.* 361–69. 1876.
A small, circular engrav., absolutely imaginary. Another ed., signed "Isr. Sylvestre in. et fc.," is a little better.

BLAEU, J.—Theatrvm civitatvm nec non admirandorvm Neapolis et Siciliæ Regnorvm.—*fol., pp.* 78+30, 34 *pls. Amstelœdami*, 1602. [C.A. and B.M.—176, h. 4.]
This is 2nd pt. of "Theatrum Civitatum et Admirandorum Italiæ."—Amstelædami, 1663.

BLAEU, J.—Nouveau Théâtre d'Italie ou description exacte de ses Villes, Palais, Églises, &c. et les Cartes Géographiques de toutes ses Provinces.—3 vols. *fol. Amsterdam, Pierre Mortier*, 1704.
In Vol. iii, No. 9 is a view of the eruption of 1631 from the Ponte della Madalena, entitled " Vesvvivs Mons, à deux Lieues de Naples." No. 10 is a redrawn reproduction of Hoefnaglius' view of Vesuvius and Naples from above the Grotto, but signed Pierre Mortier.
Another ed., title same as last, 4 vols. *fol. La Haye*, 1724.
Latin ed., entitled : " Novum Italiæ Theatrum, sive accurata descriptio ipsius Urbium, Palatiorum, Sacrarum Ædium, &c."—4 vols. *fol. Hagæ Comitum R. Ch. Alberts*, 1724.

BLAKE, J. F.—A Visit to the Volcanoes of Italy.—*Proc. Geol. Assoc. ix, pp.* 145–76. *London*, 1889.

BLAKIE, W. G.—On the top of Mount Vesuvius (with two figs. from photos by Johnston-Lavis).—" *The Quiver,*" *pp.* 45–49, 3 *figs. Nov.* 1891.

BLASIIS, G. DE.—Una seconda congiura di Campanella.—*Giorn. Napoletano, i, pp.* 425–68. *Napoli*, 1875.

BLONDI, F. F.—De Roma instaurata, de Italia illustrata, de gestis Venetorum, Imperatorum Rom. Vitæ, et conflagratio Vesævi Montis ex Dione.—*fol., pp.* 3+146. *Venetiis*, 1510.

BOCANGEL Y VNÇUETA, G.—Epitafio al Vesuvio, y svs incendios. — *See* QUINONES.—El Monte Vesvvio.

BOCCAGE, MME DU.—Sur le Vésuve. Deux lettres en date des 8 et 15 oct. 1757.—*Extr. du Recueil de ses œuvres*, 3 vols. 8°. *Lyon*, 1770. [C.A.]
See Vol. iii, pp. 265–86.

BOCCOSI, F.—Centurie poetiche. Centuria I e II, piacevole.—8°, *pp.* 8+100+5. *Napoli*, 1712–14.
See Sonetto LXXX.

BOECKER, J.—Krystallographische Beobachtungen am Idokras vom Monte Somma.—*Zeitschr. f. Kryst. xx, p.* 225. *Leipzig*, 1892.

BOERNSTEIN, H.—Der Ausbruch des Vesuvs vom 16. bis 20. Novemb. 1868.— " *Die Gartenlaube,*" *p.* 808. *Leipzig*, 1868.

BOLLETTINO TRIMESTRALE DELLA SOCIETÀ ALPINA MERIDIONALE pubblicato per cura del consiglio direttivo. Anno I–IV.—8°. *Napoli*, 1893–96.
Contains the reports of the Society's expeditions to Vesuvius and M. Somma.

BOMARE, DE.—Articolo di . . . Sopra il Vesuvio ed altri Vulcani.—*See* ANON.— Dei Vulcani o Monti Ignivomi, etc.

BONITO, M.—Terra tremante ovvero continuazione dei Terremoti dalla creatione del mondo sino al tempo presente.—4°, *pp.* 822. *Napoli*, 1691.
See pp. 758–63, eruption of 1631.

BONNEY, T. G.—Volcanoes, their structure and significance.—8°, *pp.* 351, 13 *pls.*, 21 *figs. London*, 1899.

BONUCCI, C.—*See* QUARANTA, B. 1845.

BORNEMANN, J. G.—Sur l'état des volcans d'Italie pendant l'été de 1856.—Transl. by De Perrey from " *Tageblatt der 32 Versam. Deutsch. Naturf. u. Aertze,*" *pp.* 114–41, *Wien*, 1856.—Original MS. *pp.* 4. [C.A.]

BORNEMANN, J. G.—Gegenwärtiger Zustand der aktiven Vulkane Italiens. (Protokoll.)—*Zeitschr. deutsch. geol. Gesellsch. viii, pp.* 534–35. *Berlin*, 1856.

BORNEMANN, J. G.—Brief an Herrn Beyrich. [Ueber Erscheinungen am Vesuv und geognostisches aus den Alpen.]— *Zeitschr. deutsch. geol. Gesellsch. ix, pp.* 21– 24. *Berlin*, 1857.

BORNEMANN, J. G.—Bericht über eine Reise in Italien. (Aus einem Briefe an Herrn v. Humboldt, dat. Neapel, den 29 August 1856.)—*Zeitschr. deutsch. geol. Gesellsch. ix, pp.* 464–69. *Berlin*, 1857.

BORY DE ST. VINCENT.—*See* DESMAREST.

BORZI.—*See* GRANVILLE, A. 1814.

BOSCOWITZ, A.—Les Volcans et les Tremblements de Terre.—8°, *pp.* 604, *tav. and illustr. Paris*, 1866.—New ed. 1884.
See pp. 227–45, 1866.

BÖSE, E., & LORENZO, G. DE.—Zur Geologie der Monti Picentini bei Neapel.— *Zeitschr. deutsch. geol. Gesellsch. xlviii, pp.* 202–15, 1 *fig. Berlin*, 1896.

BOSSIS, DESSOULAVY, & SANTORELLI, F.—Raccolta di Vedute del regno di Napoli e suoi contorni disegnate dal vero.— *obl.* 8°. *Roma*, 1829. [B.M. S. 136 (22).]
Shows Vesuvius truncated by the great crater of 1822 and smoking.

BOSSOLI, C. (dis.).—Napoli. Milano, A.Vallardi, etc. N. 1118. [Vienna lib.]
A stipple sepia engraving, panorama of Naples and Vesuvius from Pizzofalcone, with inscript. at foot of principal buildings : 890 × 325 mm.

BOTTIS, G. DE.—Ragionamento istorico intorno ai nuovi vulcani comparsi nella fine dell' anno scorso 1760 nel territorio della Torre del Greco.—4°, *pp.* 67, 2 *pls. Napoli*, 1761. [C.A.]

BOTTIS, G. DE.—Ragionamento istorico dell' incendio del Vesuvio accaduto nel mese di Ottobre del 1767.—8°, *pp.* lxxiv, 1 *pl. Napoli*, 1768. [B.M. 664. b. 25(2), bound up with Anon. [Serao, F.]—Neap. Scient. Acad. de Vesuvii conflag. etc. 1738.]
A fine engrav.

BOTTIS, G. DE.—Ragionamento istorico dell' incendio del Monte Vesuvio, che cominciò nell' anno 1770 e delle varie eruzioni che ha cagionate.—*Napoli*, 1774. —Another ed. 4°, *pp.* 84+iii, 4 *pls. Napoli*, 1776. [C.A.]
Fine engravings of much interest.

BOTTIS, G. DE.—Ragionamento istorico intorno all' eruzione del Vesuvio che cominciò il dì 29 luglio dell' anno 1779 e continuò fino al giorno 15 del seguente mese di agosto.—4⁰, *pp.* 117+*iii*, 4 *pls. Napoli*, 1779. [C.A.]
Very fine engravings.

BOTTIS, G. DE.—Istoria di varii incendi del Monte Vesuvio.—4⁰, *pp.* 344, 11 *pls. Napoli*, 1786.
Reproduction of the plates in his other books.

BOTTONI, D. L.—Pyrologia Topographica, id est de igne dissertatio juxta loca cum eorum descriptionibus.—4⁰, 3 *pls., foll.* 19, *pp.* 245. *Neapolis*, 1692.—Also *Messanæ*, 1721.

BOUR.—Vue du Palais des Princes d'Anjou à Naples (dit le Palais de la Reine Jeanne). Lith. de Langlumé. [B.N.P. Vb. 119.]
A redrawn reduction of that by Isabey.

BOURDARIAT, A.—Recrudescence d'activité du Vésuve.—" *La Nature*," *p.* 25, 1 *fig. Paris, mai,* 1895.

BOURKE, E. DE.—Le Mont Somma et le Vésuve.—*In* : " Notice sur les ruines les plus remarquables de Naples et ses environs," 8⁰, *pp.* 167–74. *Paris*, 1823. [C.A.]

BOURLOT, J.—Étude sur le Vésuve, son histoire jusqu'à nos jours.—8⁰, *pp.* 206, 1 *topogr. map. Paris, Colmar et Strasbourg*, 1867.

BOURLOT, J.—Réactions de la haute température et des mouvements de la mer ignée interne sur la croûte extérieure du globe. Étude sur le Vésuve.—8⁰. *Paris*, 1867.

BOVE, V.—Decima relatione, nella qvale piv dell' altre si dà breue, e soccinto ragguaglio dell' incendio risvegliato nel Monte Vesuuio o di Somma, etc.—4⁰, *pp.* 11. *L. Scoriggio, Napoli*, 1632.

BOVE, V.—Nuove osservationi fatte sopra gli effetti dell' incendio del Monte Vesuuio. Aggiunti alla " Decima Relatione," etc.—8⁰, *pp.* 31. *Napoli*, 1632.

BOVE, V.—Il Vesvvio acceso.—12⁰, *foll.* 12, 1 *pl. -Napoli, P. S. Roncagliolo*, 1632.

BOVE, V.—Nota di tutte le relationi stapate sino ad hoggi del Vesuuio.—*See* MORMILE, G.—L'incendio del Monte Vesuvio.

BOVIO, G.—La Geologia dell' Italia meridionale rispetto all' indole degli abitatori.—8⁰, *pp.* 31. *Napoli, Ernesto Anfossi*, 1883. [C.A.]

BOZZI, C., & PAGLIANO, A.—Exposition Universelle de 1900 : Paris-Naples.—4⁰, *pp.* 11, 4 *pls. Napoli*, 1899.
Panorama of Naples and of Vesuvius in eruption.

BRACCHI, D. A.—Una gita al Vesuvio nella notte del 19 al 20 Maggio (1855).—" *Poliorama Pittoresco*," *xvi, figs. Napoli*, 1855.

BRACCI, G.—Veduta del Vesuvio interiore nel 1755.—pl. 4⁰. [O.V.]
It is the 22nd pl. of the " Raccolta delle più interessanti vedute della città di Napoli e luoghi circonvicini disegnate da Giuseppe Bracci ed incise in 30 rami da Antonio Cardoni."

BRACCI, G. (del.), CARDON, A. (scul.).— Icon Crateris Neapolitani uti nuper videb. Nobil. D. D. Gulielmo. Hamilton, etc. P. H. D. H. Lubens C. V. D., A. Cardon scul.—Appo F. Morgh. Con. Priv. Reg. 1772. [B.M.—K. 83. 55.]
Engrav. map of bay of Naples in ancient times, with idealized view of Vesuvius and Temples. Explanation in Latin : 900× 617 mm.

BRACCINI, G. C.—Relazione dell' incendio fattosi nel Vesuuio alli 16. di Decembre 1631. Scritta dal Signor Abbate Givlio Cesare Braccini da Giouiano di Lucca, in vna lettera diritta all' Eminentissimo, e Reuerendissimo Signore Il Sign. Card. Girolamo Colonna.—16⁰, *pp.* 40. *Napoli, Per Secondino Roncagliolo.* 1631.
This rare account was referred to by P. G. M. della Torre under the title : " Colonna Girolamo Cardinale. Lettera sopra l'incendio del Monte Vesuvio del 1631."

BRACCINI, G. C.—Dell' incendio fattosi nel Vesvvio a XVI. di Dicembre MDC.XXXI e delle sue cause, ed effetti. Con la narrazione di quanto è seguito in esso per tutto Marzo 1632. E con la Storia di tutti gli altri incendij nel medesimo monte auuenuti. Discorrendosi in fine delle Acque, le quali in questa occasione hanno danneggiato le campagne, e di molte altre cose curiose. Dell' Abbate Givlio Cesare Braccini Da Giouiano di Lucca Dottor di Leggi, e Protonotario Appostolico.—4⁰, *pp.* 104. *Napoli, Per Secondino Roncagliolo*, 1632.

BRARD.—Une éruption du Vésuve.—*Feuilleton de l'Écho de Numidie*, 15–29 *mai et* 5 *juin* 1861. [C.A.]

BRAUN, G., HOHENBERG, F.—Civitates Orbis Terrarum.—6 vols. *fol. Coloniæ Agrippinæ*, 1523 [?1573]–1618.—Other ed. : 5 vols. *fol.* 1612.—6 vols. *fol.* 1582 [–1618]. —1 or 2 vols. *Coloniæ*, 1572. [*Cologne ?*, 1575 ?]—In French : 6 vols. *fol. Brussels*, 1574–1617.
The numbering of the plates is often erroneous; thus plate 65 in Vol. v of one ed. is marked 56. It is a view of Vesuvius and Naples from Posilippo, with a rather fantastic view of that volcano, entitled " Elegantissimus ad Mare Tyrrhenum ex Monte Pausilipo Neapolis Montisque Vesuvii Prospectus," with text at back.

BRAUNS, R.—Vesuvasche an der Ostsee. Gips in der in Italien gefallenen Vesuvasche. Salzkruste auf frischer Vesuvlava. —*Centralbl. f. Min. pp.* 321–27. *Stuttgart*, 1906.

BREISLAK, S., e WINSPEARE, A.— Memoria sull' eruzione del Vesuvio accaduta la sera de' 15 giugno 1794.—*pp.* 88, 1 *tab. Napoli*, 1794.—*Giorn. Lett. xvii, pp.* 58–80. *Napoli*, 1794.

BREISLAK, S., und WINSPEARE, A.— Fortgesetzte Berichte vom Ausbruche des Vesuvs am 14 Junius 1794. Nebst einer meteorolog. Abhandlung vom Hagel von A. d'Onofrio. Aus dem Italien übersetzt.— 4⁰, *pp.* 96. *Dresden*, 1795.

BREISLAK, S.—Topografia fisica della Campania. [With a map drawn by Rizzi-Zannoni, G. A.]—*Napoli*, 1797. [B.M. —K. 83. 52. 2.]
Should be consulted for lava streams.
Another ed. 8⁰, *pp. xii*+368, 3 *pls. Firenze*, 1798.
See pp. 104–203.

BREISLAK, S.—Carta Topografica del cratere di Napoli e dei Campi Flegrei, colla pianta speciale del Vesuvio, secondo le ultime osservazioni del Abte. Breislak.— *See his* : Topografia fisica della Campania, 1798.

BREISLAK, S.—Voyages physiques et lithologiques dans la Campanie suivis d'un mémoire sur la constitution physique de Rome.—*Vol. i, pp. xvi*+300, 3 *pls.* ; *Vol. ii, pp.* 324, 3 *pls. Paris*, 1801.
Cont. map of Vesuvius.

BREISLAK, S.—Physische und lithologische Reisen durch Campanien, nebst mineralogischen Beobachtungen über die Gegend von Rom. Uebers. von F. A. Reuss.

Zwey Theile in einem Bande.—8⁰, *tav. Leipzig*, 1802.

BREISLAK, S.—Mineralogia dell' Isola di Capri.—*In* ROMANELLI.—Isola di Capri. —8⁰, *pp.* 111–22. *Napoli*, 1816.

BREISLAK, S.—Institutions géologiques.— 3 vols. 8⁰, 56 *pls. Milan*, 1818.

BREISLAK, S.—Lehrbuch der Geologie. Deutsche Uebers. m. Anmerk. von F. K. von Strombeck.—*Braunschweig*, 1819.

BREISLAK, S.—Traité sur la structure extérieure du Globe, ou institutions géologiques.—3 vols. atlas, 56 *pls. Milan*, 1822.

BREWSTER, SIR D.—Account of Comptonite, a new mineral from Vesuvius.— *Edinb. Phil. Journ. iv, pp.* 131–33. 1821. —*Jahrb. f. Chem. Phys. xxxiii, pp.* 278–81. *Nürnberg*, 1821.

BRIGNOLE, COMTE DE.—Lettre à S.E. le Comm. Bianchini, avec réponse.—8⁰, *pp.* 3. — ?, 1858.

BRIGNONE, F.—Versi sulla eruzione Vesuviana del 1872.—8⁰, *pp.* 7. *Napoli*, 1872.

BRITISH ASSOCIATION COMMITTEE.— Report on the Volcanic Phenomena of Vesuvius.—*See* JOHNSTON-LAVIS.

BROCCHI, G. B.—Catalogo ragionato di una raccolta di rocce disposto con ordine geografico per servire alla geognosia dell' Italia.—8⁰, *pp. xl*+346. *Milano*, 1817.

BROCCHI, G. B.—Sull' eruzione del Vesuvio del 1812.—*Bibl. Ital. Giorn. Lett. Sci. vi, pp.* 275–90. *Milano*, 1817.

BROCKEDON, W.—Traveller's Guide to Italy, or Road-book from London to Naples.—16⁰, *pp. vi*+208. *Paris*, 1835.

BROCKEDON, W.—*See* MAPEI, C.—Italy, Classical, Historical and Picturesque.

BROEGGER, W. C., u. BÄCKSTRÖM, H.— Die Mineralien der Granatgruppen. [Sodalith vom Vesuv, Aetzfiguren.]—*Zeitschr. f. Kryst. xviii, pp.* 209–76, 8 *figs., taf. ii. Leipzig*, 1891.
See pp. 215 *et seq.*

BROGHI.—5231. Contorni di Napoli. Versante della Ferrovia funicolare sul Vesuvio. [1st June, 1880.]
Photo. : 374×276 mm.

BROGHI.—5236. Contorni di Napoli. Cratere del Vesuvio. [1st June, 1880, looking East across crater plain of 1872, filled with lava, and from E. edge of 1872 crater.]
Photo. : 370×274 mm.

BROGHI.—5236. Contorni di Napoli. Cratere del Vesuvio. [1 June, 1880. View of cone of eruption and plain of lava filling crater of 1872, taken from its S.W. edge.]
Photo. : 374 × 276 mm.

BROGHI.—5238. Contorni di Napoli. Vesuvio visto dal Monte Somma. [June, 1880.]
Photo. : 374 × 276 mm.

BROGHI.—5239. Contorni di Napoli. Vesuvio, vallata di Massa-Somma. [Atrio del Cavallo eastwards ; summer, 1880.]
Photo. : 374 × 276 mm.

BROMEIS, T.—Analyse eines Glimmers vom Vesuv.—*Ann. Phys. Chem.* lv, *pp.* 112–13. *Leipzig,* 1842.

BRONZUOLI, G.—Veduta del Monte Vesuvio dalla parte di mezzogiorno, 24 Ottobre 1751.—*fol., with descript., in* CORAFÀ, G.—Dissertazione, 1752.

BROOKE, H. J.—On the Comptonite of Vesuvius, the Brewsterite of Scotland, the Stilbite, and the Heulandite.—*Edinb. Phil. Journ.* vi, *pp.* 112–15. *Edinburgh,* 1822.

BROOKE, H. J.—On the identity of Zeagonite and Phillipsite, etc. ; and other Mineralogical Notices.—*Phil. Mag. N.S.* x, *pp.* 109–11. *London,* 1831.

BROOKE, H. J.—On Monticellite, a new species of Mineral.—*Phil. Mag. N.S.* x, *pp.* 265–67. 1831.

BROOKE, N.—Observations on the Manners and Customs of Italy, with remarks on the vast importance of British Commerce on that continent ; also particulars of the wonderful explosion of Mount Vesuvius, taken on the spot at midnight, in June, 1794, when the beautiful and extensive city of Torre del Greco was buried under the blazing river of lava from the mountain ; Likewise . . . cures . . . opium, etc.—8⁰, *pp.* viii+269. *London and Bath,* 1798.
See pp. 184–85.

BROOKE, N.—Voyage à Naples et en Toscane avant et pendant l'invasion des Français en Italie, avec des observations critiques, sur les Mœurs et Coûtumes de l'Italie, des détails sur la terrible explosion du Mont-Vésuve, pris sur les lieux à minuit, en Juin 1794, lorsque la belle ville de Torre del Greco fut détruite par la lave brûlante qui se précipitoit de la montagne. On y a joint un récit des cures merveilleuses, produites par une préparation d'opium, suivant la méthode asiatique. Traduit de l'anglais.—8⁰, *pp.* 275. *Paris, an* VII [1799].

BROWN, I. (sculp.).—Mount Vesuvius in eruption. Published by T. Kinnersley, May 7, 1817.
Fantastic outline of Vesuvius ; figures praying before crucifix in foreground. Engrav. : 197 × 174 mm.

BRUCE.—Voyage to Naples and journey up Mount Vesuvius, giving an account of the strange disaster on his arrival at the summit, the discovery of a central world with the laws, customs, and manners of that nation, described, etc.—16⁰, *pp.* 41, 1 *pl. London,* 1802.
Rubbish.

BRUN, A.—L'éruption du Vésuve de septembre 1904.—[Extr.] *Arch. Sci. phys. nat.* 4ᵉ *pér., xviii, pp.* 2. *Genève,* 1904.—*Journ. de Genève du* 10 *oct.* 1904.—*Bull. Soc. Belge Géol. pp.* 228–31. *Bruxelles,* 1904.

BRUN, A.—Quelques recherches sur le Volcanisme. Première partie.—*Archiv. Sci. phys. nat. pp.* 24, 1 *pl. Mai–juin,* 1905.—Deuxième partie.—*pp.* 24, 1 *pl. Nov.* 1906.

BRUN, A.—Verhalten des Schwefels in tätigen Solfataren. — *Chemiker-Zeitung,* 15, *pp.* 2. *Cöthen,* 1909.

BRUN, A.—Exhalaison volcanique secondaire.—*Arch. Sci. phys. nat.* 4ᵉ *pér., xxix,* p. 1. *Genève, janv.* 1910.

BRUN, A.—Recherches sur l'Exhalaison Volcanique.—*fol., pp.* 277, 34 *pls.,* 17 *figs. Genève, Paris,* 1911.

BRUNHUBER, A.—Beobachtungen über die Vesuveruption im April 1906.—*Ber. Naturwissensch. Ver.* x, *pp.* 16, 1 *pl. Regensburg,* 1906.

BRUNI, A.—Canzone sull' incendio del Vesuvio (1631).—*See* GIORGI URBANO. [C.A.]

BRUNO, F. S.—L'Osservatore di Napoli ossia rassegna delle istituzioni civili, de' pubblici stabilimenti, dei monumenti storici ed artistici, e delle cose notevoli di Napoli, con una breve descrizione de' suoi contorni, etc.—12⁰, *pp.* 8+592, 25 *pls. Napoli,* 1854.
See pp. 376–86 and pls. at pp. 74, 205, 381.

BRUNO, F. S.—Regolamento del Prefetto di Polizia per le Guide volgarmente dette " Ciceroni."— " *L'Osservatore di Napoli,*" 1854.

BRYDONE, P.—A Tour through Sicily and Malta ; in a series of letters to W. Beckford, Esq.—8⁰. *London*, 1773.——2nd ed., corrected. 2 vols. 8⁰. *London*, 1774.——3rd ed. 2 vols. 8⁰. *London*, 1774.—New ed. 2 vols. 8⁰. *London*, 1776.—Another ed., MS. notes [by J. Mitford]. 2 vols. 12⁰. *Paris*, 1780.—New ed., with engrav., etc. 2 vols. 12⁰. *Perth*, 1799.—New ed. 12⁰. *London*, 1807.—Another ed. 12⁰. *Edinburgh*, 1809.—New ed. 2 vols. 12⁰. *Glasgow*, 1817.—In French, " traduit de l'anglois par M. Demeunier " : 2 tom. 12⁰. *Amsterdam*, 1776.—[Supplement] 8⁰. 1782. —In German : Zweyte nach der neuesten Englischen Ausgabe verbesserte Auflage. Nebst einer Charte von Sicilien und Malta. —2 Thle. 8⁰. *Leipzig*, 1777.—*See also* CAMPE, J. H.—Sämmtliche Kinder- und Jugend-schriften, etc.—*Bd. xxiii*, 8⁰. 1831, *etc.—See* corresponding entry under ETNA.

BRYDONE, P.—Lettre au P. Della Torre sur l'éruption du Vésuve en 1770.—*In his :* " Voyage en Sicile et à Malthe," *Pt. ii, pp.* 265–72. *Neuchâtel*, 1776. [B.S.]

BUCH, C. L. VON.—Ueber die Formation des Leucits.—*Ann. Phys. vi, pp.* 53–66. 1800.

BUCH, C. L. VON.—Bocche nuove. Fragment aus einer Reihe von Briefen über den Vesuv.—*Jahrb. Berg.- und Hüttenkunde, v, pp.* 1–10. *Salzburg*, 1801.

BUCH, C. L. VON.—Lettre à M. Pictet sur les volcans. [Dated Neuchâtel, 30 jan. 1801.] —*Bibl. Britann. Part. Sci. and Arts, xvi, pp.* 227–49. *Genève*, 1801.

BUCH, C. L. VON.—Geognostische Beobachtungen auf Reisen durch Deutschland und Italien.—*2 vols. with plates. Berlin*, 1802–9. *See* Vol. ii, pp. 85–224.

BUCH, C. L. VON.—Lettre sur la dernière éruption du Vésuve et sur une expérience galvanique nouvelle.—*Bibl. Britann. Part. Sci. et Arts, xxx, pp.* 247–63, 1 tav. *Genève*, 1805.

BUCH, C. L. VON.—Physikalische Beschreibung der Canarischen Inseln.—*2 figs. Berlin*, 1825.—*Gesammelte Schriften, iii, pp.* 524 *et seq. Berlin*, 1877.—In French : 8⁰, *pp. vii+*525. *Paris*, 1836. *See* pp. 338–47. 1825.

BUCKINGHAM, DUKE OF.—[Extract of a letter upon the eruption of Mount Vesuvius on Apr. 3, 1828.]—*Proc. Geol. Soc. i, p.* 86. *London*, 1834.

BULIFON, A.—Lettere storiche politiche ed erudite.—12⁰, *pp.* 482+10. *Pozzuoli*,1685. *See* Vol. iv, pp. 177–88.

BULIFON, A.—Carte de' Regni di Napoli con le sui provincie distinte. Nuovamente date in luce. Accuratissima e nuova delineazione.—*21 maps. Napoli*, 1692. 365×265 mm., with engraved cover by Fran. de Grado. On map 20 is a good outline sketch of Vesuvius, but reversed in position.

BULIFON,A.—Lettere memorabili, istoriche, politiche, ed erudite.—2nd ed., ded. F. D. Cocco-Palmieri, 3 vols. 12⁰. *Vol. i, pp.* 24+460+11, 4 *pls. ; Vol. ii, pp.* 12+ 399+8, 8 *pls. ; Vol. iii, pp.* 12+355+5, 5 *pls. Pozzuoli*, 1693.—Also 4 vols. 12⁰. *Pozzuoli e Napoli*, 1693–98.—4 vols. 12⁰. *Pozzoli e Napoli*, 1696–97.—4 vols. 12⁰. *Pozzoli e Napoli*, 1698. *See* Vol. ii, pp. 166–74, 1693 ; Vol. ii, pp. 131–35, 1 pl., 1696–97, and 1698.

BULIFON, A.—Campagna Felice (map).— *Neapoli* [1692]. [B.M.—K. 83. 52. 1.] ⸴ Shows Vesuvius about 1690. This has been photographed by Dr. Johnston-Lavis.

BULIFON, A.—Ragguaglio dello spaventevole moto del Vesuvio succeduto il mese di Dicembre 1689. Lettera al R. P. Mabillon. —*In his :* " Lettere memorabili," *Vol. ii, pp.* 174–81, 1 woodcut. *Napoli*, 1693.

BULIFON, A.—Esattissima Delineazione del Monte Vesuvio altrimenti di Somma data in luce da Antonio Bulifon, nel 1694. Incendio soccedato nel mese d'Aprile dell' anno 1694.—*Napoli*, 24 *Giugno*, 1694. With insets of Vesuvius before and after the eruption of 1631.

BULIFON, A.—Lettera nella quale si dà distinta raguaglio dell' incendio del Vesuvio succeduto nel mese di Aprile 1694.—16⁰, *pp.* 84, 1 pl. *Napoli*, 1694.

BULIFON, A.—Raguaglio istorico dell' incendio del Monte Vesuvio succeduto nel mese d'Aprile 1694, con breve notizie degl'incendij antecedente.—16⁰, *pp.* 81–90 +80, 2 pls. *Napoli*, 1696. [B.M. 662. a 22.] Two very interesting plates.

BULIFON, A.—Compendio istorico del Monte Vesuvio in cui si ha piena notizia di tutti gl'incendj ed eruzioni accadute in esso fino a quindici di Giugno del 1698.— 16⁰, *pp.* 106. *Napoli*, 1698.——2nd ed. 12⁰, *pp.* 116, 1 pl. (of erupt. 1631 and 1698). *Napoli*, 1701.

BULIFON, A., LUIGI, DR. (nipote).—Carte de' Regni di Napoli, e di Sicilia, loro provincie, ed isole adjacenti fatte esattamente incidere nel 1692.—4^0, pp. 7, 19 maps. Napoli, 1734. [B.M.—118. C. 10, also 661 k. 1.]

A good sketch of Vesuvius is given on the map of the " Campagna Felice."

BULIFON, A.—Campagna Felice. Della bella Prov^a di Terra di Lavoro per dimostrarne le parte più considerabili, etc. [B.M.—K. 83. 52–1.]

BULWER-LYTTON.—The Last Days of Pompeii.—num. ed. 1834 . . . etc.

BUNONIS, JOH.—See CLUVERIUS, PH.

BURFORD, R.—Description of a View of the City and Bay of Naples by Moonlight with an Eruption of M. Vesuvius, now exhibiting at the Panorama, Leicester Square (assisted by H. C. Selous from drawings taken on the spot during one of the great eruptions).—16^0, pp. 16, 1 pl. (includ. 2 panoramas in woodcut). London, 1845.

Very poor and of no scientific value.

BURIOLI, P.—Vera relazione del terremoto, e voragine occorso nel Monte Vesuvio il 16 Dicembre 1631 a ore 12 etc.—4^0, foll. 4. Bologna, 1632. [C.A.]

BURMANNUS, P.—See GRÆVIUS, J. G.— Thesavrvs Antiqvitatvm et Historiarvm Italiæ. 1725, etc.

BURNET, G.—Some Letters. Containing, an account of what seemed most remarkable in Switzerland, Italy, etc.—12^0, pp. 310. Rotterdam, 1686.—Another ed. 2 pts. 12^0. Amsterdam, 1686.——2nd. ed. 8^0, pp. 336. Rotterdam, 1687.——3rd ed. 12^0, pp. 321. Rotterdam, 1687.—Another ed. 3 pts. 12^0. Amsterdam, 1687.——3rd ed., with appendix, 12^0, pp. 232. Amsterdam, 1688.—Other ed. : 12^0, pp. 400. London, 1689.—8^0, pp. 322. [London ?] 1708.—8^0, pp. xxvi+355. London, 1724.—12^0, pp. 24+264. London, 1737.—12^0, pp. xxiv+258. Edinburgh, 1752.—In French : 2 tom. in 1 vol. 12^0. T. i, pp. 235 ; T. ii, pp. 312.- Rotterdam, 1687.—2nd ed. 12^0, pp. 536. Rotterdam, 1688.—Another ed. [last, B.M.] 12^0, pp. 468. Rotterdam, 1690. ——3rd ed. 2 tom. in 1 vol. 12^0, pp. 546. 1718.

BUSCA, D.—Sonetto (1631).—See GIORGI URBANO. [C.A.]

BUSSO, G.—Ansicht der Stadt Pompei mit dem Ausbruche des Vesuvs im Jahr 1838. Veduta degli Scavi di Pompei coll' eruzione del Vesuvio nell' anno 1838. nach d. Nat. gem. u. ges. v. G. Busso in Verlag bei dem Autor. inc. a Roma 1840.

A very fine engrav. on double tinted paper : 565×391 mm.

BYLANDT PALSTERCAMP, A. DE.—Résumé préliminaire de l'ouvrage sur le Vésuve.—8^0. Naples, 1833. [B.N.]

BYRNE, W.—See WRIGHT, J. 1788.

BYRNE, W.—See SMITH, JOHN. 1796.

CACCABO, G. B.—Januarius poema sacrum —4^0, foll. 4, pp. 46. Napoli, 1635. [O.V.]

CADET, L. C.—Analyse chimique d'une lave de Vésuve.—Mem. Acad. Sci. 1761 ; Hist. pp. 63–65. Paris, 1763.

CADET, L. C.—Materiæ e voragine ignivoma montis Vesuvii ejectæ analysis.—Nova Acta Acad. Nat. Curios. iii, p. 268.

Quoted by Reuss.

CÆSIUS, B.—Mineralogia, sive Naturalis Philosophiæ Thesauri, etc.—fol., pp. 16 + 626+69. Lugduni, 1636.

See pp. 118–22.

CAGNAZZI, LUCA DE SAMUELE.—Discorso meteorologico dell' anno 1794.—[Extr. fr.] Giorn. Lett. xxx, pp. 3–29. Napoli, 1794.

CAGNAZZI, LUCA DE SAMUELE.—Lettera sull' elettricismo della cenere lanciata dal Vesuvio, diretta al P. Em. Taddei.—[Extr. fr.] Giorn. Enciclop. pp. 8. Napoli, June 10th, 1806. [C.A.]

CALÀ, C.—Memorie historiche dell' apparitione delle Croci prodigiose.—4^0, pp. 12+ 189+25. Napoli, per Novello de Bonis Stampator della Corte arcivescovile, 1661.

See Cap. 15. A rare book.

CALABRESE.—See CIRILLO. 1834.

CALLOW, W. (pinx^t).—Naples. R. Wallis, sculp^t. H. Mandeville, Paris.

Steel-engrav. : 258×207 mm.

CALVERT, F.—Bay of Naples from Château St. Elme, N° 12.—London, published by William Cole, Newgate Street, 1824.

This is a reversed print of the view by Batty. A rough litho. : 360×244 mm.

CAMERLENGHI, G. B.—Incendio di Vesuvio. Poema.—4^0, foll. 2, pp. 190, frontisp. Napoli, 1632.

CAMERON, H. C.—The great eruption of Vesuvius in 1631.—" *Hours at Home*," iv, *pp.* 74–82 *and* 130–39. *New York*, 1866.
Abbrev. transl. from H. Le Hon : Histoire complète de la grande éruption du Vésuve de 1631.

CAMOLA, G. P. — Sonetto (1631). — *See* GIORGI URBANO. [C.A.]

CAMPAGNE, E. M.—Volcans et Tremblements de Terre.—8⁰. *Limoges*, 1885.

CAMPO, D.—Histoire des phénomènes du Vésuve.—*Naples*, 1771.

CAMPO, D.—*See* TORRE, G. M. DELLA.—Incendio trentesimo del Vesuvio, etc. 1779.

CAMPOLONGO, E.—La Vulcaneide.—8⁰, *pp.* 52. *Napoli*, 1766.

CAMPONESCHI, F.—De Vesevo monte. Epigramma.—*See* GIORGI URBANO. [C.A.]

CANDIDUS, P.—*See* LUCRETIUS CARUS.

CANEVA, S. (Hermit priest).—Lettera dell' Eremita del S. S. Salvatore sito alle falde del Vesuvio per dare ad un amico suo un succinto ragguaglio dell' accaduta Eruzione la sera del 15 Giugno1794.—8⁰, *foll.* 2. — ?, — ? [C.A.]—German transl. in ÒNOFRIO.—Ausführlicher Bericht, etc.——Another ed. 8⁰, *foll.* 4. — ?, — ?

CANGIANO, L.—Sur la hauteur du Vésuve.—*C.R. Acad. Sci. xxii, p.* 736. *Paris,* 1846.

CANTALUPO, G.—Reminiscenze Vesuviane di un profugo.—8⁰, *pp.* 66. *Napoli*, 1872.

CANTALUPO, R.—Il Vesuvio in vetrina.—*La Lettura, pp.* 9, 12 *figs. Milano, Luglio,* 1913.

CAPACCIO, A.—Il Vesuvio nel Luglio, Agosto e Settembre 1893.—*Boll. Oss. Moncalieri, S.* 2, *xiii, pp.* 152, 174, 191. *Torino,* 1894.

CAPACCIO, G. C.—Neapolitanæ Historiæ a J. C. Capaccio eivs vrbis . . . conscriptæ, tomvs primvs. In quo antiqvitas ædificio, ciuibus, republica, ducibus, religione, bellis, lapidibus, locis adiacentibus, qui totam ferè amplectuntur Campaniam, continetur.—4⁰ *pp.* 900, *figs. of coins, views of Solfatare, Avernus, Tritoli, Pausilippe. Neapoli, Apud Jo. Jacobum Carlinum.* M.DCVII.
See pp. 443–60.

CAPACCIO, G. C.—Il Forastiero, dialoghi ne' quali oltre a quel, che si ragiona dell' origine di Napoli, ecc. siti e corpo della città con tutto il contorno da Cuma al Promontorio di Minerva, varietà e costumi di habitatori, famiglie nobili, e popolari, con

molti Elogii d'huomini illustri, aggiuntavi la cognitione di molte cose appartenenti all' istoria d'Italia, con particolari relationi per la materia politica con brevità spiegate.—*pp.* 56+1024.
Bound up with : Incendio del Vesuvio, Dialogo.—4⁰, *pp.* 86. *Napoli, per Gio. Dom. Roncagliolo,* 1634.

CAPACCIO, G. C.—Incendio del Vesvvio, Dialogo.—*See* " Il Forastiero Dialogo."—4⁰, *pp.* 86. *Napoli,* 163[4].

CAPACCIO, G. C.—Antiquitates et Historiæ Neapolitanæ : in quibus antiquitas ædificii, civium, reipublicæ, ducum, religionis, bellorum, lapidum, adjacentiumque locorumque continetur : Novissima editione a mendis corruptelisque, quibus scatebant plurimis, repurgatæ, locisque compluribus restitutæ : & Nummis figurisque accuratissimè ornatæ. Cui Vita auctoris effigiesque additæ sunt.—*foll.* 4, *pp.* 194+6 *in two cols., portrait,* 2 *maps,* 8 *pls.*—*See* GRÆVIUS, J. G.—Thesaurus Antiquitatum . . . Italiæ, *T. ix, Pt.* 2. 1725, *etc.*

CAPACCIO, G. C.—Historiæ Neapolitanæ libri duo in quibus antiquitas ædificii, civium, reipublicæ, ducum, religionis, bellorum, lapidum, locorumque adjacentium, qui totam fere Campaniam complectuntur, continetur.—4⁰. *Liber primus, foll.* 4, *pp.* 312; *Liber secundus, pp.* 500, *figs. Neapoli Sumptibus Joannis Gravier Typographi, et Bibliopolæ Galli,* MDCCLXXI.

CAPASSO, B.—Topografia storico-archeologica della Penisola Sorrentina e raccolta di antiche iscrizioni edite ed inedite appartenenti alla medesima.—8⁰, *foll.* 4, *pp.* 99. *Napoli,* 1846.

CAPECE, P. A.—Lettere scritte al P. A. Capece della Comp. di Gesù a Roma. (Erupt. 1631.)—MS. *in library of the Faculty of Medicine of Montpellier.* Copy [C.A.]—*See* RICCIO, L.—Nuovi documenti.

CAPECELATRO, F.—Historia della città, e regno di Napoli, detto di Cicilia. Da che peruenne sotto il dominio de i Re. Parte Prima. La qual contiene ciò che auuenne in esso da Ruggieri I. sino alla morte di Costanza Imperatrice vltima del legnaggio de Normandi.—4⁰, *pp.* 7+186+9. *Napoli, O. Beltrano,* MDCXXXX.—Other ed. : 2 pts. 8⁰. *Napoli,* 1724.—2 tom. 4⁰. *Napoli,* 1769.—4 tom. 8⁰. *Pisa,* 1820, 21.—2 vols. 16⁰. *Napoli,* 1834.—8⁰. *Napoli,* 1840.
See p. 42, 1640.

CAPECE-MINUTOLO, F.—Al sempre invitto pretettore della città di Napoli, S. Gennaro. Sonetto.—*loose sheet.* —?, 1794. [B.N.]

CAPECE-MINUTOLO, F. — Per l'eruzione del Vesuvio accaduta a' 15 Giugno 1794. Canzone.—*loose sheet.* — ?, — ? [B.N.]

CAPMARTIN DE CHAUPY, B.—Découverte de la maison de Campagne d'Horace. —2 vols. 8°, *topogr. map. Rome*, 1767–69. *See* Vol. i, pp. 102 *et seq.* de' Vulcani, del Vesuvio, etc.

CAPOA, L. Di.—Lezioni intorno alla natura delle Mofete.—4°, *foll.* 8, *pp.* 179, *foll.* 8. *Napoli*, 1683.——Another ed. 8°. *Cologna*, 1714.

CAPOCCI, E.—Viaggio alla Meta, al Morrone ed alla Majella.—*Ann. Civ. Reg. Due Sicilie, vi, pp.* 112–25. *Napoli*, 1833–47.

CAPOCCI, E.—Su di un raro fenomeno vulcanico, che il Vesuvio ha offerto nel mese scorso.—*Rend. Acc. Sci. v, p.* 6. *Napoli*, 1846.

CAPOCCI, E.—Su di un poco noto fenomeno vulcanico.—*Rend. Acc. Sci. v, pp.* 14–18. *Napoli*, 1846.

CAPOCCI, E.—Relazione del fenomeno delle corone di fumo e di cenere presentato dal Vesuvio nella eruzione del Dicembre del 1845, e ne' mesi seguenti.—*Rend. Acc. Sci. v, pp.* 20–23. *Napoli*, 1846.

CAPOCCI, E.—Investigazioni delle interne masse vulcaniche dai loro effetti sulla gravità.—*Atti R. Ist. Incorag. ix, pp.* 215–29. *Napoli*, 1861.

CAPOCCI, E.—Catalogo de' Tremuoti avvenuti nella parte continentale del regno delle Due Sicilie, posti in raffronto con le eruzioni vulcaniche ed altri fenomeni cosmici, tellurici e meteorici.—*Atti R. Ist. Incorag. ix, pp.* 335–78, 379–421, *Napoli*, 1861 ; x, *pp.* 293–327, 1863.—4°, *pp.* 45. *Napoli*, 1859.

CAPOCCI, E.—*See* PALMIERI, L. (relatore). 1862.

CAPOCCI, E.—Sulla eruzione del Vesuvio degli 8 Dicembre 1861.—*At pp.* 23–25 *of* " Raccolta di Scritti varii per cura di C. Rinaldo de Sterlich."—8°. *Napoli*, 1863. [C.A.]

CAPPA, R.—Delle proprietà fisiche, chimiche e terapeutiche dell' acqua termo-minerale Vesuviana Nunziante.—8°, *pp.* 12. *Napoli*, 1847. [C.A.]

CAPPA, R.—*See* PALMIERI, L. (relatore). 1862.

CAPPA, R.—*See* BALDACCHINI, M. 1862.

CAPRADOSSO, A.—Il lagrimevole avvenimento dell' incendio del Monte Vesuvio per la città di Napoli e luoghi adiacenti, etc.— 4°, *foll.* 4. *Napoli, E. Longo*, 1632.—Also an ed. 1631. [O.V.]

CAPUANO, G. A.—*See* SANFELICIUS. 1779. [C.A.]

CARAFA, G.—In opusculum de novissima Vesuvii conflagratione. Epistola isagogica.—8°, *foll.* 64, 1 *pl. Neapolis*, 1632. ——Also 2nd ed. 4°, *pp.* 93, *foll.* 4, 1 *pl.* 1632.
Interesting view of eruption with St. Gennaro presiding.

CARAFA, PADRE.—[In the bibliographical notice by Galiani in " Dei Vulcano o Monti ignivomi," p. 144, occurs : " accuratamente l'ha descritta il pad. Carafa al cap. 2, a Francesco Petrarca nel suo Itinerar. ital., pag. 3."]

CARDASSI, S.—Relazione dell' irato Vesuvio, dei sui fulminanti furori ed avvenimenti compassionevoli.—12°, *pp.* 46. *Bari*, 1632.

CARDON, ANT. (scul.).—Veduta interiore del Vesuvio nel 1755. 22 [— ?] [S. Martino Mus. 5947. *Also* B.N.P. Vb. 121.]
Good engraving.

CARDON, A. (inv. sculp.), PICCININO, F. (Math. Arch. Del. L.).—Icon Crateris Neapolitani.—*Napoli*, 1765. [B.M.—K. 83.56.]

CARDON, A.—Veduta di Ponte Nuovo, D.D.A.S. il Conte di Cobenze, Ministro Plenipot°. della Maesta dell' Imperatrice Regina nei Paesi Bassi Ec.,- . . . . , intagliata dal Quadro Originale di Gabriele Ricciardelli 1765. [S. Martino Mus. No. 2433.]

CARDON, A.—Napoli e Vesuvio nel 1765.— 2 tav. fol., *with Ital. and Lat. explan., engrav. by A. Cardon, jun., and dedicated to Sir W. Hamilton.*

CARDON, A.—Veduta di Chiaja dalla parte de Levante D.D. a S.E. Mme. Hamilton incisa dal quaddro originale di Gabriele Ricciardelli 1767. [S. Martino Mus. A. 2401. *Also* B.M.—K. 83.60–e.]
A fine view of this eruption.

CARDON, A.—[Four views of Naples by Ricciardelli.] [B.M.—K. 83.60–c–f.]

CARDON, A. (sculp.).—*See* BRACCI, G. (del.).—Icon Crateris Neap.

CARDONE, A.—Saggio di poetici componimenti. (Sull' ultima eruzione del Vesuvio. [Poem.])—8°, *fol.* 1, *pp.* 25. *Napoli*, 1828. [C.A.]

CARDOSO, F.—Discurso sobre el Monte Vesvvio, insigne por sus rvinas, famoso por la muerte de Plinio. Del prodigioso incendio del año passado de 1631, y de sus causas naturales, y el origen verdadero de los terremotos, vientos, y tempestades, etc. —4°. *Madrid, por Francisco Martinez*, 1633.

CARDOSO, F.—Al Vesuvio. Soneto.—*See* QUINONES.—El Monte Vesvvio. [C.A.]

CAREGA DI MURICCE, F.—*See* MURICCE, F. CAREGA DI.

CARLES, FLAMINIO MARTINO DI.—Ottave sopra l'incendio del Monte Vesuvio.—12°. *Napoli*, 1632. [B.N.]

CARLETTI, N.—Storia della regione abbruciata in Campagna Felice in cui si tratta il suo sopravvenimento generale, e la descrizione de' Luoghi, de' Vulcani, de' Laghi, de' Monti, delle Città litorali, e de' Popoli che vi furono e vi sono, etc.—4°, *pp.* xliii+ 382, 1 *pl. Napoli*, 1787. [B.N.]

CARLYLE, REV. GAVIN.—*See* MAPEI, C. 1864.

CARMINA.—Lycii.—8°. — ?, 1647. [O.V.]

CARNOVALE, G. A.—Brevi e distinti raguagli de i nuovi e meravigliosi successi nella città di Napoli e suo distretto.—4°, *pp.* 11. *Napoli*, 1631.
Quoted by V. Bove, Soria and Bucca.

CARPANO, G.—Giornale dell' incendio del Vesuvio nell' anno 1660.

CARREY, E.—Carteggio di due amanti alle falde del Vesuvio.—8°, *pp.* 45. *Pompej*, 1783.

CARREY, E.—Le Vésuve.—*Feuilleton du "Moniteur,"* Appendice, 16, 17, 18 *Octobre*, 1861. [C.A.]

CARROZZARI, R.—Leo Gladiator, seu Pompei Vesuvii montis conflagratione obruti. Carmen Raphælis Carrozzari Ferrariensis in certamine poetico Hoeufftiano magna laude ornatum.—8°, *pp.* 27. *Amstelodami*, 1899.

CARUSI, G. M.—Tre passeggiate al Vesuvio ne' di' 3 e 21 Giugno e 27 Settembre 1858. —8°, *pp.* 44. [On wrapper :] *Napoli, stab. tip. di Gaet. Nobile.* 1858.
No proper frontispiece. This is the 1st ed., published only in " La Verità."

CARUSI, G. M.—Tre passeggiate al Vesuvio ne' di' 3 e 21 Giugno e 27 Settembre 1858 ovvero osservazioni sulla eruzione Vesuviana del detto anno e sulla influenza sua verso gli esseri organizzati. Edizione seconda, corretta dall' autore, ed accresciuta della storia della eruzione Vesuviana dal 1855 a tutto Settembre del 1858.—8°, *pp.* iv+68. *Napoli, dalla Stamp. del Vaglio*, 1858.

CASARTELLI, L. C.—A wave of volcanic disturbance in the Mediterranean.—*Geol. Mag.* iv, *pp.* 239–40. *London*, 1867.

CASORIA, E.—Studi e ricerche chimiche sul terreno del podere Sta. Croce in Ponticelli (presso Napoli).—*Ann. R. Scuola Agric. pp.* 26. *Portici*, 1884.

CASORIA, E.—L'acqua della fontana pubblica di Torre del Greco ed il predominio della potassa nelle acque Vesuviane.— *Idrol. e Climatol. Med.* vii, 9, *pp.* 12. *Firenze*, 1885. [C.A.]

CASORIA, E.—Composizione chimica e mineralizzazione delle acque potabili Vesuviane.—*Idrol. e Climatol. Med.* ix, 3, *pp.* 11. *Firenze*, 1887. [C.A.]

CASORIA, E.—Sopra due varietà di Calcari Magnesiferi del Somma.—*Boll. Soc. Naturalisti, i, pp.* 45–46. *Napoli*, 1887.

CASORIA, E.—Composizione chimica di alcuni Calcari Magnesiferi del Monte Somma.—*Boll. Soc. Naturalisti, ii, pp.* 207–10. *Napoli*, 1888.

CASORIA, E.—Sulla presenza del Calcare nei terreni Vesuviani.—*Boll. Soc. Naturalisti, ii, pp.* 211–12. *Napoli*, 1888.

CASORIA, E.—Mutamenti chimici che avvengono nelle lave Vesuviane per effetto degli agenti esterni e delle vegetazione.— *Boll. Soc. Naturalisti, ii, pp.* 214–31. *Napoli*, 1888.

CASORIA, E.—Predominio della Potassa nelle acque termo-minerali Vesuviane (Nunziante e Montella).—*Idrol. e Climatol. Med.* xi, 8, *pp.* 5. *Firenze*, 1889.

CASORIA, E.—L'analisi dell' acqua termo-minerale Montella a Torre Annunziata, pubbl. dal Prof. Silvestro Zinno, confutata. —*Idrol. e Climatol. Med.* xi, 11–12. *Firenze*, 1889.

CASORIA, E.—Le acque della regione Vesuviana.—8°, *pp.* 86. [Extr. from] *Ann. R. Scuola Agric.* vi, 3. *Portici*, 1891.

CASORIA, E.—I nitrati nelle acque dei pozzi nei comuni Vesuviani. Analisi chimiche e considerazioni igieniche.—*L'agric. Merid.* *xiv*, 5. *Portici*, 1 *Marzo* 1891.—Reprinted in " *Vesuvio.*" *Portici*, 8 *Marzo* 1891.

CASORIA, E.—L'acqua Carbonico-Alcalina della Bruna di Torre del Greco. Studii e ricerche.—8⁰, *pp.* 26. *Torre Annunziata*, 1895.

CASORIA, E.—Le produzioni saline Vesuviane dell'Atrio del Cavallo e la presenza in esse del Molibdeno, del Bismuto, del Cobalto e delle Zinco.—*Boll. Oss. Moncalieri*, S. 2, *xix*, 11–12, *pp.* 80–89 ; *xx*, 1–3, *pp.* 2–7. *Torino*, 1900.

CASORIA, E.—Sul poterie incrostante e sui metodi di depurazione delle acque della regione Vesuviana. — ?, 1901.

CASORIA, E.—Sui processi di mineralizzazione delle acque in rapporto con la natura geologica dei terreni e delle rocce.—*Ann. R. Scuola Agric. S.* 2, *iv*, *pp.* 1–196. *Portici*, 1903.—8⁰, *pp.* 197. *Portici*, 1902. *See* pp. 123–53.

CASORIA, E.—Studio analitico dei prodotti delle ultime eruzioni Vesuviane (1891–94 e 1895–99).—*Ann. R. Scuola Agric. S.* 2, *iv*, *pp.* 1–44. *Portici*, 1903.

CASORIA, E.—Le terre vecchie della regione del Monte Somma.—*Ann. R. Scuola Agric. S.* 2, *vi*, *pp.* 13. *Portici*, 1906.

CASORIA, E.—Sulle alterazioni chimiche che subiscono le Lave Vesuviane a contatto delle acque marine.—*Ann. R. Scuola Agric. S.* 2, *vi*, *pp.* 10. *Portici*, 1906.

CASORIA, E.—Conglomerato vulcanico degli scavi di Ercolano.—*Ann. R. Scuola Agric. S.* 2, *vi*, *pp.* 5. *Portici*, 1906.

CASORIA, E.—Lava preistorica del sottosuolo di Pompei.—*Ann. R. Scuola Agric. S.* 2, *vi*, *pp.* 4. *Portici*, 1906.

CASORIA, E.—Sulla presenza del Bario e dello Strontio nelle Lave Vesuviane ed in alcune rocce vulcaniche.—*Ann. R. Scuola Agric. S.* 2, *vi*, *pp.* 5. *Portici*, 1906.

CASORIA, E.—Condizione che influiscono sul diverso rapporto fra il Potassio ed il Sodio nei prodotti salini Vesuviani.—*Ann. R. Scuola Agric. S.* 2, *vi*, *pp.* 5. *Portici*, 1906.

CASORIA, E.—Sulla presenza del Fluore in un prodotto Vesuviano.—*Ann. R. Scuola Agric. S.* 2, *vi*, *pp.* 1–4. *Portici*, 1906.

CASORIA, E.—L'Acqua Solfurca Carbonica di Contursi (Prov. di Salerno).—*Ann. R. Scuola Agric. S.* 2, *vi*, *pp.* 1–18. *Portici*, 1906.

CASORIA, E.—Analisi della sabbia vulcanica del littorale di Torre del Greco.—*Ann. R. Scuola Agric. S.* 2, *vi*, *pp.* 1–7. *Portici*, 1906.

CASORIA, E.—Azione dell' Anidride Solforosa sopra le Lave Vesuviane, ed origine dei Solfati.—*Ann. R. Scuola Agric. S.* 2, *vi*, *pp.* 1–11. *Portici*, 1906.

CASORIA, E.—Sulla composizione chimica delle ceneri Vesuviane cadute a Portici nei giorni 9 e 10 Aprile 1906. (Prima memoria.) —*Ann. R. Scuola Agric. S.* 2, *vi*, *pp.* 1–11. *Portici*, 1906.—*Chemiker-Zeitung*, *xxx*, 61. 1906.

CASORIA, E.—*See* MATTEUCCI, R. V. 1907.

CASORIA, E.—La Lava di Boscotrecase ed il Lapillo di Ottaiano.—*Ann. R. Scuola Agric. S.* 2, *vii*, *pp.* 1–14. *Portici*, 1908.

CASORIA, E.—Sopra un nuovo minerale di Nichelio nei prodotti dell' eruzione Vesuviana dell' Aprile 1906.—*Ann. R. Scuola Agric. S.* 2, *vii*, *pp.* 1–6. *Portici*, 1908.

CASORIA, E.—Sulla presenza dell' Allume, allo stato libero, nel prodotti delle fumarole del cratere Vesuviano.—*Ann. R. Scuola Agric. S.* 2, *vii*, *pp.* 1–7. *Portici*, 1908.

CASORIA, E.—Sulla presenza di un nuovo Solfato nei prodotti delle fumarole del cratere Vesuviano.—*Ann. R. Scuola Agric. S.* 2, *vii*, *pp.* 1–5. *Portici*, 1908.

CASORIA, E.—Sulla Thenardite, nuovo prodotto delle fumarole del cratere Vesuviano.—*Ann. R. Scuola Agric. S.* 2, *vii*, *pp.* 1–6. *Portici*, 1908.

CASORIA, E.—Le Sabbie e le Ceneri Vesuviane cadute a Portici nel mese d'Aprile dell' anno 1906. (Seconda memoria.)— *Ann. R. Scuola Agric. S.* 2, *ix*, *pp.* 26. *Portici*, 1910. (Posthumous.)

CASORIA, F. — Mineralogia Vesuviana. Osservazioni sul rame ossidato.—*Il Lucifero*, *i*, *p.* 171. *Napoli*, 1838.

CASSANO (ARAGONA, PRINCE OF).—*See* ARAGONA (PRINCE OF CASSANO).

CASSIANUS DE SILUA (sculp. D. F.).— Naples.

A map with a sketch of Vesuvius about 1700 ; it also gives details of the different water supplies of Naples from the Carmignano.

CASSINI, G.—[Relation de l'incendie du Mont Vésuve, 1694.]—*Hist. Acad. R. Sci. ii, p.* 204. *Paris*, 1733.

CASSOLA, F.—*See* PILLA, L. 1832–33.

CASTALDI, G. e F.—Storia di Torre del Greco. Con prefazione di Raffaele Alfonso Ricciardi.—8⁰, *pp. xv+294. Torre del Greco*, 1890.

CASTALDI-CERASI, J.—Inscriptiones in solenni celebritate Divi Januarii Curiæ Montanæ vertente secennio.—4⁰. *Napoli*, 1798.

CASTALIÆ STILLULÆ.—Florentiæ apud Samartello.—8⁰. 1667.

CASTELLAN, A. L.—Lettres sur l'Italie, 'faisant suite aux lettres sur la Morée, l'Hellespont et Constantinople.—3 vols. 8⁰. *Vol. i, pp.* 367, *Pls. i–xvi ; Vol. ii, pp.* 307, *Pls. xvii–xxxiv ; Vol. iii, pp.* 365, *Pls. xxxv–l. Paris*, MDCCCXIX. *See* Pls. ix and xiii, views of Vesuvius drawn by Castellan.

CASTELLI, P.—Incendio del Monte Vesuvio. Nel quale si tratta di tutti gli luoghi ardente, delle differenze delli Fuoghi ; loro Segni ; Cagioni ; Prognostici ; e Rimedij, con metodo distinto, historico, e filosofico.—4⁰, *foll. iv, pp.* 92, *foll.* 4. *Roma*, 1632.

CASTERA, DUPERRON DE.—*See* DUPERRON DE CASTERA.

CASTRUCCI, G.—Breve cenno della eruzione Vesuviana del Maggio 1855. —4⁰, *pp.* 3, 1 *pl. Napoli*, 1855.

CASTRUCCI, G.—Catalogo delle materie appartenenti al Vesuvio.—*See* GALIANI.

CATALANO, G.—*See* PALMIERI, L.— Incend. Vesuv. 1872.

CATANI, A.—Lettera critica filosofica su della Vesuviana eruttazione accaduta il 19 Ottobre 1767.—4⁰, *foll.* 3, *pp.* 42. *Catania*, 1768.

CATANTI, C. G.—Introduzione al Catalogo delle eruzioni del Vesuvio.—*See* MECATTI.—Racconto storico-filosof. del Vesuvio. *Napoli*, 1752.

CATANTI, C. G.—Osservazioni fatte sul Vesuvio nel 1750 e 1751.—*Idem. pp.* 55 *et seq.*

CATANTI, C. G.—Catalogo dell' eruzioni fatte dal Vesuvio, delle quali n'è rimasta memoria, insieme colle materie vomitate, lave, pietre, lapilli, cenere, ec.—*Idem, p.* 163.

CATOZZI, F. (dis.).—Veduta della trentessima eruzione di Cenere delli 9 Agosto 1779. Vue de la trentième éruption de Cendre arrivée à 9 Août 1779. Gennaro Bartolo inc. l'anno 1804. T. XIV. In Napoli, presso Franc. Scafa Str. S. Biagio de' Librari. N⁰ 117.
Engrav. : 257 × 196 mm.

CATOZZI, F. (dis. dal vero).—Veduta del principio della 32ᵐᵃ eruzione de' 15 Giugno dell' Anno 1794. Vue du commencement de la 32ᵉ éruption arrivée le 15 guin [*sic*] 1794. Gennaro Bartolo inc. 1804. T. XVI. In Napoli, presso Franc. Scafa. Str. S. Biagio de' Librari. N⁰ 117.
Engrav. : 257 × 198 mm.

CATOZZI, F. (del.).—Veduta della grande Eruzione delli 15 Giugno del 1794. Vue de la grande Éruption de 15 Juin du 1794. Gen. Bartolo inc. T. XVII. In Napoli presso Franc. Scafa. Str. S. Biagio de' Librari. N⁰ 117.
Engrav. : 258 × 197 mm.

CATOZZI, F. (del.).—Veduta della grande Eruzione delli 15 Giugno del 1794. Vue de la grande Éruption de 15 Jouin [*sic*] du 1794. Gen. Bartolo inc.
View by night from Naples. Fine engrav. : 257 × 172 mm.

CATOZZI, F. (dis.).—Eruzione di Cenere accaduta alli 19 Giugno de 1794. Vue du Mont Vésuve dans son Éruption du 19 Juin 1794. Gen. Bartolo incise. T. XIX. In Napoli presso F. Scafa. Str. S. Biagio de' Librari. N⁰ 117.
Engrav. : 257 × 197 mm.

CATOZZI, F. (dis.).—Veduta della Eruzione di Fuoco principiᵃ la notte de' 12 Agosto 1804 a ore 6. e disᵗᵃ la sera de' 13 di dᵉ mese. Vue de l'Éruption de Feu commencée la nuit 12 du mois d'Août 1804 à une heure et demi et dessinée aux 13 du dit mois. Vinc. Scarpata inc. T. XXI. In Napoli presso Filippo Spano. Str. S. Biagio de' Librari. N⁰ 20.
Engrav. : 253 × 205 mm.

CATOZZI, F. (dis. dal vero).—Grande Eruzione di Fuoco e Lava accaduta e disegnata li 9 Settembre 1804. Grande Éruption de Feu et débordement des matières vulcaniques arrivé ce 9 Septembre 1804 et dessiné dans le même instant. Gennaro Bartolo inc. nel 1804. T. XXII. In Napoli presso Franc. Scafa. Str. S. Biagio de' Librari. N⁰ 117.
Engrav. : 254 × 195 mm.

CATOZZI (dis.).—Veduta dell' eruzione del Vesuvio dis. dalle Masserie de Camandoli la notte delli 11 7bre 1804. Vue de l'Éruption du Vésuve prise de la vigne des Camaldules la nuit du 11 7bre 1804. Vinc. Scarpati inc. T. XXIV. In Napoli presso Franc. Scafa. Str. S. Biagio de' Librari. N⁰ 117.
Engrav. : 250×205 mm.

CATTANEO DE FIGINI, G. (dep. ad nat.).—Der Krater des Vesuvs. Il Cratere del Vesuvio. J. Alt. lith.—Ged. b. Mansfeld & Comp. [Vienna lib.]
Rough litho. of crater and cone of erupt. : 232×178 mm.

CATTANEO DE FIGINI, G. (dep. ad nat.).—Neapel vom Grabmale des Virgil's. Napoli preso della tomba di Virgilio. J. Alt. lith.—Ged. b. Mansfeld & Comp. [Vienna lib.]
Litho. : 232×184 mm.

CAVALLERI, G. M.—Considerazioni sul vapore e conseguente calore che manda attualmente (8 Ottobre 1856) il vulcano di Napoli.

CAVALLI, A.—Il Vesuvio, poemetto storico-fisico con annotazioni.—8⁰, *pp.* 157, 2 *pls.* *Milano*, 1769.
Two interesting plates.

CAVAZZA, G.—Sonetto che l'incendio del Vesuvio è stato per salute dell' anime nostra.—*loose sheet. Napoli*, 1632. [B.N.]

CAVAZZA, G.—Sonetto in lode di S. Gennaro nell' incendio del Vesuvio.—*p.* 1. *Napoli ?*, 1632 ?

CAVOLINI, F.—Saggio di storia naturale dell' estremo ramo degli Appennini che termina di rimpetto l'Isola di Capri.—8⁰. *Napoli*, 1853.

CAVOLINI, F.—Piano del Vulcano di Napoli denominato il Vesuvio colle più rimarche-voli eruzioni seguite in più tempi.—pl. *fol., published about* 1854 *in his " Opere postume."* [O.V.]

CAVOLINI, F.—Cenno storico dell' eruzione del Vesuvio dell' Ottobre 1822.—8⁰, *pp.* 29. *Napoli*, — ? [O.V.]

C. D. (dis. lit.).—Vue de Naples du Tombeau de Virgile. C. D. dis. dal vero e in Lit.
Fine outline litho. of Naples and Vesuvius : 356×238 mm.

C. D.—Vue de Naples prise du Tombeau de Virgile.—*Lit. Marras, ab.* 1828 ? [B.M.— 4045.19.]
A good outline view of Vesuvius.

CECI, G. (editore).—Il Vesuvio. Strenna pel 1869 pubblicata a pro de' dannegiati dall' eruzione.—8⁰, *pp.* 200, 1 *map. Napoli*, — ?

CELANO, C.—Notizie del bello, dell' antico, e del curioso della città di Napoli, etc.— 6 vols. 12⁰. *Napoli*, 1692.——Other ed. : 3 vols. 12⁰, *num. pls. Napoli*, 1724 (called 2nd ed.).——3rd ed. 4 vols. 8⁰, *num. figs. Napoli*, 1758-59 (Coll. H. Elliott, Esq.).— 5 vols. 8⁰, *num. figs. Napoli*, 1792.—5 vols. 8⁰, *figs. Napoli*, 1856-60.
See Vol. i, pp. 317-18 ; Vol. v, pp. 729-82. 1856-60.

CENSORINUS.—Index operum quæ in hoc volumine continentur. Censorini de die natali liber aure' . . . antiqua lectioni restitutus Neruæ Traianiq; et Adriani Cæsaris uitæ ex Dione in Latinum uersæ : a G. Merula. Item Vesæui montis conflagratio ex eodem Merula interprete. Cebetis Thebani tabula . . . Plutarchi . . . de differentia, etc.—8⁰, *pp.* 177+8. *Medeolani*, 1503 *or* 1505.

CERASI.—*See* CASTALDI-CERASI.

CERASO, F.—L'opere stupende e meravigliosi eccessi dalla natura prodotti nel Monte Vesuvio, etc.—8⁰, *foll.* 18. *Napoli, Secondino Roncaliolo*, 1632.

CERMENATI, M.—Una Lettera geologica e patriottica di A. Volta. [On Vesuvius.]— *Rend. R. Ist. Lomb. S.* 2, *xxxiv, pp.* 681-91. *Milano*, 1902.

CERTAIN, G.—Il Vesuvio a mezza attezza. —" *Poliorama pittoresco*," xvi, 8, 1 *illustr. lithogr. by* G. Festa. *Napoli*, 1855.

CESARE, F. DE.—Le più belle ruine di Pompei descritte, misurate, e disegnate . . . colle notizie de' scavi da che ebbero principio sino al 1835.—44 *tav.*

CESARE, O. DI.—Sonetto per l'Eruzione del 1794.
Referred to by Duca della Torre.

CESARI, C.—Saggio di Idrografia sotterranea alle Falde del Vesuvio.—*Giorn. Geol. Prat. Perugia, v, pp.* 104–7, *tav.* 1907.

CESARO, G.—Contribution à l'étude des Minéraux du Vésuve et du Mont Somma. —*Mém. Acad. Roy. Belg. S.* 2, *iii,* 2, *pp.* 1-122, *figs.,* 1 *pl. Bruxelles*, 1911.

CETTO, A.—Pompei e il Golfo di Napoli nell' antichità. (L'eruzione Vesuviana del 79 d.C.)—2 *maps. Trento*, 1907.

C. F. C. H.—*See* SALVADORI, G. B.— Notizen über den Vesuv.

C. H. (ex Nat. Del.).—The Hermitage of Mount Vesuvius. Island of Capri (in distance). London : Published by C. Hullmandel, Gt. Marlbro' St. June, 1818.
A rough litho. with good details of cone : 312 × 230 mm.

C. H. (ex Nat. Del.).—Naples viewed from the new Road of Posilipo. London : Published by C. Hullmandel, Gt. Marlbro' Street. July 10, 1818.
Litho. with fair view of Vesuvius ; three men in foreground, one drinking.

C. H. (ex Nat. Del.).—The Castle del Uovo at Naples.
Vesuvius in distance.—Probably published by C. Hullmandel, Gt. Marlbro' Str. July 10th, 1818. Litho. : 312 × 246 mm.

C. H. (ex Nat. Del.).—The Fort of Granatello built on the lava which covers Herculaneum. [In distance] Ischia. Cap Misenum.
Probably published by C. Hullmandel, Gt. Marlbro' St. July 10th, 1818. Litho. : 312 × 218 mm.

C. H. (ex Nat. Del.).—The Hermitage of Mount Vesuvius. Island of Capri.
Litho. after pencil drawing of Hermitage with cone of Vesuvius behind it and Capri to right : 350 × 190 mm.

CHAIX, E.—Une course à l'Etna.—*Genève,* 1890.—*Bull. Amer. Geog. Soc. xxiii, pp.* 92–101, 3 *pls. New York,* 1891.

CHAMPIN. — Maison de l'Ermitage du Vésure.
View of Hermitage and cone of Vesuvius (sea on wrong side). Woodcut from French illust. paper : 132 × 75 mm.

CHAPUY, J. B. (sculp.).—*See* ANNA, A. D'.
—Éruption du Mont Vésuve de 1779.

CHARDON, F. (imp.).—Naples. Imp[ie] F. Chardon aîné, 30 R. Hautefeuille, Paris. Publié par Furne, à Paris.
View from above Grotto over town and Vesuvius ; personages, donkey and 7 trees in foreground. This is similar to one by Rouargue, with smoke of Vesuvius and clouds retouched. Fine engrav. : 149 × 102 mm.

CHARRIN, P. J.—*See* RICHARD DE SAINT-NON. 1829.

CHASTELET (del.).—Naples. Vue d'après nature dans les environs de Portici sur le bord de la mer. C. B. Racine sculp.
A picturesque engrav., but too idealized to be of value : 222 × 148 mm.

CHASTELET (des.).—Naples. Vue du Mosle de Naples ou Fort de la Lanterne. Gravé par Nicollet.
Vesuvius in distance, but much idealized. Quay, personages, bales and boats in foreground. Fine line engrav. : 233 × 164 mm.

CHASTELET (del.). — Naples. Vue du Vésuve prise du côté de Mare Piano près de Pouzzuole. Vangelisti sculp.
Line engrav. : 214 × 148 mm.

CHASTELET (des.). — Naples. Vue du Vésuve prise du Mont St Angelo, où est située une maison de Camaldules. Dessinée d'après Nature par C. Gravé à l'eau forte par Desmoulins. Terminé au burin par Née. N⁰ 35, A.P.D.R.
Vesuvius in distance; Camaldoli, woods and personages in foreground. *Circa* 1780. Line engrav. : 346 × 211 mm.

CHASTELET (del.).—Vue de l'Église de Résina, petit village situé au pied du Vésuve et bâtie à 120 pieds au-dessus du sol d'Herculaneum. Dequevauviller sculp. N⁰ 53, A.P.D.R.
View of Sta Maria de Pugliano ; ruins, trees and personages in foreground. Line engrav. : 222 × 150 mm.

CHASTELET.—Vue d'une partie de la Ville et du Golfe de Naples, prise du Château St. Elme.—Gravé par Desmoulins & J. B. Racine. [B.N.P., Vb. 119.]
Col. engrav.

CHASTELET.—Vue prise près de Portici. Dequevauviller sculp. Naples.
A picturesque engrav. of Vesuvius.

CHASTELET.—Vue de Vésuve prise du Côté de Mare Piano près Pouzzuole. Vangelisti sculp. Naples. [B.N.P., Vb. 121.]
Col. engrav.

CHÂTEAUBRIAND.—Le Vésuve.—*See his :* Voyage en Italie, 1804.

CHÂTELET.—*See* CHASTELET.

CHAVANNES, M. DE.—Le Vésuve.—*pp.* 127, 1 *pl. Tours,* 1859 *and* 1867. [C.A.]
——Another ed. 32⁰, *pp.* 126. *Tours,* 1882.

CHAVANNES, M. DE.—Histoire du Vésuve. —*In :* AUDOT : Voyage de Naples.

CHERBUIN, L. (gravé).—Le Vésuve à Naples. Le Daguerréotype. Exécuté d'après le Daguerréotype. Milan, chez Ferd. Artaria et Fils, Éditeurs. [Vienna lib.]
Stipple engrav. in sepia : 215 × 206 mm.

CHERUBINI, Cav. C.—Carta Fisica dell' Italia.—*Pub. G. B. Paravia e C., Torino, Roma, Milano, Firenze, Napoli,* 1876.
Raised map, 1 : 750,000 horiz. ; 1 : 150,000 vert.

CHEVALIER, Abbé G.—Naples, le Vésuve et Pompéi. Croquis de voyage.—4⁰, *pp.* 288, 1 *engrav. Tours,* 1887.

CHEVALLEY DE RIVAZ.—Analyse et propriétés médicinales des Eaux Minérales de Castellamare par MM. les Profs. Sementini, Vulpes et Cassola. Trad. de l'Italien et accompagnées de notes par . . .—8⁰, *pp.* 4+80. *Naples,* 1834.
Usually bound up with his other books.

CHIARINI, G., e PALMIERI, L.—Il Cratere del Vesuvio nell di 8 Novembre 1875.—*Rend. R. Acc. Sci. xv, pp.* 9–10. *Napoli,* 1876.

CHICCHIO, F. X. De.—Dissertatio de Vesuvio—sub disciplina d. Josephi Vairo Academiæ Neapolitanæ Lectoris qui finem imposuit Kalendis Iuniis in vesperis corporis Christi anno bisextili 1768.—MS. [O.V.]

CHIKHACHEV, or CHIKHATCHEFF, P. A. De.—*See* TCHIHATCHEFF, P. A. De.

CHODNEW, A. — Untersuchungen eines schwärzlich-grünen Glimmers vom Vesuv. —*Ann. Phys. Chim. lxi, pp.* 381–85. *Leipzig,* 1841.

CHOISEUIL, Vicomte.—*See* GIRAUD, E.— Le grand Golfe de Naples (for an engraving after a painting by the former).

CHOULOT, Comte P. De.—Le Vésuve (fragment).—[Estr.] *Mém. Soc. Antiq. du Centre,* 1867, *pp. ii*+18. *Bourges,* 1868.

CHRISTIAN, F. [Prince of Denmark].— Beobachtungen am Vesuv angestellt im Jahre, 1820.—*Taschenb. f. gesammt Min. xvi, pp.* 3–10. *Frankfurt-am-Main,* 1822. —*Atti R. Acc. Sci. ii, Pt.* 2, *Mem. Class. Fis. Stor. Nat. pp.* 3–8. *Napoli,* 1825.

CHRISTIANI, P.—De Vesevo Monte, epigramma.—*See* GIORGI URBANO.

CICADA, H.—De Vesevi conflagratione.—*In* " Carmina," 8⁰, *pp.* 206. *Lycii,* 1647. [O.V.]

CICCONI, M.—Il Vesuvio, canti anacreontici, etc. dopo l'eruzione degli 8 Agosto, 1779.— 8⁰, *pp.* 96. *Napoli,* 1779. [C.A.]

CILLUNZIO, N.—Versi per la ervzione del Vesvvio accaduta a' 12. Agosto. 1805. Il Sincero. — *Reale Accademico Neante,* 8⁰, *foll.* 5. — ?, 1805 ?

CINITANO, G. — Sonetto (1631). — *See* GIORGI URBANO. [C.A.]

CIOFFI DI PERUGIA, Ant.—Pianta fatta dall' architetto . . . dopo l'Eruzione del Giugno 1794.—*Giorn. Lett. xv, pp.* 94–95. *Napoli,* 1794.

CIOFFI [DI PERUGIA], A.—Dimostrazione scenografica e iconografica di tutti gli effetti prodotti dall' eruzione del Vesuvio de'15 Giugno 1794.
Copper-pl. in fol. with description.

CIRILLI.—Vita S. Januarii.—4⁰, *pp.* 48. *Venetiis,* 1776.

CIRILLO, CALABRESE e SEVASTANO.— Raccolta di osservazioni cliniche sul' uso dell' acqua termo-minerale Nunziante del 1832.—Fasc. 1⁰, 8⁰. *Napoli,* 1834.

C. J. R.—Eruption of Mount Vesuvius. Extract of private letter. Naples, October 25th, 1822.
Cutting from an English newspaper, 78 lines.

CLARKE, E. D.—Life of . . .—4⁰. *London,* 1824.
See account of erupt. of 1793, also repeated in " Library of Entertaining Knowledge." Pompei.

CLARKE, W. B.—" Pompeii, a Poem."— *Ipswich,* 1819.—*See* MACAULAY : Pompeii, 1819.

CLARO, F.—Humanæ calamitatis considerationes.—4⁰, *foll.* 14, *pp.* 87. *Neapoli,* 1632. [O.V.]

CLASSENS DE JONGSTE, A.—Souvenirs d'une promenade au Mont Vésuve.—8⁰, *pp.* 61. *Naples,* 1841. [C.A.]

CLENNELL.—Interior View of the Crater of Mount Vesuvius as it was before the Great Eruption of 1767. Engraved by Scott from a drawing by C. for the Gallery of Nature and Art. London : Published by R. Wilks, 89, Chancery Lane, Janʳ 1, 1813. Line engrav. : 174×95 mm.

CLERKE, E. M.—Il Vesuvio in eruzione.— [Estr.] *Rivista Europea,* An. 6, *iii, pp.* 441–49. *Firenze,* 1875.

CLERMONT.—*See* WEBERT, C. 1778.

CLIFTON, C. E.—*See* VALERY, M.

CLUVERIUS, Philippus.—Italia antiqua . . . Ejusdem Sicilia, Sardinia et Corsica . . . (Cum epistola dedicatoria Danielis Heinsii).—3 pts. in 2 vols. *fol. Vol. i, pp.* 786 ; *Vol. ii, pp.* 787–1338+510, *portrait, maps and plans. Lugduni Batavorum,* 1624.

" Sicilia antiqua " is dated 1619 and has special title and pagination.

Another ed. 2 vols. *fol.* 1624. [B.N.P.] In this " Sicilia antiqua " is missing.

CLUVERIUS, PHILIPPUS.—Italia Antiqua auctoris methodo, verbis, et tabulis geographicis retentis contracta opera Ioh. Bunonis.—4⁰, *pp.* 12+773+48 (*index*), 5 *maps. Guelferbyti,* 1659.
See p. 652.

C. M. F.—Great Eruption of Mount Vesuvius (from a private correspondent).—*Naples, October* 25, 1822.
Cutting from an English newspaper, 179 lines.

C. M. F.—Further accounts of the Great Eruption of Vesuvius (from a private correspondent).—*Naples, October* 29, 1822.
Cutting from English newspaper, 139 lines.

COCCHIA, E.—La Forma del Vesuvio nelle Pitture e Descrizioni antiche.—*Atti R. Acc. Archeol. xxi, Pte.* 1, *pp.* 1–66, 8 · *figs. Napoli,* 1901.

COCHIN, C. N., BELLICARD, J. C.—Observations sur les antiquités d'Herculaneum, avec quelques reflexions, etc.—8⁰, *pp.* 36+ 98+10, *num. figs. Paris,* 1754.
See pl. showing crater in 1754.
2nd ed. 12⁰, *pp. xxxviii*+6+104. *Paris,* 1755.—A reprint, 8⁰, *pp. xli*+84, 40 *pls. Se trouve à Naples chez Jean Gravier,* 1757.
This is called 2nd ed., but is a reprint of the 2nd ed. All the plates are badly redrawn, except Pl. 24, a new, fine, folding plate of the Grotto, and Pl. 30, a fine one of Temple of Serapis ; Pl. 25 is missing, and there are two Pl. 30. *See also* BELLICARD.

COCHIN.—Vue de Vésuve, dessiné d'après Nature. Chedel sculp.—*Paris,* — ? [B.N.P., Vb. 121.]

COCKBURN, MAJOR [J. P.] (drawn by).—Temple of Venus, otherwise called Bacchus. Engraved by W. B. Cooke. London : Published July 1, 1826, by W. B. Cooke, 9, Soho Square.
Engrav., Vesuvius in distance : 424 × 298 mm.

COCKBURN, J. P.—Pompeii, illustrated with picturesque views . . . from the original drawings of Lieut.-Col. Cockburn . . . and with plans and details of the public and domestic edifices . . . and a descriptive letterpress to each plate, by T. L. Donaldson.—2 vols. *gd. fol., pls., figs. London,* 1827.

COCKBURN, COL. [J. P.].—*See* WRIGHT, G. N.—The Rhine, Italy and Greece.

COIGNET, M.—Vues Pittoresques de l'Italie, dessinées d'après Nature par . . . et lithographiées par Mlle. Villeneuve, MM. Allaux, Bichebois, Deroy, Enfantin, Gué, Gudin, Joly, Sabatier, Villeneuve, etc. etc. 6me livraison.—*fol.,* 36 *pls. Paris, chez Sazerac et Duval, Dondey-Dupré et fils, Mme. Brossier,* MDCCCXXV. [B.N.P., Vb. 45.]

COIGNET.—Voyage en Italie en 60 pièces, dessiné sur les lieux par . . . et lithographié avec les plus grands soins par MM. Villeneuve, Bichebois, Tirepenne, Joli, Sabatier, Victor Adam, Jacotet.—*imp. fol.,* 60 *pls. Paris, Decrouan, circa* 1830.

COIGNET (del.).—Château de Castelamare. Villeneuve Lith. N⁰ 70. Imp. Lith. de Langlumé.
Vesuvius in distance, Castello di Lettere in foreground. Litho. on single · paper : 288 × 200 mm.

COIGNET (del.).—Château de Castelamare. Villeneuve Lith. Imp. Lith. de Langlumé.
Vesuvius in distance. Castello di Lettere in foreground. Lith. on double paper : 290 × 198 mm. Embossed mark with harp and inscript.

COIGNET (del.).—Pausilippe. Route de Pouzzole. Lith. Langlumé. S. Sabatier, Lith. et V. Adam.
Litho., Vesuvius in distance, rocks, road and ox-cart in foreground. Dr. Johnston-Lavis' copy bears in pencil the inscript. " 3ᵐᵉ Livᵒⁿ " : 341 × 222 mm.

COIGNET (del.).—Pausilippe, Route de Pouzzole. S. Sabatier Lith. et V. Adam (?). K. . . . Ligny, Rue Quincampoix 38 [undecipherable].
A bad and rough relith. of same view as above, by same author and engrav. Langlumé : 342 × 226 mm.

COLAMARINO, D., e MAZZEI-MEGALE, G.—Ragioni del comune di Torre del Greco contro il comune di Resina in materia di circoscrizione territoriale.—8⁰. *Portici,* 1887.

COLAO, B.—Carta della regione perturbata dai fenomeni Vesuviani cominciati il di 8 Dicembre, 1861. 1 : 20,000.—Officio superiore di Stato Maggiore, Sezione di Napoli. [1862 ?] [B.M., K. 24058.3.]
A well-drawn, detailed map of the vents and rifts and raised coast formed by the lava.

COLLENUCCIO, PANDOLFO. — Compendio delle Historie del regno di Napoli composto da Messer Pandolpho Collenutio iurisconsulto in Pesaro. [Figure of Sibilla on title-page. At end :] Et infino a qui si troua scritto della historia di Napoli dal presente Auttore. Fine delle historie Napolitane, composte per lo Egregio Dottore messer Pandolpho Collenutio Iurisconsulto da Pesaro. Stampate in Vineggia per Michele Tramezino, Nel anno. M.D.XXXIX. Nel mese di Maggio.—8⁰, *foll.* 204. *Venetia*, MDXXXIX. [B.N.P.] This ed. is extremely rare. *See* pp. 32–33.

[Also] 8⁰, *foll.* iv+196. 1541.—8⁰, *foll.* 216. 1543.—8⁰, *foll.* iv+196. 1548.

Another ed. " nuovamente emendato da Girolamo Rvscelli, con un brieue discorso del medesimo sopra l'istesso autore."—8⁰, *foll.* iv+215. *Vinegia, G. M. Bonelli,* M.D.LII.

See pp. 25–26.

Another ed.—" Con la givnta di M. Mambrino Roseo da Fabriano delle cose notabili successe dopo. [On title-page figure of Sibylla with the foll. inscription on three sides :] Qval piv fermo è il mio foglio è il mio presaggio."—2 vols. 8⁰. *Vol. i, foll.* vi+344 ; *Vol. ii, foll.* 312. *Vinegia, xv di Ottobre,* MDLVII.

The date at end of 2nd vol. is 1558.

Another ed.—Del Compendio dell' Istoria del regno di Napoli, prima parte, di M. Pandolfo Collenuccio, . . . e di Mambrin Roseo da Fabriano . . . seconda parte, di Mambrin Roseo da Fabriano, col settimo libro del Pacca . . . con la Giunta (overo terza parte) . . . scritta da Tomaso Costo. . . .—3 pts. in 1 vol. 4⁰. *Venezia, B. Barezzi,* 1591.

Another ed.—Compendio dell' Istoria del regno di Napoli, di Pandolfo Collenvccio da Pesaro, di Mambrino Roseo da Fabriano, et di Tomaso Costo Napolitano. [Lib. vii, Pt. 2 by C. Pacca.] Diuiso in tre parti. Con le Annotationi del Costo. Aggiuntovi in questa vltima editione il quarto libro alla terza parte, che serue per tutto l'anno MDCX.—3 pts. in 1 vol. 4⁰, *pp.* 443+407+264 *and index. Venetia, i Giunti,* 1613.

Another ed.—Raccolta di tutti i più rinomati Scrittori dell' Istoria . . . di Napoli, etc.—*tom. xvii–xix,* 4⁰, 1769, *etc.*

Another ed.—3 vols. 4⁰. *Napoli, stamp. G. Gravier,* 1771.

[In Latin.]—Historiæ Neapolitanæ ad Herculem I, Ferrariæ ducem, libri VI. . . . Omnia ex Italico sermone in Latinum

conuersa. Ioann. Nicol. Stvpano, Rheto Interprete, etc.—4⁰, *pp.* 325 *and index, portrait. Basileæ, P. Pernam,* 1572.

Another ed.—8⁰, *pp.* 716 *and index. Roterodami, typis J. L. Berevvont,* 1617.

See pp. 46–47.

[In French.]—Sommaire des Histoires du royaume de Naples, qui traicte de toutes choses advenues en iceluy . . . composé . . . en langage italien par M. P . . . C . . ., et depuis n'aguères mis en françois par Denis Sauvage. . . . Avecques annotations. . . .—8⁰, *foll.* 320. *Paris, A. L'Angelier,* 1546. [B.N.P.]

See foll. 40–41. Another copy is on ruled paper with mosaic binding.

Another ed.—" Contenant les choses mémorables advenues depuis l'empire d'Auguste jusques à nostre temps . . . nouvellement traduite en langage vulgaire, reveue et augmentée de ce qui est advenu depuis l'année 1459 jusques à présent."—8⁰, *pp.* 509. — ?, 1586. [B.N.P.]

Incomplete.

Other ed.—8⁰, *pp.* 509. *Tournon, G. Linocier,* 1595.—8⁰, *pp.* 609. 1596.

[In Spanish.]—" Traduzido por Nicolas Spinosa . . ."—8⁰, *foll.* 274. *Valecia, impr. de J. Nauarro,* 1563.

Another ed.—Traduzida de lengua Toscana por Juan Vasquez del Marmol, etc.—*fol., foll.* 167, *figs. Seville, F. Diaz,* 1584.

COLLETTA, P.—Storia del reame di Napoli dal 1734 sino al 1825.—2 vols. 8⁰. *Capolago,* 1834.——Another ed. 4 vols. 12⁰. *Capolago,* 1834.——Another ed. " Con una notizia intorno alla vita dell' autore, scritta da G. Capponi," 2 vols. 12⁰. [*Bastia*] 1846.——Another ed. 2 vols. 8⁰. *Milano,* 1861.

COLLETTA, P.—L'eruzione del Vesuvio del 1794.—*In his* " Istoria del reame di Napoli," *Lib.* III, *Cap.* 1.

COLLETTA, P.—Histoire du royaume de Naples . . . Traduite de l'Italien sur la 4ᵉ édition, par C. Lefèvre, et L . . . B . . .—4 tom. 8⁰. *Paris,* 1835.

COLLETTA, P.—The History of Naples from the accession of Charles of Bourbon to the death of Ferdinand I. Translated from the Italian, with a supplementary chapter by S. Horner.—2 vols. 8⁰. *Edinburgh,* 1860.—Earlier ed. *Edinburgh,* 1858. *See* Vol. i, 1860.

COLLEZIONE DI MONOGRAFIE ILLUSTRATE.—Italia Artistica.—*See* RICCI, C.

COLLI.—Éruption de Nuit du Mont Vésuve en 1812. Gravé par Levacher.—Paris. [B.N.P., Vb. 121]. A fine sepia engrav.

COLLINI, C. M.—Considérations sur les Montagnes Volcaniques, etc.—4°, *pp. viii*+ 61, 1 *pl. Mannheim*, 1781. See pp. 43 *et seq.* In German : 4°. *Dresden*, 1783.

COLOMBA, L.—La Leucite del tufo di Pompei.—*Boll. Soc. Geol. Ital. xxiii, pp.* 379-91, *tav. Roma*, 1905.

COLOMBO, A.—La fauna sottomarina del Golfo di Napoli.—*Rivista Marittima, xx, pp.* 5-32, 413-43, *tav. i-vii. Roma, Ottobre-Dicembre*, 1887.

COLONNA, C.—Lettera sopra l'incendio del Vesuvio nel 1631.—*Napoli*, 1632.—*See* BRACCINI.

COLUMBRO, G.—Rime e prose.—2 vols. 8°. *Napoli*, 1817. See Vol. i, pp. 72-75 : a poem " Il Vesuvio " (erupt. 1794); Vol. ii, pp. 202-11 : letter to a friend at Resina, speaking of Vesuvius.

COMANDUCCI, E., e PESCITELLI, L.—Analisi chimica della Cenere caduta in Napoli la notte del 2 Ottobre 1904.—*Rend. R. Acc. Sci. S. 3, xi, pp.* 249-53. *Napoli*, 1905.

COMANDUCCI, E., e ARENA, M.—Analisi chimica della Cenere caduta in Napoli la notte del 4-5 Aprile 1906.—*Rend. R. Acc. Sci. S. 3, xii, pp.* 267-80. *Napoli*, 1906.— *Gazz. Chim. Ital. xxxvi, Pt. 2, pp.* 797-812. *Roma*, 1906.

COMES, O.—Le Lave, il terreno Vesuviano e la loro vegetazione.—*Lo spettatore del Vesuvio e dei Campi Flegrei, N.S. i. Napoli*, 1887.—16°. *Portici*, 1888.—In German, transl. by J. J. Mohrhoff : 8°, *pp.* 40. *Hamburg*, 1889.

COMITÉ D'ORGANISATION DU 2ME CONGRÈS GÉOLOGIQUE INTERNATIONAL À BOLOGNE, 1881.—Bibliographie Géologique et Paléontologique de l'Italie.—8°, *pp. viii*+630. *Bologne*, 1881. See No. XII. ZEZI, G. P.—Le Vesuvio. (Nos. 2538-3205.)

COMPENDIO DELLE TRANSAZIONI FILOSOFICHE DELLA SOCIETA REALE DI LONDRA.—[Treats of various earthquakes and eruptions of Etna, Vesuvius, etc.]—*Giorn. Lett. v, pp.* 78-89. *Napoli*, 1793.

COMPTE, A. C.—Lettera critico-filosofica sull' eruzione del Vesuvio del 1767.— *Catania*, 1868.

CONDAMINE, M. DE LA.—Journal of a Tour in Italy with accounts of the eruption of Vesuvius, curiosities discovered at Herculaneum, remarks on the mountains and ice valleys of Switzerland, etc.—8°, *pp.* 24+167. *Dublin*, 1763.—[Extr.] *Hist. Acad. R. Sci., Mém. Math.* 1757, *pp.* 6-16. *Paris*, 1762. See pp. 78-89 : state of Vesuvius, June 4th, 1755.

CONDE DE CORVÑA.—Sonetto (1631).— *See* QUINONES. [C.A.]

CONFORTI, L.—Il Vesuvio nella Storia. Per le vittime dell' ultima eruzione.—8°, *pp.* 64, *fig. on cover. Napoli*, 1906. Gives a list of eruptions, and at end refers to researches by boring on plain of Sarno.

CONRAD, M. G.—Am Fusse des Vesuvs.— *Illustrirte Welt, pp.* 556-58, 1 *illustr. Stuttgart*, 1872.

CONRAD, M. G.—Die jüngste Eruption des Vesuvs.—*Ueber Land u. Meer, xxvii,* 36, *pp.* 18-19, 1 *illustr. Stuttgart*, 1872.

CONSTANTIN (fecit).—[Erupt. of Vesuvius by night from Naples. 1 May, 1817.] Oil painting on panel : 232×182 mm.

CONTARINO, F.—Sull' altezza delle Polveri Vesuviane cadute in Napoli dopo le eruzione del 22 Ottobre 1822 e dell' 8 Aprile 1906 e sull' abbassamento subito dal cratere per le stesse eruzioni.—*Rend. R. Acc. Sci. S. 3, xii, pp.* 333-35. *Napoli*, 1906.

COOMANS, J.—Sur l'éruption du Vésuve en 1858.—" *Moniteur," pp.* 6, 10 *Juin*, 1858. [C.A.]

COPPOLA, M.—Contribuzione alla storia chimica dello " Stereocaulon Vesuvianum." Notizie preliminari.—*Rend. R. Acc. Sci. xviii, pp.* 232-35. *Napoli*, 1879.

COPPOLA, M.—Produzione artificiale dell' oligisto sulla lava Vesuviana.—*Gazz. Chim. Ital. ix, pp.* 452-55. *Palermo*, 1879. [C.A.]

CORAFÀ, G.—Veduta del Vesuvio dalla parte di mezzogiorno 25 Ottobre, 1751.— *pl. fol., with descript.* [O.V.]

CORAFÀ, G.—Osservazioni da lui fatte il dì 26 Ottobre 1751 e seg.

CORAFÀ, G.—Dissertazione istorico-fisica delle cause e degli effetti delle eruttazioni del Monte Vesuvio negli anni 1751-52.— 4°, *foll. ii, pp.* 86. *Napoli*, 1752.

CORAGGIO, G. P.—Breve trattato e discorso di quello, che successe di bene al regno di Napoli, etc.—4⁰, *pp.* 30. *Napoli*, 1769. [B.M. 1316.i.17.]

CORBONE.—Veduta dell' eruzione del Vesuvio nel 1631 con illustrazione stampata dei danni prodotti. — ?, — ? [C.A.]

CORCIA, N.—Il Vesuvio.—*In his* " Storia delle due Sicilie," *Tom. ii, pp.* 404–7. *Napoli*, 1843–52.

CORDIER, P. L. A.—Rapport sur le voyage de M. Constant Prévost à l'Île Julia, à Malte, en Sicile, aux Îles Lipari et dans les environs de Naples.—*C.R. Acad. Sci. ii, pp.* 243–55. *Paris*, 1836.—*Nouv. Ann. Voyages, lxx (S. 2, x), pp.* 43–64. *Paris*, 1836.

CORNELIUS, T.—De sensibus.—8⁰, *foll.* 7, *pp.* 119. *Neapoli*, 1638.

CORNELIUS, T.—Opera quædam posthuma nunquam antehac edita.—*See Chap.* " De sensibus progymnas postum," *pp.* 39 *et seq. Neapoli*, 1688.

CORRADO, M.—Descrizione del fenomeno cagionato dal Monte Vesuvio nella sera del dì 15 di Giugno dell' anno 1794 de' fatti occorsi in seguito e della somma religiosità de' cittadini Napolitani. Verses.—8⁰, *pp.* 7. *Napoli*, 1794. [C.A.]

CORRADO, M.—Descrizione (Nuova) de' danni cagionati dal Monte Vesuvio dalla sera de' 15, sino al giorno 28 di Giugno dell' anno 1794, e della somma religiosità de' cittadini Napolitani.—12⁰. *Napoli*, 1794. [B.N.]

CORVÑA, CONDE DE.—*See* QUINONES.— El Monte Vesvvio.

COSENZA, G.—Der Bahnhof auf dem Vesuv. Nach einer Zeichnung von G. Cosenza. (S. 406.) Canedi [inc. ?]—*Illustrirte Welt, xxix, p.* 401. *Stuttgart u. Leipzig*, 1881. Woodcut of road with carriages ascending to lower station of funicular rail on Vesuvius, which had just blown a big smoke-ring : 320 × 216 mm.

COSSA,˜ A.—Sulla Predazzite Periclasifera del Monte Somma.—*Atti R. Acc. Lincei, S. 2, iii, Pt. 2, pp.* 3–8. *Roma*, 1876.

COSSA, A.—Ricerche chimiche e microscopiche su Roccie e Minerali d'Italia (1875–80).—4⁰, *pp. vii*+302, 12 *pls.* (11 *col.*). *Torino*, 1881.—*Boll. R. Com. Geol. Ital. xiii, notiz. bibliog. pp.* 57–58. *Roma*, 1882.

COSSOVICH, E.—Il Vesuvio.—*See* BOURCARD : " Usi e costumi di Napoli e contorni," *Vol. ii, pp.* 85–118, *tav.* 1. *Napoli*, 1853–58.

COSSOVICH, E.—Cenni geologici e topografici sulle eruzioni, sui ricchi prodotti, e gita al Vesuvio. — ?, — ?

COSTA, A.—Osservazioni sugl'insetti che rinvengonsi morti nelle fumarole del Vesuvio.—*Il Giambattista Vico, i, pp.* 39–44. *Napoli*, 1857.—*Ann. R. Oss. Meteor. Vesuv. ii, pp.* 21–27. *Napoli*, 1862.

COSTA, A.—Fenomeni osservati nella vita delle Api in seguito alla eruzione Vesuviana dell' Aprile 1872.—*Rend. R. Acc. Sci. xi, pp.* 108–9. *Napoli*, 1872.

COSTA, A.—Le incrostazioni gialle della lava Vesuviana del 1631.—*Rend. R. Acc. Sci. xix, pp.* 40–41. *Napoli*, 1880.

COSTA, O. G.—Fauna Vesuviana, ossia descrizione degl'Insetti che vivono ne' fumajoli del Cratere del Vesuvio.—*Atti Acc. Sci. iv* (1826), *pp.* 21–53, 2 *pls. Napoli*, 1839.—*See also* " Giambattista Vico," i, *pp.* 39–44. *Napoli*, 1857.

COSTA, O. G.—Rapporto sull' escursioni fatte al Vesuvio in Agosto-Dicembre 1827. —*Atti Acc. Sci. iv* (1826), *pp.* 55–60. *Napoli*, 1839.

COSTA, O. G.—Memoria da servire alla formazione della Carta Geologica delle provincie Napoletanc.—4⁰, 13 *tav. Napoli*, 1864.

COSTA, O. G.—*See* PALMIERI, L., ET ALII. 1859.

COSTANZO, G.—Intorno all' eruzione del Vesuvio durante il Maggio˜del 1900.—*Riv. Fis. Mat. Sci. Nat. ii, 14, pp.* 97–107. *Pavia*, 1901.

COSTO, T.—Ragionamenti di . . . intorno alla descrizzione del regno di Napoli, et all' antichita di Pozzuolo di Scipione Mazzella. —4⁰, *pp.* 82. *Napoli*, 1595.

COSTO, T.—*See* COLLENUCCIO, P.

COSYNS, M.—Analyse des cendres volcaniques tombées à Ottajano (Vésuve) le 14 avril 1906.—[Extr.] *Bull. Soc. chim. Belgique, xx,* 5–6, *pp.* 4. *Bruxelles*, 1906.

COTTA.—Der Ausbruch des Vesuv am 17 December 1867.—*Illustrirte Zeitung,* No. 1283, *p.* 81, 4 *illustr. Leipzig*, 1868.

COVELLI, N.—Débit des Minéraux du Vésuve. Catalogue pour 1826.—8⁰, *pp.* 16. *Naples*, 1826.

COVELLI, N.—Sur le Bisulfure de Cuivre qui se forme actuellement dans le Vésuve (1826).—*Ann. Chim. xxxv, pp.* 105–11. *Paris,* 1827.—*Bull. Sci. nat. et Géol. xi, pp.* 335–38. *Paris,* 1827.—*Ann. Phys. Chem. x, pp.* 494–98. *Leipzig,* 1827.— *Quart. Journ. Sci. Lit. and Arts, ii, pp.* 226–27. *London,* 1827.—*Atti Acc. Sci. iv, pp.* 9–16. *Napoli,* 1839.

COVELLI, N.—Cenno sullo stato del Vesuvio dalla grande eruzione del 1822 in poi (1824). —" *Il Pontano,*" *i, pp.* 19–27, 145–54. *Napoli, Marzo* 1828.

COVELLI, N.—Su la natura de' fummajoli e delle termantiti del Vesuvio dove vivono e si moltiplicano varie specie d'Insetti (1826). —*Atti R. Acc. Sci. iv, pp.* 3–8. *Napoli,* 1839.

COVELLI, N.—Su la Beudantina, nuova specie minerale del Vesuvio (1826).—*Atti R. Acc. Sci. iv, pp.* 17–32. *Napoli,* 1839.

COVELLI, N.—Memoria per servire di materiale alla costituzione geognostica della Campania [1827].—*Atti Acc. Sci. iv, pp.* 33–69. *Napoli,* 1839.

COVELLI, N.—Relazione di due escursioni fatte sul Vesuvio e di una nuova specie di solfuro di ferro, che attualmente producesi in quel vulcano [1827].—*Atti Acc. Sci. iv, pp.* 71–86. *Napoli,* 1839.

COVELLI, N.—Rapporto sopra due gite fatte sul Vesuvio.—*Atti R. Acc. Sci. iv, pp.* 87–95. *Napoli,* 1839.

COVELLI, N.—*See* MONTICELLI. 1822, 1823, 1825 (2), 1839, — ? (2).

COX, J. C.—Hints for Invalids about to visit Naples ; being a sketch of the Medical Topography of that city. Also an account of the Mineral Waters of the Bay of Naples ; with Analyses of the most important of them derived from authentic sources.—8⁰, *pp.* 6+190, 2 *pls. London, Paris, Nottingham,* 1841.

COZZA, P.—Eruption of Vesuvius A.D. 787. —*Archiv. Stor. xv,* 3, *pp.* 642–46. *Napoli,* 1890.

COZZOLINO, P.—La Barra e sue origini nella Napoli suburbana, con note e documenti epigrafici.—8⁰, *pp.* 44, 1 *tav. Napoli,* 1889.

COZZOLINO, V.—Cataloghi di Minerali Vesuviani.—3 *sheets.* 1844–46.

CRAIG.—Excavation leading to the Remains of Herculaneum. Engraved by Lacey from a drawing by C. for the Gallery of Nature and Art.—London. Published by R. Wilks, 89, Chancery Lane, Nov. 1st, 1814.
Line engrav. : 156×96 mm.

CRAVEN, A.—Studii sull' antico Sebeto.— 4⁰, *pp. xii*+103. *Napoli,* 1863.

[CRAVEN, K.]—Italian Scenes, a series of Interesting Delineations of Remarkable Views and of the most Celebrated Remains of Antiquity.—4⁰, 27 *pls.* (*des. by author, T. Ruiz, etc., engrav. by Chas. Heath, Taylor, etc., with explan. text*). *London,* 1825.
See Pl. 14 : erupt. 1751, and Pl. 15 : lava of 1751.

CRESWICK, THOMAS (paint.).— Bay of Naples and Vesuvius taken from above Pausilippo. Engraved by W. B. Cooke.— London. Published March 1, 1833, by W. B. Cooke, 27, Charlotte Street, Bloomsbury.
Fine line engrav. on highly glazed paper : 164×118 mm.

CRISCOLI, P. A.—Vesevi montis elogica inscriptio.—1 *leaf, fol., fig. Vesuvius. Neapoli,* 1632. [O.V.]

CRISCONIO, P.—Il Vesevo : Ode.—12⁰, *pp.* 12. *Napoli,* 1828. [C.A.]

CRISTIANO, FRED.—*See* CHRISTIAN, F.

CRISTIANO, P.—*See* CHRISTIANI, P.

CRIVELLA, ANTONIO (detto il " Monaciello " improvissante). — Il fumicante Vesevo, ovvero il Monte di Somma bruggiato. Con diverse Terre, Casali, e luoghi situati nella sua falda. Con esservi anco un minuto ragguaglio di quanto in quello è successo. Composto in ottava rima.—12⁰, *foll.* 6. *Napoli,* 1632. [C.A.]

CROIX, G. DE LA (Peint sur les lieux en 1757 par), élève de Mr. Vernet.—Vue du Mont Vézuve tel qu'il étoit en 1757. Dedié à Monsieur Blondel Dazaincourt Lieutenant Colonel d'infanterie. Chevalier de l'ordre Royal et Militaire de St. Louis par son très humble et très obéissant Serviteur Noel le Mire à Paris chés l'auteur rue Pavée St. André des Arts. N. Le Mire Sculp. 1762.
Engrav. : 333×438 mm.

CROSBY, E. C.—Vesuvius and the surrounding country.—*Kansas City Review, ii, pp.* 77–91. 1878–79.

CROSET-MOUCHET, P. B.—Proposta ed utilità di una carta topografica del Vesuvio.—*Atti Sett. Adun. Sci. Ital. p.* 1141. *Napoli,* 1845.

CRUSIUS, V.—Vesuvius ardens.—4°, *pp.* 319. *Rome,* 1632.

CUCCURULLO, G.—Torre Annunziata : Cenni intorno alle terme, in occasione del congresso internazionale d'idrologia.—8°, *pp. xiii. Torre Annunziata,* 1894.

CUCINIELLO,Dom., BIANCHI, L.—Viaggio pittorico nel regno delle due Sicilie (with drawings by R. Müller, L. Jely, F. Horner, G. Forino, F. Dura, F. Wenzel, P. de Leopold, C. Goetzloff, G. Gigante, A. Vianelly, A. Marinoni, A. Carelli).—*gd. fol. Vol. i, Pt.* 1, *pp.* 128, *pls.* 60 ; *Vol. ii, Pt.* 1, *pp.* 122, *pls.* 60 ; *Vol. iii, Pt.* 2, *pp.* 122, *pls.* 60. *Napoli* [1833].

CUCINIELLO, [D.].—*See* VIANELLY.

CUOMO, V.—L'Isola di Capri come stazione climatica. Con una carta geografico-geologica dell' isola.—8°, *pp. viii*+155, 1 *col. geol. map. Napoli,* 1894.

CURTIS, L. M. DE.—Saggio sull' elettricità naturale diretto a spiegare i movimenti e gli effetti dei Vulcani.—8°, *pp.* 88. *Napoli,* 1780. [O.V.]

CYRILLUS, N.—An account of an extraordinary eruption of Mount Vesuvius in the month of March, in the year 1730.—*Phil. Trans. R. Soc. xxxvii, pp.* 336–38. *London,* 1733.—In Ital. : *Compend. Trans. filos. Londra, pp.* 72–73. *Venezia,* 1793.

DALBONO, C.—*See* QUARANTA, B. 1845.

DALLAS, R. C.—*See* ORDINAIRE, C. N.

DAMIANO, P.—Breve narratione de' meravigliosi esempi occorsi nell' incendio del Monte Vesuvio circa l'anno 1038, cavata dall' opera del B° Pietro Damiano.—12°, *foll.* 4. *Napoli,* 1632. [C.A.]

DAMIANO, P.—Il Vesuvio considerato qual bocca dell' Inferno.—*Opera Parissiis* (4 vols. bound together),*fol., Opusc. xix,* 6, 9, *and* 10, *pp.* 191–92. 1663. [C.A.]
Refers to an eruption A.D. 993.

DAMOUR, A. A.—Analyse de la Périclase de la Somma.—*Bull. Soc. géol. France, S.* 2, *vi, pp.* 311–15. *Paris,* 1849.

DAMOUR, A. A.—Relation de la dernière éruption du Vésuve en 1850.—8°. — ?, 1851.

DANA, J. D.—On the condition of Vesuvius in Italy, 1834.—*Amer. Journ. Sci. xxvii, pp.* 281–88. *New Haven,* 1835.

DANA, J. D.—Abstract of a paper on the Humite of Monte Somma ; by A. Scacchi, with observations.—*Amer. Journ. Sci. S.* 2, *xiv, pp.* 175–82. *New Haven,* 1852.

DANA, J. D.—[On volcanic eruptions of Barren Island, Vesuvius, and Kilauea.]— *Amer. Journ. Sci. S.* 3, *xxxi, pp.* 394–97. *New Haven,* 1886.

DANA, J. D.—Contrast between Mount Loa and volcanoes of the Vesuvian type.—*In* " Characteristics of Volcanoes,"*pp.* 265–69. *New York,* 1890.

DANZA, E.—Breve discorso dell' incendio succeduto a 16 Dicembre 1631 del Vesuvio e luoghi circonvicini e dei terremoti della città di Napoli.—8°, *foll.* 24. *Trani,* 1632. [O.V.]

DARBIE, F. (or DARBES).—Istoria dell' incendio del Vesuvio accaduto nel mese di Maggio dell' anno 1737, scritta per l'Accademia delle Scienze. 2nda. Ediz. Riveduta ed accresciuta di alquante annotazioni.—8°, *pp.* 14+226, 2 *pls. Napoli,* 1740.—*See also* ANON.—Dei Vulcani o Monti Ignivomi.—*Livorno,* 1779. '

DARBIE, F.—Delle mofete eccitate dell' incendio del Monte Vesuvio.—*See* ANON. —Dei Vulcani o Monti Ignivomi, *T. i, pp.* 125–57.

DARONDEAU, GAUSSIN, VIARD, MANEN, E. PLOIX, LAROUSSE et VIDALIN.—Carte particulière des côtes d'Italie ; partie comprise entre la tour Patria et le Cap Sottile, Golfe de Naples et Îles. (Nr. 2058.)—*Paris, Dépôt de la Marine,* 1865.

DARONDEAU and GAUSSIN.—Gulf of Naples with soundings in fathoms (and surface outlines).—*London,* 1867. [B.M. Sec. 5 (1728).]
A fine chart ; height of Vesuvius given as 4,100 ft., and Somma as 3,630 ft.

DASCHER.--Éruptions Volcaniques. Notices abrégées relevées par . . . dans les ouvrages spéciaux.—16°, *pp.* 16. *Paris,* 1902.

DAU, L.—Lettere al Barone Durini intorno ad una nuova teoria spiegatrice dei fenomeni dei Vulcani.—8°, *pp.* 32. — ?, 1835. [O.V.]

DAUBENY, C. G. B.--*See* RAFFLES. 1825.

DAUBENY, C. G. B.—A Description of active and extinct Volcanos ; with remarks on their origin, their chemical phenomena, and the character of their products, as determined by the condition of the earth during the period of their formation.—8⁰, *pp.* 466, *figs.*, 2 *maps*, 1 *pl. London*, 1826.
——2nd ed., greatly enlarged, with pls. by Lorory, 8⁰, *pp.* 743, *figs.*, 10 *maps*, 4 *pls. London*, 1848.
Last 14 pp. give a copious bibliog. of works on vulcanology.

DAUBENY, C. G. B.—Some account of the eruption of Vesuvius which occurred in the month of August 1834, extracted from the MS. notes of the Cav. Monticelli, foreign member of the Geological Society, and from other sources ; together with a statement of the products of the eruption, and of the condition of the Volcano subsequently to it.—*Phil. Trans. R. Soc. pp.* 153–59. *London*, 1835.

DAUBENY, C. G. B.—On the Volcanic Strata exposed by a section made on the site of the new Thermal Spring discovered near the town of Torre dell' Annunziata, in the Bay of Naples ; with some remarks on the Gases evolved by this and other springs connected with the Volcanoes of Campania. —*Edinb. New Phil. Journ. xix, pp.* 221–31. 1835.—*Proc. Geol. Soc. ii, pp.* 177–79. 1838.

DAUBENY, C. G. B.—Die Vulkane, Erdbeben und heissen Quellen, etc. Erster Abschnitt : Die noch thätigen und erloschenen Vulkane. Bearb. von Gust. Leonhard.—8⁰. *Stuttgart*, 1850.

DAUBENY, C. G. B.—Remarks on the recent eruption of Vesuvius in December, 1861.—8⁰. *London*, 1862.—*Edinb. Phil. Journ. xvii, pp.* 1–14. *Edinburgh*, 1863.

DAVENPORT ADAMS, W. H.—The buried cities of the Campania, or Pompeii and Herculaneum, their history, their destruction, and their remains.—8⁰, *pp. viii*+282, 57 *figs.*, *and pls. London*, 1873.
See pls. at pp. 24, 36.

DAVID, P.—Le Vésuve et Pompeïa, poème. —*Mém. Soc. Acad. pp.* 91–98. *Falaise*, 1838.

DAVY, Sir Humphry.—On the phenomena of Volcanoes.—*Phil. Trans. R. Soc. pp.* 241–50. *London*, 1828.—*Phil. Mag. S.* 2, *iv, pp.* 85–94. *London*, 1828.—*Ann. Chim. Phys. xxxviii, pp.* 133–50. *Paris*, 1828.

DAWKINS, W. B.—Vesuvius in January, 1877.—" *Good Words*," *xviii, pp.* 243–48. *London*, 1877.

DAWKINS, W. B.—The condition of Vesuvius in January, 1877.—*Trans. Manchester Geol. Soc. xiv, pp.* 169–76. *Manchester*, 1878.

DAWSON, J. W.—Note on a paper on " Eozoonal Structure of the Ejected Blocks of Monte Somma."—4⁰, *pp.* 4. 1895.
A proof with corrections sent by the author to Dr. Johnston-Lavis, signed, and dated Montreal, March, 1895.

DAWSON, J. W., JOHNSTON-LAVIS, H. J., GREGORY, J. W.—Eozoon and the Monte Somma Blocks.—*Nat. Sci. vi, pp.* 398–404. 1895.

D. B.—L'Italia descritta e depinta con le sue Isole di Sicilia, Sardegna, Elba, Malta, Eolie, di Calipso, ecc. Collected from numerous authors by D. B.—2nd ed. 5 vols. 8⁰, *many* [*good*] *engravings. Turin, Gius. Pomba e.c.*, 1837.

DEBUCOURT, P. L. (gravé par).—Éruption du Mont-Vésuve à la nuit, d'après dessin fait à Naples.
Stipple engrav. of Vesuvius as seen from sea to the S. ; moon in sky : 247 × 174 mm.

DEECKE, J. E. W.—Bemerkungen über Bau- und Pflastermaterial in Pompeji — ?, 1888 ?

DEECKE, J. E. W.—Ueber den Sarno in Unteritalien (Prov. Neapel.).—*Jahresb. geog. Gesellsch. v. Greifswald*, 1892.

DEECKE, J. E. W.—Italien.—*Bibl. der Länderkunde, iii u. iv, pp.* 519, 33 *pls. and maps*, 79 *figs. Berlin*, 1899.

DEECKE, J. E. W.—Ueber die kohlereichen gebänderten Sommablöcke (1901).—[Separatabdr.] *Centralbl. f. Min. pp.* 309–11. *Stuttgart*, 1901.

DELAIRE.—Osservazioni sul Vesuvio negli anni 1745-1752.—*In* MECATTI.—Discorso storico filosofico del Vesuvio.—*Napoli*, 1752.

DELESSE, A. E. O. J.—Recherches sur l'origine des roches.—[Extr.] *Bull. Soc. géol. France, S.* 2, *xv, pp.* 728–82. *Paris*, 1858.—8⁰, *pp.* 74. *Paris*, 1865.
See p. 753. 1858.

DELTA (Δ) [FORBES, J. D.].—Remarks on Mount Vesuvius.—*Edinb. Journ. Sci. vii, pp.* 11–18. 1827.—*Cf.* FORBES.

M

DELTA (Δ) [FORBES, J. D.].—Remarks on the climate of Naples and its vicinity ; with an account of a visit to the Hot Springs of La Pisavella, Nero's Baths.—*Edinb. Journ. Sci. vii, pp.* 263–67. 1827.

DELUC, J. A.—Lettres physiques et morales sur l'histoire de la Terre, etc.—5 vols. 8º. *La Haye, Paris,* 1779, 1780.
Vol. v is in 2 pts.   Another copy has 6 vols.   *See* Vol. ii, pp. 416–27.

DELUC, J. A.—Formation des Montagnes Volcaniques.   Observations au Vésuve et à l'Etna.—8º, *pp.* 19.   *La Haye et Paris,* 1780.

DELUC, J. A.—Observations sur les prismes ou schorls volcaniques, et particulièrement sur ceux de l'Etna.—*Journ. Phys. lii, pp.* 195–205.   *Paris,* 1801.

DELUC, J. A. (fils).—Remarks on the geological theory supported by Mr. Smithson in his paper on a Saline Substance from Mount Vesuvius.—*Phil. Mag. xliii, pp.* 127–40.   *London,* 1814.—*Journ. Phys. Chim., Hist. nat. lxxviii, pp.* 386–98. *Paris,* 1814.

DELVAUX.—Vue du Vésuve et d'une partie du Golfe de Naples. —?, —?   [C.A.]

DEMARD, E.—Extinction des Volcans. Étude sur les Volcans en général et principalement sur les Monts Vésuve et Etna.— *Rouen,* 1873.

DEMBOUV et GAUGEL.—Ombres Chinoises.   Décor de Pleine Mer.—*Metz,* 1843 ?
A litho intended as a transparency ; very fantastic view of Vesuvius.

DEMEUNIER, M.—*See* BRYDONE, P. —A Tour through Sicily and Malta.—(In French.)   1776.

DENZA, F.—Eruzioni del Vesuvio.—*Ann. Scient. Industr. xxviii.   Milano,* 1892.

DEPRAT, J.—Modifications apportées au Cône Vésuvien par l'éruption d'avril 1906. —*Bull. Soc. géol. France, S.* 4, *vi, pp.* 253–55, *figs.   Paris,* 1906.

DEQUEVAUVILLER. — Vue du Vésuve prise sur le bord de la mer et du côté de Portici. —?, —?   [C.A.]

DEQUEVAUVILLER (sculp.).—*See* CHASTELET (del.).—Vue de l'église de Résina, etc., *and* Vue prise près du Portici.

DERHAM, G.—Delle Caverne Sotterranee e de' Monti che vomitano fuoco.—*See* ANON.—Dei Vulcani o Monti Ignivomi, etc.

DEROY.—Naples, Vue prise de Pausilippe. Imp. Lemercier, Paris [1843 ?].

DEROY (lithographiées par).—Vues de Naples.—No. 20.   Paris, Bulla frères, imp. Lemercier.
Six small views : each 121 × 83 mm. The second shows " Palais de la Reine Jeanne," with Vesuvius in the distance. Titles in French and Italian.

DEROY.—Naples, Palais de la Reine Jeanne (Italie No. 116).   Imp. Lemercier à Paris. [B.N.P., Vb. 119.] .
An effective view of Vesuvius by night.

DEROY (des. et lith.).—Italie No. 118. Naples.   Vue prise de Capo di Monte.— Napoli.   Veduta presa da Capo di Monte. Imp. Lemercier, à Paris.   Paris : publié par Jeannin, Place du Louvre 20.   London : publ. by Gambart, Junin & Co., 25, Berner's St., Oxford St.
Litho. on straw ground : 271 × 240 mm.

DESMAREST, N., et BORY DE ST. VINCENT, J. B. M. G., BARON.—Atlas Encyclopédique contenant les cartes et les planches relatives à la Géographie Physique.—4º, *pp.* 120, 48 *pls.   Paris,* 1827.   (*See* Pl. 35.)

DESMOULINS (gravé).—*See* CHASTELET (des.).—Naples.   Vue du Vésuve prise du Mont St. Angelo, etc., *and* Vue d'une partie de la Ville et du Golfe de Naples, etc.

DESPREZ, L. J. (des.).—Naples.   Vue du Bourg de Torre del Greco situé au pied du Vésuve.   Gravé p. Queverdo, Terminé au burin par d'Embrun.   No. 43.   A.P.D.R.
Engrav. : 350 × 233 mm.

DESPREZ, L. J.—*See* PIRANESI.

DESSOULAVY. — [24 pen, pencil-and-ink sketches of S. Italy and Sicily.]—*obl. fol.* 1826.
See No. 5.

DESSOULAVY.—*See* BOSSIS.

DESVERGERS, N.—Sur l'éruption du Vésuve en janvier 1839.—*Nouv. Ann. Voyages, pp.* 197 *et seq.   Paris,* 1839.— *N. J. f. Min. pp.* 720–21.   *Stuttgart,* 1839.

DEVILLE, C. J. SAINTE-CLAIRE.—Quatre lettres à M. Élie de Beaumont sur l'éruption du Vésuve du 1r. mai.—*Bull. Soc. géol. France, xii, pp.* 1065–82.   *Paris,* 1854–55. —*C.R. Acad. Sci. xl, pp.* 1228–29, 1247–64 ; *xli, pp.* 62–67, 487, 593–98.   *Paris,* 1855.— *Zeitschr. deutsch. geol. Gesellsch. vii, pp.* 511–25.   *Berlin,* 1855.   (Transl. by C. Rammelsberg.)

DEVILLE, C. J. SAINTE-CLAIRE.—Observations sur la nature et la distribution des fumeroles dans l'éruption du Vésuve du 1 mai 1855.—*Bull. Soc. géol. France, xiii, pp.* 606–45. *Paris*, 1855–56.

DEVILLE, C. J. SAINTE-CLAIRE.—Recherches sur les produits des Volcans de l'Italie méridionale.—*C.R. Acad. Sci. xlii, pp.* 1167–71. *Paris*, 1856.

DEVILLE, C. J. SAINTE-CLAIRE.—Lettres sur les phénomènes éruptifs du Vésuve et de l'Italie méridionale.—*C.R. Acad. Sci. xliii, pp.* 204–14, 431–35, 533–38, 606–10, 681–86, 745–51, *Paris*, 1856; *liv, pp.* 99–109, 241–52, 328–39, 473–83, 1862.

DEVILLE, C. J. SAINTE-CLAIRE.—Mémoire sur les émanations volcaniques.—*Bull. Soc. géol. France, S.* 2, *xiv, pp.* 254–79. *Paris*, 1856–57. — *C.R. Acad. Sci. xliii, pp.* 955–58, 1856; *xliv, pp.* 58–62. *Paris*, 1857.

DEVILLE, C. J. SAINTE-CLAIRE, et LEBLANC, F.—Sur les émanations gazeuses qui accompagnent l'acide borique dans les Soffioni et Lagoni de la Toscane. (Extr. d'une lettre à M. Élie de Beaumont.)—*C.R. Acad. Sci. xlv, pp.* 750–52. *Paris*, 1857.

DEVILLE, C. J. SAINTE-CLAIRE.—Rapport sur les mémoires relatifs à la composition des gaz rejetés par les évents volcaniques de l'Italie.—*C.R. Acad. Sci. xlv, p.* 1029. *Paris*, 1857.

DEVILLE, C. J. SAINTE-CLAIRE, et LEBLANC, F.—Sur la composition chimique des gaz rejetés par les évents volcaniques de l'Italie Méridionale.—*Bull. Soc.géol.France, S.* 2, *xv, pp.* 310–13. *Paris*, 1858 (2ᵉ *Mém.*). —*C.R. Acad. Sci. xliv, pp.* 769–73. *Paris*, 1857 (1ʳ *Mém.*); *Id. xlv, pp.* 398–402 (2ᵉ *Mém.*).—*Ann. Chim. lii, pp.* 5–63. *Paris*, 1858.—*Journ. Pharm. S.* 3, *xxxiii, pp.* 128–32. *Paris*, 1858.—*Mém. Sav. Étrang. xvi, pp.* 225–76. *Paris*, 1862.

DEVILLE, C. J. SAINTE-CLAIRE.—M. Ch. Sainte-Claire Deville communique l'extrait d'une lettre de M. de Verneuil sur l'état actuel, janvier 1858, du Vésuve et appelle l'attention sur les changements qui se sont opérés depuis 1854 dans le plateau supérieur du volcan.—*C.R. Acad. Sci. xlvi, p.* 117. *Paris*, 1858.—*Bull. Soc. géol. France, S.* 2, *xv, pp.* 369–70. *Paris*, 1858.

DEVILLE, C. J. SAINTE-CLAIRE.—Éruption du Vésuve. — *C.R. Acad. Sci. liii, pp.* 1231–39. *Paris*, 1861.

DEVILLE, C. J. SAINTE-CLAIRE, LEBLANC, F., et FOUQUÉ, F.—Sur les émanations à gaz combustibles, qui se sont échappées des fissures de la lave de 1794, à Torre del Greco, lors de la dernière éruption du Vésuve.—*C.R. Acad. Sci. lv, pp.* 75–76, 1862; *lvi, pp.* 1185–89. *Paris*, 1863.

DEVILLE, C. J. SAINTE-CLAIRE.—[Remarques sur les émanations volcaniques et métallifères.]—*C.R. Acad. Sci. lviii, pp.* 329–33. *Paris*, 1864.

DEVILLE, C. J. SAINTE-CLAIRE.—Remarques [à l'occasion de diverses communications de M. Fouqué concernant les phénomènes éruptifs de l'Italie Méridionale].—*C.R. Acad. Sci. lxi, pp.* 567, 737. *Paris*, 1865.

DEVILLE, C. J. SAINTE-CLAIRE.—M. Ch. Sainte-Claire Deville donne, d'après une lettre que lui écrit de Naples M. Pignant, quelques détails sur une éruption du Vésuve qui paraît avoir commencé le 11 mars 1866.—*C.R. Acad. Sci. lxii, p.* 749. *Paris*, 1866.

DEVILLE, C. J. SAINTE-CLAIRE.—Rapport sur un mémoire de M. Fouqué, intitulé : Recherches sur les phénomènes chimiques des volcans. — *C.R. Acad. Sci. lxii, pp.* 1366–77. *Paris*, 1866.

DEVILLE, C. J. SAINTE-CLAIRE.—Quinzième lettre à M. Élie de Beaumont sur les phénomènes éruptifs de l'Italie méridionale. —*C.R. Acad. Sci. lxiii, pp.* 77–85, 146–54. *Paris*, 1866.

DEVILLE, C. J. SAINTE-CLAIRE.—De la succession des phénomènes éruptifs dans le cratère supérieur du Vésuve après l'éruption de décembre, 1861.—*C.R. Acad. Sci. lxiii, pp.* 237–43. *Paris*, 1866.

DEVILLE, C. J. SAINTE-CLAIRE. — Remarques . . . à l'occasion des deux précédentes communications.—*C.R. Acad. Sci. lxv, pp.* 900–1. *Paris*, 1867.

DEVILLE, C. J. SAINTE-CLAIRE.—[Observations relatives à une communication de M. Diego Franco, intitulée : Faits pour servir à l'histoire éruptive du Vésuve.]—*C.R. Acad. Sci. lxvi, p.* 162. *Paris*, 1868.

DEVILLE, C. J. SAINTE-CLAIRE.—[Observations relatives à une communication de M. Palmieri, intitulée : Faits pour servir à l'histoire éruptive du Vésuve.]—*C.R. Acad. Sci. lxvi, p.* 207. *Paris*, 1868

M 2

DEVILLE, C. J. SAINTE-CLAIRE.—Observations relatives à une communication de M. Silvestri, sur l'éruption actuelle du Vésuve. —*C.R. Acad. Sci. lxvi, p.* 680. *Paris,* 1868.

DEVILLE, C. J. SAINTE-CLAIRE. — Réflexions au sujet des deux communications de M. Diego Franco sur l'éruption actuelle du Vésuve. — *C.R. Acad. Sci. lxvii, pp.* 29–32. *Paris,* 1868.

DEVILLE, C. J. SAINTE-CLAIRE. — Remarques sur une communication de M. Palmieri pour servir à l'histoire éruptive du Vésuve.—*C.R. Acad. Sci. lxvii, p.* 803. *Paris,* 1868.

DEVILLE, C. J. SAINTE-CLAIRE.—Observations relatives à une note de M. H. de Saussure, sur l'éruption du Vésuve en avril 1872.—*C.R. Acad.' Sci. lxxv, p.* 154. *Paris,* 1872.

DEVILLE, C. J. SAINTE-CLAIRE.—M. Ch. Sainte-Claire Deville communique des extraits de lettres de MM. Guiscardi et H. de Saussure, sur la dernière éruption du Vésuve.—*C.R. Acad. Sci. lxxv, p.* 504. *Paris,* 1872.

DEVILLE, C. J. SAINTE-CLAIRE.—Observations sur la prochaine phase d'activité probable du Vésuve.—*C.R. Acad. Sci. lxxvi, p.* 1428. *Paris,* 1873.

DICKENS, CH.—Pictures from Italy (1846). —8⁰, *pp.* 180. *London,* 1892.

DICKERT, T.—*See* NOEGGERATH.— Vesuv und Monte Somma im Relief.

DIDEROT et ALEMBERT, D'.—Encyclopédie ou dictionnaire raisonné des Sciences, des Arts et des Métiers par une société de gens de lettres.—32 vols. *fol.,* 3130 *pls. Paris,* 1751–77.
    See "Minéralogie." 6me Collection : Volcans. 5 pls.
    Pl. I. Æ s. Histoire naturelle : Volcans. Vue génénalle du Vésuve en 1757. 142, 143. 418×308 mm.
    Pl. II. Éruption du Vésuve en 1754. Monaco fecit. 144, 145. 418×312 mm.
    Pl. III. Laves qui sortoient des flancs du Vésuve à la suitte de l'éruption de 1754. Æ s. 146, 147. 428×320 mm.
    Pl. IV. (2 figs.) Sommet du Vésuve. Autre vue du même sommet durant une petite éruption. Æ s. 148. 206×158 mm.

Pl. V. Vue de la Soufrière qui est près de Pouzzole au royaume de Naples appellée Solfatara. 1. Atteliers où l'on travaille pour obtenir l'alun. 2. Source qui bouillonne et qui paraît enflammée. 149, 150. Coarse engrav. : 428×318 mm.

DIDIER, CH.—*See* NORVINS. 1737.

DIEFFENBACH, F.—Die Erdbeben und Vulkanausbrüche des Jahres 1872.—*N. J. f. Min. pp.* 155–63. *Stuttgart,* 1874.

DIEMER, M. ZENO.—Im Krater des Vesuv. —" *Vom Fels zum Meer,*" xv, *p.* 252, *woodcut. Stuttgart,* 1896.

DIEMER, M. ZENO.—Vesuvausbruch. Boscotrecase, 9 April, 1906. [Deutsch. Mus. ; geol. dept. Munich.]
    Water-colour sketch of good quality : 386×490 mm.

DIETRICH, DE [? P. F. VON].—*See* FERBER, J. J. 1776.

DINGESTEDT, C. VON.—Olivin vom Vesuv analysirt.—*Min. Mitth. p.* 130. *Wien,* 1873.

DIODORUS SICULUS.—De Antiquitatibus. Lib. IV.

DIONIS CASSIUS.—Vesævi montis conflagratio, Giorgio Merula interprete.—4⁰, *foll. lxxvi. Milano,* 1503. (Very rare.) [C.A.]

DIONIS CASSIUS. — Historia Romana. Lib. XXVI.

[DOCTOR MYSTICUS.]—Vesuvio. Appunti di viaggio di un congressista della pace venuto a Napoli per verdere Partenope, il Vesuvio e Pompei.—*Gazz'. Com. Vesuv.* xiv. *Portici,* 29 *Nov.,* 1891.

DOELTER, C.—Zur Kenntniss der chemischen Zusammensetzung des Augits.— *Min. Mitth. pp.* 278–96. *Wien,* 1877.— *Zeitschr. f. Kryst. ii, p.* 525. *Leipzig,* 1878.

DOELTER, C. — Krystallographisch-chemische Studien am Vesuvian.—*Zeitschr. f. Kryst. v, pp.* 289–94. *Leipzig,* 1881.— [Abstr.] *N. J. f. Min. (Bd. i, Ref.), pp.* 8–9. *Stuttgart,* 1883.

DOELTER, C. — Erhitzungsversuche an Vesuvian, Apatit, Turmalin.—*N. J. f. Min. ii, pp.* 217–21. *Stuttgart,* 1884.

DOELTER, C.—Ueber einige Beobachtungen bei der Vesuveruption 1906.—*Anz. k. Akad. Wissensch. pp.* 295–98. *Wien,* 1906.

DOGLIONI, N.—Anfiteatro d'Europa, etc.— 4⁰, *pp.* 72 + 1377, *portrait. Venetia*, 1623. *See* p. 694 : Del Monte di Somma, e sua historia.

DOHRN, F. A.—Besteigung des Vesuv während des Ausbruchs in der Nacht vom 1 zum 2 November 1871.—*Westermann's Monatshefte, xxxii, pp.* 53–58. *Braunschweig*, 1871.

DOLOMIEU, D. G. S. T. G. DE.—Mémoire sur les Îles Ponces et catalogue raisonné des produits de l'Etna, pour servir à l'histoire des volcans.—8⁰. *Paris*, 1788. *See* p. 450.

DOLOMIEU, D. G. S. T. G. DE.—Distribution méthodique de toutes les matières dont l'accumulation forme les montagnes volcaniques.—*Journ. Phys. xliv, pp.* 102–25 ; *xlv, pp.* 81–105. *Paris*, 1794.

DOLOMIEU, D. G. S. T. G. DE.—Sur la Leucite ou Grenat blanc.—*Journ. Mines, v, pp.* 177–84. 1796–97.

DOLOMIEU, D. G. S. T. G. DE.—Sur l'éruption du Vésuve de l'an 2.—*Journ. Phys. liii, p.* 1. *Paris*, 1801.

DOMENICHI, J.—Montis Vesuvii alluvio ; ad Lillam. 4 Epigrams in " Castaliæ Stillulæ." — 8⁰, *pp.* 187–90. *Florentiæ*, 1667. [C.A.]

DOMENICIS, G. DE.—[Eruption 1631.] *See* PALOMBA, D., *pp.* 39 and 106. 1881.

DOMIZI, F. S. (RINALDO).—Prodigioso miracolo del nostro gran difensore S. Gennaro d'averci liberati dall' incendio del Vesuvio, e dal terremoto la sera del dì 15 Giugno, 1794.—8⁰, *pp.* 8. *Napoli*, 1794. [B.N.]

DOMNANDO.—[Extract of a letter communicated by M. C. Prévost, dated from Nauplie, 25 novembre 1834, describing the ascents of Etna and Vesuvius.]—*Bull. Soc. géol. France, vi, pp.* 124–25. *Paris*, 1835.

DONALDSON, T. L.—*See* COCKBURN, J. P.—Pompeii.

DONATI, E.—Phenomena observed at the last eruption of Mount Vesuvius in 1828.— *Journ. R. Inst. Gt. Britain, i, pp.* 296–306. *London*, 1831.—*Bibl. univ., Part. Sci. ii, pp.* 73–89. *Genève*, 1831.

DONATO DA SIDERNO. (Attributed to POLIENO DONATO.)—Discorso filosofico et astrologico, nel quale si mostra quanto sia corroso il Monte Vesuvio dal suo primo incendio sino al presente, e quanto habbi da durare detto Incendio.—4⁰, *foll. iv. Napoli*, 1632. [C.A.]

DONNA, V. DI.—L'Università della Torre del Greco nel secolo XVIII.—4⁰, *figs.*, 20 *pls., plan of Torre. Torre del Greco*, 1912.
Refers to the customs and industries of the locality and to the eruptions of Vesuvius during the eighteenth cent., and specially to that of 1794.

DORMAN, H.—Ein Vesuvausbruch. Erinnerung an den April 1872.—8⁰, *pp.* 14. *Naples*, 1882. [C.A.]

DRAGON, DEMETRIO (inc.).—Veduta della eruzione del Vesuvio accaduta la notte dei 14 venendo il 15 di Giugno di quest' anno 1794 e della rovina della Torre del Greco che faceva circa 18 mila anime, e resto quasi tutta atterrata della lava della eruzione. Tav. XI. [B.N.P., Vb. 121.]

DUCHANOY.—Détails sur la dernière éruption du Vésuve 1779.—*Observ. s. la phys. xvi, pp.* 3–16. *Paris*, 1780.

DUCHANOY. — Esatta descrizione dell' ultima eruzione del Vesuvio.—*Osservazione appartenente alla fisica, alla storia naturale ed alle arti*, 8⁰, *pp.* 36. 1780. [C.A.]

DUCLOS, C. P.—Voyage en Italie, ou Considérations sur l'Italie.—8⁰, *pp. viii*+412. *Paris*, 1791.

DUCOS, B.—Itinéraire et souvenirs d'un Voyage en Italie en 1819 et 1820.—4 vols. 8⁰, *maps. Paris*, 1829. *See* Vol. ii.

DUFRÉNOY, O. P. A. P.—Mémoire sur les terrains volcaniques des environs de Naples. *C.R. Acad. Sci. i, pp.* 353–56. *Paris*, 1835. —*Notiz. aus d. Geb. d. Natur- u. Heilkunde, xlvi, coll.* 225–30. *Erfurt und Weimar*, 1835.—*Edinb. New Phil. Journ. xx, pp.* 126–30. *Edinburgh*, 1836.—*Ann. Mines, S. 3, xi, pp.* 113–58, 369–86, 389–434, *pls. ii and viii. Paris*, 1837.—*Proc. Verb. Acad. Philom. pp.* 61–64. *Paris*, 1837.— *Mém. pr. servir à une description géologique de la France*, 8⁰, *foll.* 4, *pp.* 227–386, 9 *pls., figs. Paris*, 1838.—*Nouv. Ann. Voyages, lxx, pp.* 64–70. *Paris*, 1836.

DUFRÉNOY, O. P. A. P.—Parallèle entre les différents produits volcaniques des environs de Naples et rapport entre leur composition et les phénomènes qui les ont produits.—*Bull. Soc. géol. France, ix, pp.* 334–37. *Paris,* 1837–38.—*Ann. Chim. lxix, pp.* 95–100. *Paris,* 1838. — *Ann. Mines, xiii, pp.* 565–84. *Paris,* 1838.— *C.R. Acad. Sci. vi, pp.* 813–16. *Paris,* 1838.

DUFRÉNOY, O. P. A. P., et ÉLIE DE BEAUMONT, J.B.A.L.L.—Recherches sur les terrains volcaniques des Deux-Siciles, comparés à ceux de la France centrale.—*See their* "Mém. pr. servir à une descript. géol. de la France," *iv, pp.* 284-386. *Paris,* 1838.

DUGIT, E.—Une ascension au Vésuve et à l'Etna.—*Ann. Soc. Touristes Dauphiné,* 6. *Grenoble,* 1880.

DULAC, A.—Compte rendu de l'histoire du Vésuve par Della Torre.—*Mélanges d'Hist. Nat. iv, pp.* 375–401, *1 pl. Lyon,* 1765.

DUMAS, ALEX.—*See* NORVINS. 1737.

DUMONT.—Plan du Mont-Vésuve, tel qu'il étoit en 1750. [B.N.P., Vb. 121.] *See* SOUFFLOT. An engraved plate.

DUNIN DE BORKOWSKY, S.—Sur la sodalite du Vésuve.—4⁰, *pp.* 7. *Paris,* 1816.—*Ann. Mines, i, pp.* 451–52. *Paris,* 1817.—*Journ. Phys. Chem. Hist. nat. lxxxiii, pp.* 428–34. *Paris,* 1816.—*Ann. Phil., or Mag. Chem. Min. x, pp.* 192–97. *London,* 1817.—*Ann. Phys. lxiii, pp.* 382–87. *Halle u. Leipzig,* 1819.

DUPERRON DE CASTERA.—Histoire du Mont Vésuve avec l'explication des phénomènes qui ont coûtume d'accompagner les embrasements de cette montagne, le tout traduit de l'Italien de l'Académie des Sciences de Naples.—8⁰, *pp. xx+iv+*361+ 3, *3 pls. Paris,* 1741. [O.V.] *See* SERAO.

DUPPA, R.—The crater of Mount Vesuvius from an original sketch made in the year 1797 by . . . Lowry, sculp. — (London) Published as the Act directs, May 1st, 1802, by Longman and Rees, Paternoster Row.
A bǎdly drawn line-engrav. of crater seen from W. edge : 228×168 mm.

DUPUY.—*See* TAVERNIER.

DURER, G.—Saggio di cataloghi per ordine di materie della libreria antica e moderna. 1⁰. Vulcani e tremuoti.—12⁰, *pp.* 104. *Napoli,* 1866.

DURIER, C.—Le Vésuve et Capri.—*Ann. Club Alp. Franç. xxii* (1895), *pp.* 404–64, *7 pls.* 1896.

DURIER, E.—Le Vésuve en septembre 1878.

DURINI, B.—Conghiettura geologica sulla cagione dei Vulcani.—*Giorn. Encicl. vii, pp.* 23. *Napoli,* 1841. [O.V.]

EASTGATE (sc.).—View of the enormous cloud of smoke, etc., from Mount Vesuvius, June 18, 1794.
Engrav. similar to plate in Hamilton's " 84 Vedute " : 184×280 mm.

EASTMAN, C. R.—Disputed Vesuvian eruptions.—" *Science,*" *N.S. xxiv, .pp.* 284–86. *London,* 1906.

EASTMAN, C. R.—Les éruptions du Vésuve pendant la première partie du Moyen-Âge. —*Rev. Scient. S.* 5, *vii, pp.* 37–42, *fig. Paris,* 1907.

ECHARDT.—*See* WUTKY.

EDWARDS, A. B.—Lord Brackenbury. A novel.—2 vols. Tauchnitz ed.—*Leipzig,* 1880.
See Vol. ii, pp. 248 *et seq.,* for a descript. of the erupt. of 1872.

EDWARDS, J.—*See* SMITH, J. 1796.

ÉLIE DE BEAUMONT, J. B. A. L. L.— [Remarques sur une note de M. Constant Prévost relative à une communication de M. L. Pilla, tendant à prouver que le cône du Vésuve a été primitivement formé par soulèvement.] — *C.R. Acad. Sci. iv, pp.* 554–55. *Paris,* 1837.

ÉLIE DE BEAUMONT, J. B. A. L. L.— Valeurs numériques des pentes des principales coulées de lave dans les différentes contrées volcaniques de l'Europe.—*Mém. pr. servir à une descript. géol. de la France, iv, pp.* 217–21. *Paris,* 1838.

ÉLIE DE BEAUMONT, J. B. A. L. L.— Note sur les émanations volcaniques et métallifères. ⊸ [Estr.] *Bull. Soc. géol. France, S.* 2, *iv, pt.* 2, *pp.* 1249–334. *Paris,* 1847.

ÉLIE DE BEAUMONT, J. B. A. L. L.— *See* DUFRÉNOY.

ELISEO, N. A.—Rationalis methodus curandi febres, flagrante Væsevo subortas.— 8⁰. Pars prima, *pp.* 160 ; Pars secunda, *foll.* 2, *pp.* 160. *Napoli,* 1634. [C.A.] ——Another ed. 8⁰, *foll.* 2, *pp.* 160, *with new frontisp. and ded.* 1645.

EMANUEL MONACUS.—Vita S. Januarii
E. M., in greco e latino.—4⁰, *pp.* 32. *Ex
typi Montis Cassini*, 1875. [C.A.]
At the end a description of the eruption
of A.D. 472, followed by another of the
eruption of 685.

EMES, J.—*See* SMITH, J. 1796.

EMILIE, F. (delin.).—The south prospect of
Mount Vesuvio with the town of Portici
and Recina built upon the ancient city
of Herculana which was destroy'd by an
earthquake and eruption of that Mountain
the first of November '81. Taken from a
fort of the sea side at a time of an eruption
Anno 1731. C. Mosley, Sculp. Publish'd according to Act of Parliament
July 3, 1749.
Four ref. nos. Engrav. : 712×356 mm.

EMILIO, L. D'.—La conflagrazione Vesuviana del 27 Aprile 1872.—8⁰, *foll. iv, pp.* 27.
Napoli, 1872. [C.A.]

EMILIO, L. D'.—Della conflagrazione Vesuviana del 26 Aprile 1872.—2a ed. [Estr. d.
giorn.] "*La Scuola Italica*," 16⁰, *pp.* 50.
Napoli, 1873.

ENFANTIN.—*See* COIGNET, M.—Vues
pittoresques de l'Italie, etc.

ENGENIO CARACCIOLO, C. D'.—*See*
BELTRANO, O.

ESPIN, C. E. [? T. E.]—The Volcanoes of
Central Italy.

ESPIN, T. E.—A Possible Factor in Volcanic
Eruptions.—*Publ. Wolsingham Observ.* 8⁰,
pp. 10, 2 *figs. Tow Law, Darlington.
Crook*, 1902.

ESQUILACHE, PRINCIPE DE. — Soneto.
(1631.) — *See* QUINONES. — El Monte
Vesvvio.

ESTATICO (pseud.).—Dissertazione intorno
all' eruzione del Vesuvio del 1751.—8⁰,
pp. 27. *Napoli*, 1752. [O.V.]

ETZOLD, DR. FRANZ.—Die jüngste Eruption des Vesuvs im Juni 1891.—*Naturwissensch. Wochenschr. vi*, 36, *pp.* 361-
63. *Berlin*, 1891.

EUGENIUS, A. DE.—Il maraviglioso e
tremendo incendio del Vesuvio detto a
Napoli la Montagna di Somma nel 1631.—
4⁰, *pp.* 20. *Napoli*, 1631.

EWALD, J. W.—Ueber Petrefakten führende
Gesteine der Somma.—*Zeitschr. deutsch.
geol. Gesellsch. vii, pp.* 302-3. *Berlin*,
1855.

EYLES STILES, SIR F. H.—An account of
an eruption of Mount Vesuvius : in a letter
to Philip Carteret Webb, Esq.; F.R.S.—
Phil. Trans. R. Soc. lii, Pt. 1 (1761), *pp.*
39-40. *London*, 1762.

EYLES STILES, SIR F. H. — Another
account of the same eruption of Mount
Vesuvius : in a letter to Daniel Wray, Esq.;
F.R.S.—*Ibidem, pp.* 41-44.

F. A. A.—Dialoghi sul Vesuvio in occasione
dell' eruzione della sera de' 15 giugno 1794.
Parlono Aletoscopo e Didascofilo.—8⁰, *pp.*
52. *Napoli*, 1794. [C.A.]

FABRIS.—[Twenty Views of Naples and
its environs.]—Engrav. by Sandby and
Robertson, 1777-82. [B.M.—K. 7, tab.
60.]
Fine views, but of little geol. interest.

FABRIS, P.—Eruzione del Vesuvio succe-
duta il giorno 8 di Agosto dell' anno 1779,
all' ora 1½ di notte o circa, veduta da un
luogo vicino al Real Casino in Posilipo.
—[B.S.]
Copper engrav. fol. by F. Giomignani.

FADDEN, W.—*See* RIZZI-ZANNONI, G. A.
1803.

FALB, R.—Gedanken und Studien über den
Vulkanismus, etc.—8⁰, *tav. Graz*, 1875.

FALCO, B. DI.—Antichità di Napoli, e del
suo amenissimo distretto.—8⁰, *pp.* 64,
1 *fig. Napoli*, 1679.—*See also* CAMPI
PHLEGRÆI.
This is the oldest guide to Naples
in which Vesuvius and the Solfatara are
mentioned.

FALCONE, N. C.—L'intera istoria della
famiglia, vita, miracoli, translazione e culto
del glorioso martire S. Gennaro.—4⁰, *foll.
viii, pp.* 526, *figs. Napoli*, 1713. [C.A.]
See Cap. IX, pp. 502 to end.

FALCONE, S.—Discorso naturale delle cause
ed effetti causati nell' incendio del Monte
Vesuvio, con relatione del tutto.—4⁰, *foll.
xxii. Napoli*, 1632.

FALCONI, B. A. DELLI.—Gli terrori del
titubante Vesuvio.—8⁰, *pp.* 24. *Napoli*,
1632.

FARIA, L.—Relacion cierta y verdadera de
el incendio de la Montaña de Somma, ecc.
—*sm. fol., pp.* 8. *Napoles*, 1631.

FARIA, L.—Relacion de l'incendio del
Vesuvio.—4⁰. *Napoles*, 1632.

FARINA, A.—Compendio delle cose piv cvriose di Napoli, e di Pozzvoli. Con alcune notitie del regno.—16⁰, *foll.* 5, *pp.* 111. *Napoli*, 1679.

FARRAR, A. S.—The earthquake at Melfi in 1851, and recent eruption of Vesuvius in 1855.—*Abst. Proc. Ashmolean Soc.* 34, *pp.* 91–96. *Oxford*, 1856.

FARRAR, A. S.—On the late eruption of Vesuvius.—*Rept. British Assoc.* (1855), *Notices and Abstracts*, p. 55. *London*, 1856.

FATA, ABATE.—Miscellanea Vesuviana. *See* XXIX, B. 142.

FAUJAS DE SAINT-FOND, B.—Recherches sur les Volcans éteints du Vivarais et du Velay ; avec un discours sur les Volcans brûlans.—*fol., foll.* 2, *pp.* 20+460, 20 *pls.*, 2 *maps. Grenoble et Paris*, 1778.

FAUJAS DE SAINT-FOND, B.—Sur l'éruption du Vésuve de l'année dernière.—*In* ROZIER et MONGEZ.—Observations sur la physique, *xv, pp.* 256–363. *Paris*, 1780.

FAUJAS DE SAINT-FOND, B.—Minéralogie des Volcans, ou description de toutes les substances produites, ou rejetées par les feux souterrains.—8⁰, *pp. xviii*+511, 3 *pls. Paris*, 1784.—German ed. 1786.

FAUJAS DE SAINT-FOND, B.—Classification des Produits Volcaniques.—4⁰, *pp.* 24. [*Paris*, 1804.]

FAVELLA, G.—Abbozzo delle ruine fatte dal Monte di Somma con il seguito incendio insino ad hoggi 23 di Gennaro 1632.—4⁰, *pp.* 16. *S. Roncagliolo, Napoli*, 1632. [C.A.]

FAZZINI, G.—Cenno sulla Pozzolana della Baja di Napoli.—4⁰, *pp.* 21. *Napoli*, 1857.

FELBER.—*See* NESTEMANN.

FENICE, I.—Lo struppio della Montagna de Somma, in rima Napoletana.—8⁰, *foll. iv. Napoli*, 1632.

FER, C. G. N. DE.—Description du Mont Vésuve tel que l'auteur l'a vu en 1667.— *fol.* 1, 1 *pl.* — ?, — ?

FER, N. DE.—Les environs de la ville de Naples dans la Province de Labour avec la routte de cette ville à Rome. Vincent de Ginville scripsit.—*Paris*, [? 1706.] [B.M. —K. 83.47.] Vesuvius is shown ejecting flames.

FER, N. DE.—Description du Mont-Vésuve, ou Montagne de Somma. —?, —? [Vienna lib.] Engraved text of 28 lines of descript.: 224×157 mm.

FER, N. DE.—Le Mont Vésuve ou Montagne de Somma près de Naples. Avec Priv. du Roi. [B.N.P. Vb. 121.] Fantastic view of Vesuvius with description and small plan of interior of crater in top right corner, entitled : " Coupe du Mont Vésuve 101," and explan. in text. Rough engrav. : 336×227 mm.

FERBER, J. J.—Briefe aus Welschland über natürliche Merkwürdigkeiten dieses Landes. —*Prag*, 1773. *See* 11th letter.

FERBER, J. J.—Lettres à Mr. le Chev. de Born sur la Minéralogie, et sur divers autres objets d'histoire naturelle de l'Italie, traduit de l'Allemand, enrichi de notes et d'observations faites sur les lieux par M. de Dietrich.—8⁰, *pp.* 16+508. *Strasburg and Paris*, 1776.—English transl. by R. E. Raspe : " With explanations, notes and a preface on the present state and future improvement of mineralogy."—8⁰, *pp. xxxiii*+377. *London*, 1776. *See* Letter XI, pp. 160–274, Napoli, 17 Feb. 1772 : long descript. of Vesuvius, etc.

FERGOLA, L[UIGI] (dis. dal vero).—Veduta della trigesima eruzione di fuoco fatta dal Vesuvio li 8 Agosto 1779. Vue de la trentième éruption de feu du Mont Vésuve arrivée à 8 Août 1779, T. XIII. Gennaro Bartoli inc. 1804. In Napoli presso Franc. Scafa. Str. S. Biagio de' Librari. N⁰ 117. Engrav. : 256×199 mm.

FERGOLA, LUIGI.—Veduta di Napoli dalla parte di Mergellina. Vincenzo Aloja inc. Napoli, 1804. [B.N.P. Vb. 116.]

FERGOLA, LUIGI.—Veduto di un sepolcro antico sopra la collina detto ' Scudillo ' a Napoli. Vincenzo Aloja inc. [Napoli ?] 1804. [B.N.P. Vb. 119.] Shows three columns of smoke over Vesuvius.

FERGOLA, L[UIGI].—*See* HACKERT, PH. —Raccolta di XXV vedute.

FERGOLA, L[UIGI].—Recueil des vues [25 and frontisp.] les plus agréables de Naples et de ses environs . . . dessinées d'après nature par L. F. et gravées par V. Aloja.— *obl. fol. Naples* [1817]. *See* Nos. 4, 8, 12, 13 (2), 24. Also HACKERT, GRASSI and FERGOLA.

FERRARA, M.—Lettera sull' analisi della cenere del Vesuvio eruttata dal 16 al 18 giugno 1794.—4⁰, *pp.* 14. *Napoli*, 1794.

FERRARI, G. B. DE.—Nuova Guida di Napoli, dei contorni, di Procida, Ischia e Capri compilata su la Guida del Vasi ed altre opere più recenti.—1st ed. 8⁰, *pp.* 320, 4 *pls. Napoli*, 1826.——Another, called also 1st ed., in English and Italian, 12⁰, *pp.* 671, 4 *pls. Napoli*, 1839.
See pp. 192-213 (eruption 1822), 1826 ; pp. 422-48 and pl., 1839.

FERREIRA-VILLARINO, G.—Vera relatione di un spaventoso prodigio seguito nell' Isola di S. Michele alli 2 di Settembre di questo presento anno 1630, tradotta dal Portoghese in Italiano.—1st ed. 8⁰. *Roma*, 1630.——2nd ed. (on the occasion of the erupt. of 1631), 12⁰, *foll.* 4. *Napoli*, 1632.

FIECHTER, A.—*See* MATTEUCCI, R. V. 1906.

FIECHTER, [A.]—Il Vesuvio [map] (a) Riduzione delle antiche levate al 10,000 riconosciuto nel 1900. (b) Riduzione della levata a 10,000 eseguito nel 1900 e riconosciuto nel 1906. Scala 1 : 25,000.—*Ist. Geog. Milit. Ital.* 1908.
Six-tinted map extending from Portici to S. Giuseppe, and Pompei to Somma Vesuviana : 660×625 mm.

FIELDING and WALKER (publ.).—View of the eruption of Mount Vesuvius, Augᵗ. 8, 1779, from Pausilipo. Published 1ˢᵗ Octoʳ, 1780, by Fielding and Walker, in Paternoster Row.
A fine engrav., contained in original copy of Hamilton's Campi Phlegræi in B.M. : 160×94 mm.

FIGUIER, L.—Revue scientifique (éruption du Vésuve).—*Feuilleton de la Presse, samedi,* 18 *janvier,* 1862. [C.A.]

FILERT, J. C.—De montibus ignovomis.— 4⁰, *foll.* 11. *Witteb.* 1661. [O.V.]

FILLICIDIO, IL.—Sul Vesuvio.—Anacreontica.—4⁰, *pp.* 8. *Naples* [*circa* 1790].

[FILOMARINO, CLEMENTE.] — Stanze a Crinatéa di Tersalgo Lidiaco P. A.—4⁰, *pp.* 10. — ?, — ?
Treats of the eruption of Vesuvius of 79 and of the death of Pliny.

FIORDELISI, N.—Lettera all' Arcidiacono Cagnazzi sulla elettricità della cenere del Vesuvio.—*Giorn. Encicl. No.* 7, *pp.* 7. *Napoli*, 1806. [C.A.]

FISCHER, L. H.—Eine Reise nach dem Vesuv.—*Oestr. Touristen-Zeitung,ii. Wien,* 1882.

FISCHER, TH.—Das Halbinselland Italien. —*In* Kirchhoff's " Länderkunde von Europa," *pp.* 285-515. *Prag, Wien, Leipzig,* 1890.

FISCHETTI, OD. (del.).—Veduta prima. Prospetto del Vesuvio innanzi l'eruzione del anno 1631. Première vue, état du Vésuve avant l'éruption de l'année 1631. Vinc. Scarpati inc. T. I. In Napoli presso Franc. Scafa. Str. S. Biagio de' Librari. N⁰ 117.
257×199 mm.

FISCHETTI, OD. (dis.).—Veduta terza. Ventiduesima eruzione del anno 1737. Troisième vue, vingt-deuxième éruption en l'année 1737. Vinc. Scarpati inc. T. III. In Napoli presso Franc. Scafa. Str. S. Biagio de' Librari. N⁰ 117.
Engrav. : 252×200 mm.

FISCHETTI, O[D]. (dis.).—Veduta della 24ᵐᵃ eruzione del Monte Vesuvio accaduta l'anno 1754. Vue de la 24ᵐᵉ éruption du Mont Vésuve en 1754. Vinc. Scarpati inc. T. VI. In Napoli presso Franc. Scafa. Str. S. Biagio de' Librari. N⁰ 117.
Engrav. : 243×203 mm.

FISCHETTI, O[D]. (dis.).—Veduta decimaterza del cratere del anno 1775 con le varie fumarole. Vue treizième du cratère en l'année 1775 avec les diverses fumaroles. Gennaro Bartoli inc. T. XII. In Napoli presso Franc. Scafa. Str. S. Biagio de' Librari. N⁰ 117.
Engrav. : 258×199 mm.

FISCHETTI, O[D]. (dis.).—Vedute dell' eruzione de' 12 Agosto 1805 disegnata il giorno 19 dello stesso mese. Vue de l'éruption arrivée le 12 août 1805. Gennaro Bartoli inc. T. XXV. In Napoli presso Nicola Gervasi al Gigante di Palazzo. N⁰ 23.
Line engrav. : 252×173 mm. Vesuvius in eruption, lava flowing near Bellavista. Man leading donkey in foreground.

FISCHETTI, O[D]. (dis.).—Veduta dell' eruzione de 12 Agosto 1805 disegnata il giorno 19 dello stesso mese. Vue de l'éruption arrivée le 12 août 1805 dessinée le jour 19 du même mois. Gennaro Bartoli inc. T. XXV. In Napoli presso Franc. Scafa. Str. S. Biagio de' Librari. N⁰ 117.
Engrav. : 254×198 mm.

FISCHIETTI, O.—*See* FISCHETTI, O.

FITZGERALD, LADY (del.).—View of Torre del Greco taken on the 8th day after the eruption of Vesuvius, on the 15th of June, 1794. J. Barnett sc.—*Cent. Mag., Pl.* I, *p.* 393. *May*, 1822.
Engrav. : 166 × 107 mm.

FLORENZANO, G.—Accanto al Vesuvio. Salmo.—8°, *pp.* 12. *Napoli*, 1872. [C.A.]

FLORES, E.—La scoperta dell' Helium nelle sublimazioni Vesuviane.—*Riv. " La Gioventù Italiana,"* i, 7, *p.* 5. *Bologna*, 1909.

FLORUS, L. A.—L'Héracléade ou Herculaneum enseveli sous la lave du Vésuve. Poème traduit en vers français avec des notes par I. F. S. Maizony de Lauréal.—8°, *foll. ii, pp. xxi+*458, 1 *map. Paris*, 1837. [C.A.]

FLOTTES, L. — Géologie des environs de Rome et du Vésuve.—*Bull. Soc. Hist. nat. xiii, pp.* 252-55. *Toulouse*, 1879.

FOERSTER, O. — Kleine illustrirte Geschichte des Vesuvs und besonders seiner Tätigkeit in den letzten 10 Jahren.—*maps and num. figs. Neapel*, 1908.

FONSECA, F. DE.—Observations géognostiques sur la Sarcolite et la Melilite du Mont Somma.—*Bull. Soc. géol. France, iv, pp.* 14-20. *Paris*, 1846-47.

FONTANELLA, GIROLAMO.—L'incendio rinovato del Vesuvio. Ode.—12°, *pp.* 24. *Napoli*, 1632. [C.A.]

FORBES, G.—The Observatory on Mount Vesuvius.—*" Nature," vi, pp.* 145-48, 4 *illustr. London and New York*, 1872.

FORBES, G. — Palmieri's Vesuvius.— *" Nature," vii, pp.* 259-61, 1 *illustr. London and New York*, 1873.

[FORBES, J. D.] (signed Δ).—Remarks on Mount Vesuvius.—*Edinb. Journ. Sci. vii,* 13, *pp.* 11-18. *Edinburgh*, 1827.—*Froriep. Notiz. xviii, coll.* 129-36. *Erfurt u. Weimar,* 1827.

FORBES, J. D.—*See* DELTA. 1827.

[FORBES, J. D.] (signed Δ).—Physical notices of the Bay of Naples : No. 1. On Mount Vesuvius.—*Edinb. Journ. Sci. ix,* 18, *pp.* 189-213, 1 *tav. Edinburgh*, 1828.

[FORBES, J. D.] (signed Δ).—Physical notices of the Bay of Naples : No. 2. On the buried cities of Herculaneum, Pompeii, and Stabiæ. [With note on Mount Vesuvius.]—*Edinb. Journ. Sci. x, pp.* 108-36. *Edinburgh*, 1829.

FORBES, J. D.—Physical notices of the Bay of Naples : No. 8. Concluding view of the volcanic formations of the district, with notes upon the whole series.—*Edinb. Journ. Sci. N.S. iii, pp.* 246-77. *Edinburgh*, 1830.

FORBES, J. D.—Sixth letter on Glaciers.— *Edinb. New Phil. Journ. pp.* 231-49. *Edinburgh*, 1844. (*See pp.* 232 *et seq.*)

FORBES, J. D.—Analogy of Glaciers to Lava Streams.—*Phil. Trans. R. Soc. pp.* 147-55. *London*, 1846.

FORBES, W. A.—A visit to Vesuvius.—*Rept. Winchester Coll. of the Nat. Hist. Soc.* 1875.

FORDYCE, W.—Memoirs concerning Herculaneum, the subterranean city lately discovered at the foot of Vesuvius, etc.—8°, *pp.* 4+68. *London*, 1750. See pp. 10-15.

FOREST, J.—Le Vésuve ancien et moderne. —8°, *pp.* 22. *Lyon*, 1858.

FORLEO, G.—Meteorico discorso sopra i segni, cause, . . . dei terremoti et incendii di diverse parti della terra . . . e causa dell' incendio della Montagna di Somma.— 4°, *foll.* 6. *Napoli, S. Roncagliolo*, 1632.

FORSTER, C. (publ.).—Literary Magazine and British Review. View of Mount Vesuvius with part of the Bay of Naples. Published according to Act of Parliament, Septber 1, 1788, by C. Forster, N° 41, Poultry.
Engrav. pl. : 167 × 119 mm.

FORTUNATO, G.—Ascensione notturna al Vesuvio.—*In* " Ricordi di Napoli," 16°, *pp.* 135-45. *Milano*, 1877.

FOUGEROUX DE BONDAROY.—Sur le Vésuve.—*Hist. Acad. R. Sci.* (1760), *pp.* 7-16 ; *Mém. pp.* 70-99. *Paris*, 1769.

FOUGEROUX DE BONDAROY.—Recherches sur les ruines d'Herculaneum et sur les lumières qui peuvent en résulter relativement à l'état présent des Sciences et des Arts.—8°, *pp. xvi+*226, 3 *pls. Paris*, 1770. [C.A.]

FOUQUÉ, F. A.—*See* DEVILLE, C. J. SAINTE-CLAIRE. 1862.

FOUQUÉ, F. A.—Sur les phénomènes éruptifs de l'Italie méridionale. Sixième lettre à Ch. Sainte-Claire Deville.—*C.R. Acad. Sci. lxi, pp.* 734-37. *Paris*, 1865.

FOUQUÉ, F. A.—Recherches sur les phénomènes chimiques des Volcans. (Résumé et conclusions.)—*C.R. Acad. Sci. lxii, pp.* 616-17. *Paris*, 1866.

FOUQUÉ, F. A.—Étude microscopique et analyse médiate d'une ponce du Vésuve.—*C.R. Acad. Sci. lxxix, pp.* 869–72. *Paris,* 1874.

FOUQUÉ, F. A., LÉVY, A. MICHEL.—Production artificielle d'une leucotéphrite identique aux laves cristallines du Vésuve et de la Somma. Formes naissantes cristallitiques de la leucite et de la néphéline ; étude optique des cristaux élémentaires de ces minéraux.—*Bull. Soc. Min. France, iii, pp.* 118–23, 4 *figs. Paris,* 1880.—*Boll. R. Com. Geol. Ital. pp.* 177–78. *Roma,* 1881.

FOUQUÉ, F. A.—Conférence sur les Volcans. —8°, *pp.* 20. *Lille,* 1885.

FOUQUÉ, F. A.—Sur les matériaux de construction employés à Pompéi.—8°, *pp.* 6. *Paris,* 1886.

FOUQUÉ, F. A.—Contribution à l'étude des Feldspaths des Roches Volcaniques.—8°, *pp.* 336. *Paris,* 1894.

FRANCESCO II.—Lettera a S⁴ Em. il Cardinale Arc° di Napoli pe' danneggiati di Torre del Greco. Eruzione del 1861.—*pp.* 14. *Napoli,* 1862. [C.A.]

FRANCO, D.—Faits pour servir à l'histoire éruptive du Vésuve.—*C.R. Acad. Sci. lxvi, pp.* 159–62. *Paris,* 1868.

FRANCO, D.—Excursion au cratère du Vésuve le 21 février 1868.—*C.R. Acad. Sci. lxvi, pp.* 1350–53. *Paris,* 1868.

FRANCO, D.—Excursion faite, le 17 mars 1868, à la nouvelle bouche qui s'est ouverte à la base orientale du Vésuve.—*C.R. Acad. Sci. lxvii, pp.* 59–60. *Paris,* 1868.

FRANCO, D.—Sur l'éruption d'avril 1872, au Vésuve.—*C.R. Acad. Sci. lxxv, pp.* 221–24. *Paris,* 1872.

FRANCO, D.—L'acido carbonico del Vesuvio. —*Atti R. Ist. Incorag. S.* 2, *ix, Appendice, pp.* 1–4. *Napoli,* 1872.—*Ann. Chim. xxx, pp.* 87–114. *Paris,* 1873.

FRANCO, P.—Memorie per servire alla Carta Geologica del Monte Somma. Memoria Prima.—*Rend. R. Acc. Sci. xxii, pp. i–xiii. Napoli,* 1883.

FRANCO, P.—Il Vesuvio ai tempi di Spartaco e di Strabone.—*Atti Acc. Pontaniana, xvii, Appendice, pp.* 1–28, 2 *pls. Napoli,* 1887.

FRANCO, P.—Ricerche micropetrografiche intorno ad una pirossenandesite trovata nella regione Vesuviana.—*Rend. R. Acc. Sci. S.* 2, *ii, pp.* 464–71. *Napoli,* 1888.

FRANCO, P.—I massi rigettati dal Monte di Somma detti lava a breccia.—4°, *pp.* 16, 1 *pl. Napoli,* 1889.

FRANCO, P.—Fonolite trasportata dalla lava del Vesuvio nell' eruzione del 1872.—*Boll. Soc. Nat. S.* 1, *iv, pp.* 25–28. *Napoli,* 1890.

FRANCO, P.—Quale fu la causa che demolì la parte meridionale del cratere del Somma. —*Atti Soc. Ital. Sci. Nat. xxxii, pp.* 65–95. *Milano,* 1890.

FRANCO, P.—Studii sull' Idocrasia del Vesuvio (Monte Somma). Nota preliminare.—*Boll. Soc. Nat. iv, pp.* 173–89. *Napoli,* 1890.—*Zeitschr. f. Kryst. u. Min. xx, p.* 616. *Leipzig,* 1892.

FRANCO, P.—Studii sull' Idocrasia del Monte Somma.—*Boll. Soc. Geol. Ital. xi, pp.* 245–91, 3 *tav. Roma,* 1892.—*Giorn. Min. Crist. Petrog. iv,* 3. *Pavia,* 1893.

FRANCO, P.—Sull' Analcime del Monte Somma.—*Giorn. Min. Crist. Petrog. iii,* 3, *pp.* 5, 2 *pls. Pavia,* 1892.

FRANCO, P.—Sull' Aftalosa del Vesuvio.—*Giorn. Min. Crist. Petrog. iv,* 2, *pp.* 5, 5 *figs. Pavia,* 1893.

FRANCO, P.—Sulle costanti geometriche dell' Ortoclasia del Vesuvio e costanti ottiche della Mizzonite.—*Giorn. Min. Crist. Petrog. v, pp.* 184–92, 4 *tab.,* 1 *pl. Pavia,* 1894.

FRANCO, P., GALDIERI, A.—L'Eruzione del Vesuvio nel mese di Luglio del 1895.—*Soc. Alp. Merid. iii,* 3, *pp.* 194–204. *Napoli,* 1895.

FRANCO, P., GALDIERI, A.—Escursioni al Vesuvii.—*Soc. Alp. Merid. iv,* 1, *pp.* 9. *Napoli,* 1896.

FRANCO, P.—La lava Vesuviana di Luglio 1895.—*Boll. Soc. Nat. xi, pp.* 82–100, 2 *tav. Napoli,* 1897.

FRANCO, P.—Le sublimazioni saline dell' ultima eruzione Vesuviana.—*Rend. R. Acc. Sci. S.* 3, *iii, pp.* 192–96. *Napoli,* 1897.

FRANCO, P.—Se il cono del Vesuvio esistesse prima del 79.—*Boll. Soc. Geol. Ital. xviii, pp.* 41–44. *Roma,* 1899.

FRANCO, P.—Sulle fiamme recentemente osservate al Vesuvio.—*Boll. Soc. Nat. xii, pp.* 70–71. *Napoli,* 1899.

FRANCO, P.—L'attività vulcanica nella Campania secondo la tradizione e la storia. —*Boll. Soc. Nat. xvi, pp.* 260–88. *Napoli,* 1903.

FRANCO, P. — *See* JOHNSTON-LAVIS, H. J.

FRAN^co LELIO, MARCHESE.—Narratione di molte cose auuenute nel regno di Napoli nel gouerno di Don Pierro di Toledo, e d'alcune fameglie nobili del regno.—MS. 8⁰, *pp.* 116. *See* p. 18.

FREDA, G.—Sulla presenza del Moliddeno nella Sodalite Vesuviana.—*Rend. R. Acc. Sci. xvii, pp.* 88–90. *Napoli,* 1878.

FREDA, G.—Altre sperienze su la Sodalite Vesuviana.—*Rend. R. Acc. Sci. xvii, pp.* 136–37. *Napoli,* 1878.

FREDA, G.—Sulla presenza dell' acido Antimonioso in un prodotto Vesuviano.—*Rend. R. Acc. Sci. xviii, pp.* 12–15. *Napoli,* 1879.

FREDA, G.—Millerite del Vesuvio.—*Rend. R. Acc. Sci. xix, pp.* 84–85. *Napoli,* 1880.

FREDA, G.—Sulla Linarite rinvenuta nel cratere Vesuviano.—*Rend. R. Acc. Sci. xxii, pp.* 141–43. *Napoli,* 1883.

FREDA, G. — Note Mineralogiche. Sulla Humite verde del Monte Somma, etc.— *Rend. R. Acc. Sci. xxii, pp.* 248–52. *Napoli,* 1883.

FREDA, G.—Breve cenno sulla composizione chimica e sulla giacitura dell Moliddenite, Galena, Pirrotina, Blenda e Pirite del M. Somma.—*Rend. R. Acc. Sci. xxii, pp.* 290–95. *Napoli,* 1883.

FREDA, G.—Intorno alla Haussmannite ed alla Scolezite del Vesuvio.—*Rend. R. Acc. Sci. xxiv, pp.* 203–6. *Napoli,* 1885.

FREDA, G.—Sulla composizione di alcune recenti lave Vesuviane.—*Gazz. Chim. Ital. xix, pp.* 10–16. *Palermo,* 1889.

FREDA, G.—Sulla costituzione chimica delle sublimazioni saline Vesuviane. — *Gazz. Chim. Ital. xix, pp.* 16–21. *Palermo,* 1889.

FREDA, G.—Sulle masse trachitiche rinvenute nei recenti trafori delle colline di Napoli.—*Rend. R. Acc. Sci. S.* 2, *iii, pp.* 38–46. *Napoli,* 1889.

FREEMAN.—An extract of a letter dated May 2, 1750, relating to the ruins of Herculaneum.—*Phil. Trans. R. Soc. xlvii, pp.* 131–42. *London,* 1751.

FREY DES LANDRES, J. R. — *See* RIEDESEL, J. H. VON. 1773.

FRIEDLAENDER, B.—Der Vulkan Kilauea auf Hawaii. Mit einigen Bezugnahmen auf die Vulkane Italiens.—*Samml. pop. Schriften herausg. v. d. Ges. Urania zu Berlin, No.* 38, 8⁰. *Berlin,* 1896.

FRIEDLAENDER, H.—Ansichten von Italien, während einer Reise in den Jahren 1815 und 1816.—2 vols. 12⁰. *Leipzig,* 1819–20.—In English : 5 vols. 8⁰. *London,* 1820. *See* Vol. ii, pp. 225–32.

FRIEDLAENDER, I.—Der Krater des Vesuvs im März 1911.—*Naturwiss. Wochenschrift, N.F. x,* 29, *pp.* 8, 4 *figs.* 1911.— *Geol. Zentr. xvi,* 14, *p.* 678. *Leipzig,* 1911.

FRIEDLAENDER, I.—Pro Vesuvio.—"*Il Mattino,*" 2 *figs. Giov.-Venerdi,* 23–24 *Marzo,* 1911.

FRIEDLAENDER, I.—Karten des Eruptionskegels des Vesuv und des Vesuvkraters. — *Peterm. Geog. Mitth. p.* 1, 2 *maps,* 2 *pls. Gotha, Nov.,* 1912.—Also French, English and Italian eds.

FRIEDLAENDER, I.—Bildung eines Einsturztrichters im Vesuv-krater (1913).— *Naturwiss. Wochenschrift, N.F. xii,* 25, *pp.* 389–91, 2 *figs.* 1913.

FRIEDLAENDER, I. — Proposition de M. I. Friedlaender relative à la création d'un Institut Volcanologique.—*Proc.-verb. Congr. Internat. Géog. pp.* 178–80. *Rome,* 1913.

FRIEDLAENDER, [I.]—Uber die Kleinformen der vulkanischen Produkte.—*Zeitschr. f. Vulk. i,* 2. *Berlin, Mai,* 1914. *See* tab. XXIV, fig. 23 ; tab. XXV, fig. 25 ; tab. XXIX, fig. 34 ; tab. XXX, fig. 36 ; tab. XXXII, fig. 39.

FROJO, G.—Osservazioni geologiche su di un ramo della lava del Vesuvio della eruzione del 1 maggio 1855.—*Ann.'Scient. iii, pp.* 5. *Napoli,* 1856.

FROMMEL, C. (pinx. et del.).—Neapel. Praemie zu Meyers Universum. Band XIV., C. Frommel aqua fort : Hoffmeister sc. Inst. Bibl. excudit. Das Original Oelgemälde bey J. Meyer in Hildburghausen. Steel engrav. : 474×350 mm. Woman, child, man playing mandoline, and dog in foreground.

FUCCI, P.—La crudelissima guerra, danni, e minacce del superbo campione Vesuvio, etc.—4⁰, *pp.* 8, *frontisp. Napoli, E. Longo,* 1632.

FUCHS, C. W. C.—Notizen aus dem vulcanischen Gebiete Neapels.—*N. J. f. Min. pp.* 31–40. *Stuttgart,* 1865.

FUCHS, C. W. C.—Die vulkanischen Erscheinungen der Erde.—8⁰. *Leipzig u. Heidelberg,* 1865.

FUCHS, C. W. C.—Die Laven des Vesuv. Untersuchung der vulcanischen Eruptions-Producte des Vesuv in ihrer chronologischen Folge, vom 11 Jahrhundert an bis zur Gegenwart.—*N. J. f. Min. pp.* 667-87, *Stuttgart,* 1866 ; *pp.* 553-62, 1868 ; *pp.* 42-59, 169-93, 1869.—*Quart. Journ. Geol. Soc. xxv (Pt. 2), p.* 9, 1869.—*Verhandl. Nat. Med. v, pp.* 12-14. *Heidelberg,* 1871.

FUCHS, C. W. C.—Die vulkanischen Erscheinungen im Jahre 1865, etc., to 1885.—*N. J. f. Min.* 1866 *to* 1872.—*Min. petr. Mitth.* 1873 *to* 1887.—*Jahrb. k. k. geol. Reichsanst. xxiii. Wien,* 1873 *et seq.*

FUCHS, C. W. C.—Ueber einen Ausflug von Ischia nach dem Vesuv.—*N. J. f. Min. pp.* 587-88. *Stuttgart,* 1870.

FUCHS, C. W. C.—Die Veränderungen in der flüssigen und erstarrenden Lava.—*Min. petr. Mitth. Heft* 2, *pp.* 65-80, *tav. Wien,* 1871.—*N. J. f. Min. pp.* 540-41. *Stuttgart,* 1872.

FUCHS, C. W. C.—Vulkane und Erdbeben.—*Internat. wissensch. Biblioth. xvii, pp.* 269-71, 1 *litho. map, figs. Leipzig,* 1873.— 8⁰, *pp. xii+*343, 1 *map col., figs. Leipzig,* 1875.

FUCHS, C. W. C.—Les Volcans et les Tremblements de Terre.—8⁰, *pp. viii+*279, *fig. and map. Paris,* 1876.——2nd ed. 1878.

FUCHS, C. W. C.—Vulcani e Terremoti.— 8⁰. *Milano,* 1881. *See* pp. 76-82 and 280-83.

FUCINI, R.—Napoli a occhio nudo. Lettere ad un amico.—8⁰. *Firenze,* 1878. *See* Lettera 8, pp. 121-38.

FUMAGALLI.—[Nine views of Vesuvius by night ; eruption of June, 1905, taken mostly from the observatory and from the Hotel Eremo, Crook. Bromophot.]

FUMAGALLI, P. (lith.).—Vue de l'éruption du Vésuve arrivée l'an . . . 1822, tirée du côté de la maison de Pauza à Pompéi. Gravé par Paul Fumagalli.
A stipple engrav. in dark umber : 290×212 mm.

FURCHHEIM, F.—Bibliotheca Pompejana. Catologo ragionato di opere sopra Ercolano e Pompei pubblicate in Italia ed all' estero, dalla scoperta delle due città fino ai tempi più recenti con appendice : Opere sul Vesuvio.—8⁰, *pp.* 37. *Napoli,* 1879. [C.A.]

FURCHHEIM, F.—Bibliografia del Vesuvio compilata e corredata di note critiche estratte dai più autorevoli scrittori Vesuviani.—8⁰, *pp. xii+*297. *Napoli,* 1897.

FURCHHEIM, F.—Bibliografia della Campania.—2 vols. 8⁰. 1897-99.

F * * * V * * *. [FILIPPO VOLPICELLA.] —Notizie storiche delle eruzioni del Vesuvio.—*Ann. Civ. Due Sicilie, vii, pp.* 31-38. *Napoli,* 1833-47.

GAIZO, M. DEL.—*See* PALMIERI, L. 1886, 1887, 1888, 1890.

GAIZO, M. DEL.—Note di storia della Vulcanologia [per l'eruzione del 1906].—*Atti Acc. Pontaniana, xxxvi (S.* 2, *xi), Mem.* 5, *pp.* 1-19. *Napoli,* 1906.

GALANTI, G. M.—Breve descrizione della città di Napoli e del suo contorno, etc. (Da servire di appendice alla descrizione geografica e politica delle Sicilie.)—8⁰, *pp. xvi+* 348. *Napoli,* 1792.——Another ed. with Appendix, *pp.* 28. *Napoli,* 1803.

GALANTI, G. M. e L.—Napoli e contorni. Nuova edizione interamente riformata dall' Abate Luigi Galanti.—8⁰, *pp.* 7+381, 11 *pls.,* 2 *maps. Napoli,* 1838.—Also 1829. *See* pp. 310-19.

GALANTI, L.—Guida per Napoli e suoi contorni.—*Napoli,* 1845.——4th ed. 8⁰, *pp.* 4+292, 11 *pls.,* 2 *maps. Napoli,* 1861. *See* pp. 220-49 and pl. erupt. 1822. Also 8⁰, *pp.* 292, 11 *pls.,* 2 *maps. Napoli,* 1872. *See* pp. 220-27, pl. 7.

GALANTI, L.—*See* GALANTI, G. M. e L. —Napoli e contorni.

GALDIERI, A.—*See* FRANCO, P. 1895, 1896.

GALDIERI, A.—*See* BASSANI, F. 1906, 1907, 1910.

GALDIERI, A.—Fiori, insetti e fumarole. Nota.—*Boll. Soc. Nat. xxvi (S.* 2, *vi), pp.* 39-43. *Napoli,* 1914.

GALENUS, CLAUDIUS.—Scripta minora.— 8⁰. *Lipsiæ,* 1884.

GALEOTA, D. ONOFRIO.—Spaventosissima descrizione dello spaventoso spavento che ci spaventò tutti coll' eruzione del Vesuvio la sera delli otto d'Agosto del corrente anno, ma (per grazia di Dio) durò poco.—8⁰, pp. 17. (On p. 18 is a sonnet in praise of the author.)—Napoli, 1779.—Other eds. 1780 and 1825.

This was written by Galiani, under the name of the above author, who was well known for his ridiculous simplicity and whose vulgar style was copied by Galiani in this work. It was republished in Galiani's "Opuscoli editi ed inediti." 1825.

GALEOTA, D. O.—Spaventosissima descrizione dello spaventoso spavento, che spaventò a tutti quanti la seconda volta colla spaventevole eruzione del Vesuvio alli 15 Giugno dell' anno 1794 a due ore scarse di notte, pure come era sortito l'anno 1779, che se ne fece la prima descrizione, che questa è la seconda.—4⁰, portrait, pp. 18. Napoli, 1794. [C.A.] (Very rare.)

This work must have been written by Galeota, though the other with similar title was really by Galiani, writing under the pseudonym of Galeota. Galiani died in 1787. (Furchheim.)

GALEOTA, D. O.—Opera estemporanea all' impronto.—4⁰, pp. viii+23. Napoli, 1795. [O.V.]

GALIANI, F.—Catalogo delle materie appartenenti al Vesuvio, contenute nel museo, con alcune brevi osservazioni. Opera del celebre autore di Dialoghi sul Commercio de Granii.—12⁰, pp. viii+184. London, 1772.——2nd ed. 4⁰, pp. 18. Napoli, 1780. ——3rd ed. 8⁰, pp. 20. Napoli, 1825.

GALIANI, F.—Osservazioni sopra il Vesuvio e delle materie appartenenti a questo Vulcano, e ad altre contenute nel Museo. —See ANON.—Dei Vulcani o Monti Ignivomi, etc., pp. x+149. 1779.

GALIANI, F.—Spaventosissima descrizione dello spaventoso spavento, etc.—See GALEOTA, D. ONOFRIO. 1779.

[GALIANI, F.]—Del dialetto Napolitano. —See "Collezione di tutti i poemi in lingua Napoletana."—28 tom. 12⁰. Napoli, 1783–89.

GALIANI, F.—Opuscoli editi ed inediti.—8⁰. Napoli, 1825. [B.M. 12226. cc. 1.]

Reproduces the "Spaventosissima descrizione . . . 1779, etc."

GALIANI, F.—Veduta del Vesuvio da mezzagiorno nella eruzione dell' anno 1754 : da . . . [B.M.—K. 83. 79–a.]

GALIANI, MARCHESE (pinxt.).—Eruption of Mount Vesuvius in 1769. (With seven reference nos.) Sutherland sculpsit.— London : Published by Dr. Thornton, 1 Sept. 1808.

Aquatint : 545×458 mm. Drawn with exaggeration.

GALIANI, MARCHESE (fece).—[View of the eruption of Vesuvius of 1760.]

This is a retouched plate of the 1754 eruption included in Mecatti. A third line of inscription has been added, making 19 nos. of reference. It bears also " 4 " as No. of plate.—Engrav. : 502×266 mm. on ochre-coloured paper. Another type is similar to the first, but bears a third line as a dedication. "A.S. Ecc. Lady Mary Fox d.d.d. G.M.M."

GALLO, M.—Cenno storico sulla fondazione di Ercolano, e sua distruzione, corredato di utili riflessioni sulla natura del Monte Vesuvio, applicabili ancora agli altri Vulcani.—1st part (published only), 8⁰, pp. xv+81. Napoli, 1829. [C.A.]—Reprinted in 1834.

GALLO, M.—Saggio storico su la fondazione e distruzione di Ercolano e Pompei.—8⁰, foll. ii, pp. 79. Napoli, 1835. [C.A.]

GAMA, G.—Descrizione del tremuoto di Napoli del 15 Giugno 1794 e successivo scoppiamento flammifero del Vesuvio, etc. Canto.—4⁰, pp. 36. Napoli, 1794. [O.V.]

GAMBA, B.—Lettere descrittive da celebri Italiani.—2nd ed. 8⁰, pp. 8+262. Venezia, 1819.—Earlier ed. 8⁰. Venezia, 1813.

GANDY, J. P.—See GELL, SIR W.

GARRUCCI, P. R.—Topografia del Vesuvio. —Bull. Arch. Nap. N.S. i, 21. Napoli, Aprile, 1853.

GARRUCCI, P. R.—Come fu interrata Pompei.—Bull. Arch. Nap. N.S. i, 26. Napoli, Agosto, 1853.

GARRUCCIO, G.—La catastrofe di Pompei sotto l'incendio vulcanico del 79 del Vesuvio colla produzione dei suoi fuochi.—8⁰, pp. 30. Napoli, 1872. [C.A.]

GARSIA, G. A.—I funesti avvenimenti del Vesuvio principiati martedì 16 Dicembre 1631.—4⁰, pp. 12. Napoli, Egidio Longo, 1632.

GASPARE (father of LUIGI).—See VANVITELLI.

GASPARIS, A. DE, e BELLINI, R.— Alcuni schiarimenti sopra una speciale produzione dell' Isola di Capri.—*Riv. Ital. Sci. Nat. xvii, pp.* 91–92. *Siena,* 1897.

GATTA, L.—L'Italia, sua formazione, suoi vulcani e terremoti.—8⁰, *pp.* 539, 32 *figs.,* 3 *maps. Milano,* 1882.—*Boll. R. Com. Geol. Ital., Notiz. Bibliog. pp.* 102–4. *Roma,* 1882.
See Cap. 7 and 8, pp. 288 *et seq.*

GATTA, L.—Vulcanismo.—16⁰, *pp.* 267, *figs. Milano,* 1885.

GAUDIOSI, T.—Sonetto per l'incendio del Vesuvio del 1660.—*Arpa Poetica, p.* 63. *Napoli,* 1671. [C.A.]

GAUDRY, A.—Sur les coquilles fossiles de la Somma.—*Bull. Soc. géol. France, S.* 2, x, *pp.* 290–92. *Paris,* 1852–53.

GAUDRY, A.—Lettre sur l'état actuel du Vésuve.—*C.R. Acad. Sci. xli, pp.* 486–87. *Paris,* 1855.

GAUGEL.—*See* DEMBOUV.

GAUSSIN.—*See* DARONDEAU.

GAUTIER, A.—La Genèse des Eaux Thermales et ses rapports avec le Volcanisme.— [Extr.] *Ann. Mines, S.* 10, *Mém. ix, pp.* 316–70. *Paris,* 1906.

GAUTIER, A.—L'intervention et le rôle de l'eau dans les phénomènes volcaniques.— 8⁰, *pp.* 20. *Paris,* 1909.

GAVAZZA, G. — Sonetto. — *See* GIORGI URBANO.

GEIKIE, A.—Text-book of Geology.—8⁰, *pp.* 971, 434 *figs. London,* 1882.
See Book III, Pt. 1.
2nd ed. *London,* 1885. —— 3rd ed. *London,* 1893.

GELL, SIR W., and GANDY, J. P.—Pompeiana. The topography, edifices and ornaments of Pompeii.—2 vols. 4⁰, *pl. and fig. London,* 1824, 1832.

GELL, SIR W., and GANDY, J. P.—Vue des ruines de Pompéi ou Pompeiana.—4⁰. — ?, 1827.

GEMMELLARO, G.—Eruzione del Vesuvio. —*fol.* 29 *dell' Album di Roma, pp.* 2. *Oct.,* 1834. [O.V.]

GENILLION (del.), GUYOT (sculp.).—Vue du Port de Naples.—Paris. [B.N.P. Vb. 118.]
Oval, coloured engraving.

GENNARO, A. DI.—Lettera sopra l'ultima eruzione del Vesuvio dell' anno 1779.— "*Antologia Romana,*" *No.* 10. 1779.— "*Poesie,*" *pp.* 53–59. *Napoli,* 1797.—See ANON.—Dei Vulcani o Monti Ignivomi. *Livorno,* 1779.

GENNARO, A. DI.—Lettera del Signore . . . Scritta al Sig. Abate Gio. Cristofano Amaduzzi in data di Napoli a Mergellina. *See* ANON.—Dei Vulcani o Monti Ignivomi, etc.

GENNARO, A. DI.—1a lettera. Raccolta di monumenti sopra l'eruzione del Vesuvio seguita nell' Agosto, 1779.—*Giorn. Arti Comm. i, pp.* 141 *et seq. Macerata,* 1780. [O.V.]

GENNARO, A. DI.—Il Vesuvio.—*In his:* "Poesie scelte," 12⁰, *foll. iv, pp.* 298+2. *Napoli,* 1795.
See Pt. I, pp. 1–60.

GENNARO, A. DI (DUCA DI BELFORTE).— Sonetto sul Vesuvio, diretto al P. Ant. Piaggio.—*loose sheet.* [C.A.]

GENNARO, B. DI.—Historica narratio incendii Vesuviani, anno 1631.—8⁰. *Napoli,* 1632.
Mentioned by Soria.

GENNARO, B. A. DI.—Lettera sopra l'ultima eruzione del Vesuvio dell' anno 1779.—See ANON.—Dei Vulcani o Monti Ignivomi, *Vol. ii.* 1779.

GENOVESI, AB.—Raccolta di lettere scientifiche ed erudite dell' Ab. [Genovesi].—8⁰, *pp.* 247. *Napoli,* 1780.
Letter 7 : Account of the last eruption of Vesuvius, 1779. At the end of this are eight verses of P. Ant. de Sanctis, selected from the work of the same entitled : Il Mostruoso parto del Monte Vesuvio ora dal volgo detto il Monte Diavolo la cui mostruosità è qui descritta.—*Napoli,* 1632.

GENTILE.—*See* ANON.—Dei Vulcani o Monti Ignivomi, etc.

GERARDI, A.—Relatione dell' horribil caso et incendio occorso per l'esalatione del Monte di Somma detto Vesuvio vicino la città di Napoli.—4⁰, *foll. iv. Roma,* 1631.

GERARDI, A.—Warhaffte Relation von dem erschröcklichen Erdbidem und Fewrsgelwalt so auss dem Berg zu Somma, Vesuvio genant, nit weit von Neaples entsprungen, im Monat Dicember 1631.—4⁰, *foll.* 4. *Augsburg,* 1632. [C.A.]

GERBINO, G.—Nota su di un pianta Vesuviana.—*Ann. Acc. Aspir. Nat. iii, pp.* 230–32. *Napoli*, 1845–46.

GEREMICCA, M.—Il Vulcanismo del Golfo di Napoli. Dispensa Ia.—8⁰. *Napoli*, 1878.

GERI, F.—Osservazioni da lui fatte il dì 21 Marzo 1752 e seg.—*See* MECATTI.—Racconto storico-filosofico del Vesuvio.—*Napoli*, 1752.

GERNING.—Nachricht von dem letzten Ausbruch des Vesuvs.—*Mag. f. Phys. v. Voigt. x. Gotha*, 1795.

GERONIMO, B. Dı.—Ragguaglio del Vesuvio.—8⁰, *pp.* 24. *Benevento*, 1737.

GERVASI, N,—Raccolta di tutte le vedute che esistevono nel Gabinetto del Duca della Torre rappresentanti l'eruzioni del Monte Vesuvio fin oggi accadute, con le respettive descrizione ora per la prima volta ricavate dalla storia e con l'aggiunta delle due lettere di Plinio il giovine nelle quale vien riferito il primo incendio avvenuto nell' anno 79 dell' Era Christiana.—*obl. fol., fol.* 1, *pp.* 20, 27 *pls. Napoli*, 15 *Nov.*, 1805.—*See also* TORRE, DUCA DELLA.

GERVASI, N.—Recueil de toutes les vues qui existoient dans le Cabinet du Duc de la Tour et qui représentoient les incendies du Mont Vésuve arrivés jusqu'à présent avec les descriptions correspondantes tirées pour la première fois de l'histoire. On y a ajouté aussi les deux lettres de Plini le jeune, où l'on parle du premier incendie arrivé l'an 79 de l'Ère Chrétienne. Au mérite très-singulier de Son Excellence Mr. Le Comte de Milltown, Pair d'Irlande, Nicolas Gervasi D.D.D., C. Zahn.—*Naples*, chez Nicolas Gervasi Marchand d'Estampes au Géant No. 23. Avec permission du Roi, 1823.—*obl.* 4⁰, *pp.* 21, *fol.* 1, *pl.* XXIX, *frontisp. and terminal fig. of erupt. of* 1779.
A better printed series of these views, identical in every way, bears the final inscription " In Napoli presso Franc. Scafa Str. S. Biagio de' Librari N° 117," or a part thereof. These have so far only been found as loose, unbound plates and with Pl. 18, which, in Gervasi's series, is erroneously marked " 6," missing. There is no text.

GEUNS, W. J. VAN.—De Vesuvius en zijne geschiedenis.—*Album der Natur*, 8⁰, *pp.* 267–87, 1 *lithogr. map, woodcuts. Groningen*, 1858.

GIACHETTI, J.—Apuliæ terræmotus defloratio.—4⁰, *pp.* 7. *Romæ*, 1632.

GIACOMO, S. Dı.—Napoli, Part. I.—192 *illustr.*—*See* RICCI, C.—Napoli, *No.* 32 *in* " Collezione di Monografie Illustrate," *S.* 1 : Italia Artistica, 1902, etc.

GIANETTI, G.—La vera relazione del prodigio novamente successo nel Monte Vesuvio, etc.—4⁰, *pp.* 8. *Napoli*, 1631.

GIANETTI, G.—Rime dell' incendio del Vesuvio.—12⁰, *foll. viii. Napoli*, 1632. [C.A].

GIANNELLI, B.—Lettera intorno alle ceneri Vesuviane piovute in Vitulano (Principiato ultra) nell' Agosto del 1779.—*See* TORCIA. —Relazione. 1779.

GIANNETTASIIS, N. P.—Æstates Surrentinæ.—12⁰, *foll.* 6, *pp.* 280, *frontisp. Neapoli*, 1696.
See pp. 77–93, erupt. 1696, and pp. 252–61.

GIANNETTASIIS, N. P.—Ver Herculaneum. —8⁰, *foll. iv, pp.* 256, *engrav. frontisp. Neapoli*, 1704. [C.A.]
See Lib. III, Cap. III.

GIANNETTASIIS, N. P.—Annus eruditus in partes quatuor, seu stata tempora distributus. Ver Herculanum, Æstates Surrentinæ, Autumni Surrentini, et Hyemes Puteolani.—4 vols. 4⁰. *Vol. i, pp.* 185 ; *Vol. ii, pp.* 193 ; *Vol. iii, pp.* 192 ; *Vol. iv, pp.* 185. *Napoli*, 1722.
See Vol. i, pp. 155–68.

GIANNONE, P.—Lettera scritta ad un amico che lo richiedeva onde avvenisse che nelle due cime del Vesuvio, in quella che butta fiamme ed è la più bassa, la neve lungamente si conservi e nell' altra che è più alta ed intera non vi duri che per pochi giorni.—4⁰, *foll.* 2. *Napoli*, 1718.

GICCA, A.—Dei prodotti minerali del regno delle Due Sicilie.—*Ann. Civ. Regno Due Sicilie, li, p.* 31. *Napoli*, 1854.

GIGANTE, [A. ?]—[View of Naples and Vesuvius from above the tunnel—a line lithograph.] 1828.

GIGANTE, A.—Friso. [Signed] Achille Gigante, 1844. [Vesuvius, Naples, and Pal. Donn' Anna.]
Open line- or etching-like engraving on dark yellow paper : 294 × 190 mm. Lady and gentleman descending steps in foreground.

GIGANTE, A.—Frisio (View of Vesuvius and Palazzo Donna Anna). 1844.
Fine line-engraving on brown-tinted paper.

GIGANTE, [A. ?]—[Good outline of Vesuvius with view of Naples from above Grotto.]
Open line - engrav. : 417×270 mm. 10 umbrella pines, shepherd, boy and sheep in foreground.

GIGANTE, GIACINTO [1821–1876].—[View of Bay of Naples from Villa Tricase at Vomero.] [S. Martino Mus.]
A pencil drawing. Another from above Mergellina shows in Vesuvius the same crater, but no eruptive cone, which is well delineated in first.

GIGANTE, G. (pin.).—Le Môle de Naples.
Litho. of Vesuvius, with Mole and lighthouse and lazzaroni in foreground : 183 × 121 mm.

GIGANTE, G. (pin.).—Sᵗᵉ Lucie.
A view from the W. end towards Vesuvius. Litho. : 193×148 mm.

GIGLI, G.—Discorso sulla Zona Vulcanica Mediterranea.—8⁰, *pp.* 146. *Napoli,* 1857.
See pp. 89–122.

GILL, H. V.—On a possible connection between the eruption of Vesuvius and the earthquake at San Francisco in April, 1906. —*Sci. Proc. R. Dublin Soc. N.S. xi, pp.* 107–10. 1906.

GIMBERNAT, C. DE.—Notizie intorno ad una sostanza particolare che trovansi presso le acque termali d'Ischia, ed intorno ai vapori del Vesuvio.—*Giorn. Fis. Chim., Stor. Nat.,* Dec. 2, *ii, pp.* 178–81. *Pavia,* 1819.

GIMMA, G.—Della storia naturale delle Gemme, delle Pietre e di tutti i Minerali, ovvero della fisica sotterranea.—4⁰. *Vol. i, pp.* 46+551 ; *Vol. ii, pp.* 603. *Napoli,* 1730.
See Vol. ii, Lib. VI, Cap. 7, pp. 493–510.

GIOENI, G.—Relazione d'una nuova pioggia [vulcanica]. — ?, 1785.—In English : Account of a new kind of rain.—*Phil. Trans. R. Soc. lxxii, Append. pp.* i–vi. *London,* 1782.

GIOENI G.—Saggio di litologia Vesuviana. —*Napoli,* 1789.—8⁰, *foll.* 6, *pp.* xcii+208, 1 *map. Napoli,* 1790.—8⁰, *foll.* 6, *pp.* 272. *Napoli,* 1791. [O.V.]

GIOENI, G.—Versuch einer Lithologie des Vesuvs. [Transl.]—8⁰, *pp.* 392. *Wien,* 1793.

GIOMIGNANI, F.—*See* FABRIS, P.

GIORDANO, FABIO.—De Vesuvio Monte. [O.V.]
Copied by Miniere M. S.

GIORDANO, G.—Sur la dernière éruption du Vésuve, du 8 déc., 1861.—" *Moniteur,*" *foll. iii.* 31 *janv.,* 1862.—*Moigno and Cosmos, xx, pp.* 50–56. 1862.

GIORDANO, G.—*See* BALDACCHINI, M. 1862.

GIORDANO, G.—*See* PALMIERI, L. (relatore). 1862.

GIORDANO, G.—Succinta relazione dell' avvenuto durante la eruzione del Vesuvio del dì 8 dicembre 1861.—*Atti R. Ist. Incorag. x, pp.* 507–16. *Napoli,* 1863.

GIORDANO, G.—Fossili Marini sul Vesuvio. — ?, — ? [O.V.]

GIORGI URBANO.—Scelta di poesie nell' incendio del Vesuvio.—4⁰, *pp.* 94, *engrav. frontisp. Roma,* 1632. [C.A.]
For contents *see* FURCHHEIM, F.— Bibliografia del Vesuvio.

GIOVANELLI, D.—Sopra la non antica apertura, o manifestazione dei Lagone di Monte Cerboli nell' agro Volterrano. Note relativa al contenuto nella presente lettera rapporto ai sassi piovuti in Siena.—*Giorn. Lett. lxi, pp.* 3–21. *Napoli.*

GIOVANNOZZI, G.—Vulcanologia.—*Ann. Scient. Ind. xxxvi, pp.* 31–33. *Milano,* 1900.

GIOVENE, G.—Discorso meteorologico-campestre per l'anno 1794.—4⁰. — ?, — ? [B.N.]

GIOVO, N.—Del Vesuvio. Song.—*fol., foll. ii, pp. xxvi. Napoli,* 1737. [C.A.]

GIRARD, A.—Geologische Reise-Bemerkungen aus Italien.—*N. J. f. Min. pp.* 769–92. *Stuttgart,* 1845.

GIRARD, A.—L'éruption du Vésuve du 1861.—" *Journal des Débats,*" *feuilleton du* 28 *mars* 1862.

GIRARDET, KARL.—[Comical sketch of tourists climbing Vesuvius.]
Woodcut in French illustr. paper : 170×145 mm.

GIRARDIN, J. P. L.—Considérations générales sur les Volcans, et examen critique des diverses théories, etc.—8⁰, *pp.* 248. *Rouen et Paris,* 1831.

N

GIRAUD, E.—Le grand Golfe de Naples par Giraud, ou Recueil des plus beaux Palais de la dite ville. Le dit ouvrage renferme les plus beaux restes d'antiquité qui existent sur la coste de Poussole, Baja et Cuma. Le tout pittoresquement gravé à un seul trait à lau [*sic*] forte dans le goût du célèbre Piranesi.—30 *views, obl. fol.* [*Naples ?*] 1771.
Dr. Johnston-Lavis' copy contains 28 pls. in one album and 6 in another ; that of the B.M. (K. 7. Tab. 59) contains 30 views. *See* Pls. 10, 11, 20, 23, 32.

GIRAUD-SOULAVIE, Abbé.—*See* HAMILTON, Sir W.—Œuvres complettes. 1781.

GIROLAMO MARIA Di S. Anna, F.—Aggiunta all' Istoria della vita, virtù e miracoli di S. Gennaro vescovo e martire principal padrone della fedelissima città, e regno di Napoli. Nella quale si rapportano varie erudizioni, e molte curiose notizie.—4°, *pp.* 70. *Napoli*, 1710. [C.A.]—There were also other ed.

GIROS, S.—Veridica relazione circa l'ultima eruzione del Vesuvio accaduta ai 15 Giugno per tutto Luglio del 1794.—8°, *pp. xxxv. Napoli*, 1794.

GIROS, S.—Continuazione delle notizie riguardanti il Vesuvio.—8°, *pp.* 24. [*Napoli*, 1795.] [B.N.]

GIROUD, A.—Mémoire historique et critique sur la ville souterraine découverte au pied du Mont-Vésuve, *etc.*—8°, *pp.* 8+74. *Avignon*, 1748.

GIUDICE, F. Del.—Dei più importanti fenomeni naturali accaduti nel regno durante l'anno 1855, seguito dalle principali notizie delle eruzioni del Vesuvio dal 79 fin oggi.—4°. *Napoli*, 1856.

GIUDICE, F. Del.—Ragguaglio dei principali fenomeni naturali avvenuti nel regno durante il 1856.—4°, *with 2 continuations for the years* 1857 *and* 1858.

GIUDICE, F. Del.—Brevi considerazioni intorno ad alcuni più costanti fenomeni Vesuviani.—*Atti R. Ist. Incorag. ix, pp.* 1–67, 7 *tab. Napoli*, 1861.
Published as a separate memoir in 1855.

GIUDICE, R.—Lettera relativa all' eruzione del Vesuvio dell' anno 1804.—*Mag. Lett. Sci. Arti, pp.* 38–44. *Firenze, feb.* 1805. [O.V.]

GIULIANI, G. B.—Trattato del Monte Vesuvio e de' suoi incendii.—4°, *pp. x*+224, 2 *pls., engrav. frontisp. Napoli*, 1632.

GIULIANI, G. B.—*See* NAUDÉ, G.—Ueber den Vesuv, etc.

GIUSTINIANI, E.—*See* MATTEUCCI, R. V.—Il Silenio . . . dell' eruzione Vesuviana, 1897.

GIUSTINIANI, L.—La biblioteca storica e topografica del regno di Napoli.—4°, *pp. xv*+241. *Napoli*, 1793.
See pp. 215–28 (ref. to Vesuvius).

GIUSTINIANI, L.—Dizionario geografico ragionato del regno di Napoli.—10 vols. 8°. *Napoli*, 1797–1805.—13 vols. 8°. *Napoli*, 1816. [2nd pt. (3 vols.) publ. sep. under title :] De Fiume, Laghi, Fonti, Golfi, Monti Promontori, Vulcani, e Boschi.

GIUSTO, L.—Diverbio del Sebeto col Vesuvio su gl'insetti microscopici del colera.—8°, *pp.* 16. *Napoli*, 1836.

GIUSTO, P.—Progetto di Associazione per compensamento dei danni che il Vesuvio può recare ai paesi messi sul suo pendio ed alla sua base.—4°, *pp.* 24. *Napoli*, 1862 *and* 1872. [C.A.]

GLADSTONE, G.—On the dust thrown up by Vesuvius during the late eruption.—*Rept. Brit. Assoc.* (1872) *Trans. pp.* 74–75. *London*, 1873.

GLASS, G.—Eruzione del 1813.
Vesuvius from Naples by night ; two men in foreground. Gouache : 415× 275 mm.

GLASS, G.—Eruzione de 25 Novembre 1819.—Giorgio Glass in Napoli.
Vesuvius by night from Naples ; a long lava stream on south slope, but no smoke from summit. Gouache : 405×275 mm.

GLIELMO, A.—L'incendio del Monte Vesuvio, etc., del 1631.—16°, *pp.* 185. *Napoli*, 1632 *and* 1634.
Two editions, the first anon.

G. Ma. C.—Lettera ragionata ad un amico nella quale si dà un esatto ragguaglio dell' eruzione del Vesuvio accaduta a' 15 Giugno 1794 e degli altri fenomeni, ecc.—8°, *pp.* 24, 2 *pls. Napoli*, 1794.

GMELIN, L.—Observationes oryctognosticæ et chemicæ de Haüyne, etc.—8°, *pp.* 6+58, 1 *pl., figs. Heidelbergæ*, 1814. [O.V.]
See Pars 2a, pp. 43–48.

GMELIN, L.—Chemische Untersuchung eines blauen Fossils vom Vesuv und des Lasursteins.—*Journ. f. Chem. Phys. xiv, pp.* 325–30. *Nürnberg u. Halle*, 1815.

GMELIN, L.—Analyse des Mejonits.—*Journ. f. Chem. Phys. xxv, pp.* 36–39. *Nürnberg u. Halle*, 1819.

GOETHE, J. W. VON.—Travels in Italy : together with second residence in Rome and fragments on Italy. Transl. from the German by the Rev. A. J. W. Morrison and Charles Nisbet.—8⁰, *pp.* 589. *London,* 1892.—Earlier ed. 8⁰. 1846, *etc.*

GOGGIA, P.—La dernière phase d'activité du Vésuve.—"*Cosmos,*" *No.* 348, *pp.* 525–29. *Paris,* 1901.

GOLDSCHMIDT, V., SCHROEDER, R.—Salmiak vom Vesuv.—*Zeitschr. f. Kryst. xlv, pp.* 221–24, *fig., pl. vii. Leipzig,* 1908.

GOOD, J. M.—*See* POLEHAMPTON, E.

GORCEIX, H.—État du Vésuve et des dégagements gazeux des Champs Phlégréens au mois de juin 1869.—*C.R. Acad. Sci. lxxiv, pp.* 154–56. *Paris,* 1872.

[GORI, A. F.]—Notizie del memorabile scoprimento dell' antica città Ercolano, etc. —8⁰, *pp. xx+*106, 2 *pls. Firenze,* 1748.

GORI, A. F.—Admiranda antiquitatum Herculanensium descripta et illustrata ad annum MDCCL.—2 tom. 8⁰. *Patavii,* 1752. ——2nd ed. 2 tom. 8⁰. *T. i, pp.* 28 (*xviii*)+ 139, 1 *pl. ; T. ii, pp,* 24+203. *Romœ,* MDCCLVI.
One good view of Vesuvius. *See* pp. 11–16.

GORINI, P.—Sull' origine dei Vulcani. Studio sperimentale.—8⁰, *pp. xxiv+*694. *Lodi,* 1871.
See Art. III : Il Vulcano Partenopeo, pp. 418–34.

GOSSELET, J.—Observations géologiques faites en Italie. (I. Vésuve ; II. Champs Phlégréens ; III. Etna ; IV. Latium.)—*Mém. Soc. Imp. Sci. S.* 3, *vi, pp.* 417–75, 7 *pls. Lille,* 1869.

GOURBILLON, M.—Travels in Sicily and to Mount Etna in 1819.—16⁰, *pp.* 120, 4 *figs. London,* 1820.

GOURDAULT, J.—L'Italie illustrée de 450 gravures sur bois.—*gd.* 4⁰, *pp. viii+*743. *Paris,* 1877.

GOURMONT, R. DE.—Un volcan en éruption. Le Vésuve.—*Librairie de vulgarisation,* 16⁰, *pp.* 70. *Paris* [1883]. (*Forms part of the "Bibliothèque du jeune âge.*")

GRABLOVITZ, G. — Fenomeni Vesuviani dell' Aprile 1906 osservati da Ischia.—*Boll. Soc. Sismol. Ital. xi,* 9, *pp.* 289–311, *tav. Modena,* 1906.

GRÆVIUS, J. G.—Thesaurus antiquitatum et Historiarum Italiæ, Neapolis, Siciliæ . . . atque adjacentium terrarum insularumque . . . digeri atque edi olim cœptus cura et studio J. G. G. . . . continuatus et ad finem perductus cum præfationibus P. Burmanni, etc.—10 tom. 45 vol. *fol. Lugduni Batavorum,* 1725.

GRANDE DE LORENZANA, F.—Breve compendio del lamentabile ynzendio del Monte di Soma.—8⁰, *pp.* 16. *En Napoles,* 1632.

GRANVILLE, A. B.—A report on a memoir of Sig. Monticelli, entitled : " Descrizione dell' eruzione del Vesuvio avvenuta ne' giorni 25 e 26 Dic. 1813."—*Journ. Sci. and Arts, ii, pp.* 25–34. *London,* 1817.

GRANVILLE EARL.—A Communication . . . enclosing a report from H.M. Minister at Rome relating to the recent eruption of Vesuvius. [Title only.]—*Quart. Journ. Geol. Soc. xxviii, p.* 396. 1872.

GRASSI, C.—*See* HACKERT, PH.—Raccolta di XXV Vedute.

GRAVIER, G.—Veduta di Napoli dalla parte di Chiaja sino al Vesuvio come si vede di Posilipo. Inc. Gius. Aloja.—*Napoli,* 1759. [B.M. copy cut and mounted on cloth. 24045 (14).]
A plate.

GRAVIER, G.—Veduta della Real Villa di Portici come si vede dal mare. Aloja inc.
An engraved plate.

GRAVINA, C.—Poesie. Il Vesuvio.—12⁰, *p.* 10. *Catania,* 1834. [B.N.]

GRAYDON, G.—On the Dykes of Monte Somma in Italy.—*Trans. Geol. Soc. iii, pp.* 233–55. 1816.

GREGORIUS, F.—Euphorion. Eine Dichtung aus Pompeji in vier Gesängen. 16 Aufl.—*Leipzig,* 1891.
See dritter Gesang : Pallas Athene, pp. 73–109.

GREGORY, J. W., JOHNSTON-LAVIS, H. J.—Eozoonal structure of the ejected blocks of Monte Somma.—*Scient. Trans. R. Dublin Soc. N.S. v, pp.* 259–86, 5 *photoengrav.* 1894.—*Abstr. Proc. Geol. Soc. London, pp.* 107–8. *London, June* 7, 1893.

GREGORY, J. W.—Eozoon and the Monte Somma blocks.—*See* DAWSON, J. W., ET ALII. 1895.

GREIM, G.—Die Veränderungen am Vesuv im Folge des Ausbruches vom April, 1906. —[Sonderabdr.] *Geogr. Zeitschr. xvi*, 1, *pp.* 2, 1 *tab. Leipzig*, 1910.

GREVTER, MATTEO.—Le XII provincie del regno [di Napoli].—*Venecia*, 1657.—*Also* " nuouamente ristampata, riuista et augmentata da Domenico de Rossi herede di Gio. Giacomo de Rossi . . . l'anno 1695."

GRIFONI, HECTOR.—Vue du cratère du Vésuve après l'éruption d'Octobre 1822 prise du côté occidental. Gravé par Ferdinand Mori. Écrit par Marco di Pietro. [Below in medallion :] Vue entière du grand cône actuel avec les scories et les débris de cette dernière lave.
A very fine stipple sepia engraving : 555 × 260 mm., or, with text, 375 mm.

GRIOLET (lith.).—[Vesuvius from Castellamare] Maladies aigues ? — Marseilles. [B.N.P. Vb. 121.]
A fine litho.

GROSS, A.—Neapel, seine Umgebung und der letzte Ausbruch des Vesuvs (April, 1906).—*Brünn*, 1908.

GROSSER, P.—Messungen an Wollastonitkrystallen v. Vesuv.—*Zeitschr. f. Kryst. xix*, 6, *pp.* 604–11. *Leipzig*, 1891.

GROSSI, G. B. G.—Ragionamento per i comuni Vesuviani, Isola del Cratere, ecc. contro il commune di Sarno, ed altri. Nel Consiglio d'Intendenza di Salerno.—4°, *pp.* 64. *Napoli*, 1817. [B.N.]

GROSSMANN, A.—Analyse quantitative des gaz occlus dans les laves des dernières éruptions de la Montagne Pelée et du Vésuve.—*C.R. Acad. Sci. cxlviii*, *pp.* 991–92. *Paris*, 1909.

GROVE, F. C.—The eruption of Vesuvius [in December, 1867].—*Macmillan's Magazine, xvii, pp.* 415–19. *London and New York*, 1868.

GUARINI, G.—Saggi analitici sopra taluni prodotti· Vesuviani (1832).—*Atti R. Acc. Sci. v, Pte.* 2, *Mem. Class. Fis. Stor. Nat. pp.* 151–56. *Napoli*, 1844.

GUARINI, G.—Analisi chimica di un prodotto Vesuviano (1833).—*Atti R. Acc. Sci. v, Pte.* 2, *Mem. Class. Fis. Stor. Nat. pp.* 161–63. *Napoli*, 1844.

GUARINI, G., SEMENTINI, L.—Saggi analitici su talune sostanze Vesuviane. [1834.]—*Atti R. Acc. Sci. v, Pte.* 2, *Mem. Class. Fis. Stor. Nat. pp.* 165–68. *Napoli*, 1844.

GUARINI, G.—Analisi chimica della sabbia caduta in Napoli la sera de' 26 Agosto 1834. [1834.]—*Atti R. Acc. Sci. v, Pte.* 2, *Mem. Class. Fis. Stor. Nat. pp.* 233–37. *Napoli*, 1844.

GUARINI, G., PALMIERI, L., SCACCHI, A. (relatore).—Memoria sull' incendio del Vesuvio.—*Rend. R. Acc. Sci. N.S. iv, pp.* 69–72. *Napoli*, 1855.

GUARINI, R.—Poemata varia.—12°, *pp.* 5–192. *Neapoli*, 1821.
See pp. 23–26.

GUARRO, R.—Il tributo di riconoscenza torrese a Maria S.S. della Neve. Sommario. Torre Annunziata et Maria S.S. della Neve ; AMMIRATI, B.—Il Vesuvio e le sue eruzioni in rapporto a Torre Annunziata ; GARGIULO, G.—L'ora triste ; ESPOSITO, R. —L'arcano della Sventura ; PRISCO, A.— Una nuova gemma alla corona di glorie di M.SS. della Neve ; VILLANI, G.—L'otto Aprile ; MAGRO, S.—Il trionfo del sopranaturala ; GUARRO, R.—Inno di ringraziamento a Maria SS. della Neve.—8°, *pp.* 31. *Torre Annunziata*, 1906.

GUDIN.—*See* COIGNET, M.—Vues pittoresques de l'Italie, etc.

GUÉ.—*See* COIGNET, M.—Vues pittoresques de l'Italie, etc.

GUEMBEL, C. W. VON.—Ueber vulcanische Erscheinungen.— *Westermann's Monatshefte, xxii, pp.* 413–27. *Braunschweig*, 1867.

GUENTHER, R. T., MERCALLI, G.— Recent changes in Vesuvius.—" *Nature*," *lxxii, pp.* 455–56, *figs.* 1905.

GUERRA, G. (inc.).—[Map of Gulf of Naples from Salerno to Lago di Patria with Capri and Ischia.]—N⁰ 14. Naples, 1794.
Map with plain border : 527 × 763 mm.

GUERRA, G. (engrav. by).—Carta de' crateri esistenti tra il Vesuvio e la spiaggia di Cuma.—*Napoli*, 1797. [C.A., B.M.— 83. 52. 2. b.]

GUESDON, [A.] (des.).—L'Italie à vol d'oiseau. Pompéi. Vue prise au-dessus de la plage de Chiaja. Lith. p. Jacottet. Paris, Imp. Lemercier. Paris, publié par A. Hauser, Boul. des Italiens 11.
Litho. : 440 × 345 mm.

GUESDON, A. (del.).—Naples. Vue prise au-dessus de la plage de Chiaja. L'Italie à vol d'oiseau. Rouargue lith. Paris, publié par A. Hauser, Boul. des Italiens. Lith. on straw-coloured background : 436×324 mm.

GUESDON, [A.] (des.).—Pompéi. Vue prise au-dessus de l'Odéon et du Théâtre tragique.—L'Italie à vol d'oiseau. Lith. par Jacottet. Paris, publié par A. Hauser, Boul^d. des Italiens, 11. Imp. Lemercier, Paris.
Litho. with fine view of Vesuvius on straw-coloured ground : 439×334 mm.

GUICCIARDINI, C.—Mercurius Campanus præcipua Campaniæ Felicis loca indicans, et perlustrans.—12⁰, *foll.* 6, *pp.* 273, 6 *figs.* *Neapoli*, 1667. [O.V.]
See pp. 66–67, 87–88.

GUIDICCIONI, L.—De Vesevo Monte, epigramma.—*See* GIORGI URBANO.

GUILLAUMANCHES-DUBOSCAGE, G. P. I. DE.—Relation de l'éruption du Vésuve en 1822, suivie 1⁰ de l'observation d'un phénomène qui constate les moyens que la Nature employe pour alimenter les volcans; 2⁰ de la comparaison de l'éruption de 1822 avec celle où Herculaneum et Pompeii furent engloutis ; à la suite est un aperçu sur les anciens volcans.—8⁰, *pp.* 54, *fol.* 1. *Aix*, 1823. [C.A.]

GUIRAUD, DR.—L'éruption du Vésuve en avril, 1872.—[Sep. publ.] *Recueil Soc. Sci. Bel. Lett. et Arts de Tarn-et-Garonne*, 8⁰, *pp.* 32. *Montauban*, 1872. [C.A.]

GUISCARDI, G.—Del Solfato Potassico trovato nel cratere del Vesuvio nel Nov. e Dic. 1848.—8⁰, *pp.* 11, 1 *pl.*, *figs.* *Napoli*, 1849.

GUISCARDI, G.—Lettera all' egregio prof. A. Scacchi sullo stato del Vesuvio.—8⁰, *foll.* 2, 1 *pl.* *Napoli*, 1855.

GUISCARDI, G.—Sopra un minerale del Monte Somma (Guarinite).—*Atti R. Acc. Sci. ii, pp. cvii–cviii and* 407–12, 3 *figs.* *Napoli*, 1855–57.—*Zeitschr. deutsch. geol. Gesellsch. x, pp.* 14–16. *Berlin*, 1858.— *Nuovo Cimento, vii, pp.* 448–52. *Pisa*, 1858.

GUISCARDI, G.—Fauna fossile Vesuviana. —8⁰, *pp.* 16. *Napoli*, 1856.

GUISCARDI, G.—Notizie del Vesuvio.— "*Giambattista Vico*," i, *pp.* 132–34 ; ii, *pp.* 139, 461–62 ; iii, *pp.* 457–61 ; iv, *pp.* 136–37, 314–15. *Napoli*, 1857.—[Sep. extr.] 8⁰, *pp.* 14. [C.A.] Reprint, 1858.

GUISCARDI, G.—Studii su i minerali Vesuviani. Ossido Ferrico Idrato.—*Giambattista Vico, ii, pp.* 137–39. *Napoli*, 1857.

GUISCARDI, G.—Sopra un minerale del Monte Somma. Memoria.—*Mem. R. Acc. Sci. ii, pp.* 408–12. *Napoli*, 1857.—[Extr.] 4⁰, *pp.* 6, 1 *woodcut.*

GUISCARDI, G.—[Ueber die neuesten Kraterveränderungen und Ausbrüche des Vesuvs.]—*Zeitschr. deutsch. geol. Gesellsch. ix, pp.* 196–97, 383–86, 562–64. *Berlin*, 1857.
Letters to Herr Roth.

GUISCARDI, G.—Ueber den Guarinit, eine neue Mineralspecies vom Monte Somma.— [Abdr.] *Zeitschr. deutsch. geol. Gesellsch. x, pp.* 14–16. *Berlin*, 1858.

GUISCARDI, G.—Briefliche Mittheilungen an J. Roth (8 Aug. und 15 Sept., 1858).— *Zeitschr. deutsch. geol. Gesellsch. x, p.* 374. *Berlin*, 1858.

GUISCARDI, G. — Sublimazioni verdiccie sulle scorie d'una fumarola apparsa nel Vesuvio.—*Ann. R. Oss. Vesuviano. Napoli*, 1859.

GUISCARDI, G.—[State of Vesuvius 21 May 1861.]—*Zeitschr. deutsch. geol. Gesellsch. xiii, p.* 147. *Berlin*, 1861.
Letter to Herr Roth, dated Neapel, 16 Juni 1861.

GUISCARDI, G.—Sulla presenza di combinazioni del Titanio e del Boro in alcune sublimazioni Vesuviane.—*Rend. R. Acc. Sci. S.* 3, i, *pp.* 59–62. *Napoli*, 1861.— *Ann. R. Oss. Meteor. Vesuv.* 1862.

GUISCARDI, G.—[Analisi chimica della Wollastonite del Monte Somma.]—*Rend. R. Acc. Sci. S.* 3, i, *pp.* 77–78. *Napoli*, 1861.

GUISCARDI, G.—[Sur l'éruption du Vésuve, lettre à M. Deville.]—*C.R. Acad. Sci. liii, pp.* 1233–36. *Paris*, 1861.

GUISCARDI, G.—Notizie Vesuviane.—*Rend. R. Acc. Sci. S.* 3, i, *pp.* 99–100. *Napoli*, 1862.

GUISCARDI, G. (relatore).—*See* BALDACCHINI, M. 1862.

GUISCARDI, G.—*See* PALMIERI, L. (relatore). 1862.

GUISCARDI, G.—[Lettre sur la dernière éruption du Vésuve.]—*C.R. Acad. Sci. lxxv, pp.* 504–5. *Paris*, 1872 .

GUISCARDI, G.—Sulla genesi della Tenorite nelle fumarole del Vesuvio.—*Rend. R. Acc. Sci. S.* 3, *xii, pp.* 46–47. *Napoli,* 1873.
    Also in : PALMIERI.—Cronaca Vesuviana, *pp.* 105–8. *Napoli,* 1874.

GUISCARDI, G.—Sulla Guarinite.—*Rend. R. Acc. Sci. S.* 3, *xv, pp.* 10–11. *Napoli,* 1876.

GUISCARDI, G.—Ueber Erscheinungen am Vesuv. Neapel den 8 Februar 1880.—*Zeitschr. deutsch. geol. Gesellsch. xxxii, p.* 186. *Berlin,* 1880.

GUISCARDI, G.—Communicazione [sopra un cristallo di Nefelina del M. Somma].—*Rend. R. Acc. Sci. S.* 3, *xxiv, p.* 181, 1 *pl. Napoli,* 1885.

GUISCARDI, G.—Descrizione dello stato attuale del cratere del Vesuvio.—*Ann. Scient. ii, pp.* 249–51.

GUSSONE, G.—*See* BALDACCHINI, M. 1862.

GUTTENBERG, H.—[A View of an eruption of Mount Vesuvius after J. A. Volaire (?).]—*Nuremberg ?,* 1771 ?—*See* VOLAIRE. [B.M. 24858 (1).]

GUTTENBERG, [H. ?] (engrav. by).—Éruption du Mont Vésuve du 14 mai 1771.—*Naples.* [C.A.]
    A plate.

GUTTENBERG, [H.?] (engrav. by).—Vue de la sommité et du cratère du Vésuve au moment de l'éruption du 8 août 1779. [C.A.]

GUYOT (sculp.).—*See* GENILLION.

G. W. M. D.—Philosophische und in der Natur gegründete Abhandlung des physikalischen Problematis : Woher dem Meere seine Saltzigkeit entstehe ? Wobey zugleich eine kurtze Nachricht von dem Ursprunge, Natur und Nahrung der drei feuerspeyenden Berge Hecla, Vesuvius und Æthna gegeben wird, von einem curieusen Besitzer der natürlichen Wissenschaften. —8⁰, *pp.* 86. *Gothenburg,* 1737.

H . . . —Sur le Vésuve.—*Two articles in the "Journal de l'Empire,"* 6 *and* 10 *Nov.* 1807. [C.A.] .

HAAS, H. J.—Unterirdische Gluten. Die Natur und das Wesen der Feuerberge im Lichte der neuesten Anschauungen für die Gebildeten aller Stände in gemeinverständlicher Weise dargestellt. 2te Auflage.—8⁰, *pp.* 316, *fig. and pl. Berlin,* 1912.

HACKERT, J.—*See* HACKERT, Ph.

HACKERT, Ph., GRASSI, C., FERGOLA, L., etc.—Raccolta di xxv vedute dell' città e regno di Napoli. Incise da Vincenzo Aloja.—*obl.* 4⁰. *Napoli e Francoforte, presso G. F. Wenner,* ? 1810. [Flor. B.N., 9, 1, 6, 26.]

HACKERT, Ph. (pinx.), HACKERT, J. (sculp.).—Veduta del Teatro di Pompei, presa dall' estremità del Portico Superiore. —Si vende a Napoli, presso l'Autore Incisore di S.M. Con Privilegio. No. 2. [B.M.—K. 83. 68–a–2.]

HAIDINGER, W. K. Von.—On the Sodalite of Vesuvius.—*Edinb. Phil. Journ. xiii, pp.* 222–24. *Edinburgh,* 1825.

HAIDINGER, W. K. Von.—Ueber Schmidt's Werke über den Vesuv.—*Mitth. geog. Gesellsch. i, pp.* 92–94. *Wien,* 1857.

HAKEWELL, J.—*See* HAKEWILL, J.

HAKEWILL, James (drawn by).—Naples from the West.—Engraved by George Cooke.
    Copper-pl. : 216×148 mm. View of Naples and Vesuvius from Posilippo through grape-vines. This was re-engraved smaller for Audot's book by Skelton *fils,* and is signed only " J. H." The large plate is in HAKEWILL, J.—A picturesque tour of Italy, from drawings made in 1816–1817 by J. . . . H . . ., Archᵗ.—*fol. London,* 1818.

HAKEWILL, J.—A picturesque tour of Italy, from drawings made in 1816–1817. —*fol.,* 63 *pls. with text. London,* 1820.

HALL, J.—Experiments on Whinstone and Lava.—*Trans. R. Soc. Edinb. v, p.* 63. *Edinburgh,* 1805.

HALL, Sidney.—[A series of sketches, with text, of Vesuvius in the eruption of 1872 in the " Graphic " newspaper as follows :]— Eruption of Mount Vesuvius. View from Pompeii (*with description on pp.* 429, 430 *and* 431, *May* 11*th*). A Lava Torrent (*p.* 448). Peasants flying from the lava (*pp.* 469–70, *May* 18*th*). House at S. Sebastiano overwhelmed and burnt by lava. Prof. Palmieri's Observatory. Sketch from the top of the Observatory, showing crater and the two courses taken by the lava. Lava current between the villages of Massa di Somma and S. Sebastiano (5 *figs. on p.* 472). Climbing the mountain (*pp.* 477 *and* 478, *May* 25*th*). A trip to the crater of Vesuvius (*text p.* 490). On the brink of the Crater (*p.* 493). The Neapolitan populace attacking San Gennaro (*p.* 516, *June* 1*st*).—" *The Graphic,*" v. *London,* 1872.

HAMEL, Du.—Regiæ scientiarium Academiæ historia in qua . . . dissertationes et experimenta digerunta.—2a ed. 8⁰, *pp.* 634. *Paris,* 1701.
Some lines describing the eruption of 5 April, 1694.

HAMILTON, Sir William.—An account of the last eruption of Vesuvius.—" *Gentleman's Magazine,*" *xxxviii, pp.* 578–79. *London,* 1768.—*Phil. Trans. R. Soc. lvii, pp.* 192–200. *London,* 1768.—*Phil. Trans. R. Soc. Abridged, xii, pp.* 417–19. *London,* 1809.

HAMILTON, Sir W.—Extract of a letter from the Hon. William Hamilton, his Majesty's Envoy Extraordinary at Naples, to the Right Hon. the late Earl of Morton, giving an account of the new eruption of Mount Vesuvius in 1767.—" *Gentleman's Magazine,*" *xxxix, pp.* 527–29, 1 *pl. London,* 1769.—*Phil. Trans. R. Soc. lviii, pp.* 1–12, 3 *pls. London,* 1769.—*Phil. Trans. R. Soc. Abridged, xii, pp.* 494–96. *London,* 1809.

HAMILTON, Sir W.—A Letter, containing some farther particulars on Mount Vesuvius and other Volcanos in the neighbourhood.—*Phil. Trans. R. Soc. lix, pp.* 18–22. *London,* 1770.

HAMILTON, Sir W.—Osservazioni sopra la natura del suolo di Napoli e quello dei suoi contorni. A Matteo Mati, Dottor di Medecina, membro della Società R. di Londra.
Consists of three MS. letters bound up in a volume in Italian with English notes and corrections. They are probably translation copies of the originals, which one would presume to be in English. The first is dated 16 Oct. 1770 and is Lettre v in Œuvres Complettes. The second is entitled " Estratto d'un altra Lettera del Signor Hamilton al Dr. Mati sullo stesso soggetto, Napoli, 5 Marzo 1771." It is not reproduced in the Œuvres Complettes. The third letter is to Lord Morton on the erupt. of Vesuvius 1767, dated 29 Dec. 1767, and is Lettre ii in his Œuvres Complettes.

HAMILTON, Sir W.—Remarks upon the nature of the soil of Naples and its neighbourhood.—*Phil. Trans. R. Soc. lxi* (1771), *pp.* 1–47, 48–50, 1 *map. London,* 1772.

HAMILTON, Sir W. — Observations on Mount Vesuvius, Mount Etna, and other Volcanos : in a series of letters, addressed to the Royal Society from the Honourable Sir W. Hamilton, K.B., F.R.S., His Majesty's Envoy Extraordinary and Plenipotentiary at the Court of Naples. To which are added explanatory notes by the Author, hitherto unpublished.—8⁰. *London,* 1772.—*Trans. R. Soc. lvii–lxi. London,* 1768–72.——2nd ed. 8⁰, *pp. iv+*179, 5 *pls.,* 1 *map, printed for T. Cadell in the Strand. London,* 1773.——3rd ed. *London,* 1774.——4th ed. *London,* 1783.

HAMILTON, Sir W.—Beobachtungen über den Vesuv, den Ætna und andere Vulcane ; in einer Reihe von Briefen an die Königl. Grossbr. Gesellsch. der Wissenschaften, etc. nebst neuen erläuternden Anmerkungen des Herrn Verfassers und mit Kupfern. Aus dem Englischen.—12⁰, *pp.* 196, *foll.* 2, 5 *pls.,* 1 *map, bei Haude und Spener. Berlin,* 1773.
This is a transl. of the original paper in the Phil. Trans. R. Soc. lvii–lxi. London, 1768–72.

HAMILTON, Sir W.—Campi Phlegræi.—*fol. Vol. i, pp.* 90, 1 *map,* 1 *pl., frontisp. ; Vol. ii,* 54 *pls. (text in Engl. and French), frontisp. Napoli,* 1776. [B.M.—Tab. 435. a.]
Br. Mus. copy contains MS. notes and the original drawings, besides 11 others and one print (of Vesuvius).

HAMILTON, Sir W.—Supplement to the Campi Phlegræi, being an account of the great eruption of Mount Vesuvius in August 1779.—*fol., pp.* 29, 5 *col. pls. (text in Engl. and French). Naples,* 1779. [B.M.—Tab. 435. a.]
Br. Mus. copy has the original drawings and 8 coloured drawings of Vesuvius in eruption.

HAMILTON, Sir W.—Account of an eruption of Mount Vesuvius which happened in August 1779.—*Phil. Trans. R. Soc. lxx, pp.* 42–84, 1 *pl. London,* 1780.

HAMILTON, Sir W.—Nachrichten von den neuesten Entdeckungen in der J.C. 79 am 24 August durch den Ausbruch des Vesuv verschuetteten Stadt Pompeji mit einigen Zusaetzen begleitet, von Cristoph Gottgeb. von Murr.—4⁰, *foll.* 2, *pp.* 26, 3 *pls. Nuernberg,* 1780.

HAMILTON, Sir W.—Œuvres complettes, traduites et commentées par l'abbé Giraud-Soulavie.—8⁰, pp. xx+506, 1 map. Paris, 1781. [C.A.]

HAMILTON, Sir W.—Neuere Beobachtungen über die Vulkane Italiens und am Rhein, nebst merkwürdigen Bemerkungen des Absts Giraud Soulavie v. G. A. R.—8⁰, pp. xvi+214, map. Frankfurt und Leipzig, 1784. [C.A.]

HAMILTON, Sir W.—Warneemingen over de Vuurbergen in Italie, Sicilie en omstreiks den Rhyn, etc.—8⁰, pp. 552. Amsterdam, 1784. [C.A.]—8⁰, pp. 16+55, foll. 4, 2 pls. Amsterdam, 1784. [O.V.]

HAMILTON, Sir W.—Some particulars of the present state of Mount Vesuvius; with the account of a journey into the province of Abruzzo, and a voyage to the Island of Ponza.—Phil. Trans. R. Soc. lxxvi, pp. 365–81, folding map and 2 pls. by Basire. London, 1786.

HAMILTON, Sir W.—Bericht vom gegenwärtigen Zustande des Vesuvs und Beschreibung einer Reise in die Provinz Abruzzo und nach der Insel Ponza.—4⁰. Dresden, 1787.

HAMILTON, Sir W.—Relazione ragionata della eruzione del Vesuvio di Napoli accaduta a' 15 Giugno 1794.

HAMILTON, Sir W.—Der Ausbruch des Vesuvs im Sommer 1794. Aus einem Schreiben des Ritters Hamilton an den Präsidenten Banks.—Neapel, 25 August, 1794. — See ANON. — Taschenbuch für Freunde der Gebirgskunde.

HAMILTON, Sir W.—An account of the late eruption of Mount Vesuvius. Letter to Sir Joseph Banks, Bart., P.R.S.—Phil. Trans. R. Soc. pp. 73–116, 7 mezzotints. London, 1795.—Also in Danish: 8⁰. Copenhagen, 1796.

HAMILTON, Sir W.—Efterretning om det sidste Udbrud af Vesuvius i et Brev fra W. H. til J. Banks, oversat efter den engelske Original ["Account of the late eruption of Mount Vesuvius"] af C. G. Rafn, og- foroget med Anmærkninger af P. C. Abildgaard.—8⁰. Kjøbenhavn, 1796.

HAMILTON, Sir W.—Campi Phlegræi, ou Observations sur les Volcans des Deux Siciles.—fol., pp. 118, 59 tav., frontisp. Paris, l'an septième [1799].
    Text in English and French.

HANSEL, V.—Mikroscopische Untersuchung der Vesuvlava vom Jahre 1878.—Min. petr. Mitth. ii, pp. 419–30. Wien, 1879.

HARDING, J. D. (drawn by).—Bay of Baiæ. Engraved by J. C. Varrall. Printed by Fenner, Sears & Co., London. Published Oct. 28, 1831, by Jennings & Chaplin, 62, Cheapside.
    Steel engrav. : 141×107 mm. Seven peasants sitting on ruins in foreground ; Vesuvius well defined in distance.

HARDING, J. D. (drawn . . . from a sketch by W. Page).—Bay of Naples. Engraved by E. Finden : London. Published 1833, by J. Murray, and sold by C. Tilt, 86, Fleet Street. [B.M., Portfolio of Naples.]
    Steel engrav. : 232×161 mm.

HARDING, [J. D.]—See MAPEI, C.—Italy, Classical, Historical and Picturesque.

HARE, A. J. C., and ST. CLAIR BADDELEY.—Cities of Southern Italy.—8⁰, pp. 237, 24 illustr., 2 plans, 1 map. London, 1911.

HAUGHTON, S., and HULL, E.—Report on the chemical, mineralogical and microscopical characters of the lavas of Vesuvius from 1631 to 1868.—Trans. R. Irish Acad. xxvi, pp. 49–164, 1 pl. Dublin, 1876.

HEARNE, [I.?] (publ.).—Interno del Vesuvio della notte 21 Marzo, 1829. Publ. by Hearne, 81, Strand.
    Hand-coloured stipple : 340×224 mm.

HEARNE, I. (publ.).—Eruzione [of Vesuvius] del 1832 [by day from Naples]. Pub. by Hearne, 81, Strand.
    Hand-coloured litho. : 330×218 mm.

HEARNE, I. (publ.).—Eruzione del 1832. Publis. by Hearne, 81, Strand.
    Two lava streams on cone of Vesuvius seen from ridge of Somma by night ; man and guide with torch in foreground. Hand-coloured litho. : 330×218 mm.

HECK, R.—Das Sicherheitsventil Italiens.— " Die Gartenlaube," p. 324. Leipzig, 1872.

HECK, R.—Der Vesuv an der Mündung vor dem groszen Ausbruch am 24 April 1872.— " Die Gartenlaube," p. 774. Leipzig, 1873.

HEIM, A.—Der Ausbruch des Vesuv im April 1872.—8⁰, pp. xv+52, 4 pls. Basel, 1873.

HEIM, A.—Der Vesuv im April 1872.— Zeitschr. deutsch. geol. Gesellsch. xxv, pp. 1–52. Berlin, 1873.

HELBIG.—Untersuchungen über die campanische Wandmalerei.—*pp.* 105. *Leipzig,* 1873.

HELBIG.—Monte Somma, from a fresco at Herculaneum.—*See his* " Le Pitture antiche d'Ercolano e contorni," *T. v. p.* 343 ; *also* FRANCO, P.—*Atti R. Acc. Pontaniana, xvii, Appendix, pp.* 1–28, 2 *pls. Napoli,* 1887.
Engrav. : 185 × 80 mm.

HELLEMANNS, J. GEORG.—De Montibus ignivomis, vulgò Feuer-speyende Berge.— 4⁰, *pp.* 22. *Marburgi Cattorum, Typis hæred. Joh. Jodoc. Kürsneri, Acad. Typogr.* 1698.

HENRICH-ERLANGEN, F.—Versuche mit frisch geflossener Vesuvlava, ein Beitrag zur Kenntnis der Fumarolentätigkeit.—*Zeitschr. f. angewandte Chemie, xix,* 30, *pp.* 1326–28. *Leipzig,* 1906.

HERBINII, J.—Dissertationes de admirandis mundi Cataractis supra et subterraneis, earumque principio, elementorum circulatione, ubi eadem occasione æstus maris reflui vera ac gemina causa asseritur, nec non terrestri ac primigenio Paradiso locus situsque verus in Palæstina restituitur, in tabula chorographica ostenditur, et contra Utopios, Indianos, Mesopotamios, aliosque asseritur.—4⁰, *pp.* 14+267+ 17, *figs. Amstelodami apud Janssonio-Wæsbergios,* 1678.

HESS, W.—Der Golf von Neapel, seine classischen Denkmale und Denkwürdigkeiten in Bildern aus dem Alterthum.— 8⁰, *tav. Leipzig,* 1878.
See Cap. XIII, pp. 244–67.

HESSENBERG, F. — Magnesia-glimmer (Biotit) vom Vesuv.—*Min. Notiz. von Hessen, N.F., H.* 1. *Frankfurt,* 1861.— *Abh. Senckenberg. naturf. Gesellsch. vi, pp.* 12–28. *Frankfurt a.M.,* 1866–67.

HESSENBERG, F.—Titanit vom Vesuv.— *Min. Notiz. v. Hessen, N.F.,* 1. *Frankfurt,* 1861.—*Abh. Senckenberg. naturf. Gesellsch. vi, pp.* 37–39. *Frankfurt a.M.,* 1866–67. —*N. J. f. Min. pp.* 364–65. *Stuttgart,* 1866.

HESSE-WARTEGG, E. V.—Drahtseilbahn auf dem Vesuv.—*Illustr. Zeitung, No.* 1924, *pp.* 414–15, 5 *illustr. Leipzig,* 1880.

HILDEBRAND, W.—Weitverbesserte und vielvermehrte MAGIA NATURALIS. Das ist Kunst- und Wunderbuch darinne begriffen wunderbahre Secreta, Geheimnisse u. Kunststücke, wie man nemlich mit den gantzen menschlichen Cörper zahmen u. wilden Thieren, Vögeln, Fischen, Unzieffern u. Insecten allerley Gewächsen, Pflanzungen und sonsten fast unerhörte wunderbarliche Sachen verrichten. Auch etliche Wunderschrifften künstlich bereiten zu Schimpff Kurtzweil löblicher u. lustiger Übung u. zu Nutz gebrauchen u. damit die Zeit vertreiben kan : beneben Erzehlung vieler wunderlichen Dingen so hin u. wieder in der Welt gefunden werden. In 4 Bücher eingetheilt, ietzo mit vielen geheimbten Kunststücklein welche bey den vorigen Exemplarien nicht zu finden u. gantz neu in Druck gegeben.—Mit Privil. begn. in 10 Jahren nicht nachzudrucken.— 4⁰, *foll.* 7+53+55+39+31. *Erffurdt, In Verl. J. Birckners Buchhandlers. Gedr. bey J. G. Hertzen,* 1664.—Earlier ed. *Leipzig,* 1610.
See Book 4, pp. 9–10 : lines on Etna and Vesuvius after the Latin lines of J. R. Rabman.

HIMMEL.—Nachricht von dem Ausbruche des Vesuvs am 15 Junius.—*Lausitz. Monatschr. Pt.* 2, *pp.* 31–41. 1794.

HINTON, I. (printed for).—A view of the late eruption of Mount Vesuvius. Printed for I. Hinton at the King's Arms in Newgate Street.
This engrav. is identical with one in Padre della Torre's account. It appeared in the " Gentleman's Magazine " in 1761 with a page of explanation : 239 × 186 mm.

HOBBS, W. H.—The grand eruption of Vesuvius in 1906.—*Journ. of Geol. No.* 7, *pp.* 636–55, *figs.* 14. *Chicago, Oct.-Nov.,* 1906.

HOCHSTETTER, FERD. C. VON.—Die Phlegräischen Felder und der Vesuv.—*Schrift. Ver. Naturw. Kennt. iv, pp.* 3–23. *Wien,* 1863–64.

HOCHSTETTER, F. C. VON.—Ueber den inneren Bau der Vulkane und über Miniatur-Vulkane aus Schwefel ; ein Versuch, vulcanische Eruptionen und vulcanische Kegelbildung im Kleinen nachzuahmen.— *N. J. f. Min. pp.* 469–78, 3 *woodcuts. Stuttgart,* 1871.

HOEFNAGLIUS, A. O. G. (depinxit).—Elegantissimus ad Mare Tyrrhenum ex Monte Pausilipo Neapolis Montisque Vesuvii prospectus 1578.—*In* BRUIN seu BRAUN.—Civitates Orbis Terrarum, etc.—*Coloniæ*, 1582–1618.—*See also:* BLAEV.—Theatrum Civitatum nec non Admirandorum.
View of Naples and Vesuvius from above entrance to Grotto, with two pages of explanation at back entitled : " L'Agréable et Plaisante veve de la Ville de Naples," etc. Engrav. map : 480 × 356 mm.

HOEPLI, U.—Catalogue Nr. 8. Bibliotheca Vesuviana. Catalogue d'une collection d'ouvrages précieux sur le Vésuve, l'Etna, les autres Volcans et les Tremblements de Terre.—8⁰. *Milan, U. Hoepli*, 1883.

HOEPLI, U.—Catalogue Nr. 14. Pompéi. Le Vésuve, Herculanum, etc. Avec un Appendice : L'Île d'Ischia.—8⁰. *Milan, U. Hoepli*, 1883.

HOERNES, DR. R.—Erdbebenkunde. Die Erscheinungen und Ursachen der Erdbeben, die Methoden ihrer Beobachtung.—8⁰, *woodcuts and pls. Leipzig*, 1893.
See pp. 240–44.

HOFF, K. E. A. VON.—Geschichte der durch Ueberlieferung nachgewiesenen natürlichen Veränderungen der Erdoberfläche.—5 vols. 8⁰. *Gotha*, 1822–41.
See Vol. ii, pp. 184–218 ; Vol. iii, pp. 394–400, 408–16.

HOFF, K. E. A. VON.—Chronik der Erdbeben und Vulcan-Ausbrüche mit vorausgehender Abhandlung über die Natur dieser Erscheinungen.—2 vols. 8⁰. *Vol. i, pp.* 6+470 ; *Vol. ii, pp.* 2+406. *Gotha*, 1840–41.

HOFFMANN, F.—Geognostische Beobachtungen. Gesammelt auf einer Reise durch Italien und Sicilien in den Jahren 1830–32.—*Archiv. F. Min. Geognos. etc. xiii, pp.* 3–726, 1 *pl.*, 1 *map. Berlin*, 1839.—[Sep. publ.] *Berlin*, 1839.
See pp. 68–69, 173–216, 304.

HOFFMANN, F.—Mémoire sur les terrains volcaniques de Naples, de la Sicile, et des Isles de Lipari.—*Bull. Soc. géol. France, iii, pp.* 170=80. *Paris*, 1833. — *C.R. Acad. Sci. xli, pp.* 872–76. *Paris*, 1855.

HOHENBERG, F.—*See* BRAUN, G.

HOLMS, CH.—*See* LAURENT, A.

HOMANN, J. B.—Urbis Neapolis cum præcipuis ejus ædificiis secundum planitiem exacta delineatio.—*coloured map and*

views. *Norimbergæ*, 1727. [B.M.—K. 83. 57, and also 24045. 12.]
Shows a sketchy, distant view of Vesuvius. This is similar to many other maps under names of different authors, as Vindelicor, etc.

HOMBRES-FIRMAS, L. A. D'.—Souvenirs de voyage aux environs du Vésuve.—*Bull. Soc. géog. S.* 2, *xvii, pp.* 205–13. *Paris*, 1842.

HON, H. LE.—*See* LE HON, H.

HOOK, C. W.—In sunny climes. Vesuvius, etc.—" The Argosy," *xlvii, pp.* 229–44, 5 *illustr. London*, 1889.

HORN, W. O. VON.—Zwei Ausbrüche des Vesuv's. Dargestellt für die Jugend und das Volk.—16⁰, *pp.* 89, 4 *copper-engrav. Wiesbaden*, 1863.

HORNADAY, W. T.—Up and down Vesuvius.—" The Cosmopolitan," *i, pp.* 102–10, 6 *illustr. London*, 1886.

HORNE, J. F.—Vesuvius and its eruptions.—*In* " The buried cities of Vesuvius," 8⁰, *pp.* 1–18, *illustr. London*, 1895.

HORNER, S.—*See* COLLETTA, P. 1860.

HOROZCO COVARRUVIAS, J. DE, Episcopus Agrigentinus.—Emblemata moralia memoriæ Sanc. D. D. Didaci Covarruvias de Leyva, Episcopi Segobiensis dedicata.—3 books in 1 vol. 8⁰, 100 *woodcuts. Lib. i, pp.* 4+256 ; *Lib. ii, pp.* 110 ; *Lib. iii, pp.* 100. *Agrigenti*, 1601.

HOSANG, E.—Am Vesuvkrater.—" Illustrirte Zeitung," No. 2185, *p.* 486, *with text. Leipzig*, 1885.
Original design, woodcut.

HOSPITAL, MARCHESE DE L'.—Memoria sopra la città sotteranea scoperta a' piedi del Monte Vesuvio.—*Raccolta di Opuscoli Sci. e Filos. xli, pp.* 1–61. *Venezia*, 1752 ?

HOUEL, J. B. (des. d'après nat.).—Vue du Vésuve et d'une partie du Golphe de Naples prise de l'endroit appellé Dogana di Terra près le Pont de la Madelaine.
Engrav. Boats, fishermen, cart, etc., in foreground ; Vesuvius with a cloud on its S. flank : 328 × 240 mm.

HOUEL, J. B.—Vue de Vésuve et d'une partie du Golfe de Naples prise de l'endroit appellé Dogana di Terra près le Pont de la Madeleine. Gravé à l'eau forte par Delvaux, terminé au burin par Longueuil. Naples (No. 31). [B.N.P., Vb. 121.]
A coloured engraving.

HOUEL, J. P. L. L.—Voyage pittoresque des Isles de Sicile, de Malthe et de Lipari ; où l'on traite des antiquités qui s'y trouvent encore ; des principaux phénomènes que la nature y offre ; du costume des habitans, et de quelques usages.—4 tom. *fol. T. i,* pp. vii+138, pls. 1–72, 1782 ; *T. ii, pp.* 148, *pls.* 73–144, 1784 ; *T. iii, pp.* 126, *pls.* 145–204, 1785 ; *T. iv, pp.* 124, *pls.* 205–64. *Paris,* 1787.—In German : 4 pts. 8⁰· *Gotha,* 1797–1805.

HOWARD, J.—Observations on the heat of the ground of Vesuvius.—*Phil. Trans. R. Soc. lxi, p.* 53. *London,* 1771.—Also in French : *Observations sur la Physique, etc., xiii, p.* 224. *Paris,* 1779.

HUBER, I. W. (fece).—Veduta di Posilipo. Roma 1814. Si vende presso Giorgio Glass dirimp¹º. S. Ferdinando. N° 54.
Outline engraving with view of Pal. Donn' Anna and Vesuvius : 320×231 mm.

HUELCKER, O.—Ein Tag auf dem Vesuv. —" *Die Gartenlaube,*" p. 841, 1 *woodcut. Leipzig,* 1875.

HUERTA, A. DE.—Soneto.—*See* QUINO-NES.—El Monte Vesvvio.

HUGHES, W. (sc.).—View of crater of Vesuvius from the South. [B.M. Portfolio of Naples.]
Panorama : 496×160 mm.

HULETT, I. (sculp.).—Mount Vesuvius with its eruption.
Engrav. in part copied from Sandrart, but with fewer figures : 186×157 mm.

HULL, E.—Composition of Vesuvian lava.—*Quart. Journ. Microscop. Sci. N.S. xv, p.* 330. *London,* 1875.

HULL, E.—Crystals of Olivine from Vesuvian Lava and Irish Basalt.—*Quart. Journ. Microscop. Sci. N.S. xv, p.* 411. *London,* 1875.

HULL, E.—Lavas of Vesuvius from 1631–1868.

HULL, E.—*See* HAUGHTON, S.

HULLMANDEL, C.—Twenty-four views of Italy, drawn from Nature, and engraved upon stone.—*obl. fol. [London]* 1818.

HUMBOLDT, A. VON.—Ueber den Bau und die Wirkungsart der Vulkane.—*Abh. k. Akad. Wiss.* (1822–23), pp. 137–55. *Berlin,* 1825. (With appendix by Oltmann, *q.v.*) —*Ansichten der Natur, ii,* pp. 251–96. *Tübingen,* 1849.—*Taschenb. gesammt. Min. xviii,* pp. 3–39. *Frankfurt,* 1824.

HUOT, J. J. N.—Coup d'œil sur les Volcans et sur les phénomènes volcaniques.—*pp.* 588, *maps* 30–46 (*bound separately*). — ?, 1831.
See Pls. 31, 34, 35.

HVRTADO DE MENDOÇA, A.—Dezimas. —*See* DE QUINONES.—El Monte Vesvvio.

IFE, A.—Fussreisse vom Brocken auf den Vesuv und Rückkehr in die Heimath.—8⁰, *pp. xii+234, 1 pl. Leipzig,* 1820. [C.A.]

ILARDI, N.—Breve cenno di Torre Annunziata.—16⁰, *pp.* 16. *Napoli,* 1861.

IMBERT DE VILLEFOSSE.—Vue du Mont Vésuve et de son éruption arrivée le 25 octobre 1751 à 10 heures du soir.—*fol.* 1. [C.A.]

IMPERATO, G.—L'enologia delle falde del Vesuvio. — *L'Agric. Merid. iii,* 19–22. *Portici,* 1880.

INCARNATO, C.—Prodigium Vesevi Montis, etc.—4⁰, *pp.* 7. *Neapoli,* 1632.——Another ed. 8⁰.

INCREDULO ACCADEMICO INCAVTO.— Incendio del Vesuvio. Ode.—12⁰, *foll.* 10. *Napoli,* 1632. [B.N.]

INCREDULO ACCADEMICO INCAVTO.— Le querele di Bacco per l'incendio del Vesuvio, ode.—8⁰, *pp.* 16. *Napoli,* 1632. [B.N.]

INOSTRANTZEV, A. A. VON.—Historische Skizze der Thätigkeit des Vesuvs vom Jahre 1857 bis jetzt. — *St. Petersburg,* 1872.

INOSTRANTZEV, A. A. VON.—Ueber die Mikrostructur der Vesuv-Lava vom Septemb. 1871, März und April 1872.—*St. Petersburg,* 1872. — *Zeitschr. gesammt. Naturw. vi,* pp. 470–71. *Halle,* 1872.— *Min. Mitth. ii,* pp. 101–6. *Wien,* 1872.

INSENSATO ACCADEMICO FURIOSO.— L'afflitta Partenope per l'incendio del Vesuvio al suo glorioso protettore S. Gennaro. — 12⁰, *foll.* 8. *Napoli,* 1632. [C.A.]

IRTON, MAJOR.—*See* WRIGHT, G. N.

ISABEY, J. B.—Voyage en Italie en 1822, 30 dessins.—*fol. Paris,* 1823.
See Pls. 4, 25.

ISABEY, J. [B. ?]—Le cratère du Vésuve après l'éruption de 1822.—pl. *fol.* [B.S.]

ITTIG, THOMAS.—De Montium Incendiis in quibus post ardentium toto passim orbe montium catalogum et historiam, ac variarum opinionum examen, non modo totius Naturæ cum in efficiendis tum in conservandis illis ignibus processus exponitur, etc. — 8⁰, *pp.* 16+347+*index. Lipsiæ,* 1671.
See pp. 70–90 and other refs.

IZZO, S.—Altra relazione del Monte Vesuvio. —*Gazz. (Suppl.) Nap. Civ. Commerc.* 76, 1804. [B.N.]

JACCARINO, DOM.—Lo Ciciarone de lo Visuvio.—*See* " Galleria di Costumi Napoletani," 8⁰, *p.* 197. *Napoli,* 1876.

JACOBUCCI, G.—Un episodio della eruzione Vesuviana del MDCCCLXXII.—8⁰, *pp.* 40. *Pomigliano d'Arco,* 1879.

JACOTET.—*See* COIGNET, M.—Voyage en Italie.

JADELOT, L'AB.—Mécanisme de la nature, ou Système du Monde fondé sur les forces du feu, etc.—8⁰, *pp.* xvi+259. *Londres,* 1787.
See pp. 209–59.

JAECKEL, O.—Bilder von der letzten Eruption des Vesuvs (1906).—[Abdr.] *Naturw. Wochenschr. N.F.* v, 36 and 37, 2 col. pls., 9 *figs.* 1906.

JAGGAR, T. A.—The volcano Vesuvius in 1906.—[Reprint from] *Technol. Quart.* xix, 2, *map, pp.* 105–15. *June,* 1906.

JAGGAR, T. A.—The eruption of Mount Vesuvius. April 7–8, 1906.—3 *figs.* — ?, — ?

JAMES, C.—Voyage scientifique à Naples avec Mr. Magendie en 1843.—8⁰, *pp.* 103. *Paris,* 1844. [O.V.]
See pp. 37–49.

JAMINEAU, J.—An extract of the substance of three letters concerning the late eruption of Mount Vesuvius.—*Phil. Trans. R. Soc.* xlix, *pp.* 24–27. *London,* 1756.—In Ital. : *Compend. Trans. Filos. Londra, pp.* 88–92. *Venezia,* 1793.

JANNACE, V.—La storia d'havere timore, e gran spavento dello foco dello inferno, lo quale si è scoperto per causa de li nostri peccati nella Montagna di Somma la quale si è aperta, e buttato lingue di foco, e cenere, e pietre che ha consumato tridece tra terre e casali intorno di se, li quali segni ci ha mostrato Iddio per nostro beneficio. E questo, e successo di martedì matino alli 16 di Decembre 1631.—12⁰, *foll.* 6. *Napoli,* 1632. [C.A.]

JANNASCH, P.—Die Auffindung des Fluors in dem Vesuvian vom Vesuv (1883).— *N. J. f. Min.* ii, *pp.* 123–35. *Stuttgart,* 1883.

JANNASCH, P.—Zur Kenntniss der Zusammensetzung des Vesuvians.—*N. J. f. Min.* ii, *pp.* 269–70. *Stuttgart,* 1883.

JANSSEN, J.—Sur une récente ascension au Vésuve.—*C.R. Acad. Sci.* cxl, *pp.* 200–2. *Paris,* 1905.

JANUARIO, F. DE. — Felicis Campaniæ Hilaritas tumvolata.—*fol. Neapoli,* 1632. [C.A.]

JANUARIO, R.—Analisi chimica qualitativa di una produzione Vesuviana.— Lettera al Prof. Palmieri.—*Rend. R. Acc. Sci.* xvii, *pp.* 147–48. *Napoli,* 1878.

JARDMET, C., AVRIL, R. DU.—Carte Géologique et Topographique du Mont Vésuve 1838. Gravé sur pierre par . . . . Lith. Roissy P. Q.
Coloured map : 278×190 mm.

JATTA, G.—Discorso sulla ripartizione civile, e chiesastica dell' antico agro Cumano, Misenese, etc.—8⁰, *pp.* viii+242. *Napoli,* 1843.

JAUCOURT, DE.—Vésuve.—*Article from* " Encyclopédie," 4⁰, *pp.* 330–34. *Genève.* [C.A.]

JEFFS, W.—Recollections of Italy, in 15 select views drawn from Nature in the years 1826 and 1827.—*fol. London,* 1829.

JERVIS, G.—*See* JERVIS, W. P.

JERVIS, W. P.—I Tesori sotterranei dell' Italia.—4 vols. 8⁰, *num. pls. and figs. Torino,* 1873–89.

JOANNE, P.—Italie.—16⁰, *pp.* 514, 10 *maps,* 80 *plans. Paris,* 1909.

JOHNS, C. A.—Vesuvius previous to, and during the eruption of 1872.—*Soc. Journ. Sci.* i, *pp.* 98–108. *Winchester,* 1874.

JOHNSEN, A.—Vesuvasche von April 1906. —*Centralbl. f. Min. No.* 13, *pp.* 385–87. *Stuttgart,* 1906.

JOHNSTON-LAVIS, H. J.—A visit to Vesuvius during an eruption.—" *Science Gossip*," xvi, *pp.* 9–10. *London,* 1880.

JOHNSTON-LAVIS, H. J.—Volcanic cones, their structure and mode of formation.— " *Science Gossip*," xvi, *pp.* 220–23, 1 *fig. London,* 1880.

JOHNSTON-LAVIS, H. J.—On the origin and structure of volcanic cones.—" *Science Gossip*," xvii, *pp.* 12–14, 4 *figs. London,* 1881.

JOHNSTON-LAVIS, H. J.—Smoke-rings, as seen from above Resina, Feb. 8th, 1881, at about 2 p.m.
Water-colour drawing : 312×235 mm.

JOHNSTON-LAVIS, H. J.—The late changes in the Vesuvian Cone.—" *Nature,*" *xxv, pp.* 294–95. 1882.

JOHNSTON-LAVIS, H. J.—Notes on the comparative specific gravities of molten and solidified Vesuvian lavas. [Abstr.]—*Quart. Journ. Geol. Soc. xxxviii, pp.* 240–41. 1882.

JOHNSTON-LAVIS, H. J.—Diary of Vesuvius from January 1 to July 16, 1882.—" *Nature,*" *xxvi, pp.* 455–56, *2 figs.* 1882.

JOHNSTON-LAVIS, H. J.—The late eruption of Vesuvius.—" *Nature,*" *xxix, pp.* 271, 291. 1884.—Also in French : " *L'Italie,*" 12 *et* 15 *janvier,* 1884.

JOHNSTON-LAVIS, H. J.—The Geology of Monte Somma and Vesuvius, being a study in Vulcanology.—*Quart. Journ. Geol. Soc. xl, pp.* 35–119, *2 figs.,* 1 *pl. London,* 1884. —[Abstr. in] *Geol. Mag. pp.* 379–80. 1883.

JOHNSTON-LAVIS, H. J.—The physical conditions involved in the injection, extrusion and cooling of Igneous Matter. [Abstr.]—*Quart. Journ. Geol. Soc. xli, Proc. pp.* 103–6. *London,* 1885.—*Geol. Mag. p.* 282. 1885.

JOHNSTON-LAVIS, H. J.—The new outburst of lava from Vesuvius.—" *Nature,*" *xxxii, pp.* 55, 108. 1885.

JOHNSTON-LAVIS, H. J.—Notice of a Geological Map of Monte Somma and Vesuvius.—*Rept. Brit. Assoc.* (1884), *p.* 730. 1885.—Also *Geol. Mag. pp.* 27–28. 1885.

JOHNSTON-LAVIS, H. J.—Some speculations on the phenomena suggested by a geological study of Vesuvius and Monte Somma.—*Geol. Mag. pp.* 302–7. 1885. —[Rept. in] *Peterm. Mitth. xxxi, p.* 401. *Gotha,* 1885.

JOHNSTON-LAVIS, H. J.—[First] Report of the Committee . . . for the Investigation of the Volcanic Phenomena of Vesuvius.—*Rept. Brit. Assoc.* (1885), *pp.* 395–96. *London,* 1886.—Also " *Nature,*" *xxxii, pp.* 505–6. 1885.

JOHNSTON-LAVIS, H. J.—Nouvelle éruption du Vésuve du 4 février, 1886.—" *L'Italie,*" Rome, 9 *février,* 1886.

JOHNSTON-LAVIS, H. J.—Vesuvian eruption of February 4th, 1886.—" *Nature,*" *xxxiii, p.* 367. 1886.

JOHNSTON-LAVIS, H. J.—The relationship of the structure of Igneous Rocks to the conditions of their formation.—*Scient. Proc. R. Dublin Soc. N.S. v, pp.* 113–55. 1886.

JOHNSTON-LAVIS, H. J.—On the Fragmentary Ejectamenta of Volcanoes.—*Proc. Geol. Assoc. ix, pp.* 421–32, 1 *pl.* 1886.

JOHNSTON-LAVIS, H. J.—Notes on Vesuvius from February 4 to August 7, 1886.—" *Nature,*" *xxxiv, pp.* 557–58. 1886.

JOHNSTON-LAVIS, H. J.—The relationship of the activity of Vesuvius to certain Meteorological and Astronomical Phenomena.—*Proc. R. Soc. xl, pp.* 248–49. *London,* 1886.

JOHNSTON-LAVIS, H. J.—L'eruzione del Vesuvio nel 2 Maggio 1885.—*Ann. Acc. Aspir. Nat. Era,* 3, i, *pp.* 87–94, *2 pls. Napoli,* 1886.

JOHNSTON-LAVIS, H. J.—Sounding a crater, fusion points, pyrometers, and seismometers.—" *Nature,*" *xxxv, p.* 197. 1886.

JOHNSTON-LAVIS, H. J.—Crater of Vesuvius, looking towards the East. End of 1886, or early in 1887.
Photo. : 377×150 mm.

JOHNSTON-LAVIS, H. J.—Diario dei fenomeni avvenuti al Vesuvio da Luglio 1882 ad Agosto 1886.—" *Lo Spettatore del Vesuvio e dei Campi Flegrei,*" nuova serie pubblicata a cura e a spese della Sezione Napoletana del Club Alpino Ital.—4°, *pp.* 81–103, 13 *photo-engrav. Napoli,* 1887.

JOHNSTON-LAVIS, H. J.—[Second] Report of the Committee . . . for the Investigation of the Volcanic Phenomena of Vesuvius and its Neighbourhood.—*Rept. Brit. Assoc.* (1886), *pp.* 226–28. *London,* 1887.—" *Nature,*" *xxxiv, p.* 481. 1886.

JOHNSTON-LAVIS, H. J.—Further observations on the form of Vesuvius and Monte Somma.—*Geol. Mag. pp.* 445–51, 1 *fig.* 1888.

JOHNSTON-LAVIS, H. J.—[Third] Report of the Committee . . . for the Investigation of the Volcanic Phenomena of Vesuvius and its Neighbourhood.—*Rept. Brit. Assoc.* (1887), *pp.* 226–29. *London,* 1888.

JOHNSTON-LAVIS, H. J.—The Ejected Blocks of Monte Somma ; Part I. Stratified Limestones. [Abstr.]—*Quart. Journ. Geol. Soc. xliv, Proc. Pt.* 4, *pp.* 94–96. 1888.—*Geol. Mag. pp.* 381–82. 1888.
Published in full in 1893.

JOHNSTON-LAVIS, H. J.—Eruptive apparatus of Vesuvius looking from W. to E. as seen from lava-plain filling 1872 crater, 31 Oct., 1888.
Photo.: 493×155 mm.

JOHNSTON-LAVIS, H. J.—Eruptive apparatus of Vesuvius looking from W. to E. as seen from lava-plain filling 1872 crater, 27 January, 1889.
Photo.: 565×150 mm.

JOHNSTON-LAVIS, H. J.—[Fourth] Report of the Committee . . . appointed for the Investigation of the Volcanic Phenomena of Vesuvius and its Neighbourhood.—Rept. Brit. Assoc. (1888), pp. 320–26. London, 1889.

JOHNSTON-LAVIS, H. J.—Nuove osservazioni fatte in Napoli e dintorni.—Boll. R. Com. Geol. Ital. xix, pp. 393–98. Roma, 1888.
Abstr. of preceding.

JOHNSTON-LAVIS, H. J.—The state of Vesuvius.—" Nature," xxxix, pp. 302–3. 1889.

JOHNSTON-LAVIS, H. J.—L'état actuel du Vésuve.—Bull. Soc. Belge Géol. Mém. iii, pp. 1–11, 3 figs. Bruxelles, 1889.

JOHNSTON-LAVIS, H. J.—Note sur les récentes manifestations du Vésuve.—Bull. Soc. Belge Géol. etc. iii, Proc.-verb. pp. 14–15. Bruxelles, 1889.

JOHNSTON-LAVIS, H. J.—Le ultime trasformazioni del Vesuvio.—Boll. R. Com. Geol. Ital. xx, pp. 136–39. Roma, 1889.
Ital. transl. of foregoing.

JOHNSTON-LAVIS, H. J.—Il pozzo Artesiano di Ponticelli.—Rend. R. Acc. Sci. S. 2, iii, pp. 142–48. Napoli, 1889.

JOHNSTON-LAVIS, H. J. — Volcans et Tremblements de Terre. Revue de ce qui a été publié sur ces sujets durant l'année 1888.—Ann. géol. univ. v, pp. 629–55. Paris, 1889.

JOHNSTON-LAVIS, H. J.—The conservation of heat in Volcanic Chimneys.—Rept. Brit. Assoc. (1888), pp. 666–67. London, 1889.

JOHNSTON-LAVIS, H. J.—Note on a mass containing Metallic Iron found on Vesuvius. —Rept. Brit. Assoc. (1888), pp. 667–68. London, 1889.

JOHNSTON-LAVIS, H. J.—The new eruption of Vesuvius.—" Nature," xl, p. 34. 1889.

JOHNSTON-LAVIS, H. J.—Viaggio scientifico alle regioni vulcaniche Italiane nella ricorrenza del centenario del " Viaggio alle due Sicilie " di Lazzaro Spallanzani.—8°, pp. 1–10. Napoli, 1889.
This is the programme of the excursion of the English geologists who visited the South Italian volcanoes under the direction of the author. It is here included since it contains various new and unpublished observations.

JOHNSTON-LAVIS, H. J.—Excursion to the South Italian Volcanoes. [Read Jan. 3, 1890.]—Proc. Geol. Assoc. xi, pp. 389–423. London, 1890.

JOHNSTON-LAVIS, H. J.—The extension of the Mellard Reade and C. Davison theory of Secular Straining of the Earth to the explanation of the deep phenomena of Volcanic Action.—Geol. Mag. pp. 246–49. 1890.

JOHNSTON-LAVIS, H. J.—Volcans et Tremblements de Terre (Revue).—Ann. géol. univ. vi, pp. 355–81. Paris, 1890.

JOHNSTON-LAVIS, H. J.—Fifty conclusions relating to the eruptive phenomena of Monte Somma, Vesuvius and Volcanic Action in general.—8°, pp. 6. Naples, 1890.

JOHNSTON-LAVIS, H. J.—[Fifth] Report of the Committee . . . for the Investigation of the Volcanic Phenomena of Vesuvius and its Neighbourhood.—Rept. Brit. Assoc. (1889), pp. 283–94, 5 figs. London, 1890.

JOHNSTON-LAVIS, H. J.—Top of Vesuvius, 3rd May, 1891, as seen from the S.W. edge of the 1872 crater.
Photo. : 365×150 mm.

JOHNSTON-LAVIS, H. J.—Geological map of Vesuvius and Monte Somma, with a short and concise account of the geology and eruptive phenomena to serve as an explanation to the map. Scale 1 : 10,000.—Philip and Son, London, 1891.—[Reviewed in] " Nature," xliv, pp. 271–72. 1891.
There were separate publications of the explanatory text as follows :

JOHNSTON-LAVIS, H. J.—A short and concise account of the eruptive phenomena and geology of Monte Somma and Vesuvius in explanation of the great Geological Map of that volcano, constructed during the years 1880 to 1888.—16°, pp. 22. London, 1891.—In Ital. 16°, pp. 24.

JOHNSTON-LAVIS, H. J.—Il Vesuvio.—
" *Il Corriere di Napoli*," 10 *Giugno*, 1891.

JOHNSTON-LAVIS, H. J.—L'Éruption du
Vésuve du 7 juin 1891.—" *L'Italie*,"
Rome, 13 *juin*, 1891.

JOHNSTON-LAVIS, H. J.—L'Éruption du
Vésuve.—" *Le Figaro*," *Paris*, 17 *juin*,
1891.

JOHNSTON-LAVIS, H. J.—The Eruption of
Vesuvius of June 7, 1891.—" *Nature*," *xliv*,
pp. 160–61; 320–22, 1 *fig.*; 352. *London*,
1891.

JOHNSTON-LAVIS, H. J.—The Eruption of
Vesuvius of June 7th, 1891.—" *The Mediterranean Naturalist*," pp. 21–22 (*July* 1);
pp. 54–57, 1 *fig.* (*Sept.* 1). *Malta*, 1891.

JOHNSTON-LAVIS, H. J. — Lettre sur
l'éruption du Vésuve du 7 juin, 1891.—
" *L'Italie*," *Rome*, 18 *juillet*, 1891.

JOHNSTON-LAVIS, H. J.—L'Éruption du
Vésuve, visites d'exploration au volcan.—
" *La Nature*," pp. 152–54, 4 *figs.* *Paris*,
8 *août*, 1891.

JOHNSTON-LAVIS, H. J.—L'Eruzione del
Vesuvio del 7 Giugno, 1891.—[Extr.]
" *Rassegna delle Scienze Geologiche*," *i*,
pp. 12, 4 *figs.* *Roma*, *Agosto*, 1891.

JOHNSTON-LAVIS, H. J. — The South
Italian Volcanoes, being the account of an
Excursion to them made by English and
other Geologists in 1889 under the auspices
of the Geologists' Association of London,
and the direction of the author, with papers
on the different localities by Messrs.
Johnston-Lavis, Platania, Sambon, Zezi
and Mme. Antonia Lavis, including the
Bibliography of the Volcanic Districts.—
8⁰, pp. vi+342, 16 *pls.* *Furchheim*, *Naples*,
1891.—[Reviewed in] " *Nature*," *xliv*, pp.
539–40. 1891.
A reprint of the account given in the
Proc. Geol. Assoc. with the addition of the
Bibliography.

JOHNSTON-LAVIS, H. J., and MME. AN-
TONIA LAVIS.—Bibliography of the
geology and eruptive phenomena of the
South Italian Volcanoes that were visited
in 1889 as well as of the submarine volcano
of A.D. 1831.—*From* " The South Italian
Volcanoes, etc." 8⁰, pp. 89–331. *Naples*,
1891.
Chapt. VII of foregoing, a number of
reprints of which were also issued.

JOHNSTON-LAVIS, H. J.—A short and
concise account of the geology of Vesuvius
and Monte Somma.—*In* " The S. Italian
Volcanoes, etc." pp. 45–58. *Naples*,
1891.

JOHNSTON-LAVIS, H. J.—[Sixth] Report
of the Committee . . . appointed for the
Investigation of the Volcanic Phenomena
of Vesuvius and its Neighbourhood.—*Rept.*
Brit. Assoc. (1890), pp. 397–410, 3 *figs.*
London, 1891.

JOHNSTON-LAVIS, H. J. — [Seventh]
Report of the Committee . . . appointed
for the Investigation of the Volcanic
Phenomena of Vesuvius and its Neighbour
hood.—*Rept. Brit. Assoc.* (1891), pp. 312–
20, 3 *figs.*, 1 *pl.* *London*, 1892.

JOHNSTON-LAVIS, H. J.—The Ejected
Blocks of Monte Somma; Part I. Stratified
Limestones.—*Trans. Edinb. Geol. Soc. vi*,
pp. 314–51, 3 *pls.*, 1 *fig.* 1893.

JOHNSTON-LAVIS, H. J.—[Remarks on
Eozoonal Structure in Ejected Blocks from
Monte Somma.]—*Quart. Journ. Geol. Soc.*
xlix, *Proc.* pp. 149–50. *London*, 1893.

JOHNSTON-LAVIS, H. J.—[Eighth] Report
of the Committee . . . appointed for the
Investigation of the Volcanic Phenomena
of Vesuvius and its Neighbourhood.—*Rept.*
Brit. Assoc. (1892), pp. 338–43. *London*,
1893.—*Geol. Mag.* pp. 507–13. 1892.

JOHNSTON-LAVIS, H. J.—The causes of
variation in the composition of Igneous
Rocks.—" *Natural Science*," *iv*, pp. 134–40.
London, 1894.

JOHNSTON-LAVIS, H. J., GREGORY,
J. W.—Eozoonal Structure of the Ejected
Blocks of Monte Somma.—*Scient. Trans.*
R. Dublin Soc. N.S. v, pp. 259–86, 5 *photo-
engrav.* 1894.—*Abstr. Proc. Geol. Soc.*
1892–93, *No.* 610, *June* 7, pp. 107–8.
London.

JOHNSTON-LAVIS, H. J.—The Science of
Vulcanology [being the introductory address to a course of lectures on that
subject in the R. University of Naples].—
" *Nature*," *l*, pp. 66–68. 1894.—" *Science*,"
16 *Mar.*, 1894.

JOHNSTON-LAVIS, H. J.—[Ninth Report
of the Committee appointed for the Investigation of] The Volcanic Phenomena of
Vesuvius and its Neighbourhood.—*Rept.*
Brit. Assoc. (1893), pp. 471–73. *London*,
1894.

JOHNSTON-LAVIS, H. J.—[Tenth Report of the Committee appointed for the Investigation of] The Volcanic Phenomena of Vesuvius and its Neighbourhood.—*Rept. Brit. Assoc.* (1894), *pp.* 315-18. *London,* 1895.—*Geol. Mag. pp.* 513-16. 1894.

JOHNSTON-LAVIS, H. J.—The Eruption of Vesuvius, July 3, 1895.—" *Nature,*" *lii, pp.* 343-45, 4 *figs.* 1895.

JOHNSTON-LAVIS, H. J.—*See* DAWSON, J. W. 1895.

JOHNSTON-LAVIS, H. J.—[Eleventh and final Report of the Committee appointed for the Investigation of] The Volcanic Phenomena of Vesuvius and its Neighbourhood.—*Rept. Brit. Assoc.* (1895), *p.* 351. 1896.

JOHNSTON-LAVIS, H. J.—Calcareous confetti and oolitic structure.—*Rept. Brit. Assoc.* (1899), *pp.* 744-46. 1900.

JOHNSTON-LAVIS, H. J.—Second cutting below Eremo Station on Railway of Vesuvius, N. side of cutting. Oct., 1903. Negat. 308, 309.
Panorama of tuffs on slopes of Vesuvius showing section of ancient ravines. Photo.: 410×155 mm.

JOHNSTON-LAVIS, H. J.—A new Vesuvian mineral, " Chlormanganokalite." — " *Nature,*" *lxxiv, pp.* 103-4. 1906.

JOHNSTON-LAVIS, H. J.—Remarks and explanation of an exhibit of views of Vesuvius, taken after the eruption of Vesuvius in April, 1906, made before the Geological Society of London.—*Proc. Geol. Soc. p.* cxxxiv, 1906.—" *Nature,*" *lxxiv, pp.* 165-66. 1906.—*Abstr. Proc. Geol. Soc. No.* 830, *pp.* 107-9. *London,* 1905-6.
Also quoted as " The recent eruptive phenomena of Vesuvius."

JOHNSTON-LAVIS, H. J.—" The New Vesuvius. — Its unrecognizable Aspect. First photographs of the altered cone, obtained and described for the ' Sphere ' by H. J. J.-L., Prof. of Vulcanology at Naples, who described to King Edward the effects of the great eruption."— " *Sphere,*" 3 *views and text. London,* 2nd *June,* 1906.

JOHNSTON-LAVIS, H. J.—Another new Vesuvian mineral, " Chlornatrokalite."— " *Nature,*" *lxxiv, p.* 174. 1906.

JOHNSTON-LAVIS, H. J.—[A reprint of the three preceding articles.]—8⁰, *pp.* 4. *St. Dizier,* 1906.

JOHNSTON-LAVIS, H. J.—Recent observations at Vesuvius. [Title only.]—*Rept. Brit. Assoc.* (1906), *p.* 579. 1907.

JOHNSTON-LAVIS, H. J.—De la relation existant entre l'activité du Vésuve et certains phénomènes météorologiques et astronomiques.—*Bull. Soc. Belge Géol. xxi, Mém. pp.* 303-24, 1 *pl. Bruxelles,* 1907.

JOHNSTON-LAVIS, H. J., SPENCER, L. J. —On Chlormanganokalite, a new Vesuvian mineral ; with notes on some of the associated minerals.—*Min. Mag. xv, pp.* 54-61. 1908.

JOHNSTON-LAVIS, H. J.—The Eruption of Vesuvius in April, 1906.—*Scient. Trans. R. Dublin Soc. S.* 2, *ix, pp.* 139-209, 21 *pls.,* 2 *figs.,* 2 *col. maps.* 1909.—[Reviewed in] *Geol. Mag. p.* 281, 1909, [and in] " *Nature,*" *lxxx, pp.* 289-90, 3 *figs.* 1909.

JOHNSTON-LAVIS, H. J.—The mechanism of Volcanic Action, being the opening address to Section III. (Vulcanology) of the Int. Geographical Congress at Geneva, 1908.—*Geol. Mag. pp.* 433-43, 2 *pls.,* 1 *fig.* 1909.—[Reprinted in] *Smithsonian Report for* 1909, *pp.* 305-15, 3 *pls. Washington,* 1910.

JOHNSTON-LAVIS, H. J.—Mécanisme de l'Activité Volcanique.—*C.R. Travaux* IX. *Congrès Internat. Géographie* (1908), *pp.* 187-200, 5 *pls. Genève,* 1910.

JOHNSTON-LAVIS, H. J.—Osmotic Metamorphism : see discussion of Dedolomitization in Marble of Port Shepstone (Natal), by F. H. Hatch.—*Quart. Journ. Geol. Soc. lxvi, pp.* 520-22. 1910.

JOHNSTON-LAVIS, H. J.—On the effects of Volcanic Action in the production of Epidemic Diseases in the Animal and in the Vegetable Creation, and in the production of Hurricanes and Abnormal Atmospherical Vicissitudes.—8⁰, *pp.* xii+67. *J. Bale, Sons and Danielsson, London,* 1914.
Parkin Prize Essay for Dec., 1913.

JOLI.—*See* COIGNET.—Voyage en Italie.

JOLY.—*See* COIGNET, M.—Vues pittoresques de l'Italie, etc.

JONGSTE DE CLASSENS, E. A.—Souvenir d'une promenade au Mont Vésuve.—8⁰, *pp.* 61. *Naples,* 1841.

JORDANUS, D. — Delectus Scriptorum rerum Neapolitanarum qui populorum, ac civitatem res antiquas, aliasque vario tempore gestas memoriæ prodirunt. Partim nunc primum editi, partim auctiores, ac emendatiores accesserunt variæ, ac accuratæ tabulæ geographicæ, ac aliæ cum indice locupletissimo, *etc.—fol., pp. 5+ 890+index, pls. Neapoli*, 1735.
Reproduces Ambrosius Leo's "De Agro Nolano," and the plates include a re-drawing of the first known view of Vesuvius.

JORDANUS FABIUS.—De Vesuvio Monte (1631).—*Copy of MS. in the Bibl. Brancacciana, 8⁰, pp.* 60. [C.A.]

JORI, V.—Portici e la sua Storia.—*8⁰, foll. 5, pp.* 178. *Napoli*, 1882.

JORIO, A. DE.—Indicazione del più remarcabile in Napoli e contorni. Giosne Russo del. 1819.
A folding map, extending from Lago di Patria to Pestum.

JORIO, A. DE.—Notizie su gli scavi di Ercolano.—*8⁰, pp.* 122+2, 5 *pls. Napoli*, 1827. [C.A.]

JOUSSET, P.—L'Italie illustrée.—*fol., pp.* 370, 14 *col. maps and plans*, 9 *engrav. maps*, 12 *pls.*, 784 *photos. Paris*, 1829.

JUDD, J. W.—Contributions to the study of Volcanoes.—*Geol. Mag. pp.* 348–56. *London*, 1875.

JUDD, J. W.—Volcanoes : what they are and what they teach.—*International Scientific Series*, 8⁰, 96 *illustr. London*, 1881.

KADEN, W.—Der Ausbruch des Vesuv am 26 April 1872.—*Illustrirte Zeitung, no.* 1507, *pp.* 360–61, 2 *illustr.; no.* 1508, *pp.* 380–81, 3 *illustr.; no.* 1512, *p.* 453, 1 *illustr. Leipzig*, 1872.

KADEN, W.—Das Observatorium auf dem Vesuv.—*Illustrirte Zeitung, no.* 1510, *p.* 418, 1 *illustr. Leipzig*, 1872.

KADEN, W.—Der Bahnhof auf dem Vesuv. —*Illustrirte Welt, xxix, pp.* 406–7, 1 *illustr.* (from a drawing by G. Cosenza). *Stuttgart u. Leipzig*, 1881.

KADEN, W.—Vesuv und Aetna. Touristische Aufzeichnungen und Randbemerkungen, I, II.—*Westermann's Monatshefte, lxiv, pp.* 529–42, 7 *figs., pp.* 599–615, 7 *figs. Braunschweig*, 1888.

KAEPPELIN (del. 1830).—Éruption en 1822. Pl. 24.
Vesuvius from the sea ; rough litho. : 200×138 mm.

KAEPPELIN (del.).—Éruption en 1822. Lith. de Engelmann. Pl. 26.
Vesuvius from sea at night ; rough litho. : 202×139 mm.

KAISER, E.—Melilith und Nephelin vom Vesuv. Mittheilungen aus dem Mineralogischen Museum der Universität Bonn, IX Theil.—*Zeitschr. f. Kryst. u. Min. xxxi*, 1, *pp.* 24–28. *Leipzig*, 1899.

KAISER, FRED.—Éruption du Vésuve le premier de l'an 1812 prise à Ste. Lucie. No. 3.—*Naples*, 1812. [B.N.P., Vb. 121.]
A beautiful coloured engraving.

KAISER, F. (dis. e inc. dal vero l'Anno 1829).—Eruzione del Vesuvio a Napoli. Veduta da Santa Lucia. N⁰ 3. Si vende in Roma da Tommaso Cuccioni Negoziante di Stampe in Via della Croce. N⁰ 25.
Outline engrav. : 188×138 mm. ; ox-wagon and goats in foreground.

KALKOWSKY, L. E.—Ueber Krystallsystem und Zwillingsbildung des Tenorites (darunter auch Tenorit vom Vesuv).— *Zeitschr. f. Kryst. u. Min. iii, pp.* 279–87, *Taf. vi, figs.* 9 *and* 10. *Leipzig*, 1879.

KARSTEN, H.—Zur Geologie der Insel Capri.—*N. J. f. Min. i, pp.* 139–61. *Stuttgart*, 1895.

KATZ (gravé par).—Vue du Mont Vésuve prise du Mont Sᵗ Angelo, où est située une Maison de Camaldules. À Augsbourg dans le Négoce de l'Académie des Arts.
A hand-painted outline engrav. : 344× 227 mm., copy of the plate by Desmoulins, N⁰ 35, A.P.D.R.

KEILHACK, F. L. H. K.—Ueber gelbe Schlacken vom Vesuv.—*Zeitschr. deutsch. geol. Gesellsch. xliv, p.* 161. *Berlin*, 1892.

KENNGOTT, J. G. A.—Bemerkungen über die Zusammensetzung einer Vesuvlava.— *Zeitschr. gesammt. Naturw. xv, pp.* 102–13. *Halle, Berlin*, 1860.

KENNGOTT, J. G. A.—Pyrit, Calcit, Anorthit vom Vesuv.—*Vierteljahrsschr. Naturf. Gesellsch. xiv, pp.* 408–9. *Zürich*, 1869.

KENNGOTT, J. G. A.—Salmiak vom Vesuv. —*Vierteljahrsschr. Naturf. Gesellsch. xv, pp.* 379–80. *Zürich*, 1870.

KENNGOTT, J. G. A.—Ueber die Zusammensetzung des Vesuvian.—*N. J. f. Min. i, pp.* 200–7. *Stuttgart*, 1891.

KENNGOTT, J. G. A.—Die Formel des Vesuvischen Meionit.—*N. J. f. Min. i, p. 47. Stuttgart, 1892.*

KERNOT, F.—L'Acqua Filangieri minerale acidolo-alcalina con l'analisi quantitativa del Prof. R. Monteferrante.—8°, *pp.* 84, 1 *map. Napoli, 1873.*
Map of lava streams of Vesuvius.

KERNOT, G.—Analisi chimica delle ceneri Vesuviane dell' Aprile, 1906.—*Rend. R. Acc. Sci. S.* 3, *xii, pp.* 449–62. *Napoli, 1906.*

KERNOT, G.—Sulla presenza di Elementi Radioattivi in alcune Incrostazioni delle Fumarole del Vesuvio.—*Rend. R. Acc. Sci. S.* 3, *xvi, pp.* 48–50. *Napoli, 1910.*

KEWITSCH, J.—Die Vulkane Pelé, Krakatau, Etna, Vesuv.—8°, *pp.* 1–35, *figs. Norden, 1902.*

KIRCHER, A.—Diatribe de prodigiosis crucibus quæ tam supra vestes hominum, quam res alias non pridem post ultimum incendium Vesuvii Montis, Neapoli comparuerunt.—8°, *foll.* 4, *pp.* 103, 1 *pl. Romæ, 1661.* [C.A.]
See also: CARAMUELIUS, A. [*i.e.* G. SCHOTT].—Ioco-Seriorum Naturæ et Artis . . . centuriæ tres.—8°. *Herbipoli* [1666]. Also in German, 1677.

KIRCHER, A.—Mundus subterraneus, in XII libros digestus ; qvo divinum subterrestris mundi opificium, mira ergasteriorum naturæ in eo distributio, verbo πανταμορφον protei regnum, universæ denique naturæ majestas et divitiæ summa rerum varietate exponuntur. Abditorum effectuum causæ acri indagine inquisitæ demonstrantur ; cognitæ per artis et naturæ conjugium ad humanæ vitæ necessarium usum vario experimentorum apparatu, nec non novo modo, et ratione applicantur.—2 vols. *fol. Vol. i, foll.* 16, *pp.* 346 ; *Vol. ii, foll.* 6, *pp.* 487, *foll.* 6, *index, num. pls. and figs. Amstelodami, apud Ioannem Janssonium, 1665.*——2nd ed. 2 tom. *fol.* 1668.——3rd ed. *T. i, pp.* 18+ 366+6 ; *T. ii, pp.* 8+507+9. 1678.
The plate of Vesuvius is a grotesque exaggeration, but still is useful as showing the summit conformation in 1638.

KIRCHER, A.—The Vulcano's : or, burning and fire-vomiting Mountains, famous in the World : with their remarkables. Collected for the most part out of Kircher's " Subterraneous World."—8°, *foll.* 4, *pp.* 64, 1 *pl. London, 1669.*

KLAPROTH, M. H.—Risultato dell' analisi di alcune sostanze minerali.—*Giorn. Lett. xc, pp.* 81–104. *Napoli, 1793.*
Referring to incrustations, etc., of sulphates in an opening in the Vesuvian cone.

KLAPROTH, M. H.—Beiträge zur chemischen Kenntniss der Mineralkörper.—6 vols. 8°. *Posen u. Berlin, 1795–1815.*
Vol. ii is entitled : " Chemische Abhandlungen gemischten Inhalt."

KLAPROTH, M. H.—Chemische Untersuchung des blauen Vesuvischen Kalksteins. —*Mag. Gesellsch. Nat.-Freunde, i, pp.* 251– 54. *Berlin, 1807.*

KLEIN, J. A., NAPOLI, A., and Nbg. 1824.
A good engrav. ; man, ox-cart, one ox reposing, and distant view of Vesuvius : 189 × 134 mm.

KLEIN, J. F. C.—[Optische Untersuchung zweier Humitkrystalle des dritten Typus vom Vesuv.]—*N. J. f. Min. pp.* 633–35. *Stuttgart, 1876.*

KLEIN, J. F. C.—Optische Studien. I : 1°. Die optischen Constanten des Anorthits vom Vesuv.—*Sitzber. k. preuss. Akad. Wiss. xix, pp.* 346–58. *Berlin, 1899.*

KLEINPAUL, R.—Neapel und seine Umgebung. Mit 142 Illustrationen.—*fol., pp.* 183. *Leipzig, 1884.*
Contains several woodcuts of Vesuvius.

KLEMM, G.—Reise durch Italien.—8°, *pp. xii*+515. *Dresden und Leipzig, 1839.*
See pp. 379–80 : description of the effect of the smaller eruption of Vesuvius in 1834 upon its crater, and how this small one led to the big eruption of August, 1838.

KLUGE, K. E.—Verzeichniss der Erdbeben und vulkanischen Eruptionen und der dieselben begleitenden Erscheinungen in den Jahren 1855 und 1856.—*Allgem. deutsch. nat. hist. Zeit. N.F. iii, pp.* 321– 43, 361–90, 401–16. *Dresden, 1857.*

KLUGE, K. E.—Ueber einige neue Forschungen auf dem Gebiete des Vulkanismus.—*Zeitschr. deutsch. geol. Gesellsch. xv, pp.* 377–402. *Berlin, 1863.*

KNOLL, F.—Wunder der feuerspeyenden Berge in Briefen an eine Frau ; für Damen und Liebhaber der Natur.—16°. *Erfurt, 1784.*
See Letters 14–20.

KNUETTEL, S.—Bericht über die vulkanischen Ereignisse im engeren Sinne während des Jahres 1893, nebst einem Nachtrag zu dem Bericht vom Jahre 1892. —*Min. u. petr. Mitth. pp.* 196 *et seq. Wien,* 1895.
See pp. 246–49.

KOBELL, W. X. F. F. VON.—Analyse eines sinterartigen Minerals vom Vesuv. — *Gelehrt. Anzeig. xxi, coll.* 305–7. *München,* 1845.

KOESTLIN, C. H.—Examen mineralogico-chemicum materiei, quæ Herculaneum et Pompejos anno 79 æræ Christ sepelivit.— *Fasciculus animadversionum phisiologici atque mineralogico-chimici argumenti,* 4°. *Stuttgardiæ,* 1780. [C.A.]

KOKSCHAROW, N. VON.—*See* KOKSHAROV, N. I.

KOKSHAROV, N. I.—Ueber den Klinochlor von Achmatowsk am Ural und den zweiaxigen Glimmer vom Vesuv (1854).— *Ann. Phys. Chem. xciv, pp.* 212–16. *Leipzig,* 1855.—*Bull. Class. Phys. Math. Acad. Imp. Sci. xiii, coll.* 149–53. *St. Pétersbourg,* 1855.—*Jahrb. k. k. geol. Reichsanst. v, pp.* 852–66. *Wien,* 1856.

KOKSHAROV, N. I.—Messungen eines besonders vollkommen ausgebildeten Anorthitcrystalls vom Vesuv.—*Bull. Class. Phys. Math. Acad. Imp. Sci. N.S. vii, coll.* 326–33. *St. Pétersbourg,* 1864.

KOKSHAROV, N. I.—[Ueber Klinochlor und den Glimmer vom Vesuv.]—*N. J. f. Min. pp.* 351–52. *Stuttgart,* 1866.

KOKSHAROV, N. I.—Ueber den Glimmer vom Vesuv.—*Materialien z. Min. Russlands, vii. St. Petersburg,* 1875.

KOKSHAROV, N. I.—[Der Biotit vom Vesuv gehört dem hexagonalen System an.]—*N. J. f. Min. pp.* 857–58. *Stuttgart,* 1875.

KOLDERUP, C. F.—Vesuvs Verksomhed vaaren 1906.—" *Naturen," xxxi, pp.* 57–63, *fig. (sketch-map). Bergen,* — ?

KOPISCH, A.—Auf dem Vesuv am 13 November, 1828. Improvisation.—*Gesammelte Werke, ii,* 12 *strophe. Berlin,* 1856.

KÖVESLIGETHY.—L'ultima eruzione del Vesuvio.—*Földrajzi Közlemenyck, nn.* 6–10. *Budapest* [1896 ?].

KRANZ, W.—Vulcanismus und Tektonik im Becken von Neapel.—*Peterm. geog. Mitth. pp.* 131–35, 203–6, 258–64, 2 *maps. Gotha,* 1912.

KRAUS, E. H.—*See* VIOLA, C. 1900.

KRENNER, J. A.—Ueber den Pseudobrookit vom Vesuv.—*Zeitschr. f. Kryst. u. Min. xvii, p.* 516. *Leipzig,* 1890.—*Földtani Közlöng, xviii, pp.* 81–83. 1888. (In Hungarian.)

KRESSNER. — Geographisch-orographische Uebersicht über das vulkanische Terrain im Neapolitanischen.—*Berg-u. Hüttenmänn. Zeitung, xxii (N.F. xvii), pp.* 236–37. *Freiberg,* 1863.

KREUTZ, F.—Mikroskopische Untersuchungen der Vesuv-Laven vom Jahre 1868.— *Anzeig. Akad. Wiss. vi, pp.* 26–27. *Wien,* 1869.—*Sitzber. Akad. Wiss. lix, Abth.* 2, *pp.* 177–88, 1 *pl. Wien,* 1869.

KREUTZ, F.—Ueber Vesuvlaven von 1881 und 1883.—*Min. u. petr. Mitth. N.F. vi, pp.* 133–50. *Wien,* 1884.

KUDERNATSCH, J.—Chemische Untersuchung einiger Abänderungen des Augits und der Hornblende.—*Ann. Phys. Chem. xxxvii, pp.* 577–88. *Leipzig,* 1836.—*N. J. f. Min. pp.* 596–98. *Stuttgart,* 1836.
See pp. 583–84.

KUDERNATSCH, J.—Analyse des Augit.— *Ann. Phys. u. Chem. xxxvii, p.* 577. *Leipzig,* 1838.

KURR, J. G. VON.—Ueber den letzten Ausbruch des Vesuvs im December 1861.— *Jahresh. Ver. f. vaterl. Naturk. in Würtemberg, xix, pp.* 45–47. *Stuttgart,* 1863.

L. [E. R.]—A night on Vesuvius in eruption. —[*Newspaper.*] 1871.

LABAT.—Le Vésuve et les sources thermo-minérales.—*Bull. Soc. géol. France, S.* 3, *xxii, C.R. pp. lxxix–lxxxi. Paris,* 1894.

LA CAVA, P.—Osservazioni sullo stato attuale del Vesuvio.—*Ann. Acc. Aspir. Nat. i, pp.* 7–10. *Napoli,* 1843.

LA CAVA, P.—Rapporto sui cambiamenti avvenuti al Vesuvio dal 27 Dicembre [1842] al 19 Marzo 1843.—8°, *pp.* 12. [O.V.]— *Ann. Acc. Aspir. Nat. i, pp.* 161–69. *Napoli,* 1843.

LACROIX, A. F. A.—Les enclaves des roches volcaniques.—*Ann. Acad. de Mâcon, S.* 2, *x, pp.* 1–710, 8 *pls.* 1893.

LACROIX, A. F. A.—Étude sur le Métamorphisme de contact des roches volcaniques.—4°, *pp.* 88. *Paris,* 1894.

LACROIX, A. F. A.—Sur un nouveau type pétrographique représentant la forme de profondeur de certaines Leucotéphrites de la Somma.—*C.R. Acad. Sci. cxli, pp.* 1188–93. *Paris,* 1905.

LACROIX, A. F. A.—Sur l'éruption du Vésuve et en particulier sur les phénomènes explosifs. — *C.R. Acad. Sci. cxlii, pp.* 941–44. *Paris,* 1906.

LACROIX, A. F. A.—Les Conglomérats des explosions vulcaniennes du Vésuve, leurs minéraux, leur comparaison avec les Conglomérats trachytiques du Mont-Dore.— *C.R. Acad. Sci. cxlii, pp.* 1020–22. *Paris,* 1906.

LACROIX, A. F. A.—Les avalanches sèches et les torrentes boueux de l'éruption récente du Vésuve [et Chlormanganokalite]. —*C.R. Acad. Sci. cxlii, pp.* 1244–49. *Paris,* 1906.

LACROIX, A. F. A.—Les cristaux de Sylvite des blocs rejetés par la récente éruption du Vésuve.—*C.R. Acad. Sci. cxlii, pp.* 1249–52. *Paris,* 1906.

LACROIX, A. F. A.—Les produits laviques de la récente éruption du Vésuve.—*C.R. Acad. Sci. cxliii, pp.* 13–18. *Paris,* 1906.

LACROIX, A. F. A.—Sur quelques produits des Fumerolles de la récente éruption du Vésuve et en particulier sur les minéraux arsénifères et plombifères.—*C.R. Acad. Sci. cxliii, pp.* 727–30. *Paris,* 1906.

LACROIX, A. F. A.—Pompéi, Saint-Pierre, Ottajano.—*Rev. scient. S.* 5, *vi, pp.* 481–89, 519–23, 551–57, *figs. Paris,* 1906.

LACROIX, A. F. A.—The eruption of Vesuvius in April, 1906.—*Ann. Rept. Board of Regents Smiths. Inst. for the Year ending June 30th,* 1906, *pp.* 223–48, *pls. i–xiv (sketch-map).* 1907.—[Abstr.] *Rev. gén. Sci. pp.* 111, 28 *figs. Paris,* 30 *oct.* and 15 *nov.,* 1906.

LACROIX, A. F. A.—Sur la constitution pétrographique du massif volcanique du Vésuve et de la Somma.—*C.R. Acad. Sci. cxliv, pp.* 1245–51. *Paris,* 1907.

LACROIX, A. F. A.—Contribution à l'étude des Brèches et des Conglomérats Volcaniques (Antilles 1902–3 ; Vésuve 1906). —*Bull. Soc. géol. France, S.* 4, *vi, pp.* 635–85, *figs., pls. xix–xxii. Paris,* 1907.

LACROIX, A. F. A.—Sur une espèce minérale nouvelle des Fumerolles à haute température de la récente éruption du Vésuve.—*C.R. Acad. Sci. cxliv, pp.* 1398–401. *Paris,* 1907.

LACROIX, A. F. A.—Étude minéralogique des produits silicatés de l'éruption du Vésuve, avril 1906, conséquences à en tirer à un point de vue général.—*Nouv. Arch. Mus. Hist. nat. ix, pp.* 1–172, *pls. i–x. Paris,* 1907.

LACROIX, A. F. A.—Les Minéraux des fumerolles de l'éruption du Vésuve en avril 1906.—*Bull. Soc. Franç. Min. xxx, pp.* 219–68. *Paris,* 1907.

LACROIX, A. F. A.—Les derniers jours d'Herculanum et de Pompéi, interprétés à l'aide de quelques phénomènes récents du Volcanisme.—*La Géographie, xviii, pp.* 281–96, *figs.* 16–25. *Paris,* 1908.

LACROIX, A. F. A.—Sur les Minéraux des fumerolles de la récente éruption de l'Etna et sur l'existence de l'Acide Borique dans les fumerolles actuelles du Vésuve.—*C.R. Acad. Sci. cxlvii, pp.* 161–65. *Paris,* 1908.

LACROIX, A. F. A.—La Montagne Pelée après ses éruptions, avec observations sur les éruptions du Vésuve en 79 et en 1906.— 4⁰, *pp. i–viii,* 1–136, *figs. Paris,* 1908.

LACROIX, A. F. A.—Sur la Tridymite du Vésuve et sur la genèse de ce minéral par fusion.—*Bull. Soc. Franç. Min. xxxi, pp.* 323–38, *figs. Paris,* 1908.

LACROIX.—Le Mont Vésuve Peint par Lacroix et gravé par Lemaire. N. Lemire sculp. A Paris chez Jean, Rue Sᵗ Jean de Beauvais, Nᵒ 10.
Very fine view of Vesuvius with eruption of 1757 ; coast near Portici. Engrav. : 457×300 mm.

LALANDE, L. J. Lebouidre De.—*See* LEBOUIDRE DE LALANDE, L. J.

LAMANNIS, G.—Memorie su la necessità di stabilire i parafulmini sulla reale polveriera della Torre dell' Annunziata.—8⁰, *pp.* 24. *Napoli,* 1808.

LAMBRUSCHINI, R.—*See* ANON.—Sur l'éruption du Vésuve . . . 1832.

LAMÉTHERIE, J. C. De.—Notes sur quelques cristaux de Ceylanite trouvés parmi les substances rejetées par le Vésuve.— *Journ. Phys. Chim. Hist. nat. li, pp.* 77–80. *Paris,* 1800.

LAMÉTHERIE, J. C. DE.—Observations sur les dernières éruptions du Vésuve.—*Journ. Phys. lxi, pp.* 218–25. *Paris,* 1805.

LAMI, GIOVANNI.—Articoli delle novelle letterarie . . . sopra le antichità di Ercolano dell' anno MDCCXLVIII.—*See* GORI.—Admiranda Antiquitatum Herculanensium, *etc. 2nd Pt. of Vol. ii, pp.* 16+68.

LAMOTHE, A. DE.—Le fou du Vésuve et autres contes.—4th ed. 12⁰, *pp.* 318. *Paris,* 1879.
Eruption of 79.

LANCEDELLI, C.—(Druck u. Verlag.)—Neapel. Wieden, Wienstrasse N⁰ 883. WIEN.
Litho., on yellow ground, of Naples from above Grotto; man and woman walking and man and woman sitting: 212× 173 mm.

LANCELLOTTI, J.—Epistolæ tres : I. De Incendio Vesuvii ; II. De Stabiis ; III. De petitione Magistratura.—8⁰, *pp.* 30. *Neapolis,* 1784.

LANDGREBE, G.—Mineralogie der Vulcane. —8⁰. *Cassel und Leipzig,* 1870.

LANELFI.—Incendio del Vesuvio.—4⁰, *foll.* 8, *figs. Napoli, O. Beltrano,* 1632.

LANG, O.—Ueber den zeitlichen Bestandwechsel der Vesuvlaven und Aetnagesteine. —*Zeitschr. f. Naturwiss. lxv,* 1–2, *pp.* 30, 6 *figs. Leipzig,* 1892.

LANG, O.—Die vulcanischen Herde am Golfe von Neapel.—*Zeitschr. deutsch. geol. Gesellsch. xlv,* 2, *pp.* 177–94, 1 *tab. Berlin,* 1893.

LANGDON, W. C.—A Vesuvian Episode.— " *The Atlantic Monthly," lxvi, pp.* 122–25. *Boston,* 1890.

LANGLUME.—*See* COIGNET.—Château de Castelamare *and* Pausilippe.

LANZA, V.—*See* LIBERATORE.

LAPPARENT, A. A. DE.—Le Vésuve et la Somma.—*Ann. Club alp. franç. xxiv, pp.* 509–23. *Paris,* 1897.

LARBELESTIER, G.—Naples. Publié par Pourret F. à Paris.
View of Vesuvius over town of Naples from above Grotto ; peasants by cistern, dog, pitcher, sheep and two trees in foreground. Very fine engrav. : 112×74 mm.

LAROUSSE.—*See* DARONDEAU.

LASALLE, E.—1. Vésuve de Strabon, ou Somma. 2. Somma et Vésuve après l'éruption de Pline. 3. Astrone vu des Camaldoli. 4. Astrone vu des bords du cratère. Lith. de C. Adrien, rue Richer 7. *See* BUCH, L. VON.—Geognostische Beobachtungen, *etc.* Pl. 9. Lith. : 385× 252 mm.

LASAULX, A. C. P. F. VON.—Dünnschliffe der Vesuv-Lava der Eruption vom April dieses Jahres.—*Sitz. niederrhein. Gesellsch. xxix, pp.* 120–25. *Bonn,* 1872.

LASAULX, A. C. P. F. VON.—[Microscopische Untersuchung der neuesten Lava vom Vesuv.]—*N. J. f. Min. xl, pp.* 408–10. *Stuttgart,* 1872.

LASAULX, A. C. P. F. VON.—[Ueber Granat und Vesuvian.]—*N. J. f. Min.* (1876), *pp.* 630–32. *Stuttgart,* 1876.

LASAULX, A. C. P. F. VON.—Der Vesuv im Jahre 1878.—*Ausland,* 52, *pp.* 541–47. *Stuttgart u. Augsburg,* 1879.

LASENA, P.—Dell' antico Ginnasio Napoletano.—4⁰, *pp.* 3+292. *Roma,* 1641.
See pp. 77–84.

LASOR A VAREA [*or* SAVANAROLA].—Universus terrarum orbis scriptorum calamo delineatus.—2 vols. *fol. Patavii,* 1713.

LASPEYRES, E. A. H.—Die Grundform des Biotit vom Vesuv. [Part of : Die Grundformen des Glimmer und des Klinochlor.] —*Zeitschr. f. Kryst. u. Min. xvii, p.* 541. *Leipzig,* 1890.

LASSELS, RICHARD.—The Voyage of Italy ; or A Compleat Iovrney Throvgh Italy, aend the Holy Laend with the Characters of the People, and the description of the chief Townes, Churches, Monasteries, Tombes, Libraries, Pallaces, Villas, Gardens, Pictures, Statues, Antiquities : as also of the Interest, Gouerment, Riches, Force, etc. of all the Princes.—Opus posthumum : Corrected and set forth by his old friend and fellow Traveller S. W. —12⁰, *pp.* 447+4. *Paris, V. Dv Movtier,* M.DC.LXX.——2nd ed. 8⁰. *London,* 1698.
See pp. 284–88 : state of Vesuvius about 1650.

LATINI, A.—Lo scalco alla moderna, overo l'arte di ben disporre li conviti.—2 vols. 4⁰. *Napoli,* 1692–94.
In Vol. ii, pp. 234–38, the eruption of Vesuvius of April 12th, 1694, is described.

LAUGEL, A. A.—Sur l'éruption du Vésuve du 8 déc. 1861.—*Moniteur de la Côte d'Or,* foll. 3. Jan. 1862.

LAUGIER, A.—Examen chimique d'un fragment d'une masse saline considérable rejetée par le Vésuve dans l'éruption de 1822.—*Mém. Mus. Hist. nat. x, pp.* 435–38. *Paris,* 1823.—*Ann. Chim. N.S. xxvi, pp.* 371–75. *Paris,* 1824.—*Quarterly Journ. Sci. Lit. and Arts, xviii, p.* 407. *London,* 1825.

LAURENT, A., HOLMS, CH.—Analyses diverses. Fer oxidulé artificiel ; Albite de Chesterfield ; Minéral des laves du Vésuve ; Cristallisation de l'oxide de zinc.—*Ann. Chim. lx, pp.* 330–33. *Paris,* 1835.—*Journ. f. prakt. Chem. vii, pp.* 339–44. *Leipzig,* 1836.

LAURENTIIS, M. DE.—Universæ Campaniæ Felicis Antiquitates.—2 vols. 4⁰. *Vol. i, pp.* 7+188, 1 *pl.* ; *Vol. ii, pp.* 303, 1 *pl. Neapolis,* 1826.
See Vol. ii, pp. 148–67.

LAURIA, G. A.—*See* POLI, G. 1872, 1873.

LAVINI, G.—Rime filosofiche colle sue annotazioni alle medesime. — 4⁰, *pp. xxxii*+232. *Milano,* 1750. [B.M. 638. i. 9.]
See pp. 74–85.

LAVINI, G.—Analyse de la cendre du Vésuve de l'éruption 1822 (1828).—*Mém. R. Acc. Sci. xxxiii, pp.* 183–98. *Torino,* 1829.

LAVIS.—*See* JOHNSTON-LAVIS.

LAWRENCE, E.—The Lands of the Earthquake.—" *Harper's Magazine,*" *xxxviii, pp.* 466–82, 2 *illustr. New York,* 1868.

L * * B * *.—*See* COLLETTA, P. 1835.

LEALE, S. (dis.).—Spiaggia di Santa Lucia. Lit. del Poliorama.
Tinted litho. : 250×163 mm., a bad copy of that by Benoist.

LEBERT, H.—Le Golfe de Naples et ses volcans, et les volcans en général.—8⁰, *pp.* 120. *Vevey, Lausanne, etc.,* 1876.

LEBLANC, F.—*See* DEVILLE, C. J. SAINTE-CLAIRE. 1857 (2), 1862.

LE BLOND.—Veue de la Montagne de Somma à Naple. [B.N.P. Vb. 121.]

LEBOUIDRE DE LALANDE, L. J.—Du Mont Vésuve et de la nature des laves.—
See his " Voyage en Italie," *Vol. vii, pp.* 153–206. *Paris,* 1779.——2nd ed. *See Vol. vii, pp.* 479–544. 1786.

LEBOUIDRE DE LALANDE, L. J.—Relation de la dernière éruption du Vésuve, août 1779.—*Journ. Savants,* 12⁰, *pp.* 103–14. *Paris, janvier,* 1781.

LECOUTOURIER.—Phénomènes observés au Vésuve (par M. Palmieri).—*Musée des Sci., mai* 1856.

LEE (sc.).—Eruption of Vesuvius in 1794. Woodcut : 106×71 mm., bears note in pencil " After Sir William Hamilton, 1794." Plate from book, 8⁰.

LEFÈVRE, C.—*See* COLLETTA, P. 1835.

LEGOUVÉ.—*See* NORVINS. 1737.

LEGRAS, A. (oléographe).—[Coloured, oleographic view of Vesuvius.] [B.M. Portfolio of Naples.]
633×440 mm.

LE HON, H.—Histoire complète de la grande éruption du Vésuve de 1631, avec la carte au 1 : 25,000 de toutes les laves de ce volcan depuis le seizième siècle jusqu'aujourd'hui.—*Bull. Acad. R. Sci. Lett. et Beaux-Arts Belgique, S.* 2, *xx, pp.* 64. *Bruxelles,* 1865–66.

LEITCH, W. L.—*See* MAPEI, C.—Italy, Classical, Historical and Picturesque.

LEITCH, W. L.—*See* WRIGHT, G. N. 1839?, 1841.

LÉMERY, L.—Sel Armoniac naturel du Mont Vésuve.—*Hist. Acad. Roy. Sci.* 1705, *p.* 66. *Paris,* 1730.

LEMME, A.—Eine neue Vulkantheorie.—8⁰, *pp. vi*+89, *fig. Essinglen a N.* 1909.

LEMMO, G.—Pietosa istoria del danno accaduto nel paese detto Somma, non già del foco ; ma di acqua, pietre, arena, e saette, che ha spianato detto paese, con Ottajano.—8⁰, *pp.* 4 (*loose sheets*). *Napoli,* 1794.
Verses.

LEMMO, G.—Prodigioso miracolo del nostro gran Santone, e Difensore S. Gennaro, d'averci liberato dall' incendio del Vesuvio, e dal terremoto nell' anno 1794.—8⁰, *pp.* 4 (*loose sheets*), dated 18 *Giugno* 1794.
Verses.

LEMONNIER.—*See* NORVINS. 1737.

LENGHI, G.—Pompei. Il Foro. Le Forum. Giacomo Lenghi editore proprietario.

Good view of Vesuvius. Litho. : 240 × 173 mm.

LEO, AMBROSIUS NOLANUS.—De Nola, opusculum distinctum, plenum, clarum, doctum, pulcrum, verum, graue, varium, et vtile. [In fine :] Incussum est hoc opus opera diligentiaque probi uiri Ioannis Rubri Vercellani. Venetiis anno Salutis. M.D. XIIII Septembris uero die IIII sub Leonardo Lauredano Duce Sapientissimo.—*fol., foll.* lviii+8, (*index*), 4 cop. *pls.* (by Girolamo Moceto, detto il Mozzeto, disciple of Giovanni Bellini). *Venetiis*, 1514. [B.M. 178. g. 14.]

Another ed. is called : " Antiquitatum nec non Historiarum urbis ac Agri Nolæ, ut et de Montibus Vesuvio, et Abella descriptionis. Libri tres.—*See* GRÆVIUS, J. G.—Thesaurus Antiquitatum et Historiarum Italiæ, etc. *Tom. ix, Pt.* 3, *col.* 92. *Lugduni Batavorum*, 1725, 1723, *etc.* [B.M. 2068 f.]

Another ed. is called : " De Agro Nolano deque Montibus Vesuvio, et Abella, cæterisque agri limitibus."—*See* JORDANUS, D.—Delectus Scriptorum Rerum Neapolitanarum, etc. — *Neapoli*, M.DCC.XXXV. [B.M. 180. g. 7.]

See coll. 1–118, 4 pls.

This is also reproduced in : JORDANUS, D.—Rarissimorum Scriptorum Rerum Neapolitanarum collectio, *etc.—Neapoli*, 1738. [B.M. 9166. k. 1.]

See coll. 1–118, 4 pls. The first plate of the 1514 ed. is the first known view of Vesuvius and a remarkably fine example of the engraver's art. It is on Leo's authority that the record rests of an eruption of Vesuvius in 1500. This plate shows Vesuvius and Somma covered with trees, and the cone of Vesuvius higher and obtusely rounded.

LEO, M. DI.—Il Vesuvio nell' ultima eruzione dell' 8 Agosto 1779. Canto.—8⁰, *pp.* 26. *Napoli*, 1779.——Another ed. *pp.* 24. [O.V.]

LEONHARD, C. C. VON.—Die Basaltgebilde in ihren Bezichungen zu normalen und abnormen Felsmassen.—2 Pts. 8⁰. *Pt. i,* pp. xxii+498 ; *Pt. ii, pp. x*+536+*Atlas* (20 col. pls.). *Stuttgart*, 1832.

See Pt. ii, pp. 80–83.

LEONHARD, C. C. VON.—Geologie oder Naturgeschichte der Erde auf allgemein faszliche Weise abgehandelt.—5 vols. 8⁰. *Vol. i, pp.* 456, *pls. i–xiv* ; *Vol. ii, pp.* 481, *pls. xv–xxxix* ; *Vol. iii, pp.* 628, *pls. xl–lxviii* ; *Vol. iv, pp.* 490, *pls. lxix–lxxx* ; *Vol. v, pp.* 712, *pls. lxxxi–lxxxxvii*. *Stuttgart*, 1836–44.

See Vol. v, pp. 161–62, 237–88, pls. lxxxvi, lxxxvii, lxxxx.

LEONHARD, C. C. VON.—Vulkanen-Atlas zur Naturgeschichte der Erde.—*obl.* 4⁰, 15 tav. (4 col.). *Stuttgart*, 1844.

LEOPARDI, G.—La Ginestra, o il fiore del deserto. Canto.—*In his :* Opere, *Vol. i, pp.* 159–68. *Firenze*, 1889.

LEPOITTEVIN, E. (pinx.).—Golfe de Naples. Galerie Durand. Ruel.

Steel engrav., two boats near rock between Capri and P. Campanella : 232 × 165 mm.

LEPOITTEVIN, E. (pinx.).—Vue prise du Golfe de Naples. L'Artiste. Doherty sc. Imprimerie de P. Dieu.

Steel engraving same as that by Lepoittevin entitled : " Golfe de Naples," except inscript. : 232 × 155 mm.

LERCY (dis.).—Veduta della città di Napoli disegnata dalla Collina di Posilipo presso il Sepolcro di Virgilis. Vue de la ville de Naples prise sur la Colline de Pausilype près le Tombeau de Virgile. Lith. Cuciniello e Bianchi.

Loose litho. plate on double paper similar to that contained in their " Viaggio Pittoresco, 1845 " : 330 × 257 mm.

LEREBOURS, [N. P.] (daguerréotype).—Italie. Le Môle à Naples. Salathé sc. Rittner et Goupil, Boulev'. Montmartre, 15, N. P. Lerebours, Place du Pont Neuf 13, Hʳ Bossange, Quai Voltaire, 11.

Stipple engraving : 204 × 142 mm. Good outline of Vesuvius in distance, and Strada Municipio, with cart and bullocks, in foreground.

LEREBOURS, N. P. (daguerréotype).—Le Môle à Naples. Salathé sc. Rittner et Goupil, Paris.

A sepia engrav.

LE RICHE, M. J.—Antiquités des environs de Naples, et dissertations qui y sont relatives par M. J. L. R.—8⁰, *pp.* 392+5, 3 *maps. Naples*, 1820.

See pp. 195–212.

LE RICHE, M. J.—Vues des Monumens antiques de Naples gravées à l'aqua-tinta accompagnées de notices de dissertations. —4⁰, *pp.* 110, 60 *pls.* [*Paris*] 1827. *See* Pl. 23.

LEVI, G.—*See* NASINI, R.

LÉVY, A. MICHEL.—*See* FOUQUÉ, F. A.

LIBERATORE, R.—Delle nuove ed antiche terme di Torre Annunziata e parere di V. Lanza sulle facoltà salutifere dell' acqua termo-minerale Vesuviana Nunziante.— *Ann. Civ. Regno Due Sicilie, vi, pp.* 95–109. *Napoli*, 1835.

LICOPOLI, G.—Storia naturale delle piante crittogame che vivono sulle lave Vesuviane. —8⁰, *foll.* 2, *pp.* 58, 3 *pls. Napoli*, 1871.— *Atti R. Acc. Sci. v,* 2, *pp.* 1–58, 3 *pls. Napoli*, 1873.

LICOPOLI, G.—Sopra alcune sementi provenienti dagli scavi di Pompei.—*Rend. R. Acc. Sci. S.* 2, *iv, pp.* 85–87. *Napoli*, 1890.

LIDIACO, T.—Stanza a Crinatea (L'eruzione del Vesuvio dell' anno 79, e la morte di Plinio).—4⁰, *p.* 12. — ?, — ?

LIGUORI, F. S.—Cenni storico-critici della città di Gragnano e luoghi convicini.—8⁰. *Napoli*, 1863. [B.N.] *See* Chapt. XI, pp. 36–37.

LINDEMANN FROMMEL (?) (pinx.).— Neapel und der Vesuv vom Posilippo aus. A. Closs. X. L. W. Werkmeister sc. Woodcut on straw-tinted background : 250×197 mm.

LINDEMANN FROMMEL.—N⁰ 32. Villa Reale. Hôtel de la Victoire. Pizzafalcone. Castel dell Uovo. Skizzen und Bilder aus Neapel und der Umgegend.—Goupil & C⁰, Paris, Berlin, London, New York. Imp. de Jacomme et Cⁱᵉ, r. Meslay 61, Paris. Litho. in two pale tints : 262×220 mm.

LINGG, H.—Auf dem Vesuv.—*Gedichte, i, pp.* 191–93. *Stuttgart*, 1871.

LINTON, W.—Sketches in Italy drawn on stone. Facsimiles of sketches during a tour in 1828–29 in various parts of Piedmont, the Milanese, Venetian and Roman States, Tuscany and the Kingdom of Naples ; 96 [very fine] views.—*imp. fol. London*, 1832. *See* Pls. 18, 77.

LIPPI, C.—Dell' utilità della parte vulcanica. —4⁰, *p.* 24. [*Napoli*] 1807.

LIPPI, C.—Qualche cosa intorno ai vulcani inseguito di alcune idee geologiche all' occasione dell' eruzione del Vesuvio del 1⁰ Gennaio 1812.—8⁰, *pp.* 167. *Napoli*, 1813. [O.V.]

LIPPI, C.—Esposizione dei fatti che da Novembre 1810 a Febbraio 1815 han avuto luogo nell' Accademia di Sci. di Napoli relativamente alla sua scoperta geologicaistorica dalla quale risulta che le due città Pompei ed Ercolano non furono distrutte e sotterrate dal Vesuvio, etc. [Also] Circolare Esaglotta.—4⁰, *pp.* 384+18, 1 *pl. Napoli*, 1815. [C.A.]

LIPPI, C.—Fu il fuoco e l'acqua che sotterrò Pompei ed Ercolano ? Scoperta geologicoistorica.—8⁰, *foll.* 2, *pp.* 384, *foll.* 2, 1 *pl. Napoli*, 1816. [At end] Circolare esaglotta inirata a tutte le Accademie di Europa ed a quella di Filadelfia a norma dell' appello alle medesime fatto nell' opera relativa al sotterramento di Pompei, e d'Ercolano, per via umida, pagina 363. Spedita colla presente a tutte le accademie suddette.—8⁰, *pp.* 14+4. *Napoli, presso Domenico Sangiacomo,* 1816. *See also* TENORE, M. — . . . Ragguaglio di alcune peregrinazioni, etc.

LIPPI, C.—Apologia sulla pretesa Zurite. Letta alla R. Acc. d. Sci. il 12 Febbraio 1819.—8⁰, *pp.* 15. *Napoli*, 1819. [C.A.]

LIPPI, C.—Il carbone fossile è la cagione de' Vulcani.—8⁰. *Napoli*, 1820.

LLORD Y GAMBOA, R.—Estudo químicogeognóstico de algunos materiales volcánicos del Golfo de Nápoles.—*Rev. R. Acad. Cienc. iv, pp.* 340–50, *figs.,* 1 *pl.,* 1906 ; *vi, pp.* 179–97, 250–57, *Madrid,* 1907.

LOBLEY, J. L.—Account of Mount Vesuvius.—*Geol. Mag. pp.* 321–25. 1868.

LOBLEY, J. L.—Mount Vesuvius ; a descriptive, historical and geological account of the volcano with a notice of the recent eruption, and an appendix containing letters by Pliny the younger, a table of dates of eruptions, and a list of Vesuvian minerals.—*Published by the Geologists' Association of London,* 8⁰, *pp.* vi+55, 3 *pls.* 1868.——2nd ed. 8⁰, *pp.* 385, 20 *figs.,* 1 *col. map. London,* 1889.

LOCCHI, ING. D.—Italia : Carta Fisica.— *Pub. G. B. Paravia e C., Torino, Roma, Milano, Firenze, Napoli,* 1876. 1 : 200,000. Raised map.

LOCCHI, ING. D.—Napoli e dintorni.— *Pub. G. B. Paravia e C., Torino, Roma, Milano, Firenze, Napoli*, 1876. 1 : 100,000. Raised map, coloured, in two ed.—1st, physical and political. 2nd, geological. (Campi Phlegræi and Vesuvius.)

LOMASTO (inc.).—Veduta della 25ᵃ eruzione, accaduta li 27 e 28 Marzo del 1759. Vue de la 25ᵐᵉ éruption arrivée le 27 et 28 mars en 1759. T. VII. In Napoli presso Franc. Scafa Str. S. Biagio de' Librari. N° 117. Engrav. : 255 × 196 mm.

LONGO, A.—Sulle cagioni probabili delle ascensioni vulcaniche subaeree.—*Atti Acc. Gioen. S.* 3, *iv, pp.* 1-35. *Catania*, 1870.

LONGO, G. B.—Il lagrimoso lamento del disaggio che a fatto il Monte di Somma, con tutte le cose occorse fino al presente giorno.—12°, *foll.* 6. *Napoli, per Dom. Maccarano*, 1632.

LONGOBARDI, P.—Musarum primi flosculi. —4°, *foll.* 8, *pp.* 132. *Napoli*, 1714. [O.V.] *See pp.* 46, 90, 129, 132.

LOPE FELIX DE VEGA.—[Sonnet.]—*See* QUINONES.—El Monte Vesvvio.

LOPEZ DE ZARATE, F.—Soneto, aludendo que en la tierra del Vesuvio fue el levantamiento de los Titanos por su mucha abundancia.—*See* QUINONES.—El Monte Vesvvio.

LOPEZ VALDERAS, FERNANDO.—Soneto. —*See* QUINONES.—El Monte Vesvvio.

LORENZANO, F. G. DE.—Breve compendio del lamentable incendio del Monte de Somma.—8°, *pp.* 16. *Napoli*, 1632.

LORENZO, G. DE.—*See* BASSANI, F. 1893.

LORENZO, G. DE.—Efflusso di lava dal gran cono del Vesuvio, cominciato il 3 Luglio 1895.—*Rend. R. Acc. Sci. S.* 3, *i*, 7, *pp.* 183-94, 3 *figs. Napoli*, 1895.

LORENZO, G. DE.—Lava Pahoehoe effluita il 24 Maggio 1895 dal cono terminale del Vesuvio.—*Atti R. Acc. Lincei, S.* 5, *Rend. iv, sem.* 2, *pp.* 10-19, *fig. Roma*, 1895.

LORENZO, G. DE.—Studi di geologia nell' Appennino meridionale.—*Napoli*, 1896.— *Atti R. Acc. Sci. S.* 2, *viii, Mem.* 7, *pp.* 128. *Napoli*, 1896.

LORENZO, G. DE.—*See* BÖSE, E. 1896.

LORENZO, G. DE.—Der Vesuv in der zweiten Hälfte des 16 Jahrhunderts.— *Zeitschr. deutsch. geol. Gesellsch. xlix, pp.* 561-67, 1 *fig. Berlin*, 1897.

LORENZO, G. DE.—Ancora del Vesuvio dei tempi di Strabone.—*Boll. Soc. Geol. Ital. xvii, pp.* 257-60. *Roma*, 1898.

LORENZO, G. DE.—Sulla probabile causa dell' attuale aumentata attività del Vesuvio.—*Rend. R. Acc. Sci. S.* 3, *vi, pp.* 127-30. *Napoli*, 1900.

LORENZO, G. DE.—Influenza dell' acqua atmosferica sull' attività del Vesuvio.— *Rend. R. Acc. Sci. S.* 3, *vi, pp.* 217-23. *Napoli*, 1900.

LORENZO, G. DE.—La pioggia e il Vesuvio. —*Rend. R. Acc. Sci. S.* 3, *vii, pp.* 125-27. *Napoli*, 1901.

LORENZO, G. DE.—Un paragone tra il Vesuvio e il Vulture.—*Rend. R. Acc. Sci. S.* 3, *vii, pp.* 315-20, 2 *figs. Napoli*, 1901.

LORENZO, G. DE.—Considerazioni sull' origine superficiale dei Vulcani.—*Atti R. Acc. Sci. S.* 2, *xi*, 7, *pp.* 19, 1 *pl. Napoli*, 1902.

LORENZO, G. DE.—I Vulcani di Napoli.— *pp.* 16. *Roma*, 1902.—*Nuova Antologia, S.* 4, *xcviii, pp.* 684-95. *Roma*, 1902.

LORENZO, G. DE.—Geologia e geografia fisica dell' Italia meridionale.—8°, *pp.* 241. *Bari*, 1904.

LORENZO, G. DE.—L'Eruzione del Vesuvio, Aprile, 1906.—*Nuova Antologia, xli, pp.* 691-98. *Rome*, 1906.

LORENZO, G. DE.—The eruption of Vesuvius in April, 1906.—*Quart. Journ. Geol. Soc. lxii, pp.* 476-83, 3 *figs.* (*sketch-map*), 1906.—*Abs. Proc. Geol. Soc.* 1905-6, *No.* 829, *pp.* 100-10.

LORENZO, G. DE.—L'Éruption du Vésuve et les Volcans.—*La Revue du Mois, ii, pp.* 385-97. 1906.

LORENZO, G. DE.—Ueber den Ursprung des Ammoniaks in den Produkten der Vesuveruption im April 1906.—*Centralbl. f. Min. pp.* 161-66. *Stuttgart*, 1907.

LORENZO, G. DE.—Come cresce il Vesuvio. —" *Natura*," *i*, 2, *pp.* 33-40, 7 *figs.* 1909

LORENZO, G. DE.—Il Seppellimento di Ercolano.—*Nuova Antologia*, 1 *Ottob. pp.* 11, 1 *fig. Roma*, 1909.

LORY, G., fils (pinx.).—Royaume de Naples. N° 21. Le Vésuve près de Torre dell' Annunziata. Vogel sculp. À Paris chez A. Bes et F. Debreuil. Impr. Éditeur. Rue Git-le-Cœur, 11.
A very dark, stippled sepia : 208 × 157 mm.

LOTTI GIOVANNI (Accad. errante).—L'incendio del Vesuvio in ottava rima.—12°, *foll.* 12. *Napoli*, 1632.

LOZZI, C.—Biblioteca istorica dell' antica e nuova Italia.—2 vols. 8°. *Imola*, 1887. *See* Vol. ii, pp. 480–83.

LUCA, F. DE.—Ricerche su' Vulcani. Memoria.—*Rend. Acc. Sci. v, pp.* 45–65. *Napoli*, 1846.

LUCA, F. DE.—Nuove considerazioni sui Vulcani e sulla loro cagione.—Memoria letta nella R. Accad. d. Sci. d. Napoli 1846 e riprodotta con qualche aggiunzione nel 1850.—8°. *Napoli*, 1850. *See* pp. 17, 18, 22 and 28.

LUCA, S. DE.—Recherches analytiques sur l'eau découverte dans un puits de Pompéi. —*C.R. Acad. Sci. lix, pp.* 467–70. *Paris*, 1864.—*Journ. Pharm. Chim. xlvi, pp.* 427– 30. *Paris*, 1864.—*Rend. R. Acc. Sci. iii, pp.* 198–200. *Napoli*, 1864.

LUCA, S. DE.—Ricerche analitiche sulle ossa trovate negli scavi di Pompei.—*Rend. R. Acc. Sci. iii, pp.* 293–97. *Napoli*, 1864.

LUCA, S. DE.—Ricerche chimiche sopra talune efflorescenze Vesuviane.—*Rend. R. Acc. Sci. x, pp.* 146–51. *Napoli*, 1871.

LUCA, S. DE.—Prime ricerche chimiche eseguite sopra talune materie raccolte in una fumarola del cratere Vesuviano.— *Rend. R. Acc. Sci. xv, pp.* 94–95. *Napoli*, 1876.

LUCA, S. DE.—Ricerche chimiche sopra una particolare argilla trovata negli scavi di Pompei.—*Rend. R. Acc. Sci. xvii, pp.* 46–47. *Napoli*, 1878.

LUCA, S. DE.—Ricerche chimiche sopra una cenere trovata negli scavi di Pompei.— *Rend. R. Acc. Sci. xvii, pp.* 47–48. *Napoli*, 1878.

LUCA, S. DE.—Ricerche chimiche sopra una materia somigliante a filo carbonizzato rinvenuta negli scavi di Pompei.—*Rend. R. Acc. Sci. xvii, pp.* 159–62, *Napoli*, 1878 ; *xviii, pp.* 44–46, 1879.

LUCA, S. DE.—Ricerche chimiche sopra una materia stratiforme rinvenuta negli scavi di Pompei.—*Rend. R. Acc. Sci. xviii, pp.* 68–70. *Napoli*, 1879.

LUCIANO (padre).—[Descript. erupt. 1631 in a parish book of S. Giorgio a Cremano.] —*See p.* 101 *of* PALOMBA, D.—Memorie storiche, etc.

LUCIFER.—Inspirations du Vésuve. Poésies volcaniques.—12°, *pp.* 125, *vignettes by David Clarens. Naples*, 1878. *See* notes pp. 121–23.

LUCRETIUS CARUS, T.—T. Lucretii Cari de rerum natura libri VI. [Edited by Petrus Candidus.]—8°, *foll.* 125. *Sumptibus P. Giuntæ: Florentiæ*, 1512.—Another copy [B.M. 11375. aa.] MS. notes.

LUDOVICI, D.—Carmina et inscriptiones. Opus posthumum.—2 pts. *Naples*, 1746. [C.A.] *See* Pt. i, pp. 42–46, relating to earthquakes, and pp. 46–47, 63–67, 143–45, relating to Vesuvius.

LUDWIG, E., et RENARD, A. F.—Analyses de la Vésuvienne d'Ala et de Monroni.— *Bull. Mus. Hist. nat. i, pp.* 131–83. *Bruxelles*, 1882.

LUIGI, DR.—*See* BOLIFONI, A.—Cárte de' Regni di Napoli, etc.

LUISE, L. DE.—Sulle Altezze della Vetta Vesuviana.—*Atti Acc. Pontaniana, xxxiii, pp.* 7, 1 *pl. Napoli*, 1904.

LULLIN DE CHATEAUVIEUX, F.— Lettres écrites d'Italie en 1812 et 1813, à M. Charles Pictet.—2 vols. 12°. *Paris*, 1816.——2nd ed. 8°. 1820. *See* Vol. ii, pp. 37–49 (1st ed.).

LYELL, C.—Principles of Geology.—12 editions. *London*, 1830 *to* 1875. *See* 12th ed. Vol. i, pp. 603–55 ; Vol. ii, pp 516–17. London, 1875. In French, transl. from 6th ed. " Principes de Géologie."—*Lyon*, 1846.

LYELL, SIR C.—On the structure of Lavas which have consolidated on steep slopes; with remarks on the mode of origin of Mount Etna, and on the theory of "Craters of Elevation."—4⁰, *tav. London*, 1859.— *Phil. Trans. R. Soc. Pt. ii, pp.* 703–86. *London*, 1858. (*See* pp. 4, 6, 27, 30, 49, 55.)—*Bibl. univ. Archiv. Sci. phys. nat. vi, pp.* 217–66. *Genève, Lausanne, Paris,* 1859.—*Zeitschr. deutsch. geol. Gesellsch. xi, pp.* 149–250. *Berlin,* 1859.—*Corrisp. Scient. vi, pp.* 181–82. *Roma,* 1863. —*Amer. Journ. Sci. xxvi, pp.* 214–19. *New Haven,* 1858.

LYELL, SIR C.—On the consolidation of Lava on steep slopes, and on the origin of the conical form of Volcanoes.—*Proc. R. Inst. iii, pp.* 125–31. *London,* 1858–62.— *Amer. Journ. Sci. xxviii, pp.* 221–26. *New Haven,* 1859.

LYTTON, B.—The last days of Pompeii.— 3 vols. *London,* 1834; *many subsequent ed.*

M*** (Avocat en Parlement).—Lettres écrites de Suisse, d'Italie, de Sicile et de Malthe, à Mlle. * * à Paris, en 1776, 1777 et 1778.— 6 tomes in 3 vols. 12⁰. *T. i, pp.* 454; *T. ii, pp.* 509; *T. iii, pp.* 536; *T. iv, pp.* 418; *T. v, pp.* 550; *T. vi, pp.* 515. *Amsterdam,* 1780.
See T. ii and iv.

MACAULAY, LORD. — Pompeii, a poem which obtained the Chancellor's Medal, July, 1819, at Cambridge.—1st ed. *Cambridge,* 1819.

MACDONALD.—*See* MACLURE.

MACDONALD, M.—Le Vésuve. Ode.—8⁰, *foll.* 4. [*Napoli, circa* 1750.]
Bound with his: "Les Richesses."—*See* MECATTI.—Raconto storico-filosofico del Vesuvio. Napoli, 1752.

MACKINLAY, R.—Letter dated at Rome the 9th January, 1761, concerning the late eruption of Mount Vesuvius, etc.—*Phil. Trans. R. Soc. lii, pp.* 44–45. *London,* 1762.

MACLURE and MACDONALD (Lithⁿ).— Naples. [6 views on same sheet :] Street, Naples; Castello d'Uovi, St. Elmo and fishmarket, Naples; In the streets, Naples. A.M.; Bay of Naples (with Vesuvius); Top of Vesuvius in 1846; A Courtyard. Maclure and Macdonald, Lithⁿ to the Queen, London.
Litho.? : 323 × 247 mm.

MACRET (sculp.).—Éruption du Vésuve. An imaginary outburst of Vesuvius; resembles an engraving on the Table de Planches in WILKINS, H. : "Vues Pittoresques," but is not the same. Fine engrav. : 134 × 86 mm.

MACRINUS, J. — De Vesuvio, item poetica opuscula ejusdem.—8⁰, *foll.* 16, *pp.* 156. *Neapoli,* 1693.

MACRINUS, J.—Vindimialium ad Campaniæ usum libri duo.—4⁰, *pp.* 12 + 36. *Neapoli,* 1716.

MADEMOISELLE * * *—Lettre sur l'éruption du Vésuve en août 1756.—"*Journ. Étrang.*" *pp.* 159–68. *Mars,* 1757. [C.A.]

M. A. D. O.—*See* ONOFRIO, MICHELE ARCANGELO D'.

MAFFEI, F. S.—Tre lettere a P. Bernardo de Rubeis.—4⁰. *Verona,* 1748. [C.A.]
The 2nd treats of the new discovery of Herculaneum.

MAFFEI, F. S.—*See* MAPHEI, F. S.

MAFFEI, G. C. DA SOLOFRA.—Scala naturale, overo fantasia dolcissima intorno alle cose occulte, e desiderate nella Filosofia.— 8⁰. *foll.* 140. *Vinegia, per Gio. Varisco e Compagni,* 1573.—Also : 8⁰. *Venetia,* 1564. —8⁰, *foll.* 140, *appresso Marco Guarischo, Venetia,* 1600.—"Di nuovo con quella più accurata diligentia che si è potuto corretta, et ristampata."—8⁰, *foll.* 126. *Venetia, appresso Lucio Spineda,* 1601.
See Cap. IV.—Cagione perchè nella falda del Vesuvio sono alcuni buchi, etc.

MAGALOTTI, CONTE L.—Lettera al Sig. Vincenzo Viviani, in cui si descrive il Vesuvio nel 1663.—*See* ANON.—Dei Vulcano o Monti ignivomi, *T. ii, p.* 11.

MAGNATI, V.—Notizie istoriche de' terremoti succeduti ne' secoli trascorsi, e nel presente.—8⁰, *foll.* 16, *pp.* 431. *Napoli,* 1688.
See pp. 16, 81, 150–52, 168.

MAIONE, D.—Breve descrizzione della regia città di Somma Vesuviana.—4⁰, *foll.* 10, *pp.* 56, 1 *pl.* (*a quaint map, of no value*), *figs. Napoli,* 1703.

MAIZONY DE LAUREOL.—L'Héracléade, ou Herculaneum enseveli sous la lave du Vésuve, poème de L'A. Florus, trad. en vers français avec des notes.—8⁰, *pp. xxiii* + 458. *Paris,* 1837. [C.A.]

MAJO.—Trattato delle acque acidule che sono nella città di Castellammare di Stabia. —*Napoli,* 1754.

MAJONE, G.—Della esistenza del Sebeto nella pendice settentrionale del Monte di Somma.—4⁰, fol. 1, pp. 34, 1 pl., 1 map. Napoli, 1865. [C.A.]

MAKOWSKY, A.—[Vortrag über seine Reise nach Unter-Italien mit besonderer Rücksicht auf die vulkanischen Gebiete] (1876). —Verhandl. xv, Heft 1, Sitzber. pp. 47–58. Brünn, 1877.

MALLADRA, A.—See STOPPANI, A.— Corso di Geologia, 3a ed.

MALLADRA, A.—Il fondo del cratere Vesuviano.—Rend. R. Acc. Sci. S. 3, xviii, pp. 223–34, 4 figs. Napoli, 1912.

MALLADRA, A.—Down into Vesuvius.— " The World Magazine," pp. 2, 4 figs. New York, 7 July, 1912.

MALLADRA, A.—Inside the fiery crater of Vesuvius.—" Nash's Magazine," 8⁰, pp. 560–70, 20 figs. London, August, 1912.
A visit to the crater in early summer of 1912.

MALLADRA, A.—Nouvelle descente au fond du Vésuve [5 August, 1913, with one-quarter page of text and good photo of new opening]. — L'Illustration, Paris, 27 sept. 1913.

MALLADRA, A.—La Solfatara dell Atrio del Cavallo.—Rend. R. Acc. Sci. S. 3, xix, pp. 153–63, pl. Napoli, 1913.

MALLADRA, A.—Il terremoto, Napoli e il Vesuvio.—Rassegna Nazionale di Firenze, pp. 8. Nov., 1913.

MALLADRA, A.—Stato del Vesuvio (Gennaio-Settemb. 1913).—Rivista di Vulcanologia di Im. Friedlaender, Lipsia No. 1. 1914.

MALLADRA, A.—Stato del Vesuvio [da Ottobre a Dicembre 1913].—Zeitschr. f. Vulk. i, 2, pp. 104–7, 2 pls. Berlin, Mai, 1914.
See Pls. xxxx and xxxxi.

MALLET, G.—Voyage en Italie dans l'année 1815.—8⁰, pp. 277. Paris, 1817.

MALLET, R.—Determination of Volcanic Temperatures.—fol., pp. 2. London, Sept. 29th, 1862.

MALLET, R.—The Great Neapolitan Earthquake of 1857.—2 vols. 8⁰, num. pls. and figs. London, 1862.

MALLET, R.—Preliminary report on the experimental determination of the temperatures of Volcanic Foci, and of the temperature, state of saturation, and velocity of the issuing Gases and Vapours.— Rept. Brit. Assoc. (1863), pp. 208–9. London, 1864. [C.A. (with autogr. letter).]

MALLET, R.—The eruption of Vesuvius in 1872, by Prof. Luigi Palmieri. [Transl.] With notes and an introductory sketch of the present state of knowledge of terrestrial vulcanicity, the cosmical nature and relations of Volcanoes and Earthquakes.— 8⁰, pp. 148, 8 pls. London, 1873. [C.A.]

MALLET, R.—On the mechanism of production of volcanic dykes, and on those of Monte Somma.—Phil. Mag. ii, pp. 395–97. London, 1876.—Quart. Journ. Geol. Soc. xxxii, pp. 472–95. London, 1876.
See PALMIERI. — The Eruption of Vesuvius in 1872.

MALLET, R.—On some of the conditions influencing the projection of discrete solid materials from Volcanoes and on the mode in which Pompeii was overwhelmed.— Journ. R. Geol. Soc. Ireland, iv, Pt. 3, pp. 144–69, pls. viii–x. Dublin, 1877.

MALPICA, C.—La notte del 3 Gennaio in cima del Vesuvio.—Poliorama Pittoresco, N. 23, pp. 181–83, figs. 19 Gennaio, 1839.

[MALPICA, C.]—Inaugurazione del Reale Osservatorio Meteorologico alle falde del Vesuvio il 28 Settembre, 1845.—Annali Civili, xxxix, pp. 125–41. Napoli, 1845.

MANEN.—See DARONDEAU. 1865.

MANFREDI, A.—See BARONIUS. 1632.

MANNI, P. — Saggio fisico-chimico della cagione de' baleni e delle pioggie che osservansi nelle grandi eruzioni vulcaniche. In occasione dell' eruzione del Vesuvio a Giugno 1794.—8⁰, pp. 16. Napoli, 1795. —See SANTOLI, V.—Narrazione de' fenomeni, etc.

MANTOVANI, P.—Un' escursione al Vesuvio durante l'eruzione del Gennaio 1871.— Boll. Naut. Geog. v, pp. 16. Roma, 1871.

MANTOVANI, P.—La pioggia di cenere caduta a Napoli e la lava del Vesuvio dell' Aprile 1872.—Boll. Naut. Geog. vi. Roma, 1872.

MANZI, A. (sculp.).—Vue de la grande éruption du Mont Vésuve de la Coletion [sic] de G. Hamilton.
Stipple engrav., hand-coloured, of Vesuvius in 1779 eruption by night. Carriage and two horses and numerous men looking across bay: 245×178 mm.

MANZO, G. B. (Marchese di Villa).—Lettera in materia del Vesuvio [Erupt. 1631] scritta da Napoli al Sig. Antonio Bruni a Roma.—*MS. in library of the Faculty of Medicine of Montpellier.—See also* RICCIO, L.—Nuovi documenti, *etc.* [C.A.]

MAPEI, C.—Italy, Classical, Historical and Picturesque. Illustrated in a series of views from drawings by Stanfield, R.A., Roberts, R.A., Harding, Prout, Leitch, Brockedon, Barnard, etc., etc., with descriptions of the scenes. Preceded by an Introductory Essay, on the recent history and present conditions of Italy and the Italians. —*fol., pp. cviii+164, 163 pls. London,* 1859.
See p. 103.
2nd ed. *pp. viii+cxlvi, 65 pls.* 1864.

MAPEI, C.—Italy, illustrated and described, in a series of views, from drawings by Stanfield, R.A., Harding, Prout, Leitch, Brockedon, Barnard, etc., etc. With descriptions of the scenes, and an introductory essay, on the political, religious, and moral state of Italy. And a sketch of the History and Progress of Italy during the last fifteen years (1847–62), in continuation of Dr. Mapei's essay, by the Rev. Gavin Carlyle, M.A.—*4°, pp. viii+cxlvi+168, 65 pls. London,* MDCCCLXIV.

MAPHEI, F. S.[MAFFEI,F.S.(Marquis)].— Admiranda Antiquitatum Herculanensium a claris Italis descripta inlustrata at que ab obtrectationibus vindicata.—*See* GORI.— Admir. Antiq. Hercul. *etc. T. i, pp.* 1–33 (*Ital. and Lat.*). *Roma,* 1756.

MARANA, G. P.—Des Montagnes de la Sicile et de Naples, qui jettent des feux perpétuels, de la nature de ces feux et de ces montagnes et de leurs effets.—*Letter xli of his :* L'Espion du Grand Seigneur, *T. ii, pp.* 124–34. *Amsterdam,* 1686.

MARAVIGNA, C.—Esame di alcune opinioni del Sig. N. Boubée contenute nelle sue opere intitolate "Géologie populaire, et tableau de l'état du globe à ces différens âges."—4th ed. 4°, *pp.* 48. 1834.—*Atti Acc. Gioen. xii, pp.* 275–323. *Catania,* 1837.

MARCHI, LUIGI DE.—Una visita al cratere del Vesuvio dopo l'eruzione.—"*Mondo Sotteraneo,*" iii, 1–2, *pp.* 12, 1 *fig. Udine,* 1906.

MARCHINÆ, M. — Virginis Neapolitanæ Musa posthuma.—12°, *pp.* 12+144. *Neapoli,* 1701.
See p. 118 : De incendio Montis Vesuvii. Ode.

MARENA, THOM. ANTONIUS.—Brevissimum terræmotuum examen, etc.—4°, *pp.* 8. *Neapoli,* 1632.

MARGERIE, E. DE.—*See* SUESS, E. 1897.

MARGOLLÉ, É.—*See* ZURCHER, F.

MARI, C.—Il Vesuvio. Canto.—16°, *pp.* 16. *Napoli,* 1869. [At end : *Napoli,* 1862.]

MARIGNAC, J. C. G. DE.—Notices minéralogiques. (Epidote, Humite ou Chondrodite du Vésuve, Pinite, Gigantolite.)—*Supplément Biblioth. Univ. et Revue Suisse, S.* 2, iv, *pp.* 148–62. *Genève,* 1847.—*Journ. Pharm. Sci. access. S.* 2, xii, *pp.* 150–52. *Paris,* 1847.

MARRA, F. LA.—Antichità di Pozzuoli. Puteolanæ Antiquitates. F. la Marra inv. et sculp.—*gd. fol., pp.* 107, *engrav. text in Italian and Latin,* 68 *pls.* [*Napoli*] ? 1768.
Includes plates by Falciatore, P., Fischetti, F., Natali, G. B., Magri, C., Cla. Nic., Rajola, T., De Dominicis, A., Ricciardelli, G., and engravers Volpato, G., Cardon, A., F., Nicole, C. F., Mogalli, N., M.P. (monogram), Fiorillo, Boily, L. *See* specially Pls. 4, 6, 12, 13, 14, 15, 40, 41, 42, 42 No. ii, 43, 44, 49, 50, 54, 55. Another copy in the Johnston-Lavis collection contains most of the plates, but these are not numbered, and there is no text.

MARRIOTT, H. P. FITZGERALD.—An ascent of Vesuvius.—"*Month,*" lxxiii (*S.* 3, liv), *pp.* 506–21. *London, December,* 1891.

MARTENS, G. M. VON.—Italien. I. Band : Italisches Land.—*Stuttgart,* 1846.

MARTIN, J. (drawn by).—[Eruption of Vesuvius 1822 ? by night from Mergellina.] Engraved by W. B. Cooke, 1827.
A beautiful steel engraving reproduced by Audot Père in his book. The actual engrav. is 152×111 mm., but was printed from a plate 240×303 mm.

MARTINIO, C. DE.—Osservationi giornali del successo nel Vesuvio, dalli 16 di Decembre 1631 sino alli 10 di Aprile 1632. —4°, *pp.* 32. *Napoli,* 1632.

MARTINO DI CARLES FLAMINIO.—
Ottave sopra l'incendio del Monte Vesuvio.
—12⁰, foll. 12. Napoli, 1632. [B.N.]

MARTINO, L. M. DE.—Eruzione del Vesuvio 29 [79] dell' Era cristiana. [Signed
M. P.]—Melphis excidium, pp. 209–13.

MARTINOZZI, V.—Sonetto.—See GIORGI
URBANO.

MARTORANI.—See VIANELLY.

MARTORELLI, J.—De Regia Theca Cala-
maria.—2 vols. 4⁰. Vol. i, pp. 8, foll. 290 ;
Vol. ii, pp. 8, foll. 291–738. Neapoli, 1756.
See pp. 417 et seq., 566.

MARZELLA, BENED⁰ (esegui).—Piante delle
Antiche Fabbriche incontrate nella cos-
truzione della strada che conduce allo
Stabilimento de' Bagni di Acqua Termo-
Minerale-Vesuviana-Nunziante fino al
giorno 1 Dicembre 1834, etc. [with leg-
genda].
Hand-col. litho. plan : 445×270 mm.

MASCULUS, J. B.—Masculi . . . de Incendio Vesvii excitato XVII kal. Januar.
an. 1631. libri X. Cum chronologia
superiorum incendiorum ; et ephemeride
ultimi, etc.—4⁰, foll. 4, pp. 312–37, foll. 5,
2 pls. Neapoli, 1633.

MASINO DI CALVELLO, M. A.—Distinta
relatione dell' incendio del sevo Vesuvio
alli 16 di Dic. 1631, successo, etc.—4⁰, pp.
36. Napoli, 1632. [C.A.]

MASSARII, J. P.—Sirenis lachrymæ effusæ
in Montis Vesevi incendio.—4⁰, pp. 28.
Neapoli, 1632. [C.A.]

MASTRACA, M. (publ. by).—Le Vésuve et
ses principales éruptions depuis 79 jusqu'à
nos jours, suivi de 120 gravures représentant les monuments les plus remarquables
de Pompéi, Herculaneum et du Musée de
Naples. Traduction française par M. H.
Sandré, testo Italiano di E. Pistolesi.
Trans. into English by Mrs. Spry Bartlett.
—4⁰. Vol. i, pp. 153 ; Vol. ii, pp. 143, 120
pls. Lagny, 1842.
The frontisp., text and index are printed
in Italian, French and English.

MASTRIANI.—L'eruzione del Vesuvio del
26 Aprile 1872.—8⁰, pp. 102, 1 col. pl., 1
map. Napoli, 1872.

MASTROJANNI, D. G.—L'incendio del
Vesuvio di Maggio e l'accensione dell' aria
di Decembre, del caduto anno, etc.—4⁰,
pp. 30. Napoli, 1738.

MATI, M.—See HAMILTON, SIR W.—
Osservazioni sopra la natura del suolo di
Napoli, etc.

MATTEUCCI, R. V.—Sulla fase eruttiva del
Vesuvio cominciata nel Giugno 1891.—
Atti R. Acc. Sci. S. 2, v, 2, pp. 31, 2 pls.
Napoli, 1893.—Id. Rend. p. 223. 1891.

MATTEUCCI, R. V.—Nuove osservazioni
sull' attuale fase eruttiva del Vesuvio.
Nov. 1891-Luglio 1892.—Boll. Mens. Soc.
Meteor. Ital. S. 2, xii, 10, pp. 8, 4 figs.
Torino, 1892.

MATTEUCCI, R. V.—Sulla fase eruttiva
del Vesuvio cominciata nel Giugno 1891.—
Atti R. Acc. Sci. S. 2, v, 2, pp. 28, 1 map,
2 pls. Napoli, 1893.

MATTEUCCI, R. V.—Due parole su l'attuale
dinamica del Vesuvio (1893).—Boll. Soc.
Meteor. Ital. S. 2, xiv, 1, pp. 6, 1 pl. Torino,
1894.

MATTEUCCI, R. V.—La fine dell' eruzione
Vesuviana (1891–94).—Boll. Mens. Osserv.
Cent. Moncalieri, S. 2, xiv, 4, pp. 8. Torino,
1894.

MATTEUCCI, R. V.—Die vulcanische Tätig-
keit des Vesuvs während des Jahres 1894.—
Min. petr. Mitth. N.F. xv, pp. 77–90, pls.
Wien, 1894.

MATTEUCCI, R. V.—Ueber die Eruption
des Vesuvs am 3 Juli 1895.—Zeitschr.
deutsch. geol. Gesellsch. xlvii, pp. 363–67.
Berlin, 1895.

MATTEUCCI, R. V.—Der Vesuv und sein
letzter Ausbruch von 1891–94.—Min. petr.
Mitth. N.F. xv, 3–4, p. 325, 4 tav. Wien,
1895.

MATTEUCCI, R. V.—L'Apparato dinamico
dell' eruzione Vesuviana del 3 Luglio 1895.
—Rend. R. Acc. Sci. S. 3, iii, pp. 89–100,
fig. Napoli, 1897.

MATTEUCCI, R. V.—Come dovrebbe essere
studiato il Vesuvio.—8⁰, pp. 17. Napoli,
1897.

MATTEUCCI, R. V., GIUSTINIANI, E.—
Il Selenio nei prodotte delle fumarole dell'
eruzione Vesuviana del 3 Luglio 1895.
Note preliminare.—Rend. R. Acc. Sci. S. 3,
iii, pp. 100–1. Napoli, 1897.

MATTEUCCI, R. V.—Iodio e Bromo nei
prodotti delle fumarole dell' eruzione Vesuviana del 1895. Nota preliminare.—Rend.
R. Acc. Sci. S. 3, iii, pp. 151–52. Napoli,
1897.

MATTEUCCI, R. V.—Sul Bicarbonato Sodico prodottosi sulle lave dell' eruzione Vesuviana principiata il 3 Luglio 1895.— *Rend. R. Acc. Sci. S.* 3, *iii, pp.* 223–32. *Napoli,* 1897.

MATTEUCCI, R. V.—La comparsa di fiamme nel cratere Vesuviano.—*Atti R. Acc. Lincei, S.* 5, *Rend. vii, sem.* 1, *pp.* 314–15. *Roma,* 1898.

MATTEUCCI, R. V.—Sull' incremento dell' attività presentata dal Vesuvio nei mesi di Aprile-Maggio 1898.—*Rend. R. Acc. Sci. S.* 3, *iv, pp.* 277–79. *Napoli,* 1898.

MATTEUCCI, R. V.—Sul sollevamento endogeno di una cupola lavica al Vesuvio.— *Rend. R. Acc. Sci. S.* 3, *iv, pp.* 285–99, 4 *figs. Napoli,* 1898.

MATTEUCCI, R. V.—Fisica delle lave fluenti —Cenno sull' arresto artificiale della cristallizzazione nella massa fondamentale.— *Rend. R. Acc. Sci. S.* 3, *iv, pp.* 350–51. *Napoli,* 1898.

MATTEUCCI, R. V.—Relazione sull' escursione al Vesuvio fatta dalla Società Geologica Italiana il 19 Febbraio 1898.—*Boll. Soc. Geol. Ital. xvii, pp. xxxi–xxxvi. Roma,* 1898.

MATTEUCCI, R. V.—Cenno sulle attuali manifestazioni del Vesuvio (fine Giugno 1899).—*Rend. R. Acc. Sci. S.* 3, *v, pp.* 173–77. *Napoli,* 1899.

MATTEUCCI, R. V.—Sur les particularités de l'éruption du Vésuve.—*C.R. Acad. Sci. cxxix, pp.* 65–66. *Paris,* 1899.

MATTEUCCI, R. V.—Sur l'état actuel des Volcans de l'Europe méridionale.—*C.R. Acad. Sci. cxxix, pp.* 734–37. *Paris,* 1899.

MATTEUCCI, R. V.—Su fenomeni magmastatici verificatisi nei mesi di Luglio-Agosto 1899 al Vesuvio.—*Atti R. Acc. Lincei, S.* 5, *Rend. viii, sem.* 2, *pp.* 168–76, 1 *fig. Roma,* 1899.

MATTEUCCI, R. V.—Sulla causa verosimile che determinò la cessazione della fase effusiva cominciata il 3 Luglio 1895 al Vesuvio.—*Atti R. Acc. Lincei, S.* 5, *Rend. viii, sem.* 2, *pp.* 276–81. *Roma,* 1899.

MATTEUCCI, R. V.—Sullo stato attuale del Vesuvio (3 Luglio 1899) e sul sollevamento endogeno della nuova cupola lavica (avvenuto nei mesi di Febbrajo-Marzo 1898). —*Boll. Soc. Sismol. Ital. v, pp.* 97–121, 4 *figs. Modena,* 1899.

MATTEUCCI, R. V.—Sulla attività dei vulcani Vesuvio, Etna, Vulcano, Stromboli e Santorino nell' autunno del 1898.— *Boll. Soc. Sismol. Ital. v, pp.* 132–44. *Modena,* 1899.

MATTEUCCI, R. V.—Sul periodo di forte attività esplosiva offerto nei mesi di Aprile-Maggio 1900 dal Vesuvio.—*Boll. Soc. Sismol. Ital. vi,* 7, *pp.* 207–38 ; 8, *pp.* 239–76 ; 9, *pp.* 277–312, 6 *tav. Modena,* 1900.—8⁰, *pp.* 110, 13 *pls.* 3 *figs. Modena,* 1901.

MATTEUCCI, [R. V.]—Photographs of the last eruption of Vesuvius 13th of May, 1900.

8 photos : N°s 1–6 : Successive eruptions. N$^{\circ}$ 7 : The ruined Guidehouse. N$^{\circ}$ 8 : Big ejected block.

MATTEUCCI, R. V.—Sur la production simultanée de deux Sels Azotés dans le cratère du Vésuve.—*C.R. Acad. Sci. cxxxi, pp.* 963–65. *Paris,* 1900.

MATTEUCCI, R. V.—Sulle carte topografiche del Somma-Vesuvio, recentemente rilevate dall' Istituto Geografico Militare. Lettera al Presidente.—*Rend. R. Acc. Sci. S.* 3, *vii, pp.* 149–50. *Napoli,* 1901.

MATTEUCCI, R. V.—Explosion of Vesuviu in May, 1900.—" *Nature," lxiv, p.* 13. 1901.

MATTEUCCI, R. V.—Salmiak vom Vesuvkrater, einem neuen Fundorte.—*Centralbl. f. Min. pp.* 45–47. *Stuttgart,* 1901.

MATTEUCCI, R. V.—Silberführender Bleiglanz vom Monte Somma.—*Centralbl. f. Min. p.* 47. *Stuttgart,* 1901.

MATTEUCCI, R. V.—Das Vorkommen des Breislakits bei der Vesuveruption von 1895–1899.—*Centralbl. f. Min. pp.* 48–49. *Stuttgart,* 1901.

MATTEUCCI, R. V.—Se al sollevamento endogeno di una cupola lavica al Vesuvio possa aver contribuito la solidificazione del magma.—*Boll. Soc. Geol. Ital. xxi, pp.* 413–35. *Roma,* 1903.

MATTEUCCI, R. V.—Cenno sul periodo effusivo del Vesuvio iniziatosi il 20 Luglio 1903.—*Boll. Soc. Geol. Ital. xxiii, pp.* 504–6. *Roma,* 1905.

MATTEUCCI, R. V., NASINI,R.,CASORIA, E., FIECHTER, A.—Appunti sull' eruzione Vesuviana 1905-1906.—*Boll. Soc. Geol. Ital. xxv, pp.* 846-56. *Roma,* 1907.

MAUGET, A.—Lettre à M. St.-C. Deville sur l'éruption du Vésuve du 27 mai 1858.— *C.R. Acad. Sci. xlvi, p.* 1098. *Paris,* 1858.

MAUGET, A.—Lettres à M. C. Laurent sur une éruption du Vésuve.—*Bull. Soc. géol. France, xv, pp.* 550-51, 569-70. *Paris,* 1857-58.—*C.R. Acad. Sci. xlvi, p.* 1221. *Paris,* 1858.

MAUGET, A.—Sur les phénomènes consécutifs de la dernière éruption du Vésuve.— *C.R. Acad. Sci. liv, pp.* 926-28. *Paris,* 1862.

MAUGET, A.—Sur les phénomènes consécutifs de l'éruption de décembre 1861 au Vésuve.—*C.R. Acad. Sci. lxiii, pp.* 97-98. *Paris,* 1866.

MAUGET, A.—Sur les phénomènes observés le 29 juin 1866, et sur les variations subites survenues dans le régime de divers cours d'eau de l'Italie méridionale.— *C.R. Acad. Sci. lxiv, pp.* 189-92. *Paris,* 1867.

MAUGET, A.—Récit d'une excursion au sommet de Vésuve, le 11 juin 1867.—*C.R. Acad. Sci. lxv, pp.* 898-900. *Paris,* 1867.

MAUGET, A.—Faits pour servir à l'histoire éruptive du Vésuve. Récit d'une excursion au sommet du Vésuve le 11 juin 1867. —*C.R. Acad. Sci. lxvi, pp.* 163-66. *Paris,* 1868.—Also see : *Revue des Cours Scientifiques de la France et de l'Étranger,* 14 Dec. 1867 [analysis of fumarole gases].

MAURI, A.—Memoria sulla eruzione Vesuviana de' 21 Ottobre 1822.—8⁰, *foll.* 6, *pp.* 22, 1 *pl., figs. Napoli,* 1823. [C.A.]

MAURINI, G.—De Vesuvio.—8⁰, *pp.* 156. *Neapoli,* 1693.

MAURION DE LARROCHE.—Une ascension au Vésuve. (Souvenirs de voyage.)— *Mém. Soc. Sci. nat. et méd. de Seine et Oise de* 1885-90, *xiv, pp.* 110-30. *Versailles,* 1891.

MAYORICA.—L'incendio di Vesuvio successo nell' anno del Signor 1631 a 16 xbre. —*MS. in the S. Martino Library, Naples.* Copy *pp.* 99. [C.A.]

MAZOCHI, A. S.—In vetus marmoreum sanctæ Neapolitanæ ecclesiæ Kalendarium commentarius.—2 vols. 4⁰, *pp. xl*+1096, *fol.* 1, 3 *pls. Napoli,* 1744. [C.A.]
See Diatriba v.—De Vesuviani incendii ceterarumque vulcaniarum flammarum origine, ex antiquorum christianorum sententia ex chronographo Gerasimo Monacho, pp. 392-402.

MAZOIS.—Plan of Vesuvius and neighbouring cities as they existed before the great eruption in the year 79. (Pl. 3) Engrav. by J. Cross. London, 1818. [B.N.P., Vb. 121.]
A beautiful, finely engraved map.

MAZZEI, D.—Sonetti due.—*See* GIORGI URBANO.

MAZZEI - MEGALE, G. — *See* COLAMARINO, D.

MAZZELLA, S.—Descrizione del Regno di Napoli.—4⁰. *Napoli, Cappelli,* 1586.

MECATTI, G. M.—Racconto storico-filosofico del Vesuvio e particolarmente di quanto è occorso in quest' ultima eruzione principiata il dì 25 Ottobre 1751, e cessata il dì 25 Febbrajo 1752, al luogo detto l'Atrio del Cavallo.—4⁰, *pp.* DCCXXXII, 2 *maps,* 10 *tav., figs. Napoli,* MDCCLII.
[Contains :] Terremoto che suol precedere, e accompagnare ogni eruzione, *p.* III.
Descrizione della Lava, *p.* IV (*interrottamente fino a p.* CXXXVI).
Diario del corso, che ha fatto la Lava, con varie osservazioni fatte nel corso della medesima, che si leggono nel Diario, *p.* VI.
Nota ideale del danno cagionato a diversi dalla Lava, *p.* XXVIII.
Altra simile, *p.* XLI.
Altra simile, *p.* LXXXVI.
Nota esatta di tutto il danno, *p.* CCCXLVII.
Lettera del Signor Francesco Geri Giardinier Maggiore di S. M. Siciliana scritta all' Autore, e dà conto di varie osservazioni da lui fatte, *p.* XLV.
Lettera del Signor D. Giovanni Morena all' Autore sopra varj dubbj scambievolmente proposti intorno alla Lava, *p.* XLIX.
Lettera prima del Signor Conte Catanti spettante alla visita da esso fatta al Vesuvio, *p.* XV.
Lettera II. del medesimo sulla medesima materia, *p.* LVIII.

Lettera III. del medesimo sul medesimo soggetto, *p.* LXII.

Lettera I. scritta da un amico di Firenze all' Autore, domandando lo scioglimento di varj dubbj, e particolarmente quello della penetrazione nel Vesuvio dell' acqua marina, *p.* LXXVIII.

Risposta dell' Autore al medesimo e intanto si difende dalle calunnie, e censure del Novellista Fiorentino, *p.* LXXX.

Lettera II. dell' amico di Firenze, *p.* XCIV.

Discorso I. dell' origine, e antichità, e situazione del Vesuvio, *p.* XCVII.

Carta significante lo stato del Vesuvio prima dell' eruzione del 1631, *p.* CVIII.

Risposta dell' Autore alla Lettera II. dell' amico di Firenze, *p.* CXXXI.

Discorso II. delle materie, e loro accensione nel Vesuvio, della loro liquefazione, eruzione, e moto, *p.* CXXXVII.

Introduzione al Catalogo delle Eruzioni del Vesuvio del Signor Conte Catanti Patrizio Pisano, *p.* CLIX.

Catalogo dell' eruzioni fatte dal Vesuvio del Signor Conte Catanti suddetto, *p.* CLXIII.

Discorso III. dell' eruzioni seguite nel Vesuvio, e massime delle due più celebri, l'una seguita l'anno del Signore LXXXI come più comunemente si vuole, e l'altra l'anno MDCXXXI, *p.* CLXXII.

Carta di come rimase il Vesuvio, e il paese adjacente al medesimo dopo la suddetta eruzione del 1631, *p.* CCXI.

Digressione sopra le due antiche città di Pompei, e d'Ercolano, *p.* CCXLIX.

Carta del Signor Francesco Geri dimostrante la presente eruzione, preso il punto di veduta proprio di dove sboccò la lava all' Atrio del Cavallo, *p.* CCCXXXVI.

Discorso IV. Dimostrazione di quanto è occorso nell' ultima eruzione del Vesuvio con le misure de' territorj, che ha occupato la lava ; colla nota de' danni cagionati ai Padroni di detti territorj, e con varie osservazioni, che si son fatte in quest' anno M.DCCLII, fino a tutto il mese di Luglio, tanto nel corso che ha fatto la lava, e sue adjacenze, quanto fuori, e dentro al cratere del Vesuvio, *p.* CCCXXXVII.

Osservazioni, che si sono fatte da diversi nel Vesuvio, avanti nel tempo, e dopo quest' ultima eruzione, fino a tutto il mese di Luglio di questo anno 1752, *p.* CCCLVIII.

Osservazioni di Mons. Delaire, *p.* CCCLX.

Osservazioni del Signor Conte Corafà Maresciallo di Campo, e Colonnello de' Macedoni, o siano Albanesi al servizio di S. M. Siciliana, *p.* CCCLXXI.

Osservazioni del Signor Francesco Geri Giardinier Maggiore di S. M. Siciliana, *p.* CCCLXXXVIII.

Carta dello Spaccato della montagna del medesimo Signor Francesco Geri preso il punto dalla parte di Napoli, *p.* CCCIC.

Osservazioni dell' Abate Mecatti Autore del Libro, *p.* CCCC.

Carta del corso della lava secondo il quadro fatto della presente eruzione dal celebre Signor Ignazio Vernet Pittore Avignonese preso il punto dalla parte di Castellamare, *p.* CCCCXI.

Osservazioni fatte sopra il Vesuvio dal mese di Marzo 1752, in cui terminò quell' eruzione, fino al mese di Luglio 1754, etc., *p.* CCCCXIII.

Descrizione della lava scorsa nel mese di Luglio dell' anno 1754, nel cratere, o sia piattaforma del Vesuvio, ed eruttata dalla cima d'una Montagnuola creatasi quasi nel mezzo di esso cratere ; come lo dimostra l'ingiunta Carta, *p.* CCCCXXXVII. (*Tav.* VI.)

Indice di tutto ciò che contiene l'Aggiunta delle Osservazioni ultimamente fatte in questi tre anni dopo l'eruzione seguita sulla fine dell' anno 1751 e nel principio dell' anno 1752. [*Another edition differs here as following :*—Indizj della nuova eruzione, che si è fatta il dì 3 del mese di Dicembre all' Atrio del Cavallo, che servono per osservazione di quel, che è seguito nel rimanente del mese di Novembre 1754 nel Vesuvio.] *p.* CCCCLIX.

Narrazione istorica di quel, che è occorso nella rottura del Vesuvio nel luogo detto l'Atrio del Cavallo dal dì 3 Dicembre 1754, in cui incominciò questa nuova eruzione fino a quanto è posteriormente avvenuto, *p.* CCCCLXI. [This is p. I in another edition, which ends 16 pages before this one, and in which the carrying-over syllable " Fi-" does not appear. The following titles are therefore also missing in the other edition :]—

Narrazione istorica di quel che è occorso nelle eruzioni, e scrosci del Vesuvio dal dì 12 Agosto 1756, in cui incominciarono, fino a quanto è posteriormente avvenuto : tutto ricavato dalle Osservazioni fatte sopra il Vesuvio, *p.* DLXXIX (*Tav.* VIII.).

Narrazione istorica di quel che è occorso nel Vesuvio nell' eruzione del mese di Gennajo del nuovo anno 1758, da aggiun-

P

gersi al libro delle Osservazioni fatte sopra il Vesuvio, *p.* DCXXXIII.

Narrazione istorica di quel che è occorso al Vesuvio nella seconda eruzione di quest' anno 1759, sequita alla fine del mese di Marzo, *p.* DCXLIII.

Discorso v.—Si pretende provare, che il Vesuvio, che si vede presentemente sia una Montagna formata appoco appoco dalle materie eruttate, e non antica al pari del Mondo, e creata da Dio, come le altre Montagne naturali. Che le acque del mare, e non le piovane siano la principalissima cagione della durazione delle materie, e delle eruzioni. Che siano infinite le materie, che finora sonosi eruttate, e infinitamente maggiori del cilindro, che manca alla Montagna pel Voto fattosi nell' evacuazione di tante materie ; e si dà notizia di varie altre importanti cose appartenenti a questa storia, *p.* DCLV.

Narrazione istorica di quel che è avvenuto al Vesuvio nell' eruzione del dì 23 Dicembre 1760, nel pendiò inverso la via, che è fra Camaldoli, e Tre Case, lontana dalla cima della Montagna circa quattro, o cinque miglia per aggiungersi al libro del Vesuvio, *p.* DCICI.

Narrazione istorica di quel ch'è occorso al Vesuvio nell' eruzione incominciata la notte del dì fra i dieci, e gli undici d'Aprile dell' anno 1766, e interrottamente proseguita nella maggior parte del rimanente dell' anno nel luogo detto l'Atrio del Cavallo, da aggiungersi al libro del Vesuvio, *p.* DCCXXIII.

The work consists of 2 tomes, the first of which is entitled as above, and the second is divided into 2 pts. and entitled ': Osservazioni, e Narrazione Istorica. It is rare ever to find two copies identical. Many errors occur in the pagination, etc. : for a careful study of these, reference should be made to Furchheim's bibliography. The information is very full and the plates, by the following authors, admirable :—D. d'Acerra, Fil. Morghen, D. G. Aguir, March. Galiani, Ig. Lucbesini (woodcut), M. S., Nic. d'Oratii. At the end of the O.V. copy of " Osservazioni che si son fatte sopra il Vesuvio dal Marzo 1752 al Luglio 1754, etc." there is a view of the eruption of Vesuvius of 1767.

MECATTI, G. M.—Racconto storico-filosofico del Vesuvio e particolarmente di quanto è occorso in quest' ultima eruzione principiata il dì 25 Ottobre 1751, e cessata il dì 25 Febbrajo 1752, al luogo detto l'Atrio del Cavallo.—4⁰, *foll. iii, pp.* 411, 5 *tav.* (I–V of 1st ed.) *and some woodcuts. Napoli,* 1752.

T. i of the above work. *See* FURCHHEIM.—Bibliografia del Vesuvio.

MECATTI, G. M.—Osservazioni che si son fatte nel Vesuvio dal mese di Agosto dell' anno 1752 fino a tutto il mese di Luglio dell' anno 1754, etc.—*foll.* 4, *pp.* 298, 5 *tav.* (VI–X of 1st ed.). *Napoli,* 1754.

T. ii of same.

MECATTI, G. M.—Osservazioni fate sopra il Vesuvio dal mese di Marzo 1752 in cui terminò quell' eruzione, fino al mese di Luglio 1754 che ne occorse un altra, della quale si da distintamente la Relazione, che serve d'Aggiunta al Racconto storicofilosofico, ed ai discorsi sopra il Vesuvio. [There are really five discorsi consecutively paged to DCCXXII.]

MECATTI, G. M.—Discorsi storici-filosofici sopra il Vesuvio estratti dal libro intitolato Racconto storico-filosofico del Vesuvio. A' quali Discorsi si sono aggiunte varie Osservazioni fatte dal medesimo nella piattaforma del Vesuvio l'anno 1753, e varie Notizie circa ai Ritrovamenti fatti in detto anno nella Real Villa di Portici.— 4⁰, *foll.* 4, *pp.* 594, with the 10 *pls.* of the 1st ed. *and some woodcuts. Napoli, Presso Giovanni di Simone,* 1754.

See FURCHHEIM. — Bibliografia del Vesuvio.

MECATTI, G. M.—Narrazione istorica di quel ch'è occorso al Vesuvio nel luogo detto l'Atrio del Cavallo dal dì 25 Ottobre 1751, in cui incomincio l'eruzione fino a quanto posteriormente è avvenuto.— 4⁰, *pp. ccxxiv,* 2 *pls.,* 2 *figs. Napoli,* 1752–54 ?

There is a gap from pp. lvi to lxxiii ; the 2 figs. are at pp. cxviii and ccxxiv, but they are the same. The Johnston-Lavis copy has at end : " Supplemento alla storia del Vesuvio del P. della Torre," pp. 15, pl. (erupt. 1760).

MECATTI, G. M.—Descrizione della lava scorsa nel mese di Luglio dell' anno 1754, nel cratere, ossia piattaforma del Vesuvio ed eruttata dalla cima di una montagnola. —*Napoli,* 1754.

MECATTI, G. M.—Storia delle ultime sei eruzioni del Vesuvio. Cioè di quella dell' anno 1754, e del 1756, delle due occorse, una nel mese di Gennajo, e l'altra nel mese di Agosto del 1758, e di due altre, la prima nel mese di Gennajo, e l'altra alla fine del mese di Marzo del 1759, da aggiungersi al Libro delle Osservazioni sopra il Vesuvio. —4°, *foll. iv, pp.* 270, 4 *tav.* (VII–X of 1st ed.). *Napoli*, 1760.
See FURCHHEIM. — Bibliografia del Vesuvio.

MECATTI, G. M.—Continuazione delle Osservazioni sopra diverse eruzioni del Vesuvio. —4°, *foll. iv, pp.* 298, *tav.* 5 (VI–X of 1st ed.) *and some woodcuts. Napoli,* 1761.
See FURCHHEIM. — Bibliografia del Vesuvio.

MECATTI, G. M. (printed Mecatri).—A view of Vesuvius and the adjacent hills, which emitted the greater part of the lava or liquid fire on the 23rd of Dec. 1760 and several days after ; in the form and condition they appeared in on the 25th of January, 1761 ; illustrated with some extracts from the account of these eruptions lately published by the Abbot Joseph Maria Mecatri of Naples.—" *Gentleman's Mag.*" 1761.

MECATTI, G. M.—Osservazioni che si sono fatte nel Vesuvio dal mese di Agosto 1752 sino alla narrazione istorica di quel che è occorso al Vesuvio nella eruzione cominciata la notte del dì fra i dieci e gli undici d'aprile dell' anno 1766.—*foll.* 4, *pp.* 298, 6 *pls. Napoli,* — ? [C.A.]

MECATTI, G. M.—Narrazioni storiche di quel che occorse alla rottura del Vesuvio dal dì 3 Dic. 1754 fino a quanto è posteriormente avvenuto.—*Napoli,* 1776.*

MECATTI, G. M.—Esame o sia confronto di ragioni adottate dall' autore delle novelle letterarie di Firenze Dᵣ Gio. Lami di Santacroce, e dall' Ab. Giuseppe M. Mecatti sopra la pretesa città di Pompei, e di Ercolano : sopra la Rettina, o sia Resina di cui parla Plinio : e sopra le scavazioni, che presentemente si fanno alla Real Villa di Portici di S. M. Siciliana, estratte tutte da alcune lettere de' medesimi.—4°, *pp.* 7–88. *Napoli,* 1752.

* All these works of Mecatti are much the same, with additional accounts of new eruptions, and rarely are two copies alike.

MEDANICH, G.—Beiträge zur experimentellen Petrographie.—*N. J. f. Min. ii, pp.* 20–32. *Stuttgart,* 1903.—*Giorn. Geol. Pract. i, pp.* 103–15. *Genova,* 1903.

MEISTERS. — Beobachtungen über den Vesuv.—*Mag. d. Wissensch. u. d. Litt. ii, pp.* 25, 1 *pl. Göttingen,* 1781.
Contains the " Osservazioni " of Deluc and Duchanoy in German.

MELCHIORRE, D.—3ᵃ Lettera. Raccolta di monumenti sopra l'eruzione del Vesuvio seguita nell' Agosto 1779.—*Giorn. d. Arti e d. Commercio, i, pp.* 141 *et seq. Macerata,* 1780. [O.V.]

MELE, F. — De conflagratione Vessevi : Poema.—12°, *foll.* 10. *Neapoli,* 1632. [C.A.]

MELI, R.—Escursioni geologiche al Vesuvio e nei dintorni di Napoli eseguite con gli allievi ingegneri della R. Scuola di Applicazione di Roma nell' anno 1909.—16°, *pp.* 15. *Roma,* 1909.

MELLONI, M., et PIRIA, R.—Recherches sur les fumeroles, les solfatares, etc. Lettre de M. Melloni à M. Arago.— *C.R. Acad. Sci. xi, pp.* 352–56. *Paris,* 1840. —*Ann. Chim. lxxiv, pp.* 331–35. *Paris,* 1840.—*Journ. f. prakt. Chem. xxii, pp.* 52–57. *Leipzig,* 1841. — *Froriep. Notiz. xvi, coll.* 33–37. *Erfurt u. Weimar,* 1840.

MELLONI, M.—Considerazioni intorno a certi fenomeni di direzione che si manifestano ne' Vulcani a doppio ricinto.— Comunicate al Settimo Congresso degli Scienziati Italiani, e pubblicati nel *Museo di Scienzi e Letterature, fasc.* 27, *pp.* 14. *Napoli,* 18 *Dicembre* 1845.

MELLONI, M.—Discorso per la inaugurazione del Reale Osservatorio Meteorologico Vesuviano.—*Atti Settima Adunanza Scienziati Ital. pp.* 1096–99. *Napoli,* 1846.

MELLONI, M.—Sulla polarità magnetica delle lave e rocce affini. Sopra la calamitazione delle lave in virtù del calore, ecc.— *Mem. R. Acc. Sci. i, pp.* 121–64. *Napoli,* 1856.—See also : *Atti Acc. Pont. N. Lincei, v, pp.* 666–85. *Roma,* 1851–54.—*Rend. R. Acc. Sci. N.S. ii, pp.* 187–88. *Napoli,* 1853.—*Ateneo Italiano, i, pp.* 197, 257.— *C.R. Acad. Sci. xxxvii, pp.* 229–31, 966–68. *Paris,* 1853. — " *Cosmos,*" *iii, p.* 273. *Paris,* 1854.

MELOGRANI, G.—Dell' origine e formazione de' Vulcani. Memoria.—*Atti R. Ist. Incorag. i, pp.* 162–85. *Napoli,* 1811.

MENARD DE LA GROYE, F. J. B.—Observations avec réflexions sur l'état et les phénomènes du Vésuve pendant une partie des années 1813-14.—*Journ. Phys. Chim. Hist. Nat. lxxx, pp.* 370–409, 442–72, *et lxxxi, pp.* 27–55, 160–69. *Paris,* 1815.—*Soc. Roy. Trans. Le Mans.* 1820 ? —" *Courcier,*" 4⁰, *foll.* 2, *pp.* 98+4. 1815. [C.A.]

MENZELA, Nᵃ DEL.—[Vesuvius from Bosco Trecase and Bosco Reale with 20 reference nos. and two insets, one of lava in the Vallone Fluscio and the other of the crater.] Ferd. Adonasio sculp. Engrav. : 419×257 mm.

MERCALLI, G.—Vulcani e fenomeni vulcanici in Italia.—*See* NEGRI, STOPPANI e MERCALLI.—Geologia d'Italia, *iii, pp.* 51–89. *Milano,* 1883.

MERCALLI, G.—Éruption de l'Etna et du Vésuve.—" *La Nature,*" *sem.* 2, *p.* 223. *Paris,* 1884.

MERCALLI, G.—Notizie sullo stato attuale dei Vulcani attivi Italiani.—[Estr.] *Atti Soc. Ital. Sci. Nat. xxvii, pp.* 184–98. *Milano,* 1884.

MERCALLI, G.—*See* TARAMELLI, T. 1886.

MERCALLI, G.—Notizie Vesuviane.—*Boll. Soc. Sismol. Ital. i,* 2, *pp.* 15, 1 *fig.,* 1894; *i,* 5, *pp.* 90–97, 112–18, 1895 ; *ii,* 1, *pp.* 28, 4 *figs.,* 1896 ; *ii,* 8, *pp.* 251–66, 1897 ; *iv, pp.* 12–29, 153–66, 1 *fig.,* 1898 ; *v,* 1, *pp.* 15, 1 *pl.,* 1899 ; *vi, pp.* 25, 1 *fig., Genn.–Giug.* 1900 ; *vi, pp.* 23, 4 *figs., Lugl.–Dicemb.,* 1900 ; *vii, pp.* 97–113, 3 *figs.,* 1901 ; *vii, pp.* 229–38, 5 *figs.,* 1902 ; *viii, pp.* 277–85, 3 *figs.,* 1903 ; *ix, pp.* 41–65, 7 *figs.,* 1903 ; *x, pp.* 41–63, 6 *pls.,* 1904 ; *xi, pp.* 24–44, 7 *figs.,* 1905 ; *xii, pp.* 225–44, 2 *pls.,* 1906 ; *xiii, pp.* 193–206, 2 *pls.,* 1907. *Modena,* 1894–1907.

MERCALLI, G.—Il terremoto sentito in Napoli nel 25 Gennajo 1893 e lo stato attuale del Vesuvio.—16⁰, *pp.* 7. *Torino,* 1893.—[Extr.] *Bull. mens. Oss. Centr. Moncalieri, S.* 2, *xiii,* 5. *Torino,* 1893.

MERCALLI, G.—L'Eruzione del Vesuvio cominciata il 3 Luglio del corrente anno.—8⁰, *pp.* 15. *Firenze,* 1895.—[Extr.] *Rassegna Nazionale, Roma,* 1 *Ottobre* 1895.

MERCALLI, G.—La presente fase eruttiva del Vesuvio.—*Natura ed Arte, n.* 21, *p.* 8. *Milano,* 1896.

MERCALLI, G.—Le Notizie sismo-vulcaniche riferite nelle cronache Napoletane apocrife o sospette.—*Arch. Stor. Prov. Napol. xxiii,* 2, *pp.* 10. 1898.

MERCALLI, G.—La nuova cupola lavica formatasi sul Vesuvio.—8⁰, *pp.* 4, *tav. Napoli,* 1899.

MERCALLI, G.—Escursioni al Vesuvio. La fine delle fase eruttiva 1895–99.—" *Appennino Meridionale,*" *Boll. Sez. Nap. Club Alp. Ital.* 3–4, *pp.* 1–4. *Napoli,* 1899.

MERCALLI, G.—Sul Vesuvio e sui Campi Flegrei.—"*Appennino Meridionale,*" *Boll. Sez. Nap. Club Alp. Ital. ii,* 1–2, *pp.* 6. *Napoli,* 1900.

MERCALLI, G.—Parosismo stromboliano ed esplosioni vulcaniane al Vesuvio nel Maggio 1900.—*Rassegna Nazionale,* 16, *pp.* 8. *Prato,* 1900.

MERCALLI, G. — Il Vesuvio. — " *Napoli d'oggi,*" 8⁰, *pp.* 18, *fig. Napoli,* 1900.

MERCALLI, G.—1. Escursioni al Vesuvio. Gennaio, Febbraio, Marzo, Maggio, Giugno 1899. 2. Le grandi esplosioni del Maggio-Giugno 1900. Escursioni di Aprile, Maggio, Giugno, Agosto ed Ottobre 1900. 3. Escursioni di Febbraio, Marzo e Giugno 1901.—[Estr.] " *Appennino Meridionale,*" *Boll. Sez. Nap. Club Alp. Ital. ii,* 3–4 ; *iii,* 1. *Napoli,* 1900, 1901.

MERCALLI, G.—Sul modo di formazione di un cupola lavica Vesuviana.—*Boll. Soc. Geol. Ital. xxi, pp.* 197–210, 3 *figs.,* 1902 ; *xxii, pp.* 421–28, *Roma,* 1903.

MERCALLI, G.—Ueber den jüngsten Ausbruch des Vesuv.—*Monatsschr.* "*Die Erdbebenwarte,*" *ii,* 11 *and* 12, *pp.* 4, 3 *pls. Laibach,* 1903.

MERCALLI, G.—Sulla forma di alcuni prodotti delle esplosioni Vesuviane recenti.—*Atti Soc. Ital. Sci. Nat. xlii, pp.* 411–17, 1 *pl. Milano,* 1903–4.

MERCALLI, G.—*See* GUENTHER, R. T. 1905.

MERCALLI, G.—Intorno alla successione dei fenomeni eruttivi del Vesuvio.—*Atti V. Congr. Geog. Ital. ii, pp.* 271–80. *Napoli,* 1906.

MERCALLI, G.—La grande eruzione Vesuviana cominciata il 4 Aprile 1906. *Mem. Pontif. Acc. Rom. N. Lincei, xxiv, pp.* 307–38, *Pl.* v. *Roma,* 1906.

MERCALLI, G.—La grande eruzione Vesuviana dell'Aprile 1906.—" *Rassegna Nazionale,*" 1, *pp.* 21. *Nov.* 1906.

MERCALLI, G.—I Vulcani attivi della terra (morfologia, dinamismo, prodotti, distribuzione geografica, cause).—8⁰, *pp. viii*+422, 82 *figs.*, 26 *pls. Milano,* 1907.

MERCALLI, G.—L'Osservatorio Vesuviano e gli indispensabile suoi miglioramenti.—*Congr. Soc. Geol. Ital. pp. cccxlii–ccclii. Sept.* 1911.

MERCALLI, G.—L'Osservatorio Vesuviano. —" *Natura,*" *iii, pp.* 5–16, 1 *fig. Pavia,* 1912.

MERCALLI, G.—Il riposo attuale del Vesuvio.—*Rend. R. Acc. Sci. S.* 3, *xix, pp.* 64–66. *Napoli,* 1913.

MERCALLI, G.—Sopra un recente sprofondamento avvenuto nel cratere del Vesuvio.—*Rend. R. Acc. Sci. S.* 3, *xix, pp.* 134–36, 1 *pl. Napoli,* 1913.

MERCALLI, G.—Il risveglio del Vesuvio.—*Rend. R. Acc. Sci. S.* 3, *xix, pp.* 137–40, 1 *fig. Napoli,* 1913.

MERCATOREM GERARDUM. — Italiæ, Sclavoniæ et Græciæ tabulæ geographicæ. —*fol.,* 23 *col. maps. Duysburgi,* 1589.

MERCEY, F. DE (del.).—Vue de Naples, prise du Môle. Eug. Ciceri lith.—Imp. Lemercier, Paris.
Litho. on straw-tinted ground : 362 × 261 mm.

MERULA, G.—*See* DION CASSIUS. [C.A.]

MÉRY, M.—Les amants du Vésuve.—12⁰, *p.* 95. *Paris,* 1856.

MESCHINELLI, L.—La flora dei tufi del Monte Somma.—*Rend. R. Acc. Sci. S.* 2, *iv, pp.* 115–20. *Napoli,* 1890.

MESSINA, N. M.—Relatione dell' incendio del Monte Vesuvio dell' anno 1682.—4⁰, *foll.* 2. *Napoli,* 1682. [C.A.]

MEUNIER, É. S.—Fer natif trouvé au Vésuve.—*Le Naturaliste,* 10ᵐᵉ *ann., pp.* 89–91, 1 *fig. Paris,* 1888.

MEUNIER, É. S.—Les Éruptions et les Tremblements de Terre.—[Extr.] *Bull. Soc. Normande Géog.* 3e *cahier de* 1906, *pp.* 173–90. *Rouen,* 1907.

MEURIS.—Great cone of Vesuvius from road below funicular station. Snowfall of March 2ⁿᵈ, 1881.
Gouache : 572 × 278 mm.

MEURIS.—Crater of Vesuvius seen from S.W:, March 13ᵗʰ, 1881.
Gouache : 245 × 182 mm.

MEURIS.—[Vesuvius from road below lower railway station by night, about 1883.]
Gouache : 525 × 325 mm.

MEYER, F. J. L.—Darstellungen aus Italien. —16⁰, *pp. xvi*+475. *Berlin,* 1792.

MEYER, F. J. L.—Voyage en Italie.—8⁰, *pp. xiv*+426. *A Paris, An* x. (1802).
See pp. 331–49.

MICHAEL, R.—Ueber Beobachtungen während des Vesuv-Ausbruches im April, 1906.—*Zeitschr. deutsch. geol. Gesellsch. lviii,* 2, *Monatsb. April, Mai, Juni, pp.* 121–43, 7 *figs. Berlin,* 1906.

MICHEL (delin. et sculp.).—Éruption du Mont Vésuve. À Paris chez Basset Md. d'Estampes Rue St. Jacques No. 670.
A good engrav. of an erupt. (? 1779) from Mergellina by night : 233 × 186 mm. Eighteen spectators on sea-wall in foreground.

MICHEL LÉVY, A.—*See* LÉVY, A. MICHEL.

MIELE, A. G.—Sulle miscele di Alite e di Silvite delle fumarole Vesuviane.—*Rend. R. Acc. Sci. S.* 3, *xvi, pp.* 235–38. *Napoli,* 1910.

MIERISCH, BR.—Die Auswurfsblöcke des Monte Somma.—*Tschermak, Min. petr. Mitth. viii, pp.* 113–89, *figs. Wien,* 1887.

MIGLIORATO.—Le dernier fouille à Herculaneum. [On a printed label stuck at back is written the title as above and :] Chez Migliorato, éditeur à Naples.
A hand-coloured litho. : 192 × 135 mm., with Vesuvius in background.

MIGLIORATO (éditeur).—Souvenir Pittoresque de Naples. La Rue de S. Lucia. Chez Migliorato éditeur, rue Tolédo 232 à Naples.
Hand-coloured, mounted lith. : 223 × 300 mm.

MILANO, N. P.—Vera relatione del crudele, misero e lacrimoso prodigio successo nel Monte Vesuvio, etc.—4⁰, *pp.* 8. *Napoli,* 1632.

MILENSIO, F.—Vesevvs . . . Carmen.—4⁰, *foll.* 6. *Napoli,* 1595.—*See appendix to author's work entitled* " *Dell'* impresa *dell'* Elefante," *pp.* 121–30. [C.A.]

MILESIO, G.—Relazione dell' incendio del Vesuvio del 1631.—2 pts. *pp.* 16, *per Gion Beltramo, Napoli,* 1631.—*See* GALIANI, F.—Osservazioni sopra il Vesuvio, Note.

MILESIO, G.—Vera relazione del miserabile e memorabile caso successo nella falda della nominatissima Montagna di Somma, *etc.*—4⁰, *pp.* 8. *Napoli,* 1631.

MILESIO, G.—La seconda parte delli avisi . . . di tutto quello ch'è successo in tutta la seconda settimana (Vesuvio).—4⁰, *pp.* 8. *Napoli,* 1632.—*See also* PONTANO.

MILESIO, G. — Warhaffte Relation dess erbaermlichen und erschroecklichen Zustands, so sich in der Seyten dess weitberühmten Bergs Vesuuij, *etc.*—4⁰, *pp.* 19. *München;* 1632.
See pp. 4–19.

MILESIO, G.—Récit véritable du misérable et mémorable accident arrivé en la descente de la très-renommée Montagne de Somma, autrement le Vésuve, environ trois lieües loing de la ville de Naples. Depuis le lundy 15 décembre 1631, sur les 9 heures du soir, jusques au mardy suivant 23 du mesme ; décrit jour par jour et heure par heure.—8⁰, *pp.* 13. *Lyon,* 1632. [C.A.]

MILL, H. R.—Report to council of the Scottish Geographical Society, giving notification of a grant of £20 by the general committee of the British Association for the advancement of science, for the investigation of the Volcanic Phenomena of Vesuvius.—*Scottish Geograph. Mag. iii,* p. 522. *Edinburgh,* 1887.

MILLTOWN.—*See* GERVASI, N. 1823.

MILNE, J.—On the form of volcanoes.— *Geol. Mag.* pp. 337–45, *illustr. London,* 1878.

MILO, D. A. DE. — All' IIᵐᵃ Sig⁴ Maria Selvaggia Borghini, ragguagliandola del Monte Vesuvio e dei suoi incendi.—*See* BULIFON.—Letter. Memor. *Vol. iii, pp.* 176–85. *Napoli,* 1698.

MILWARD, A.—On the motion of a lava stream observed on the side of Mount Vesuvius.—*Edinb. New Phil. Journ. xlviii,* pp. 46–55. 1850.

MINERVINI, G.—*See* BALDACCHINI, M. 1862.

MINERVINO, C. S.—Articolo di lettera dei Sig. Abate. . . . Al medesimo Sig. Amaduzzi sopra lo stesso argomento, che riferiamo, perchè aggiugne qualche altra notizia di più.—*See* ANON.—Dei Vulcani o Monti Ignivomi, *etc.* 1779.

MINERVINO, C. S.—Lettere due al P. Ab. D. Pier M. Rosini Olivetano [sull' eruzione del Vesuvio del 1794].—*Giorn. Lett. xi, pp.* 86–97. *Napoli,* 1794.

MINTO, EARL OF.—Notice of the barometrical measurements of Vesuvius, and the new cone which was formed in the eruption of February 1822.—*Edinb. Journ. Sci. vii,* pp. 68–72. *Edinburgh,* 1827.

MIOLA, A.—Ricordi Vesuviani, Carmen pel centenario di Pompei.—4⁰, *pp.* 7. *Napoli,* 1879. [C.A.]

MIRANDA, D. DE, PACI, G. M.—Osservazioni di meteorologia elettrica sulle vulcaniche esalazioni.—4⁰, *pp.* 14. *Napoli,* 1845. [C.A.]

MIRON, F.—Étude des phénomènes volcaniques, tremblements de terre, éruptions volcaniques, le cataclysme de la Martinique, 1902.—8⁰, *pp.* viii+320, *fig. and map. Paris,* 1903.

MISCELLANEA POETICA.—" Parthenope terræmotu vexata." *foll.* 6. " Vesuvius morum magister," *foll.* 3. " De Vesuvio semper ignum ejactante," *fol.* 1. " Fontis descriptio : ubi Vulcani statica diaculantis," *fol.* 1. [C.A.]

MISSON, F. M.—Nouveau voyage d'Italie, fait en l'année 1688. Avec un mémoire contenant des avis utiles à ceux qui voudront faire le mesme voyage.—2 pts. 8⁰. *La Haye,* 1691.——2nd ed. " beaucoup augmentée," etc. 3 vols. 12⁰, *copper engrav. La Haye,* 1694.——3rd ed. 3 vols. 12⁰. *La Haye,* 1698.——4th ed. 3 vols. 12⁰. *La Haye,* 1702.——Another ed., also called 4th ed., 3 vols. 12⁰. *La Haye,* 1727. [*See* Vol. ii, pp. 60–72 ; Vol. iii, pp. 391–418.]—— 5th ed. . . . " augmentée d'un quatrième volume traduit de l'Anglois, et contenant les Remarques que Monsieur Addisson a faites dans son voyage d'Italie," 4 vols. 12⁰. *Utrecht,* 1722.——Another ed., also called 5th ed., 3 vols. 8⁰. *La Haye,* 1731. ——Another ed. 4 vols. 12⁰. *Amsterdam,* 1743.
See Vol. i, pp. 311–20, 1694 ; Vol. ii, pp. 114–24 ; Vol. iv, pp. 205–26, num. pls. (erupt. June, 1688). 1743.

MISSON, F. M.—A new voyage to Italy: with a description of the chief towns, libraries, palaces, statues, and antiquities of that country. Together with useful instructions for those who shall travel thither. . . . Done into English, and adorn'd with figures.—2 vols. 8⁰. *London*, 1695.——Another ed. " with . . . observations on several other countries, as Germany, Switzerland, Savoy, Geneva, Flanders and Holland. . . . Done out of French. The second edition, enlarg'd above one third," *etc.* 2 vols. 8⁰. *London*, 1699.——4th ed. 2 vols. (4 pts.) 8⁰. *London*, 1714.——Another ed. 4 vols. 8⁰. — ?, 1739.—*See also :* HARRIS, J.—Navigantium atque Itinerantium Bibliotheca, etc. *Vol. ii, pp.* 339 [639]–702. *London*, 1705.

MITFORD, J.—*See* BRYDONE, P.—A Tour through Sicily, *etc.*, ed. 1780.

MITROWSKY, I. G. VON.—Physikalische Briefe ueber den Vesuv und die Gegend von Neapel.—8⁰, *pp.* 142. *Leipzig*, 1785.

MITSCHERLICH, R.—Ueber eine Vesuvianschlacke.—*Zeitschr. deutsch. geol. Gesellsch.* xv, *pp.* 375–76. *Berlin*, 1863.

MIXELLE (gravé).—*See* ANNA, A. D'.— Éruption du Mont Vésuve, 1794.

M. J. L. R.—*See* LE RICHE, M. J.

MOCCIA, P.—Ad Andream Fontanam de Vesuviano incendio anni 1767. Epistola. —4 *loose leaves.* [Soria.]

MODESTO, P.—All' Eccellentissimo D. Francesco Conte Esterhazy [concerning the controversy about the presence of Metallic Iron in Vesuvian Sand between D. Tata and F. Viscardi].—4⁰, *pp.* 26. *Napoli*, 1795. [O.V.]

MOEHL, H.—Erdbeben und Vulkane.— *Samml. gemeinverst. wissenschaft. Vorträge,* H. 202, 1 *tav. Berlin*, 1874.

MOHRHOFF, J. J.—*See* COMES, O. 1889.

MOLES, F.—Relacion tragica del Vesuvio.— 8⁰, *pp.* 68. *Napoles*, 1632.

MOLTEDO, F. T.—Sulle origini di Torre del Greco.—8⁰, *pp.* 20. *Napoli*, 1870.

MONACO.—Éruption du Vésuve en 1754. [C.A.] A plate.

MONACO, E.—Su di una blenda cadmifera del Monte Somma e su di un solfuro arsenicale della Solfatara di Pozzuoli.— *Ann. R. Scuol. Agric. S.* 2, iv, *pp.* 1–12. *Portici*, 1903.

MONACO, V. DI.—Lettera analitica sull' acqua della Torre del Greco, comunemente creduta prodigiosa al Sig. Ant. Sementini, *etc.* [Dated Aug. 4th, 1789.]—12⁰. *Napoli*, 1789. [B.N.]

MONFORTI, F. A.—Ad divum Januarium, elogium.—*See* GIORGI URBANO.

MONGES, G.—Sulla terribile eruzione del Vesuvio accaduta ai 15 Giugno 1794.— Lettera responsiva a N. N. [dated from Salerno].—*pp.* 24. *Salerno*, 1794.

MONITIO, C.—La Talia dove si contiene la Fiasca con le lagrime del Vesbo furioso.— 16⁰, *pp.* 208, *fol.* 1. *Napoli*, 1645. [C.A.] ——2nd ed. 8⁰, *pp.* 208. 1647. [O.V.]— [Another copy of the " Fiasca " only, at the end of which is a leaf, not numbered in the work, with a view of Vesuvius and some lines of verse], *pp.* 74, *fol.* 1. [O.V.]

MONNIER, M.—Le Vésuve et les tremblements de terre.—*L'Illustration, Paris, janvier*, 1858.

MONNIER, M.—Pompéi et les Pompéiens.— 8⁰. *Paris*, 1864.—Éd. abrégée, *etc.* 12⁰. *Paris*, 1865.

MONNIER, M.—Promenades aux environs de Naples (éruption du Vésuve, destruction de Torre del Greco).—" Le Tour du Monde," 3ᵐᵉ an., N. 124, *pp.* 305–19, *with illust. Paris*, 1864.

MONNIER, M. — Le Vésuve en 79.—*Biblioth. Univ. et Revue Suisse,* 3me pér., vii, *pp.* 193–214. *Lausanne*, 1880.

MONTALLEGRI, M. DE.—Sur l'éruption du Vésuve de l'année 1737.—*See* DE BOMARE in ANON.—Dei Vulcani o Monti ignivomi, *Vol. ii, pp.* 113 *et seq.*

MONTANI, B.—Catechismo geologico ovvero elementi della Scienza della terra per gli studj generali dell' Alta : istruzione del Regno di Napoli.—8⁰, 11 *pls.*, one coloured. *Napoli*, 1850. Treats much of Vesuvius.

MONTÉALÈGRE, DE.—[Observation sur une violente éruption du Vésuve.]—*Hist. Acad. Roy. Sci.* 1737, *pp.* 7–8. *Paris*, 1740.

MONTEFERRANTE, R.—*See* KERNOT, F.

MONTEFUSCOLI, GAET. — Pianta topografica dell' interno del cratere del Vesuvio formato nel mese di Giugno dell' Anno 1805 e diretta dal Duca della Torre. (R. Aloja inc.) [O.V.]

MONTEIRO, I. A.—Mémoire sur la chaux fluatée du Vésuve.—*Ann. Mus. Hist. Nat. xix, pp.* 36–50, 1 *pl. Paris,* 1812.—*Journ. Mines, xxxii, sem.* 2, *pp.* 171–86. *Paris,* 1812.

MONTÉMONT, A.—Des volcans en général et plus spécialement du Vésuve et de l'Etna.—*Bull. Soc. Géog. S.* 2, *xvi, pp.* 137–58. *Paris,* 1841.

MONTICELLI, T., e RICCIARDI, Fr.—Qual sia l'influenza del Vesuvio, colle sue varie eruttazioni, sulle meteore, e sulla vegetazione del Circondario. Programmi due per la Real Accademie delle Scienze. —4⁰, *pp.* 4. *Napoli,* 1810.

MONTICELLI, T.—Descrizione dell' eruzione del Vesuvio avvenuta nei giorni 25 e 26 Dicembre 1813.—4⁰, *pp.* 47. *Napoli,* 1815.——2nd ed. ?, 4⁰, *pp.* 40. [*Napoli,* 1842.] [O.V.]—*See also his:* " Opere," *Vol. ii, pp.* 1–40.

MONTICELLI, T.—Extrait d'une lettre . . . sur un phénomène particulier, observé dans l'éruption actuelle du Vésuve.—*Bibl. univ. ii, p.* 87. *Genève,* 1816.

MONTICELLI, T.—Substances volcaniques nouvelles.—*Bibl. univ. vi, pp.* 199–201. *Genève,* 1817.

MONTICELLI, T.—Descrizione delle eruzioni del Vesuvio nel 1813 e rapporto di quelle accadute nel 1817 (?).—*Giorn. Enciclop. pp.* 47. *Napoli,* — ?

MONTICELLI, T.—Rapporto sull' eruzione del Vesuvio del dì 22 a 26 Dicembre 1817. —*Giorn. Enciclop. pp.* 323–29. *Napoli,* 1818.

MONTICELLI, T.—Report on the eruption of Vesuvius in Decemb. 1817.—*Quart. Journ. Sci. v, pp.* 199–201. *London,* 1818.

MONTICELLI, T.—Altre escursioni fatte nel Vesuvio dal 1817 al 1820. — ?

MONTICELLI, T.—[Fenomeni osservati sul Vesuvio.]—*Giorn. Enciclop. i, p.* 366. *Napoli,* 1820.

MONTICELLI, T.—Notizia di una escursione al Vesuvio e dell' avvenimento che vi ebbe luogo il giorno 16 Gennajo 1821 ; in cui il Francese Coutrel si precipitò in una di quelle nuove bocche.—8⁰, *pp.* 7. [O.V.] —[Extr.] *Giorn. Enciclop. i, pp.* 62–68. *Napoli,* 1821.—*See also his:* " Opere," *Vol. ii, pp.* 67–71.

MONTICELLI, T., e COVELLI, N.—Osservazioni ed esperienze fatte al Vesuvio in una parte degli anni 1821 e 1822.— *Giorn. Arcad. Sci. ecc. xvi, pp.* 293–97. *Roma,* 1822.—*Froriep., Notizen, vi, coll.* 81–84. 1824.—*Quart. Journ. Sci. xvi, pp.* 180–83. 1823.—*Tilloch, Phil. Mag. lxii, pp.* 90–93. 1823.—In French : 8⁰, *pp.* 66. *Naples,* 1822.

MONTICELLI, T., e COVELLI, N.—Storia de fenomeni del Vesuvio avvenuti negli anni 1821, 1822 e parte del 1823, con osservazioni e sperimenti.—*Giorn. Arcad. xx, pp.* 327–37. *Roma,* 1823.—8⁰, *pp. xix*+208+3, 4 *pls. Napoli,* 1823.—— 2nd ed. 4⁰, *pp.* 170, *foll.* 3, 2 *pls.' Napoli,* 1842. [O.V.]—In German, transl. by Dr. Nöggerath and Dr. Pauls : 8⁰, *pp.* 30+234, *fol.* 1, 4 *pls. Elberfeld,* 1824. [C.A.]

MONTICELLI, T.—Collections des substances volcaniques du Royaume de Naples. —8⁰, *pp.* 16. *Naples,* 1825.

MONTICELLI, T.—Memoria sopra delle sostanze vulcaniche rinvenute nella lava di Pollena discoperta dalle ultime alluvioni del Vesuvio.—*Atti R. Acc. Sci. ii, Pt.* 1, *pp.* 77–86. *Napoli,* 1825.—*See also his :* " Opere," *Vol. ii, pp.* 81–89.

MONTICELLI, T., e COVELLI, N.—Nuove specie minerali del Vesuvio.—*Brugnatelli, Giorn. viii, pp.* 342–68. 1825.—*Amer. Journ. Sci. xi, pp.* 250–67. *New Haven,* 1826.

MONTICELLI, T., e COVELLI, N.—Prodromo della mineralogia Vesuviana. Vol. i. Orittognosia. Con atlante.—8⁰, *pp.* 34+ 483, 19 *pls. Napoli,* 1825.——2nd ed. 1843.

MONTICELLI, T.—Catalogo de' minerali esotici della collezione del Cav. . . . —4⁰. [*Napoli, circa* 1825.]

MONTICELLI, T.—Memoria sopra il disegno dell' eruzione del Vesuvio nel Marzo 1827.— 4⁰, 1 *pl.* 1827.

MONTICELLI, T.—Lettera sullo stato del Vesuvio nel prossimo passato mese di Marzo.—*Ateneo, Giorn. Sci. Lett. i, pp.* 84–87. *Napoli,* 1831. [C.A.]

MONTICELLI, T.—Sull' origine delle acque del Sebeto di Napoli antica, di Pozzuoli, etc. (1828).—*Atti R. Ist. Incorag. v, pp.* 1– 56, 2 *figs. Napoli,* 1834.

MONTICELLI, T.—[Ausbrüche des Vesuvs seit April 1835.]—*N. J. f. Min. iii, pp.* 522–23. *Stuttgart,* 1835.

MONTICELLI, T., e COVELLI, N. —
Appendici al Prodromo della Mineralogia
Vesuviana.—8°, *pp.* 28. *Napoli,* 1839.
[C.A.]

MONTICELLI, T.—Memoria [sulle vicende
del Vesuvio]. Letta . . . nella tornata
de' 19 di Agosto 1827, *etc.—Atti R. Acc.
Sci. iv, Mineralogia, pp.* 97–104. *Napoli,*
1839.

MONTICELLI, T.—Rapporto del Segretario
perpetuo della R. Accad. d. Sci. sulla
eruzione del Vesuvio del dì 22 a 26 Dic. 1817
letto nella tornata de' 9 Marzo 1818.—4°,
pp. 15. *Napoli,* 1841.

MONTICELLI, T.—Opere.—3 vols. 4°. *Vol.
i, foll.* 4, *pp.* 295, 2 *pls.* ; *Vol. ii, pp.* 335,
7 *pls.* ; *Vol. iii, pp.* 432, 19 *pls.,* 1 *map.
Napoli,* 1841–43.
For contents *see* FURCHHEIM.—Bibliografia del Vesuvio.

MONTICELLI, T.—Osservazioni dello stato
del Vesuvio dal 1823 al 1829.—*See his :*
" Opere," *Vol. ii, pp.* 106–12.

MONTICELLI, T.—Sopra alcuni prodotti
del Vesuvio ed alcune vicende di esso (1832).
—*Atti R. Acc. Sci. v, Pt.* 2, *pp.* 141–45,
1 *pl. Napoli,* 1844.

MONTICELLI, T.—Sulle sublimazioni del
Vesuvio (1832).—*Atti R. Acc. Sci. v, Pt.* 2,
pp. 147–49. *Napoli,* 1844.

MONTICELLI, T.—Memoria sopra talune
nuove sostanze Vesuviane (1832).—*Atti
R. Acc. Sci. v, Pt.* 2, *pp.* 157–59. *Napoli,*
1844.

MONTICELLI, T.—Memoria sopra la eruzione del 28 Luglio 1833 (1833).—*Atti R.
Acc. Sci. v, Pt.* 2, *pp.* 169–77. *Napoli,*
1844.

MONTICELLI, T.—Muriato Ammoniacale
sublimato dal Vesuvio (1834).—*Atti R. Acc.
Sci. v, Pt.* 2, *pp.* 179–81. *Napoli,* 1844.

MONTICELLI, T.—Memoria sopra altre
vicende del Vesuvio del 1835 (1835).—
Atti R. Acc. Sci. v, Pt. 2, *pp.* 183–86.
Napoli, 1844.

MONTICELLI, T.—Memoria sopra i danni
che il fumo del Vesuvio reca ai vegetabili
(1835).—*Atti R. Acc. Sci. v, Pt.* 2, *pp.* 187–
89. *Napoli,* 1844.

MONTICELLI, T.—Introduzione alla Monografia delle pelurie lapidee del Vesuvio
(1837).—*Atti R. Acc. Sci. v, Pt.* 2, *pp.*
191–94. *Napoli,* 1844.

MONTICELLI, T.—Monografia delle pelurie
lapidee del Vesuvio (1837).—*Atti R. Acc.
Sci. v, Pt.* 2, *pp.* 195–205. *Napoli,* 1844.

MONTICELLI, T.—Continuazione alla Mono-
grafia delle pelurie lapidee del Vesuvio.—
Atti R. Acc. Sci. v, Pt. 2, *pp.* 207–10, 1 *pl.
Napoli,* 1844.

MONTICELLI, T.—Storia e giacitura del
ferro di Cancarone (1840).—*Atti R. Acc.
Sci. v, Pt.* 2, *pp.* 211–15. *Napoli,* 1844.

MONTICELLI, T.—Monografia del ferro di
Cancarone (1841).—*Atti R. Acc. Sci. v,
Pt.* 2, *pp.* 217–27, 3 *tav. Napoli,* 1844.

MONTICELLI, T.—Genesi del ferro di
Cancarone (1842).—*Atti R. Acc. Sci. v,
Pt.* 2, *pp.* 229–32. *Napoli,* 1844.

MONTÙ, C.—Il Vesuvio e le sue eruzioni.
Conferenza.—8°, *pp.* 32. *Torino,* 1906.

MORAWSKI, T., und SCHINNERER, L.—
Analysen von vulcanischen Producten,
welche Prof. Kornhuber gelegentlich einer
Besteigung des Vesuvs im Jahre 1871
gesammelt hat.—*Verhandl. geol. Reichsanst. pp.* 160–62. *Wien,* 1872.

MORELLI, F.—Raccolta degli antichi Monu-
menti esistenti fra Pozzuolo, Cuma e Baja.
—*Tip. Agapito Franzetti, Roma* [? 1810].
The first view is marked as drawn by
Hackert, and it is to be presumed that the
rest are by him also.

MORENA, G.—Lettera all' Abate Mecatti.—
See MECATTI.—Racconto storico-filosofico
del Vesuvio. *Napoli,* 1752.

MORENO.—*See* SANZ Y MORENO.

MORGAN, LADY.—Italy.—3 vols. 8°. *London,*
1821.
See Vol. iii, Chapt. XXIII.

MORGAN, O.—On some phenomena of
Vesuvius.—*Quart. Journ. Sci. i, pp.* 132–34.
1829.—*Journ. f. Chem. Phys. lvii (Jahrb.
XXVII), pp.* 405–7. *Halle,* 1829.

MORGHEN, F.—[A Collection of 84 views
and plans of Naples and the Vicinity.]—
fol. [*Naples,*] 1772–77. [B.N.P. Vb. 221
and B.M., S. 107. 12.]
See 16, 17 (2), 18 (3), 20 (5), 21 (6),
72 (22), 79 (33), 80 (34), 81 (35), 82 (36)
(of the Johnston-Lavis collection).

MORGHEN, F.—[A Map of the Gulf of Naples and Vesuvius in classical times with references to authors. — *Naples* ?, 1772 ?] [B.M., S. 107. 12. Better copy 24043. 1.]
There is a view of Vesuvius in eruption. The plate signed Félix Piccinino. Math. Arch. Del. and S. Cardon Sculp. is a modern map of the same. [B.M., S. 107. 12.] These maps are similar to the last plates in Morghen's collection of 84 views of Naples and vicinity. There is added the inscription : " Appo F. Morghen. Con Priv. Reg. 1772."

MORGHEN, F. (engrav. by).—Eruzione del Vesuvio seguita la notte degli 8 Agosto, nel 1779 . . . 5 . . .—pl. *gd. fol.* [B.N.P. Vb. 221.]

MORGHEN, F. (scp.).—Piano del volcano di Napoli denominato il Vesuvio ; colle vieppiu rimarchevoli eruzioni seguite in piu tempi. A.S.A. Mad^{ma} la Principessa Jablonouka, *etc.*
Circa 1779. Similar to Pl. 16 in Morghen's 84 views. Engrav. map : 375×250 mm.

MORHOF, D. G. — Polyhistor. literarius philosophicus et practicus.—2 vols. 4⁰. *Lubecæ*, 1714.
See Vol. ii, pp. 338 *et seq.*

MORI, F.—Ricordi di alcuni rimarchevoli oggetti di curiosità e di belle arti di Napoli (erupt. 1822).—8⁰, *foll.* 31, 23 *pls., figs. Napoli*, 1837. [O.V.]

MORMILE, C.—Del dialetto Napoletano. [By F. Galiani.] Edizione seconda, corretta ed accresciuta [by C. Mormile and others].—*See* " Collezione di tutti i poemi in lingua Napoletana."—28 tom. 12⁰. *Napoli*, 1783–89.

MORMILE, G.—Descrittione della città di Napoli e del suo amenissimo distretto e dell' antichità della città di Pozzuoli.—*Napoli*, 1617.——2nd ed. 8⁰, *pp.* 248, 3 *pls., figs.* 1625.——3rd ed. 8⁰, *foll.* 4, *pp.* 251+3, *num. figs. Napoli*, 1670.

MORMILE, G.—Nuovo discorso intorno all' antichità di Napoli, e di Pozzuolo.—8⁰, *pp.* 69. ‾ *Napoli*, 1629.
See pp. 31–32.

MORMILE, G. (Napolitano).—L'incendio del Monte Vesuvio e delle straggi, e rovine, che hà fatto ne' tempi antichi, e moderni insino a' 3 di Marzo 1632.—8⁰, *pp.* 48. *Napoli*, 1632. [C.A.]

At p. 47 there is a " Nota di tutte le relazioni stampati fino ad hoggi del Vesuvio raccolte da Vincenzo Bove," containing 56 entries : the earliest bibliographical list of Vesuvian literature.

MORREN.—Le Vésuve, poésie. — ?, 1843.

MORRISON, A. J. W.—*See* GOETHE.

MORSELLI, G.—Napoli antica, descritta co' luoghi che abbellivano il suo delizioso cratere.—8⁰. *Napoli*, 1832.

MORTIER, P. (publ.).—Elegantissimus ad Mare Tyrrhenum ex Monte Pausilipo. Neapolis et Vesuvii Montis Prospectus. Veüe très agréable de Naples du M. Veüe et du Posilipo et sa grotte, etc. 10. Amsterdam par Pierre Mortier. [Vienna lib.]
This is a copy of Hoefnaglius' drawing : 521×411 mm.

MORTIER, P.—Vesuvius Mons à deux lieues de Naples. Chez Pierre Mortier avec privil. à Amsterdam.—*From* BLAEU.—Theatrvm Civitatvm, etc. 1663.
A fine view of Vesuvius during the eruption of 1631 with people flocking over the Maddelena bridge. Very fine engraving : 515×450 mm.

MORYSON, Fynes.—An Itinerary written . . . First in the Latine Tongue, and then translated by him into English : Containing His Ten Yeeres Travell Throvgh the twelve Dominions of Germany, Bohmerland, Sweitzerland, Netherland, Denmarke, Poland, Jtaly, Turky, France, England, Scotland and Ireland. Divided into III Parts.—4⁰, *foll.* 6, *Pt. i, pp.* 285 ; *Pt. ii, pp.* 301 ; *Pt. iii, pp.* 292. *London*, 1617.
See Pt. i, Bk. 2.

MOURLON, M.—Recherches sur l'origine des phénomènes volcaniques et des tremblements de terre.—8⁰. *Bruxelles*, 1867.

MOUSSINOT, ARTHENAY, D' (edited by). —Mémoire sur la ville souterraine découverte au pied du Mont Vésuve. Suivant la copie imprimée à Paris.—4⁰. *Gottingæ*, 1748.——Another ed. 8⁰, *pp.* 51. *Paris*, 1748.——Another ed. *Museum Helveticum. partic.* 11. 8⁰, 1746, *etc.*

MOUTON.—[Four views of Vesuvius.] 1. Eruzione del 1820. [By day from E. of Camaldoli.] 2. [Same by night.] 3. Ermitaggio del Vesuvio 1830. [By night with slight erupt.] 4. [Same by day.] M' Mouton, strada S. Carlo. N° 32.
4 gouaches : 200×140 mm.

MOUTON.—[Four views of Vesuvius in 1830.] 1. Neve di 2 Gennajo 1830. [By day from Naples ; three fishermen in foreground.] 2./ [Same by night.] 3. Cratere di 2 Novembre 1830. [By night.] 4. [Same by day.] M' Mouton, strada S. Carlo. N° 32.
4 gouaches, each : 22×142 mm.

MOUTON.—Neve di 29 Xbre. 1831. M' Mouton, Strada S. Carlo. N° 32.
Vesuvius from Naples by day with snow mantle. Three figures, one with rod in foreground, Gouache : 450×320 mm.

MUECKE, H.—*See* NOEGGERATH, J J.—Der Ausbruch des Vesuv. 1868.

MUELLER (del.).—Naples with Mount Vesuvius. Neapel und der Vesuv. A. H. Payne Sc.
Picturesque, but incorrectly drawn view ; man on donkey and one on foot in foreground. Steel engrav. : 144×108 mm.

MUELLER, A.—Ueber das Vorkommen von reinem Chlorkalium am Vesuv.—*Verhandl. i, pp.* 113–19. *Basel,* 1857.

MUELLER, R.—Les Volcans.—12⁰. *Rouen,* 1882.

MUNICIPIO DI NAPOLI.—Relazione della Giunta al Consiglio sui provvedimenti adottati per la eruzione del Vesuvio 1872 ed atti relativi.—4⁰, *pp.* 31. *Napoli,* 1872. [C.A.]

MUNSON, M. A.—About Vesuvius.—" *The Lakeside Monthly,*" *vii, pp.* 193–96. 1872.

MUNTERUS, M. T. L.—Parerga historico-philologica.—8⁰, *pp.* 12+128+14, 1 *fig. Gottingæ,* 1749. [O.V.]
See pp. 1–64 : View of Vesuvius, 1749 ; *also pp.* 103–22.

MURATORI, L. A.—Rerum Italicarum Scriptores, etc.—28 vols. *fol. Mediolani,* 1723–51.
See Vol. i, Pte. i, p. 278.

MURICCE, F. CAREGA.—I vulcani d'Italia (Etna, Vesuvio, Campi Flegrei, Isole Eolie, Stromboli).—1877.

MUSSET, P. DE.—Voyage Pittoresque en Italie, partie méridionale, et en Sicile. Illustrations de MM. Rouarge Frères.—4⁰, *pp.* 524. *Paris,* 1856.
See pls. at pp. 351 and 407 and text pp. 405–11.

MUSUMECI, M.—Sopra l'attitudine delle materie vulcaniche alle arti susidiarie dell' architettura.—*Atti Acc. Gioen. xv, pp.* 43–58. *Catania,* 1839.

NANSOUTY, M. DE.—Actualités scientifiques. Volcans et volcanisme . . . etc.—16⁰, *pp.* 361. *Paris,* 1906.

NAPOLI, A.—*See* KLEIN, J. A. 1824.

NAPOLI, R.—Nota sopra alcuni prodotti minerali del Vesuvio.—*Bull. Acc. Aspir. Nat. pp.* 62–65. *Napoli,* 1861.

NAPOLI, R. — Sulla produzione del Sale Ammoniaco nelle fumarole Vesuviane.—*Rend. R. Acc. Sci. i, pp.* 239–40. *Napoli,* 1862.—*Nuovo Cimento, xvi, pp.* 338–39. *Pisa,* 1862.

NAPOLI, R.—La cenere Vesuviana dell' eruzione del 1855.—*Ann. R. Osserv. Meteor. Vesuv. i, pp.* 74–75. — ?, — ?

NASINI, R., ANDERLINI, F., e SALVADORI, R.—Sulla probabile presenza del Coronio e di nuovi elementi nei gas della Solfatara di Pozzuoli e del Vesuvio.—*Atti R. Acc. Lincei, S.* 5, *Rend. vii, sem.* 2, *pp.* 73–74. *Roma,* 1898.—*Atti R. Ist. Veneto, S.* 7, *ix, disp.* 10, *pp.* 1371–72. *Venezia,* 1898.

NASINI, R.—Terrestrial Coronium. (Gases of Vesuvius.)—*Chem. News, lxxviii, p.* 43. 1898.

NASINI, R., e LEVI, G. — Radioattività di alcuni prodotti vulcanici dell' ultima eruzione del Vesuvio (Aprile 1906) e confronto con quella di materiali più antichi.—*Atti R. Acc. Lincei, S.* 5, *Rend. xv, sem.* 2, *pp.* 391–97. *Roma,* 1906.

NASINI, R., ANDERLINI, F., SALVADORI, R.—Ricerche sulle emanazioni terrestri Italiani. II. Gas del Vesuvio e dei Campi Flegrei, delle Acque Albule di Tivoli, del Bulicame di Viterbo, di Pergine, di Salsomaggiore.—*Gazz. Chim. Ital. xxxvi, Pte.* 1, *pp.* 429–57, 9 *tav. Roma,* 1906.

NASINI, R.—*See* MATTEUCCI, R. V. 1906.

NAUDÉ, G.—Sur les divers incendies du Mont Vésuve et particulièrement sur le dernier qui commença le 16 décembre 1631.—12⁰, *pp.* 37. *Paris,* 1632.

NAUDÉ, G., und GIULIANI, G. B.—Ueber den Vesuv und Aetna. — ?, 1632.

NBG.—*See* KLEIN, J. A. 1824.

NECKER DE SAUSSURE, L. A.—Description du cône du Vésuve le 15 avril 1820.—*Biblioth. univ. Sci. xxiii, pp.* 223–28. *Genève,* 1823.

NECKER DE SAUSSURE, L. A.—Storia de fenomeni del Vesuvio. C'est-à-dire, Histoire des phénomènes offerts par le Vésuve dans les années 1821 et 1822, avec des observations et des expériences, par T. Monticelli, . . . et N. Covelli. Naples, février 1823.—*Bibl. Univ. Sci. Arts, xxiii, pp,* 197–231. *Genève,* 1823.

NECKER DE SAUSSURE, L. A.—Mémoire sur le Mont-Somma.—*Mem. Soc. Phys. Hist. nat. ii, Pt.* 1, *pp.* 155–203, 2 *tav. Genève,* 1823.—[Sep. publ.] *Genève,* 1828.

NECKER DE SAUSSURE, L. A.—Ueber den Monte Somma.—" *Sammlung von Arbeiten ausländischer Naturforscher über Feuerberge und verwandte Phänomene. Deutsch bearb. von Dr. Nöggerath und Dr. J. P. Pauls,*" Vol. ii, *pp.* 111–200, *tav.* 2 *and* 3. *Elberfeld,* 1825.
Transl. of foregoing.

NECKER DE SAUSSURE, L. A.—*See* RAFFLES.

NÉE.—*See* CHASTELET (des.).—Naples. Vue du Vésuve prise du Mont St. Angelo, etc.

NEGRONI, O.—Lettera al Sig. D. Michele Torcia intorno alla pioggia delle ceneri Vesuviane nell' eruzione del 1779.
Referred to by Torcia in his " Relazione."

NEGRONI, O.—Sulle ceneri Vesuviane del 1779.
Mentioned by Duca della Torre.

NEMINAR, E. F. — Ueber die chemische Zusammensetzung des Mejonits vom Vesuv. —*Jahrb. geol. Reichsanst. xxv, Min. Mitth. pp.* 51–56. *Wien,* 1875.

NESTEMANN und FELBER. — Notizen über den Vesuv im Mai 1830.—*Archiv. f. Min. Geogn. Bergbau, und Hüttenkunde, iv, pp.* 121–24. *Berlin,* 1831.

NETTI, F.—Il Vesuvio.—Article in " *L'Illustrazione Italiane,*" *with figs.,* 19–26 *Dic.* 1875, *and* 2, 9, 16 *and* 23 *Gen.* 1876. [C.A.]

NEUMAYR, M. — Erdgeschichte. — *Allgemeine Naturkunde, i, pp.* 42+*xii*+653, *very num. illustr. Leipzig,* 1886.

NIBBY, A.—*See* VASI, M. 1826.

NICCOLINI, A.—Tavolametrica-cronologica delle varie altezze tracciate dalla superficie del mare fra la costa di Amalfi ed il promontorio di Gaeta nel corso di diciannove secoli. —4⁰, *pp.* 52. *Napoli,* 1839. [C.A.]

NICCOLINI, A.—Descrizione della Gran-Terma Puteolana, volgarmente detta Tempio di Serapide.—4⁰, *pp.* 95, *num. col. and uncol. pls., maps, etc. Napoli,* 1846.

NICOLAI, A.—De Vesevo Monte, epigramma. —*See* GIORGI URBANO.

NICOLLET (gravé).—*See* CHASTELET.— Naples. Vue du Mosle, etc.

NIERIKER, J.—Sorrent gegen Monte S. Angelo und Vesuv. Originalzeichnung von J. N. . . . (S. 367). G. Raux s.
Woodcut from a German illustr. paper : 238×160 mm.

NIGLIO, M.—Saggio di Poesia.—8⁰, *pp.* 120. *Napoli,* 1825. [C.A.]
See pp. 70–74.

NISBET, C.—*See* GOETHE.

N. N.—Lettera scritta dal Sig. N. N. al Sig. N. N. in Calabria sulle cagioni delle tante mosse e minacce fatte dagli edificj di Napoli nella fine del prossimo scorso anno 1766, e nel principio del corrente.—4⁰, *pp.* 16. *Napoli,* 1767. [B.N.]

NOBILI, G. DE.—Analisi chimica ragionata del lapillo eruttato dal Vesuvio nel dì 22 Ottobre 1822, etc.—8⁰, *pp.* 20. *Napoli,* 1822.

NOCERINO, N.—La Real Villa di Portici illustrata.—8⁰, *pp.* 157+3. *Napoli,* 1787.

NODIER, CH.—*See* NORVINS. 1737.

NOEGGERATH, J. J.—*See* MONTICELLI e COVELLI. 1824.

NOEGGERATH, J. J.—Vesuv u. Monte Somma im Relief mit geognostischer Bezeichnung verfertigt von Thomas Dickert.—*Anzeige. Rheinl. u. Westphal. Verhandlungen, vi, pp.* 266–68. *Bonn,* 1849.

NOEGGERATH, J. J.—Der Ausbruch des Vesuv im Jahre 1834.—*Illustrirte Zeitung, Nr.* 1290, *pp.* 199–200, 1 *illustr. by Prof. H. Mücke. Leipzig,* 1868.

NOLLET (Abbé).—Plusieurs faits d'histoire naturelle observés en Italie.—*Hist. Acad. Roy. Sci.* (1750), *pp.* 7–25. *Paris,* 1754.

NORTHALL, J.—Travels through Italy, containing new and curious observations on that country ; *etc.*—8⁰, *pp.* 476 *and index. London,* 1766.

NORVINS, NODIER, CH., DUMAS, ALEX., DIDIER,CH.,WALCKNAER,LEGOUVÉ, ROYER, AL., BERLIOZ, H., BEAU-VOIR, ROGER DE, AUGER, H., LEMONNIER. — L'Italie pittoresque. Tableau historique et descriptif de l'Italie, du Piémont, de la Sardaigne, de Malte, de la Sicile et la Corse. Orné de dessins inédits de Mme. Haudebourt-Lescot, MM. le Comte de Forbin, Gravet, Deveria, Storelli, Coignet, Girard et Lambrouste.— 2 vols. 8⁰, *num. pls. and maps. Paris,* 1737.—8⁰. *Paris,* 1846.

NOTO, S.—Cenno storico della Cappella di S. Maria della Bruna in Torre del Greco.— 12⁰, *pp.* 36. *Napoli,* 1851. Eruption 1631.

NOUGARET, J.—Herculanum.—*Le Moniteur universel, No.* 116, *p.* 500, *coll.* 4–5. *Paris,* 26 *avril,* 1865.

NOVI, G.—Degli Scavi fatti a Torre del Greco dal 1881 al 1883, primi indizii del probabile sito di Veseri, Tegiano, Taurania e Retina.—*Atti Acc. Pontaniana, xvi,* 1, *pp.* 1–36, 3 *tav. Napoli,* 1885.

NOVI, G.—Gl'Idrocarburi liquidi e solidi.— *Atti Acc. Pontaniana, xvi,* 1, *pp.* 57–136. *Napoli,* 1885.

NOVI, G.—Idrologia, acque irrigue, balneari e potabili in Torre del Greco, ecc.—*Atti Acc. Pontaniana, xxiii,* 9, *pp.* 24. *Napoli,* 1893.

NOVI, G.—Il Vesuvio. I prodromi della presente eruzione ed i materiali da costruzione.—" *Polytechnicus,*" *iv,* 7, *pp.* 49–50. *Napoli,* 1 *Aprile,* 1896.

NOVI, G.—Il Vesuvio e l'apparizione di vegetali esotici sulle sue pendici.—" *Polytechnicus,*" *iv,* 9, *pp.* 66–67. *Napoli,* 1 *Maggio,* 1896.

NUNZIANTE, MARCHESE VITO.—Dimanda di privativa per la fabbricazione di lastre e cristalli, facendo uso per essa delle lave vulcaniche Vesuviane.—4⁰, *pp.* 8. *Napoli,* 1826.

NUNZIANTE, MARCHESE VITO.—Eau Vésuvienne.—*fol., pp.* 2. — ?, — ? [C.A.]

NUZZO MAURO, A.—Un Papiro, ossia i gladiatori nella Caverna del Vesuvio.—8⁰, *p.* 197. *Venezia,* 1826.

OBERBECK, C.—Pompeji et le Vésuve.— *Leipzig,* 1866.

OBERMANN, X. A. V. W. (sc.). — Vogelansicht von Pompeji. Woodcut from a German illustr. paper : 411 × 271 mm.

OBLIEGHT, E.—Vesuv-Eisenbahn aus der Vogelschau.—*Illustrirte Zeitung,* 1614, *p.* 437, 2 *illustr. Leipzig,* 1874.

O'CONNOR, B.—Mirabilis viventium interitus in ᵃ Charonea Neapolitana crypta. Novissimum Vesuvii montis incendium anni aere salutis 1694.—12⁰, *pp.* 68. *Coloniæ Agrippinæ,* 1694. [O.V.]

O'CONNOR, B.—DeMontis Vesuvii incendio. Dissertationes med.-phis. Auxonisi, 1695. —*Acta Eruditorum, Lipsiæ,* 1696.

ODELEBEN, E. G. VON.—Beiträge zur Kenntniss von Italien vorzügl. in Hinsicht auf die mineralogischen Verhältnisse dieses Landes.—2 vols. 8⁰, *maps. Freiberg,* 1819–20. *See* Vol. ii, pp. 253–343.

ODELEBEN, E. G. VON.—Reise in Italien. —2 vols. — ?, 1821.

OGLIALORO-TODARO, A.—Poche Notizie sulle Sabbie emesse dal Vesuvio.—*Rend. R. Acc. Sci. S.* 3, *xii, pp.* 135–36. *Napoli,* 1906.

OGLIALORO-TODARO, A., BAKUNIN, M., ARENA, F.—La Sorgente minerale di Valle di Pompei.—*Rend. R. Acc. Sci. S.* 3, *xiv, p.* 160. *Napoli,* 1908.—*Id. Atti, S.* 2, *xiv,* 3, *pp.* 1–20. *Napoli,* 1910.

OHNESORGE, T.—Ueber Vesuvaschenfälle im nordöstlichen Adriagebiete im April 1906.—*Verh. k. k. geol. Reichsanst. pp.* 296–97. *Wien,* 1906.

OLEARIUS, T.—Feuer-flammen des Vesuv. —4⁰. *Halle,* 1650.

OLIVA, N. M.—Lettera scritta all' abbate Flavio Ruffo nella quale si dà vera e minuta relazione degli segni, terremoti ed incendii del Monte Vesuvio, cominciando dal dì 10 del mese Dicembre 1631, per sino alli 5 Gennaio 1632.—4⁰,*foll.* 4. *Napoli,* 1632.

OLIVA, N. M.—La ristampata lettera con aggiunta di molte cose notabili, nella quale dà vera e minuta relazione delli segni, etc. —4⁰, *pp.* 8. *Napoli,* 1632. [C.A.]

OLIVI, AB.—Risposta al Sig. Ab. Tomaselli. —*Giorn. Lett. i, pp.* 88–93. *Napoli,* 1793.

OLIVIERI, G. M.—Breve descrizione istorico-fisica dell' eruzione del Vesuvio del 15 Giugno 1794.—4⁰, *pp.* 22. *Napoli,* 1794.

OLTMANNS, J.—Darstellung der Resultate welche sich aus den am Vesuv von A. von Humboldt und anderen Beobachtern angestellten Höhenmessungen ableiten lassen. —*Abh. k. Akad. Wiss.* (1822–23), *pp.* 137–57. *Berlin,* 1825.

OLTMANNS, J.—Humboldts Barometer-Messungen am Vesuv (1827). 4.

OMBONI, G.—Geologia dell' Italia.—8⁰, 5 *tav. Milano,* 1869. *See* No. 12.

ONOFRII, P. DEGLI.—Elogii storici di alcuni servi di Dio, che vissero in questi ultimi tempi e si adoperarono pel bene spirituale e temporale della città di Napoli. —8⁰, *pp. xvi+*472. *Napoli,* 1803. [C.A. and O. V.]
   In the life of P. Gregoris Mᵃ Rocco, on pp. 432–61, some Vesuvian eruptions are described, particularly those of 1794 and 1799.

ONOFRIO, M. A. D'.—Nuove riflessioni sul Vesuvio, con un breve dettaglio de' paraterremoti, premessi i luoghi degli antichi scrittori, che han parlato di questo vulcano. —12⁰, *pp.* 20. *Napoli,* 1794.——2ᵃ ed. 8⁰, *pp.* 16, 1 *pl., figs. Napoli,* 1794. [O.V.]

[ONOFRIO, M. A. D'.]—Relazione ragionata della eruzione del nostro Vesuvio accaduta a' 15 Giugno 1794, in seguito della storia completa di tutte le eruzioni memorabili sino ad oggi con una breve notizia della cagione de' terremoti. Dal Professore di Medicina M.A.D.O.—4⁰, *pp.* 8. [*Napoli,* 1794.]—Also 4⁰, *pp.* 2. [*Napoli,* 1794.] [B.V.]—Another ed.: " Corretta dall' autore M. A. D'Onofrio, ed. accresciuta di note in fin di questa."—*Napoli, li 7 Luglio,* 1794.

ONOFRIO, M. A. D.'—Ausführlicher Bericht von dem letzten Ausbruche des Vesuvs, am 15ten Juni 1794, die Geschichte aller vorhergegangenen Ausbrüche und Betrachtungen über die Ursachen der Erdbeben ; von Herrn M. A. D. O. Professor der Ärzneygelahrtheit zu Neapel. Nebst einem Schreiben des Einsiedlers am Vesuv und zwey Briefe des Duca della Torre über den nämlichen Gegenstand. Als ein Anhang zu des Ritters Hamilton Bericht vom Vesuv. Aus dem Italienischen übersetzt. Mit einem nach der Natur gezeichneten Kupfer.—4⁰, *pp.* 88, 1 *copperengrav. Dresden,* 1795. [O.V.]
   German transl. of foregoing.

ONOFRIO, M. A. D'.—*See* BREISLAK, S., and WINSPEARE, A. 1795.

ONOFRIO, M. A. D'.—Lettera ad un amico in provincia sul tremuoto accaduto ai 26 di Luglio e seguito dalla eruzione Vesuviana dell' Agosto 1805, etc.—8⁰, *pp.* 44. *Napoli,* 1805. [O.V.]

OPITZ, M.—Vesuvius Poëma Germanicum. —8⁰, *foll.* 6, *pp.* 33+2. *David Müller, Bresslaw,* 1633.

OPITZ, M.—Vesuvius, Gedichte (1631).— 8⁰, *Vol. i, pp.* 19–44. *Frankfurt am Mayn,* 1746. [C.A.]

ORATY, C. (engrav. by).—Pianta e veduta del Monte Vesuvio dalla parte meridionale. Co' varj corsi più recenti del Bitume, e colla situazione de' villaggi, ed altri luoghi circonvicini, secondo lo stato dell' anno 1761, e coll' accurata descrizione della eruzione fatta in Xᵇʳᵉ 1760. [In margin :] Fatta a spese di Nicola Petrini e da lui si vendono.—*fol.* [B.S.]

ORATY (?), NIC. D'.—Veduta del Monte Vesuvio dalla parte di Oriente con le nuove bocche, e corsi di bitume nel 1751. [B.N.P. Vb. 121.]
   An engraving with section of crater and restoration of Vesuvius before 1631.

ORDINAIRE, C. N.—Histoire naturelle des volcans, comprenant les volcans soumarins, ceux de boue, et autres phénomènes analogues.—8⁰, 1 *topogr. map. Paris,* 1802.—Eng. ed., transl. fr. orig. French MS. by R. C. DALLAS : 8⁰, *pp. xxiv+*328. *London,* 1801.
   See Cap. 25, 30 and 36.

O'REILLY, REV. A. J.—Alvira, the heroine of Vesuvius.—16⁰, *pp.* 228. *Dublin,* 1884.

ORIMINI, P.—Poesie.—8⁰, *fol.* 1, *pp.* 174. *Napoli,* 1771. [O.V.]

ORIMINI, P.—Nell' eruttazione della Montagna di Somma del 1767.—*See pp.* 158–63 *of his :* " Degli antichi signori del Gaudo. Poesie."—4⁰, *pp.* 174. *Napoli,* 1771.

ORLANDI, G.—Dell' incendio del Monte di Somma.—4⁰, *pp.* 15. *Napoli,* 1631.

ORLANDI, G.—Miserando successo, e spaventeuole occorso nelli 16 dixᵇʳᵉ nel Monte Veseuo detto Soma.—[*Napoli,* 1631.]
   An engraved plate with engraved text showing the eruption of Vesuvius, and, above text, the 12 protecting saints of Naples with the Virgin and Child : 520× 390 mm.

ORLANDI, G.—La cinquatesima e bellissima relatione del Monte Vesuvio in stile accademico.—4º, *pp.* 12. *Napoli*, 1632.

ORLANDI, G.—Nuova e compita relatione del spaventevole incendio del Monte di Somma, detto il Vesuvio. Dove s'intende minutamente tutto quello che è successo fin' al presente giorno. Con la nota di quante volte detto Monte si sia abbrugiato. Aggiuntovi un rimedio denotissimo contro il terremoto.—4º, *figs., pp.* 16. *Napoli*, 1632. [C.A.]

ORLANDI, G.—La Morte de Plinio nel incendio del Monte Vesvvio, e l'effetto che fece.—4º, *foll.* 2. *In Napoli, Appresso Matteo Nucci. Con licenza de' Superiori. Ad instanza de Giouanni Orlando alla Pietà.* M.DC.XXXII.

ORLANDI, P. P.—Tra la belle, la bellissima, esquisita, et intiera e desiderata relatione dell' incendio del Monte Vesuuio detto di Somma, con dedica di Giov. Orlandi.—4º, *foll.* 4. *Napoli, per Secondino Roncagliolo,* MDCXXXII.
Another ed. is identical but for the frontispiece.

ORLANDI, S.—La tregua senza fede del Vesuvio.—4º, *foll.* 4. *Napoli*, 1632. [C.A.]

ORLANDI DI ROMANO, JIOS.—Miserando successo, e spaventeule occorso nelli 16 di Xbre nel Monte Veseuo detto Soma. [A view of Vesuvius from W. early in the eruption. Text on left and under view; at head of text, twelve Saints flanking the Madonna and Child, and above the inscription in large characters :] La Madonna de Costatinopoli con le dodici Protettori de Napoli. Napoli li 24 Xbre 1631.
Engrav. view : 317×356 mm. ; total, with engrav. text : 521×388 mm.

ORME, WM.—This View of the last eruption of Mount Vesuvius to Sir Wm. Hamilton, K.B., etc., etc., etc., drawn by Wm. Orme from an Original Painted at Naples, is most respectfully Dedicated by his most Obᵗ Hᵇˡ Servᵗ Edwᵈ Orme. Sold and published as the Act directs, June 4, 1800, by Edwᵈ Orme, Printseller to the King, 59, New Bond Street, corner of Brook Street, London.
Mezzotint, coloured and varnished at back to make it transparent : 513× 301 mm

ORME, W.—View of the last eruption of Mount Vesuvius from an original painted at Naples. Dedic. to Sir W. Hamilton. Probably erupt. 1794. Col. transparency of a steel engraving in roy. fol. in the collection of Mr. L. Sambon, Naples.

ORRIGONE, C. G.—Pensieri poetici (erupt. 1631). — 8º, *pp.* 108–19. *Genova*, 1636. [C.A.]

ORSO DI LIERANO, G. B.—[Erupt. 1631.] —*See* PALOMBA, D., p. 108.

ORTELIUS, A.—Theatrum Orbis Terrarum. —*fol., maps* 1–53. *Antwerpiæ*, 1570.
For further ed. see CAMPI PHLEGRÆI.

OSTERLAND, C., WAGNER, P.—Beitrag zur Kenntniss der Vesuvasche. — *Ber. deutsch. chem. Gesellsch.* vi, *pp.* 285–86. *Berlin*, 1873.—*Bull. Soc. Chim. Paris*, oct. 1873.

OTTAVIANO, C.—Alla Maestà di Ferdinando IV, Re delle Due Sicilie, per la terribile eruzione del Vesuvio. Sonetto. —*loose sheet.* — ?, — ? [B.N.]

OTTO, E.—Auf den Vesuv. Vortrag in der Section Strassburg i. E. des deut.-österr. Alpenvereins.—8º, *pp.* 24. *Strassburg*, 1886.

OVIEDO Y VALDES, G. F.—An account of the ascent of Vesuvius in 1501. Storia di Nicaragua.—*See* TERNAUX-COMPANS.— Voyages pour servir à l'histoire de la découverte de l'Amérique.—*Paris*, 1840.

OWENSON, S.—*See* MORGAN, LADY.

P.—Una Visita al Vesuvio.—[Estr. d. Giorn.] " *Il Panaro*," 23, 24, 25, 26, 27, *pp.* 35. *Modena*, 1879.

PACCA.—*See* COLLENUCCIO, P.

PACI, G. M.—*See* MIRANDA, D. DE.

PACICHELLI, G. B.—Memorie de' Viaggi per l'Europa Christiana scritte a diversi in occasione de' suoi Ministeri.—5 pts. 12º. *Pt.* i, *pp.* 40+743+53 ; *Pt.* ii, *pp.* 8+827+ 40 ; *Pt.* iii, *pp.* 8+761+27 ; *Pt.* iv, *Vol.* i, *pp.* 4+541+20 ; *Pt.* v, *Vol.* 2, *pp.* 4+438+ 18. *Napoli*, 1685.
See Pt. iv, Vol. 2, pp. 255 *et seq.*

PACICHELLI, G. B.—Lettere familiare, istoriche ed erudite, *etc.*—2 vols. 12º. *Napoli*, 1695. [B.N.]
See Vol. ii, pp. 343–53.

PACICHELLI, G. B.—Il regno di Napoli in prospettiva diviso in dodeci provincie, *etc.* —3 vols. 8º. *Napoli*, 1703.
See Vol. i.

PADAVINO, M. A. (according to Castelli, P.).—Lettera narratoria a pieno la verità dei successi del Monte Vesuvio detto di Somma, seguiti dalli 16 Dicembre fin alli 22 dell' istesso mese.—8°, *pp.* 14. *Roma,* 1632. [C.A.]

PADERNI, C.—An account of the late discoveries of Antiquities at Herculaneum. Translated from the Italian by Robert Watson.—*Phil. Trans. R. Soc. xlix,* 2, *pp.* 490–508. *London,* 1757. [C.A.]

PADERNI, C.—An account of the late discoveries of Antiquities at Herculaneum, and of an Earthquake there.—*Phil. Trans. R. Soc. l,* 2, *pp.* 619–23. *London,* 1759.

PAGLIANO, A.—*See* BOZZI, C.

PALATINO, L.—Storia di Pozzuoli e con-torni con breve trattato istorico di Erco-lano, Pompei, Stabia e Pesto.—8°, *pp.* 336, 9 *pls. Napoli,* 1826.

PALMERI, P.—Osservazioni sulle acque piovane raccolte all' Osservatorio Vesu-viano ed alla Specola dell' Università di Napoli.—*Rend. R. Acc. Sci. iv, pp.* 58–59. *Napoli,* 1865.

PALMERI, P.—Sulla cenere lanciata dal Vesuvio a Portici e a Resina la notte del 3 a 4 Aprile 1876. Ricerche chimiche.— *Rend. R. Acc. Sci. xvi, pp.* 73–74, 87–95. *Napoli,* 1877. [C.A.]—*Ann. R. Scuol. Agric. Portici, i, pp.* 101–15. *Napoli,* 1878.

PALMERI, P.—Studii sul pulviscolo atmos-ferico piovuto il 25 Febbrajo 1879 in Portici.—*Rend. R. Acc. Sci. xviii, pp.* 112–13. *Napoli,* 1879.—*Ann. R. Scuol. Agric. Portici, ii, pp.* 363–85. *Napoli,* 1880.

PALMERI, P.—Il pozzo artesiano dell' Arenaccia del 1880 confrontato con quello di Palazzo Reale di Napoli del 1847.—*Lo Spettatore del Vesuvio e dei Campi Flegrei,* ｝ *N.S. i, pp.* 53–58, 1 *col. pl. Napoli,* 1887. [C.A.]

PALMIERI, L.—L'eruzione del Vesuvio del 1850.—*Giorn. Costituz. Reg. Due Sicilie, Napoli,* 9 & 11 *Febbrajo,* 1850.

PALMIERI, L.—Studj Meteorologici fatti sul Real Osservatorio Vesuviano.—4°, *pp.* 22. *Napoli,* 1853.

PALMIERI, L.—Disquisizioni accademiche sulle scoperte Vesuviane attinenti alla elettricità atmosferica. Mem. letta all' Accad. d. Scienze.—4°, *pp.* 33, 3 *figs. Napoli,* 1854.

PALMIERI, L. — Elettricità atmosferica. Continuazione degli studii meteorologici fatti sul Reale Osservatorio Vesuviano.— *Poliorama Pittoresco, xv,* 23, 24, 25, *pp.* 8– 11, *pl. Napoli,* 1854.

PALMIERI, L.—Eruzione del Vesuvio del 1° Maggio 1855, studiata dal R. Osserva-torio Meteorologico Vesuviano. — *Nuovo Cimento, i, pp.* 421–32. *Pisa,* 1855.— *Giorn. Reg. Due Sicilie, p.* 1. *Napoli,* 25 *Mag.* 1855.

PALMIERI, L. — *See* GUARINI, G.— Memoria sull' incendio del Vesuvio, 1855.

PALMIERI, L.—Relazione del direttore del Reale Osservatorio Meteorologico diretta al presidente della Regia Università.— *Giorn. Reg. Due Sicilie,* 58. 1856.

PALMIERI, L.—Alcune osservazioni sulle temperature delle fumarole che si generano sulle lave del Vesuvio.—*Il Nuovo Cimento, v, pp.* 241–44. *Pisa,* 1857.—*Rend. Acc. Pontaniana, v, pp.* 12–16. *Napoli,* 1857.

PALMIERI, L.—Sur l'éruption actuelle du Vésuve. Lettre à M. Sainte-Claire Deville. —*C.R. Acad. Sci. xlv, pp.* 549–50. *Paris,* 1857.

PALMIERI, L.—Osservazioni di meteoro-logia e di fisica terrestre fatte durante l'eruzione del Vesuvio del Maggio 1855.— *Il Nuovo Cimento, v, pp.* 17–48. *Pisa,* 1857.

PALMIERI, L.—Sur le Vésuve. Lettre à Deville.—*C.R. Acad. Sci. xlvi, pp.* 1219–20, *Paris,* 1858 ; *l, p.* 726, 1860.

PALMIERI, L.—Annali del Reale Osserva-torio Meteorologico Vesuviano. Anno I, II, III, IV.—*Napoli,* 1859–70.—Nuova Serie Anno I.—*Napoli,* 1874.
This Nuova Serie is also called : Cronaca del Vesuvio, *q.v.*

PALMIERI, L.—Biblioteca Vesuviana.—4°, *pp.* 18.
This is a catalogue of the books in the Vesuvian Observatory, which is contained in the 1st vol. of the Annali del Reale Osservatorio Meteorologico Vesuviano. 1859.

PALMIERI, L., COSTA, O. G., SCACCHI, A., TENORE, M.—Rapporto alla R. Accademia delle Scienze intorno a taluni alberi trovati nel bacino del Sarno.—8°, *pp.* 19, *tav. Napoli,* 1859.

PALMIERI, L.—[Sur l'éruption du Vésuve.] Lettre à Deville.—*C.R. Acad. Sci. liii, pp.* 1232-33. *Paris,* 1861.

PALMIERI, L. (relatore), CAPOCCI, E., GIORDANO, G., SCHIAVONI, F., CAPPA, R., GUISCARDI, G.—Intorno allo incendio del Vesuvio cominciato il dì 8 Dic. 1861.—8°, *pp.* 36, 1 *tab. Napoli,* 1862.—*Il Nuovo Cimento, xv, pp.* 392–419. *Pisa,* 1862.—*Rend. Acc. Pontaniana, x, pp.* 40–61, 72–83. *Napoli,* 1862.

PALMIERI, L.—Notizie sulle scosse di terremoto segnate dal sismografo elettro-magnetico dopo l'incendio del Vesuvio cominciato il dì 8 Dic. 1861.—*Rend. R. Acc. Sci. i, p.* 144. *Napoli,* 1862.

PALMIERI, L.—Sur les phénomènes électriques qui se sont produits dans la fumée du Vésuve pendant l'éruption du 8 décembre 1861.—*C.R. Acad. Sci. liv, pp.* 284–85. *Paris,* 1862.

PALMIERI, L.—Sur les secousses de tremblement de terre ressenties à l'Observatoire du Vésuve pendant les mois de décembre 1861 et janvier 1862.—*C.R. Acad. Sci. liv, pp.* 608–11. *Paris,* 1862.

PALMIERI, L.—On some Volcanic Phenomena lately observed at Torre del Greco and Resina. [Abstr.]—*Quart. Journ. Geol. Soc. xviii, p.* 126. 1862.

PALMIERI, L.—*See* BALDACCHINI, M. 1862.

PALMIERI, L.—Scosse risentite al Vesuvio in occasione dell' ultima eruzione dell' Etna.—*Rend. R. Acc. Sci. ii, p.* 199. *Napoli,* 1863.

PALMIERI, L.—Delle scosse di terremoto avvenute all' Osservatorio Meteorologico Vesuviano nell' anno 1863, quali furono registrate dal sismografo elettro-magnetico. —*Rend. R. Acc. Sci. iii, pp.* 35–36. *Napoli,* 1864.

PALMIERI, L.—Il Vesuvio dal 10 Febbraio al 5 Marzo del 1865.—*Rend. R. Acc. Sci. iv, pp.* 67–70. *Napoli,* 1865.

PALMIERI, L.—Il Vesuvio dal 10 Febbraio al 1 Aprile 1865. Relazione.—*Rend. Acc. Pontaniana, xiii, pp.* 47–51. *Napoli,* 1865.

PALMIERI, L.—Il Vesuvio, il terremoto di Isernia e l'eruzione sottomarina di Santorino.—*Rend. R. Acc. Sci. v, pp.* 102–3. *Napoli,* 1866.

PALMIERI, L.—Di alcuni prodotti trovati nelle fumarole del cratere del Vesuvio.— *Rend. R. Acc. Sci. vi, pp.* 83–84. *Napoli,* 1867.

PALMIERI, L.—Nuove corrispondenze tra i terremoti del Vesuvio e l'eruzioni di Santorino.—*Rend. R. Acc. Sci. vi, pp.* 130–31. *Napoli,* 1867.

PALMIERI, L.—Lettre à St.-Claire Deville. Revue des Cours Scientifiques de la France et de l'Étranger.—*Paris,* 14 *déc.,* 1867.

PALMIERI, L.—Ueber den neuen Ausbruch des Vesuv.—*Verhandl. k. k. geol. Reichsanst. pp.* 373–75. *Wien,* 1867.

PALMIERI, L.—Sur les produits ammoniacaux trouvés dans le cratère supérieur du Vésuve.—*C.R. Acad. Sci. lxiv, pp.* 668–69. *Paris,* 1867.

PALMIERI, L.—Sur une nouvelle éruption du Vésuve.—*C.R. Acad. Sci. lxv, pp.* 897–98. *Paris,* 1867.

PALMIERI, L.—Faits pour servir à l'histoire éruptive du Vésuve.—*C.R. Acad. Sci. lxvi, pp.* 205–7, 756–57, 917–18, *Paris,* 1868 ; *lxvii, pp.* 802–3, 1109, 1869.—"*Cosmos,*" *iii, pp.* 485–86. *Paris,* 1868.

PALMIERI, L.—Ueber die Tätigkeit des Vesuv.—*Verh. k. k. geol. Reichsanst. pp.* 7–9, 23–26, 45–48, 63–66, 89–92, 116–18. *Wien,* 1868.

PALMIERI, L.—Dell' incendio del Vesuvio cominciato il 13 Novembre del 1867. Sunto di una relazione dell' Autore.— *Rend. R. Acc. Sci. vii, pp.* 76–77. *Napoli,* 1868.—*Id. Atti, iv, pp.* 29, 1 *pl.* 1869.

PALMIERI, L.—Ultime fasi delle conflagrazioni Vesuviane del 1868.—*Rend. R. Acc. Sci. viii, pp.* 44–48. *Napoli,* 1869.— *Id. Atti, iv, 9, pp.* 17. 1869.—*Il Nuovo Cimento, S. 2, iii, pp.* 29–47. *Pisa,* 1870.

PALMIERI, L.—Osservazioni sul terremoto del 26 Agosto (1869).—*Rend. R. Acc. Sci. viii, pp.* 146–47. *Napoli,* 1869.

PALMIERI, L.—Nuovi fatti di corrispondenza tra le piccole agitazioni del suolo al Vesuvio ed i terremoti lontani.—*Rend. R. Acc. Sci. viii, p.* 179. *Napoli,* 1869.

PALMIERI, L.—Il Vesuvio nel 1868.—*See* "Il Vesuvio, Strenna pel 1869," *pp.* 8–11.

PALMIERI, L.—Qualche osservazione spettroscopica sulle sublimazioni Vesuviane.— *Rend. R. Acc. Sci. ix, pp.* 58–59. *Napoli,* 1870.

PALMIERI, L.— Il terremoto di Calabria ed il sismografo Vesuviano.—*Rend. R. Acc. Sci. ix, p.* 176. *Napoli,* 1870.

Q

PALMIERI, L.—Il solfato di zinco fra le sublimazioni Vesuviane.—*Rend. R. Acc. Sci. x, pp.* 13–14. *Napoli,* 1871.

PALMIERI, L.—Indicazioni del sismografo dell' osservatorio Vesuviano del 1° Dic. 1869 al 31 Dic. 1870.—*A note inserted in* " Memoria sopra i terremoti della Prov. di Cosenza nell' anno 1870 del Sig. Dott. Conti."—*Rend. R. Acc. Sci. x, pp.* 16–17. *Napoli,* 1871.

PALMIERI, L.—Le lave del Vesuvio guardate con lo spettroscopio.—*Rend. R. Acc. Sci. x, pp.* 33–34. *Napoli,* 1871.

PALMIERI, L.—Osservazioni microscopiche sulle sabbie eruttate dal Vesuvio nei mesi di Gennaio e Febbraio del 1871.—*Rend. R. Acc. Sci. x, pp.* 34–35. *Napoli,* 1871.

PALMIERI, L.—Intorno ad un Lapillo filiforme eruttato dal Vesuvio.—*Rend. R. Acc. Sci. x, pp.* 51–52. *Napoli,* 1871.

PALMIERI, L.—Sopra qualche legge generale cui obbediscono le sublimazioni delle fumarole delle lave del Vesuvio.—*Rend. R. Acc. Sci. x, pp.* 90–93. *Napoli,* 1871.

PALMIERI, L.—Trasformazione di alcuni cannelli di vetro rimasti per lungo tempo in una fumarola.—*Rend. R. Acc. Sci. x, p.* 124. *Napoli,* 1871.

PALMIERI, L.—Il Litio ed il Tallio nelle Sublimazioni Vesuviane.—*Rend. R. Acc. Sci. x, p.* 124. *Napoli,* 1871.

PALMIERI, L.—Di alcuni effetti del fulmine caduto sull' Osservatorio Vesuviano. —*Rend. R. Acc. Sci. x, p.* 180. *Napoli,* 1871.

PALMIERI, L.—L'Acido Carbonico al Vesuvio.—" *Il Criterio," periodico settimanale di scienze, ecc. Napoli,* 18 *Agosto* 1872.

PALMIERI, L.—Der Ausbruch des Vesuv's vom 26 April, 1872. Besorgt und bevorwortet von C. Rammelsberg.—8⁰. *Berlin,* 1872.

PALMIERI, L.—Sur l'éruption du Vésuve (avril 1872).—*C.R. Acad. Sci. lxxiv, pp.* 1298–99. *Paris,* 1872.

PALMIERI, L.—Sepolcri antichi scoperti sul Vesuvio.—*Rend. R. Acc. Sci. xi, pp.* 42–43. *Napoli,* 1872.

PALMIERI, L. — Sopra alcuni fenomeni notati nell' ultimo incendio Vesuviano del 26 Aprile 1872.—*Rend. R. Acc. Sci. xi, p.* 108. *Napoli,* 1872.

PALMIERI, L.—L'Incendio Vesuviano del 26 Aprile 1872. Conferenza tenuta nel di 9 Maggio coll' analisi chimica delle ceneri cadute il 28 Aprile, del Prof. C. Catalano.—12⁰, *pp.* 16. *Napoli,* 1872.— Another ed. *pp.* 24.—*Rend. R. Acc. Sci. xi, pp.* 157–58. *Napoli,* 1872.—*Id. Atti, v,* 17, *pp.* 64, *Pls.* I–V. 1873.—[Sep. publ.] 4⁰, *pp.* 64, 5 *pls. Napoli,* 1873.— In German, transl. by C. Rammelsberg: 8⁰, *pp.* 60, 7 *tav. Leipzig und Berlin,* 1872.— In English, with introduction by R. Mallet: 8⁰, *pp.* iv+148, 8 *tav. London,* 1873.

PALMIERI, L.—Le Vittime del Vesuvio.— *See* ANON.—Convito di Carità, etc., *pp.* 32–33. *Napoli,* 1872.

PALMIERI, L.—Eruption of Vesuvius in 1872. With notes and introductory sketch of present knowledge of terrestrial vulcanicity, the cosmical nature and relation of Volcanoes and Earthquakes.—8⁰, *pp.* 148, 8 *pls. London,* 1873.

PALMIERI, L.—Indagini spettroscopiche sulle sublimazioni Vesuviani.—*Rend. R. Acc. Sci. xii, pp.* 47–48. *Napoli,* 1873.— *Cronaca Vesuviana, pp.* 109–11. 1874.

PALMIERI, L.—Sul ferro oligisto trovato entro le bombe dell' ultima eruzione del Vesuvio.—*Rend. R. Acc. Sci. xii, p.* 48. *Napoli,* 1873. —*Cronaca Vesuviana, pp.* 112–13. 1874.

PALMIERI, L.—Carbonati Alcalini trovati tra' prodotti Vesuviani.—*Rend. R. Acc. Sci. xii, p.* 92. *Napoli,* 1873.—*Cronaca Vesuviana, pp.* 114–15. 1874.

PALMIERI, L.—Del Sale Ammoniaco giallo e della Cotunnia gialla. Continuazione delle indagini spettroscopiche sopra i prodotti Vesuviani.—*Rend. R. Acc. Sci. xii, pp.* 92–94. *Napoli,* 1873.—*Cronaca Vesuviana, pp.* 116–21. 1874.

PALMIERI, L.—Sulle fumarole eruttive osservate nell' incendio Vesuviano del 26 Aprile 1872.—*Rend. R. Acc. Sci. xii, p.* 143. *Napoli,* 1873.

PALMIERI, L.—L'Antimonio tra le sublimazioni Vesuviane.—*Rend. R. Acc. Sci. xii, p.* 156. *Napoli,* 1873.

PALMIERI, L.—Il Sismografo dell' Osservatorio Vesuviano ed i terremoti contemporanei.—*Rend. R. Acc. Sci. xii, p.* 156. *Napoli,* 1873.

PALMIERI, L.— Recherches spectrosco-
piques sur les fumerolles de l'éruption
du Vésuve en avril 1872 et état actuel de ce
volcan.—*C.R. Acad. Sci. lxxvi, pp.* 1427-28.
Paris, 1873.

PALMIERI, L.—Cronaca del Vesuvio, sommario della storia dei principali accendi-
menti del Vesuvio dal 1840 fino al 1871,
seguita da estesa relazione dell' ultimo
incendio del 1872.—8⁰, *pp. iv*+164, 5 *pls.*
Napoli, 1874.

PALMIERI, L.—Il Sismografo dell' Osservatorio Vesuviano e quello della Specola
Universitaria nell' ultimo terremoto della
Valle del Liri.—*Rend. R. Acc. Sci. xiii,
p.* 177. *Napoli,* 1874.

PALMIERI, L.—Del peso specifico delle
Lave Vesuviane nel più perfetto stato di
fusione.—*Rend. R.Acc. Sci. xiv,pp.* 214-15.
Napoli, 1875.—*Riv. Scient. Napoli,* 1876.

PALMIERI, L.—Il terremoto del 6 Dic.
1875.—*Rend. R. Acc. Sci. xiv, pp.* 215-16.
Napoli, 1875.

PALMIERI, L.—Il cratere del Vesuvio nel di
8 Novembre 1875. (Estratto di una lettera
del giovane Alpinista, G. Chiarini.)—
Rend. R. Acc. Sci. xv, pp. 9-10, 1 *fig.*
Napoli, 1876.

PALMIERI, L.—Sulla cenere lanciata dal
Vesuvio a Portici e Resina la notte dal
3 al 4 Aprile 1876.—*Rend. R. Acc. Sci. xv,
pp.* 73-74. *Napoli,* 1876.—*Ann. R. Scuol.
Agric. Portici. Napoli,* 1878.

PALMIERI, L.—Cronaca Vesuviana (Decembre 1875-Maggio 1877).—*Bull. Vulc. Ital.
iii, pp.* 14-15, 51-52, 1876 ; *iv, p.* 43,
Roma, 1877.

PALMIERI, L.—*See* CHIARINI, G. 1876.

PALMIERI, L.—Il Tallio nelle presenti
sublimazioni Vesuviane.—*Rend. R. Acc.
Sci. xvi, pp.* 179-80. *Napoli,* 1877.

PALMIERI. L.—Il Litio trovato in alcune
recenti produzioni Vesuviane.—*Rend. R.
Acc. Sci. xvii, p.* 118. *Napoli,* 1878

PALMIERI, L.—Sismographes électro-mag-
nétiques.—8⁰, *pp.* 12. *Naples,* 1878.

PALMIERI, L.—Del Vesuvio dei tempi di
Spartaca e di Strabone e del precipuo
cangiamento avvenuto nell' anno 79 dell'
Era volgare.—*See* "Pompei e la Regione
Sotterrata," etc. *pp.* 91-93, 1 *tav. Napoli,*
1879.

PALMIERI, L.—Specchio comparativo della
quantità di pioggia caduta nell' anno
meteorico 1880 nelle stazioni di Napoli
(Università) e Vesuvio (O.V.).—*Rend. R.
Acc. Sci. xix, pp.* 179-80. *Napoli,* 1880.

PALMIERI, L.—Il Vesuvio e la sua storia.—
pp. 79, 25 *figs. Milano,* 1880.—*See also :
Lo Spettatore del Vesuvio e dei Campi
Flegrei, N.S. i. Napoli,* 1887.

PALMIERI, L.—Della riga dell' Helium
apparsa in una recente sublimazione Vesuviana.—*Rend. R. Acc. Sci. xx, p.* 233.
Napoli, 1881.

PALMIERI, L.—L'attività del Vesuvio ai
29 Dicembre 1881.—*Bull. Vulc. Ital. ix,
p.* 26. *Roma,* 1882.

PALMIERI, L.—Ueber das Erdbeben am
6 Juni 1882.—*Deutsche Revue, J.* 7, *iii,
pp.* 401-2. *Breslau,* 1882.

PALMIERI, L., e GAIZO, M. DEL. — Il
Vesuvio nel 1885.—*Ann. Meteor. Ital. i,
pp.* 183-91. *Torino,* 1886.

PALMIERI, L.—Nuove esperienze che rifer-
mano le antecendi sull' origine dell' elettricità atmosferica. Appendice alla memoria inserita nel tomo IV della Società
Italiana delle Scienze.—*Atti R. Acc. Sci.* ?,
pp. 24. *Napoli,* 1886.
Reference cannot be verified.

PALMIERI, L.—L'elettricità negl'incendi
Vesuviani studiata dal 1855 fin' ora con
appositi istrumenti.— *Lo Spettatore del
Vesuvio e dei Campi Flegrei, N.S. pp.*
77-79. *Napoli,* 1887.

PALMIERI, L., e GAIZO, M. DEL. — Il
Vesuvio nel 1886, ed alcuni fenomeni vul-
cano-sismici del Napoletano.—*Ann. Meteor.
Ital. ii, pp.* 227-36. *Torino,* 1887.

PALMIERI, L.—Azione de' terremoti dell'
eruzioni vulcaniche e delle folgori sugli
aghi calamitati.—*Rend. R. Acc. Sci. S. 2, ii,
pp.* 454-56. *Napoli,* 1888.

PALMIERI, L.—Der gegenwärtige Zustand
der süditalienischen Vulkane.—*Deutsche
Revue, J.* 13, *iv, p.* 230. *Breslau,* 1888.

PALMIERI, L., e GAIZO, M. DEL.—Il
Vesuvio nel 1887.—*Ann. Meteor. Ital. iii,
pp.* 303-8. *Torino,* 1888.

PALMIERI, L., e GAIZO, M. DEL. — Il
Vesuvio nel 1888.—*Ibid. iv, pp.* 312-15.
1889.

PALMIERI, L.—Le correnti telluriche all'
Osservatorio Vesuviano.—*Rend. R. Acc.
Sci. S. 2, iii, pp.* 250-53. *Napoli,* 1889.

Q 2

PALMIERI, L.—La corrente tellurica ed il dinamismo del cratere Vesuviano durante l'ecclisse solare del dì 17 Giugno 1890.—*Rend. R. Acc. Sci. S.* 2, *iv, p.* 164. *Napoli,* 1890.

PALMIERI, L., e GAIZO, M. DEL. — Il Vesuvio nel 1889.—*Ann. Meteor. Ital. v, pp.* 263–66. *Torino,* 1890.

PALMIERI, L. — Osservazioni simultanee sul dinamismo del cratere Vesuviano e della grande fumarola della Solfatara di Pozzuoli, fatte negli anni 1888–89–90.—*Rend. R. Acc. Sci. S.* 2, *iv, pp.* 206–8. *Napoli,* 1890.—*Ann. Meteor. Ital. vi, pp.* 141–44. *Torino,* 1891.

PALMIERI, L.—Le correnti telluriche all' Osservatorio Vesuviano osservate per un anno intero non meno di quattro volte al giorno.—*Rend. R. Acc. Sci. S.* 2, *iv, pp.* 228–33. *Napoli,* 1890.

PALMIERI, L., e GAIZO, M. DEL. — Il Vesuvio nel 1890.—*Ann. Meteor. Ital. vi, pp.* 210–15. *Torino,* 1891.

PALMIERI, L.—Ripetizione, del dì 7 Giugno di questo anno, dei fenomeni notati nello scorso anno il 17 dello stesso mese, all' Osservatorio Vesuviano, in occasione delle due ecclissi solari avvenute in detti giorni.—*Rend. R. Acc. Sci. S.* 2, *v, p.* 161. *Napoli,* 1891.

PALMIERI, L.—Il Vesuvio e la Solfatara contemporaneamente osservati.—*Rend. R. Acc. Sci. S.* 2, *v, pp.* 161–62. *Napoli,* 1891.

PALMIERI, L.—Le osservazioni sulla corrente tellurica fatte all' Osservatorio Vesuviano dal mese di Agosto del 1889 fino al dì 1 Novembre del 1891.—*Rend. R. Acc. Sci. S.* 2, *v, pp.* 216–23. *Napoli,* 1891.

PALMIERI, L.—Sull' ultimo periodo eruttivo del Vesuvio.—*Ann. Meteor. Ital. vii, pp.* 257–63. *Torino,* 1892.

PALMIERI, L. — L'Atrio del Cavallo. Strenna della Tipografia Giannini, Anno IV, Capodanno 1892.—8⁰. *Napoli,* 1892.

PALMIERI, L.—Il Vesuvio nel 1892.—*Boll. Mens. Osserv. Centr. Moncalieri, S.* 2, *xii,* 12. *Torino,* 1892.

PALMIERI, L.—Continuazione degli studi della corrente tellurica all' Osservatorio Vesuviano.—*Rend. R. Acc. Sci. S.* 2, *vii, pp.* 207–8. *Napoli,* 1893.

PALMIERI, L.—Il Vesuvio nel 1893.—*Boll. Mens. Osserv. Centr. Moncalieri, S.* 2, *xiii,* 12. *Torino,* 1893.

PALMIERI, L.—Continuazione degli studii della corrente tellurica osservata all' Osservatorio Vesuviano con fili inclinati all' orizzonte in diversi azimut.—*Atti R. Acc. Sci. S.* 2, *vi,* 12, *pp.* 7, 2 *figs. Napoli,* 1894.

PALMIERI, L.—Sulle presenti condizioni del Vesuvio.—*Boll. Soc. Alp. Merid. ii,* 2, *pp.* 53–57. *Napoli,* 1894.

PALMIERI, L.—Rivelazioni delle correnti telluriche studiate all' Osservatorio Vesuviano con fili inclinati all' orizzonte.—*Rend. R. Acc. Sci. S.* 2, *viii, p.* 207. *Napoli,* 1894.

PALMIERI, L. — A proposito della riga dell' Helium apparsa nello spettro di una sublimazione Vesuviana nel 1881, ed ora riveduta da Ramsay e da Clève nella Clevite o Cleveite.—*Rend. R. Acc. Sci. S.* 3, *i, pp.* 121–22. *Napoli,* 1895.

PALMIERI, L.—Rivelazioni delle correnti telluriche studiate all' Osservatorio Vesuviano con fili inclinati all' orizzonte e disposti in qualsiasi azimut.—*Atti R. Acc. Sci. S.* 2, *vii,* 6, *pp.* 7. *Napoli,* 1895.

PALMIERI, L.—Le correnti telluriche all' Osservatorio Vesuviano osservate con fili inclinati all' orizzonte durante l'anno 1895. —*Atti R. Acc. Sci. S.* 2, *viii,* 4, *pp.* 6. *Napoli,* 1897.

PALMIERI, L.—Il Vesuvio dal 1875 al 1895.—*Boll. Soc. Meteor. Ital. S.* 2, *xvi,* 45–46, *pp.* 29–34. *Torino,* 1896.—*Atti R. Acc. Sci. S.* 2, *viii,* 5, *pp.* 1–8. *Napoli,* 1897. —*Id. Rend. S.* 3, *i, p.* 313. 1895.

PALMIERI, L.—*See* ANON.—Luigi Palmieri.

PALOMBA, D.—Memorie storiche di S. Giorgio a Cremano raccolte da . . .— 8⁰, *foll.* 5, *pp.* 452. *Napoli,* 1881.

PANICHI, U.—Sulla Breislakite.—*Rend. R. Acc. Sci. S.* 3, *xix, pp.* 141–51, 1 *fig. Napoli,* 1913.

PAOLI, F.—Per l'andata al Vesuvio de Marchese di Palombara. Sonetti due.—*See* GIORGI URBANO. [C.A.]

PAPACCIO, G. S. (venditor d'oglio).—Relatione del fiero, et iracondo incendio del Monte Vesuviano flagello occorso a 16 di Decembre 1631, nella Montagna di Somma all' incontro sei miglia della fedelissima e famosissima città. In ottava rima.—4⁰, *foll.* 4. *Napoli, F. Sanio e D. Maccarano,* 1632. [C.A.]

PARAGALLO, G. — Istoria naturale del Monte Vesuvio, divisa in 2 libri.—4⁰, *foll.* 10, *pp.* 430. *Napoli,* 1705.

PARAT, ABBÉ A.—Volcans et Tremblements de Terre, conférence faite à l'hôtel
de ville d'Avallon, le 21 mars 1909.—16°,
pp. 29. *Avallon*, 1909.

PARETO, L.—Corso al Vesuvio 26 Settembre 1845, ed osservazioni intorno alla
natura del Conglomerato nella Valle del
Fosso Grande.—*Atti Sett. Adun. Scienz.
Ital. pp.* 1132–40. *Napoli*, 1846.

PARETO, L.—Della posizione delle roccie
pirogene ed eruttive dei periodi terziario
quaternario ed attuale in Italia.—8°, *pp.* 35.
Genova, 1852.

PARISIO, N.—Monte Somma (Punta del
Nasone m. 1137).—*Boll. Soc. Alp. Merid.
ii*, 4, *pp.* 183–87. *Napoli*, 1894.

PARISIO, P.—Convitto nazionale di Genova.
Escursioni e viaggio d'istruzione nell' anno
1891.—8°.
On cover : Dalle Alpi al Vesuvio. *See*
pp. 134–79.

PARKER, J.—Part of a letter . . . concerning the late eruption of Mount Vesuvius 1751.—*Phil. Trans. R. Soc. xlvii, pp.*
474–75. *London*, 1753.—In Ital. : *Compendio d. Trans. filos. d. Londra, pp.* 86–88.
Venezia, 1793.

PARKIN, J.—The remote cause of epidemic
diseases ; or, the influence of volcanic
action in the production of general pestilences. Part II.—8°, *pp.* 16, *foll.* 4, 3 *pls.*
London, 1853.

PARRINO, A.—Fidelissima Vrbis Neapolitana cvm omnibvs locis accvrata et nova
delineatio 1691. [B.M. Portfolio of
Naples.]
Vesuvius in background : 331×214 mm.

PARRINO, A.—Relazione dell' eruzione del
Vesuvio nel 1694.—*Napoli*, 1694.

PARRINO, A.—Succinta relazione dell' incendio del Vesuvio nel 1696.—*Napoli*, 1696.

PARRINO, A.—Moderna distintissima descrizione di Napoli, città nobilissima, antica
e fedelissima, e del suo seno cratere.—
Aggiunte, osservazioni, e correzioni a
questo primo tomo della nuova descrizione
di Napoli.—2 vols. 12°. *Vol. i, pp.* 20+
438+54+46+2 ; *Vol. ii, pp.* 16+292+
23, 28 *pls., fig. Napoli*, 1703–4.
See Vol. ii, pp. 205–35.

PARRINO, A.—Nuova Guida dei Forestieri
per osservare e godere della fedelissima gran Napoli.—
38 *pls. Napoli*, 1709.—12°, *pp.* 16+371,
index, 28 *figs., frontisp.* 1714. (No views
of Vesuvius.)

PARRINO, A.—Nuova Guida de' Forastieri
per osservare, e godere le curiosità più
vaghe, e più rare della Real Fedeliss.
Gran NAPOLI, città antica, e nobilissima,
In cui si dà distinto ragguaglio delle varie
opinioni dell' origine di essa, e Strade,
Fabbriche, Chiese, Pitture, Statue, Dogi
regnanti, Vescovi, & Arcivescovi, che la
governarono, con tutto ciò, che di più bello,
e di più buono della medesima città si
trova ; Ricavato dagl' Autori impressi, e
manoscritti che di essa trattano ; Adornata
con Figure delle sue più nobili Vedute,
intagliate in Rame. Opera . . . consecrata Agl'Illustriss. ed Eccellentiss. Signori Li Signori ELETTI Della Fedelissima
Gran Città di Napoli.—12°, *foll.* 17+*pp.*
371+*foll.* 30, 17 *pls. Napoli, Appresso
Domenico-Antonio Parrino*, MDCCXII.

PARRINO, A.—Nuova Guida de' Forastieri,
per l'Antichità Curiosissime di Pozzuoli ;
dell' Isole aggiacenti d'Isca, Procida,
Nisida, Capri, Colline, Terre, Ville, e Città,
che giaccioni intorno alle Riviere dell' uno,
e l'altro lato di Napoli, detto Cratero.
Colla descrizione della città di Gaeta. Il
tutto epilogato dagli Autori impressi, e
manoscritti, che ne han trattato. Adornata
di 38. bellissime Figure intagliate in Rame.
Dedicata all' Illustrissimo Signore Il Signor
D. Diego Ripa De' Baroni di Pianchetella.
—12°, *pp.* 257, *foll.* 4, 30 *pls. Napoli,
Presso il Parrino*, MDCCXXV.
See pp. 181–219.

PARRINO, A.—Nuova Guida de' Forastieri per l'Antichità Curiosissime di Pozzuoli : dell' Isole adjacenti d'Ischia, Procida,
Nisida, Capra, . . . e città, che sono
intorno alle Riviere dell' uno, e l'altro lato
di Napoli, detto Cratero. Colla descrizione
della città di Gaeta.—8°, *pp.* 4+269+14,
30 *pls., map. Dédié à Diego Ripa di Pianchetella. Napoli, Parrino*, 1727. [B.M.
719.]

PARRINO, A.—Nuova Guida de' Forestieri
per l'Antichità di Pozzuoli, e di tutte le
città, e Luoghi, et Isole, che sono alla veduta
presso il mare dalla parte destra della città
di Napoli.—12°, *num. figs.* 1727.
See Parte II, pp. 182–242. The views of
Vesuvius are poor and sketchy.

PARRINO, A.—Nuova Guida de' Forastieri
per osservare, e godere la curiosità più
vaghe, e più rare della Fedelissima Gran
NÁPOLI città antica, e nobilissima, In cui
si dà anco distinto ragguaglio delle varie
opinioni dell' origine di essa ; Dogi

regnanti, Vescovi, ed Arcivescovi, che la governarono : Con tutto ciò, che di più bello, e di più buono nella medesima si ritrova. Ricavato dagl'Autori impressi, e manoscritti, che di essa trattano. Adornata con Figure delle sue più nobili Vedute, intagliate in Rame. Accresciuta con moderne notizie da NICCOLO' suo Figlio. —12⁰, foll. 2, pp. 409, foll. 14, 35 pls. Napoli, A spese di Giuseppe Buono, MDCCLI.

PARRINO, A.—Nuova Guida de' Forastieri per l'Antichità Curiosissime di Pozzuoli ; Dell' Isole adjacenti d'Ischia, Procida, Nisida, Capri, Colline, Terre, Ville, e Città, che sono intorno alle Riviere dell' uno, e l'altro lato di Napoli, detto Cratero. Colla descrizione della città di Gaeta. Il tutto epilogato dagli Autori impressi e manoscritti, che ne han trattato. Adornate di 30. bellissime Figure intagliate in Rame. Ed in questa ultima Edizione di nuovo ricorretta, ed aumentata.—12⁰, foll. 2+ pp. 269+foll. 9, 29 pls. Napoli, A spese di Giuseppe Buono, MDCCLI.
See pp. 181–217. The views of Vesuvius are poor and sketchy.

PARTENIO (accademico). — La morte ; Idillio fatto in occasione dell' incendio del Monte Vesuvio, ed una canzonetta sopra la stella apparsa nel medesimo tempo sopra detto monte.—4⁰, foll. 4. Roma, 1632.

PASQUALE, F.—Ancora del Vesuvio ai tempi di Spartao e di Strabone.—Bol. Soc. Geol. Ital. xvii, pp. 76–80. Roma, 1898.

PASQUALE, G. A.—Flora Vesuviana, o catalogo ragionato delle Piante del Vesuvio confrontate con quelle dell' Isola di Capri e di altri luoghi circostanti.—Esercitazioni accademiche degli Aspiranti Naturalisti, ii, 2, Napoli, 1842.—Atti R. Acc. Sci. iv, 6, pp. 142. Napoli, 1869.—Id. Rend. vii, pp. 161–65. 1868.

PASQUALE, G. A.—Di alcuni effetti della caduta di cenere sulle piante, nell' ultima eruzione Vesuviana, osservati in Napoli.— Rend. R. Acc. Sci. xi, pp. 110–17. Napoli, 1872.

PASSARI, G. B.— Vero disegno dell' Incendio nella Montagna di Somma altrimente detto Mons Vesvvii distante da Napoli sei Miglia a 16 Decemb. nel 1631. Gio. Battista Passaru Formis Neap. [B.N.P. —Vb. 121.]

Engrav. similar to ANON. — " Vero Ritratto," etc., with engrav. text. In this one there are reference letters up to I, but differently located : 332 × 185 mm.

PASSE, C. DE.— Waerachtige Af-beeldinge van den schricklijcken brandende Bergh Somma (anders genoemt Vesuvi,) gelegen vande wijtberoemde Stadt Neepolis een Uyre gaens, die meteen onuytspreechenlijck Dyer en Water noch dagelijer der Stadt groolelijer beschadicht, als blijckt uit dit nae-volgende. As ghebeeldt ende overgeset uyt het Italiens nae de Roomsche Copye. [C.A.]
Engraved plate of erupt. 1631, with 3 columns of explanation.

PASSERI, G.—Saggio di Poesie.—8⁰, pp. 7+202+1. Napoli, 1766.
Cantata sul Vesuvio : pp. 114–26.

PASSERINI, N.—Contributo allo studio della composizione delle ceneri e dei lapilli eruttati dal Vesuvio durante il periodo di attività dell' Aprile 1906.—Atti R. Acc. Georgofili, S. 5, iii, pp. 14. Firenze, 1906.—Le Stazioni Sper. Agr. Ital. xl, 1, pp. 40–53. Modena, 1907.

PASTORE, À.—Eruzione del Vesuvio (Aprile 1906). Descritta in tutta i suoi spaventevoli episodi.—16⁰, pp. 32, 2 figs. (on cover). Napoli [1906 ?].

PAYAN, D.—Notice sur quelques Volcans de l'Italie méridionale.—Bull. Soc. Stat. Arts Utiles, Sci. Nat. du Départ. Drôme, iii, pp. 145–63. 1842. [C.A.]

PEDRETTI.—Der Ausbruch des Vesuv am 2 Mai 1855.—Illustrirte Zeitung, 622, p. 353, 1 illustr. Leipzig, 1855.

PELLÉ, C.—Il Mediterraneo illustrato, le sue Isole, etc., preceduta da un saggio storico sul Mediterraneo, e compilata dal bibliofilo M. Malagoli Vecchi, etc.—4⁰, pp. 512, num. pls. Firenze, 1841.

PELLEGRINI, A.—Vesuvio nel Novembre 1893.—Boll. Mens. Osserv. Centr. Moncalieri, xiii, p. 191. Torino, 1894.

PELLEGRINI, G.—Il Vesuvio, poemetto. —8⁰, pp. 112, frontisp. Bassano, 1785. [C.A.]—8⁰, fol. 1, pp. 301. Bassano, 1798. [O.V.]—8⁰, pp. 108, fol. 1. Palermo, 1814. [O.V.]

PELLEGRINO, CAMILLO (figl. di ALESS.).— Descrittione della Campania Felice nella maniera dimostrata ne' suoi Discorsi. Jacob' Thoneno Lotharing (?) sculp. 1651. [B.N.P.—Vb. 113. No. 3.]

Vesuvius is represented as a symmetrical, large-mouthed crater. See also GRÆVIUS, J. G. — Thesaurus Antiquitatum et Hist. Italiæ.

PELLEGRINO, C.—Apparato alle Antichità di Capva overo Discorsi della Campania Felice di Camillo Pellegrino figlio di Aless.—4⁰. *Napoli*, 1651.
See pp. 309–28.

PELLEGRINO, C.—Discorso istorico dell' incendii naturali del Monte Vesuvio ed altri luoghi di Terra di Lavoro detti anticamente Campania, raccolto in un manoscritto a dì 16 Dicembre 1631.—MS. *foll.* 15. [C.A.]
Copy of a MS. belonging to Signor Adolfo Parascandolo.

PELLICER DE TOUAR, J.—Estancias al Vesuuio ed un epigrama.—*See* QUINONES.

PENCK, F. C. A.—Studien über lockere vulcanische Auswürflinge.—8⁰, *pp.* 33, 1 *pl. Leipzig*, 1878.—*Zeitschr. deutsch. geol. Gesellsch. xxx, pp.* 97–129, 1 *tav. Berlin*, 1878.

PENINO, D. A.—Part XI. S. XIII. 1698. —*See* FORDYCE, *pp.* 13–14.

PENTLAND, B.—Osservazioni intorno alla natura de' conglomerati nella Valle del Fosso Grande.—*Atti Sett. Adun. Scienz. Ital. p.* 1135. *Napoli*, 1846.

PENTLAND, B.—Pensieri intorno alle Pomice ond' è coperta Pompei.—*Atti Sett. Adun. Scienz. Ital. p.* 1166. *Napoli*, 1846.

PEPE, A.—Il medico clinico o sia dessertazione fisico-medica.—4⁰, *foll.* 6, *pp.* 178, *fol.* 1. *Napoli*, 1768. [C.A.]
Speaks in Chapt. I of the eruption of Vesuvius 1767.

PÈRE, G. LE.—Deuxième recueil de divers mémoires sur les Pouzzolanes naturelles et artificielles.—4⁰, *pp.* 8+62, 1 *pl. Paris*, 1807.
See pp. 25–26 (pozzolana of Vesuvius).

PERENTINO GIANO (Pietro Giannone).— Lettera ad un suo amico che lo richiedeva onde avvenisse che nelle due cime del Vesuvio, ecc.—4⁰, *pp.* 3. *Napoli*, 1718. [O.V.]

PEREZ DE MONTALUAN, I.—Soneto. [Erupt. 1631.]—*See* QUINONES.—El Monte Vesvvio.

PERI, D.—Sull' eruzione del Vesuvio del 15 Giugno 1794. Anacreontica.—4⁰, *pp.* 24. [O.V.]

PERILLO, D.—Vero e distinto ragguaglio di ciò etc., spaventevole fiumana di fuoco scoppiato dal Monte Vesuvio incaminavasi al di lei danno e sterminio.—4⁰, *pp.* 76. *Napoli*, 1755. [O.V.]

PERRET, F. A. (photo.).—Vesuvius. Eruption of April 1906. View of Great Cone from the West, 12 April. Naples, Raggozino, 1906.
Sepia photo-engrav. : 570×445 mm.

PERRET, F. A. (photo.).—Vesuvius. Eruption of April, 1906. A great Avalanche of Fragmentary Ejecta, 13 April. Naples, Raggozino, 1906.
Sepia photo-engrav. : 515×355 mm.

PERRET, F. A. (photo.).—Vesuvius. Eruption of April, 1906. Ejection of sand and dust as seen from the Observatory, 16 April. Naples, Raggozino, 1906.
Sepia photo-engrav. : 515×353 mm.

PERRET, F. A. (photo.).—Vesuvius. Eruption of April, 1906. Ejection of lapilli, sand and dust as seen from S.S.W. of Pedimentina. Naples, Raggozino, 1906.
Sepia photo-engrav. : 510×355 mm.

PERRET, F. A.—Vesuvio. 30 photos., with descriptive letterpress in Ital. and Fr.— 4⁰. *Napoli* [1907].

PERRET, F. A.—Notes on the electrical phenomena of the Vesuvian eruption, April, 1906.—*Scient. Bull. Brooklyn Inst. Arts and Sci. ii, pp.* 307–12, 2 *figs.*, 1 *pl. Dec.*, 1907.

PERRET, F. A.—Vesuvius : characteristics and phenomena of the present repose-period.—*Amer. Journ. Sci. S.* 4, *xxviii, pp.* 413–30, 13 *figs. New Haven*, 1909.

PERRET, F. A.—The Flashing Arcs : A volcanic phenomenon.—*Amer. Journ. Sci. S.* 4, *xxxiv, pp.* 329–33, 2 *figs. New Haven*, 1912.

PERREY, A.—Mémoire sur les Tremblements de Terre de la Pénisule Italique, etc. —*pp.* 145, 1 *pl.*—*See Acad. Roy. Sci., Mém. couronnés, etc. xxii. Bruxelles*, 1848.

PERREY, A.—Bibliographie Séismique. Catalogue de livres, mémoires et notes sur les tremblements de terre et les phénomènes volcaniques.—3 pts. 8⁰. *Pts. i and ii* (together), *pp.* 161 ; *Part iii, pp.* 70. —[Extr. :] *Mémoires de l'Acad. de Dijon*, 1855–65.

PERROT, FERD.—Mont Vésuve. No. 13.—
Imp. Lemercier, Benard et Cie. Paris
[1838 ?] [B.N.P. Vb. 121.]
A good litho.

PERROT, FERD.—Naples. Vue prise du
Capo di Monti. Lemercier.—[*Paris ?*,
1838 ?] [B.N.P. Vb. 117.]

PERROT, FERD.—Pêcheurs Napolitains sur
le Golfe de Naples.—Imp. Lemercier,
Benard et Cie., Paris. [B.N.P. Vb. 121.]
A fine litho. plate of large size.

PERROTTA, F.—Relatione del nuovo incendio del Monte Vesuvio delli 3 Luglio 1660
del medico fisico Francesco Perrotta di
Piedimonte d'Alife, medico della Torre del
Greco.—MS. *in* [O.V.]

PERROTTI, A. — Discorso astronomico
sopra li quattro Ecclissi del 1632 et una del
1633.—4⁰, *foll*. 26. *Napoli*, 1632. [C.A.]

PESCE, D.—Il povero lacrimante sopra
alcune dimostrazioni di Fisica Naturale del
Gran Monte Vesuvio.—MS. 4⁰, *foll*. 34.
1767. [O.V.]

PESCITELLI, L.—*See* COMANDUCCI, E.
1905.

PESSINA, L. G.—Questioni naturali e
ricerche meteorologiche.   Memorie.—8⁰.
Firenze, 1870.
See pp. 97 *et seq.*

PETERMANN, A. H.—Uebersicht des vulkanischen Heerdes im Mittelmeer. Maasstab 1 : 15,000,000.—*Peterm. Mitth. Taf.* 7.
Gotha, 1866.

PETINO, N.—Il nobile creduto contadino
da' suoi compatrutti per la continuata
dimora in campagna illuminato dal filosofo.
—8⁰. *Napoli*, 1794.

PETITON, A. J. C.—Nature géologique et
forme du Vésuve.—*Assoc. franç. p. l'Avance-
ment d. Sci. Compt. Rend.* (1880), *pp.*
588–92, *section and plan*. 1881.

PETIT-RADEL, P. — Voyage historique,
chorographique et philosophique dans les
principales villes de l'Italie, en 1811 et 1812.
—3 vols. 8⁰.   *Vol. i, pp. xlviij*+348, 1 *map* ;
Vol. ii, pp. 578 ; *Vol. iii, pp.* 592. *Paris*,
1815.
See T.-iii, pp. 140–55 : concerning state
of crater in 1811–12.

PETRINI, N.—Pianta e veduta del Monte
Vesuvio dalla parte meridionale, secondo
lo stato dell' anno 1761 ; e coll' accurata
descrizione della eruzione fatta in Decembre 1760. [B.M.—K. 83. 79b.]

PETRINI, PAOLO.—Vedute delle antichità
dell' città di Pozzuoli, etc.—*obl.* 4⁰, 16 *pls.*
and frontisp. Napoli, 1718. [B.N.P.]
" Vesuvius " is a very distinct plate with
details well shown.

PETRIS, FR. DE.—De Vesuvij conflagratione.—*See* MORMILE, C.—Del Dialetto
Napoletano.

PETRIZZI, ANT. DA.—Lettera a Sua Eccellenza il Signor D. Francesco Ant. Marmi-
gola Duchino di Petrizzi sulla lava eruttata
dal fianco, o pendici del Vesuvio ad ore due,
e minuti 10, di notte circa, del dì 15 Giugno,
1794.—ed. 12⁰ *and* 4⁰. — ?, — ?   [B.N.]

PEZANT, A.—Voyage pittoresque à Pompéi,
Herculaneum, au Vésuve, à Rome et à
Naples.—8⁰, *fig. Paris*, 1839.

PFAFF, A. B. I. F.—Die vulkanischen
Erscheinungen.—*Die   Naturkräfte, vii,
illustr. München*, 1871.

PHILIPPI, E.—Beobachtungen über die
Vesuveruption März (April) 1906.—*Briefliche Mitteilung an den Oberrheinischen
geologischen Verein, Sitzung in Worth, pp.*
13, 4 *figs. Napoli*, (14, IV.) 1906.

PHILIPPI, E.—Ueber die Vesuveruption
April 1906.—*figs.* 1906.

PHILIPPI, E.—Einige Bemerkungen über
seine Beobachtungen am Vesuv im April
1906.—*Zeitschr. deutsch. geol. Gesellsch.
lviii, Monatsb. pp.* 143–51, 7 *figs. Berlin*,
1906.

PHILIPPI, E.—Ueber die Vesuveruption,
April 1906.—*Ber. Oberrhein. Geol. Ver.
No.* 39, *pp.* 1–13, 4 *figs.* (*sketch-map*). 1907.

PHILIPPI, R. A.—Nachricht über die letzte
Eruption des Vesuvs (am 1 Jan. 1839).—
N. J. f. Min. pp. 59–69. *Stuttgart*, 1841.—
See ROTH.—Der Vesuv, etc.

PHILIPPI, R. A.—Relief des Vesuvs und
seiner   Umgegend.—*Bericht   Versamml.
deutsch. Naturforsch. u. Aerzte. vii, pp.*
135–42. 1842.

PHILLIPS, J.—Vesuvius.—8⁰, *pp. xvi*+355,
11 *pls., text illustr. Oxford*, 1869.—*pp.*
xvii+355, 10 *pls.*, 1 *map*, 35 *figs. London*,
1872.

PIAGGIO, [P. ?] A. — Furentis anno
MDCCLXXIX Vesuvii prospectus Ferdinando
IV Siciliarum Regi Antonius Piaggius ex
scholarum piarum clericis regularibus.
Plate engrav. by Cataneus, at the back
of which is a sonnet by the Duca di Belforte.   Engraving : 600×494 mm.

PIAGGIO, P. A.—Idea dell' incendio del Vesuvio dell' anno 1779, abbozzata dal P. Antonio Piaggio delle Scuole Pie, e dedicata a S.E. la Signora D. Giulia Duchessa Giovane nata Baronessa di Mudersbach. [B.S.] Copper-engrav., fol.

PIAZZAI, S. — Sonetti due (1631). — *See* GEORGI URBANO. [C.A.]

PICCININI, D.—Per la eruzione del Vesuvio, accaduta nell' anno 1822. Poesie italiane e in dialetto napolitano.—8°, *pp.* 49–64. *Napoli*, 1827. [C.A.]

PICCININO, F. (del.).—*See* CARDON, A.—Icon Crateris Neapolitani.

PICHETTI, F.—Notizia di scavi fatti alle falde del Vesuvio nel 1689.—*See* BIANCHINI, F.—Istoria Universale, *p.* 174. *Roma*, 1747.

PIERAGGI, E.—*See* SCROPE, G. POULETT. 1860.

PIETRO, FR. DI.—I problemi accademici ove le più famose quistioni proposte nell' ill. Accademia degli Otiosi di Napoli si spiegano.—4°, *pp.* 40+317+25. *Napoli*, 1642. *See* Problema LXXX: Dell' incendio del Monte Vesuvio avvenuto ai 16 di Decembre 1631, pp. 217–20.

PIETRO, M. DI.—*See* GRIFONI.

PIETROSIMONE, N.—Descrizione istorica-cronologica delle principali eruzioni del Vesuvio tolte dalle opere di Luigi Galante e riportate nell' istoria dei monumenti di Napoli da Camillo, Napol. e Sasso, con due sonetti sul Vesuvio del Pietrosimone.—" *L'Ateneo Popolare,*" *pp.* 80, 62 *pls.* *Napoli*, 1868. [C.A.]

PIGHIUS, S. V.—Hercules Prodicius, seu principis juventutis vita et peregrinatio, *etc.*—8°. *Antuerpiæ*, 1587. [O.V.] Few MS. notes. [B.M. 1050. d. 1.]—Nova editio, *etc.* 8°. *Coloniæ*, 1609.

PIGNANT.—Sur une éruption du Vésuve le 11 mars 1866.—*C.R. Acad. Sci. lxii, p.* 749. *Paris*, 1866. [C.A.]

PIGONATI, A.—Descrizione delle ultime eruzioni del Vesuvio dai 25 Marzo 1766 fino a' 10 Dicembre dell' anno medesimo.—8°, *foll.* 4, *pp.* 28, 3 *pls.* *Napoli*, 1767. [O.V.] Various other ed.

PIGONATI, A.—Descrizione dell' ultima eruzione del Vesuvio dei 19 Ottobre 1767, in seguito dell' altra del 1766.—8°, *pp.* 23, 4 *pls.*, *fig.* *Napoli*, 1768.—Various other ed., one, 4°.

PIGONATI, [A. ?]—Relazione della straordinaria eruzione del Monte Vesuvio nel dì 8 Aprile 1779.—*Opuscoli Scelti sulle Scienze e sulle Arti*, ii, 4, *pp.* 310–12. *Milano*, 1778. [C.A.]

PILLA, L.—Cenno biografico su Nicola Covelli.—8°, *pp.* 43. *Napoli*, 1830.

PILLA, L.—Narrazione d'una gita al Vesuvio fatta nel dì 26 Gennaio 1832.—*Il Progr. Sci.* i, *pp.* 232–40. *Napoli*, 1832.

PILLA, L., e CASSOLA, F.—Lo Spettatore del Vesuvio e dei Campi Flegrei.—8°. *Fasc.* 1, *Nos.* 1–3, *pp.* 35+24+31 ; *Fasc.* 2, *Nos.* 1–3, *pp.* 92. *Napoli*, 1832–33. This was continued under the title : " Bolletino geologico del Vesuvio," etc.

PILLA, L.—Catalogue des collections de minéraux et de laves du Vésuve à vendre. —8°, *foll.* 2. [C.A.]—*See* " Lo Spettatore del Vesuvio e de' Campi Flegrei," *Napoli*, 1832–33.—*Bull. Geol. del Vesuvio e dei Campi Flegrei*, *Napoli*, 1833–34.—CAMPANI : Biografia del prof. L. Pilla, *Siena*, 1849.—FERRUCIUS : De laudibus L. Pillæ, *Pisa*, 1862.

PILLA, L.—Cenno storico su i progressi della Orittognosia e della Geognosia in Italia.—*Il. Progr. Sci.* v, *pp.* 5–40. *Napoli*, 1833.

[PILLA, L.]—Sur l'éruption du Vésuve en juillet et août 1832.—*L'Osservatore del Vesuvio, No.* 3.—*Bibl. Univ. lii, pp.* 350–56. *Genève, Paris*, 1833.

PILLA, L.—Osservazioni intorno a' principali cangiamenti e fenomeni avvenuti nel Vesuvio nel corso dell' anno 1832.—*Annali Civili*, i, *pp.* 185–86. *Napoli*, 1833.

PILLA, L.—Bollettino geologico del Vesuvio e dei Campi Flegrei, destinato a far seguito allo Spettatore del Vesuvio.—*Ann. R. Oss. Vesuv.* 8°, 1–5, *pp.* 35+30+28+31+40. *Napoli*, 1833–34. [Complete, O.V.]—*Il Progr. Sci. viii, pp.* 129–56 ; *ix, pp.* 126–49, 1834 ; *x, pp.* 262–89 ; *xvi, pp.* 223–53, 1837. *Napoli*, 1834–37.—German transl. in ROTH.—Der Vesuv, *etc.*

PILLA, L.—Ausbrüche des Vesuvs im Anfange Aprils 1835.—*N. J. f. Min. pp.* 454–55. *Stuttgart*, 1835.

PILLA, L.—Parallelo fra i tre Vulcani ardenti dell' Italia.—*Napoli*, 1835.—*Atti Acc. Gioen. xii, pp.* 89–127. *Catania*, 1837. —*N. J. f. Min. p.* 347. *Stuttgart*, 1836.

PILLA, L.—Sur des coquilles trouvées dans la Fosse Grande de la Somma.—*Bull. Soc. géol. France, viii, pp.* 199–201, 217–24. *Paris*, 1837. [C.A.]

PILLA, L.—Observations tendantes à prouver que le cône du Vésuve a été primitivement formé par soulèvement.—*C.R. Acad. Sci. iv, p.* 527. *Paris*, 1837.

PILLA, L.—Relazione de' principali fenomeni avvenuti nella eruzione del Vesuvio del corrente mese di Agosto.—*Il Lucifero, i, p.* 114. *Napoli, 22 Agosto*, 1838.

PILLA, L.—Ventitresima gita al Vesuvio nella notte del 13 al 14 Settembre, 1834.— *Il Progr. Sci. N.S. xix, pp.* 230–41. *Napoli*, 1838.—*Lo Spettatore del Vesuvio, Fasc.* 11. *Napoli*, 1838.

PILLA, L.—[Ausbruch des Vesuvs Anfangs Januar 1839.]—*N. J. f. Min. pp.* 309–14. *Stuttgart*, 1839.

PILLA, L.—Sur l'éruption du Vésuve en janvier, 1839. Lettre à M. Élie de Beaumont.—*C.R. Acad. Sci. viii, pp.* 250–53. *Paris*, 1839.

PILLA, L.—Relazione dei fenomeni avvenuti nel Vesuvio nei primi di del corrente anno 1839.—*Il Progr. Sci. xxii, pp.* 29–41. *Napoli*, 1839.—German transl. in ROTH : Der Vesuv und die Umgebung von Neapel. —*Berlin*, 1857.

PILLA, L.—Applicazione della teorica dei Crateri di Sollevamento al vulcano di Rocca Monfina.—*Atti 3a Riun. Sci. Ital. pp.* 169–71. *Firenze*, 1841.—*Mém. Soc. géol. France, S.* 2, *i, Pt.* 1, *pp.* 163–79, *Pls. iv–vi. Paris*, 1844.—[Extr.] *Bull. id. xiii, pp.* 402–3. 1842.—German transl. in ROTH : Der Vesuv und die Umgebung von Neapel.—*Berlin*, 1857.

PILLA, L.—Observations relatives au Vésuve. —*C.R. Acad. Sci. xii, pp.* 997–1000. *Paris*, 1841.

PILLA, L.—Sopra la produzione delle Fiamme nei vulcani e sopra le consequenze che se ne possono tirare.—4⁰. *Pisa*, 1837.—4⁰, *pp.* 28, 2 *pls. Lucca*, 1844.—*Atti Riun. Scienz. Ital. pp.* 293–318.—*Padova*, 1843. —*Museo, ii, pp.* 211–36. *Napoli*, 1844.— [Estr.] *Nuov. Ann. Sci. Nat. di Bologna, Nov.* 1844.—*Bull. Soc. géol. France, viii, p.* 262. *Paris*, 1837.—*Bibl. univ. xlviii,*

pp. 175–83. *Genève*, 1843.—*C.R. Acad. Sci. xvii, pp.* 889–95. *Paris*, 1843.—ROTH : Der Vesuv, *etc. p.* 350. *Berlin*, 1857.— *Edinb. New Phil. Journ. xxxvi, pp.* 231–36. 1844.—*Polytechn. Mag. i, pp.* 341–44. *London*, 1844.

PILLA, L.—Aggiunte al discorso sopra la produzione delle Fiamme ne' vulcani.— *Il Cimento, pp.* 380–96. *Pisa*, 1844.— *Museo, v, pp.* 152–66. *Napoli*, 1845.— *Nuov. Ann. Sci. Nat. iii, pp.* 161–78. *Bologna*, 1845.—*Atti Congr. Lucca, pp.* 16, 1 *fig.*

PILLA, L.—Sur quelques Minéraux recueillis au Vésuve et à la Rocca Monfina.—*C.R. Acad. Sci. xxi, pp.* 324–27. *Paris*, 1845.

PILLA, L.—Trattato di Geologia.—2 vols. 8⁰. *Vol. i, pp. xiv*+549, *num. figs., Pisa,* 1847 ; *Vol. ii, pp.* 614, *num. figs., Pisa,* 1847–51. *See* Vol. i.

PILLA, L.—Besteigung des Vesuvs am 26 Jan. 1832.—Bulletino geologico del Vesuvio e de' Campi Flegrei destinato a far seguito allo Spettatore del Vesuvio.— Bericht über die am Vesuv am 1 Jan. 1839 beobachteten Erscheinungen.—Ueber die Flammen der Vulkane.—*See* ROTH : Der Vesuv, *etc.* 1857.

PILLA, L.—Catalogue des principaux Minéraux du Vésuve qu'on vend, ou qu'on échange avec d'autres minéraux exotiques dans le cabinet de M. L. Pilla à Naples.— 16⁰, *pp.* 8. — ?, — ? [B.V.]

PILLA, N.—Primo viaggio geologico per la Campania, ecc.—8⁰. *Napoli*, 1814. *See pp.* 56 *et seq.*

PILLA, N.—Geologia vulcanica della Campania.—2 vols. 8⁰. *Vol. i, pp. xix*+124+ 1 ; *Vol. ii, pp.* 159+1. *Napoli*, 1823.

PINA, IVAN DE.—Al Bolcan de Soma. Soneto.—*See* QUINONES.—El Monte Vesvvio.

PINELLI, B.—Nuova raccolta di ventiquattro vedute de' contorni di Napoli incise da Bartolomeo Pinelli.—*obl.* 8⁰. *Roma*, 1823. Outline engraving No. 1 is the more interesting view of Vesuvius.

PIRANESI.—Vue de la dernière éruption du Vésuve vue du Pont de la Magdaleine. Par Desprez. [B.M.—K. 83. 79c. Portfolio 11, tab.]

PIRIA.—*See* MELLONI. 1840.

PISAN.—[Comical sketch of tourists descending Vesuvius.] Woodcut in French illustr. paper : 170×145 mm.

PISANI, F.—Rapport sur l'éruption du Vésuve du 24 au 30 avril 1872.—*Bull. Soc. géol. France, S.* 2, *xxix, pp.* 334–36. *Paris,* 1872.

PISANI, M. P.—Lettre . . . au sujet d'une éruption qui a eu lieu au Vésuve, le 13 novembre 1867.— *C.R. Acad. Sci. lxv, sem.* 2, *p.* 871. *Paris,* 1867.

PISTOJA, G.—Monte Vesuvio modellato nell' Istituto Topografico Militare da . . . col sistema del Maggiore Pistoja 1878. Scala per le orizzontali 1 a 25,000 ; per le verticali 1 a 20,000. Eseguito in bronzo da Emilio Benini, Firenze 1878.

PISTOLESI, E.—Il Vesuvio.—*Real Museo Borbonico, i, pp.* 5–91. *Roma,* 1836.

PISTOLESI, E.—Guida metodica di Napoli e suoi contorni per vedere con nuovo metodo la città adornata di piante e vedute litografate.—12⁰, *pp.* 11+706, *num. pls. Napoli,* 1845. *See* pp. 483–98.

PITARO, A.—Esposizione delle sostanze costituenti la cenere vulcanica caduta in questa ultima eruzione de' 16 del prossimo passato Giugno 1794.—8⁰, *pp.* 22. *Napoli,* 1794.

PIUTTI, A.—L'Elio nell' Aria di Napoli e nel Vesuvio.—*Rend. R. Acc. Sci. S.* 3, *xv, pp.* 203–4. *Napoli,* 1909.

PIUTTI, A.—L'Elio nei minerali recenti.— *Rend. R. Acc. Sci. S.* 3, *xvi, pp.* 30–32, 1 *tab. Napoli,* 1910.

PIUTTI, A., e COMANDUCCI, E.—Analisi chimica dell' acqua minerale "Minerva" di Torre Annunziata.—*Rend. R. Acc. Sci. S.* 3, *xviii, pp.* 159–61. *Napoli,* 1912.

PLACIDO, F.—Dialogo sopra il miracolo del gloriosissimo protettore della città e del regno di Napoli S. Gennaro. — ?, — ? [B.N.]

PLANGENETO, U. (pseud. Ugo Bassi).— La lacrima del Monte Vesuvio volgarmente Lacryma Christi. Ditirambo.—12⁰, *pp.* 67+3. *Napoli,* 1841.

PLATEN, A. GRAF VON.—Der Vesuv im December 1830. Ode.—*Gedichte, Meyer's Volksbüche, Nr.* 269–70, *p.* 118. *Leipzig,* — ?

PLINIUS SECUNDUS, CAIUS.—C. Plinii Secundi epistolæ lib. ix. Ejusdem et Trajani imp. epist. etc. adjunctæ sunt Isaaci Casauboni notæ in epist. variæ lectiones ultra precedentes, in hac posteriori editione marginis acceserunt.—2 pts. 16⁰. [*Geneva* ?] 1620.—16⁰, *pp.* 862. 1632.

PLINIUS SECUNDUS, C.—[Letter to Tacitus giving an account of his uncle's death and his own danger from an eruption of Vesuvius.]—" *Gentleman's Magazine,*" *xvii, pp.* 421–23. *London,* 1747.

PLINIUS SECUNDUS, C.—Letters, with observations on each letter, and an essay on Pliny's Life, addressed to Charles Lord Boyle by John Earl of Orrery.—2 vols. 8⁰, *figs. Vol. i, pp.* iv+lxx+397+34 ; *Vol. ii, pp.* 2+450+53. *London,* 1751.

PLINIUS SECUNDUS, C.—Lettera di . . . a Tacito ove descrive la morte di Plinio suo zio presso il Vesuvio, cagionata dalla eruzione di esso.—*See* ANON.—Dei Vulcani o Monti Ignivomi, etc. 1779.

PLOIX, E.—*See* DARONDEAU. 1865.

PLUEMICKE, C. M.—Fragmente, Skizzen und Situationen auf einer Reise durch Italien. — *Görlitz,* 1795. — Reprint in RITTER : Beschreibung merkw. Vulkane. —*Breslau,* 1847.

POLEHAMPTON, E., and GOOD, J. M.—The Gallery of Nature and Art, in six volumes, illust. with one hundred engravings.— 2nd ed. 8⁰. *Vol. i, pp.* vi+x+527 ; *Vol. ii, pp.* vi+488 ; *Vol. iii, pp.* v+411 ; *Vol. iv, pp.* vi+552 ; *Vol. v, pp.* vi+688 ; *Vol. vi, pp.* vi+624+iv. *London,* 1818. *See* Vol. i, pp. 330–403 : crater before erupt. 1767.

POLI, G., e LAURIA, G. A.—Prosa Elegiaca per Giacinto Poli e fotografia morale del giovane Vitangelo Poli vittima della esiziale eruzione del Vesuvio nella notte del 25 Aprile 1872.—4⁰, *pp.* 20. *Napoli,* 1872. [C.A.]

POLI, G., e LAURIA, G. A.— Prose e versi pubblicati nella ricorrenza delle esequie solenni alle cinque vittime del Vesuvio . . .—8⁰. *Bari,* 1873.

POLI, G. S. [1746–1825].—Dissertazione intorno al Vesuvio in cui si ragiona del suo stato sì antico che recente.—*Extr. works of author,* 8⁰, *pp.* 46.

POLI, G. S.—Saggio di Poesie.—2 vols. in 4 pts. 4⁰. *Vol. i, Pts.* 1 *and* 2, *pp.* 10+337 ; *Vol. ii, Pts.* 1 *and* 2, *pp.* 366+6. *Palermo,* — ?
See Vol. i, Pt. 1, pp. 1–21 : Il Vesuvio, poemetto ; Vol. ii, Pt. 2, pp. 247–92 : Dissertazione intorno al Vesuvio, etc.

POLL, T. V.—Vue de Naples vers le Vésuve et la Somma. Gravé et se vend chez T. V. Poll.
View of Naples from beyond Mergellina. Hand-coloured litho. of no importance : 208×158 mm.

POLLERA, G. D.—Relatione dell' incendio del Monte di Somma successa [*sic*] nell' anno 1631, nella quale si rendono le ragioni di molte cose le più desiderabili.—8⁰, *foll.* 8. *Napoli,* 1632. [B.N.]

POMBA, CAV. C.—L'Italia nel suo aspetto fisico.—*Pub. G. B. Paravia e C., Torino, Roma, Milano, Firenze, Napoli,* 1890.
Scale, 1 : 100,000 horizont. and vert. Raised map on section of globe.

PONTANO.—La seconda parte delli Avisi del Rev. Pad. Pontano, etc. Di tutto quello, ch'è successo in tutta la seconda settimana. Et cosl l'haverete d'ogni sette in sette giorni.—4⁰, *foll.* 4. *Napoli,* 1632. [B.N.]

PORENA, F.—Sulla forma del Vesuvio prima del 79 d.C.—" *Giro pel Mondo," i, p.* 71. *Bologna,* 1899.

PORRATA SPINOLA, G. F.—Discorso sopra l'origine dei fuochi gettati dal Monte Vesevo, ceneri, etc.—4⁰, *foll.* 3, *pp.* 55. *Lecce,* 1632.

PORZIO, L. A.—Lettere e discorsi accademici.—4⁰, *pp.* 8+347. *Napoli,* 1711.— *See also his :* Opera Omnia, *Vol. ii.*
See pp. 174, 181, 185, 186, 196, 198, 228, 233, 241, 243.

POULETT SCROPE, G.—*See* SCROPE.

P. R.—Seconda lettera. Raccolta di monumenti sopra l'eruzione del Vesuvio seguita nell' Agosto, 1779.—*Giorn. Arti e Commercio, i, pp.* 141 *et seq. Macerata,* 1780. [O.V.]

PRELLER, [FR. ?]—Collection of plans and views in Italy. Photos. of M.S., 1860–61. [B.M. 20660/2101]
A carefully drawn sketch of Vesuvius, 17th May, 1860, from " Trattoria sulla strada Nuova (di Posilippo)."

PRÉVOST, L. C.—Sur la mode de formation des cônes volcaniques, et sur celui des chaînes de montagnes.—*Nouv. Ann. Voy. lxx, pp.* 74–80. *Paris,* 1836.

PRÉVOST, L. C.—Voyage à l'Île Julia, à Malte, en Sicile, aux Îles Lipari et dans les environs de Naples.—*C.R. Acad. Sci. ii, pp.* 243–54. *Paris,* 1836.

PRÉVOST, L. C.—Sur les Coquilles marines trouvées à la Somma.—*C.R. Acad. Sci. iv, pp.* 552–54, 586–89. *Paris,* 1837.

PRÉVOST, L. C.—Théorie des soulèvements.—*Bull. Soc. géol. France, xi, pp.* 183–203. *Paris,* 1839–40.

PRÉVOST, L. C.—Études des phénomènes volcaniques du Vésuve et de l'Etna.— *C.R. Acad. Sci. xli, pp.* 794–97. *Paris,* 1855.

PRÉVOST, L. C.—*See* DOMNANDO.

PRINA, L. G.—Ascensione al Vesuvio.—8⁰, *pp.* 15. *Novara,* 1874. [C.A.]

PRINZ, W.—Analyse des sédiments atmosphériques d'avril et de mai 1906.—[Extr.] *Revue, " Ciel et Terre," an.* 27, *pp.* 7, 1 *fig. Bruxelles,* 1906.

PRINZ, W.—L'éruption du Vésuve d'avril 1906.—8⁰, *pp.* 49, 4 *pls.,* 8 *figs. Bruxelles,* 1906.—[Extr.] *Revue, " Ciel et Terre," an.* 27, *pp.* 115–21, 169–75, 243–49, 323–30, 401–8, 485–96, *pls. and figs. Bruxelles,* 1906.

PRIOR, G. T.—*See* ZAMBONINI, F.—On the identity of Guarinite and Hiortdahlite, etc. 1909.

PRISCO, C.—Componimento in versi latini sull' incendio del Vesuvio.—4⁰, *pp.* 31. *Napoli,* 1832. [O.V.]

PROCOPIUS OF CÆSAREA.—De belló Gothorum. Lib. II.

PROCTER, W. C.—The Vesuvian Railway. —" *Good Words," xxii, pp.* 312–15, 4 *illustr. London,* 1881.

PROCTOR, R. A.—Le Vésuve et Ischia.— *Rev. mens. Astron. pop. pp.* 340–43. *Paris,* 1883. [C.A.]—In English : " Knowledge," *iv, pp.* 81–82. *London,* 1883.

PROST.—Trépidations du sol à Nice pendant l'éruption du Vésuve. — *C.R. Acad. Sci. xliv, pp.* 511–12. *Paris,* 1862. [C.A.]

PROUT.—*See* MAPEI, C.—Italy, Classical, Historical and Picturesque.

PRZYSTANOWSKI, R. VON.—Ueber den Ursprung der Vulkane in Italien.—8⁰. *Berlin,* 1822.

PULSINII, V.—Sonetto [erupt. Vesuvius, Aug. 12th, 1805].—*See* CILLUNZIO, N. [B.N.]

PUOTI, F.—*See* QUARANTA, B. 1845.

PUTIGNANI, J. D.—De redivivo sanguine D. Januarii Episcopi ed Martyris.—3 vols. in 4 pts. 4⁰. *Napoli*, 1723–26.
See Pt. 1, pp. 155–88, and Pt. 4, pp. 130–54.

QUARANTA, A.—Tre fugitivi, Dialogo, ove brevemente si dà ragguaglio dei principali successi, nell' incendio di Vesuvio.—12⁰, *pp.* 35. *Napoli*, 1632. [C.A.]

QUARANTA, B., AJELLO, G., ALOE, S. D', AMBRA, R., AYALA, M., BONUCCI, C., DALBONO, C., PUOTI, F.—Napoli e sue vicinanze. Napoli e luoghi celebri, etc.—*Sett. Cong. Scient. Ital.* 4⁰. *Vol. i, pp.* 12+542, 15 *pls.*, 1 *map* ; *Vol. ii, pp.* 602+ *xxii*, 11 *pls.*, 1 *map. Napoli*, 1845.

QUATTROMANI, G.—Itinerario delle Due Sicilie.—8⁰, *pp.* 249+*xxii*, 1 *map. Napoli*, 1827.

QUATTROMANI, L.—Per Napoli salvata dal terremoto, e dalle lave del Vesuvio, ad intercessione di S. Gennaro. Sonetti.— 8⁰, *pl.* — ?, — ? [B.N.]

QUENSEL, P. D.—Untersuchungen an Aschen, Bomben und Laven des Ausbruches des Vesuv 1906.—[Separatabdr. a.d.] *Centralblatt f. Min. pp.* 497–505, 3 *figs. Stuttgart*, 1906.

QUEUEDO VILLEGAS, F. DE.—Al Vesvvio qve interpoladamente es jardin, y Bolcan. Soneto.—*See* QUINONES.—El Monte Vesvvio.

QUINONES, I. DE.—El Monte Vesvvio. Aora la Montaña de Soma.—8⁰, *foll.* 2+ 56+15, 1 *pl. Madrid*, 1632.
Contains in 2nd pt. :

CORVÑA, CONDE DE.—Soneto.

LOPE FELIX DE VEGA.—[Sonnet.]

VALDIUIELSO, J. DE.—Silva.

QUEUEDO VILLEGAS, F. DE.—Al Vesvvio, qve interpoladamente es jardin, y Bolcan.

PEREZ DE MONTALUAN, I.—Soneto.

BOCANGEL Y VNÇUETA, G.—Al Vesvvio, y svs Incendios.

ESQUILACHE, PRINCIPE DE.—Soneto.

LOPEZ DE ZARATE, F.—Soneto.

SOLIS MESSIA, I. DE.—Soneto.

VILLAYÇAN GARCES, G. DE.—Al Bolcan qve aborto la Montaña de Soma.

REMIREZ DE AVELLANO, L.—Soneto.

CARDOSO, F.—Al Vesuuio. Soneto.

SILVEYRA.—Soneto.

LOPEZ VALDERAS, F.—Soneto.

VELEZ DE GUEVARA, L.—A la Montaña de Soma. Soneto.

ANDOSILLA LARRAMENDI, I. DE.— Al Vesvvio. Soneto.

PINA, I. DE.—Al Bolcan de Soma. Soneto.

HUERTA, A. DE.—Soneto.

PELLICER DE TOUAR, J.—Estancias al Vesuuio & Epigrama.

RUIZ DE ALARCON Y MENDOÇA.— Al Bolcan,y Incendios delVesuuio. Soneto.

HVRTADO DE MENDOÇA, A.—Dezimas.

QUINONES, I. DE.—Epigramma.

CORVÑA, CONDE DE.—[Versi.]

QUINONES, I. DE.—Epigramma. Acrostico.—*See* QUINONES.—El Monte Vesvvio.

QUIRINI, CARD. A. M.—Epistola de Herculaneo ad Jo. Math. Gesnerum, cum observationibus Munteri.—*See* GORI.—Admiranda Antiquitatum Herculanensium, *etc.* i, *pp. vii–xviii* [24]. *Roma*, 1756.

QUIRINI, CARD. A. M.—De Herculaneo Epistola.—*See* MUNTERUS.

RAAB, L.—Ueber Versuche, *etc.* (Expériences sur de la lave fraîche du Vésuve, *etc.*) —8⁰, *pp.* 28. *Erlangen*, 1907.

RABMAN, JOHAN RUDOLPH.—*See* HILDEBRAND, Book IV, p. 9.

RACINE, C. B. (sculp.).—*See* CHASTELET (del.).—Naples. Vue d'après nature, *etc.*

RACINE, J. B. (gravé).—*See* CHASTELET. —Vue d'une partie de la ville et du golfe de Naples, *etc.*

RADCLYFFE, E. (engraved by).—Naples from Monte Martino. W. R. M°Phun and Son, Publishers, Glasgow.
Engrav. : 197×147 mm. Shepherd and twelve sheep in foreground.

RAFFELSBERGER, F.—Gemälde aus dem Naturreiche Beyder Sicilien.—8⁰, *foll.* 4, *pp.* 164, 8 *pls. Wien*, 1824.
Treats principally of Spallanzani's voyage. *See* p. 1 and Pl. 1.

RAFFLES, NECKER [DE SAUSSURE], und DAUBENY.—Ueber die Vulkane auf Java, in den Auvergne und über den Monte Somma.—*Elberfeld,* 1825.

RAMES, J.-B.—Études sur les Volcans.—16⁰. *Aurillac,* 1866.

RAMMELSBERG, C. F. A.—Ueber die mineralogischen Gemengtheile der Laven, insbesondere der Isländischen, im Vergleich mit den älteren Gebirgsarten und den Meteorsteinen. — *Zeitschr. deutsch. geol. Gesellsch. i, pp.* 232–44. *Berlin,* 1849.
See p. 234.

RAMMELSBERG, C. F. A.—Ueber die krystallographischen und chemischen Verhältnisse des Humits (Chondrodits) und Olivins.—*Ann. Phys. Chem. lxxxvi, pp.* 404–17. *Leipzig,* 1852.

RAMMELSBERG, C. F. A.—Chemische Zusammensetzung des Vesuvians.—*Ber. Verh. k. preuss. Akad. Wiss. pp.* 593–97. *Berlin,* 1854.—*Journ. f. prakt. Chem. lxiv, pp.* 305–9. *Leipzig,* 1855.—*Ann. Phys. Chem. xciv, pp.* 92–114. *Leipzig,* 1855.

RAMMELSBERG, C. F. A.—Ueber die Eruption des Vesuvs vom 1 Mai 1855.—*Zeitschr. deutsch. geol. Gesellsch. vii, pp.* 511–25. *Berlin,* 1855.
Transl. of the four letters of Ch. Sainte-Claire Deville to Élie de Beaumont.

RAMMELSBERG, C. F. A.—*See* DEVILLE, C. J. SAINTE-CLAIRE. 1855.

RAMMELSBERG, C. F. A.—Ueber die chemische Zusammensetzung des Leucites, und seiner Zersetzungsprodukte.—*Monatsb. k. preuss. Akad. Wiss. pp.* 148–53. *Berlin,* 1856.—*Ann. Phys. Chem. xcviii, pp.* 142–61. *Leipzig,* 1856.

RAMMELSBERG, C. F. A.—Sur les rapports cristallographiques et chimiques de l'Augite, de l'Hornblende et des minéraux analogues. Trad. p. Delesse.—8⁰.—[Estr. d.] *Ann. Mines, S.* 5, *Mém. xiv, pp.* 1–30. *Paris,* 1858.

RAMMELSBERG, C. F. A.—Ueber den Magnoferrit vom Vesuv und die Bildung des Magneteisens und ähnlicher Verbindungen durch Sublimation.—*Monatsb. k. preuss. Akad. Wiss. pp.* 362–63. *Berlin,* 1859.—*Journ. f. prakt. Chem. lxxvii, pp.* 71–72. *Leipzig,* 1859.—*Ann. Phys. Chem. cvii, pp.* 451–54. *Leipzig,* 1859.

RAMMELSBERG, C. F. A.—Ueber die mineralogische Zusammensetzung der Vesuvlaven und das Vorkommen des Nephelins in denselben.—*Zeitsch. deutsch. geol. Gesellsch. xi, pp.* 493–506. *Berlin,* 1859.

RAMMELSBERG, C. F. A.—Ueber die chemische Zusammensetzung einiger Mineralien des Vesuvs.—*Ann. Phys. Chem. cix, pp.* 567–83. *Leipzig,* 1860.

RAMMELSBERG, C. F. A.—Ueber den letzten Ausbruch des Vesuvs vom 8 December 1861.—*Zeitschr. deutsch. geol. Gesellsch. xiv, pp.* 567–74. *Berlin,* 1862.

RAMMELSBERG, C. F. A.—Ueber die chemische Natur der Vesuvasche des Ausbruchs von 1872.—*Zeitschr. deutsch. geol. Gesellsch. xxiv, pp.* 549–50. *Berlin,* 1872.

RAMMELSBERG, C.F.A.—*See* PALMIERI, L.—Der Ausbruch des Vesuv's, *etc.* 1872.

RAMMELSBERG, C. F. A.—*See* SCACCHI, A.—Ueber den Ursprung, *etc.* 1872.

RAMMELSBERG, C. F. A.—Ueber die Zusammensetzung des Vesuvians.—*Monatsb. k. preuss. Akad. Wiss. pp.* 418–36. *Berlin,* 1873.—*Ber. deutsch. chem. Gesellsch. vi, pp.* 783–84. *Berlin,* 1873.—*Zeitschr. deutsch. geol. Gesellsch. xxv, pp.* 421–35. *Berlin,* 1873.

RAMMELSBERG, C. F. A.—Ueber die chemische Natur des Vesuvians.—*N. J. f. Min. ii, pp.* 157–64. *Stuttgart,* 1896.

RAMONDINI, V.—Rapporto di un Minerale del Vesuvio non ancora descritto.—*See* MONTICELLI e COVELLI.—Prodromo della Mineralogia Vesuviana.

RANIERI, A.—Sale ammoniaco marziale raccolto sulla lava del Monte Vesuvio.— *Ann. Chim. xlix, pp.* 61–62. *Milano,* 1869. —*Atti R. Ist. Veneto, S.* 3, *xiv, pp.* 925–31. *Venezia,* 1869.

RANIERI, A.—Il Vesuvio ed Ottajano attraverso la Storia.—4⁰, *pp.* 79, 10 *figs. Napoli,* 1907.

RAPOLLA, D.—Portici Cenni Storici.—16⁰, *pp. iv*+72+2. *Napoli,* 1878.——3rd ed. [entitled :] Memorie Storiche di Portici.— 4⁰, *foll.* 7, *pp.* 173+1. *Portici,* 1891.

RASPE, R. E.—*See* FERBER.—Lettres à M. Le Chev. de Born, *etc.*

RATH, J. J. G. Vom.—Ueber die Zusammensetzung des Mizzonits vom Vesuv.— *Zeitschr. deutsch. geol. Gesellsch. xv, p.* 246. *Berlin,* 1863.

RATH, J. J. G. VOM.—Der Zustand des Vesuv am 3 April 1865.—*Sitzber. niederrhein. Gesellsch. pp.* 72–75. *Bonn*, 1865.

RATH, J. J. G. VOM.—Olivin-Zwilling vom Vesuv.—*Ann. Phys. Chem. cxxxv, pp.* 581–83. *Leipzig*, 1868.

RATH, J. J. G. VOM.—Ueber die Zwillingsbildungen des Anorthit vom Vesuv.— *Ann. Phys. Chem. cxxxviii, pp.* 449–64. *Leipzig*, 1869.

RATH, J. J. G. VOM.—Oligoklas vom Vesuv. —*Ann. Phys. Chem. cxxxviii, pp.* 464–84. *Leipzig*, 1869.—*N. J. f. Min. pp.* 347–48. *Stuttgart*, 1870.

RATH, J. J. G. VOM.—Ueber den Wollastonit vom Vesuv.—*Ann. Phys. Chem. cxxxviii, pp.* 484–91. *Leipzig*, 1869.— *N. J. f. Min. pp.* 478–79. *Stuttgart*, 1870.

RATH, J. J. G. VOM.—Crystallisirter Lasurstein vom Vesuv.—*Ann. Phys. Chem. cxxxviii, pp.* 491–92. *Leipzig*, 1869.

RATH, J. J. G. VOM.—Orthit vom Vesuv.— *Ann. Phys. Chem. cxxxviii, pp.* 492–96. *Leipzig*, 1869.—*N. J. f. Min. pp.* 346–47 *Stuttgart*, 1870.

RATH, J. J. G. VOM.—[Ueber Orthit und Oligoklas in den alten Auswürflingen des Vesuvs.]—*Sitzber. niederrhein. Gesellsch. pp.* 108–9. *Bonn*, 1869.—*Zeitschr. gesammt. Naturwiss. xxxv, pp.* 517–18. *Halle*, 1870.

RATH, J. J. G. VOM.—Ueber Humitcrystalle des zweiten Typus vom Vesuv.—*Ann.Phys. Chem. cxxxviii, pp.* 515–29. *Leipzig*, 1869.

RATH, J. J. G. VOM.—Ueber die Zwillingsgesetze des Anorthits vom Vesuv.—*Sitzber. niederrhein. Gesellsch. p.* 144. *Bonn*, 1869.

RATH, J. J. G. VOM.—Ueber den Babingtonit von Herbornselbach (Nassau), sowie über den Humit vom Vesuv.—*Sitzber. niederrhein. Gesellsch. pp.* 130–31. *Bonn*, 1870.—*Ann. Phys. Chem. Erg.-Bd. v, pp.* 420–25. *Leipzig*, 1871.—*N. J. f. Min. pp.* 513–14. *Stuttgart*, 1871.

RATH, J. J. G. VOM.—Ein interessanter Wollastonit–Auswürfling vom Monte Somma.—*Sitzber. k. Bayr. Akad. Wiss. iii, math. phys. Class. pp.* 228–31. *München*, 1871.—*N. J. f. Min. pp.* 217–18. *Stuttgart*, 1872.

RATH, J. J. G. VOM.—Ueber die letzte Eruption des Vesuv und über Erdbeben von Cosenza.—*Verh. naturh. Ver. preuss. Rheinl. xxviii, pp.* 66–68, 101–2. *Bonn*, 1871.

RATH, J. J. G. VOM.—Der Vesuv am 1 und 17 April, 1871.—*Zeitschr. deutsch. geol. Gesellsch. xxiii, pp.* 702–33. *Berlin*, 1871.— *Zeitschr. gesammt. Naturwiss. xxxix, pp.* 254–59, *Taf.* XVIII. *Halle*, 1872.

RATH, J. J. G. VOM.—Beitrag zur Kenntniss der chemischen Zusammensetzung des Humits.—*Ann. Phys. Chem. cxlvii, pp.* 246–63. *Leipzig*, 1872.—*Sitzber. niederrhein. Gesellsch. pp.* 109–12. *Bonn*, 1872.— *N. J. f. Min. pp.* 945–46. *Stuttgart*, 1872.

RATH, J. J. G. VOM.—Tridymit im Neapolitanischen Vulkan-Gebiete.—*Ann. Phys. Chem. cxlvii, pp.* 280–81. *Anm.* 2. *Leipzig*, 1872.—*N. J. f. Min. p.* 320. *Stuttgart*, 1873.

RATH, J. J. G. VOM.—Ueber den Zustand des Vesuv vor der letzten Eruption.— *Sitzber. niederrhein. Gesellsch. pp.* 115–18. *Bonn*, 1872.

RATH, J. J. G. VOM.—Ueber Vesuvische Auswürflinge der Eruption vom 26 April 1872.—*Sitzber. niederrhein. Gesellsch. pp.* 134–38. *Bonn*, 1872.

RATH, J. J. G. VOM.—Ueber einen merkwürdigen Lavablock ausgeschleudert vom Vesuv bei der grossen Eruption im April 1872.—*Sitzber. niederrhein. Gesellsch. pp.* 139–41. *Bonn*, 1872.—*N. J. f. Min. pp.* 738–40. *Stuttgart*, 1872.—*Ann. Phys. Chem. cxlvi, pp.* 562–68. *Leipzig*, 1872.— *Rept. Brit. Assoc.* 1872, (*Sect.*) *pp.* 120–22. 1873.

RATH, J. J. G. VOM.—Ueber Tridymit vom Vesuv und von Tumbaco bei Quita.— *Sitzber. niederrhein. Gesellsch. p.* 141. *Bonn*, 1872.

RATH, J. J. G. VOM.—Ueber das Krystalsystem des Leucits.—*Sitzber. niederrhein. Gesellsch. pp.* 146–47. *Bonn*, 1872.— *Monatsber. k. preuss. Akad. Wiss. pp.* 623–33. *Berlin*, 1872.—*N. J. f. Min. pp.* 113–14. *Stuttgart*, 1873.—*Rept. Brit. Assoc.* 1872, (*Sect.*) *pp.* 79–82. 1873.

RATH, J. J. G. VOM.—Ueber einige Leucit-Auswürflinge vom Vesuv.—*Ann. Phys. Chem. cxlvii, pp.* 263–72. *Leipzig*, 1872.— *N. J. f. Min. pp.* 188–90. *Stuttgart*, 1873.

RATH, J. J. G. VOM.—Der Aetna und der Vesuv.—2 vols. *figs. Bonn*, 1872–73.

RATH, J. J. G. VOM.—Ueber den Mikrosommit.—*Sitzber. k. preuss. Akad. Wiss. pp.* 270–73. *Berlin*, 1873.—*N. J. f. Min. pp.* 544–46. *Stuttgart*, 1873.

RATH, J. J. G. VOM.—Geognostische mineralogische Fragmente aus Italien. XI. Ein Beitrag zur Kenntniss des Vesuv's.—Zeitschr. deutsch. geol. Gesellsch. xxv, pp. 209–36. Berlin, 1873.

RATH, J. J. G. VOM.—Der Vesuv. Eine geologische Skizze.—8°, pp. 55, 2 pls. Berlin, 1873.—[Extr. fr.] Samml. gemeinv. wissens. Vorträge, viii, Heft 185.

RATH, J. J. G. VOM.—Ueber die chemische Zusammensetzung der durch Sublimation in Vesuvischen Auswürflingen gebildeten Krystalle von Augit und Hornblende.—Ann. Phys. Chem. Erg.-Bd. vi, pp. 229–40. Leipzig, 1874.

RATH, J. J. G. VOM.—Ueber die verschiedenen Formen der Vesuvischen Augite.—Ann. Phys. Chem. Erg.-Bd. vi, pp. 337–49. Leipzig, 1874.

RATH, J. J. G. VOM.—Ueber die Glimmerkrystalle vom Vesuv.—Ann. Phys. Chem. Erg.-Bd. vi, pp. 366–68. Leipzig, 1874.

RATH, J. J. G. VOM.—Ueber den angeblichen Epidot vom Vesuv.—Ann. Phys. Chem. Erg.-Bd. vi, pp. 368–72. Leipzig, 1874.

RATH, J. J. G. VOM.—[Ueber Sanidinumrindete Leucite in einem Vesuvischen Auswürflinge.] (Fortsetz.)—Ann. Phys. Chem. Erg.-Bd. vi, pp. 381–82. Leipzig, 1874.

RATH, J. J. G. VOM. — Mineralogische Notizen über die chemische Zusammensetzung des gelben Augits vom Vesuv.—Monatsber. k. preuss. Akad. Wiss. pp. 523–40. Berlin, 1875.—Ann. Phys. Chem. clviii, pp. 387–406, 412–14. Leipzig, 1876. —N. J. f. Min. p. 201. Stuttgart, 1876.

RATH, J. J. G. VOM.—Ein merkwürdiger Glimmerkrystall vom Vesuv.—Ann. Phys. Chem. clviii, pp. 420–22. Leipzig, 1876.

RATH, J. J. G. VOM.—[Ueber die oktaëdrischen Krystalle des Eisenglanzes vom Vesuv, über die Verwachsungen von Biotit, Augit und Hornblende mit grösseren Augitkrystallen vom Vesuv . . . und über Augit von Traversella.] Brief an Prof. Leonhard.—N. J. f. Min. pp. 386–405, 1 tav. Stuttgart, 1876.

RATH, J. J. G. VOM.—Ueber die sogenannten oktaëdrischen Krystalle des Eisenglanzes vom Vesuv.—Verh. naturh. Ver. preuss. Rheinl. xxxiv, pp. 131–44. Bonn, 1877.

RATH, J. J. G. VOM.—Ueber einige durch vulkanische Dämpfe gebildete Mineralien des Vesuv.—Verh. naturh. Ver. preuss. Rheinl. xxxiv, pp. 144–67. Bonn, 1877.— N. J. f. Min. pp. 826–27. Stuttgart, 1877.

RATH, J. J. G. VOM.—Studien am Mt. Somma.—B.M. No. 1. 1877.

RATH, J. J. G. VOM.—[Cuspidin-ähnliches Mineral vom Vesuv.]—Sitzber. niederrhein. Gesellsch. pp. 69–70. Bonn, 1881.—N. J. f. Min. i, (Ref.) p. 177. Stuttgart, 1882.

RATH, J. J. G. VOM.—[Ueber den Zustand des Vesuv am 18 März 1881.]—Sitzber. niederrhein. Gesellsch. pp. 198–200. Bonn, 1881.

RATH, J. J. G. VOM.—[Ueber mit weisser Zersetzungsrinde bedeckte Lavastücke aus dem Centralkrater des Vesuv.]—Sitzber. niederrhein. Gesellsch. 1882, pp. 229–31. Bonn, 1882.

RATH, J. J. G. VOM.—Mineralien von Monte Poni und Montevecchio auf Sardinien.—Vesuvische Mineralien ; gelber Augit, Sarkolith, Leucit, Humboldtilith. —Ueber den Zustand des Vesuvs im December 1886.—Ueber die Tuffbrüche von Nocera.—Sitzber. niederrhein. Gesellsch. pp. 130–48. Bonn, 1887.—Zeitschr. f. Kryst. u. Min. xvii, pp. 101–4. Leipzig, 1890.

RAUFF, N.—Ueber die chemische Zusammensetzung des Nephelins.—Zeitschr. f. Kryst. u. Min. ii, p. 445. Leipzig, 1878.

RAUFF, N.—Ueber die chemische Zusammensetzung des Mikrosommits.—Zeitschr. f. Kryst. u. Min. ii, p. 468. Leipzig, 1878.

RAUSCH VON TRAUBENBERG, H.— Ueber die elektrische Zerstreuung am Vesuv.—Physikal. Zeitschr. 4 Jahrgang. No. 16, pp. 460–61. Leipzig, 1903.

RAYMOND, J.—An Itinerary contayning a Voyage made through Italy in the yeare 1646 and 1647 illust. with divers figures of Antiquities.—12°. London, 1648.
Describes his excursion to Vesuvius : the crater or " Vorago " is estimated by him as 3 miles in circumference and 1½ in depth ; " in the midst is a new hill that still vomits smoke." An engraving is given of the most impossible view of Vesuvius from Naples.

RAZZANTI, F.—Récit véritable d'un misérable et mémorable accident arrivé en la descente de la très renommée Montagne de Somma autrement le Vésuve environ trois lieues loin de la ville de Naples depuis le Lundy 15 Décembre 1631 sur les neuf heure du soir jusque au Mardi suivant 23 du mesme, par un Observantin reformé du Couvent Royal de Naples.—[Extr. du] *Mercure François*, 2ᵐᵉ *pte., pp.* 67–73. 1631. —*pp.* 478–80, *foll.* 11. *Paris*, 1632. [C.A.]

READ, S.—The Bay of Naples, from Posilipo. Drawn by S. Read, Oct., 1856.— "*The Illustrated London News,*" *p.* 542, *Nov.* 29, 1856. [B.M. Portfolio of Naples.] *See* p. 544. 383×255 mm.

READ, S.—The Bay of Naples. From above the Grotto looking towards Vesuvius. Litho. in colours : 446×308 mm.

REBUFFAT, O.—Analisi di alcune malte a pozzolana.—8⁰. *Napoli*, 1893.

REBUFFAT, O.—Studi sull' analisi tecnica delle Pozzolane.—*Rend. R. Acc. Sci. S.* 3, ii, *pp.* 165–70. *Napoli*, 1896.

RECLUS, J. J. É.—Les Volcans de la Terre, trois fasc. (tout ce qui en a paru).—Asie antér. : Iranie, Arménie, Syrie ; Asie Mineure : Caucase ; Méditerranée : Égéide, Italie, Sicile. (With bibliog.) — *Soc. Astronom. 9 pls. and maps. Bruxelles,* 1906.

RECUPITO, G. C.—De Vesvviano incendio nvntivs. Auctore Ivlio Cæsare Recvpito Neapolitano e societate Iesv.—4⁰, *pp. viii+* 119+1. *Neapoli, ex Regia Typographia Egidij Longhi* MDCXXXII. 2a ed. 16⁰, *pp.* 124. *Neapoli, apud Lazarum Scorigium*, 1632. Another ed. 8⁰, *pp.* 124, *fol.* 1. *Sumptibus Andreæ Carbonis Bibliopolæ. Neapoli, apud Ægidium Longum* 1632. *Et denuo per Octavium Béltranum*, 1633. Another ed. 4⁰, *pp. viii+*114, *foll.* 3. *Mediolani, Ex Regia, & Duc. Typographia Io. Bapt. Malatestæ Anno Dni.* M.DC.XXXIII. Another ed. 16⁰, *pp. vi+*196. *Pictavis,* 1636. 3a ed. 8⁰, *pp.* 180. *Lovanii, typ. Everardi de Witte.* 1639. Another ed. 8⁰, *pp.* 140, *foll.* 5. *Romæ, ex Typographiæ Manelphi Manelphij.* M.D.C.XLIV. Ultima ed. 8⁰, *pp.* 140. *Romæ, typ. Philippi de Rubeis*, 1670.

RECUPITO, G. C.—Avviso dell' incendio del Vesvvio. Composto dal P. Givlio Cesare Recvpito Napolⁿᵒ della Campagnia di Giesù. Tradotto dalla lingva Latina all' Italiana ad istanza dell' Illᵐⁱ Principe ; & Academici Otiosi.—16⁰, *pp. iv+*264. *In Napoli, per Egidio Longo*, 1635.

REGALDI, G.—Le ruine di Pompei.—*See* ANON.—Convito di Carità . . . etc. *pp.* 35–37. *Napoli*, 1872.

REGNAULT, H. V.—Ascension au Vésuve, le 10 janvier 1868.—*C.R. Acad. Sci. lxvi, pp.* 166–69. *Paris*, 1868.

REIMER, H.—Die Ausbrüche des Vesuv.— 8⁰, *pp.* 16. 1872.

REMIREZ DE AVELLANO, Lvis.—Soneto. —*See* QUINONES, I. Dᴇ.

REMOND.—Château neuf et entrée du Port. 1831. I. Lith. de Delpech. Vesuvius emitting smoke. Litho. : 235×189 mm.

REMOND.—Vue de l'Église de Sᵗ Anastase près Naples. I. lith. de Delpech 25. Litho. : 235×255 mm.

REMOND.—Vue d'une fabrique en allant au Vésuve. 33. I. lith. de Delpech. Litho. : 230×205 mm.

REMONDINI, G.—Della Nolana ecclesiastica istoria.—3 tom. *fol., tav. Napoli,* 1747–57. *See* T. i, pp. 130 *et seq.*

RENARD, A. F.—*See* LUDWIG, E.

REQUIER.—Recueil général, historique, et critique de tout ce qui a été publié de plus rare sur la ville d'Hercolane.—4⁰, *pp.* 135. *Paris*, 1754. [C.A.]

REUSS, F. A.—*See* BREISLAK, S.

REY, S.—Naples et Rome ou Souvenirs de l'Italie.—12⁰, *pp.* 252. *Genève*, 1869. *See* pp. 116–21, erupt. 20th March, 1828.

REYER, Eᴅ.—Beitrag zur Fysik der Eruptionen und der Eruptivgesteine.—8⁰, *pp. xv+*225, 9 *col. pls. Wien*, 1877.

REYER, Eᴅ.—Ueber Vulkane. Vortrag.— *Volksthüm. Vorträge, Nr.* 17. *Wien*, 1892.

REYER, Eᴅ.— Geologische und geographische Experimente. Zweites Heft. Vulkanische und Massen-Eruptionen. — 8⁰, *illustr. Leipzig*, 1892.—Transl. in Ital. by F. Virgilio. *Torino*, 1893.

REYNAUD, J. D.—On the ancient and present state of Vesuvius (1831).—*Proc. Geol. Soc. i, pp.* 337–38. *London*, 1834.

REYNOLDS, SIR J.—Letters from a young painter abroad to his friend in England.— 5 photos. 8º. London, 1748. See pp. 128–74.

REZZONICO, C. C.—Viaggio al Vesuvio.— Opere del . . . T. vii, pp. 52–61. Como, 1825.

RICCI, C.—Napoli.—See COLLEZIONE DI MONOGRAFIE ILLUSTRATE. — S. 1. Italia Artistica, 1902, etc.

RICCI, G.—Analisi chimica dell' Acqua Ferrata, e Solfurea di Napoli, . . . con un appendice sopra un nuovo liquido Vesuviano.—8º, fol. 1, pp. 27. Napoli, — ? [C.A.]—Giorn. enciclop. iii, pp. 285–301. Napoli, 1820.—[Estr.] Giorn. Arcad. Sci. xii, pp. 313–15. Roma, 1821.

RICCI, G.—Analisi dell' acqua termo-minerale della Torre dell' Annunziata.—4º, pp. 32. Napoli, 1831. [C.A.]

RICCI, G.—Raccolta di osservazioni cliniche sull' uso dell' acqua termo-minerale Vesuviane Nunziante.—8º, Fasc. 1, pp. 76, 1 map; Fasc. 2, pp. xxxix+x+145, 1 map, 1 pl. Napoli, 1833–34. [C.A.]

RICCI, G., ET ALII.—Raccolta di osservazioni intorno gli effetti terapeutici e le cure per l'acqua termo-minerale Vesuviana-Nunziante.—Fasc. 10 ed 20. Naples, 1833–34.

RICCI, G.—Analisi dell' acqua termo-minerale Vesuviana-Nunziante.—8º, pp. 49. Napoli, 1834.

RICCIARDELLI.—See CARDON, A.— [Four Views of Naples.]

RICCIARDI, FR.—See MONTICELLI, T. . 1810.

RICCIARDI, L.—Sulla composizione chimica delle pomici Vesuviane raccolte sul Monte Sant' Angelo. Ricerche chimiche.—Atti Acc. Gioen. xvi, pp. 185–88. Catania, 1882. —Gazz. Chim. Ital. xii, pp. 130–32. Palermo, 1882.—Journ. Chem. Soc. xlii, p. 814. London, 1882.—C.R. Acad. Sci. xciv, pp. 1321–22. Paris, 1882.

RICCIARDI, L.—Sulla origine delle ceneri vulcaniche e sulla composizione chimica delle lave e ceneri delle ultima conflagrazioni Vesuviane. (1868–1882.)—Gazz. Chim. Ital. xii, pp. 305–28. Palermo, 1882.

RICCIARDI, L.—I tufi vulcanici del Napolitano. Ricerche ed osservazioni.—Atti Acc. Gioen. S. 3, xviii, pp. 37–46. Catania, 1885.

RICCIARDI, L.—Sull' allineamento dei Vulcani italiani. Sulle roccie eruttive subaeree e submarine e loro classificazione in due periodi. Sullo sviluppo dell' acido cloridrico, dell'anidride solforosa e del jodio dai vulcani. Sul graduale passaggio delle roccie acide alle roccie basiche.—8º, pp. 1–45, tav. Reggio-Emilia, 1887.

RICCIARDI, L.—Genesi e successione delle rocce eruttive.—Atti Soc. Ital. Sci. Nat. xxx, pp. 212–37. Milano, 1887.

RICCIARDI, L.—Sull' azione dell' acqua del mare nei Vulcani. — Dal Laboratorio Chimico del Regio Istituto tecnico di Bari, Dicembre 1887.—Atti Soc. Ital..Sci. Nat. xxxi, pp. 129–34. Milano, 1888.

RICCIARDI, L.—Genesi e composizione chimica dei Terreni Vulcanici Italiani.— L'Agricoltura Italiana, xiv–xv, pp. 155. Firenze, 1889.

RICCIARDI, L.—Per una critica del Prof. Sigismondo Guenther. Earthquakes and Volcanoes.—Boll. Soc. Nat. xxiii (S. 2, iii), pp. 17–50. Napoli, 1909.

RICCIO, L.—Un altro documento sulla eruzione del Vesuvio del 1649.—Lo Spettatore del Vesuvio e dei Campi Flegrei, N.S. i, pp. 61–64. Napoli, 1887.

RICCIO, L.—Prodigiosi portenti del Monte Vesuvio. Invettiva di Camillo Tuttini contro gli Spagnuoli, in occasione dell' incendio dell' anno 1649. E note riguardanti quella eruzione.—Archiv. Stor. Prov. Nap. ii, 1, pp. 28. Napoli, 1887. [C.A.]

RICCIO, L.—Nuovi documenti sull' incendio Vesuviano dell' anno 1631 e bibliografia di quella eruzione.—Archiv. Stor. Prov. Nap. xiv, 3, pp. 489–555. Napoli, 1889.

RICCIO, M.—L'Eruzione del 1632.—See " Il Vesuvio, Strenna pel 1869," pp. 21–23.

RICHARD DE SAINT-NON, J. C.—Voyage pittoresque, ou description des royaumes de Naples et de Sicile.—gd. fol. Vol. i, Naples et Vésuve, foll. 11, pp. 252, 2 engrav. frontisp., 4 maps, 16 figs., 50 pls. ; Vol. ii, Herculaneum, Phlegrean Fields and Campania, foll. 16, pp. 283, 2 maps, 26 figs., 24 col. figs., 80 pls. ; Vol. iii, Italie Méridionale, foll. 24, pp. 201, 15 figs., 4 maps, 57 pls. ; Vol. iv, Sicile, Pt. 1, foll. 14, pp. 266, 13 figs., 65 pls., 2 maps ; Pt. 2, foll. v, pp. 267–430, frontisp., 4 figs., 32 pls. Paris, 1781–86.

RICHARD DE SAINT-NON, J. C.—Éruption du Vésuve de l'année 1779.—*In his* "Voyage . . . de Sicile."

RICHARD DE SAINT-NON, J. C.—Neapel und Sizilien. Ein Auszug aus dem groszen und kostbaren Werke : Voyage pittoresque de Naples et Sicile.—12 pts. 8⁰. *Pt. i, foll.* 6, *pp. xv*+200, 4 *pls.*, 1 *map* ; *Pt. ii, pp.* 220, 4 *pls.* ; *Pt. iii, pp.* 196, 7 *pls.* ; *Pt. iv, pp.* 202, 5 *pls.*, 1 *map* ; *Pt. v, pp.* 180, 6 *pls.; Pts. vi, vii, viii, pp.* 128, 8 *pls.* ; *Pt. ix, pp.* 123, 7 *pls.*; *Pt. x, pp.* 155, 8 *pls.*; *Pts. xi, xii, pp.* 308. *Gotha,* 1789–1806.

RICHARD DE SAINT-NON, J. C.—Voyage pittoresque à Naples et en Sicile (compr.: Naples et ses environs, toute la partie méridionale de l'Italie, connue autrefois sous le nom de Grande-Grèce, et la Sicile). Nouvelle édition, corrigée, augmentée, mise dans un meilleur ordre, par P. J. Charrin.—4 vols. 8⁰. *Paris, Dufour,* 1829. Atlas, *fol.,* 558 *engrav.* [consisting of : I, Naples et ses environs, *Pls.* 1–285 ; II, Grande-Grèce, *Pls.* 286–400 ; III, Sicile, *Pls.* 401–558, by the following artists : Berteaux, Nicollet, Germain, Deny, Longueil, Marillier, Desmoulins, Berthault Queverdo, Cochin, de St. Aubin, Fraganard, Varin, Desprez, etc., etc.]—Another ed. 4 vols. 8⁰. *Paris, Houdaille,* 1836.

RIDDELL, R. A.—*See* WILSON, J.

RIEDESEL, J. H. VON.—Voyage en Sicile et dans la Grande Grèce, adressé par l'auteur à son ami Mr. Winckelmann, traduit de l'allemand [by J. R. Frey des Landres].—12⁰, *pp.* 12+370. *Lausanne,* 1773.

RIEDL.—Der Vesuv im Mai 1900. [Separat-Abdruck a. d.] "*Carinthia,*" *ii,* 4–5, *pp.* 11. *Klagenfurt,* 1901.

RINNE, F. W. B.—Ueber Olivin und Olagioklasskelette.—*N. J. f. Min. ii, pp.* 272–85, 1 *tav. Stuttgart,* 1891.

RISO, B. DE.—Relazione della pioggia di cenere avvenuta in Calabria ulteriore nel dì 27 Marzo 1809.—*Atti Acc. Pontaniana, i, pp.* 163–65. *Napoli,* 1810.

RISSLER, J. B.—Neuer Ausbruch des Vesuv. Ein feuerspeihender Berg des Königreichs Neapel in der Nähe von dessen Hauptstadt. — 4⁰, *pp.* 8. *Mülhaussen, gedruckt bei J. B. Rissler,* 1855. [C.A.]

RITTER.—Vue du Sommet du Vésuve dessinée sur les lieux au mois de Novembre 1755. A. Zingg sculp. Very fine engrav. of interior of crater.

RITTER, C. W. J.—Beschreibung merkwürdiger Vulkane.—8⁰. *Breslau,* 1847. *See* pp. 62–113. Earlier ed. 2 pts. in 1 vol. illustr.—8⁰. *Posen u. Leipzig,* 1806.

RIVINUS, A. [BACHMANN].—Vesuvius, in promotione XVI Bataliarorum VI *idus Martii* MDCXXXII, Lipsiæ, declamatus.— 4⁰, *foll.* 22. *Lipsiæ,* 1632. [C.A.]

RIVINUS, A.—Tripus Delphichus de Monte Campaniæ Somma ejusque fatitidico incendio.—4⁰. *Lipsiæ,* 1635. *See* SORIA.

RIZZI-ZANNONI, G. A.—Topografia del Agro Napolitano con le sue adjacenze. Gius. Guerra inc.—[*Naples*] 1793. A very good map from Scafata di N. of Lago di Patria, Vesuvius and Campi Phlegræi, with lava-streams of the former. No islands shown. Has an elaborate border-title : 870×584 mm.

RIZZI-ZANNONI, G. A.—Carte del Littorale di Napoli e di luoghi antiche più remarchevoli di quei contorni. Gius. Guerra Nap. Reg. Inc. — ?, 1794. A good map for the period, extending from Majori to Licola, with Ischia and Capri : 821×517 mm.

RIZZI-ZANNONI, G. A.— [Map of Vesuvius in 1794 in his album.]

RIZZI-ZANNONI, G. A.—Chart of the Bay of Naples and of a part of the Bay of Salerno. Drawn and published in 1785 . . . republished with additions by W. Fadden.—*London, May 1st,* 1803. [B.M. —Sec. 5 (159). *See also* Mar. v. 61.]

RIZZI-ZANNONI, G. A.— Carta del regno di Napoli, indicante la divisione delle XV sue Provincie.—[*Naples,*] 1807. [B.M.— 23880 (25).] A smaller scale map than in " Topografia del Agro," *etc.*

RIZZI-ZANNONI, G. A.— Carte du royaume de Naples.—[*Paris ?,* 1830 ?]

RIZZI-ZANNONI, G. A.—Topografia fisica della Campania.—*See* BREISLAK, SC.

R * * * L * * *.—*See* LIBERATORE, R.

R 2

ROBERT (Peintre du Roi, des.).—Vue de la sommité et du cratère du Vésuve, au moment de la dernière éruption arrivée le 8 d'Août 1779, à 9 heures du soir, *etc.* Gravé par Ch. Guttenberg. [Above, printed on top of plate :] 208 "Voyage Pittoresque," et de pierres qui, malgré un vent violent, *etc.* [being continuation of text on back of plate].
Steel engrav. : 250 × 360 mm.

ROBERT, L. E.—Rapprochement géologique entre le Vésuve et l'Hekla.—*Les Mondes, lv, pp.* 16–18. 1881.—*Sézanne, [Mem. Soc. Sci. Vitry ?] pp.* 12. 1881.

ROBERTS, R. A.—*See* MAPEI, C.—Italy, Classical, Historical and Picturesque.

ROCCA, F.—Osservazioni [sull' acqua Vesuviana-Nunziante].—*See* RICCI, G.

ROCCA ROMANA.—Cratere del Vesuvio.— pl. *fol. Napoli,* 1805.

ROCCO, A.—Lettera, nella quale si dà vera, e minuta relatione delle Gratie fatte dalla Gloriosissima Vergine e Madre di Dio dell' Arco Maggiore, a beneficio della sua Casa e della Gente, che in essa si salvò in questi travagliati tempi del nuovo incendio del Monte Vesuvio nel 1631, e della carità usatali dai Padri dell' Arco.—8⁰, *pp.* 40. *Napoli,* 1632. [C.A.]

ROCCO, A. — Oratione devotissima alla Gloriosa Vergine Maria dell' Arco.—8⁰ (frontisp. wanting). *Napoli,* 1632. [B.N.] Descript. of erupt. 1631.

ROCCO, E.—Al Vesuvio ! Bizzarria.—*Il Salvator Rosa, i,* 10. *Napoli,* 13 *Gennaio,* 1839.

ROCKILLY, E.—Der Ausbruch des Vesuvs. —*Illustrirte Welt, pp.* 111–14, 1 *illustr. Stuttgart,* 1862.

RODWELL, G. F.—South by East : Notes of travel in Southern Europe.—8⁰, *pp.* 274. *London,* 1877.

RODWELL, G. F.—The History of Vesuvius during the last ten years.—*Journ. of Sci. i, pp.* 463–71. *London,* 1879.

RODWELL, G. F.—La récente éruption du Vésuve et son état actuel.—" *La Nature,*" *sem.* 1, *pp.* 217–19. *Paris,* 1879.— In English : " *Nature,*" *xix, pp.* 343–45, 1 *illustr. London,* 1879.—"*The Academy,*" 354, *p.* 149. *Feb.* 15, 1879.

RODWELL, G. F.—The History of Vesuvius during the year 1879.—"*Nature,*" *xxi, pp.* 351–53, 1 *illustr. London,* 1880.

ROGADEI, G. D.—Carmen de Vesuvio.—*In* " Epigrammata leges et carmina insculpta in villula et hortulo."—4⁰. — ?, — ?

ROGATI, F. S. DE.—Il Tremuoto. Ode a Dio.—16⁰, *foll.* 6. *Colle,* 1783.
See Stanza XI.

ROGGERO, CAV. G.—Carta in rilievo dell' Italia.—*Pub. G. B. Paravia e C., Torino, Roma, Milano, Firenze, Napoli,* 1876.
Raised map, 1 : 2,800,000 horiz. ; 1 : 320,000 vert.

ROGISSARD, DE.—Les Délices de l'Italie ou description exacte de ce Pays, de ses principales villes, et de toutes les raretez, qu'il contient.—3 vols. 12⁰. *Vol. i, foll.* 8, *pp.* 275, *num. pls. ; Vol. ii, pp.* 277–554, *num. pls. ; Vol. iii, pp.* 555–718, *foll.* 31, *pp.* 10. *Leide,* 1706.
See pl. at p. 548 : eruption 1631.
Another ed. 6 tom. 12⁰. *Leide,* 1709.
Another ed. 4 tom. 8⁰. *Amsterdam,* 1743.
In German : *Berlin,* — ?

ROJAS, A.—El rey de los volcanos.—4⁰, *pp.* 42. *Caracas,* 1869.

ROMANELLI, D.—Viaggio a Pompei, a Pesto, e di ritorno ad Ercolano ed a Pozzuoli.—8⁰, *pp.* 248, 1 *pl. Napoli,* 1811.—— 2nd ed. 12⁰. *Vol. i, pp.* 288, 2 *pls. ; Vol. ii, pp.* 276, 2 *pls. Napoli,* 1817.——3rd ed. *Milano,* 1831.
See pp. 53–63, 2nd ed.

ROMANELLI, D.—Napoli antica e moderna. —3 pts. 12⁰. *Pt. i, pp.* 8+182, 1 *map ; Pt. ii, pp.* 189 ; *Pt. iii, pp.* 212. *Napoli,* 1815.
See Pt. i, pp. 163–80.

ROMANO, E.—Eruption of Vesuvius by night, June 1st, 1881.
Gouache : 261 × 182 mm.

ROOKER (sculp.).—Mount Vesuvius.
Line engrav. (in engrav. frame) of Vesuvius in eruption (1757), similar to many others, with boat and fishermen in foreground : 197 × 121 mm.

ROOKER (sculp.).—Mount Vesuvius.
A copy of Vernet's picture of 1767.

ROSATI, A.—Notizie riassuntive di uno studio cristallografico dell' Idocrasio del Vesuvio.—*Atti R. Acc. Lincei, S. 5, Rend. xix, sem.* 2, *pp.* 75–77. *Roma,* 1910.

ROSATI, A.—Contributo allo studio cristallografico dell' Idocrasio del Vesuvio.—*Atti R. Acc. Lincei, S. 5, Mem. viii, pp.* 558–73, 1 *pl. Roma,* 1911.

ROSE, G.—Sur la composition du Feldspath vitreux et du Rhyacolithe.—*Ann. Mines, S.* 3, *v, pp.* 541-43. *Paris,* 1834.—*Ann. Phys. Chem. xxviii, pp.* 143-56. *Leipzig,* 1833.

ROSE, G.—Abhandlung des Herrn C. Rammelsberg über die chemische Zusammensetzung des Chondrodits, Humits und Olivins, etc.—*Ann. Phys. Chem. lxxxv, pp.* 345-50. *Leipzig,* 1851.

ROSE, H.—Untersuchung einiger Mineralien. (Lithionglimmer von Zinnwald ; schwärzlichgrüner Glimmer vom Vesuv ; Saccharit ; Crystallisirter Albit von Schreibershau. u.s.w.) — *Ann. Phys. Chem. lxi, pp.* 377-96. *Leipzig,* 1844.

ROSENTHAL-BONIN.—Al Vesuvio ! Ein touristisches Albumblatt.—*Ueber Land u. Meer, xviii,* 21, *illustr. Stuttgart,* 1876.

ROSEO DA FABRIANO, MAMBRINO.—*See* COLLENUCCIO, P. 1591, 1613, 1771.

ROSINI, C. — Dissertationis isagocicæ ad Herculanensium voluminum explanationem. Pars prima [all published].—*fol., foll.* 3, *pp.* 104, 2 *maps,* 20 *pls. Neapoli,* 1797. [C.A.]

ROSSI, D. DE.—Maps of Italy.—*Rome,* 1693-96.

ROSSI, G.—Sulla radioattività della Cotunnite Vesuviana.—*Atti R. Acc. Lincei, S.* 5, *Rend. xvi, sem.* 2, *pp.* 630-38. *Roma,* 1907.

ROSSI, G. J. DE.—Fidelissimæ urbis Neapolitanæ cum omnibus viis accurate nova delineatio anno 1649. Roma alla Pace. [B.M.]—24045 (3).]
Engrav. bird's-eye view of Naples and Campi Phlegræi : 708×290 mm.

ROSSI, M. S. DE.—Intorno ai fenomeni concomitanti l'ultima eruzione Vesuviana, avvenuti nella zona vulcanica dell' Italia.—*Atti Acc. Pont. N. Lincei, xxv, pp.* 378-82. *Roma,* 1872.

ROSSI, M. S. DE.—Bullettino del Vulcanismo Italiano e di geodinamica generale.—*Anno i-xvii. Roma,* 1874-90.
According to Bolton, there were 14 vols., 1874-87, and to the Club Alp. : 1873-88.

ROSSI, M. S. DE.—Quadro generale statistico topografico giornaliero dei terremoti avvenuti in Italia nell' anno meteorico 1874 [& 1877] col confronto di alcuni altri fenomeni.—*Atti Acc. Pont. N. Lincei, xxviii, pp.* 514-36. *Roma,* 1875. [& *xxxi, pp.* 479-82. 1878.]

ROSSI, M. S. DE.—Cronaca Vesuviana con confronti d'altri fenomeni.—*Bull. Vulc. Ital. iii, pp.* 50-51, 1876 ; *iv, pp.* 43-44, 111-12, 1877 ; *v, pp.* 137-40, 1878 ; *vi, pp.* 39-41, 144-49, 1879 ; *vii, pp.* 57-59, 79-80, *Roma,* 1880.

ROSSI, M. S. DE.—Studii intorno al terremoto che devastò Pompei nell' anno 62 e ad un basso-rilievo votivo Pompeiano che lo rappresenta.—*Bull. Vulc. Ital. vi,* 8, 11, *pp.* 109-18. *Roma,* 1879.

ROSSI, M. S. DE.—Cranaca dell' Etna e del Vesuvio dal Gennaio al Febbraio 1880 con confronti. (Notizie varie riunite del Prof. Palmieri e Silvestri.) — *Bull. Vulc. Ital. vii, pp.* 80-82. *Roma,* 1880.

ROSSI, M. S. DE.—L'Eruzione del Vesuvio. —*Bull. Vulc. Ital. xii,* 10-12. *Roma,* 1885.

ROSSI, M. S. DE.—Massimi sismici Italiani dell' anno meteorico 1887.—*Ann. Meteor. Ital. vi, pp.* 192-209, *Torino,* 1891 ; *vii, pp.* 239-56, 1892.

ROSSMANN, W.—Vom Gestade der Cyklopen und Sirenen. Reisebriefe. 2te. Auflage.—16⁰. *Leipzig,* 1880.
See pp. 233-39.

ROTH, J. L. A.—Analysen : I. Dolomitischer Kalkstein, sogenannter Auswürfling vom Rio della Quaglia von der Somma.—II. Dolomitischer Kalkstein von der Punta delle Coglione an der Somma.—III. Stängliger Braunspath aus Mexico.—IV. Kluftgestein aus dem Gypse des Schildsteins bei Lüneburg.—V. Stinkstein von Segeberg.— *Zeitschr. deutsch. geol. Gesellsch. iv, pp.* 565-70. *Berlin,* 1852.—*Journ. f. prakt. Chem. lviii, pp.* 82-86. *Leipzig,* 1853.

ROTH, J. L. A.—Litteratur über den Vesuv, besonders der Ausbrüche.—8⁰, *pp.* 98. *Berlin,* 1857. [C.A.]

ROTH, J. L. A.—Der Vesuv und die Umgebung von Neapel.—8⁰, *pp. xliv*+540, 9 *pls., figs. Berlin,* 1857.

ROTH, J. L. A.—[Ueber den Ausbruch des Vesuv vom Jahre 1861.]—*Zeitschr. deutsch. geol. Gesellsch. xv, pp.* 11-12. *Berlin,* 1863.

ROTH, J. L. A.—Geschichte des Vesuvs.— *Berlin,* 1869.

ROTH, J. L. A.—*See* SCACCHI, A. 1872.

ROTH, J. L. A.—[Ueber Vesuv und Aetnalaven.]—*Zeitschr. deutsch. geol. Gesellsch. xxv, p.* 116. *Berlin,* 1873.

ROTH, J. L. A.—Ueber eine neue Berechnung der Quantitäten der Gemengtheile in den Vesuvlaven.—*Zeitschr. deutsch. geol. Gesellsch. xxviii, pp.* 439–44. *Berlin,* 1876.

ROTH, J. L. A.—Ueber die Gänge des Monte Somma.—[Title only] *Monatsb. k. preuss. Akad. Wiss.* 1877, *p.* 74. *Berlin,* 1878.

ROTH, J. L. A.—Studien am Monte Somma. —*Abh. k. preuss. Akad. Wiss.* 1877 (*Physik., pp.* 1–47). *Berlin,* 1878.—[Abstr. in Ital.] *Boll. R. Com. Geol. Ital. viii, pp.* 440–51. *Roma,* 1877.

ROTH, J. L. A.—Zur Geologie der Umgebung von Neapel.—*Monatsb. k. preuss. Akad. Wiss.* 1881, *pp.* 990–1006. *Berlin,* 1882.

ROTTMAN (gemalt).— Golf von Baje. Der Kunstverein in München seinen Mitgliedern 1832. Gedr. unter der Leitung v. W. Flachnecker u. Fr. Hoke. Auf Stein gez. v. C. Lebschée.
Litho. : 303 × 280 mm.

ROUARGUE (del. and sc.).—Naples. Imp. F. Chardon aîné. 30 r. Hautefeuille, Paris. Publié par Furne à Paris.
Fine engraving : 149 × 102 mm. View from above Grotto over town and Vesuvius ; personages, a donkey, 7 trees in foreground. This is similar to one, unsigned, in which sky and smoke of Vesuvius have been retouched.

ROUARGUE (del. et sc.).— Naples. (Vue générale.) Publié par Furne, Paris. View from above grotto over town and Vesuvius ; 5 women, 3 men and a donkey and trees in foreground. [B.M. Portfolio of Naples.]
Engraving : 275 × 178 mm.

ROUARGUE.—Naples. Imp. F. Chardon aîné. Par Furne, Paris.
View from above the Grotto. Another plate is identical but for the clouds and smoke of Vesuvius.

ROUILLET, A¹ᵉ (del. et lith.).—Naples. Italie. Paris, chez Gosselin, ed imp. r. Sᵗ Jacques, 71, chez Forgues à Montrejeau, à Lyon, chez Gadola.
Naples with Vesuvius ; a rough litho. on tinted ground, very square and inaccurate : 274 × 182 mm.

ROUX, H.—Pompéi: vue générale. Frontispiece. Imp. de Senefelder.
Fine engrav. : 184 × 104 mm.

ROZET, C. A.—Mémoire sur les Volcans d'Italie.—*Mém. Soc. géol. France, S.* 2, i, *pp.* 131–62. *Paris,* 1844.

ROZET, C. A.—Sur les Volcans des environs de Naples.—*Bull. Soc. géol. France, S.* 2, i, *pp.* 255–66. *Paris,* 1844.

RUDOLPH, E.—Bericht über die vulcanischen Ereignisse während des Jahres 1894.—*Min. u. petr. Mittheil. xvi,* 5, *pp.* 365–464. *Wien,* 1896.

RUE, DE LA.—Laves qui sortaient des flancs du Vésuve à la suite de l'Éruption de 1754. Minéralogie, 6me collection, Volcans. Histoire Naturelle. Bénard fecit. [B.N.P. Vb. 121.]
A rather fantastic engraving.

RUE, DE LA.—Histoire Naturelle; Volcans. Vue Générale du Vésuve en 1757. Bénard fecit. Minéralogie, 6me collection, Volcans. Pl. 1. [B.N.P. Vb. 121.]

RUECKERT, F.—Lied am Vesuv. Gedichte. Auswahl des Verfassers. — *pp.* 326–27. *Frankfurt a. M.* 1843.

RUGGIERO, M. — Sopra una massa di pomici trovata in Pompei, con una lettera del Prof. Scacchi.—*Atti R. Acc. Archeol. viii,* Pt. 2, *pp.* 195–97, 1 *pl. Napoli,* 1877.

RUGGIERO, M.—Della eruzione del Vesuvio nell' anno LXXIX.—*In* : Pompei e la regione sotterrata dal Vesuvio nell' anno LXXIX, *pp.* 1–4. *Napoli,* 1879.

RUIZ, TOMASO (pinxᵗ).—Distant view of Mount Vesuvius in Eruption A.D. 1751. Taylor excudᵗ. Landscape Plate XXXII. —*See* [CRAVEN, K.] Italian Scenes.
Line engrav. : 148 × 98 mm.

RUIZ, TOMASO (pinxᵗ).—View of the lava of Mount Vesuvius in its course, A.D. 1751. Landscape Plate XXXIII.
Fine engrav. : 150 × 98 mm.

RUIZ DE ALARCON Y MENDOÇA, J.— Al Bolcan, y incendios del Vesuuio. Soneto.—*See* QUINONES. — El Monte Vesvvio.

RUSCELLI, G.—*See* COLLENUCCIO, P. 1552.

RUSH, DR. J.—Der Ausbruch des Vesuv.— *Illustrirte Zeit,* 2723, *p.* 282, 1 *illustr. Leipzig,* 1895.

RUSSEGGER, J. VON. — Geognostische Beobachtungen in Rom, Neapel, am Aetna, auf den Cyclopen, dem Vesuv, Ischia, etc. —*N. J. f. Min. pp.* 329–32. *Stuttgart,* 1840.

RUSSO, G. DEL.—Pianta della città di Napoli delineata nel 1815 da Giosuè Russo. Inc. da Dom. Guerra, Gen. Galiani scris. Scala 1 : 20,000.—[*Napoli,* 1815.]

Finely engraved map extending from Sebeto to La Grotta and Castel dell' Uovo to Pal. Reale di Capodimonte; distant view of Vesuvius on dedication; 104 references : 255 × 323 mm.

SABATIER.—*See* COIGNET, M.—" Vues pittoresques de l'Italie," *etc. Also :* " Voyage en Italie " *and* " Pausilippe."

SABATINI, V.—Sull' attuale eruzione del Vesuvio.—*Boll. R. Com. Geol. Ital. xxvi,* 2, *pp.* 149–64. *Roma,* 1895.

SABATINI, V.—Vulcani e terremoti.—*Riv. Ital. An.* 5, *ii, pp.* 353–79, 10 *figs. Roma,* 1902.

SABATINI, V.—L'attuale eruzione e l'Osservatorio Vesuviano. — " *La Tribuna,*" 112, 22 *Aprile* 1906.

SABATINI, V.—Sull' eruzione del Vesuvio dell' Aprile 1906.—*Boll. R. Com. Geol. Ital. xxxvii, pp.* 158–62, 169–229, 25 *figs., Pls.* IV *and* V, *geol. map* (of S.E. Vesuv. 1 : 25,000). *Roma,* 1906.

SABATINI, V.—Eine Vesuv-Expedition.— *Die Zeit, Wien,* 8 *Mai,* 1906.

SABATINI, V.—I diversi modi di attività dei vulcani italiani e l'ultima cruzione del Vesuvio.—*Atti Soc. Ligustica Sci. Nat. e Geogr. xviii,* 3–4, *pp.* 161–66. *Genova,* 1907.

SABATINI, V.—I Vetri forati di San Giuseppe e d'Ottaiano durante l'eruzione Vesuviana del 1906.—*Boll. R. Com. Geol. Ital. xxxviii, pp.* 277–316, *figs., Pls.* VII–VIII. *Roma,* 1907.

SACCO, G.—Ragguaglio storico della calata nel Vesuvio e relazione del suo stato dei 16 Luglio 1794.—8⁰, *pp.* 14. *Portici,* 1794.

SACHERI, G.—La ferrovia funicolare del Vesuvio.—*pp.* 7, 12 *figs. Torino,* 1881. —[Estr. d. Period. mens.] " *L'Ingegneria Civile e le Arti Industriali," Anno* VII. Of no vulcanological interest.

ST. CLAIR BADDELEY.— *See* HARE, A. J. C.

SAINT-LAURENT, JOANNON DE. — Risposta di . . . ad un amico in difesa delle scoperte di Ercolano.—*See* GORI.—Admiranda Antiquitatum Herculanensium, *etc. T. ii, pp.* 158–88.

SALATHÉ (dis. e inc.).—Vue de Naples près du Tombeau de Virgile.—Chez C. T. Muller à Naples.

Fine view of Naples and Vesuvius from above the Grotto ; peasant woman on donkey with dog in foreground. Line litho. : 575 × 420 mm.

SALLE, DE LA.—*See* ARTAUD.

SALMON, C. G.—Lo stato presente di tutti i paesi e popoli del mondo.—*Venezia,* 1761. *See* Vol. xiii, pp. 86–102.

SALMON, C. G.—Storia del regno di Napoli antica e moderna descritta dal Salmon.— 8⁰. *Napoli,* 1763.

SALMON, C. G.—Descrizione del Monte Vesuvio.—*See his :* " Storia del Regno di Napoli," *pp.* 65–79. [B.N.]

SALVADORI, G. B.—Notizie sopra il Vesuvio e l'eruzione dell' Ottobre 1822.— *Napoli,* 1823.

SALVADORI, G. B.—Notizen über den Vesuv, und dessen Eruption v. 22 Oct. 1822, verdeutscht durch C. F. C. H.—4⁰, *pp.* 75, 3 *pls. Neapel,* 1823. [C.A.]

SALVADORI, R.—*See* NASINI, R., ET ALII. 1906.

SALVATOR ROSE (pinxit). — Le Mont Vésuve. Peint par Salvator Rose, de l'École Romaine et gravé par René le Charpentier. Le Tableau original a 36 pouces de long sur 23 de haut. Le Charpentier sc. A Paris, chez l'Auteur, rue la Harpe, vis à vis celle des Cordeliers. Baisier scripsit.

Fine engrav. of Vesuvius, much idealized, from Castellamare ; ship, boats, personages, donkeys, barrels, etc., in foreground : 570 × 402 mm.

SAMBIASI, O.—Soneto (1631).—*See* GIORGI URBANO. [C.A.]

SANCHEZ, G.—Il Monte Vesuvio deificato. —*Il Progr. Sci. xii, pp.* 145–49. *Napoli,* 1835. [C.A.]

SANCTIS, A. DE.—Il mostruoso parto del Monte Vesevo hora dal volgo detto, Monte Diavolo, la cui mostruosità e crudeltà è qui descritta.—12⁰. *Napoli,* 1632.

SANCTIS, A. DE.—*See* GENOVESI, AB.

SANDBY, P. (fecit). — Castello dell Ovo at Naples. Vue du Château des Œufes à Naples. Fabris pinxt. Published as the Act directs by P. Sandby, Sᵗ Georges Row,

Oxford Turnpike, Jany 1st, 1778. [B.M. Portfolio of Naples.]
Vesuvius in background to the right : 515 × 352 mm.

SANDMAN (lith. von).—Neapel. Ged. bei Höfelich.—Verlag u. Eigenthum von L. T. Neumann in Wien.
Two women talking to a woman sitting in foreground, taken from over Grotto. Litho. on yellow ground : 403 × 322 mm.

SANDRART, J.—Warhaffte Contrafaktur des Bergs Vesuuij und desselbigen Brandt sambt der umbligenden Gegend nach dem Leben gezeichnet. 1631. Vesuvius Mons Neapolcos.
Engraving with man talking to woman, also man on horse and dog in foreground : 324 × 203 mm. Another, earlier ed. occurs without the inscription " Vesuvius Mons Neapoleos."

SANDULLI, P.—Gli Eroi del Virginiano celebrati con epistole, idilli, ed altre rime eroiche sagre.—8⁰, *p*. 134. *Napoli*, 1708.
See pp. 60–65 : Il Vesuvio a posteri.

SANDYS, G.—A Relation of a Iourney begun An. Dom. 1610. Fovre Bookes. Containing a description of the Turkish Empire, of Ægypt, of the Holy Land, of the Remote parts of Italy, and Islands adioyning.—4⁰, *pp.* 309+1, *figs., frontisp. portrait of author. London*, 1615.

SANFELICIUS, A. — Campania Antonii Sanfelicii Monachi. [At end :] " A partu Virginis anno MDLXII (1562) descripsit Matthias Cancer."—4⁰, *foll.* 20. *Neapoli*, 1562.
First edition, extremely rare. *See* Pl. 15.

SANFELICIUS, A.—Campania.—12⁰, *pp.* 8+64, 1 *map, frontisp. Amstelædami, Typis Ioannis Blaeu*, 1656. [C.A.]

SANFELICIUS, A.—Campania notis illustrata.—4⁰, *pp.* 26+158, 1 *pl. Neapoli*, 1726.

SANFELICIUS, A.—La Campana recata in volgare italiano da Girolamo Aquino Capuano.—8⁰, *pp. lxxi*+117+3, 1 *map, portrait. Napoli*, 1779. [C.A.]—*Also* 1796.

SAN MARTIN, A.—Un viaje al Vesubio. Novela originale, histórica.—8⁰, *pp.* 236. *Madrid*, 1880. [C.A.]

SANNICOLA,G.—Biografia di Nicola Covelli. —8⁰, *pp.* 16. *Palermo*, 1845.—Another ed., with portrait : 8⁰, *pp.* 19. *Napoli*, 1846.

SANTAGATA, S.—[Descript. erupt. 1631 in Pt. v of Storia della Compagnia de Gesù.] Unpublished MS. cited by Palomba, D., p. 102.

SANTA MARIA, AGNELLO DI.—Trattato scientifico delle cause che concorsero al fuoco cd al terremoto del Monte Vesuuio vicino Napoli.—8⁰, *pp.* 100. *Napoli*, 1632.

SANTA MARIA, ANDREA. — Sonetti tre (1631).—*See* GIORGI URBANO.

SANTELET DE LAGRAVIÈRE, M.—Étude sur les pierres précieuses, suivie de l'éruption du Vésuve en 1872.—8⁰, *pp.* 74, 2 *maps. Avellino*, 1876. [C.A.]

SANTELIA, A.—Contentio inter Coridonem Partenopeum et Moeridem ex Septemtrione. An Vesuvius Neapolitanis deliciis obstet, an vero sit emolumento. Egloga.— MS. *fol., foll.* 4. *Circa* 1681. [C.A.]

SANTOLI, V. M.—De Mephiti et vallibus Auxanti, libri 3. Cum observationibus super nonnullis urbibus Hirpinorum, quorum lapides et antiquitatum reliquiæ illustr.—4⁰, *pp. viii*+99+1, 6 *pls. Neapoli*, 1783.

SANTOLI, V. M.—Narrazione de' fenomeni osservati nel suolo Irpino, contemporanei all' ultimo incendio del Vesuvio accaduto a Giugno di questo anno 1794.—*Giorn. Lett. xxx, pp.* 84–85. *Napoli*, 1794.—8⁰, *pp. vi*+160+43, 1 *pl. Napoli*, 1795.

SANTOLINI, G. M.—Egloga in lode di S. Gennaro difensore contro l'incendio Vesuviano.—*See* " Carmina Latina et Italica." —4⁰, *pp.* 55 *et seq. Napoli*, 1784. [O.V.]

SANTORELLI, A.—Discorsi della natura, accidenti e pronostici dell' incendio del Monte di Somma nell' anno 1631.—4⁰, *foll.* 2, *pp.* 58, *fol.* 1. *Napoli*, 1632. [C.A.]

SANTORELLI, F.—*See* BOSSIS.

SANZ Y MORENO, F.—Ampla, copiosa y verdadera relacion dell' incendio della Montaña de Soma o Vesubio, *etc.* — 4⁰, *foll.* 8, *pp.* 80. *Napoles*, 1632.—*See also* PALOMBA, D.

SARACINELLI, M.—Guerra della Montagna o sia eruzione del Vesuvio del dì 24 Agosto 1834.—*loose sheet, fol.* [C.A.]

SARNELLI, P.—La vera Guida de' Forestieri curiosi di vedere e d'intendere le cose più notabili della Real città di Napoli e del suo amenissimo distretto, *etc.*—12⁰, *pp.* 22+3+8, *num. pls. Napoli*, 1685.

Another ed. 12⁰, *foll.* 17+*pp.* 401+*foll.* 15, 51 *pls., frontisp.* 1692.

Contains on title-page the addition : " In questa nuova edizione da Antonio Bulifon di vaghissime figure abbellita, e dedicata all' Illustriss. e Reverendiss. Monsignor Francesco Maria Pignatello, Arcivescovo di Taranto, e Regio Consigliero. A spese di Antonio Bulifon."

See p. 378.

Another ed. 12⁰, *fol.* 1+*pp.* 302. 1752. (Separate vol. of pls.)

Has the addition : " con annotazioni di tutto il circuito del Regno, e numero delle città, terre, casali, e castelli d'esso, come pure de' Fiumi, e Laghi. Vescovati Regj, e Papalini : e il numero, e titoli de' Baroni di esso Regno : con una distinta descrizione di tutte l'eruzioni da volta in volta fatte dal Monte Vesuvio. . . . Questa nuova edizione viene ampliata con molte moderne fabriche secondo lo stato presente, ed arrichita con un altro tomo di Figure, per magior comodo de' diletanti, che si dà separato. A spese di Nicolò Petrini."

See p. 256.

Another ed. 12⁰, *fol.* 1+*pp.* 312, 11 *pls., frontisp.* 1772.

Is entitled : " Nuova Guida de' Forestieri, e dell' Istoria di Napoli, con cui si vede, e si spiegano le cose più notabil della medesima, e del suo amenissimo distretto ; con annotazioni di tutto il circuito del Regno, etc. [as in the 1752 edit.]. In questa nuova edizione ampliata delle molte moderne fabbriche secondo lo stato presente, ed arricchita di varie figure. A spese di Saverio Rossi."

See p. 262.

Another ed. 12⁰, *pp.* viii+364, 12 *pls., frontisp.* 1788.

Is entitled : " Guida de' Forestieri per la città di Napoli. In cui si contengono tutte le notizie topografiche della città, e degli Edificj sacri, e pubblici da' tempi antichi infino al dì di oggi, per istruire brevemente l'umano, e prestante leggitore. Nuovamente spurgata dalle suiste, ed accresciuta di quanto si osserva in sì famosa città. A spese del Librajo Nunzio Rossi." (Anon., attributable to Sarnelli.)

Another ed. 12⁰, *fol.* 1+*pp.* 394, 10 *pls., figs.* 1791. [O.V.]

SARNELLI, P.—Gvida de' Forestieri, curiosi di vedere, e considerare le cose notabili di Pozzoli, Baja, Miseno, Cuma, ed altri luoghi convicini. Ritrovata colla lettura de' buoni Scrittori, e colla propria diligenza dall' Abate. . . .—Nova edit. 12⁰, *foll.* 10+*pp.* 160+*foll.* 4, 13 *pls., frontisp. In Napoli, a spese di Antonio Bulifon.* 1688.

Another ed. 12⁰, *foll.* 5+*pp.* 305+*foll.* 6, 32 *pls.*, 2 *frontisp.* 1697.

This ed. is in Italian and French, the title-page having the addition : " Tradotta in Francese, accresciuta, e di vaghe figure abbellita da Antonio Bulifon, giontovi ancora li Bagni d'Ischia. Dedicata all' Illustrissimo Signor D. Giacomo Farelli Cavalier Gerosolimitano. Per Giuseppe Roselli."

Another ed. 12⁰, *foll.* 4+*pp.* 368+*foll.* 7, 34 *pls., frontisp.* 1702.

Also in Italian and French, but whereas edit. of 1697 had first title-page in Italian and second in French, this edit. has both in French, the first bearing the dedication to Victor Marie Comte d'Estrées by the translator (Antoine Bulifon), the second the addition : " Traduite en François par Antoine Bulifon, qui l'a enrichie de plusieurs figures en taille douce, et augmentée de quelques particularitez très-curieuses, et de la Description des Bains, et Étuves de l'Isle d'Ischia très-salutaires pour la guérison de diverses maladies." This ed. contains J. C. Capaccio's " Description des Vertus, et Proprietez des Bains d'Ischia " [French transl. by A. Bulifon] (pp. 313-45), and also " Brieve Descrittione delle cose più notabili della città di Gaeta cavata da quella di D. Pietro Rossetto " (pp. 346-68).

Another ed. 12⁰, *foll.* 7, *pp.* 192 (*pp.* 1-192 *in double*), 32 *pls., frontisp.* 1709.

Also in Italian and French, 2 title-pages, bearing the addition " Ed in quest' impressione data in luce da Michele-Luigi Muzio, arricchita di molte figure in Rame, ed accresciuta di alcune curiosissime particolarità, con la Descrizione de' Bagni, e Stufe dell' Isola d'Ischia molto salutevoli per guarire d'ogni sorte d'Infermità. Dedicata all' Eccellentiss. Sig. D. Girolamo Capece. A spese di Michele-Luigi Muzio."

Another ed. in French, 12⁰, *pp.* x+324, 15 *pls.*, 1 *map.* 1769.

Is called the 4th ed.

Another ed. 12⁰, *foll.* 2+*pp.* 190+*fol.* 1, 23 *pls.* 1770.

In Italian only, and with the addition : " E arricchita da Antonio Bulifone di molte figure in Rame, ed accresciuta di alcune curiosissime particolarità, con la Descrizione de' Bagni, e Stufe dell' Isola d'Ischia molto salutevoli per guarire ogni sorte d'Infermità. A spese di Saverio Rossi." Is also called the 4th ed.

Another ed. 12⁰, *foll*. 2, *pp*. 190, *fol*. 1, 23 *pls*. 1782.

In Italian only, with the same addition as the 1770 edit., is : " A spese del Librajo Nunzio Rossi," and is called : " Nuova Guida . . . di Pozzuoli, Baja, Cuma, Misena, Gaeta, e dell' Isole adjacenti d'Ischia, Procida, Nisita, Capri, colline, terre, ville, e città, che sono intorno alle Riviere dell' uno, e l'altro lato di Napoli, detto Cratero."

Another ed. in Italian and French, 12⁰, *pp*. 12+324+*xxiii*, *pls*.   *Naples, Ant. Spano, Eritier di Xavier Rossi,* 1784.

Is called the 5th ed. and has the same addition as the 1770 and 1782 editions.

Another ed. 12⁰, *pp*. *xi*+215, 20 *pls*. 1789.

Is called : " Guida de' Forestieri per Pozzuoli, Baja, Cuma, e Miseno. Si dà conto preciso di molti Edifizj sacri, pubblici, e privati non meno Greci, che Romani. Si descrivono i Bagni, e le Terme che vi esistono, colle regole necessarie per usarle ne' disgraziati successi. Edizione novissima corretta con diligenza ed arricchita di molte Note. A Spese del Librajo Nunzio Rossi." All these ed., excepting those of 1688, in Italian, and 1769, in French, contain J. C. Capaccio's " Descrizione delle Virtù, e Proprietà de' Bagni d'Ischia," and all but the 1688, 1697 and 1789 have the " Brieve Descrittione delle cose più notabili della città di Gaeta cavata da quella di D. Pietro Rossetto."

SARNELLI, V.—La violenta eruzione del Vesuvio nel di 8 Maggio 1855.—*Terzine nel Poliorama Pittoresco, xvi,* 8. *Napoli,* 1855.

SASS, H.—A Journey to Rome and Naples, performed in 1817 ; *etc*.—8⁰, *pp*. 345. *London,* 1818.

SASSO, C. N.—Il Vesuvio, Ercolano e Pompei, con una pianta geometrica della città di Pompei e con l'indicazione di quanto ivi si è rinvenuto sino a tutto il 1855.—*Storia dei Monumenti di Napoli,* 8⁰, *Fasc.* 16, 17, 18, *pp*. 60, 1 *pl*. *Napoli,* 1857. [C.A.]

SASSO, G.—Cronaca dell' eruzione del Vesuvio, Aprile, 1906.—8⁰, *pp*. 41. *Portici,* 1906.

SASSONE, A. F.—Sonetto (1631).—*See* GIORGI URBANO. [C.A.]

S. A. T.—*See* TATA.—Relazione dell' ultima eruzione del Vesuvio, *etc*.

SAUSSURE, DE.—Copie d'une lettre de Mr. De Saussure à Sʳ W. Hamilton, a 17 Decᵐ, 1774.—MS. *fol., foll.* 107–28. [B.M. 19309 (viii).]

SAUSSURE, H. [L. F.] DE.—Promenade au Vésuve.—" *Journal de Genève,*" 7 *juillet* 1872.—" *Débats,*" 8 *août*.—" *La France.*" —" *Le Sémaphore,*" *etc*.

SAUSSURE, H. [L. F.] DE.—La dernière éruption du Vésuve en 1872.—*Actes Soc. Helvét. Sci. nat., Sess.* 55, *pp*. 196–220. *Fribourg,* 1873. — *C.R. Acad. Sci. lxxv, pp*. 151–54, 505. *Paris,* 1872.

SAUTELET DE LA GRAVIÈRE, E. M.— Étude sur les pierres précieuses suivie de l'éruption du Vésuve en 1872.—8⁰, *pp*. 74. *Avellino,* 1876.

SAVARESE.—Troncs d'arbres trouvés à Pompéi.—*Feuilleton de la Presse,* 19 *mai* 1860. [C.A.]

SAVARESE, A.—Lettera sui Vulcani al Sig. Gugl. Thomson.—*Giorn. Lett. xcvii, foll.* 12. *Napoli,* 1798. [O.V.]

SAVARESE, A.—Lettera seconda sui Vulcani.—*Giorn. Lett. xcvii, pp*. 195–226. *Napoli,* 1798. [O.V.]

SAVASTANO, G.—Tavola sinottica di osservazioni mediche relative alle acque termominerali Vesuviane Nunziante. — 8⁰. *Napoli,* 1832.

SAVONAROLA.—*See* LASOR A VAREA.

SAVVALLE.—Relazione del Mongibello e del Vesuvio.—*Targioni Tozzetti dei progressi delle Scienze in Toscana, ii, Pt.* 1, *p*. 338.

Thus quoted by Reuss.

SCACCHI, A.—Della periclasia, nuova specie di minerale del Monte Somma.—*Antologia di Sci. Nat. i, pp*. 274–83. *Napoli,* 1841.— *Mem. Min. pp*. 16. *Napoli,* 1841.—In French, transl. by Damour : *Ann. Mines, S.* 4, *iii, pp*. 369–84. *Paris,* 1843.

SCACCHI, A.—Memorie mineralogiche e geologiche.—8⁰, *pp*. 132, 1 *tav*. *Napoli,* 1841–43.

See pp. 22–32.

SCACCHI, A.—Esame cristallografico del Ferro Oligisto e del Ferro Ossidulato del Vesuvio.—8⁰, *pp*. 34, *figs*. *Napoli,* 1842.

SCACCHI, A.—Nota sulle forme cristalline della Sommite.—*Rend. R. Acc. Sci. i, pp*. 129–31. *Napoli,* 1842.

SCACCHI, A.—Notizie geologiche e conchiliologiche ricavate da una lettera del Dr. R. A. Philippi ad A. Scacchi.—*Rend. R. Acc. Sci. i, pp.* 86–90 (186–90). *Napoli,* 1842.

SCACCHI, A.—Lezioni di geologia : Vulcani di Roccamonfina, Campi ed Isole Flegree, M¹ᵉ Somma e Vesuvio.—8⁰, *pp.* 178. *Napoli,* 1843.
See pp. 155–74.

SCACCHI, A.—Osservazioni critiche sulla maniera come fu seppellita l'antica Pompei. Lettera al Cav. Avellino.—8⁰. *Napoli,* 1843.—*Bull. Archeol. Nap. i,* 6, *pp.* 41–45. *Napoli,* 1843. [C.A.]

SCACCHI, A.—Voltaïte und Periklas, zwei neue Mineralien ; mit Bemerkungen von Kobell.—*Gel. Anz. xvi, coll.* 345–48. *München,* 1843.—*Journ. f. prakt. Chem. xxviii, pp.* 486–89. *Leipzig,* 1843.

SCACCHI, A.—Notizie geologiche dei Vulcani della Campania estratte dalle Lezioni di Geologia.—8⁰. *Napoli,* 1844.
See pp. 135–56.

SCACCHI, A.—Campi ed Isole Flegree, Vesuvio. Specie orittognostiche del Vesuvio e del Monte Somma.—*See :* Napoli e i luoghi celebri delle sue vicinanze, *ii, pp.* 361–413. *Napoli,* 1845.

SCACCHI, A.—Sopra una straordinaria eruzione di cristalli di Leucite. *etc.—Racc. Lett. etc. i, pp.* 185–89. *Roma,* 1845.—*Ann. Civ. Reg. Due Sicilie, xliv,* 87, *pp.* 62–66. *Napoli,* 1847.

SCACCHI, A.—Osservazioni intorno alla natura de' conglomerati nella valle del Grande.—*Atti Sett. Adun. Scienz. Ital. p.* 1141. *Napoli,* 1846.

SCACCHI, A.—I Vulcani. Notizie sull' ultima eruzione del Vesuvio.—*Il Propagatore delle Scienze Naturali, i, pp.* 150–52, 175–76, 182–84. *Napoli,* 1846.

SCACCHI, A.—Istoria delle eruzioni del Vesuvio accompagnata dalla bibliografia delle opere scritte su questo vulcano.—*Il Pontano, i, pp.* 16–21, 106–31. *Napoli,* 1847.
—*See also* ROTH, J. L. A.—Der Vesuv u. die Umgebung von Neapel. 1857.

SCACCHI, A.—Notice sur le gisement et sur la cristallisation de la Sodalite des environs de Naples. (Transl. by Damour.)—*Ann. Mines, S.* 4, *xii, pp.* 385–89, *figs.* 11–14 *of Pl.* 3. *Paris,* 1847.

SCACCHI, A.—Notizie su l'ultima eruzione del Vesuvio, composizione della lave, delle cenere, de' lapilli, emanazioni gassose, *etc.* —*Il Propagatore delle Scienze Naturali, pp. viii*+416, 4 *pls. Napoli,* 1847.
See pp. 150–84.

SCACCHI, A.—Memorie geologiche sulla Campania e relazione dell' incendio accaduto nel Vesuvio nel mese di Febbrajo del 1850.—4⁰, *pp.* 131, 4 *pls. Napoli,* 1849.—*Rend. R. Acc. Sci. viii, pp.* 41–65, 1849 ; *ix, pp.* 84–114, 1 *pl., Napoli,* 1850.

SCACCHI, A.—Relazione dell' incendio accaduto nel Vesuvio nel mese di Febbraio del 1850, seguita dai giornalieri cambiamenti osservati in questo vulcano dal 1840 sin ora.—*Rend. R. Acc. Sci. ix, pp.* 13–48, 3 *pls. Napoli,* 1850.—*Ann. Mines, S.* 4, *xvii, pp.* 323–80, *Pl.* IV, 6 *figs. Paris,* 1850.

SCACCHI, A.—Della Humite e del Peridoto del Vesuvio (1850).—*Atti R. Acc. Sci., Mem. Class. Sci. Nat. vi, pp.* 241–73. *Napoli,* 1852.—*Journ. f. prakt. Chem. liii, pp.* 156–60. *Leipzig,* 1851.—*Ann. Phys. Chem. Erg.-Bd. iii, pp.* 161–87, 1 *pl. Leipzig,* 1853.—*Amer. Journ. Sci. S.* 2, *xiv, pp.* 175–82. *New Haven,* 1852.

SCACCHI, A.—Sopra le specie di Silicati del Monte di Somma e del Vesuvio le quali in taluni casi sono state prodotte per effetto di sublimazioni.—*Rend. R. Acc. Sci. N.S. i, pp.* 104–12. *Napoli,* 1852.—German transl. in ROTH : Der Vesuv und die Umgebung von Neapel.

SCACCHI, A.—Notiz über den Sommit (Nephelin), Mizzonit und Mejonit. (Transl.) —*Ann. Phys. Chem. Erg.-Bd. iii, pp.* 478–79, *figs.* 16–18 *of Pl.* 2. *Leipzig,* 1853.— *N. J. f. Min. pp.* 61–62. *Stuttgart,* 1853.

SCACCHI, A.—Uebersicht der Mineralien, welche unter den unbezweifelten Auswürflingen des Vesuvs und des Monte di Somma bis jetzt mit Bestimmtheit erkannt worden sind.—*N. J. f. Min. pp.* 257–63. *Stuttgart,* 1853.

SCACCHI, A.—*See* GUARINI, G.—Memoria sull' incendio del Vesuvio. 1855.

SCACCHI, A.—[Sur la Cotunnite du Vésuve.] (Extract of a letter, communicated by C. J. Sᵗᵉ Claire Deville.)—*Bull. Soc. géol. France, S.* 2, *xv, pp.* 376–77. *Paris,* 1858. —*C.R. Acad. Sci. xlvi, pp.* 496–97. *Paris,* 1858.

SCACCHI, A.—*See* PALMIERI, L., ET ALII. 1859.

SCACCHI, A.—Note mineralogiche. Memoria Prima. Cristalli geminati di Ortosa del Monte Somma. Leucite del Monte Somma metamorfizzata, *etc.* Nuove specie di Solfati di Rame. (Dolerfano, Aftalosa, o Solfato Potassico, Cottunnia o Cloruro di Piombo.)—*Atti R. Acc. Sci. v,* 3, *pp.* 39, 1 *pl. Napoli,* 1873.—*Id. Rend. ix, pp.* 43-53. 1870.

SCACCHI, A.—Dell' Eriocalco e del Melanotallo, nuove specie di minerali del Vesuvio. —*Rend. R. Acc. Sci. ix, pp.* 86-89. *Napoli,* 1870.

SCACCHI, A.—Sulla origine della cenere vulcanica.—*Rend. R. Acc. Sci. xi, pp.* 180-91. *Napoli,* 1872.

SCACCHI, A.—Durch sublimationen entstandene Mineralien bei dem Vesuvausbruch im April 1872. [Transl. by J. Roth.] —*Zeitschr. deutsch. geol. Gesellsch. xxiv, pp.* 493-504. *Berlin,* 1872.—*Zeitschr. gesammt. Naturwiss. xl, pp.* 530-32. *Halle,* 1872.

SCACCHI, A.—Vorläufige Notizen über die bei dem Vesuvausbruch, April 1872, gefundenen Mineralien. [Extr. transl. by J. Roth.]—*Zeitschr. deutsch. geol. Gesellsch. xxiv, pp.* 505-6. *Berlin,* 1872.

SCACCHI. A.—Ueber den Ursprung der vulkanischen Asche. [Extr. transl. by C. Rammelsberg.] — *Zeitschr. deutsch. geol. Gesellsch. xxiv, pp.* 545-48. *Berlin,* 1872.

SCACCHI, A.—Contribuzioni mineralogiche per servire alla storia dell' incendio Vesuviano nel mese di Aprile 1872. Parte Ia : —*Rend. R. Acc. Sci. xi, pp.* 203-4. *Napoli,* 1872. — *Id. Atti, v,* 22, *pp.* 35, 1 *tav. lith. Napoli,* 1873. Parte IIa :—*Atti R. Acc. Sci. vi,* 9, *pp.* 69. *Napoli,* 1875.—*Id. Rend. xii, pp.* 164-68. 1873 ; Appendice, *Id. xiii, pp.* 179-80, 1874 ; Seconda Appendice, *Id. xiv, pp.* 77-79, 1875.

SCACCHI, A.—Notizie preliminari di alcune specie mineralogiche rinvenute nel Vesuvio dopo l'incendio di Aprile 1872.—*Rend. R. Acc. Sci. xi, pp.* 210-13. *Napoli,* 1872.— *Ann. R. Oss. Meteor. Vesuv. i, pp.* 122-28.— *Zeitschr. deutsch. geol. Gesellsch. xxiv, pp.* 505-6. *Berlin,* 1872.—*Also in* : PALMIERI, L.—Cronaca Vesuviana, *pp.* 122-28. 1874.

SCACCHI, A.—Leucite del Monte Somma metamorfizzata in baritina (1870). — *Atti R. Acc. Sci. v,* 3, *pp.* 14-17. *Napoli,* 1873.

SCACCHI, A.—Cotunnia o Clorurodi Piombo (1870).—*Atti R. Acc. Sci. v,* 3, *pp.* 37-39. *Napoli,* 1873.

SCACCHI, A. — [Humitkrystalle des III. Typus, regelmässig mit Olivin verwachsen. Ueber die Verwachsung des Eisenglanz mit Magneteisen.]—*N. J. f. Min. pp.* 637-40. *Stuttgart,* 1876.

SCACCHI, A.—Microsommite del Monte Somma.—*Rend. R. Acc. Sci. xv, pp.* 67-69, 1 *fig. Napoli,* 1876.

SCACCHI, A.—Della Cuspidina e del Neocrisolito, nuovi minerali Vesuviani.—*Rend. R. Acc. Sci. xv, pp.* 208-9. *Napoli,* 1876. · —*Zeitschr. f. Kryst. u. Min. i, pp.* 398-99, 2 *figs. Leipzig,* 1877.

SCACCHI, A.—Sulla regolare scambievole posizione dei cristalli di Olivina cóngiunti a quelli di Humite e dei cristalli di Oligisto congiunti a quelli di Magnetite. Lettera al Prof. vom Rath (versione tedesca).—*N. J. f. Min. pp.* 637-40, 3 *figs. Stuttgart,* 1876.

SCACCHI, A.—Dell' Anglesite rinvenuta sulle lave Vesuviane.—*Rend. R. Acc. Sci. xvi, pp.* 226-30. *Napoli,* 1877.

SCACCHI, A.—Sopra un masso di pomici saldate per fusione trovato in Pompei.— *Atti R. Acc. Archeol. viii, Pt.2, pp.* 199-207, 1 *pl. Napoli,* 1877.

SCACCHI, A.—*See* RUGGIERO, M. 1877.

SCACCHI, A.—Le case fulminate di Pompei. —*Pompei e la Regione sotterata dal Vesuvio nell' anno* LXXIX, *fol., pp.* 117-29, 3 *col. pls. Napoli,* 1879. [C.A.]

SCACCHI, A.—Ricerche chimiche sulle incrostazioni gialle della lava Vesuviana del 1631. Memoria prima.—*Atti R. Acc. Sci. viii,* 10, *pp.* 15. *Napoli,* 1879.—*Id. Rend. xviii, pp.* 296-98. 1879.—*Gazz. Chim. Ital. x, pp.* 21-37. *Palermo,* 1880.

SCACCHI, A.—Le incrostazioni gialle della lava Vesuviana del 1631. Risposta del socio A. Scacchi alla domanda rivoltagli dal Collega A. Costa.—*Rend. R. Acc. Sci. xix, pp.* 40-41. *Napoli,* 1880.

SCACCHI, A.—Sulle incrostazioni gialle della lave Vesuviana del 1631.—*Atti R. Acc. Lincei, S.* 3, *Trans. iv, pp.* 150-51. *Roma,* 1880.

SCACCHI, A.—Lapilli azzurri del Vesuvio. —*Rend. R. Acc. Sci. xix, pp.* 175-79. *Napoli,* 1880.

SCACCHI, A.—Nuovi sublimati del cratere Vesuviano trovati nel mese di Ottobre del 1880. Memoria. [1880.]—*Atti R. Acc. Sci. ix,* 5, *pp.* 10, 2 *figs. Napoli,* 1882.—*Id. Rend. xx, pp.* 11-14. 1881.

SCACCHI, A.—Della silice rinvenuta nel cratere Vesuviano nel mese di Aprile del 1882.—*Rend. R. Acc. Sci. xxi, pp.* 176–82. *Napoli,* 1882.

SCACCHI, A.—Breve notizia dei Vulcani Fuoriferi della Campania.— *Rend. R. Acc. Sci. xxi, pp.* 201–4. *Napoli,* 1882.

SCACCHI, A.—Della lava Vesuviana dell' anno 1631. Memoria prima.—*Mem. Mat. Fis. Soc. Ital. Sci. (detta dei* XL), *S.* 3, *iv,* 8, *pp.* 34+*xi,* 2' *pls. Napoli,* 1882.—*Roma,* 1882.—*Napoli,* 1883.

SCACCHI, A., e SCACCHI, E.—Sopra un frammento di antica roccia vulcanica inviluppato nella lava Vesuviana del 1872. Memoria.—*Rend. R. Acc. Sci. xxii, pp.* 281–83. *Napoli,* 1883.

SCACCHI, A.—La regione Vulcanica Fluorifera della Campania.—*Rend. R. Acc. Sci. xxiv, pp.* 155–61. *Napoli,* 1885.—Seconda appendice, *S.* 2, *ii, pp.* 130–33. 1888.— *Id. Atti, S.* 2, *ii,* 2, *pp.* 108, 3 *figs. Napoli,* 1888.——2a ed. 4⁰, *pp.* 48+1, 1 *col. map,* 3 *lithos. Firenze,* 1890. [Extr. fr. *Mem. p. serv. descriz. carta geol. Ital. pubbl. R. Com. Geol. Ital. iv, Pt.* 1, *pp.* 48+1. *Firenze,* 1891.]

SCACCHI, A.—Le eruzioni polverose e filamentose dei Vulcani.—*Atti R. Acc. Sci. S.* 2, *ii,* 10, *pp.* 7. *Napoli,* 1888.—*Id. Rend. xxv, p.* 258. 1886.

SCACCHI, A.—Catalogo dei minerali Vesuviani con la notizia della loro composizione e del loro giacimento.—*Lo Spettatore del Vesuvio e dei Campi Flegrei, N.S.* 1, *pp.* 13. *Napoli,* 1887.

SCACCHI, A.—Katalog der Vesuvischen Mineralien mit Angabe ihrer Zusammensetzung und ihres Vorkommens.—*N. J. f. Min. ii, pp.* 123–41. *Stuttgart,* 1888.—*Riv. Min. e Crist. Ital. iii, pp.* 58–73. *Padova,* 1888.

SCACCHI, A.—Sopra un frammento di antica roccia vulcanica inviluppato nella lava Vesuviana del 1872.—*Atti R. Acc. Sci. S.* 2, *i,* 5, *pp.* 19, 1 *pl.* (by E. Scacchi). *Napoli,* 1888.

SCACCHI, A.—Catalogo dei Minerali e delle Rocce Vesuviane per servire alla storia del Vesuvio ed al commercio dei suoi prodotti. —*Atti R. Ist. Incorag. S.* 4, *i,* 5, *pp.* 57, 4 *pls. Napoli,* 1888.—*Riv. Min. e Crist. Ital. v, pp.* 34–87, 4 *pls. Padova,* 1889.

SCACCHI, A.—I projetti agglutinanti dell' incendio Vesuviano del 1631.—*Rend. R. Acc. Sci. S.* 2, *iii, pp.* 220–25. *Napoli,* 1889.

SCACCHI, A.—Appendice alla prima memoria sulla lava Vesuviana del 1631.—*Mem. Mat. Fis. Soc. Ital. Sci. (detta* XL), *S.* 3, *vii,* 7, *pp.* 26, 1 *pl. Napoli,* 1890.

SCACCHI, E.—Lapilli azzurri del Vesuvio.— *Rend. R. Acc. Sci. xix, pp.* 175–79. *Napoli,* 1880.

SCACCHI, E.—Notizie cristallografiche sulla Humite del M. Somma.—*Rend. R. Acc. Sci. xxii, pp.* 303–9. *Napoli,* 1883.

SCACCHI, E.—*See* SCACCHI, A. 1883.

SCACCHI, E.—Contribuzioni mineralogiche. (1. Idrogiobertite. 2. Aragonite metamorfizzata. 3. Fluorite di una lava Vesuviana. 4. Leucite metamorfizzata in ortoclasia vitrea.)—*Rend. R. Acc. Sci. xxiv, pp.* 310–18. *Napoli,* 1885.

SCACCHI, E. — Contribuzioni mineralogiche. Memoria terza.—*Rend. R. Acc. Sci. S.* 2, *i, pp.* 50–54. *Napoli,* 1887.

SCACCHI, E.—Contribuzioni mineralogiche. No. 1. Facellite, nuovo minerale del Monte Somma. No. 2. Carbonato Sodico della lava Vesuviana del 1859. No. 3. Zeolite alterata dei conglomerati del M. Somma.— *Rend. R. Acc. Sci. S.* 2, *ii,* 12, *pp.* 486–94. *Napoli,* 1888.

SCAFA, F. (publ.).—Veduta della stessa 23ᵃ eruzione del 1751.

SCAFA, F. (publ.). — Veduta della 28ᵃ eruzione accaduta li 19 Ottobre del 1767. Vue de la 28ᵃ éruption arrivée le 19 Octobre en 1767., T. x. In Napoli presso Franc. Scafa. Str. S. Biagio de' Librari. N° 117.

Engrav. : 253×198 mm.

SCAFA, F. (publ.).—Pianta della Torre del Greco distrutta dall' eruzione del 1794. Scala di palmi 5000 Napolitani. Plan de la Tour du Grec qui fut détruite par l'érupⁿ du 1794. T. XX. In Napoli presso Frances Scafa. Str. S. Biagio de' Librari. N° 117.

Engrav. : 187×184 mm.

SCAFA, F.—Vedute del Monte Vesuvio sino al 1822.—*fol. Napoli,* — ?
Album of 29 pls.

SCARPA, O.—Sulla radioattività delle lave del Vesuvio.—*Atti R. Acc. Lincei, S.* 5, *Rend. xvi, sem.* 1, *pp.* 44–51. *Roma,* 1907.

SCHAFHAEUTL, K. E. F. Von.—Ueber den gegenwärtigen Zustand des Vesuv und sein Verhältniss zu den Phlegräischen Gefilden. —*Gel. Anz. xx, coll.* 247–54, 257–67. *München*, 1845.—*Bull. k. Akad. Wiss. coll.* 87–94, 97–107. *München*, 1845.

SCHIAVONI, F.—Osservazioni geodetiche sul Vesuvio.—*Rend. Acc. Pontaniana, iii, pp.* 22–27, 1 *tav.*, 1855 ; *vi, pp.* 114–18, 1 *lith.*, 1858; *xvi,pp.* 29–34, 1 *lith.*, *Napoli*, 1868.—*Ann. Scient. ii,pp.* 418–22. *Napoli*, 1855.—8⁰, *pp.* 6, *pls. Naples*, 1872. [Extr. of :] " Per la solenne commemorazione in Bassano del primo centenario dell' insign. naturalista G. Brocchi, offerta dall' Accademia Pontaniana."—4⁰, *pp.* 107–11, 1 *lith.*

SCHIAVONI, F. — *See* PALMIERI, L. (relatore). 1862.

SCHILBACH, A.—Ein unerwarteter Ausbruch des Vesuvs.—*Ueber Land u. Meer, xxxi*, 41, *illustr. Stuttgart*, 1891.

SCHINDLER,J. (del.).—Neapel.S. Langer sc. Small steel engrav. of Vesuvius and Naples from Posilippo : 74×56 mm.

SCHINNERER, L.—*See* MORAWSKI, T.

SCHIRLITZ, [L.] P.—*See* WALTHER, J. 1886.

SCHMIDT, J. F. J.—Die Eruption des Vesuv im Mai 1855 nebst Beiträgen zur Topographie des Vesuv, der Phlegräischen Crater, Roccamonfina's und der alten Vulkane im Kirkenstaate mit Benützung neuer Charten und eigener Hohenmessungen.—8⁰, *pp.* xii+212, 37 *figs. Wien u. Olmütz*, 1856.—*Peterm. Mitth. pp.* 125–35. *Gotha*, 1856.

SCHMIDT, J. F. J.—Die Eruption des Vesuv in ihren Phänomaenen im Maj 1855, nebst Ansichten und Profilen der Vulkane des Phlegräischen Gebietes, Roccamonfina's und des Albaner Gebirges. Nach der Natur aufgenommen und durch Winkelmessungen berichtigt.—*gd.* 4⁰, 9 *pls. Wien und Olmütz*, 1856. Album to foregoing.

SCHMIDT, J. F. J.—Neue Höhen-Bestimmungen am Vesuv, in den Phlegräischen Feldern, zu Roccamonfina und im Albaner-Gebirge.—4⁰, *pp.* 41. *Wien u. Olmütz*, 1856.

SCHMIDT, J. F. J.—Vulkanstudien. Santorin 1866–1872 ; Vesuv, Bajæ, Stromboli, Aetna, 1870.—8⁰, *foll.* 4, *pp.* 235, 1 *map*, 7 *col. pls.*, 13 *figs. Leipzig*, 1874.——2nd ed. 8⁰. 1881.

SCHMITT, G.—Ein Blick in den Krater des Vesuvs.—*Ueber Land u. Meer, lxxii, p.* 722, 1 *illustr. Stuttgart*, 1894.

SCHNEER, J., und STEIN-NORDHEIM, Von.—Der Vesuv und seine Geschichte von 79 n. Chr.—1894.——2nd ed. 8⁰, *pp.* 70, 15 *illustr. Karlsruhe*, 1895. — In English : [*Napoli*, 1895.]

SCHNEIDER, K.—Die vulkanischen Erscheinungen der Erde.—4⁰, *pp.* viii+272, 50 *figs.*, *maps. Berlin*, 1911.

SCHNETZER, C.—Sur l'éruption du Vésuve du 22 octobre 1822 (traduction).— *Bull. Sci. Nat. Géol. i, pp.* 115–16. *Paris*, 1824.

SCHOOK, M.—De Vesuvio ardente disputationes (1631).—*See* MORHOF. — Polyhistor, *etc.* [C.A.]

SCHOTTI, Andreas. — *See* SCHOTTUS, Andreas.

SCHOTTUS, Andreas. — Itinerario ovvero nova descrittione de' viaggi principali d'Italia . . . di A. Scoto [or rather of F. Schottus].—8⁰. *Vincenza, Bolzetta*, 1622.—Another ed. 2 pts. 8⁰. *Padoa, Vicenza*, 1629, 28.

Has the addition : " Novamente tradotto del Latino . . . & accresciuto," etc. Another ed. 3 pts. in 1 vol. 8⁰. *Pt.* 1, 64 *pls. and frontisp.* ; *Pt.* 2, 43 *pls.* ; *Pt.* 3, 25 *pls.* (*pls.* by F. Bertelli). *Vicenza, Bolzetta*, 1638. [On engrav. title : " *Padova*, 1642."]

Another ed. 3 pts. in 2 vols. 8⁰. *Vol. i, Pt.* 1, *pp.* 10+20, *foll.* 165, 98 *pls.* ; *Vol. ii, Pt.* 2, *foll.* 115, 47 *pls.*, *Padova, Fr. Bolzetta*, MDCXLVIII ; *Vol. ii, Pt.* 3, *foll.* 83, 25 *pls.*, *Padova, Fr. Bolzetta*, M.DC.XLVII (*with error of pag.*).

Has the addition : " nella quale si ha piena notitia di tutte le cose più notabili, & degne d'esser vedute. Et aggiuntoui in quest' ultima impressione la Descrittion dell' Isole di Sicilia, & di Malta. [At begin. :] *Padova* appresso *Francesco Bolzetta* Libraro. M.DC.XXXXIX. [At end :] *Padova*, nella Stamparia del Crivellari, 1648."

Another ed. Itinerarum Italiæ.—12⁰, *pp.* 606+11, 19 *pls. Amstelodami*, 1655. *See pp.* 529–70.

SCHOTTUS, Franciscus.—Itinerario ovvero nova descrittione de' viaggi principali d'Italia . . . di A. Scoto [or rather of F. Schottus].—*See* SCHOTTUS, Andreas.

Another ed. " Corretta, . . . abbellita, . . . & accresciuta della quarta parte."— 8⁰. *Roma*, 1650.

Another ed. 3 pts. 8⁰. *Padova*, 1654.

Another ed. 8⁰. *Padova*, 1659.

Another ed. 12⁰. *Venetia*, 1665.

Another ed. 8⁰, *maps and pls. Padova, Bolzetta,* 1669.

Another ed. 8⁰. *Cadorin, Padova,* 1670.

Another ed. 8⁰. *Padova,* 1688.

Another ed. 12⁰. *Roma,* 1717.

Another ed. 12⁰. *Roma,* 1737.

Another ed. — Itinerario d'Italia. In questa nuova Edizione abbellito di rami, accresciuto, ordinato, ed emendato, ove si descrivono tutte le principali città d'Italia, e luoghi celebri, con le loro origini, antichità, e monumenti singolari, che nelle medesime si ammirano.—3 pts. in 1 vol. 8⁰, *foll. 4, pp. 479, foll. 8, 1 map, 25 pls., frontisp. Roma, a spese di Fausto Amidei Mercante di Libri al Corso. Nella Stamperia del Bernabo, e Lazzarini,* MDCCXLVII.
See pp. 444-48, pl. of Pozzuoli and of Cuma.

Another ed. *Roma,* 1761.

SCHOTTUS, F.—Visite de Pighius (Étienne) au Vésuve vers 1575.—*See his:* Itin. Italiæ.—8⁰, *pp.* 222-25. *Vicentiæ,* 1601.

SCHRAMM, DR. R.—Italienische Skizzen.— 8⁰. *Leipzig,* 1890.
See pp. 230-53, 261-76.

SCHROEDER, R.—*See* GOLDSCHMIDT, V.

SCHWAHN, P.—Der Vesuvausbruch, 1906. —18 *figs. Berlin,* 1906.

SCLOPIS, I.—Prospetto Generale della città di Napoli dedicato a Sua Ecc^za Georgiana, Vicecontessa Spencer.—*Two panorama in 6 sheets, engraved.* [Collect. of Mr Tell Meuricoffre of Naples.]
Eruption 1760.

SCLOPIS, I.—Veduta di Napoli dalla parte di Chiaja dedicata a Sua Ecc^za Georgiana Vicecontessa Spencer. Napoli, 25 Genn. 1764. Dal suo Umil^mo serv. Ignazio Scolpis, Conte del Borgo.
Panoramic engrav. in 3 sections showing W. end of Naples and Vesuvius : 1950× 420 mm.

SCLOPIS, I.—Veduta di Napoli dalla parte di Chiaja.—*Napoli,* Genn. 1764. [B.M. 24045. 16.]
A very fine panoramic view with ref. nos.

SCORIGGIO, L.—L'incendio del Monte Vesuvio, rappresentazione spirituale, composta da un devoto saccerdote e data in luce da Lazaro Scoriggio.—12⁰, *pp.* 185. *Napoli,* 1632. [C.A.]

SCOTO, A.—*See* SCHOTTUS, ANDREAS.

SCOTO, F.—*See* SCHOTTUS, FRANCESCUS.

SCOTTI, E.—Ragionamento della eruzione del Vesuvio accaduta il dì 15 Giugno 1794. —*Gazz. (Suppl.) Nap. Civ.-Comm. pp.* 48. *Napoli,* 1794.—*See also his :* Elementi di Fisica, 1831.

SCOTTI, E.—Lettera a Dom. Cotugno sulla eruzione del Vesuvio del 1804.—*Gazz. (Suppl.) Nap. Civ.-Comm. N.* 70. *Napoli,* 4 *settembre,* 1804.

SCOTTI, E.—Del tremuoto e dell' eruzioni vulcaniche.—*Extr. of foregoing,* 8⁰, *foll.* 17. *Napoli,* 1805.

SCOTTO, F.—*See* SCHOTTUS, FRANCESCUS.

SCOTTO DI PAGLIARA.—*See* ALFANI, P. G.

SCROPE, G. J. POULETT.—An account of the eruption of Vesuvius in October 1822.— *Quart. Journ. Lit. Sci. and Arts, xv, pp.* 175-83, 1 *tav. London,* 1823.

SCROPE, G. J. POULETT.—Considerations on Volcanos, the probable causes of their phenomena . . . and their connection with the present state and past history of the globe ; leading to the establishment of a new Theory of the earth.—8⁰, *pp. xxxi+* 270, 2 *pls.,* 1 *map. London,* 1825.——2nd ed. entitled : Volcanos : the character of their phenomena. . . . With a descriptive Catalogue of all known Volcanos, *etc.* 8⁰, *pp. xi+*490, 1 *pl.,* 1 *col. map. London,* 1862. —Another copy, 1872. [Reviewed in :] *Amer. Journ. Sci. xiii, pp.* 108-45. *New Haven,* 1828.—In French (transl. by Endymion) : 2 *col. pls. Paris,* 1864.—In Germ. (transl. by G. A. v. Klöden) : 1 *pl.,* 65 *figs. Berlin,* 1872.—[Extr. in Ital. :] *Bibl. Ital. xlv, pp.* 70-83, 211-26. *Milano,* 1827.

SCROPE, G. J. POULETT.—On the volcanic district of Naples (1827).—*Proc. Geol. Soc. i, pp.* 17-19. *London,* 1834.—*Trans. Geol. Soc. ii, pp.* 337-52, 1 *pl. London,* 1829.— *Bull. Sci. nat. xiv, pp.* 412-14. *Paris,* 1828.

SCROPE, G. J. POULETT.—On the mode of production of Volcanic Craters, and on the nature of the liquidity of Lavas (1856).— *London, Edinb. and Dublin Phil. Mag. and Journ. Sci. S.* 4, *xi, pp.* 477-79. 1856.— *Quart. Journ. Geol. Soc. xii, pp.* 326-50. *London,* 1856.

SCROPE, G. J. POULETT.—On the mode of formation of Volcanic Cones and Craters.— *Quart. Journ. Geol. Soc. xv, pp.* 505–49. *London,* 1859.—[Sep. publ.] 8⁰, *pp.* 45. *London,* 1859.—In French, transl. by Pieraggi: 8⁰, *tav. Paris,* 1860.—In German, transl. by C. L. Griesbach. *Berlin,* 1873. *See* pp. 541–44 with 4 illustr., 1859.

SCROPE, G. J. POULETT.—On the supposed internal fluidity of the Earth. (Second notice.)—*Geol. Mag. pp.* 145–47. *London,* 1869.

SCROPE, G. J. POULETT.—Notes on the late eruption of Vesuvius (Apr.–May, 1872).— *Geol. Mag. pp.* 244–47. 1872.

SEEBACH, C. A. L. VON.—Vorläufige Mittheilung über die typischen Verschiedenheiten im Bau der Vulkane und über deren Ursache.—*Zeitschr. deutsch. geol. Gesellsch. xviii, pp.* 643–47. *Berlin,* 1866.

SEGONIUS.—De Regno. Ital. *See* Lib. II.

SEGONIUS.—De Imp. Occident. *See* Lib. XIV and XVI.

SEMENTINI, L., GUARINI, G.—Saggi analitici su talune sostanze Vesuviane. [1834.]—*Atti R. Acc. Sci. v,* Pte. 2, *pp.* 165–68. *Napoli,* 1844.

SEMMOLA, E.—La cattedra di fisica terrestre dell' Univ. di Napoli, la specola meteorologica della stessa Univ., il R. Osservatorio Vesuviano.—*pp.* 4. 1860.

SEMMOLA, E.—Sulle emanazioni aeriformi delle fumarole collocate a diversa distanza dall' attuale bocca d'eruzione del Vesuvio. —*Rend. R. Acc. Sci. xvii, pp.* 125–26. *Napoli, Agosto e Settembre,* 1878.

SEMMOLA, E.—Sulle presenti condizioni del Vesuvio. Relazione al Sig. Diret. dell' Osserv. Vesuviano, Prof. Palmieri.—*Rend. R. Acc. Sci. xviii, pp.* 109–10. *Napoli,* 1879.—*Boll. R. Com. Geol. Ital. x, pp.* 181–82. *Roma,* 1879.—*Riv. Scient. Ind.* 10. *Firenze,* 1879.—In French: *C.R. Acad. Sci. lxxxviii, pp.* 860–61. *Paris,* 1879.

SEMMOLA, E.—Relazione sulle condizioni del Vesuvio a dì 11 Génnaio (e a dì 24 Febbraio) 1882.—*Bull. Vulc. Ital. ix, pp.* 135–39. *Roma,* 1882.

SEMMOLA, E.—Le altezze barometriche a Napoli e all' Osservatorio del Vesuvio.— *Ann. Meteor. Ital. vi, pp.* 190–91. *Torino,* 1891.

SEMMOLA, E.—Le fiamme nel cratere del Vesuvio in Aprile 1898.—*Rend. R. Acc. Sci. S.* 3, *iv, pp.* 215–19. *Napoli,* 1898.

SEMMOLA, E.—La pioggia ed il Vesuvio nel Maggio 1900.—*Rend. R. Acc. Sci. S.* 3, *vi, pp.* 232–36, *Napoli,* 1900 ; *vii, pp.* 122–25, 1901.— *Boll. Soc. Sismol. Ital. vii,* 4, *pp.* 139–50. *Modena,* 1901.

SEMMOLA, E.—Quando ebbe fine la fase esplosiva del Vesuvio nel Maggio 1900 ?— 8⁰, *pp.* 10, 2 *figs.,* 1 *pl. Napoli,* 1901.

SEMMOLA, E.—Il nuovo cono eruttivo Vesuviano nell' Aprile 1901.—*Rend. R. Acc. Sci. S.* 3, *vii, pp.* 143–44. *Napoli,* 1901.

SEMMOLA, E.—Il Vesuvio nel Maggio 1900. —*Rend. R. Acc. Sci. S.* 3, *vii, pp.* 222–27. *Napoli,* 1901.

SEMMOLA, F.—Relazione ragionata dell' analisi chimica delle ceneri Vesuviane eruttate nell' ultima deflagrazione de' 16, 17 e 18 Giugno dell' anno 1794. — 4⁰, *pp.* 15. [*Napoli,* 1794.]

SEMMOLA, G.—Du Cuivre oxidé natif (Ténorite).—*Bull. Soc. géol. France, xiii, pp.* 206–11. *Paris,* 1841–42.

SEMMOLA, G.—Del Rame ossidato nativo, nuova specie minerale del Vesuvio (Tenorite).—"*Opere Minore,*" 8⁰, foll. 2, *pp.* 42–491. *Napoli,* 1845.

SEMMOLA, M.—Analisi chimica delle acque potabili dei dintorni del Vesuvio e del Somma.—*Il Giambattista Vico, i,* 3, *pp.* 413–28. *Napoli,* 1857.

SEMMOLA, V.—Delle varietà de' Vitigni del Vesuvio e del Somma. Ricerche ed annotazioni nelle quali si ragiona de' terreni, della coltivazione della vite, e dell' enologia Vesuviana.— 4⁰, *pp.* viii+136. *Napoli,* 1848.—*Atti R. Ist. Incorag. viii, pp.* 1–134. *Napoli,* 1855.

SEMPLE, R.—Observations on a journey through Spain and Italy to Naples ; and thence to Smyrna and Constantinople, *etc.*—2 vols. 12⁰. *London,* 1807. *See* Vol. ii.

SENAPE, A.—Panorama di Napoli preso dal Casino Ruffo al Vomero.
Pen-and-two-ink sketch, *circa* 1858, in 4 sections, mounted on linen : 1195 × 173 mm.

SENAPE, A.—Panorama di Napoli presa dalla Strada Nuova di Posilipo.
View of Naples, Vesuvius and peninsula of Sorrento, *circa* 1858. Pen-and-two-ink sketch : 1337 × 236 mm.

SENAPE, A. (Romano).—Dis^{ne} di Paesi con la penna da Lezione nel' istesso genere. Abita Gradoni di Chiaja. No. 59, 2° piano. Napoli.

28 pen-and-ink sketches of Naples and vicinity, obl. fol. *See* Nos. 2, 6, 10, 13 and 14.

SENEBIER, J.—Réflexions générales sur les Volcans pour servir d'introduction aux Voyages volcaniques de M. L'Abbé Spallanzani.—*See ed.* "Voyages," etc. *Berne*, 1795.

[SERAO, FRANCESCO.]—Istoria dell' incendio del Vesuvio accaduto nel mese di Maggio dell' Anno MDCCXXXVII. Scritta per l'Accademia delle Scienze.—4°, *foll. iv, pp.* 122, 2 *copper-pls.* [entitled] "Vesuvii prospectus ex ædibus regiis," and "Vesuvius a vertice dissectus." *Napoli, nella stamperia di Novello de Bonis*, MDCCXXXVIII.

Anon., but recognized as being that of Francesco Serao (Delle Torre writes it Serrao), prof. of medicine at the Univ. of Naples and medical officer to Her Majesty the Queen. Monticelli writes of him (Opere, vol. iii) : "Francesco Serao is without doubt the first writer who, in narrating the phenomena of the eruption of 1737, speaks, as far as those times permitted, in scientific language."

[SERAO, FRANCESCO.]—Neapolitanæ Scientiarum Academiæ de Vesuvii Conflagratione quæ mense Majo anno MDCCXXXVII accidit commentarius.—4°, *foll. iv, pp.* 118, 2 *pls.* [same as in Ital. ed.]. *Napoli, typis Novelli de Bonis*, MDCCXXXVIII.

Latin ed., likewise anonymous.

Another ed. 4°, *pp. viii+163, 2 pls.* (same as in 1st ed.). *Napoli, nella stamperia di Novello de Bonis*, 1738.

This ed., also anonymous, contains the Italian and Latin text side by side, and is exactly the same as the two ed. above.

Seconda edizione riveduta ed accresciuta di alquante annotazioni.—8°, *pp. xvi+226, 2 pls.* (same as 1st ed.) *In Napoli. Nella Stamperia di Angelo Vocola a Fontana Medina. A spese di Francesco Darbes*, MDCCXL.

The B.V. contains a copy, roy. fol., in which the last page is numbered 192 instead of 226. The above ed., the first in 8°, may be called 4th ed., there having been published already three ed. in 1738. For that reason the ed. of 1778 is called 5th ed., unless it is that the three preceding translations (Latin, French and English) are counted as 2nd, 3rd and 4th ed. *See* FURCHHEIM.

5th ed. 4°, *pp. viii+244. Napoli, presso il de Bonis*, MDCCLXXVIII.

Reprint of the Ital.-Lat. ed. of 1738. These each contain a meteorological chart.

[SERAO, FRANCESCO.]—Histoire du Mont Vésuve, avec l'explication des phénomènes qui ont coûtume d'accompagner les embrasements de cette Montagne. Le tout traduit de l'Italien de l'Académie des Sciences de Naples. Par M. Duperron de Castera. Dédiée à Monseigneur le Dauphin. —12°, *pp. xx+361, 2 pls. A Paris, chez Nyon fils, ruë du Hurepois, à l'Occasion.* M.DCC.XLI.

This ed. has the two plates and the "Explication de la figure représentant le Mont Vésuve vu du Palais du Roi" at the beginning, whereas another ed., also Paris, 1741, but "Chez Despilly, ruë Saint Jacques, dans la Vieille Poste," has these at the end, and a third (Furchheim), 8°, has : "A Paris, chez Le Clerc 1741." The pagination of all three is the same. This French translation is also anonymous, but is usually found under the heading of the translator.

[SERAO, FRANCESCO.]—The natural history of Mount Vesuvius, with the explanation of the various phænomena that usually attend the eruptions of this celebrated Volcano. Translated from the original Italian, composed by the Royal Academy of Science at Naples, by order of the King of the Two Sicilies.—8°, *pp. vi+231, 2 pls. Printed for E. Cave at St. John's Gate, London*, 1743.

Same as first ed., reduced in size. An anonymous literal translation.

SERIO.—Ottave sul Vesuvio.—4°, *pp.* 24. *Napoli*, 1775. [C.A.]

SEUTTERI, M. — Neapolis, regni hujus maxima, ornatissima, siti amœnissima, multisque castellis munita Metropolis et Emporium maratimum florentissimum cum illustrissimis ædificiis delineata cura et cælo Matthæi Seutteri, Sac. Cæs. Majest. Geogr. Augusta Vindelicor. [B.M.24045. 4.]

Hand-col. engrav. plan of town with 7 views, one being of Vesuvius : 568× 490 mm.

SEVASTANO.—*See* CIRILLO. 1834.

S. FR. S.—*See* SILVESTRO, F. S.

S

SHURY, J. (sculp.). — Mount Vesuvius. London : Published by Thomas Tegg, 73, Cheapside. Line engrav. of Vesuvius from the sea to the south : 200×115 mm. Heights greatly exaggerated. Copied, no doubt, from a sketch by Duppa in 1797.

SICA FRA GERONIMO DE GIFONI.— Morale discorso fatto tra l'effeti cagionati dalla voragine del Vesuvio, e li motivi visti nelli Cristiani.—8°, foll. 8. Napoli, 1632. [C.A.]

SICOLA, S.—La nobilta gloriosa nella vita di S. Aspremo primo Christiano, e primo Vescovo di Napoli.—4°, pp. 38+576+40. Napoli, 1696.
See pp. 177 et seq.

SICURO, F.—Prospetto della Villa del Principe di Aci (oggi Favorita) con veduta del Vesuvio.—2 pls. largest fol. [O.V.]

SIDERNO, D. Da.—Discorso filosofico, et astrologico. Nel quale si mostra quanto sia corroso il Monte Vesuuio dal suo primo incendio fino al presente, e quanto habbi da durare detto incendio.—8°, foll. 4. Napoli, Matteo Nucci, 1632.

SIEMENS, W. — Physikalisch-mechanische Betrachtungen, veranlasst durch einige Beobachtungen der Thätigkeit des Vesuvs im Mai 1878.—Monatsb. k. preuss. Akad. Wiss. pp. 558–82. Berlin, 1878.—See also his "Gesammt Abhandl. u. Vorträge," Berlin, 1881, and his "Scientif. & Techn. Papers," London, 1895 (transl.).

SIGISMONDO, G.—Descrizione della città di Napoli e suoi Borghi.—3 vols. 8°. Vol. i, pp. 8+287, 1 map ; Vol. ii, pp. 8+367 ; Vol. iii, pp. 8+320, foll. 2. [Napoli,] 1788–89.
See Vol. iii, pp. 209 et seq.

SIGISMONDO, G.—Lettera ad un suo amico di Benevento con la quale gli dà notizia dell' ultima eruzione del Vesuvio seguita nella sera del 15 Giugno 1794, e con un confronto della medesima con quella accaduta nel 1631.—MS. in [O.V.]

SIGONIO, C.—C. Sigonii Historiarum de regno Italiæ libri quindecim . . . qui libri historiam ab anno DLXX. usque ad MCC. continent.—fol. Venetiis, 1574.— Another ed. fol. Francofurti ad Mœnum, 1575.—4°, pp. 591. Basileæ, 1575.—fol., pp. 359. Francofurti ad Mœnum, 1755.— 2 pts. fol. Francofurti, 1591.—fol. Venetiis, 1591. (See Lib. II.)

SIGONIO, C.—C. Sigonii Historiarum de occidentali imperio, libri xx.—8°. Basileæ, 1579.—Another ed. fol. Francofurti, 1593. See Lib. XIV and XVI.

SILLIMAN, B.—Miscellaneous notes from Europe : 1. Present condition of Vesuvius. 2. Grotta del Cane and Lake Agnano. 3. Sulphur Lake of the Campagna, near Tivoli. 4. Meteorological Observatory of Mount Vesuvius, etc.—Amer. Journ. Sci. S. 2, xii, pp. 256–61. New Haven, 1851.

SILOS, M.—Vesuvius erumpens. Ode.—In the "Pinacotheca sive Romana pictura et scultura," 8°, pp. 344–46. Romæ, 1673. [C.A.]

[SILVESTRE, I.?]—Veve de la Montagne de Somme à Naples. Le Blond excudit cum priuil. Regis.—[1647 ?] Circular engrav. : 115 mm.

SILVESTRE, Isr. (inc. et sc.).—Veüe de la Montaigne de Sommes et partie de Naples. A. de Fer ex eü priuit.2. [B.N.P. Vb. 116.] A line engrav. : 253×112 mm. (?) from "Gravures de 129 vues en 83 planches."

SILVESTRI, O.—Sur l'éruption actuelle du Vésuve.—C.R. Acad. Sci. lxvi, pp. 677–80. Paris, 1868.

SILVESTRI, O.—Ricerche chimiche sulla eruzione del Vesuvio.—Atti Acc.Gioen. S.3, ii, pp. 31–44, 1 fig. Catania, 1868.

SILVESTRI, O.—Sulla eruzione del Vesuvio incominciata il 12 Nov. 1867 [1868].—Atti Acc. Gioen. S. 3, iii, pp. 29–44. Catania, 1869.

SILVESTRO, F. S.—All' inclito Martire S. Giorgio, singolar protettore del villaggio S. Giorgio a Cremano. Ringraziamento per aver fermato la lava del Vesuvio nella notte del 12 Maggio (1855) alle ore 12 p.m. dopo la processione fatta nello stesso giorno. Ode.—8°, pp. 4. Napoli, 1855. [C.A.]

SILVEYRA, Dr.—Soneto.—See QUINONES.—El Monte Vesvvio. [C.A.]

SIMOND, L.—Voyage en Italie et en Sicile. —2nd ed. 2 vols. 8°. Vol. i, pp. 8+405 ; Vol. ii, pp. 4+420, figs. (Vesuvius 11 April, 1818.) Paris, 1828.—Earlier ed. 2 vols. 8°. Paris, 1827–28.—8°, pp. 624. London, 1828.—N. J. f. Min. pp. 348–51. Stuttgart, 1833.

SINCERO ACCADEMICO INSENSATO.—
Il Vesuvio fiammeggiante. Poema.—8⁰,
foll. 8, *pp.* 155. *Per Secondino Roncagliolo,
Napoli,* 1632.—Another ed. 16⁰, *appresso
Ottauio Beltrano, Napoli,* 1632.
See FURCHHEIM.

SINIGALLIA, LUIGI.—Ueber einige glasige
Gesteine vom Vesuv.—[Sep.–Abdr.] *N. J. f.
Min. Beil.-Bd. vii, pp.* 417–29, 1 *fig.
Stuttgart,* 1891.

SINISCALCO, C.—Compendio delle principali Eruzioni Vesuviane dall' anno 79
E.V. infino alla descrizione delle recenti.—
8⁰, *pp.* 28. *Napoli,* 1863.
In the text mention is made of plates
which were never published. [C.A.]

SINISCALCO, C.—Notizie del Vesuvio e del
Monte di Somma con la descrizione delle
principali eruzioni Vesuviane dall' anno
79 E.V. fino alle recenti.—8⁰, *pp.* 36 (no
pls.). *Napoli,* 1881.
New ed. of the " Compendio."

SINISCALCO, C.—Istoria del Vesuvio e del
Monte di Somma con la descrizione delle
principali eruzioni Vesuviane dall' anno 79
E.V. fino alle recenti.—8⁰, *pp.* 72, 57 *pls.
and portrait. Napoli,* 1890.
Very poor reproductions in litho. of old
views and engravings, text equally poor,
mostly historic, though some references to
ancient authors are important. This is
the 3rd ed. of the " Compendio." *See* :
Archiv. stor. per. le prov. Napol., xvi,
p. 242. 1891.

SINISCALCO, C.—Histoire du Vésuve et du
Mont de Somma. Avec la description des
principales éruptions Vésuviennes par
l'anne 79 E.V. jusqu'aux récentes.—8⁰,
pp. 72, 57 *views. Naples,* 1890. [B.S.]
French transl. of foregoing.

SINISCALCO, C.—History of Vesuvius and
Mount of Somma. With the description
of the principal Vesuvian eruptions from
the year 79 E.V. till the recent.—8⁰, *pp.*
69, 57 *views. Naples,* 1890.
English transl. of foregoing.

SINISCALCO, C.—De Vesuvii Montisque
Summæ historia. Cum descriptione
superiorum conflagrationum Vesuvianum
ab anno 79 E.V. usque ad recentes.—8⁰,
pp. 66, 57 *views. Napoli,* 1890.
Latin transl. of foregoing.

SJÖGREN, S. A. H.—The Eruption of
Vesuvius.—" *Nature,*" *lxxiv, p.* 7. 1906.

SKIPPON, P.—An Account of a journey
made through part of the Low Countries,
Germany, Italy, and France.—*See* A. & J.
Churchill's collection of voyages and travels,
Vol. vi, p. 599. *London,* 1732.

SLAVIK, F.—Ueber Salmiakkristalle vom
Vesuv. a. d. J. 1906 [31 Mai 1907].—*Bull.
Internat. Acad. Sci. xii, pp.* 50–54, 5 *figs.
Prag,* 1908.—*Česká Akad. Císaře Fran-
tiška Josefa, etc. S.* 2, *xvi,* 15, *pp.* 6, 5 *figs.
Praze,* 1907.

SLAVIK, F.—Mineralogische Notizen.—*Bull.
Internat. Acad. Sci. xvii, pp.* 122–29, 3 *figs.
Prague,* 1912.—*Česká Akad. Císaře Fran-
tiška Josefa, etc. S.* 2, *xxi,* 16, *pp.* 9, 3 *figs.
Praze,* 1912.

SMITH, J.—Select Views in Italy, with
topographical and historical descriptions
in English and French.—2 tom. *obl.* 4⁰, 72
pls. and text. Tom. i, *London,* 1792 ;
Tom. ii, *London,* 1796.
See Pl. 59 : " On Mount Vesuvius, above
Portici " ; Pl. 60 : ' " Summit and Crater of
Mount Vesuvius." T. i contains the
inscript. : " Printed for John Smith,
Williaᵐ Byrne and John Emes," while
T. ii has : " . . . J. Smith, W. Byrne
and J. Edwards."

SMITH, J.—On Mount Vesuvius above
Portici. Engraved by B. T. Pouncy.—
London, published 24 March, 1798, by
Willᵐ Byrne, John Smith and James
Edwards. Pl. 59.
Line engrav. : 190×128 mm. Identical
with Pl. 59 in Smith's " Views in Italy,"
but with details of publication.

SMITHSON, J.—On a saline substance from
Mount Vesuvius.—*Phil. Trans. R. Soc. ciii,
Pt.* 2, *pp.* 256–62. *London,* 1813.

SMITHSON, J.—A discovery of Chloride of
Potassium in the Earth.—*Annals of Philos.
N.S. vi, p.* 258. *London,* 1823.

SOGLIANO, A.—Di un luogo dei libri Sibil-
lini relativo alla catastrofe delle città
Campane sepolte dal Vesuvio.—*Atti R.
Acc. Archeol. xvi, Pte.* 1a, *pp.* 165–79.
Napoli, 1894.

SOGLIANO, A.—Studi di topografia storica
e di storia antica della regione sotterata dal
Vesuvio nel LXXIX.—*Rend. R. Acc. Archeol.
xv, pp.* 45. *Napoli, Genn. ad Aprile,* 1901.

SOLIS MESSIA, IVAN DE.—Soneto.—*See*
QUINONES.—El Monte Vesvvio.

SOMMA, A. DI.—Historico racconto dei terremoti della Calabria dall' anno 1638 fin' anno 41.—*Napoli*, 1641.

SOMMER, E.—Eine wunderbare Werkstätte der Naturforschung.—" *Die Gartenlaube*," pp. 774–78, 1 *woodcut. Leipzig*, 1873.

SOMMER, G. (photo.).—Der Vesuv am 26 April 1872. Nach einer Aufnahme des Photographen. G. Sommer in Neapel. (S. 18.)
Woodcut from a German illust. paper : 314×222 mm.

SORIA, F. A.—Scrittori Vesuviani. Memorie storico-critiche degli storici Napoletani.—2 vols. 4⁰. *Napoli*, 1731, reprinted in 1781.
See Vol. ii, pp. 621–41, 1781.

SORRENTINO, I.—Istoria del Monte Vesuvio divisata in due libri.—4⁰, *foll.* 8, *pp.* 224, *foll.* 2. *Napoli*, 1734.

SOTIS, B.—Dissertazione fisico-chimica dell' ultima eruzione Vesuviana dei 12 Agosto 1804.—8⁰, *pp.* 55. *Napoli*, 1804.

SOUFFLOT et DUMONT.—Plan du Mont-Vésuve, tel qu'il étoit le vi Juin en 1750, à deux heures du matin. [B.N.P. Vb. 121.]
A note on the margin says " au mois d'octobre 1750 la montagne s'entreouvrée [*sic*] et vomit une quantité prodigieuse de lave."—A water-colour sketch of a cone of eruption. Another sketch is given on 9 June 1750 at 2 a.m.

SOUFFLOT et DUMONT.—Plan du Mont-Vésuve parcouru et mesuré. Voyez l'histoire et phénomènes du Vésuve par l'abbé Peton. [B.N.P. Vb. 121.]
A water-colour plan of crater in 1750, which is the original of the engraving by Dumont (*q.v.*).

SOYE, L. R.—Ode cantada no felis die natalicio d'Augusta Maria Carolina d'Austria Rainha das Duas Cecilias.—8⁰, *pp.* xx, 2, *figs. Napoles*, 1792.

SPALLANZANI, L.—Viaggi alle due Sicilie e in alcune parti dell' Appennino.—6 vols. 8⁰. *Vol. i, pp.* 55+292, *tav.* 1–2 ; *Vol. ii, pp.* 351, *tav.* 3–9 ; *Vol. iii, pp.* 364 ; *Vol. iv, pp.* 356, *tav.* 10–11 ; *Vol. v, pp.* 371 ; *Vol. vi, pp.* 288. *Pavia*, 1792–97.—Another ed. 3 vols. 8⁰, *portrait and pls. Milano, Tip. Classici It.*, 1825–26.—In German : 8 vols. *Leipzig*, 1794–96.—Another ed. 5 vols. *Leipzig*, 1795–98.
In French : Voyages dans les deux Siciles et dans quelques parties des Appennins.—2 tom. 8⁰. *Tom. i, pp.* 44+299, *pls.* 1–2 ; *Tom. ii, pp.* 273, *pls.* 3–9. *Berne*, 1795.
Another ed. " Traduit de l'Italien par G. Toscan. Avec des Notes du cit. Faujas-de-St.-Fond."—6 tom. 8⁰. *Tom. i, pp.* 10+311, *pls.* 1–2 ; *Tom. ii, pp.* 280, *pls.* 3–5 ; *Tom. iii, pp.* 291 ; *Tom. iv, pp.* 272, *pls.* 6–7 ; *Tom. v, pp.* 309 ; *Tom. vi, pp.* 215. *Paris, An* VIII [1800].
In English : Travels in the two Sicilies, and some parts of the Apennines. Translated from the original Italian.—4 vols. 8⁰. *Vol. i, pp.* 50+315, *pls.* 1–2 ; *Vol. ii, pp.* 389, *pls.* 3–7 ; *Vol. iii, pp.* 402, *pls.* 8–9 ; *Vol. iv, pp.* 394, *pls.* 10–11. *London*, 1798.
—*See also* Pinkerton's Collection of Voyages and Travels, *Vol. v. London*, 1809.

SPALLANZANI, L.—Lettera nella quale si tratta de' Sassi caduti dall' aria nella Campagna Sanese il dì 16 Giugno 1794.—*Giorn. Lett. xxxi, pp.* 81–102. *Napoli*, 1794.

SPALLANZANI, L. — Lettera scritta al Wilseck sul fenomeno della pioggia di pietre avvenuta a Siena nel 1794. [C.A.]
The original MS. letter presented by Prof. G. Uzielli.

SPALLANZANI, L.—Relation de l'éruption du Vésuve arrivée le 15 juin 1794.

SPALLANZANI, L.—*See* RAFFELSBERGER.

SPENCER, L. J.—*See* JOHNSTON-LAVIS, H. J.—On Chlormanganokalite, *etc.* 1908.

SPINA, D. (ing.).—Pianta, e Veduta del Monte Vesuvio dalla parte meridion : co' varj Corsi più recenti del Bitume, e colla situazione de Villaggi ed altri luoghi circonvicini secondo lo stato dell' anno 1761. E coll' accurata descrizione della eruzione fatta in Xbre 1760. Cor. Oratj. inc. Petrini, N. [*Napoli* ?, 1761 ?] [B.M.]
Bird's-eye view of the 1760 eruption. The lavas of 1737 and others up to that date are indicated.

SPINOSA, S.—Dichiarazione genealogica, fisico-chimica, naturale apologetica, ed epidemica del Signor Vesuvio.—4⁰, *foll.* 8. [*Napoli*, 1794 ?]—*See* VESUVINO, CRISIPPO.

SPUHLER, A.—Mon Voyage en Italie.—800 *photos. Paris, Leipzig*, — ?

STAIBANO, V.—Risolutiones forenses.—*fol. Napoli*, 1654.

In Centuria II, Resolutio CXLIV describes the eruption of 1631 of Vesuvius and contains the decisions of the Sacro R. Consiglio in cases of disputes arising from this eruption.

STANFIELD, R. A.—*See* MAPEI, C.—Italy, Classical, Historical and Picturesque.

STAS.—Sur la découverte par le Prof. Scacchi, de Naples, d'un corps simple nouveau dans la lave du Vésuve.—*Bull. Acad. R. Sci. de Belgique, S.* 2, *xlvi, xlvii, xlviii, xlix,* 1–4. *Bruxelles*, 1878–80.

STEFANI, C. DE.—Sull' opportunità di un completo Istituto Vesuviano.—*Atti R. Acc. Lincei, S.* 5, *Rend. xix, sem.* 2, *pp.* 90–93. *Roma*, 1910.

STEFANO, G. DI.—Nuove osservazioni sulla geologia del Monte Bulgheria in provincia di Salerno.—*Boll. Soc. Geol. Ital. xiii,* 2, *pp.* 170, 191–98. *Roma*, 1895.

STEFANO, R. DE, e SOCI.—Contratto costitutivo della Compagnia Vesuviana.—8⁰, *pp.* 30. *Napoli*, 1836.

STEIN-NORDHEIM, VON.—*See* SCHNEER, J.

STELLA STARRABBA, F.—Sul rapporto esistente fra le precipitazioni atmosferiche annuali e l'attività dei vulcani Vesuvio ed Etna.—*Rend. R. Acc. Sci. S.* 3, *xvii, pp.* 216–25, 8 *figs. Napoli*, 1911.

STIELER, C.—Italy from the Alps to Mount Etna. Translated by F. E. Trollope and edited by T. A. Trollope.—*fol., pp. xiii+* 468, *num. pls. London*, 1877.

STILES, F.—Eruption of Mount Vesuvius on 23 December, 1760.—*Phil. Trans. R. Soc. lii, pp.* 39–44. *London*, 1761.

STILLINGFORD, R.—Die Flucht vor dem Ausbruch des Vesuvs.—" *Ueber Land u. Meer,*" *iii, p.* 217, 1 *illustr. Stuttgart*, 1860.

STOKLASA, J.—Chemische Vorgänge bei der Eruption des Vesuvs im April 1906.—*Chemiker-Zeitung, Nr.* 61. 1906.

STOKLASA, J.—Ueber die Menge und den Ursprung des Ammoniaks in den Producten der Vesuveruption im April 1906.—*Ber. deutsch. chem. Gesellsch. xxxix,* 13, *pp.* 3530–37. *Berlin*, 1906.

STOKLASA, J.—Ueber den Ursprung des Ammoniaks in den Produkten der Vesuveruption in April 1906.—*Centralbl. f. Min. pp.* 161–66. *Stuttgart*, 1907.

STOLBERG, F. L.—Reise in Deutschland, der Schweiz, Italien und Sicilien.—4 vols. 8⁰. *Königsburg und Leipzig*, 1794. Atlas, 4⁰.—In English : 2 vols. 4⁰. *London*, 1796–97.

See Vol. ii.

STOPPA, G.—Memorie istorico-fisiche sulle eruzioni Vesuviane, *etc* —4⁰, *pp.* 92, 1 *pl. Napoli*, 1806.

STOPPANI, A.—Corso di Geologia.—3 vols. 8⁰. *Milano*, 1871–73.

See Vol. i : Dinamica Terrestre. *Milano*, 1871.

STOPPANI, A.—Osservazioni sulla eruzione Vesuviana del 24 Aprile 1872.—*Atti R. Ist. Lomb. S.* 2, *v, Pt.* 2, *pp.* 814–17. *Milano*, 1872.

STOPPANI, A.—Il Bel Paese. Conversazioni sulle bellezze naturali, la geologia e la geografia fisica d'Italia.—8⁰. *Milano*, 1876. —24a ediz. 16⁰, *fig. Milano* [1894].

See pp. 430–85.

STOPPANI, A.—Corso di Geologia. 3a ediz. con note ed aggiunte per cura di Allessandro Malladra.—3 vols. 8⁰. *Vol. i, pp.* 695, 178 *figs.,* 1 *map, Milano*, 1900 ; *Vol. ii, pp.* 883, 217 *figs.,* 2 *maps,* 1903 ; *Vol. iii, pp.* 714, 60 *figs.,* 1903.

See Vol. ii.

STRABO.—Della Geografia di S. libri XVII.—8⁰. 1819, *etc.*

STRANGE, G.—*See* STRANGE, J.

STRANGE, J.—Catalogo ragionato di varie produzioni naturali del regno Lapideo, raccolte in un viaggio per i Colli Euganei nel mese di Luglio 1771.—*See* ANON.—Dei Vulcani o Monti Ignivomi, *etc.*

STRANGE, J.—Lettera geologica scritta al Dottor Gio. Targioni Tozzetti.—*See* ANON.—Dei Vulcani o Monti Ignivomi, *etc.*

STROMBECK, F. K.VON.—*See* BREISLAK, S. 1819.

STROZZI, N.—Soneto.—*See* GIORGI URBANO. [C.A.]

STRUEVER, G.—*See* STRUEVER, J. K. T.

STRUEVER, J. K. T.—Sodalite pseudomorfa di Nefelina del Monte Somma [1871]. —*Atti R. Acc. Sci. vii, disp.* 3, *pp.* 329–35. *Torino*, 1871–72.

STRUEVER, J. K. T.—[Ueber das Albaner Gebirge und über Somma-Bomben mit der schönsten Zonen-Structur.]—*N. J. f. Min. pp.* 619–20. *Stuttgart*, 1875.

STRUEVER, J. K. T.—Die Mineralien Latiums (darunter Sanidin vom Vesuv).— *Zeitschr. f. Kryst. u. Min. i, p.* 246. *Leipzig,* 1877.

STRUEVER, J. K. T.—Notizie riassuntive di uno studio cristallografico dell' Idocrasio del Vesuvio.—*Atti R. Acc. Lincei, S.* 5, *Rend. xix, sem.* 2, *pp.* 75-77. *Roma,* 1910.

STUEBEL, M. A.—Die Laven der Somma bei Neapel.—*Sitz.-Ber. naturwiss. Gesellsch. Isis,* 1861, *pp.* 113-14. *Dresden,* 1862.

STUEBEL, M. A.—Der Vesuv. Eine vulkanologische Studie für jedermann. Ergänzt und herausgegeben von W. Bergt.— 1 *map,* 9 *figs. and* 10 *col. prints. Leipzig,* 1909.

SUAREZ, F. M.—De Monte Vesuvio.—MS. *Bibl. Brancacciana,* 8⁰, *pp.* 21. Copy [C.A.]

SUESS, E.—Die Erdbeben des südlichen Italien [1873].—4⁰. *Wien,* 1874.—*Denkschr. k. Akad. Wiss. xxxiv (Abth.* 1), *pp.* 1-32, *taf. i-iii. Wien,* 1875.—[Abstr.] *Boll. R. Com. Geol. Ital. vi, pp.* 111-13. *Roma,* 1875.—*Bull. Vulc. Ital. fasc.* 1-3, *p.* 42. *Rome,* 1875.

SUESS, E.—Das Antlitz der Erde.—3 vols. 8⁰. *Prag, Wien, Leipzig,* 1883-1909.— In French, transl. by E. de Margerie: 3 tom. in 5 pts. 8⁰. *Paris, A. Colin,* 1897.— In English: 8⁰. *Oxford,* 1904. *See* T. i and ii.

SUESS, E.—L'aspetto della Terra.—8⁰. *Pisa,* 1894.
    Translation from the German by P. E. Vinassa de Regny. *See* Pt. I, Cap. 4, *pp.* 173 *et seq.*

SUETONIUS TRANQUILLUS, C.—C. S. T. Cæsarum XII. Vitæ.—12⁰. *Dresdæ,* 1677.

SUPO (Padre Gesuita Matematico et Meteorista, nel collegio di Napoli).—Relation del nuovo incendio del Vesuvio ai 3 di Luglio 1660.—MS. *in* [O.V.]
    This fixes the authorship of the articles under ANON.: " Continuatione de' successi," etc., referring to this eruption.

SUPPLE, R.—An account of the eruption of Mount Vesuvius, from its first beginning to the 28 Oct. 1751.—*Phil. Trans. R. Soc. xlvii, pp.* 315-17. *London,* 1753.—In Italian : *Compendio Trans. filos. Soc. Reale d. Londra, pp.* 81-84. *Venezia,* 1793.

SURGENS, MARC. ANT. — M. A. Surgentis . . . de Neapoli illustrata. Lib. I. Cum adnot. Mutii Fratris.—4⁰, *pp.* 30 + 456, *portrait. Neapoli, Stelliolæ,* M.D.XCVII.

SURGENS, MUTIUS.—Adnotationes illustratæ Neapolis primum librum. — *See* SURGENS, M. A.—M. A. Surgentis . . . de Neapoli illustrata, pp. 317-456.

SWINBURNE, H.—Travels in the Two Sicilies in the years 1777-80.—2 vols. 4⁰, *num. pls. London,* 1783-85.—— 2nd ed. 2 vols. 8⁰. *Vol. i, pp.* lxviii+307, 5 *pls. ; Vol. ii, pp.* xi+359, 3 *pls. London, Nichols,* 1790. [*See* Vol. i, pp. 73-92.]——3rd ed. 1795.—In French : 4 vols. 4⁰. *Paris, Didot,* 1785.—In German, transl. by I. R. Forster: 2 pts. *Hamburg,* 1785.

SZATHMÁRY, L. VON.—Chemische und petrographische Untersuchung des Lavastromes des Vesuvs.—*Földt. Közl. xxxvii, pp.* 131-33, 180-83. *Pest,* 1907.

SZEMBECH, F.—Relazione composta di varie relazioni intorno all' ultimo incendio del Vesuvio.—(In Polish) 4⁰. *Cracovia,* 1632.

TADINI, CONTE F.—*See* T., C. F. [C.A.]

TAMAGNON, EMÉRIE DE.—Île de Nisida (Naples). Imp. Lemercier, Paris. [B.N.P. Vb. 119.]
    Lithograph in two tints ; Vesuvius with a flat truncated top.

TARAMELLI, T., e MERCALLI, G.—I Terremoti Andalusi cominciati il 25 Dicembre 1884.—*Atti R. Acc. Lincei, S.* 4, *Mem. iii, pp.* 116-222, *tav. i-iv. Roma,* 1886. *See* p. 98.

TARDIEU, B. (gravé par).—Carte du Vésuve et de la Plage comprise entre Naples et la Torre dell' Annunziata. Écrit par Miller.— *See* BREISLAK, S.—Voyages Physiques et Lithologiques . . . *Tom. i, p.* 122, *Pl. ii. Paris,* 1801.

TARGIONI TOZZETTI, G.—Estratto di una annotazione ai Viaggi del celebre Dott. . . . Al Tomo IX. di detti Viaggi.—*See* ANON.—Dei Vulcani o Monti Ignivomi, *etc.*

TARGIONI TOZZETTI, G.—Dei Monti Ignivomi della Toscana e del Vesuvio.—*See* ANON.—Dei Vulcani o Monti Ignivomi, *etc.*

TARGIONI TOZZETTI, G.—Notizie istoriche delle Mofete che si trovano nei monti della Toscana somministrate dall' Eccell. . . . Ne' suoi Viaggi ristampati in Firenze l'anno 1769.—*See* ANON.—Dei Vulcani o Monti Ignivomi, *etc.*

TARI, A.—Reliquie di lava sul lido di Resina. —12⁰, *foll.* 3. — ?, — ? [O.V.]

TARINO, G. A.—Continuatione de' successi del prossimo incendio del Vesuvio, con gli effetti della cenere, e pietre da quello vomitate, e con la dichiaratione, ed espressioni delle croci maravigliose apparse in varii luoghi dopo l'incendio.—4⁰, 1 *pl. Napoli,* 1661. [B.N.]
This work is anon., but has a preface by G. A. Tarino. *See* ANON., SUPO and ZUPO.

TASCONE, L. — Somma-Vesuvio. Modello eseguito dall' ingegnere . . . coadiutore del R. Osservatorio Vesuviano e del Gabinetto di fisica terrestre nella R. Università di Napoli. 1894.
250 × 320 mm.

TASCONE, L.—Diario Vesuviano (Luglio-Ottobre 1898).—*Portici,* 1898.

TASCONE, L.—Il fenomeno delle fiammi apparse entro il cratere Vesuviano nel 1898. —8⁰, *pp.* 7. *Napoli,* 1898.

TASCONE, L.—Sull' utilità della pubblicazione d'un diario Vesuviano. Breve nota preliminare.—*pp.* 4. *Portici,* 1898.

TASCONE, L.—Il Vesuvio nei primi sette mesi del 1899.—*Boll. Oss. Moncalieri, S.* 2, *xix,* 6–7, *pp.* 42–43. *Torino,* 1899.

TASCONE, L.—Il Vesuvio e la fine del periodo eruttivo 1895–99.—*Boll. Oss. Moncalieri, S.* 2, *xix,* 8–10, *pp.* 58–59. *Torino,* 1899.

TASCONE, L.—Il Vesuvio e la sua ultima fase eruttiva.—*Boll. Oss. Moncalieri, S.* 2, *xx,* 1–2–3, *pp.* 8–9. *Torino,* 1900.

TASCONE, L.—10 anni al Osservatorio Vesuviano e le dimissioni.—1900.

TASCONE, L.—Per i domanda sibillina sulla fase esplosiva del Vesuvio di Maggio 1900. —*Portici,* 1901.

TASCONE, L.—Pelée e Vesuvio. Ferrovia elettrica e la distruz. d. R. Osserv. Vesuviano. Eruz. d. Martinica.

TATA, D.—Descrizione del grande incendio del Vesuvio successo nel giorno otto del mese di Agosto del corrente anno 1779.— 8⁰, *pp.* 38. *Napoli,* 1779.

TATA, D. (S. A. T.).—Relazione dell' ultima eruzione del Vesuvio accaduta in Agosto di quest' anno.—*Giorn. Enciclop. Ital. v,* 24, *pp.* 185–200. *Napoli,* 1787. [O.V.]

TATA, D.—Breve relazione dell' ultima eruttazione del Vesuvio (Agosto e Settembre 1790), *etc.*—8⁰, *pp.* 24. *Napoli,* 1790.

TATA, D.—Continuazione delle notizie riguardanti il Vesuvio.—12⁰, *pp.* 24. [*Naples,* 1790.] [C.A.]

TATA, D.—Lettera al Sig. Barbieri sull' eruzione del Vesuvio.—8⁰, *pp.* 26. *Napoli,* 1790.

TATA, D.—Relazione dell' ultima eruzione del Vesuvio nel 15 Giugno 1794.—8⁰, *pp.* 42. *Napoli,* 1794.

TATA, D.—Memoria sulla pioggia di pietre, avvenuta nella Campagna Sanese il dì 16 di Giugno di questo corrente anno (1794).— 8⁰, *pp.* 74. *Napoli,* 1794.

TATA, D.—Lettera sulla figura, ecc. del Vesuvio, 21 Agosto 1794. Con breve risposta di F. Viscardi. — ?, 1794.

TAVERNA, E.—Cenni descrittivi di Torre del Greco.—8⁰, *pp.* 12, 8 *woodcuts.* [Extr. of] " *La Patria,*" *Geografia dell' Italia. Torino,* 1896.

TAVERNIER et DUPUY (lith.).—Éruption du Mont Vésuve. Maggio 10, 1834 [or 1854 ?].—*Metz,* — ? [B.N.P. Vb. 121.]
A very rough litho.

TAYLOR, LE BARON.—Lettre à M. Charles Nodier sur les villes de Pompéi et d'Herculanum.—*Nouv. Ann. Voy. xxiv, pp.* 424–25. *Paris,* 1824.

T., C. F. (TADINI, CONTE FRANC.).—L'Eruzione del Vesuvio della notte de' 15 Giugno 1794, poeticamente descritta.—8⁰, *pp.* 30, 1 *pl.* [*Napoli,* 1794 ?] [C.A.]

TCHIHATCHEFF, P. DE.—Lettre sur l'éruption du Vésuve du 1er mai 1855.—*C.R. Acad. Sci. xl, pp.* 1229–38. *Paris,* 1855.

TCHIHATCHEFF, P. DE.—Nouvelle éruption du Vésuve.—*C.R. Acad. Sci. liii, pp.* 1090–92. *Paris,* 1861.—*Zeitschr. deutsch. geol. Gesellsch. xiii, pp.* 453–58. *Berlin,* 1861.

TCHIHATCHEFF, P. DE.—Der Vesuv im Dezember 1861.—*Verh. k. k. geol. Reichsanst. xii, pp.* 179–81. *Wien,* 1861–62.

TCHIHATCHEFF, P. DE.—Ausbruch des Vesuv.—*N. J. f. Min. pp.* 69–73. *Stuttgart,* 1862.

TCHIHATCHEFF, P. DE.—On the recent eruption of Vesuvius in December, 1861. Communicated by Sir R. I. Murchison. [Abstract.]—*Quart. Journ. Geol. Soc. xviii, pp.* 126–27. *London*, 1862.

T. D.—Éruption du Volcan. [B.N.P. Vb. 121.]
An effective litho. of no value scientifically.

T. D.—Sommet du Vésuve, intérieur du cratère. [B.N.P. Vb. 121.]
A very effective litho.

T. D.—Vue de Vésuve et d'une maison de plaisance du Cardinal Bernetti.
A good litho.

T. D.—Vues . . . dessinées d'après nature, *etc.*
1. Vue du Vésuve et d'une maison de plaisance du Cardinal Bernetti.
2. Sommet du Vésuve, intérieur du cratère.
[At back] À Paris, chez Aumont, rue J. J. Rousseau, N⁰ 10.
Two lithos. : 178×115 mm.

TEMPLE, SIR G.—*See* WRIGHT, G. N.

TENORE, G.—Notizia di una gita al Vesuvio fatta nel giorno 10 Febbraio 1850.— *Rend. R. Acc. Sci. viii, pp.* 379–80. *Napoli* [1850].—*Ann. Fis. Chim. ii, pp.* 169–71. *Torino*, 1850.

TENORE, G.—Il tufo vulcanico della Campania e le sue applicazioni alle costruzioni. —*Boll. Coll. Ing. ed Arch. x,* 5–8. *Napoli,* 1892.

TENORE, M.—Ragguagli di alcune peregrinazioni effettuate in diversi luoghi delle provincie di Napoli e di Terra di Lavoro, nella primavera, e nell' està del 1832.— *Il Progr. Sci. vi, pp.* 187–211. *Napoli,* 1833.

TENORE, M.—Notizia sullo spruzzolo vulcanico caduto in Napoli il dì 1 Gennajo 1839.—" *Il Lucifero," i, p.* 198, coll. 1–2. *Napoli,* 1839.

TENORE, M.— Relation de l'éruption du Vésuve dans les premiers jours de janvier 1839.—*Bull. Soc. géol. France, x, pp.* 166–68. *Paris,* 1839.

TENORE, M.—Congetture sull' abbassamento altra volta avvenuto nel Vesuvio e l'innalzamento avuto luogo successivamente nelle posteriori eruzioni. Nota letta nella tornata d. R. Acc. Sci. Napoli, 16 Giugno, 1846.—*Ann. Civ. Reg. Due Sicilie, xlii,* 83, *p.* 40, *col.* 2. *Napoli,* 1846.

TENORE, M.—Storia del Vesuvio intorno ad un passo del Cosmos concernente l'altezza del Vesuvio.—" *Il Lucifero," ix, p.* 287, col. 1, *p.* 288, col. 2. *Napoli,* 1846.

TENORE, M.—*See* PALMIERI, L., ET ALII. 1859.

TERSALGO LIDIACO. — Stanze a Crinatéa.—*See* FILOMARINO.

T., F. M. D. C. A.— Dettaglio su l'antico stato ed eruzioni del Vesuvio colla ragionata relazione della grande eruzione accaduta ai 15 Giugno 1794.—8⁰, *pp.* 16. [*Napoli,* 1794.] [C.A.]—*See* ANON.

THOMAS (sc.).—Environs de Naples: (Vue du Vésuve.) Imp. F. Chardon Aᵉ 30 r. Hautefeuille.
Fine engrav. : 147×102 mm. View of Vesuvius from slopes of Capodimonte. Palm, one umbrella-pine and pergola in foreground, with women dancing, musicians playing and woman fetching water.

THOMAS, T. H.—A Visit to the Volcanoes of South Italy. Pt. II, The Neapolitan District.—*Trans. Cardiff Nat. Soc. xxiii, pp.* 10–19. *Cardiff,* 1892.

THOMPSON, G.—*See* THOMSON, W.

THOMSON.—*See* ARAGO.

THOMSON, W.—Notizia sul marmo bianco del Vesuvio.—*Giorn. Lett. lxxxix, pp.* 98–102. *Napoli,* 1781.—In French : *Bibl. Britan. vii. Paris,* 1798.—8⁰, *pp.* 5. 1797. [O.V.]

THOMSON, W.—Breve catalogo di alcuni prodotti ritrovati nell' ultima eruzione del Vesuvio.—*Giorn. Lett. cii. Napoli,* 1794.

THOMSON, W.—Breve notizia di un viaggiatore sulle incrostazioni silicee termali d'Italia, e specialmente di quelle dei Campi Flegrei nel regno di Napoli.—8⁰, *pp.* 35. *Napoli,* 1795. [O.V.]—[Reprinted in :] *Giorn. Lett. cii, pp.* 51–55. *Napoli,* 1794.
See pp. 28–35.

THOMSON, W.—Abbozzo di una classificazione de prodotti vulcanici.—*See* ANCORA, G. D' : Prospetto storico-fisico degli scavi di Ercolano e di Pompei.— Reprinted in the anon. ed. of *Firenze,* 1795, and in the *Giorn. Lett. xli, pp.* 59–81. *Firenze.*

THOMSON, W.—Sur l'origine de l'oxigène nécessaire pour entretenir le feu souterrain du Vésuve.—*Giorn. Lett. cvi, pp.* 3–46. *Napoli,* 1798.

THORPE, A.—Recent analyses of Leucite Basalt from Vesuvius.—*Chem. News, lxxii,* p. 53. *London,* 1895.

THUGUTT, S. J.—Ueber einen Apophyllit-Analcim-Auswürfling des Monte Somma. —*Centralbl. f. Min. pp.* 761-65, 1 *fig. Stuttgart,* 1911.

THUILLIER (fils) (gravé par). — Carte Physique de la Campanie. Écrit par Miller.—*See* BREISLAK, S. — Voyages Physiques et Lithologiques.—*T. i, pl.* 1. *Paris,* 1801.

TIERCE, I. B. (des.).—Naples. Vue des Laves anciennement sorties du Vésuve et amoncelées sur le bord de la mer près du Palais de Portici. Dessiné d'après nature par I. B. T., gravé par Carl Guttenberg. Nº 117. A. P. D. R.—[*Circa* 1780.]
Lava of 1631 on sea-shore ; fishermen and boats in foreground. Line engrav. : 350×214 mm.

TIREPENNE.—*See* COIGNET.—Voyage en Italie.

TIREPENNE (litho.).—Chiatamone, Naples Imp. Imbert, etc.
A lithograph view of Vesuvius in floral frame.

TOFANO (?).—Gedächtnissfeier der Zerstörung von Pompeji. (79 n. Chr.) [Centenary meeting at Pompei in 1879.]
Woodcut from a German illust. paper : 221×163 mm.

TOMASELLI, AB.—Ricerche sulla natura e generi delle lave compatte, lettera al Ab. Olivi.—*Giorn. Lett. i, pp.* 85-87. *Napoli,* 1793.

TOMMASI, DOM DE.—Avviso al pubblco [*sic*] sull' analisi della cenere eruttata dal Vesuvio.—*fol., fol.* 1. [*Napoli,* 16 *Giugno* 1794.]

TOMMASI, D. DE.—Esperienze et osservazioni del Sale Ammoniaco Vesuviano.— 8º, *pp.* 3-15. *Napoli,* 1794. [C.A.]—*Also* 4º, *pp.* 16. 1794. [O.V.]

TOMMASI, D. DE.—Altro avviso al pubblico sulla nuova analisi delle ceneri eruttate dal Vesuvio ne' dì 16, 17, 18 del corrente mese di Giugno 1794.—4º, *p.* 1. [O.V.]

TONDI, M.—Catalogo della Collezione Orittologica et Oreognosica del fù chiarissimo Professore Cav. Matteo Tondi Direttore del Museo di Mineralogia di Napoli.—8º, *pp. viii*+243. *Napoli,* 1837.

TONIOLO, A. — L'eruzione del Vesuvio [Aprile 1906].—*Riv. Fis. Mat. Sci. Nat. vii,* 77, *pp.* 426-33. *Pavia,* 1906.

TORCIA, M.—Relation de la dernière éruption du Vésuve, arrivée au mois d'août 1779.—12º, *pp.* 135. *Naples,* 1779.—Also in Italian : 8º, *foll.* 5, *pp.* 136, 1 *col. pl., fig. Napoli,* 1779. [O.V.]

TORCIA, M.—Breve cenno di un giro per le provincie meridionali ed orientali del regno di Napoli.—8º. *Napoli,* 1795.

TORCIA, M.—Lettere al Sig. D. Biagio Michitelli Regio Assessore nella Piazza di Longone.—8º, *pp.* 16. *Napoli,* 1795. [B.N.] —*Antologia, xxx.* 1796. [B.N.]—*Giorn. Lett.* 89.

TORRE, G. M. DELLA. — Scienza della natura.—2 vols. 4º, *tav. Napoli,* 1748.
See Vol. i, pp. 250-71.

TORRE, G. M. DELLA.—Narrazione del torrente di fuoco uscito dal Monte Vesuvio nel 1751.—8º, *pp.* 23. *Napoli,* 1751. [O.V.]—Reprinted in the " *Storia e fenomeni* " and in the " *Novelle letterarie fiorentine,*" coll. 230 *et seq.* 1752.

TORRE, G. M. DELLA.—Storia e fenomeni del Vesuvio.—4º, *foll.* 4, *pp.* 120, 8 *pls., figs. Napoli,* 1755.—In German, 1755 ?

TORRE, G. M. DELLA.—Supplemento alla Storia del Vesuvio fino all' anno 1759.—4º. *Napoli,* 1759.

TORRE, G. M. DELLA.—Histoire et phénomènes du Vésuve. [Transl. from the Ital. by M. l'Abbé Péton and followed by] Dissertation critique sur les opinions courantes touchant les phénomènes du Vésuve et des autres volcans. [By P. G. d'Amato, and] Supplément [by G. M. Della Torre].—12º, *pp.* xxiv+399, 5 *pls.,* 1 *map. Paris,* 1760. —Another ed., ed. by D. Campo, 8º, *pp. xii*+298, *foll.* 3, 11 *pls. Naples,* 1771.

TORRE, G. M. DELLA.—Supplemento alla Storia del Vesuvio, ove si descrive l'incendio del 1760.—4º, *fig., pp.* 15. 1 *pl. Napoli,* 1761.

TORRE, G. M. DELLA.—Histoire du Mont Vésuve et exposition de ses phénomènes.— [Extr. from :] *Mélanges d'histoire naturelle,* 8º, *fig., foll.* 14, 1 *pl. Lyon,* 1765. [O.V.] —*Journ. Étrang. janv. pp.* 182-208. *Paris,* 1756.

TORRE, G. M. DELLA.—Incendio del Vesuvio accaduto l'anno 1766.— 4º. *Napoli,* 1766.

TORRE, G. M. DELLA.—Incendio del Vesuvio accaduto li 19 d'Ottobre del 1767.—4⁰, *pp.* 30, 1 *pl.*, *figs. Napoli,* 1767.—Reprinted in " *Storia e fenomeni.*"

TORRE, G. M. DELLA.—Storia e fenomeni del Vesuvio con supplemento.—4⁰, *foll.* 3, *pp.* 120+39, 10 *pls.*, *figs. Napoli,* 1768. [O.V.]

TORRE, G. M. DELLA.—Incendio trentesimo del Vesuvio accaduto gli 8 Agosto 1779. [Edited by D. Campo.]—4⁰, *foll.* 2, *pp.* 15. *Napoli* [1779].

TORRE, G. M. DELLA.—Geschichte und Naturbegebenheiten des Vesuvs von den ältesten Zeiten bis zum Jahr 1779. Aus dem Italienischen. Nebst einer Vorrede und vielen Anmerkungen von L * * [*i.e.* L. F. B. Lentin]. Mit Kupfern.—8⁰, *pp.* *xlviii*+222+60+4, 2 *tav. Altenburg,* 1783. —*Gel. Zeit.* p. 515, 1783 ; p. 201, *Leipzig,* 1785.—*Götting. gel. Anz.* p. 857. 1783.— *Hall. Zeit.* p. 417. 1783.—*Allgem. d. Bibl. lviii, p.* 152.—*Beckm. physik. ökon. Bibl. xiii, p.* 90.

TORRE, DUCA DELLA (sen.).—Lettera prima sull' eruzione del Vesuvio de' 15 Giugno 1794.—8⁰, *pp.* 14. [*Naples* ?, 1794.]

TORRE, DUCA DELLA (sen.). — Lettera seconda sull' eruzione del Vesuvio de' 15 Giugno, 1794.—8⁰, *pp.* 52. *Napoli,* 1794.

TORRE, DUCA DELLA (sen.).—Lettera prima e seconda sulla eruzione del Vesuvio del 15 Giugno 1794.—8⁰, *pp.* 8+34. *Napoli,* 1794.—Several ed. (*See* Furchheim's Bibliography.)—In German. *Dresden,* 1795.

TORRE, DUCA DELLA (sen.).—Estratto dalla prima lettera sulla eruzione del Vesuvio dei 15 Giugno 1794.—8⁰, *pp.* 8. *Napoli,* 1794. [C.A.]

TORRE, DUCA DELLA (sen.).—Auszug eines Briefes aus Neapel über die Eruption des Vesuvs in der Nacht vom 15 Juni 1794.— *Deutscher Merkur, p.* 420. 1794.—*Reprinted in :* SPALLANZANI.—Reise in Beide Sicilien.

TORRE, DUCA DELLA (sen.).—Breve descrizione dei principali incendi del Monte Vesuvio e di molte vedute di essi, ora per la prima volta ricavata dagli storici contemporanei, ed esistenti nel gabinetto del Duca della Torre.—8⁰, *pp.* 46, *foll.* 3. *Napoli,* 1795.

TORRE, DUCA DELLA (sen.).—Il Gabinetto Vesuviano.—1a ed. *Napoli,* — ?——2a ed. 8⁰, *fol.* 1, *pp.* 108, *foll.* 4, 22 *pls.* 1796. ——3a ed. 8⁰, *foll.* 2, *pp.* 86, *fol.* 1, 22 *pls.* 1797.

TORRE, DUCA DELLA (sen.).—*See* TOUR, DUC DE LA, 1805.

TORRE, DUCA DELLA (sen.).—Atlante di Vedute de' principali incendij del Monte Vesuvio ricavate dagli storici contemporanei ed esistente nel gabinetto del Duca della Torre.—22 *pls.* 4⁰. — ?, — ? [C.A.] *See also* GERVASI, N.

TORRE, DUCA DELLA (sen.).—Descrizione dei principali incendi del Monte Vesuvio e di molte vedute di essi.—4⁰, *pp.* 86+2. — ?, — ? *See* pp. 55–63 : Catalogo delle pietre Vesuviane ; pp. 67–86 : Biblioteca Vesuviana esistente nel Gabinetto.

TORRE, DUCA DELLA (jun.).—Relazione prima dell' eruzione del Vesuvio dagli 11 Agosto fino ai 18 Sett. 1804.—8⁰, *pp.* 61, *fol.* 1. *Napoli,* 1804.

TORRE, DUCA DELLA (jun.).—Veduta di una apertura formatasi all'orlo del Vesuvio nell' eruzione del 22 Novembre 1804.—*pl.* 4⁰, *with descript. Napoli,* 1804. [O.V.]

TORRE, DUCA DELLA (jun.).—Éruption du Vésuve.—*Ann. Mus. Hist. Nat.* v, *pp.* 448–61. *Paris,* 1804.

[TORRE, DUCA DELLA (jun.).]—Observations sur les dernières éruptions du Vésuve. —*Journ. Phys. Chim. lxi, pp.* 218–25. *Paris,* 1805.

[TORRE, DUCA DELLA (jun.).]—Détails sur le tremblement de terre du 26 juillet 1805. —*Journ. Phys. lxi, pp.* 225–28. *Paris,* 1805.

TORRE, DUCA DELLA (jun.).—Pianta topografica dell' interno del cratere del Vesuvio formata nel mese di Giugno 1805.—*pl.* 4⁰, *with descript. Napoli,* 1805. [O.V.]— *Reproduced in* ROTH : Der Vesuv u. die Umgebung von Neapel.

TORRE, DUCA DELLA (jun.).—Descrizione della eruzione del Maggio e Giugno 1806. —*Giorn. Enciclop.* 7. *Napoli,* 1806.

TORRE, DUCA DELLA (jun.).—Lettera a Domenico Catalano sulla eruzione del 1806. —*Giorn. Enciclop. pp.* 155–71. *Napoli,* 1806. [C.A. and B.V.]

TORRE, Duca Della (jun.).—Catalogue abrégé de la Collection Vésuvienne de Mr. le Duc de la Torre de Naples 1820.—*fol.*, *foll.* 2. [*Napoli*, 1820.] [C.A.]

TORTALETTI, B.—Sonetto (1631).—*See* GIORGI URBANO.

TORTORELLI, L.—Lettera al Sig. D. Michele Torcia intorno alla pioggia delle ceneri e lapilli Vesuviani accaduta in Foggia ec. nell' eruzione del 1779.—*See* TORCIA.—Relazione, *p.* 61.

TOSCAN, B.—Précis du Journal de l'éruption du Vésuve depuis le 11 août jusqu'au 18 sept. 1804.—*Ann. Mus. xv, pp.* 448–61. *Paris*, 1810. [B.S.]

TOSCAN, G. L. G. (transl. by). — *See* SPALLANZANI, L.—Voyage dans les Deux Siciles, etc.—*Paris, An* VIII [1800].

TOSI, C.—De incendio Vesevi. Ode ed un sonetto (1631).—*See* GIORGI URBANO.

TOULA, F.—Die vulkanischen Berge.—16⁰, 1 view, 1 map. *Wien*, 1879.
   See pp. 14–37, 38–67. Forms part of the Geogr. Jugend-und-Volks-Bibliothek.

TOUR, Duc De La.—*See* ANON. 1805.

TRANSARELLI, O. — *See* GIORGI URBANO. 1631. [C.A.]

TRAUBENBERG, H.—*See* RAUSCH VON TRAUBENBERG.

TRAVAGLINI, Fed. (dis.).—Italia, Napoli, Pompei. Avanzi del Tempio di Venere. Pemié inc., Tav. XLV.
   Small line engrav.: 170×111 mm.

TREGLIOTTA, L.—Descrittione dell' incendio del Monte Vesuvvio, e suoi marauigliosi effetti. Principiato la notte delli 15 di Decembre MDCXXXI.—8⁰, *pp.* 40. *Napoli*, 1632. [B.N.]

TRENTINAGLIA, J. Von. — Ueber die Thätigkeit des Vesuv's seit dem Jahre 1870 (1876).—*Nat. Med. Berichte, vii, Heft* 1, *pp.* 122–36. *Innsbruck*, 1877.

TROJAN, E.—[An account of a visit to Vesuvius after the eruption, with views of cone before and after.]—"*Nature,*" lxxiv, *p.* 305. *July* 26th, 1906.—*Deutsche Arbeit, v, p.* 352.

TROLLOPE, F. E.—*See* STIELER, C.

TROLLOPE, T. A.—*See* STIELER, C.

TROMBELLI, G.—Sonetto (1631). — *See* GIORGI URBANO.

TROYBI, D. P.—Istoria generale del reame di Napoli.—11 vols. 4⁰. *Napoli*, 1747 et seq.
   See Vol. i, pp. 119–36.

T., S. A. [Tata, according to A. Scacchi].—Relazione dell' ultima eruzione del Vesuvio accaduta in Agosto di quest' anno.—*Giorn. Enciclop. Ital. Mem. Scient. Lett. v,* 24 e 25. *Napoli*, 1787.—8⁰, *pp.* 16. *Napoli*, 1788. [C.A.]

TSCHERMAK, G. Von.—Biotit-Zwillinge vom Vesuv.—*Jahrb. deutsch. geol. Reichsanst. xxvi, Min. Mittheil. p.* 187. *Wien*, 1876.

TSCHERMAK, G. Von.—Die Glimmergruppe. (Meroxen vom Vesuv.)—*Zeitschr. f. Kryst. u. Min. ii, p.* 18. *Leipzig*, 1878.

TURBOLI, D.—Supplica et memoria al Sig. Duca di Caivano, *etc.* Con un brevissimo racconto d'alcune sentenze di Seneca, cavata dai libri de beneficiis, e providentia, e d'altre materie gradibili. [Erupt. 1631.]— 4⁰. *Napoli*, 1632. [B.N.]

TURGIS (lith.).— Golfe du Torre del Greco . . . rue Sᵗ Jacques 16 . . . rue Sᵗ Rome 36.
   A poor view of Vesuvius through trees above Castellamare. Rough litho. on straw-tinted paper: 140×107 mm.

TURLERUS, H.—De peregrinatione et agro Neapolitano libri II . . . Omnibus peregrinantibus utiles ac necessarii : ac in eorum gratiam nunc primum editi.—8⁰. *Argentorati*, 1574. [B.N.]
   See pp. 104–7.

TURPIN DE CRISSÉ, Cte.—Souvenirs du Golfe de Naples recueillis en 1808, 1818 et 1824.—4⁰, *pp.* 65, *frontisp.*, 10 *figs.*, 2 *maps*, 38 *pls.* (fine steel engrav.). *Paris*, 1828.

TURPIN DE CRISSÉ. Cte. (peint par).— [View of Vesuvius from Castello di Lettere.] Gravé par Lemaître.
   Engrav. on double paper : 135×105 mm.

TUTINI, C.—Memorie della vita, miracoli e culto di S. Giannuario martire.—4⁰, *foll.* 4, *pp.* 141, *foll.* 3, 1 *pl.*, *figs.* *Napoli*, 1633. [C.A.]—Another ed. 4⁰. 1703. [B.N.]— Another ed. *Napoli*, 1710.
   See Cap. x. ed. 1703.

TUTINI, C.—Prodigiosi portenti del Monte Vesuvio. Invettiva contro g'i Spagnuoli in occasione dell' incendio dell' anno 1649. E note riguardanti quella eruzione per Luigi Riccio.—*Archiv. Stor. Prov. Nap. ii,* 1, *pp.* 28. *Napoli*, 1877. [C.A.]

ULLOA SEVERINO, N.—Lettere erudite.—12⁰, *pp.* 24+451+25. *Napoli*, 1700.
See pp. 166–94.

ULLOA SEVERINO, N.—Relazione dell' incendio Vesuviano del 1698. Descrizione del Vesuvio, sue eruzioni, effetti ecc. —*See* " Lettere erudite," *pp.* 149, 166.

UNGERN-STERNBERG, W. H. C. R. A. Von.—Werden und Seyn des vulkanischen Gebirges. Mit 8 Abbildungen.—8⁰, *pp.* xi+320. *Carlsruhe*, 1825.
See pp. 64–92.

URCIUOLI, A.—Relazione di ciò, che accadde in questa Provincia di Principato ultra nell' eruzione del Vesuvio in Agosto 1779.— *See* TORCIA.—Relazione, p. 84.

URSUS, J. B.—Vesevi montis epitaphium.—8⁰, *fol.* 1. *Napoli*, 1632. [C.A.]

URSUS, J. B.—Inscriptiones.—*fol., foll.* 11, *pp.* 350, *engrav. frontisp. Napoli*, 1642.
See pp. 14, 24, 26, 39, 99, 100, 101, 111, 331, 332, 333, 334, 336.

UVOLO, B.—Lettera intorno alla nuvola di ceneri Vesuviane per l'incendio del 1779.— *See* TORCIA.—Relazione, p. 81.

VACHMESTER, M.—Analyse de la Sodalite du Vésuve.—*Ann. Mines, x, pp.* 262–63. *Paris*, 1817.

VAIL, H. D.—Description of the appearance of Mount Vesuvius during an eruption (1868).—*Proc. Amer. Phil. Soc. x, pp.* 421–23, 425–28. *Philadelphia*, 1869.

VALDIUIELSO, J. DE.—Silva.—*See* QUINONES.—El Monte Vesvvio.

VALENTI, S.—Lezioni tre sopra il tremoto (1729).—8⁰, *foll. viii, pp.* 86. *Roma*, 1748.

VALENTIN, L.—Voyage médical en Italie fait l'année 1820, précédé d'une excursion au volcan du Mont Vésuve, et aux ruines d'Herculanum et Pompéi.—8⁰, *foll.* 2, *pp.* 166. *Nancy*, 1822.——2nd ed. " corrigée et augmentée de nouvelles observations faites dans un second voyage en 1824."—8⁰, *pp.* 400. *Paris*, 1826.
See pp. 11–26, 1822.

VALENZIANI, M.—Indice spiegato di tutte le produzioni del Vesuvio, della Solfatara e d'Ischia.—4⁰, *pp. lii*+135. *Napoli*, 1783.

VALENZIANI, M.—Dissertazione della vera raccolta o sia Museo di tutte le produzioni del Monte Vesuvio.—4⁰, *pp.* 12. *Napoli, circa* 1790.

VALENZIANI, M.—Note de la collection complète des diverses espèces de productions du Mont Vésuve.—*fol., fol.* 1. — ?, — ? [O.V.]

VALÉRY, M.—Voyages historiques et littéraires en Italie, pendant les années 1826, 1827 et 1828 ; ou l'indicateur italien.—8⁰, *pp.* 606. *Bruxelles*, 1835. —— 2nd ed. *Paris*, 1838.

VALÉRY, M.—Historical, literary and artistical travels in Italy, a complete and methodical guide for travellers and artists. Translated . . . from the second corrected and improved edition, by C. E. Clifton, with a copious index and a road-map of Italy.—8⁰, *pp. vii*+781. *Paris*, 1842.—Also *Paris*, 1852.
Transl. of above.

VALETTA, J.—Epistola . . . de incendio et eruptione Montis Vesuvii, anno MDCCVII. —*Phil. Trans. R. Soc. xxviii, pp.* 22–25. *London*, 1714.—*Compend. Trans. Filos. d. Londra, pp.* 59–61. *Venezia*, 1793.

VALETTA, J.—An account of the eruption of Mount Vesuvius in 1707. Translated from the Latin.—*Phil. Trans. R. Soc. (Abridged), vi* (1713–23), *pp.* 12–14. *London*, 1809.

VALMONT DE BOMARE, J. C.—Dictionnaire raisonné universel d'Histoire Naturelle ; *etc.*—5 tom. 8⁰. *Paris*, 1765.—9 tom. 8⁰. *Paris*, 1775.——4th ed. 8 tom. 4⁰. *Lyon*, 1791.
See Tom. ix, 1775.

VALMONT DE BOMARE, J. C. (?)—*See* BOMARE, DE.

VANDER AA, PIERRE.— Le Mont Vésuve comme il étoit en 1631, La Gallerie Agréable du Monde. Leide. [B.N.P. Vb. 121.]
A small, damaged print of much later date than the eruption.

VANDER BURCH.—Le Vésuve prise au côté de Portici. (Planche II.) Lith. Lemercier, Paris. [B.N.P. Vb. 121.]
A very bad litho.

VANGELISTI (sculp.).—*See* CHASTELET (del.).—Naples. Vue du Vésuve, prise du côté de Mare Piano, *etc.*

VANVITELLI (Van Witel), GASPARE (father of Luigi).—[Panorama of the Arsenal and Mole of Naples from Pizzofalcone.]— *San Martino Museum, Naples, No.* 5965.
A pen-and-ink drawing of about the 17th century.

VARONIS, S. — Vesuviani incendii historiæ libri tres.—4⁰, *foll.* 8, *pp.* 400, *foll.* 6. *Neapoli*, 1634.

VASI, M.—Itinerario istruttivo da Roma a Napoli ovvero descrizione generale de' più insigni monumenti antichi, e moderni, e delle opere più rimarchevoli di pittura, scultura, ed architettura di questa celebre città.—3rd ed. 12⁰, *pp. ix+*264, *pls.*, 2 *plans. Roma*, 1816.—Other ed. : 2 tom. *Roma*, 1814.—2 tom. *Roma*, 1818.——5th ed. 8⁰, *pp.* 282, *num. figs. Roma*, 1819. [Coll. H. Elliott, Esq.]—2 tom. *Roma*, 1820, 19.—2 tom. *Roma*, 1824.—2 tom. *Roma*, 1830.—2 tom. *Roma*, 1844. Poor figures of Vesuvius.

VASI, M.—A New Picture of Naples, and its environs ; in the form of an itinerary.— 16⁰, *pp. xii+*364, *pls.*, 1 *map*, 1 *plan. London* [1820 ?].

VASI, M.—Itinéraire instructif de Rome à Naples et à ses environs, tiré de celui de feu M. Vasi, et de la Sicile, tiré de celui de M. de Haraczay [by A. Nibby].—12⁰, *pp.* 399. *Rome*, 1826.—Other ed. : 2 tom. *Rome*, 1797.—2 tom. *Rome*, 1816.—(4th.) *Rome*, 1817.—2 tom. *Rome*, 1820.—2 tom. *Rome*, 1824 ; *Naples*, 1824.—2 tom. *Rome*, 1829. —2 tom. *Rome*, 1838, 39.

VAUQUELIN, L. N.—Analyse des cendres du Vésuve, *etc.—Mém. Mus. Hist. Nat. ix, pp.* 381–84. *Paris*, 1822.—*Ann. Chim. xxv, pp.* 72–75. *Paris*, 1824.

VAUQUELIN, L. N.—Chemische Untersuchung der Asche des Vesuv's.—*Arch. f. gesammt. Naturl. i, pp.* 343–45. *Nürnberg*, 1824.

VECCHI, MALAGOLI.—*See* PELLÉ, C. 1841.

VEGA, F. and P.—Topographia Herculanensis, qua ejus agri facies, prout olim, ante quam celeberrima Vesuvii eructatione, anno primo Titi Imperatoris obrueretur, erat spectabilis, ex varia multiplicum ad gestionum altitudine et situ investigata exhibetur. Cataneus inc.
A beautiful, detailed engraved map of coast near Resina : 855×404 mm.

VEGA, P. and F.—Topographia dei villaggi di Portici, Resina, e Torre del Greco, e di porzione de' loro territorj, per quanto serve a rischiarare altra carta dell' antico stato dell' agro Ercolanese. Aniello Cataneo incise.
A beautifully engraved map of the coast, later than 1794 : 404×858 mm.

VELAIN, C.—Les Volcans, ce qu'ils sont et ce qu'ils nous apprennent.—8⁰, *pp.* 127, 1 *pl., figs. Paris*, 1884.—*Bull. hebd. Assoc. Scient. France, S.* 2, *viii and ix.* 1883–84.

VELEZ DE GUEVARA, LUIS.—À la Montaña de Soma. Soneto (1613).—*See* QUINONES.—El Monte Vesvvio.

VENTIGNANO, DUCA DI. — Il Vesuvio. Poema.—8⁰, *pp.* 126, *fol.* 1. *Napoli*, 1810. [C.A.]

VENUTI, D. M. DE.—Descrizione delle prime scoperte dell' antica città di Ercolano.—4⁰, *pp. xxiii+*146. *Roma*, 1748.— 8⁰, *pp. xx+*138. *Venezia*, 1749.

VERNEAU, F. (levò.).—Cratere del Vesuvio in Febbraio 1862. Scala 1 : 10,000. B. Colao litografo.—[*Naples*, 1862 ?] [B.M. 24058 (4).]

VERNET (painted from a drawing on the spot by G. de la Croix).—A night sea piece with a view of the eruptions of Mount Vesuvius. Vue du Mont Vézuve tel qu'il étoit en 1757. Dixon fecit. London, printed for John Bowles in Cornhill.
Hand-coloured engrav. : 340×246 mm.

VERNET, JGN.—Éruption du Mont Vésuve, 1779. Gravé d'après le tableau de Monsieur Jgn. Vernet, élève de son frère aîné. Werroter sculp. A Paris chez la Chausée rue St. Jacques vis à vis la fontaine S. Severin.
Engrav. : 377×525 mm.

VERNEUIL, P. É. P. DE.—[Lettres sur la dernière éruption du Vésuve.]—*Bull. Soc. géol. France, S.* 2, *xv, pp.* 369–70, 376–77. *Paris*, 1858. — *C.R. Acad. Sci. xlvi, pp.* 117–18. *Paris*, 1858.

VERNEUIL, P. É. P. DE.—[Sur l'éruption du Vésuve de 1867–68.]—*Bull. Soc. géol. France, S.* 2, *xxv, pp.* 802–10. *Paris*, 1868.

VERNEUIL, P. É. P. DE.—Sur les phénomènes récents du Vésuve.—*C.R. Acad. Sci. lxvi, pp.* 1020–24. *Paris*, 1868.

VERNEUIL, P. É. P. DE.—Note sur l'altitude du Vésuve le 26 avril, 1869. — *C.R. Acad. Sci. lxviii, pp.* 1309–10. *Paris*, 1869.

VERNEUIL, P. É. P. DE.—Note sur l'éruption du Vésuve (avril 1872).—*C.R. Acad. Sci. lxxiv, pp.* 1373–76. *Paris*, 1872.— *Bull. Soc. géol. France, S.* 2, *xxix, pp.* 415–21. *Paris*, 1872.

VERRI, A.—Studio geologico delle sorgenti del Sarno.—" *Sorgenti, estuario e canale del fiume Sarno,*" 4⁰, *pp.* 119–51, *tav.* Roma, 1902.

VERRI, A.—Sul Vesuvio e sul Vulcano Laziale.—*Boll. Soc. Geol. Ital. xxi, pp. xxxi–xxxv,* 411–12. *Roma,* 1902.

VESUVINO CRISIPPO.—Dichiarazione genealogica fisico-chimica naturale, apologetica ed epidemica del Signor Vesuvio Frottola.—8⁰, *pp.* 16. [*Napoli,* 1794 ?] [C.A.]

VETRANI, A.—Sebethi vindiciæ, sive dissertatio de Sebethi antiquitate, nomine, fama, cultu, origine, prisca magnitudine, decremento, atque alveis, adversus Jacobum Martorellium.—8⁰, *pp.* 8 + 213, 2 *pls. Neapoli,* 1767.

VETRANI, A.—Il prodromo Vesuviano in cui oltre al nome, origine, etc. del Vesuvio s'esaminano tutti i sistemi dei filosofi, etc.—8⁰, *foll.* 4, *pp.* 238. *Napoli,* 1780.

VIANELLI.—*See* VIANELLY, A.

VIANELLO.—*See* VIANELLY, A.

VIANELLY, [A.] (dis.).—Il foro di Pompeia. Napoli, 1845. Lit. Wenzel.
Similar to pl. at p. 516 in Vol. ii of ANON.—" Napoli e . . . sue vicinanze."
Fine view of Vesuvius. Litho. : 213 × 141 mm.

VIANELLY, [A.] (pinx.).—Royaume de Naples, Nº 24. Naples vue du Champ de Mars. Salathé scᵗ. A Paris chez A. Bis et F. Debrucil. Imp. Edit., Rue Git le Cœur, 11.
Stipple engrav. : 210 × 198 mm.

VIANELLY, A. (dis.).—Vue de Naples prise de la mer. Dˢ dis a pen.—Lit. Marras.
Outline litho. of Naples from the sea ; fisherman smoking in boat in foreground : 357 × 256 mm.

VIANELLY, [A.]—[View looking towards Naples from the Hermitage on Vesuvius.] 1825.
Line litho. : 420 × 273 mm.

VIANELLY, A.—[88 views of the neighbourhood of Naples. A series of lithographs coloured by Martorani and some by Vianelly.]—[Coll. H. Elliott, Esq., of Naples.]
Publ. by Cuciniello and Bianchi, some only by the latter. Naples ?, 1825–30 ?

VIANELLY [A.] and GIGANTE.—[52 coloured engravings of views and scenes in the neighbourhood of Naples. Eight original water-colours of Neapolitan types.] —4⁰. *Naples,* 1827.
Most are signed and dated 1827, and many show good outlines of Vesuvius.

VIANELLY, [A.]—[View of Bay of Naples and Vesuvius from summit of M. Epomeo in Ischia.] 1828.
Peasant and monk with pitcher in foreground. Line litho. plate : 415 × 270 mm.

VIANELLY, A.—[12 line engravings on tinted paper, retouched by hand, of Naples and Pæstum. From drawings by the author and Ercole and Achille Gigante.] —*obl. fol.* [*Naples*] 1842.
Contains letter from Vianelly himself to M. A. Delanoy, from whose collection it came. *See* Pls. 7 and 8.

VIANELLY, A. (dis.).—Veduta di Napoli disegnata dal Casino della Margravia di Anspach sulla strada di Posilipo. Vue de Naples dessinée de la maison de plaisance de la Margrave d'Anspach sur la route nouvelle de Pausilipe.—Litˢ Cuciniello e Bianchi.
Similar to a plate in their " Viaggio Pittorico," 1845. Litho. on double paper : 336 × 253 mm.

VIARD.—*See* DARONDEAU.

VIDALIN.—*See* DARONDEAU.

VIENNELLY.—*See* VIANELLY, A.

VILLAYÇAN GARCES, G. DE.—Al Bolcan que aborto la Montaña de Soma. Soneto (1631).—*See* · QUINONES.—El Monte Vesvvio.

VILLEFORE, [I. DE] (des.).—Veduta 'del Monte Vesuvio, e dell' eruzione accaduta a' xxv d'Ottobre 1751 ad ore 10 della sera dell' orinolo Franzese, ed alle 4 ore d'Italia, etc.—*Napoli* ?, 1752 ?
Engrav. pl. with printed title, etc., and 27 ref. nos. : 410 × 263 mm.

VILLEFORE, I. DE.—Vue du Mont Vésuve et de son éruption arrivée le 25 Oct. 1751.
Plate fol. with engraved description.

VILLENEUVE.—*See* COIGNET, M.—Vues pittoresques de l'Italie, *etc., and* Voyage en Italie, *etc.*

VILLENEUVE (lith.).—*See* COIGNET, M. —Château de Castelamare.

VILLENEUVE, MLLE.—*See* COIGNET, M. —Vues pittoresques de l'Italie, *etc.*

VINALLY.—*See* VIANELLY, A.

VINDELICOR, AUG.—Neapolis regni hujus maxima ornatissima siti amœnissima mutisque castellis. . . . Napoli, 1720. [B.M. —24045 (4).]
Coloured engraving and views. A too fantastic view of Vesuvius, very similar to publications by Homanni. The crater and cone are probably of this earlier date.

VIOLA, C.—Per l'Anortite del Vesuvio.— *Atti R. Acc. Lincei, S.* 5, *Rend. viii, sem.* 1, *pp.* 400-4, 463-69, 490-97. *Roma,* 1899.

VIOLA, C.—Zur Kenntniss des Anorthits vom Vesuv.—*Zeitschr. f. Kryst. u. Min. xxxi, pp.* 484-98, *figs. Leipzig,* 1899.

VIOLA, C., und KRAUS, E. H.—Ueber Fedorowit (nuovo minerale della provincia di Roma).—*Zeitschr. f. Kryst. u. Min. xxxiii,* 1, *pp.* 36-38. *Leipzig,* 1900.

VIOLA, S. (Nap.).—Historia del Monte Vesuvio nella quale diffusamente si tratta di tutto lo che è occorso in esso dal principio del mondo sino all' anno 1631 et 1649. Con occasione del ultima eruttatione di fuoco fatta dal detto Monte a 16 Decembre 1631, e a 28 Novembre 1649.—Original MS. *fol., foll.* 3+132. [C.A.]

VIRGILII, P. DE.—Al Vesuvio. Poesia.— *See* ANON.—Il Vesuvio. Strenna pel capo d'anno del 1844, *pp.* 1-4.

VIRGILIO, F.—*See* REYER, ED. 1893.

VISCARDI, F.—Risposta alla lettera dell' Abate Tata de' 21 Agosto per l'eruzione del 1794.—8°, *pp.* 16, *fol.* 1. *Napoli,* 1794.

VISSCHER, N.—Totius Italiæ. Tabula.

VITO, C. DE (dis.).—Veduta della 34ᵘᵃ eruzione, accaduta li 13 Settembre 1810. Vue de la 34ᵐᵉ éruption arrivée le 13 septembre 1810. P. Toro inc. T. XXVI. In Napoli presso Franc. Scafa. Str. S. Biagio de' Librari. N⁰ 117.
Engrav.: 252×193 mm.

VITO, C. DE (dis.).—Veduta della 35ᵐᵃ eruzione accaduta il 1 Gennaro 1812. Vue de la 25ᵐᵉ éruption arrivée le 1 janvier 1812. P. Toro incise. T. XXVII. In Napoli presso Franc. Scafa. Str. S. Biagio de' Librari. N⁰ 117.
Engrav.: 250×191 mm.

VITOLO-FIRRAO, A.—La città di Somma Vesuviana illustrata nelle sue famiglie nobile, con altre notizie storico-araldiche. —8°, *foll.* 2, *pp.* 106. *Napoli,* 1886.

VITRIOLI, D.—I due scheletri [di Pompei]. —*See* ANON.—Convito di Carità . . . *etc. pp.* 13-19. *Napoli,* 1872.

VITRIOLI, D.—Un cretese a Pompei nell' ultima giornata.—*See* ANON.—Convito di Carità . . . *etc. pp.* 28-31. *Napoli,* 1872.

VITRUVIUS POLLIO, M.—De Architectura libri decem.—*See* CLEONIDAS.— Hoc in volumine . . . continentur . . . Cleonidæ Harmonicum, *etc.—fol.* — ?, 1497.

VITTORIA, G.—Studi sulla resistenza delle lave Vesuviane.—8°, *pp.* 11. *Napoli,* 1870.

VOCOLA, A.—Istoria dell' eruzione del Vesuvio accaduta nel mese di Maggio 1737 scritta per l'Accademia delle Scienze.— *Napoli,* 1738.

VOGEL, J. H.—Ueber die chemische Zusammensetzung des Vesuvians.—8°, *pp.* 58. *Göttingen,* 1887.

VOGT, C. C.—Ueber Vulkane. Vortrag.—8°, *pp.* 48. *Basel,* 1875.
See pp. 6, 10-12.
Öffentl. Vorträge gehalt. in der Schweiz, iii, 2.

VOLAIRE, J. A.—Ausbruch des Vesuv am 14 Mai 1771.
This fine oil painting is the original from which the engraving by Guttenberg and others was made. It is No. 872 in the Akad. d. Bildenden Künste in Vienna.

VOLAIRE, [J. A.]—Éruption du Mont Vésuve du 14 Mai 1771. Naples, No. 32. Gravé par H. Guttenberg. [B.N.P. Vb. 121.]
A beautiful engraving showing the junction of Somma and the ridge of the Salvatore. Original in Vienna, No. 872 in the Akad. d. Bildenden Künste.

VOLAIRE, [J. A.]—Éruption du Vésuve 14 Mai 1771. Prise sur le Vésuve même de la partie appelée Monte di Somma; l'espace qui est entre les spectateurs e la sommité de la Montagne, d'où l'on voit couler la lave, est le Vallon Atrio di Cavallo, il se trouve au deux tiers environ du Vésuve. Peint d'après nature par Volaire. Gravé par H. Guttenberg. N⁰ 60 N.
Very fine engraving: 375×220 mm.

VOLAIRE, [J. A.]—Veduta dell' eruzione del Vesuvio accaduta a 1½ di notte la sera degli 8 Agosto 1779.—*fol.* engraved on copper by L. Boilly.—*See* TORCIA.— "Relazione," etc. [B.S.]

VOLPE, C.—Breve discorso dell' incendio del Monte Vesuvio e degli suoi effetti.—8⁰, pp. 60. Napoli, 1632. [O.V.]

VOLPI, A. Von.—Der Ausbruch des Vesuvs im April 1872.—" Unsere Zeit," N.F. viii, pp. 393–403. Leipzig, 1872.
See his : " Neapel und die Internat. Maritime Ausstellung."—Ibid. vii, pp. 637 et seq. Leipzig, 1871.

VOLPICELLA, S.—Gita ad Amoretto S. Giorgio a Cremano, S. Sebastiano, Massa di Somma e Pollena Trocchia.—In " Albo artistico Napoletano per cura di Mariano Lombardi." Napoli, 1853.—[Reprinted in :] " Studi di letteratura, storia ed arti." Napoli, 1876.

VOLPICELLA, S.—Studi di letteratura, storia ed arti, con le poesie e vita del Costanzo, vita del Tansillo, la Madonna di Atella, il palazzo Donnanna a Posilipo, antichita di Amalfi, cenni storici su Amoretto, San Giorgio, San Sebastiano, Massa di Somma, Pollena, Trocchia, Lacco, Casamicciola, etc.—12⁰, pp. 534+2. Napoli, 1876.

VOLPICELLI, F.—Il Vesuvio bocca dell' inferno. Leggenda.—8⁰, pp. 20. Napoli, 1871. [C.A.]

VOLPICELLI, F.—See F . . . V . . .

VOLTA, A.—See CERMENATI, M.

VOLZ (sculp.).—Éruption du Mont Véssuve, de la coletion [sic] de G. Hamilton. Chez V. Zanna & Comp.
A stipple engrav. hand-col. ; two women, a man and boy in foreground, looking across bay at erupt. of Vesuvius by night : 241 × 193 mm.

VUOLO, P.—Lettera sull' eruzione del Vesuvio nel 1779.—See TORCIA.—Relazione, etc.

WAGNER, P.—See OESTERLAND.

WAGNER, P.—Ueber den Vesuv.—Sitzber. naturwiss. Gesellsch. Isis, 29 Juni, 1905, p. 12. Dresden, 1906.

WAIBLINGER, W.—Der Vesuv im Jahre 1829. — " Abendzeitung," 212, 213, pp. 845–47, 849–51. Dresden, 1829.—Gesammelte Werke, ix. Hamburg, 1839.

WALCHIO, JOANNE ERNESTO IMM.—Antiquitates Herculanenses litterariæ oratione auspicali memoratæ et inlustratæ.—See GORI.—Admiranda Antiquitatum Herculanensium, etc. i, pp. 100–39.

WALCKNAER.—See NORVINS.

WALDO, C. A.—A Vesuvian cycle.—Proc. Ind. Acad. Sci. 1898, pp. 72–74. Indianapolis, Ind., 1899.

WALKER.—See FIELDING.

WALKER, GIO.—Lettera scritta all' erudito Sig. Ab. Tata in Napoli.—Giorn. Lett. iii, pp. 95–98. Napoli, 1793.

WALKER, K. C.—Vesuvius and Pozzuoli.— " Harper's Magazine," xxxi, pp. 756–61. New York, 1865.

WALLNER, F.—Am ewigen Feuerheerd.— " Die Gartenlaube," pp. 548–49, 2 figs. 1866.

WALLNER, F.—Wenn Jemand eine Reise thut. Flüchtige Reiseskizzen von der Spree bis zur Tiber, von der Tiber bis zum Vesuv.—8⁰, pp. viii+350. Berlin, 1866.
See pp. 144–48.

WALTHER, J. K.—Brief an Herrn Beyrich. Ueber geologische Beobachtungen im Golf von Neapel.—Zeitschr. deutsch. geol. Gesellsch. xxxvii, pp. 537–39. Berlin, 1885.

WALTHER, J. K., SCHIRLITZ, [L.] P.— Studium zur Geologie des Golfes von Neapel.—Zeitschr. deutsch. geol. Gesellsch. xxxviii, pp. 295–341. Berlin, 1886.—Boll. R. Com. Geol. Ital. pp. 383–96. Roma, 1886.

WARBURTON, M.—Dissertation sur les tremblements de terre et les éruptions de feu.—2 vols. 8⁰. Paris, 1764.

WARD, I.—Vue de Véssuv. 3.—Augsbourg, etc. [B.N.P. Vb. 121.]
A sepia engraving of unknown date.

WARD, I. (peint.).—Vue du Vésuve à Augsbourg dans le négoce de l'Académie des Arts. Gravé par Tinimal.
An imaginary view of Vesuvius in eruption. Stipple sepia engrav., hand-coloured : 190 × 140 mm.

WARREN (sc.).—The suburbs of Naples with a distant view of Mount Vesuvius.
Obviously in part imaginary. Engraving : 203 × 133 mm.

WASHINGTON, H. S.—Italian petrological sketches. v. Summary and Conclusion.— The Journ. of Geology, v, 4, pp. 349–77. Chicago, 1897.

WASHINGTON, H. S.—Some analyses of Italian Volcanic Rocks.—Amer. Journ. Sci. S. 4, viii, 31, pp. 286–94. New Haven, 1899.

WASHINGTON, H. S.—Chemical analyses of Igneous Rocks published from 1884 to 1900, with a critical discussion of the character and use of analyses.—*U.S. Geol. Surv. Prof. Paper* 14, *pp*. 495. *Washington*, 1903.

WASHINGTON, H. S.—The superior analyses of Igneous Rocks from Roth's Tabellen, 1869–1884, arranged according to the Quantitative System of Classification.—*U.S. Geol. Surv. Prof. Paper* 28, *pp*. 61. *Washington*, 1904.

WATSON, R.—*See* PADERNI, C. 1757.

WEBER, FRID. (Gestochen u. verlegt.).— [A rather good series of col. engraving reproductions of Sir W. Hamilton's plates in his " Campi Phlegræi."] There is one in the Johnston-Lavis collection, which is probably the eruption of 1760 by night.

WEBER, FRID.—Vesuv. Welche schrökbare Illumination mach er nan nicht ! als wollte er das halbe Erdenrunde beleuchten, u. die ewigen Eissgebürge schmelzen ! Gibt vielleicht Vulcan ein Götter-Fest in seiner Werkstätte ! Mag er immerhin dies schöne Schauspiel uns geben, schont nur sein zerstörendes Toben der umherliegenden friedlichen Palläste und Hütten. Gestochen u. verlegt von Frid. Weber. Col. engrav. after Sir W. Hamilton : 382×280 mm.

WEBER, F. R.—*See* ANNA, A. D'.—Éruption du Mont Vésuve. [1779.]

WEBERT, C., CLERMONT.—Carte des environs de la ville et du Golfe de Naples. [As insets :] Plan du cratère. Dessiné le 2 janvier 1778. Coupe du cratère sur la ligne A.B. Dessiné le 2 janvier, 1778. A good, engraved map of Vesuvius : 480×367 mm.

WEBERT, C.—Bay of Naples and Salerno. Map. Plan of crater of Mount Vesuvius, Jan. 1778. 2nd. 1778. — ?, 1803. [B.M.— Sec. 5 (159).] A good map and section.

WEDDING, G. T. A.—Beitrag zu den Untersuchungen der Vesuvlaven.—*Zeitschr. deutsch. geol. Gesellsch. x, pp*. 375–411. *Berlin*, 1858.

WEDDING, G. T. A.—De Vesuvii montis lavis.—4⁰, *pp*. 30+2. *Berolini*, 1859.

WEGNER, T. H.—Beobachtungen über den Ausbruch des Vesuv im April 1906.— *Centralbl. f. Min. pp*. 506–18, 529–40, 11 *figs*. (*geol. map*). *Stuttgart*, 1906.

WELSCH, H.—Warhafftige Reiss-Beschreibung aus eigener Erfahrung von Teutschland, Croatien, Italien denen Inseln Sicilia, Malta, ecc. Nicht venigen bey dennen wunderbahren brennenden Bergens als dem Vesuvio bey Naples, ecc. Erupt. 1631 *etc*. —4⁰, *foll*. 12, *pp*. 427, 1 *portrait. Stuttgart*, 1658. [C.A.]

WENTRUP, F.—Der Vesuv und die vulcanische Umgebung Neapels.—8⁰, *pp*. 35. *Wittemberg*, 1860. [C.A.]

WENTZEL, FR. (lith.).—Naples. Neapel. Lith. de Fr. Wentzel à Wissembourg. Deposé 2.—Depôt chez Vᵛᵉ Humbert, rue Sᵗ Jacques 65, Paris. View of Naples and Vesuvius from above the Grotto of Posilippo, *circa* 1832. Litho. on highly tinted background : 366× 250 mm.

WENTZEL, FR. (dis.).—Riviera di Chiaja. Le Rivage de Chiaja. G. Gigante dip. Litho ̇ Cuciniello e Bianchi. Litho. on double paper of Naples from Mergellina ; wall, crucifix and boats in foreground : 313×220 mm. It is pl. at p. 112, Vol. i, of Cuciniello e Bianchi's " Viaggio Pittoresco," 1845.

WERNLY, R.—Von den Alpen zum Vesuv. Reisebilder aus Italien.—8⁰. *Aarau*, 1892.

WESTPHAL, G. E.—Carta de' contorni di Napoli per uso de' Forestieri e Viaggiatori rettificata ed accresciuta in Napoli a tutto il 1880.—*Napoli, Detken e Rocholl*, 1880. Scale, 1 : 90,000.

WESTPHAL, G. E.—Guide pour accompagner la Carte des environs de Naples, à l'usage des Voyageurs.—12⁰, *pp*. 43 *and large map with line-shading. Rome*, 1828. The Pedimentina is shown as a ridge.

WIET.—Reprise actuelle d'activité du Vésuve.—*C.R. Acad. Sci. cxi, p*. 404. *Paris*, 1890.

WILKINS, H.—Suite de vues pittoresques des ruines de Pompéi et un précis historique de la ville avec un plan des fouilles qui ont été faites jusqu'en février 1819, et une description des objets les plus intéressants.—*pp. viii*+23, 30 *pls*., 1 *map*, 1 *plan. Rome*, 1819. *See* Pls. 1, 14, 15, 18 and 19.

WILSON, J.—A History of Mountains, Geographical and Mineralogical. Accompanied by a picturesque view of the principal mountains of the World, in their respective proportions of height above the level of the sea by Robert Andrew Riddell. —3 vols. *Vol. i, pp. lv+368+176, London,* 1807 ; *Vol. ii, pp.* 735, *London,* 1809 ; *Vol. iii, pp.* 906*+index, London,* 1810. *See* Vol. ii. (Vols. ii and iii read : " A History . . . to accompany a picturesque view," *etc.*)

WILSON, W. R. (sketch.).—Eruption of Vesuvius, Dec‍ʳ, 1833. Engraving.—*Publ. by Longman & Co.* 12⁰. *London,* 1835. [Potter's collect.]

WINCKELMANN, J. J.—Critical account of the situation and destruction by the first eruptions of Mount Vesuvius, of Herculaneum, Pompeii and Stabia, etc.—8⁰, *pp. vi+125. London,* 1771.

WINGARD, F. C. Von.—Die chemische Zusammensetzung der Humitmineralien. (Chondrodit vom Vesuv.)—*Zeitschr. f. analyt. Chem. xxiv, pp.* 344–56. *Wiesbaden,* 1886.—*Zeitschr. f. Kryst. u. Min. xi, p.* 444. *Leipzig,* 1886.

WINSPEARE, Ant.—*See* BREISLAK, S.

WISBECH, F. (sc. Nbg.).—Neapel's Golf. Carlsruhe durch Kunst Verlag. W. Creuzbauer.
Small steel engrav. from above Grotto ; man sitting on log in foreground : 133×97 mm.

WIT, F. De.—Novissima et accuratissima totius Italiæ Corsicæ et Sardiniæ descriptio.—*Amstelodami,* — ?

WITZANI (gest.).—Ansicht von Neapel bei der Grotte von Posilipo. Im Kunstverlag v. L. v. Kleist in Dresden.
Very poor and incorrect view of no value ; hand-coloured litho. : 536×412 mm.

W. L. W.—Mount Vesuvius during the recent eruption. The Vesuvius Railway (inset). From an instantaneous photograph.—" *The Graphic," p.* 536. *London, May* 30, 1885.

WOLF, H.—On the lavas of Mount Vesuvius. —*Quart. Journ. Geol. Soc. xxv, p.* 16. *London,* 1869.

WOLF, H.—Vesuvlaven, eingesendet von Frau Marie Schmetzer in Brünn.—*Verhandl. deutsch. geol. Reichsanst. p.* 53. *Wien,* 1869.

WOLF, H.—Das Schwefelvorkommen zwischen Altavilla und Tufo O.N.O. von Neapel.—*Verhandl. deutsch. geol. Reichsanst. p.* 195. *Wien,* 1869.

WOLF, H.—Il giacimento zolfifero di tufo ad Altavilla all' E.N.E. di Napoli.—*Boll. R. Com. Geol. Ital. i, pp.* 160–62. *Firenze,* 1870.

WOLF, H.—Suite von Mineralien aus dem vulcanischen Gebiete Neapels und Siciliens.—*Verhandl. k. k. geol. Reichsanst. pp.* 219–20. *Wien,* 1870.

WOLFENSBERGER (drawn by).—The Forum, Pompeii, Italy. Le Forum à Pompéia, Italia. Das Forum, .Pompeii, Italien. Engraved by E. Radclyffe.— Fisher, Son & Co., London and Paris.
Fine steel engrav.,with view of Vesuvius : 188×163 mm.

WOLFFSOHN, L.—The Railway up Vesuvius.—" *The Daily News," London, March* 30, 1880.

WOLFFSOHN, L.—A night ascent of Vesuvius by rail.—*Ibid. June* 30, 1880.

WOLFFSOHN, L.—Mount Vesuvius.—*Ibid. Jan.* 13, 1882.

WOLFFSOHN, L.—Geological Survey on Monte Somma.—*Ibid. June* 1, 1882.

WOLFFSOHN, L.—Vesuvius : new breathing forth of lava.—*Ibid. May* 10, 1889.

WOLFFSOHN, L.—A visit to Vesuvius in eruption.—*Ibid. June* 17, 1891.

WOOD, H. (del.).—Naples. Dickinson & Co. Lith.
Vesuvius in distance. A very bad litho. on tinted background : 412×292 mm.

WRIGHT, E.—Some observations made in travelling through France, Italy, etc. in the Years 1720, 1721, and 1722.—2 vols. 4⁰. *London,* 1730.——2nd ed. 2 vols. [in 1] 4⁰, *pp. xvi+516, 41 pls., figs. London,* 1764.
See Vol. i, pp. 165–73, 1730.

WRIGHT, G. N.—The Shores and Islands of the Mediterranean drawn from Nature by Sir Grenville Temple, Bart., W. L. Leitch, Esq., Major Irton, and Lieut. Allen, R.E., with an analysis of the Mediterranean and description of the plates by the Rev. G. N. Wright.—4⁰, *pp.* 156, 65 *pls. London and Paris,* 1839 ?
See Pl. 149.

WRIGHT, G. N.—The Rhine, Italy and Greece illustrated. In a series of views from drawings on the spot. By W. L. Leitch, Col. Cockburn and Major Irton. With descriptions by the Rev. G. N. Wright.—2 vols. in 18 pts. 4⁰, 73 [beautiful] *steel-engraved pictures. London, Fischer, and Paris,* 1841.

WRIGHT, J.—Distant view of Mount Vesuvius, from the shore of Posilipo at Naples. Painted by Jos. Wright of Derby. Engraved by Wm. Byrne. Published as the Act directs 1 Nov.ʳ 1788, by Wm. Byrne, N° 79 Titchfield Street, London.
Line engraving in Johnston-Lavis collection : 320 × 230 mm. *See also* B.M.—K. 83. 79. d.

WUTKEY, MICHAEL (1738–1822).—Die Spitze des Vesuv beim Ausbruche.
Oil painting in the Akad. d. Bildenden Künste, Vienna. A cascade of lava, without date. Another, similar, shows lava flowing on cone : *circa* 1450 × 1000 mm. A third, much larger picture, No. 355, is a view from Naples with lava flowing on N. side of cone to the Atrio.

WUTKY (pinx.), ECHARDT (del.).—Prospect des Vesuvs und Baijs von Neapel. — ?, — ? [B.N.P. Vb. 121.]
A simple view of Naples and Vesuvius of no interest.

WYLD, J.—[A map of Vesuvius and the surrounding country, with a list of the principal eruptions from the year 79 to the present date.]—*fol. London,* 1872. [B.M. 24058 (5).]

WYLD, W.—Vue de Naples.
View of Vesuvius, badly drawn, over Naples from a terrace, with part of house to left. Woodcut in illustrated French paper : 146 × 125 mm.

WYNDHAM, T. HEATHCOTE.—The recent eruption of Vesuvius.—*" Oxford Undergraduates' Journal," Oxford,* 5 Dec., 1872.

XIFILINUS.—Storia Romana.
Thus quoted by J. Schneer and von Stein-Nordheim at end of " The History of Vesuvius," *etc.*

Z.—Das neue geheime Buch Chevilla von den wunderseltsamen Veränderungen der Erde, des Meeres, der Berge, des Himmels, von der Structur der Sonne, u.s.f. Herausge-

geben von Z.—4 pts. 8⁰. [? *Leipsic*] 1786. —Earlier ed. 1784.
See Pt. 2.

ZACCARIA DA NAPOLI.—Discorso filosofico sopra l'incendio del Monte Vesuvio cominciato a' 16 Decembre 1631, nell' apparir dell' alba.—4⁰. *Napoli,* 1632. Printed together with PERROTTI, A.—Discorso astronomico. [C.A.]

ZACHER, A.—Im Lande des Erdbebens. Vom Vesuv zum Aetna. Land und Leute in Sizilien und Kalabrien. Die vulkanischen Katastrophen von 1905 bis 1908. Zerstörung von Messina und Reggio.—*pp.* 316. *Stuttgart,* 1908.

ZAMBONINI, F.—Sul Sanidino (Viterbese, Tombe dei Nasoni, Lazio, Vesuvio).—*Riv. Min. e Crist. Ital. xxv,* 3–6, *pp.* 33–69, 6 *tav. Padova,* 1900.

ZAMBONINI, F.—Sulla Galena formatasi nell' ultima eruzione Vesuviana dell' Aprile 1906.—*Atti R. Acc. Lincei, S.* 5, *Rend. xv, sem.* 2, *pp.* 235–38. *Roma,* 1906.

ZAMBONINI, F.—Notizie mineralogiche sull' eruzione Vesuviana dell' Aprile 1906.—*Rend. R. Acc. Sci. S.* 3, *xii, p.* 397. *Napoli,* 1906.—*Id. Atti, S.* 2, *xiii,* 8, *pp.* 1–40, 1 *pl. Napoli,* 1908.

ZAMBONINI, F.—Sur la présence de la Galène parmi les minéraux produits par les fumerolles de la dernière éruption du Vésuve.—*C.R. Acad. Sci. cxliii, pp.* 921–22. *Paris,* 1906.

ZAMBONINI, F.—Sulla radioattività della Cotunnite Vesuviana.—*Atti R. Acc. Lincei, S.* 5, *Rend. xvi, sem.* 1, *pp.* 975–78. *Roma,* 1907.—*Riv. Min. e Crist. Ital. xxxix, pp.* 88–92. *Padova,* 1909.

ZAMBONINI, F.—Sulla Disanalite del Monte Somma.—*Rend. R. Acc. Sci. S.* 3, *xiv, pp.* 134–35. *Napoli,* 1908.—*Riv. Min. e Crist. Ital. xxxiv, pp.* 93–95. *Padova,* 1908.

ZAMBONINI, F.—Su alcuni Minerali non osservati finora al Vesuvio.—*Rend. R. Acc. Sci. S.* 3, *xiv, pp.* 156–59. *Napoli,* 1908.

ZAMBONINI, F.—Sulla identità della Belonesite con la Sellaite.—*Atti R. Acc. Lincei, S.* 5, *Rend. xviii, sem.* 1, *pp.* 305–8. *Roma,* 1909.

ZAMBONINI, F.—On the identity of Guarinite and Hiortdahlite with a note on the chemical composition of Guarinite by G. T. Prior.—*Min. Mag. xv,* 70, *pp.* 247–59, *figs. London,* 1909.

ZAMBONINI, F.—I Minerali del Somma e del Vesuvio.—" Natura," i, 1, pp. 9+21, 4 figs. Milano, 1909.

ZAMBONINI, F.—Mineralogia Vesuviana.— Atti R. Acc. Sci. S. 2, xiv, 6, pp. 1–368, figs. Napoli, 1910.

ZAMBONINI, F.—Baddeleyite e Pirrite del Monte Somma.—Atti R. Acc. Lincei, S. 5, Rend. xx, sem. 2, pp. 129–30. Roma, 1911.

ZAMBONINI, F.—Appendice alla Mineralogia Vesuviana.—Atti R. Acc. Sci. S. 2, xv, 12, pp. 51. Napoli, 1912.

ZANNICHELLI, G. J.—Considerazioni intorno ad una pioggia di terra caduta nel Golfo di Venezia, e sopra l'incendio del Vesuvio.—Racc. Opusc. Scient. Filos. xvi, pp. 87–124. Venezia, 1727.

ZECH, A.—Das Observatorium auf dem Vesuv.—Illustrirte Welt, p. 392, 1 illustr. (p. 381). Stuttgart, 1876.

ZEZI, G. P.—See COMITÉ D'ORGANISATION, etc.—Bibliographie Géologique, etc. No. XII. 1881.

ZEZZA, BARON M.—Na chiamata alli peccature. Canzona ncopp'a l'eruzione de lo Vesuvio a l'anno 1855.—fol., foll. 2. Napoli, 1855. [C.A.]

ZINNO, S.—Analisi chimica sopra una importante sublimazione, ecc.—Ann. R. Oss. Meteor. Vesuv. iv. 1870.

ZINNO, S.—Analisi di alcuni prodotti vulcanici dell' ultima eruzione del Vesuvio.— Riv. Sci. Ind. iv, pp. 184–88. 1872.

ZINNO, S.—Acqua termo-minerale Montella acidola-alcalina-ferrugginosa di Torre Annunziata. Analisi chimica.—Atti R. Ist. Incorag. S. 4, i, 8, pp. 8. Napoli, 1888.— See CASORIA. 1889.

ZINNO, S.—Analisi della cenere caduta nei giorni 5, 6, 7 Aprile corrente della eruzione Vesuviana.—Atti Acc. Pontaniana, xxxvi (S. 2, xi), Mem. 4, pp. 4. Napoli, 1906.

ZITO, V.—Sonetti due (1631). Per lo incendio del Vesuvio negli scherzi lirici.—12⁰. Napoli, 1538 [1638]. [B.M.—1062. a. 39 (1).]
The original date, which appears to have been misprinted 1538, has since been altered with the pen to 1638. See pp. 401–2.

ZORDA, G.—Discorso contro l'opinione dell' assorbimento vulcanico dell' acqua de' pozzi e del mare.—8⁰, pp. 15. Napoli, 1805.

ZORDA, G.—Relazione dell' eruzione del Vesuvio del 31 Maggio 1806.—4⁰, pp. 22. Napoli, 1806.

ZORDA, G.—Continuazione dei fenomeni del Vesuvio dopo l'eruzione del 1806 fino al principio della primavera del 1810.—8⁰, pp. 16. Napoli, 1810.

ZUCCAGNI-ORLANDINI, A.—Atlante illustrativo ossia raccolta dei principali Monumenti Italiani antichi, del medio evo e moderni e di alcune vedute pittoriche per servire di corredo alla ' Corografia Fisica, Storica e Statistica dell' Italia.'—3 vols. of pls. gd. fol. Firenze, 1845.
The first two are views of N. and Central Italy, the third of Naples and Sicily.

ZUCCAGNI-ORLANDINI, A. — Corografia Fisica, Storica e Statistica dell' Italia e delle sue Isole corredata di un atlante di mappe geografiche e topografiche, e di altre tavole illustrative.—12 pts. in 17 vols. 8⁰. Firenze, 1845. Also Atlas.—4 vols. fol., maps and views.
See Vol. ii.

ZUCHERIO NORICO, M.—Vesevj Montis vulgo Montagna di Somma versus plagam occidentalem prospectus post ultimam eruptionem a D.XX. Maj anni MD.CCXXXVII ex adverso Blanchiniano a Marco Zucherio Norico del. et æri incisus Neapoli MD.CCXXXVIII. [Vienna lib.]
Road up Vesuvius near S. Vito. Men, mules and dogs in foreground. Engrav. : 207×145 mm.

ZUPO, G. B.—Giornale dell' incendio del Vesuvio dell' anno 1660 con le osservationi matematiche A. C.—4⁰, pp. 15. Roma, 1660. [C.A.]

ZUPO, G. B.—Principio, e progreſsi del fvoco del Vesvvio osseruati giorno per giorno dalli tre fin' alli venticinque di Luglio in quest' anno 1660, et esposti alla curiosità de' Forestieri.—4⁰, foll. 8. 1660.

ZUPO, G. B.—Continuatione de' successi del prossimo incendio del Vesuvio, con gli effetti della cenere e pietre da quello vomitate, e con la dichiarazione, ed espressione delle croce maravigliose apparse in varii luoghi dopo l'incendio.—4⁰, foll. 11, 1 pl. Napoli, 1661. [C.A.]
See SUPO.

ZURCHER, F., et MARGOLLÉ, E.— Volcans et tremblements de terre.—16⁰, figs. Paris, 1866.—5th ed. 8⁰, pp. 311, figs. Paris, 1886. (Biblioth. des Merveilles.)

ISOLE EOLIE, OR LIPARI ISLANDS

ANON.—Bibliographie géologique et paléontologique de l'Italie, par les soins du Comité d'Organisation du 2e Congrès Géologique International à Bologne.—8⁰, *pp.* 630. *Bologne,* MDCCCLXXXI.

ANON.—Breve descrizione geografica del regno di Sicilia.—4⁰, *pp.* 293. *Palermo,* 1787.
See pp. 272 *et seq.* Isole Eolie, *etc.*

ANON.—Carta (Corografica) d'Italia.—*Ist. Geog. Milit. Ital.* 1889.
1 : 1,000,000, in 7 sheets.—3 ed. 1st, in 3 colours, with mountains shaded in brown and water in blue ; 2nd, mountains in grey ; 3rd, without mountain shading. *See* sheet 6. (Etna and Lipari Is.)

ANON.—Carta (Corografica) d'Italia.—*Ist. Geog. Milit. Ital.* 1889.
1 : 1,800,000, in 6 sheets.—2 ed. 1st, in 3 colours as in preceding ; 2nd, without the mountains shaded. *See* sheet 6.

ANON. — Carta Corografica del regno d'Italia e delle regioni adiacenti.—*Ist. Geog. Milit. Ital.* 1889.
1 : 500,000, in 35 sheets.—3 ed. 1st, in 3 colours ; 2nd, in 2 colours ; 3rd, in black, without mountain shading. *See* sheet 29.

ANON. [CORTESE, E.]—Carta Geologica della Isola di Sicilia.—*R. Uffic. Geol. Ital. Roma,* 1886, 1890.
Scale 1 : 100,000. *See* sheet 244.

ANON.—Carta Geologica della Sicilia.—*R. Uffic. Geol. Ital. Roma,* 1886, 1890.
Scale 1 : 500,000. Etna and Lipari Islands.

ANON.—Carta delle Isole Eolie.—*Uffic. Idrograf. R. Mar. Ital.* 1881.
Scale 1 : 150,000.

ANON.—Carta del Mare Jonio e Mar Tirreno.—*Uffic. Idrograf. R. Mar. Ital.* 1878.
1 : 1,000,000.

ANON.—Carta della Sicilia.—*Ist. Geog. Milit. Ital.* 1885.
Scale 1 : 500,000, in 1 sheet, in black, mountains shaded. Includes Etna and Lipari Islands.

ANON. — Carta Topografica del regno d'Italia.—*Ist. Geog. Milit. Ital.* 1889.
1 : 100,000. Chromolithographic ed. in 3 colours without line shading of mountains. *See* sheet 244.

ANON. — Carta Topografica del regno d'Italia.—*Ist. Geog. Milit. Ital.* 1889.
1 : 100,000, in 277 photo-engraved sheets, in course of publication (1889). The orography is shown by contour lines of 50 m. as well as by zenith-light shading. *See* sheet 244.

ANON. — Carta Topografica del regno d'Italia.
1 : 75,000. Economic edition similar to above.

ANON.—Carte de la Sicile et des Isles adjacentes, réduite et rédigée d'après la grande carte qui a été faite en 1720 par le Baron Sam. Schmettau, et corrigée sur les observations récentes de plusieurs voyageurs. — ?, 1784.
Vulcano and Vulcanello are represented as two isles.

ANON. — Description des estats Naples, Sicille, Sardagne.—*fol., pp.* 320, *num. plans, maps and engrav.* — ?, — ?

ANON.—Description historique et géographique de la ville de Messine, etc., etc., et détails météorologiques du désastre que cette ville vient d'éprouver (le 5 février 1783) par le tremblement de terre. Avec des notes curieuses et intéressantes sur la Calabre ultérieure, la Sicile et les Îles de Lipari, etc., etc., avec carte.—4⁰, *pp.* 25. *Paris,* 1783.

ANON.—Extrait du " Journal d'Angleterre " contenant une description curieuse de la montagne d'Eole en Italie.—*Journal des Sçavans,* 12⁰, *pp.* 419–20. *Paris,* 1685. [C.A.]

ANON.—[Graham's Island, Isola Julia or Isola Ferdinandea, 1831.]
Oil painting on copper : 253×183 mm.

ANON.—A Handbook for Travellers in Southern Italy and Sicily ; comprising the description of Naples and its environs, Pompeii, Herculaneum, Vesuvius, Sorrento ; the Islands of Capri and Ischia ; Amalfi, Pæstum, and Capua, the Abruzzi and Calabria ; Palermo, Girgenti, the Greek Temples, and Messina.—9th ed. in 2 pts. 8⁰ ; *Pt. i*, South Italy, *pp.* 288+20, *maps, plans, etc.* ; *Pt. ii*, Sicily, *pp.* 289–418+11, *maps, plans, etc. London*, 1890.

ANON.—Un incendio sconosciuto del Vesuvio.—*Archiv. Stor. Prov. Nap.* xv, *pp.* 642–46. *Napoli*, 1890.

ANON.— Die Insel Stromboli. — *Museum des Wundervollen u. Auszerordentlichen in Natur, Kunst, ecc.* ix, 3. *Leipzig*, 1806–10.
Contains a large engraved view of Stromboli.

ANON.—L'Italia.—4⁰, *pp.* 326, *num. maps. Torino*, 1896.

ANON.—L'Italie.—8⁰, *pp.* 608, 243 *engrav.*, 5 *maps. Paris*, — ?

ANON.—Notes on the production of Pumicestone in the Island of Lipari.—*Journ. Soc. Arts*, xxx, 1527, *pp.* 398–99. *London*, 1882.

ANON.—Piano degli Ancoraggi di Vulcano, Lipari e Panaria.—*Uffic. Idrograf. R. Mar. Ital.* 1882.
Scale 1 : 25,000.

ANON.—Raccolta di Storia naturale.—4⁰, 1 *pl. Roma*, 1784.

ANON.—Stromboli [1854 ?].
Woodcut illustration out of a book : 156×100 mm.

ANON.—Tavolette rilevate per la costruzione della carte del regno d'Italia.—*Ist. Geog. Milit. Ital.* 1873–79.
Part to the scale of 1 : 50,000, and part 1 : 25,000. *See* sheet 244, i–iv.

ANON.—Vulcani di Europa.—*Il Propagatore Sci. Nat. i*, pt. 2, *pp.* 328.

ABICH, O. W. H. Von.—Geologische Beobachtungen über die vulkanischen Erscheinungen und Bildungen in Unter- und Mittelitalien.—Bd. i, Lief. 1.—Ueber die Natur und den Zusammenhang der vulkanischen Bildungen.—4⁰, *pp.* viii+134+xi, 3 *maps*, 2 *lith. pls.* (Atlas to same bound separately, 5 *pls.*) *Braunschweig*, 1841.

ABICH, O. W. H. Von.—Besuch des Kraterbodens von Stromboli am 25 Juli 1836.—*Zeitschr. deutsch. geol. Gesellsch. ix, pp.* 392–406, 1 *fig.*, *Taf.* xv. *Berlin*, 1857.

ACUNTE, Gennaro.—Veduta del fondo del Cratere del volcano nell' Isola di Vulcano il 31 Agosto 1840.
A pencil and sepia sketch-plan in the Johnston-Lavis collection.

ACUNTE, Gennaro.—Veduta del fondo del Cratere del vulcano nell' Isola di Vulcano il 31 Agosto 1840.
Water-colour and pen sketch of the crater bottom : 220×205 mm.

AGAMENNONE, G. — Terremoto siculo-calabro della notte dall' 11 al 12 Febbraio 1897.—*Boll. Soc. Sismol. Ital. iii*, 2, *pp.* 42–59 *delle* " Notizie sui terremoti, ecc." *Modena*, 1897.

AGATIO DI SOMMA.—Historico racconto dei terremoti della Calabria dell' anno 1638, etc.—*pp.* 189. *Napoli*, 1641.

AGUILAR, E.—*See* FRIEDLAENDER, B.

ALBERTI, F. L.—Isole appartenenti all' Italia. Di nuovo ricorrette e con l'aggionta in più luoghi di diverse cose occorsi fino a nostri tempi adornate.—4⁰, *foll.* 96+ *index, foll.* 4. *Venetia*, 1581.—Earlier ed. 4⁰. *Venetia*, 1567.
See foll. 66–70.

ALBERTI, F. L.—Descrittione di tutta Italia. Aggiuntavi la Descrittione di tutte l'Isole all' Italia appartenenti . . . (Edizione curata da Antonio Cheluzio da Colle.)—4⁰, *foll.* 42+504+100+5, 7 *maps. Venetia*, 1568.—Other ed.: 1576 ; 4⁰, *foll.* 32+501+ 69+4, 1577.

ALBERTI, F. L.—Descrittione di tutta l'Italia . . . Aggiontovi di nuovo . . . tutto quello chè successo sino l'anno 1581. E di più accresciutà d'altre additioni . . . da M. Borgaruccio Borgarucci.—4⁰, *foll.* 32+501+96+4. *Venetia*, 1581.—4⁰, *foll.* 34+495+100+5. *Vinegia*, 1588. — 4⁰, *foll.* 34+495+91+4. *Venetia*, 1596.

ALEXANDER, C.—Practical remarks on the lavas of Vesuvius, Etna and the Lipari Islands.—*Proc. Scient. Soc. i, pp.* 31–32. *London*, 1839.

ALLAN, R.—Abstract of a paper accompanying a suite of Volcanic Rocks from the Lipari Islands.—*Trans. Roy. Soc. Edinburgh, xii, pp.* 531–37. 1834.

AMICO E STATELLA, V. M.—Lexicon topographicum Siculum, *etc.*—3 vols. 4⁰. *Catanæ*, 1759–60. See Vol. iii, Pt. 1, pp. 45–52.

ANDERSON, T.—The Volcanoes of the two Sicilies. — *Geol. Mag. p.* 473. 1888.— *Rept. Brit. Assoc.* 1888, *pp.* 663–64. *London*, 1889.

ANDERSON, T., and JOHNSTON-LAVIS, H. J.—Notes on the late eruption in the Island of Volcano.—*Rept. Brit. Assoc.* 1888, *pp.* 664–66. *London*, 1889.

ANDERSON, T.—Volcanic studies in many lands.—8⁰, *pp.* xxii+202, *Pl.* cv. *London*, 1903.

ANDERSON, T.—On certain recent changes in the crater of Stromboli.—*Ann. Rept. Yorks. Phil. Soc.* 1904, *pp.* 123–38, 12 *pls.* (*chart*). 1905.—*Geogr. Journ. xxv, pp.* 123–38, 12 *pls.* (*chart*). 1905.—*Scot. Geogr. Mag. xxi, pp.* 345–47, 1 *pl. Edinburgh*, 1905. —*See also* YELD, G.

ANGELIS D'OSSAT, G. DE.—Riunione straordinaria della Società Geologica Italiana tenuta alle Isole Eolie ed a Palermo nell' Aprile 1900.—*Boll. Soc. Geol. Ital. xix*, 2, *pp.* xli–lxxiv. *Roma*, 1900.

ARAGO, D. F. J.—Liste des Volcans actuellement enflammés. — *Ann. Bur. Longit. pp.* 167–89. *Paris*, 1824. [C.A.]—Engl. transl. by Thomson : *Ann. Phil. N.S. vii*, *pp.* 201–14. *London*, 1824.

ARANCIO, F.—Guida statistica su la Sicilia e sue Isole adjacenti, con Carta coroidrografica-doganale-statistica anche di Malta e Gozo.—*fol., pp.* xi+132 *and index, map* (bound separately). *Palermo*, 1844.

ARCIDIACONO, S.—*See* RICCO, A., MERCALLI, G. 1889–92, 1893.

ARCIDIACONO, S.—*See* SILVESTRI, O. 1890.

ARCIDIACONO, S.—Rassegna dei principali fenomeni eruttivi avvenuti in Sicilia e nelle Isole adiacenti durante il quadrimestre Gennaio-Aprile 1895 [-l'anno 1902]. —*Boll. Soc. Sismol. Ital. i*, 3. *Modena*, 1895. [*ii*, 3 e 7, *pp.* 122–24, 229–32, 1896 ; *iii*, 4, *pp.* 57–60, 1897 ; *iii*, 9, *pp.* 203–13, 1897 ; *iv*, 5, *pp.* 107–13, 1898 ; *iv*, 9, *pp.* 261–75, 2 *tav.*, 1898 ; *vi*, 4, *pp.* 101–14, 1900 ; *vii*, 2, *pp.* 82–91, 1901 ; *x*, 2, *pp.* 65–71, 1904 ; *xi*, 1 e 2, *pp.* 45–53, 1906.]

ARCIDIACONO, S.—Il terremoto di Nicolosi dell' 11 Maggio 1901 e le sue repliche.— *Boll. Acc. Gioen. lxx, pp.* 2–15. *Catania*, 1901.

ARROSTO, G.—Analisi chimica delle acque termo-minerali della Grotta di S. Calogero in Lipari.—8⁰, *pp.* 20. *Messina*, 1872.

AUDOT, L. E. (père).—L'Italie, la Sicile, les Îles Éoliennes, *etc.*—2 vols. of text, 2 vols. of steel engrav. 8⁰. *Vol. i, pp.* 370, 1 *map ; Vol. ii, pp.* 280+128 ; *Vol. iii*, *pls.* 140 ; *Vol. iv, pls.* 141–291. *Paris*, 1834. See Vol. i, pp. 277–84 and Pl. 95. For other editions *see* VESUVIUS.

BÄCKSTRÖM, H.—Ueber Leucitführende-Gesteine von den Liparischen Inseln.— *Geol. Fören i Stockholm Forhandl. xviii*, 3, *pp.* 155–64. 1896.

BACOT, L.—Notizie sulla pietra pomice di Lipari.—*Messina*, 1878.—In French : *Messina*, 1878.

BAEDEKER, K.—Italien. Handbuch für Reisende. 3 Theil : Unter-Italien und Sicilien nebst Ausflügen nach den Liparischen Inseln.—8th ed. 16⁰, *pp.* xlviii+ 412, 26 *maps*, 17 *plans. Leipzig*, 1887. See pp. 322–25.

BALDACCI, L.—*See* TOSO, P.

BALTZER, R. A.—Ueber die jüngsten Eruptionen auf der Insel Vulcano und ihre Producte. — *Vierteljahrschr. Zürch. naturf. Gesellsch. xix, pp.* 306–13. *Zürich*, 1874.

BALTZER, R. A.—Eruption von tridymitischen Aschen am Insel Vulcano den 7 Sept. 1873.—*Neue Züricher Zeitung*, 21, 13 *Jan.* 1875.—*Ref. naturw. Gesellsch. Zürich*, 4 *Jan.* 1875.—*Boll. R. Com. Geol. Ital. vi, p.* 197. *Roma*, 1875.—*N. J. f. Min. pp.* 316–17. *Stuttgart*, 1875.

BALTZER, R. A.—Geognostisch-chemische Mittheilungen über die neuesten Eruptionen auf Volcano und die Producte derselben.—*Zeitschr. deutsch. geol. Gesellsch. xxvii*, *pp.* 36–62, 3 *pls. Berlin*, 1875.—*N. J. f. Min. p.* 93. *Stuttgart*, 1876.

BALTZER, R. A.—[Ueber eine eigenthümliche Gruppe vulcanischer Aschen, von einer Eruption des Craters auf der Insel Vulcano im Jahre 1873.]—*Verh. Schweiz. naturf. Gesellsch. lviii, pp.* 51–54. *Andermatt* (*Luzern*), 1875.

BALTZER, R. A.—Ueber ein neues massenhaftes Vorkommen von Tridymit in den Liparen.—*Vierteljahrsschr. naturf. Gesellsch. xx, pp.* 182–84. *Zürich,* 1875.

BALTZER, R. A. — [Ueber vulcanische Aschen von Vulcano.]—*Zeitschr. deutsch. geol. Gesellsch. xxx, pp.* 365–68. *Berlin,* 1878.

BARATTA, M.—Carta sismica d'Italia per l'anno 1892.—*Boll. Soc. Geog. Ital. S.* 3, *vi, pp.* 313–23. *Roma,* 1893.

BARATTA, M.—Sulla distribuzione topografica dei terremoti in Italia durante il quinquennio 1887–91.—*Atti Primo Congr. Geog. Ital., Mem. Sez. Scient. ii,* 1, *pp.* 180–89, *tav. v. Genova,* 1894.

BARATTA, M.—Sullo stato presente dei Vulcani Eolici.—*Boll. Soc. Geog. Ital. xxxvii, pp.* 542–47. *Roma,* 1900.

BARATTA, M.—I Terremoti d'Italia.—8⁰, *pp.* 950, *pls. Torino,* 1901.

Gives, in Pt. III, an extensive bibliography of the earthquakes of Italy.

BARVÍŘ, J. L.—[Ueber einige Zwillingscristalle v. Augit v. d. Insel Stromboli.]— O nĕkterých srostlicích augitu z ostrova Stromboli.—*Sitzber. k. bohm. Gesellsch. Wiss.* 1902, 40, *pp.* 11, 1 *pl. Prag,* 1903. (*Vĕstnik královské České Společnosti Náuk,* 1902, 40, *pp.* 11, 1 *pl. Praze,* 1903.)

BERGEAT, A.—Cordierit- und granatführender Insel Lipari.—*N.J.f. Min. ii, pp.* 148–49. *Stuttgart,* 1895.

BERGEAT, A.—Der Stromboli. — *Habilitationsschrift, etc.* 4⁰, *pp.* 42, 3 *pls.,* 1 *map. München,* 1896.

BERGEAT, A.—Der Stromboli als Wetterprophet.—*Zeitschr. deutsch. geol. Gesellsch. xlviii, pp.* 153–68. *Berlin,* 1896.

BERGEAT, A.—Mineralogische Mitteilungen über den Stromboli.—*N. J. f. Min. ii, pp.* 109–23, *Taf.* I *and* II. *Stuttgart,* 1897.

BERGEAT, A.—Die äolischen Vulkaninseln bei Sicilien.—" *Globus,*" *lxxiii, pp.* 169–74, 3 *figs. Braunschweig,* 1898.

BERGEAT, A.—Von den äolischen Inseln.— *Zeitschr. f. prakt. Geol.* 1899, 2, *pp.* 43–47. *Berlin,* 1899.

BERGEAT, A.—Die äolischen Inseln (Stromboli, Panaria, Salina, Lipari, Vulcano, Filicudi und Alicudi) geologisch beschrieben.—*Abh. k. bayer. Akad. Wiss. xx,* 1, *pp.* 1–274, 24 *tav., geol. map. München,* 1899.

BERGEAT, A.—Pumici of Monte Pelato, Lipari Islands, Italy.—*Trans. North of England Inst. of Min. and Mech. Engineers, xlviii, pt.* 4, *pp.* 26. *Newcastle-upon-Tyne,* 1899.

BERTELLI, F. (Apresso).—Italia nouamente posta in luce et da molti errori emendata in Venetia. MDLXV.

Map of Italy, part of Sicily and the Lipari Is., the last fancifully arranged.

BIANCHI, L.—*See* CUCINIELLO, D.

BIOT, J. B.—Bemerkungen zu letzterem Briefe.—*See* DEVILLE.—Huitième lettre, etc.

BLAKE, J. F.—A Visit to the Volcanoes of Italy.—*Proc. Geol. Assoc. xi, pp.* 145–76. *London,* 1891.

BONNEY, T. G.—Volcanoes, their structure and significance.—8⁰, *pp.* 351, 13 *pls.,* 21 *figs. London,* 1899.

BORCH, M. J. DE.—Lettres sur la Sicile et sur l'Île de Malthe, 1777. Pour servir de supplément au voyage en Sicile et à Malthe de M. Brydonne [*sic*].—2 tom. 8⁰, *num. pls. Turin,* 1782.—German by Werther: *Berne,* 1796.

BORNEMANN, J. G.—Sur l'état des Volcans d'Italie pendant l'été de 1856.—[Transl. by De Perrey from] *Tageblatt der 32 Versam. deutsch. Naturf. u. Aertze in Wien, pp.* 114–41. *Wien,* 1856. Original MS. *pp.* 4. [C.A.]

BORNEMANN, J. G.—Bericht über eine Reise in Italien.—*Zeitschr. deutsch. geol. Gesellsch. ix, pp.* 464–72. *Berlin,* 1857.

BORNEMANN, J. G.—Ansichten von Stromboli.—*Zeitschr. deutsch. geol. Gesellsch. xiv, pp.* 696–701, *Taf.* VII–X. *Berlin,* 1862.

BORNEMANN, J. G.—Ueber Schlackenkegel und Laven. Beitrag zur Lehre von Vulcanismus.—*Jahrb. k. preuss. Landesanst. Berlin,* — ?

BOUÉ, A.—Ueber Solfataren und Kratererlöschener Vulcane.—*Sitzber. k. Akad. Wiss. xlviii, Abth.* 1, *pp.* 361–80. *Wien,* 1863.

BOWYER, R. (publ.).—Crater in the Island of Volcano. Published by R. Bowyer, 80, Pall Mall, 1809.

Delicately hand-coloured aquatint: 331 × 264 mm.

BRUN, A.—Excursion géologique au Stromboli.—*Bibl. univ., Archiv. Sci. phys. nat.* 4e *pér., xii, pp.* 86–88. *Genève,* 1901.— *N.J.f. Min. ii, pp.* 345–46. *Stuttgart,* 1903.

BRUN, A.—Sur la constitution du Basalte du Stromboli.—*Bibl. univ., Archiv. Sci. phys. nat.* 4e pér., xiii, pp. 85–87. *Genève,* 1902.

BRUN, A.—Quelques recherches sur le Volcanisme. 1re partie.—*Bibl. univ., Archiv. Sci. phys. nat.* 4e pér., xvi, pp. 30, 1 pl. *Genève,* 1905.

BRUN, A.—Cristallisation de l'Obsidienne de Lipari.—*Bibl. univ., Archiv. Sci. phys. nat.* xxiv, pp. 97–98. *Genève,* 1907.

BRUN, A.—Recherches sur l'Exhalaison Volcaniqué.—*fol., pp.* 277, 34 pls., 17 figs. *Genève, Paris,* 1911.

BRYDONE, P.—A Tour through Sicily and Malta ; in a series of letters to William Beckford, Esq.—2 vols. 8°. *London,* 1773. For other editions *see* ETNA. Contains observations on eruption of Stromboli, 17 May, 1770.

BUCCA, L.—Le Andesiti dell' Isola di Lipari. Studio micrografico.—*Boll. R. Com. Geol. Ital.* xvi, pp. 285–98. *Roma,* 1885.

BUCH, C. L. VON.—Einige Bemerkungen über eine Sammlung aus den Liparischen Inseln.—*Mag. Gesellsch. naturf. Freunde, iii, pp.* 299–303. *Berlin,* 1809.

BUCH, C. L. VON.—Ueber die Natur der vulkanischen Erscheinungen auf den Canarischen Inseln und ihre Verbindung mit andern Vulcanen der Erdoberfläche.— *Ann. Phys. Chem.* x, pp. 1–46. *Leipzig,* 1827.

BUCH, C. L. VON.—Description Physique des Îles Canaries, suivie d'une indication des principaux Volcans du Globe. Traduite par C. Boulanger.—8°, pp. vii+525. *Paris,* 1836.

BULIFON, A., LUIGI, DR. (nipote).— Carte de' regni di Napoli e di Sicilia loro provincie ed Isole adjacenti.—4°, pp. 7, 19 maps. *Napoli,* 1734. [B.M.—118. c. 10 ; also 661. k. 1.] Vulcano is represented in several maps as separate from Vulcanello.

BURMANNUS, P.—*See* GRÆVIUS, J. G.— Thes. Antiq. et Hist. Sic.

BUTLER, G. W. See COLE, GRENVILLE A. J.

BYLANDT PALSTERCAMP, A. DE.— Théorie des Volcans.—3 vols. 8°. Atlas, 17 pls. fol. *Paris,* 1835. See pp. 261–315 and atlas.

CABELLA, A.—Risultati dell' analisi dell' acqua termo-minerale della sorgente San Calogero nell' Isola di Lipari.—*Boll. Soc. Nat.* xxii, pp. 38–44. *Napoli,* 1909.

CALCARA, P.—*See* PRESTANDREA, A.

CALLEGARI, G. V.—Una leggenda delle Lipari secondo lo scoglio al verso 761 del libro IV dell' Argonautica d'Apollonio Rodio.—[Estr. d. vol.] " *In memor. di Oddone Ravenna,*" pp. 5. *Padova,* 1904.

CAMPI, P.—Istoria di Lipari. Cited by Mongitore and Mercalli. MS. in the Ex-convento dei Capucini at Lipari.

CANDIDE, ACCIPE (?).—Elegantioris Italiæ Topographium. Map of Italy with the Lipari Is. and part of Sicily. Vulcano and Vulcanello are represented as two islands far apart.

CANTELLI, G. — L'Italia. — *Roma,* 1694. [B.M.—28. e. 4.] Map. Vulcano is represented as detached from Vulcanello—at least, two islands are marked.

CAPACCIO, G. C.—Neapolitanæ Historiæ a J. C. Capaccio . . . tomus primus. In quo antiqvitas ædificio, ciuibus, republica, ducibus, religione, bellis, lapidibus, locis adiacentibus, qui totam ferè amplectuntur Campaniam, continetur.—4°, pp. 21+900, figs. *Neapoli, apud Jo. Jacobum Carlinum.* M.DCVII. See p. 750. For other editions *see* CAMPI PHLEGRÆI.

CAPOCCI, E.—Catalogo de' tremuoti avvenuti nella parte continentale del regno delle Due Sicilie, posti in raffronto con le eruzioni vulcaniche ed altri fenomeni cosmici, tellurici e meteorici.—*Atti R. Ist. Incorag.* ix, pp. 335–78, 379–421, 1861 ; x, pp. 293–327, *Napoli,* 1863.—4°, pp. 45. *Napoli,* 1859.

CASORIA, F.—Sopra un Minerale di Rame dell' Isola di Lipari.—*Rend. R. Acc. Sci. iii, pp.* 335–36. *Napoli,* 1844.

CASORIA, F.—Memoria sopra un minerale di Lipari (Liparite, CuS^3+Aq^5).—*Atti Sett. Adun. Scienz. Ital. pp.* 1156–57. *Napoli,* 1846.

CASTALDO, J.—Italiæ novissima descriptio.—[B.M.—S. 69 (13).] Vulcano is represented as two islands.

CHAIX, C.—The Past History of Vulcano.— *Bull. Amer. Geogr. Soc.* xx, pp. 464–69. *New York,* 1888.

CHASTELET (des.).—P^{re} vuĕ de l'Isle de Vulcano, une des Isles de Lipari, à 30 mille Nord-Est, des côtes de la Sicile. Gravée par de Ghendt. No. 133, S^{de} vuĕ de l'Isle Vulcano, prise du côté où est situé le Vulcanello. No. 134. A.P.D.R.
Two engrav., each : 238×164 mm.

CHASTELET (des.).—Pre. vuĕ de l'Isle de Vulcano, une des Isles de Lipari, à 30 mille Nord-Est, des côtes de la Sicile. Gravée par de Ghendt, No. 133. A.P.D.R.
Engrav. : 243×182 mm.

CHASTELET (des.).—S^{de} vuĕ de l'Isle Vulcano, prise du côté où est situé le Vulcanello. Gravé par Quaivilliers. No. 134. A.P.D.R.
Engrav. : 236×180 mm.

CHASTELET (des.).—P^{re} vuĕ du Stromboli prise en y arrivant du côté du midy. No. 135. Gravée par de Ghendt. S^{de} vuë du Stromboli dans la partie opposée au Nord-Est. No. 136. Gravée par Licnard. A.P.D.R.
Two engrav. : 235×162 mm.

CHASTELET (del.).—(1) Vulcano [fr. Lipari]. (2) Stromboli [fr. Panaria ?]. E. Rouargue sc., 95. Audot edit.
Two engrav., each : 113×78 mm.

CHÂTELET.—*See* CHASTELET.

CHERUBINI, Cav. C.—Carta Fisica dell' Italia.—*Pub. G. B. Paravia e C., Torino, Roma, Milano, Firenze, Napoli,* 1876.
1 : 750,000 horiz. ; 1 : 150,000 vert. Raised map.

CHIRONE, V.—Le terme di S. Calogero nell' Isola di Lipari.—*Napoli,* 1880.

CIANCIO, A.—Ragionamento sulla privativa del Marchese Nunziante nella fabbricazione dell' Allume Vulcanico.—4^0, *pp.* 60. *Napoli ?, — ?*

CLERICI, E.—[Studio sui fenomeni di carattere meccanico e fisico della fase eruttiva di Vulcano.] Lavoro meccanico e calorie sviluppate nella caduta dei grossi massi. [Studî sulla perforazione dei vetri nelle finestre di Casa Narlian da scheggie angolose di projetti. Considerazioni sulla rottura del cavo sottomarino tra Lipari e Milazzo.]—*Ann. Uffic. Centr. Meteor. x* (*pt.* 4), *pp.* 208–10, 210–11, 211–13. *Roma,* 1891.

CLUVERIUS, Ph.—Sicilia Antiqua ; cum minoribus Insulis ei adjacentibus. Item Sardinia et Corsica, *etc.—fol. Lugduni Batavorum,* 1619.— *See also* GRÆVIUS, J. G.—Thesaurus Antiquitatum . . . Italiæ, *etc. T. x, Vol.* 1. 1725, *etc.*

COLE, Grenville A. J., and BUTLER, G. W.—On the Lithophyses in the Obsidian of the Rocche Rosse, Lipari.—*Quart. Journ. Geol. Soc. pp.* 438–46, *Pl.* XII. *London,* 1892.

COLOMBA, L.—Sul deposito d'una fumarola silicea alla fossa delle Rocche Rossi (Lipari).—*Boll. Soc. Geol. Ital. xix, pp.* 521–34. *Roma,* 1900.

COLOMBA. L.—Sopra alcune lave alterate di Vulcanello.—[Estr.] *Boll. Soc. Geol. Ital. xx, pp.* 233–46. *Roma,* 1901.

COMITÉ D'ORGANISATION DU 2$_{ME}$ CONGRÈS GÉOLOGIQUE INTERNATIONAL À BOLOGNE, 1881.—Bibliographie Géologique et Paléontologique de l'Italie.—8^0, *pp. viii*+630. *Bologne,* 1881.
See No. XVI. SILVESTRI, O.—L'Etna . . . les Îles Lipari, l'Île Pantellaria et l'Île Ferdinandea (nos. 3763–4643).

CONSIGLIO-PONTE, S.—*See* SILVESTRI, O., ET ALII. 1889.

CONSIGLIO-PONTE, S. — Contribuzione alla Vulcanologia delle Isole Eolie. Fine del periodo eruttivo di Vulcano e stato attuale del cratere.—*Atti Acc. Gioen. S.* 4, *iii, pp.* 317–33. *Catania,* 1891.

CONSIGLIO-PONTE, S. — Contribuzione alla Vulcanologia delle Isole Eolie. I proiettili e l'interno meccanismo eruttivo di Vulcano.—*Atti Acc. Gioen. S.* 4, *v, Mem.* 12, *pp.* 33, 1 *pl. Catania,* 1892.

CONSIGLIO-PONTE, S.—Morfologia dei proietti di Vulcano.—*Boll. Soc. Geol. Ital. xxiii, pp.* 398–402. *Roma,* 1905.

CONSIGLIO-PONTE, S.—Eruzione dell' Isola di Vulcano.—*Ann. Meteor. ix, pte.* 3.

CORDENONS, F.—Sul Meccanismo delle Eruzioni Vulcaniche e Geiseriane. Part I. —8^0, *pp.* 43, *figs. Venezia,* 1885.

CORDIER, P. L. A.—Rapport sur le voyage de M. Constant Prévost à l'Île Julia, à Malte, en Sicile, aux Îles Lipari, et dans les environs de Naples.—*Nouv. Ann. Voy. lxx* (*S.* 2, *x*), *pp.* 43–64. *Paris,* 1836.—*C.R. Acad. Sci. ii, pp.* 243–55. *Paris,* 1836.

CORTESE, E.—Sulla costituzione geologica dell' Isola di Lipari.—*Boll. R. Com. Geol. Ital. S.* 2, *ii, pp.* 501–23. *Roma,* 1881.

CORTESE, E.—L'Eruzione dell' Isola Vulcano veduta nel Settembre 1888.—*Boll. R. Com. Geol. Ital. S.* 2, *ix, pp.* 214–23. *Roma,* 1888.

CORTESE, E., SABATINI, V.—Descrizione geologico-petrografica delle Isole Eolie.—*Mem. descritt. Carta Geol. Ital. vii, pp.* 130, 11 *figs.,* 9 *pls.,* 8 *geol. maps col.* (1 : 50,000 *and one of* 1 : 500,000). *Roma,* 1892.

COSSA, A.—Ricerche chimiche su minerali e roccie dell' Isola di Vulcano [1877].—*Atti R. Acc. Lincei, S.* 3, *Mem. ii, disp.* 1, *pp.* 117–25. *Roma,* 1878.—*Gazz. Chim. Ital. viii, pp.* 235–46. *Palermo,* 1878.

COSSA, A.—Ricerche chimiche e microscopiche su Roccie e Minerali d'Italia (1875–1880).—4⁰, *pp. vii*+302, 12 *pls.* (11 *col.*). *Torino,* 1881.—*Boll. R. Com. Geol. Ital., Notiz. Bibliog. pp.* 57–58. *Roma,* 1882.

COSSA, A.—Sur la Hiératite, nouvelle espèce minéralogique.—*C.R. Acad. Sci. xciv, pp.* 457–58. *Paris,* 1882.

COSSA, A.—Sulla presenza del Tellurio nei prodotti dell' Isola Vulcano (Lipari).—*Atti R. Acc. Sci. xxxiii, disp.* 8, *pp.* 449–50. *Torino,* 1898.—*Zeitschr. f. anorg. Chemie, xvii, pp.* 205–6. *Hamburg,* 1898.

CRAIG.—The Island of Stromboli. Engraved by White from a Drawing by Craig. London. Published by R. Wilks, Chancery Lane, June 1st, 1814. For the Gallery of Nature and Art.
Engrav. : 156 × 98 mm.

CROTTI, C.—Viaggio per la Sicilia eseguito nell' anno 1830. Poemetto.—*fol., pp.* 20. *Napoli,* 1830.
See p. 6 : Stromboli, Vulcano, etc.

CUCINIELLO, D., BIANCHI, L.—Viaggio pittorico nel regno delle Due Sicilie. [With drawings by R. Müller, L. Jely, F. Horner, G. Forino, F. Dura, F. Wenzel, P. de Leopold, C. Goetzloff, G. Gigante, A. Vianelly, A. Marinoni, A. Carelli.]—*gd. fol. Vol. i, Pt.* 1, *pp.* 128, 60 *pls. ; Vol. ii, Pt.* 1, *pp.* 122, 60 *pls. ; Vol. iii, Pt.* 2, *pp.* 122, 60 *pls. Napoli* [1833].

DANCKERTS, J.—Regnum Neapolis, Siciliæ et Lipariæ insulæ. — *Amstelodami* [1670?]. [B.M.—23880 (2).]

DANKERO, C.—Tabula Italiæ Corsicæ, Sardiniæ et adjacentium regnorum noua et accurata discriptio a . . . — ?, — ?

DAUBENY, C. G. B.—A Description of active and extinct Volcanos ; with remarks on their origin, their chemical phenomena, and the character of their products, as determined by the condition of the earth during the period of their formation. —8⁰, *pp.* 466, *figs.,* 2 *maps,* 1 *pl. London,* 1826.—8⁰, *pp.* 743, *figs.,* 10 *maps,* 4 *pls. London,* 1848.

D. B.—L'Italia descritta e depinta con le sue Isole di Sicilia, Sardegna, Elba, Malta, Eolie, di Calipso, ecc. Collected from numerous authors by D. B.—2nd ed. 5 vols. 8⁰, *with many* (good) *engravings. Turin, Gius. Pomba, e.c.* 1837.

DEECKE, J. E. W.—Italien.—*Bibl. der Länderkunde, iii and iv, pp.* 519, 33 *maps and pl.,* 79 *figs. Berlin,* 1899.

DELUC, J. A.—Observations sur les prismes, ou schorls volcaniques, et particulièrement sur ceux de l'Etna.—*Journ. Phys. lii, pp.* 195–205. *Paris,* 1801.

DENZA, F.—Etna, Sicilia ed isole vulcaniche adiacenti dal Dicembre 1889 all' Ottobre 1890.—*Ann. Meteor. Ital. vi, pp.* 216–20. *Torino,* 1891.

DENZA, F.—Etna, Sicilia ed isole adiacenti dal Novembre 1890 all' Ottobre 1891.—*Ann. Meteor. Ital. vii, pp.* 264–69. *Torino,* 1892.

DENZA, F.—Stromboli.—*Ann. Scient. Ind. xxviii. Milano,* 1892.

DESNOYERS, J. P. F. S.—Notice sur l'Île Julia, le Stromboli, les colonnes du Temple de Pozzuoli.—*Bull. Soc. géol. France, ii, pp.* 238–46. *Paris,* 1831–32.

DESSOULAVY, J.—Island of Vulcano seen from Monte della Guardia on the Island of Lipari.—*Rome,* 1826.
A fine original water-colour drawing.

DEVILLE, C. J. SAINTE-CLAIRE.—Sur quelques produits d'émanations de la Sicile.—*C.R. Acad. Sci.* [extr.] *xli, pp.* 887–94, 1855 ; *xliii, pp.* 359–70, *Paris,* 1856.

DEVILLE, C. J. SAINTE-CLAIRE.—Huitième lettre à Élie de Beaumont sur les phénomènes éruptifs de l'Italie méridionale.—*C.R. Acad. Sci. xliii, pp.* 606–10. *Paris,* 1856.

DEVILLE, C. J. SAINTE-CLAIRE.—Mémoire sur les émanations volcaniques.—*C.R. Acad. Sci. xliv, pp.* 58–62. *Paris,* 1857.—*Bull. Soc. géol. France, S.* 2, *xiv, pp.* 254–79. *Paris,* 1856–57.

DEVILLE, C. J. SAINTE-CLAIRE, et LE-
BLANC.—Sur la composition chimique des
gaz rejetés par les évents volcaniques de
l'Italie méridionale. — *Bull. Soc. géol.
France, S.* 2, *xv, pp.* 310–13. *Paris,* 1858
· 2ᵉ *Mém.).—C.R.Acad. Sci. xliv, pp.* 769–73,
Paris, 1857 (1ʳ *Mém.*) ; *id. xlv, pp.* 398–402
(2ᵉ *Mém.).—Ann. Chim. lii, pp.* 5–63. 1858.
—*Journ. Pharm. S.* 3, *xxxiii, pp.* 128–32.
1858.—*Mém. Sav, Étrang. xvi, pp.* 225–76.
Paris, 1862.

DEVILLE, C. J. SAINTE-CLAIRE, et LE-
BLANC.—Sur les émanations gazeuses qui
accompagnent l'Acide Borique dans les
Soffioni et Lagoni de la Toscane. (Extr.
d'une Lettre à M. Élie de Beaumont.)—
C.R. Acad. Sci. xlv, pp. 750–52. *Paris,*
1857.

DEVILLE, C. J. SAINTE-CLAIRE.—Note sur
la nature des éruptions actuelles du Volcan
de Stromboli.—*Bull. Soc. géol. France, S.* 2,
xv, pp. 345–62. *Paris,* 1858.

DEVILLE, C. J. SAINTE-CLAIRE.—Remarques [à l'occasion de diverses communications de M. Fouqué concernant les phénomènes éruptifs de l'Italie Méridionale].—
C.R. Acad. Sci. lxi, pp. 567, 737. *Paris,*
1865.

DEVILLE, C. J. SAINTE-CLAIRE.—Rapport
sur un mémoire de M. Fouqué, intitulé ;
" Recherches sur les phénomènes chimiques
des volcans."—*C.R. Acad. Sci. lxii, pp.*
1366–77. *Paris,* 1866.

DOLOMIEU, D. G. S. T. G. DE.—Voyage
aux Îles de Lipari fait en 1781, ou notice
sur les Îles Æoliennes pour servir à l'histoire des volcans.—8⁰, *pp. viii*+208. *Paris,*
1783.

DOLOMIEU, D. G. S. T. G. DE.—Reise nach
den Liparischen Inseln, oder Nachricht von
den Aeolischen Inseln zur näheren Aufklä-
rung der Geschichte der Vulkane. Deutsch
v. L. Chr. Lichtenberg.—8⁰. *Leipzig,*
1783.

DONATI, E.—Notice sur l'Île de Stromboli.
—*Bull. Soc. géol. France, i, pp.* 242–45.
Paris, 1830.

ESCARD, J.—Les Phénomènes volcaniques,
leurs causes, leurs effets.—[Extr.] " *Science
Catholique,*" Oct. 1903, *pp.* 22, *fig. Arras,*
1904.

FAUJAS DE SAINT-FOND, B.—Classification des Produits Volcaniques.—*Ann. Mus.
Hist. nat. v, pp.* 325–48. *Paris,* 1804.

FER, N. DE.—Le Royaume de Naples avec
l'Isle de Sardaigne ; et une description.
1701. [B.M.—K. 83. 17.]
Vulcano is represented as two islands
with their respective names.

FERRARA, F.—I Campi Flegrei della Sicilia
e delle Isole che le sono intorno, o descrizione fisica e mineralogica di queste Isole.—
4⁰, *pp. xix*+434, 1 *pl.,* 6 *maps. Messina,*
1810.

FERRARA, F.—Volcanologia Geologica della
Sicilia e delle Isole che le sono intorno.—
Atti Acc. Gioen. S. 2, *ii, pp.* 229–307.
Catania, 1845.

FIORE, O. DE.—I Fenomeni avvenuti a
Vulcano (Isole Eolie) dal 1890 al 1913.
Parte I con 3 tavole (xx, xxi, xxii).—
Zeitschr. f. Vulk. i, 2, *pp.* 57–73. *Berlin,*
Mai, 1914.

FISCHER, TH.—Das Halbinselland Italien.
—*In* Kirchhoff's " Länderkunde von
Europa," *pp.* 285–515. *Prag, Wien, Leip-
zig,* 1890.

FOUQUÉ, F. A.—Sur les phénomènes éruptifs de l'Italie Méridionale. Sixième lettre
à Ch. Sainte-Claire Deville.—*C.R. Acad.
Sci. lxi, pp.* 564–67. *Paris,* 1865.

FOUQUÉ, F. A.—Recherches sur les phénomènes chimiques des Volcans. (Résumé
et conclusions.)—*C.R. Acad. Sci. lxii, pp.*
616–17. *Paris,* 1866.

FRIEDLAENDER, B., AGUILAR, E.—
Una visita a Stromboli.—*Boll. Soc. Nat.
xix, pp.* 40–47. *Napoli,* 1905.

FRIEDLAENDER, E.—Ueber die Kleinformen der vulkanischen Produkte.—*Zeitschr. f. Vulk. i,* 2. *Berlin, Mai,* 1914.'
See Tab. xxii, figs. 18 and 19 ; Tab. xxx,
fig. 35 ; Tab. xxxi, fig. 38.

FUCHS, C. W. C.—Die vulkanischen Erschei-
nungen im Jahre 1867 [*etc.* to 1885].—
N. J. f. Min. 1868 [1870.—*Tschermak's
Min. Mitth.* 1875, 1876, 1883, 1887].

FUCHS, C. W. C.—Vulkane und Erdbeben.—
Internat. wissensch. Biblioth. xvii, pp. 269–
71, 1 *map, figs. Leipzig,* 1873.—8⁰, *pp.
xii*+343, 1 *map col., figs. Leipzig,* 1875.
—In French, 8⁰, *pp. viii*+279, *fig., map.
Paris,* 1876.——2nd ed. 1878.—In Italian,
8⁰. *Milano,* 1881.

FULCHER, L. W.—A Visit to the Lipari
Islands and Mount Etna.—*Journ. City of
London College Science Soc.* 16, *pp.* 9.
April, 1890.

FULCHER, L. W.—¹Vulcano and Stromboli. —*Geol. Mag. pp.* 347–53. 1890.

GALVANI, D.—Memoria geologica e mineralogica su le Isole Eolie e classificazione de' prodotti volcanici delle medesime.—*N. Ann. Sci. Nat. Bologna, vi, pp.* 18. 1841. [C.A.]—*R. Ist. Naz. Ital., Sez. Bolognese, p.* 95. *Bologna,* 1840.

GATTA, L.—L'Italia, sua formazione, suoi vulcani e terremoti.—8⁰, *pp.* 539, 32 *figs.,* 3 *lith. maps. Milano,* 1882.—*Boll. R. Com. Geol. Ital., Notiz. Bibl. pp.* 102–4. *Roma,* 1882.

GATTA, L.—Vulcanismo.—16⁰, *pp.* 267, *figs. Milano,* 1885.

GAUDIN, C. T., et PIRAINO DI MANDRALISCA.—Contributions à la Flore Fossile Italienne. Cinquième Mémoire : Tufs volcaniques de Lipari.—*Nouv. Mém. Soc. Helv. Sci. nat. xvii, pp.* 1–12, 3 *pls. Zürich,* 1860.

GAUTIER, A.—La Genèse des Eaux Thermales et ses rapports avec le Volcanisme.— [Extr.] *Ann. Mines, S.* 10, *ix, pp.* 316–70. *Paris,* 1906.

GEMMELLARO, C.—Sui vulcani di Sicilia ed Isole vicine.—*Catania,* 1831.

GENOVESI.—Sull' acque termo-minerali e sulla Grotta di Lipari, 1879.—*Idrol. Med. xiv,* 15, *pp.* 94–95. 1880.

GIANNETTASIIS, N. P.—Æstates Surrentinæ.—12⁰, *foll.* 6, *pp.* 280, *frontisp. Napoli,* 1696. *See pp.* 111–25.

GOOD, J. M.—*See* POLEHAMPTON, E.

GRABLOVITZ, G.—*See* MERCALLI, G., ET ALII.—Le eruzioni dell Isola di Vulcano, *etc.* 1888.

GRÆVIUS, J. G.—Thesaurus Antiquitatum et Historiarum Siciliæ, *etc.*—15 vols. *fol.*— *See Tom. x of his :* " Thes. Antiq. et Hist. Italiæ." *Lugduni Batavorum,* 1725–4–25. Also cited as " Thesaurus scriptorum Siciliæ," *etc.* (Cura P. Burmanni), and as " Thesaurus Siculus."

HAAS, H. J.—Unterirdische Gluten. Die Natur und das Wesen der Feuerberge im Lichte der neuesten Anschauungen für die Gebildeten aller Stände in gemeinverständlicher Weise .dargestellt. 2te. Auflage.— 8⁰, *pp.* 316, *fig. and pl. Berlin,* 1912.

HAMILTON, SIR W.—Observations on Mount Vesuvius, Mount Etna and other Volcanos : In a series of letters, addressed to the Royal Society . . . to which are added explanatory notes by the Author, hitherto unpublished.—*Trans. R. Soc. lvii–lxi. London,* 1768–72. — 8⁰. *London,* 1772. ——2nd ed. 8⁰, *pp. iv*+179, 6 *pls. London,* 1773.——3rd ed. *London,* 1774.——4th ed. *London,* 1783.

HAMILTON, SIR W.—Campi Phlegræi. Observations on the Volcanos of the Two Sicilies . . . to which a . . . map is annexed, with 54 plates illuminated, from drawings taken and colour'd after Nature, under the inspection of the Author, by the Editor . . . P. Fabris, *etc.* [English and French].—2 vols. *fol. Naples,* 1776.

HEERL, J. L.—*See* HOUEL, J. P. L. L.— Reisen durch Sicilien, *etc.*

HELLEMANNS, J. GEORG.—De montibus ignivomis, vulgò Feuer-speyende Berge.— 4⁰, *pp.* 22. *Marburgi Cattorum, Typis hæred. Joh. Jodoc. Kürsneri, Acad. Typogr.* 1698.

HOBBS, W. H.—Notes on a Trip to the Lipari Islands in 1889.—*Trans. Wisconsin Acad. Sci. ix, pp.* 21–32, 1 *pl.,* 3 *figs.* 1892.

HOBBS, W. H.—Volcanite, an Anorthoclase-Augite rock chemically like the Dacites (bread-crust bombs of Vulcano).—*Bull. Geol. Soc. Amer. v, pp.* 598–602. *Boston,* 1893.

HOBBS, W. H.—The grand eruption of Vesuvius in 1906.— *Journ. Geol. xvii, pp.* 636–55, *figs. Chicago,* 1906.

HOFF, K. E. A. VON.—Geschichte der natürlichen Veränderungen der Erdoberfläche.—3 vols. *Gotha,* 1822, 1824, 1834. *See* Vol. ii, § 11, *pp.* 252–67.

HOFF, K. E. A. VON.—Chronik der Erdbeben und Vulcan-Ausbrüche mit vorausgehender Abhandlung über die Natur dieser Erscheinungen.—2 vols. 8⁰. *Vol. i, pp.* 6+470 ; *Vol. ii, pp.* 2+406. *Gotha,* 1840–41.

HOFFMANN, F.—Ueber die geognostische Beschaffenheit der Liparischen Inseln.— *Ann. Phys. Chem. xxvi, pp.* 31 *et seq. Leipzig,* 1832.—*N. J. f. Min. pp.* 67–77. *Stuttgart,* 1834.

HOFFMANN, F.—Mémoire sur les terrains volcaniques de Naples, de la Sicile, et des Îles de Lipari.—*Bull. Soc. géol. France, iii, pp.* 170–80. *Paris,* 1835.—[Extr.] *C.R. Acad. Sci. xli, pp.* 872–76. *Paris,* 1855.

HOFFMANN, F.—Physikalische Geographie. (Erhebungskratere, Vegetation Siciliens, Aetna u. A.)—*Berlin,* 1837.

HOFFMANN, F.—Geognostische Beobachtungen, gesammelt auf einer Reise durch
Italien und Sicilien, in den Jahren 1830-
1832.—*Archiv. f. Min. Geognos. etc. xiii,
pp.* 3-726, 1 *pl.*, 1 *map. Berlin,* 1839.—[Sep.
publ.] *Berlin,* 1839.

HOFFMANN, F.—Geognostische Karte von
Sicilien.—*Berlin,* 1839.
Scale 1 : 500,000.

HÖRSTEL, W.—Die Erdbeben in Kalabrien.
—" *Himmel und Erde,*" *xviii,* 3, *pp.* 97-117,
tav. Berlin, 1905.

HOUEL, J. P. L. L.—Voyage Pittoresque des
Isles de Sicile, de Lipari et de Malte, où
l'on traite des Antiquités qui s'y trouvent
encore ; des principaux Phénomènes que
la Nature y offre ; du Costume des Habitans, et de quelques Usages.—4 tom. *fol.*
T. i, pp. vii+138, *pls.* 72, 1782 ; *T. ii,
pp.* 148, *pls.* 73-144, 1784 ; *T. iii, pp.* 126,
pls. 145-204, 1785 ; *T. iv, pp.* 124, *pls.*
205-64, *Paris,* 1787.

HOUEL, J. P. L. L.—Reisen durch Sicilien
u. Malta etc. übersetzt. v. J. L. Heerl, mit
Kpft.—4 vols. 8⁰. *Gotha,* 1797-1805.

HOUEL, J. [? P. L. L.] (des. et grav.).—Vue
des deux bouches de Volcanello de l'Isle de
Lipari et de l'Isle appellée Saline. Pl. LXV.
Sepia engrav. : 350×222 mm.

HOVEY, E. O.—The volcanic condition of
Stromboli [1897]. — *Nature, lvii, p.* 100.
1897-98.

IDDINGS, J. P., PENFIELD, S. L.—
Fayalite in the Obsidian of Lipari.—*Amer.
Jour. Sci. xl, pp.* 75-78. *New Haven,* 1890.

ITTIG, THOMÆ.—De Montium incendiis, in
quibus post ardentium toto passim orbe
montium catalogum et historiam, ac variarum opinionum examen, non modo totius
naturæ cum in efficiendis tum in conservandis illis ignibus processus exponitur,
etc.—8⁰, *pp.* 16+347, *index. Lipsiæ,* 1671.
See pp. 65-70 and other refs.

JANSSEN.—Sur la composition des gaz émis
par le volcan de Santorin.—*C.R. Acad. Sci.
lxiv, pp.* 1303-4. *Paris,* 1867.
See p. 1304.

JERVIS, G.—*See* JERVIS, W. P.

JERVIS, W. P.—I Tesori sotterranei dell'
Italia.—4 vols. 8⁰, *num. pls. Torino,*
1873-89.

JERVIS, W. P.—Guida alle acque minerali
d'Italia.—*Torino,* 1876.

JOHNSTON-LAVIS, H. J.—Volcanic Cones,
their Structure and Mode of Formation.—
" *Science Gossip,*" *xvi, pp.* 220-23, 1 *fig.
London,* 1880.

JOHNSTON-LAVIS, H. J.—On the Origin
and Structure of Volcanic Cones.—" *Science
Gossip,*" *xvii, pp.* 12-14, 4 *figs. London,*
1881.

JOHNSTON-LAVIS, H. J.—The Relationship of the Structure of Igneous Rocks
to the Conditions of their Formation.—
Scient. Proc. R. Dublin Soc. N.S. v, pp.
113-55. 1886.

JOHNSTON-LAVIS, H. J.—On the Fragmentary Ejectamenta of Volcanoes.—*Proc.
Geol. Assoc. ix, pp.* 421-32, 1 *pl.* 1886.

JOHNSTON-LAVIS, H. J.—Lo Sciarra and
Crater of Stromboli, Sept. 1887.
Photo. : 290×187 mm.

JOHNSTON-LAVIS, H. J.—Vulcano and
Vulcanello from Lipari in 1887.
Photo. : 370×140 mm.

JOHNSTON-LAVIS, H. J.—The Islands of
Vulcano and Stromboli. — " *Nature,*"
xxxviii, pp. 13-14. *London,* 1888.

JOHNSTON-LAVIS, H. J.—Further Notes
on the Late Eruption at Vulcano Island.—
" *Nature,*" *xxxix, pp.* 109-11. 1888.

JOHNSTON-LAVIS, H. J.—The Recent
Eruption at Vulcano.—" *Nature,*" *xxxix,
p.* 173. 1888.

JOHNSTON-LAVIS, H. J.—Il Pozzo Artesiano di Ponticelli.—*Rend. R. Acc. Sci. S.* 2,
iii, pp. 142-48. *Napoli,* 1889.

JOHNSTON-LAVIS, H. J.—Volcans et
Tremblements de Terre. Revue de ce qui
a été publié sur ces sujets durant l'année
1888.—*Ann. géol. univ. v, pp.* 629-55.
Paris, 1889.

JOHNSTON-LAVIS, H. J.—The Excursion
to the Volcanoes of Italy.—Seismology in
Italy.—" *Nature,*" *xl, p.* 294. 1889.

JOHNSTON-LAVIS, H. J., and ANDERSON,
T.—Notes on the late eruption in the
Island of Vulcano.—*Rept. Brit. Assoc.* 1888,
pp. 664-66. *London,* 1889.

JOHNSTON-LAVIS, H. J.— On the Con-
servation of Heat in Volcanic Chimneys.—
Rept. Brit. Assoc. 1888, *pp.* 666-67.
London, 1889.

JOHNSTON-LAVIS, *I* H. J.—Viaggio scientifico alle regioni vulcaniche Italiane nella ricorrenza del centinario del " Viaggio alle due Sicilie " di Lazzaro Spallanzani.—8°, *pp. 1–10. Napoli, 1889.*
This is the programme of the excursion.

JOHNSTON-LAVIS, H. J.—The Eruption of Vulcano Island.—" *Nature,*" *xlii, pp.* 78–79. 1890.

JOHNSTON-LAVIS, H. J.—Excursion to the South Italian Volcanoes.—*Proc. Geol. Assoc. xi, pp.* 389–423. *London,* 1890.

JOHNSTON-LAVIS, H. J.—The State of the Active Sicilian Volcanoes in September 1889.—*Scóttish Geog. Mag. vi, pp.* 145–49. *Edinburgh,* 1890.

JOHNSTON-LAVIS, H. J.—The Extension of the Mellard Reade and C. Davison theory of Secular Straining of the Earth to the explanation of the deep phenomena of Volcanic Action.—*Geol. Mag. pp.* 246–49. 1890.

JOHNSTON-LAVIS, H. J.—Volcans et Tremblements de Terre (Revue).—*Ann. géol. univ. vi, pp.* 355–81. *Paris,* 1890.

JOHNSTON-LAVIS, H. J.—The South Italian Volcanoes, being the account of an Excursion to them made by English and other Geologists in 1889 under the auspices of the Geologists' Association of London, and the direction of the author, with papers on the Different Localities by Messrs. Johnston-Lavis, Platania, Sambon, Zezi and Mme. Antonia Lavis, including the Bibliography of the Volcanic Districts.—8°, *pp. vi+342, 16 pls.—Furchheim, Naples,* 1891.—Reviewed in " *Nature,*" *xliv, pp.* 539–40. 1891.
A reprint of account given in Proc. Geol. Assoc. with addition of Bibliography.

JOHNSTON-LAVIS, H. J.—Bibliography of the Geology and Eruptive Phenomena of the South Italian Volcanoes, that were visited in 1889, as well as of the submarine volcano of A.D. 1831. Compiled by Madame A. Lavis and Dr. Johnston-Lavis. —8°, *pp.* 89–331. *Naples,* 1891.
Chapt. VII of foregoing, a number of reprints of which were also issued.

JOHNSTON-LAVIS, H. J.—Note on the Lithophyses in Obsidian of the Rocche Rosse, Lipari.—*Geol. Mag. pp.* 488–90. *London,* 1892.

JOHNSTON-LAVIS, H. J.—Stromboli.— " *Nature,*" *xlvii, p.* 453. 1893.

JOHNSTON-LAVIS, H. J.—The Causes of variation in the composition of Igneous Rocks.—" *Natural Science,*" *iv, pp.* 134–40. *London,* 1894.

JOHNSTON-LAVIS, H. J.—Sulle Inclusione di Quarzo nelle lave di Stromboli, ecc. e sui cambiamenti da ciò causati nella composizione della lava.—*Boll. Soc. Geol. Ital. xiii, pp.* 32–41, 1 *pl. Roma,* 1894.

JOHNSTON-LAVIS, H. J.—On Quartz Enclosures in Lavas of Stromboli and Strombolicchio, and their Effect on the Composition of the Rock.—*Rept. Brit. Assoc.* 1893, *pp.* 759–60. *London,* 1894.— *Geol. Mag. pp.* 47–48. 1894.—*Quart. Journ. Geol. Soc. l, Proc. p.* 2. 1894.

JOUSSET, P.—L'Italie illustrée.—*fol., pp.* 370, 14 *col. maps and plans,* 9 *engrav. maps,* 12 *pls.,* 784 *photos. Paris,* 1829.

JUDD, J. W.—Contributions to the Study of Volcanoes.—*Geol. Mag. pp.* 1–16, 56–70, 145–52, 206–14, *pls. and figs. London,* 1875.

KIRCHER, A.—The Vulcano's : or, burning and fire-vomiting Mountains famous in the World : with their remarkables, *etc.* —8°, *foll.* 4, *pp.* 64, 1 *pl. London,* 1669.

LA CHAVANNE, DE.—Histoire des Îles de Lipari.—*See* AUDOT, L. E. (père).— Royaume de Naples.—8°, *pp.* 370, 117 *pls. Paris,* 1835. [C.A.] — Also *Paris,* 1855.

LACROIX, A. F. A.—Les enclaves des roches volcaniques.—*Ann. Acad. Mâcon, S.* 2, *x, pp.* 1–710, 8 *pls.* 1893.

LACROIX, A. F. A.—Sur le Tremblement de Terre ressenti le 8 septembre à Stromboli et sur l'état actuel de ce Volcan.— *C.R. Acad. Sci. cxli, pp.* 575–79. *Paris,* 1905.

LACROIX, A. F. A.—Les Laves des dernières éruptions de Vulcano (Îles Éoliennes).—*C.R. Acad. Sci. cxlvii, pp.* 1451–56. *Paris,* 1908.

LANZA DI TRABIA, S.—Novissima Guida pel viaggiatore in Sicilia.—16°, *pp.* 358. *Palermo,* 1884.

LASAULX, A. C. P. F. VON.—*See* SARTORIUS VON WALTERSHAUSEN. 1880.

LEANTI, A.—Dello Stato presente della Sicilia o sia breve e distinta descrizione di essa. Accresciuta colle notizie delle Isole adiacenti.—2 vols. 8°, *portrait and num. pls. Palermo,* 1761.

LEBLANC, F.—See DEVILLE, C. J. SAINTE-CLAIRE.—Sur la composition chimique des Gaz, etc.

LEBLANC, F.—See DEVILLE, C. J. SAINTE-CLAIRE.—Sur les émanations gazeuses, etc.

LEONHARD, C. C. Von.—Geologie, oder Naturgeschichte der Erde auf allgemein faszliche Weise abgehandelt.—5 vols. 8⁰. Stuttgart, 1836-44.
See Vol. v, pp. 221-33.

LÉVESQUE DE BURIGNY, J.—Histoire générale de Sicile.—2 vols. 4⁰, 2 maps. La Haye, 1745.
In Ital. : " dalla lingua francese tradotta, . . . accresciuta, . . . dal Signor E. Scasso e Borrello."—6 tom. 4⁰. Palermo, 1792-94.
—Also printed separately in the " Descrizione Geografica della Sicilia."—8⁰. Palermo, 1806.
See Vol. ii, pp. 272-75.

LICHTENBERG, L. C.—See DOLOMIEU, D. G. S. T. G. De.—Reise nach den Liparischen Inseln, etc.

LOCCHI, Ing. D.—Italia ; Carta Fisica. 1 : 200,000.—Pub. G. B. Paravia e C., Torino, Roma, Milano, Firenze, Napoli, 1876.
Raised map.

LOMBARDO-BUDA, G.—Lettera monitoria d'un Accademico Etneo.—8⁰. Catania, 1791.

LOMBARDO-BUDA, G.—Lettere sull' antichita di vari vulcani dirette al p. priore D. Salv. M. di Blasi.—Nuova Raccolta di Opuscoli di Autori Siciliani, v. Palermo, 1792.

LONGO, A.—Sulle cagioni probabili delle ascensioni vulcaniche subaeree.—Atti Acc. Gioen. S. 3, iv, pp. 1-35. Catania, 1870.

LUCA, S. De.—Ricerche analitiche sull' Acido Borico dell' Isola di Vulcano.—Rend. R. Acc. Sci. ii, pp. 105-9, 120-21. Napoli, 1863.

LUIGI, Dr. (nipote).—See BULIFON, A.—Carte de' regni di Napoli, etc.

LYELL, C.—Principles of Geology.—12 editions. London, 1830 to 1875.
See 12th ed. Vol. ii, p. 135. London, 1875.
In French, transl. from 6th ed., " Principes de Géologie."—Lyon, 1846.
See Pt. III, p. 357.

MALAGOLI VECCHI, M.—See PELLÉ, C.—Il Mediterraneo illustrato, le sue Isole, ecc.

MALLADRA, A.—See STOPPANI, A.—Corso di Geologia. 3a ediz.

MALLET, R.—On the mechanism of Stromboli.—Proc. R. Soc. xxii, pp. 496-514, 5 figs. London, 1874.—Amer. Journ. Sci. S. 3, viii, pp. 200-2. New Haven, 1874.—Transl. in Ital. by Prof. O. Silvestri : Bull. Vulc. Ital. vii, viii, ix, x. Roma, 1876.

MALLET, R.—Note on Mr. Mallet's Paper on the Mechanism of Stromboli.—Proc. R. Soc. xxiii, p. 444. London, 1875.

MARGOLLÉ, E.—See ZURCHER, F.

MASSA, G. A.—La Sicilia in prospettiva.— 2 pts. 4⁰. Pte. 1, pp. 12-359 ; Pte. 2, pp. 503. Palermo, 1709 [i.e. 1708].

MATTEUCCI, R. V.—Sulla attività dei vulcani Vesuvio, Etna, Vulcano, Stromboli e Santorino nell' autunno del 1898.—Bull. Soc. Sismol. Ital. v, pp. 132-44. Modena, 1899.

MATTEUCCI, R. V.—Sur l'État actuel des volcans de l'Europe Méridionale.—C.R. Acad. Sci. cxxix, pp. 734-37. Paris, 1899.

MATTIROLO, E.—[Esame di una varietà impura di Opale, di Timpone Patasso (Lipari).]—See CORTESE, E., e SABATINI, V.—Descriz. geol.-petrograf. d. Isole Eolie.—Mem. descr. Carta Geol. Ital. vii, pp. 39-42. Roma, 1892.

MERCALLI, G.—Le ultime eruzioni dell' Isola di Vulcano.—Bull. Vulc. Ital. iv, p. 28. Roma, 1879.

MERCALLI, G.—Le ultime eruzioni [delle isole Vulcano e Stromboli].—Bull. Vulc. Ital. vi, pp. 27-28, 95-96, 96-97. Roma, 1879.

MERCALLI, G.—Contribuzioni alla Geologia delle Isole Lipari.—Atti Soc. Ital. Sci. Nat. xxii, pp. 367-80. Milano, 1879.—[Estr.] Boll. R. Com. Geol. Ital. S. 2, i, pp. 315-17. Roma, 1880.

MERCALLI, G.—Natura delle eruzioni dello Stromboli ed in generale dell' attivita sismo-vulcanica nelle Eolie.—Atti Soc. Ital. Sci. Nat. xxiv, pp. 105-34. Milano, 1881.

MERCALLI, G.—Notizie sullo stato attuale dei vulcani attivi Italiani.—Atti Soc. Ital. Sci. Nat. xxvii, pp. 184-98. Milano, 1884.

MERCALLI, G.—La fossa di Vulcano e lo Stromboli dal 1884 al 1886.—Atti Soc. Ital. Sci. Nat. xxix, pp. 352-60. Milano, 1886.

MERCALLI, G.—L'Isola Vulcano e lo Stromboli dal 1886 al 1888.—Atti Soc. Ital. Sci. Nat. xxxi, pp. 407-19. Milano, 1888.

MERCALLI, G., SILVESTRI, O., e GRAB-
LOVITZ, G.—Le Eruzioni dell Isola di
Vulcano incominciate il 3 Agosto 1888 e
terminate il 22 Marzo 1890.—*Ann. Uffic.
Cent. Meteor. Geodinam. x, pte.* 4, *pp.* 210,
14 *pls. Roma,* 1888.—[Estr.] *Roma,* 1891.

MERCALLI, G.—Osservazioni fatte allo
Stromboli nel 1888-89.—*Ann. Uffic. Cent.
Meteor. Geodinam. x, pte.* 4. *Roma,* 1888.

MERCALLI, G.—Studio comparativo dei
fenomeni vulcanici osservati nell' arcipelago
Eolio durante il periodo eruttivo di Vulcano.—*Ann. Uffic. Cent. Meteor. Geodinam.
x, pte.* 4. *'Roma,* 1888.

MERCALLI, G.—Le Eruzioni dell' Isola Vulcano.—*Rassegna Nazionale, An.* 11, *xlv,
pp.* 51-66. *Firenze,* 1889.

MERCALLI, G.—Sopra alcune Lave antiche
e moderne dello Stromboli.—*Rend. R. Ist.
Lomb. S.* 2, *xxiii, pp.* 863-73. *Milano,*
1891.—*Giorn. Min. ii,* 3. *Milano,* 1891

MERCALLI, G.—Le Lave antiche e moderne
dell' Isola Vulcano.—*Giorn. Min. Crist.
Petr. iii,* 2, *pp.* 16. *Pavia,* 1892.

MERCALLI, G.—I Vulcani attivi della terra
(morfologia, dinamismo, prodotti, distribuzione geografica, cause).—8°, *pp. viii+*
422, 82 *figs.,* 26 *pls. Milano,* 1907.

MERCALLI, G.—*See* RICCÒ, A.

MERCALLI, G.—*See* SILVESTRI, O.

MERCALLI, G.—*See* TARAMELLI, T.

MINÀ-PALUMBO, F.—Cenno topografico
delle Isole adiacenti alla Sicilia.—*L'Empe-
docle, i, pp.* 419-36, 465-92. *Girgenti,* 1851.

MIRON, F.—Étude des phénomènes volcaniques, tremblements de terre, éruptions
volcaniques, le cataclysme de la Martinique, 1902.—8°, *pp. viii+*320, *fig. and
map. Paris,* 1903.

MURICCE, F. CAREGA.—I vulcani d'Italia
(Etna, Vesuvio, Campi Flegrei, Isole Eolie,
Stromboli).—1877.

MUZIO, C. D.—Saggio sull' origine de' fuochi
vulcanici e de' loro fenomeni, recitato
nell' Accademia del Buongosto, e ripertato
nel T. II. dei suoi Saggi.—4°. *Palermo,*
1800.

NEUMAYR, M. — Erdgeschichte. — *Allgemeine Naturkunde, i, pp.* 42+xii+653, *very
num. illustr. Leipzig,* 1886.

NOLIN, J. B.—Le Royaume de Naples,
divisé en ses douze Provinces.—*Paris,* 1702.
Very imaginary maps. Vulcano is represented as a single island and Palmarola as
two.

OMBONI, G.—Geologia dell' Italia.—8°,
5 *tav. Milano,* 1869.
See No. 14.

ORTELIUS, A.—Theatrvm Orbis Terrarvm.
—*fol.,* 53 *col. maps. Antverpiæ,* 1570.
—For other editions *see* CAMPI PHLEGRÆI.
In map of Italy, Vulcano and Vulcanello
are represented as separated, Lipari
coming in between them. A small island,
where Vulcanello should have been, is
unnamed.

OTTÉ, E. C.—*See* QUATREFAGES DE
BRÉAU, J. L. A. DE.—The Rambles of a
Naturalist. 1857.

PALMIERI, L.—Intorno ad una recente
eruzione nell' Isola di Vulcano ed alla continuazione del terremoto in Corleone.—
Rend. R. Acc. Sci. xv, p. 123. *Napoli,*
1876.

PANICHI, U.—Solfo di Muthmann osservato
all' Isola di Vulcano.—*Geol. Zentr. xviii,* 6,
p. 253. *Leipzig,* 1912.

PANICHI, U.—Sullo Zolfo di Vulcano
(Isole Eolie).—*Atti Acc. Gioen. S.* 5, *v, Mem.*
15, *pp.* 15, 1 *pl. Catania,* 1912.

PAPARCURI, S. (1743).—Discorso fisico-
matematico sopra la variazione de' venti
pronosticata ventiquattr'ore prima dalle
varie e diverse qualità, ed effetti de' fumi
di Vulcano.—*See* Opuscoli di Autori Siciliani, *v, pp.* 76-120. *Catania, Palermo,*
1758-78.

PARETO, L.—Della posizione delle roccie
pirogene ed eruttive dei periodi terziario
quaternario ed attuale in Italia.—8°, *pp.*
35. *Genova,* 1852.

PARTHEY, G. F. C.—Wanderungen durch
Sicilien und die Levante.—2 pts. 12°.
Pt. i, pp. 8+458+32 (*of music*) ; *Pt. ii,
pp. x+*594. *Berlin,* 1834-40.
See Pt. i, pp. 309-19.

PAYAN, D.—Notice sur quelques volcans de
l'Italie méridionale.—*Bull. Soc. Stat. Arts
Utiles, Sci. Nat. du Départ. Drôme, iii,
pp.* 145-63. 1842. [C.A.]

PELLÉ, C.—Il Mediterraneo illustrato, le
sue Isole, etc. preceduta da un saggio
storico sul Mediterraneo, e compilata dal
bibliofilo M. Malagoli Vecchi, etc.—4°,
pp. 512, *num. pls. Firenze,* 1841.

U

PENFIELD, S. L.—*See* IDDINGS, P.

PEREIRA, A. Von.—Sieben Tage auf den Aeolischen Inseln. — ?, 1880.

PEREIRA, A. Von.—Im Reiche des Aeolus. Ein Bordleben von hundert Stunden an den Liparischen Inseln.—8⁰, *pp.* 168, *num. illustr.,* 1 *map. Wien,* 1883.

PERRET, F. A.—Notes on the eruption of Stromboli, April, May, June, 1907.— *Scient. Bull. Brooklyn Inst. Arts and Sci. ii, pp.* 313–23, 8 *figs.* 1907.

PERREY, De.—*See* BORNEMANN, J. G. 1856.

PETERMANN, A. H.—Uebersicht des vulkanischen Heerdes im Mittelmeer. Maasstab 1 : 15,000,000.—*Peterm. Mitth. Taf.* 7. *Gotha,* 1866.

PILLA, L.—Paralello fra i tre Vulcani ardenti dell' Italia.—*Napoli,* 1835.—*Atti Acc. Gioen. xii, pp.* 89–127. *Catania,* 1837. —*N. J. f. Min. p.* 347. *Stuttgart,* 1836.

PILLA, L.—Osservazioni fisiche sopra il Vulcano di Stromboli.—*Il Lucifero, i, pp.* 30, 54, 89, 106. *Napoli,* 1838.

PILLA, L.—Trattato di Geologia.—2 vols. 8⁰. *Vol. i, pp.* xiv+549, *num. figs.* ; *Vol. ii, pp.* 614, *num. figs. Pisa,* 1847–51. *See Vol.* i.

PIRAINO DI MANDRALISCA. — *See* GAUDIN, Ch. T.

PLATANIA. Gaet.—Sui projettili squarciati di Vulcano (Isole Eolie) nell' eruzione del 1888–90.—*Ann. Uffic. Cent. Meteor. Geodinam. x, pte.* 4, *pp.* 7. *Roma,* 1888. —[Estr.] *Roma,* 1891.

PLATANIA, Gaet.—Stromboli e Vulcano nel Settembre del 1889.—8⁰. *Riposto,* 1889.

PLATANIA, Gaet.—I Fenomeni sottomarini durante l'eruzione di Vulcano (Isole Eolie) nel 1888–89.—8⁰. *Acireale,* 1890.

PLATANIA, Gaet. e Giov.—Le Interruzioni del Cavo telegrafico Milazzo-Lipari e i fenomeni vulcanici sottomarini nel 1888–92.—*Atti Acc. Gioen. S.* 4, *vii, Mem.* 10, *pp.* 13, 3 *tav.* 1894.—*Bull. id. xxxvi, pp.* 2–3. *Catania,* 1894.

PLATANIA, Gaet.—Il Terremoto Calabrese dell' 8 Settembre 1905 a Stromboli.— *Rend. e Mem. R. Acc. Sci. d. Zelanti, S.* 3, *v, Mem. Class. Sci. pp.* 79–87. *Acireale,* 1909.

PLATANIA, Gaet.—Effetti magnetici del fulmine sulle lave di Stromboli.—*Rend. e Mem. R. Acc. Sci., Lett. ed Arti d. Zelanti, S.* 3, *v, Mem. Class. Sci. pp.* 163–67. *Acireale,* 1909.

PLATANIA, Gaet.—I Fenomeni eruttivi dello Stromboli nella primavera 1907. Appendice : Il cratere di Stromboli nell' Aprile 1908–9.—*Ann. Uffic. Cent. Meteor. Geodinam. xxx, pte.* 1, *pp.* 27, *pl. vii. Roma,* 1910.

PLATANIA, Gaet.—Stromboli.—*Rend. e Mem. R. Acc. Sci., Lett. ed Arti d. Zelanti, S.* 3, *vi, pp.* 11, 4 *pls. Acireale,* 1912.— *C.R. 9e Congrès internat. Géog,. (1908), ii, pp.* 235–45. *Genève,* 1910.

PLATANIA, Gaet.—Effetti magnetici del Fulmine.—*Rend. e Mem. R. Acc. Sci., Lett. ed Arti d. Zelanti, S.* 3, *vi,* 1908–11, *pp.* 21–25. *Acireale,* 1912.

PLATANIA, Giov.—Éruptions volcaniques aux Îles Lipari, du 3 au 6 août 1888.— " *La Nature*," 16e *Ann.,* 795, *pp.* 198–99. *Paris,* 1888.—*Bull. Soc. Belge Géol. etc. ii, Proc.-verb., p.* 355. *Bruxelles,* 1888.

PLATANIA, Giov.—Éruption volcanique à l'Île Vulcano.—" *La Nature*," 16e *Ann.,* 805, *pp.* 359–63, *fig. Paris,* 1888.

PLATANIA, Giov.—Stromboli e Vulcano nel Settembre del 1889.—*Boll. Oss. Meteor. R. Ist. Naut. Riposto, xv,* 9–12, *pp.* 14. *Riposto,* 1889.

PLATANIA, Giov.—I Fenomeni sottomarini durante l'eruzione di Vulcano (Eolie) nel 1888–89.—*Atti e Rend. R. Acc. Sci., Lett. ed Arti d. Zelanti, N.S. i, pp.* 63–76, 3 *tab. Acireale,* 1890.

PLATANIA, Giov.—La récente éruption volcanique à l'Île Vulcano (1888–90).— "*La Nature*," 19e *Ann.,* 927, *pp.* 211–14, *fig. Paris,* 1891.

PLATANIA, Giov.—Una nuova interruzione del Cavo telegrafico Milazzo-Lipari. —*Atti e Rend. Acc. Sci. Acireale, N.S. v, Class Sci. pp.* 47–53, 1 *diag. Acireale,* 1894.

PLATANIA, Giov.—Intorno ad alcune sorgenti termali nelle Isole Eolie.—*Boll. Acc. Gioen. S.* 2, *xv, pp.* 19–24, 1 *fig. Catania,* 1911.

POLEHAMPTON, E., and GOOD, J. M.—Gallery of Nature and Art, in six volumes, illustrated with one hundred engravings. —2nd ed. 8⁰. *Vol. i, pp. vi+x+527 ; Vol. ii, pp. vi+488 ; Vol. iii, pp. v+411 ; Vol. iv, pp. vi+552 ; Vol. v, pp. vi+688 ; Vol. vi, pp. vi+624+iv. London,* 1818. *See* Vol. i, pp. 435-45.

POMBA, Cav. C.—L'Italia nel suo aspetto fisico.—*Pub. G. B. Paravia e C., Torino, Roma, Milano, Firenze, Napoli,* 1890. 1 : 100,000 horiz. and vert. Raised map on section of globe.

PRESTANDREA, A., e CALCARA, P.—Breve cenno sulla geognosia ed agricoltura delle Isole di Lipari e Vulcano.—*Giorn. Commess. Agric. e Pastor. per l. Sicilia, pp.* 28. *Palermo,* 1853.

PRÉVOST, L. C.—Voyage à l'Île Julia, à Malte, en Sicile, aux Îles Lipari, et dans les environs de Naples.—*C.R. Acad. Sci. ii, pp.* 243-54. *Paris,* 1836.

QUATREFAGES DE BRÉAU, J. L. A.—Souvenirs d'un Naturaliste. Les Côtes de Sicile. IV. Stromboli.—*Revue des Deux Mondes, N.S. xvii, pp.* 120-49. *Paris,* 1847.—2 tom. in 1 vol. 12⁰. *Paris,* 1854.

QUATREFAGES DE BRÉAU, J. L. A.—Note sur l'état du cratère du Stromboli en juin 1844.—*C.R. Acad. Sci. xliii, pp.* 610-11. *Paris,* 1856.

QUATREFAGES DE BRÉAU, J. L. A.—The Rambles of a Naturalist on the Coasts of France, Spain and Sicily. Translated [from " Souvenirs d'un Naturaliste "] by E. C. Otté.—2 vols. 8⁰. *London,* 1857.

RAFFELSBERGER, F.—Gemälde aus dem Naturreiche Beyder Sicilien.—8⁰, *pp.* 164, 8 *pls. Wien,* 1824. *See* pp. 12–19 and Pls. 2 and 3.

RAMMELSBERG, C. F. A.—Ueber die Natur der gegenwärtigen Eruptionen des Vulkans von Stromboli.—*Zeitschr. deutsch. geol. Gesellsch. xi, pp.* 103–7. *Berlin,* 1859.

RATH, J. J. G. Vom.—[Ueber den Eisenglanz von Stromboli.]—*Ann. Phys. Chem. cxxviii, p.* 30. *Leipzig,* 1866.

RATH, J. J. G. Vom.—[Besuch der Insel Vulcano.]—*N. J. f. Min. pp.* 63–66. *Stuttgart,* 1874.

RATH, J. J. G. Vom.—Ueber eine Tridymit Eruption auf der Insel Vulcano.—*Sitzber. niederrhein. Gesellsch. xxxii, p.* 14. *Bonn,* 1875.

RECLUS, Élisée.—Les Volcans de la Terre. 3 fasc. (Asie antér. : Iranie, Arménie, Syrie ; Asie Mineure : Caucase ; Méditerranée : Egéide, Italie et Sicile.)—*Soc. Astronom.* 9 *pls. and map. Bruxelles,* 1906–10. *See* Vulcano, Etna, etc., with the bibliography.

RICCIARDI, L.—Sull' allineamento dei vulcani Italiani. Sulle roccie eruttive subaeree e submarine e loro classificazione in due periodi. Sullo sviluppo dell' acido cloridrico, dell' anidride solforosa e del jodio dai vulcani. Sul graduale passaggio delle roccie acide alle roccie basiche.—8⁰, *pp.* 1–45, *tav. Reggio-Emilia,* 1887.

RICCIARDI, L.—Sull' azione dell' acqua del mare nei Vulcani.—*Dal Laboratorio Chimico del Regio Istituto Tecnico di Bari, xxxi, pp.* 129–34. 1887.

RICCIARDI, L.—Genesi e successione delle rocce eruttive.—*Atti Soc. Ital. Sci. Nat. xxx,* 3, *pp.* 212–37. *Milano,* 1887.

RICCIARDI, L.—Genesi e composizione chimica dei Terreni Vulcanici Italiani.—*L'Agricoltura Italiana, xiv-xv, pp.* 155. *Firenze,* 1889.

RICCIARDI, L.—La recente eruzione dello Stromboli in relazione alla frattura Capo Passero-Vulture e sulla influenza lunisolare nelle eruzioni.—8⁰, *pp.* 12. *Reggio Calabria,* 1893.

RICCIARDI, L.—Su le relazioni delle Reali Accademie delle Scienze di Napoli e dei Lincei di Roma sui Terremoti Calabro-Siculi del 1783 e 1908.—*Boll. Soc. Nat. xxiv (S. 2. iv), pp.* 23–75. *Napoli,* 1910.

RICCÒ, A.—Fumo di Vulcano veduto dall' Osservatorio di Palermo durante l'eruzione del 1889 ed applicazioni della Termodinamica alle eruzioni vulcaniche.—[Estr.] *Ann. Uffic. Cent. Meteor. Geodinam. S. 2, xi, pte.* 3. *Roma,* 1889.—*pp.* 8, 1 *tab.* (VI). *Roma,* 1892.

RICCÒ, A., MERCALLI, G.—Sopra il periodo eruttivo dello Stromboli cominciato il 24 Giugno 1891. Con Appendice dell' Ingegn. S. Arcidiacono.— *Ann. Uffic. Cent. Meteor. Geodinam. S. 2, xi, pte.* 3, *pp.* 37, 2 *pls. Roma,* 1892.—*Giorn. Min. Crist. Petrog. iv,* 15. *Milano,* 1893.

RICCÒ, A.—Stato presente dei fenomeni endogeni nelle Eolie.—*pp.* 13, 2 *figs. Modena,* 1896.—[Estr. *Boll. Soc. Sismol. Ital. ii,* 3, *pp.* 96–106.]

RICCÒ, A.—Stato attuale dell' attività endogena nelle Eolie.—*Boll. Acc. Gioen.* lv, pp. 12–14. *Catania*, 1898.

RICCÒ, A.—Riassunto della Sismografia del Terremoto del 16 Novembre 1894.—Parte I.—*Atti R. Acc. Lincei, S.* 5, *Rend.* viii, sem. 2, pp. 3–12, *fig., map, Roma*, 1899 ; Parte II.—*Ibid.* pp. 35–45, 1899.

RICCÒ, A.—Il Vulcano Stromboli.—*Boll. Soc. Sismol. Ital.* x, 1, pp. 37–40. *Modena*, 1904.

RICCÒ, A.—Attività dello Stromboli.—*Boll. Acc. Gioen.* xciv, pp. 7–12. *Catania*, 1907.

RICCÒ, A.—Les Paroxysmes de Stromboli. —*C.R. Acad. Sci.* cxlv, pp. 401–4. *Paris*, 1907.

RICHARD DE SAINT NON, J. C.— Voyage Pittoresque, ou Description des royaumes de Naples et de Sicile.—*gd. fol. Vol.* i [Naples and Vesuvius], *foll.* 11, pp. 252, 2 *engrav. frontisp.*, 4 *maps*, 16 *figs.*, 50 *pls.* ; *Vol.* ii [Herculaneum, Phlegrean Fields and Campania], *foll.* 16, pp. 283, 2 *maps*, 26 *figs.*, 24 *col. figs.*, 80 *pls.* ; *Vol.* iii [Southern Italy], *foll.* 24, pp. 201, 15 *figs.*, 4 *maps*, 57 *pls.* ; *Vol.* iv [Sicily], *Pt.* i, *foll.* 14, pp. 266, 13 *figs.*, 65 *pls.*, 2 *maps* ; *Pt.* ii, *foll.* v, pp. 267–430, *frontisp.*, 4 *figs.*, 32 *pls. Paris*, 1781–86.

RICHARD DE SAINT NON, J. C.—Neapel und Sizilien. Ein Ausug aus dem grossen und kostbaren Werke: "Voyage Pittoresque de Naples et Sicile."—12 vols. 8°. *Gotha*, 1789–1806.

RIDDELL, R. A.—*See* WILSON, J.

RODWELL, G. F.—The Lipari Islands.— "*Nature*," xxi, pp. 400–2, 1 *fig. London*, 1880.

ROGGERO, CAV. G.—Carta in relievo dell' Italia.—*Pub. G. B. Paravia e C., Torino, Roma, Milano, Firenze, Napoli*, 1876. 1 : 2,800,000 horiz.; 1 : 320,000 vert. Raised map.

ROSSI, DOM DE.—Maps of Italy.—10 *maps*, *gd. fol. Roma*, 1694.
In map 1 Vulcano and Vulcanello are marked as two islands.

ROSSI, DOM DE.—L'Italia. Dedicata all' Ill*mo* Reu*mo* Sig*re* Monsig*r* Gio. Batista Spinola. . . . Descritta da Giacomo Cantelli Geografo del Ser*mo* di Modena, e data in luce da Domenico de Rossi erede di Gio. Giac° de Rossi in Roma alla Pace con

Priuil. del S.P. e Licenza de Sup. l'anno 1694 il 15 Luglio.
Vulcano and Vulcanello are represented as two isles.

ROSSI, M. S. DE.—Cronaca dei vulcani delle Isole Eolie. (Informazione di A. Picone ed E. Rodriguez.)—*Bull. Vulc. Ital.* ix, pp. 200–3. *Roma*, 1882.

ROSSI, M. S. DE.—Massimi sismici Italiani dell' anno meteorico 1887.—*Ann. Meteor. Ital.* iv, pp. 283–305, 1889 ; v, pp. 253–62, 1890 ; vi, pp. 192–209, 1891 ; vii, pp. 239–56, *Torino*, 1892.

RUDOLPH, E.—Bericht über die vulcanischen Ereignisse während des Jahres 1894. —*Tschermak's min. u. petr. Mittheil.* xvi, pp. 365–464. *Wien*, 1896.

RUSSELL, G.—A Tour through Sicily in the year 1815.—8°, pp. x+289, 10 *col. pls.* (with views of Stromboli), 9 *plans and map. London*, 1819.

SABATINI, V.—*See* CORTESE, E. 1892.

SABATINI, V.—Sui Basalti labradoritici di Strombolicchio.—*Boll. Soc. Geol. Ital.* xiii, pp. 160–61. *Roma*, 1895.

SABATINI, V.—Vulcani e Terremoti.—*Riv. Ital. An.* 5, ii, pp. 353–79, 10 *figs. Roma*, 1902.

SALINO, F.—Le Isole Lipari.—*Boll. Club Alp. Ital.* viii, pp. 135–81. *Torino*, 1874.

SALINO, F.—Le Eruzioni di Vulcano.— *Cosmos*, x, pp. 45–56. *Torino*, 1890.

SALVATOR, LUDWIG. — Die Liparischen Inseln Vulcano, Salina, Lipari, Panaria, Filicudi, Alicudi, Stromboli.—8 vols. *fol.*, *num. pls., maps, figs., plans.* — ?, 1893.

SAMBON, L. W.—Eolie.—pp. 60. *Napoli*, 1891.—*See also : Pro Patria. ᵎ Napoli*, 1890.

SAMBON, L. W.—Notes on the Eolian Islands and on Pumice.—*See* JOHNSTON-LAVIS.—South Italian Volcanoes.

SANDWICH, JOHN MONTAGU, EARL OF.— A Voyage performed by the late Earl of Sandwich round the Mediterranean in the years 1738 and 1739.—4°, pp. xl+539, *pls.*, 1 *map. London*, 1799.

SANDYS, G.—A Relation of a Iourney begun An. Dom. 1610. Fovre Bookes. Containing a description of the Turkish Empire, of Ægypt, of the Holy Land, of the Remote parts of Italy, and Islands adioyning.—4°, pp. 309+1, *figs., frontisp.* (portrait of author). *London*, 1615.

SANSON, S^r.—Le Royaume de Naples divisé en douze Provinces.—*Amsterdam* [1705 ?]. [B.M.—23880 (7).]
Vulcano is represented as one island and Palmarola as two.

SARTORIUS VON WALTERSHAUSEN, W.—Ueber die vulkanischen Gesteine in Sicilien und Island und ihre submarine Umbildung.—8⁰, *pp. xvi+532, 1 pl. Göttingen, 1853.*

SARTORIUS VON WALTERSHAUSEN, W. — Der Aëtna . . . Herausgegeben, selbständig bearbeitet und vollendet von . . . A. von Lasaulx.—2 vols. 4⁰, *illustr. Leipzig, 1880.*

SAYVE, A. DE.—Sur les Volcans : voyage en Sicile, fait en 1820-1821.—3 tom. 8⁰. *Paris, 1822.*

SCACCHI, A.—Sabbia eruttata da Vulcano dal dì 11 al 26 Gennaio 1886.—*Boll. Oss. R. Coll. Carlo Alberto, S. 2, vi, 8. Torino, 1886.*

SCACCHI, A.—Le Eruzioni polverose e filamentose dei Vulcani.—*Atti R. Acc. Sci. S. 2, ii, 10, pp. 7. Napoli, 1888.—Id. Rend. xxv, p. 258. 1886.*

SCASSO E BORRELLO, M.—Descrizione geografica dell' Isola di Sicilia e dell' altre sue adiacenti.—*Palermo, 1798.*——3rd ed. 8⁰. *Palermo, 1806.*

SCASSO E BORRELLO, M.—*See* LÉVESQUE DE BURIGNY.

SCHENK, P. — Continentis Italiæ pars australior sive regnum Neapolitanum, *etc.* —*Amsterdam, 1703.* [B.M.—23880 (5).]
Both Vulcano and Palmarola are represented as double islands.

SCHLEE, P.—Die Liparischen Inseln und ihre Vulkane.—*Mitth. Geogr. Gesellsch. xxi, pp. 202-5. Hamburg, 1906.—Mitth. k. k. geogr. Gesellsch. xlviii, pp. 82-84. Wien, 1905.*

SCHMIDT, J. F. J.—Vulkanstudien. Santorin, 1866-1872. Vesuv, Bajae, Stromboli, Aetna, 1870.—8⁰, *foll. 4, pp. 235, 7 pls., 1 map, 13 figs. Leipzig, 1874.*——2nd ed. 8⁰. *1881.*

SCROPE, G. J. POULETT.—Considerations on Volcanos, the probable causes of their phenomena . . . and their connection with the present state and past history of the globe ; leading to the establishment of a new Theory of the Earth.—8⁰, *pp. xxxi+270, 2 pls., 1 map. London, 1825.*——[2nd

ed. entitled :] Volcanos : the character of their phenomena. . . . With a descriptive Catalogue of all known Volcanos, etc.—8⁰, *pp. xi+490, 1 pl., 1 col. map. London,* 1862.—Another copy 1872 [reviewed in] *Amer. Journ. Sci. xiii, pp. 108-45. New Haven,* 1828.—In French (transl. by Endymion) : 2 *col. pls. Paris,* 1864.—In Germ. (transl. by G. A. v. Klöden) : 1 *pl.,* 65 *figs. Berlin,* 1872.—[Extr. in Ital.] *Bibl. Ital. xlv, pp.* 70-83, 211-26. *Milano,* 1827.

SCROPE, G. J. POULETT.—The mechanism of Stromboli.—*Geol. Mag. pp.* 529-42. *London,* 1874.

SECCHI, A.—Lezioni elementari di fisica terrestre.—8⁰, *pp.* 218. *Torino e Roma,* 1879.

SEGUENZA, G.—Dell' arsenico nei prodotti vulcanici delle Isole Eolie.—*Eco Peloritano, iii, 7, pp.* 8. *Messina,* 1856.

SEGUENZA, G.—Di certe rocce vulcaniche interstratificate fra rocce di sedimento.—*Rend. R. Acc. Sci. xv, pp.* 112-15, 1 *pl. Napoli,* 1876.

SENTIERI, M.—Neapolis regnum quo continentur Aprulium Ulterius et Citerius. Augusta Vind[elicorum, 1740 ?] [B.M.—23880 (13).]
Vulcano represented as a single island.

SIEBERG, A.—Ein Besuch des Stromboli. —6 *figs.* — ?, 1912.

SILVESTRI, A.—*See* SILVESTRI, O. 1889.

SILVESTRI, O.—Fenomeni eruttivi dell' Isola di Vulcano e Stromboli nel 1874.— *Boll. Vulc. Ital. ix e x, p.* 117. *Roma,* 1874.

SILVESTRI, O.—Il Meccanismo nel vulcano attivo di Stromboli.—*Boll. Vulc. Ital. vii, viii, ix, x, Roma,* 1876.
Translation into Italian of work by R. Mallet.

SILVESTRI, O.—Bibliografia generale riguardante la vulcanologia, geologia, mineralogia della Provincia di Catania e delle Isole vulcaniche adiacenti alla Sicilia.—*pp.* 64. *Bologna,* 1881.

SILVESTRI, O.—*See* COMITÉ D'ORGANISATION, *etc.* — Bibliographie Géologique, *etc. No. xvi.* 1881.

SILVESTRI, O.—L'Eruzione dell' Isola di Vulcano.—*Boll. Oss. R. Coll. Carlo Alberto, S. 2, viii, 10. Torino, 1888.—*[Estr.] *Ann. Uffic. Cent. Meteor. e Geodinam. x, pte. 4, pp. 3. Roma, 1888.*

SILVESTRI, O.—Sull' attuale eruzione di Vulcano nelle Isole Eolie incominciata il 3 Agosto 1888.—*Ann. Uffic. Cent. Meteor. e Geodinam. ix, pte.* 4, *pp.* 13. *Roma,* 1889.

SILVESTRI, O., CONSIGLIO PONTE, S., SILVESTRI, A.—Sulla attuale eruzione scoppiata il dì 3 Agosto 1888 all' Isola Vulcano nell' arcipelago Eolio.—*Bull. Acc. Gioenia, N.S. viii, pp.* 5–10. *Catania,* 1889.

SILVESTRI, O.— Sur l'éruption récente de l'Île de Vulcano.—*C.R. Acad. Sci. cix, pp.* 241–43. *Paris,* 1889.—*Bull. Soc. Belge Géol. etc. iii, Proc.-verb. pp.* 354–56. *Bruxelles,* 1889.

SILVESTRI, O.—Etna, Sicilia ed Isole vulcaniche adiacenti, sotto il punto di vista dei fenomeni eruttivi e geodinamici avvenuti durante l'anno 1888.—*Atti Acc. Gioen. S.* 4, *i, pp.* 291–331. *Catania,* 1889.—*Ann. Meteor. Ital. iv, pp.* 316–55. *Torino,* 1889.

SILVESTRI, O.—L'Isola di Vulcano ed l'attuale suo risveglio eruttivo.—*Nuova Antologia, xxi, pp.* 569–76. *Roma,* 1889.

SILVESTRI, O., ARCIDIACONO, S.—Etna, Sicilia ed Isole vulcaniche adiacenti sotto il punto di vista dei fenomeni eruttivi e geodinamici avvenuti durante l'anno 1889. —*Atti Acc. Gioen. S.* 4, *ii, pp.* 221–49. *Catania,* 1890.—*Ann. Meteor. Ital. v, pp.* 267–70. *Torino,* 1890.—*Boll. Oss. Moncalieri, S.* 2, *x,* 2. *Torino,* 1890.

SILVESTRI, O.—Discussione dei fatti osservati [nell' eruzione di Vulcano 1888–90] e criteri sui quali si può fondare qualche giudizio sul meccanismo eruttivo di Vulcano.—*Ann. Uffic. Centr. Meteor. e Geodinam. x, pte.* 4. *Roma,* 1891.

SILVESTRI, O., e MERCALLI, G.—Modo di presentarsi e cronologia delle esplosioni eruttive di Vulcano, cominciate il 3 Agosto 1888.—*Ann. Uffic. Centr. Meteor. e Geodinam. x, pte. iv. Roma,* 1891.

SILVESTRI, O., e MERCALLI, G.—Studio fisico-chimico-petrografico sul materiale delle dejezioni eruttive di Vulcano, 1888–90.—*Ann. Uffic. Centr. Meteor. e Geodinam. x, pte.* 4. *Roma,* 1891.

SILVESTRI, O.—*See* MERCALLI, G.—Le Eruzioni dell Isola di Vulcano, *etc.*

SMYTH, W. H.—Memoir descriptive of the resources, inhabitants and hydrography of Sicily and its Islands, *etc.*—4°, *map, num. fine aquatint engrav. London,* 1824.

SOMMA DI AGATIO.—*See* AGATIO DI SOMMA.

SPALLANZANI, L.—Viaggi alle due Sicilie e in alcune parti dell'Appennino.—6 vols. 8°. *Pavia,* 1792–97.—Another ed. 3 vols. 8°, *portrait and pls. Milano,* 1825.—In German : 8 vols. *Leipzig,* 1794–96.— Another ed. 5 vols. *Leipzig,* 1795–98.— In French : 2 tom. 8°. *Berne,* 1795.— Another ed., transl. by G. Toscan : "Avec des notes du cit. Faujas-de-Saint Fond," 6 tom. 8°. *Paris, An* VIII [1800].—In English : 4 vols. 8°. *London,* 1798.—*See also* Pinkerton's collection of voyages and travels, *Vol. v. London,* 1809.

STAGNO, S. F.—Ragionamento sopra il nascimento dell' Isola di Vulcano.—*Opusc. di Autori. Sic. Vol. ii, pp.* 93–121. *Palermo,* 1759.

STARK, M.—Die Gesteine Usticas und die Beziehungen derselben zu den Gesteinen der Liparischen Inseln.—*Tschermak's Min. u. Petr. Mitth. xxiii, pp.* 469–532, *tav. Wien,* 1904.

STEFANI, C. DE.—Le Acque atmosferiche nelle Fumarole a proposito di Vulcano e di Stromboli.—*Boll. Soc. Geol. Ital. xix, pp.* 295–320. *Roma,* 1900.

STOPPANI, A.—Corso di Geologia.—3 vols. 8°. *Milano,* 1871–73.
   See Vol. i : Dinamica Terrestre, pp. 504. Milano, 1871.
   3a ediz. con note ed aggiunte per cura di Allessandro Malladra.—3 vols. 8°. *Milano,* 1900–3.
   See Vol. i.

STRENG, A.—Ueber die geologischen Verhältnisse der Inseln Lipari und Vulcano.— XXV *Ber. Oberhess. Gesellsch. Nat. u. Heilkunde, Giessen,* 1887.

STRUEVER, G.—*See* STRUEVER, J. K. T.

STRUEVER, J. K. T.— Ematite di Stromboli.—*Atti R. Acc. Lincei, S.* 4, *Mem. vi, pp.* 153–60, 1 *pl. Roma,* 1889.—*Riv. Min. Crist. Ital. vii, pp.* 21–32. *Padova,* 1890.

STURDZA, D. DIM.—Insulele Liparice. Conferintá tinutá in sedinta Adunári generale de la 25 Februarie 1890.—*Bul. Soc. Geogr. Románá, Anul. al* XI*, Trim.* 1, *pp.* 78–91. *Bucuresci,* 1890.

SWINBURNE, H.—Travels in the Two Sicilies in the years 1777-80.—2 vols. 4⁰. *London*, 1783-85.——2nd ed. 2 vols. 8⁰. *London, Nichols*, 1790.——3rd ed. 1795.— In French : 5 vols. 8⁰. *Paris, Didot*, 1785. —In German, transl. by I. R. Forster : 2 pts. *Hamburg*, 1785.

TACCHINI, P.—Sulle attuali eruzioni di Vulcano e Stromboli.—*Atti R. Acc. Lincei, S.* 4, *Rend. v, sem.* 1, *pp.* 327-29. *Roma*, 1889.

TARAMELLI, T., e MERCALLI, G.—I Terremoti Andalusi, cominciati il 25 Dicembre 1884.—*Atti R. Acc. Lincei, S.* 4, *Mem. iii, pp.* 116-222, *Tav.* I-IV. *Roma*, 1886. *See* p. 98.

TARAMELLI, T.—Sulle bombe di Vulcano e sulla forma dello Stromboli.—*Rend. R. Ist. Lomb. S.* 2, *xxxiii, pp.* 790-803. *Milano*, 1900.

THOMAS, T. H.—A Visit to the Lipari Isles and Etna.—*Trans. Cardiff Naturalists' Soc. xxii*, 1, *pp.* 11-26. 1891.

THOMAS, T. H.—A Visit to the Volcanoes of South Italy.—*Trans. Cardiff Naturalists' Soc. xxiii, pp.* 10-19. 1892.

THOMSON.—*See* ARAGO.

TISCHBEIN (fec. ?).—Vue de l'intérieur du cratère. [In the distance] Volcanello, les Isles de Lipari, de Saline, Alicudi et Felicudi.—[*Circa* 1770.] Water-colour painting : 375×240 mm.

TOSO, P., e BALDACCI, L.—Notizie sui giacimenti e prodotti minerali dei Monti di Messina e delle Isole di Lipari.—*Ann. Agric., Relaz. sul servizio minerario nel* 1879. *Roma*, 1882.

TROVATINI, G. M.—Dissertazione chimico-fisica sull' analisi dell' acqua minerale dell' Isola di Vulcano nel Porto di Levante detta volgarmente l'acqua del Bagno.—4⁰. *Napoli*, 1786. [B.N.]

UNGERN-STERNBERG, W. H. C. R. A. VON.—Werden und Seyn des vulkanischen Gebirges. Mit 8 Abbildungen.—8⁰, *pp. xi*+320. *Carlsruhe*, 1825.

VALK, G.—Italiæ pars Meridionalis ; quæ nunc Sceptri Hispanici Regnum Neapolitanum, in 12 Provincias divisum.—[*Amsterdam*, 1704 ?] [B.M.—23880 (18).] Palmarola appears as two islands and Vulcano as one.

VARENIUS, B.—Geografia generalis, in qua affectiones generales telluris explicantur. —*Amstelodami*, 1664. *See* Lib. I, Cap. X : on Etna and the Island of Vulcano.

VECCHI, MALAGOLI.—*See* PELLÉ, C. 1841.

VEGNI, L. DE (inc.).—Veduta dell' Isola Vulcano in Sicilia. No. 2. From Corografia Ital*, Pl. 19. Engrav.: 285×198 mm.

VILLANOVA, J.—Observations géologiques sur la Sicile et les Îles Lipari.—*Bull. Soc. géol. France, S.* 2, *xi, pp.* 80-86. *Paris*, 1854.

VIRLET [D'AOUST, T.].—[Remarks upon DEVILLE, C. J. Sainte-Claire : Note sur la nature des éruptions actuelles, *etc.*]— *Bull. Soc. géol. France, S.* 2, *xv, p.* 362. *Paris*, 1858.

VISSCHER, N.—Totius Italiæ Tabula.

WASHINGTON, H. S.—Italian petrological sketches. v. Summary and Conclusion.— *The Journ. of Geology, v, pp.* 349-77. *Chicago*, 1897.

WASHINGTON, H. S.—Some Analyses of Italian Volcanic Rocks.—*Amer. Journ. Sci. viii, Art.* 31, *pp.* 286-94. *New Haven*, 1899.

WASHINGTON, H. S.—Chemical Analyses of Igneous Rocks published from 1884 to 1900, with a critical discussion of the character and use of analyses.—*U.S. Geol. Surv. Prof. Paper* 14, *pp.* 495. *Washington*, 1903.

WEGNER, T. H.—Der Stromboli im Mai 1906.—*Centralbl. f. Min. pp.* 561-66, *fig. Stuttgart*, 1906.

WENZEL (dis.).—L'Isola di Vulcano con veduta di Lipari in distanza ; Isola di Vulcano con eruzione del 13 Ottobre 1834 ; Cratere del Vulcano. Lit. Wenzel. Three views on same sheet. Lith. : 240×190 mm. (total).

WILSON, J.—A History of Mountains, Geographical and Mineralogical. Accompanied by a picturesque view of the principal mountains of the World, in their respective proportions of height above the level of the sea by Robert Andrew Riddell. —3 vols. 4⁰. *Vol. i, pp.* lv+368+176, 1807 ; *Vol. ii, pp.* 735, 1809 ; *Vol. iii, pp.* 906+ *index, London*, 1810. *See* Vol. iii. Vols. ii and iii read : " A History . . . to accompany a picturesque view," *etc.*

YELD, G.—In the Lipari Islands.—*Scot. Geogr. Mag. xxi*, pp. 348–52, 1 *pl.* *Edinburgh*, 1905.—*See also* ANDERSON, T.

ZUCCAGNI-ORLANDINI, A. — Corografia fisica, storica e statistica dell' Italia e delle sue Isole corredata di un atlante di mappe geografiche e topografiche e di altre tavole illustrative.—12 pts. in 17 vols. 8⁰. *Firenze,* 1845. Atlas.—4 vols. *fol., containing maps and views.*
   See Vol. xii.

ZURCHER, F., MARGOLLÉ, E.—Volcans et tremblements de terre.—16⁰, *figs. Hachette et Cie, Paris*, 1866.——5th ed. 8⁰, pp. 311, *figs. Paris*, 1886. (*Bibl. des Merveilles.*)
   Etna and Stromboli.

ETNA

ANON.—Abbildung des Erschrecht : brands dess bergs Aetna so gesehen Anno 1669. Engraving : 348×259 mm.

ANON.—[Account of the eruption of Etna of July 19, 1899.]—"*Nature*," p. 185. 1899.

ANON.—Ætna.
A Poem in 644 hexameters, ascribed variously to Vergil, Severus, Manilius and others, but probably written, at the invitation of Seneca, by Lucilius. Probable date between A.D. 65 and 79. [Walter Woodburn Hyde : "The Volcanic History of Etna."—Geograph Review, i, 6, p. 410. New York, 1916.]

ANON.—Ætna. Mons Siciliæ.
A beautiful engrav. of the erupt. of 1669. The crater-top is enclosed in a semicircular dotted line : 293×181 mm.

ANON.—Der Aetna auf Sizilien.—*Museum des Wundervollen u. Ausserordentlichen in Natur, Kunst, etc.* v, 2. *Leipzig*, 1806–10.
Contains a large view of Etna.

ANON.—An Answer to some inquiries concerning the eruptions of Mt. Ætna, 1669, communicated by some inquisitive English merchants now residing in Sicily.—*Phil. Trans. R. Soc.* iv, pp. 1028–34. *London*, 1669.—*Coll. Accad.* i, pt. 2, pp. 201–5. [? *Dijon*, 1755.]—*Gibelin*, i, pp. 4–13.

ANON.—Archivio dei Benedettini in Catania. —*Arca I. Lit. B. p.* 100.
Eruptions of 1536, 1682 and others.

ANON.—Bibliographie géologique et paléontologique de l'Italie, par les soins du Comité d'Organisation du 2e. Congrès Géologique International à Bologne.—8°, pp. 630. *Bologne*, MDCCCLXXXI.

ANON.—Breve descrizione geografica del regno di Sicilia.—4°, pp. 293. *Palermo*, 1787.
See pp. 209–11 : L'Eruzioni del Mongibello, etc.

ANON.—Carta (Corografica) d'Italia.—*Ist. Geog. Milit. Ital.* 1889.
1 : 1,800,000, in 6 sheets.—2 ed. 1st, in three colours as in preceding ; 2nd, without mountain-shading. *See* sheet 6.

ANON.—Carta (Corografica) d'Italia.—*Ist. Geog. Milit. Ital.* 1889.
1 : 1,000,000, in 7 sheets.—3 ed. 1st, in three colours, with mountains shaded in brown and water in blue ; 2nd, mountains in grey ; 3rd, without mountain shading. *See* sheet 6.

ANON.—Carta Corografica del regno d'Italia e delle regioni adiacenti.—*Ist. Geog. Milit. Ital.* 1889.
1 : 500,000, in 35 sheets.—3 ed. 1st, in three colours ; 2nd, in two colours ; 3rd, in black, without mountain shading. *See* sheet 34.

ANON.—Carta Geologica dell' Isola di Sicilia. Cenni alla Carta Geologica dell' Isola di Sicilia, 1885.—*Ist. Geog. Milit. Ital. Roma*, 1884–85.
Four sheets : Messina, Etna, Palermo, Catania.

ANON.—Carta Geologica dell' Isola di Sicilia alla scala di 1 a 100,000, con memoria descrittiva dell' ing. L. Baldacci.—*R. Uffic. Geol. Ital. Roma*, 1886.

ANON.—Carta Geologica della Sicilia.— *R. Uffic. Geol. Ital. Roma*, 1886, 1890.
1 : 500,000. Etna and Lipari Islands.

ANON.—Carta Geologica della Isola di Sicilia. 1 : 100,000, in 28 fogli e 5 tavole di sezioni, con quadro d'unione e copertina. —*R. Uffic. Geol. Ital. Roma*, 1886, 1890.
See sheets 261, 262, 269, 270, and Section II.

ANON.—Carta della Sicilia.—*Ist. Geog. Milit. Ital.* 1885.
1 : 500,000, in 1 sheet, in black ; mountains shaded. Includes Etna and Lipari Islands.

ANON.—Carta di Sicilia, Provincia di Catania, fogl. IX. 1 : 50,000.—*Stato Maggiore d'Italia.*
The region of Etna was made by the help of the map of Sartorius von Waltershausen.

ANON. — Carta Topografica del regno d'Italia.—*Ist. Geog. Milit. Ital.* 1889.
1 : 100,000. Chromo-lithographic ed. in three colours without line shading of mountains. *See* sheets 261, 262, 269, 270.

ANON. — Carta Topografica del regno d'Italia.—*Ist. Geog. Milit. Ital.* 1889.
1 : 100,000, in 277 photo-engraved sheets, in course of publication (1889). The orography is shown by contour lines of 50 m. as well as by zenith-light shading. *See* sheets 261, 262, 269, 270.

ANON. — Carta Topografica del regno d'Italia.
1 : 75,000. Economic edition, similar to above.

ANON.—Carte Géologique Internationale de l'Europe.
Scale 1 : 1,500,000.

ANON. [Clermont ?].—Carte de l'Italie méridionale et de la Sicile ancienne, pays autrefois connus sous le nom de Grande Grèce. Rédigée et corrigée d'après les observations les plus récentes, et que l'on croît les plus certaines. — ?, — ?

ANON.—Carte de la Sicile et des Isles adjacentes, réduite et rédigée d'après la grande carte qui a été faite en 1720 par le Baron Sam. Schmettau, et corrigée sur les observations récentes de plusieurs voyageurs. — ?, 1784.

ANON.—Catana Urbs Siciliæ clarissima Patria Sc[tæ] Agathæ Virginis et Mart.
View of Catania and Etna before eruption of 1669. Engraved map : 420×370 mm.

ANON.—Catania Tutrix Regum.
Ancient view of Catania and Etna before the eruption of 1669. Engraving : 288× 200 mm.

ANON.—Chronicon Siciliæ complectens accuratam regni Siciliæ historiam.—*See* GRÆVIUS, J. G.—*Thes. Antiq. Sic.*

ANON.—A Chronological Accompt of the several Incendium's or Fires of Mt. Ætna. —*Phil. Trans. R. Soc. iv, pp.* 967–69. *London,* 1669.—Transl. in Ital. by Oldenbourg : *Compend.-Trans. Filos. Anno* 1669, *pp.* 1–4. *Venezia,* 1793. [C.A.]

ANON.—Compendio delle Transazioni filosofiche, *etc.* Tom. i. Venezia, 1793.— *Giorn. Lett. v, pp.* 78–89. *Napoli,* 1793.
Speaks of various earthquakes and volcanic eruptions of Etna, Vesuvius, etc.

ANON.—Congrès des Clubs Alpins à Catane en 1880 et ascension de l'Etna.—*Bull. trim. Club Alp. franç. 3e trim. Paris,* 1880.

ANON.—Description des estats Naples, Sicille, Sardagne.—*fol., pp.* 320, *num. plans, maps and engrav.* — ?, — ?

ANON.—Description historique et géographique de la ville de Messine, etc., etc., et détails météorologiques du désastre que cette ville vient d'éprouver (le 5 février 1783) par le tremblement de terre. Avec des notes curieuses et intéressantes sur la Calabre ultérieure, la Sicile et les Îles de Lipari, etc., etc., avec carte.—4⁰,· *pp.* 25. *Paris,* 1783.

ANON.—Descrizione di Catania e delle cose notevoli dei dintorni di essa.—6⁰, *pp.* 277. *Catania,* 1841.

ANON.—Descrizione della eruzione dell' Etna di quest' anno.—*Gazz. Britannica,* 73, *mercoledì,* 13 *Nov.* 1811.

ANON.—Distinto ragguaglio del spaventevole terremoto accaduto nel regno di Sicilia li 9 e 11 del mese di Gennaio 1693.—*Roma,* 1693.

ANON. (DI SCIACCA).— [Éruption de cendres, 1408.]
Cited by Recupero.

ANON.—Éruption de l'Etna. Poussière rougeâtre transportée d'au-delà des mers en Italie par le vent.—*Bull. Soc. géog. France, xiii, pp.* 307–8. *Paris,* 1830.

ANON.—L'Éruption de l'Etna.—*Rev. scient. S.* 2, *xvii, p.* 144. *Paris,* 1879.

ANON. — Les Éruptions volcaniques de l'Etna.—*Rev. scient. S.* 2, *xvii, p.* 884. *Paris,* 1879.

ANON.—Eruption of Etna 1865.—*Amer. Journ. Sci. S.* 2, *xl,* 118, *p.* 122. *New Haven,* 1865.

ANON.—[Eruption of Mount Etna, March–April, 1910.]—" *Nature,*" *pp.* 135–36, 165. 1910.

ANON.—[Eruzione dell' Etna, Luglio 1787.]
Mezzotint : 445×317 mm.

ANON.—Eruzione dell' Etna dell' anno 1879. —*Gazzetta di Catania,* 16 *numbers, May and June,* 1879.—*Gazzetta di Messina,* 17 *numbers, Maggio e Giugno,* 1879. [C.A.]

ANON.—L'Eruzione dell' Etna.—*Boll. Soc. Geog. Ital. pp.* 569–72. *Roma,* 1886.

ANON. [U. C.].—L'Eruzione dell' Etna del Luglio 1892.—*Boll. R. Com. Geol. Ital. S.* 3, *iii, pp.* 306–7. *Roma,* 1892.

ANON.—Sulla eruzione dell' Etna del 1879. Tre disegni sopra schizzi autentici del Prof. Orazio Silvestri.—*Illustrazione Italiana, sem.* 2, *p.* 5. *Milano,* 1879.

ANON.—Sulla eruzione di fango a Paternò nelle adiacenze dell' Etna. Disegno e testo sopra comunicazione autentica del Prof. Orazio Silvestri.—*Illustrazione Italiana, sem.* 1, *p.* 113. *Milano,* 1879.

ANON.—L'Etna et ses éruptions.—*L'Univers Illustré, pp.* 99–100, 3 *figs.* 15 *février,* 1865. [C.A.]

ANON.—Extrait du Journal d'Angleterre contenant une relation chronologique des embrasemens du Mont Etna.—*Journal des Sçavans, pp.* 103–5. 1683. [C.A.]

ANON.—La fine della eruzione dell' Etna 1879. Disegno e testo sopra comunicazioni di Nicola Lazzaro.—*Illustrazione Italiana, sem.* 2, *p.* 5. *Milano,* 1879.

ANON.—De gestis Gallorum et Aragonensium.—*Mem. Stor. d. Città d. Catania.* i, 2, *c.* 2.
  Cited by Carrera.

ANON.—Giornale della presente eruzione dell' Etna.—*Rend. R. Acc. Sci.* i, *pp.* 466–68. *Napoli,* 1842.

ANON.—Gita a Catania ed ai dintorni (Ricordi di Viaggio).—"*Innominato,*" i, 21, 22, *Messina,* 21 *Giugno,* 1 *Luglio* 1836.

ANON.—A Handbook for Travellers in Southern Italy and Sicily ; comprising the description of Naples and its environs, Pompeii, Herculaneum, Vesuvius, Sorrento ; the islands of Capri and Ischia ; Amalfi, Pæstum, and Capua, the Abruzzi and Calabria ; Palermo, Girgenti, the Greek Temples, and Messina.—9th ed. in 2 pts. 8⁰. *Pt.* i, South Italy, *pp.* 288+20, *maps, plans, etc.* ; *Pt.* ii, Sicily, *pp.* 289–418 +11, *maps, plans, etc. London,* 1890.

ANON.—L'Italia.—4⁰, *pp.* 326, *num. maps. Torino,* 1896.

ANON.—L'Italie.—8⁰, *pp.* 608, 243 *engrav.,* 5 *maps. Paris,* — ?

ANON.—Kurze Beschreibung des letzten Ausbruches des Aetna, welcher im November 1832 an der westlichen Seite des Berges Statt gefunden hat.—*Froriep. Notiz. xxxvi, pp.* 23–26. *Erfurt,* 1833.—*N. J. f. Min. p.* 583. *Stuttgart,* 1833.

ANON.—Lagrimoso spectacolo della misera città di Catania nell' Isola di Sicilia, la quale fu distrutta li 15 Gennaio del corrente anno 1693 da un spaventoso terremoto, etc.—16⁰, *foll. vi. Viterbo,* 1693. [C.A.]

ANON.—Manuscriptum ex libro in Ecclesia majori Nicholosorum asservato, *etc.* Notices on the erupt. of 1766.

ANON.—Map of Naples and Sicily with part of the Roman States and Tuscany.—*Stanford, London,* 1860. [B.M.—23880 (29).]

ANON.—Mont Etna in Catania. Etna in eruption by night from over Catania ; early 19th cent. Gouache : 402×265 mm.

ANON.—Le Mont Etna en éruption. A small engraving of Etna as seen from the Cyclopean (?) Islands : 108×89 mm.

ANON.—Mount Ætna or Mongibello in Sicily beeing a true draught of yᵉ Eruption in 1669. View of Etna from sea in front of Catania ; five letters of ref. Engrav. : 224×140 mm.

ANON.—Mount Etna. From the Lava of 1669. [B.M. Portfolio of Sicily.] Engraving : 258×174 mm.

ANON.—Mute History or Documentary Ruins of Nature and Art in Italy ; illustrated by a volcanic and antiquarian map of the Italian continent and islands.— "*Gentleman's Magazine,*" vii, *pp.* 249–56, 468–70, 1 *map. London,* 1837.

ANON.—Nicolosi and Mount Etna. [B.M. Portfolio of Sicily.] Engraving : 258×174 mm.

ANON.—[Note sur l'ouverture de nouvelles bouches d'éruption à l'Etna, et sur quelques trépidations du sol ressenties à Messine, août et septembre 1874.]—*C.R. Acad. Sci.* lxxix, *pp.* 655–56, 790–91. *Paris,* 1874.

ANON.—Nouveau Dictionnaire de Géographie Universelle.—*Paris,* 1884. *See* Vol. ii, p. 224.

ANON.—Observations diverses sur les Volcans.—*MS. fol., pp.* 125. *After* 1808. Many notes from other authors on Vesuvius, Campi Phlegræi, Etna, etc.

ANON.—L'Observatoire de L'Etna.—*Rev. scient. S.* 2, *xvii, pp.* 599, 884. *Paris,* 1879.

ANON.—Plan du Mont Etna, communément dit Mont Gibel en l'Isle de Sicile, et l'incendie arrivé par un tremblement de terre le 8 mars 1669. [B.N.P.]

ANON.—A Prospect of Mount Ætna, with its irruption in 1669.
Explanation in four lines.   Engrav. : 197 × 153 mm.

ANON.—Raccolta di storia naturale.—4⁰, 1 *pl*. *Roma*, 1784.

ANON.—Raised Model of Etna and neighbourhood.—*Ist. Geog. Milit. Ital.* 1876.
Scale 1 : 50,000 horizontal and 1 : 25,000 vertical, cast in zinc and plated with copper.

ANON.—Relation (an exact) of the famous Earthquake and Eruption of Mt. Etna.— —*London*, 1775.

ANON.—Relazione de' danni cagionati da terremoti sentiti nel regno Sicilia, cavata dall' ultime lettere di Messina, sotto li 28 Gennaro 1693.—8⁰, *pp*. 4. *Roma and Perugia*, 1693. [B.M.]

ANON.—Relazione del danno cagionato dal terremoto successo à di 7 Giugno 1695 nelle città di Bagnara, Orvieto e luoghi convicini.—8⁰, *pp*. 4. *Roma*, 1695. [B.M.]

ANON.—Relazione dell' incendio di Mongibello dell' anno 1669.
Cited by Massa : Etna.

ANON.—Relatione (vera) del nuovo incendio della Montagna di Mongibello cavata da una lettera scritta da Tauramina ad un Signore dimorante in Roma.—12⁰, *foll*. 4. *Roma and Napoli*, 1669. [C.A.]

ANON.—Relazione del nuovo incendio fatto da Mongibello con rovina di molti casali della città di Catania e dei miracoli e prodigi operati dal sacro velo dell' invittissima V. e M. S. Agata.—*Catania, presso Bonaventura La Rocca*, 1669.—*pp*. 45. *Messina, presso G. Bisagni*, 1670.

ANON.—Relazione dei danni cagionati nel territorio di Catania per causa della eruzione del Monte Etna (27 Aprile 1766). —*Palermo,-*1766.

ANON.—Relazione degli Ingegneri del R. Corpo delle Miniere addetti al rilevamento geologico della zona solfifera di Sicilia, sulla eruzione dell' Etna avvenuta nei mesi di Maggio e Giugno 1879.—4⁰, *pp*. 7, 1 *map*. *Roma*, 1879. [C.A.]

ANON.—Rerum Sicularum scriptores ex recentioribus præcipui, in unum corpus nunc primum congesti, diligentiq. ; recognitione plurimus in locis emendati.—4⁰, *pp*. 705 *and index*. *Francofurti ad Mœnum*, 1579.

ANON. (del.) [name illegible].—Ruines du Thᵗʳᵉ de Taormina. Galerie du Palais Royal (Michallon) Litho. de C. Motte.
Litho. : 315 × 242 mm.

ANON.—Della Sicilia, grand' isola del Mediterraneo, in prospettiva il Mont' Etna, o Mongibello, esposto in veduta da un Religioso della Compagnia di Giesù.— 8⁰, *pp*. viii+126. *Palermo*, 1708.

ANON.—Sopra una lapide rinvenuta in Catania sotto la lava.—*Giorn. Gab. Lett. Acc. Gioen. N.S. ii, pp*. 51–56. *Catania*, 1859.

ANON.—Sunto di un viaggio in Sicilia : Catania - Etna. — " *Gondoliere*," iii, 83. *Venezia*, 17 *Ottobre* 1835.

ANON.—Tavolette rilevate per la costruzione della carte del regno d'Italia.—*Ist. Geog. Milit. Ital.* 1873–79.
Part to the scale of 1 : 50,000 and part 1 : 25,000. *See* sheets 261, 262, 269, 270.

ANON.—Terza relatione dell' incendio di Mongibello, et de mirabili successi nella città di Catania e altri luoghi circonvicini, cavata da una lettera scritta à Roma da un personaggio qualificato sotto li 27 Aprile 1669.—12⁰, *pp*. 4. *Roma*, 17 *Maggio*, 1669. [B.M.]

ANON. — Trattati dei Terremoti. — 8⁰. *Bologna*, 1571. [B.M. 444. b. 20.] ,

ANON.—A true design of the late eruption of Mount Ætna in Sicily. A. 1669.
Engraved view, from before Catania with five letters of reference : 200 × 138 mm.

ANON.—Vera relatione del nuovo incendio della Montagna di Mongibello.—12⁰. *Roma and Naples*, 1669.
May be a transl. of FINCH, H.—A true and exact relation of the late . . . earthquake and eruption of Mount Ætna, of which the original edition is in the B.M.

ANON.—Untergang der Stadt Messina. Ingleichen eine kurze Beschreibung von den beiden feuerspeyenden Bergen Vesuv und Aetna.—4⁰, *pp*. 28, 2 *pls*. — ?, 1783.

ANON.—Veduta generale del Monte Etna e della città di Catania, e porto, di doppo l'eruzioni di 1669. 89.— (? *17th cent.*)
Sepia sketch : 302×254 mm.

ANON.—Veduta della parte meridionale del Canale di Messina pressa la Calabria ove si vede la gran spiaggia di Messina sino a Catania. 90.
Etna in distance, ? 17th cent. Sepia sketch : 320×252 mm.

ANON.—Vera relatione di quello che è successo nell' *l*ultimo terremoto in Sicilia. [In Italian and French.]—*Toulon*, 1693.

ANON.—V,erissima e distinta relatione del terribile e spaventoso terremoto seguito in Siracusa, Augusta, Cattania, Messina et altre città e luoghi della Calabria, principiato alli 6 di Gennaro 1693 con il danno di molti milioni e morti di più di cento mila persone.—*Venezia, Bergamo*, 1693.

ANON.—View of the Crater of Etna ; from the Ruins of the Philosopher's Tower. Publishᵈ Sepʳ 1, 1804, by C. Taylor, No. 118, Hatton Garden, London.
Engrav.: 154×104 mm.

ANON.—[View of Etna from low coast some miles south of Catania. Shepherd and goats in foreground.]
Dark sepia stippled engrav.: 293×212 mm.

ANON.—[View of Etna from an old bridge over a stream. Three men, two horses and a donkey in foreground.]
Dark sepia stippled engrav.: 292×213 mm.

ANON.—[View of Etna from ruins of Roman aqueduct.]
Engraving without title ; man on mule and two cows in foreground. Of no scientific value : 316×226 mm.

ANON.—Vulcani di Europa.—*Il Propagatore Sci. Nat. i, pt. 2, pp.* 328.

ANON.—Dei Vulcani o Monti Ignivomi più noti, e distintamente del Vesuvio. Osservazioni fisiche e notizie istoriche di Uomini insigni di varj tempi, raccolte con diligenza. Divise in due Tomi.—12⁰. *Tom. i, pp.* lxx+149 ; *Tom. ii, pp.* viii+228, 1 *pl.* [? Vesuvius, 1737].
Contains contributions from Targioni Tozzetti (Dei Monti Ignivomi della Toscana e del Vesuvio), Galiani, F., Plinio il Giovine, Magalotti, L., Strange, G., De Bomare, Darbie, F., Derham, G., Mead, R., Gennaro, A., Minervino, C. S. This work is attri-

buted by some to Galiani, by others to Gentile. There are two copies in the Johnston-Lavis collection, one with the two tomes in one vol., containing a plate " Prospetto del Vesuvio dal Palazzo Regio " ; the other in two vols., from which the plate is missing.

ABICH, O. W. H. VON.—Sur les phénomènes volcaniques du Vésuve et de l'Etna.—*Bull. Soc. géol. France, vii, pp.* 40–48. *Paris*, 1835.

ABICH, O. W. H. VON.—Vues illustratives de quelques phénomènes géologiques prises sur le Vésuve et l'Etna, pendant les années 1833 et 1834.—*gd. fol., pp.* 4, 10 *pls. Paris*, 1836.

ABICH, O. W. H. VON.—Erlaüternde Abbildungen geologischer Erscheinungen beobachtet am Vesuv und Aetna in den Jahren 1833 und 1834.—With French and German text, *roy. fol., pp.* 8, 10 *pls. Berlin*, 1837.—Also *Braunschweig*, 1841.
Very fine and correct views.

ABICH, O. W. H. VON.—[Vulkanische Phaenomene am Aetna.]—*N. J. f. Min. pp.* 550–52. *Stuttgart*, 1839.

ABICH, O. W. H. VON.—Beiträge zur Kenntniss des Feldspathes.—*N. J. f. Min. pp.* 468–74. *Stuttgart*, 1841.—*Ann. Phys. Chem. l, pp.* 125–49, 341–63. *Leipzig*, 1840.

ABICH, O. W. H. VON.—Geologische Beobachtungen über die vulkanischen Erscheinungen und Bildungen in Unter- und Mittel-Italien.—Bd. i, Lief. 1. Ueber die Natur und den Zusammenhang der vulkanischen Bildungen.—4⁰, *pp.* viii+134+xi, 3 maps, 2 lith. pls. *Braunschweig*, 1841. Atlas to same, bound separately, 5 *pls.*

ABICH, O. W. H. VON.—On some points in the history and formation of Etna.—*Quart. Journ. Geol. Soc. xv, pp.* 117–28, 11 *figs. London*, 1859.

ABICH, O. W. H. VON.—Vues illustrées . . . sur le Vésuve et l'Etna.—*Paris*, 1887.

ABU-HAMID DA GRANADA.—*See* AMARI.
—Biblioteca Arabo-Sicula, *p.* 74. *Torino, Roma*, 1880–81.
Erupt. of XII century.

ACCARIAS DE SERIONNE, J.—Dissertation sur le Mont Etna.—12⁰, *pp.* 179–223. *Paris*, MDCCXXXVI. [C.A.]

ACCARIAS DE SERIONNE, J.—L'Etna de P. Cornelius Severus et les sentences de Publius Syrus. Traduit en français avec des remarques, des dissertations critiques, historiques, géographiques.—12⁰, *pp. xxxix* +358, *2 maps. A Paris, chez Chaubert et Clousier,* MDCCXXXVI.

ÆLIAN.—[Συμμικτός ἱστορια.]—*In Stobæus Flov.* 79, 38.
Erupt. of 693 B.C.

ÆLIAN.—Var. Hist. *viii*, 11.

ÆSCHYLUS.—Prometheus.
Erupt. of 364 B.C.

AGAMENNONE, G.—Terremoto Siculo-Calabro della notte dall' 11 al 12 Febbraio 1897.—*Boll. Soc. Sismol. Ital. iii*, 2, " *Notizie sui terremoti,"* ecc. *pp.* 42–59. *Modena,* 1897.

ALBERT, H.—Taormina. A. H. Payne. London : Brain & Payne, 12, Paternoster Row.
Fine line engrav. : 156×104 mm.

ALBERTI, F. L.—Descrittione di tutta Italia. Aggiuntavi la descrittione di tutte l'Isole all' Italia appartenenti . . . (Edizione curata da Antonio Cheluzio da Colle.) —4⁰, *foll.* 42+504+100+5, *7 maps. Venetia,* 1568.—Other ed. : 1576 ; 4⁰, *foll.* 32+ 501+69+4, 1577.

ALBERTI, F. L.—Descrittione di tutta l'Italia . . . Aggiontovi di nuovo . . . tutto quello chè successo sino l'anno 1581. E di più accresciutà d'altre additioni . . . da M. Borgaruccio Borgarucci.—4⁰, *foll.* 32+501+96+4. *Venetia,* 1581.—4⁰, *foll.* 34+495+100+5. *Vinegia,* 1588.—4⁰, *foll.* 34+495+91+4. *Venetia,* 1596.

ALBERTI, F. L.—Isole appartenenti all' Italia, di nuovo ricorette, e con l'aggionta in più luoghi di diverse cose accorse fino a nostri tempi adornate.—8⁰, *foll.* 97+*iv. Venetia,* 1581.
See foll. 84 [34] to 38.

ALBERTI, [? F.] L.—Descrizione di Sicilia.
Cited by Massa.

ALESSI, G.—Elogio del cav. Gius. Gioeni.— 4⁰. *Palermo,* 1824. [B.N.]

ALESSI, G.—Storia critica delle eruzioni dell' Etna. Otto discorsi.—*Atti Acc. Gioen. iii, pp.* 17–75, 1829 ; *iv, pp.* 23–75, 1830 ; *v, pp.* 43–72, 1831 ; *vi, pp.* 85–116, 1832 ; *vii, pp.* 21–66, 1833 ; *viii, pp.* 99–149, 1834 ; *ix, pp.* 121–206, 1835. *Catania,* 1829–35.

ALESSI, G.—Sopra gli Ossidi di Silicio ed i Silicati appartenenti alla Sicilia.—*Atti Acc. Gioen. v, pp.* 95–139. *Catania,* 1831.

ALESSI, G.—Relazione accademica per l'anno IX.—*Atti Acc. Gioen. x, pp.* 1–29. *Catania,* 1833.

ALEXANDER, C.—Practical remarks on the Lavas of Vesuvius, Etna, and the Lipari Islands.—*Proc. Scient. Soc. i, pp.* 31–32. *London,* 1839.

ALLEN.—*See* WRIGHT.

ALOI, A.—L'Eruzione dell' Etna del Luglio 1892 con cenni storici sui precedenti eruzioni.—*Riv. Mens. Club Alp. Ital. xi,* 7, 8, 9, 10 e 11.—*Boll. Club Alp. Ital. xxvi, pp.* 247–84, *2 pls.,* 1 *map. Torino,* 1893.

ALZINGER, L.—Studia in Ætnam collata. —*Lipsiæ,* 1896.

AMARI, M.—Storia dei Musulmani in Sicilia. —*See* AMARI.—Biblioteca Arabo-Sicula, *i, pp.* 85–218. *Torino, Roma,* 1880–81.
Erupts. of VII–IX cent.

AMARI, M.—*See* DUFOUR, A. H.

AMICO, C.—Cronologia Universale.
Cited by Ferrara and by Amico, V. M., in " Catana Illustr." iv, p. 252. 1740. (Unpublished.)

AMICO, F. D'.—[Eruzione dell' Etna cominciata il 18 Maggio 1886.]— *Boll. Oss. Moncalieri, vi, p.* 98. *Acireale,* 1886.

AMICO E STATELLA, V. M.—Catana Illustrata sive sacra et civilis urbis Catanæ Historia.—*fol. Catania,* 1740.

AMICO E STATELLA, V. M.—*See* FAZELLUS.—De rebus Siculis.—*Catania,*1749–53.

AMICO E STATELLA, V. M.—Lexiçon topographicum Siculum, *etc.*—3 vols. 4⁰. *Panormi, et Catanæ,* 1757–60.
See Vol. iii, Pt. 1, pp. 45–52.

AMICO [E STATELLA], V. [? M.]—Discorso intorno alla materia de' fuochi di Mongibello. (Serbasi, una colla lettera suddetta, nella libreria comunale di Palermo.)

AMORE, A.—Sull' Etna.—16⁰, *illustr. Catania,* 1906.

ANDERSON, T.—The Volcanoes of the Two Sicilies.— *Geol. Mag. p.* 473. 1888.— *Rept. Brit. Assoc.* 1888, *pp.* 663–64. *London,* 1889.

ANDERSON, T.—Volcanic Studies in many lands.—8⁰, *pp. xxii*+202, *pls. cv. London,* 1903.

ANDREÆ, J. L.—Disßertatio inauguralis de montibus ignivomis sive Vulcanis, etc.— 4º, *pp.* 32. *Altdorpi*, 1710.

ANNA, A. D'.—Eruption of Mount Etna.— *London, June*, 1800.
Col. transparency on steel engrav., roy. fol., in collection of Mʳ L. Sambon, Naples.

ANNA, A. D'.—The Eruption of Mount Etna from a painting done at Naples by Alexander D'Anna. Orme Excut. 59, Bond Street, removed from Conduit Street. Sold and published June, 1800, by Edwᵈ Orme, Nˢ 59, New Bond Street, corner of Brook Street, London. Where may be had a great variety of Transparencies and every new Publication.
Mezzotint varnished and coloured at back : 510×299 mm.

ANNA, A. D'.—Éruption du Mont Etna. Gravé d'après le dessin original de Signor Alexandre d'Anna, peintre à Naples. Gravé par Fr. Weber. Zu finden bei Steingriebell Junior in Augsburg.
Hand-col. engrav. : 545×389 mm. A similar one, but inscr. " Se vend chez Ferrari & Comp. et chez Fr. Weber," is on straw-yellow paper and is for sale (1913) by Ludwig Rosenthal, Lenbach Plaz, München : 541×387 mm.

ANSTED, D. T.—Notes on a winter visit to Mount Etna. The eruption of 1669.— " *Intellectual Observer,*" *ix, pp.* 125–31. *London*, 1866.

ANSTED, D. T.—Notes on a winter visit to Mount Etna. The Eruption of 1865.— " *Intellectual Observer,*" *ix, pp.* 268–76. *London*, 1866.

APARES, J.—De in universa Calabria terræmotu, eius causis, signis, effectibus, temporibus et locis.—*Messanæ*, 1639.

APPIANUS, A.—Bellor. civil.—*Edit. Amstelodami*, 1660.
Erupt. 34 B.C.

APRILE, Francesco. — Della Cronologia Universale della Sicilia. Libri tre al serenissimo Principe Eugenio di Savoia.—*fol. Palermo, Gaspare Bayona*, 1725.
See pp. 13, 360.

APRILE, Z.—Cronaca di Sicilia.— *Vol. i. Palermo*, 1725.

ARABICUS, Cᴴ. [Cited by Carrera.]

ARACRI, G.—Relazione della pioggia di cenere avvenuta in Calabria ulteriore il dì 27 Marzo 1809.—*Atti Acc. Pontaniana, i, pp.* 167–70. *Napoli*, 1810.

ARADAS, A.—Un' Abbozzo del panorama Etneo.—*Atti Soc. Ital. Sci. Nat. xii, pp.* 499–534. *Milano*, 1869.

ARADAS, A.—Brevissimo sunto della Conchigliologia Etnéa.—*Atti Soc. Ital. Sci. Nat. xii, pp.* 535–44. *Milano*, 1869.

ARADAS, A.—Ricerche sulle variazioni in media delle Acque del Golfo di Catania rispetto ai littorali che lo formano.—*Atti Acc. Gioen. xvii, pp.* 1–15. *Catania*, 1883.

ARAGO, D. F.—Liste des Volcans actuellement enflammés.—*Ann. Bur. Longit. pp.* 167–89. *Paris*, 1824. [C.A.] — English transl. by Thomson, *Ann. Phil. N.S. vii, pp.* 201–14. *London*, 1824.

ARANCIO, F. — Guida statistica su la Sicilia e sue Isole adjacenti, con Carta coroidrografica - doganale - statistica anche di Malta e Gozo.—*fol., pp. xi*+132 *and index. Palermo*, 1844. Map, bound separately.

ARCIDIACONO, S.—*See* SILVESTRI, O. 1890.

ARCIDIACONO, S.—Fenomeni geodinamici che precedettero, accompagnarono e seguirono l'eruzione Etnea del Maggio-Giugno 1886.—*Atti Acc. Gioen. S. 4, vi, Mem. 21, pp.* 49, 1 tav. *Catania*, 1893.

ARCIDIACONO, S.—*See* RICCÒ, A. 1894, 1902, 1903, 1904.

ARCIDIACONO, S.—Rassegna dei principali fenomeni eruttivi avvenuti in Sicilia e nelle Isole adiacenti, durante il quadrimestre Gennaio-Aprile 1895, [*etc.*]—*Boll. Soc. Sismol. Ital. i,* 3, 1895 ; [*ii, pp.* 122–24, 229–32, 1896 ; *iii, pp.* 57–60, 203–13, 1897 ; *iv, pp.* 107–13, 261–75, 1898 ; *v, pp.* 122–31, 1899 ; *vi, pp.* 101–14, 1900 ; *vii, pp.* 82–91, 1901 ; *x, pp.* 65–71, 1904 ; *xi, pp.* 45–53, 1906.]

ARCIDIACONO, S.—L'Esplosione centrale dell' Etna del 19 Luglio 1899.—*Boll. Soc. Sismol. Ital. v. Modena*, 1899.

ARCIDIACONO, S.—Sui terremoti del 3 Maggio 1899.—*Boll. Acc. Gioen. lx, pp.* 28–33. *Catania*, 1899.

ARCIDIACONO, S.—Sul periodo eruttivo dell' Etna dal 19 Luglio al 5 Agosto 1899. —*Atti Acc. Gioen. S. 4, xiii, Mem. 17, pp.* 42. *Catania*, 1900. — *Osserv. Geodinam. Catania, Maggio* 1900.

ARCIDIACONO, S.—Sui recenti terremoti Etnei.—*Boll. Acc. Gioen. lxxix, pp.* 5–12. *Catania*, 1904.

ARCIDIACONO, S.—Il Terremoto di Massa Annunziata del 2 Giugno 1906.—*Boll. Acc. Gioen. S.* 2, *iii–iv, pp.* 32–36. *Catania,* 1908.

ARCIDIACONO, S.—*See* VINASSA DE REGNY ET ALII.

ARCONATI, G. M.—Appunti relativi all' eruzione dell' Etna, 1863.—*Nuovo Cimento, xvii, pp.* 104–8. *Pisa,* 1863.

ARDINI, L.—Carta agronomica dell' Etna. —*Catania,* 1878.
This map is not published, but can be obtained from the author.

AREZZO, C. M.—C. M. Aretii de situ insulæ Siciliæ libellus.—*See* FAZELLUS, TH.— Rerum Sicularum, *pp.* 572–600. *Francofurti ad Mœnum,* 1579.—*Also* CARUSO, G. B.—Bibl. Hist. Reg. Siciliæ, *Tom.* 1.— *Also* GRÆVIUS, J. G.—Thesaurus Antiquitatum et Historiarum . . . Italiæ, *Tom.* 10, *Vol. i.*
Etna mineral waters, etc.

AREZZO, C. M.—Cl. Marii Aretii . . . Siciliæ chorographia accuratissima.—*See* GRÆVIUS, J. G.—Thesaurus Antiquitatum . . . Italiæ, *Tom.* 10, *i, etc.*

AREZZO, C. M.—Siciliæ chorographia inter Rer. Sic. Script. in unum congestos.— *Wechel Francofurtii.*—*See* ANON.—Rerum Sic. Script. etc. 1579.

ARGAND, E.—*See* LUGEON, M.

ARISTOTELES. — Περὶ Κοσμου. — *p.* 365. General treatise.

ARISTOTELES.—*C.* 38, *p.* 832. *Edit. Boeckh.* [B.C.] ·
Erupt. of IV century.

AUDOT, L. E. (père).—L'Italie, la Sicile, les Îles Eoliennes, *etc.*—5 pts. 8⁰. *Pt. i, pp.* 113, 26 *pls., Paris,* 1834 ; *Pt. ii, pp.* 370, *pls.* 27–118, 1835 ; *Pt. iii, pp.* 280, *pls.* 119– 207, 1836 ; *Pt. iv, pp.* 108, *pls.* 208–52, 1836 ; *Pt. v, pp.* 111–28, *pls.* 253–91, 1 *map,* 1837.——2nd ed. ? 8⁰, *pp.* 267, 94 *pls. Paris,* 1835. [B.M.].
See Pt. ii, pp. 293–305, Pls. 98–99. 1835. Various ed. *See* VESUVIUS.

AUGER, H.—*See* NORVINS.

AURIA, DON V.—Storia Cronologica dei Vicerè di Sicilia. 1409–1597.—*Palermo, Coppola,* 1797.
Eruption of 1669, earthquake of 1663. *See* p. 143.

AURIA, DON V.—Diario delle cose occorse nella città di Palermo e nel regno di Sicilia 1631–74.—*Bibl. del Di Marzo, iii and v* [? *iv*]. Eruption 1669.

AUTORI SICILIANI.—Opuscoli I–XX.— *Palermo,* 1785–88.

AZOUR, A.—Sulla materia dei fuochi Etnei. —*Giorn. Litt. p.* 183. *Roma,* 1676. Cited by Massa, Etna.

BACCARINI, P.—Studio comparativo sulla Flora Vesuviana e sulla Etnea.—*Nuov. Giorn. Bot. Ital. xiii,* 3, *pp.* 150 *et seq.* 1881.

BACCI, A.—De Thermis, libri septem, *etc.*— *fol., pp. xxxii+*509. *Venetiis,* 1571.— Other ed. : *fol., foll. xxiii, pp.* 493.·*Venetiis,* 1588.—*fol., pp. viii+*425*+xviii. Romœ,* 1622.—*fol., pp. viii+xxviii+*366. *Patavii,* 1711.

BACCI, A —De Thermis veterum liber singularis.—*See* GRÆVIUS, J. G.—*Thes. Antiq. Sic. xii.* 1694, *etc.*
Contains indication of mineral sources of Paternò, near Catania.

BAEDEKER, K.—Italien. Handbuch für Reisende. 3. Theil : Unter-Italien und Sicilien nebst Ausflügen nach den Liparischen Inseln.—8th ed. 16⁰, *pp. xlviii+*412, 26 *maps,* 17 *plans. Leipzig,* 1887. *See* pp. 341–48, map.

BALDACCI, L., MAZZETTI, L., e TRAVAGLIA, R.—Relazione sull' eruzione dell' Etna.—*Boll. R. Com. Geol. Ital. x, pp.* 195– 201, 1 *geol. map. Roma,* 1879.

BALDACCI, L. (Ing.).—Descrizione geologica dell' Isola di Sicilia.—*Mem. descritt. Carta Geol. Ital. i, pp. xxxii+*403, 2 *maps,* 10 *tav., figs. Roma,* 1886.

BALTZER, R. A.—Wanderungen am Aetna. —[Sep.-Abdr.] *Jahrb. Schweiz. Alpen-Clubs, ix, pp.* 261–323. *Zürich,* 1874.
Contains view of Etna and topogr. map of Val del Bove.

BALTZER, R. A.—Die Etna-Eruption von 1892.—*N. J. f. Min. i, pp.* 75–88. *Stuttgart,* 1893.

BAMMARATA, C.—Quarta relatione de lu lacrimusu successu alle 30 de Maiu 1669, di lu focu di Mongibeddu, in terza rima Siciliana.—8⁰. *Naples,* 1669 (?).

BARATTA, M.—Sull'eruzione eccentrica dell' Etna scoppiata il 9 Luglio 1892.—*Rassegna Scient. Geol. Ital. ii, pp.* 81–86, *map.* 1892.

BARATTA, M.—Carta' sismica d'Italia per l'anno 1892.—*Boll. Soc. Geog. Ital. S.* 3, *vi, pp.* 313–23. *Roma,* 1893.

BARATTA, M.—La Vulcanologia e la recente eruzione dell' Etna.—*Il Pensiero Italiano, ii,* 24. *Milano, Dicembre,* 1893.

BARATTA, M.—Sulla distribuzione topografica dei terremoti in Italia durante il quinquennio 1887-91.—*Atti Primo Congr. Geog. Ital. Settembre* 1892, *Mem. sez. scient. ii, pt.* 1, *pp.* 180–89, *Tav.* v. *Genova,* 1894.

BARATTA, M.—Intorno ai recenti fenomeni endogeni avvenuti nella regione Etnea, con due diagrammi.—*Boll. Soc. Geog. Ital. xxxi, pp.* 740–60,'2 *figs. Roma,* 1894.

BARATTA, M.—Materiali per un catalogo dei fenomeni sismici avvenuti in Italia (1800–72).—*Mem. Soc. Geog. Ital. vii, pt.* 1, *pp.* 81–164. *Roma,* 1897.

BARATTA, M.—Saggio dei materiali per una storia dei fenomeni sismici avvenuti in Italia raccolti dal Prof. Michele Stefano de Rossi.—*Boll. Soc. Geol. Ital. xviii, pp.* 432–60. *Roma,* 1899.

BARATTA, M.—I Terremoti d'Italia.—8º, *pp.* 950, *pls. Torino,* 1901.
Gives, in Pt. III, an extensive bibliography of the earthquakes of Italy.

BARBAGALLO, J.—Descriptio montis Ætnei ignem vomentis 1766 die Aprilis 27.—*Catanæ,* 1766.
In hexameter verses.

BARDI, G.—Sommario cronologico.
Cited by Mongitore.

BARONIUS (Cardinalis).—Historiæ annales. —*pp.* 667–82. *Romæ,* 1675.
Eruption of 1169, etc.

BARTELS, J. H.—Briefe über Kalabrien und Sicilien.—3 vols. 8º. *Vol. i, pp. xv+* 428, 1787; *Vol. ii, pp. xxiii+*500, 1 *map,* 1789; *Vol. iii, Pt.* 1, *pp.* 38+472, 1792; *Pt.* 2, *pp.* 475–902, 1 *plan. Göttingen,* 1787–92.

BARTLETT, W. H.—Pictures from Sicily.— 8º, *pp.* 200, 33 *steel engrav.,* 16 *woodcuts. London,* 1853.

BARTOLI, A.—Sul calore specifico fino ad alta temperatura delle lave dell' Etna e di altri vulcani.—*Atti Acc. Gioen. S.* 4, *iii, pp.* 61–66. *Catania,* 1891.

BARTOLI, A.—Sul calore specifico fino ad alta temperatura di alcune roccie della Sicilia. Nota II [1893].—*Riv. Min. Crist. xii, pp.* 56–60. *Padua,* 1892.

BARTOLI, A.—Sulla temperatura delle Lave dell' attuale eruzione dell' Etna.—*Bull. Acc. Gioen. xxix, pp.* 2–4. *Catania,* 1892.—*Riv. Min. Crist. xii, pp.* 61–63. *Padua,* 1892. —*Riv. Sci. Ind. xxiv, pp.* 218–20. *Firenze,* 1892.

BARTOLI, A.—Sull' eruzione dell' Etna, scoppiata il 9 Luglio 1892.—*Boll. Soc. Meteor. Ital. S.* 2, *xii,* 11, *pp.* 169–79. *Torino,* 1892.

BARTOLI, A.—Etna.—*Boll. Oss. Moncalieri, xiii, p.* 11. *Torino,* 1893.

BARTOLI, A., e LUNGO, C. DEL.—Etna. La fine dell' eruzione dell' Etna [Gennaio 1893].—*Boll. Oss. Moncalieri, xiii, pp.* 28–29. *Torino,* 1893.

BARTOLI, A.—Sullo stato dell' Etna dopo la fine della grande eruzione del 1892.— *Boll. Oss. Moncalieri, xiv, pp.* 33–35. *Torino,* 1894.

BARTOLI, A.—Trasmissibilità delle radiazioni solari attraverso l'atmosfera carica di cenere vulcanica, nell' eruzione dell' Etna del 1892.—*Atti Acc. Gioen. S.* 4, *vii, Mem.* 15, *pp.* 6. *Catania,* 1895.

BARTOLI, A., STRACCIATI, E., RAFFO, G., e PETTINELLI, P.—Studi pireliometrici fatti nel 1894 sullo Stelvio e loro confronto con quelli compiuti sull' Etna.— *Rend. R. Ist. Lomb. xxviii, pp.* 583–99. *Milano,* 1895.—*Boll. Oss. Moncalieri, xv, pp.* 57–63. *Torino,* 1896.—*Nuovo Cimento, ii, pp.* 5–17. *Pisa,* 1895.

BARTOLI, A.—Sopra alcuni data termici riguardanti la Fisica terrestre. (Misura della temperatura, della capacità calorifica delle lave e del calore da loro emesso nelle eruzione.)—*Rend. R. Ist. Lomb. S.* 2, *xxix, pp.* 363–67, *figs. Milano,* 1896.

BARTOLOMEO A PATERNIONE, DON.— Chronica in monasterio Sanctæ Mariæ de Licordia Auctore don Bartolomeo a Paternione.
Eruption of XV century.

BASILE, G.—Ricerche di chimica agraria sopra i principali vitigni coltivati sul suolo dell' Etna.—*Atti Acc. Gioen. S.* 3, *ix, pp.* 139–87. *Catania,* 1874.

BASILE, G.—Note di fenomeni vulcanici presentati dall' Etna dal Settembre 1874 a tutto l'anno 1875.—*Atti Acc. Gioen. S.* 3, *x, pp.* 289–93. *Catania,* 1876.

BASILE, G.—L'Elefante fossile nel terreno vulcanico dell' Etna.—*Atti Acc. Gioen. S.* 3, *xi, pp.* 221–36. *Catania,* 1877.

BASILE, G.—Sulla presenza del Quarzo con inclusioni di Magnetite in una Trachite dell' Etna.—*Atti Acc. Gioen. S.* 3, *xvi, pp.* 157–66. *Catania,* 1882.

BASILE, G.—Le Bombe vulcaniche dell' Etna.—*Atti Acc. Gioen. S.* 3, *xx, pp.* 29–110, 3 *pls. Catania,* 1888.

BASILE, G.—Sulle acque potabili di Acireale.—*Atti e Rend. Acc. Sci. d. Zelanti, N.S. iv, pp.* 97–170. *Acireale,* 1893.

BASILE, G.—Di un nuovo Minerale trovato in una lava dell' Etna 1892.—*Atti Acc. Gioen. S.* 4, *vi, Mem.* 6, *pp.* 14. *Catania,* 1893.

BASILE, G.—Di un antica Ascia di pietra trovata ad Aci Catena.—*Atti Acc. Gioen. S.* 4, *vii, Mem.* 9, *pp.* 10, 1 *pl. Catania,* 1894.

BAUDRAND.—[Article on Etna.]—*See his*: Geographia, *T. i, p.* 22. *Parisiis,* 1682. Cited by Massa.

BEAUREGARD, J. DE.—Du Vésuve à l'Etna et sur le littoral de l'Adriatique . . . (1er juin 1895).—8⁰, *pp. vii*+328, *fig. Lyon,* 1895.

BEAUVOIR, ROGER DE.—*See* NORVINS.

BECKE, F. J. K.—Ueber den Herschelit von Aci Castello.—*Tschermak's Min. Mitth. ii,* 5, *p.* 413. *Wien,* 1880.

BELAR, A.—Ein Ausflug nach dem Aetna.— *Laibacher Zeitung, pp.* 54, 1 *map,* 1 *fig. Laibach,* 1898.

BELLEVUE, FLEURIAU DE.—*See* FLEURIAU DE BELLEVUE.

BELLIA, C.—Sulla radioattività dei prodotti gasosi Etnei.—*Il Nuovo Cimento, S.* 5, *xiii, pp.* 526–36. *Pisa,* 1907.

BEMBO, P.—Liber de Ætna, edit. Theod. suæ J. Clericus.—*Amstelodami,* 1703, *and David Martier,* 8⁰, 1718.—Other ed.: 4⁰. *Venetiis,* 1495 *and* 1530. *Also* 1818.—*See* ALBINOVANUS, C. P.—C. P. Albinovani elegiæ, *etc.* 8⁰. 1703. Eruption of 1494 and preceding ones.

BEMBO, P.—Omnia opera.—3 tom. *Basiliæ,* 1567.

BEMBO, P.—P. Bembi de Ætna ad Angelum Chabriélem liber.—*Amstelædami,* 1703.— *See* SEVERUS, C.—Ætna, et quæ supersunt fragmenta, *etc. pp.* 187–224.

BENOIST, PH. (des. d'après nature).— Catane: Vue Générale. 174. Lith. par Jacottet. Imp. par Lemercier à Paris.

Paris, Bulla Éditeur, rue Tiquetonne 18 et (Mᵒⁿ Aumont) François Delarue Succ. rue J. J. Rousseau 10. Hand-coloured litho. : 293×246 mm.

BERGH, TH.—Die Eruptionen des Aetna. —*p.* 138. *Philologus,* 1873. Proofs of the eruption of 693 B.C.

BERLIOZ, H.—*See* NORVINS.

BERNARDO, GIOVANNI DI S.—Vita, e Miracoli di Santa Rosalia, Vergine Palermitana. (I terremoti di Sicilia.)—12⁰, *foll. viii, pp.* 274. *Palermo,* 1693. *See pp.* 231, 272.

BERTACCHI, C.—Dal Ruvenzori all' Etna. —" *Scienza e Diletto,*" xiv, 9.

BERTELLI, P. D. T.—Delle cause probabili del Vulcanismo presente ed antico della Terra.—4⁰, *pp.* 28, 8 *figs. Torino,* 1886.

BERTELLI, P. D. T.—Di alcuni moti tromometrici osservati in Sicilia nelle eruzioni Etnee del 1883 e 1892, e di quella sottomarina della Pantelleria nell' Ottobre 1891. —*Boll. Oss. Moncalieri, S.* 2, *xii, pp.* 133–36. *Torino,* 1892.—*Atti Acc. Pont. N. Lincei, xlvi, pp.* 17–24. *Roma,* 1893.

BERTELLI, P. D. T.—In occasione dell' eruzione dell' Etna [Novembre 1892]. Lettera.—*Boll. Oss. Moncalieri, S.* 2, *xii, pp.* 194–95. *Torino,* 1892.

BERTHIER.— *See* DEVILLE, CH. SAINTE-CLAIRE. 1865.

BEVACQUA, S.—Terremoti ed eruzione dell' Etna. [Sulle pioggie di cenere avvenute in reggio Calabria, il 20 Marzo 1883.] —*Boll. Oss. Moncalieri, iii, p.* 56. *Torino,* 1883.

BIANCHI.—*See* CUCINIELLO.

BIANCONI, G. G.—Storia naturale dei terreni ardenti, dei Vulcani fangosi, *etc.*— 8⁰, *tav. Bologna,* 1840.

BIRMAN.—*See* FORBIN.

BISCARI, E. G.—Memoria sul suolo di Catania.—*Catania,* 1771.

BISCHOF, C. G. C.—Lehrbuch der chemischen und physikalischen Geologie.—2 Bd. in 4 vols. 8⁰, *illustr. Bonn,* 1847–55.— 2nd ed. 3 Bd. *illustr.* 8⁰. *Bonn,* 1863–66.— Supplement-Band, 8⁰, *pp. viii*+214, *illustr. Bonn,* 1871. *See* Supplement (ed. by F. Zirkel), chapt. XIII, XIV, XV.

BLAEU, Caesius (Willem Janszoon).—
Atlas major.—*Tom. i–ii.* 1662.
Cited by Massa, Etna.

BLAEU, J. A.—Theatrvm Civitatvm nec
non admirandorvm Neapolis et Siciliæ
regnorvm.—*fol., pp.* 78+30, 34 *pls. Amstelædami,* 1602. [C.A. and B.M.—176.
h 4.]

BLAEU, J. A.—Nouveau Théâtre d'Italie, ou
description exacte de ses Villes, Palais,
Églises, etc., et les Cartes Géographiques de
toutes ses Provinces.—3 vols. *fol. Amsterdam, Pierre Mortier,* 1704.
See Vol. iii, No. 27 : " Regium inter et
Messinam. Elegantissimus Freti Siculi
prospectus. Veüe très belle entre Rhege
et Messine, etc." (redrawn from Braun);
No. 30 : "Catana Patria S. Agathæ Virg.
et Mart. Catana or Catania, Ville de la
Sicile, etc." (with 46 reference nos.).
Another ed. 4 vols. *fol. La Haye,* 1724.
Latin ed. entitled : "Novum Italiæ Theatrum, sive accurata descriptio ipsius Urbium, Palatiorum, Sacrarum, Ædium,"
etc.—4 vols. *fol. Hagæ Comitum, R. Ch.
Alberts,* 1724.

BLAKE, J. F.—A Visit to the Volcanoes of
Italy.—*Proc. Geol. Assoc. ix, pp.* 145–76.
London, 1889.

BLASERNA, P. — *See* COMMISSIONE
GOVERNATIVA.

BLASI, A. Di.—La Sicilia geologica e la vulcanologia dell' Etna.—*Rassegna Sci. Geol.
Ital. i, p.* 245. *Torino,* 1891.

BLASI E GAMBACORTA, G. E. Di.—
Storia cronologica.—3 tom., 5 pts., 4⁰.
Palermo, 1790–91.
See Vol. i in " Appendice " : eruptions of
Etna 1787–1842.

BLUNDUS, P.—De Siciliæ mirandis.—*i,* 3,
Cap. 20.
Cited by Massa.

BOCCARDO, G.—Le Terre e le acque dell'
Italia.—*Milano,* 1865.
Eruption 1865 (pp. 49 *et seq.*).

BOCCARDO, G.—Sismopirologia, terremoti,
vulcani e lente oscillazioni del suolo.—
Genova, 1869.
Etna, p. 215.

BOCCONE, P. [afterwards S.].—L'Embrasement du Mont Etna.—*Paris,* 1672.

BOCCONE, P. [afterwards S.].—Recherches
et observations naturelles touchant le
Corail, la pierre Étoilée, les pierres de
figure de Coquilles, les Dents de Poissons
pétrifiées, l'Embrasement du Mont Etna,
etc.—12⁰, *figs., pls. Amsterdam,* 1674.

BOCCONE, P. [afterwards S.].—Museo di
fisica, e di esperienze variato, *etc.*—4⁰, *pp.
viii*+319, 18 *pls. Venetia,* 1697.
Eruption and earthquakes in 1693.

BODENEHR, G. (fec. et ex. Cum. Gr. et Pr.
S.C.M.).—Catania vor ihrem Untergang.
Catanca eine feine und alte Stadt so im
Königreich Sicilien am Meer gelegen, und
mit einem sehr guten Hafen versehen ist.
Anno 1719. Sich aber, hat an die Käyserl.
ergeben müssen.
Engraving with reference text and nos. :
190×152 mm.

BOECKH, A.—Corpus Inscriptionum Græ-
carum.—*Soc. Reg. Scient. fol., iii, fasc.* 1.
Berolini, 1828–44.
Eruption of 475 B.C.

BOECKH, A.—Edit. Pindar. Pyth.—*Odes, i,
p.* 224.

BOLANUS.—De Igne Ætneo.
Dissertation lost. Cited by Amico.

BOLLANDUS.—*See* GHESQUIÈRE, J.—
Acta Sanctorum, *etc. Tom. i* and *ii.
Bruxellis,* 1783–94.
Eruption of 252.

BOLTSHAUSER, J. A.—Éruption dans
l'intérieur du cratère central de l'Etna.—
Revue Savoisienne, pp. 78–79. *Annecy,*
15 *sept.,* 1874.

BOLTSHAUSER, J. A.—Nouveau Guide de
Catane.—*Catane,* 1874.

BOMARE, De.—Sopra il Vesuvio ed altri
vulcani.—*See* ANON.—Dei Vulcani o
Monti Ignivomi. *Livorno,* 1775.

BOMBARA, N. (del.).—Veduta da Catania
dell' Eruzione del 1787 la notte dei 18
Luglio. Ant. Zacco incise Cat.—*See* FER-
RARA.—Stor. gen. dell' Etna, *Cart.* v.
1793.
A view of Etna from over Catania.
Engraving : 245×132 mm.

BONITO, M.—Terra tremante, ovvero continuazione dei terremoti dalla creazione
del mondo fino al tempo presente.—4⁰.
Napoli, 1691.

BONNEY, T. G.—Volcanoes, their structure
and significance.—8⁰, *pp.* 351, 13 *pls.,* 21
figs. London, 1899.

BORBERA, G.—Relazione ed analisi dell' acqua della sorgente termale " Acetosa " presso Mineo.—*Boll. Oss. Moncalieri, S. 2, xi, 8. Torino,* 1891.

BORCH, M. J. DE.—Lithographie Sicilienne, ou catalogue raisonné de toutes les pierres de la Sicile propre à embellir le cabinet d'un amateur.—4°, *foll. iv, pp.* 50. *Naples,* 1777.

BORCH, M. J. DE.—Lithologie Sicilienne, ou connaissance de la nature des pierres de la Sicile, suivie d'un discours sur la Calcara de Palerme.—4°, *pp.* xvi+228. *Rome,* 1778.

BORCH, M. J. DE.—Minéralogie Sicilienne docimastique et métallurgique, ou connaissance de tous les minéraux que produit l'Île de Sicile avec les détails des mines et des carrières, et l'histoire des travaux anciens et actuels de ce pays. Suivie de la minérhydrologie Sicilienne.—8°, *pp.* 80+264, 12 *pls., portrait of author. Turin,* 1780.

BORCH, M. J. DE.—Lettres sur la Sicile et sur l'Île de Malthe, 1777.—2 tom. 8°, *num. pls. Turin,* 1782. — German by Werther. *Bern,* 1796.
    See Lettera VII.

BORELLI, G. A.—Historia et Meteorologia incendii Ætnæi anno 1669 ac responsio ad censuras Honoratii Fabri contra librum de vi percussionis.—*pp.* 162+vi, 1 *pl.,* 1 *map. Regio Julio,* 1670.

BORELLO.—*See* BURIGNY. 1786–94.

BORMANS, DE.—Collation des 168 premiers vers de l'Ætna de Lucilius junior, avec un fragment manuscrit du XIᵉ siècle.—*Bull. Acad. R. de Belgique, xxi, 2, pp.* 258–379. *Bruxelles,* 1854.

BORNEMANN, J. G.—[Aetnakrater.]— *Zeitschr. deutsch. geol. Gesellsch. viii, p.* 535. *Berlin,* 1856.

BORNEMANN, J. G.—Sur l'état des Volcans d'Italie pendant l'été de 1856.—Transl. by De Perrey from " *Tageblatt der 32 Versam. Deutsch. Naturf. u. Aerzte,*" *pp.* 114–41. *Wien,* 1856.—Original MS. *pp.* 4. [C.A.]

BORNER et MUELLER (des. et publ.).— Cratère de l'Etna, Sicile. Lit. Moschiano, Strada del Gigante n. 17.
    Lith. : 317×218 mm.

BORZI, G.—L'Etna nelle sue ultime fasi vulcaniche degli anni 1883–1886–1892. Quinta ediz. corretta ed accresciuta d'un appendice intorno al vulcanismo strom-

boliano nell' antico terremoto delle Calabrie e di Messina anno 1783, e dell' ultimo degli anni 1894 e 1895.—[? ed.] 8°, *pp.* 180. *Catania,* 1900.——3rd ed. *Catania,* 1896.

BOSIO, G.—Historia Gerosolimitana. Cited by Mongitore.

BOTTONI, DOM L.—Pyrologia Topographica ; id est, de igne dissertatio juxta loca, cum eorum descriptionibus.—4°, *foll.* 18, *pp.* 245, 3 *pls. Neapolis,* 1692. (Date at end is 1691.)—— 2nd ed. 8°, *foll.* 6, *pp.* 326. *Messanæ,* 1721.
    See pp. 142 *et seq.* 1692.

BOTTONI, DOM L.—D. B. de immani Trinacriæ terræmotu idea historico-physica, *etc.* —4°. *Messanæ,* 1718. (*Ital. transl. by Marcello Malpighi.*)

BOULANGER, C.—*See* BUCH, C. L. VON. 1836.

BOURDELOT, ABB.—Responsio Abbatis Bourdelot ad Dn. Boccone, de incendio Montis Ætnæ, 12 Maii, 1670.—MS. *foll.* 18. [B.M. 15076.]

BOURQUELOT, J.—Viaggio in Sicilia.— *Bibl. d. Viaggi, x. Milano, Frat. Treves,* 1873.

BOUSSINGAULT.—*See* ÉLIE DE BEAUMONT. 1866.

BRAUN, G., HOHENBERG, F.—Civitates Orbis Terrarum.—6 vols. *fol. Coloniæ Agrippinæ,* 1523 [? 1573]–1618.—Other ed. : 5 vols. *fol.* 1612.—6 vols. *fol.* 1582 [-1618].—1 or 2 vols. *Coloniæ,* 1572. [*Cologne ?,* 1575 ?]—In French : 6 vols. *fol. Brussels,* 1574–1617.
    The numbering of the plates is often erroneous. In the ed. of 1582–1618, Pl. 69 of Vol. v is " Catana Urbs Siciliæ Clarissima Patria. SCⁱᵉ Agathæ Virginis et Mart." (with 45 reference nos. and 2 pp. of text : 494×371 mm.) Pl. 58, Vol. vi, is entitled " Prospectus Freti Siculi vulgo il Faro di Messina," with view of Etna by Pietri Bruegelii and Georgius Houfnaglius 1617, and with 2 pp. of text with same heading. The plate is 475×305 mm. In the Brussels ed. 1574, the Catana pl. is No. 69 (Vol. v) with 2 pp. of text, and Pl. 21 (? 58) is the same as in the Latin ed., but entitled " Le Regard de la Mer de Sicile, communément il Faro di Messina."

BREISLAK, S.—Institutions Géologiques.— 3 vols. 8°, 56 *pls. Milano,* 1818.

BRÉON, R.—L'Éruption de l'Etna.—*Rev. Scient. S.* 2, *xvii, pp.* 150–54. *Paris,* 1879.

BRIET, PH.—Annales Mundi, *etc.*—*Venetiis,* 1692. Also *Augustæ Vindel. et Dilingæ,* 1696.
Fiovanti. Description of the earthquake of 1169.

BROCCHI, G. B.—Osservazioni naturali fatte alle Isole de' Ciclopi, e nella contigua spiaggia di Catania.—*Bibl. Ital. xx, pp.* 217–28. *Milano,* 1820.

BROCCHI, G. B.—Sulle diverse formazioni di Rocce della Sicilia.—*Bibl. Ital. xxiii, pp.* 357–73. *Milano,* 1821.—*L'Iride, Giorn. Sci. Lett. e Art. An.* 1, *ii,* 7, *p.* 21. *Palermo,* 1822.

BROCCHI, G. B.—Sulle geognostiche relazioni delle Rocce calcarie e vulcaniche in Val-di-Noto nella Sicilia.—*Bibl. Ital. xxvii, pp.* 53. *Milano,* 1822.

BRUN, A.—Recherches sur l'Exhalaison Volcanique.—*fol., pp.* 277, 34 *pls.,* 17 *figs. Genève, Paris,* 1911.

BRYDONE, P.—A Tour through Sicily and Malta ; in a series of letters to William Beckford, Esq.—2 vols. 8⁰. *London,* 1773. ——2nd ed., corrected, 2 vols. 8⁰. *London,* 1774.——3rd. ed. 2 vols. 8⁰. *London,* 1774. —Another, called also 3rd ed., 12⁰. *Dublin,* 1775.—Other ed.: 2 vols. 8⁰. *London,* 1776. —2 vols. 12⁰. [MS. notes by J. Mitford.] *Paris,* 1780.—2 vols. 12⁰. 1781.—2 vols. 8⁰. *London,* 1790.—2 vols. 12⁰, *with engrav. Perth,* 1799.—12⁰. *London,* 1807.—12⁰. *Edinburgh,* 1809.—2 vols. 12⁰. *Glasgow,* 1817.—In French : " traduit de l'Anglois par M. Demeunier," 2 tom. 8⁰. *Amsterdam, Paris, chez Pissot et Panckoucke,* 1775.— 2 tom. in 1 book, with notes by Derveil. *Neuchatel,* 1776.—2 tom. in 1 vol. 12⁰. *Amsterdam,* 1776.—[Supplément] 8⁰. 1782. —12⁰, *pp.* 428. *Francfort-sur-le-Mein,* 1793.—In German : 2 tom. in 1 book. *Leipzig,* 1774.—" Zwcyte nach der neuesten englischen Ausgabe verbesserte Auflage. Nebst einer Charte von Sicilien und Malta."—2 Th. 8⁰. *Leipzig,* 1777.— *See also :* CAMPE, J. H.—Sämmtliche Kinder- und ·Jugendschriften, *etc. Bd. xxiii.* 1831, *etc.*

BUCCA, L.—Primo rapporto sulla eruzione dell' Etna, scoppiata il 9 Luglio, 1892.— 1 *map. Catania,* 1892.—*N. Rassegna Sci. Geol. Ital. ii,* 3, *pp.* 124–26.

BUCCA, L.—Sopra le linee di accrescimento dell' Ematite dell' Etna.—*Boll. Acc. Gioen. xxxiii, pp.* 10–11. *Catania,* 1893.

BUCCA, L.—Sopra una nuova località di Ferro Oligisto dell' Etna.—*Atti Acc. Gioenia, S.* 4, *vi, Mem.* 5, *pp.* 3. *Catania,* 1893. —*Riv. Min. Crist. xiii, pp.* 12–14. *Padova,* 1893.

BUCCA, L.—Gli ultimi terremoti delle regioni Etnee.—*Giorn. di Sicilia, Palermo,* 11, 12 e 13 *Settembre,* 1894.

BUCCA, L.—Osservazioni sugli ultimi terremoti Etnei nello scorso Agosto.—*Bull. Acc. Gioen. xxxviii, pp.* 8–12. *Catania,* 1894.

BUCCA, L.—Contributo allo studio delle Lave dell' Etna. (Nota preventiva.)—*Boll. Acc. Gioen. xcii, pp.* 13–14. *Catania,* 1907.

BUCH, C. L. VON.—Ueber die Zusammensetzung der basaltischen Inseln und über Erhebungs-Cratere.—*Abh. phys. Klass. k. preuss. Akad. Wiss.* (1818–19), *pp.* 51–68. *Berlin,* 1820.—*Gesammelte Schriften, iii, p.* 15. *Berlin,* 1877.

BUCH, C. L. VON.—Physikalische Beschreibung der Canarischen Inseln.—4⁰, 2 *figs. Berlin,* 1825.—*Gesammelte Schriften, iii, pp.* 524 *et seq. Berlin,* 1877.

BUCH, C. L. VON.—Ueber die Natur der vulkanischen Erscheinungen auf den Canarischen Inseln und ihre Verbindung mit andern Vulcanen der Erdoberfläche.— *Ann. Phys. Chem. x, pp.* 1–46. *Leipzig,* 1827.

BUCH, C. L. VON.—Description physique des Îles Canaries, suivie d'une indication des principaux Volcans du Globe. Traduite par C. Boulanger.—8⁰, *pp. vii*+525. *Paris,* 1836.

BUCH, C. L. VON. — Ueber Erhebungscratere und Vulcane.—*Ann. Phys. Chem. xxxvii, pp.* 169–90. *Leipzig,* 1836.

BUCH, C. L. VON.—Gesammelte Schriften. —*Berlin,* 1877.
See Vol. iii, pp. 513–16.

BULIFON, A., LUIGI, DR. (nipote).—Carte de' regni di Napoli e di Sicilia, loro provincie ed Isole adjacenti.—4⁰, *pp.* 7, 19 *maps. Napoli,* 1734. [B.M.—118. c. 10.] Etna is poor.

BUONFIGLIO E COSTANZO, G.—Messanæ urbis nobilissimæ descriptio. — *See* GRÆVIUS, J. G.—Thesaurus Antiquitatum . . . Italiæ, *T.* 10, *vol. ix.* 1725, *etc.*
See p. 35 : Ætnæ incendium 1537.

BUONFIGLIO E COSTANZO, G.—Historia Siciliana.—Vols. I–II. *Messina*, 1738–39.

BURGIS.—Lettre du 10 avril 1536 sur la dernière éruption.
Cited by Palgrave.

BURGOS, A.—Distinta relazione dello spaventoso eccidio cagionato dai terremoti ultimamente con replicate scosse, accaduto a 9 e 11 Gennaro 1693 nel regno di Sicilia.— 4°. *Napoli*, 1693. [C.A.]—In Latin :— *See* GRÆVIUS, J. G.—Thes. Antiq. Sic. *Vol. ix, p.* 88.

BURGOS, A.—Sicilia piangente su le rovine delle sue più belle città atterrate da' tremuoti agli undici di Gennaio dell' anno 1693, *etc.*—4°, *pp.* 19. *Palermo*, 1693. [C.A.]

BURGOS, A.—Descriptio Terræ Motus Siculi anni 1693.—*See* GRÆVIUS, J. G.—Thesaurus Antiq. Sic. *T.* 10, *Vol. ix, col.* 87 (*from Carrera*). *Lugduni Batavorum*, 1723.

BURMANNUS, P.—*See* GRÆVIUS, J. G. —Thesavrvs Antiqvitatvm et Historiarvm Siciliæ.—1725, *etc.*

BYLANDT PALSTERCAMP, A. DE.— Théorie des volcans.—3 vols. 8°. Atlas, 17 *pls. fol. Paris*, 1835. *See* Vol. ii, pp. 185–260, 1 pl.

CÆSARIUS HEISTERBACHENSIS.— Illustria Miracula. [Erupt. of 1200.]—*Lib.* 12, *c.* 12, *p.* 857. *Colon. Agrip. Offic. Birckmannica*, 1599.

CÆSIUS, B.—Mineralogia, sive Naturalis Philosophiæ thesauri, *etc.*—*fol., pp.* 16+ 626+69. *Lugduni*, 1636. *See* pp. 118–22.

CAFICI, I.—Stazione della età della pietra a S. Cono in provincia di Catania.—*Boll. Paleontol. Ital.* 3–4. 1879.

CAFIERO, F.—[Terremoti ed eruzione nell' Etna.] Riposto.—*Boll. Oss. Moncalieri, S.* 2, *iii, pp.* 69–71. *Torino*, 1883.

CAFIERO, F.—Attività sismica dell' Etna [nei mesi di Aprile, Maggio e Giugno 1883]. Riposto.—*Boll. Oss. Moncalieri, S.* 2, *iii, pp.* 84, 102–3, 118. *Torino*, 1883.— *Giarre*, 1883.

CAFIERO, F.—Attività sismica dell' Etna in Riposto e paesi vicini. [1883.]—*Spettrosc. Ital. Mem.* 12, *pp.* 31–35. 1884.

CAFIERO, F.—Pioggia di polvere all' Etna. —*Boll. Oss. Moncalieri iv, p.* 195. *Torino*, 1884.

CAFIERO, F.—Terremoto del 5 Dicembre [1884. Riposto].—*Boll. Oss. Moncalieri, v, p.* 9. *Torino*, 1885.

CAFIERO, F.—Eruzione dell' Etna [cominciata il 18 Maggio 1886].—*Boll. Oss. Moncalieri, vi, pp.* 96–98. *Torino*, 1886.— " *Astronomie*," *pp.* 304–7. *Paris*, 1886.

CAFIERO, F., ET ALII.—[Terremoto del 27 Agosto 1886. Italia Bassa.] Sicilia.— *Boll. Oss. Moncalieri, vi, pp.* 161–62. *Torino*, 1886.

CAFIERO, F.—Eruzione dell' Etna. [Riposto, 31 Maggio e 1 Giugno 1887.]— *Boll Oss. Moncalieri, vii, p.* 104. *Torino*, 1887.

CAFIERO, F.—[Eruzione dell' Etna.]— *Boll. Oss. Moncalieri viii, pp.* 89–90. *Torino*, 1888.

CAIETANUS, OCTAVIUS.—P. Octavii Cajetani Syracusani Isagoge ad Historiam Siculam illustrandam.—*See* GRÆVIUS, J. G.—Thes. Sic. *Vol. ii.*

CALCARA, P.—Esposizione metodica delle Rocce e dei Terreni del Globo con indicazione dei principali esempii della Sicilia.— 8°, *tav. Palermo*, 1847.

CALÌ, R.—Un' Ascensione sull' Etna fatta nell' Agosto del 1882.—*Acireale*, 1883.

CALÌ SARDO, A.—Relazione accademica per gli anni I e II dell' Accademia dei Zelanti di Acireale.—*Palermo*, 1836.
Contains synopses of : GRASSI, G. R.— Discorso sull' Etna, pp. 16–18, and DI MARZO RIGGIO, M.—I basalti di Aci-Castello, pp. 33–35.

CALLEJO Y ANGULO, PIERRE DEL.— Description de l'Isle de Sicile et de ses côtes maritimes, avec les plans des forteresses. Avec le portrait de Charles III. d'Espagne, et beaucoup de cartes et plans pliées. J. A. Pfeffel et C. Engelbrecht sc.— *fol., pp.* 26. *Vienne*, 1719.—8°, 17 *plans. Amsterdam*, 1734.

CAMILIANO, C.—Descrizione della Sicilia. —*See* MARZO, G. DI.—Opere storiche, *Vol. xxvi.*

CAMPAILLA, TOM. MODICANO.—L'Apocalisse dell' Apostolo S. Paolo Poema sacro, gl'opuscoli filosofici, e tutte l'altre opere. —*fol., pp.* 16+466, 4 *tav. Siracusa nelle stampe di D. Francesco Maria Pulejo*, 1784.—An earlier ed. : *Palermo*, 1738. *See* pp. 88–102.—Discorso dell' incendio del Monte Etna, e del come si accende.

/
CAMPAILLA, T. [M.]—Muticensis dissertatio.
Cited by Amico.

CANEDI (?).—Schauplatz des Schlamm-Ausbruchs bei Paternò am Fusse des Aetna (S. 422).
Woodcut from a German illust. paper : 214 × 155 mm.

CANTANI, A.—Acireale considered as a climatic station and a bathing town.— *Naples, Riv. Morgagni, Marzo*, 1880.
Treats of waters of Santa Venere.

CAPECELATRO, F.—Historia della città, e regno di Napoli, *etc.*—2 vols. 8⁰. *Napoli*, 1724.
For other ed. see VESUVIUS.

CAPOZZO, G. — Memorie sulla Sicilia.— *Palermo*, 1840.

CAPPA, U.—L'Eruzione dell' Etna del Luglio 1892.—*Boll. R. Com. Geol. Ital. xxiv, pp.* 12–17, 2 *pls. Roma*, 1893.

CARAFA, P.—Notucæ Descriptio.—*See* GRÆVIUS, J. G.—Thes. Antiq. Sic.

CARCACI, PATERNO-CASTELLO F., DUCA DI.—Descrizione di Catania e delle cose notevoli ne' dintorni di essa.—8⁰, *pp.* 284. *Catania, Giuntini*, 1841.——2a ed. *Catania*, 1847.
See pp. 253–56. 1841.

CAREGA DI MURICCE, F.—*See* MURICCE, CAREGA DI.

CARNEVALE, G.—Historia e descrizione del regno di Sicilia.—4⁰. *Napoli, Salviani*, 1591.

CARRERA, P.—Il Mongibello descritto in tre libri nel quale oltre diverse notitie si spiega l'historia degl'incendii e la cagione di questi.—4⁰. *Catania*, 1636.

CARRERA, P.—Poesie pertinente alle materie di Mongibello, e del sacro vito della gloriosa S. Agatha.—8⁰, *pp.* 177–203. *Catania*, 1636. [C.A.]

CARRERA, P.—Memorie storiche della città di Catania.—2 vols. *fol. Catania*, 1639.— *See* GRÆVIUS, J. G.—Thes. Sic. *Tom. x, Vol. i.*

CARRERA, P.—Descriptio Ætnæ.—*See* GRÆVIUS, J. G.—Thes. Sic. *Vol. ix.*

CARRERA, P.—Monumentorum historicorum Urbis Catanæ.—*See* GRÆVIUS, J. G. —Thes. Sic. *Vol. ix.*

CARREY, E.—L'Etna.—[Extr. du] " *Moniteur," foll. xxviii.* 1863. [fide C.A.]

CARUSO, G. B.—Bibliotheca historica Regni Siciliæ, *etc.*—2 vols. *fol. Panormi*, 1719–23.
See p. 18.

CARUSO, G. B.—Memorie Istoriche [up to 1654].—3 pts. 4⁰. *Palermo*, 1742–45.

CASAGRANDI, V.—Su due antiche città Sicule (Vesse-Inessa, sive Ætna).—*Atti Acc. Zelanti, N.S. vi, pp.* 1–46. *Acireale*, 1895.

CASSAS, L. F. (des.).—Vue des Ruines du Proscenium ou avant-scène de l'ancien Théâtre de Taorminum. Dessinée d'après Nature par L. F. Cassas, en 1783. Gravée à l'eauforte [*sic*] par Berthault. Terminée au burin par De Ghendt. No. 15 Sicile. A.P.D.R.
Fine engrav. : 394 × 246 mm.

CASTIGLIONE, C. — Panormitani terræ motus descriptio (carmen).—*Panormi, Aiccardo*, 1726.

CASTONE, C.—Viaggio della Sicilia.—12⁰. *pp.* 3+240, 1 *pl. Palermo*, 1828. [B.N.]
See pp. 163 *et seq.* (erupt. 1787).

CASTORINA, P. DI-G., e GAETANI, G. DE. —Catalogo di alcune Piante medicinali dei dintorni di Catania e del suo monte ignivomo che fa seguito alla Flora Medica Catanese.—*Atti Acc. Gioen. xviii, pp.* 161– 79, 1842 ; *xx, pp.* 383–98. *Catania*, 1843.

CASTORINA, PASQUALE.—Sulla eruzione dell' Etna del 1669 e su d'un ignoto documento relativo alla stessa.—*Archiv. Stor. Sic. N.S. xvi,* 3–4, *pp.* 392–409. *Palermo*, 1892.

CATHOLY, C.—De Ætnæ ætate . . .—8⁰, *pp.* 64. *Gryphiæ*, 1908.

CATTANEO, L.—L'Eruzione dell' Etna del 1879.—*Illustr. Ital. d. Treves, sem.* 1, *p.* 371. *Milano*, 1879.

CAVASINO, A.—Sui recenti terremoti Etnei. —*Boll. Acc. Gioen.* 3–4, *pp.* 26–31. *Catania*, 1908.

CHAIX, E.—Une course à l'Etna.—*Genève*, 1890.—*Bull. Amer. Geog. Soc. xxiii, pp.* 92–101, 3 *pls. New York*, 1891.

CHAIX, E.—La Vallée del Bove et la végétation de la région supérieure de l'Etna.—*Le Globe, Journ. géog. xxx (S.* 5, *ii), Mém. pp.* 1–32, 3 *pls. Genève*, 1891.

CHAIX, E.—Eine Besteigung des Etna, 9. VII. 1892.—*map. Catania*, 1892.

CHAIX, E.—Carta volcanologica e topografica dell' Etna. 1 : 100,000. (With explanation.)—*Genève*, 1892.—*See also :* *Bibl. Univ., Archiv. Sci. phys. nat.* 3e *pér., xxvii, pp.* 343–44. *Genève*, 1892.

CHAIX, E.—[Éruption actuelle de l'Etna.] —*Bibl. Univ., Archiv. Sci. phys. nat. xxviii, pp.* 488–90, 501–2. *Genève*, 1892.

CHASTELET (des.).—Vuë du Phare, ou détroit de Messine prise du côté de la Calabre et en arrivant à Reggio. Gravée par Varin. No. 69. G^{de} Grèce. A.P.D.R.

CHASTELET (des.).—Vue des Rochers et de la Marine de Bova près le Cap Spartivento. On apperçoit l'Etna dans l'éloignement.— Gravé par Guttemberg. No. 67. G^{de} Grèce. A.P.D.R.
     Engrav. : 342×232 mm.

CHÂTELET.—*See* CHASTELET.

CHERUBINI, CAV. C.—Carta Fisica dell' Italia.—*Pub. G. B. Paravia e C., Torino, Roma, Milano, Firenze, Napoli,* 1876.
     Raised map, 1 : 750,000 horiz. ; 1 : 150,000 vert.

CHIAVETTA, B. ABB. BASILIANO.—Memoria dell' ultima eruzione dell' Etna accaduta il 27 Marzo 1809.—8⁰. *Messina,* 1809.

CHILDREN, J. B.—*See* PALGRAVE. 1835.

CHISARI, V.—Breve notizie sulle acque termali di Paternò da lui scoperte.—8⁰. *Catania,* 1736.—*Prospetto della storia letteraria di Sicilia, Vol. i, p.* 137. *Palermo,* 1824.
     Cited by Scina.

CHRIST, W. VON.—Der Aetna in der Griechischen Poesie.—*pp.* 50. — ?, 1888.

CICERO, M. T.—De natura Deorum lib. II, cap. 38, 96.—*In :* CAIETANUS, OCTAVIUS.—Isagoge ad Hist. Sic. *cap. xii.*

CIMARELLI, A.—Risoluzioni filosofiche. *See* Cap. 12, p. 104, description of the mineral springs of Paternò.—Cit. by De Gregorio.

CLAUDIANUS, C.—Opus de raptu Proserpinæ, etc.——2nd ed. *fol., pp.* 656. *Nicolæ Bizzi Nobili Bergomensi, Lucæ,* 1751.
     See Vol. i, pp. 158–76.

CLENNELL.—Summit of Mount Etna. Engraved by Owen from a drawing by Clennell for the Gallery of Nature and Art. London : Published by R. Wilks, 89, Chancery Lane, Jan. 15th, 1813.
     Engrav. : 167×91 mm.

CLERICI, E.—Sul Giacimento diatomeifero de S. Tecla, presso Acireale.—*Boll. Soc. Geol. Ital. xxiii, pp.* 430–34. *Roma,* 1905.

CLERICI, E.—Sopra due Campioni raccolti nella Valle del Bove.—*Boll. Soc. Geol. Ital. xxviii, pp. ccvi–ccvii, fig. Roma,* 1910.
     Volcanic dust of Etna.

CLUB ALPIN FRANÇAIS (Bulletin Trimestriel).—Congrès des Clubs Alpins à Catane en 1880 et ascension de l'Etna.—3ᵉ *Trim. Paris,* 1880.

CLUVERIUS, PH.—Geologia. De creatione et formatione Globi terrestris.—4⁰. *Lugd. Bat.* 1619.

CLUVERIUS, PH.—Sicilia antiqua, cum minoribus insulis ei adjacentibus, item Sardinia et Corsica . . .—*fol., pp.* 510 *and index,* 4 *maps. Lugduni Batavorum,* 1619. —Editio novissima, *fol., coll.* 687 *and index, portrait, maps and plans.* 1723.—*See* GRÆVIUS, J. G.—Thesaurus Antiquitatum . . . *Italiæ, etc. Tom.* 10, *Vol. i.*
     See pp. 97–124. 1619.

CLUVERIUS, PH.—Italia antiqua . . . Ejusdem Sicilia, Sardinia et Corsica . . . (Cum epistola dedicatoria Danielis Heinsii.) —3 pts. in 2 vols. *fol. Vol. i, pp.* 786 ; *Vol. ii, pp.* 787–1338+510, *portrait, maps and plans. Lugduni Batavorum,* 1624. (" Sicilia antiqua " is dated 1619 and has special title and pagination. *See* preceding.)—Also 2 vols. *fol.* 1624. (In this " Sicilia antiqua " is missing.) [B.N.P.]

CLUVERIUS, PH.—Sicilia antiqua, auctoris methodo . . . contracta, opera Joh. Bunonis . . . Ejusque Sardinia et Corsica antiqua.—4⁰, *pp.* 293 *and index, maps, engraved title. Guelferbyti,* 1659.

COCCO-GRASSO, L.—Su la eruzione dell' Etna.—*Palermo,* 1838.

COCCO-GRASSO, L.—Parere ragionato sur una memoria del prof. Rob. Sava intorno alcuni Prodotti Minerali formati in una spelonca a piè dell' Etna.—" *Il Gran Sasso d'Italia,*" *Aquila,* 1843.

COCO, G.—L'Etna. Saggi Poetici.—8⁰, *pp.* 142+2. *Acireale,* 1859. [C.A.]
     See pp. 90–93.

CODEX DIPLOMATICUS SICILIÆ.— [Eruption of 760 A.D.]—*Dipl.* CCLXXIV. *Panormi,* 1743.

COLLIGNON, F.—Vero disegno del novo incendio della Montagna di Mongibello in Sicilia hauendo aperto diuersi bocche nel Monpelieri con gran spauento è rouina del territorio di Catania, cominciato li 11 Marzo 1669. Franᶜᵒ Collignon formis Romæ nel Parioⁿᵉ. Romæ con privᵃ si stampa nel Parione.

Fine engrav. of the epoch, with names of towns and villages inscribed under each, lava flowing into the sea at Catania, ships in foreground and compass in left lower corner : 348 × 293 mm.

COLLINI, M.—Considérations sur les Montagnes Volcaniques, *etc.*—4⁰, *pp. viii*+61, 1 *pl. Mannheim*, 1781.—In German : 4⁰. *Dresden*, 1783.

COLLOTTI, G.—Un'Ascensione sull'Etna.— "*Natura e Arte,*" 9–12. *Milano*, 1894.

COMITÉ D'ORGANISATION DU 2ᴹᴱ CONGRÈS GÉOLOGIQUE INTERNATIONAL À BOLOGNE, 1881.— Bibliographie Géologique et Paléontologique de l'Italie. — 8⁰, *pp. viii*+630. *Bologne*, 1881.

See No. XVI. SILVESTRI, O.—L'Etna . . . les Îles Lipari, l'Île Pantellaria et l'Île Ferdinandea (nos. 3763–4643).

COMMISSIONE GOVERNATIVA [BLASERNA, P., GEMMELLARO, G. G., SILVESTRI, O.].—Relazione della eruzione dell'Etna del 26 Maggio 1879.—*Gazz. Uffic. Regno, i*, 152. *Roma, Luglio,* 1879.—*Boll. Soc. Geog. Ital. xvi, pp.* 550–59, *map. Roma,* 1879.—*Boll. R. Com. Geol. Ital. x, pp.* 309–20, 1 *pl. Roma,* 1879.

COMPAILLA, T. — Discorso diretto all' Accademia del Buon-gusto, dell' incendio dell' Etna, e del come si accende.—4⁰. *Palermo,* 1738.

COMPENDIO DELLE TRANSAZIONI FILOSOFICHE DELLA SOCIETÀ REALE DI LONDRA.—[Speaks of various earthquakes and eruptions of Etna, Vesuvius, etc.]—*Giorn. Lett. v, pp.* 78–89. *Napoli,* 1793.

CONSIGLIO - PONTE, S. — Ricerche dei blocchi eruttati dal cratere centrale dell' Etna durante l'eruzione del 1879.—*Boll. Acc. Gioen. xxxvii, pp.* 24–25. *Catania,* 1894.

CONSIGLIO-PONTE, S.—Studio mineralogico dei blocchi eruttati dal cratere centrale nell' eruzione Etnea del 1879.—*Boll. Acc. Gioen. lxxvi, pp.* 17–30. *Catania,* 1903.

CONTEJEAN, CH. L.—Une Ascension de l'Etna. (Extrait du journal d'un Voyageur.)—*Riv. Alp. Ital. pp.* 14. *Torino, février,* 1884.

CONTI, C.—Sull' eruzione dell' Etna incominciata il giorno 19 Maggio 1886.—*Boll. R. Com. Geol. Ital. xvii, pp.* 149–55, 1 *map. Roma,* 1886.

COOKE, J. H.—Eruption of Etna, July 1892. —"*The Mediterranean Naturalist,*" ii, 15, *pp.* 219–21. *Malta,* 1892.

COPLEY FIELDING (des.).—[Etna (?) from a lake.] Peint par Copley Fielding, d'après l'esquisse de Cassas. Gravé par Théodore Fielding.

Stipple engrav. : 428 × 300 mm.

CORDENONS, F.—Sul Meccanismo delle Eruzioni Vulcaniche e Geiseriane. Part I. —8⁰, *pp.* 43, *figs. Venezia,* 1885.

CORDIER, P. L. A.—Rapport sur le voyage de M. Constant Prévost à l'Île Julia, à Malte, en Sicile, aux Îles Lipari et dans les environs de Naples.—*C.R. Acad. Sci. ii, pp.* 243–55. *Paris,* 1836.—*Nouv. Ann. Voy. lxx (S.* 2*, x), pp.* 43–64. *Paris,* 1836.

CORONELLI, P.—Isolarium Atlantis Veneti. —*Venetii,* 1696.

See Pt. i : Eruptions of Etna 1535–1683.

CORRAO, ALB.—Memoria sopra i Tremuoti di Messina accaduti in quest' anno 1783.— *Messina,* 1783.

CORTESE, E.—Brevi cenni sulla geologia della parte N.E. della Sicilia.—*Boll. R. Com. Geol. Ital. S.* 2, *iii, pp.* 105–37, 161–89, 308–52. *Roma,* 1882.

See Tav. VIII.

CORTI, E.—Da Catania alla cima dell' Etna. Notizie ed impressioni, etc.—8⁰. *Milano,* 1876.

COSENTINI, F.—Colpo d'occhio sulle produzioni vegetali dell' Etna.—*Atti Acc. Gioen. iv, pp.* 125–36. *Catania,* 1830.

COSSA, A.—Osservazioni chimico-microscopiche sulla Cenere dell' Etna caduta a reggio di Calabria il 28 Maggio [1879] e sulla Lava raccolta a Giarre il 2 Giugno, 1879. Note preliminare.—*Atti R. Acc. Lincei, S.* 3, *Trans. iii, pp.* 248–50. *Roma,* 1879.—*Boll. R. Com. Geol. Ital. x, pp.* 329–32. *Roma,* 1879.—*C.R. Acad. Sci. lxxxviii, pp.* 1358–59. *Paris,* 1879.

COSSA, A.—Ricerche chimiche e microscopiche su Roccie e Minerali d'Italia (1875–80).—4⁰, *pp. vii*+302, 12 *pls. Torino,* 1881.—*Boll. R. Com. Geol. Ital. xiii, notiz. bibliog. pp.* 57–58. *Roma,* 1882.

COUSIN, G.—Cognatus Nozerenus (Gilbertus) de incendio Ætnæ anni MDXXXVI.— *See his:* De Sylva Narrationum, 8⁰, *pp.* 35–39. *Basileæ*, 1560 (?).

COVELLI, N.—*See* MONTICELLI.

[CRAVEN, K.]—Italian Scenes, a series of interesting delineations of remarkable views and of the most celebrated remains of Antiquity.—4⁰, 27 *pls., des. by Author, T. Ruiz, etc., and engrav. by C. Heath, Taylor, etc., with explan. text. London,* 1825. *See* Pl. 16 : Philosopher's tower, Etna.

CREMONENSIS, L.—Annales 1868.—*See* GRÆVIUS, J. G.—Thes. Sic.
Eruption of 1570. Cited also by Alessi.

CRINÒ, S.—Un nuovo documento sull' eruzione dell' Etna del 1669.—*Archiv. Stor. Sic. N.S. xxx,* 1. *Palermo,* 1905.

CRINÒ, S.—Bibliografia storico-scientifica della " Regione Etnea."—*Atti Acc. Gioen. S.* 4, *xx, Mem.* 6, *pp.* 69. *Catania,* 1907.

CRINÒ, S.—L'Etna. Carta altimetrica e filoantropica. 1 : 125,000. Con un saggio antropogeografico.—*Atti Acc. Peloritana, xxii,* 1. *Palermo,* 1907.

CROCE, G. A. DELLA.—La tranquillità di Catania conturbata dai vomiti di Mongibello per l'inondazione del fuoco degli 11 Marzo 1669.—12⁰. *Palermo,* 1670.

CUCINIELLO, D., e BIANCHI, L. — Viaggio pittorico nel regno delle due Sicilie [with drawings by R. Müller, L. Jely, F. Horner, G. Forino, F. Dura, F. Wenzel, P. de Leopold, C. Goetzloff, G. Gigante, A. Vianelly, A. Marinoni, A. Carelli].—*gd. fol. Vol. i, Pt.* 1, *pp.* 128, 60 *pls.* ; *Vol. ii, Pt.* 1, *pp.* 122, 60 *pls.* ; *Vol. iii, Pt.* 2, *pp.* 122, 60 *pls. Napoli* [1833].

DALTON, R. (delin.).—A View of Mount Ætna in Sicily (now called Mon Gibello) from Lo Strozzo ; with the range of huge black Rocks which is continued along the sea coast for sixteen miles. Some of these rocks have been at diffcrent eruptions thrown with great violence from the cavity of the Mountain, others have been formed from the liquid fiery matter, called by the Sicilians la Sciarra, that issued from the Mouñtain in torrents and, cooling, grew hard. Chatelain & Basire junʳ Sculp.—Publish'd according to Act of Parliament, April 12th, 1751.
Text also in French. Dedicated to Sir John Frederick, Bart. A fine engraving with careful detail : 584 × 392 mm.

DAL VERME, L.—Una Escursione al nuovo cratere sull' Etna.—*Boll. Soc. Geog. Ital. S.* 2, *xi, p.* 679. *Roma,* 1886.

DAMOUR, A. A.—Analyse de la Herschélite. —*Ann. Chim. Phys. S.* 3, *xiv, pp.* 97–101. *Paris,* 1845.—*Racc. Lett. Fis. Mat. i, pp.* 127–28. *Roma,* 1845.

DANCKERTS, J.—Regnum Neapolis, Siciliæ et Lipariæ Insulæ.—*Amstelodami* [1670 ?]. [B.M.—23880 (2).]

DASCHER.—Éruptions Volcaniques. Notices abrégées relevées . . . dans les ouvrages spéciaux.—16⁰, *pp.* 16. *Paris,* 1902.

DAUBENY, C. G. B.—Sketch of the Geology of Sicily.—*Jameson's Phil. Journ. xiii, pp.* 107–18, 254–69, *geol. map. London,* 1825. —*Amer. Journ. Sci. x, pp.* 230–56. *New Haven,* 1826.

DAUBENY, C. G. B.—A description of active and extinct Volcanos : with remarks on their origin, their chemical phenomena, and the character of their products, as determined by the condition of the earth during the period of their formation.—8⁰, *pp.* 466, *figs.,* 2 *maps,* 1 *pl. London,* 1826. —8⁰, *pp.* 743, *figs.,* 10 *maps,* 4 *pls. London,* 1848.

DAUBENY, C. G. B.—Die noch thätigen und erlöschenen Vulkane ; Bearb. von G. Leonard.—*Stuttgart,* 1851.
See Chapt. XIV.

DAUBRÉE.—La Chaleur intérieure du Globe. Conférences populaires faites à l'Asile Impérial de Vincennes.—*Paris, Hachette et Cie,* 1866.

DAUBRÉE.—Note accompagnant le rapport de M. Silvestri, sur l'éruption de l'Etna, des 18 et 19 mai 1886. — *C.R. Acad. Sci. cii, pp.* 1221–23. *Paris,* 1886.

DAUBRÉE.—*See* ÉLIE DE BEAUMONT. 1866.

DAVISON, C.—The Eruption of Etna.— " Nature," *lxxxvii, p.* 384. *London,* 1911.

DAVY, SIR HUMPHRY.—On the phænomena of Volcanoes.—*Phil. Trans. R. Soc. pp.* 241–50. *London,* 1828.—*Phil. Mag. S.* 2, *iv, pp.* 85–94. *London,* 1828.—*Ann. Chim. Phys. xxxviii, pp.* 133–50. *Paris,* 1828.

D. B.—L'Italia descritta e depinta con le sue isole di Sicilia, Sardegna, Elba, Malta, Eolie, di Calipso, ecc. Collected from numerous authors by D. B. — 2nd ed. 5 vols. 8⁰, *many* (good) *engravings. Turin, Gius. Pomba, e. c.* 1837.

D. C. G. G.—Relazione dell' eruzione dell' Etna nel mese di Luglio 1787, scritta da D. C. G. G.— 4⁰, *fol.* 1, *pp.* 40. *Catania,* 1787. [C.A.]

DEECKE, J. E. W.—Über die Sicilianischen Schlammvulkane.—[Sonder-Abdr.] " *Globus,*" *lxxi, pp.* 69–71.

DEECKE, J. E. W.—Italien.—*Bibl. der Länderkunde, iii and iv, pp.* 519, 33 *pls. and maps,* 79 *figs. Berlin,* 1899.

DELESSE, A.—Recherches sur l'origine des Roches.—[Extr.] *Bull. Soc. géol. France,* S. 2, *xv, pp.* 728–82. *Paris,* 1858.—8⁰, *pp.* 74. *Paris,* 1865. *See* p. 749, 1858.

DELUC, J. A.—Formation des Montagnes volcaniques. Observations au Vésuve et à l'Etna.—8⁰, *pp.* 19. *La Haye, Paris,* 1780.

DELUC, J. A.—Observations sur les prismes, ou schorls volcaniques, et particulièrement sur ceux de l'Etna.—*Journ. Phys. lii, pp.* 195–205. *Paris,* 1801.

DELUC, J. A.—Nouvelles Observations sur les Volcans et sur leurs laves.—*Journ. Mines, xvi, pp.* 329–54, 1804 ; *xx, pp.* 5–40, *Paris,* 1806.

DELUTHO, Abbé.—L'Etna, poème de Cornelius Severus. Traduction nouvelle.— 8⁰, *pp.* xxvii+105. *Paris,* 1842. [C.A.]

DEMARD, E.—Extinction des Volcans. Étude sur les Volcans en général et principalement sur les monts Vésuve et Etna.— *Rouen,* 1873.

DENZA, F.— Notizie di Meteorologia e Fisica Terrestre. (Le lucicrepuscolari e le eruzioni dell' Isola Ferdinandea e dell' Etna.)—*Ann. Meteor. Ital. ii, pp.* 256–58. *Torino,* 1887.

DENZA, F.—Etna, Sicilia ed Isole vulcaniche adiacenti, dal Dicembre 1889 all' Ottobre 1890.—*Ann. Meteor. Ital. vi, pp.* 216–20. *Torino,* 1891.

DENZA, F.—Etna, Sicilia ed Isole adiacenti dal Novembre 1890 all' Ottobre 1891.— *Ann. Meteor. Ital. vii, pp.* 264–69. *Torino,* 1892.

DEROY (del.).—Ruines du Thᵗʳᵉ de Taormina. Galerie du Palais Royal (Michallon) J. P. Quénot : direx. Litho. de C. Motte. Hand-tinted on straw-col. film ; man standing and another prone in foreground : 313×268 .mm.

DERVEIL.—Voyage en Sicile et Malte.— *Neufchâtel,* 1776.

DESPRET (des.).—Vue de la ville et du port de Reggio avec une partie des côtes de la Sicile et de l'Etna que l'on apperçoit de l'autre côté du détroit. Gravée à l'eauforte [sic] par Berteaux. Terminée par d'Embrun. No. 71. Gᵈᵉ Grèce. A.P.D.R.

DESSOULAVY.—[24 pen, brush and ink drawings of S. Italy.]—*obl. fol.* 1826. *See* No. 16.

DEVILLE, C. J. Sainte-Claire.—Relation sur l'Etna.—*See* ARCHIAC, E.-J.-A. D. DE S.-S., Vicomte D'.—Histoires des progrès de la Géologie, *Vol. i, p.* 579. *Paris,* 1847.

DEVILLE, C. J. Sainte-Claire.—Sur quelques produits d'émanations de la Sicile. Deux lettres à M. Dumas.—*C.R. Acad. Sci.* [extr.] *xli, pp.* 887–94, 1855 ; *xliii, pp.* 359–70, *Paris,* 1856.

DEVILLE, C. J. Sainte-Claire.—Sur les produits des Volcans de l'Italie méridionale. —*C.R. Acad. Sci. xlii, pp.* 1167–71. *Paris,* 1856.

DEVILLE, C. J. Sainte-Claire.—Septième Lettre à M. Élie de Beaumont sur les phénomènes éruptifs de l'Italie méridionale. —*C.R. Acad. Sci. xliii, pp.* 533–38. *Paris,* 1856.

DEVILLE, C. J. Sainte-Claire.—Neuvième Lettre à M. Élie de Beaumont sur les phénomènes éruptifs de l'Italie méridionale. —*C.R. Acad. Sci. xliii, pp.* 681–86. *Paris,* 1856.

DEVILLE, C. J. Sainte-Claire.—Mémoire sur les émanations volcaniques.—2 pts. *Paris,* 1856-62.—*C.R. Acad. Sci. xliii, pp.* 955–58, 1856; *xliv, pp.* 58–62, *Paris,* 1857.—See also : *Bull. Soc. géol. France,* S. 2, *xiv, pp.* 254–79. *Paris,* 1856-57.

DEVILLE, C. J. Sainte-Claire, et LEBLANC, F.—Sur les émanations gazeuses qui accompagnent l'Acide Borique dans les Soffioni et Lagoni de la Toscane. (Extr. d'une lettre à M. Élie de Beaumont.) —*C.R. Acad. Sci. xlv, pp.* 750–52. *Paris,* 1857.

DEVILLE, C. J. Sainte-Claire.—Gaz de la Salinelle de Paternò.—*Ann. Chim. Phys.* S. 3, *lii, p.* 51. *Paris,* 1858.

DEVILLE, C. J. Sainte-Claire, LEBLANC, F.—Sur la composition chimique des gaz rejetés par les évents volcaniques de l'Italie méridionale.—*Bull. Soc. géol. France,* S. 2, *xv, pp.* 310–13. *Paris,* 1858. (2e Mém.) —*C.R. Acad. Sci. xliv, pp.* 769–73. *Paris,* 1857. (1r Mém.)—*Id. xlv, pp.* 398–402. (2e Mém.)—*Ann. Chim. lii, pp.* 5–63. *Paris,* 1858.—*Journ. Pharm. S.* 3, *xxxiii, pp.* 128–32. *Paris,* 1858.—*Mém. Sav. Étrang. xvi, pp.* 225–76. *Paris,* 1862.

DEVILLE, C. J. SAINTE-CLAIRE, et GRAND-JEAN.—Analyse de la Lave de l'Etna. —*C.R. Acad. Sci. xlviii, p.* 21. *Paris,* 1859.

DEVILLE, C. J. SAINTE-CLAIRE.—Remarques à l'occasion d'une lettre de M. Longobardo relative à une récente éruption de l'Etna.—*C.R. Acad. Sci. lx, p.* 384. *Paris,* 1865.

DEVILLE, C. J. SAINTE-CLAIRE.—Réflexions à l'occasion d'une Note de M. Fouqué relative à l'éruption de l'Etna du 31 janvier 1865.—*C.R. Acad. Sci. lx, p.* 555. *Paris,* 1865.

DEVILLE, C. J. SAINTE-CLAIRE.—Remarques à l'occasion de deux lettres de M. Fouqué relatives à l'éruption de l'Etna du 31 janvier 1865.—*C.R. Acad. Sci. lx, pp.* 1140, 1189. *Paris,* 1865.

DEVILLE, C. J. SAINTE-CLAIRE.—M. Ch. Sainte-Claire Deville présente, au nom de M. Berthier, un Atlas photographique relatif à l'éruption de l'Etna.—*C.R. Acad. Sci. lx, p.* 1334. *Paris,* 1865.

DEVILLE, C. J. SAINTE-CLAIRE.—Extrait de deux lettres de M. O. Silvestri sur l'éruption de 1865.—*C.R. Acad. Sci. lxi, pp.* 212–13. *Paris,* 1865.

DEVILLE, C. J. SAINTE-CLAIRE.—Notes à une lettre de M. Fouqué relative au même phénomène.—*C.R. Acad. Sci. lxi, pp.* 423–24. *Paris,* 1865.

DEVILLE, C. J. SAINTE-CLAIRE.—Remarques à l'occasion de diverses communications de M. Fouqué concernant les phénomènes éruptifs de l'Italie Méridionale.— *C.R. Acad. Sci. lxi, pp.* 567, 737. *Paris,* 1865.

DEVILLE, C. J. SAINTE - CLAIRE. — Remarques à l'occasion d'une communication de M. Silvestri sur une éruption boueuse des salses de Paterno, en Sicile.—*C.R. Acad. Sci. lxii, p.* 648. *Paris,* 1866.

DEVILLE, C. J. SAINTE-CLAIRE.—Rapport sur un Mémoire de M. Fouqué, intitulé : Recherches sur les phénomènes chimiques des volcans.—*C.R. Acad. Sci. lxii, pp.* 1366–77. *Paris,* 1866.

DEVILLE, C. J. SAINTE - CLAIRE. — [Remarks upon FOUQUÉ, F.—Sur les phénomènes éruptifs, *etc.*]—*C.R. Acad. Sci. lxi, pp.* 567–69. *Paris,* 1865.

DEVILLE, C. J. SAINTE-CLAIRE.—*See* ÉLIE DE BEAUMONT. 1866.

DEWINT, P. (drawn by).—Catania from the West. Engraved by Cha⁵ Heath. London. Published May 1, 1821 : by Rodwell & Martin, 1, New Bond Street.
    Engraving, showing Etna in background : 275 × 186 mm., from " Sicilian Scenery," from drawings by P. Dewint. The original sketches by Major Light. [B.M.]

DEWINT, P. (drawn by).—View of Ætna. From the Theatre at Taormina. Engraved by Robᵗ Wallis, London. Published Sept. 1, 1821 : by Rodwell & Martin, New Bond Street. [B.M.]
    275 × 186 mm. *See* " Sicilian Scenery."

DEWINT, P.—View from the Capuchin Convent, at Franca Villa, looking towards Etna. Engraved by Robᵗ Wallis, London. Published Decʳ 1, 1822, by Rodwell & Martin, New Bond Street. [B.M.]
    275 × 186 mm. *See* " Sicilian Scenery."

DEWINT.—*See* LIGHT, MAJOR.—Sicilian Scenery.

DIACONO, W. P. (WARNEFRIDUS PAOLO DIACONO).—Historiæ Miscellanea.—*Basileæ,* 1569.

DICKERT, TH.—Relief à couleurs de l'Etna. (Les couleurs géologiques d'après la carte de M. Sartorius de Waltershausen.)

DIDIER, CH.—*See* NORVINS.

DIODORUS SICULUS. — Diodori Bibliothecæ Historicæ libri xv.—*fol.* (*Gr. and Lat.*) *Basileæ,* 1578.
    See Vol. iii, p. 6, Vol. xiv, p. 59 : Erupt. of 475, 425, 394 B.C.

DOGLIONI, N.—Anfiteatro d'Europa, in cui si ha la descrittione del mondo celeste, *etc., etc.*—4⁰, *with portrait, pp.* 72+1377. *Venetia,* 1623.
    See p. 993 : Dell' Ethna detto Mongibello e sua historia.

DOLOMIEU, D. G. S. T. G. DE.—Mémoire sur les Îles Ponces et catalogue raisonné des produits de l'Etna ; . . . description de l'éruption de l'Etna du mois de juillet 1787. . . . Suite au voyage aux Îles de Lipari [1788].—8⁰, 2 *pls. Paris,* 1788.—In German : 8⁰, *pp.* 4+412, 4 *pls. Leipzig,* 1789.

DOLOMIEU, D. G. 'S. T. G. DE.—Abhandlung über das Erdbeben in Calabrien im Jahre 1783.—8°, *pp.* 80. *Leipzig*, 1789.

DOLOMIEU, D. G. S. T. G. DE.—Distribution méthodique de toutes les matières dont l'accumulation forme les montagnes volcaniques.—*Journ. Phys. xliv, pp.*102–25 ; *xlv, pp.* 81–105. *Paris*, 1794.

DOMNANDO.—[Extract of a letter communicated by M. C. Prévost, dated from " Nauplie, 25 novembre 1834," describing the ascents of 'Etna and Vesuvius.]—*Bull. Soc. géol. France, vi, pp.* 124–25. *Paris*, 1835.

DRYDEN, J.—Voyage to Sicily and Malta, *etc.*—8°. *London*, 1776.

DUFOUR, A. H., et AMARI, M.—Carte comparée de la Sicile moderne avec la Sicile au XII siècle d'après Edrisi et d'autres géographes Arabes.—4°. *Paris*, 1859.

DUFRÉNOY et ÉLIE DE BEAUMONT.—Recherches sur les terrains volcaniques des Deux-Siciles, comparés à ceux de la France centrale.—*See their :* " Mém. pour servir à une descript. géol. de la France," *iv. Paris*, 1838.

DUMAS, ALEX.—*See* NORVINS.

DUPARC, L., et MRAZEC, L. — Sur quelques bombes volcaniques de l'Etna des Éruptions 1886 et 1892.—*Bibl. Univ., Arch. Sci. phys. nat. xxix, p.* 256. *Genève*, 1893.—*C.R. Acad. Sci. cxv, pp.* 529–31. *Paris*, 1892.

DURIER, C.—L'Etna.—*C.R. réun. Clubs Alpins à Genève, août* 1879. *Genève*, 1880.

E * * *, W. B.—1. A Mountain of Pumices formed in yᵉ Year 1763. 2. The Eruption wᶜʰ began on yᵉ 27 of April 1766. 3. A Mountain which fell in, while we were present on yᵉ 19ᵗʰ of June 1766, at night.
A water-colour drawing of some adventitious cones and a lava stream on Etna : 252×157 mm.

E * * *, W. B.—A letter to the late Lord Lyttelton, containing a description of the last great eruption, etc., of Mount Ætna, A.D. 1766.—8°. *London*, 1772.

EICHWALD, C. E. VON.—Beitrag zur vergleichenden Geognosie auf einer Reise durch die Eifel, Tyrol, Italien, Sicilien u. Algier.—4°, 4 *pls. Moskau*, 1851.

ELIDRIS, SHERIFF.—Descrizione della Sicilia, tradotta da Franc. Tardia.—*Opuscoli di autori Siciliani, viii, p.* 233. 1788.

ÉLIE DE BEAUMONT, J. B. A. L. L.—Recherches sur la structure et sur l'origine du Mont Etna.—*Ann. Mines, S.* 3, *ix, pp.* 175–216, 575–630, *Paris*, 1836 ; *x, pp.* 351–70, 507–76, 1836.—*C.R. Acad. Sci. i, pp.* 429–32. *Paris*, 1835.—*Mém. pr. serv. à une descript. géol. de la France* (by Dufrénoy and Élie de Beaumont), *iv, pp.* 1–226. *Paris*, 1838.—*Edinb. New Phil. Journ. xx, pp.* 185–87, 376–93. 1836.—*Froriep. Notiz. xlvii, coll.* 33–40. *Erfurt u. Weimar*, 1836.

ÉLIE DE BEAUMONT, J. B. A. L. L.—[Maps and views of Etna.]—*Ann. Mines, S.* 3, *ix, pls.* 1–5. *Paris*, 1836.
Pl. 1. Esquisse Topographique et Géologique du Mont Etna. Chartier sculp. Échelle ₁/₁₁₁₁₁.
Col. map : 395×390 mm.
Pl. 2. L'Etna vu de Lentini à 12 lieues de distance.
Lith. : 423×165 mm.
Pl. 3. Gibbosité Centrale de l'Etna. Vue des Monti Rossi à 4 lieues du grand Cratère.
Lith. : 315×220 mm.
Pl. 4. Gibbosité Centrale de l'Etna. Vue du Pont d'Alcantara.
Lith. : 474×258 mm.
Pl. 5. Gibbosité Centrale de l'Etna. Vue d'un point situé à une demi-lieue à l'E. de Zafferana (point B de la carte).
Lith. : 405×300 mm.

ÉLIE DE BEAUMONT, J. B. A. L. L.—Remarques comparatives sur les cendres de l'Etna et sur celles du volcan de la Guadeloupe.—*C.R. Acad. Sci. iv, pp.* 743–49. *Paris*, 1837.—*Froriep. Notiz. iii, coll.* 133–36. *Jena*, 1837.

ÉLIE DE BEAUMONT, J. B. A. L. L.—*See* DUFRÉNOY. 1838.

ÉLIE DE BEAUMONT, J. B. A. L. L.—Sur les émanations volcaniques et métallifères.—*Bull. Soc. géol. France, S.* 2, *iv, pp.* 1249–333. *Paris*, 1846–47.—*Edinb. New Phil. Journ. xlviii, pp.* 94–98. 1850.—*Zeitschr. deutsch. geol. Gesellsch. ii, pp.* 388–401. *Berlin*, 1849.

ÉLIE DE BEAUMONT, J. B. A. L. L.—Remarques à l'occasion d'une Lettre de M. Longobardo sur une nouvelle éruption de l'Etna, du 31 janvier 1865.—*C.R. Acad. Sci. lx, pp.* 354–55. *Paris*, 1865.

ÉLIE DE BEAUMONT, J. B. A. L. L.—Remarques à l'occasion d'une communication de M. Fouqué sur la même éruption.—*C.R. Acad. Sci. lx, p.* 556. *Paris*, 1865.

ÉLIE DE BEAUMONT, BOUSSINGAULT, DAUBRÉE, SAINTE-CLAIRE DE-VILLE.—[Rapport sur un Mémoire de M. Fouqué, intitulé : Recherches sur les phénomènes chimiques des volcans.]—*C.R. Acad. Sci. lxii, pp.* 1366-77. *Paris,* 1866.

ÉLIE DE BEAUMONT, J. B. A. L. L.—Carte du relief de l'Etna.—*École d. Mines, Paris.*

EREDIA, F.—La pioggia nella regione Etnea.—*Atti Acc. Zelanti, S.* 3, *i, pp.* 1-6. *Acireale,* 1901-2.

ERRICO, S.—Ode di Mongibello. Cited by Massa.

ESPIN, T. E.—A possible factor in volcanic eruptions.—*Publications of the Wolsingham Observatory, pp.* 10, 2 *figs. Tow Law, Darlington, Crook,* 1902.

F., C. F.—Eruzione dell' Etna in Ottobre 1832.—*Effemeridi scient. e lett. vii,* 19, *pp.* 3-7. *Palermo,* 1833.

FALB, R.—Gedanken und Studien über das Vulkanismus, mit besonderer Beziehung auf . . . die Eruption des Aetna am 29 August 1874.—8⁰. *Gratz,* 1875. *See* Cap. III, p. 46 : Der Ausbruch des Aetna am 29 August, 1874.

FALCANDUS, H.—Historia . . . de rebus gestis in Siciliæ regno.—4⁰. *Parisiis,* 1550.

FALCON (del.).—Catania. Lava del 1669. E. Rouargue sc., 99. Audot edit. Engrav. : 148×99 mm.

FAUJAS DE ST.-FOND, B.—Discours sur les Volcans brûlants.—*fol. Grenoble et Paris,* 1778.

FAUJAS DE ST.-FOND, B.—Minéralogie des Volcans, ou description de toutes les substances produites ou rejetées par les feux souterrains.—8⁰, *pp. xviii*+511, 3 *pls. Paris,* 1784.—German ed. 1786.

FAUJAS DE ST.-FOND, B.—Essai sur l'histoire naturelle des Roches de Trapp, etc.—8⁰, *foll.* 2+160. *Paris,* 1788. *See* pp. 68-71.

FAUJAS DE ST.-FOND, B.—Essai de Géologie, ou Mémoires pour servir à l'histoire naturelle du Globe.—3 tom. 8⁰. *Paris,* 1803-9. — Another ed. 1 tom. *illustr.* 8⁰. *Paris,* 1805. *See* Tom. i.

FAYE, H. A. E. A.—Sur les orages volcaniques.—*C.R. Acad. Sci. xci, pp.* 708-12. *Paris,* 1880.

FAZELLUS, T.—De Rebus Siculis decades duæ, nunc primum in lucem editæ ; his accessit totius operis index locupletissimus. —*fol., pp.* 618 *and index. Panormi, apud Joannem Matthæmum Maidam, et Franciscum Carraram,* 1558. Fine woodcut on title. Another ed. *fol. Panormi,* 1568.

FAZELLUS, T.—De Ætna monte et ejus ignibus.—*See his :* De Rebus Siculis, *Lib.* II, *Cap.* 4, *p.* 616. 1558. [C.A.]

FAZELLUS, T.—Le due deche dell' Historia di Sicilia . . . divise in venti libri, tradotte dal latino in lingua toscana dal P. M. Remigio.—4⁰, *pp.* 919 *and table. Venetia,* 1573.—*Also* 1574.

FAZELLUS, T.—De Rebus Siculis decades duæ.—*fol., pp.* 705+*index. Francofurti ad Mœnum,* 1579. *See :* Rerum Sicularum scriptores, ex recentioribus præcipui. [B.N.P.]

FAZELLUS, T.—Le due deche dell' Historia di Sicilia . . . tradotte dal latino in lingua toscana dal R. P. M. Remigio, . . . e . . . ricorrette dall' abate D. Martino Lafarina, etc.—*fol., pp. x*+625, *tab. Palermo,* 1628.

FAZELLUS, T.—De Rebus Siculis decades duæ, quarum prior . . . descriptionem, posterior vero historiam Siciliæ . . . continet. Editio de novo revisa.—*fol., coll.* 712, *index and portrait. Lugduni Batavorum,* 1723.

FAZELLUS, T.—De Rebus Siculis decas prima (secunda), criticis animadversionibus atque auctario (ab anno 1556 ad 1750) ab S.T.D.D. Vito M. Amico e Statella, . . . illustrata.—3 vols. *fol. Catanæ,* 1749-53.

FER, Sᵃ DE.—Catane et le Mont Gibel en Sicile. Paris, 1672 (?). Palerme. Capitale de la Sicile. View of Etna over Catania and another, a plan of Palermo. Engrav., each : 200× 165 mm.

FERLITO FARO, C.—Sunto delle osservazioni meteorologiche per l'anno 1837.—*Atti Acc. Gioen. xiv, pp.* 301-19. *Catania,* 1837.

FERRARA, F.—Storia generale dell' Etna, che comprende la descrizione di questa montagna : la storia delle sue eruzioni, e dei suoi fenomeni.—8⁰, *pp. xliv*+359, 5 *pls. Catania,* 1793.

FERRARA, F.—Memoria sopra il Lago Naftia nella Sicilia Meridionale, e sopra l'Ambra Siciliana.—4⁰. *Palermo*, 1805.

FERRARA, F.—I Campi Flegrei della Sicilia e delle Isole che le sono intorno.—4⁰, *pp. xix+434, 1 pl.,* 6 *maps. Messina,* 1810.

FERRARA, F.—Memoria sopra le acque della Sicilia, loro natura, analisi e usi.—*Londra*, 1811.

FERRARA, F.—[Eruption 1811.]—" *Fa per tutti." Catania,* 1812.

FERRARA, F.—Storia naturale della Sicilia, che comprende la Mineralogia.—4⁰, *pp. lxiv+159. Catania,* 1813.

FERRARA, F.—Sur la Minéralogie de la Sicile.—*Journ. Phys. lxxxv, pp.* 31–42. *Paris,* 1817.

FERRARA, F.—Descrizione dell' Etna con la storia delle eruzioni e il catalogo dei prodotti, *etc.—*8⁰, *pp. xvi+256, 5 pls. Palermo,* 1818.
This is a corrected and extended edition of his " Storia generale dell' Etna."
In French : Extr. par M. le Docteur Foderà.—*Journ. Phys. lxxxviii, pp.* 283–|89, 364–72. *Paris,* 1819.

FERRARA, F.—Guida dei viaggiatori agli oggetti più interessanti a vedersi in Sicilia.—8⁰, *pp.* 304, 8 *pls. Palermo,* 1822.
See pp. 113–18 and pl. of erupt. 1787.

FERRARA, F.—Memoria sopra i tremuoti della Sicilia in Marzo 1823.—8⁰, *foll. iv, pp.* 51, 1 *pl. Palermo,* 1823.—[Analysis in :] *Edinb. Journ. Sci. vi, pp.* 362–70. 1826. *—Amer. Journ. Sci. ix, pp.* 216–39. *New Haven,* 1825.—*Tilloch. Phil. Mag. lxv, pp.* 92–100, 168–79. *London,* 1825.

FERRARA, F.—Notices of the Geology and Mineralogy of Sicily. (Transl.)—*Amer. Journ. Sci. viii, pp.* 201–13. *New Haven,* 1824.

FERRARA, F.—Della influenza dell' aria alla sommità dell' Etna sopra l'economia animale.—*Giorn. Sci. Lett. ed Arti per la Sicilia, xxvi, pp.* 17. *Palermo,* 1825. [C.A.] *—See also* CAPOZZO, G.—Memorie sulla Sicilia, *Vol. i, pp.* 309–19.—In French : *Journ. Univ. Sci. Méd. xxxiv.*

FERRARA, F.—Storia di Catania sino alla fine del XVIII secolo.—*Catania,* 1829.

FERRARA, F.—Sopra l'eruzione dell' Etna, segnata da Orosio nell' anno 122 B.C. [1833]. *—Atti Acc. Gioen. x, pp.* 141–58. *Catania,* 1835.

FERRARA, F.—Storia generale della Sicilia. *—Palermo,* 1838.

FERRARA, F.—Volcanologia geologica della Sicilia e delle Isole che le sono intorno.— *Atti Acc. Gioen. S.* 2, *ii, pp.* 231–307. *Catania,* 1845.

FERRARA, F.—Boschi dell' Etna.—*Atti Acc. Gioen, S.* 2, *iii, pp.* 187–209. *Catania,* 1846.

FICHERA, S.—Acqua minerale di S. Venera di Acireale.—*Relaz. Acc. Sci. Lett. ed. Arti dei Zelanti di Acireale, pp.* 37–38. *Palermo,* 1836.

FINCH, H.—A true and exact relation of the late . . . earthquake and eruption of Mount Ætna, or, Monte-Gibello. . . . Together with a more particular narrative of the same, as it is collected out of severall relations sent from Catania.—4⁰, *pp.* 30, 1 *pl.* [*London*] 1669.—Other ed. : 4⁰. [*London*] 1669.—4⁰. *Edinburgh,* 1669.— *See* SOMERS, J.—A second collection of scarce and valuable tracts, *etc. Vol. iii,* 4⁰. 1750.—8⁰. *London,* 1775.—*See* SOMERS, J.—A collection of scarce . . . tracts, *etc. Vol. viii,* 4⁰. 1809, *etc.*

FIORE, O. DE.—Il periodo hawaiano dell' Etna nel 1910–1911.— *Riv. Geog. Ital. xviii,* 4, *pp.* 205–12. *Firenze,* 1911.

FIORE, O. DE.—Il periodo di riposo dell' Etna 1893–1907.—*Rend. e Mem. R. Acc. Sci. Lett. ed Arti d. Zelanti, S.* 3, *vi, pp.* 57–128. *Acireale,* 1912.

FIORE, O. DE.—*See* VINASSA DE REGNY ET ALII.

FISCHER, TH.—Das Halbinselland Italien. *—In* Kirchhoff's " Länderkunde von Europa," *pp.* 285–515. *Prag, Wien, Leipzig,* 1890.

FLEURIAU DE BELLEVUE.—Mémoire sur l'action du feu dans les volcans.— *Journ. Phys. lx, pp.* 409–70. *Paris,* 1804.

FODERA, DR.—[Extrait de la] Description de l'Etna, avec l'histoire de ses éruptions et le catalogue de leurs produits par M. l'Abbé François Ferrara.—*Journ. Phys. Chim. Hist. nat. lxxxviii, pp.* 283–89, 364–72. *Paris,* 1819.

FOERSTNER, H.—Das Gestein der Insel Ferdinandea (1831) und seine Beziehungen zu den jüngsten Laven Pantellerias und des Aetnas.—*Tschermak's min. u. petr. Mitth. N.F. v, pp.* 388–96. *Wien,* 1883.

FORBES, J. D.—Analogy of Glaciers to Lava Streams.—*Phil. Trans. R. Soc. pp.* 147–55. *London.* 1846.

FORBIN, Cᵀᴱ DE, et BIRMAN.—Vue du Cratère de l'Etna. Gravé par Newton Fielding.
Dark sepia stippled engrav.: 295 × 212 mm.

FORNARI.—*See* PAOLUCCI, D.

FOUQUÉ, F. A.—Sur l'éruption de l'Etna du 31 janvier 1865. Lettres . . . à M. Ch. Sainte-Claire Deville.—*C.R. Acad. Sci. lx, pp.* 548–55, 1135–40, 1185–89. *Paris,* 1865.

FOUQUÉ, F. A.—Sur l'éruption de l'Etna du 1er février 1865. 4me lettre . . . à M. Ch. Sainte-Claire Deville.—*C.R. Acad. Sci. lx, pp.* 1331–34 ; *lxi, pp.* 210–12. *Paris, 1865.—Archiv. Missions scient. litt. S. 2, ii, pp.* 321–57. *Paris,* 1865.—*Zeitschr. deutsch. geol. Gesellsch. xvii, pp.* 606–8. *Berlin,* 1865.

FOUQUÉ, F. A.—Sur l'éruption de l'Etna en 1865 et sur les phénomènes éruptifs de l'Italie méridionale. 5me lettre . . . à M. Ch. Sainte-Claire Deville.—*C.R. Acad. Sci. lxi, pp.* 421–24. *Paris,* 1865.

FOUQUÉ, F. A.—Ueber den Ausbruch des Aetna vom 31 Januar 1865.—*Zeitschr. deutsch. geol. Gesellsch. xvii, pp.* 606–8. *Berlin,* 1865.

FOUQUÉ, F. A.—Eruption of Etna [1865]. —*Amer. Journ. Sci. S.* 2, *xl, p.* 122. *New Haven,* 1865.—*See also* " *Les Mondes,*" 6 *avril,* 1865.

FOUQUÉ, F. A.—Recherches sur les phénomènes chimiques des volcans.—*C.R. Acad. Sci. lxii, pp.* 616–17. *Paris, 1866.—Archiv. Missions scient. litt. S.* 2, *iii, pp.* 165–246, 5 *pls. Paris,* 1866.

FOUQUÉ, F. A.—Sur la récente éruption de l'Etna (1879). Lettre à M. le Secrétaire perpétuel. — *C.R. Acad. Sci. lxxix, pp.* 33–35. *Paris, 1879.—Rev. scient. S.* 2, *xvii, p.* 45. *Paris,* 1879.

FOUQUÉ, F. A.—Santorin et ses éruptions. —4⁰, *pp. xxi*+440+*vii,* 61 *pls.* (19 *col.*). *Paris,* 1879.
See Cap. xx.

FOUQUÉ, F. A.—Conférence sur les Volcans. —8⁰, *pp.* 20. *Lille,* 1885.

FOUQUÉ, F. A.—Contribution à l'étude des Feldspaths des Roches Volcaniques.—8⁰, *pp.* 336. *Paris, 1894.—Bull. Soc. Franç. Min. xvii, pp.* 283–611. *Paris,* 1894.

FOUQUÉ, F. A.— L'Etna.—*Rev. gén. Sci. pp.* 65–81. *Paris,* 30 *janvier,* 1901.

FRAAS, E.—Vortrag über Reiseerinnerungen aus Sizilien und Sardinien.—*Jahresh. Ver. vaterl. Naturkunde in Würtemberg, liii, pp. xxxv–xxxvi. Stuttgart,* 1897.

FRANCIS, J. G.—Notes from a Journal kept in Sicily and Italy.—8⁰, *num. views. London,* 1847.

FRANCO, L.—*See* RICCÒ, A. 1900.

FRANCO, S. DI.—L'Herschelite déi Basalti Siciliani.—*Atti Acc. Gioen. S.* 4, *xv, Mem.* 3, *pp.* 13, 1 *tav. Catania, 1902.—N. J. f. Min. i, p.* 363. *Stuttgart,* 1904.

FRANCO, S. DI.—Studio cristallografico sull' Ematite dell' Etna.—*Boll. Acc. Gioen. lxxiv, pp.* 18–19. *Catania, 1902.—Id. Atti, S.* 4, *xvii, Mem.* 1, *pp.* 16, 2 *tav. Catania,* 1904.

FRANCO, S. DI.—La Gmelinite di Aci Castello.—*Atti R. Acc. Lincei, S.* 5, *Rend. xiii, sem.* 1, *pp.* 640–42, *figs. Catania, 1904.— Riv. Min. e Crist. Ital. xxxii, pp.* 7–9, *figs. Padova,* 1905.

FRANCO, S. DI.—La Phakolite dell' Isola dei Ciclopi.—*Boll. Acc. Gioen. lxxxiii, pp.* 7–10. *Catania,* 1905.

FRANCO, S. DI.—Le Inclusioni nel Basalte dell' Isola dei Ciclopi.—Note preventiva.— —*Boll. Acc. Gioen. lxxxiv, pp.* 17–18. *Catania,* 1905.

FRANCO, S. DI.—Gli Inclusi nel Basalto dell' Isola dei Ciclopi.—*Atti Acc. Gioen. S.* 4, *xix, Mem.* 18, *pp.* 8, 1 *tav. Catania,* 1906.

FRANCO, S. DI.—La Tenorite dell' Etna.— *Atti Acc. Gioen. S.* 5, *iii, Mem.* 8, *pp.* 5, 1 *tav. Catania,* 1910.

FRANCO, S. DI.—Le Lave ad Orneblenda dell' Etna.—*Atti Acc.Gioen. S.* 5, *iv, Mem.* 3, *pp.* 12, 2 *tav. Catania,* 1911.

FRANCO, S. DI.—Struttura columnare della lava Etnea nella valle dell' Alcantara.— *Boll. Soc. Geol. Ital. xxix, pp. cxxv–cxxvi. Roma,* 1911.

FRANCO, S. DI.—Gli Inclusi nella Lava Etnea di Rocca S. Paolo presso Paternò.— *Atti R. Acc. Lincei, S.* 5, *Rend. xxi, sem.* 2, *pp.* 249–56, *pls. i–ii. Catania,* 1912.

FRANKLYN, Dr.—On the Eruption of Mount Etna. MS. 1809.

FREDA, G.—Sulla crisocolla dei Monti Rossi all' Etna.—*Gaz. Chim. Ital. xiv, pp.* 339–40. *Palermo,* 1885.

FRESENIUS, W.—Der Phillipsit von Aci Castello in Sicilien.—*Zeitschr. f. Kryst. iii, pp.* 52–54. *Leipzig,* 1879.

FRIDRICH (sc.), HAFN.—Aetna's Crater 1785.
    Engrav. with two men in cloaks in foreground : 210×140 mm.

FRIEDLAENDER, E.—Ueber die Kleinformen der vulkanischen Produkte.—*Zeitschr. f. Vulk. i,* 2. *Berlin, Mai,* 1914.
    See Taf. xxiv, fig. 22 ; Taf. xxv, fig. 24 ; Taf. xxvi, fig. 26 ; Taf. xxvii, fig. 30 ; Taf. xxviii, fig. 31 ; Taf. xxxi, fig. 37.

FROMONDUS LIBERTUS.—Meteorologia, eorum Libr. VI. I, I, cap. II.—*Antwerpen,* 1627.
    Cited by Massa, Etna.

FUCHS, C. W. C., u. GRAEBE, C.—Die Lava der Aetna-Eruption des Jahres 1865. —*N. J. f. Min. pp.* 711–15. *Stuttgart,* 1865.

FUCHS, C. W. C.—Die vulkanischen Erscheinungen der Erde.—8⁰, *pp. viii*+582, 2 *pls., figs. Leipzig u. Heidelberg,* 1865.

FUCHS, C. W. C.—Die vulkanischen Erscheinungen im Jahre 1865 [*etc.* to 1885].— *N. J. f. Min.* 1866 [*to* 1872].—*Tschermak's min. petr. Mitth.* 1873 [*to* 1887].

FUCHS, C. W. C.—[Aetna Ausbruch 27 Nov. 1868.]—*N. J. f. Min. pp.* 694–95. *Stuttgart,* 1869.

FUCHS, C. W. C.—Vulkane und Erdbeben. —*Internat. wissensch. Biblioth. xvii, pp.* 269–71, 1 *map, figs. Leipzig,* 1873.—8⁰, *pp. xii*+343, 1 *map col., figs. Leipzig,* 1875.
    See p. 274.
    In French : 8⁰, *pp. viii*+279, *fig., map. Paris,* 1876.——2nd ed. 1878.
    See p. 217, 1876.
    In Italian : 8⁰. *Milano,* 1881.

FULCHER, L. W.—A Visit to the Lipari Islands and Mount Etna.—*Journ. City of Lond. Coll. Sci. Soc.* 16, *pp.* 9. *April,* 1890.

GAETANI, G. De.—Sopra l'acqua minerale solforosa del Pozzo di S. Venera.—*Atti Acc. Gioen. xvi, pp.* 35–48. *Catania,* 1841.

GAETANI, G. De.—Analisi fisico-chimica sopra l'Acqua Santa (acqua minerale presso Catania).—*Atti Acc. Gioen. xvi, pp.* 89–106. *Catania,* 1841.

GAETANI, G. De.—Sulla analisi fisicochimica e proprietà mediche dell' Acqua Acidola della Valle di S. Giacomo.—*Atti Acc. Gioen. xvi, pp.* 381–95. *Catania,* 1841.

GAETANI, G. De.—Intorno alle Acque Solforose del Pozzo di S. Venera. Nuove Osservazioni.—*Atti Acc. Gioen. xx, pp.* 187-222. *Catania,* 1843.

GAETANI, G. De.—*See* CASTORINA, P. Di-G.

GALANTI, G. M.—Della descrizione geografica e politica delle Sicilie.—4 tom. 8⁰. *Napoli,* 1793–94.—German transl. by C. J. Jagemann, 8⁰. *Leipzig,* 1795.

GALDIERI, A.—Fiori, insetti e fumarole. Nota.—*Boll. Soc. Nat. xxvi (S. 2, vi), Atti, pp.* 39–43. *Napoli,* 1914.

GALLIANO, D.—Liste des éruptions de l'Etna. —[*Extr.*] HOUEL, J. — Voyage Pittoresque des Isles de Sicile, de Malte et de Lipari, *T. ii, pp.* 115–20. *Paris,* 1782– 87.

GALLO, A.—Lettera per li terremoti del 1783, con un giornale meteorologico de' medesimi. Aggiuntasi anche la relazione di qui di Calabria con li paesi distrutti ed il numero dei morti.—*Messina,* 1784.

GALVAGNI, G. A.—Sopra una Malattia endemica che stanzia nei contorni dell' Etna.—*Atti Acc. Gioen. xi, pp.* 129–76. *Catania,* 1836.

GALVAGNI, G. A.—Fauna Etnea.—*Atti Acc. Gioen. xii, pp.* 25–57, 377–411 ; *xiii, pp.* 163–205 ; *xiv, pp.* 137–77, 241–300 ; *xvi, pp.* 107–30 ; *xvii, pp.* 239–53 ; *xix, pp.* 243–59 ; *xx, pp.* 165–85. *Catania,* 1837-43.

GALVAGNI, G. A.—Sopra un nuovo fenomeno sonoro accaduto sul sommo giogo dell' Etna.—*Atti Acc. Gioen. xii, pp.* 325- 32. *Catania,* 1837.

GALVAGNI, G. A.—Storia naturale fisiologica e medica del villagese dell' Etna.— *Atti Acc. Gioen. xiii, pp.* 75–113 ; *xv, pp.* 121–85. *Catania,* 1839.

GALVAGNI, G. A.—Memorie di Geografia Fisico-Medica sulle principali acque stagnanti di Sicilia. Memoria Prima : Delle Acque Stagnanti dei contorni dell' Etna e

Y

della piana di Catania.—*Atti Acc. Gioen. xiv, pp.* 65–85. *Catania,* 1839.

GALVAGNI, G. A.—Elogio di Mario Gemmellaro.—*Atti Acc. Gioen. xvi, pp.* 17–47. *Catania,* 1841.
Treats of his writings upon Etna, etc.

GALVAGNI, G. A.—Saggio di geografia medica per la Sicilia.—Mem. IV. Sopra una nuova malattia endemica dell' Etna.—*Atti Acc. Gioen. S.* 2, *x, pp.* 231–64. *Catania,* 1854.

GATTA, L.—L'Italia, sua formazione suoi vulcani e terremoti.—8°, *pp.* 539, 32 *figs.,* 3 *maps. Milano,* 1882.—*Boll. R. Com. Geol. Ital. notiz. bibliog. pp.* 102–4.—*Roma,* 1882.

GATTA, L.—Vulcanismo.—16°, *pp.* 267, *figs. Milano,* 1885.

GAUTIER, A.—La Genèse des Eaux Thermales et ses rapports avec le Volcanisme.—[Extr.] *Ann. Mines, S.* 10, *ix, pp.* 316–70. *Paris,* 1906.

GAUTIER, A.—L'Intervention et le rôle de l'Eau dans les phénomènes volcaniques.—8°, *pp.* 20. *Paris,* 1909.

GEIKIE, A.—Text-book of Geology.—8°, *pp.* 971, 434 *figs. London,* 1882.
See Book III, Pt. 1.
2nd ed. *London,* 1885. —— 3rd ed. *London,* 1893.

GELLIUS, AULUS.—[Noctes Atticæ.]—*Lib. xvii, Cap.* 10.

GEMMA, F.—L'Incendio di Mongibello del 1669. Poema in cento stanze.—8°, *pp.* 50. *Catania,* 1674.

GEMMELLARO, CARLO. — Giornale dell' eruzione dell' Etna avvenuta alli 27 Maggio 1819.—*pp.* 30, 5 *pls. Catania,* 1819.

GEMMELLARO, C.—Sopra alcuni pezzi di granito e di lava antica trovati presso la cima dell' Etna.—*Catania,* 1823.

GEMMELLARO, C. — Descrizione orittognostica di alcuni pezzi di granito e di lavo rinvenuti presso la cima dell' Etna nel piano del lago vicino al Ciglioni de Balzo del Trifoglietto.—*Giorn. Fis. Chim. Stor. Nat. vii, pp.* 109–13. *Pavia,* 1824.—*Giorn. Arcad. xxiv, pp.* 284–86. *Roma,* 1824.

GEMMELLARO, C.—Prospetto d'una topografia fisica dell' Etna e suoi contorni.—*Atti Acc. Gioen. i, pp.* 19–34. *Catania,* 1825.

GEMMELLARO, C.—Memoria sopra le condizioni geologiche del tratto terrestre dell' Etna.—*Atti Acc. Gioen. i, pp.* 183–211. *Catania,* 1825.

GEMMELLARO, C.—Rapport sur l'éruption de l'Etna du 27 mai 1819.—*Bull. Sci. Nat. ix, pp.* 151–52. *Paris,* 1826.—*Quart. Journ. Sci. xix, pp.* 227–34. *London,* 1825.

GEMMELLARO, C.—Sopra il Basalto e gli effetti della sua decomposizione naturale.—*Atti Acc. Gioen. ii, pp.* 49–66. *Catania,* 1827.

GEMMELLARO, C.—Extrait d'un mémoire géologique sur le terrain occupé par l'Etna.—*Bull. Sci. Nat. xvi, pp.* 374–78, *Paris,* 1829.

GEMMELLARO, C.—[Ueber Basalt u. basaltische Lava.]—*N. J. f. Min. pp.* 246–49. *Stuttgart,* 1830.

GEMMELLARO, C.—Cenno sulla vegetazione di alcune Piante e varie altezze del cono dell' Etna [1827].—*Atti Acc. Gioen. iv, pp.* 77–86. *Catania,* 1830.

GEMMELLARO, C.—Sopra il confine marittimo dell' Etna [1828].—*Atti Acc. Gioen. iv, pp.* 179–93. *Catania,* 1830.

GEMMELLARO, C.—Sopra la fisionomia delle montagne di Sicilia [1828].—*Atti Acc. Gioen. v, pp.* 73–93. *Catania,* 1831.

GEMMELLARO, C.—Relazione accademica per l'anno VII dell' Accademia Gioenia, letta nella seduta ordinaria dei 12 Maggio 1831.—8°, *p.* 29. *Catania,* 1831.
Etna, eruption of 1494.

GEMMELLARO, C.—Sui vulcani di Sicilia ed Isole vicine.—*Catania,* 1831.

GEMMELLARO, C.—Sopra un masso di lava dell' Etna corroso dalle acque marine.—*Atti Acc. Gioen. vi, pp.* 71–83. *Catania,* 1832.—*N. J. f. Min. pp.* 64–69. *Stuttgart,* 1832.

GEMMELLARO, C.—Saggio sopra il clima di Catania, abbozzato dietro un decennio di osservazioni meteorologiche [1830].—*Atti Acc. Gioen. vi, pp.* 133–75. *Catania,* 1832.

GEMMELLARO, C.—[Aetna-Eruption 31 Oct. 1832.]—*N. J. f. Min. pp.* 182–84. *Stuttgart,* 1833.

GEMMELLARO, C.—Alcuni fenomeni osservati all' eruzione del 31 Ottobre 1832. Oratio habita in Physicorum Congressu Stuttgardiæ, 1834.
This is the original of the following.

GEMMELLARO, C.—Uber einige, bei dem Ausbruche des Aetna am 31 Oktober 1832 beobachtete, Phänomene. (Transl.)— *N. J. f. Min. pp.* 641–62. *Stuttgart*, 1833.

GEMMELLARO, C.—Descrizione di una nuova tavola geologica di Sicilia.—*Poligrafo, N.S. iv, pp.* 68–75. *Verona*, 1834.— *Bull. Soc. géol. France, vi, p.* 14. *Paris*, 1834–35.

GEMMELLARO, C.—De Vallis de Bove in Monte Ætna geognostica constitutione.— *Atti Acc. Gioen. xi, pp.* 351–59. *Catania*, 1836.

GEMMELLARO, C.—Sulla costituzione fisica della Valle del Bove.—*Atti Acc. Gioen. xii, pp.* 163–81. *Catania*, 1837.—*Isis, coll.* 177–81. *Jena*, 1836.

GEMMELLARO, C.—Sopra il terreno giurassico di Sicilia. Memoria prima sul terreno giurassico di Tauromina.—*Atti Acc. Gioen. xii, pp.* 353–75. *Catania*, 1837.—*Congrès scient. France, pp.* 368–71. *Metz*, 1837. Speaks of Etna and its lavas.

GEMMELLARO, C.—[Aetna-Eruption 1838.] —*N. J. f. Min. pp.* 531–32. *Stuttgart*, 1838.

GEMMELLARO, C.—Cenno sull' attuale eruzione dell' Etna.—8°, *pp.* 37. *Catania*, 1838.

GEMMELLARO, C.—Cenno geologico sul terreno della piana di Catania.—*Atti Acc. Gioen. xiii, pp.* 117–31. *Catania*, 1839.

GEMMELLARO, C.—Sulla causa geognostica della fertilità di Sicilia.—*Atti Acc. Gioen. xiv, pp.* 71–80. *Catania*, 1839.

GEMMELLARO, C.—Elementi di Geologia. —*Catania*, 1840.

GEMMELLARO, C.—Sulla varietà di superficie nelle correnti vulcaniche.—*Atti Acc. Gioen. xix, pp.* 173–98. *Catania*, 1842.

GEMMELLARO, C.—Cenno storico sulla eruzione dell' Etna del 27 Novembre 1842. —*Atti Acc. Gioen. xix, pp.* 227–42. *Catania*, 1842.

GEMMELLARO, C.—Sulla eruzione del 17 Novembre 1843.—*Atti Acc. Gioen. xx, pp.* 225–57. *Catania*, 1843.

GEMMELLARO, C.—[Aetna-Eruption 1843.] —*N. J. f. Min. pp.* 180–81. *Stuttgart*, 1844.

GEMMELLARO, C.—Détails sur l'éruption de l'Etna en novembre 1843. (Transl.)— —*L'Institut, xii, pp.* 286–87. *Paris*, 1844.

GEMMELLARO, C.—Sulla costa marittima meridionale del Golfo di Catania.—*Atti Acc. Gioen. S.* 2, ii, *pp.* 67–79. *Catania*, 1845.

GEMMELLARO, C.—Sul Basalto decomposto dell' isola de' Ciclopi.—*Atti Acc. Gioen. S.* 2, ii, *pp.* 311–19. *Catania*, 1845.

GEMMELLARO, C.—Memoria intorno all' Etna ed alla costa di Aci.—*Atti Sett. Adun. Scienz. Ital. pp.* 1112–13. *Napoli*, 1846.

GEMMELLARO, C.—Memoria intorno al Basalte degli scogli de' Ciclopi in Catania.— *Atti Sett. Adun. Scienz. Ital. pp.* 1149–50. *Napoli*, 1846.

GEMMELLARO, C.—Sui crateri di sollevamento e di eruzione.—*Atti Acc. Gioen. S.* 2, iii, *pp.* 109–33, 1 *pl. Catania*, 1846.

GEMMELLARO, C.—Saggio sulla costituzione fisica dell' Etna.—*Atti Acc. Gioen. S.* 2, iii, *pp.* 347–409. *Catania*, 1846.

GEMMELLARO, C.—Saggio di storia fisica di Catania.—*Atti Acc. Gioen. S.* 2, v, *pp.* 91–268. *Catania*, 1848.

GEMMELLARO, C.—Sunto del giornale della eruzione dell' Etna del 1852.—*Atti Acc. Gioen. S.* 2, ix, *pp.* 115–41, *map. Catania*, 1854.

GEMMELLARO, C.—Breve ragguaglio della eruzione dell' Etna del 21 Agosto 1852 [1853].—*Atti Acc. Gioen. S.* 2, ix (*suppl.*), *pp.* i–xxx, 3 *pls. Catania*, 1854.

GEMMELLARO, C.—Una corsa intorno all' Etna in Ottobre [1853].—*Atti Acc. Gioen. S.* 2, x, *pp.* 53–72. *Catania*, 1854.

GEMMELLARO, C.—Sulla struttura del cono de' Monti Rossi e de' suoi materiali.— *Atti Acc. Gioen. S.* 2, xi, *pp.* 57–76. *Catania*, 1855.

GEMMELLARO, C.—La Vulcanologia dell' Etna che comprende la topografia, la geologia, la storia delle sue eruzioni, non che la descrizione e lo esame de' fenomeni vulcanici [1857].—4°, *pp.* xiv+266, 1 *map*, 2 *pls. Catania*, 1858. [C.A.]—*Atti Gioen. S.* 2, xiv, *pp.* 183–349, 1859 ; xv, *pp.* 27–140, 1 *map.* 2 *tav., Catania*, 1860.

GEMMELLARO, C.—Sul profondamento del suolo nel cratere dell' Etna [1857].—*Atti Acc. Gioen. S.* 2, xiv, *pp.* 149–60. *Catania*, 1859.

GEMMELLARO, C.—Ulteriori considerazioni sul Basalto in appendice alla volcanologia dell' Etna.—*Atti Acc. Gioen. S.* 2, xvi, *pp.* 149–72. *Catania*, 1860.

GEMMELLARO, C.—Dell' Eruzione dell' Etna 1863.—*Catania*, 1863.

GEMMELLARO, C.—Sulla cima dell' Etna considerata sotto il rapporto dell' utile che appresta al viaggiatore istruito e allo scienziato [1863].—*Atti Acc. Gioenia, S. 2, xix, pp.* 223-33. *Catania*, 1864.

GEMMELLARO, C.—Breve ragguaglio della eruzione dell' Etna negli ultimi di Gennaio 1865.—*Catania*, 1865.

GEMMELLARO, C.—Un' addio al maggior vulcano di Europa.—*Catania*, 1866.—2ª ed. con aggiunte. *Catania*, 1866.

GEMMELLARO, GAETANO GIORGIO.—Sui modelli esterni della Quercia in contrada Pinitella sull' Etna. Lettera al Prof. Guiscardi.—*Giorn. Gab. Lett. Acc. Gioen. Fasc.* 6º, *pp.* 6. *Nov.-Dic.* 1858. [C.A.]

GEMMELLARO, G. G.— Nota sul Ferro oligisto di Monte Corvo su l'Etna.— *Atti Acc. Gioen. S. 2, xiv, pp.* 105-12. *Catania*, 1859.

GEMMELLARO, G. G.—On the volcanic cones of Paternò and Motta (S. Anastasia) Etna.—*Quart. Journ. Geol. Soc. xviii, Proc. pp.* 20-24. *London*, 1862.

GEMMELLARO, G. G. — *See* COMMISSIONE GOVERNATIVA.

GEMMELLARO, GIUSEPPE.—Quadro istorico topografico delle eruzioni dell' Etna.— *fol.* 1. *Catania*, 1824.—*London*, 1828.

GEMMELLARO, G. — Sunto del giornale dell' eruzione dell' Etna nel 1852 [1853]. —*Atti Acc. Gioen. S. 2, ix, pp.* 113-41. *Catania*, 1854.

GEMMELLARO, MARIO. — Memoria dell' eruzione dell' Etna nel 1809.—8º. *Messina*, 1809.——2ª ed. *pp.* 41, 1 *pl. Catania*, 1820.

GEMMELLARO, M.—Tavole sinottiche dell' Etna.—8º. *Catania*, 1811.

GEMMELLARO, M.—Giornale dell' eruzione dell' Etna avvenuta al 27 Maggio 1819. —*Catania*, 1819.

GEMMELLARO, M.—Giornale dell' eruzione dell' Etna avvenuta a 27 Ottobre 1811.— MS. *with appendix.*

GEMMELLARO, M.—Curiosi venuti all' Etna. (Number of visitors to the Casa Inglese.)—Auto. MS. *fol., no date.*

GEMMELLARO, M.—Extrait d'un Journal tenu à Catane pendant quatorze ans.— MS. copy, *foll. ii.* [C.A.]

GEMMELLARO, M.—Registro di osservazioni.—*See* GEMMELLARO, C.—La Vulcanologia dell' Etna. 1858.

GEMMELLARO, RAIMONDO.—Manoscritto sulla eruzione del 1766 con appendice.

GENTILE-CUSA, B.—Sulla eruzione dell' Etna di Maggio-Giugno 1886.—8º, *foll. ii, pp.* 210, 2 *plans,* 7 *pls.,* 9 *figs. Catania*, 1886.

GEREMIA, G.—Vertunno Etneo ovvero stasulegrafia storia delle varietà delle uve che trovansi nel d'intorno dell' Etna.— *Atti Acc. Gioen. x, pp.* 201-21, 1835 ; *xi, pp.* 313-40, 1836 ; *xiv,* 2, *pp.* 3-68, *Catania*, 1839.

GHIGI, I. B.—Nuova carta della Sicilia. Fogli I-IV.—*Roma*, 1779.

GIACOMO, A. DI.—Idrologia generale dell' Etna. Discorso per servire d'introduzione allo studio delle acque minerali di quella regione [1832].—*Atti Acc. Gioen. ix, pp.* 23-40. *Catania*, 1835.

GIACOMO, A. DI.—Relazione accademica per l'anno XIII.—*Atti Acc. Gioen. xiv, pp.* 3-39. *Catania*, 1839. *See* pp. 5-9.

GIANNETTASIIS, N. P.—Æstates Surrentinæ.—12º, *foll.* 6, *pp.* 280, *frontisp. Neapoli*, 1696.

GIARDINA, F. S.—Note di geografia Siciliana, con rilievi e schizzi cartografici (fasc. 1-11).—*Catania*, 1899.

GIARDINA, F. S.—La Sicilia.—*In* MARINELLI, G.—" La Terra, trattato popolare di Geografia Universale," *Vol. iv,* Italia, *Pte.* 2 : Etna, *Cap.* XV, *pp.* 1426-37.

GIMMA, G.—Fisica sotterranea.—2 vols. *Napoli*, 1730.

GIOENI, C.—Relazione di una nuova Pioggia, scritta dal Conte de Gioeni abitante della 3ª Reggione dell' Etna ; communicated by Sir William Hamilton, K.B., F.R.S.—*Phil. Trans. R. Soc. lxxii, pp.* 1-7. *London*, 1782.—*Opusc. Scelt. Sci. Arti, viii. Milano*, 1785.

GIOENI, G.—Relazione dell' eruzione dell' Etna avvenuta nel Luglio del 1787. Scritta d. C. G. G. abitante della prima regione del monte.—*Catania*, 1787.—*See also* DOLOMIEU.—Mém. s. les Îles Ponces et Catalogue raisonné, *etc.* 1789.

GIOENI, S.—Alcune lettere di uomini illustri nella storia naturale dirette al Cav. G. Gioeni. Aggiuntavi la descrizione data dall' ab. Spallanzani del Gabinetto di St. Nat. Siciliana in casa del medesimo Gioeni. —*4⁰, foll. iii, pp.* 41. *Catania*, 1815. [C.A.]

GIOVANNOZZI, G.—Vulcanologia.—*Ann. Scient. Industr. xxxvi* (1899), *pp.* 31–33. *Milano*, 1900.

GIUFFRIDA, A.—Quaesita medica.—*Catania*, 1753.
With notes on the mineral waters of Paternò.

GIULIANI, G. B.—*See* NAUDÉ, G. 1632.

GIUSTI, G.—Lettera intorno all' ultima eruzione (1819) dell' Etna.—*Giorn. Enciclop., Fasc. vii. Napoli*, 1819.

GIUSTI, G.—Lettre à M. Monticelli sur la dernière éruption de l'Etna.—*Bull. Sci. Nat. iii, pp.* 159–60. *Paris*, 1824.

GOLDICUTT, J. (drawn by).—Mount Etna. Etched by Pinelli.
An outline engrav. with woman on donkey, man and a shepherd with sheep in foreground : 332×242 mm.

GOLZIUS, H.—De vita rebusque gestis regum Siciliæ.—Pars II.—*See* GRÆVIUS, J. G.—Thes. script. Sic. *viii, p.* 1144.

GOOD, J. M.—*See* POLEHAMPTON, E.

GORINI, P.—Sull' origine dei Vulcani.—*8⁰, pp. xxiv+*694. *Lodi*, 1871.—*8⁰. Napoli*, 1872.

GOSSA, A.—[Sur la cendre et la lave de la récente éruption de l'Etna.]—*Rev. scient. S.* 2, *xvii, p.* 45. *Paris*, 1879.

GOSSELET, J. A. A.—Observations géologiques faites en Italie.—*Mém. Soc. Imp. Sci. Agric. Lille, S.* 3, *vi, pp.* 417–75, 7 *pls. Lille*, 1869.
See N⁰ III : Etna.

GOURBILLON, J. A. DE.—Voyage critique à l'Etna en 1819.—2 vols. 8⁰, *engraved title. Vol. i, pp.* 1+541, 1 *pl.; Vol. ii, pp.* 1+ 463, 1 *pl. Paris*, 1820.

GOURBILLON, J. A. DE.—Travels in Sicily and to Mount Etna in 1819.—16⁰, *pp.* 112, 3 *pls.*, 1 *fig. London*, 1820.

GOUTOULAS, J.—Universalis historia profana a Christo nato ad annum 1640, *etc.*— 2 vols. *fol. Parisiis*, 1653–59.
See Dec. IV, Sect. 14, Dec. VI, Sect. 12.

GRAEBE, C.—*See* FUCHS, C. W. C. 1865.

GRÆVIUS, J. G.—Thesaurus Antiquitatum et Historiarum Siciliæ, *etc.*—15 vols. *fol.* —*See Tom. x of his :* "Thes. Antiq. et Hist. Italiæ." *Lugduni Batavorum*, 1725–4– 25.
Also cited as "Thesaurus scriptorum Siciliæ," *etc.* (Cura P. Burmanni), and as "Thesaurus Siculus."

GRANDJEAN. — *See* DEVILLE, C. J. SAINTE-CLAIRE. 1859.

GRASSI, M.—Relazione storica ed osservazioni sulla eruzione dell' Etna del 1865 e sui terremoti flegrei che la seguirono.—8⁰, *pp.* 92. *Catania*, 1865.

GRASSI, M.—Relation historique de l'éruption de l'Etna en 1865.—*Bull. Soc. géog. S.* 5, *xii, pp.* 5–29. *Paris*, 1866. [C.A.]

GRASSI, M.—Relazione dell' eruzione dell' Etna nel Novembre e Dicembre 1868.—*Il Nuovo Cimento, S.* 2, *i, pp.* 186–91. *Pisa*, 1869.
Translated by J. Roth, *q.v.*

GRASSI, M.—Ueber den jüngsten Ausbruch des Aetna (25 Sept. 1869).—*Verh. Geol. pp.* 289–90. *Wien*, 1869.

GRASSI, M.—Ueber die Ausbrüche des Aetna im November und December 1868.— *Zeitschr. deutsch. geol. Gesellsch. xxii, pp.* 189–90. *Berlin*, 1870.

GRASSI, M.—Sull' eruzione dell' Etna del 1879.—*Giorn. d. Sicilia,* 154. *Palermo,* 7 *Giugno*, 1879.

GRASSO, A.—Li spaventosi incendi di Mongibello scampati dalla città di Catania per la protezione della sua beata concittadina S. Agata.—8⁰. *Venezia*, 1670.

GRAVINA, C. (PRINCIPE DI VALSAVOYA).— Poesie. Sonetto per la eruzione dell' Etna del 1832.—12⁰, *pp.* 72. *Catania*.

GRAVINA, M. B.—Notes sur les terrains tertiaires et quaternaires des environs de Catane.—*Bull. Soc. géol. France, S.* 2, *xv, pp.* 391–421. *Paris*, 1859.

GREGORI, A.—*See* MANTOVANI. 1879.

GREGORI SANCTI PAPÆ. — I. Dialog.— *Lib.* IV, *Cap.* 30, *n⁰* 35.

GREGORIO, A. DE.—Una Gita sulle Madonie e sull' Etna.— *Boll. Club Alp. Ital.* 48, *pp.* 38. *Torino*, 1882.

GREGORIO, G. DI.—Lettera sulle acque acidoledi Paternò.—*Opusc. di Aut. Siciliani, iii,* 269. *Palermo*, 1788.

GREGORIO, R.—Storia delle eruzioni del Mongibello.—*See his* " Discorsi sulla Sicilia," *Vol. i, pp.* 47–54. *Palermo,* 1821.

GREVTER, M.—Regno di Sicilia.—*Venecia,* 1657. — *Also* " nuouamente ristampata, riuista et augmentata da Domenico de Rossi Herede di Gio. Giacomo de Rossi . . . l'anno 1695."

GRISEBACH, A. H. R.—La Végétation du Globe . . . Ouvrage traduit de l'allemand par P. de Tchihatchef.—2 tom. 8⁰. *Paris,* 1877–78.
See Tom. i, pp. 466–67.

GROSSO, D. J. B. DE.—Catana sacra.—*Cataniæ,* 1654.
Eruption of 1654.

GROSSO, D. J. B. DE.—Catanense decachordum sive novissima sacræ Catanensis Ecclesiæ notitia.—*See* GRÆVIUS, J. G.— *Thes. Sic. x. Cataniæ,* 1654.

GROSSO, D. J. B. DE.—Agatha catanensis. —*Cataniæ,* 1656.
Eruption of 1656.

GSELL FELS, TH.—Sicilien aus Meyers Reisehandbüchern. Cap. XVIII. Etna.— *Leipzig,* 1877.
Short, detailed description of Etna and its eruptions, with a history of the latter.

GUALTERIUS, G.—Siciliæ objacent, insularum et Brutiorum antiq. tabulæ.— *Messanæ,* 1664.

GUARNERII, G. B.—Le Zolle narrationi storiche Catanesi.—3 tom. *Catania,* 1651. —Reprinted in Latin in GRÆVIUS, J. G. —Thes. antiq. Sic.
Cited by Massa, Etna.

GUARNERII, G. B.—Dissertationes historicæ Catanenses.—*See* GRÆVIUS, J. G. —Thes. antiq. Sic. XI.

GUEMBEL, C. W. VON.—Ueber das Eruptionsmaterial des Schlammvulkanes von Paternò am Aetna und der Schlammvulkane im Allgemeinen.—8⁰. *Wien,* 1879.— *Sitzber. Bayr. Akad. Wiss. ix, pp.* 217–37. *München,* 1879.—[Abstr.] *Boll. R. Com. Geol. Ital. x, pp.* 506–30, 561–66. *Roma,* 1879.

GUEMBEL, C. W. VON.—Vulkanische Asche des Aetna von 1879.—*N. J. f. Min. i, pp.* 859–61. *Stuttgart,* 1879. — [Abstr.] *Boll. R. Com. Geol. Ital. x, pp.* 605–8. *Roma,* 1879.

GUGLIELMINI, D.—Catania distrutta dal terremoto nel 1693.—*Palermo,* 1695.

GUIDO, V. A. DI PATERNÒ.—Breve istorica descrizione del portentoso miracolo della gloriosa vergine e martire Santa Barbara, principale patrona della fedelissima città di Paternò, operato al 27 Maggio dell' anno 1780. Della liberazione del feudo di Villabona o sia Ragalna dall' incendio di Mongibello.—*Catania,* 1785.

GULLI, S.—Ricerche sulla profondità dei Vulcani.—*Atti Acc. Gioen. xi, pp.* 39–57. *Catania,* 1836.

GUSTANAVILLA, P. DE.—Notæ in Petrum Blesensem.   .·
Cited by Massa, Etna.

GUZZANTI, C.—A proposito dei terremoti Etnei.—" *Corriere di Catania,*" *an. xvi,* 247. *Catania,* 21 *Agosto* 1894.

G. W. M. D.—Philosophische und in der Natur gegründete Abhandlung des physikalischen Problematis : Woher dem Meere seine Saltzigkeit entstehe ? Wobey zugleich eine kurtze Nachricht von dem Ursprunge, der Natur und Nahrung der drei feuerspeyenden Berge Hecla, Vesuvius und Aethna gegeben wird, von einem curieusen Besitzer der natürlichen Wissenschaften.— 8⁰, *pp.* 86. *Gothenburg,* 1737.

HAAS, H. J.—Unterirdische Gluten. Die Natur und das Wesen der Feuerberge im Lichte der neuesten Anschauungen für die Gebildeten aller Stände in gemeinverständlicher Weise dargestellt. 2te. Auflage.— 8⁰, *pp.* 316, *fig. and pl. Berlin,* 1912.

HAFN.—*See* FRIDRICH, sc.   ʼ

HAMILTON, SIR W. — Observations on Mount Vesuvius, Mount Etna, and other Volcanos : In a series of letters, addressed to the Royal Society . . . to which are added Explanatory Notes by the Author, hitherto unpublished.—*Trans. R. Soc. lvii-lxi. London,* 1768–72.—8⁰, *pp. iv+*179, 6 *pls. London,* 1772.——2nd ed. 8⁰. *London,* 1773.——3rd ed. *London,* 1774. ——4th ed. *London,* 1783.

HAMILTON, SIR W.—Account of a Journey to Mount Etna in a letter . . . to Mathew Maty.—*Phil. Trans. R. Soc. lx, pp.* 1–20. *London,* 1771.—*Phil. Trans. R. Soc. Abridged, xiii, pp.* 1–7. *London,* 1809.

HAMILTON, Sir W.—Voyage au Mont Ethna, et observations par M. H., *etc.* [Transl. from " Account of a journey to Mount Etna."]—12⁰. 1773. [B.M. 10130. bb. 15.]

HAMILTON, Sir W.—Beobachtungen über den Vesuv, den Aetna und andere Vulkane ; in einer Reihe von Briefen an die Königl. Grossbr. Gesellsch. der Wissenschaften, etc. nebst neuen erläuternden Anmerkungen des Herrn Verfassers und mit Kupfern. Aus dem Englischen.—12⁰, *pp.* 196, 5 *pls.*, 1 *map. Berlin,* 1773. This is a transl. of the original paper in the Phil. Trans. R. Soc. London, vols. 57–61. 1768–72.

HAMILTON, Sir W.—Voyage au Mont Etna en juin 1769.—[Extr. fr.] " *Voyage en Sicile et dans la Grande Grèce* " (*addressed to Winckelmann and translated from the German*), 12⁰. *Lausanne,* 1773. MS. Copy. [C.A.]

HAMILTON, Sir W.—Voyage au Mont Etna en 1769 (trad. en français par M. de Villebois).—*See* WINCKELMANN, J. J. —Voyage en Sicile, 12⁰. 1773.

HAMILTON, Sir W. — Campi Phlegræi. Observations on the volcanoes of the two Sicilies.—*fol. Vol. i, pp.* 90, 1 *pl.*, 1 *map ; Vol. ii,* 54 *pls. Naples,* 1776. [C.A.] [B.M.—Tab. 435a, with MS. notes, contains the original drawings, besides 11 others and 1 print.]

HAMILTON, Sir W.—Œuvres complètes, traduites et commentées par l'Abbé Giraud-Soulavie.—8⁰, *pp. xx+*506, 1 *map. Paris,* 1781.

HAMILTON, Sir W.—An account of the Earthquake in Calabria, Sicily, etc.—8⁰. *Colchester* [1783].

HAMILTON, Sir W.—First letter to Sir Joseph Banks upon the earthquakes in Calabria Ultra and Sicily, dated Naples, Feb. 18, 1783.—MS. 4⁰, *foll.* 2. [B.M. 8967. ff. 34–5.]

HAMILTON, Sir W.—Account of the Earthquakes in Italy.—*London,* 1783.—(Tradotto ed illustrato da G. Seila.) *Firenze,* 1783.

HAMILTON, Sir W.—Relation des derniers Tremblemens de Terre arrivés en Calabre et en Sicile. Traduit de l'anglois, et enrichie de notes traduites de l'Italien du Doct. G. Stella.—8⁰. *Geneva,* 1784.

HAMILTON, Sir W.—Waarneemingen over den Vuurbergen in Italie, Sicilie, en omstreiks den Rhyn als mede over de Aardbeevingen, voorgevallen in Italie, 1783. —8⁰, *pp.* 552. *Amsterdam,* 1784. [C.A.]

HAUER, K. Von.—Ueber die Beschaffenheit der Lava des Aetna von der Eruption im Jahre 1852.—*Sitzber. k. Akad. Wiss. xi, pp.* 87–92. *Wien,* 1854.—*Journ. prakt. Chem. lx, pp.* 224–30. *Leipzig,* 1854.

HEERL, J. L.—*See* HOUEL, J. P. L. L.— Reisen durch Sicilien u. Malta, *etc.*

HELLEMANNS, J. Georg.—De Montibus ignivomis, Vulgò Feuer-speyende Berge.— 4⁰, *pp.* 22. *Marburgi Cattorum, Typis hæred. Joh. Jodoc. Kürsneri, Acad. Typogr.* 1698.

HERBERGER, J. E.—Chemische Analyse der körnigen Lava vom Aetna.—*Brandes' Archiv. d. Apoth. Vereins, xxxiii, pp.* 10–17. 1830.—*N. J. f. Min. p.* 426. *Stuttgart,* 1832.

HERBERGER, J. E.—Lithion in der Lava vom Aetna.—*Repert. f. Pharm. xxxiv, pp.* 150–51. *Nüremberg,* 1830.

HERBINII, J.—Dissertationes de admirandis mundi Cataractis supra et subterraneis, earumque principio, elementorum, etc. etc.—*4⁰, pp.* 14+267+17, *fig. Amstelodami,* 1678.

HILDEBRAND, W.—Weitverbesserte und vielvermehrte Magia naturalis. Das ist Kunst- und Wunderbuch darinne begriffen wunderbahre Secreta, Geheimnisse u. Kunststücke, wie man nemlich mit dem gantzen menschlichen Cörper zahmen u. wilden Thieren, Vögeln, Fischen, Unzieffern u. Insecten allerley Gewächsen, Pflanzungen und sonsten fast unerhörte wunderbarliche Sachen verrichten. Auch etliche Wunderschrifften künstlich bereiten zu Schimpff Kurtzweil löblicher u. lustiger Übung u. zu Nutz gebrauchen u. damit die Zeit vertreiben kan : beneben Erzehlung vieler wunderlichen Dingen so hin u. wieder in der Welt gefunden werden. In 4 Bücher eingetheilt, ietzo mit vielen geheimbten Kunststücklein welche bey den vorigen Exemplarien nicht zu finden u. gantz neu in Druck gegeben.—Mit Privil. begn. in 10 Jahren nicht nachzudrucken.— 4⁰, *foll.* 7+53+55+39+31. *Erffurdt, In Verl. J. Birckners Buchhandlers. Gedr. bey J. G. Hertzen,* 1664.—Earlier ed. *Leipzig,* 1610.

See Book 4, pp. 9–10 : lines on Etna and Vesuvius after the Latin of J. R. Rabman.

HILL.—Observations and Remarks in a journey through Sicily and Calabria, in the year 1791 : etc.—8⁰, pp. xvi+306, 1 map. London, 1792.

HOEPLI, U.—Bibliotheca Vesuviana. Catalogue d'une collection d'ouvrages précieux sur le Vésuve, l'Etna, les autres Volcans et les Tremblements de Terre. (Catalogue Nr. 8.)—8⁰. *Milan, U. Hoepli,* 1883.

HOFF, K. E. A. Von.—Geschichte der natürlichen Veränderungen der Erdoberfläche.—3 vols. *Gotha,* 1822, 1824, 1834. *See* Vol. ii, § 10, pp. 221-52.

HOFF, K. E. A. Von.—Chronik der Erdbeben und Vulcan-Ausbrüche mit vorausgehender Abhandlung über die Natur dieser Erscheinungen.—2 vols. 8⁰. *Vol. i, pp.* 6+470 ; *Vol. ii, pp.* 2+406. *Gotha,* 1840-41.

HOFFMANN, F.—[Ueber das Albaner Gebirge, den Aetna, den Serapis-Tempel von Pozzuoli, und die geognostischen Verhältnisse der Umgegend von Catania.]—*Archiv. f. Min. iii, pp.* 361-412. *Berlin,* 1831.

HOFFMANN, F.—On the Scenery of Italy as contrasted with that of Germany ; the Geognosy of Albano, near Rome ; and the General Structure and Trachytic Rocks of Etna.—*Edinb. New Phil. Journ. xii, pp.* 370-78. *Edinburgh,* 1832.

HOFFMANN, F.—Verhältnisse der in den letzten 40 Jahren zu Palermo beobachteten Erdstösse.—*Ann. Phys. Chem. xxiv, pp.* 49-64. *Leipzig,* 1832.

HOFFMANN, F.—Mémoire sur les terrains volcaniques de Naples, de la Sicile, etc.— *Bull. Soc. géol. France, iii, pp.* 170-80. *Paris,* 1833.—*C.R. Acad. Sci. xli, pp.* 872-76. *Paris,* 1855.

HOFFMANN, F.—Physikalische Geographie. (Erhebungskratere, Vegetation Siciliens, Aetna u. a.)—*Berlin,* 1837.

HOFFMANN, F.—Geschichte der Geognosie u. Schilderung der vulkanischen Erscheinungen.—*Hinterlassene Werke, Bd. ii,* 8⁰. *Berlin,* 1838. *See* pp. 273 et seq.

HOFFMANN, F.—Geognostische Beobachtungen. Gesammelt auf einer Reise durch Italien und Sicilien, in den Jahren 1830 bis 1832.—*Archiv. f. Min. xiii, pp.* 3-726, 1 *pl.,* 1 *map. Berlin,* 1839.—[Sep. publ.] 8⁰. *Berlin,* 1839. The map is identical with the following.

HOFFMANN, F.—Geognostische Karte von Sicilien aus den hinterlassenen Materialen v. . . . F. Hoffmann. Maasstab 1 : 500,000. Map in preceding work. Etna and lava-streams.

HOFFMANN, F.—Lettera al signor E. Repetti (sull' altezza dell' Etna).—*Giorn. Lett. Sicilia, xxxv, pp.* 54.

HOFFMANNUS, G.—Lexicon topographicum Siculum. Cited by Massa, Etna.

HOHENBERG, F.—*See* BRAUN, G.

HOLM, A.—Geschichte Siciliens im Alterthum.—2 vols. *Vol. i,* 1869 ; .*Vol. ii, Leipzig,* 1874.

HOLM, A.—Das alte Catania, mit Plan.— *Lübeck,* 1873.

HOROZCO COVARRUVIAS, J. De. Episcopus Agrigentinus. — Emblemata moralia memoriæ Sanc. D.D. Didaci Covarruvias de Leyva, etc. etc.—3 books in 1 vol. 8⁰, 100 *pls. Book i, pp.* 4+256 ; *Book ii, pp.* 110 ; *Book iii, pp.* 100. *Agrigenti,* 1601.

HOUEL, J. P. L. L.—Voyage Pittoresque des Isles de Sicile, de Malthe et de Lipari, où l'on traicte des Antiquités qui s'y trouvent encore ; des principaux Phénomènes que la Nature y offre ; du Costume des Habitans, et de quelques Usages.—4 tom. *fol. T. i, pp.* vii+138, *pls.* 72, 1782 ; *T. ii, pp.* 148, *pls.* 73-144, 1784 ; *T. iii, pp.* 126, *pls.* 145-204, 1785 ; *T. iv, pp.* 124, *pls.* 205-64, *Paris,* 1787.—In German : 4 Th. 8⁰. *Gotha,* 1797-1805. *See* Vol. ii, pp. 99-148, 1784.

HUGHES, T. S.—Travels in Sicily, Greece and Albania. Illustrated with engravings of maps, scenery, plans, etc.—2 vols. 4⁰. *London,* 1820. *See* Vol. i, pp. 115-20.

HUMBOLDT, F. H. A. Von.—Ueber den Bau und die Wirkungsart der Vulcane in verschiedenen Erdstrichen.—*Abh. k. Akad. Wiss. pp.* 137-56. *Berlin,* 1822-23.— *Froriep. Notiz. iv, coll.* 49-54. *Jena,* 1823. —*Taschenb. f. Gesammt. Min. xviii, pp.* 1-39. *Frankfurt a. M.,* 1824.—*Ann. Phil. vi, pp.* 121-35. *London,* 1823.

HUMBOLDT, F. H. A. Von.—Ansichten der Natur.—2 vols. *Tübingen,* 1839. Notices on Etna, without historical date.

HUOT, J. J. N.—Coup d'œil sur les Volcans et sur les phénomènes volcaniques considérés sous les rapports minéralogiques, géologiques et physiques.—*pp.* 588, *maps* 30–46 (*bound separately*). — ?, 1831. *See* Pl. 30.

HUPFER, P.—Die Regionen am Aetna.— [Sep.-Abdr.] *Wissensch. Verhoff. Ver. f. Erdkunde zu Leipzig, ii, pp.* 299–362, 1 *map.* 1894.

IDACII.—Chronica. Eruption of *A.D.* 72.

ILMONI, I.—Misceller an Vulcanen Aetna [1841].—*Föredr. för Vet. Soc. d.* 4 *Mars* 1839 *och d.* 26 *Apr.* 1841, 4⁰, *pp.* 4. [C.A.] —*Acta Soc. Sci. Fenn. i, pp.* 749–54. *Helsingfors,* 1840.

INTERLANDI E SIRUGO, P.—Osservazioni geognostiche e geologiche sopra i terreni di Avola.—*Atti Acc. Gioen. xii, pp.* 333–52. *Catania,* 1837.

INTERLANDI E SIRUGO, P.—Sopra i Basalti globulari del Morgo.—*Atti Acc. Gioen. xiv, pp.* 41–64. *Catania,* 1839.

INTERLANDI E SIRUGO, P.—Sopra i terreni di Lognina, Aci Trezza e Castello.— *Atti Acc. Gioen. xv, pp.* 255–86. *Catania,* 1839.

INTERLANDI E SIRUGO, P.—Osservazioni geognostico-geologiche sul poggio di S. Filippo e sui dintorni in Militello.—*Atti Acc. Gioen. S.* 2, *i, pp.* 35–55. *Catania,* 1844.

IRTON.—*See* WRIGHT.

ISSEL, A.—Saggio di una Teoria dei Vulcani. —*N. Antologia, xxviii, pp.* 58–88. *Firenze,* 1875.—[In abstr. :] *Boll. Vulc. Ital. Fasc.* I, II, III, *pp.* 13. *Roma,* 1875.

ISSEL, A.—Sullo stato sferoidale dell' acqua nelle lave incandescenti.—*Boll. Vulc. Ital. Fasc.* IV *e* V, *pp.* 57. *Roma,* 1876.

ITTAR, S.—Viaggio pittorico all' Etna contenente le vedute più interessanti di questo Monte, e gli oggetti più rimarchevoli che nelle sue regioni esistono, con una Carta Topografica, che indica con numeri i punti dai quali il disegnatore le ha espresse, ed una breve descrizione di esso e del suo itinerario.—25 *pls. obl.* 4⁰. — ?, — ? [B.N.]

ITTIG, THOMAS.—De Montium Incendiis, in quibus post ardentium toto passim orbe montium catalogum et historiam, ac variarum opinionum examen, non modo totius Naturæ cum in efficiendis tum in conser-

vandis illis ignibus processus exponitur, *etc.* — 8⁰, *pp.* 16+347+*index. Lipsiæ,* 1671. *See* pp. 7–65 and many other references.

JERVIS, G.—*See* JERVIS, W. P.

JERVIS, W. P.—I Tesori sotterranei dell' Italia.—4 vols. 8⁰, *num. pls. Torino,* 1873–89.

J. H. C.—The Eruption of Etna.—" *Mediterranean Naturalist,*" *ii, pp.* 239–40. *Malta,* 1892.

JOANNE, P.—Italie.—16⁰, *pp.* 514, 10 *maps,* 80 *plans. Paris,* 1909.

JOHNSTON-LAVIS, H. J.—Volcanic Cones, their Structure and Mode of Formation.— " *Science Gossip,*" xvi, pp. 220–23, 1 *fig. London,* 1880.

JOHNSTON-LAVIS, H. J.—The Relationship of the Structure of Igneous Rocks to the Conditions of their Formation.— *Scient. Proc. R. Dublin Soc. N.S. v, pp.* 113–55. 1886.

JOHNSTON-LAVIS, H. J.—On the Fragmentary Ejectamenta of Volcanoes.— *Proc. Geol. Assoc. ix, pp.* 421–32, 1 *pl. London,* 1886.

JOHNSTON-LAVIS, H. J.—Note on the occurrence of Leucite at Etna.—*Rept. British Assoc.* 1888, *p.* 669. *London,* 1889. —*Geol. Mag. p.* 564. *London.* 1888.— [Rept. in :] *Zeitschr. f. Kryst. xix, p.* 484. *Leipzig,* 1891.

JOHNSTON-LAVIS, H. J.—Su una roccia contenente Leucite trovata sull' Etna.— *Boll. Soc. Ital. Microscopisti, i, pp.* 26–29, 1 *photo-engrav. Acireale,* 1889.

JOHNSTON-LAVIS, H. J.—Il Pozzo Artesiano di Ponticelli.—*Rend. R. Acc. Sci. S.* 2, *iii, pp.* 142–48. *Napoli,* 1889.

JOHNSTON-LAVIS, H. J. — Volcans et tremblements de terre. Revue de ce qui a été publié sur ces sujets durant l'année 1888.—*Ann. géol. univ. v, pp.* 629–55. *Paris,* 1889.

JOHNSTON-LAVIS, H. J.—Viaggio scientifico alle regioni vulcaniche Italiane nella ricorrenza del centenario del " Viaggio alle Due Sicilie " di Lazzaro Spallanzani.—8⁰, *pp.* 1–10. *Napoli,* 1889. This is the programme of the excursion of the English geologists who visited the South Italian Volcanoes under the direction of the author. It is here included as it contained various new and unpublished observations.

JOHNSTON-LAVIS, H. J.—Excursion to the South Italian Volcanoes.—*Proc. Geol. Assoc. xi, pp.* 389–423. *London*, 1890.

JOHNSTON-LAVIS, H. J.—The State of the active Sicilian Volcanoes in September 1889.—*Scottish Geog. Mag. vi, pp.* 145–49. *Edinburgh*, 1890.

JOHNSTON-LAVIS, H. J. — Volcans et tremblements de terre (Revue).—*Ann. géol. univ. vi, pp.* 355–81. *Paris*, 1890.

JOHNSTON-LAVIS, H. J. — The South Italian Volcanoes, being the account of an Excursion to them made by English and other Geologists in 1889 under the auspices of the Geologists' Association of London, and the direction of the author, with papers on the different localities by Messrs. Johnston-Lavis, Platania, Sambon, Zezi and Mme Antonia Lavis, including the Bibliography of the Volcanic Districts.— *8°, pp. vi+342, 16 pls. Furchheim, Naples,* 1891.—Reviewed in " *Nature,*" *xliv, pp.* 539–40. 1891.
A reprint of account given in Proc. Geol. Assoc. with the addition of the Bibliography.

JOHNSTON-LAVIS, H. J., and MME. ANTONIA LAVIS.—Bibliography of the Geology and Eruptive Phenomena of the South Italian Volcanoes that were visited in 1889, as well as of the submarine volcano of A.D. 1831.—*From* " The South Italian Volcanoes, etc." 8°, *pp.* 89–331. *Naples*, 1891.
Chapt. VII of foregoing, a number of reprints of which were also issued.

JOUSSET, P.—L'Italie illustrée.—*fol., pp.* 370, 14 *col. maps and plans,* 9 *engrav. maps,* 12 *pls.,* 784 *photos. Paris,* 1829.

JOY.—[Analysis of the Lava of the flow of 124 B.C.]—*See* RAMMELSBERG, C. F.—Handwörterbuch.—*Supplem.* 5, *Seite* 157, 1853.

JULLIEN, JOHN J.—L'Etna et le troisième congrès du Club Alpin Italien à Catane.— —*Echo d. Alpes, publ. Club Alpin Suisse, N° 4, pp.* 263. *Genève*, 1880.

JUSTINUS.—Historiæ Philippicæ. Lib. IV, cap. 1, 5, 14.

KADEN, W.—Vesuv und Aetna. Touristische Aufzeichnungen und Randbemerkungen, I, II.—*Westermann's Monatshefte, lxiv, pp.* 529–40, 7 *figs., pp.* 599–615, 7 *figs. Braunschweig,* 1888.

KARACZAY, F.—Manuel du Voyageur en Sicile, avec une carte.—*Stuttgart,* 1826.

KEMPF, P.—*See* MUELLER, G.

KENNEDY, ROBT.—A chemical analysis of three species of Whinstone . . . and two of Lava [Lava of Catania; Lava St. Venere, Piedemonte, Ætna]. [1798.]— *Trans. Edinb. R. Soc. v, pp.* 76–98. 1805.— *Ann. Chim. xli, pp.* 225–41. *Paris,* 1801. —*Nicholson, Journ. Nat. Phil. etc. iv, pp.* 407–15, 438–42. *London,* 1801.

KENNGOTT, J. G. A.—[Chlornatriumhydrat am Aetna.]—*N. J. f. Min. pp.* 500–1. *Stuttgart,* 1871.

KEPHALIDES, M. A. W.—Voyage à l'Etna. —*Nouv. Ann. Voyages, S.* 2, *iv, pp.* 289– 306. *Paris,* 1827.

KEWITSCH, G.—Die Vulkane Pelé, Krakatau, Etna, Vesuv.—8°, *pp.* 1–35, *figs. Norden,* 1902.

KIRCHER, A.—Mundus Subterraneus.— 2 vols. *fol. Amstelodami,* 1665.——2nd ed. 1668.——3rd ed. 1678.
See Vol. i, Lib. IV, Cap. 8 and 9. 1678.

KIRCHER, A.—The Vulcano's : or, burning and fire-vomiting Mountains, famous in the World : with their remarkables. Collected for the most part out of Kircher's " Mundus Subterraneus " and exposed to more general view in English, upon the late wonderful and prodigious eruptions of Ætna.—8°, *foll.* 4, *pp.* 64, 1 *pl. London,* 1669. [B.M.—B. 395.]

KLUGE, K. E.—Ueber Synchronimus u. Antagonimus von vulkanischen Eruptionen.—*Leipzig,* 1863.

KOELLIKER, R. A. VON.—Die Eruption des Aetna von 1852.—*Verhandl. iv, pp.* 37–43. *Würzburg,* 1854.

KUDERNATSCH, J.—Chemische Untersuchung einiger Abänderungen des Augits und der Hornblende.—*Ann. Phys. Chem. xxxvii, pp.* 577–88. *Leipzig,* 1836.—*N. J. f. Min. pp.* 596–98. *Stuttgart,* 1836.
See p. 583.

LACROIX, A. F. A.—Les Enclaves des Roches volcaniques.—*Ann. Acad. Mâcon, S.* 2, *x, pp.* 1–710, 8 *pls.* 1893.

LACROIX, A. F. A.—Sur la récente éruption de l'Etna (Taormina, 15 mai, 1908).— *C.R. Acad. Sci. cxlvi, pp.* 1071–76. *Paris,* 1908.

LACROIX, A. F. A.—Nouvelles Observations sur l'Etna.—*C.R. Acad. Sci. cxlvi, pp.* 1134–37. *Paris,* 1908.

LACROIX, A. F. A.—Sur la Lave de la récente éruption de l'Etna.—*C.R. Acad. Sci. cxlvii, pp.* 99–103. *Paris*, 1908.

LACROIX, A. F. A.—Sur les Minéraux des Fumerolles de la récente éruption de l'Etna et sur l'existence de l'Acide Borique dans les Fumerolles actuelles du Vésuve.— *C.R. Acad. Sci. cxlvii, pp.* 161–65. *Paris*, 1908.

L'ALLEMANT.—*See* LALLEMEN.

LALLEMEN [? L'ALLEMANT]. — [Letters to Dolomieu upon the eruption of Etna of [1792.]—*Observ. s. l. Phys. xl, p.* 482 ; *xli, pp.* 120–22. *Paris*, 1792.

LANDGREBE, G.—Naturgeschichte der Vulkane.—2 vols. *Gotha*, 1855.

LANG, O.—Ueber den zeitlichen Bestandwechsel der Vesuvlaven und Aetnagesteine.—*Zeitschr. f. Naturwiss. lxv,* 1–2, *pp.* 30, 6 *figs. Leipzig*, 1892.

LANGLEY, S. P.—Observations on Mount Etna.—*Amer. Journ. Sci. xx, pp.* 33–44. *New Haven*, 1880.

LANZA. P.—Eruzione del 1646. Cited by Recupero.

LANZA DI TRABIA, S.—Novissima Guida pel viaggiatore in Sicilia.—8°, *pp.* 358. *Palermo*, 1884.

LASALLE, A. É. GIGAULT DE.— Voyage pittoresque en Sicile [edited by J. F. D'Osterwald].—2 tom. *fol.*, 92 *pls. Paris*, 1822–26.

LASALLE, A. É. GIGAULT DE.—Sicile.— *See* L'Univers, ou Histoire et description de tous les peuples, etc. *pp.* 96, 24 *pls. Paris*, 1835.
Bound with " Italie," by Artaud de Montor. *See* Pl. 5.

LASAULX, A. C. P. F. VON.—Etnabesteigung am 2 Okt. 1878.—Letter to *Schlesische Zeitung,* 15 *Okt.* 1878.

LASAULX, A. C. P. F. VON.—Der Aetna und seine neueste Eruption von 1879.— *Deutsche Rev. Septemberheft. Berlin*, 1879.

LASAULX, A. C. P. F. VON.—Mineralogische Notizen. (1. Szabóit von Biancavilla am Etna. 2. Szabóit von Riveau grand im Mont Dore. 3. Eisenglanz von Biancavilla.) [1879.]—*Zeitschr. f. Kryst. iii,* 3, *pp.* 288–98. *Leipzig*, 1879.—*N. J. f. Min. i, Ref. pp.* 43–45. *Stuttgart*, 1880.— [Abstr.] *Boll. R. Com. Geol. Ital. x, pp.* 372–82. *Roma*, 1879.

LASAULX, A. C. P. F. VON.—Ueber die Salinellen von Paternò am Etna und ihre neueste Eruption.—*Zeitschr. deutsch. geol. Gesellsch. xxxi, pp.* 457–72. *Berlin*, 1879. —*Jahresber. schles. Gesellsch. pp.* 172–73. *Breslau*, 1879.

LASAULX, A. C. P. F. VON. — Sicilien, ein geographisches Charakterbild.—*Bonn*, 1879.
See pp. 13–26.

LASAULX, A. C. P. F. VON. — Ueber die letzte Eruption des Schlammvulkans von Paterno am Südfusse des Aetnas.—*Jahresber. schles. Gesellsch. pp.* 172, 173. *Breslau*, 1880.

LASAULX, A. C. P. F. VON.—Der Aetna, 1880.—*See* SARTORIUS VON WALTERSHAUSEN.

LASAULX, A. C. P. F. VON.—Mineralogische. (1. Ueber einige Aetnäische Mineralien. 2. Albit von der Butte du Monte Cau in den Pyrenäen. 3. Ein fossiles Harz aus den Steinkohlen von Oberschlesien.)—*N. J. f. Min. (Bd. i, Ref.) pp.* 12–16. *Stuttgart*, 1882.—*Zeitschr. f. Kryst. v, pp.* 326–47. *Leipzig*, 1881.

LASAULX, A. C. P. F. VON.—Die neueste Eruption des Aetna vom 22 Marz 1883. (Zum Teil nach Mitteilungen von Prof. O. Silvestri.)—" Humboldt," *ii, pp.* 213–15. *Stuttgart*, 1883.

LAUBE, G. C.—[Ueber den Aetna.] [1877.] —*Jahresber. Nat.-hist. Ver. " Lotos," xxvii, pp.* 18–34. *Prag*, 1878.

LAVINI, CONTE G.—Rime filosofiche colle sue annotazioni alle medesime.—4°, *pp. xxxii*+232. *Milano*, 1750.
See pp. 74–85.

LAVIS.—*See* JOHNSTON-LAVIS.

LAZZARO, N.—Da Napoli all' Etna.—*Due corrispondenze all' Illustraz. Ital. di Trèves. Sem.* 1°, *pp.* 388 ; *Sem.* 2°, *pp.* 6, *con una incisione. Milano*, 1879.

LEANTI, A.—Dello stato presente della Sicilia o sia breve e distinta descrizione di essa. Accresciuta colle notizie delle Isole adiacenti.—2 vols. 8°. *Vol. i, pp.* 21+222, *num. pls. ; Vol. ii, pp.* 223 + 407 + 45 (*index*). *Palermo*, 1761.
With a few notes on Etna.

LEBLANC, F.—*See* DEVILLE.—Sur la composition chimique des gaz, *etc.* 1858.

LEBLANC, F. — *See* DEVILLE.—Sur les émanations gazeuses, *etc.* 1857.

LEGOUVÉ.—*See* NORVINS.

LEITCH,ʾ W. L.—The City of Catania and Mount Ætna, Sicily. Città di Catania ed Mont Ætna. W. Floyd. Peter Jackson, London and Paris.
Steel engraving : 191×156 mm.

LEITCH, W. L.—Ruins of the Theatre at Taormina, and Mᵗ Etna. Rovine del Teatro a Taormina, et il Monte Etna. H. Adlard.
Steel engrav.: 189×152 mm.

LEITCH, W. L.—*See* WRIGHT.

LEMONNIER.—*See* NORVINS.

LENZ, O.—Ueber die vulcanischen Ausbrüche bei Pantellaria 1891 und am Etna 1892.—" *Lotos,*" *N.F. xiv, pp.* 19–32. *Prag, Wien, Leipzig,* 1894.

LEONHARD, C. C. Von.—Die Basalt Gebilde in ihren Beziehungen zu normalen und abnormen Felsmassen.—2 vols. 8⁰. *Stuttgart,* 1832.

LEONHARD, C. C. Von.—Geologie, oder Naturgeschichte der Erde auf allgemein faszliche Weise abgehandelt.—5 vols. 8⁰. *Vol. i, pp.* 456, *lith. pls. i–xiv ; Vol. ii, pp.* 481, *pls. xv–xxxix ; Vol. iii, pp.* 628, *pls. xl–lxviii ; Vol. iv, pp.* 490, *pls. lxix–lxxx ; Vol. v, pp.* 712, *pls. lxxxi–lxxxxvii. Stuttgart,* 1836–44.
See Pl. LXXXXI, pp. 180–219.

LEONHARD, C. C. Von.—Geologisches Atlas.—*Stuttgart,* 1841.
Two maps of Etna, the one showing the lava-streams from G. Gemmellaro's " Quadro Istorico."

LEOPOLDO DEL RE.—Relazione di una Gita in Catania e all' Etna durante la eruzione del Dicembre 1842 per eseguirvi alcune magnetiche osservazioni.—*Atti R. Acc. Sci. v, pt.* 1, *pp.* 46. *Napoli,* 1843.

LÉVESQUE DE BURIGNY, J.—Histoire générale de Sicile.—2 vols. 4⁰, 2 *maps. La Haye,* 1745.
In Ital.: " dalla lingua francese tradotta, . . . accresciuta, . . . dal Signor E. Scasso e Borrello."—6 tom. 4⁰. *Palermo,* 1792–94.—*Also printed separately in the* " Descrizione Geografica della Sicilia," 8⁰. *Palermo,* 1806.
See Vol.¨ii, p. 209.

LIGHT, Major, and DEWINT.—Sicilian Scenery.—8⁰. *London,* 1823.
62 fine engraved pls. drawn by Dewint, averaging 228 to 212 × 155 to 146 mm. Short explanations in French and English.

LOCCHI, Ing. D.—Italia ; Carta Fisica. —*Publ. G. B. Paravia e C., Torino, Roma, Milano, Firenze, Napoli,* 1876.
1 : 200,000. Raised map.

LOEWE, A.—Analyse des Basaltes und der Lava vom Aetna von 1669.—*Ann. Phys. Chem. xxxviii, pp.* 151–60. *Leipzig,* 1836. —*Edinb. New Phil. Journ. xxiv, pp.* 22–29. 1838.—*Ann. Pharm. xx, pp.* 237–38. *Lemgo,* 1836.—*N. J. f. Min. pp.* 48–50. *Stuttgart,* 1837.

LOMBARDO-BUDA, G.—Vulcania Lithosylloge Ætnea in classes digesta.—*Nuova Raccolta Opusc. Autori Siciliani, iii, pp.* 145–70. *Palermo,* 1789.

LONGO, A.—Memoria storico-fisica sul tremuoto de' 20 Febbraio 1818.—*Catania,* 1818.—Transl. *Bibl. univ. Sci. Arts, ix, pp.* 228–36. *Genève,* 1818.—*Bibl. Ital. ix, pp.* 343–55. *Milano,* 1818.

LONGO, A.—Delle accensioni volcaniche e della ipotesi del calore centrale della terra. Memoria letta all' Acc. Gioenia 8 Maggio 1862.—4⁰, *pp.* 47. *Catania,* 1862.

LONGO, A.—Colpo d'occhio geologico sul terreno di Caltagirone.—1864.

LONGO, A.—Ad un addio del Prof. Cav. Ufficiale C. Gemmellaro. Parole di Risposta del vecchio Mongibello.—*Catania,* 1866.

LONGO, A.—Sul bisogno di determinare il vero e reale perimetro dell' Etna.—*Atti Acc. Gioen. S. 3, ii, pp.* 103–14. *Catania,* 1868.

LONGO, A.—Un apostrofe all' Etna oggi Mongibello (in versi).—*Catania,* 1869.

LONGO, A.—Dell' età dell' Etna ossia del primo esordio dei volcani estinti, memoria in appendice alla precedente.(Nuove vedute sulle formazione del Globo.)—*Atti Acc. Gioen. S. 3, iii, pp.* 151–69. *Catania,* 1869.

LONGO, A.—Sulle cagioni probabili delle accensioni vulcaniche subaeree.—*Atti Acc. Gioen. S. 3, iv, pp.* 1–35. *Catania,* 1870.

LONGO, A.—Sulle interpretazioni dei fenomeni chimici in rapporto alle leggi della Natura.—*Atti Acc. Gioen. S. 3, v, pp.* 187–219. *Catania,* 1871.

LONGO, A.—Osservazioni sopra alquanti squarci della memoria del Sig. Mallet " Volcanic Energy."—*Atti Acc. Gioen. S. 3, xiv, pp.* 119–45. *Catania,* 1879.

LONGO, A.—L'Etna al cospetto della Scienza.—4⁰, *pp.* 63, 1 *map. Catania,* 1886. [C.A.]

LONGOBARDO, A.—Extrait d'une lettre adressée à M. Ch. Sainte-Claire Deville (éruption de l'Etna 7 juillet 1863).—*C.R. Acad. Sci. lvii, p.* 157. *Paris,* 1863.

LONGOBARDO, A.—Extrait d'une lettre adressée à M. Ch. Sainte-Claire Deville (éruption de l'Etna, 31 janv. 1865).—*C.R. Acad. Sci. lx, p.* 354. *Paris,* 1865.

LONGUS, J.—Continuation du Maurolycus. —*See* MAUROLICO.

LOPERFIDO, A.—Sull' Etna.—*Ist. Geog. Milit. Ital., many pls. and views. Firenze,* 1901.
Frontisp., exaggerated view of Etna crater, and distant view of Etna from W. in plate of Catania.

LORENZO, G. DE.—L'Etna. With 153 illustr.—*See* RICCI, C.—No. 32 in "*Collezione di Monografie Illustrate.*"—*Italia Artistica.—S.* 1. 1902, *etc.*

LORENZO, G. DE.—La Basi dei Vulcani Vulture ed Etna.—*Internat. Geol. Congress, pp.* 6, 1 *pl. Mexico,* 1906.

LORENZO, G. DE.—L'Etna.—*Ist. Ital. Arti Graf.* 4⁰, *pp.* 154, 150 *figs.,* 3 *tav. Bergamo,* 1907.

LORENZO, G. DE.—Il Neck subetneo di Motta Sant' Anastasia.—*Atti R.Acc. Lincei, S.* 5, *Rend. xvi, sem.* 2, *pp.* 15–25. *Roma,* 1907.

LUCA, P. DE.—Memoria sull' eruzione del 1832.—"*Nuova Antologia,*" *xlviii, p.* 155. *Firenze,* 1832.

LUCA, P. DE.—Relazione sommaria delle nuove eruzioni accadute nel lato occidentale dell' Etna, nel corrente mese di Novembre 1832.—*Antologia, xlviii* (*S.* 2, *viii*), *pp.* 155–58. *Firenze,* 1832.

LUCA, P. DE.—Eruzione dell' Etna in Novembre del 1843, e suoi effetti nell' industria dei Brontesi.—8⁰, *pp.* 27, 1 *pl. Napoli,* 1844. [B.N.]—*Museo Sci. Lett. ii, pp.* 145–69. *Napoli,* 1844.

LUCA, P. DE.—Lettera sul miserando caso della esplosione avvenuta addì 25 Nov. 1843 durante la eruzione dell' Etna con osservazioni del Luigi Saitta da Bronte.— *Rend. R. Acc. Sci. iii, pp.* 177–78. *Napoli,* 1844.

LUCAS e MARESCHINI. — Estratto del giornale del Viaggio in Sicilia.—*Giorn. Fis. Chim. Stor. Nat. ii, pp.* 358–60. *Pavia,* 1819.

LUCILIUS JUNIOR. — Lucilii Junioris (vulgo Cornelii Severi) Ætna. — *See* WERNSDORF, J. C.—Poctæ Latini Minores, 8⁰, *Tom.* 4. 1780, *etc.*
See "Satires de Lucilius Junius." For all other editions of this work *see* B.M. Catalogue.

LUCRETIUS.—T. Lucretii Cari de Rerum Natura, Lib. VI, 639–702.—[*Florentiæ,* M.D.XII.]

LUDOVICUS AURELIUS. — Eruption of 1169.—*Ex Baronio in epist. Lib. XI.*

LUDOVICUS CREMONENSIS.—*See* CREMONENSIS.

LUEBECK, A. VON.—Cronica Slavorum.— *Written in* 1209.
See Vol. XIX : Pertz. Monument. Historic. Germanic. Scriptorum. Cap. XXI, p. 159 : Epistola Conradi cancellarii episcopi electi Hildeseimensis. Anno 1195. Notice on Etna and an erupt. of the period.

LUGEON, M., et ARGAND, E.—La Racine de la Nappe Sicilienne et l'arc de charriage de la Calabre.—*C.R. Acad. Sci. cxlii, pp.* 1107–9. *Paris,* 1906.

LUIGI, DR. (nipote).—*See* BULIFON, A.— Carte de' regni di Napoli, *etc.*

LUNGO, C. (del.).—L'Etna e le sue eruzioni. —"*La Rassegna nazionale,*" *lxvii. Firenze,* 1⁰ *sett.,* 1892.

LUNGO, C. (del.).—*See* BARTOLI, A. 1893.

LYCURGOS.—Contra Leokrates 95. Eruz. dei Fratelli pii.

LYELL, SIR C.—Principles of Geology.— 12 editions. *London,* 1830 *to* 1875.
See Vol. ii, chapt. XXVI. *London,* 1875. In French, transl. from 6th ed. : "Principes de Géologie." *Lyon,* 1846. *See* Pt. i, *pp.* 137–205.

LYELL, SIR C.—On the Structure of Lavas which have consolidated on steep slopes ; with Remarks on the Mode of Origin of Mount Etna, and on the Theory of "Craters of Elevation."—4⁰, *tav. London,* 1859. —*Phil. Trans. R. Soc. pt. ii, pp.* 703–86. *London,* 1858.—*Bibl. univ. Archiv. Sci. phys. nat. vi, pp.* 217–66. *Genève, Lausanne, Paris,* 1859.—*Zeitschr. deutsch. geol. Gesellsch. xi, pp.* 149–250, *Taf.* VI–IX. *Berlin,* 1859.—[Abstr.] *Corrisp. Scient. vi, pp.* 181–82. *Roma,* 1863.—*Amer. Journ. Sci. xxvi, pp.* 214–19. *New Haven,* 1858.

LYELL, SIR C.—On the Consolidation of Lava on steep slopes, and on the origin of the Conical Form of Volcanoes.—*Proc. R. Inst. iii, pp.* 125–31. *London,* 1858–62.—*Amer. Journ. Sci. xxviii, pp.* 221–26. *New Haven,* 1859.

M * * * (Avocat en Parlement).—Lettres écrites de Suisse, d'Italie, de Sicile et de Malthe, à Mlle. * * à Paris, En 1776, 1777 et 1778.—6 tom. in 3 vols. 12⁰. *T. i, pp.* 454 ; *T. ii, pp.* 509 ; *T. iii, pp.* 536 ; *T. iv, pp.* 418 ; *T. v, pp.* 550 ; *T. vi, pp.* 515. *Amsterdam,* 1780.
See T. iii.

MACRI, V. (DI NICOLOSI).—[Eruption of XVII century.]—MS.
Cited by Recupero ; abstr. printed in the appendix to his work.

MACROBIUS.—Macrobii Ambrosii Avrelii Theodosii, etc., In somnium Scipionis, Lib. II. Saturnaliorum, Lib. VII.—16⁰. *Lvgduni, Apud Seb. Gryphivm,* 1556.
See Lib. V, pp. 446 *et seq.*

MAGINI, G. M.—Descrizione della Sicilia.
Cited by M. Di Gregorio in : " Sur les eaux minérales de Paternò."

MAGLI, G.—*See* PIUTTI, A.

MAGNETI, V.—Notitie istor. di Terremoti.
Cited by Mongitore.

MAKOWSKY, A.—Reise nach Unter-Italien und Sizilien mit besd. Rücksicht auf der vulcanischen Gebiete.—*Verhandl. xv,* 1877 (*Heft* 1, *Sitzber.*), *pp.* 47–58, 70–78. *Brünn,* 1876.

MALAGOLI VECCHI, M.—Il Mediterraneo illustrato, le sue Isole.—*See* PELLÉ, C.

MALATERRA, G.—De rebus gestis Roberti Guiscardi Ducis Calabriæ et Rogeri comitis Siciliæ, libri quatuor.—*See* GRÆVIUS, J. G.—Thes. Antiq. . . . . Sic. *viii, lib.* II, *cap.*
Eruption of 11th cent.

MALHERBE, A.—Ascension à l'Etna.—[Extr. d.] *Mém. Acad. xxii, pp.* 96–121. *Metz,* 1841.

MALLET, R.—On the mechanism of production of Volcanic Dykes.—*Quart. Journ. Geol. Soc. xxxii, p.* 472. *London,* 1876.

MALVICA, F.—Gita alle Madonie.—*Effemeridi Scientifiche e Letteraria per la Sicilia, Fasc.* 35. *Palermo,* 1835. [B.N.]

MANCINO, C.—Narrativa del fuoco uscito dal Mongibello il dì undici Marzo del 1669, etc.—4⁰. *Messina,* 1669.

MANCUSI, P. ANT.—Istoria di Sᵗᵃ Rosalia, etc.—4⁰. *Vol. i, pp.* 17+456 ; *Vol. ii, pp.* 19+221. *Palermo,* 1721.
See Vol. i, pp. 117–37.

MANDALARI, M.—Riccordi di Sicilia. I. Caltagirone. II. Randazzo. III. Le popolazioni dell' Etna.—3 vols. 16⁰. *Vol. i, pp.* 59, 1897 ; *Vol. ii, pp.* 150, 1897 ; *Vol. iii, pp.* 77, 1899. *Catania,* 1897–99.

MANGINI, F.—L'Eruzione dell' Etna nel 1879.—*Ann. Soc. Meteor. Ital. ii,* 41–44, *pp.* 306.

MANNERT, H.—Geographie der Griechen und Römer.—8⁰. *Leipzig,* 1832.
See Bd. IX, p. 2 : Geogr. v. Sicilien. Ancient notes upon Etna.

MANONI, A.—L'Etna. Una gita durante l'ultima eruzione.—*Venezia,* 1886.

MANTOVANI, P.—Sulla formazione basaltica delle Isole dei Ciclopi presso Catania.—*Roma,* 1870.

MANTOVANI, P., e GREGORI, A.—La Eruzione dell' Etna nel 1879.—*Bull. Club Alp. Ital. N.* 37. *Torino,* 15 *Giugno,* 1879.

MANZELLA, E.—Contributo allo studio delle Pozzolane Italiane. Ricerche su una Pozzolana di Sicilia.—*Gazz. Chim. Ital. xli, pte.* 2, *pp.* 730–47. *Roma,* 1913.

MARANA, G. P.—Des Montagnes de la Sicile et de Naples, qui jettent des feux perpétuels, de la nature de ces feux et de ces montagnes et de leurs effets.—*Letter* XLI *of his :* L'Espion du Grand Seigneur, *T. ii, pp.* 124–34. *Amsterdam,* 1686.

MARANO, A.—L'Etna e le sue eruzioni. Discorso.—*Riposto,* 1891.

MARASCHI, G.—Lettera sulla costruzione della Gratissima e della Casa Inglese detta altrimenti di Mario Gemmellaro, fabbricata sopra l'Etna sin dal 1804.—8⁰, *pp.* 13. *Palermo,* 1829. [C.A.]

MARAVIGNA, C.—Descrizione dell' eruzione dell' Etna del 1802.—8⁰. *Catania,* 1803.

MARAVIGNA, C.—Memorie compendiose dell' ultima eruzione dell' Etna, accaduta nel mese di Novembre 1802.—4⁰, *pp.* 19. *Catania,* 1803.

MARAVIGNA, C.—Tavole sinottiche dell' Etna che comprendono la topografia, la storia delle eruzioni, la descrizione delle materie eruttate ed di alquanti fenomeni di questo vulcano dietro le recenti fisicochimiche scoverte.—4⁰, 10 *engrav. tables and frontisp. Catania,* 1811.——2nd ed. 5 *pls. folio. Paris,* 1838.

MARAVIGNA, C.—Istoria dell' incendio dell' Etna del mese di Maggio 1819.—8⁰, *pp.* 102, 2 *pls. Catania*, 1819.—*Bibl. Ital. xviii, pp.* 198–204. *Milano*, 1820.

MARAVIGNA, C.—Della Causa dei vulcani, dei loro fenomeni, e delle sostanze eruttate. —*Giorn. Sci. Lett. ed. Arti, i, pp.* 223–29 ; *ii, pp.* 3–9. *Palermo*, 1823.

MARAVIGNA, C.—Note alle considerazioni generali sui Vulcani, e particolari sopra l'Etna, del Signor Sayve.—*Giorn. Sci. Lett. ed Arti, iv, pp.* 140–46. *Palermo*, 1823.

MARAVIGNA, C.—Materiali per servire alla compilazione dell' Orittognosia Etnea. —*Atti Acc. Gioen. v, pp.* 141–61, 1831 ; *vi, pp.* 205–14, 1832 ; *viii, pp.* 25–51, 1834 ; *ix, pp.* 231–95, 1835. *Catania*, 1831–35.

MARAVIGNA, C.—*See* ZUCCARELLO. 1831.

MARAVIGNA, C.—Su i miglioramenti che le recenti scoverte chimiche hanno apportato alla soluzione di alcuni fenomeni geologici e particolarmente alla teoria de' vulcani.—*Atti Acc. Gioen. vii, pp.* 139–84. *Catania*, 1833.

MARAVIGNA, C.—Alcune idee sull' azione del fuoco nella produzione di alcuni membri della serie geognostica, sui rapporti del terreno trachitico e basaltico con quello dei vulcani estinti ed attivi, *etc.*—*Atti Acc. Gioen. viii, pp.* 177–201. *Catania*, 1834.

MARAVIGNA, C.—Esame di alcune opinioni del Sig. N. Boubée contenute nelle sue opere titolate " Géologie populaire, et tableau de l'état du Globe à ces différens âges."— 4e éd. 4⁰, *pp.* 48. 1834.—*Atti Acc. Gioen. xii, pp.* 275–323. *Catania*, 1837.

MARAVIGNA, C.—Cenno sul Ferro Oligisto ottaedrico del Monte del Corvo [vicino a Biancavilla.]—*Atti Acc. Gioen. xi, pp.* 307–12. *Catania*, 1836.

MARAVIGNA, C.—Sulla Jalite del Basalte della Motta, sulla Tremolite dell' Isola dei Ciclopi, sull' Idroclorato di ammoniaca della eruzione di Bronte anno 1832.—*Atti Acc. Gioen. xii, pp.* 81–88. *Catania*, 1837.

MARAVIGNA, C.—Sul Solfato di Calce che formasi nell' interno del cratere dell' Etna, sulla genesi di altri sali che ivi rinvengonsi, e specialmente di una sostanza molto rassomigliante al Caolino, prodotte dalla decomposizione delle lave [1835].—*Atti Acc. Gioen. xii, pp.* 149–61. *Catania*, 1837.

MARAVIGNA, C.—Description des Minéraux simples qui se trouvent à l'Etna, et monographie des formes diverses du soufre cristallisé en Sicile.—8⁰, *pp.* 87, 4 *pls. Paris*, 1838.

MARAVIGNA, C.—Examen de la question suivante : Peut-on prouver les rapports qui existent entre le Basalte et Téphrine, d'après l'inspection de leurs caractères orictognostiques et de leur gisement, pour établir quelque théorie sur l'origine et le moyen de leur formation ? Que pourrait-on dire de probable sur cette question, à l'égard des trachytes de l'Etna ?—*Mém. Congr. scient. France, pp.* 350–55. *Clermont-Ferrand*, 1838.

MARAVIGNA, C.—Mémoires pour servir à l'histoire naturelle de la Sicile. (Orictognosie Etnéenne, Soufre, Célestine, Mollusques et Coquilles, Basalte et Téphrine de l'Etna.)—8⁰, *pp.* 86, 6 *pls. Paris, Londres*, 1838.

MARAVIGNA, C. — Memorie di Orittognosia Etnea e dei Vulcani estinti della Sicilia.—8⁰, *pp.* 203, 2 *pls. Parigi*, 1838. [C.A.]—[An abridged form of the above appears in the report of :] *Congr. scient. de France*, 8⁰, *pp.* 331–49. *Clermont*, 1838.

MARAVIGNA, C.—Su i rapporti che passano fra le rocce dell' Etna e sul modo di loro emissione.—VII *Congr. Scienz. Ital. pp.* 40. *Napoli*, 1845. [C.A.]—*Atti Acc. Gioen. S.* 2, *ii, pp.* 337–67. *Catania*, 1845.

MARAVIGNA, C.—Osservazioni di Trachite sull' Etna.—*Atti Sett. Adun. Scienz. Ital. p.* 1130. *Napoli*, 1846.

MARESCHINI.—[Sull' Eruzione dell' Etna della notte 27–28 Maggio 1819.]—*Giorn. Fis. Chim. Stor. Nat. ii, pp.* 358, 502–3. *Pavia*, 1819.

MARGERIE, E. DE.—*See* SUESS, E.

MARGOLLÉ, E.—*See* ZURCHER, F.

MARINELLI, D.—Dal Canino all' Etna (con tre illustr.).—*Udine*, 1881.

MARINELLI, O.—Alcune particolarità morfologiche della regione Circumetnea.—*Riv. Geog. Ital. Agosto*, 1896.

MARINI, N.—De formidabilissimo terræmotu, *etc.* Poema.—8⁰. *Panormi*, 1729.

MARMOR PARIUM (pseud. ?).—Marmora Oxoniensia ex Arundellianis. Seldenianis aliisque conflata.—*Oxonii*, 1676. Eruption of 475 B.C.

MARTINES, A. M.—De situ Siciliæ et insularum adjacentius.—1580.

MARTINORI.—*See* PAOLUCCI, D.

MARZACHI, L. — Terremoti in Catania.—
" *Lanterna di Messina,*" *Giorn. Sci. Lett. e Arti, i, pp.* 26–29. *Messina,* 1848.

MARZO, G. DE.—Biblioteca storica e letteraria di Sicilia.—*Vols. i–xxvi. Palermo,* 1869–76.

MASCARI, A.—Il Cratere dell' Etna dopo l'esplosione del 19 e 25 Luglio 1899.—*Boll. Soc. Sismol. Ital. v,* 4, *pp.* 145–52. *Modena,* 1899.

MASCULUS, J. B.—I. B. Masculi . . . de incendio Vesuvii excitato xvii Kal. Januar. an. 1631 . . . libri x. Cum chronologia superiorum incendiorum ; et ephemeride ultimi, etc.—2 pts. 4⁰, *pp.* 312+37, 2 *pls. Neapoli,* 1633.
Eruption 1631.

MASSA, G. A.—Della Sicilia grand' Isola del Mediterraneo in prospettiva e il Monte Etna o il Mongibello esposto in veduta da un religioso della Compagnia di Gesù.—
4⁰, *pp.* 126. *Palermo,* 1708.—2 vols. 4⁰. *Vol. i, pp.* 12+359 ; *Vol. ii, pp.* 503. *Palermo,* 1709.
See Cap. xviii, 1708.

MATTEUCCI, R. V.—Sulla attività dei vulcani Vesuvio, Etna, Vulcano, Stromboli e Santorino nell' Autunno del 1898.—*Boll. Soc. Sismol. Ital. v, pp.* 132–44. *Modena,* 1899.

MATTEUCCI, R. V.—Sur l'État actuel des Volcans de l'Europe méridionale.—*C.R. Acad. Sci. cxxix, pp.* 734–37. *Paris,* 1899.

MAUGINO, F.—L'Eruzione dell' Etna 1879. Lettera al prof. Ragona.—*Ann. Soc. Meteor. Ital. ii,* 41–44, *pp.* 306.

MAURO, M. DI.—Osservazioni Geologiche ed Orittologiche dei dintorni di Aci Reale.—*Atti Sett. Adun. Scienz. Ital. pp.* 1167–68. *Napoli,* 1846.

MAURO, M. DI.—Memoria sugli scogli dei Ciclopi.—*Atti Sett. Adun. Scienz. Ital. p.* 1168. *Napoli,* 1846.

MAURO CIRINO.—Lentini abbattuta dai terremoti.—*Messina,* 1700.

MAUROLICO, F. — Cosmographia . . . in tres dialogos distincta.—4⁰. *Venetiis,* 1543.
Cited by Massa, Etna.

MAUROLICO, F.—Sicanicarum Rerum Compendium.—4⁰. *Messanæ,* 1562.——2nd ed. *Messanæ,* 1716.—*See also* GRÆVIUS, J. G.
—Thes. Antiq. . . . Ital. *T. iv.* 1725, *etc.*

MAZZA.—Storia di Adernò.—4⁰, *figs., pls. Catania,* 1820.

MAZZARA, G.—Poema del Mongibello.—*Poeti Siciliani, Cap.* 30.
Reported by Ventimiglia.   Cited by Massa, Etna.

MAZZETTI, L.—*See* BALDACCI.   1879.

MELLONI, M.—Sulla polarità magnetica delle Lave e rocce affini.   Sopra la calamitazione delle Lave in virtù del calore, ecc.—*Mem. R. Acc. Sci. i, pp.* 121–64.   *Napoli,* 1856.—For notices thereon *see* VESUVIUS.

MERCALLI, G.—Sull' eruzione Etnea del 22 Marzo 1883.—*Atti Soc. Ital. Sci. Nat. xxvi, pp.* 111–21.   *Milano,* 1883.

MERCALLI, G.—Éruption de l'Etna et du Vésuve.—" *La Nature,*" sem. 2, *p.* 223. *Paris,* 1884.

MERCALLI, G.—Notizie sullo stato attuale dei Vulcani attivi Italiani.—[Estr.] *Atti Soc. Ital. Sci. Nat. xxvii, pp.* 184–98.   *Milano,* 1884.

MERCALLI, G.—Le ultimi eruzioni dell' Etna del 22 Marzo 1883 e del 18 Maggio 1886.—4⁰, *pp.* 8.   *Firenze, M. Cellini,* 1887. [C.A.]

MERCALLI, G.—L'Etna.—*Natura ed Arte,* 1 *Novembre* 1892.

MERCALLI, G.—Sopra l'eruzione dell' Etna cominciata il 9 Luglio, 1892.—*Atti Soc. Ital. Sci. Nat. xxxiv, pp.* 137–62, 2 *figs. Milano,* 1893.

MERCALLI, G.—I Vulcani attivi della terra (morfologia, dinamismo, prodotti, distribuzione geografica, cause).—8⁰, *pp. viii+* 422, 82 *figs.,* 26 *pls. Milano,* 1907.

MERCALLI, G.—*See* TARAMELLI, T.

MERCATOREM   GERARDUM. — Italiæ, Sclavoniæ et Græcia tabulæ geographicæ.—*fol.,* 23 *col.* maps. *Duysburgi,* 1589.

MERCURIO, G. A.—Sulla salsa di Fondachello nel comune di Mascali, del profondamento parziale del cono argilloso e dell' apparizione di un' acqua minerale gasosa.—*Catania,* 1847.

MERCURIO, G. A.—Relazione della grandiosa eruzione Etnea della notte dal 20 al 21 Agosto 1852.—*Catania*, 1853.—1 *pl. Palermo*, 1853.—[A short abstract in :] RATH.—Aetna, *p.* 32.—*Also in* BALTZER.—Wanderungem am Aetna, *p.* 38.

METAPHRASTUS, S.—Editio Migre.—*Vol. i, p.* 346. *Paris*, 1864.
  Eruption of A.D. 251.

METAPHRASTUS, S.—Vitæ Sanctorum.— *In Neander's Historia Ecclesiæ, Vol. i.*
  Eruption of A.D. 253.

MICHALLON.—Ruines du Théâtre de Taormine. Renoux del.—Publié par Lami Denozan, Libraire-éditeur, rue des Fossés Montmartre, no. 4.—*From his* " Vues d'Italie et de Sicile dessinées d'après Nature."—*Paris*, 1827.
  Lith. on straw-col. film : 272 × 223 mm.

MICHALLON.—Vues d'Italie et de Sicile dessinées d'après Nature et lithographiées par MM. Villeneuve, Deroi et Renoux.— *fol. Paris*, 1827.
  Of no scientific interest.

MINASI, G.—Relazione de' Tremuoti di Sicilia. — *Messina*, 1783. — Supplemento. *Messina*, 1785.

MIRON, F.—Étude des phénomènes volcaniques, tremblements de terre, éruptions volcaniques, le cataclysme de la Martinique, 1902.—*8⁰, pp. viii+320, fig. and map. Paris*, 1903.

MIRONE. G.—Sopra un' acqua minerale (Acqua Santa) nelle vicinanze di Catania.— *Catania*, 1786.

MIRONE, G., e PASQUALI, G.—Descrizione del fenomeni osservati nell' eruzione dell' Etna accaduta in quest' anno 1787 e d'alcuni vulcanici prodotti che gli appartengono.—*12⁰, pp.* 29. *Catania*, 1788.
  There is also a descript. of the Aurora Borealis of 13 July 1787 during the erupt. French transl. on page facing Ital. text.

MODONI, A.—Su per l'Etna : ricordi del XIII Congresso Alpina Italiano.—16⁰, *pp.* 84. *Milano*, 1881.

MOLL, H.—Map of Italy, containing a representation of Etna, during the eruption of 1669.—*London*, 1714.

MOMPILERI.—Relazione MS. dell' eruzione del 1536.
  Cited by Massa.

MONACO, F.—Cataclysmus Ætnæus, sive inundatio ignea Ætnæ montis anni 1669.— 4⁰, *foll.* 6, *pp.*60,*figs. Venetiis*,1669. [C.A.]

MONCORNET, VESUE.—Plan du Mont Etna, communément dit Mont Gibel, en l'Isle de Scicille et de l'jncendie arriué par un Treblement [*sic*] de Terre le 8me mars dernier 1669. À Paris ches la Vesue Moncornet rue St. Jacque avec privilège du Roy.
  Engrav. : 411×328 mm., with seven lines of text below.

MONGITORE, A.—La Sicilia ricercata nelle cose più memorabili.—2 vols. 4⁰. *Palermo*, 1742-43.
  See Tom. ii, *p.* 286 : Etna, ovvero Mongibello, p. 345 : Istoria cronologica dei terremoti in Sicilia, etc.

MONGITORE, A.—Cronologia de Tremuoti di Sicilia.—4⁰. *Palermo*, 1743.

MONGITORE, A. — Diario Palermitano 1640-1743. — *Biblioteca de Marzo, Vols. vii, ix e xii.*

MONTÉMONT, A.—Des Volcans en général et plus spécialement du Vésuve et de l'Etna.—*Bull Soc. Géog. S.* 2, *xvi, pp.* 137-58. *Paris*, 1841.

MONTICELLI, T., e COVELLI, N.—Analisi del fango dell' Etna.— *Bibl. Analit. Sci. Lett. ed Arti, pp.* 143-48. *Napoli, Agosto,* 1823. — Also : *Giorn. Lett. di Palermo*, 1823.

MONTICELLI, T., e COVELLI, N.—Esame chimico d'una pioggia di polvere caduta il 21 di Giugno, 1822.—*Giorn. di Sicilia, N.* 5. 1823.

MORELLI, F.—Raccolta degli antichi monumenti esistenti nella città di Pesto e di alcune altre vedute appartenenti alla medesima città.—Roma, nella calcografia di Agapito Franzetti a Torsanguigna, ecc. —20 *pls. obl.*
  The last two refer to Sicily and Etna. The first is signed F. Hackert, and it may be presumed that the others were by him also. *See* last plate.

MORICAND, S.—Éruption de l'Etna (en 1819).—" *Nouv. Ann. Voyages,*" *N.S. iii, pp.* 455-62. *Paris*, 1819.

MORICAND, S.—Notice sur une éruption récente de l'Etna.—*Bibl. Univ. xi, pp.* 191-99. *Genève*, 1819.

MORICAND, S.—Die geognostische Beschaffenheit Siciliens.—*Ann. Phys. vi, pp.* 200-12. *Leipzig*, 1820.—*Journ. Britann.* 1819.

MORIS, A.—Account of the eruption of 1822. —*See* RODWELL, G. F.—Etna, *p.* 106.

MORTILLARO, B. V.—Discorso su la vita, e su le opere dell' Abbate Domenico Scinà. —8⁰, p. 61. Palermo, 1837. Etna in 1811.

MORTILLARO, B. V.—Dizionario geografi-costatistico Siciliano-lat-ital. dell' Isola di Sicilia e delle sue adiacenze.—pp. 62. Palermo, 1850.

MOTTURA, S.—Sulla formazione Solfifera della Sicilia.—Mem. per serv. descriz. carta geol. Ital. pubbl. R. Com. Geol. Ital. i, pp. 51–140, tav. i–iv. Firenze, 1871.—Mem. Acc. Sci. xxv, pp. 363–444. Torino, 1871.

MRAZEC, L.—See DUPARC, L.

MUELLER.—See BORNER.—Cratère de l'Etna, Sicile. Lit.

MUELLER, C. F. (Chromolithographie von).—Ausbruch des Aetna. II Bd. 9. A chromo. on dark buff paper : 240 × 184 mm.

MUELLER, G., und KEMPF, P.—Unter-suchungen über die Absorption des Ster-nenlichts in der Erdatmosphäre, angestellt auf dem Aetna und in Catania.—See VOGEL, H. (editor).—Publicationen des Astrophisikalischen Observatoriums zu Potsdam, xi, pp. 213–79. Potsdam, 1898.

MUELLER, G. A. (sculp.).—Aetna. Durch Kunst Verlag. W. Creuzbauer in Carlsruhe. Small steel engrav. with shepherds, goats and bridge in foreground : 128 × 97 mm.

MUENSTER, S.—Cosmographia, etc.—fol. Basel, 1545.—Lat. trans.fol. Basileæ, 1550. See Lib. I, Cap. vii, pp. 5–6: De Igne in terræ visceribus flagranti, and Lib. II, pp. 257–58 : De Monte Ætna. Description of the changes in crater of Etna since the time of Strabo to the erupt. of 1537.

MUENTER, F.—Viaggio in Sicilia. (Transl. from German, with notes by F. Peranni, and including " Viaggio al Monte Etna fatta da L. Spallanzani nell' anno 1788.") —2 vols. 12⁰, 2 col. pls. Milano, 1831.

MURABITO, F.—Catania liberata dall' in-cendio dell' Etna del 1669 in x canti.— Catania, 1675. Cited by Ferrara : Storia di Catania.

MURATORI.—Annales. See Tom. v, p. 743 ; Tom. vii, p. 342 ; Tom. x, p. 921, etc.

MURICCE, F. CAREGA DI.—Etna. Confe-renza tenuta presso il Club Alpino di Bologna.—Bologna, 1877.

MURICCE,F.CAREGA DI.—I Vulcani d'Italia (Etna, Vesuvio, Campi Flegrei, Isole Eolie, Stromboli).—1877.

MURICCE, F. CAREGA DI.—Il nuovo Monte Etneo (Umberto-Margherita) studiato e descritto dal prof. Orazio Silvestri.—Rass. Alp. ii, 1, p. 7. RoccaSan Casciano(Firenze), Marzo, 1880.

MUSSET, P. DE.—Voyage pittoresque en Italie, partie méridionale, et en Sicile. Illustrations de MM. Rouargue Frères.—4⁰, pp. 524. Paris, 1856.

MUSUMECI, M.—Memoria sopra la eruzione apparsa nella plaga occidentale dell' Etna nelle notti del 31 Ottobre, 1 e 3 Novembre dell' anno 1832 per cui fu in pericolo il comune di Bronte.—Atti Acc. Gioen. ix, pp. 207–18. Catania, 1835.

MUSUMECI, M.—Sopra una colonnella nella Lava.—Opere Archeol. ed Art.i,p.59 (Nota).

NANSOUTY, M. DE.—Actualités scienti-fiques. Volcans et Volcanisme . . . etc. —16⁰, pp. 361. Paris, 1906.

NARBONE.—Bibliographia Sicula.—Paler-mo, 1854. See Vol. iii, p. 139 : descript. of Auria during the eruption of Etna, 1669.

NATALIS COMITIS.—Universæ historiæ sui temporis libri triginta ab anno salutis 1545 usque ad annum 1581.—Acta Sanct. ii, p. 650. Venetiis, 1581. See Lib. XVII, p. 370 : eruption 1566.

NAUDÉ, G., und GIULIANI, G. B.—Ueber den Vesuv und Aetna. —?, 1632.

NEGRI, F.—Pianta del Monte Etna. Cited by Massa, Etna.

NEUMAYR, M. — Erdgeschichte. — Allge-meine Naturkunde, i, pp. 42+xii+653, very num. illustr. Leipzig, 1886.

NIBBY, A.—See VASI, M. 1826.

NIGER, M.—Siciliæ insulæ descriptio.—See ANON.—Scriptores Rer. Sicul. iii.

NODIER, CH.—See NORVINS.

NORVINS, NODIER, CH., DUMAS, ALEX., DIDIER,CH.,WALCKNAER,LEGOUVÉ, ROYER, AL., BERLIOZ, H., BEAU-VOIR, ROGER DE, AUGER, H., LEMONNIER.—L'Italie pittoresque. Tab-leau historique et descriptif de l'Italie, du Piémont, de la Sardaigne, de Malte, de la Sicile et la Corse. Orné de dessins inédits de Mme. Haudebourt-Lescot, MM. le Comte de Forbin, Gravet, Deveria, Storelli, Coignet, Girard et Lambrouste.—2 vols.

8⁰, *many pls. and maps. Paris,* 1737.—8⁰. *Paris,* 1846.

NOUGARET, J.—Lettres de Sicile. Excursion à l'Etna.—*Le Moniteur universel, No.* 77, *p.* 283, *col.* 6—*p.* 284, *col.* 2. *Paris,* 18 *mars,* 1865.

OBSEQUENS, J.—Iulii Obsequentis Prodigiorum liber.—16⁰. *Basileæ,* 1589.
See p. 64, cap. 82 ; p. 66, cap. 85 ; p. 69, cap. 89.

ODDONE, E.—L'Éruzione Etnea del Marzo-Aprile 1910.—*Boll. Soc. Sismol. Ital. xiv,* 4–5, *pp.* 141-204. *Modena,* 1910.

ODELEBEN, E. G. VON.—Beiträge zur geologischen Kenntniss von Italien.—2 Th. *Freiberg,* 1819.

OMBONI, G.—Geologia dell' Italia.—8⁰, 5 *tav. Milano,* 1869.
See No. 14.

OMODEI, ANTONIO FILOTEO DEGLI.—A. P. de Homodeis . . . Ætnæ topographia.—4⁰, *pp.* 56. [*Perugia ?*] 1590.—Another ed. "incendiorumque Ætnæorum historia," 4⁰. *Venetiis,* 1591.—*Also in* ANON.— Italiæ illustratæ . . . scriptores varii, *etc. fol.* 1600.—*Also in* GRÆVIUS, J. G.— Thes. Antiq. et Hist. Ital. *etc. T.* 10. 1725, *etc.*

OMODEI, ANTONIO FILOTEO DEGLI.—La Descrittione Latina del sito di Mongibello, trad. in Italica.— 4⁰, *foll. iv, pp.* 85, *with view of Etna at back of frontisp. Palermo,* 1611.—*See* ORLANDINI.

OMODEI, ANTONIO FILOTEO DEGLI.— Descrizione della Sicilia.—*MS. in the Biblioteca Communale di Palermo.*—*See* MARZO, G. DI.—Bibl. Stor. e Lett. di Sic. *xxiv and xxv* (*S.* 2, *vi and vii*).

ORLANDINI, L.—La Descrittione Latina del sito di Mongibello di Ant. Filoteo degli Homodei tradotta in Lingua Italiana.— 4⁰, *foll. iv, pp.* 85, 1 *pl. Palermo,* 1611.

OROSIUS, P. — P. Orosii . . . adversus Paganos historiarum libri septem.—4⁰, *pp.* 142. *Coloniæ,* M.D.XXVI.
See Lib. II, Cap. xiv, xviii ; Lib. v, Cap. v, x, xiii : erupt. 425, 134, 126, 122 B.C.

ORTOLANI, G. E.—Prospectus of the Minerals of Sicily.—1808.

ORTOLANI, G. E.—Prospetto dei Minerali di Sicilia.—2⁰ ediz. 8⁰, *pp.* 17–18, 30–31. *Palermo,* 1809.

ORTOLANI, G. E.—Nuovo Dizionario geografico, statistico, e biografico della Sicilia antica e moderna.—8⁰, *pp.* 8+156, 1 *map. Palermo,* 1819.

ORVILLE, J. PH. D'.— Jacobi Philippi d'Orville Sicula, quibus Siciliæ veteris rudera illustrantur.—*fol., many figs. and pls. Amstelodami,* 1764.

OSTERVALD, J. F. D. (ed. by).—Voyage Pittoresque en Sicile.—2 vols. *fol. Paris,* 1822-26.
See Vol. ii, 7 views of Etna with explan. notes. *See also* LASALLE.

OTTAVIO, PADRE G.—Isag. ad hist. Sic.— *See* CAIETANUS, OCTAVIUS.
Cited by Mongitore. *See* Cap. XIII, N. 15: Earthquake at Etna.

OTTAVIO, PADRE G.—Sicul. in animad.
See T. i, fol. 22 : Earthquake of 1619. Cited by Mongitore.

OTTÉ, E. C.—*See* QUATREFAGES, J. L. A. DE.

OVIDIUS.—Metamorph. Lib. xv, pp. 299 *et seq.,* 340-55.

PACICHELLI, G. B.—Memorie di viaggi per l'Europa Christiana scritte a diversi in occasione de' suoi Ministeri.—5 vols. 12⁰. *Pt. i, pp.* 40+743+53 ; *Pt.* 2, *pp.* 8+ 827+40 ; *Pt.* 3, *pp.* 8+761+27 ; *Pt.* 4, *Vol. i, pp.* 4+541+20 ; *Vol. ii, pp.* 4+ 438+18. *Napoli,* 1685.
See Pt. 4, Vol. ii, pp. 66 *et seq.* : Del Mongibello.

PACICHELLI, G. B. — Lettere familiari istoriche ed erudite.—2 vols. 12⁰. *Vol. i, pp.* 12+490 ; *Vol. ii, pp.* 20+432+34. *Napoli,* 1695.

PAGLIA, B.—Epigrammata in XII. Suetoni Cæsaris.—8⁰, *pp.* 200. *Neapoli,* 1693.
Messana fugit, Ætna teritus, pp. 65.

PALAZZO, L.—Risultati delle determinazioni magnetiche in Sicilia, e cenni sulle perturbazioni nelle Isole Vulcaniche e nei dintorni dell' Etna.—*Atti R. Acc. Lincei, S.* 5, *Rend. vi, sem.* 2, *pp.* 331-37. *Roma,* 1897.

PALGRAVE, SIR F.—An Account of the eruption of Mount Etna in the year 1536, from an original contemporary document, communicated in a letter to J. G. Children, Esq., Secretary of the Royal Society.— *Proc. R. Soc. iii,* 19, *p.* 316. *London,* 1835.

PALGRAVE, SIR F.—Sac. Dr. Children communique une lettre de Sir Francis Palgrave contenant le récit d'une éruption du Mont Etna dans l'année 1536 d'après les documents originaux contemporains, trouvés parmi les papiers qui renferment la correspondance de Henry VIII avec les princes d'Italie, dans les archives de Westminster. — *L'Institut. Journ. général, N.* 5, 1835.

PALMERI, N.—Somma della Storia di Sicilia.—5 vols. 8⁰. *Palermo,* 1834-40.
See Vol. ii, pp. 274-75. 1835.
Another ed. 4⁰. *Palermo,* 1850.

PALMIERI, L.—Un Fatto che merita di essere registrato. (Relazione tra i terremoti di S. Nicandro del 1865 e del 1866, e le eruzioni dell' Etna degli stessi anni.)— *Rend. R. Acc. Sci. xxv,* p. 125. *Napoli,* 1886.

PANVINI, P.—Saggio di Tufo Calcareo di forma somigliante alle organiche, trovato in Comiso e Monte Etna.—*Atti Sett. Adun. Scienz. Ital.* p. 1151. *Napoli,* 1846.

PAOLUCCI, D., MARTINORI, FORNARI. —La Salita degli Alpinisti Romani sull' Etna. Disegni di D. Paolucci, sopra schizzi originali di Fornari e testo di Martinori.— *Illustrazione Italiana,* sem. 2, *p.* 123. *Milano,* 1879.

PAPIN, S.—Theb. XII, 274 ; Silv. III, I. 130.

PARETO, L.—Osservazioni sopra l'Etna e la costa di Aci.—*Atti Sett. Adun. Scienz. Ital. p.* 1111. *Napoli,* 1846.

PARETO, L.—Della posizione delle Roccie pirogene ed eruttive dei periodi terziario quaternario ed attuale in Italia.—8⁰, *pp.* 35. *Genova,* 1852.

PARKIN, J.—The remote cause of epidemic diseases ; or, the influence of volcanic action in the production of general pestilences. Part II.—8⁰, *pp.* 16, *foll.* 4, *3 pls. London,* 1853.

PARTHEY.—Wanderungen durch Sicilien und die Levante.—2 pts. 12⁰. *Pt. i, pp.* 8+458+32 (*of music*) ; *Pt. ii, pp.* x+594. *Berlin,* 1834-40.
See Pt. i, pp. 226-81, 333.

PARUTA, F.—La Sicilia descritta.—*fol. Lione,* 1617.
Cited by Carrera.

PASCALE, V.—Descrizione storico-topografico-fisica delle Isole del regno di Napoli.— 8⁰, *pp.* 138, *1 pl. Napoli,* 1796. [C.A.]

PASQUALI, G.—*See* MIRONE, G.

PASS, J. (sc.).—Eruption of Mount Etna in July 1787.—London, Published as the Act directs, March 5, 1808, by J. Wilkes.
Engrav. : 218×180 mm. Another copy, hand-coloured, framed.

PATERNIO, J.—Matricula monasteriorum S. Mariæ, S. Leonis.—*Catanæ,* 1693.

PATERNÒ, A.—Cronaca di Sicilia.
Cited by Auria.

PATERNÒ, I. (Principe di Biscari).—Viaggio per tutte le antichità della Sicilia.—4⁰, *pp.* 200, 2 *pls. Napoli,* 1817. [C.A.]

PAULY-WISSOWA.—Realencyclopädie.
See article : " Aitne," Vol. i, pp. 1111 *et seq.*

PELLÉ, C.—Il Mediterraneo illustrato, le sue Isole e le sue Spiagge comprendente la Sicilia, ecc. ecc. compilata dal bibliofilo M. Malagoli Vecchi.—4⁰, *pp.* 512, *num. pls. Firenze,* 1841.
See pp. 215-67.

PENK, A.—Ueber Palagonit u. Basalttuffe. —*Zeitschr. deutsch. geol. Gesellsch. xxxi, pp.* 504-77. *Berlin,* 1879.

PERANNI, F.—*See* MUENTER.

PEREIRA, A.—Die Aetna-Eruption (1879). —*Verh. k. k. geol. Reichsanst. Nr.* 10, *pp.* 231-32. *Wien,* 1879.

PÉROU, Du.—Notice sur l'Etna, formation et composition de son massif. Éruption de février 1865, précédée d'une histoire des anciennes éruptions, etc.—*Catane,* 1865.

PERREY, DE.—*See* BORNEMANN, J. G. 1856.

PETAVIUS, D.—Dionysii Petavii Aurelianensis . . . variarum dissertationum ad Uranologion . . . libri octo in quibus pleraque ad cœlestium rerum ac temporum scientiam necessaria tractantur. — *See* PETAU. — *Uranologion, etc. fol. Paris,* 1630.
Cit. by Massa, Etna.

PETERMANN, A. H.—Uebersicht des vulkanischen Heerdes im Mittelmeer, Maasstab 1 : 15,000,000.—*Peterm. Mitth. Taf.* 7. *Gotha,* 1866.

PETERS, C. E. F.—Di alcune osservazioni su Magnetismo all' Etna. Lettera a Leopoldo del Re.—*Atti R. Acc. Sci. v, pt.* 1, *appendice, pp.* 19-46, 1 *pl. Napoli,* 1843.

PETRARCA, F.—Chronica delle vite de Pontefici et Imperatori Romani.—8⁰, *foll.* xc+1. *Venetia,* MDVII.
See p. lxviii : earthquake of 1159.

PETRONIUS, A.—Satyr 119.
Eruption of 49 B.C., cited by Massa.

PETRUS, BLESENSIS.—Ætna mons. (Cronica manoscritta dei Re di Sicilia ; epistola 46 ad Richard.)—*Opera Omnia, p.* 683. *Parisiis,* 1667.
Eruption of 1169, cited by Massa and Amico.

PETTINELLI, P.—*See* BARTOLI, A.

PHILOSTRATUS.—Vita Apoll.—*v, cap.* 16 and 17.

PHILOTHEUS.—*See* OMODEI, ANTONIO FILOTEO DEGLI.

PIAZZA, F. M. DI.—Cronaca. MS.
Earthquake of 1176, cited by Massa, Etna.

PIGNATELLI, M.—Estratto della relazione, che il Sigᵣ Maresciallo Pignatelli ha rassegnata alla Corte, dando esatto conto di quanto ha egli potuto sinora appurare sulle avvenute rovine nella Calabria ulteriore, *etc.* [On the back :] Copy of an authentic paper which Marquis Squillace, the Spanish Ambassador at Venice, received from Naples.—MS. *fol., foll.* 2. *Napoli,* 11 *Marzo,* 1783. [B.M. 8967. ff. 36–7.]

PILLA, L.—Parallelo fra i tre Vulcani ardenti dell' Italia.—*Napoli,* 1835.—*Atti Acc. Gioen. xii, pp.* 89–127. *Catania,* 1837.—*N. J. f. Min. p.* 347. *Stuttgart,* 1836.

PILLA, L. — Sopra la produzione delle fiamme nei Vulcani e sopra le consequenze che se ne possono tirare.—4⁰. *Pisa,* 1837.— 4⁰, *pp.* 28, 2 *pls. Lucca,* 1844.—*Atti Riun. Scienz. Ital. pp.* 293–318. *Padova,* 1843. —*Museo, ii, pp.* 211–36. *Napoli,* 1844.— [Estr.] *Nuov. Ann. Sci. Nat. di Bologna, Nov.* 1844.—*Bull. Soc. géol. France, viii, p.* 262. *Paris,* 1837.—*Bibl. univ. xlviii, pp.* 175–83. *Genève,* 1843.—*C.R. Acad. Sci. xvii, pp.* 889–95. *Paris,* 1843.— ROTH.—*Der Vesuv, etc. p.* 350. *Berlin,* 1857.—*Edinb. New Phil. Journ. xxxvi, pp.* 231–36. 1844.—*Polytechn. Mag. i, pp.* 341–44. *London,* 1844.

PILLA, L.—Studii di Geologia.—*Napoli,* 1841.

PILLA, L.—Aggiunte al discorso sopra la produzione delle fiamme ne' Vulcani.— *Il Cimento, pp.* 380–96. *Pisa,* 1844.— *Museo, v, pp.* 152–66. *Napoli,* 1845.— *Nuov. Ann. Sci. Nat. iii, pp.* 161–78. *Bologna,* 1845.—*Atti Congr. Lucca, pp.* 16, 1 *fig.*

PILLA, L.—Trattáto di Geologia.—2 vols. 8⁰. *Vol. i, pp. xiv*+549, *num. figs., Pisa,* 1847 ; *Vol. ii, pp.* 614, *num. figs., Pisa,* 1847–51.
See Vol. i.

PILLA, L.—Cenno storico sui progressi della Orittognosia e della Geognosia in Italia.— *Progr. Sci. Lett. ed Arti, ii, pp.* 37–81. *Napoli,* 1832.

PINDARUS.—Pythia.
See Ode 1, 36–38, 40–46, also Ode 29 *et seq.*

PINELLI.—*See* GOLDICUTT, J.

PINET, A. DU.—Plantz, povrtraitz et descriptions de plusieurs villes et forteresses, tant de l'Evrope, Asie, et Afrique, que des Indes, et terres neuues : leurs fondations, antiquitez, et manières de viure : *etc.* —*obl. fol., foll.* 4, *pp. xxxvi*+308+*index. Lyon,* 1564.

PIRRI, ROCCO.—Catanensis Ecclesiæ Notitiæ.—*See* GRÆVIUS, J. G.—Thes. Antiq. Sic. *i, Lib.* III.

PIRRI, ROCCO.—R. Pirri Chronologia regum Siciliæ.—*See* GRÆVIUS, J. G.—Thes. Antiq. Sic. *v.*

PIRRI, ROCCO.—Sicilia Sacra.—MS. notes, 4 vols. 4⁰. *Panormi, Catanœ [Salerno printed],* 1644–33–1734.—Another ed. of vols. 1 and 2.—*See* GRÆVIUS, J. G. Thes. Antiq. . . . Ital. *ii and iii.*— 3rd ed. 2 tom. *fol. Panormi,* 1733. [B.M.]

PIRRI, ROCCO.—Annales Panormi sub annis D. Ferdinandi de Andrada archiepiscopi Panormitani . . . ab anno 1646.—*See* MARZO, G. DI.—Bibl. Stor. e Lett. *iv, pp.* 58–252. 1869.

PISTOIA, C. F.—Carta dell' Etna in rilievo per uso dell' Istituto Topografico Militare a Firenze (colorata geol.). Scala verticale 1 : 25,000 ; scala orizzontale 1 : 50,000.
Constructed on the basis of the map of Sartorius von Waltershausen.

PIUTTI, A., e MAGLI, G.—Sulla Radioattività dei prodotti della recente eruzione dell' Etna.—*Rend. R. Acc. Sci. S.* 3, *xvi, pp.* 159–63. *Napoli,* 1910.

PLATANIA, GAET.—Geological notes on Acireale. — *See* JOHNSTON-LAVIS.— South Italian Volcanoes, *pp.* 37–44, 2 *pls. Napoli,* 1891.

PLATANIA, GAET.—Sulla presenza di Filliti nei tufi della Scala (Acireale).—_Atti e Rend. Acc. Sci. Lett. ed Arti di Acireale, N.S. iii, pp._ 157-60. _Acireale_, 1892.

PLATANIA, GAET.—The recent eruption of Etna.—_fig._ — ?, 1892.—_Rept. Brit. Assoc._ 1899, _p._ 750. 1900.—"_Nature,_" _xlvi, pp._ 542-47, 8 _figs. London_, 1892.

PLATANIA, GAET.—Su alcuni Minerali di Aci Catena. Communicazione preliminare. —_Atti e Rend. Acc. Sci. Lett. ed Arti di Acireale, N.S. iv, pp._ 209-12. _Acireale_, 1893.

PLATANIA, GAET.—Su la Xiphonite, nuovo Amfibolo dell' Etna.—_Atti e Rend. Acc. Sci. Lett. ed Arti di Acireale, N.S. v, Class. Sci. pp._ 55-62. _Acireale_, 1894.—_N. J. f. Min. ii, pp._ 236-37. _Stuttgart_, 1895.

PLATANIA, GAET. e GIOV.—Sui recenti terremoti nella regione orientale dell' Etna. —_Rend. Acc. Sci. Lett. ed Arti dei Zelanti, N.S. vi, Class. Sci. pp._ 97-99. _Acireale_, 1895.

PLATANIA, GAET.—Aci Castello : Ricerche geologiche e vulcanologiche.—_Rend. e Mem. R. Acc. Sci. Acireale, S._ 3, _ii, pp._ 23-56, _pls._ i, ii, iia, _and_ iii [_geol. map_]. 1903.

PLATANIA, GAET.—Sur les anomalies de la gravité et les bradysismes dans la région orientale de l'Etna. — _C.R. Acad. Sci. cxxxviii, pp._ 859-60. _Paris_, 1904.

PLATANIA, GAET.—Su un moto differenziale della spiaggia orientale dell' Etna.— _Atti_ v _Congr. Geog. Ital._ 1904, _ii, sez._ 1, _pp._ 214-19. _Napoli_, 1905.

PLATANIA, GAET.—Origine della Timpa della Scala. Contributo allo studio dei burroni vulcanici.—_Boll. Soc. Geol. Ital. xxiv, pp._ 451-60. _Roma_, 1905.

PLATANIA, GAET.—Sulla velocità dei microsismi vulcanici.— _Mem. Acc. Sci. Lett. ed Arti Zelanti, N.S._ (3), _iv, pp._ 8. _Acireale_, 1905.—_N. J. f. Min. ii, p._ 188. _Stuttgart_, 1906.

PLATANIA, GAET.—Sul Magnetismo delle lave dell' Etna.—_Atti_ v _Congr. Naturalisti. Ital. ii, pp._ 208-13. _Milano_, 1907.

PLATANIA, GAET.—Su alcuni avanzi di Cervo nei tufi dell' Etna.—_Rend. e Mem. R. Acc. Sci. Acireale, S._ 3, _v_, 1906-7, _pp._ 169-71. _Acireale_, 1909.

PLATANIA, GAET.—L'Erosione marina all' Isola di Aci Trezza.—_Mem. R. Acc. Zelanti, S._ 3, _v_, 1906-7, _pp._ 35, 4 _pls. Acireale_, 1909.

PLATANIA, GAET.—Il Terremoto Calabrese dell 8 Settembre 1905 a Stromboli.—_Mem. R. Acc. Zelanti, S._ 3, _v_, 1906-7, _pp._ 79-87. _Acireale_, 1909.

PLATANIA, GAET.—Sull' Eruzione dell' Etna del 29 Aprile 1908. Prima relazione. —_Rend. e Mem. R. Acc. Sci. Lett. ed Arti Zelanti, S._ 3, _v_, 1906-7, _pp._ 89-96. _Acireale_, 1909.

PLATANIA, GAET.—L'Eruzione dell' Etna del 1910.—_Riv. Geog. Ital. xvii, pp._ 293-403. _Firenze_, 1910.

PLATANIA, GAET.—L'Istituto Etneo di Vulcanologia della R. Università di Catania. Sunto della communicazione presentata alla Quinta Riunione della Società Italiana per il Progresso delle Scienze.—8⁰, _pp._ 4. _Acireale_, 1911.

PLATANIA, GAET.—La recente eruzione dell' Etna.—_Atti_ VII _Congr. Geog. Ital._ 1910, _pp._ 16, 10 _figs. Palermo_, 1911.

PLATANIA, GAET.—Le recente fasi eruttive dell' Etna.—8⁰, _pp._ 8. _Acireale_, 1911.

PLATANIA, GAET.—La grande eruzione Etnea del Settembre 1911.—_Riv. Geog. Ital. xix, pp._ 511-29, 9 _figs. Firenze_, 1912.

PLATANIA, GAET.—Il Terremoto del 7 Dicembre 1907.—_Rend. e Mem. R. Acc. Sci. Lett. ed Arti Zelanti, S._ 3, _vi_, 1908-11, _pp._ 13-20. _Acireale_, 1912.

PLATANIA, GAET.—Effetti Magnetici del Fulmine.—_Rend. e Mem. R. Acc. Sci. Lett. ed Arti Zelanti, S._ 3, _vi_, 1908-11, _pp._ 21-25. _Acireale_, 1912.

PLATANIA, GAET.—I singolari terremoti di S. Caterina (Acireale).—_Rend. e Mem. R. Acc. Sci. Lett. ed Arti Zelanti, S._ 3, _vi_, 1908-11, _pp._ 27-33. _Acireale_, 1912.'

PLATANIA, GAET.—Su l'emanazione di anidride carbonica nel fianco orientale dell' Etna.—_Pubbl. Ist. Geog. Fis. Vulc. R. Univ. Catania, N._ 1, _pp._ 7. _Acireale_, 1914.

PLATANIA, GAET.—L'Esportazione della lava dell' Etna.—_Boll. Comiz. Agrar. di Acireale_, "_Agricoltore Etneo,_" _anno_ xvi, _trim._ 3, _pp._ 7.

PLATANIA, GIOV.—Le Typhon du 7 octobre 1884 à Catane, en Sicile.—"_La Nature,_" _xiii_, 1, _pp._ 97-98, 2 _figs. Paris_, 1885.

PLATANIA, GIOV.—Les Tremblements de terre de Nicolosi (Sicile).—"_La Nature,_" _xiii_, 2, _p._ 350. _Paris_, 1885.

PLATANIA, Giov.—La récente éruption de l'Etna.— " *La Nature,*" *xiv,* 2, *pp.* 97–99, 1 *fig.,* 1 *map. Paris,* 1886.

PLATANIA, Giov.—L'Éruption de l'Etna. —" *La Nature,*" *xx, sem.* 2, *pp.* 278–82, 4 *figs. Paris,* 1892.

PLATANIA, Giov.—Radioattività di materiali Etnei.—*Boll. Acc. Gioen. S.* 2, *fasc.* 15, *pp.* 25–28. *Catania,* 1911.

PLATANIA, S.—Sul Carbonato di Soda nativo nelle Lave dell' Etna [1832].—*Atti Acc. Gioen. viii, pp.* 153–78. *Catania,* 1834.

PLATTNER, C. F.—Analyse des Gesteins von Serra Giannicola in Val del Bove.— *Mitgeth. in Fr. Hoffmann's Beobacht. Karsten's Archiv, xiii, p.* 702. 1839.

PLINIUS.—Historia natur.—II, 103, 106, 110, *and* III, 8, 14.

POHLIG, H.—Untersuchung des neuesten Aetna-Ausbruches.—*Verhandl. naturh. Vereins preuss. Rheinl. S.* 5, *ix,* 2 *Sitz. Bonn,* 1893.

POLEHAMPTON, E., GOOD, J. M.—The Gallery of Nature and Art, in six volumes, illustrated with one hundred engravings.— —2nd ed. 8⁰. *Vol. i, pp. vi+x+*527 ; *Vol. ii, pp. vi+*488 ; *Vol. iii, pp. v+*411 ; *Vol. iv, pp.* 6+552 ; *Vol. v, pp. vi+*688 ; *Vol. vi, pp. vi+*624+*iv. London,* 1818. *See* Vol. i, pp. 403–35.

POLEMONE. — De admirabilibus Siciliæ Fluminibus. Cited by FERRARA, F., in " Mem. sulle acque d. Sicilia," p. 7. Londra, 1811.

POLI, I.—A Short and ffaithful Account of the Earthquakes lately happen'd in the province of Calabria Ultra.—*fol.* [B.M. 8967. ff. 39–44.] MS. of an account sent to the Royal Society, dated Naples, May 13, 1783.

POMBA, Cav. C.—L'Italia nel suo Aspetto Fisico.—*Publ. G. B. Paravia e C., Torino, Roma, Milano, Firenze, Napoli,* 1890. 1 : 100,000 horiz. and vert. Raised map on section of globe.

POMPONIUS MELA.—De situ orbis II, 7. Eruption of first century B.C.

PONTE, G.—Deflazione prodotta dalle sabbie vulcaniche nella Valle del Bove.—*Boll. Acc. Gioen. S.* 2, 5 e 6, *pp.* 13–15. *Catania,* 1909.

PONTE, G.—Gita attorno all' Etna 11 Settembre 1909.—*Boll. Soc. Geol. Ital. xxviii, pp. clxxxiii–clxxxviii,* 3 *figs. Roma,* 1910.

PONTE, G.—Gita ad Acireale ed alle Isole dei Ciclopi.—*Boll. Soc. Geol. Ital. xxviii, pp. ccix–ccxv,* 6 *figs. Roma,* 1910.

PONTE, G.—Fase hawaiana dell' attività dell' Etna.—*Atti R. Acc. Lincei, S.* 5, *Rend. xx, sem.* 1, *pp.* 257–59. *Roma,* 1911.

PONTE, G.—Nota preventiva sulla violenta eruzione Etnea del 10 Settembre 1911.— 8⁰, *pp.* 13. *Catania,* 1911.

PONTE, G.—Studii sull' eruzione Etnea del 1910.—*Atti R. Acc. Lincei, Mem. Cl. Sci. Fis. S.* 5, *viii, pp.* 665–92, *pl. viii. Catania,* 1911.

PONTE, G.—Sulla cenere vulcanica dell' eruzione Etnea del 1911.—*Atti R. Acc. Lincei, S.* 5, *Rend. xxi, sem.* 2, *pp.* 209–16. *Roma,* 1912.

PORTAL, P.—Osservazioni sopra il Ferro Speculare vulcanico trovato nell' Etna.— 8⁰, *pp.* 10. — ?, — ?

PORTIUS, S.—Physiologicum opus. De Ætnæ ignibus eorumque causis.— *Messinæ,* 1618.

POWER, Jeannette.—Itinerario della Sicilia riguardante tutt' i rami di storia naturale, e parecchi di antichità che essa contiene.—4⁰, *pp. viii+*249, *pl. Messina,* 1839. Etna : pp. 63–82.

POWER, Jeannette.—Guida per la Sicilia. —8⁰, *pp. xxvi+*380, 3 *maps. Napoli,* 1842. *See* pp. 74–82.

PRÉVOST, L. C.—Lettres sur Malte et la Sicile.—*Bull. Soc. géol. France, ii, pp.* 112–16. *Paris,* 1831–32.

PRÉVOST, L. C.—[Extrait de son mémoire sur la géologie de la Sicile.]—*Bull. Soc. géol. France, ii, pp.* 403–7, 1 *map. Paris,* 1831–32.

PRÉVOST, L. C.—Rapport fait à l'Académie Royale des Sciences sur le voyage à l'Île Sicilia en 1831–32.—*Paris,* 1832.

PRÉVOST, L. C.—Voyage à l'Île Julia, à Malte, en Sicile, aux Îles Lipari, et dans les environs de Naples.—*C.R. Acad. Sci. ii, pp.* 243–54. *Paris,* 1836.

PRÉVOST, L. C.—Théorie des soulèvements. —*Bull. Soc. géol. France, xi, pp.* 183–203. *Paris,* 1839–40.

PRÉVOST, L. C.—Étude des phénomènes volcaniques du Vésuve et de l'Etna.—*C.R. Acad. Sci. xli, pp.* 794–98. *Paris,* 1855.

PRÉVOST, L. C.—Sur un projet d'exploration de l'Etna et des formations volcaniques de l'Italie.—*C.R. Acad. Sci. xxxv, pp.* 409-13. *Paris,* 1852.

PRIVITERA, F.—Annuario Catanese.—*Catania,* 1690.
Eruptions 1536-37.

PRIVITERA, F.—Succinta relazione del Tremuoto del 1693.—*Catania,* 1694.

PRIVITERA, F.—Dolorosa tragedia, . . . di Catania distrutta nel 1693. . . . Con le memorie de passati tremoti causati del Gran Mongibello con suoi incendij, ecc.—*4⁰, fol. i, pp.* 98. *Catania,* 1695.
Earthquake of 1693.

PROCOPIUS.—[Eruption 550.]—*De bello Gothico, iv,* 35.

PROVANA DI COLLEGNO, G.—Osservazioni intorno alla Trachita dell' Etna.—*Atti Sett. Adun. Scienz. Ital. pp.* 1130-31. *Napoli,* 1846.

PRZYSTANOWSKI, R. VON.—Ueber den Ursprung der Vulkane in Italien.—*8⁰. Berlin,* 1822.

PUBLIUS SYRUS.—*See* ACCARIAS DE SERIONNE, J.—L'Etna.

PURSER, W. (drawn by, from a sketch by T. Little, Esq.).—Mount Ætna. Engraved by E. Finden. London, published 1832 by J. Murray and sold by C. Tilt, 86, Fleet Street.
Steel engrav. : 130 × 108 mm.

QUATREFAGES DE BRÉAU, J. L. A. DE.—Souvenirs d'un Naturaliste. Les Côtes de Sicile. v. L'Etna.—*Revue des Deux Mondes, N.S. xix, pp.* 9-36. *Paris,* 1847. —2 tom. in 1 vol. 12⁰. *Paris,* 1854.

QUATREFAGES DE BRÉAU, J. L. A. DE.—The Rambles of a Naturalist on the Coasts of France, Spain and Sicily. Translated [from " Souvenirs d'un Naturaliste "] by E. C. Otté.—2 vols. 8⁰. *London,* 1857.

QUATTROMANI, G.—Itinerario delle Due Sicilie.—*8⁰, pp.* 249+*xxii,* 1 *map. Napoli,* 1827.

QUINGLES, I. F. DE.—Lettera sopra alcuni fenomeni del Monte Etna, ai 24 Nov. 1723. — ?, — ?

RAFFELSBERGER, F.—Gemälde aus dem Naturreiche Beyder Sicilien.—*8⁰, foll.* 4, *pp.* 164, 8 *pls. Wien,* 1824.
See pp. 60-86 and pls. 4 and 5.

RAFFO, G.—Ancora sulla densità di alcune lave dell' Etna, del Vesuvio e di alcuni mattoni.—*Boll. Acc. Gioen. S.* 2, 18, *pp.* 4-10. *Catania,* 1911.

RAFFO, G.—*See* BARTOLI, A.

RAMMELSBERG, C. F. A.—Ueber die mineralogischen Gemengtheile der Laven, etc. (Aetnalava).—*Zeitschr. deutsch. geol. Gesellsch. i, pp.* 232-44. *Berlin,* 1849.

RAMMELSBERG, C. F. A.—Ueber den Ausbruch des Aetna vom 31 Januar 1865.— *Zeitschr. deutsch. geol. Gesellsch. xvii, pp.* 606-8. *Berlin,* 1865.

RANZANO, P.—De auctore et primordiis urbis Panormi.—*Opusc. di Autori Siciliani, ix, p.* 1. *Palermo,* 1747.
Eruption 1444.

RATH, J. J. G. VOM.—Der Aetna in den Jahren 1863-66, nach O. Silvestri's " I fenomeni Vulcanici presentati dall' Etna negli anni, *etc.*"—[Uebertragen im] *N. J. f. Min. pp.* 51, 257. *Stuttgart,* 1870.

RATH, J. J. G. VOM.—Der Aetna, Vortrag gehalten am 21 Mai 1872.—*Verh. naturhistor. Vereins f. Rheinl. u. Westf. xxix, pp.* 49-81. *Bonn,* 1872.—*N. J. f. Min. p.* 200. *Stuttgart,* 1873.

RATH, J. J. G. VOM.—Der Aetna.—*Bonn,* 1872.
View in foregoing work.

RATH, J. J. G. VOM.—Der Aetna und der Vesuv.—2 vols., *figs. Bonn,* 1872-73.

RATH, J. J. G. VOM.—[Referat über Silvestri's " La doppia eruzione dell' Etna scoppiata il 26 Maggio 1879."]—*Sitzber. niederrhein. Gesellsch. pp.* 198-209. *Bonn,* 1879.

R. B.—The General History of Earthquakes, being an account of the most remarkable and tremendous earthquakes that have happened in diverse parts of the world and particularly those lately in Naples, Smyrna, Jamaica and Sicily. With description of Mount Ætna, etc.—12⁰, *pp.* 177. *London,* 1734.

RE, L. DEL.—Relazione di una gita in Catania e all' Etna durante la eruzione del Dicembre 1842 per eseguirvi alcune magnetiche osservazioni.—*Atti R. Acc. Sci. v, Pte.* 1, *App. pp.* 46. *Napoli,* 1843.

RE, L. DEL.—Relazione del viaggio all' Etna ed in altri luoghi di Sicilia.—*Rend. R. Acc. Sci. ii, pp.* 201-4. *Napoli,* 1843.

RECLUS, J. J. É.—La Sicile et l'éruption de l'Etna en 1865.—" *Le Tour du Monde*," *xiii, sem.* 1, *pp.* 353–416, 35 *figs.*, 3 *maps. Paris*, 1866.—*Bibl. di Viaggi, x* (*La Sicilia*), *pp.* 53. *Milano*, 1873.

RECLUS, J. J. É.—La terre.—2 vols. *Paris*, 1877.
See Vol. i, p. 575: eruption of Etna in 1856 with coloured geol. map.

RECLUS, J. J. É.—Les Volcans de la Terre, trois fasc. (tout ce qui en a paru).—Asie antér. : Iranie, Arménie, Syrie ; Asie Mineure : Caucase ; Méditerranée : Égéide, Italie, Sicile (Vulcano, Etna, etc.). With bibliog.—*Soc. Astronom.* 9 *pls. and maps. Bruxelles*, 1906–10.

RECUPERO, A.—*See* RECUPERO, G. 1815.

RECUPERO, G.—Discorso storico sopra l'acque vomitate da Mongibello e suoi ultimi fuochi avvenuti nel mese del Marzo 1755, recitato nell' Accademia degli Etnei.—*4⁰, pp.* 79, 1 *pl. Catania*, 1755.

RECUPERO, G.—Storia naturale e generale dell' Etna. Opera postuma con annotazioni del suo nipote Agatino Recupero.—2 tom. 4⁰. *Vol. i, pp. xx*+244+*lxiv*+15, 3 *pls., portrait; Vol. ii, pp.* 236+*xii*+22, 1 *map*, 4 *pls. Catania*, 1815.

RECUPITUS, J. C.—De novo in universa Calabria terræmotu congeminatus nuncius.—*4⁰. Neapoli*, 1633.

REYER, E.—Beitrag zur Fysik der Eruptionen und der Eruptiv-Gesteine.—*8⁰, pp. xv*+225, 9 *pls. col. Wien*, 1877.

RIBIZZI.—Eruzione del 1646.
Cited by Recupero.

RICCI, G.—Rapporto a S.E. il Ministro della Guerra intorno alla misura di una base nella Piana di Catania.—*With a plate of triangulation. Torino*, 1867.

RICCIARDI, L.—Ricerche chimiche sulle lave dei dintorni di Catania indicate nella carta geologica di Sciuto Patti.—*Atti Acc. Gioen. S.* 3, *xv, pp.* 147–79, *map and pl. Catania*, 1881.—*Gazz. Chim. Ital. xi, pp.* 138–65. *Palermo*, 1881.—*Journ. Chem. Soc. xl, pp.* 701–3. *London*, 1881.

RICCIARDI, L., e SPECIALE, S.—Sui Basalti della Sicilia. Ricerche Chimiche. (Nota preliminare.)—*Atti Acc. Gioen. S.* 3, *xv, pp.* 181–83. *Catania*, 1881.—*Gazz. Chim. Ital. xi, pp.* 169–71. *Palermo*, 1881.

RICCIARDI, L., SPECIALE, S.—I Basalti della Sicilia. Ricerche chimiche.—*Gazz. Chim. Ital. xi, pp.* 359–92. *Palermo*, 1881. —*Atti Acc. Gioen. S.* 3, *xv, pp.* 211–51, 2 *maps. Catania*, 1881.

RICCIARDI, L.—Sopra un' alterazione superficiale osservata sulla selce piromaca dei dintorni di Vizzini.—*Atti Acc. Gioen. S.* 3, *xv, pp.* 273–74. *Catania*, 1881.

RICCIARDI, L.—Sur le rôle de l'Acide Phosphorique dans les sols volcaniques.— *C.R. Acad. Sci. xcii, pp.* 1514–16. *Paris*, 1881.

RICCIARDI, L.—Analyse d'une cendre volcanique rejetée par l'Etna le 23 janvier 1882.—*C.R. Acad. Sci. xciv, pp.* 586–87. *Paris*, 1882.

RICCIARDI, L.—Sulla cenere caduta dall' Etna il giorno 23 Giugno 1882.—*Gazz. Chim. Ital. xii, pp.* 57–59. *Palermo*, 1882.

RICCIARDI, L.—Composition chimique des diverses couches d'un courant de lave de l'Etna.—*C.R. Acad. Sci. xciv, pp.* 1657–59. *Paris*, 1882.

RICCIARDI, L.—Sulla composizione chimica di diversi strati di una stessa corrente di lava eruttata dall' Etna nel 1669. Ricerche chimiche [1882].—*Gazz. Chim. Ital. xii, pp.* 454–59. *Palermo*, 1882.—*Atti Acc. Gioen. xvii, pp.* 17–24. *Catania*, 1883.

RICCIARDI, L.—L'Etna e l'eruzione del mese di Marzo 1883. Ricerche e relazione. —*Atti Acc. Gioen. S.* 3, *xvii, pp.* 195–229, 2 *pls. Catania*, 1883.

RICCIARDI, L.—Sulla composizione chimica della cenere lanciata dall' Etna il 16 Novembre 1884.—*Atti Acc. Gioen. S.* 3, *xviii, pp.* 223–27. *Catania*, 1885.

RICCIARDI, L.—Sull' Eruzione dell' Etna del Maggio-Giugno 1886.—*4⁰, pp.* 8. *Chieti*, 1886. [C.A.]

RICCIARDI, L.—Recherches chimiques sur les produits de l'éruption de l'Etna aux mois de mai et de juin 1886.—*C.R. Acad. Sci. cii, pp.* 1484–87. *Paris*, 1886.—*The Chemical News, liv, p.* 23. *London*, 1887.

RICCIARDI, L.—Sull' azione dell' acqua del mare nei Vulcani.—*Dal Laboratorio Chimico del Regio Istituto tecnico di Bari, xxxi, pp.* 129–34. 1887.

RICCIARDI, L.—Sull' allineamento dei Vulcani italiani. Sulle roccie eruttive subaeree e submarine e loro classificazione in due periodi. Sullo sviluppo dell' acido cloridrico, dell' anidride solforosa e del jodio dai vulcani. Sul graduale passaggio delle roccie acide alle roccie basiche.—8°, *pp.* 1–45, *tav. Reggio-Emilia,* 1887.

RICCIARDI, L.—Genesi e successione delle Rocce Eruttive.—*Atti Soc. Ital. Sci. Nat. xxx, pp.* 212–37. *Milano,* 1887.

RICCIARDI, L.—Genesi e composizione chimica dei Terreni Vulcanici Italiani.—*L'Agricoltura Italiana, xiv–xv, pp.* 155. *Firenze,* 1889.

RICCIARDI, L.—L'attuale eruzione dell' Etna e il terremoto del 28 Dicembre 1908. —" *Il Giorno*," 13–14 *Aprile, Napoli,* 1909.

RICCIARDI, L.—Il vulcanismo nel terremoto Calabro-Siculo del 28 Dicembre 1908.— *Boll. Soc. Nat. xxiii* (*S.* 2, *iii*), *pp.* 65–120, *figs. Napoli,* 1909.

RICCIARDI, L.—Su le relazioni delle Reali Accademie delle Scienze di Napoli e dei Lincei di Roma sui terremoti Calabro-Siculi del 1783 e 1908.—*Boll. Soc. Nat. xxiv* (*S.* 2, *iv*), *pp.* 23–75. *Napoli,* 1910.

RICCIOLI, B.—Chronologia reformata Seti. —*Bononiæ,* 1669.
Eruptions from 1321–23.

RICCÒ, A.—Phénomènes atmosphériques observés à Palerme pendant l'éruption de l'Etna.—*C.R. Acad. Sci. ciii, pp.* 419–21. *Paris,* 1886.

RICCÒ, A.—L'Eruzione dell' Etna.—*Nuova Antologia, xli,* 1 *Sett., pp.* 18,1 *pl., and* 16 *Sett., pp.* 18. *Roma,* 1892.—*C.R. Acad. Sci. cxv, pp.* 687–89. *Paris,* 1892.

RICCÒ, A.—Der gegenwärtige Ausbruch des Aetna.—8°. *Berlin,* 1892.

RICCÒ, A.—La Lava incandescente nel cratere centrale dell' Etna e fenomeni geodinamici concomitanti (1893).—*Ann. Uffic. Centr. Meteor. e Geodinam. xv, pt.* 1, *pp.* 9, 1 *pl. Roma,* 1893.

RICCÒ, A.—Notizie sullo stato dell' Etna.— *Boll. Soc. Sismol. Ital. i,* 2, *pp.* 4. *Roma,* 1894.

RICCÒ, A.—Breve relazione sui terremoti del 7 e 8 Agosto 1894 avvenuti nelle contrade Etnee.—*Boll. Oss. Moncalieri, S.* 2, *xiv,* 10. *Torino,* 1894.

RICCÒ, A., ARCIDIACONO, S.—Osservazioni puteometriche eseguite nell' Osservatorii di Catania.— *Boll. Acc. Gioen.* 37, *pp.* 8–12. *Catania,* 1894.

RICCÒ, A.—All' Osservatorio Etneo.—*Rassegna Siciliana, pp.* 53. *Catania,* 1895.

RICCÒ, A., e SAIJA, G.—Saggio di meteorologia dell' Etna.—4°, 3 *tav. Roma,* 1896.

RICCÒ, A.—Stato del cratere centrale dell' Etna dal 2° semestre 1895 al 1° semestre 1897.—*Boll. Soc. Sismol. Ital. iii,* 4, *pp.* 61–63. *Modena,* 1897.

RICCÒ, A.—Determinazioni della Gravità relativa fatte nelle regioni Etnee e nella Sicilia orientale.—*Atti R. Acc. Lincei, S.* 5, *Rend. vii, sem.* 2, *pp.* 3–14, *fig.* (*map*). *Roma,* 1898.

RICCÒ, A.—Rilievo topografico e variazioni del cratere centrale dell'·· Etna.— *Boll. Acc. Gioen.* 51, *pp.* 2–6. *Catania,* 1898.

RICCÒ, A.—Terremoto Etneo del 14 Maggio 1898.—*Boll. Acc. Gioen.* 53–54, *pp.* 19–22. *Catania,* 1898.—*Boll. Soc. Sismol. Ital. v,* 7, *pp.* 220–30. *Modena,* 1899.—*tav. Modena,* 1900.

RICCÒ, A.—Riassunto della sismografia del terremoto del 16 Novembre 1894.—Pte. i : *Atti R. Acc. Lincei, S.* 5, *Rend. viii, sem.* 2, *pp.* 3–12, *fig.* [*map*], 1899 ; Pte. ii : *Ibid. pp.* 35–45, 1899.

RICCÒ, A., e FRANCO, L.—Stabilita del suole all' Osservat. Etneo.—4°. 1900.

RICCÒ, A.—Cratere centrale dell' Etna.— *Boll. Soc. Sismol. Ital. vii,* 3, *p.* 136, 5 *figs.,* 2 *tav. Modena,* 1901.

RICCÒ, A., e ARCIDIACONO, S.—L'Eruzione dell' Etna del 1892. Parte I. L'Etna dal 1883 al 1892.—*Atti Acc. Gioen. S.* 4, *xv, Mem.* 5, *pp.* 1–62, *fig.*—*Boll. Acc. Gioen.* 72, *pp.* 6–7. *Catania,* 1902.

RICCÒ, A., e ARCIDIACONO, S.—L'Eruzione dell' Etna del 1892. Parte II. Diario dell' eruzione.—*Atti Acc. Gioen. S.* 4, *xvi, Mem.* 8, *pp.* 1–86, 3 *tav. Catania,* 1903.

RICCÒ, A.—Fondo del cratere centrale dell' Etna.—*Boll. Soc. Sismol. Ital. ix,* 2, *pp.* 9–12, *tav. Modena,* 1903.

RICCÒ, A.—Rilevamento topografico della lava dell' eruzione Etnea del 1892.—*Boll. Acc. Gioen.* 75, *pp.* 5–8. *Catania,* 1903.

RICCÒ, A., e ARCIDIACONO, S.—L'Eruzione dell' Etna nel 1892. Parte III. Visite all' apparato eruttivo e al cratere centrale.—*Atti Acc. Gioen. S.* 4, *xvii, Mem.* 5, *pp.* 1–51, 3 *tav. Catania,* 1904.

RICCÒ, A.—Eruzioni e pioggie.—*Boll. Soc. Sismol. Ital. x*, 2, *pp.* 95–109. *Modena,* 1904.—*Atti Acc. Gioen. S.* 4, *xvii, Mem.* 17, *pp.* 1–13. *Catania,* 1904.

RICCÒ, A.—Eruzione di cenere dell' Etna nella sera del 5 Giugno 1906.—8⁰, *pp.* 2. *Catania,* 1906.

RICCÒ, A.—Sur l'activité de l'Etna.—*C.R. Acad. Sci. cxlv, pp.* 289–91. *Paris,* 1907.

RICCÒ, A.—Periodi di riposo dell' Etna.— *Boll. Acc. Gioen.* 94, *pp.* 2–6. *Catania,* 1907.

RICCÒ, A.—Eruzione Etnea del 28 Aprile 1908.—*Boll. Acc. Gioen. S.* 2, 5 *e* 6, *pp.* 11–12. *Catania,* 1909.

RICCÒ, A.—Un' altra visita alla eruzione Etnea del 29 Aprile 1908. III. Nota.— *Boll. Acc. Gioen. S.* 2, 10, *pp.* 11–14. *Catania,* 1910.

RICCÒ, A.—Sur l'Éruption de l'Etna du 28 mars 1910.—*C.R. Acad. Sci. cl, pp.* 1078–81. *Paris,* 1910.—" *Nature," lxxxiii, pp.* 399–400, *figs. London,* 1910.

RICCÒ, A.—Eruzione dell' Etna al 23 Marzo 1910. Note preliminare.—*Boll. Acc. Gioen. S.* 2, 12, *pp.* 2–7. *Catania,* 1910.—*Boll. Soc. Sismol. Ital. xiv,* 3, *pp.* 101–7. *Modena,* 1910.

RICCÒ, A.—Eruzione Etnea del 1911.— *Boll. Soc. Sismol. Ital. xv,* 6–7, *pp.* 273–80, 4 *figs. Modena,* 1911.

RICCÒ, A.—La Nuova Bocca a N.E. del Cratere dell' Etna.—*Atti Acc. Gioen. S.* 5, iv, *Mem.* 11, *pp.* 6, 1 *pl. Catania,* 1911.

RICCÒ, A.—Fenomeni geodinamici consecutivi alla eruzione Etnea del Settembre 1911. —*Boll. Soc. Sismol. Ital. xvi,* 1–2, *pp.* 9–38, 7 *figs. Modena,* 1912.

RICCÒ, A.—*See* VINASSA DE REGNY.

RICHARD DE SAINT-NON, J. C.—Voyage pittoresque, ou description des royaumes de Naples et de Sicile.—*fol. Vol. i* [Naples and Vesuvius], *foll. ii, pp.* 252, 2 *engrav. frontisp.,* 4 *maps,*16 *figs.,* 50 *pls. ; Vol. ii* [Herculaneum, Phlegrean Fields and Campania], *foll.* 16, *pp.* 283, 2 *maps,* 26 *figs.,* 24 *col. figs.,* 80 *pls. ; Vol. iii* [Southern Italy], *foll.* 24, *pp.* 201, 15 *figs.,* 4 *maps,* 57 *pls. ; Vol. iv* [Sicily], *Pt.* 1, *foll.* 14, *pp.* 266, 13 *figs.,* 65 *pls.,* 2 *maps ; Pt.* 2, *foll. v, pp.* 267–430, *frontisp.,* 4 *figs.,* 32 *pls. Paris,* 1781–86.

RICHARD DE'SAINT-NON, J. C.—Travels in Sicily and Malta, translated from the French of M. de Non.—8⁰, *foll.* 2, *pp.* 427. *London,* 1789.

RICHARD DE SAINT-NON, J. C.—Neapel und Sizilien. Ein Auszug aus dem grossen kostbaren Werke : " Voyage pittoresque de Naples et Sicile."—12 pts. 8⁰, *num. pls. Gotha,* 1789–1806.

RICHARD DE SAINT-NON, J. C.—Voyage pittoresque à Naples et en Sicile. Nouvelle édition, corrigée, augmentée, mise dans un meilleur ordre par P. J. Charrin.—4 vols. 8⁰, and one atlas, *fol.* [containing 558 very fine large engraved plates divided into :] I, Naples et ses environs, *pls.* 1–285 ; II, Grande-Grèce, *pls.* 286–400 ; III, Sicile, *pls.* 401–558. *Paris, Dufour,* 1828–29.

The plates are engraved by Berteaux, Nicollet, Germain, Deny, Longueil, Marillier, Desmoulins, Berthault Queverdo, Cochin, De St. Aubin, Fraganard, Varin, Desprez, and many others, most of whom engraved " all' acqua forte."

Another ed. 4 vols. 8⁰. *Paris,* 1836.

RICHARDUS, S. G. DE.—Chronicon Siculum ab anno 1189–1243.—*See* CARUSO, G. B.—Memorie storiche.

RIDDELL, R. A.—*See* WILSON, J.

RIEDESEL, J. H. VON.—Reise durch Sicilien und Gross-Griechenland.—*Zürich,* 1771.—In French (transl. par Frey des Landes) : 12⁰, *pp.* xii+353. *Lausanne,* 1773.

RIEGEL, G.—Der Unter Theil von Italia darinen die Königreiche Neapolis und Sicilien sich befindet.—*Nürnberg* [1730 ?]. [B.M.—23880 (12).]

A badly constructed map.

RIEP (f[ecit]).—Prospeckt des Etna, von Kalabriens Küste.

Engraving of no interest : 92×82 mm.

RIO, M. DEL.—Disquisitiones magic. 1, 2 quest. 10.

Cited by Massa, Etna.

RIOLO, V.—Delle acque minerali di Sicilia. —8⁰. *Palermo,* 1794.

RISO, B. DE.—Relazione della pioggia di cenere avvenuta in Calabria Ulteriore nel di 27 Marzo 1809.—*Atti Soc. Pontaniana, i, pp.* 163–65. *Napoli,* 1810.

RITIUS, M.—De regibus Siciliæ usque ad 1497. Scriptore Sic.—*See* GRÆVIUS, J. G.—Thes. Sic. v.

RITTER, C. W. J.—Beschreibung merkwürdiger Vulkane.—*Breslau*, 1847.—Earlier ed. : 2 pts. in 1 vol., *illustr.* 8⁰. *Posen u. Leipzig*, 1806.

RITTER VON HAUER, K.—Ueber die Beschaffenheit der Lava des Aetna von der Eruption im Jahre 1852.—*Sitz. k. Akad. Wiss. xi, pp.* 87–92. *Wien*, 1854.

RIZZI-ZANNONI, G. A.—Carta Geograf. della Sicilia prima o sia regno di Napoli.—*foll.* 4. *Parigi*, 1769. [B.M.—23880 (21).]
A fine map of Palmarola, well-drawn.

RIZZI-ZANNONI, G. A.—Carta del regno di Napoli con parte della Sicilia e l'Isola di Malta.—*Vienna*, 1806. [B.M.—23880. (24).]
Much the same as his " General-Karte von dem Koenigreiche Neapel."

ROBERTO, F. DE.—L'Eruzione dell' Etna. —*Riv. Mens. Club Alp. Ital.* 6, *p.* 170. *Giugno*, 1886.

ROBINS, J. (publ.).—Mount Etna as it appeared in July 1787. Published by J. Robins and Co., London and Dublin, Feb. 1, 1825.
Small engrav. hand-coloured: 83 × 62 mm.

ROCCAFORTE.—Relazione sui terremoti di Val di Noto.
Cited by Mongitore.

ROCCATI, A.—Escursione sull' Etna compiuta dalla Società Geologica Italiana durante il Congresso in Sicilia (13 e 14 Settembre 1909).—*Boll. Soc. Geol. Ital. xxviii*, 3, *pp. clxxxix–ccv. Roma*, 1910.

RODWELL, G. F.—Etna, a history of the Mountain and of its eruptions.—8⁰, *pp. xi*+142, *maps. and pl. London*, 1878.

ROGGERO, CAV. G.—Carta in rilievo dell' Italia.—*Pub. G. B. Paravia e C., Torino, Roma, Milano, Firenze, Napoli*, 1876.
Raised map, 1 : 2,800,000 horiz. ; 1 : 320,000 vert.

ROMANO, S.—Le più recenti eruzioni dell' Etna.—" *Geografia per tutti*," *iv*, 11. *Milano*, 1894.

ROMUALDUS.—Ex Romualdi . . . Chronico postrema pars, ab anno 1159 ad annum 1177.—*See* ˜CARUSO, G. B.—Bibl. Hist. Reg. Siciliæ, *ii*. 1719, *etc.*
Eruption A.D. 1169.

ROSENBUSCH, H.—Die Aetna-Eruption vom Frühjahr, 1879.—*map. Stuttgart*, 1880.

ROSENBUSCH, H.—[Referat über die Eruption des Aetna 1879.]—*N. J. f. Min. i, pp.* 390–94. *Stuttgart*, 1880.

ROSSI, D. DE.—[Maps of Italy.]—*Rome*, 1693-96.

ROSSI, M. S. DE.—Fenomeni concomitanti l'eruzione dell' Etna nel suolo d'Italia.—*Bull. Vulc. Ital. i, pp.* 118–20. *Roma*, 1874.

ROSSI, M. S. DE.—Quadro generale statistico topografico giornaliero dei terremoti avvenuti in Italia nell' anno meteorico 1874 [and 1877] col confronto di alcune altri fenomeni.—*Atti Acc. Pont. N. Lincei, xxviii, pp.* 514–36. *Roma*, 1875 [and *xxxi, pp.* 479–82. 1878].

ROSSI, M. S. DE.—Terremoti presso l'Etna dal 7 al 20 Gennaio 1875.—*Bull. Vulc. Ital. ii*, 1–3. *Roma*, 1875. — *Boll. R. Com. Geol. Ital. vi, p.* 113. *Roma*, 1875.

ROSSI, M. S. DE.—Insegnamento di fisicochimica terrestre nella R. Università di Catania ed Osservatorio Vulcanologico nell' Etna. Lettera di M. S. de Rossi al Prof. Orazio Silvestri.—*Bull. Vulc. Ital. vi*, 1–3, *p.* 5. *Roma*, 22 *Gennaio*, 1879.

ROSSI, M. S. DE.—La Meteorologia endogena.—*Bibl. Scient. Internaz. xix, i, pp.* 360, 5 *lith. taf. Mailand*, 1879. — [Extr.] *N. J. f. Min. pp.* 911–12. *Stuttgart*, 1879.

ROSSI, M. S. DE.—Cronaca dell' Etna e del Vesuvio dal Gennaio al Febbraio 1880 con confronti. Notizie varie riunite dei prof. Palmieri e Silvestri.—*Bull. Vulc. Ital. vii, pp.* 80–82. *Roma*, 1880.

ROSSI, M. S. DE.—Massimi sismici Italiani dell' anno meteorico 1887.—*Ann. Meteor. Ital. iii, pp.* 297–302, 1888 ; *iv, pp.* 283–305, 1889 ; *v, pp.* 253–62, 1890 ; *vi, pp.* 192–209, 1891 ; *vii, pp.* 239–56, *Torino*, 1892.

ROTH, J. L. A. (transl. by).—Ueber die auf steilgeneigter Unterlage erstarrten Laven des Aetna und über die Erhebungskratere. (Transl. of the original by Lyell.)—*Zeitschr. deutsch. geol. Gesellsch. xi, pp.* 149–250. *Berlin*, 1859.

ROTH, J. L. A.—O. Silvestri, Ueber die vulkanischen Phänomene des Aetna in den Jahren 1863-66, mit besonderer Bezugnahme auf den Ausbruch von 1865.—*Atti Acc. Gioen. S.* 3, *i, pp.* 56–285. *Catania*, 1867.—*Zeitschr. deutsch. geol. Gesellsch. xxi, pp.* 221–38, *taf. iv. Berlin*, 1869.

ROTH, J. L. A. (transl. by).—Ueber die Ausbrüche des Aetna im November und December 1868, von Herrn Mar. Grassi in Acireale.—*Zeitschr. deutsch. geol. Gesellsch. xxii, pp.* 189–90. *Berlin,* 1870.

ROTH, J. L. A.—[Ueber Vesuv u. Aetnalaven.]—*Zeitschr. deutsch. geol. Gesellsch. xxv, p.* 116. *Berlin,* 1873.

ROTH, J. L. A.—Der Ausbruch des Aetna am 26 Mai 1879 (nach Silvestri, Baldacci, etc.).—*Zeitschr. deutsch. geol. Gesellsch. xxxi, pp.* 399–404. *Berlin,* 1879.

ROUARGUE (des.).—Italie. Vue Générale de Catane. Feulut sc.
Woodcut : 322×222 mm.

ROVERE, C. A.—La Sicilia sotto l'aspetto geologico e fisico con annesse nozioni elementari di Geologia : conferenze.— *Roma,* 1895.

ROVERETO, G.—Relazione dell' ascensione sull' Etna compiuta dalla Società Geologica Italiana il 21 e il 22 Settembre 1904. —*Boll. Soc. Geol. Ital. xxiii, pp. clxvi-clxx. Roma,* 1905.

ROYER.—*See* NORVINS.

ROZET.—Mémoire sur les volcans de l'Auvergne avec un appendice sur les Volcans d'Italie.—*Mém. Soc. géol. France, S.* 2, *i* (*see pp.* 131–62). *Paris,* 1844.

RUDOLPH. E.—Bericht über die vulcanischen Ereignisse während des Jahres 1894.—*Tschermak's min. u. petr. Mittheil. xvi,* 5, *pp.* 365–464. *Wien,* 1896.

RUFFO, S.—Istoria dell' orrendo terremoto accaduto in Palermo 1 Settembre 1726.— 4⁰. *Palermo,* 1726.

RUSSEGGER, J. Von.—[Geognostische Beobachtungen in Rom, Neapel, am Aetna, auf den Cyclopen, dem Vesuv, Ischia, etc.]—*N. J. f. Min. pp.* 329–32. *Stuttgart,* 1840.

RUSSEGGER, J. Von.—Reise in der Levante und in Europa mit besonderer Berücksichtigung der naturwissenschaftlichen Verhältnisse der betreffenden Ländern.— *Stuttgart,* 1851.
See pp. 255–363.

RUSSELL, G.—A Tour through Sicily in the year 1815.—*pp.* x+289, 10 *col. pls.,* 9 *plans and map. London,* 1819.

RUSSO, A.—[Manoscritto che possiede don Ludovico Toscano di Aci Reale.]
Cited by Recupero II, p. 58. Eruptions 1651–53.

RUSSO (GRASSI), G.—Acqua di Santa Venera.—*Aci Reale,* 1878.—Traduction française par Ingigliardi. *Lyon,* 1878.

RUTLEY, F.—The mineral constitution and microscopic characters of some of the Lavas of Etna.—*See* RODWELL.—Etna, *etc. p.* 135. *London,* 1878.

SABATINI, V.—L'Eruzione dell' Etna del Marzo-Aprile 1910.—*Boll. R. Com. Geol. Ital. xli, pp.* 71–92, *figs., pl. ii* (*topogr. map*). *Roma,* 1910.

SACCO, F.—Dizionario geografico del regno di Sicilia.—2 tom. in 1 vol. 4⁰. *Tom. i, pp.* xi+380; *Tom ii, pp.* 312. *Palermo,* 1799–1800.

SAIJA, G.—*See* RICCÒ, A.

S. BERNARDO.—*See* BERNARDO.

SAITTA DA BRONTE, L.—Sul miserando caso della esplosione avvenuta addì 25 Nov. 1843.—*See* LUCA, P. De.

SALATHÉ (del.).—Taormina, Theatro. Etna, E. Rouargue sc. Audot edit.
Fine engrav. : 172×118 mm.

SALIS-MARSCHLINS, K. U. Von.—Beiträge zur natürlichen u. ökonomischen Kenntniss beider Sicilien.—2 Bde. [in 1] 8⁰, *illustr. Zürich,* 1790.

SALOMONE, S.—Le Provincie Siciliane studiate sotto tutti gli aspetti.—8⁰. *Acireale,* 1884.

SALOMONE, S.—L'Eruzione dell' Etna del 19 Maggio 1886.—8⁰, *pp.* 52 *and index. Catania,* 1886.

SALOMONE, S.—Catania illustrata.—8⁰, *pp.* 264. *Catania* [1907 ?].
See pp. 189–203.

SANCHEZ, G.—La Campania sotterranea, e brevi notizie degli edificii scavati entro Roccia nelle Due Sicilie, ed in altre regioni. —2 vols. 8⁰, *pp.* 2–656. *Napoli,* 1833.
See pp. 78 *et seq.* Etna.

SANDWICH, JOHN MONTAGU, EARL OF.—A Voyage performed by the late Earl of Sandwich round the Mediterranean in the years 1738 and 1739.—4⁰, *pp. xl+539, pls., 1 map. London, 1799.*

SANDYS, G.—A Relation of a Iourney begun An. Dom. 1610. Fovre Bookes. Containing a description of the Turkish Empire, of Ægypt, of the Holy Land, of the Remote parts of Italy, and Islands adioyning.—4⁰, *pp. 309+1, figs., frontisp. portrait of author. London, 1615.*

SANSON, Sʳ.—Carte nouvelle des royaumes de Naples : et de Sicile.—*Covens et Mortier, Amsterdam* [1730 ?]. [B.M.— 23880 (11).]

SARTORIUS VON WALTERSHAUSEN, W.—Ueber die submarinen vulkanischen Ausbrüche in der Tertiär-Formation des Val di Noto im Vergleich mit verwandten Erscheinungen am Aetna.—8⁰, *pp. 63. Göttingen, 1846.*

SARTORIUS VON WALTERSHAUSEN, W.—Atlas des Aetna . . . mit Beihülfe von S. Cavallari, C. F. Peters und C. Roos.— *obl. fol., 31 pls. (6 col.), 26 maps (13 col.). Göttingen, 1848.—Weimar, 1848–64.*

SARTORIUS VON WALTERSHAUSEN, W.—Ueber die vulkanischen Gesteine in Sicilien und Island und ihre submarine Umbildung.—8⁰, *pp. xvi+532, 1 pl. Göttingen, 1853.*

SARTORIUS VON WALTERSHAUSEN, W.—Ein Vortrag über den Aetna und seine Ausbrüche gehalten in der ersten allgemeinen Sitzung der XXXII Versammlung der deutschen Naturforscher zu Wien am 16 September 1856.—8⁰, *pp. 23. Leipzig, 1857.*

SARTORIUS VON WALTERSHAUSEN, W.—Ueber den Aetna u. seine Ausbrüche. —8⁰, *pp. 23. Leipzig, 1857.—Allgemeine deutsch. naturhist. Zeitung, iii, Literaturblatt, p. 18. Dresden, 1857.*

SARTORIUS VON WALTERSHAUSEN, W.—Eine kurze Beschreibung der geodätischen und topographischen Vermessungen, welche der Ausarbeitung der Karte des Etna voraufgegangen sind.—*Peterm. Mitth. pp. 102–7. Gotha, 1864.*

SARTORIUS VON WALTERSHAUSEN, W., und LASAULX, A. VON.—Der Aetna nach den Manuscripten des verstorbenen B. Sartorius von Waltershausen herausgegeben und vollendet von . . . A. von

Lasaulx.—2 vols. *fol. Vol. i, pp. xviii+371, 1 map, 14 pls., portrait, figs. ; Vol. ii, pp. viii+540, 1 map, 23 pls., figs. Leipzig, 1880.—See also* ROSENBUSCH.—[Referat, etc.]

SAUSSURE, H. DE. — Mount Etna. — "*Nature,*" *xx, pp. 544–45. London, 2 Oct. 1879.*

SAUSSURE, H. DE.—Sur la récente éruption de l'Etna.—*C.R. Acad. Sci. lxxxix, pp. 35–41. Paris, 1879.—Journ. de Genève, 15, 17, 20, 21, 26, 27 juin, 3 et 4 juillet, 1879.—*[Abstr. in] *Boll. R. Com. Geol. Ital. x, pp. 323–29. Roma, 1879.—Rev. scient. S. 2, xvii, p. 72. Paris, 1879.*.

SAUSSURE, H. DE.—L'Etna et ses dernières éruptions.—"*Le Globe,*" *S. 4, vii, pp. 211. Genève, 1888.*

SAUSSURE, H. DE.—[Détails sur les dernières éruptions de l'Etna.]—*Bibl. Univ., Archiv. Sci. phys. nat. 3e pér., xxvii, pp. 344–47. Genève, 1892.*

SAUSSURE, [H. B.] DE.—Copie d'une lettre de M. de Saussure à Sʳ W. Hamilton, à 17 Décʳᵉ 1774. — MS. *fol., foll.* 107–28. [B.M. 19309 (viii).]

SAUSSURE, H. B. DE.—Voyages dans les Alpes.—4 vols. 4⁰. *Neuchâtel, 1779–96.*

SAVA, R.—Sopra alcuni prodotti minerali che si formano in una spelonca dell' Etna. —*Ann. Civ. Reg. Due Sicilie, xxx, pp. 89– 102. Napoli, 1842.*

SAVA, R.—Sull' accidentale Arsione umana per l'eruzione dell' Etna di Novembre 1843.—*Rend. R. Acc. Sci. ii, pp. 444–47. Napoli, 1843.*

SAVA, R.—Lucubrazioni sulla Flora e Fauna dell' Etna e sopra l'origine delle spelonche nelle lave di questo Vulcano.—*obl. 8⁰, pp. 36. Milano, 1844.—Congr. Scient. Ital. pp. 36. Milano, 1844.—*In German: *Tübingen, — ? Also in :* BALBI, A.— "Miscellanea Italiana," *Milano, 1845.*

SAVERIO, C.—De Ætna. Poem cited by Mongitore.

SAYVE, A. DE.—Voyage en Sicile, fait en 1820 et 1821.—3 tom. 8⁰. *Paris, 1822.*

SCALIA, S.—Una nuova località fossilifera del Post-pliocene Subetneo.—*Atti Acc. Gioen. S. 4, xiv, Mem. 12, pp. 1–9. Catania, 1901.*

SCALIA, S.—Sopra le Argille Postplioceniche della Vena, presso Piedimonte Etneo (Prov. di Catania).—*Rend. R. Acc. Sci. S.* 3, *xii, pp.* 110–12. *Napoli,* 1906.

SCALIA, S.—Il Postpliocene dell' Etna.— *Atti Acc. Gioen. S.* 4, *xx, Mem.* 13, *pp.* 43, 1 *pl. Catania,* 1907.

SCALIGERI, J.— *See* SEVERUS, COR- NELIUS.—Ætna et quæ supersunt, *etc.*

SCANELLO, C.—Descrizione di Sicilia. Eruption 1536. Cited by Filoteo and Massa.

SCASSO E BORELLO, M.—Descrizione geografica dell' Isola di Sicilia e dell' altre sue adiacenti.—*Palermo,* 1798.——3rd ed. 8⁰. *Palermo,* 1806.

SCASSO E BORELLO, M.—*See* LÉVESQUE DE BURIGNY.

SCHMID, C. A.— *See* SEVERUS, COR- NELIUS, 1769.

SCHMIDT, J. F. J.—Vulkanstudien. San- torin, 1866–1872. Vesuv, Bajæ, Stromboli, Aetna, 1870.—8⁰, *foll.* 4, *pp.* 235, 1 *map,* 7 *pls.,* 13 *figs. Leipzig,* 1874.——2nd ed. 8⁰. 1881.

SCHOENBERG, A. VON.—Lettre sur la dernière éruption de l'Etna.—*Bull. Sci. Nat. iii, p.* 160. *Paris,* 1824.

SCHOTT, G.—Magia universalis naturæ et artis. IV.—4 pts. 4⁰. *Herbipoli,* 1657–59.— In German : 4⁰. *Bamberg,* 1671.—*Frank- furt a. M.* 1677.
See l. 1, capt. X, *et seq.* Cited by Massa, Etna.

SCHOTTUS, ANDREAS.—Itinerario overo nova descrittione de' viaggi principali d'Italia, nella quale si ha piena notitia di tutte le cose più notabili, e degne d'esser vedute. Et aggiuntoui in quest' ultima impressione la Descrittion dell' Isole di Sicilia, e di Malta.— 3 pts. in 2 vols. 8⁰. [At beginning :] Padova appresso Fran- cesco Bolzetta Libraro. M.DC.XXXXIX. [At end :] Padova, nella Stamparia del Criucl- lari, 1648.—*See* CAMPI PHLEGRÆI.

SCHOUW, J. F.—Observations météoro- logiques sur le Mont Etna.—*Bibl. Univ. Sci. et Arts, xii, pp.* 34–42. *Genève,* 1819.

SCHOUW, J. F.—L'ultima eruzione dell' Etna 1819.—*Giorn. Enciclop. di Napoli,* 1819.—*Goetting. Wochenblatt.* 18 te. Woche, *pp.* 71–75. 1819.

SCIACCA, E.—Eruzione dell' Etna del 1669.—8⁰. *Napoli,* 1671.
Cited by Gemmellaro, C., in : Origine e progressi delle scienze naturali in Sicilia, Catania, 1833.

SCIACCA, E.—Narrazione dell' incendio di Mongibello nel 1669.—8⁰. *Napoli,* 1671.

SCIGLIANO, A.—Pomona Etnea.—*Atti Acc. Gioen. viii, pp.* 53–97. *Catania,* 1834.

SCINA, D.—[Palermitano trovandosi in Catania. Copia di lettera scritta ad un suo amico 2 Nov. 1811.]—*Catania,* 1811.— " *Fa per Tutti,*" 27 *Ottobre,* 1811.
Eruptions October 1811.

SCIUTO-PATTI, C.—Della utilità del Dren- aggio in talune terre della Piana di Catania. —*Atti Soc. Econ. Prov. di Catania.* 1857.

SCIUTO-PATTI, C.—Sull' età probabile della massa subaerea dell' Etna.—*Atti Acc. Gioen. S.* 3, *i, pp.* 25–52. *Catania,* 1867.

SCIUTO-PATTI, C.—Carta geologica della città di Catania e dintorni di essa.—*Atti Acc. Gioen. S.* 3, *vii, pp.* 141–217, 8 *tav. Catania,* 1872.—[Notice in] *Atti Soc. Ital. Sci. Nat. xii, p.* 460. *Milano,* 1869.

SCIUTO-PATTI, C.—Sulla temperatura del mare nel Golfo di Catania.—*Atti Acc. Gioen. S.* 3, *v, pp.* 33–51. *Catania,* 1871.

SCIUTO-PATTI, C.—Carta idrografica della città di Catania e dei dintorni immediati di essa.—*Atti Acc. Gioen. S.* 3, *xi, pp.* 267– 91, 1 *map. Catania,* 1877.

SCIUTO-PATTI, C.—Sul sito dell' antica città di Symaetus.—*Atti Acc. Gioen. Sci. Nat. S.* 3, *xv, pp.* 127–36. *Catania,* 1881.

SCIUTO-PATTI, C. — Contribuzione allo studio dei tremuoti in Sicilia.—*Atti Acc. Gioen. S.* 4, *ix, Mem.* 16, *pp.* 34, 1 *map. Catania,* 1896.

SCOTO, A.—*See* SCHOTTUS, ANDREAS.

SCROPE, G. J. POULETT.—Considerations on Volcanos, the probable causes of their phenomena . . . and their connection with the present state and past history of the Globe ; leading to the establishment of a new Theory of the Earth.—8⁰, *pp.* xxxi+ 270, 2 *pls.,* 1 *map. London,* 1825.——[2nd ed. entitled :] Volcanos : the character of their phenomena. . . . With a descriptive Catalogue of all known Volcanos, *etc.* 8⁰, *pp.* xi+490, 1 *pl.,* 1 *col. map. London,* 1862.—Another copy, 1872 [reviewed in :] *Amer. Journ. Sci. xiii, pp.* 108–45. *New Haven,* 1828.—In French (transl. by

Endymion) : 2 *col. pls. Paris*, 1864.—In Germ. (transl. by G. A. v. Klöden) : 1 *pl.*, 65 *figs. Berlin*, 1872.—Extr. in Ital. : *Bibl. Ital. xlv, pp.* 70–83, 211–26. *Milano*, 1827.

SCROPE, G. J. POULETT.—On the mode of formation of volcanic cones and craters.— *Quart. Journ. Geol. Soc. xv, pp.* 505–49. *London*, 1859.—[Sep. publ.] 8⁰, *pp.* 45. *London*, 1859.—In French, transl. by Pieraggi : 8⁰, *tav. Paris*, 1860.—In German, transl. by C. L. Griesbach. *Berlin*, 1873.

SCUDERI, R.—Memoria su la Meteorologia in generale, e su i segni naturali meteorologici dell' Etna.—*Atti Acc. Gioen. iii, pp.* 193–210. *Catania*, 1829.

SCUDERI, S.—Trattato dei Boschi dell' Etna.—*Atti Acc. Gioen. i, pp.* 41–80, 241–92, *Catania*, 1825 ; *ii, pp.* 19–48, 1827 ; *iii, pp.* 3–16, 1829.

SECCHI, A.—Lezioni elementari di Fisica Terrestre.—8⁰, *pp.* 218. *Torino e Roma*, 1879.

SEGUENZA, G.—Di certe rocce vulcaniche interstratificate fra rocce di sedimento.— [Nota ove è illustrata una serie stratigrafica di Salice netta provincia di Messina nella quale s'incontrano materiali vulcanici delle isole Eolie interstratificati nel pliocene antico. (Astiano.)]—*Rend. R. Acc. Sci. xv. pp.* 112–15, 1 *pl. Napoli*, 1876.

SELVAGGIO, M.—Descriptio Montis Ætnæi cum horrendis emanationibus ignium a retro seculis usque da tempora nostra.— 12⁰. *Venetiis*, 1541.—*It is Chap.* XLIII of : De partibus Mundi, *etc. Venetiis*, 1542.

SELVAGGIO, M.—Colloquium trium Peregrinorum.
    See p. 143 : earthquake 1169. Cited by Mongitore and Massa, Etna, *ibid*. Cronaca Siciliana.

SENECA, L. A.—L. A. Senecæ Naturalium Quæstionum.—II, 1 ; *epist.* 51 *et* 79 ; *de benefic.* III, 37, 2 ; VI, 36, 1.

SERPETRO, N.—Il Mercato delle Maraviglie della Natura, ovvero Istoria Naturale.— 4⁰. *Venezia*, 1653.

SERPETRO, N.—Trattato della Geografia dell' Etna.
    Cited by Massa, Etna. Not edited.

SETO. — Opera chronologica. — *For the* " Chronologia reformata Seti auctore Joanne Baptista Riccioli," *see* RICCIOLI.

SEVASTA, F.—Istoria dell' orrendo terremuoto di Sciacca nell' anno 1727 ; colla relazione di altri terremuoti.—8⁰. *Palermo*, 1729.

SEVERUS, CORNELIUS.—Le Poème d'Etna, accompagné de quelques autres sur le même sujet, traduit en vers.—*See* MAROLLES, ABBÉ DE.—Traductions en vers de Virgile et de plusieurs autres poètes célèbres des Anciens, *etc*.—8⁰. *Paris*, 1671. [B.N.P., Yc. 13565.]

SEVERUS, CORNELIUS.—Ætna et quæ supersunt fragmenta cum notis et interpretatione Jos. Scaligeri, Frid. Lindenbruchii et Theod. Goralli accessit Petri Bembi.— 8⁰, *foll.* 3, *pp.* 186, *foll.* 12 (*index*), 1 *pl. Amstelædami*, 1703.—*See* BEMBUS, P.— Ætna, *etc*.—Ital. transl. by Gargiulli. *Venice*, 1701. [C.A.]—French transl. by Accarias de Sérionne. *Paris*, 1736.—*See also* ALBINOVANUS, C. P.—C. P. Albinovani Elegiæ, *etc*. 1703, 1715.

SEVERUS, CORNELIUS.—L'Etna . . . tradotto del dottor Claudio Nicola Stampa.—4⁰. *Mediolani*, 1735. [B.N.P., Yc. 893.]
    See Tomus decimus : Corpus omnium veterum poetarum Latinorum, cum eorundem italica versione.

SEVERUS, CORNELIUS.—L'Etna . . . et les Sentences de Publius Syrus, traduits en François, avec des remarques . . . (par Accarias de Sérionne) et le texte latin de ces deux auteurs.—12⁰, *pp.* 359. *Paris*, 1736.

SEVERUS, CORNELIUS.— Der Aetna . . . übersetzt von Conrad Arnold Schmid.— 8⁰, *pp.* 104. *Braunschweig*, 1769.

SEVERUS, CORNELIUS.—L'Etna, poème de Cornélius Séverus, traduction nouvelle par M. l'Abbé Delutho.—8⁰, *pp.* xxvii+105. *Paris*, 1842.

SEVERUS, CORNELIUS. — L'Etna. — *See* Petits Poèmes latins . . . traduits en Français par le traducteur de Claudien . . . et par M. l'Abbé Delutho.—8⁰. *Paris*, 1842. [B.N.P., Yc. 11689 and 11690.]

SEVERUS, CORNELIUS.—Lucilius Junior. L'Etna . . . suivi d'un fragment de Cornelius Severus sur la mort de Cicéron, *etc*. —8⁰. *Paris*, 1845.

SEVERUS, CORNELIUS.—Aetna, erklaert von Siegfried Sudhaus.—8⁰, *pp.* x+230. *Leipzig*, 1898.

SEVERUS, CORNELIUS.—Ætna, texte établi et traduit en français par J. Vessereau . . . —8⁰, *pp.* 48. *Paris*, 1905.

SEVERUS, CORNELIUS.—Ætna, texte Latin publié avec traduction 'et commentaire, par J. Vessereau.—8⁰, *pp. li+105. Paris,* 1905.

SEVERUS, CORNELIUS.—L'Etna. Poema di Cornelio Severo, traduzione di Onofrio Gargiulli colle notizie biografiche dell' autore.—*Giorn. Lett. xxxi, pp.* 3–32. *Napoli.*

SHURY, J. (sculp.).—Mount Ætna. Pl. I. [View of Etna and Catania with 1669 lava flow.] Pl. II. [Crater of Etna.] Published as the Act directs, April 5, 1820, by Longman, Hurst, Rees, Orme & Brown, Paternoster Row.

SICKLER.—Aetna.—*Allg. Encyclop. d. W. u. k.* 2ᵃ, *pp.* 123–35, 1 *pl.* (representing the panorama of Etna of Gemmellaro). [C.A.]

SIEBERG, A.—Die topographischen Umgestaltungen auf dem Aetna, hervorgerufen durch die Eruption in der Zeit vom 9 bis 26 September 1911.—*Beitr. Geophys. xi, kleine Mitth. pp.* 162–76, *figs., pls. ix–xi. Leipzig,* 1912.

SIEGERT.—Panorama des Etna und der umliegenden Gegend.—8⁰, *pp.* 8, 1 *pl. Breslau,* 1822. [C.A.]

SILIUS ITALICUS, C.—*Lib.* XIV, 59 *et seq.*

SILLIMAN, B.—An Excursion on Etna.— *Amer. Journ. Sci. S.* 2, *xiii, pp.* 178–84. *New Haven,* 1852.

SILVESTRI, A.—L'Eruzione dell' Etna del 1886. [2 pts.] I. Fenomeni, scoppio, cronaca, lava, fumaioli, *etc.* II. Studio del materiale eruttivo.—*Atti Acc. Gioen. S.* 4, *vi, Mem.* 11, *pp.* 36, 19 *pls.,* 1 *map ; Mem.* 20, *pp.* 44, *col. pls. xx–xxii (by O. Silvestri). Catania,* 1893.—*Boll. Acc. Gioen. N.S.* 32, *pp.* 9–10. *Catania,* 1893.

SILVESTRI, A.—Sulla Molibdenite delle Isole dei Ciclopi.—*Boll. Acc. Gioen.* 32, *pp.* 13–20. *Catania,* 1893.

SILVESTRI, A.—Sulla Pirrotite delle Isole dei Ciclopi.—*Boll. Acc. Gioen.* 33, *pp.* 25–30. *Catania,* 1893.

SILVESTRI, O.—Analisi chimica di un prodotto minerale di un vulcano spento della Toscana. Studiato in paragone a un prodotto analogo dell' Etna.—*Atti Acc. Gioen. S.* 2, *xix, pp.* 159–70. *Catania,* 1864.

SILVESTRI, O.—Sulla Eruzione dell' Etna nel 1865. Prima relazione al Prefetto della Provincia.—*Giorn. Prov. di Catania.* 1865. —In French : *C.R. Acad. Sci. lxi, pp.* 212–13. *Paris,* 1865.

SILVESTRI, O.—*See* VIOTTI, G. 1865.

SILVESTRI, O.—Sulla Eruzione dell' Etna nel 1865, studj geologici e chimici.—*Atti Soc. Ital. ix, pp.* 50–67. *Milano,* 1866.— *Il Nuovo Cimento, xxi–xxii, pp.* 167–84. *Pisa,* 1865–66.

SILVESTRI, O.—Le Salse e la eruzione fangosa di Paternò in Sicilia incominciata a dì 7 Febbraio 1866. Ricerche chimico-geologiche.—*Catania,* 1866.—*Il Nuovo Cimento, xxi–xxii, pp.* 225–46. *Pisa,* 1865–66.

SILVESTRI, O.—Découverte du Vanadium dans les laves de l'Etna.—*Journ. Min. Géol. Paris,* 1866.

SILVESTRI, O.—Sur une récente éruption boueuse des Salses de Paternò en Sicile.— *C.R. Acad. Sci. lxii, pp.* 646–48. *Paris,* 1866.—*Les Mondes, x, pp.* 586–87. *Paris,* 1866.—*N. J. f. Min. pp.* 277–81. *Stuttgart,* 1870.

SILVESTRI, O.—Relazione scientifica sugli ultimi fenomeni vulcanici presentati dall' Etna fatta al Congresso della Società Italiana di Scienze Naturali, tenuto alla Spezia nell' autunno 1866.—*Atti* 2ᵃ *Riun. Straord. Soc. Ital. Sci. Nat. ix, fasc.* 1. 1866.

SILVESTRI, O.—Sur un tremblement de terre ressenti en Sicile le 26 mars 1866.— *C.R. Acad. Sci. lxii, pp.* 1122–23. *Paris,* 1866.

SILVESTRI, O.—I Fenomeni vulcanici presentati dall' Etna nel 1863–66, considerati in rapporto alla grande eruzione del 1865. Studii di geologia-chimica.—*Atti Acc. Gioen. S.* 3, *i, pp.* 53–319, *tav. i–v. Catania,* 1867.—[Abstr.] *Zeitschr. deutsch. geol. Gesellsch. xxi, pp.* 221–38. *Berlin,* 1869.— *N. J. f. Min. pp.* 51–79, 257–77. *Stuttgart,* 1870.—*Verh. k. k. geol. Reichsanst. pp.* 391–92. *Wien,* 1868.

SILVESTRI, O.—Sull' eruzione dell' Etna del 27 Novembre 1868 dal cratere centrale. Relazione.—*Catania,* 30 *Novembre* 1868.— *Gazz. Piemontese, N.* 342. *Torino,* 10 *Dicembre* 1868.

A A

SILVESTRI, O.—Fenomeni eruttivi Etnei in seguito alla eruzione scoppiata il 27 Novembre 1868 dal cratere centrale. Relazione.—*Gazz. d. Provincia d. Catania, N° 147, Dicembre* 1868.

SILVESTRI, O.—[Processi chimici e di dissociazione studiati nella lava fluente e nei fumajoli a elevatissima temperatura sul cratere centrale dell' Etna nel 1868. Lavoro comunicato al Congresso della Società Italiana di Scienze Naturali tenuto in Catania nell' Agosto 1869.]—*Atti Soc. Ital. xii, pp.* 463–64. *Milano,* 1869.

SILVESTRI, O.—Ascensione dell' Etna.— *Atti Soc. Ital. xii, pp.* 495–98. *Milano,* 1869.

SILVESTRI, O.—Sopra un supposto nuovo vulcano della Sicilia. Studio chimico-geologico di una eruzione idrogassosa accompagnata da fango e bitume.—*Atti Acc. Gioen. S.* 3, *v, pp.* 239–52. *Catania,* 1871.— *Gazz. Chim. Ital. i, pp.* 501–8. *Palermo,* 1871.

SILVESTRI, O.—Ambrogio Soldani e le sue opere (con osservazioni del Soldani sulle sabbie dell' Etna. Discorso fatto nella R. Accademia dei Fisiocritici a Siena in occasione del Congresso della Società Italiana di Scienze Naturali).—*Atti Soc. Ital. Sci. nat. xv, pp.* 273–89. *Milano,* 1872.

SILVESTRI, O.— Fumarolenbildungen. — *Min. Mitth. i, p.* 54. *Wien,* 1872.
Notice upon Silvestri's researches.

SILVESTRI, O.—Osservazioni fatte sull' Etna durante la ecclisse totale di sole del 22 Dicembre 1870.—*Atti Acc. Gioen. S.* 3, *vii, pp.* 219–22, 1 *table. Catania,* 1872.

SILVESTRI, O.—Sulle Sorgenti Idrogassose Solfuree dette di S. Venera al Pozzo alla base orientale dell' Etna.—*Atti Acc. Gioen. S.* 3, *viii, pp.* 47–146, 2 *pls. Catania,* 1873.—*Gazz. Chim. Ital. iii, pp.* 35–37. *Palermo,* 1873.—*Journ. Chem. Soc. xi, pp.* 863–64. *London,* 1873.

SILVESTRI, O.—Emissione di fumo eruttivo straordinario dal cratere centrale dell' Etna.—*Bull. Vulc. Ital. fasc.* 2 *e* 3, *pp.* 44. *Roma,* 1874.

SILVESTRI, O.—Éruption dans l'intérieur du cratère central de l'Etna.—*Revue Savoisienne,* 15 *sept.* 1874. (Résumé by M. Boltshauser.)

SILVESTRI, O.—Fenomeni eruttivi dell' Etna nell' interno del cratere centrale. (Col presagio di una prossima grande eruzione laterale.)—*Boll. R. Com. Geol. Ital. v, pp.* 244–47. *Roma,* 1874.—*Bull. Vulc. Ital. fasc.* 6 *e* 7, *pp.* 73. *Roma,* 1874.

SILVESTRI, O.—Notizie sulla eruzione dell' Etna del 29 Agosto, 1874.—*Boll. R. Com. Geol. Ital. v, pp.* 312–22. *Roma,* 1874.— *Gazz. di Catania, Suppl. al N°* 75 [? 1874]. —*Bull. Vulc. Ital. fasc.* 9 *e* 10, *pp.* 105. *Roma,* 1874.—*N. J. f. Min. pp.* 36–42. *Stuttgart,* 1875.—*Phil. Mag. xlix, pp.* 126–34. *London,* 1875.

SILVESTRI, O.—La Scombinazione chimica (dissociazione) applicata alla interpretazione di alcuni fenomeni vulcanici. Sintesi ed analisi di un nuovo composto minerale dell' Etna e di origine comune nei vulcani.— *Gazz. Chim. Ital. v, pp.* 301-7. *Palermo,* 1875.—*Journ. Chem. Soc. i, p.* 200. *London,* 1876.—*Atti Acc. Gioen. S.* 3, *x, pp.* 17–27. *Catania,* 1876.—*Rev. Scient. ix, pp.* 565–68. *Paris,* 1875.—*Ann. Phys. Chem. clvii, pp.* 165–72. *Leipzig,* 1876.

SILVESTRI, O.—Terremoti presso l'Etna e conati eruttivi del medesimo dal 7 al 20 Gennaio 1875.—*Bull. Vulc. Ital. fasc.* 1, 2 *e* 3, *pp.* 19. *Roma,* 1875.

SILVESTRI, O.—Sopra due grandi perdite che ha fatto la vulcanologia. Cenni sulla vita scientifica e sulle opere di C. Sainte-Claire Deville e W. Sartorius v. Waltershausen.—*Bull. Vulc. Ital. fasc.* 11 *e* 12, *pp.* 179. *Roma,* 1876.

SILVESTRI, O.—La Scienza della Terra. Discorso d'inaugurazione al corso di Chimico-fisica terrestre, Mineralogia e Geologia nella R. Università di Catania nell' anno 1877.—*Catania,* 1877.
Read after the foundation of the chair of terrestrial physics and chemistry with special application to the vulcanology of Etna.

SILVESTRI, O.—Sopra alcune Paraffine ed altri Carburi d'Idrogeno omologhi che trovansi contenuti in una lava dell' Etna [1876].—*Atti Acc. Gioen. S.* 3, *xii, pp.* 69-97. *Catania,* 1878.—*Vorträge u. Mitth. v. G. v. Rath, pp.* 8. *Bonn,* 1877.—*Sitzber. niederrhein. Gesellsch. pp.* 40–45. *Bonn,* 1877.—*Gazz. Chim. Ital. vii, pp.* 1–21. *Palermo,* 1877.—*Journ. Chem. Soc. i, pp.* 704-5. *London,* 1877.

SILVESTRI, O.—Sulla Eruzione di fango a Paternò nelle adiacenze dell' Etna dal suo principio fino alla data del 25 Maggio 1879.—*Relazioni al Giorn. d. Sicilia, N. 304, 25 Dicembre 1878; N. 314, 25 Dicembre 1878; N. 18, 15 Gennaio 1879; N. 56, 8 Aprile 1879; N. 146, 30 Maggio 1879.*

SILVESTRI, O.—Importante eruzione di fango comparsa a Paternò nelle adiacenze dell' Etna ai primi Dicembre 1878.—*Bull. Vulc. Ital. v, pp. 131-32, Roma, 1878; vi, pp. 28-31, 97-98, 1879. — Riv. Sci. Ind. xi, pp. 29-31 (part only). 1879.*

SILVESTRI, O.—I Terremoti di Mineo, in Provincia di Catania, dell' Ottobre e Novembre 1878, accompagnati da singolari fenomeni di rombi. Relazione presentata al Prefetto della Provincia (in commissione col Prof. Boltshauser).—*Catania, Novembre, 1878.*

SILVESTRI, O.—Lettera (sopra una eruzione di fango dell' Etna) comunicata dal Socio Ordinario Luigi Palmieri.—*Rend. R. Acc. Sci. xvii, p. 162, 1878; xviii, pp. 110-11. Napoli, 1879.*

SILVESTRI, O.—Cronaca dei fenomeni Etnei del 1878-1879. Osservazioni meteoriche fatte nelle stazioni presso le Alpi e gli Apeninni, pubblicate per cura del Club Alpino Italiano.—*Ann. viii. Torino, 1878-79.*

SILVESTRI, O.—Atlante di grandi fotografie sulla eruzione ed effetti dei terremoti dell' Etna nel 1879.—*Diretto e pubblicato per cura del R. Governo Italiano. Catania, 1879.*

SILVESTRI, O.—Continuazione della eruzione fangosa a Paternò nelle adjacenze dell' Etna e sua fase in data del 20 Dicembre 1878.—*Bull. Vulc. Ital. vi, p. 28. Roma, 1879.*

SILVESTRI, O.—Andamento della eruzione fangosa di Paternò nelle adiacenze dell' Etna in data del 14 Gennaio 1879.—*Bull. Vulc. Ital. vi, p. 30. Roma, 1879.*

SILVESTRI, O.—L'Attuale eruzione di fango, termale, salato, petrolifero dell' Etna presso Paternò.— *Illustrazione Ital. di Trèves, N. 8, fig. and text. Milano, 23 Febbraio, 1879.*

SILVESTRI, O.—La doppia eruzione dell' Etna scoppiata il 26 Maggio 1879. Relazione ai Ministri di Istruzione pubblica, Agricoltura, Industria e Commercio, pub-

blicata il 31 Maggio 1879, con una carta topografica.—*4°, pp. 19, 1 pl. Catania, 1879.—Bull. Vulc. Ital. vi, 4-7, p. 67. Roma, 1879.—Sitzber. niederrh. Gesellsch. pp. 198-209. Bonn, 1879.—Vorträge und Mitth. von G. vom Rath, 1880. [Abstr.]*

SILVESTRI, O.—Sulla doppia eruzione e i terremoti dell' Etna nel 1879. 2ª ediz., ampliata del primo rapporto presentato al R. Governo.—*4°, pp. 46, 1 pl. Catania, 1879.—[Abstr.] Boll. R. Com. Geol. Ital. x, pp. 590-604. Roma, 1879.*

SILVESTRI, O.—L'Eruzione dell' Etna.—*Bull. Vulc. Ital. vi, pp. 61-75. Roma, 1879.*

SILVESTRI, O.—Sulla Eruzione dell' Etna del 1879.—Tre incisioni sopra disegni originali fatti sul teatro eruttivo e che rappresentano : 1°. Un gruppo di bocche eruttive formatosi a 1950 metri di altitudine sul livello del mare alla base del Monte Nero.—2°. Eruzione dell' Etna sul fianco nord-nord-est osservato da Randazzo la notte del 28 Maggio a ore 3 ant.—3°. Fenditure ed avvallamenti di suolo che fanno capo alle bocche eruttive situate tra il Monte Timparossa e il Monte Nero.—*Illustr. Ital. sem. 2, pp. 5. Milano, 1879.*

SILVESTRI, O.—Fenomeni dell' Etna successivi all' ultima eruzione del Maggio-Giugno 1879.—*Bull. Vulc. Ital. vi, pp. 119-24. Roma, 1879.*

SILVESTRI, O.—[Lettera al Prof. Palmieri per la eruzione dell' Etna del Maggio 1879.]—*Rend. R. Acc. Sci. xviii, p. 154. Napoli, 1879.*

SILVESTRI, O.—Il Nuovo monte Umberto-Margherita comparso in 5 giorni sull' Etna durante la eruzione del Maggio-Giugno 1879.—*Illustr. Ital. di Trèves, sem. 2, pp. 309, woodcuts. Milano, 1879.*

SILVESTRI, O.—Un Viaggio all' Etna. Vol. I, con la descrizione storica, topografica, geologica, altimetrica e pittoresca del grande vulcano, con una carta topografica e un' appendice, con le norme e tariffe per i viaggiatori all' Etna, stabilite dalla Sezione Catanese del Club Alpino Italiano. —*16°, 1 map. Torino-Roma-Firenze, 1879.*

SILVESTRI, O.—Ricerche chimiche sulla composizione delle acque del Fiume Simeto in Sicilia e delle acque potabili di Catania eseguite negli anni 1871 e 1872 (per 18 mese). Memoria.—*2 tav. Catania, 1880.—Atti Acc. Gioen. S. 3, xiii, pp. 125-242, 2 tav. Catania, 1879.*

A A 2

SILVESTRI, O.—*See* COMMISSIONE GOVERNATIVA. 1879.

SILVESTRI, O.—*See* GEMMELLARO, G. G. 1879.

SILVESTRI, O.—Continuazione della eruzione fangosa di Paternò e sulle condizioni attuali dell' Etna (25 Dicembre 1879). Lettera diretta da O. Silvestri al Prof. Luigi Palmieri, direttore dell' Osservatorio Vesuviano.—*Bull. Vulc. Ital. vii, pp.* 9-12. *Roma,* 1880.

SILVESTRI, O.—Sulle condizioni attuali dell' Etna.—*Bull. Vulc. Ital. vii, pp.* 9-12. *Roma,* 1880.—*L'Incorag. vii,* 2.

SILVESTRI, O.—Fenomeni vulcanici dell' Etna avvenuti dal Gennaio a tutto Aprile 1880.—*Bull. Vulc. Ital. vii, pp.* 80-83. *Roma,* 1880.

SILVESTRI, O.—Più recenti fenomeni vulcanici dell' Etna nel Maggio e Giugno 1880.—*Bull. Vulc. Ital. vii, pp.* 86-89. *Roma,* 1880.

SILVESTRI, O.—Programma per il XIII congresso degli Alpinisti Italiani da tenersi a Catania il 15 Settembre 1880 con ascensione all' Etna.—*Catania,* 1880.—*Boll. Club Alp. Ital. Torino,* 1880.

SILVESTRI, O.—Sullo Sfeno trovato per la prima volta tra i prodotti minerali dell' Etna.—*Riv. Scient. e Industr.* 12. *Firenze, Giugno,* 1880.

SILVESTRI, O.—Cronaca della eruzione di fango a Paternò e dei fenomeni vulcanici generali dell' Etna durante l'anno 1880. An. IX, 1879-80.—*Osservazioni meteorologiche fatte nelle stazioni presso le Alpi e gli Appennini e pubblicate per cura del Club Alpino Italiano, Torino,* 1880.—*Bull. Vulc. Ital.* 3. *Roma,* 1881.

SILVESTRI, O.—Continuazione del periodo eruttivo (con eruzione di fango) presso Paternò e cronaca dei fenomeni vulcanici generali dell' Etna durante l'anno 1881.— *Boll. Assoc. Meteor. Ital. x. Torino,* 1880-81.—*Bull. Vulc. Ital. Roma,* 1881.

SILVESTRI, O.—Bibliografia generale riguardante la vulcanologia, mineralogia, geologia della provincia di Catania e delle Isole vulcaniche adiacenti alla Sicilia.— *pp.* 64. *Bologna,* 1881.

SILVESTRI, O.—Progetto di una rete sismica estesa dal centro alla periferia dell' Etna con a capo l'Osservatorio Centrale a 3000 metri di elevazione e l'Istituto Vulcanologico di Catania a 10 metri sopra il mare. Presentato al R. Ministero di Agricoltura, Industria e Commercio nel 1881.—*Giorn. Sicilia,* 137. *Palermo,* 20 *Maggio* 1881.

SILVESTRI, O.—Sulla natura chimica di alcune inclusioni liquide contenute in cristalli naturali di Solfo della Sicilia.— *Boll. R. Com. Geol. Ital. xii, pp.* 576-78. *Roma,* 1881.—*Gazz. Chim. Ital. xii, pp.* 7-9. *Palermo,* 1882.

SILVESTRI, O.—Sulla presenza della Paraffina naturalmente cristallizzata nelle geodi di una Lava Basaltica di Paternò nelle adiacenze dell' Etna.—*Boll. R. Com. Geol. Ital. xii, pp.* 578-79. *Roma,* 1881.—*Gazz. Chim. Ital. xii, pp.* 9-11. *Palermo,* 1882.

Appendix to " Sopra alcune paraffine ed altri carburi, etc." 1877.

SILVESTRI, O.—Petrografia e mineralogia micrografica delle roccie eruttive dell' Etna e degli altri centri vulcanici (ora spenti) della Sicilia.—[Estr.] *Boll. R. Com. Geol. Ital. xii, pp.* 583-85. *Roma,* 1881.

SILVESTRI, O.—*See* COMITÉ D'ORGANISATION, *etc.*—Bibliographie Géologique, *etc.* No. XVI. 1881.

SILVESTRI, O.—Sulle acque che circolano e scaturiscono nella regione dell' Etna. III : Sorgente idrogassose minerali acidule di Paternò.—4⁰, *pp.* 89, 3 *pls. Catania,* 1882.

SILVESTRI, O.—Eruzioni stromboliane dell' Etna.—*Bull. Vulc. Ital. ix, pp.* 139-41. *Roma,* 1882.

SILVESTRI, O.—Ricerche chimiche sulla composizione dell' acqua minerale acidulo-alcalino-magnesiaco-ferruginosa, detta, del Fonte Halimonide e volgarmente la Grassa, delle sorgenti idrogassose di Paternò alla base S.-O. dell' Etna ; 3ª memoria per servire ad un' opera completa di Idrologia generale dell' Etna sotto il punto di vista della chimica geologica [1881].—*Atti Acc. Gioen. S.* 3, *xvi, pp.* 189-277, 2 *pls.,* 1 *map,* 1 *tab. Catania,* 1882.

SILVESTRI, O.—Sulla eruzione dell' Etna scoppiata il 22 Marzo 1883. Rapporto al R. Governo.—*pp.* 8, 1 *map. Catania,* 1883.

SILVESTRI, O.—Album fotografico di 12 fotografie che riproducono i fatti più caratteristici della eruzione suddetta.— *Catania,* 1883.

SILVESTRI, O.—Sulla esplosione Etnea del 22 Marzo 1883, in relazione ai fenomeni vulcanici (geodinamici ed eruttivi) presentati dall' Etna durante il quadriennio compreso dal Genn. 1880 al Dec. 1883.—*Atti Acc. Gioen. S.* 3, *xvii, pp.* 237–431, *pls. i–iv, and map of Etna* 1 : 250,000. *Catania*, 1883.

SILVESTRI, O.—Sopra una particolare specie di Quartzite semivetrosa a struttura pomiceo-granulare contenuta nell' interno di alcune bombe projettate dall' Etna nella recente eruzione eccentrica del 22 Marzo 1883.—*Atti Acc. Gioen. S.* 3, *xvii, pp.*ᐟ167–72. *Catania*, 1883.

SILVESTRI, O.—Osservazioni geodinamiche fatte nella R. Università di Catania durante il mese di Luglio 1883.—*Gazz. di Sicilia,* 9 *Agosto* 1883.

SILVESTRI, O.—Sulla esplosione eccentrica dell' Etna avvenuta il 22 Marzo 1883 e sul contemporaneo parossismo geodinamico-eruttivo. Saggio di nuovi studi (che comprende tutti i fenomeni vulcanici presentati dall' Etna, dal 1 Gennaio 1880 al 1 Gennaio 1884).— 4⁰, *pp.* 195, 6 *pls.,* 1 *map. Catania*, 1884. [C.A.]

SILVESTRI, O.—Fenomeni Etnei.—*Boll. Soc. Meteor. Ital. v. Torino,* 1885.

SILVESTRI, O.—I Terremoti di Nicolosi avvenuti nel Settembre e Ottobre 1885.—*Boll. Soc. Meteor. Ital. v. Torino,* 1885.

SILVESTRI, O.—Sulle acque che circolano e scaturiscono nella regione dell' Etna. Monografie chimico-geologiche. Sorgente dell' acqua potabile detta Reitana presso Acireale.—*Atti Acc. Gioen. S.* 3, *xix, pp.* 229–45. *Catania*, 1886.

SILVESTRI, O.—Sur l'Éruption de l'Etna de mai et juin 1886. Lettre à M. Daubrée. —*C.R. Acad. Sci. cii, pp.* 1589–92. *Paris,* 1886.

SILVESTRI, O.—Sulle Eruzioni centrale ed eccentrica dell' Etna del Maggio-Giugno. 1⁰. Rapporto al R. Governo.—*with map. Catania,* 22 *Maggio,* 1886.
    IDEM. 2⁰. Rapporto.—12 *Giugno,* 1886.
    2ᵃ Edizione dei due detti rapporti.—*pp.* 32. *Catania,* 1886.

SILVESTRI, O.—L'Etna nel 1885.—*Ann. Meteor. Ital. i, pp.* 192–201. *Torino,* 1886.

SILVESTRI, O.—Der letzte Ausbruch des Aetna. Brief des Prof. O. Silvestri in Catania an Prof. E. Suess in Wien.—*Neue Freie Presse,* 7855, *p.* 1, *col.* 1–*p.* 4, *col.* 3. *Wien,* 10 *Juli,* 1886.

SILVESTRI, O.—Observations sur les phénomènes éruptifs de l'Etna depuis le 18 mai jusqu'au 7 juin 1886.—*Bull. Soc. Sci. Flammarion, ii, p.* 97. *Marseille,* 1886.

SILVESTRI, O.—La recente eruzione dell' Etna.—*Nuova Antologia, S.* 3, *iv, pp.* 22–36. *Roma,* 1886.

SILVESTRI,O.—[Sunti di fatti più rimarchevoli dell' eruzione dell' Etna del Maggio-Giugno 1886.]—*Boll. Soc. Geogr. Ital. S.* 2, *xi, pp.* 569–72. *Roma,* 1886.

SILVESTRI, O.—Sull' eruzione dell' Etna del Maggio e Giugno 1886.—*Ann. Meteor. Ital. ii, pp.* 237–41. *Torino,* 1887.

SILVESTRI, O.—Etna e Sicilia nel 1887, sotto il punto di vista dei fenomeni eruttivi e geodinamici.—*Ann. Meteor. Ital. iii, pp.* 309–23. *Torino,* 1888.

SILVESTRI, O.—Etna, Sicilia ed Isole vulcaniche adiacenti, sotto il punto di vista dei fenomeni eruttivi e geodinamici avvenuti durante l'anno 1888.—*Atti Acc. Gioen. S.* 4, *i, pp.* 291–331. *Catania,* 1889. —*Ann. Meteor. Ital. iv, pp.* 316–55. *Torino,* 1889.

SILVESTRI, O., ARCIDIACONO, S.—Etna, Sicilia ed Isole vulcaniche adiacenti sotto il punto di vista dei fenomeni eruttivi e geodinamici avvenuti durante l'anno 1889. —*Atti Acc. Gioen. S.* 4, *ii, pp.* 221–49. *Catania,* 1890.—*Ann. Meteor. Ital. v, pp.* 267–70. *Torino,* 1890.—*Boll. Oss. Moncalieri, S.* 2, *x,* 2. *Torino,* 1890.

SILVESTRI, O.—Sopra un importante fatto di *litoclasi* sotterranea, messo in evidenza dalla acque meteoriche torrenziali nella bassa regione est dell' Etna.— *Boll. Acc. Gioen. N.S.* 11–13, *pp.* 11–15. *Catania,* 1890.

SILVESTRI, O.—Sul terremoto Etneo del 25 Dicembre 1889.—*Boll. Acc. Gioen. N.S.* 11–12, *p.* 15. *Catania,* 1890.

SILVESTRI, O.—Proposta di un' Osservatorio sull' Etna in servizio alla Vulcanologia e Meteorologia. Presentata manoscritta al R. Ministero della Pubblica Istruzione.
    See note at p. 112 of " I Fenomeni vulcanici presentati dall' Etna, etc."

SILVESTRI, O.—I Fenomeni vulcanici presentati dall' Etna dal 1866 al 1880. Studi di geologia chimica. [Sequel to " I Fenomeni presentati dall' Etna 1863 al 1866," which appeared in 1867.]
    In the preface to his work " Sulla es-

plosione Etnea del 22 Marzo 1883, etc."
(Atti Acc. Gioen. S. 3, xvii, pp. 237–
431, 1883) the author states that the Acc.
Gioenia di Sci. Nat. intended to give a
whole volume of the Atti for the publication of the above, but it cannot be
verified that it was ever published.

SIMOND, L.—A Tour in Italy and Sicily.—
8⁰, *pp. xi*+624. *London*, 1828.—In French :
2 vols. 8⁰. *Paris*, 1827–28.——2nd ed.
2 vols. 8⁰. *Paris*, 1828.—*N. J. f. Min. pp.*
348–51. *Stuttgart*, 1833.

SIMONE DA LENTINI.—Chronicon o
Chronaca in Rosario di Gregorio.—*Biblioth.
script. Arag. Panormi*, 1691.
　Cited by Ferrara and Caruso.

SIMONE DA LENTINI.—Historia MS.
del Conte Rogero.—*Biblioth. script. Arag.
Vol. ii. Panormi*, 1691.
　Cited by Massa, Etna.

SINCELLO, G.—Chorographia.—*Tip. Reg.
pp.* 257. *Paris*, 1652.
　Eruption of Etna.

SMITH, J. (drawn by).—Distant View of
Mount Etna, near Catania, in Sicily.
Engraved by W. Byrne and T. Medland.
This is in the Johnston-Lavis collection
in another stage (especially of the sky),
without any inscription. Man on mule-back
with two cows and an aqueduct ruin in
foreground : 308 × 244 mm. (with inscription).

SMYTH, W. H.—Carta generale dell' Isola
di Sicilia, compilata, disegnata ed incisa
nell' Ufficio Topografico di Napoli sui
migliori materiali esistenti e sulle recenti
operazioni fatte dal Cav. G. E. Smyth.—
Napoli, 1814.

SMYTH, W. H.—Memoir descriptive of the
resources, inhabitants, and hydrography
of Sicily and its Islands, etc.—4⁰, *map and
num. fine aquatint engravings by Daniell.
London*, 1824.

SOLDANI, A.—Testaceographiæ ac Zoophy-
tographiæ parvæ et microscopicæ. tomus
primus (secundus), *etc.*—2 tom. fol. *Senis*,
1789–98.
　See Tom. ii, Cap. 2 : Volcanic sand of
Etna.

SOLINUS, C. J.—C. J. Solini Collectanea
rerum memorabilium.—8⁰, *pp. xciv*+287.
Berolini, 1864.
　See pp. 54, 56, 57, 60, 183.

SOMMA, AGAT. DI.—Historico racconto dei
terremoti della Calabria dall' anno 1638
fin' anno 41.—*Napoli*, 1641.

SOMMA, ANT. — Osservazioni vulcanologiche sulle fenditure esistenti in Mas-
calucia volgarmente chiamate Cavòli.—
Atti Acc. Gioen. xvi, pp. 19–34. *Catania*,
1841.

SOMMA, ANT.—Sopra le stratificazioni al-
luviali del Fasano.—*Catania*, 1845.

SOMMA, ANT.—Sul luogo e tempo in cui
avvenne l'eruzione dell' Etna appellata
dei Fratelli Pii.—*Atti Acc. Gioen. S. 2. xx,
pp.* 61–84. *Catania*, 1865.

SPALLANZANI, L.—Viaggi alle due Sicilie
e in alcune parti dell' Appennino.—6 vols.
8⁰. *Vol. i, pp.* 55+292, *tav.* 1–2 ; *Vol. ii,
pp.* 351, *tav.* 3–9 ; *Vol. iii, pp.* 364 ;
Vol. iv, pp. 356, *tav.* 10–11 ; *Vol. v, pp.*
371 ; *Vol. vi, pp.* 288. *Pavia*, 1792–97.—
Another ed. 3 vols. 8⁰, *portrait and pls.
Milano*, 1825.—In German : 8 vols. *Leipzig*, 1794–96.—Another ed. 5 vols. *Leipzig*,
1795–98.—In French : 2 tom. 8⁰. *T. i,
pp.* 44+299, *pls.* 1–2 ; *T. ii, pp.* 273, *pls.*
3–9. *Berne*, 1795.—Another ed., transl. by
G. Toscan : " Avec des notes du cit.
Faujas-de-St. Fond," 6 tom. 8⁰. *T. i, pp.*
10+311, *pls.* 1–2 ; *T. ii, pp.* 280, *pls.* 3–5 ;
T. iii, pp. 291 ; *T. iv, pp.* 272, *pls.* 6–7 ; *T. v,
pp.* 309 ; *T. vi, pp.* 215. *Paris, an* VIII
[1800].—In English : 4 vols. 8⁰. *Vol. i,
pp.* 50+315, *pls.* 1–2 ; *Vol. ii, pp.* 389,
pls. 3–7 ; *Vol. iii, pp.* 402, *pls.* 8–9 ;
Vol. iv, pp. 394, *pls.* 10–11. *London*,
1798.—See also Pinkerton's collection of
voyages and travels, *Vol. v. London*, 1809.

SPALLANZANI, L.—*See* MUENTER.

SPECIALE, S.—All' Etna ! Escursione del
6 Agosto 1876. Relazione.—*Musumeci-
Papale, Catania*, 1876.

SPECIALE, S.—*See* RICCIARDI, L. 1881
(2).

SPECIALIS, N.—Rerum Sicularum libri
octo (1282–1337).—*See* GRÆVIUS, J. G.—
Thes. Antiq. Sic. v.

SPEZIA, G.—Sull' origine del Solfo nei
giacimenti solfiferi della Sicilia.—*Torino*,
1892.

SPUHLER, A.—Mon Voyage en Italie.—
800 *photos. Paris, Leipzig*, — ?

SQUILLACI, P.—Progressi portentosi dell'
incendio di Mongibello.—8⁰, *foll.* 8. *Catania*,
1669.

STAMPINATO, B.—Osservazione sui tremuoti in occasione del tremuoto che scosse
orribilmente la città di Catania la sera del
20 Febbrajo 1818.—4⁰, *pp.* 64, 1 *pl.
Catania*, 1818. [C.A.]

STANGHI, V. (inc.).—Vedute delle Grotte di Calypso in Sicilia.—*No.* 2 *of Tavola* 44 *in Corografia dell' Italia, etc.* 1845. Engraving : 256×191 mm.

STARK, M.—Die Gesteine Usticas und die Beziehungen derselben zu den Gesteinen der Liparischen Inseln.—*Min. u. petr. Mitth. xxiii, pp.* 469–532, *tav. Wien,* 1904.

STELLA STARRABBA, F. — L'Eruzione dell' Etna nel Marzo-Aprile 1910.— [Estr.] " *Natura," pp.* 8. *Pavia,* 1910.

STELLA STARRABBA, F.— L'Eruzione Etnea del 1910, dal 23 al 31 Marzo.—*Atti R. Acc. Lincei, S.* 5, *Rend. xix, sem.* 1, *pp.* 495–500, *fig.* [*plan*]. *Roma,* 1910.

STELLA STARRABBA, F.—La Melilite negli inclusi delle Lave Etnee.—*Atti R. Acc. Lincei, S.* 5, *Rend. xix, sem.* 1, *pp.* 755–58. *Roma,* 1910.

STELLA STARRABBA, F.— Ueber das Vorkommen des Tridymit in einigen Gesteineinschlüssen der Laven des Aetnas.— *Centrabl. f. Min.* 20, *pp.* 627–29. *Stuttgart,* 1911.

STELLA STARRABBA, F.—Sull' esistenza di bocche eruttive a sud-est di Mompilieri formatesi durante l'eruzione dell' Etna del 1669.—*Atti Acc. Gioenia, S.* 5, *iv, Mem.* 13, *pp.* 7, 1 *fig. Catania,* 1911.

STELLA STARRABBA, F.—Sul rapporto esistente fra le precipitazioni atmosferiche annuali e l'attività dei vulcani Vesuvio e Etna.—*Rend. R. Acc. Sci. S.* 3, *xvii, pp.* 216–25, 8 *figs. Napoli,* 1911.

STELLA STARRABBA, F.—*See* VINASSA DE REGNY.

STIELER, C.—Italy from the Alps to Mount Etna. Transl. by F. E. Trollope and edited by T. A. Trollope.—*fol., pp. xiii*+ 468, (ca.) 400 engrav. *London,* 1877. *See pp.* 463–68.

STOBÆUS.—Flor. 79, 38. Cited by Ælian.

STOLBERG, F. L.—Reise in Deutschland, der Schweiz, Italien und Sicilien.—4 vols. 8⁰. *Königsburg und Leipzig* 1794. Atlas, 4⁰.—In English : 2 vols. 4⁰. *London,* 1796–97. *See* Vol. ii.

STOPPANI, A.—Sull' opuscolo " Esperimenti vulcanici del Prof. Gorini di Arturo Issel." Nota.—*Rend. R. Ist. Lomb. S.* 2, *vi, pp.* 213–36. *Milano,* 1873.

STOPPANI, A.—Corso di Geologia.—3 vols. 8⁰. *Bernardoni e Brigola, Milano,* 1871-73. *See* Vol. i, § 585, 596, 602, 603, 611, 617, 618, 650, 651, 683 ; Vol. ii, § 599 ; Vol. iii, § 137. 3ᵃ ediz. con note ed aggiunte per cura di Allessandro Malladra.—3 vols. 8⁰. *Vol. i, pp.* 695, 178 *figs.,* 1 *map, Milano,* 1900 ; *Vol. ii, pp.* 883, 217 *figs.,* 2 *maps,* 1903 ; *Vol. iii, pp.* 714, 60 *figs,* 1903. *See* Vol. i.

STRABO.—Geogr. 6, 2 ; De natura Rerum. Lib. VI.

STRACCIATI, E.—*See* BARTOLI, A., ET ALII.

SÜDHAUS, S. — *See* SEVERUS, CORNELIUS.—Ætna.—*Leipzig,* 1898.

SUESS, E.—Die Erdbeben des südlichen Italien [1873].— 4⁰. *Wien,* 1874.—*Denkschr. k. Akad. Wiss. xxxiv* (*Abth.* 1), *pp.* 1–32, *taf. i–iii. Wien,* 1875.—[Abstr.] *Boll. R. Com. Geol. Ital. vi, pp.* 111–13. *Roma,* 1875.—*Bull. Vulc. Ital. fasc.* 1, 2 e 3, *p.* 42. *Roma,* 1875.

SUESS, E.—Das Antlitz der Erde.—3 vols. 8⁰. *Prag, Wien, Leipzig,* 1883-1909.—In French, transl. by E. de Margerie : 3 tom. in 5 pts. 8⁰. *Paris, A. Colin,* 1897.—In English : 8⁰. *Oxford,* 1904. *See* T. i and ii.

SURITA.—Annales Rerum Aragonensium.— I, III, *c.* 86.

SVETONIUS, C.—Caligula c, 51. Eruption A.D. 38–40.

SWINBURNE, H.—Travels in the Two Sicilies in the years 1777-80.— 2 vols. 4⁰, *with many fine pls. London,* 1783–85. ——2nd ed. 2 vols. 8⁰. *Vol. i, pp. lxviii*+307, 5 *pls.* ; *Vol. ii, pp. xi*+359, 3 *pls. London,* 1790.——3rd ed. 1795.— In French, transl. by Mlle. de Keralio, 4 vols. 4⁰. *Didot, Paris,* 1785.—In German, I. R. Forster : 2 pts. *Hamburg,* 1785. *See* Vol. ii, *p.* 246, 1790 : view of Etna.

SYMONDS, J. A.—Sketches and studies in Italy and Greece.—3 vols. 8⁰. *London,* 1898. *See* Vol. iii.

TACCHINI, P.—Della convenienza ed utilità di erigere sull' Etna una stazione astronom,- meteorologica.—4⁰, 3 *tav. Catania,* 1876.

TACCHINI, P.—Terremoti Calabro-Messinesi del 16 Novembre 1894.—*Atti R. Acc. Lincei, S.* 5, *Rend. iii, sem.* 2, *pp.* 275–78. *Rome,* 1894.

TAFFARA, L.—*See* VINASSA DE REGNY ET ALII.

TARAMELLI, T., e MERCALLI, G.—I Terremoti Andalusi cominciati il 25 Dicembre, 1884.—*Atti R. Acc. Lincei, S.* 4, *Mem. iii, pp.* 116–225, *tav.* I–IV. *Roma,* 1886.
See p. 98.

TARCAGNOTTA.—Istoria del Mondo. Earthquake of 1169. Cited by Mongitore.

TEDESCHI DI ERCOLE, V.—Extrait d'une lettre [sur la condition de l'Etna en 1879–80 et sur les conditions de l'éruption de lave].—*Ann. Chim. xx, pp.* 226–30. *Paris,* 1880.

TEDESCHI DI ERCOLE, V.—Éruption de boue au pied de l'Etna.—" *La Nature,*" *sem.* 1, *pp.* 363–64. *Paris,* 1880.

TEDESCHI DI ERCOLE, V.—L'État actuel de l'Etna.—" *La Nature,*" *sem.* 2, *p.* 231. *Paris,* 1880.

TEDESCHI DI ERCOLE, V.—L'État actuel du Mont Etna ét la Vallée del Bove.—" *La Nature,*" *sem.* 2, *pp.* 116–19, 2 *figs. Paris,* 1881.

TEDESCHI DI ERCOLE, V.—Sur le sol volcanique de Catane.—*C.R. Acad. Sci. xcii, pp.* 1516–17. *Paris,* 1881.

TEDESCHI [DI ERCOLE], V.—À propos des recherches chimiques faites par MM. Ricciardi et Speciale sur les laves des environs de Catane et sur les Basaltes de la Sicile.—*Acad. des Sciences de Paris,* 1882, 4⁰, *pp.* 7. [*fide* C.A.]

TEDESCHI DI ERCOLE, V.—La récente éruption de l'Etna [March 20–22, 1883].— " *La Nature,*" *sem.* 1, *pp.* 305–6, 1 *fig. Paris,* 1883.

TEDESCHI E PATERNÒ, T.—Breve ragguaglio degl'incendi di Mongibello, avvenuti in quest' anno 1669, con tre piante : una di Catania antica in tempo della gentilità, altra della medesima prima degli incendii e la terza dell' istessa già deformata dal fuoco.—4⁰, *pp.* 76, 3 *pls., portrait. Napoli,* 1669.

TEMPLE, G.—*See* WRIGHT, G. N.

TENORE, M.—Ragguagli di alcune peregrinazioni effettuate in diversi luoghi delle provincie di Napoli, e di Terra di Lavoro, nella primavera e nell' està del 1832.—8⁰. — ?, — ?.—*Il Progr. Sci. iv, pp.* 177–95 ; v, *pp.* 41–63, 161–75 ; vi, *pp.* 187–211. *Napoli,* 1833.

THOMAS, T. H.—A Visit to the Lipari Isles and Etna.—*Trans. Cardiff Nat. Soc. xxii, pt.* 1, *pp.* 11–26. 1891.

THUCYDIDES.—III. 116. Eruptions 475 and 425 B.C.

TOLOMEO DI LUCCA.—Bibl. Part. Tom. XXV. Earthquake of 1669. Cited by Mongitore.

TORNABENE, F.—Come si rendano coltivabili le lave dell' Etna.—*Rend. Acc. Sci. i, pp.* 425–29. *Napoli,* 1842.

TORNABENE, F.—Lettera sull' attuale eruzione dell' Etna di Nov. 1843, etc.— *Rend. Acc. Sci. ii, pp.* 441–44. *Napoli,* 1843.

TORNABENE, F.—Intorno ad alcuni resti di Vegetabili che trovansi nella formazione dell' Argilla presso Catania.—*Atti Acc. Gioen. S.* 2, ii, *p.* 380. *Catania,* 1846.— *Rend. R. Acc. Sci. v, pp.* 394–96. *Napoli,* 1846.

TORNABENE, F.—Sulla Eruzione presente dell' Etna.—*Rend. R. Acc. Sci. S.* 2, i, *pp.* 113–20, 146–54. *Napoli,* 1852.

TORNABENE, F.—Flora fossile dell' Etna. —*Atti Acc. Gioen. S.* 2, xvi, *pp.* 1–147, 10 *pls. Catania,* 1860.

TORNABENE, F.—Sull' arginazione del Simeto.—*Giorn. Agric. Ind. e Comm. d. Regno d'Italia,* 30 *Novembre* 1864.

TORNABENE, F.—Condizioni della provincia di Catania in rapporto alle Acque potabili.—*Giorn. Agric. Ind. e Comm. d. Regno d'Italia,* 31 *Ottobre,* 1865.

TRAVAGLIA, R.—*See* BALDACCI. 1879.

TRAVERSO, S.—Contribuzioni allo studio delle Rocce Vulcaniche.—*Giorn. Min. Crist. e. Petrog. v, pp.* 194–207. *Milano,* 1894.

TRITHEMIUS. — Chronologia monasteriorum. Cited by Massa, Etna, and by Mongitore.

TROLLOPE, F. E.—*See* STIELER, C.

TROLLOPE, T. A.—*See* STIELER, C.

TROVATO-CASTORINA, G.—Effetti magnetici del fulmine sulle lave dell' Etna.— *Atti Acc. Gioen. S.* 4, xix, *Mem.* 15, *pp.* 12, 5 *figs. Catania,* 1906.

TROVATO CASTORINA, G.—Sulla radio-attività di prodotti vulcanici dell' ultima eruzione Etnea, Marzo-Aprile 1910.— *Boll. Acc. Gioen. S.* 2, 12, *pp.* 21-26. *Catania*, 1910.

U. C.—*See* ANON.—L'Eruzione dell' Etna ... 1892.

UGHELLI.—Cronica Pisana.
Earthquake of 1169. Cited by Mongitore.

UNGERN-STERNBERG, W. H. C. R. A. VON.—Werden und Seyn des vulkanischen Gebirges. Mit 8 Abbildungen.—8⁰, *pp. xi+320. Carlsruhe*, 1825.
See p. 66.

VAGLIASINDI, P. DI RANDAZZO.—Memoria sull' eruzione accaduta nella pioggia accidentale dell' Etna al primo Novembre 1832.—8⁰. *Palermo*, 1833, and " *Giorn. Lett.*" No. 128.

VALERIUS FLACCUS, C.—Argonauticon.
See *Lib.* II, 24, 33.

VALGUARNERA.—Origine di Palermo.
Cited by Massa, Etna.

VALMONT DE BOMARE, J. C.—Dictionnaire raisonné universel d'Histoire Naturelle, *etc.*— 5 tom. 8⁰. *Paris*, 1765.— 9 tom. 8⁰. *Paris*, 1775.——4th ed. 8 tom. 4⁰. *Lyon*, 1791.
See Tom. IX. 1775.

VALMONT DE BOMARE, J. C. (?).—*See* BOMARE, DE.

VANDER AA (publ.).—L'Île de Sicile suivant les nouvelles observations de Messʳˢ de l'Académie Royale des Sciences, *etc.* Augmentées de nouveau.—À Leide, chez Pierre Vander Aa.
Map with engravings of Etna, Messina and Vesuvius (1631) on sides of title : 298×228 mm.

VARENIUS, B.—Geographia generalis, in qua affectiones generales telluris explicantur. —*Amstelodami*, 1664.
See *Lib.* I, cap. X : Etna and Vulcano.

VASI, M.—Itinéraire instructif de Rome à Naples et à ses environs, tiré de celui de feu M. Vasi, et de la Sicile, tiré de celui de M. de Haraczay [by A. Nibby].—12⁰, *pp.* 399. *Rome*, 1826.

VAUQUELIN, L. N.—Analyse du Pyroxène de l'Etna.—*Journ. Mines, vii, pp.* 172-80. *Paris*, 1797-98.

VAUQUELIN, L. N.—Analyse chimique des cendres de l'Etna.—*Journ. Pharm. xi, pp.* 553-58. *Paris*, 1825.—*Ann. Chimie, xxxii, pp.* 106-11. *Paris*, 1826.

VECCHI, E. DE.—Notizia su di alcune altitudine determinati geodeticamente nella regione dell' Etna.—*G. G. Casson, Torino,* 1866.

VECCHI, MALAGOLI.—*See* PELLÉ, C. 1841.

VENTIMIGLIA, D. C.—Pianta del Monte Etna.
Cited by Massa, Etna.

VESSEREAU, J. — *See* SEVERUS, CORNELIUS, 1905.

VETRANI, A.—Sebethi vindiciæ, sive dissertatio de Sebethi antiquitate, nomine, fama, cultu, origine, prisca magnetudine, decremento, atque alveis, adversus Jacobum Martorellium.—8⁰, *pp.* 8+213, 2 *pls. Neapoli*, 1767.

VIESSE DE MARMONT (DUC DE RAGUSE). —Voyage en Sicile.—*See his :* Voyage en Hongrie, *etc.* 2ᵉ éd. *Tom. v. Paris,* 1838.——3ᵉ éd. 8⁰, *pp.* 372. *Paris*, 1839. [C.A.]

VIESSE DE MARMONT.—Carte des Éruptions du Mont Etna.—*Appended to his work :* " Voyage en Sicile." *The original MS. in library* [C.A.]

VIGO, L.—Poesie e prose.—4⁰, *pp. v*+171+3. *Palermo*, 1823.

VIGO, L.—La Eruzione Etnea del 1852. Testimonianza.—*Atti Acc. Sci. Lett. N.S. ii,* 2, *pp.* 28. *Palermo*, 1853. [C.A.]

VILLANOVA, J.—Observations géologiques sur la Sicile et les Îles Lipari.—*Bull. Soc. géol. France, S.* 2, *xi, pp.* 80-86. *Paris,* 1854.

VILLEBOIS, DE.—*See* HAMILTON, SIR W. 1780.

VINASSA DE REGNY, P. E.—La Colata lavica dell' eruzione Etnea del 23 Marzo 1910.—*Boll. Acc. Gioen. S.* 2, 13, *pp.* 5-10. *Catania*, 1910.

VINASSA DE REGNY, P. E., RICCÒ, A., ARCIDIACONO, S., STELLA STARRABBA, F., TAFFARA, L., FIORE, O. DE.—L'Eruzione Etnea del 1910.—4⁰, 11 *pls. Catania*, 1912.—*Atti Acc. Gioen. S.* 5, *iv. Mem.* 17, *pp.* 65+24+23+5+57+34+ 35+*ii*, 11 *tav. Catania*, 1911.

VINASSA DE REGNY, P. E.—Relazione sull' eruzione Etnea del 1910.—*Boll. Acc. Gioen. S.* 2, 15, *p.* 17. *Catania*, 1911.

VIOTTI, G., e SILVESTRI, O.—Eruzione dell' Etna, Febbraio 1865.—4⁰. *Catania,* 1865.

VIOTTI, G.—Cenni sulla eruzione del Gennaro 1865.—*See* GEMMELLARO, C.—Breve ragguaglio, *etc. p.* 13. 1865.

VIRGILIUS MARO, P.—Georgica.—*i,* 471-73.

VIRGILIUS MARO, P.—Æneis.—*iii,* 571 *seq., viii,* 418 *seq.*

VISCIO, G. DEL.—Il Gargano in mezzo ai moti sismici d'Europa ed alle eruzioni dell' Etna.—*Bull. Soc. Meteor. Ital.* 1888.

VISSCHER, N.—Totius Italiæ. Tabula.

VITALE, P.—Relazione dell' orribile tremuoto successo in Palermo nel primo giorno di Settembre 1726.—4⁰. *Palermo,* 1726.

WAGLER, P. R.—De Ætna poemata questiones criticæ.—8⁰, *pp.* 107. *Berolini,* 1884. [C.A.]

WALCKNAER.—*See* NORVINS.

WALLERANT, F.—Sur l'éruption actuelle de l'Etna. Extrait d'une lettre à M. Fouqué.—*C.R. Acad. Sci. cxv, pp.* 370–73. *Paris,* 1892.

WALLERANT, F.—Sur l'âge des plus anciennes éruptions de l'Etna.—*C.R. Acad. Sci. cxvi, pp.* 29–31. *Paris,* 1893.

WARD, I. (peint.).—Vue de l'Etna. Gravé par Tinimal. A Augsbourg dans le Négoce de l'Académie des Arts.
View of Etna in eruption ; very untruthful. Sepia engraving, hand-coloured : 190×140 mm.

WASHINGTON, H. S.—Some analyses of Italian Volcanic Rocks.—*Amer. Journ. Sci. viii,* Art. XXXI, *pp.* 286–94. *New Haven,* 1899.

WASHINGTON, H. S.—Chemical analyses of Igneous Rocks published from 1884 to 1900, with a critical discussion of the character and use of analyses.—*U.S. Geol. Surv.Prof. Paper* 14, *pp.*495. *Washington,* 1903.

WASHINGTON, H. S.—The superior analyses of Igneous Rocks from Roth's Tabellen, 1869–1884, arranged according to the Quantitative System of Classification.—*U.S. Geol. Surv. Prof. Paper* 28, *pp.* 61. *Washington,* 1904.

WATERS, A. W.—Remarks on the recent geology of Italy. Suggested by a short visit to Sicily, Calabria and Ischia (1877).—*Trans. Geol. Soc. xiv, pp.* 251–82, *pl. Manchester,* 1878.

WENTHERN POLYCARPUS.—Krieg der Elementen, wider das baimmerus-würdige Sicilia oder Beschereibung des erschruklichen Bebens und Erschüttern der Erder grausamen Ubelauffs und Sturm des Meers auch höchstensselichen Toben und siedenden Wültur des Jener-auspeinden Bergs Aetna.—4⁰, *pp.* 52. —?, 1693. [C.A.]

WERTHER.—*See* DE BORCH. 1796.

WHITE, J.—Eruption of Mount Etna.—" *Nature,*" *xxxiv, pp.* 82–83, 108. *·London,* 1886!

WILSON, J.—A History of Mountains, geographical and mineralogical. Accompanied by a picturesque view of the principal Mountains of the World, in their respective proportions of height above the level of the sea, by Robert Andrew Riddell. —3 vols. *Vol. i, pp. lv*+368+176, *London,* 1807 ; *Vol. ii, pp.* 735, *London,* 1809 ; *Vol. iii, pp.* 906+*index. London,* 1810.
See Vol. iii. Vols. ii and iii read : " A History . . . to accompany a picturesque view," *etc.*

WINCHILSEA, EARL OF.—A true and exact relation of the late prodigious earthquake and eruption of Mount Etna or Montegibello, as it came in a letter written to his Majesty from Naples. Together with a more particular narrative of the same, as it is collected out of several relations sent from Catania.—4⁰, *pp.* 30, *with a sketch of the eruption by Hollar* (?). *Published by Authority. Printed by Newcomb in the Savoy,* 1669.   ,

WRIGHT, G. N.—The Shores and Islands of the Mediterranean drawn from Nature by Sir Grenville Temple, Bart., W. L. Leitch, Esq., Major Irton, and Lieut. Allen, R.E., with an Analysis of the Mediterranean and description of the plates.—4⁰, *pp.* 156, 65 *pls. London and Paris,* 1839 ?
See pls. and pp. 97, 142.

Z.—Das neue geheime Buch Chevilla von den Wunderseltsamen Veränderungen der Erde, des Meeres, der Berge des Himmels, von der Structur der Sonne, u.s.f. Herausgegeben von Z.—4 pts. 8⁰. [?*Leipsic*] 1786.—Earlier ed. 1784.
See Pt. 2.

ZACHER, A.—Im Lande des Erdbebens. Vom Vesuv zum Aetna. Land und Leute in Sizilien und Kalabrien. Die vulkanischen Katastrophen von 1905 bis 1908. Zerstörung von Messina und Reggio.—*pp.* 316. *Stuttgart*, 1908.

ZEILLER, R.—L'Éruption de l'Etna.— *Rev. scient. S.* 2, *xvii, pp.* 35–38. *Paris*, 1879.

ZUCCAGNI-ORLANDINI, A.—Atlante illustrativo ossia raccolta dei principali Monumenti Italiani antichi del medio evo e moderni e di alcune vedute pittoriche per servire di corredo alla Corografia fisica storica e statistica dell' Italia.—3 vols. *gd. fol. Firenze*, 1845. *See* Vol. iii.

ZUCCAGNI-ORLANDINI, A.—Corografia fisica, storica e statistica dell' Italia e delle sue Isole corredata di un atlante di mappe geografiche e topografiche e di altre tavole illustrative.—12 books in 17 vols. 8⁰. *Firenze*, 1845.—*Also* Atlas, 4 vols. *fol., containing maps and views. See* Vol. xii.

ZUCCARELLO e MARAVIGNA.—Memoria su di un Sotto-Carbonato di Soda scoperto nelle lave del litorale di Catania.—*Giorn. Sci. Lett. e Arti per la Sicilia, xxxiii, pp.* 50–59. *Palermo*, 1831.

ZURCHER, F., MARGOLLÉ, E.—Volcans et tremblements de terre (Etna et Stromboli).—16⁰, *figs. Paris*, 1866.——5th ed. 8⁰, *pp.* 311, *figs. Paris*, 1886. (*Bibl. des Merveilles.*)

ISOLA GIULIA

Otherwise known as NERITA, FERDINANDEA, GRAHAM, HOTHAM or CORAO ISLAND

ANON.—Breve ragguaglio del novello Vulcano.—*Effemeridi scient. e lett. p. l. Sicilia,* i, 3, pp. 136–65. *Palermo,* 1832.

ANON. [? GLOCKER, E. F.].— L'Écueil reconnu dans la Méditerranée, à la place qu'occupait l'Île Julia.—*Bull. Soc. géol. France, iv, p.* 71, *Paris,* 1833 ; *p.* 410, 1834.—[Extr. from] " *Le Temps,*" 4 *nov.* 1833.

ANON.—Formation soudaine d'une Île nouvelle sur les côtes de l'Italie, à la suite d'éruptions volcaniques.—*Bull. Soc. Géog. xvi, pp.* 87–95. *Paris,* 1831.

ANON. [? PARROT, G. F.].—Die Grahams-Bank.—*Ann. erd.- völker- u. staatenkunde, xxv (S.* 4, *i), pp.* 184–85. *Breslau,* 1842.

ANON. [? ALLOTTA, V.].—[L'Isola Ferdinandea.]—*Antologia, S.* 2, *iv, pp.* 78–79. *Firenze,* 1831.

ANON. [? ALLOTTA, V.].—[L'Isola Ferdinandea.]—*Giorn. Reg. Due Sicilie,* 1831, *Pte.* 2, *p.* 1166. *Napoli,* 1831.

ANON.—L'Italia.—4⁰, *pp.* 326, *num. maps. Torino,* 1896.

ANON.—New Volcanic Island, elevated by submarine eruption, on the south-west coast of Sicily, in Lat. 37 deg. 7 min. 30 sec. North, Long. 12 deg. 14 min. East, and first observed July 12th, 1831. From a sketch sent August 6th by an officer of His Majesty's Flag Ship St. Vincent to H.R.H. the Duke of Sussex, K.G., President of the Royal Society. To whom this plate is, with permission, humbly dedicated by His Royal Highness's most obedient and devoted servant R. Ackermann. On stone by L. Haghe. London, published Septr. 9th by R. Ackermann, 96 Strand. Day and Haghe, Lithⁿ to the King, 17, Gate S', Linc. Inn Fⁿ'. [B.M. Portfolio of Sicily.]

Coloured lith. : 493×135 mm.

ANON.—Réapparition de l'Île Ferdinandea (ou Julia) dans la Méditerranée.—*Bull. Soc. géog. S.* 2, *i, p.* 62. *Paris,* 1834.

ANON.—Om den vulcanske Öe, Isola Ferdinandea, der i 1831 fremkom i Nærheden af Sicilien.—*Magazin for Naturvidenskaberne. Anden Rækkes,* 1ᵗᵉ *Binds,* 2ᵈᵉᵗ *Hefte.*—8⁰, *pp.* 204–15. *Christiania,* 1832–33.

ANON. [? ALLOTTA, V.].—Vulcano sottomarino.—*Antologia, S.* 2, *ii, pp.* 137–38. *Firenze,* 1831. (*Estr. d. Gazz. Piemontese, No.* 102. *Agosto,* 1831.)

ANON. [? GLOCKER, E. F.].—Wieder-Erscheinen der Insel Ferdinandea, im Mittelmeer.— *Ann. erd.- völker- u. staatenkunde, viii, p.* 416. *Berlin,* 1833.—*N. J. f. Min. p.* 710. *Stuttgart,* 1835.

AINSWORTH, W.—Notice of the volcanic Island lately thrown up between Pantellaria and Sciacca.—*Mag. Nat. Hist. iv, pp.* 545–50. *London,* 1831.—*Amer. Journ. Sci. xxi, pp.* 399–408. *New Haven,* 1832. —*N. J. f. Min. p.* 220. *Stuttgart,* 1839.

ALLOTTA, V. (?) — See ANON.— [L'Isola Ferdinandea] *and* Vulcano sotto-marino.

ARAGO, D. F. J.—Considerations concerning the manner in which was formed in the Mediterranean in July 1831 the new Island which was successively called Ferdinandia, Hotham, Graham, Nerita and Julia.—*Edinb. New Phil. Journ. xxiii, p.* 204. 1837.

ARAGO, D. F. J.—*See* PRÉVOST, L. C. 1837.

AUDOT, L. E. (père).—L'Italie, la Sicile, les Îles Éoliennes, l'Île d'Elbe, *etc.,* d'après les inspirations, les recherches et les travaux de Chateaubriand, Lamartine, R. Rochette, Piranezi, Napoléon, Denon,

St. Non, Goethe, etc. Recueillis et publiés par Audot père.—5 pts. 8⁰. *Paris*, 1834–37. [B.M.]
See Pt. 2, p. 325. For other ed. *see* CAMPI PHLEGRÆI.

BALLINGAL.—On the new insular Volcano, named Hotham-Island, which has just appeared off Sicily ; with a view of the volcano, by one of the officers of the Philomel.—*Edinburgh New Phil. Journ. xi, pp.* 365–73, *Pl.* VI. 1831.—*Monthly Amer. Journ. of Geol. i, pp.* 314–17. *Philadelphia*, 1831.—*N. J. f. Min. p.* 335. *Stuttgart*, 1832.

BONNEY, T. G.—Volcanoes, their structure and significance. —8⁰, *pp.* 351, 13 *pls.,* 21 *figs. London*, 1899.

BOUÉ, A.—Etwas über Vulkanismus und Plutonismus, in Verbindung mit Erdmagnetismus, sowie ein Aufzählungsversuch der submarinischen brennenden Vulkane.—*Sitzber. k. Akad. Wiss. lix, Abth.* 1, *pp.* 65–103. *Wien*, 1869.

BRUN, T.—Formation soudaine d'une Île nouvelle sur les côtes de l'Italie, à la suite d'éruptions volcaniques.—*Bull. Soc. géog. xvi, pp.* 87–95, 185–88. *Paris*, 1831.

BUTLER, G. W.—The October eruption North-West of Pantelleria [1891].— " *Nature,*" *xlv, p.* 154. *London*, 1892.

BUTLER, G. W.—On the matter thrown up during the submarine eruption north-west of Pantelleria, October, 1891.—" *Nature,*" *xlv, pp.* 251–52. *London*, 1892.

CAPOCCI, E.—Considérations sur la manière dont se forma dans la Méditerranée, en juillet 1831, l'Île nouvelle qui a été tour à tour appelée Ferdinandea, Hotham, Graham, Nerita et Julia. — *C.R. Acad. Sci. iv, pp.* 753–57. *Paris*, 1837.

CAPOCCI, E.—Un nuovo Vulcano in Sicilia. Dialogo.—*Il Propagatore Sci. Nat., Pt. i, pp.* 185–86. *Napoli*, 1847–48.

CHRISTIE, A. T.—[Hotham Island Volcano.]—*In* BALLINGAL : On the new insular Volcano, *etc. pp.* 366–67.

COMITÉ D'ORGANISATION DU 2ME CONGRÈS GÉOLOGIQUE INTERNATIONAL À BOLOGNE, 1881.—Bibliographie Géologique et Paléontologique de l'Italie.—8⁰, *pp. viii+*630. *Bologne*, 1881.
See No. XVI. SILVESTRI, O.—L'Etna . . . les Îles Lipari, l'Île Pantellaria et l'Île Ferdinandea (nos. 3763–4643).

CORDIER, P. L. A.—Rapport sur le voyage de M. Constant Prévost à l'Île Julia, à Malte, en Sicile, aux Îles Lipari et dans les environs de Naples.—*Nouv. Ann. Voy. S. 2, x, pp.* 43–64. *Paris*, 1836.—*C.R. Acad. Sci. ii, pp.* 243–55. *Paris*, 1836.

COURTOIS, H.—L'Île Julia [Graham's I.] son apparition au sud de la Sicile en juillet 1831.—*Bull. Soc. géog. comm. Bordeaux, ix, pp.* 481–88. 1882.

DAUBENY, C. G. B.—Note on a paper by Dr. John Davy entitled " Notice on the remains of the recent Volcano in the Mediterranean."—*Phil. Trans. R. Soc. pp.* 545–48. *London*, 1833.

DAUBENY, C. G. B.—*See* DAVY, J.

DAVY, J., DAUBENY, C. G. B.—Account of a new Volcano in the Mediterranean.— 4⁰. *London, Paris*, 1831.

DAVY, J.—Some account of a new Volcano in the Mediterranean. 1831.—*Phil. Trans. R. Soc. pp.* 238–50. *London*, 1832.

DAVY, J.—Further notice of the new Volcano in the Mediterranean.—*Phil. Trans. R. Soc. pp.* 251–54. *London*, 1832.

DAVY, J.—Notice of the remains of the recent Volcano in the Mediterranean.— *Phil. Trans. R. Soc. pp.* 143–46. *London*, 1833.

DAVY, J.—Some remarks in reply to Dr. Daubeny's note on the air disengaged from the sea over the site of the recent Volcano in the Mediterranean.—*Phil. Trans. R. Soc. pp.* 551–54. *London*, 1834.

DEECKE, J. E. W.—Italien.—8⁰, *pp. xii+* 514, *maps, pl. and fig. Berlin*, 1898.

DENZA, F.—Notizie di Meteorologia e Fisica Terrestre. (Le lucicrepuscolari e le eruzioni dell' Isola Ferdinandea e dell' Etna.)—*Ann. Meteor. Ital. ii, pp.* 256–58. *Torino*, 1887.

DESNOYERS, J. P. F. S.—Notice sur l'Île Julia, le Stromboli, les colonnes du Temple de Pozzuoli.—*Bull. Soc. géol. France, ii, pp.* 238–46. *Paris*, 1831–32.

EHRENBERG, C. G.—Ueber die bei Sicilien sich neuerlich wieder hebende, 1831 zuerst als thätiger Vulkan erschienene und bald wieder zurückgesunkene Ferdinands- oder Grahams-Insel.—*Monatsb. k. preuss. Akad. Wiss. pp.* 486–89. *Berlin*, 1863.—*Peterm. Mitth. p.* 277. *Gotha*, 1864.

EHRENBERG, C. G.—Im Febr. 1864, 10 Fuss unter Wasser.—*Wochenschr. f. Astron. Meteor. vii, p.* 40. *Halle,* 1864.

EHRENBERG, C. G.—Eruption den 12 Aug. 1864, 25 Meilen von Sicilien, zwischen Pantellaria und Sciacca.—*Amer. Journ. Science, N.F. xxxvii, p.* 442. *New Haven,* 1864.

FISCHER, TH.—Das Halbinselland Italien. —*In* Kirchhoff's " Länderkunde von Europa," *pp.* 285–515. *Prag, Wien, Leipzig,* 1890.

FOERSTNER, H.—Das Gestein der Insel Ferdinandea (1831) und seine Beziehungen zu den jüngsten Laven Pantellerias und des Aetnas.—*Min. u. petr. Mitth. N.F. v, pp.* 388–96. *Wien,* 1883.

FOERSTNER, H.—Das Gestein der 1891 bei Pantelleria entstandenen Vulcaninsel und seine Beziehungen zu den jüngsten Eruptivgesteinen der Nachbarschaft.— *Min. u. petr. Mitth. N.F. xii, pp.* 510–21. *Wien,* 1891–92.

FUCHS, C. W. C.—Vulkane und Erdbeben. —*pp. xii*+343. *Leipzig,* 1875.—*Internat. wissensch. Bibl. xvii,* 1879, 74, *etc.*

FUCHS, C. W. C.—Les Volcans et les Tremblements de Terre.—8°, *pp. viii*+279, *fig. and map. Paris,* 1876.——2nd ed. 1878. *See p.* 220. 1876.

GEIKIE, A.—Text-Book of Geology.—8°, *pp.* 971, 434 *figs. London,* 1882. *See p.* 250.

GELCICH, E.—Die Insel Ferdinandea.— *Deutsche Rundsch. f. Geog. u. Statist. viii, pp.* 225–27, 2 *figs. Wien, Pest, Leipzig,* 1886.

GEMMELLARO, C.—Relazione dei fenomeni del Nuovo Vulcano, sorto dal mare fra la costa di Sicilia e l'Isola di Pantelleria nel mese di Luglio 1831.—8°, *pp.* 48, *Appendix, pp. xxiv,* 11 *pls. Catania,* 1831. —*Atti Acc. Gioen. viii, pp.* 271–98. *Catania,* 1834.

GEMMELLARO, C.—Vulkanischer Ausbruch im Sicilischen Meere im Jahre 1831, beobachtet von . . .—*N. J. f. Min. pp.* 64–69, 201–2. *Heidelberg,* 1832.

GLOCKER, E. F.—Systematischer Bericht über die Fortschritte der Mineralogie im Jahr 1835. Mit Berücksichtigung der Geologie und Petrefactenkunde.—8°. *Nürnberg,* 1837. *See pp.* 228–32 : Entstehung der vulcanischen Insel Julia oder Ferdinandea.

Folgerungen über die Art der Entstehung der Vulcane überhaupt. (Theorie der Erhebungskratere.)

GLOCKER, E. F. (?)—*See* ANON.—" Wieder-Erscheinen der Insel Ferdinandea " *and* " L'Écueil reconnu," *etc.*

GRAVINA, C. (PRINCIPE DI VALSAVOYE).— Poesie. La eruzione del Vulcano sottomarino tra Sciacca e Pantelleria nel Luglio del 1831. Sonetto.—12°, *pp.* 72. *Catania,* 1834. [B.N.] *See p.* 11.

HAAS, H. J.—Unterirdische Gluten. Die Natur und das Wesen der Feuerberge im Lichte der neuesten Anschauungen für die Gebildeten aller Stände in gemeinverständlicher Weise dargestellt. 2te. Auflage.—8°, *pp.* 316, *fig. and pl. Berlin,* 1912.

HOFFMANN, F.—Nuova Isola sorta presso la città di Sciacca in Sicilia per opera di un vulcano sotto marino.—*Ann. univ. statist. xxx, pp.* 99–103, 1 *taf. Milano,* 1831.

HOFFMANN, F.—Intorno al Nuovo Vulcano presso la città di Sciacca. Lettera al Duca di Serradifalco.—*Giorn. Sci. Lett. e Arti, xxxiv, pp.* 138–48, 1 *pl. Palermo,* 1831.— *Ann. Phys. Chem. xxiv, pp.* 65–109. *Leipzig,* 1832.

HORNER, L.—On the New Volcanic Island in the Mediterranean, and its connection with the extinct volcanic island of Pantellaria, and the hot springs of Sciacca on the coast of Sicily.—*Proc. Geol. Soc. i, pp.* 338–39. *London,* 1834.—*Phil. Mag. xi, p.* 57. *London,* 1832.

KERR SCOURGE (Kapit).—3 Meter unter dem Wasser.—*Unterh. f. Astr. Metr. p.* 239. *Leipzig,* 1853.

LAPIERRE, LIEUT.—Rapport adressé à M. le vice-amiral Comte de Rigny, ministre de la marine et des colonies, par M. Lapierre, lieutenant de vaisseau, commandant le brick la Flèche.—*Le Moniteur universel, No.* 295, *p.* 1918, *col.* 2–*p.* 1919, *col.* 1. *Paris,* 22 *oct.* 1832.—*Ann. erd.-völker- u. staatenkunde, iv, pp.* 635–50, 1831 ; *v, pp.* 124, 198, 411, *Berlin,* 1832.

LENZ, O.—Ueber die vulcanischen Ausbrüche bei Pantelleria 1891 und am Aetna 1892.—" Lotos," *N.F. xiv, pp.* 19–32. *Prag, Wien, Leipzig,* 1894.

LEONHARD, C. C. Von.—Geologie, oder Naturgeschichte der Erde auf allgemein faszliche Weise abgehandelt.—5 vols. 8⁰. *Stuttgart*, 1836–44. See pp. 179–86.

LYELL, Sir C.—Principles of Geology.— 12 editions. *London*, 1830 *to* 1875. See Vol. ii, pp. 58–63. London, 1875. In French, transl. from 6th ed. : " Principes de Géologie."—*Lyon*, 1846.

MAZZOLLA, B.—Descrizione dell' Isola Ferdinandea al mezzogiorno della Sicilia. —12⁰, *pp.* 4, 8 *pls. Napoli*, 1831.—Also other ed. [C.A.]

MERCALLI, G.—I Vulcani attivi della terra (morfologia, dinamismo, prodotti, distribuzione geografica, cause).—8⁰, *pp.* *viii*+422, 82 *figs.*, 26 *pls. Milano*, 1907.

MEUNIER, É. S.—Description d'une série de Roches rapportées en 1831 de l'Île Julia par Constant Prévost et conservées dans les collections géologiques du Muséum d'Histoire Naturelle de Paris.—*"Le Naturaliste,"* n. 387, *pp.* 92–95. *Paris*, 1903.

MEUNIER, É. S.—Sur une série de Roches rapportées en 1831, de l'Île Julia, par Constant Prévost et conservées dans les Collections Géologiques du Muséum.— *Bull. Mus. Hist. Nat. ix*, 1902, *pp.* 46–52. *Paris*, 1903.

NEUMAYR, M.—Erdgeschichte.—" *Allgemeine Naturkunde,*" *i*, pp. 42+xii+653, very num. illustr. *Leipzig*, 1886.

OMBONI, G.—Geologia dell' Italia.—8⁰, 5 *tav. Milano*, 1869. See No. 14.

PARETO, L.—Della posizione delle Roccie pirogene ed eruttive dei periodi terziario quaternario ed attuale in Italia.—8⁰, *pp.* 35. *Genova*, 1852.

PARROT, G. F.—Notice sur l'Île Julia et les cratères de soulèvement [1837].—*Bull. Acad. Sci. iii, coll.* 274–88. *St. Pétersbourg*, 1838.

PARROT, G. F.—*See* ANON.—Die Grahams-Bank.

PASINI, L.—L'Isola Ferdinanda, o il Nuovo Vulcano di Mediterraneo.—*Ann. Sci.Lomb.-Veneto, ii, pp.* 3–10. *Padua, Vicenza*, 1832.

PETERMANN, A. H.—Uebersicht des vulkanischen Heerdes im Mittelmeer. Maasstab 1 :15,000,000.—*Peterm. Mitth. Taf.* 7. *Gotha*, 1866.

PILLA, L.—[Phénomènes volcaniques récents dans un des points de la mer qui baigne les côtes de la Sicile. Lettre à Mons. Arago.] —*C.R. Acad. Sci. xxiii, pp.* 988–90. *Paris*, 1846.

PILLA, L.—Trattato di Geologia.—2 vols. 8⁰. *Vol. i, pp. xiv*+549, num. figs.; Vol. ii, pp. 614, num. figs. Pisa, 1847-51. See Vol. i.

PLATANIA, Giov.—L'Éruption sous-marine près de l'Île Pantellaria.—" *La Nature,*" *xix, sem.* 2, *pp.* 397–98, 2 *figs. Paris*, 1891.

POGGENDORFF. J. C.—Ueber das im Mittelländischen Meer entstandene vulcanische Eiland, genannt Corao, Nerita, Isola Ferdinandea, Graham Island, Hotham Island und Julia, nebst einigen Nachrichten über craterförmige Inseln ähnlichen Ursprungs.—*Ann. Phys. Chem. xxiv, pp.* 65–108. *Leipzig*, 1832.

PRÉVOST, L. C.—Description de l'Île volcanique sortie récemment du sein de la Méditerranée.—*Nouv. Ann. Voyages, S.* 2, *xxii, pp.* 288–303. *Paris*, 1831. [C.A.]

PRÉVOST. L. C.—[Observations sur le nouvel Îlot volcanique qui s'est formé en juillet 1831 dans la mer de Sicile.]—*Bull. Soc. géol. France, ii, pp.* 32–38. *Paris*, 1831.—*Ann. Sci. nat. xxiv, pp.* 103–13. *Paris*, 1831.

PRÉVOST, L. C.—Introduction au rapport fait à l'Académie Royale des Sciences sur le voyage à l'Île Julia en 1831 et 1832.— 8⁰, *pp.* 47. *Paris*, 1832. [C.A.]

PRÉVOST, L. C.—Documents pour l'histoire des terrains tertiaires. Avec voyage à l'Île Julia, 1831 et 1832.—8⁰. *Paris*, 1833 (?).

PRÉVOST, L. C.—Notes sur l'Île Julia pour servir à l'histoire de la formation des montagnes volcaniques.—*Mém. Soc. géol. France, ii, pp.* 91–124, 3 *pls. Paris*, 1835.—[Résumé in :] GLOCKER, E. F.— Systematischer Bericht, *etc.*

PRÉVOST, L. C.—Voyage à l'Île Julia, à Malte, en Sicile, aux Îles Lipari, et dans les environs de Naples.—*C.R. Acad. Sci. ii, pp.* 243–54. *Paris*, 1836.

PRÉVOST, L. C.—Sur le mode d'apparition de l'Île Julia.—*Bull. Soc. géol. France, viii, pp.* 282–90. *Paris*, 1836–37.

PRÉVOST, L. C., et ARAGO, D. F. J.— Formation de l'Île Julia.—*Soc. Philom. Proc.-verb. pp.* 112–15. *Paris*, 1837.— *Edinb. New Phil. Journ. xxiii, pp.* 204–6. 1837.

PRÉVOST, L. C.—Lettre au sujet de l'Île Julia.—*iv, pp.* 857–62. *Paris*, 1837.

PRÉVOST, L. C.—Théorie des Soulève-ments.—*Bull. Soc. géol. France, xi, pp.* 183–203. *Paris*, 1839–40.

RICCIARDI, L.—Per una critica del Prof. Sigismondo Guenther. [Earthquakes and Volcanoes.]—*Boll. Soc. Nat. xxiii (S.* 2, *iii), pp.* 17–50. *Napoli*, 1909.

RICCÒ, A.—L'Île Ferdinandea, le soleil bleu et les crépuscules rouges de 1831.—*C.R. Acad. Sci. cii, pp.* 1060–63. *Paris*, 1886.

RUSSO FERRUGGIA, S.—Storia dell' Isola Ferdinandea sorta nella costa meridionale della Sicilia.—4⁰, *pp.* 58. *Trapani*, 1831. [C.A.]

SAINT-LAURENT, DE.—Détails sur l'Île volcanique nouvellement apparue dans la Méditerranée.—*Bull. Soc. Geog. xvi, pp.* 185–88. *Paris*, 1831.—*Bull. univ. sci. industr. xxvi, pp.* 235–42. *Paris*, 1831.— *Edinb. New Phil. Journ. xii, pp.* 197–98. 1832.

SCHULZ, A. W. F.—Nerita.—*Kastner's Archiv. f. Naturl. xxii, pp.* 50, 279–85, 429. 1831.—*Guido u. Meyer's Taschenbuch d. neuesten Reisen, iii, pp.* 205–30. 1831.

SCINA, D.—Breve ragguaglio del Novello Vulcano (apparso e disparso nel mare di Sciacca).—*Effemeridi Siciliane, i.*

SILVESTRI, O.—*See* COMITÉ D'ORGAN-ISATION, *etc.*—Bibliographie Géologique, *etc.* No. XVI. 1881.

SMYTH, W. H.—Some Remarks on an error respecting the site and origin of Graham Island.—*Phil. Trans. R. Soc. pp.* 255–58, 1 *pl. London*, 1832. [C.A.]

SMYTHE, G. W.—Views and Description of the late Volcanic Island off the coast of Sicily.—4⁰. *London*, —?

STOPPANI, A.—Corso di Geologia.—3 vols. 8⁰. *Milano*, 1871–73. *See* Vol. i, Dinamica Terrestre, pp. 504. Milano, 1871. 3ª ediz. con note ed aggiunte per cura di Allessandro Malladra.—3 vols. 8⁰. *Milano*, 1900–3. *See* Vol. i.

STOWE.—Account of a New Volcano which rose from the sea between Sicily and the Island of Pantellaria, in July, 1831 : a translation of a paper read by Dr. Carlo Gemmellaro, Professor of Natural History, in the Royal University at Catania, on 28 Aug. 1831, in the hall of that University, and published the same year. Followed by an Appendix, containing letters, ·etc., on the same subject. — MS. Paper, 4⁰, *foll.* 36. XIX*th century.* [B.M. 1072.] The paper appears to have been origin-ally read before the " Accademia Gioenia di Scienze Naturali " at Catania on 18 Aug. 1831 : it is printed in the Atti of that society, Vol. viii (1834), p. 271.

SWINBURNE, H.—On the New Insular Volcano named Hotham Island, off Sicily. —*Edinb. New Phil. Journ. xi, pp.* 365–73. 1831.

WASHINGTON, H. S.—Chemical Analyses of Igneous Rocks published from 1884 to 1900, with a critical discussion of the character and use of analyses.—*U.S. Geol. Surv. Prof. Paper* 14, *pp.* 495. *Wash-ington*, 1903.

WASHINGTON, H. S.—The Superior Ana-lyses of Igneous Rocks from Roth's Tabellen, 1869–1884, arranged according to the Quantitative System of Classification.— *U.S. Geol. Surv. Prof. Paper* 28, *pp.* 61. *Washington*, 1904.

WASHINGTON, H. S.—The Submarine Eruptions of 1831 and 1891 near Pantel-leria I. (Mediterranean).—*Amer. Journ. Sci. S.* 4, *xxvii, pp.* 131–50, *fig. (chart). New Haven*, 1909.

PANTELLERIA

ANON.—L'Eruzione sottomarina di Pantelleria : brano di rapporto del Comandante della spedizione idrografica.—*Riv. marit. xxv*, 12. *Roma*, 1892.

ANON.—L'Italia.—4º, *pp.* 326, *num. maps. Torino*, 1896.

ANON.—The late eruption of Pantelleria.— *"The Mediterranean Naturalist," ii, pp.* 286–87. *Malta*, 1892.

ABICH, O. W. H. VON.—Geologische Beobachtungen über die vulkanischen Erscheinungen und Bildungen in Unter- und Mittel-Italien : Bd. i, Lief. 1 : Ueber die Natur und den Zusammenhang der vulkanischen Bildungen.—4º, *pp. viii+* 134+*xi*, 3 *maps*, 2 *lith. pls. Braunschweig*, 1841.—Atlas to same, bound separately, 5 *pls.*

AUDOT, L. E. (père).—L'Italie, la Sicile, les Îles Éoliennes, *etc.*—5 pts. 8º. *Pt. i, pp.* 113, *pls.* 1–26, *Paris*, 1834 ; *Pt. ii, pp.* 370, *pls.* 27–118, 1835 ; *Pt. iii, pp.* 280, *pls.* 119–207, 1836 ; *Pt. iv, pp.* 108, *pls.* 208–52, 1836 ; *Pt. v, pp.* 111–28, *pls.* 253–91, 1 *map*, 1837. *Paris*, 1834–37. [B.M.] *See* Pt. 2, p. 325. For other ed. *see* VESUVIUS.

BAEDEKER, K.—Italien. Handbuch für Reisende. 3. Theil : Unter-Italien und Sicilien nebst Ausflügen nach den Liparischen Inseln. 8th ed.—16º, *pp. xlviii+*412, 26 *maps*, 17 *plans. Leipzig*, 1887. *See* pp. 227, 381.

BARATTA, M.—Sulle Bombe esplodenti dell' eruzione sottomarina di Pantelleria [1891]. —*Ann. Uff. Cent. Meteor. Geodinam. S.* 2, *xi, pt.* 3, *pp.* 5–7. *Roma*, 1892.

BARATTA, M.—Gli odierni fenomeni di Pantelleria.—*Milano*, 1892.

BERTELLI, T.—Intorno ad un articolo dei periodici " Nature " e " Cosmos " sui moti microsismici di Rocca di Papa in ordine al terremoto di Aquila dell' 8 Febbraio 1892. —*Atti Acc. Pont. N. Lincei, xlv, pp.* 121–35. *Roma*, 1892.—*Boll. Oss. Moncalieri, xii, pp.* 103–8, 117–19. *Torino*, 1892.

BERTELLI, T.—Di alcuni Moti Tromometrici osservati in Sicilia nelle eruzioni Etnee del 1883, 1886 e 1892 e di quella sottomarina della Pantelleria nell' Ottobre 1891.—*Atti Acc. Pont. N. Lincei, xlvi, pp.* 17–24. *Roma*, 1893.—*Boll. Oss. Moncalieri, xii, pp.* 133–36. *Torino*, 1892.

BONNEY, T. G.—Volcanoes, their structure and significance.—8º, *pp.* 351, 13 *pls.*, 21 *figs. London*, 1899.

BRIGNONE, G.—Analisi di un Acqua Termominerale nell' Isola di Pantelleria. 1884.—*Gazz. Chim. Ital. xiv, pp.* 42–54. *Palermo*, 1885.

CALCARA, P.—Descrizione dell' Isola di Pantellaria.—*Atti Acc. Sci. Lett. ii, pp.* 1–44. *Palermo*, 1853.

COMITÉ D'ORGANISATION DU 2ME CONGRÈS GÉOLOGIQUE INTERNATIONAL À BOLOGNE, 1881.—Bibliographie Géologique et Paléontologique de L'Italie.—8º, *pp. viii+*630. *Bologne*, 1881. *See* No. XVI. SILVESTRI, O.—L'Etna . . . les Îles Lipari, l'Île Pantellaria et l'Île Ferdinandea (nos. 3763–4643).

CONSIGLIO-PONTE, S.—Primi appunti lito-paleontologici [in appendice alla relazione del Prof. Riccò : Terremoti, sollevamenti ed eruzione sottomarina a Pantelleria]. — *Ann. Uff. Cent. Meteor. e Geodinam. S.* 2, *pte.* 3, *xi. Roma*, 1892.

DAUBENY, C. G. B.—A Description of active and extinct Volcanos ; with remarks on their origin, their chemical phenomena, and the character of their products, as determined by the condition of the earth during the period of their formation.— 8º, *pp.* 743, *figs.*, 10 *maps*, 4 *pls. London*, 1848.

DEECKE, J. E. W.—Italien.—8º, *pp. xii+* 514, *maps, pl. and fig. Berlin*, 1898.

DENZA, F.—Etna, Sicilia, ed Isole vulcaniche adiacenti dal Novembre 1890 all' Ottobre 1891.—*Ann. Meteor. Ital. vii, pp.* 264–69. *Torino*, 1892.

DENZA, F.—Terremoti, sollevamento ed eruzioni sottomarine a Pantelleria.—*Ann. Scient. Ind. xxviii. Milano*, 1892.

FISCHER, TH.—Das Halbinselland Italien. —*In* Kirchhoff's "Länderkunde von Europa," *pp.* 285–515. *Prag, Wien, Leipzig*, 1890.

FOERSTNER, H.—Ueber Natronorthoklas von Pantellaria.—*Zeitschr. f. Kryst. i, pp.* 547–61. *Leipzig*, 1877.

FOERSTNER, H.—Ortose Sodico di Pantellaria.—*Boll. R. Com. Geol. Ital. viii, pp.* 460–61. *Roma*, 1877.

FOERSTNER, H.—Carta geologica dell' Isola di Pantelleria, con sezioni.—*Boll. R. Com. Geol. Ital. S.* 2, *ii, p.* 554. *Roma*, 1881.
        Scale 1 : 100,000.

FOERSTNER, H.—Ueber Cossyrit, ein Mineral aus den Liparitlaven der Insel Pantellaria.—*N. J. f. Min. Ref.-Bd. ii, pp.* 332–34. *Stuttgart*, 1881.—*Zeitschr. f. Kryst. v, pp.* 348–62. *Leipzig*, 1881.

FOERSTNER, H.—Nota preliminare sulla geologia dell' Isola di Pantelleria.—*Boll. R. Com. Geol. Ital. S.* 2. *ii, pp.* 523–56. *Roma*, 1881.

FOERSTNER, H.—Das Gestein der Insel Ferdinandea (1831) und seine Beziehungen zu den jüngsten Laven Pantellerias und des Aetnas.—*Min. u. petr. Mitth. N.F. v, pp.* 388–96. *Wien*, 1883.

FOERSTNER, H.—Ueber die Feldspäthe von Pantelleria.—*Zeitschr. f. Kryst. viii, pp.* 125 *et seq., Leipzig*, 1883 ; *xix, pp.* 560–70, *Leipzig*, 1891.

FOUQUÉ, F. A.—Contribution à l'Étude des Feldspaths des Roches Volcaniques.— 8⁰, *pp.* 336. *Paris*, 1894.

FUCHS, C. W. C.—Les Volcans et les Tremblements de Terre.—8⁰, *pp. viii*+279, *fig. and map. Paris*, 1876.——2nd ed. 1878.
        See p. 219. 1876.

GATTA, L.—L'Italia, sua formazione suoi vulcani e terremoti.—8⁰, *pp.* 539, 32 *woodcuts and* 3 *lith. maps. Milano*, 1882.— *Boll. R. Com. Geol. Ital. Notiz. Bibliog. pp.* 102–4. *Roma*, 1882.

GEMMELLARO, C.—Sopra l'Isola vulcanica di Pantelleria e sopra le osservazioni ivi fatte dal socio corrispondente Conte F. Beffa Negrini.—*Atti Acc. Gioen. v, pp.* 209–23. *Catania*, 1831.

HAAS, H. J.—Unterirdische Gluten. Die Natur und das Wesen der Feuerberge im Lichte der neuesten Anschauungen für die Gebildeten aller Stände in gemeinverständlicher Weise dargestellt. 2te Auflage. —8⁰, *pp.* 316, *fig. and pl. Berlin*, 1912.

HOFFMANN, F.—Geognostische Beobachtungen. Gesammelt auf einer Reise durch Italien und Sicilien, in den Jahren 1830–1832.—*Archiv. f. Min. Geognos. xiii, pp.* 3–726, 1 *pl.,* 1 *map. Berlin*, 1839.—[Sep. publ.] *Berlin*, 1839.

JERVIS, G.—*See* JERVIS, W. P.

JERVIS, W. P.—Sketch of the Geology of Pantelleria, importance of its thermal springs to the Maltese.—" *The Mediterranean Naturalist,*" i, *pp.* 93–96. *Malta*, 1891.

JOUSSET, P.—L'Italie illustrée.—*fol., pp.* 370, 14 *col. maps and plans,* 9 *engrav. maps,* 12 *pls.,* 784 *photos. Paris*, 1829.

KLEIN, J. F. C.—Ueber den Feldspath im Basalt vom Hohen Hagen bei Göttingen und seine Beziehungen zu dem Feldspath von Mte. Gibele auf der Insel Pantellaria.— *Nachrichten, pp.* 449–66. *Göttingen*, 1878.

KLEIN, J. F. C.—Mineralogische Mittheilungen. 15. Ueber den Feldspath von Mte. Gibele auf Pantellaria.—*N. J. f. Min. pp.* 518–32. *Stuttgart*, 1879.

LEONHARD, C. C. VON.—Geologie, oder Naturgeschichte der Erde auf allgemein faszliche Weise abgehandelt.—5 vols. 8⁰. *Stuttgart*, 1836–44.
        See p. 220.

MACCHI, E.—L'Isola di Pantelleria.—*map.* —?, 1895.

MAYR, A.—Pantellaria.—" *Globus,*" *lxxvii,* 9, *pp.* 137–43. *Braunschweig*, 1900.

OMBONI, G.—Geologia dell' Italia.—8⁰, 5 *tav. Milano*, 1869.
        See No. 14.

PARETO, L.—Della posizione delle Roccie pirogene ed eruttive dei periodi terziario quaternario ed attuale in Italia.—8⁰, *pp.* 35. *Genova*, 1852.

PETERMANN, A.—Uebersicht des vulkanischen Heerdes im Mittelmeer. Maasstab 1 : 15,000,000.—*Peterm. Mitth. Taf.* 7. *Gotha*, 1866.

RECLUS, E.—Les Volcans de la Terre.— *Soc. Astronom. Bruxelles*, 1906.

RICCIARDI, L.—Sulle roccie eruttive sub-aeree e submarine e loro classificazione in due periodi. Sul graduale passaggio delle roccie acide alle roccie basiche.—8⁰, *pp.* 11–40. *Reggio-Emilia,* 1887.

RICCIARDI, L.—Genesi e successione delle rocce eruttive.—*Atti Soc. Ital. Sci. Nat. xxx, pp.* 212–37. *Milano,* 1887.

RICCIARDI, L.—Ricerche di chimica vul-canologica. Confronto tra le rocce degli Euganei, del Monte Amiata e della Pantel-leria.—*R. Is:. Tec. di Bari,* 8⁰, *pp.* 195–207. *Palermo,* 1888.—*Atti Soc. Ital. Sci. Nat. xxxi, pp.* 195–211. *Milano,* 1888.— *Gazz. Chim. Ital. xviii, pp.* 32–43. *Palermo,* 1888.

RICCIARDI, L.—Genesi e composizione chimica dei Terreni Vulcanici Italiani.— 8⁰, *pp.* 155. *Firenze,* 1889.

RICCÒ, A.—Terremoti, sollevamenti ed eru-zioni sottomarine a Pantelleria nella seconda metà dell' Ottobre 1891 : con appendice di S. Consiglio Ponte.—*Ann. Uffic. Cent. Meteor. e Geodinam. S.* 2, *xi, pt.* 3. 1889.—*Boll. Soc. Geog. Ital. S.* 3, *v,* 2. *Roma,* 1892.—In French : *C.R. Acad. Sci. cxiii, pp.* 753–55. *Paris,* 1891.

RIDDELL, R. A.—*See* WILSON, J.

RUDOLPH, E.—Bericht über die vulcan-ischen Ereignisse während des Jahres 1894.—*Min. u. petr. Mitth. xvi,* 5, *pp.* 365–464. *Wien,* 1896.

SILVESTRI, O.—*See* COMITÉ D'ORGAN-ISATION, *etc.*—Bibliographie Géologique, *etc.* No. XVI. 1881.

SOELLNER, J.—Beiträge zur Kenntnis des Cossyrits von Pantelleria.—*Zeitschr. f. Kryst. xlvi, pp.* 518–62, *figs. Leipzig,* 1909.

SOELLNER, J.—Fayalit von der Insel Pantelleria.—*Zeitschr. f. Kryst. xlix, pp.* 138–51, *pls. Leipzig,* 1911.

STOPPANI, A.—Corso di Geologia. 3a ediz. con note ed aggiunte per cura di Alles-sandro Malladra.—3 vols. 8⁰. *Vol. i, pp.* 695, 178 *figs.,* 1 *map, Milano,* 1900 ; *Vol. ii, pp.* 883, 217 *figs.,* 2 *maps,* 1903 ; *Vol. iii, pp.* 714, 60 *figs.,* 1903.—Earlier ed. *Milano,* 1871–73. *See* Vol. i.

WASHINGTON, H. S.—Some Analyses of Italian Volcanic Rocks.—*Amer. Journ. Sci. viii, Art.* 31, *pp.* 286–94. *New Haven,* 1899.

WASHINGTON, H. S.—The Superior Analy-ses of Igneous Rocks from Roth's Tabellen, 1869–1884, arranged according to the Quantitative System of Classification.— *U.S. Geol. Surv. Prof. Paper* 28, *pp.* 61. *Washington,* 1904.

WILSON, J.—A History of Mountains, Geographical and Mineralogical. Accom-panied by a picturesque view of the prin-cipal mountains of the World, in their respective proportions of height above the level of the sea by Robert Andrew Riddell. —3 vols. *Vol. i, pp.* lv+368+176, *London,* 1807 ; *Vol. ii, pp.* 735, *London,* 1809 ; *Vol. iii, pp.* 906+*index, London,* 1810. *See* Vol. iii. Vols. ii and iii read : " A History . . . to accompany a pictur-esque view," *etc.*

GENERAL MAPS

ANON.—Carta Topografica ed Idrografica dei Contorni di Napoli levata per ordine di S.M. Ferdinando I. . . . dagli uffiziali dello Stato Maggiori e degli Ingegneri topografi negli anni 1817, 1818, 1819.—12 *large maps.* *Ca.* 1 : 25,000. The plan of the crater was altered from time to time. 1828.

ANON.—Map of Naples and Sicily with part of the Roman States and Tuscany.— *Stanford, London,* 1860. [B.M.—23880 (29).]

ANON.—Regno di Napoli.—*Venetia,* 1557. [B.M.—K. 83. 2.]

ANON.—Regno di Napoli.—[*Venice* ?, 1580 ?] [B.M.—23880 (15).]
Quite fantastic.

ANON.—Regno di Napoli. — ?, — ? [B.M.—K. 83. 7.]

ARTARIA, F. e FIGLIO.—Nuova Carta delle due Sicilie . . . Scala 1 : 1,382,400 del naturale.—*Milano,* 1860. [B.M.—23880 (28).]

BERTELLI, F.—Disegni di alcune più illustri città et fortezza del Mondo, con aggionta di alcune Isole principali.— 4°. *Venetiis,* 1568. [B.M.—S. 30 (2).] Same map as that of Camocium.

[BLAEU. ?]—Regno di Napoli.—*Amsterdam* ?, 1660 ? [B.M.—23880 (1).]

BODENEHR, G.—Das Königreich Napoli in dessen XII Haupt Provincien.—*Augsburg* [1720 ?] [B.M.—23880 (19).]

CAMOCIUM, F.—La vera descrittione del regno di Napoli di novo emendata et ampliata.—*Venice,* 1562. [B.M.—S. 10 (1).]—Another ed. *Venice,* 1666. [B.M.— S. 30 (2).]

CANTELLI DA VIGNOLA, G.—Regno di Napoli nuovamente descritto.—*G. G. Rossi, Roma,* 1689. [B.M.—S. 108 (4).]

DANCKERTS, J.—Regnum Neapolis, Siciliæ et Lipariæ insulæ.—*Amstelodami* [1670 ?]. [B.M.—23880 (2).]

FABRIS.—Twenty views. 1777. [B.M.— K. 7. Tab. 60.]

FER, N. DE.—Le Royaume de Naples avec l'Isle de Sardaigne ; et une description. — ?, 1701. [B.M.—K. 83. 17.]

GASTALDI, G. DI.—Descrittione del regno di Napoli. [B.M.—K. 83. 5.]

HOMANNO, J. B.—Novissima et exactissima totius regni Neapolis tabula.— *Norimbergæ* [1720 ?] [B.M.—23880 (9).]— Another ed. [B.M.—K. 83. 13.]

JAILLOT, A. H.—Le Royaume de Naples. —2 *foll.* — ?, 1703–6. [B.M.—K. 83. 19. a and b.]

JANSSONII, S. J.—Neapolitanum Regnum. —*Amstelodami* [1635]. [B.M.—23880 (16).]

LOEHORN, P. VAN.—Neapolitanum Regnum.—*Paris* [1650 ?] [B.M.—23880 (17).]

MAGINI, FABIO DI GIOV. ANT.—Recueil de 54 cartes. Regno di Napoli. — ?, 1600. [B.M.—95. 9.]

NOLIN, J. B.—Le Royaume de Naples, divisé en ses douze provinces.—*Paris,* 1702.
Very imaginary maps.

PARISIO, P.—Carta del regno di Napoli. —2 *foll.* — ?, 1591. [B.M.—K. 83. 6.]

PYRRHO LIGORIO.—Nova Regni Neapolit. — ?, 1558. [B.M.—K. 83. 3.]

[RIEGEL, G. ?]—Die Königreiche Sicilien und Neapolis. — [*Nuremberg* ?, 1710 ?] [B.M.—23880 (8).]

RIEGEL, G.—Der unter Theil von Italia darin die königreiche Neapolis und Sicilien sich befindet.—*Nürnberg* [1730 ?] [B.M.—23880 (12).]
A badly made map.

RIZZI-ZANNONI, G. A.—Atlante Geografico del regno di Napoli compito e rettificato.—*Naples,* 1788–1812. [B.M.—S. 17 (20).]—Another ed. [B.M.—S. 104 (7).]

RIZZI-ZANNONI, G. A.—Topografia . . . 1793. [B.M.—23890 (4).]

RIZZI-ZANNONI, G. A.—Chart of the Bay of Naples and of part of the Bay of Salerno. —*London,* 1803.

RIZZI-ZANNONI, G. A.—Atlante del regno di Napoli, ridotto in VI fogli.—[*Napoli*, 1807 ?] [B.M.—23875 (1).]—Another ed. *Napoli* [1808–64]. [B.M.—S. 108 (6).]

RIZZI-ZANNONI, CAV.—Carta degli itinerari militari da Bologna a tutto il regno di Napoli.—*Napoli*, 1809. [B.M.—S. 121. 9.]

RIZZI-ZANNONI, CAV.—Carta itineraria delle stazioni militari del regno di Napoli. —[*Naples*] 1810.

SANSON, S.—Royaume de Naples. — ?, 1648. [B.M.—K. 83. 9.]—Another ed. 2*foll.* 1679. [B.M.—K. 83. 10.]—Another ed. *Amstelodami* [1680 ?] [B.M.—23880 (3).] —Another ed. *Covens & Mortier, Amstelodami* [1720 ?] [B.M.—K. 83 (12).]

SANSON, S.—Le Royaume de Naples divisé en douze Provinces.—*Amsterdam* [1705 ?] [B.M.—23880 (7).]

SANSON, S. — Carte nouvelle des royaumes de Naples, et de Sicile.—*Covens & Mortier, Amsterdam* [1730 ?] [B.M.—23880 (11).]

SCHENK, P.—Continentis Italiæ pars Australior sine Regnum Neapolitanum, *etc.*— *Amsterdam*, 1703. [B.M.—23880 (5).]

SCHOEL, H. VAN.—[Another edition of ANON.—Regno di Napoli.—*Venetia*, 1557.] —*Romæ*, 1602. [B.M.—S. 69. 13.]

VALK, G.—Italie pars meridionalis, quæ nunc sceptri Hispanici Regnum Neapolitanum, in 12 provincias divisum.— [*Amsterdam*, 1704 ?] [B.M. — 23880 (18).]

VALK, G. & L.—Regnum Neapolis, subdivisum in suas peculiares provincias.— [*Amsterdam*, 1705 ?] [B.M.—23880 (6).]

WIT, F. DE.—Regnum Neapolis in quo sunt Aprulium ulterius et citerius. — *Amstelodami* [1670]. [B.M.—S. 64 (28).]

ZEZI, P.—Elenco delle Carte Geologiche in grande scala eseguite finora in Italia. (*See :* Cenni intorno ai lavori per la Carta Geologica d'Italia in grande scala.—8⁰, *pp.* 39–40. *Roma*, 1875.)

The following Bibliographies, not incorporated in the present work, should also be consulted :—

CRINÒ, S.—Bibliografia storico-scientifica della " Regione Etnea."—*Atti Acc. Gioen. Sci. Nat. S. 4, xx, Mem.* 6, *pp.* 7–69. *Catania*, 1907.

FURCHHEIM, F.—Bibliografia della Campania.—2 vols. 8⁰, 1897–99. (For maps and views of Capri.)

SILVESTRI, O.—Bibliografia generale riguardante la Vulcanologia, Mineralogia, Geologia della provincia di Catania e delle Isole vulcaniche adiacenti alla Sicilia.—*pp.* 64. *Bolo na*, 1881.

APPENDIX

CAMPI PHLEGRÆI.

MORGHEN, F.—Le Antichità di Pæstum, Pozzuoli, Baja e Cuma.—*gd. fol. obl.* *Napoli,* 1764–69.

27 engravings on white paper such as occur in Morghen's 84 views of Naples, but containing a page of text entitled : " Spiegazione delle VI tavole delle Antichità di Pesto." Pl. xviii is entitled : " Vedute d'altri Bagni di Tritoli " and differs from that in the 84 views, in which Pl. xviii is " Veduta interiore del Truglia," etc.

SAUSSURE, H. B. DE.—Copie d'une lettre de M. de Saussure à Sr. W. Hamilton, à 17 Dec^re, 1774.—MS. *fol., foll.* 107–28. [B.M. 19, 309 (viii).]

[TORRE, DUCA DELLA (jun.).]—Détails sur le tremblement de terre du 26 juillet, 1805.—*Journ. Phys. lxi, pp.* 225–28. *Paris,* 1805.

VESUVIUS.

ANON.—Notice sur une éruption récente du Vésuve, tirée d'une lettre particulière communiquée aux éditeurs de ce Recueil.—*Bibl. univ. Sci. Arts, xxi, pp.* 190–91. *Genève,* 1822.

ANON.—Nouveaux détails sur l'éruption du Vésuve, tirés d'une lettre de Naples communiquée aux Redacteurs.—*Bibl. Univ. Sci. Arts, xxi, pp.* 226–28. *Genève,* 1822.

DENZA, F.—Notizie di Meteorologia e Fisica Terrestre.—*Ann. Meteor. Ital. ii, p.* 244. *Torino,* 1887.

DUPPA, R.—Mount Vesuvius as seen from the Bay of Naples, from an original sketch made in the year 1797 . . . Lowry sculp. [London] Published as the Act directs, Sept^bre 2d, 1802, by Longman and Rees, Paternoster Row.

Vesuvius seen from sea to the South. Line engraving : 226×169 mm.

X.—Raccolta di osservazioni cliniche sull' uso dell' acqua termo-minerale Vesuviana Nunziante, fatte da varj professori.—*Effemeridi scient. e lett. p.* 1, *Sicilia, vii,* 19, *pp.* 20–21. *Palermo,* 1833.

LIPARI.

BUCH, C. L. VON.—Gesammelte Schriften.—*Berlin,* 1877.

See Vol. iii, pp. 516–20.

ETNA.

PLATANIA, GAET.—Aci Castello, *etc.*—[Also in] *N. J. f. Min. pp.* 48–50. *Stuttgart,* 1905. (*See* entry in ETNA.)

PLATANIA, GIOV.—Ascensione dell' Etna. Gita alla Valle del Bove.—*See* ROMEO, V.

RACITI.—Guida di Acireale, *pp.* 244–58. *Acireale,* 1897.

PRINTED IN GREAT BRITAIN BY
RICHARD CLAY AND SONS, LTD.,
BRUNSWICK STREET, STAMFORD STREET, S.E. 1,
AND BUNGAY, SUFFOLK.

ImTheStory.com

Lightning Source UK Ltd.
Milton Keynes UK
UKOW05f2101300115

245438UK00013B/364/P